International Economic Law

ANDREAS F. LOWENFELD

Herbert and Rose Rubin Professor
of
International Law
New York University School of Law

OXFORD
UNIVERSITY PRESS

OXFORD

UNIVERSITY PRESS

Great Clarendon Street, Oxford OX2 6DP

Oxford University Press is a department of the University of Oxford.
It furthers the University's objective of excellence in research, scholarship,
and education by publishing worldwide in

Oxford New York

Auckland Bangkok Buenos Aires Cape Town Chennai
Dar es Salaam Delhi Hong Kong Istanbul Karachi Kolkata
Kuala Lumpur Madrid Melbourne Mexico City Mumbai Nairobi
São Paulo Shanghai Taipei Tokyo Toronto

Oxford is a registered trade mark of Oxford University Press
in the UK and in certain other countries

Published in the United States
by Oxford University Press Inc., New York

© Andreas F. Lowenfeld, 2002

The moral rights of the author have been asserted
Database right Oxford University Press (maker)

First published 2002
Published new as paperback 2003

British Library Cataloguing in Publication Data
Data available

Library of Congress Cataloging in Publication Data
Data available

ISBN-10: 0–19–825667–1 (hbk.)
ISBN-13: 978–0–19–825667–0 (hbk.)

ISBN-10: 0–19–926411–2 (pbk.)
ISBN-13: 978–0–19–926411–7 (pbk.)

9 10 8

Typeset by Hope Services (Abingdon) Ltd.
Printed in Great Britain
on acid-free paper by
Biddles Ltd, King's Lynn, Norfolk

Preface

It is not inappropriate to begin by asking whether there is such a thing as international economic law, a body of law that can be subjected to systematic treatment between the covers of a book. Similar questions have, of course, been asked for years about international law in general, and that field has survived not only as an intellectual discipline but as a relevant (not to say conclusive) factor in the behaviour of nations. In fact nations, as well as the other relevant actors, behave rather more according to law in the economic sphere than they do, for instance, in respect to the use of force or the observance of human rights.

This book is not founded on a claim that all states and all economic enterprises behave at all times according to all the rules, nor that the rules are clear and universally agreed at all levels. But one would not say that there is no criminal law because crimes continue to be committed and are not always punished, or that there is no family law because marriages break up, husbands beat their wives, and children are abused. In fact international conventions, collaborative arrangements, roughly uniform national laws, and customary laws apply to much of the international economy; while there is no global sheriff, and the system of remedies does not reach as far as the system of rules, there are a surprising number of consequences of deviant behaviour, and a growing number of fora for resolving disputes among states and between states and private participants in the international economy.

The problem in undertaking a project such as this one is not a lack of material, but rather how to make a selection, and—more ambitious—how to link the apparently diverse topics with some general concepts that serve to explain, guide, limit, and predict the development of an international economic law.

Beyond the rules and practices of international economic law, there is an even more basic question: To what extent is economic law man-made—through legislation, treaties, conventions, decisions of courts and panels—and to what extent is economic law eternal—to be discovered and explored like the laws of physics but not capable of being altered? This question is not really addressed here: this is a book about law, not (except incidentally) about economic science. Nevertheless it is worth keeping in mind that at least to some extent, attempts by governments to achieve specific results through legislation or command—for instance by trying to force up the price of commodities or by attempting to govern agricultural output by inadequate or excessive incentives—run up against economic forces incapable of being tamed.

Apart from the particular rules and arrangements explored throughout the volume, it is useful to set out some concepts of general application against which all the particular arrangements are to be tested. Non-discrimination, for example, runs through the entire subject; national treatment and most-favoured-nation treatment are different aspects of the principle, which turns out to be surprisingly technical in implementation. Once the world learned that all nations were not created equal, and that some states perhaps should receive (or were entitled to) better than non-discriminatory treatment, a further question arose whether some legal content could be given to 'special and differential treatment,' and whether states claiming or enjoying such treatment—typically less developed countries—have obligations of their own—toward one another and toward developed countries. A related concept of wide application is reciprocity. What that term means and whether it can be reconciled with non-discrimination requires exploration and analysis here.

Sovereignty—an elusive and often misunderstood concept—needs to be discussed in the context of economic law: to what extent have states joined in yielding to collective decision-making, to what extent may states take particular issues into their own hands, or resist the will of the community of states; to what extent can they—legally and practically—opt out of the consensus? Are these questions the same for states, such as the United States of America, whose every move has worldwide impact, and for states whose actions or failure to act affects only a few other states? Indeed, do the answers vary according to the particular issue, so that, for instance, Brazil's actions with respect to coffee matter a great deal but its actions with respect to wine matter hardly at all?

This book does not offer firm answers to these questions. Where specific answers may be derived from international agreements, of course, these answers are primary sources. Even there, however, one needs to be careful: to take a well-known example, the Articles of Agreement of the International Monetary Fund provide that member states may not impose exchange controls on payments and transfers for current international transactions, except in the transitional period following World War II. Who could have foretold that the exception from the general principle is still operative more than fifty years after the Articles of Agreement entered into effect, and for states that had no involvement whatever in the War? Many such examples could be cited throughout the law of international trade, finance, or investment. One of the persistent challenges of this work is to steer a rational course between focusing only on the written documents and regarding all departures from them as illegal, and on the other hand focusing so heavily on the practice of states that cynicism overwhelms all respect for agreement and principle.

Though this book is primarily about law, it is intended not only for lawyers, but equally for persons engaged in business or government confronted with the laws that govern economic activity across national frontiers. Moreover, though the book is not destined in the first instance for economists, increasingly economists have come to realize that the laws of economics are not the same as economic law, and that in the real world it is useful to understand the latter as well as the former. This volume undertakes to make this possible.

Finally, this book seeks to teach, not to preach. If there is a message in these pages, it is that everything is related to everything else—trade to investment to monetary affairs, dispute settlement to sanctions and to unilateral vs. collective action, economic law to 'public international law' and to 'private international law'. These fields are not separately treated here, but it is worth keeping in mind that international economic law influences, and is influenced by, both of these fields, and that the boundaries between them are invevitably blurred. It is useful for students of the international economic system—and for the participants—to see the forest as well as the trees. While it is not expected that everyone (or indeed anyone) will want to read the book from cover to cover, the book is designed not primarily as a work of reference but rather as an integrated whole. The hope here is that the text will illuminate some of the forests as well as some of the trees.

A.F.L.

Acknowledgements

When the editors of the Oxford University Press first came to me with the proposal for a treatise on International Economic Law, I thought the task was too big for any one person. I turned to a brilliant younger scholar, Professor David W. Leebron (as he then was) to be co-author, and we planned out the book together and provisionally divided up the tasks. To my regret, Professor Leebron turned to administration, became Dean of the Columbia University School of Law, and eventually felt obliged to withdraw from the project. This not only lengthened the time required to complete the book, but deprived the end-product of many insights and much knowledge. Nevertheless, Dean Leebron's contributions, though not separately identified, are gratefully acknowledged. If the time ever comes when he is no longer Dean, and revision of this book is called for, the invitation to return to the project remains open.

My colleague and friend Professor Eleanor M. Fox graciously contributed a chapter on the place of competition law in International Economic Law, a field in which she has been not only a commentator but an energetic pioneer.

In a real sense, all my students over more than three decades contributed to my understanding of the subjects here treated. Jonathan Filas, Alexia Herwig, John W. Konstant, Bruce Price, and Miranda Stewart helped with research and also read drafts of particular chapters and made valuable suggestions. My colleagues Professor Rochelle Cooper Dreyfuss, Philippe Sands, and Richard B. Stewart were kind enough to read sections of the book about which they know much more than I do. The New York University Law Library, and in particular Elizabeth Evans, Radu Popa, Jeanne Rehberg, and Mirela Roznovschi, were indispensable not only in finding source material, but in patiently guiding me into the modern world of data retrieval. The writing would never have resulted in a book without the patient work of my secretaries, first W. Lee Baer and later Mary Edster. Last but not least, I acknowledge with thanks the support of the Filomen d'Agostino and Max E. Greenberg Research Fund at New York University Law School, which supported my work over more summers than I had any right to expect.

A.F.L.

Summary Table of Contents

Part VI. International Investment

Part VII. The International Monetary System

Part VIII. Economic Controls for Political Ends

Contents

Part IV. The Rules of International Trade in Detail

Part V. Beyond the World Trade Organization

Table of Cases

GATT AND WTO CASES

INTERNATIONAL COURT OF JUSTICE CASES

UNITED KINGDOM CASES

UNITED STATES CASES

EUROPEAN COMMUNITY CASES

MISCELLANEOUS NATIONAL COURT CASES

INTERNATIONAL ARBITRAL AWARDS

Ad Hoc Arbitrations

Iran–US Claims Tribunal Cases

Table of International Agreements

INTERNATIONAL TREATIES AND AGREEMENTS

Table of Statutes and Regulations

UNITED KINGDOM STATUTES

UNITED STATES STATUTES

LEGISLATION OF OTHER STATES

ARGENTINA

AUSTRALIA

CANADA

PART I
International Economic Law

1

Economic Law and the Laws of Economics

1.1   INTRODUCTION

If international economic law is not necessarily congruent with the laws of international economics, it is nevertheless true that economics—knowledge, faith, skepticism included—has had a strong influence on the shape and evolution of the international law of international trade, investment, and financial transactions. Indeed, the General Agreement on Tariffs and Trade, which forms much of the foundation for the subjects addressed in this volume, is clearly based on the perception that international trade is beneficial, that the gains to society from trade outweigh the losses to those who are hurt by competition from abroad, and that value is created through specialization and exchange in open markets. It is this perception that leads to the overriding principle of the GATT/WTO system that barriers to trade imposed by government should be subjected to international discipline, and that regular procedures should be established looking to reduction or elimination of such barriers.

In short, the doctrine of comparative advantage has informed, if not quite dominated, the GATT since its creation in the early post-war years, and has sustained that fragile enterprise for half a century, climaxed by establishment of the World Trade Organization in 1994.[1] But the doctrine of comparative advantage is not self-evident, and doubts about its validity, as well as about its political sustainability, have also informed the GATT, as well as the behaviour of its member states.[2] It seems useful therefore to begin this

[1] See Ch. 5.

[2] Jacob Viner, one of America's leading economists a generation ago, wrote in mid-century:

The contrast is striking between the almost undisputed sway which the protectionist doctrine has over the minds of statesmen and its almost complete failure to receive credentials

volume with a brief exegesis of the theory of comparative advantage, not with a view to making a contribution to the literature of economics, but as an introduction for those readers not schooled in that subject and as background to the detailed exploration of tariffs and quotas, subsidies and dumping, non-discrimination and preferences that make up the public law of international trade.

1.2   A First Look at Comparative Advantage

We may begin, as Adam Smith did, with the analogy of a state to a household. Smith wrote:

It is the maxim of every prudent master of a family, never to attempt to make at home what it will cost him more to make than to buy. The tailor does not attempt to make his own shoes, but buys them of the shoemaker. The shoemaker does not attempt to make his own clothes, but employs a tailor. The farmer attempts to make neither the one nor the other, but employs those different artificers. All of them find it for their interest to employ their whole industry in a way in which they have some advantage over their neighbours, and to purchase with a part of its produce, or what is the same thing, with the price of a part of it, whatever else they have occasion for.

What is prudence in the conduct of every private family, can scarce be folly in that of a great kingdom. If a foreign country can supply us with a commodity cheaper than we ourselves can make it, better buy it of them with some part of the produce of our own industry, employed in a way in which we have some advantage. The general industry of the country, being always in proportion to the capital which employs it, will not thereby be diminished, no more than that of the above mentioned artificers; but only left to find out the way in which it can be employed with the greatest advantage. It is certainly not employed to the greatest advantage, when it is thus directed towards an object which it can buy cheaper than it can make.[3]

This statement is not yet comparative advantage, but is an important step toward the doctrine. It makes clear that if Patria is more efficient or productive (whether measured in unit labour cost, or dollars, or any other relevant commitment of resources) in a given industry (say farming) than

of intellectual respectability from the economists. The routine arguments of the protectionist politician differ somewhat from country to country . . .capturing their audiences in spite of—or perhaps by—the absence of any visible means of intellectual support. . . . They are fairly adequately disposed of in any one of a large number of elementary textbooks, and what importance they have is due mainly to the fact that the general public does not read economic textbooks. (Jacob Viner, 'The Tariff Question and the Economist', *International Economics: Studies*, ch. 6, p. 109 (1951))

While it is probably still true that the general public does not read economics textbooks, both of the major propositions stated by Viner—that politicians are typically protectionist and that economists are united in support of free trade—would need substantial qualifications at the start of the twenty-first century.

[3] Adam Smith, *The Wealth of Nations* 1776, Book IV, ch. 2, repr. Modern Library edn., 414 (1937).

Xandia, and Xandia is more efficient or productive in another industry (say weaving), and both countries have need of the product of both industries, Patria should specialize in one, Xandia in the other. Trade between the two countries in the two products will be beneficial (i.e. will conserve resources and create value) for both.

David Ricardo took the theory one major step further.[4] Even if Patria is more efficient at producing both wheat and cloth (or the tailor is more skilled at making shoes than the shoemaker), the critical question, as he showed, is the relative or comparative advantage in producing wheat vs. cloth in Patria, as compared to producing wheat vs. cloth in Xandia, or to come back to the simplest example, how much more efficiently the tailor can make suits than the shoemaker, compared with how much more efficiently the tailor can make shoes compared with the shoemaker. Even if the tailor performs both tasks with less commitment of resources than the shoemaker, Ricardo demonstrated, the tailor should concentrate on making suits, and buy the shoes he needs from the shoemaker.

> To take Ricardo's own example, suppose in England a gallon of wine costs 120 and a yard of cloth 100 units of work, while in Portugal a gallon of wine costs 80 units and a yard of cloth costs 90 units. Portugal has an *absolute cost advantage* in both wine and cloth; but England has a *comparative advantage* in cloth, since the production of a yard of cloth in England involves giving up production of ⅚ (100/120) of a gallon of wine, whereas production of a yard of cloth in Portugal involves giving up 1⅛ (90/80) of a gallon of wine. Assuming constant costs, prices accurately reflecting costs, and ignoring transport and handling, a price of cloth anywhere between ⅚ and 1⅛ of the price of wine would make it profitable for Portugal to import cloth and export wine, and for England to export cloth and import wine. If the same amount of resources as before trade are committed, the output for the two countries will be both more wine and more cloth.[5]

1.3 SOME COMPLICATIONS

Ricardo's demonstration has retained its validity for almost two centuries as the starting point for analysis of the gains from trade, and in particular for distinguishing between *absolute advantage* which would compare, say, steel from Patria with steel from Xandia without taking opportunity cost into

---

[4] David Ricardo, *The Principles of Political Economy and Taxation* (1817).

[5] Ricardo's discussion appears in ch. VII 'On Foreign Trade', 82–7 of the Everyman's Edition (repr. 1987). The presentation here follows the reformulation by Harry G. Johnson in the entry on 'International Trade: Theory', in the *Encyclopedia of the Social Sciences*, Vol. 4 (1968). The reformulation uses 'units of work' rather than hours of work, in order to get away from Ricardo's labour theory of value in favour of a more generalized opportunity cost of resources.

account, and *comparative advantage*, which compares ratios between two products in the two countries and leads to the analysis that even the country that is more efficient and productive in both products gains from specialization and trade.

It is evident, however, that Ricardo's illustration is a vast simplification. *First*, it assumes one homogeneous level of input (for Ricardo it was hours of labour) and perfect ability and willingness on the part of the units of input to shift from creating one product (wine in England, cloth in Portugal) to creating another (cloth in England, wine in Portugal). *Second*, it assumes two products and two countries—far from the real world. *Third*, it assumes constant costs and constant prices, also improbable over time. *Fourth*, it takes no account of variation within products, of the role of firms, and of the fact that increasingly the subjects of exchange are themselves combinations of ingredients from various sources.[6]

Numerous economists in the twentieth century have endeavored to refine and build on the Ricardo model. The best-known model, developed by two Swedish economists, Eli Hekscher and Bertil Ohlin, focused on differences in endowment among countries in the several factors of production. The Hekscher–Ohlin model[7] also works with two countries, two products, and assumes a perfectly competitive economy, as well as constant returns to scale, but looks at two factors of production, say K (for capital) and L (for labour). Hekscher–Ohlin predicts that each country will export the product that uses its relatively abundant factor more intensively. Thus if Patria is comparatively better endowed with K, it will export K-intensive products, and will import products that call for a greater proportion for input of L, in which Patria is comparatively less endowed than, say Xandia. By 'well endowed', Hekscher–Ohlin means that the country in question has a higher ratio of the factor in question to other factors than other countries do; by 'factor- intensive' product, Hekscher–Ohlin means a product whose costs in the country in question of the factor focused on are a greater share of its value than they are of the value of other products.

Thus cloth, for instance would be labor-intensive, wheat land-intensive. A country such as the United States, with relatively larger land supply compared to the rest of the world than labor supply compared to the rest of the world, ought to export land-intensive products such as wheat, and import labor-intensive products such as cloth. In conditions of trade, the land-intensive country has a comparative advantage in wheat, the labor-intensive country, a comparative advantage in cloth, and trade benefits both.

---

   [6] It also assumes, like the other models discussed in this chapter, a single invariable currency. For more on this subject, see Ch. 2.

   [7] See Eli Hekscher, 'The Effects of Foreign Trade on the Distribution of Income' (1919), English translation in *Readings in the Theory of International Trade* (H. S. Ellis and L. M. Metzler (eds.), 1949); Bertil Ohlin, *Interregional and International Trade* (1933). See also Paul H. Samuelson, 'International Trade and the Equalization of Factor Prices', 58 *Economic Journal* 163 (1948) and later writings by Samuelson.

Hekscher–Ohlin pushes the analysis further, suggesting that trade will tend to equalize product prices and eventually factor prices, with the conditions of trade determined by relative factor endowments and factor intensities. Of course focusing on land and labour (or even on one or two additional factors of production) conceals differences among different areas of land, and among different classes of labour—skilled, semi-skilled and unskilled, plus scientists, engineers, and managers, and among different skills as well. As in the Ricardian model, it assumes mobility of factors of production, so that clothmakers will become wheat farmers and less productive farmland will be used to locate factories.

1.4   From Economic Theory to Policy, Politics, and Law

At some level, most persons who have thought about policy or politics in connection with international trade accept the theory sketched in the preceding pages, even when attempts to prove the various formulations of the propositions stated are only partly successful. Compare Professor Paul Samuelson's famous dictum:

There is essentially only one argument for free trade or freer trade, but it is an exceedingly powerful one, namely: Free trade promotes a mutually profitable division of labor, greatly enhances the potential real national product for all nations, and makes possible higher standards of living all over the globe.[8]

But the theory of comparative advantage has never been wholly satisfying. One major shortcoming, even when expanded beyond the two-country, two-product, two-factor model, is that it would lead to the expectation that countries with similar levels of economic development would trade little with each other, apart from goods directly linked to geography, such as the products of agriculture or mining. In fact, industrial countries trade in great volume with one another, often in the same sector and products. Of course the preceding sentence, though it may reflect annual or monthly statistics, is seriously misleading: with some (diminishing) exceptions, countries do not engage in trade, firms do, and firms differ from one another not only in the classical factors—labour, land, and capital—but in such factors as marketing, management, and innovation, plus economies of scale. Also, the rise of multinational enterprises has led to vast amounts of trade among affiliated firms in different countries, and to international investment as an alternative and supplement to trade, to a degree wholly unforeseen by the economists who developed and explored theories of international trade.

Perhaps a more serious concern for policy-makers has been that while the theory of comparative advantage predicts, with fair accuracy, that global

[8] Paul A. Samuelson, *Economics*, p. 692 (10th edn., 1976).

welfare will be enhanced over time by expanded exchange of goods and services, it gives less assurance to individual countries and particularly to comparatively disadvantaged sectors within countries. In the long term, the answer is adjustment, that is commitment of factors of production to economic activity in which they are comparatively more advantaged; not all factors of production, however, are equally mobile, or equally patient. How to give some time for adjustment without creating permanent distortions is one of the themes of the law of international trade.[9]

Another matter of concern is the extent to which the factor endowments that make up comparative advantage can be altered by government intervention. For instance, if technical skill and innovation are important factors, may governments sponsor research and development targeted to particular industries? What about making university education free to students? Should other countries be permitted to counteract such efforts to alter comparative factor endowments?[10] More generally, is the teaching of the economists that trade must be free limited by a proviso that it must be fair? And if it is indeed *fair trade* to which countries are prepared to commit themselves, what is, and what is not fair?[11]

In short, economic theory, and statements such as the one quoted above from Samuelson, do not provide clear guidelines for international economic law. But it would be wrong to dismiss the theory as too abstract, too removed from the 'real world' to matter. In fact a good case can be made that most of the rules of international economic law have been developed against the backdrop of the theory of international trade, and of the question—sometimes explicit, at other times tacit—how far deviations from the theory should be allowed.

One significant factor—generally not considered in discussion of the theory of comparative advantage—has been omitted thus far—the role of money, exchange rates, and the balance of payments. This subject is addressed—again only by way of introduction, in Chapter 2.

---

[9] See in particular Ch. 5, Sect. 5.4 on Safeguards.   [10] See Ch. 9 on Subsidies.
[11] See, in particular, Ch. 10 on Dumping and Anti-Dumping.

2

Money, Exchange Rates, and the Balance of Payments

2.1 INTRODUCTION

Louis XIV and his advisers, Mazarin and Colbert, believed that a nation's wealth (and not incidentally its power) depended on its store of gold and silver. The way to increase that store would be to maximize exports paid for in hard currency, and to limit imports. The heritage of that belief, generally referred to as mercantilism, has survived, even when the theory has failed to withstand analysis. Nations still seek to promote exports and restrain imports by a variety of means, and when they lower barriers to imports, for instance by reducing tariffs, they think of such action as concessions. A brief introduction to the role of international exchange and payments is presented here, as a complement to the discussion of the theory of international trade introduced in Chapter 1. The legal rules of the international monetary system are discussed in Part VII.

2.2   THREE APPROACHES TO EXCHANGE RATES AND THE ADJUSTMENT PROCESS

(a)   The Gold Standard

It is perhaps easiest to understand the international system of payments by beginning with a description of the gold standard, though such a system existed only for short periods, and never in as complete a form as the textbook model suggests.

In a pure gold standard system, each national currency is defined in terms of a stated weight of gold, and thus stands in a fixed ratio to each other currency. If money were all specie (and disregarding the costs of smelting and recasting), a given number of pounds could be converted without loss of value into francs or dollars or roubles, and back again. Of course money was generally expressed in paper—i.e. in notes issued by national treasuries or central banks—and a more accurate description of the system would be a gold exchange standard—i.e. a system based on promises by the national treasury or central bank to exchange notes for gold at the proclaimed rate. The nation's gold supply need not be in a ratio of 1:1 with the amount of notes outstanding, but the understanding was that there was to be a fixed ratio of gold to currency in circulation.

For purposes of international exchange, the fixed ratio was to be maintained. Thus, for instance, when the value of the British pound was fixed at 1/4 ounce of gold, the US dollar at 1/20 ounce of gold, and say the French franc at 1/80 ounce of gold, one pound sterling would equal five US dollars, one US dollar would equal four French francs, and so on. Under this system, the demonstrations of Ricardo and those who came after him, as described in Chapter 1, could be carried out without distortion by substituting dollars or pounds for the abstract units of value in the model. Even if the workers in Portuguese vineyards are paid in escudos and the workers in English textile mills are paid in pounds, so long as both currencies represented a fixed weight of gold, their relation to each other could be easily calculated, and payment for each country's exports to the other could be made in either currency or in a third currency.

If an exporter of cloth from England was paid in escudos, he could exchange them at an English bank for gold or, more likely, for pounds. The Portuguese treasury or central bank was obligated at any given time or at the end of an accounting period to exchange the escudos held by foreigners for gold, or for the equivalent in a currency that the holder was willing to accept—e.g. pounds—because he knew that the issuer of that currency was willing and able to perform its promise to pay gold on demand.

If a country—Portugal in our example—were unable to make the exchange promised, the value, that is the external value, of the escudo would inevitably decline, to reflect the extent to which persons outside Portugal were now willing to hold escudos, or to accept payment in escudos for their goods or services. If Portugal declared that it would no longer offer one pound for 30 escudos but only, say, 18 shillings (or one pound for 33⅓ escudos), that would constitute a devaluation of the escudo. The effect on international trade would be that a given product, say a case of wine with a domestic value of 360 escudos, would now cost 10.8 pounds, instead of 12 pounds as before. If Portuguese wine competed in England with Spanish or Italian wine, the expectation would be that Portuguese wine would have gained an advantage; conversely, a Portuguese merchant considering the cost in his own currency of a purchase from abroad would find that £100 worth of cloth would now cost not 3000 escudos as before but 3333 escudos. The effect—expected and often intended—would be to discourage imports into Portugal in favour of purchase of local products.

The theory of the gold standard, however, went a significant step beyond this simple example. To return to the hypothetical countries Patria and Xandia, the theory, as developed first by the philosopher David Hume writing even before Adam Smith,[1] posited that if Patria exported more to Xandia than Xandia exported to Patria, then at the end of the year gold would flow out of Xandia and into Patria. As a result, since the money supply in Xandia depended on its store of gold, (i) Xandia's money supply would be reduced; (ii) it followed that prices and wages in Xandia would be reduced; (iii) imports by Xandia would be reduced because foreign goods had become more expensive in comparison with domestic goods; and (iv) exports from Xandia would increase, because its products had become relatively less expensive when expressed in foreign currency.

The opposite effects would be occurring in Patria—an increase in money supply, increase in prices and wages, increased imports and reduced exports. Hume argued that these processes would reverse the prior trend, and thus that the system was self-correcting, toward equilibrium. Accordingly, tariffs and similar restraints on international trade imposed by governments were unnecessary and counterproductive.

The pure gold standard had two major difficulties. For one thing, the downward shift in prices and wages in Xandia predicted by the theory often did not occur. Wages, in particular, are difficult to reduce. For another, governments were unlikely to pursue the hands-off policy assumed by the theory in the face of economic contraction, unemployment, and even depression in Xandia, and inflation in Patria. Typically, states imposed trade barriers and exchange controls, or devalued their currency rather than awaiting the results of the 'self-correcting mechanism'. To a considerable extent such intervention through changes in the exchange rate or restrictions on the use

---

[1] See David Hume, 'Of the Balance of Trade' (1752), in *Essays Moral, Political and Literary* (repr. Oxford 1963). Also in R. N. Cooper (ed.), *International Finance: Selected Readings*, ch. 1 (1969).

of foreign exchange had similar aims and similar effects as tariffs and import quotas. But whereas tariffs could be imposed to protect a given industry or sector, interference with the value or use of currencies tended to affect the entire economy of a nation, and perhaps several nations. It is worth adding while there were certain undertakings and conventions among central banks participating in the system (for instance about the purity of gold and about the exchange rates reflecting the declared values of the currencies), no international treaties or institutions restricted the actions of individual states in the field of finance in the age of the gold standard.[2]

The gold standard was never followed as regularly as would be required to test the theory of self-correction toward equilibrium, and the system, anchored by the British pound, collapsed with the onset of World War I. Traces of the system, however, survived or were re-established in the system put in place after World War I.

The period between World War I and World War II saw a largely unchecked and chaotic pattern of government intervention in the use of currencies across national frontiers. Only the United States, among major countries, maintained the promise to exchange its notes for a fixed quantity of gold, and that promise was substantially impaired when the United States changed the rate from $20 = 1 ounce to $35 = 1 ounce in 1934. Other countries adopted a variety of measures—often discriminatory—that were believed by the architects of the post-World War II system to have contributed to the causes of the war. It is not necessary in the present context to describe these measures, except to point out that one objective of the post-war system was to avoid such measures in the future. The post-war monetary system, therefore, was a system of rules, designed in significant part to prevent the unilateralism of the inter-war period.

(b)   Fixed Exchange Rates and the Bretton Woods Scheme

Following World War II, a different system was introduced by the victorious powers and eventually by almost every other country except the Soviet Union, the People's Republic of China, and some of their satellite states. The details of the system and its demise in the 1970s are described in Chapter 16. For this introduction, we focus only on the theory.

The nations that gathered at Bretton Woods, New Hampshire a year before the end of World War II to plan the post-war monetary system were concerned above all to avoid the monetary practices of the inter-war period. They insisted on a multilateral regulatory system with fixed exchange rates, pegged to the US dollar. Only the dollar was linked expressly to gold. All other member states of the International Monetary Fund were required to

---

[2] For a description of the relevant national statutes, particularly in Great Britain, see Kenneth W. Dam, *The Rules of the Game: Reform and Evolution in the International Monetary System*, ch. 2, esp. pp. 24–9 (1982).

define the rate of exchange of their national currency in terms of the dollar. Member states were forbidden to change the par value of their currency without approval of the IMF, and approval was to be given only in case of 'fundamental disequilibrium'.

As in the gold standard, if Patria held more Xandian crowns than it chose to hold, Xandia was obliged to redeem its crowns in return for Patrian pesos, or dollars, or other currencies acceptable to Patria. If Xandia did not have sufficient resources to redeem its crowns, it could draw on the resources of the IMF, on the basis of undertaking to adopt policies designed to return its balance of payments to equilibrium within a stated period. Furthermore, member states were prohibited from imposing multiple exchange rates or discriminatory practices, and (with important exceptions) from imposing exchange controls.

Thus the emphasis was on stability and equilibrium. States were encouraged (not to say required) to achieve equilibrium in their balance of payments, and not to rely on changes in exchange rates or on the supply of money to do so. From the point of view of commerce, fixed exchange rates were a great convenience: a typical export/import transaction had no (or very slight) risk of a change in the value of the currencies involved, and indeed it did not make much difference, so long as the system worked, whether a given transaction between Patria and Xandia was denominated in Patrian pesos or Xandian crowns or US dollars. As under the gold standard, the Ricardian model of comparative advantage discussed in Chapter 1 could be illustrated without distortion in terms of dollars, or pounds, or escudos, because each of these currencies, by definition and international agreement, bore a fixed relationship to each other's currency.

(c) Floating Exchange Rates

The system of fixed exchange rates with infrequent changes, as noted above, had significant advantages for persons engaged in commercial transactions, and (not incidentally) for the establishment and analysis of economic statistics. But by the end of the 1960s, it had become clear that the system of fixed exchange rates involved predictions about the relative growth of different countries and regions, predictions that were in practice impossible to make with any degree of accuracy. Furthermore, when changes in the value of major currencies did occur—notably the devaluation of the British pound in 1967—the shocks were too sharp, the disruptions too massive, to be tolerated in the long run.

Moreover, it became clear at about the same time that the system that had functioned relatively well for a quarter century (1946–71) depended increasingly on the willingness of certain creditor countries, particularly Japan and West Germany, to hold US dollars (line 22, Table III, page 17 infra), and that this willingness was wearing thin. The events that led to the demise of the Bretton Woods system and its partial reconstruction are set out in Chapters 16 and 17. For this introduction it is necessary only to describe in general terms a third monetary system, based neither on gold nor on par values, but (at least in theory) solely on market forces.

The basic concept is that governments no longer have an obligation to maintain their currencies at any particular value, and that there is no prearranged ratio between the value of any currency and any other. Of course such a system cannot function without an active market, and for many lightly traded currencies it proved more practical to be pegged to one of the major currencies—the dollar, the yen, the D-mark, the pound, and later certain baskets of currencies. But for the major currencies, the concept was to treat them like cotton or copper or coffee—with spot and futures markets and no fixed anchor. If the market pushed up Patrian pesos and pushed down Xandian crowns, the expectation—similar to the vision of Hume (Sect. 2.2(a) supra)—was that the consequences would be self-correcting, with Xandian goods and services becoming cheaper and therefore in greater demand, Patrian goods becoming more expensive in terms of Xandian (and other) currencies and therefore less in demand.

The market in currencies soon developed, not in a stock or commodities exchange, but in a system of electronic transfers among financial institutions linked by computers and almost instantaneous communications, largely free of governmental controls. It was also true that the need to achieve 'balance'—a feature and obligation of the fixed rate system—was not as pressing, as there was no longer an *obligation* to redeem one's currency held abroad. But the self-correcting mechanism predicted by the advocates of freely floating exchange rates did not develop, and indeed the market for currencies often showed patterns quite different from the pattern of movement of goods and services, of internal prices for comparable goods, of the flow of investment, or of the real growth of the economies of the issuing countries. On and off the major countries—alone or in coordinated moves—sought to intervene in the market, that is to participate as buyers or sellers to counter market movements deemed to be excessive when compared to underlying facts.

The European Community, disturbed at the distortions in commerce of the volatile exchange movements, attempted, with mediocre success, to establish a mini-Bretton Woods system, with fixed rates among the participants;[3] when the Community changed its name to the European Union in the Treaty of Maastricht in the early 1990s, the principal symbol of the 'union' was to be the common currency, which would bind all the member states—or all the participating member states—to a single monetary and fiscal policy and common interest rate, in the way that all the states of the United States are bound together by the dollar. After some delay, the common currency, named the *euro*, entered into effect as of 1 January 1999,

---

[3] See Ch. 20, Sects. 20.1–20.2.

with eleven (and later twelve) of the fifteen member states of the European Union as full participants. This meant that there could be no movement in the exchange rate among the currencies of the participating states, and indeed the separate currencies were eliminated in the early months of 2002. The euro itself floated against the dollar, the yen, and other currencies, including (as of year-end 2001) the British pound. Thus elements of both a fixed rate and a floating rate system seem likely to survive, with residual influences of the gold standard as well.

2.3   THE BALANCE OF PAYMENTS

The balance of payments, it is important to bear in mind, includes much more than the balance of trade as contemplated by David Hume, Adam Smith, and even, it appears the designers of the Bretton Woods system. The components of Patria's balance of payments include not only receipts for exports and expenditures for imports, but remittances for pensions, expenditures by troops stationed outside their own country, foreign assistance and credits, and investment across national frontiers, as well as dividends, interest, and royalties attributable to investments. Various versions of balance of payments accounting are discussed in economic literature, and changes of detail have been made in the way different countries account for their international transactions. For present purposes, the critical fact is that an outflow of funds on current account can be offset by an inflow of funds on capital accounts and vice versa.

(a)   Balance of Payments Accounting Illustrated

In highly stylized fashion, Patria's balance of payments for a given year might be presented as follows:

I. Current Account ($ million)	*Credit*	*Debit*	*Net*
Private transactions			
1. Merchandise	550	700	
2. Freight on merchandise	25	35	
3. Trade balance (lines 1 & 2)			−160
4. Travel expenditures	15	25	
5. Income on investments (interest & dividends)		40	
6. Remittances	15	4	
7. Miscellaneous services	30	66	
8. Balance on services			−75
9. Balance on goods & services (lines 3 & 8)			−235

I. Current Account ($ million)	Credit	Debit	Net
Governmental transactions			
10. Short-term loans	12	4	
11. Misc. receipts & repts.	5	7	
12. Current govt. trans.			+6
13. Balance on current acct. (lines 9 and 12)			–229

II. Capital account	Credit	Debit	Net
14. Direct private investment	20		
15. Private loans (long-term)	53	12	
16. Govt. bonds (long-term)	22	8	
17. Miscellaneous	4	7	
18. Loans received by govt. and Central Bank	145	20	
19. Balance on capital acct. (lines 14 to 18)			+197
20. Balance on Current and capital acct. (basic balance) (lines 13 and 19)			–32

Adapted from Paul Host-Madsen, *Balance of Payments, Its Meaning and Uses*, IMF Pamphlet Series No. 9 (1967).

One can draw a number of inferences from these figures, which would be still more accurate if some of the aggregates were broken down further. For instance we see that Patria has a merchant marine, but that it also patronizes foreign ships (line 2). It has substantial exports, but less than its imports. It has some private inward but no significant outward investments, and it receives substantial government credits.[4] Whether the statement represents a healthy economy or not cannot be told from a single year, but if the figures were compared with prior years and showed, for instance, a sharp increase in imports over the prior years, the government of Patria might consider taking steps to stimulate exports or reduce imports—steps that might run into restraints imposed by the GATT.[5]

The most important lesson, however, from the above figures is that a comparatively large deficit on current account is largely offset by the surplus on capital account. This phenomenon explains (at least in part) why Great Britain was able for many years to cope with its current account deficit by selling off its overseas investments and repatriating the proceeds, and why the United States throughout the 1970s to 1990s has been able to cope with

---

[4] In fact the model is based on Colombia in 1965.   [5] See Ch. 3.

a large deficit on current account by attracting both direct and portfolio investment, as well as sales of US government securities (lines 14–18). Other countries, for instance Japan, experienced the opposite phenomenon—with capital outflow offsetting surpluses on current account.

While current and capital accounts may largely offset one another, it is apparent from the figures presented that there is not a perfect equality between the current and the capital accounts. For accounting purposes, there is therefore a third, offsetting account. Continuing with the figures presented above, the account might look as follows:

III. Cash and Reserve Account	*Credit*	*Debit*	*Net*
21. Transfer of gold (export = credit)	8		
22. Foreign holdings of Patrian pesos (increase = credit)	24		
23. Patria holdings of foreign currency (increase = debit)	<u>7</u>		
24. Balance on cash and reserve account (lines 21 to 23)			<u>+39</u>
25. Errors and omissions		<u>–7</u>	
26. Balance (lines 20, 24, and 25)			0

Table III calls for some explanation. Line 21 is similar to the assumptions of David Hume. If Patria spends more than it takes in, it must transfer gold to redeem its pesos held abroad. But if its position is generally sound (and it is prepared to pay interest), foreign holders of Patrian pesos may not insist on redeeming them. In effect these foreign holders (public and private) are extending credit to Patria (line 22); conversely, reduction of Patrian holdings of foreign currencies (line 23) serves to offset the deficit in the basic balance. The fact that the accounts still do not balance—the ever-present entry of errors and omissions—may be attributable to unreported transactions, some criminal, such as the drug trade or arms smuggling or tax avoidance, and some simply not caught by the record keepers.

(b)   The Balance of Payments and the Bretton Woods Scheme

The balance of payments as presented here is consistent with the fixed exchange system as created at Bretton Woods. If the movements toward deficit in Patria's current and capital account reinforced rather than offsetting each other, the system stood ready to help. As set out in detail in Chapter 16, the international community was prepared to help by exchanging reserve currencies for Patrian pesos, thus extending credit to Patria—usually on medium term (lines 18 and 22). If that strategy failed, but only if it failed, were more radical steps, that is a change in the value of the Patrian peso, supposed to take place. Overall, the assumption of the Bretton Woods fixed exchange rate system was that member states were to aim for equilibrium, that is to keep the entries shown on Table III as small as possible. Whether the obligation to strive for equilibrium applied equally to countries with a surplus in their basic balance (line 20) became an important issue—but only ambiguously part of a rule of law—in the 1970s.[6]

2.4   Some Preliminary Observations

Two observations may usefully conclude this introductory part, prior to plunging into the legal descriptions and analysis that occupy the bulk of this volume.

First, money—including foreign exchange—has turned out to be not only a medium of exchange and a storehouse of value, but an investment asset, with auctions, futures markets, derivative and index trading, and other traits that one would not associate with a unit of account. Each international transaction, public or private, is to some extent involved with exchange risk; statistics over time are less reliable than they once were; and governments are less able than they once were to govern the outcome of international transactions.

Second, in 1950 or 1965 the institutions created in the wake of World War II devoted to international finance—the International Monetary Fund and the World Bank—seemed strong not only as resource bases but as sources of law, while the agreement on trade issues—the GATT—seemed vulnerable, without a full-fledged institution, with an incomplete membership, and with a legal structure both fragile and ambiguous. At the beginning of the twenty-first century the situation is the reverse. The International Monetary Fund no longer administers a code of conduct applicable to the major developed states, while the GATT has grown into the World Trade Organization, with enforcement powers, almost universal membership, and an agenda that has expanded well beyond trade in goods, to include services, investment, intellectual property, and perhaps competition law and the environment as well.

It seems that micromanagement, particular laws for particular problems, is becoming more sophisticated, and more representative of consensus; macromanagement—that is taming the laws of economics into economic law by treaty—no longer holds the appeal that it did at the close of World War II.

---

[6] See Ch. 17.

PART II
The GATT/WTO System

3

The General Agreement on Tariffs and Trade: Origins and Overview

3.1 THE ANTECEDENTS

The modern law of international trade may fairly be described as a product of World War II, or to be more precise, of the perceptions of the Allied planners of the post-war world. While the details do not fully conform to the general perceptions, the architects of the post-war settlement saw the nineteenth century as a time of relatively open trade, and of peace, in contrast to the first half of the twentieth century, a time of high tariffs, discriminatory economic arrangements, import quotas, unilateralism and bilateralism—plus a global depression and barely two decades between two devastating world wars. As with other aspects of post-war planning—the creation of the United Nations, the trial of war criminals, the exaction of reparations—there was a determination not to repeat the mistakes following World War I.[1]

In the trade field, this determination called for a regime of non-discrimination—i.e. a generally applicable regime of most-favoured-nation treatment, a prohibition of quantitative restrictions, and a commitment to reduction of trade barriers and opening of markets. Moreover, there was a perception among the post-war planners, led by Churchill and Roosevelt, that the failure of the United States to join the League of Nations and the failure of the League itself had been a disaster, and that the prospects for peace and prosperity were linked to establishment of multilateral (if possible universal) organizations that could serve both as a forum for negotiations and as a guardian of the rules. Agreement on the creation of two such organizations, the International Monetary Fund and the World Bank, was reached as early as July 1944 at Bretton Woods;[2] agreement on creating an International Civil Aviation Organization was reached in Chicago in December 1944.[3] Agreement on the United Nations Charter was reached in San Francisco in April 1945. The effort to reach agreement on a trade organization only came later, as described below, but there is no doubt that the post-war planners at all times had in mind the creation of such an organization.[4]

Discussions on trade took place between officials of the United Kingdom and the United States from 1943 on. As with regard to international financial relations, it was always understood that the objectives were a set of rules applicable to all states, and an organization to develop and administer those rules.[5] The details remained to be filled in, and there were some real differences

---

[1] Perhaps the first important example of planning for the end of the war was the Atlantic Charter, signed by President Roosevelt and Prime Minister Churchill aboard an American cruiser near Newfoundland in August 1941, four months before the United States entered the war and indeed while the outcome of the war was still in doubt. The President and the Prime Minister, making known 'certain common principles . . . on which they base their hopes for a better future for the world,' wrote:

> Fourth, they will endeavor with due respect for their existing obligations, to further the enjoyment by all states, great or small, victor or vanquished, of access on equal terms, to the trade and to the raw materials of the world which are needed for their economic prosperity.

Roosevelt sought to insert the words 'without discrimination and on equal terms' in Churchill's draft. Churchill resisted, on the basis that these words might call in question the Imperial (or Commonwealth) Preferences, and the phrase 'with due respect for their existing obligations' resolved the issue. See Winston S. Churchill, *The Second World War*: Vol. III, *The Grand Alliance*, 433–44 (1950).

[2] See Ch. 16.

[3] See e.g. A. Lowenfeld, *Aviation Law*, Ch. 2, § 1.12; Ch. 6, § 6.12 (2nd edn., 1981).

[4] See e.g. Clair Wilcox, *A Charter for World Trade*, pp. 37–41 (1949, repr. 1972).

[5] It is striking, and to some extent puzzling, that different negotiators at different times focused on the trade issues and on the financial issues. Possibly the explanation is that both in the United Kingdom and in the United States, different officials were responsible for the Treasury from those charged with Trade and Commerce, and they answered to different constituencies, in and out of government.

between the British and American priorities.[6] The basic assumptions, however, were clear. Trade across national frontiers was to be encouraged; it was to be conducted primarily by private firms, not by state enterprises; and government intervention was to be subject to a code of conduct designed to limit interference with the movement of goods. These assumptions have remained the essential premises for the law of international trade ever since.

3.2   THE BIRTH OF GATT: ALMOST BY ACCIDENT[7]

In November 1945, the United States government issued a document entitled 'Proposals for Expansion of World Trade and Employment' for consideration by an International Conference on Trade and Employment, purporting to represent a consensus resulting from the United States–United Kingdom discussions over the preceding two years.[8] The *Proposals* called for a detailed charter or code of conduct relating to governmental restraints on international trade, and for creation of an International Trade Organization. The proposed code affirmed the principle of unconditional most-favored-nation treatment and the prohibition of quantitative restrictions (subject to several exceptions including agriculture). It also dealt in principle with limitations on subsidies, conforming state trading to market conditions, prevention of cartels, limited resort to commodity agreements, and it contemplated exceptions for countries with balance of payments difficulties. There was no explicit mention of economic development. As for the proposed International Trade Organization, it was to administer the code, to provide a forum for settlement of disputes, and to perform related functions such as collection and dissemination of trade statistics and preparation of guidelines for customs valuation.

---

[6] One major area of controversy concerned the future of the system of Imperial or Commonwealth preferences created in the early 1930s. In accordance with the Ottawa agreements of August 20, 1932, 135 *British and Foreign State Papers* 151 (1932), the United Kingdom had raised its duties on some raw materials originating outside the Empire and Commonwealth, in return for preferences in the participant countries for manufactured products originating in the United Kingdom. See e.g. Howard P. Whidden, Jr., *Preferences and Discrimination in International Trade* (Comm. on Int'l Econ. Policy 1945). Eventually the preferences were preserved, but frozen, in GATT Article I(2)(a) and (4), Article XIV(5)(b), and Annex A.

[7] For two contemporaneous accounts of the events here described, see Clair Wilcox, *A Charter for World Trade* (1949, repr. 1972); William Adams Brown, *The United States and the Restoration of World Trade* (1950). For later accounts, see Gerard Curzon, *Multilateral Commercial Diplomacy* (1965); Richard N. Gardner, *Sterling-Dollar Diplomacy: The Origins and the Prospects of Our International Economic Order* (2nd edn., 1969, repr. 1980); Robert E. Hudec, *The GATT Legal System and World Trade Diplomacy*, Pt. I (2nd edn., 1990); John H. Jackson, *World Trade and the Law of GATT*, ch. 2 (1969).

[8] US Dept. of State Press Release of 6 Dec. 1945, 13 *Dept. State Bull.* 912–29 (1945); US Dept. of State, *Commercial Policy Series* 79, Publ. 2411 (1945).

A few days after issuing the *Proposals* looking to long-term arrangements, the United States issued an invitation to fifteen countries to enter into negotiations looking to early conclusion of a multilateral trade agreement.[9] Every invited country except the Soviet Union accepted the invitation. Eventually this initiative turned out to have long-term consequences, while the long-term initiative failed to survive.

The proposal for an International Conference on Trade and Employment was taken up by the United Nations Economic Council at its first meeting in Paris in February 1946;[10] in accordance with a resolution introduced by the United States, ECOSOC appointed a Preparatory Committee of 19 countries to draft the document to be considered at such a conference. The Preparatory Committee met in London in October–November 1946, working from a Suggested Charter drafted by the United States. A first draft of a Charter for an International Trade Organization was produced at the London meeting, and a second draft was produced by a technical drafting committee that met in January–February 1947 at the temporary seat of the United Nations in Lake Success, New York. The full Preparatory Committee met again in Geneva from April to August 1947 and produced a third draft, which became the basis for a Plenary Conference on Trade and Development convened by the United Nations in Havana in November 1947.

At the same time as these negotiating and drafting sessions were in progress, representatives of the countries that had been invited by the United States to negotiate a trade agreement,[11] plus eight others that had been invited subsequently, were engaged in a tariff-cutting negotiation. Typically the negotiations were one-on-one sessions focusing on products for which one side was an important market and the other side was the principal supplier, with concessions on such products 'paid for' by concessions in which the roles were reversed. A total of 123 sets of such negotiations took place in Geneva in the period April–October 1947 among 23 countries, including 22 involving the United States (i.e. one with each potential negotiating partner) and 101 between other pairs of countries. Altogether more than a thousand meetings were held over a period of six months, considering some 50,000 items of trade. As to some of the products, substantial reductions were negotiated; on others, low rates of duties or duty-free entry were made subject to binding obligations.[12]

---

[9] US Dept. of State Press Release 13 Dec. 1945, 13 *Dept. State Bull.* 970 (1945). The countries invited were the United Kingdom, the Soviet Union, France and China; also Canada, Australia, New Zealand, South Africa and India; The Netherlands, Belgium, Luxembourg, and Czechoslovakia; and Brazil and Cuba.

[10] The Economic and Social Council is a 'principal organ' of the United Nations, consisting of 27 members of the United Nations elected by the General Assembly. See UN Charter Articles 7(1) and 61–72. As it turned out, ECOSOC has subsequently played no significant role in international economic relations. ECOSOC has had significant roles in the 'social' aspects of its mission, particularly in the area of human rights.

[11] See n. 9 supra.

[12] See e.g. Clair Wilcox, *A Charter for World Trade*, pp. 46–7 (1949, repr. 1972).

Apart from the details, these negotiations had several consequences still significant more than half a century later. *First*, it seems clear that the pace and volume of the negotiations could not have been maintained had they not been held all at the same time and (figuratively speaking) all in the same room, spurred on by a United States statute that gave the executive branch negotiating authority but was due to expire in June of 1948.[13] The Geneva negotiations of 1947 set the precedent for subsequent 'Rounds'—eight in all as of year-end 1999—that played a major part in the development of international trade law in the second half of the twentieth century. *Second*, as was understood from the initial invitation, all the 'concessions', i.e. the negotiated reductions and bindings with respect to tariffs, were generalized to all the participants, in implementation of the most-favoured-nation principle. *Third*, the concessions were recorded in a single document—the General Agreement on Tariffs and Trade, which not only comprised the schedules of tariff bindings but contained a code of conduct designed to safeguard, at least provisionally, the undertakings given and to commit the participants to a common (if incomplete) standard of behaviour with respect to international trade. Since the countries participating in the tariff negotiations were for the most part the same ones participating—in the same city—in the preparation of the proposed charter for the International Trade Organization, the code of conduct largely paralleled the commercial policy sections of the draft of the ITO Charter as it then stood. The General Agreement was opened for signature on October 30, 1947, and entered into effect—provisionally—on January 1, 1948.

Meanwhile, the Havana Conference on Trade and Employment opened on November 21, 1947, with more than twice as many participants as had negotiated at Geneva, and with an agenda that included employment, economic development, restrictive business practices, commodity agreements, as well as trade (labeled 'commercial policy') and an elaborate structure for the International Trade Organization. After much debate and acrimony, the Final Act of the Havana Conference embodying the ITO Charter, was signed on March 24, 1948 on behalf of 53 states. For various reasons, however, the ITO Charter never entered into effect. Most governments waited for the United States before beginning their own ratification procedures, and the United States Congress showed little enthusiasm for the ITO. For some, the ITO charter was too favourable to state intervention in the economy, for others it was too favourable to free trade, and for still others the creation of yet another international organization clashed with the disillusion setting in about the United Nations, as well as about some of the other organizations established at the end of the war. The United States administration was itself ambivalent about the ITO, at least to the extent that support for the Havana Charter might impair support for higher-priority issues of foreign affairs

---

[13] See US: Trade Agreements Extension Act of 1945, 59 Stat. 410, July 5, 1945.

such as the Marshall Plan for the reconstruction of Europe, the establishment of a program of controls on the export of strategic materials,[14] and (from the summer of 1950 on) pursuit of the war in Korea. In December 1950, the US State Department issued a press release announcing that the proposed Charter would not be resubmitted to the new Congress.[15] The ITO was never formally rejected, but it faded away.[16] What remained was the GATT, essentially as drafted as an interim arrangement in the summer of 1947, with some rectifications agreed to at Havana or just after the close of the Havana Conference. GATT 1947, conceived as a provisional agreement not requiring parliamentary approval, remained in effect from January 1948 to January 1995. When a World Trade Organization was eventually established almost half a century later, as described in Chapter 4, GATT 1947 remained the basic text and the point of departure for the new agreements embodied in the WTO.

3.3   AN OVERVIEW OF THE GATT

(a)   The Architecture

The architecture of the General Agreement was dictated by the problem of ratification (or rather the effort to get around the need for formal ratification), particularly by the United States. The Reciprocal Trade Agreements Act of 1934,[17] as amended and extended most recently in July 1945,[18] delegated to the President authority to negotiate and implement 'trade agreements', i.e. modifications in tariffs, but did not authorize changes in substantive law, which would have to be submitted to Congress. Since the object was to achieve effectiveness of the duty reductions being negotiated before expiration of the delegated authority, the General Agreement was designed so as to avoid having to submit it to the US Congress, as well as to other parliaments that might well have concerns about substantive changes in the respective national laws concerning international trade.

The solution had three aspects. *First*, in place of a Final Act that normally records the undertakings at the close of a law-making international conference, the signatory states signed a Protocol of *Provisional* Application, the idea being that definitive application, with formal ratification, would be

---

[14]   See A. Lowenfeld, *Trade Controls for Political Ends*, ch. I (2nd edn. (1983)).

[15]   State Dept. Press Release 6 Dec. 1950, 23 *Dept. State Bull.* 977 (1950).

[16]   For an account of the fate of the ITO in the United States, including discussion of the reasons for lack of support by groups that might have been expected to favour it, see William Diebold, Jr., 'The End of the I.T.O.,' *Princeton Essays in International Finance* No. 16 (1952). See also Gardner (n. 7 supra), pp. 348–80.

[17]   48 Stat. 943, approved June 12, 1934.

[18]   An Act to Extend the Authority of the President under Sect. 350 of the Tariff Act of 1930 and for Other Purposes, 59 Stat. 410 (5 July 1945).

directed to the forthcoming Charter of the ITO. This technique had been used in other contexts that called for prompt action before the full ratification process had been completed, for instance in the creation of a Provisional International Civil Aviation Organization (PICAO) by the Chicago Conference of 1944, to last until the convention creating a permanent organization—ICAO—was ratified by the requisite number of states.[19] In the case of civil aviation, the period of provisional application of the convention lasted just over two years; in the case of international trade, the period of 'provisional application' of the principal agreement lasted for 47 years.

Second, the Protocol of Provisional Application bound the signatories to apply Parts I and III of the General Agreement without reservation, but Part II only 'to the fullest extent not inconsistent with existing legislation.'[20] Part I contained the most basic provisions—most-favored-nation treatment (Art. I) and binding of scheduled concessions (Art. II); Part III contained 'procedural provisions', though following several amendments in the early years of the GATT, some of these, notably those concerned with customs unions and free trade areas (Art. XXIV), with waivers (Art. XXV(5)), and with tariff negotiations (Art. XXVIII*bis*), became highly significant. Part II contained most of the substantive provisions of the code of conduct—about national treatment with respect to internal taxation and regulation (Art. III), about anti-dumping and countervailing duties (Art. VI), about valuation for customs purposes (Art. VII), about quantitative restrictions (Art. XI), about measures to safeguard the balance of payments (Arts. XII–XV), and about subsidies (Art. XVI)—important elements in the emerging law of international trade, but subject to a giant 'grandfather clause' which provided that national measures inconsistent with the GATT provision were not unlawful if they were required by legislation existing as of October 30, 1947 for the original members, and as of the date of of accession for states that joined later.[21]

Third, the GATT was established without any text that looked as if an organization was being created. Of course if the Agreement were to last any appreciable time, there would be some need for collective action—to call meetings, to grant waivers, to hire staff, and to conduct formal or informal dispute settlement. All of these functions were assigned (explicitly or by default) to the CONTRACTING PARTIES, written in capital letters, as contrasted

---

[19] See Interim Agreement on International Civil Aviation, repr. in *Proceedings of the International Civil Aviation Conference*, Chicago, Vol. I, pp. 132–46 (US Dept. of State 1948).

[20] Part IV of the GATT, concerned with economic development, was not drafted until the 1960s, and was opened for signature in February 1965. It entered into force—provisionally—on June 17, 1966.

[21] See John H. Jackson, *World Trade and the Law GATT*, §4.10 (1969) for confirmation both as to the effective date and of the use in the text of the term 'required', in contrast to 'authorized'. For the origin and meaning of the term 'grandfather clause' see Sect. 3.4(b), note 39 infra.

with 'contracting parties' in small letters when referring to some or all of the state parties to the General Agreement.[22]

As it turned out, the founders of the GATT proved to be sufficiently agile to keep the organization alive despite its structural shortcomings. Indeed, the early growth of the GATT to some extent took the wind out of the sails of those who were pushing for the ITO in the late 1940s. Likewise when the United Nations created the UN Conference on Trade and Development (UNCTAD) in the 1960s, that body did not succeed in replacing GATT as the principal international organization concerned with trade. Not until completion of the Uruguay Round in 1994 did the GATT officially become a permanent organization, with a new name, similar to, but not quite the same as the organization that was stillborn in the 1940s.

(b)   The Major Principles[23]

The brief Preamble to the GATT looks to raising standards of living, ensuring full employment and a 'large and steadily growing volume of real income and effective demand', by expanding the production and exchange of goods. The participating states aim to accomplish these goals by entering into

reciprocal and mutually advantageous arrangements directed to the substantial reduction of tariffs and other barriers to trade, and to the elimination of discriminatory treatment in international commerce.

Thus:

(1)   *Universal MFN. Trade should be conducted on the basis of non-discrimination*, that is, all contracting parties undertake in Article I the obligation to apply duties and similar charges on the import of goods equally, without regard, as among contracting parties, to the origin of the goods.[24]

(2)   *No Increased Trade Barriers. Governmental restraints on the movement of goods should be kept to a minimum, and if changed, should be reduced, not increased.* All contracting parties undertake in Article II to apply to all other contracting parties the duties set forth in the Schedules submitted at the close of the tariff negotiations, i.e. to bind the accepted offers reflected in these schedules. Bound duties may be unbound every three

---

[22] The term 'member states' was also avoided, again because that term would have given the impression that an organization had been created.

[23] Though the GATT as negotiated in 1947–8 has been superseded by GATT 1994, as described in Ch. 4, the latter document is virtually the same as the original agreement, and thus it makes sense to describe the major obligations in the present tense. Of course, many of the obligations were explained and developed further in the ensuing decades, as discussed in subsequent chapters.

[24] Note that throughout this discussion, and of the GATT through 1994, the focus is solely on *goods*. Services and intellectual property did not enter into the discussion until the Uruguay Round, 1986–94, as described in Ch. 4.

years, but the balance of concessions is to be maintained, either by agreement with the original beneficiary of the concession or other principal supplier, or subject to reciprocal withdrawal of concessions by the beneficiary.[25]

(3) *Tariffs Only. The accepted form of trade restraint is the customs tariff,* i.e. a tax imposed by the importing state as a condition of importation of goods into its territory. The unstated assumption has always been that though the importer pays the tariff, the foreign producer/exporter bears the burden, in reduced market for its product in competition with producers in the importing country, or in reduced profit from sales in that country. Tariffs are generally easy to understand (compared, for instance with license schemes), and are suitable for negotiation with other contracting parties. In principle, tariffs are to be formulated as a percentage of the value of the goods imported—the so-called *ad valorem* tariff; specific tariffs, i.e. tariffs imposed per unit or other measure—10 cents per pair of shoes, or 5 pesetas per metre of cloth—are not excluded;[26] other bases of setting tariffs, for instance measured by the value of competing products of domestic origin, are prohibited (Art. VII).[27] Most important—and most controversial—other forms of governmental restraints on trade, in particular quantitative restrictions (quotas) on imports and exports and licensing schemes are expressly prohibited, subject, like much of the GATT, to numerous exceptions (Art XI).[28]

(4) *National Treatment. Internal taxes, charges, and other regulations must not be imposed so as to discriminate between domestically produced and imported products.* States are not disabled from imposing sales or consumption taxes, or regulatory and labeling requirements on imported goods; but neither in motive nor in effect may there be a distinction between the burden borne by imported goods and the burden borne by domestic goods. There are exceptions to this, as to other principles, and a good many nuances, but the objective is clear, and was insisted on by the United States

---

[25] See para. (5) infra.

[26] Combinations of specific and *ad valorem* tariffs—e.g. 25 pence per pound plus 10 percent *ad valorem*—are also not excluded.

[27] Still other forms of import duties, such as the variable levies imposed by the European Economic Community on agricultural imports, measured by the difference between the landed price and a target price set by the Community, were apparently not thought of when the GATT was drafted, and are thus neither expressly permitted nor expressly prohibited.

[28] Clair Wilcox, the principal trade negotiator for the United States in the period 1945–50, wrote in 1949:

Quantitative restrictions present the major issue of commercial policy. . . . If uncontrolled, they promise to become universal and permanent. Freedom to employ them is not readily to be surrendered. The proposal that this freedom be limited evoked a debate that went on for many months. The toughest problem in the trade negotiations came to be known by its initials: Q.R. It would not be inaccurate to describe the meetings at London, Geneva, and Havana as the United Nations Conferences on Q.R. (*A Charter for World Trade*, p. 82 (1949, repr. 1972))

at Havana over substantial objection. Together with principle (1) and (3), the national treatment principle establishes the emphasis on tariffs as the sole accepted instrument of trade protection, and the commitment against discriminatory treatment of goods based on their country of origin. It is worth pointing out that the national treatment provision applies not only to goods on which tariffs have been bound in GATT schedules, as many states advocated in Geneva and Havana,[29] but to all goods.

(5) *Regular Negotiations. Contracting parties are to meet regularly to engage in negotiations looking to lower trade barriers on the basis of reciprocity within a multilateral framework* (Art. XXVIII*bis*). Since the GATT was originally expected to be folded into and succeeded by the Charter of the International Trade Organization, the article calling for negotiations directed to the 'Substantial reduction of the general level of tariffs . . . from time to time' was not introduced into the text of the General Agreement until a Review Session held in Geneva in 1954–5. In the mean time two other rounds of multilateral negotiations had been held,[30] in connection with the accession of additional contracting parties. The GATT text does not prescribe a specific interval between the 'rounds' of multilateral trade negotiations, nor the duration of these rounds. Moreover, there has been a substantial expansion in the subject matter considered in successive rounds—eight altogether from 1947 to 1994.[31] An attempt to launch a ninth round (the 'Millennium Round') did not succeed in Seattle in November 1999, but a decision to launch a new round of trade negotiations was approved at a Ministerial Conference held at Doha, Qatar in November 2001.[32] There is no doubt that the periodic convening of the contracting parties of GATT for detailed negotiation of the conditions of international trade has become a fundamental ingredient of the law of international trade.

3.4   A First Look at the Qualifications

If one stopped looking at GATT after surveying only the principles set out in the preceding section, the picture that emerged would not only be incomplete, but would be severely distorted. Each of the principles is subject to exceptions, some spelled out in the text of the General Agreement, others understood at the time or developed subsequently. Yet a conclusion that the exceptions have overtaken the principles would be an even greater distortion. Indeed, the fact that the principles have survived for over half a century and have attracted nearly all of the world's commercial states suggests that,

---

[29] See John H. Jackson, *The Law of GATT*, §12.2.
[30] Annecy, France 1949; Torquay, England 1950–1.
[31] See Ch. 4, Sect. 4.2 infra.
[32] See WTO Ministerial Declaration adopted at Doha, Qatar November 14, 2001, WT/MIN(01)DEC/1 (20 Nov. 2001).

despite the mercantilist instincts reflected in every state's trade laws, the commitment to non-discrimination and coordinated reduction of trade barriers has become the foundation of the international law of international trade.[33]

(a) Preservation of Existing Preferences

The debate between British and American negotiators, going back to the wartime discussions,[34] was resolved by qualifying Article I, the fundamental MFN article, by explicit authorization to maintain the Imperial or Commonwealth preferences[35] as well as comparable arrangements for overseas territories or affiliated states of France, Belgium, and the Netherlands.[36] It was understood that permitting continuation of these preferences was a significant inroad into the principle of most-favoured nations treatment. In the early post-war years, however, the desire of the principal colonial powers to preserve by economic means some of the ties that were dissolving, and likely to dissolve further, at the political level, proved strong enough to persuade the drafters of the GATT to permit this substantial undercutting of the MFN principle. Article I stated, however, that the margin of preference could not be increased from the margin prevailing at the start of the Geneva conference, April 10, 1947.[37] The failure of United States negotiators to secure elimination of Commonwealth and other preferences was one of grounds raised by critics of the proposed ITO Charter. In the event, the preferences permitted by Article I have played a declining role in international trade,[38] except as they might be seen as precursors of arrangements by the European Community and others, to be discussed later on.

---

[33] As of year-end 2001, after the entry of China and Taiwan was approved during the Ministerial Conference at Doha, 144 states were members of the World Trade Organization, which, as set forth in the following chapters, retains the GATT as its principal agreement and code of conduct. Only Russia, among major countries in the international economy, was not a member state, but it continued to negotiate its admission.

[34] See Sect. 3.1 supra.   [35] See n. 6 supra.

[36] Also preferential arrangements between the United States and Cuba and the Philippines, between Chile and several South American states, and between Lebanon/Syria and Palestine and Transjordan.

[37] An explanatory note to Article I, para. 4 makes clear that margin of preference means the absolute difference between the MFN rate and the preferential rate, not the proportional rate. Thus if the MFN rate of duty on a given product is 36 percent *ad valorem* and the preferential rate is 24 percent, the margin of preference is 12 percent *ad valorem*; if the MFN rate is reduced to, say, 18 percent, the preferential rate could be set at anywhere between 6 and 18 percent, but not at zero. For various permutations of the margin of preference rules, whose importance has diminished as nearly all duties have come down, see John H. Jackson, *The Law of GATT*, §11.5.

[38] See e.g. Gerard Curzon, *Multilateral Commercial Diplomacy*, 75-6 (1969).

(b) 'Existing Legislation' and the Protocol of Provisional Application

As pointed out above, the contracting states were not obligated to change existing legislation with respect to the rules contained in Part II of the General Agreement, which include provisions or subsidies, dumping, state trading, and customs valuation, as well as the provisions on national treatment and quantitative restrictions discussed on the preceding section. This 'grandfather clause'[39] made it possible for several states, notably including the United States, to join the GATT without submitting the Agreement to their respective parliaments.[40] Comparable provisions were inserted in most of the subsequent protocols of accession as close to 100 countries became contracting parties.

'Not inconsistent with existing legislation' was interpreted by several GATT panels or working parties to justify implementation of a measure contrary to a provision of the GATT only when such a measure was *required* under pre-existing law, as contrasted as merely being *authorized*.[41] Also, a GATT panel held that when a pre-existing law expired and was re-enacted with a brief gap, the new law could not regain the benefit of the Protocol of Provisional Application.[42]

A significant illustration of the effect of the Protocol of Provisional Application was the anti-subsidy statute that was first adopted by the United States in 1897 and remained in effect as part of the Tariff Act of 1930 until

[39] The term 'grandfather clause', now generally used in the United States to describe any law or regulation that permits existing arrangements to remain in place notwithstanding new laws or regulations, got its name from the practice of several Southern states of the United States to condition the right to vote on proof that a prospective voter had a male ancestor entitled to vote in 1868, prior to adoption of the Fifteenth Amendment to the Constitution. The practice was declared unconstitutional by the Supreme Court in 1915, *Guinn* v. *United States*, 238 US 347 (1915); *Myers* v. *Anderson*, 238 US 368 (1915), but the expression 'grandfather clause' has remained in the language.

[40] For a detailed account, see John H. Jackson, 'The General Agreement on Tariffs and Trade in United States Domestic Law', 66 *Mich. L. Rev.* 249 (1967).

[41] See in particular the *Belgian Family Allowances* case, (*Norway and Denmark* v. *Belgium*), GATT Basic Instruments and Selected Documents (hereafter BISD), 1st Supp. 59 (1953), discussed in detail in Robert E. Hudec, *The GATT Legal System and World Trade Diplomacy*, pp. 135–57 (2nd edn. 1990); see also *Norway, Restrictions on Imports of Apples and Pears* (*United States* v. *Norway*) BISD, 36th Supp. 306 (1989).

[42] This was the well-known *United States Manufacturing Clause* case (*European Community* vs. *United States*), BISD, 31st Supp. 75 (1984), discussed in Robert E. Hudec, *Enforcing International Trade Law* at 171–2 (1993) and at greater length in Frieder Roessler, 'The Provisional Application of the GATT: Note on the Report of the GATT Panel on the Manufacturing Clause in the US Copyright Legislation', 19 *J. World Trade Law* 289 (1985). The gap in US law came about because in 1976 Congress first adopted a sunset law that would have abolished the statute in question on June 30, 1982; shortly before the scheduled expiration date, Congress passed a bill that would postpone the sunset by four years, but on July 8, the President vetoed that bill. Thereafter, on July 13, 1982, Congress enacted the bill over the President's veto by a two-thirds majority in each House of Congress. The GATT panel held that the 1976 statute had been a move toward greater conformity with the GATT, and that the 1982 statute had constituted a reversal of this move and therefore was not protected by the Grandfather clause.

1979.[43] The statute provided for imposition of a countervailing duty upon dutiable imports found to have benefited from a subsidy, with no reference to any finding of injury to a competing domestic injury. But for the Protocol of Provisional Application, imposition of countervailing duties without a finding of material injury would have violated Article VI(6) of the General Agreemen;[44] given the Protocol, there was no legal obligation on the United States to amend its countervailing duty statute, but failure to bring its law into conformity with the law applicable to nearly all the other parties was a principal matter held against the United States in the course of the Tokyo Round negotiations (1973–9).[45] Commitment by the United States to a change in its legislation, giving up reliance on the Protocol of Provisional Application, became a critical element in negotiation of the Subsidies Code that became a centerpiece of the Tokyo Round.

Like temporary barracks that become a permanent part of the landscape, the Protocol of Provisional Application lasted for 48 years. The effect was that the code of conduct was something less than a universally applicable set of laws. However, the Protocol was important in overcoming resistance on the part of a substantial number of countries to joining the GATT, both initially and as the Agreement attracted some hundred states over five decades. When the GATT was folded into and replaced by the World Trade Organization, as described in Chapter 4, the device of provisional application was discarded, along with the device adopted in the 1960s and expanded in the Tokyo Round whereby some codes, asserted to be in 'implementation' or 'interpretation' of the General Agreement, were permitted to go into effect only for those contracting parties that chose to adhere to them.

(c) Political Exclusions (Art. XXXV)

As pointed out in Section. 3.3, the idea of the GATT rested, more than on any other principle, on the commitment by all parties to treat all other parties on terms of entire equality. Could this commitment be squared with deeply felt animosities going well beyond considerations of trade? Could India and South Africa, for instance, be compelled to open their markets to each other, or else be excluded from the GATT? Or Israel and Egypt, Portugal (when it was a colonial power) and neighbouring African countries, the United States and Hungary and Romania at the height of the Cold War?

The solution to this problem, first proposed by India, was a practical one. Article XXXV, added to the text of the General Agreement in 1948 during the Havana Conference, provided that when a state joins the GATT, it could announce that it would not enter into tariff negotiations with another state and intended not to apply the GATT in relations with that state.

---

[43] 19 U.S.C. §1303 (1930–75).   [44] See Sect. 3.5(c).   [45] See Ch. 4, Sect. 4.3 infra.

Correspondingly, contracting parties were not entitled to veto the accession of a new contracting party, as had been the original design,[46] but any existing contracting party could announce at the time of accession of a new party that it would not apply the GATT to that party.

The decision on invocation of Article XXXV could be made only at the time of accession of a party to the GATT, but could be rescinded at any time. Article XXXV was abused when Japan acceded to the GATT in 1955, as some 15 states that had no current political reason for not establishing commercial relations with Japan—including Australia, Belgium, France, the Netherlands, and the United Kingdom—invoked Article XXXV to avoid granting MFN status to Japanese products. Eventually all of these states rescinded their invocation of Article XXXV, but in a number of instances did so as part of a negotiation in which Japan had to agree to some import liberalization or export restraint.[47]

As of year-end 2001, Article XXXV had not played a major role, but the substance of the article was retained in the Agreement Establishing the World Trade Organization, and indeed made subject to an understanding that a contracting party and a new party may enter into tariff negotiations with each other without thereby waiving the right to invoke Article XXXV against the other party.[48]

(d) National Security (Art. XXI)

Another important exception to the GATT code of conduct had political as well as economic aspects. According to Article XXI, nothing in the Agreement is to prevent a contracting party from taking any action 'which it considers necessary for the protection of its essential security interests.'[49] Since Article XXI is a self-judging measure and no procedure has ever been created to subject a contracting party's assertion of national security to international scrutiny, the provision had the potential to become a significant means for evading GATT obligations.

---

[46] To be precise, under the original version of Article XXXII, accession of a new contracting party required unanimous consent of the existing parties. At the same time that Article XXXV was added to the General Agreement, Article XXXII was modified to require a two-thirds majority for approval of new contracting parties.

[47] See e.g. Treaty of Commerce, Establishment and Navigation between Great Britain and Japan signed at London, 14 Nov. 1962, 53 T.S. 1963, Cmnd. 2085, 478 U.N.T.S. 29, 86.

[48] See Agreement Establishing the World Trade Organization Art. XIII, and accompanying understanding on the Interpretation of Article XXXV of GATT 1947.

[49] GATT Article XXI(b). The quoted phrase is followed by three conditions, relating to fissionable materials, traffic in arms or other goods used for the purpose of supplying a military establishment, or actions taken in time of war or other emergency in international relations. A separate provision, Article XXI(c), states that nothing precludes any action taken pursuant to an obligation under the United Nations Charter for the maintenance of international peace and security.

The Chairman of the commission that drafted Article XXI at the Geneva Conference of 1947, recognizing the danger, said that the spirit in which Members of the Organization would interpret the provisions was the only guarantee against implementations that really have a commercial purpose under the guise of security.[50] In the event, on this issue, the spirit of the parties to the GATT held up, and the abuse did not take place. All the known instances of invocation of Article XXI have grown out of genuine political confrontations—e.g. EC, Canada, Australia/Argentina during the Falklands/Malvinas war of 1982; US/Nicaragua during the Sandinista control of Nicaragua and guerrilla activity in neighbouring countries (1984–5); EC/Yugoslavia after the break-up of the former Yugoslav federation and beginning of hostilities in the former constituent territories (1991–2).[51] The maintenance by the United States for many years of import controls on oil under a national security provision of US domestic law[52] was not challenged in the GATT, but when advocates for other industries, notably the steel industry, urged resort to the national security authority for import restraints, successive American administrations resisted the effort. The question has come up from time to time whether a contracting party affected by a trade measure taken for political reasons could resort to the complaint procedure under Article XXIII. In one of the complaints arising out of the United States imposition of an embargo against Nicaragua, a dispute panel was established, but its report stated that 'both by the terms of Article XXI and by its mandates [the Panel] was precluded from examining the validity of the United States invocation of Article XXI'.[53]

(e) 'General Exceptions'

Many kinds of restrictions and prohibitions imposed by states for reasons of health, safety, and public morals may result in restraints on imports that could be regarded as inconsistent with the General Agreement, particularly Article XI, even when they were not intended as restrictions on trade. On the other hand, safety, health, and similar grounds might be asserted as justification for measures that were actually protectionist measures in disguise. To some extent the national treatment provision of the GATT, Article III, can sort out the mixture of motives in such measures, but some border measures—for instance regulations requiring inspection of meat imports—would

---

[50] Quoted in GATT, *Analytical Index of the GATT*, 554 (6th edn., 1993).

[51] For these and other cases with citations to the GATT documentation, see, GATT, *Analytical Index*, Article XXI, 552–64 (6th edn. 1993). See also Ch. 23, Sect. 23.5 infra.

[52] Trade Expansion Act of 1962 §232, 19 U.S.C. §1862. For discussion of the US Mandatory Oil Import Program as it existed from 1959 to 1973, see Kenneth W. Dam, 'Implementation of Import Quotas: The Case of Oil', 14 *J. Law & Economics* 1 (1971).

[53] *Nicaragua* v. *United States: Trade Measures Affecting Nicaragua*, Report of Panel [not adopted by GATT Council], GATT Doc. L/6053 (13 Oct. 1986). For more on this and similar cases, see Ch. 23, Sect. 23.5.

not qualify as internal regulations.[54] Article XX is designed specifically to justify—but to limit—exceptions to the general provisions of the GATT. 'Nothing in this Agreement,' it states, 'shall be construed to prevent the adoption or enforcement of measures' listed in ten subparagraphs.

Some of the listed exceptions simply exclude subjects not addressed in the GATT—trade in gold and silver, national artistic treasures, products of prison labour—as well as intergovernmental commodity agreements.[55] The critical provisions which have gained in importance as governments have become increasingly concerned with environmental controls as well as with protection of intellectual property, refer to measures necessary to protect human, animal or plant life or health (para. (b)); measures necessary to secure compliance with laws relating to . . . protection of patents, trademarks and copyrights, and prevention of deceptive practices (para. (d)); and measures relating to the conservation of exhaustible natural resources (para. (g)).

All of the measures authorized (or rather exempted from prohibitions) in Article XX are subject to maintenance of the principle of non-discrimination among supplying countries, and to the requirement that the measures are not applied in a manner that would constitute a disguised restriction on international trade. Several GATT panels have taken the position that as Article XX authorizes departure from the generally applicable rules, the burden is on the importing country to show not only that a challenged measure was not imposed for protectionist motives, but that it is *necessary* to accomplish the stated purpose, i.e. that less trade restrictive measures could not accomplish the purpose.

Article XX remains a problematic provision in the GATT, but as part of the resolution of the Uruguay Round, some of the issues raised by Article XX have been addressed in agreements relating to Technical Barriers to Trade, and to Sanitary and Phytosanitary Measures.[56]

(f)   Permissible Quantitative Restrictions

Almost all states intervene to some extent in their agricultural economy. In many instances the intervention takes the form of limits on output or on land under cultivation, as part of a program to adjust output to estimated

---

[54] The example is given in John H. Jackson, *The Law of GATT*, pp. 743–4.

[55] The relation of commodity agreements to the GATT is complicated. Article XX(h) and an explanatory note thereto refer to the provisions of the Havana Charter, which contained an entire chapter (Arts. 53–70) on the subject. In general, in order to satisfy the criteria of the Havana Charter, commodity agreements must be open to all producers and must reflect the interests of importers as well as exporters. Commodity agreements have not been the subject of activity under the GATT. See e.g. B. S. Chimni, *International Commodity Agreements: A Legal Study* (1987).

[56] See e.g. the *Beef Hormones* case, discussed in Ch. 11, Sect. 11.7.

demand and thereby to raise (or to maintain) the price of a given commodity. If the commodity in question could be imported freely, such a program could well be seriously undermined. Accordingly, though Article XI sets out in paragraph (l) the principle that all quantitative restrictions are prohibited (see Section 3.3(b) para. (4) supra), paragraph (2)(c) permits contracting parties to impose restrictions on imports on any agricultural or fishing product when 'necessary to the enforcement' of a governmental program restricting production.

Article XI(2)(c) provides that the permitted quota 'shall not be such as will reduce the total of imports relative to the total of domestic production, as compared with the proportion which might reasonably be effected . . . in the absence of restrictions.' Thus increased domestic output or increased domestic market share are not acceptable motives for imposition of import restrictions. Moreover, several GATT panels have pointed out that Article XI(2)(c) authorizes import *restrictions*, not *prohibitions*. Efforts to add domestic price support programs to output limitations as permissible justification for a quantitative restrictions on imports constitute an inroad into the principle of Article XI(i), and have led to the perception (and to a considerable extent the reality) that the GATT does not fully apply to trade in agricultural products.

A second condition permitting import quotas, less important than it was in the early days of GATT, authorizes a contracting party to impose import restrictions 'in order to safeguard its external financial position and its balance of payments', (Article XII). At first, critics of the GATT/ITO feared that since most countries other than the United States were in balance of payments difficulties, Article XII could significantly undercut Article XI. In fact, by the early 1960s all major currencies had become convertible, and while balance of payments difficulties did not cease, Article XII did not destroy the thrust of the basic principle of Article XI.

One reason why quotas were so vigorously opposed as a generally acceptable device for import restrictions was that it is very difficult to administer quotas without violating the principle of non-discrimination. Quotas based on historical market shares disfavour new entrants, global quotas disfavour suppliers that cannot meet a 'first come . . .' test, and licensing systems invite favouritism and worse. Having permitted inroads into the prohibition of quotas in Articles XI and XII, the architects of the GATT stated in Article XIII that any quantitative restrictions on imports shall be applied on a non-discriminatory basis, with provision for public notification to and consultation with interested suppliers.[57]

---

[57] Article XIV in turn authorizes limited exceptions to the rule of non-discrimination by developing countries or in connection with balance of payments restrictions.

3.5   Rounding Out the Overview

Considering that they expected their text to last only a short time,[58] the drafters of the General Agreement in 1947 covered a surprisingly large number of topics. On some of these topics—for instance on subsidies—the drafting, and indeed the understanding, was incomplete; on others, later events showed that the experience in 1947 and 1948 was insufficient. Many (though not all) of the specific topics that make up the public law of international trade as it has developed are addressed in separate chapters of this volume—devoted to dumping, subsidies, safeguards, and dispute settlement. Only a brief first look is presented in this chapter.

(a)   The Escape Clause

The architects of the GATT understood that they would have difficulty persuading the respective states to permanent arrangements reducing the barriers to imports without some means to reverse a process that turned out differently from what was expected. 'Escape clauses' had been included in bilateral trade agreements made by the United States under its Reciprocal Trade Agreements program, and these served as a model for what became Article XIX of the GATT. In addition to the 'open season' in Article XXVIII which permitted contracting parties to withdraw any binding at three-year intervals, provided that the overall balance of concessions was maintained (Section 3.3(b)(2) supra), Article XIX authorizes emergency action to impose a restriction on imports of a particular product if, 'as a result of unforeseen developments and of the effect of the obligations incurred by a contracting party under this Agreement, including tariff concessions, any product is being imported into the territory of that contracting party in such increased quantities and under such conditions as to cause or threaten serious injury to domestic producers . . . of like or directly competitive products.'

As under the open season provision, Article XIX contemplates a rebalancing of concessions, preferably by agreement between the exporting and importing country. In fact the procedures set out in Article XIX were often not used, though import relief of various kinds through 'safeguards' was common in situations that came to be known as 'market disruption'.[59]

---

[58] Article XXIX(2) stated that part A of the GATT 'shall be suspended on the day on which the Havana Charter enters into force', and the remaining paragraphs of Article XXIX (retained intact as part of GATT 1994 although they have no current application) make various other provisions all focused on the relation of the General Agreement to the entry with force of the Havana Charter.

[59] Article XIX contains a requirement for notification to the Contracting Parties, if practicable in advance of any import relief action taken under Article XIX. A list of 150 such notifications in the period 1950–93 appears in the *Analytical Index of the GATT*, 500–16 (6th edn., 1993). Many other instances, in particular 'voluntary restraint agreements' were not notified to the Contracting Parties.

Efforts to introduce more specific standards concerning the use of safe-guards—in particular with respect to defining *serious injury*, describing the permitted measures, determining whether the measures were subject to most-favoured-nation requirements or could be applied to imports from selected countries—failed in the Tokyo Round (1973–9), but succeeded in the Uruguay Round (1986–94).[60] One issue that occupied negotiators as well as national legislatures over the years was the extent to which, if the elements of unforeseen developments and market disruption were present, the cause must be attributed to tariff concessions or other obligations of a party under the General Agreement.[61] Eventually, as injury and causation were defined and the rules on safeguards were more specifically set out, the requirement of a causal link between injury and trade agreement concession eroded, and was not restated in the 1994 Safeguards Code.

(b) Customs Unions and Free Trade Areas

The drafters of the GATT had mixed feelings about customs unions. On the one hand a customs union—that is an arrangement whereby sovereign states undertake not to impose duties or comparable charges on imports of goods from one another—is by definition inconsistent with the principle of most-favoured-nation treatment. On the other hand, a customs union (as well as a free trade area)[62] entails elimination of barriers to trade *inter se*, and is thus consistent with the objectives of the GATT. Moreover, even in 1947–8, the Netherlands, Belgium, and Luxembourg, all founding parties of the GATT, had formed a customs union, and the idea of a 'unified and democratic Greater Europe' had already been put forward and was being discussed in the context of the reconstruction of Europe. The solution, embodied in Article XXIV of the GATT, as revised at the first session of the Contracting Parties during the Havana Conference in 1948, was to permit contracting parties to enter into customs unions (as well as free trade areas) provided (i) that the arrangement must cover substantially all the trade between or among the parties (to avoid the aspects of preferential or discriminatory

---

[60] See Ch. 5, Sect. 5.4.

[61] In §201(b)(1) of the Trade Act of 1974, Pub.L.93-618, 19 U.S.C. §2251(b)(1), the domestic import relief provision corresponding to GATT Article XIX, the US Congress omitted the phrase 'as a result in major part of concessions granted under trade agreements' contained in the predecessor legislation, §301(b)(l) of the Trade Expansion Act of 1962, Pub.L. 87-794. Professor Jackson has suggested that GATT obligations in this context includes not only tariff concessions but elimination or reduction of quantitative restrictions and even the obligation not to impose such restrictions. But if substantial time passed between entry into force of the GATT and the market disruption in question, it would be difficult to claim that the promise not to impose a quota was the cause that justified import relief. See John H. Jackson, *The Law of GATT*, pp. 559–60.

[62] In a customs union, the member states both eliminate trade barriers *inter se* and adopt a common set of trade barriers to products originating in non-member states. In a free trade area, only the trade barriers *inter se* are eliminated.

deals of the kind seen in the inter-war years); (ii) that on the whole the tariffs and other barriers to trade be no higher or more restrictive than the average of tariffs of the constituent territories before the formation of the customs union or free trade area. Further, (iii) if the formation of the customs union leads to the unbinding of bound duties, there is an obligation to negotiate with the beneficiaries of the concession, in order to re-establish the prior balance; and (iv) if the customs union is to be phased in, there must be a plan and schedule to do so within a reasonable time period. The drafters of the Treaty of Rome Establishing the European Economic Community, the most important customs union in the Age of the GATT, clearly had Article XXIV of the GATT in mind, and on the whole the EEC complied with the requirements of that article. Half a century later much more law—and a good deal of improvisation—have gone into the interpretation of the relation between regional arrangement and the universal organization.

(c)   Dumping and Subsidies

The drafters of the GATT were generally agreed that dumping, defined as sales by an exporter at prices less than the home market price,[63] was an unfair trade practice, and that a proper defense by an importing country was an anti-dumping duty designed to offset the unfair pricing. The drafters were not in agreement about the fairness or unfairness of government subsidies to exporters or producers of goods exported abroad, but they did agree that an importing country was entitled to impose a so-called countervailing duty to offset the effect of the subsidization. The architects of the GATT were concerned, however, that anti-dumping and countervailing duties might be abused for protectionist purposes.[64] Import quotas as a defense to dumping, as advocated by some states, were not accepted, and neither were punitive tariffs, i.e. duties greater than needed to offset the effect of the dumping or subsidy.

Accordingly, dumping was 'condemned' but not prohibited, since the assumption was that it was private firms, not states, that engaged in the practice. Subsidies were neither condemned nor prohibited in the original versions of the GATT, which contained only a notification requirement and no clear definition (Art. XVI). But both anti-dumping and countervailing (i.e. anti-subsidy) duties were permitted as an exception to the most-favoured nation and bound duty obligations, provided the duties did not exceed the amount of dumping or subsidy and provided that the authorities of the importing country had made an explicit determination that as a result of the dumping or subsidy an industry in the importing country had suffered

---

[63] Or, where there was no home market, at prices lower than the price at which the product in question is sold to a third country. For a detailed discussion, see Ch. 10.

[64] See Clair Wilcox, *A Charter for World Trade*, pp. 55–6; William Adams Brown, Jr. *The United States and the Restoration of World Trade*, pp. 110–11.

or was threatened with material injury (Art. VI(6)). As a result of the 1954–5 review session of the GATT contracting parties, the subsidies article of the General Agreement was expanded to include a statement that a subsidy on the export of a product may have harmful effects for other contracting parties, a statement that contracting parties *should seek to avoid* subsidies on primary products, but that in any event such subsidies shall not be applied to bestow *more than an equitable share* of world export trade in that product, and that for other products contracting parties *shall cease* to grant subsidies on any product which results in an export price lower than the domestic price.

As ordinary duties were reduced over time in consequence of negotiations under GATT auspices, the subject of 'unfair trade' became increasingly important and controversial, and the law was not only clarified but in several respects was significantly altered from the original understanding. These developments are described in Chapters 9 and 10.

(d) Waivers

All of the versions of what became the General Agreement, as well as the Havana Charter, contained a provision for waiver of obligations undertaken by contracting parties. Under Article XXV(5), waivers could be granted by the CONTRACTING PARTIES, i.e. by all the states acting together, upon approval by a two-thirds majority, 'in exceptional circumstances not elsewhere provided for in this Agreement'.[65] The waiver provision did not lead to erosion of the GATT—some 100 waivers were granted in the first forty years—but it did permit the GATT to avoid conflicts of priorities that might have threatened its existence. For example, the CONTRACTING PARTIES granted a waiver in 1952 to the European Coal and Steel Community,[66] though it was plainly a customs union limited to certain sectors, contrary to Article XXIV of the GATT. The waiver, a negotiated document, was subject both to detailed annual reporting requirements and to a commitment that the customs duties and other regulations of the Community shall be lower and less restrictive than the general incidence of duties and regulations previously applicable. When the same six states formed the European Economic Community in 1958, the criteria of Article XXIV were met, and no waiver was sought or granted.

---

[65] When waivers have been granted, no special effort has been made to define 'exceptional circumstances'. In one of the few cases in which an application for a waiver was denied, involving an application by Greece in 1970 to grant a preferential tariff quota to the Soviet Union to offset the competitive disadvantage that Soviet products faced as a result of the Association Agreement between the EEC and Greece, a GATT working party wrote that members 'were not convinced that exceptional circumstances as required under Article XXV(5) existed and were therefore opposed to granting of a waiver.' GATT Doc. L/3447. BISD, 18th Supp. 129, paras. 6, 13 (2 Dec. 1970).

[66] Decision of 10 Nov. 1952, GATT BISD, 1st Supp. 17 (1952).

A waiver covering restrictions on imports of virtually all agricultural products was granted to the United States in 1955,[67] and remained in effect for forty years, until phased out pursuant to the agricultural settlement reached in the Uruguay Round. Without the waiver, it was believed, the United States Congress might not have continued to support (or at least tolerate) America's participation in the GATT. The existence of the waiver, and its long duration, doubtless led other contracting parties, and later the European Community, to disregard the principles of the GATT in formulating their agricultural policies, with or without waivers. Although the United States exercised its rights under the waiver with moderation, continuation of the waiver inevitably led to the charge of hypocrisy on the part of the United States in its efforts to reduce export subsidies and import restraints by the European Community, Japan, and others. Whether without the waiver the GATT would have been more successful in applying its rules to the products of agriculture may be doubted. With the waiver granted to the United States and similar waivers to others, it was possible to maintain the overall integrity of the GATT code of conduct, without imposing the code on an unwilling world.[68]

The waiver authority was essentially retained when GATT 1947 was folded into the World Trade Organization, but subject to approval by a three-quarters majority, and to a requirement that all waivers shall have a terminal date, and if a waiver extends beyond one year, that it will be subject to annual review.[69]

(e)   Dispute Settlement in GATT

As originally conceived, the GATT (as well as the ITO) could function as a forum for resolution of disputes among the contracting parties, if possible through direct consultations, and if necessary with the help of the secretariat or a small group of neutral GATT experts to act as a kind of arbitration panel. Article XXII states that each contracting party 'shall accord sympathetic consideration' to representations regarding *any matter* that may be made by another contracting party. Article XXIII states that if any contracting party should consider that 'any benefit' accruing directly or indirectly under the Agreement is being 'nullified or impaired', the matter may be

---

[67] Decision of 5 Mar. 1955, GATT BISD, 3d Supp. 32 (1955), authorizing imposition of import restrictions under Section 22 of the US Agricultural Adjustment Act.

[68] Professor Hudec has catalogued complaints under the GATT dispute settlement process, and demonstrates that, taking only the formal complaints, the success rate in controversies concerning agriculture is about the same as in respect to other products. However, as Hudec points out, most of the important restrictions on trade in agriculture are either outside the rules altogether, including US restraints under the section 22 waiver and the EEC's Common Agricultural Policy, or else have not been effectively regulated by the GATT code. See Robert E. Hudec, *Enforcing International Trade Law*, pp. 326–37 (1993).

[69] Agreement Establishing the World Trade Organization, Article IX.

referred to the CONTRACTING PARTIES (i.e. the collective body) which shall make recommendations or give a ruling on the matter 'as appropriate'. Nothing was stated about how the recommendation or rulings should be arrived at, and no procedure was set out in the Agreement. Article XXIII does say, however, that if they consider that the circumstances are serious enough, the CONTRACTING PARTIES may authorize a contracting party [i.e. the successful complainant] to suspend the application to any other contracting party [i.e. the respondent found to be out of compliance] of 'such concessions or other obligations under [the] Agreement as they determine to be appropriate in the circumstances.'

Out of these rudimentary provisions there developed over time a kind of dispute settlement mechanism, similar in some ways to arbitration, in others to a club keeping members in line. The GATT as a dispute resolution forum had ebb and flow, as prevailing views moved back and forth between a desire to compose disputes and keep controversies from spreading and a desire to arrive at clear rules with law-making effect. In fact more than 200 formal complaints were filed over the first 45 years of the GATT, alleging either violation of the General Agreement or one of the codes subsequently adopted, or in some instances 'non-violation' nullification and impairment.[70] In the period 1948–89 analysed in detail by Professor Hudec, a GATT panel and/or plenary assembly ruled on the legal validity of the complaint in 88 cases; in 64 other cases, the respondent state settled or otherwise conceded the validity of the complaint (at least by implication) without a legal ruling, and in 55 cases the complaint was withdrawn or abandoned, without either a legal ruling or a settlement.[71]

A detailed discussion of the evolution of dispute settlement as a major element of the GATT/WTO system is presented in Chapters 7 and 8. In this introductory overview, only a few points need to be made. *First*, when it is determined that a challenged measure violates a provision of the GATT (or one of the later GATT codes), the preferred solution is a recommendation that the respondent state modify or withdraw the measure. Retaliation, by way of suspension by the complainant state of a corresponding concession is disfavoured, because the result would be not one but two barriers to trade.

Second, for many years disputes were presented by the contestants' delegates to GATT, typically to panels or working parties made up of other delegates from third countries. The GATT secretariat usually participated, but until 1981, the GATT did not have a legal division. More recently, the role of lawyers has grown both as representatives of parties and as panelists, reflecting a trend in the direction of rule-based decisions.

Third, until 1995 panels or working parties were authorized only to make recommendations, not decisions. Their reports were circulated to the GATT

---

[70] See Ch. 7, Sect. 7.3 infra.
[71] See Hudec, *Enforcing International Trade Law*, pp. 274–6.

Council, where they could be approved, disapproved, or action could be postponed. Since the GATT Council operated by consensus, it happened not infrequently that a losing party succeeded in postponing consideration of a panel report, or even in blocking its approval. In some instances, the parties in question worked out a settlement in the interval; in other instances, the process was stymied. Overall, however, the process worked in over half the cases, as losing parties considered that next time around they might be complainant, and as self-judging became unattractive to the GATT community.[72]

Fourth, the object of settlement of trade disputes in the GATT, as in the various provisions authorizing withdrawal of concessions (e.g. under the escape clause[73] or the open season[74]) was a restoration of the prevailing balance of concessions. Even when retaliation was authorized—which rarely occurred, the purpose was compensation, not punishment or damages.

Summary

It is evident that no first look or overview can give a complete picture of a complex institution such as the GATT. It is remarkable, however, that the GATT, always fragile and controversial, and designed to be 'provisional' only, survived for five decades with relatively little change, compared for example with its older and originally much stronger sister, the International Monetary Fund.[75] Many of the rules of the GATT were made more explicit, some were changed by design or practice, and not all were obeyed with equal ardour. New mechanisms and indeed a new institution have grown up, and the agenda has grown wider in scope. But the principles have remained standing, despite ambivalence within almost every contracting party and continuing tensions among the various parties. The details of these tensions and ambivalences, as well as analyses and precedents that make up the public law framework of international trade, are set out in the succeeding chapters of this book.

---

[72] Proposals to modify the procedure to require participants in GATT panel proceedings to abstain from voting on panel reports were made from time to time, but were not accepted. See Ch. 7, Sect. 7.4.

[73] See Sect. 3.5(a).   [74] See Sect. 3.3(b) para (2).   [75] See Ch. 17.

4

Evolution of the GATT and GATT Law

4.1 INTRODUCTION

When the GATT was being drafted and negotiated in 1947–8, the Cold War between the Western democracies and the Soviet bloc was just beginning; the recovery of Western Europe from the ravages of World War II was in its early stages; Japan was essentially outside the international economy; most of Africa and major parts of Asia and Oceana were subject to colonial rule; and the European Common Market was a decade away. The United States was the unchallenged leader of the world economy—in capital, technology, and resources, and with an apparently permanent trade surplus. Indeed, the United States was a net exporter of petroleum, and the price of crude oil stood at well under $3 a barrel. The US dollar itself stood as a firm anchor of the international trading system, tied to gold, and most other currencies were linked to the dollar by the par value system, established pursuant to the Articles of Agreement of the IMF.[1]

---

[1] See Ch. 16.

Six decades later, the par value system is gone; the Cold War is over, but so is the United States' unchallenged dominance of the international economy. The European Common Market has grown to fifteen states and has become at least equal to the United States in matters of trade. Oil-producing nations in the Middle East have become major participants in the international economy, though not in the rule-making bodies such as the WTO. Japan has become the world's second largest trading nation, and its seemingly permanent trade surplus has drawn the international rules into question. The developing countries—at first ignored, then patronized, have turned out not all to belong to a single class, with some active participants in the global trade system, others largely outside that system.

Given all these changes, it is surprising that the GATT—rules and institution—did not change more than it did. But no Great Depression took place, as had occurred in the 1930s, and no Great War broke out, as had occurred twice in the first half of the twentieth century. Moreover, except for some portions of Africa, standards of living rose everywhere. There were of course changes in the subjects here addressed. But the changes came largely in the form of filling in the gaps—again both in the rules and in the institution. The principles, on the whole, remained intact.

4.2   MFN, Reciprocity and the Negotiating Rounds

(a)   The First Five Rounds (1947–61)

As pointed out in the preceding chapter, one of the governing themes of the GATT was that the Contracting Parties should meet regularly to negotiate about reducing tariffs and other trade barriers. The first such round, as we saw, was held in Geneva contemporaneously with the drafting of the General Agreement in April–October 1947. The two succeeding rounds (Annecy, France, 1949; Torquay, England 1950–1) combined modest tariff-cutting with negotiation of the conditions of accession of new entrants, including at Torquay the recently established Federal Republic of Germany. A fourth round of tariff-cutting was held in Geneva in 1955–6. The typical pattern in these rounds was for each pair of countries first to exchange 'request lists', and subsequently to exchange 'offer lists'. After the lists were exchanged, they were made available to all the participants, which would take them into account in their own bilateral negotiations and preparation of revised lists. If two exporting countries might benefit from a proposed concession, the importing country might make its offer subject to being 'paid' by both of the potential beneficiaries.[2]

---

[2] See e.g. John W. Evans, *The Kennedy Round in American Trade Policy*, 10 (1971).

As it turned out, each of the rounds after the first one had small, but not very significant, results in terms of duty reductions. The Fourth Round was restrained by the fact that in the Trade Agreements Extension Act of 1955,[3] the US Congress had authorized the President to negotiate duty reductions of only 15 percent of the duties in effect on January 1, 1955 or to 50 percent *ad valorem*. If the United States could not offer greater reductions, the combination of the MFN principle and the reciprocity principle meant that other states could not offer more substantial reductions either.

Just after the close of the Fourth GATT Round in May 1956, the Foreign Ministers of the Benelux countries, France, Italy, and the Federal Republic of Germany met in Venice to consider and approve the Spaak Report commissioned a year earlier, looking to establishment of the European Common Market. If the GATT could not be the vehicle for significant tariff cuts, the six European countries—without the United Kingdom and without the United States—could and would do so among themselves. Some observers thought at the time that the Western European states were turning their back on the GATT concept, and that that concept had essentially failed.[4] In the event, the creation of the European Common Market in 1958 changed, but did not weaken the international law of international trade as embodied in the GATT. On the one hand, the Treaty of Rome creating the European Economic Community on the whole conformed to the requirements for customs unions prescribed in the GATT.[5] On the other hand, the European Community came to be a principal force within the GATT, negotiating and acting as a unit and on substantially equal terms with the United States.

The Fifth Round, named after Douglas Dillon, at the time the US Under Secretary of State for Economic Affairs under President Eisenhower,[6] came to have two aspects. In one aspect it was another effort to engage in multilateral tariff-cutting along the lines of the prior rounds, but spurred on by new United States negotiating authority, permitting duty reductions of up to 20 percent from the level of January 1958. The other aspect was a negotiation between the European Community and other GATT contracting parties pursuant to Article XXIV(6) about compensation for unbinding of duties of member states of the EEC bound in prior GATT rounds. The initial position of the EEC was that a common external tariff on a given item created by arithmetic average of the previous duties of the constituent countries, as called for (with some exceptions) by the Treaty of Rome,[7] did not require any compensation to third countries.

Thus suppose on a given item the pre-existing duties, all bound in GATT schedules pursuant to Article II, were:

---

[3] 65 Stat. 162 (1955).
[4] See Gerard Curzon, *Multilateral Commercial Diplomacy*, pp. 94–7.
[5] See in particular Article XXIV, discussed in Ch. 3, Sect. 3.5(b).
[6] And later Secretary of the Treasury under Presidents Kennedy and Johnson.
[7] See Treaty of Rome Establishing the European Community, (1957), Art. 19.

> Benelux   12 percent *ad valorem*
> Germany   15 percent *ad valorem*
> France   20 percent *ad valorem*
> Italy   25 percent *ad valorem*

An arithmetic average, without weighting for the amount of trade moving over the tariff, would result in a common tariff of 18 percent *ad valorem*. The initial position of the Community was that the rise in the Benelux duty from 12 to 18 percent was compensated to beneficiaries of the Benelux Concession by the reduction in the duty on the same item on the part of France and Italy.

That position was rejected, and the principle was established that third parties were entitled to make item-by-item claims for compensation pursuant to Article XXIV(6) when a customs union was established or—as occurred frequently with respect to the EEC—enlarged by admission of new members.[8]

Putting aside agriculture (as the contracting parties did), the Dillon/XXIV(6) Round was regarded as successful, in that the EEC was integrated into the GATT without major friction. But the actual reduction of duties was once again modest, and the process of product-by-product negotiation was tedious. The members of the EEC had utilized across-the-board adjustment of duties in the transition to complete elimination of duties *inter se*, and had proposed a similar technique for use by GATT in the Dillon Round negotiations. For the United States, such a proposal was inconsistent with its negotiating authority, which seemed to require individual reports by the US Tariff Commission before an item of import could be placed on an offer list, and so the idea was abandoned during the Dillon Round. Both the United States and the European Community, however, were determined to find a better way to conduct multilateral trade negotiations in the next round.[9] The objective remained to preserve the twin principles of reciprocity and non-discrimination. The impetus had to come from the United States, and it did, in the Trade Expansion Act of 1962, which in turn stimulated what came to be known as the Kennedy Round of Trade Negotiations.[10]

---

[8] The principle was formally stated in a Dispute Panel Report three decades later. *EEC—Payments and Subsidies Paid to Processors and Producers of Oil Seeds and Related American Feed Proteins* (*United States* v. *EEC*) 'Soya Panel', paras. 144–6, GATT BISD, 37th Supp. 86, 126–8 (25 Jan. 1990).

[9] Note that Article XXVIII*bis* of the GATT states that 'Negotiations under this Article may be carried out on a selective product-by-product basis *or by application of such multilateral procedures as may be accepted by the contracting parties concerned.*' (emphasis added)

[10] According to Theodore Sorensen, President Kennedy's counsel and later biographer, the designation 'Kennedy Round' originated in Europe, and did not altogether please the President. See T. Sorensen, *Kennedy*, 412 (1965). A brief movement to name the next round (1973–9) the 'Nixon Round' foundered as President Nixon had doubts about the future of the negotiations, and others—in the United States and elsewhere—had doubts about the future of President Nixon. Accordingly, the Seventh Round became known as the Tokyo Round after the site of the ministerial conference that launched it, though the negotiations, as always, were held primarily in Geneva. That precedent was followed for the Eighth Round as well (1986–94), which was launched at a ministerial meeting in Punta del Este, Uruguay. See Sect. 4.4 infra.

(b)   The Kennedy Round

The United States government was at first divided about how to respond to the creation of the European Economic Community. From a political standpoint, the United States welcomed the EEC, as a promising way to solve the problem of Germany in Europe, and as a way to strengthen the defense of the Western democracies against the threat of communism. From an economic standpoint, however, there was fear in some quarters that the EEC might become an inward-directed, high-tariff area, inimical to the trading interests of the United States.

The Trade Expansion Act of 1962,[11] in the words of President Kennedy, was to be 'a new and modern instrument of trade negotiations'.[12] The architects of the Trade Expansion Act understood that the effect of a customs union, even when it meets the requirements of Article XXIV of the GATT, may be to deprive an outsider, such as the United States (and at the time the United Kingdom) of the benefits of most-favoured-nation treatment, as well as the benefits of concessions previously negotiated and paid for.

> Suppose, for instance, that prior to creation of the customs union a machine made in the United States competed in the Italian market on equal terms with a machine originating in the Federal Republic of Germany. Once the customs union or common market is in effect, the machine originating in Germany can come into Italy free of duty, whereas the machine originating in the United States could come in only over the common external tariff, and may therefore no longer be able to compete in the Italian market.

The significance of this effect—i.e. the trade diversion effect—will depend, other things being equal, on the height of the common external tariff. The response of the United States government was to seek to negotiate a reduction in that tariff. In the context of the GATT, this meant seeking to launch a new round of trade negotiations with a broad mandate to reduce duties. In the context of United States law, it meant getting away from the prior confinement to article-by-article negotiation and securing authority for across-the-board or linear negotiations.[13] Moreover, the President sought, and after some controversy, the Congress granted, the authority 'through trade agreements affording mutual trade benefits', to decrease any rate of duty by up to 50 percent of the rate existing on July 1, 1962. The authority,

[11] Pub L. 87-794, 76 Stat. 872, approved 11 Oct. 1962.

[12] *Special Message to the Congress on Foreign Trade Policy*, 25 Jan. 1962, Public Papers of the Presidents, John F. Kennedy, 1962, 68 (1963).

[13] In fact the Trade Expansion Act does not expressly authorize or direct linear negotiations, but the section containing the basic authority, §201, unlike the predecessor statute, did not contain the words 'of any article', and the President's message, the legislative debates, and the committee reports made the intention clear.

which determined the duration of the subsequent negotiations, was granted for five years, that is until June 30, 1967.[14]

Shortly after passage of the Trade Expansion Act by the United States Congress, the Contracting Parties to GATT made a tentative decision to hold a new round of trade negotiations—in principle on the basis of linear or across-the-board tariff reductions. The decision was finalized—that is recorded in a formal Ministerial Decision, in May 1963.[15] But translating the idea of linear reductions into actual negotiating procedures while retaining the principle of reciprocity proved to be a task that occupied the participants for many months, and ultimately resulted in a Kennedy Round rather different from what the planners in Europe and the United States had foreseen.

> Suppose, for instance, that Patria maintains an average level of duties of 30 percent, and Xandia maintains an average level of duties of 20 percent *ad valorem*. If both countries reduce all their duties by 50 percent, the average level of Patria's duties (after phasing) will be 15 percent and the average level of Xandia's duties will be 10 percent *ad valorem*. Patria has reduced its duties by 15 percentage points, Xandia only by 10 percentage points. Has the principle of reciprocity been violated?[16]

The question was never answered in a definitive way during the Kennedy Round, or indeed in succeeding negotiating rounds.[17] But the pull of the concept of reciprocity exercised a strong influence on the negotiations, and may fairly be said to have become a permanent aspect of the ground rules—not to say the law—of international trade.

Reciprocity became a dominant issue in several other aspects of the Kennedy Round. In negotiating with the United States and the United Kingdom, the European Community pointed out that its tariffs on industrial products—as a result of averaging member countries' tariffs in the process of forming the common external tariff[18]—were nearly all in the medium range of 10–20 percent *ad valorem*, whereas British and American tariffs were widely distributed, with some quite low but others in the 30–50 percent range. The EEC argued in the Kennedy Round that even if the overall average of its tariffs, compared, say, with United States tariffs, was roughly equal, so that the Patria/Xandia problem illustrated above would not arise, a 50 percent linear cut would leave most of its tariffs at relatively low levels, whereas many British and American (as well as Japanese and others) duties

---

[14] For low-rate articles, with a starting duty of 5 percent *ad valorem* or less, there was no limit on the authority to negotiate duty reductions, so that the duty could be reduced to zero.

[15] Ministerial Meeting May 1963, GATT BISD, 12th Supp., 36 at 47 (21 May 1963).

[16] For variations on how to state this question, see e.g. John B. Rehm, 'The Kennedy Round of Trade Negotiations', 62 *Am. J. Int'l L.* 403 at 410 (1968).

[17] Nor did any dispute settlement panel render an authoritative definition of the requirement of reciprocity.

[18] See Ch. 3, Sect. 3.5(b).

would continue to constitute substantial restraints on trade. The solution proposed by the EEC, which came to be known as '*écrêtement*', meaning leveling of the peaks,[19] was a formula whereby contracting parties would agree on target rates by major categories, and then would undertake to cut their duties by an agreed percentage of the difference between the actual rate and the target rate.

Thus suppose the target rate for manufactured products was 10 percent *ad valorem*, and the parties agreed to reduce applicable duties by 50 percent of the difference between the actual and the target rate. Assume on the starting date four different industrial products imported by four different countries with four different rates of duty. Each importing country would be required to reduce the duty in question by half the difference between its original duty and the uniform target set for industrial products, 10 percent *ad valorem* in the example[20] (see Table 4.1).

TABLE 4.1.

	Starting rate (%)	Target rate (%)	Percentage pts. above target	Required reduction in pctge. pts	Reduction as pctge. of starting rate
(a)	50	10	40	20	40
(b)	30	10	20	10	33.3
(c)	15	10	5	2.5	16.6
(d)	10	10	0	0	0

The United States took the position that conformity of the formula with reciprocity would be defined by the last column in the Table, and the discrepancy there displayed showed that the formula was unacceptable—inconsistent with the agreed procedures for the Kennedy Round and inconsistent with the requirement in United States law of 'mutual trade benefits'. Quite apart from the legal argument, of course, the products subject to the highest rates of duty (category *a* in Table 4.1) were likely to be the most sensitive items for the importing country imposing the tariff. Without more information—much more than could ever be assembled on a range of thousands of products originating in or destined for tens of countries—it would be impossible to make a truly balanced assessment of duty reductions from application of the EEC's proposed formula or any of its variations. But though the point was made that 'linear reductions' might fall unevenly on

[19] From the French *crête*, crest or peak.
[20] Adapted from a more detailed illustration in John W. Evans, *The Kennedy Round in American Trade Policy*, 186–89.

different products, tariff structures, or countries, the *écrêtement* formula was not accepted, and the concept of reciprocity was not further refined.

A second aspect in which reciprocity became significant was attributable in the first instance to the negotiating authority granted by Congress to the United States executive branch. Though as we saw the authority was very broad—up to 50 percent reduction for a five-year period, it excluded products on which actions had been taken under the escape clause and national security provisions of United States law, or on products on which escape clause action had been recommended by the US Tariff Commission but rejected by the President.[21] The United States delegation announced that this restriction would exclude some 12 percent of United States imports from the negotiations.[22] Other participants in the negotiations, again in reliance on the reciprocity principle, thereupon reserved the right to present their own exceptions. After strenuous discussions, a compromise Ministerial Declaration was agreed to, stating that the tariff negotiations would be based

upon a plan of substantial linear tariff reductions *with a bare minimum of exceptions* which shall be subject to confrontation and justification. The linear reductions shall be equal. In those cases where there are significant disparities in tariff levels, the tariff reductions will be based upon special rules of general and automatic application.[23] (italics added)

The formulation concerning disparities suggested that a deviation from linear reductions might be justified for individual products or groups of products, and in fact the EEC came up with several proposed triggers for exceptions or partial exceptions to linear reductions, focusing on differences between high and low duties on given product categories.[24] The requirement for justification of exceptions, that is reservations from a plan for across-the-board reductions, seemed to suggest that Xandia could not table an exception just because Patria had done so, but it also seemed to invite negotiations about balancing of concessions. The disparities issue and the exceptions issue led not only to an inroad in the principle of linear reductions, but also to partial return to the pattern of prior rounds of bilateral negotiations, with offers subject to reservations, including reservations based on the offers or reservations of third parties.

Thus the Kennedy Round became a hybrid of product-by-product and linear negotiations. Reciprocity remained a pervasive principle of trade

---

[21] US Trade Expansion Act of 1962, §225.

[22] GATT Doc. L/1982 (14 Mar. 1963), p. 5. Among the goods reserved by reason of prior escape clause actions were lead and zinc, sheet glass, safety pine, and chemical thermometers. The national security reservation related to petroleum and its derivatives. See Rehm, 'The Kennedy Round', note 16 supra, at 411.

[23] GATT Ministerial Meeting 16–21 May 1963, *Resolution on Arrangements for the Reduction or Elimination of Tariffs and Other Barriers to Trade, and Related Matters* para. A(4), GATT BISD, 12th Supp. 36 at 47, para. 4 (1964).

[24] See Evans, *The Kennedy Round*, note 2 supra, pp. 191–200.

negotiations. It was not defined in the Kennedy Round, or in subsequent rounds, nor has it ever been defined by a dispute settlement panel.[25] To the extent there is an agreed definition of reciprocity, or mutual exchange of benefits, it is only that there are to be no free rides, that is that each contracting party (putting aside developing countries) is to open its markets in return for gaining access for its exporters to the markets of other contracting parties.

Overall, negotiation in the Kennedy Round came within that definition. And while the Kennedy Round took longer than expected, and was more of an economic tug-of-war as contrasted with a political statement than had been hoped,[26] it did result in duty reductions on 20 percent of the dutiable products of the industrial countries, about two-thirds by 50 percent or more.[27] But the shortcomings of the Kennedy Round compared with the initial expectations demonstrated how difficult it is to move away from equating reciprocity with symmetry, and how ingrained is the concern of contracting states and their representatives that they may be 'giving away' more than they are 'receiving'.

> When Patria and Xandia agree to exchange ambassadors or consuls on the basis of reciprocity, they do not attempt to measure how large the respective embassies will be or how many visas each consulate will issue. When they agree to recognize each others' civil judgements or arbitral awards or extradition requests, they do not seek to establish in advance which country will 'come out ahead.' In the trade context, however, the participants start out with some numbers, and the temptation is to construct others. Thus figures are usually available on (a)

[25] A GATT Working Party Report on Schedules and Customs Administration submitted to the 1955 Review Session stated:

> The representative of Brazil invited the Working Party to discuss . . . the proposals which had been put forward by his delegation. His delegation wished to establish certain rules for the conduct of tariff negotiations and, in particular, for the measurement of concessions. The Working Party considered that governments participating in negotiations should retain complete freedom to adopt any method they might feel most appropriate for estimating the value of duty reductions and bindings. . . . The Working Party noted that there was nothing in the Agreement, or in the rules for tariff negotiations which had been used in the past, to prevent governments from adopting any formula they might choose, and therefore considered that there was no need for the CONTRACTING PARTIES to make any recommendation in this matter. (GATT Doc L/329, 26 Feb. 1955, BISD, 3rd Supp. 205 at 219–20, para. 38)

A later report, prepared in connection with the Dillon Round, cited this report as 'the traditional attitude of the CONTRACTING PARTIES . . . that governments participating in negotiations should retain complete freedom to adopt any method they might feel most appropriate for estimating the value of duty reductions and bindings.' GATT Doc. COM. I/3, 19 Nov. 1959, BISD, 8th Supp. 103 at 110, para. 10.

[26] It may be noted that shortly before the opening of the Kennedy Round, Britain's application for membership in the European Economic Community was vetoed by President de Gaulle, thus not only undermining President Kennedy's vision of the Grand Alliance, but also causing a major rift within the EEC that was not healed until de Gaulle's resignation in 1969.

[27] For a detailed summary of the results of the Kennedy Round including the text of the Director General's closing statement see Ernest H. Preeg, *Traders and Diplomats* (1970).

the amount or value of Patria's imports of a given product; (b) the duty that Patria imposes on that product; and (c) the amount or value of the product imported by Patria from Xandia. The tendency is to attach a specific value to an offer to reduce (b) as predictive of an increase in (a) and (c), and to compare this calculation with an offer from Xandia on another product in the light of (d) the value of the imports by Xandia of that other product; (e) Xandia's duty on that product; (f) the amount or value of Xandia's imports of that product originating in Patria.

Multilateral trade negotiations from the time of the Kennedy Round, and in particular linear or across-the-board duty reductions subject to various formulas, have taken as their point of departure that the attempt to make predictions on a product-by-product basis is not only massively burdensome but is inevitably illusory. Further, to the extent that Patria is restrained or dissuaded from offering to reduce a trade barrier until it is satisfied that Xandia, as well as other potential suppliers, have made reciprocal offers, the effort to aim for reciprocity in arithmetic estimates of increased exports is inconsistent with a regime based on access, not outcomes. The experience of the Kennedy Round and of the succeeding rounds suggests, however, that reciprocity remains a deeply felt element in the economic relations of states, and that a perception of that term without reference to trade statistics—past and projected—is difficult to escape.

4.3   THE TOKYO ROUND AND THE SEPARATE CODES

(a)   An Expanded Agenda

Though Article XVIII*bis* of GATT refers explicitly only to negotiations directed to reduction of tariffs and similar changes, the Kennedy Round was the last round of GATT negotiations in which tariff reduction was the major focus. By the time that the results of the Kennedy Round had became fully effective in the early 1970s, tariffs on industrial products had been reduced substantially and no longer appeared to be the major impediment to trade that they had once been. Other restraints and distortions on trade—known collectively as non-tariff barriers or NTBs—had taken on increasing importance. Accordingly, the focus of the GATT, and of the negotiating rounds, shifted to the substantive rules of international trade, many of which had been only sketchily addressed in the General Agreement drafted a generation earlier.

Some of the NTBs were based on formal statutory constraints, such as 'buy national' laws and regulations for government procurement; others were less visible governmental practices such as subsidies of various kinds, including export credits and tax rebates; still others had begun as health or safety standards, but with no international scrutiny or attempt at harmonization. Perhaps most ominous was the spread of so-called 'voluntary export restraints' which seemed to be spreading without reference to the GATT, though they affected major industrial sectors such as steel and automobiles.[28]

By the early 1970s, the major trading countries, particularly the United States and the European Community had reached the conclusion that if the gains of the Kennedy Round were not to be dissipated and the momentum for liberalization of international trade was not to be reversed,[29] a new round of trade negotiations should be undertaken, with a broader and more creative agenda. A Joint Declaration by the United States and the European Community to the Director-General of GATT urging a new round of negotiations was issued in February 1972,[30] and a formal Ministerial Meeting in Tokyo in September 1973 declared the 'comprehensive multilateral trade negotiations' officially open.[31] The declaration stated that as before,

The negotiations shall be conducted on the basis of the principles of mutual advantage, mutual commitment and overall reciprocity, while observing the most-favored-nation clause . . . [looking to achievement of] an overall balance of advantage at the highest possible level.[32]

The Ministers' expressed aim that the negotiations be concluded in 1975[33] proved unattainable by more than three years.[34] Among their other aims, reduction or elimination of non-tariff measures, or 'where this is not appropriate, . . . to bring such measures under more effective international discipline' proved possible, in part, but by means of a significant departure from the initial model.

(b) Separate Codes and the Question of MFN

Overall reciprocity and a well-balanced package suggested that not every agreement must favour the interest of all the negotiating parties equally, as long as the overall settlement is satisfactory to all the participants. Thus, for instance, one party might agree to open up opportunities for non-nationals to bid for its government procurement projects to a greater extent than it expected its nationals to benefit from government procurement abroad if it considered that this 'concession' would enable it to prevail on a contentious

---

[28] Textiles and apparel were also subject to restraint, going back to the early 1960s, but these were, at least nominally, subject to rules approved by the GATT. See e.g. Gary H. Perlow, 'The Multilateral Supervision of International Trade: Has the Textiles Experiment Worked?', 75 *Am. Int'l L.* 93 (1981).

[29] Recall that this was the period of the collapse of the Bretton Woods monetary regime (Ch. 16, Sect. 16.9 infra) as well as of the rise of the Middle East oil-producing states to economic power.

[30] See 66 *Dept. State Bull.* 515 (1972).   [31] GATT BISD, 20th Supp. 19 (1974).

[32] Id., para. 5.   [33] Id., para. 11.

[34] In fact the negotiations did not start in earnest until 1977, by which time the European Community had more or less integrated the United Kingdom into its decision-making process, and the United States had recovered from the Watergate crisis and the deposition of President Nixon.

issue in regard to, say, dumping. On the other hand, it soon became clear that while the principal participants from the industrial countries—the United States, the European Community (since 1973 including the United Kingdom), Canada, and Japan—were interested in all the subjects proposed for negotiation and legislation, many other states had no interest in NTBs or had interests opposed to those of the major industrial countries. But the GATT had actively sought out new contracting parties, and close to a hundred states participated in the Tokyo Round, twice as many as had taken part in the Kennedy Round. The prospect of securing a series of amendments to the GATT within a reasonable time period seemed dim and might well have given influence to some states out of proportion to their participation in the international economy.[35] The idea grew up, accordingly, to develop a number of 'codes', nominally in implementation or interpretation of provisions of the General Agreement, that would create more specific understanding and more precise undertakings with respect to particular topics. The codes would be open to all contracting parties, but no particular number of signatories would be required to bring them into effect. The codes would be binding only on the signatories, and contracting parties could pick and choose among the codes. One such code—on Anti-Dumping—had been signed by 18 states at the close of the Kennedy Round, though as precedent for the program contemplated in the Tokyo Round the legal status of the code was ambiguous.[36]

The contracting parties and particularly the industrial states that sponsored and negotiated the codes—as usual predominantly the European Community and the United States—understood that a regime of non-compulsory codes to some extent undermined the claim of the GATT as a universal organization. Moreover, at least for those codes that conferred benefits on the signatories, notably the Government Procurement Code and the Subsidies Code, the principle of unconditional most-favoured-nation treatment was to some extent replaced by a form of conditional MFN, whereby in order to gain the benefits, a state had to sign on to the code in question and to undertake to abide by the commitments set out in that code.[37]

---

[35] Article XXX of the General Agreement requires unanimous consent to amend Articles I and II (the MFN and Tariff-binding articles), and approval of two-thirds of the contracting parties for all other amendments. Weighted voting, such as prevails in the Bretton Woods organizations and some commodity agreements, was never introduced into the GATT.

[36] In November 1968, at the 25th Session of the Contracting Parties, the Director-General was asked for a ruling on whether parties to the Anti-Dumping code had a legal obligation under Article I of the General Agreement to apply the provisions of the code in their trade with all GATT contracting parties. The Director General replied in the affirmative. The European Community representative, however, took the position that the parties were under no obligation to apply the provisions of the code to non-signatories. See *GATT Analytical Index*, 46, 30 (1993).

[37] For government procurement, a signatory had the right to have its firms bid for contracts of state agency set out in a schedule; for subsidies, a signatory faced with a countervailing duty had the right, important in view of the prior United States practice, to have an independent determination of injury to an industry before the countervailing duty could be imposed. For all

The advantage of the emphasis on the separate codes was that international legislation could be completed within a given time frame, and as suggested earlier, that a package deal could be put together in which advantages for one state on one subject could be used to offset a perceived unsatisfactory result for that state in another, since the understanding was that 'nothing is agreed until everything is agreed'.

In addition, the strategy of conditional MFN—no 'free rides'—was designed to offer incentives to sign on to contracting states that might be wavering. To cite the clearest example, in return for stricter definitions of subsidy and a prohibition on export subsidies on non-primary products in the Subsidies Code, the United States agreed to amend its law to require an independent finding of material injury to a domestic injury before imposing a countervailing duty.[38] The amendment applied, however, only to signatories to the Agreement. Brazil, which had the ability to compete in the American market but maintained a vast program of subsidies, signed on, in order to make it more difficult for the United States to impose countervailing duties against its exports.[39] So, eventually, did most of the developing countries whose exports had realistic chances in the United States. But at least for a time, the resort to separate codes left a bad taste in the GATT community, as it seemed to depart—probably more in theory than in fact— from the most-favoured-nation principle.[40] Moreover, creation of the separate codes demonstrated in a readily visible way the disparity in influence and importance between the developed and the developing countries.

When the issue came up again in the Uruguay Round in the early 1990s, as discussed hereafter, the opposite decision was taken, and all states that wished to be part of the GATT/WTO system were required to sign all the agreements, except those that clearly could have no relevance for them.[41] But from the point of view of legislation to fill in the gaps in the law of international trade left in 1947, the Tokyo Round codes were the point of departure. The Tokyo

the codes there were consultative committees that would give interpretations and shape consultations, oversee dispute settlement, and recommend other measures; non-signatories were unable to participate in these activities, but a decision adopted by the CONTRACTING PARTIES before the codes entered into effect gave assurance that non-signatory contracting parties could receive regular reports and could follow the proceedings of the relevant Committees or Councils in an observer capacity.
Action by the CONTRACTING PARTIES on the Multilateral Trade Negotiations 28 Nov. 1979, GATT BISD, 26th Supp. 201 (1980).

[38] The details of the 1979 Subsidies Code, and its substantial revision in the Uruguay Round are addressed in Ch. 9.

[39] For a long and complicated controversy covering imports of shoes from Brazil into the United States, involving two GATT panel decisions and more than a decade of litigation in the United States, see *Footwear Distributors and Retailers of America* v. *United States*, 852 F. Supp. 1078 (Ct. Int'l Trade 1994).

[40] For an interesting, though not wholly, convincing attempt to demonstrate that the United States could comply with its MFN obligations while changing its laws only for benefit of signatories to the codes, see G. C. Hufbauer, J. Shelton Erb, H. P. Starr, 'The GATT Codes and the Unconditional Most-Favored-Nation Principle', 12 *Law & Policy in Int'l Business* 59 (1980).

[41] See Ch. 5, Sect. 5.2 infra.

Round codes were revised—in some instances significantly—in the Uruguay Round, but they served as the bridge between GATT 1947 and GATT 1994.

(c)   Achievements and Failures of the Tokyo Round

After a slow start and various ups and downs,[42] the Final Act of the Tokyo Round was submitted for signature on April 12, 1979. All the industrial countries signed, but at first only Argentina among developing countries did so, apparently in a silent boycott designed to show disappointment that despite their numerical majority, they had played a relatively minor role, particularly in the law-making aspects of the Tokyo Round. Later in the year, however, a number of developing countries signed one or more of the codes, after a resolution by the CONTRACTING PARTIES had been adopted 'reaffirm[ing] their intention to ensure the unity and consistency of the GATT system', and 'not[ing] that existing rights and benefits under the GATT of contracting parties not being parties to the [specialized] Agreements, including those derived from Article I [i.e. MFN], are not affected by these Agreements.'[43]

Seen a generation later, the greatest achievement of the Tokyo Round was maintenance of the 'unity and consistency' of the GATT system in the face of the strenuous differences expressed during the six-year negotiations, as well as the outside pressures—involving collapse of the international monetary system and recessions and energy crises throughout both the developed and less developed world. Maintenance of unity and consistency, it was understood, meant bringing the Tokyo Round to a successful conclusion, however success was defined, for failure—the break-up of the conference without agreement on at least a major portion of the items on the agenda— could well have led to the disintegration of the still-fragile GATT. It appears that the GATT, and with it the public law of international trade, had a need to be renewed every few years, like a slow-burning fire, lest the flames go out. The same can probably be said about the World Trade Organization created in the last round held under the GATT, as set forth in the next section.[44] The need to keep the momentum going was certainly present during the Tokyo Round in the 1970s, as well as during the Uruguay Round in the 1980s and 1990s. Still, the Director General of the GATT, Olivier Long, could fairly state, at the signing ceremony for the Tokyo Round:

---

[42] See Gilbert R. Winham, *International Trade and the Tokyo Round Negotiation* (1986), an account focusing on the process of negotiations by a Canadian Political scientist.

[43] Decision of November 28, 1979 on Action by the Contracting Parties on the Multilateral Trade Negotiations, GATT BISD, 26th Supp. 201, cited also in n. 37 supra.

[44] A first effort to launch a 'Millenium Round' at a Ministerial Conference of the WTO in Seattle in November–December 1999 proved unsuccessful, partly because of a failure to agree in advance on an agenda, partly because of organized opposition and demonstrations by a variety of non-governmental groups. A commitment to a new Round was agreed to in November 2001 in Doha, Qatar, based both on better preparation and on a location deliberately chosen to be inconvenient to potential demonstrators and protesters.

Never before have there been trade negotiations so ambitious in aim, so complex in structure and subject matter, or, perhaps so long-drawn-out over time. But the enormous effort in them has paid off.[45]

If the Director-General was understandably anxious to stress the positive achievements of the Tokyo Round, he could point first to international legislation on Subsidies and Countervailing Duties, on Dumping and Anti-Dumping (revised from 1967), on Government Procurement, on Technical Standards, on Customs Valuation, and on Import Licensing. Each of these agreements or codes contains substantive rules, and each established committees of signatories to oversee their implementation and in most cases, dispute settlement as well. The details of the more important of the agreements, as well as their revision, in the Uruguay Round are presented in subsequent chapters of this book. The fact of creation of a large body of law—much of it technical but nonetheless important—is without doubt the major achievement of the Tokyo Round.

Against these achievements must be set the one great failure of the Tokyo Round, the failure to achieve agreement on a Code on Safeguards. Safeguards, as mentioned earlier, was the name applied to measures of relief against sudden or unforeseen imports of a given product, usually in the form of some kind of quantitative restraint. In some instances safeguards were applied by importing states acting alone; in other instances safeguards were applied by agreement between the importing and exporting states, or by the industries in one or both countries with the tacit approval of the respective governments. Most 'grey area' measures were made public; others were kept secret as long as possible.[46] The GATT secretariat estimated that such arrangements outnumbered Article XIX actions by about ten to one.[47]

Most of the participants in the Tokyo Round agreed that some kind of international discipline should be imposed on safeguards which were clearly 'managed trade' and made up a significant portion of all trade. Indeed several versions of a draft code, or rather an 'Outline of an Arrangement' on safeguards were published near the close of the Tokyo Round. There appeared to be agreement that safeguard measures as defined could be taken only in the case of *serious* injury to domestic producers, but whether imports

[45] GATT: Press Release containing Statement by Director-General, April 12, 1979, GATT Doc. GATT 1234.

[46] For instance, the US steel industry initiated a proceeding in 1976 before the United States Special Representative for Trade Negotiations seeking retaliation by the United States for the consequence of a secret agreement between the Japanese and European steel industries, apparently with official sanction both in Tokyo and Brussels, to restrict and divide up steel exports from Japan to the European Community. The US Special Trade Representative investigated, and concluded that such a Japanese–EC understanding had in fact been reached, but he found insufficient impact on the American market to justify counteraction by the United States. See A. Lowenfeld, *Public Controls on International Trade*, 247–51 (2nd edn., 1983) and sources there cited.

[47] See John Croome, *Reshaping the World Trading System: A History of the Uruguay Round*, 53–4 (2nd edn. 1999).

must be 'the cause', or 'the principal cause' of serious injury was left blank and the overall duration permitted listed 3 years and 8 years as alternatives. The most contentious issue—stated to be the reason for inability to reach agreement—was what came to be known as 'selectivity', that is whether safeguards must be imposed on an MFN basis or could be imposed against a particular source of increased or excessive imports only.

The European Community insisted on the opportunity to impose safeguards selectively; the developing countries (as well as Japan) resisted, and the United States appeared to be in the middle, attempting without success to promote some kind of compromise. It is not clear whether inability to resolve this issue was the cause, or the excuse for failure to agree on a Safeguards Code, as had been called for by the Tokyo Declaration of 1973.[48] Everyone understood, however, that this was a major unfinished issue. If there was to be another round after the Tokyo Round, safeguards would be high on the agenda.[49]

Amid the many debates, working groups and task forces on the codes, it was almost forgotten that the Tokyo Round was also a tariff-cutting round. This time, once it was understood that agricultural tariffs would not be subjected to whatever tariff-cutting formula emerged, agreement on a formula for linear reductions proved comparatively easy. The principle was that the higher the initial tariff, the higher the percentage by which it would be cut, subject to an eight-year period of staging.[50] There were of course exceptions, which gave rise to other exceptions, and indeed some of the details were not filled in until November 1979, seven months after the formal close of the Tokyo Round. But the principle of linear tariff reductions was accepted (again excepting agricultural products), and 'overall reciprocity' was understood to comprehend harmonization. In contrast to the Kennedy Round, negotiations about tariffs in the Tokyo Round were neither the main event nor the object of protracted legal conflict.

---

[48] Tokyo Ministerial Declaration of September 14, 1973 (n. 31 supra), para. 1(d).

[49] See Ch. 5, Sect. 5.4 for the outcome.

[50] The formula, proposed by Switzerland, provided that if an initial duty was x percent, the final duty, after staging, would be $\frac{A(x)}{A+x}$.

For the United States and Japan, A was set at 14, so that, for example, a 30 percent duty would be reduced in stages until it came to rest at $\frac{14(30)}{44} = 9.54\%$; a 15 percent duty would be reduced to $\frac{14(15)}{29} = 7.24\%$.

For the European Comunity and the Nordic countries, A was set at 16, so that, to take just the second example, a 15 percent duty would be reduced to $\frac{16(15)}{31} = 7.74\%$.

4.4 THE URUGUAY ROUND[51]

(a) The Exploding Agenda

As early as 1982, well before the results of the Tokyo Round had been fully implemented and tested, the United States urged that a new round of GATT negotiations be undertaken. In part the supporters of the proposal sought to counter protectionist trends in the United States and elsewhere, stimulated by large and apparently growing trade deficits vis-à-vis Japan and other East Asian countries. But proponents of a new round of negotiations had in mind an agenda significantly broader than any that had previously come before the GATT. Up to now, the GATT had been focused exclusively on trade in goods—first, as we saw, on tariffs, and in the Tokyo Round on non-tariff measures as well. The global economy, however, consisted of much more than trade in goods. For all its imperfections, ambivalence, and fragility, the GATT seemed to combine the right principles and the right techniques to serve as the arena for negotiation about what came to be known as the New Areas—services, intellectual property and investment. The United States now urged that these subjects be added to the agenda of the GATT, along with the unfinished subject from prior rounds, notably safeguards and agriculture.

At first the United States was unsuccessful in persuading its potential negotiating partners to launch a new round or to adopt a new agenda. Opposition, or at least reluctance, came both from the developing countries, which had felt let down in the Tokyo Round, and from the European Community whose trade officials feared that a new round would present a new opportunity to attack the Common Agricultural Policy. But the United States persisted, and late in 1985 a Preparatory Committee was established to draft a program for a new GATT round, for submission to a Ministerial Meeting in the following year.[52]

The Ministerial Meeting was convened in September 1986 at Punta del Este in Uruguay, almost forty years after a conference with a comparably broad agenda had convened in Havana. The Ministerial Meeting was far from harmonious,[53] but after five days of arguments, a Ministerial Declaration was agreed to initiating the Eighth Round of Multilateral Trade Negotiations.[54] The Declaration stated that the 'launching, the conduct and

---

[51] A comprehensive account of the Uruguay Round through 1992, including the principal documents, is *The GATT Uruguay Round: A Negotiating History* (1986–92), Terence P. Stewart (ed.), 3 vols., 1993.

[52] GATT BISD, 32d Supp. 9 (1986).

[53] See e.g. the account of the meeting based on numerous interviews, in Steve Dryden, *Trade Warriors: USTR and the American Crusade for Free Trade*, 321–5 (1995).

[54] Ministerial Declaration on the Uruguay Round, 20 Sept. 1986, GATT BISD, 33d Supp., 19–30 (1987).

the implementation of the outcome of the negotiation shall be treated as part of a single undertaking', which seemed to invite the kinds of considerations that played a crucial role as the negotiations were winding up five, six and seven years later.[55] However, the Declaration also stated that 'Balanced concessions should be sought within broad trading areas and subjects to be negotiated, in order to avoid unwarranted cross-sectional demands.'

Judging by the topics listed as subjects for negotiation, the Uruguay Round was to be by far the most ambitious round of trade negotiations ever, dealing not only with tariffs, as had the first six rounds, or non-tariff barriers, as had the Tokyo Round, but also with trade-related aspects of investment regulations; of intellectual property rights (i.e. patents, trademarks, copyright, and counterfeiting); and of services, including perhaps, banking, accounting, insurance, shipping, and even legal services. In addition, another effort was to be made to reform trade in agriculture, and to reduce the bizarre system of subsidies and overproduction that had developed in many countries at the same time as horrifying famine prevailed in others. The Ministers also undertook once again to address the problem of safeguards, and to try to bring trade in textiles back more than nominally into the GATT framework. Also, they committed themselves to two immediate actions—so-called *standstill*— i.e. not to take any trade restrictive or distorting measure inconsistent with the GATT, or to take measures in exercise of GATT rights 'that would go beyond that which is necessary' to remedy specific situations; and *rollback*, i.e. to eliminate such trade restrictive or distorting measures previously taken, without requesting GATT concessions in return. Interestingly enough in the light of the eventual outcome, nothing in the Ministerial Declaration addressed the creation of a new organization, to supplement or supplant the GATT. Also, the Ministers separated out negotiation on trade in services into a separate part II of the Declaration, apparently because the developing countries, led by Brazil and India, wanted to make sure at the outset that if rules were to be established to open up access to service providers and they were accused of violating these rules, retaliation would not be permitted against their exports of manufactured products. One other subject became more important in the Uruguay Round than it had ever been before, again with the United States as principal proponent. If states were prepared, as they declared at Punta del Este, to draft rules on such a large number of subjects, there must be a more definite and predictable method of enforcing the rules

---

[55] Oversimplifying for illustrative purposes only, as the negotiations developed, the United States and the developing countries were allied on issues of access for agricultural products, with the European Community and Japan on the other side; the EC and the United States were allied on issues of intellectual property and (to a lesser extent) on services, with the developing countries on the other side; and the developing countries and EC were, if not allied, at least resistant to American positions on dumping and subsidies. Of course this list does not include all the issues before the Uruguay Round, and the positions of participants shifted from time to time, both as particular issues arose in the negotiations, and as new administrations came into office in the participating countries and sent new representatives to the negotiations.

and resolving disputes. Without giving any indication in which direction the solution would go, the Declaration stated:

[N]egotiations shall aim to improve and strengthen the rules and the procedures of the dispute settlement process . . . [including] the development of adequate arrangements for overseeing and monitoring . . . compliance with adopted recommendations.

(b) The Ups and Downs of the Uruguay Round

Negotiating groups were established on some 15 topics, concerning the various old and new subjects to be taken up in the Uruguay Round. Most of these groups met in 1987, but a few had their first meetings early in 1988. In December 1988, a Mid-term Ministerial Meeting was held in Montreal, and agreement was said to have been reached on 11 of the 15 topics being negotiated. But agreement could not be reached on four subjects—agriculture, textiles, protection of intellectual property, and safeguards—and doubts began to arise whether it would be possible to complete the Uruguay Round.

In April 1989, at a late-night bargaining session in Geneva at 'senior official' level (i.e. not the ministers themselves), guidelines were adopted for continuing negotiations on the four topics on which no agreement had been reached at Montreal. It seemed that the deadlock at Montreal had been broken, and that the chances were good that the Uruguay Round could be successfully concluded by the 1990 target date. In July 1989, the Trade Negotiations Committee agreed that the final Ministerial Meeting of the Uruguay Round would be held in Brussels in December 1990.

As the many negotiating groups and drafting groups continued to meet on the fifteen major items on the agenda of the Uruguay Round, it was not clear that a package deal could be achieved, but increasingly clear that partial deals—say on tariffs or dispute settlement or amendments to the Subsidies Code—were not acceptable to the major actors. In July 1990, the Group of Seven Economic Summit, meeting in Houston, said in its closing communiqué: 'The successful outcome of the Uruguay Round has the highest priority on the international economic agenda.' But reports from Houston disclosed that the Summit had been stormy, with the American delegates maintaining that the European Community was 'not engaged' in the negotiations on agriculture, and insisting that without agreement on planned reduction (if not elimination) of the subsidies of the Common Agricultural Policy, there could be no successful conclusion of the Uruguay Round. The United States sought commitments on substantial reduction in all three elements of the Common Agricultural Policy—the levels of domestic support, import barriers (i.e. the variable levy),[56] and export subsidies. It did not get them.

[56] The variable levy, a device employed by the EEC since the formation of the Common Agricultural Policy, was an import duty measured by the difference between the landed cost of a given commodity such as wheat or corn and a target price negotiated among the member states of the Community and between producers and consumers, but not with non-member

In the course of fall 1990, the attention of several of the principal participants in the Uruguay Round was directed elsewhere—notably the unification of Germany, the crisis in the Persian Gulf, and the replacement after nearly a dozen years in office of Prime Minister Thatcher of Great Britain. While the trade delegations kept meeting and exchanging drafts, it became clear that if there was to be a breakthrough, it would have to come from commitment of the political leaders.

The press reported the issue as United States versus Europe; in fact the deadlock was more complicated. Not only was Japan challenged on its support of inefficient growers of rice and soya beans; the Cairns group[57] and developing countries generally made it clear that if they were not assured of greater access for their agricultural and other primary products in the markets of the industrial countries, they would not accept other parts of the proposed package, i.e. they would not agree to open their markets to Western services, liberalize their investment regimes, or agree to grant protection to the industrial world's intellectual property rights (including patents on pharmaceutical and protection for computer software). Without these concessions from the developing countries, the United States said, the whole project of the Uruguay Round would fall apart.

For two more years, the parties negotiated about the many issues in the Uruguay Round. The warning in the Punta del Este Declaration against 'unwarranted cross-sectoral demands' was regularly disregarded. One party or another always asserted that its 'concession'—on services, on TRIPs (Trade-related Intellectual Property Issues) or TRIMs (Trade-related Investment Measures), or Textiles, or whatever—would be taken off the table if agreement could not be reached on the most divisive issues, which seemed to be agricultural subsidies and trade in agriculture in general.

In November 1990, the trade ministers from 107 countries met in Brussels to attempt a final push to bring the Uruguay Round to conclusion. In this first test of economic cooperation in the post-Cold War world, the United States appeared to behave more combatively than in prior rounds, less willing, it seemed, to subordinate economic aims to security concerns. The European Community, on the other hand, with three more members than in

---

states. The higher the target price the higher the levy, and over time, the higher the proportion of crops produced within the Community rather than imported from lower-cost producers such as the United States, Canada or Australia. The variable levy seemed to be inconsistent with several articles of the GATT but had never been directly challenged in the GATT or in bilateral controversies, except when it affected entry of new members, such as Spain and Portugal in 1986.

[57] This was a group of 14 food-exporting countries that had met in Cairns, a resort city in North-east Australia, a month before the meeting at Punta del Este. The group formulated and on the whole maintained a joint policy throughout the Uruguay Round, looking to open up markets for their products and reduce subsidization and other devices that distorted the flow of agricultural products. The members of the Cairns Group were Argentina, Australia, Brazil, Canada, Chile, Colombia, Hungary, Indonesia, Malaysia, New Zealand, Philippines, Thailand, Uruguay, and Fiji.

the last round (Greece, Portugal, and Spain) as well as a reunited Germany that had problems of its own, seemed to find it more difficult than ever to make a political decision. The developing countries played a substantially greater role than in prior rounds, and efforts by the European Community to buy off members of the Cairns group by individual offers—more flowers from Colombia, more beef from Argentina—on the whole proved unavailing. In midweek of the Brussels Conference, the Latin American countries withdrew their delegates from working groups on Intellectual Property and on Services to protest the lack of progress on agriculture. The United States almost walked out as well, but decided to stay till the end of the conference. But, as the *Financial Times* put it, the GATT session broke off in disarray.[58]

Many observers thought the failure of the Brussels Ministerial Conference meant the end of the Uruguay Round, and perhaps of the GATT itself. But none of the participants were willing to go that far, and for two months the Director-General of the GATT, Arthur Dunkel, struggled to keep the Uruguay Round alive.[59]

GATT working groups continued to meet throughout 1991, but no breakthrough was achieved. At year-end 1991, the Director-General issued a Comprehensive Draft Final Act, a document of 436 pages containing what he thought were either agreed texts or feasible compromises. The Dunkel Draft, as it came to be known, was impressive in demonstrating how much had been (almost) achieved, and how much would be given up if it all came to naught. In an accompanying statement, Mr. Dunkel asked the participants to provide a first appraisal of his draft at a meeting scheduled for January 1992. The meeting was held, and much of the text was tacitly accepted, but each of the major participants had major objections, and all concurred that nothing is agreed unless everything is agreed.

Agriculture, and particularly efforts to limit the subsidy programs of the European Community, turned out to be the major and continuing obstacle throughout 1992; the effort to complete the negotiations while President

---

[58] *Financial Times*, 7 Dec. 1990, p. 1.

[59] The Director-General's task was made urgent by the fact that the 'fast track' negotiating authority under United States law expired May 31, 1991, and in order to meet the strictures of that legislation, the President had to submit proposed agreements 90 days before June 1, 1991. 19 U.S.C., § 2903 (b)(1), as enacted in the Omnibus Trade and Competitiveness Act of 1988, Publ. L. 100-318 (23 Aug. 1988). However, the statute added that if the President was of the opinion that the fast-track procedures (which permit no amendments once the implementing bill is introduced and set a timetable for action by each House of Congress) should be extended, he could request an extension of the authority for two years, provided his request was submitted by March 1, 1991, accompanied by a description of the progress made to date and a statement of the reasons why the extension is needed to complete the negotiations. President Bush made such a request on March 1, 1991, and (with difficulty) secured a two-year extension until May 31, 1993. As it turned out, the Round was not completed by that date either, and President Clinton was obliged to seek another extension, which the Congress reluctantly granted through April 16, 1994, but with a 120-advance notice requirement, so that the effective deadline for completing the Uruguay Round became December 15, 1993.

Bush remained in office almost succeeded—but not quite.[60] It is interesting to note that three elements of the Dunkel Draft that eventually effected major changes in the law and organization of international trade attracted little notice or public attention in the two years between the publication of the Dunkel Draft and the final agreement. Dunkel proposed (i) that the Balkanization of GATT law that had taken place in the Tokyo Round[61] be reversed, and that all agreements should be signed by all parties; (ii) that an integrated system of binding dispute settlement be instituted covering not only the General Agreement but all the associated agreements and codes, and including authority for retaliation; and (iii) that the GATT be placed on a firm organizational footing by creation of what the draft called a Multilateral Trade Organization and eventually became the WTO. Of course these proposals did not emerge full-blown from the Director General's head.[62] But they had not been the subject of the sharp and acrimonious debate devoted to subsidies, to trade in services, to agriculture, and to the many others that had divided the contracting parties for more than half a decade.

(c)   The Final Stage

The negotiations continued throughout 1992, prodded by a new Director-General, Peter Sutherland, an energetic Irishman who had previously served as Competition Commissioner of the European Community and as the chairman of a major bank. In the United States, much of the new Clinton administration's energy in the summer and fall of 1993 was focused on the North American Free Trade Agreement, which proved to be much more controversial in the United States than the Uruguay Round, or than the predecessor Canada–US Free Trade Agreement. After NAFTA made it through the US Congress, all the major participants made a renewed effort to complete the Uruguay Round by the deadline set by the Congress.[63] Even the controversy over agriculture was eventually resolved, with agreement by the EEC to cut back its export subsidies more slowly than had previously been understood, in return for imposed access to the European market for the

---

[60] The key was a long-running dispute between the United States and the EC over soybeans, which appeared to be settled at an agreement at Blair House (the Presidential guest house in Washington) in November 1992, negotiated for the Community by its Commissioner for Agriculture. But France blocked the agreement, and with it the possibility of concluding the Uruguay Round in 1992.

[61] See Sect. 4.3(b) supra.

[62] The suggestions about making final decisions of dispute panels binding, and about establishment of a Multilateral Trade Organization, had been included in an earlier Draft Final Act circulated by the Secretariat at the Brussels Conference in December 1990. But the proposals had been in alternative form or in brackets, and were not debated intensively. In the Dunkel draft, the proposals were made in an affirmative, not an optional form, substantially as they appeared in the final text.

[63] See n. 59 supra.

United States and other suppliers. New issues kept coming up,[64] but on December 15, 1993, the last day for the 'fast track' authority of the United States executive branch, it was announced that the Uruguay Round had been successfully concluded. 'Today', the new Director-General said, 'the world has chosen openness and cooperation instead of uncertainty and conflict.'[65] While in the enthusiasm of the moment the Director-General may have exaggerated the promise of decline of uncertainty and conflict, Mr. Sutherland was surely right to point out that 'important new areas of the World economy have been brought under multilateral disciplines, and that added together, the achievements amount to a major renewal of the world trading system.'[66] He did not add, though many must have felt, that the effort had come very close to failure, and that the commitment to the original principles, now covering a much wider area, was still fragile and not free from ambivalence in any country.

SUMMARY

The GATT evolved unevenly from its almost accidental beginnings in the 1940s to a vastly greater organization and corpus of law. In the first five rounds of multilateral trade negotiations (1947–61), the emphasis was largely on reduction of tariffs on the basis of most-favoured-nation treatment and 'mutual exchange of benefits'. Beginning with the Kennedy Round (1964–7) and more particularly in the Tokyo Round (1973–9), the contracting parties turned their attention to crafting rules applicable to non-tariff measures that affected trade in goods, including dumping and anti-dumping, subsidies and countervailing duties, government procurement, and various techniques of valuation of merchandise for purposes of assessing customs duties. In the Uruguay Round (1986–93), the GATT contracting states, by now over 100, continued the practice of negotiating rules to govern international trade, but moved well beyond trade in goods to address also intellectual property and aspects of services and transnational investment. They also reached agreements that previously eluded them concerning so-called 'safeguards', and concerning trade in agriculture, they formally established a new World Trade Organization, and they created a system of binding dispute settlement designed to be applicable to the vast new body of law developed by the Uruguay Round and its predecessors.

An overview of the law and institutions of international trade at the beginning of the twenty-first century is presented in Chapter 5. The succeeding chapters address the principal subjects in more detail.

---

[64] One issue that almost scuttled the agreement at the last moment concerned a box office tax imposed by France on (largely American) motion pictures, the proceeds of which were used to subsidize French films. Eventually this controversy, which had emerged very late in the negotiations, was put over without resolution.

[65] See GATT, *News of the Uruguay Round*, 21 Dec. 1993, 1.   [66] Id.

5

The GATT/WTO System after the Uruguay Round: A Preliminary Survey

5.1   A First Look at the System

The Final Act of the Uruguay Round was formally signed at a Ministerial Meeting in Marrakesh, Morocco on April 15, 1994. The Ministers, representing 111 nations, declared the work of the Trade Negotiations Committee to be complete and the Uruguay Round concluded. They committed themselves to seek to complete all steps necessary to establish the new World Trade Organization by January 1, 1995, and (in contrast to all prior deadlines) that deadline was kept.

Altogether, the Agreements, Annexes, Ministerial Decisions and Declarations, and Understandings take up 558 printed pages, not counting the schedules of tariff concessions, specific commitments and MFN exemptions submitted by contracting parties in the course of the Uruguay Round. In some ways the conclusion of the Uruguay Round and the establishment of the World Trade Organization constitute a new start for the international law of international trade. But there is no doubt that the WTO is a continuation of the GATT system, a ratification and formalization of close to fifty years of development of rules of an institution—written and customary—and of attitudes of the participating states. To seal this fundamental point, Article XVI(1) of the Marrakesh Agreement Establishing the World Trade Organization states:

Except as otherwise provided under this Agreement or the Multilateral Trade Agreements, the WTO shall be guided by the decisions, procedures and customary practices followed by the Contracting Parties to GATT 1947 and the bodies established in the framework of GATT 1947.

Thus in a real sense, what the world agreed to in the Uruguay Round was to subject a great many aspects of international economic activity to the principles that had been agreed to half a century earlier by far fewer states and in the context of a far smaller agenda. Not all areas of the international economy were included—competition law and the environment being two notable topics left for the next round—and not all the areas covered were the subject of equal commitments—the General Agreement on Services (GATS), for instance, is little more than a skeleton for future growth. But the principles are essentially the same as set out in Chapter 3—most-favoured-nation treatment, binding commitments that can be unbound only against compensation, national treatment with regard to most internal regulations affecting trade, regular joint efforts to reduce barriers to trade—plus more international scrutiny than ever before over the acts of individual states that may distort trade flows, and a system of dispute settlement focused both on requiring compliance by states with the decisions of impartial tribunals and on establishing legal interpretations with value as precedent, as contrasted with merely defusing particular controversies.[1]

The GATT/WTO system as of the turn of the century may be described as having four principal elements. *First*, the traditional GATT concerning trade in goods, fortified after more than seven years of struggle by a renewed commitment, and augmented by twelve multilateral agreements binding on all members,[2] plus two 'plurilateral agreements', binding only on these states that have accepted them.[3]

Second, separate from the GATT but embraced within the WTO, the 111 members of the WTO are parties of GATS, the General Agreement on Trade in Services.[4] GATS is an agreement to begin to apply to trade in services the basic principles of the GATT—non-discrimination and progressive liberalization—but subject to numerous exemptions and guaranteeing national

---

[1] Not all of the Uruguay Round Agreements are here discussed, on the ground that some of the agreements are not primarily law-making in content. Thus, for instance, the Agreement on Agriculture was in some sense the most important accord in the Uruguay Round, since without it, as shown in the previous chapter, the Uruguay Round might well have ended in failure, and the effort to seal the agreement on agriculture delayed completion of the Round by at least one, and perhaps as many as three years. The Agreement on Textiles and Clothing, which provided for integrating trade in those sectors into the overall GATT regime over a ten-year period, also was necessary to reach the eventual package deal. But neither of these agreements is primarily rule-based, as contrasted with mercantile in content, and indeed both may be regarded as long and complicated exceptions to the rules making up the GATT/WTO system.

An Agreement on Rules of Origin created a 'work programme' designed to develop over a three-year period a harmonized system of 'objective, understandable and predictable' rules of origin, addressed primarily to the problem of goods in whose creation more than one country is involved—e.g. an automobile assembled in Patria containing an engine manufactured in Xandia and a transmission made in Tertia. See Joseph A. LaNasa III, 'Rules of Origin and the Uruguay Round's Effectiveness in Harmonizing and Regulating Them', 90 *Am. J. Int'l L.* 625 (1996); Frederic P. Cantin and Andreas F. Lowenfeld, 'Rules of Origin, the Canada–U.S. FTA, and the *Honda* Case', 87 *Am. J. Int'l L.* 375 (1993). As of year-end 2001, the target dates under the Agreement had been extended several times, but the effort at harmonization was still a work in progress.

An Agreement on Preshipment Inspection addresses the practice by some developing countries as importers to employ specialized private companies to conduct surveillance in the country of export to control overinvoicing, underinvoiceing, misclassification, misappropriation of donor funds, and similar problems. Again, while the PSI Agreement is not unimportant, it does not, it seems, justify discussion in the present volume.

The Agreement on the Application of Sanitary and Phytosanitary Measure is discussed in the chapter on Trade and the Environment, Ch. 11.

[2] Since the WTO, in contrast to the GATT, see Ch. 3, Sect. 3.2, is clearly and unashamedly an international organization, the terms 'member' or 'member states' may now be used in place of 'contracting states', as was the practice from 1947 to 1994.

[3] Two other plurilateral agreements concluded as part of the Uruguay Round—an International Dairy Agreement and an International Bovine Meat Agreement—were terminated at the end of 1997.

[4] Recall that a separate track was established for negotiation concerning services, initially because of concern by developing countries that denial of access for providers of services would lead to trade sanctions. See Ch. 4, Sect. 4.4(a); Ch. 6, Sect. 6.1(b).

treatment only for sections listed on each member's schedule, i.e. subject to future negotiation.[5]

Third, the Agreement on Trade Related Aspects of Intellectual Property Rights (TRIPs) for the first time brings intellectual property—including patents, copyright, trademark, and counterfeit goods—within the orbit of the public law of international trade, thus making the basic principles of most-favoured-nation and national treatment applicable to intellectual property law and lending the enforcement (and even retaliation) capacities of the GATT/WTO system to the century-old system of the Paris and Berne Conventions and more recent conventions negotiated within the orbit of the World Intellectual Property Organization (WIPO).

Fourth, an Understanding on Dispute Settlement builds on the dispute settlement mechanism that had grown up pursuant to Articles XXII and XXIII of the GATT, but makes it applicable (with minor exceptions) to all agreements embraced within the GATT/WTO system, and provides for binding decisions in state-to-state disputes and compensation or retaliation in the event of non-compliance.

In addition, the agreement establishing WTO creates, for the first time, a Trade Policy Review Body, to provide systematic surveillance of measures taken by member states that may affect the functioning of the multilateral trading system.[6] The four countries (or groups of countries) with the greatest impact on international trade are subject to review every two years, the next 16 countries in importance every four years, and the remainder every six years. How well the Trade Policy Review Mechanism will work is not yet clear.[7] In concept, however, it appears that at the same time that the dispute settlement mechanisms are being fortified, the WTO will endeavour to anticipate problems before they arise in a contentious context, an authority not granted to the largely improvised secretariat of the prior GATT.[8]

---

[5] See Chapter 6 for a description of the GATS and more detailed discussion of its application to financial services and to telecommunications.

[6] Marrakesh Agreement Establishing the World Trade Organization, Art. IV(4) and Annex 3 thereto.

[7] Compare the largely unsuccessful program of surveillance established in the Amended Articles of Agreement of the International Monetary Fund, Ch. 17, Sect. 17.4.

[8] The official explanation of the Trade Review Policy Mechanism states:

These 'peer reviews' by other WTO members encourage goverments to follow more closely the WTO rules and disciplines and to fulfil their commitments. In practice the reviews have two broad results: they enable outsiders to understand a country's policies and circumstances, and they provide feedback to the reviewed country on its performance in the system.

For each review the government concerned prepares a policy statement, and the WTO secretariat prepares a detailed report, written independently. These two reports are submitted to the Trade Policy Review Body (in principle representatives of all member states), and the reports and the results of the discussion are subsequently published.

5.2   THE TOKYO ROUND AGREEMENTS REVISED I:
THE 'UNFAIR TRADE' REGIMES

All of the Tokyo Round agreements were reconsidered in the course of the Uruguay Round. Four of these agreements—on Civil Aircraft, Government Procurement, Dairy Products, and Bovine Meat, were renegotiated as 'Plurilateral Agreements', i.e. binding only on those states that accepted them. All the others, known as Multilateral Agreements, were 'integral parts of the Agreement Establishing the WTO', i.e. in contrast to the optional character of the agreements negotiated in the Tokyo Round,[9] all members of the GATT/WTO system—143 as of year-end 2001—were parties to all the agreements.

(a)   Subsidies and Countervailing Measures[10]

The 1979 Subsidies Code, as discussed in the preceding chapter had been viewed as a major achievement of the Tokyo Round. The Code had firmly established the rule that (primary products aside) export subsidies were unacceptable for developed countries, a rule only ambiguously stated in Article XVI of the GATT. Furthermore, the Code had confirmed that countervailing duties on imported products must be founded not only on a determination of subsidization but also on a determination of material injury (or threat of injury) to a domestic industry. Also, the 1979 Code established a dispute settlement procedure, designed to afford remedies not only to importing countries, but also to exporting countries asserting injury to their industries as a result of other countries' program of subsidies.

In practice, the 1979 Subsidies Code had proved disappointing, partly because the outcome of complaints under the dispute settlement procedure had been inconclusive,[11] and partly because the subsidies that caused the most controversy, including a major confrontation between the European Coal and Steel Community and the United States,[12] were not export subsidies as defined, but consisted in large part of governmental measures that many states regarded as not only justifiable but indeed desirable.

The Uruguay Round Agreement departs from the sharp distinction between export and domestic subsidies, and instead defines subsidies in terms of financial contribution by a government conferring a benefit on the recipient, and then divides subsidies as defined into three categories—

---

[9] See Ch. 4, Sect. 4.3(b).

[10] Agreement on Subsidies and Countervailing Measures. For a more detailed and analytical treatment, see Ch. 9.

[11] See Robert E. Hudec, *Enforcing International Trade Laws*, pp. 145–64 (1993).

[12] See e.g. A. Lowenfeld, *Public Controls on International Trade*, pp. 427–49 and supporting documents (2nd. edn. 1983).

prohibited (known as the 'red light' category), non-actionable (known as the 'green light' category), and in between (known as the 'yellow light' category). Further, whereas the Tokyo Round Subsidies Code had essentially exempted developing countries from the discipline of the Code, the revised Agreement exempts only the least developed countries from the prohibition on subsidies contingent on export performance, and makes most of its other provisions, with some modifications and grace periods, applicable to all developing countries.

Red light or prohibited subsidies include the previously condemned subsidies contingent on export performance, but also import substitution subsidies, i.e. subsidies contingent upon the use of domestic over imported goods. *Yellow light* or actionable subsidies are not expressly defined, except that they must meet a test of specificity—*de jure* or *de facto*, and that they do not come within the other two categories. *Green light* or protected subsidies—the major innovation in the 1994 Subsidies Code—are subsidies that may not be challenged in the WTO dispute settlement mechanism or be subjected to countervailing duties under national law, reflecting a recognition that many governments undertake certain kinds of expenditures that have a relation to the production of goods—some more direct than others—but are not viewed as unfair trade practices.

The Uruguay Agreement states that no Member *should cause*, through the use of any subsidy, *adverse effects* to the interests of other members, and provides both for international challenge under the strengthened dispute settlement mechanism and for countervailing duty proceedings under national law. In another innovation compared to the prior code, the revised Agreement on Subsidies divides 'adverse effects' into three classes—traditional injury to the domestic industry of another member which is up to the complainant to establish; nullification or impairment of benefits accruing to other Members, also with the burden on the complainant; and what some observers have called 'dark amber' subsidies, i.e. four kinds of subsidies *presumed to cause serious prejudice*, with the burden shifted to the respondent state to show that no adverse effects were caused by the challenged measure.[13] Among the 'dark amber' subsidies are total subsidization of a product exceeding 5 percent *ad valorem*; subsidies to cover operating losses sustained by an industry or an enterprise; and direct forgiveness of a debt.

Five years after the new Subsidies Agreement entered into effect, it was too early to tell whether the solutions agreed on were the right ones, and whether they would prove more successful than prior attempts in this area to subject the political value judgments of governments to a regime of legal rules and remedies. There was no doubt, however, that the Uruguay Subsidies Agreement constituted a major legislative effort to move beyond the original GATT and beyond the steps taken in the Tokyo Round.

---

[13] See Ch. 9, Sect. 9.6.

(b)   Dumping and Anti-Dumping[14]

The GATT Anti-Dumping Code, as noted in the preceding chapter, dates back to the Kennedy Round, and was amended in the Tokyo Round to conform as closely as possible to the Subsidies Code.[15] Though drafting the Uruguay Round Agreement on Anti-Dumping proved unexpectedly difficult and contentious, the final product, in contrast to the Agreement on Subsidies, contains no striking innovations. It essentially follows the scheme of the prior versions, but spells out in more detail terms that had been left undefined in 1967 and 1979.

The basic definition of dumping, set out in Article VI(1) of the GATT, remains: Contrary to the layman's conception that dumping means getting rid of overproduction or oversupply at whatever price is obtainable, dumping in international trade law means introduction of a product into the commerce of another country at less than normal value. *Normal value* means in the first instance home market price; if home market price is not available or is insignificant, the comparison of the challenged import price is with sales for export to a third country, or with cost of production in the country of origin, plus a reasonable addition for overhead and profit. Article VI(1) of the GATT says that dumping as thus defined is to be condemned if it causes or threatens material injury to an established industry in the importing country. The traditional remedy if dumping and injury are found (typically by administrative agencies) is an anti-dumping duty equal to the margin of dumping, applied to products of the exporter against which the finding runs.[16] Motive has no bearing on dumping as governed by the GATT and the Anti-Dumping Agreement; thus the presence or absence of 'predatory intent', is not relevant in dumping proceedings consistent with the GATT.[17]

The Uruguay Round Anti-Dumping Code, building on its predecessors, gives instructions on how to make the various findings necessary to reach a determination in a dumping case. For example, the Agreement provides that home market sales may normally be disregarded for purposes of the comparison with the challenged price if such sales constitute less than 5 percent

[14] Agreement on Implementation of Article VI of the General Agreement on Tariffs and Trade 1994. For a more detailed and analytical treatment, see Ch. 10.

[15] For example, the provisions in the 1979 Anti-Dumping Code concerning determination of injury were amended to track the corresponding provision of the 1979 Subsidies Code, as both codes in this respect interpret Article VI(6) of the GATT.

[16] The margin of dumping is the difference (after various adjustments) between the price at which the product is sold in the importing country and the 'normal value', determined as described in the text. For a more detailed explanation, see Ch. 10, Sects. 10.1, 10.5(c).

[17] GATT Article VI and the codes in implementation of that article were based on the United States Anti-Dumping Act of 1921, 42 Stat. 11 (1921), 19 U.S.C. §160 (1921–70). An earlier United States statute, the Anti-dumping Act of 1916, 39 Stat. 798 (1916) requires proof that the challenged importation was not only made at a price below that prevailing in the country of origin, but was made *with intent* to destroy or injure a domestic industry. The remedy is a civil or criminal penalty. The 1916 Act is rarely used and even more rarely successful, and is outside the GATT scheme.

of sales of the product in question to the importing country.[18] Sales below cost in the domestic market or a third country market may be disregarded for purposes of the comparison if, but only if, the authorities determine that such sales are made within an extended period of time (normally a year) in substantial quantities (normally at least 20 percent of total sales) and at prices that do not provide for the recovery of all costs within a reasonable time.[19] Detailed provisions spell out how records are to be kept, how costs are to be allocated, and how changes in exchange rates are to be dealt with. Also, the Agreement contains important provisions concerning the gathering of evidence in anti-dumping proceedings and introducing more 'transparency' into the process.[20] As in the prior codes, the Uruguay Round Anti-Dumping Agreement sets out detailed requirements for a determination of injury to an industry, and for establishing the required causal link between importation of dumped products and injury, 'including an evaluation of all relevant economic factors'.

The 1979 Code stated that anti-dumping duties were to remain in force only as long as they were necessary to counteract dumping that was causing injury. The 1994 Agreement repeats this provision but adds that anti-dumping duties shall be terminated not later than five years from their imposition (or from a review) unless a new determination is made that removal of the duty would be likely to lead to continuance or renewal of dumping and injury.[21]

In addition to anti-dumping duties imposed by the importing country, the 1994 Anti-Dumping Code, like the Tokyo Round Code, makes provision for dispute settlement. But whereas under the prior agreement a dispute not resolved by consultation would be referred to the Committee on Anti-Dumping Practices, under the integrated WTO, disputes concerning dumping are to be referred to the new Dispute Settlement Body for binding decision.

As explored in Chapter 10, the whole subject of dumping and anti-dumping is controversial, and as it came out of the Uruguay Round seems to be governed more by law than by economics. Taken together, the Agreement on Subsidies and the Agreement on Anti-Dumping reflect the concern of the major countries that reduced trade barriers will lead to 'unfair trade' as defined, balanced against the concern that defense against unfair trade does not become defense against trade in general.

---

[18] Anti-Dumping Agreement, Art. 2.2, n. 2.   [19] Id., Article 2.2.1.
[20] Id., Article 6.1–6.14 plus two Annexes (evidence); Article 12.1–12.3 (public notice and explanation of determinations).
[21] Id., Article 11.3.

5.3   The Tokyo Round Agreements Revised II:
The Lesser Agreements

(a)   Customs Valuation[22]

Tariffs—the principal subject in the first six GATT rounds and on the agenda of the Tokyo and Uruguay Rounds as well—are generally expressed as a percentage of the *value* of the product being imported—a rate *ad valorem*. Article VII of the GATT states that the value for customs purposes of imported merchandise 'should be based on the actual value of the . . . merchandise . . . and should not be based on the value of the merchandise of national origin or on arbitrary or fictitious values.' 'Actual value' is defined (again with use of the word 'should') as 'the price at which, at a time and place determined by the legislation of the country of importation, such or like merchandise is sold or offered for sale in the ordinary course of trade.' Article VII made an important statement—an exporter from Patria could reduce the duty imposed by Xandia by reducing its export sales price, which would not be possible if the duty were based on a competing domestic price.[23] But the method of assessing the 'actual value' of imported merchandise for customs purposes is left vague in Article VII, and prior to the Tokyo Round there had been wide variation among Contracting Parties as to how this function was performed. The West European countries had moved to harmonization on customs matters even before formation of the Common Market—on issues of tariff nomenclature[24] and definition of value, and had established a Customs Cooperation Council designed to insure uniform application of customs practices of signatory states. Neither the United States nor Canada had participated in these efforts, and prior to the Tokyo Round at least three approaches to customs valuation were in use on the part of developed countries, plus a variety of approaches—not all of them published or consistent—on the part of developing countries.[25] The European approach, adopted by the Community, was to focus on a uniform *notional* concept

---

[22] Agreement on Implementation of Article VII of the General Agreement on Tariffs and Trade 1994.

[23] This was the vice of the notorious American Selling Price, a formula written into law by the Congress in 1922 and applicable to benzenoid chemicals and a few other products which could result in tariffs of more than 100 percent *ad valorem* in certain instances. The United States delegation in the Kennedy Round had agreed *ad referendum* to eliminate ASP, but Congress had not adopted the implementing legislation. The issue arose again during the Tokyo Round, and this time Congress went along as part of the Tokyo Round Agreements Act. Pub. L. 96-39, §204(b), amending 19 U.S.C. §1401a.

[24] e.g. is an automobile lamp an 'auto part' or a 'lamp' for purposes of tariff classification.

[25] By the 1970s, customs duties were regarded in developed countries as a trade regulation device, and not primarily as a source of government revenue. For some developing countries, in contrast, customs duties were an important source of revenue.

of valuation, that is a price at which goods ought to be sold, regardless of particular transactions between a given exporter and a given importer.[26] The American approach, in contrast, was based on a *positive* concept of valuation, that is on the price at which the imported goods or like goods are in fact sold under specified conditions. However, the American procedures for customs valuation were a product of several statutes that were not always consistent with one another, and, it was alleged, had been subject of lobbying for protectionist purposes.[27] Canada, whose imports frequently involved transactions between parents and subsidiaries, had used an approach for customs valuation similar to that used in dumping investigations (but without comparable procedures), that is, it looked to fair market value in the country of export. For Canada this was relatively easy, since more than two-thirds of its imports originated in the United States. No other country was prepared to accept this approach.

The issues were hard fought in the Tokyo Round, but agreement on a Customs Valuation Code was eventually reached.[28] The key to agreement was that all sides concurred that their existing methods of valuation were unsatisfactory and in need of reform, and that an international code could be a vehicle for such reform. In essence, the American approach looking to transaction value was accepted, in return for commitment by the United States to abandon American Selling Price,[29] and to modernize its legislation to conform to the agreement. Article 1 of the Tokyo Round Code, retained almost verbatim in Article 1 of the Uruguay Round Agreement, provides that 'the customs value of imported goods shall be the transaction value, that is the price actually paid or payable for the goods when sold for export to the country of importation', subject to stated adjustments for costs separately invoiced but payable by the buyer.[30] If actual transaction value cannot be determined, for example because the seller and buyer are related, the Agreement provides a hierarchy of alternative methods of valuation, looking to the transaction value first of identical goods, then of similar goods,

---

[26] This was the concept of the so-called Brussels Definition of Value (BDV), established by Annex I of the Convention on the Valuation of Goods for Customs Purposes, signed at Brussels on 15 Dec. 1950, 171 U.N.T.S. 305. All the European states became parties to this Convention, and Japan and later Australia also joined.

[27] In fact there were nine different methods of valuation, without clear distinctions as to when a given method was applicable.

[28] For a detailed description of the negotiations, including a discussion of the difference in position in some countries between the commercial or export-oriented interests and the importing or financial interests, see Gilbert R. Winham, *International Trade and the Tokyo Round Negotiation*, pp. 105–9, 177–89, 223–9, 352–3 (1986). For a discussion by American expert on customs valuation, see Saul L. Sherman, 'Reflections on the New Customs Valuation Code', 12 *Law & Policy in Int'l Bus.* 119 (1980).

[29] See n. 23, supra. The process was to convert ASP duties to *ad valorem* equivalents, and then to negotiate their reduction.

[30] These adjustments, listed in Article 8 of both the 1979 Code and the 1994 Agreement, include, *inter alia* the cost of brokerage, containers, and packing, royalties, engineering, plus, at the option of the importing country, cost of transportation, handling charges, and insurance.

and finally to deducted or computed value, at the option of the importer.[31] The Agreement expressly states, however, that the fact that the buyer (importer) and seller (exporter) are related 'shall not in itself' be grounds for rejecting the primary transaction value method.[32]

The developing countries, led in this as in other controversies in the GATT by India and Brazil, were disappointed by the outcome of the Tokyo Round negotiations on customs valuation, and succeeded in obtaining a five-year grace period under the heading of 'Special and Differential Treatment'. In the Uruguay Round the issues were again debated, but with the European Community, the United States, Canada, and Australia all supporting the 1979 agreement, and only the developing countries opposed, the Customs Valuation Agreement as it emerged from the Uruguay Round was unchanged in all essentials.[33] The principal difference between the 1979 and the 1994 Agreement is that whereas only some 40 countries had joined the Tokyo Round Customs Valuation Code, all member states of the WTO (as well as any future members) are now bound under the integrated GATT/WTO system, and that the WTO Dispute Settlement mechanism is expressly made applicable to controversies concerning customs valuations.[34]

(b)   Technical Barriers to Trade

In contrast to subsidies, dumping, and customs valuation, the subject of technical barriers to trade or 'standards' has no express provision in the GATT on which to hang an agreement. At least two articles of the General Agreement recognize that industrial standards, design or safety requirements, and the like, can have the effect—and sometimes the purpose—of impeding the flow of trade across national boundaries. Article III of the GATT, the National Treatment article, provides that imported products shall be accorded treatment no less favourable than that accorded to like products of national origin in respect of all laws, regulations, and requirements affecting

---

[31] Deducted value (Art. 5) is based on the price at which the imported goods (or identical or similar imported goods) are sold in the greatest aggregate quantity, minus cost of sales and other charges payable within the country of importation; *computed value* is based on the cost of materials and labour employed in producing the imported goods, plus an amount for overhead and profit equal to that usually reflected in the industry in question in the country of export. The Agreement itself contains elaborate explanatory notes and illustrations; for detailed description and analysis, see Saul L. Sherman and Hinrich Glasshoff, *Customs Valuation; Commentary on the GATT Customs Valuation Code* (2nd. edn. 1988).

[32] Customs Valuation Agreement, Article 1(2)(a). Article 15(4) states that for purposes of the Agreement persons shall be deemed to be related only if they fall into one of eight categories, including partnership, common ownership or control and membership in the same family.

[33] Like the 1979 Agreement, the 1994 Agreement contains a five-year grace period, applicable to developing country members that were not parties to the 1979 Agreement.

[34] The Agreement on Customs Valuation is an important aspect of the law of international trade, but it is a highly specialized subject, and is not explored further in this volume. For a book-length treatment, see Sherman and Glasshoff, n. 31 supra.

their internal sale. This is an important provision, but a testing standard, or required design, or mandatory inspection may nominally be applied to domestic and imported products on terms of entire equality, yet have the effect—intended or not—of restricting or even precluding imports.[35] Article XX, the General Exceptions article,[36] lists measures necessary to protect human, animal, or plant life or health (para. (b)) and measures relating to the conservation of exhaustible natural resources (para. (g)) as justification for otherwise prohibited measures, 'subject to the requirement that such measures are not applied in a manner which would constitute a means of arbitrary or unjustifiable discrimination . . . or a disguised restriction on international trade.'[37]

The question of product standards as impediments to international trade has two, not necessarily related aspects. On one level, the thrust of international legislation as reflected in the GATT/WTO system is to strive to harmonize technical standards so that discrepancies in standards do not impede the flow of international trade. On another level, one increasingly stressed by advocates for the environment, the rules of international trade should not be used to compromise genuine concerns with safety, health or conservation. The Agreement on Technical Barriers to Trade, concluded during the Tokyo Round and amended in the Uruguay Round, seeks to balance these concerns.

First, the TBT Agreement provides that standards and regulations shall not discriminate—either between domestic and imported products, or among products originating in different countries (Art. 2.1). *Second*, the agreement provides that standards shall be public and open, and notice of proposed standards and requirements for certification that may have significant effect on trade shall be given sufficiently in advance to permit affected persons to submit written comments on the proposed regulations and to have them taken into account (Art. 2.9). Further, except in emergency circumstances, member states are required to allow a reasonable time between publication of a technical regulation and its entry into force to allow producers from other countries to adapt their products or methods of production to the new standard. Similar requirements are laid down for what the TBT Agreement calls 'conformity assessment', i.e. testing for compliance with the standards in force (Arts. 5.1, 5.6).

---

[35] An obvious illustration would be a requirement by the United States that all specifications be expressed in inches, feet, pounds, and degrees Fahrenheit, or a requirement by, say, the European Community that all specifications be expressed in the metric system. Mandatory use of Japanese for instructions accompanying products sold in Japan may or may not be a trade barrier, but would not constitute a violation of Article III of GATT.

[36] See Ch. 3, Sect. 3.4(e).

[37] Also, Article XI(2), the provision containing exceptions to the prohibition on quantitative restrictions, lists, in para. (b), prohibitions or restrictions necessary to the application of standards or regulations for the classification, grading, or marketing of commodities in international trade.

In contrast to the Agreement on the Application of Sanitary and Phytosanitary Measures (the SPS Agreement) discussed in Chapter 11, the TBT Agreement does not call for subjecting regulatory measures to scientific testing. The concern of the TBT Agreement is to prevent discrimination or standard setting that may interfere with the free flow of goods, so that even if a particular regulation is scientifically unsound, if it is applied equally to domestic and imported products, and is not inconsistent with another regulation widely applied elsewhere, it will not violate the TBT Agreement. But like the SPS Agreement and Article XX of the GATT, the TBT Agreement provides that 'Members shall ensure that technical regulations are not prepared, adopted or applied with a view to or with the effect of creating unnecessary obstacles to international trade' (Art. 2.2).

Annex 3 of the Uruguay Round TBT agreement, an innovation not in the prior version, is a Code of Good Practice for the Preparation, Adoption and Application of Standards. Central governments are required to comply with the Code of Good Practice, but the Code is open also to others that may promulgate standards, including local government bodies, regional standardizing bodies, and non-governmental bodies such as laboratories and testing organizations whose certificates of approval are required before certain products may be offered for sale.[38] In addition to repeating the principles of non-discrimination and openness, the Code of Good Practice states that whenever international standards exist or their completion is imminent the standardizing body 'shall use them . . . as a basis for the standards it develops', unless the standard would be ineffective or insufficient (para. F). Correspondingly, standardizing bodies, whether governmental or non-governmental, and whether national, regional, or local 'shall, in an appropriate way, play a full part . . . in the preparation . . . of international standards' by relevant international standardizing bodies (para. G). Article 2.5 of the TBT Agreement, added in the Uruguay Round, states that whenever a technical regulation is prepared, adopted or applied in accordance with the legitimate objectives for technical regulations listed in the Agreement and is in accordance with relevant international standards, it shall be presumed, subject to rebuttal, not to create an unnecessary obstacle to international trade.[39]

A continuing difficulty with a standards agreement among sovereign states is that a great many product standards are set at other levels of government or by industry associations of various kinds. Moreover, this problem falls unevenly on federal states, such as Australia, Canada, and the United States,

---

[38] Like most of the Uruguay Round Agreements, the TBT Agreement calls for periodic review of its operation and implementation. In its first triennial review in 1997, the TBT Committee reported that 84 standardizing bodies had notified their acceptance of the Code of Good Practice, a total that the Committee regarded as unsatisfactory.

[39] 'Legitimate objective' is not defined in the Agreement, but Article 2.2 contains an illustrative list, including national security requirements; the prevention of deceptive practices; and protection of human health or safety, animal or plant life or health, or the environment.

as compared with unitary states, such as France, Italy, and Japan.[40] For federal states, the domestic political considerations cut in both directions. In some instances, national governments are reluctant to commit constituent states or provinces to international obligations; in other instances, national governments are reluctant to seem to impair enforcement at local level of environmental, safety or health regulations imposed by constituent states on the ground that they go beyond those agreed on internationally.

The solution in the TBT Agreement is to obligate member states to 'take such reasonable measures as may be available to them'[41] to ensure compliance by local governmental bodies with the provisions of the Agreement concerning preparation, adoption, and enforcement of technical regulations.[42] The TBT Agreement states that Members are 'fully responsible' for the observance of the relevant provisions of the agreement by local governmental bodies and non-governmental bodies (Arts. 3.5, 7.5), and further that the dispute settlement provisions can be invoked if a Member state considers that another Member state 'has not achieved satisfactory results' by resort to the 'reasonable measures' obligation with respect to subordinate units of government or non-governmental bodies, and that the complainant state's trade interests are significantly affected.

As of this writing, it was too early to state with certainty how the unique federal/state issues in the TBT Agreement would be implemented.[43] One may imagine the following situation:

> Suppose the state of California, or the province of Ontario, each with 30 percent of the national consumption of the product in question, issues a regulation subjecting the product to more stringent requirements than are contained in an internationally recognized standard. Patria brings a complaint under the Dispute Settlement Understanding against the United States/Canada; it shows (i) that its product complies with the international standard; and (ii) that the sales of its product in the respondent country have been significantly affected, because the product could not meet the state/provincial standards.

The United States/Canadian government establishes that it called the international standard to the attention of the authorities of the state or

---

[40] In contrast to most of the other Multilateral Agreements, which were signed on behalf of the members of the European Community or Union only, the TBT Agreements in the Tokyo Round and in the Uruguay Round were signed both by the EC/EU and by the individual member states.

[41] The phrase is drawn from Article XXIV(12) of the GATT, the article concerning formation and customs unions and free trade areas.

[42] Member states also retain the obligation of notification of proposed or actual regulations and standards imposed by subordinate units of government or non-governmental bodies within their territories.

[43] Federal/state issues arise also in connection with the Government Procurement Code, which was not concluded as a Multilateral Agreement. Application of that Code to sub-central units of government is dependent on separate negotiations, not on a general MFN obligation.

province in question and gave the required notice to other countries including Patria, which submitted comments to the state/province. Nonetheless, the state or province persisted in its regulation, asserting that it is necessary to meet an essential health or environmental standard. Patria points out that since the regulation is not in accordance with a relevant international standard, the presumption that the regulation has not created an unnecessary obstacle to international trade is not applicable.

It seems that the United States or Canada, as the case may be, could be held responsible, and given a reasonable time to persuade its state or province to bring the regulation into conformity with the international standard. If that effort proved unsuccessful, the national government, i.e. the member state of the WTO, could be held to be in violation of the TBT Agreement and required to give compensation or (subject to the procedures set out in the Understanding on Dispute Settlement)[44] suffer retaliation. The WTO panel could not order a state or province to comply with the international standard, however, and it would not be concerned with the relationship of the national to the state/provincial governments under the constitution of the WTO member state.

(c) Import Licensing Procedures

A requirement that imports into a country be licensed may have several purposes and effects. In some instances, import licensing systems are used simply as a census or surveillance device. If import licenses are issued automatically as soon as a completed application is filed, no trade restrictive effect is created and no international agreement is violated. In other cases, for instance when licensing systems are used to administer import quotas and approval is not automatic, import licensing systems can have trade restrictive effects, even beyond the quota system itself. A licensing system may create uncertainty about which applications will be granted, about the time it will take to secure the license, and about the criteria used to grant the license. In addition, licensing systems, particularly as administered in some developing countries, can have the effect of a trade restriction just by the mass of paperwork and number of approvals required. Article XIII of the GATT, the article governing administration of quotas permitted under the exceptions to Article XI(1),[45] contains a provision requiring states that issue import licenses in connection with import restrictions to furnish to other interested contracting parties 'all relevant information' concerning administration of the licensing system. But GATT Article XIII(3)(a) contains no guidelines or criteria for import license systems. Even before the Tokyo Round began, efforts had begun under GATT auspices to develop an Import Licensing Code, but no agreement had been reached.

---

[44] See Ch. 8.   [45] See Ch. 3, Sect. 3.4(f).

For a time during the Tokyo Round, import licensing was debated in the context of quantitative restrictions; when it became clear that no progress on that subject was likely, import licensing procedures became a relatively non-controversial topic, resulting in a code consisting of five articles. Nineteen contracting parties subscribed to the Code on Import Licensing procedures at the outset, and ten more parties joined over the next decade. In the Uruguay Round, some drafting changes were made, the Agreement was made binding on all members of the GATT/WTO system, and like all the other agreements, it was made subject to the Understanding on Dispute Settlement. Apart from some drafting changes, the Agreement on Import Licensing Procedures emerged from the Uruguay Round substantially as it had been developed in the Tokyo Round.

The basic principle is that 'import licensing procedures shall be neutral in application and administered in a fair and equitable manner' (Art. 1(3)). For automatic licensing systems, applications are to be approved immediately if administratively feasible, but in any event within ten working days (Art. 2(a)(iii)). Non-automatic systems 'shall not have trade-restrictive or -distortive effects on imports additional to those caused by the imposition of the restriction', and shall be no more administratively burdensome than absolutely necessary (Art. 3(2)). Further, the period for processing applications shall not be longer than 30 days if applications are considered as and when received, or 60 days if all applications are considered simultaneously (Art. 3(5)(f)). If a license application is denied, the applicant shall be given an explanation, and shall have a right of appeal (Art. 3(5)(e)). In principle, an applicant shall have to approach only one administrative body in connection with a license application. The Tokyo Round Code provided that where it is strictly indispensable that more than one administrative body be approached, these shall be kept to the 'minimum number possible'. The Uruguay Round Agreement provides that applicants shall not need to approach more than three administrative bodies (Art. 1(6)).

(d) Government Procurement

Prior to the Tokyo Round, government procurement had usually been handled outside of normal GATT rules, on the assumption that each country preferred its own suppliers for the needs of the government, just as its civil servants traveled, when possible, on the national airline. Both Article III(8)(a), of the GATT, concerning national treatment, and Article XVII(2), concerning state trading, essentially excluded purchases for the government's own use, as contrasted with purchases for resale, from the national treatment requirements of the GATT. But with governments owning and operating railroads, telecommunication systems, national oil companies, mines, and even steel industries, the impact on international trade of national preferences was substantial. For certain industries, such as road building, dam and bridge construction, electric power generation, air traffic control systems, and the like governments at various levels were virtually the only customers.

Discussion of a government procurement code began as early as 1962 in the Organization for Economic Cooperation and Development, and in fact the OECD had drafted a proposed code, but partly at the urging of the United States and partly because the developing countries were not members of the OECD, the work on a government procurement code shifted to the GATT in the early 1970s. In the Tokyo Round, the United States, with fewer state enterprises (apart from the military) than most other contracting parties and many high-tech global contractors, pressed hard for a code on government procurement practices, which would cover such subjects as publicity for purchases by government entities, elimination of margins of preference for home-made products, and definition of permissible exceptions for national security—for instance tanks and artillery for the army as contrasted with shoes and blankets.

Once one gets over an instinctive feeling that taxpayers' funds should be spent at home, and looks at government procurement as an aspect of rational allocation of resources, the aims of a Government Procurement Code are not hard to articulate: (1) Procurement should be open and transparent, subject to stable and published rules; (2) There should be no discrimination against foreign suppliers (i.e. national treatment), or as among foreign suppliers (i.e. most favoured-nation treatment). In fact, the Tokyo Round Government Procurement Code did call for both national treatment and most-favoured nation treatment with respect to all laws, regulations procedures, and practices regarding government procurement, but only for entities subject to the Agreement, and only on the basis of reciprocity, i.e. as among parties to the Code. This statement is repeated in the revised Agreement on Government Procurement adopted in the Uruguay Round (Art. III(1)). In contrast to the other agreements adapted from the Tokyo Round codes, however, the Agreement on Government Procurement is exempt from the rule that all members of the GATT/WTO system must be parties to all the agreements coming within the system, and in fact as of year-end 2001, only 28 states (counting the members of the European Community individually) were parties to the revised Procurement Agreement.[46] On this subject, reciprocity prevailed over unconditional most-favoured-nation treatment, so that the Uruguay Round Agreement on Government Procurement is in the form of a 'plurilateral' rather than a 'multilateral' agreement, thus reproducing the Tokyo Round approach of

---

[46] 25 other members of the WTO plus several non-members had observer status, as did the IMF and the OECD.

conditional most-favoured nation (and national) treatment.[47] Disputes under the Government Procurement Code, however, are subject to the binding system of dispute settlement created as an integral part of the new GATT/WTO system.

It became clear during the Tokyo Round negotiations concerning government procurement that the controversies among the potential parties concerned not so much the principles, but the entities to be included. The Tokyo Round Code set a fairly modest threshold for coverage—SDR150,000 (approximately $195,000 at the time)[48]—subject to further negotiation, but each party was to set out the entities which it agreed to place under the procurement rules set out in the Code. The United States announced that pursuant to a statutory mandate, it would have to exclude all defense procurement—not only armaments but textiles, shoes, and food. Other United States statutes provided for so-called 'set-asides'—preferences for small business and minority-owned business, and these preferences had to be honoured before bids could be opened up to international procurement procedures. Other parties reduced their offers correspondingly, and negotiations of the Annex became similar to item-by-item tariff negotiations. By the time the Tokyo Round Procurement Code was concluded, the exceptions both by industry and by governmental level meant that not more than 10–15 percent of purchases of the participating governments were actually covered by the Code. By way of illustration, the United States excluded the Departments of Transportation and Energy, the Army Corps of Engineers, the Tennessee Valley Authority, as well as the federally owned railways and the Postal Service, but included the Smithsonian Museum and the Federal Deposit Insurance Corporation; the United Kingdom excluded British Railways and the telecommunications services of the Post Office, but included the Royal Commission on Gardening and the British Museum. France also excluded its railways, but included hundreds of schools, institutes, and museums.

The Tokyo Round Code contained one provision that proved important in development of the international law of government procurement. Article IX(6)(b) called for further negotiations within three years of entry into force

---

[47] See the Marrakesh Agreement establishing the World Trade Organization, Article II(2) and (3), which distinguish between agreements listed in Annexes 1, 2, and 3—the multilateral agreements—and agreements listed in Annex 4, the plurilateral agreements. Apart from government procurement, the plurilateral agreements were concerned with subjects in which only some of the member states have an interest—civil aircraft, dairy products, and bovine meat. The Uruguay Round Agreement on Government Procurement, like the prior Tokyo Round Agreement, also contains a mini-Article XXXV (see Ch. 3, Sect. 3.4(c)), authorizing any party to announce at the time that it accedes to the Agreement that it does not consent to its application between it and any other named party. Under the Tokyo Round Code, the United States initially announced that it did not consent to application of the agreement between itself and Japan; subsequently the two countries negotiated a bilateral agreement whereby Japan opened up competitive bidding for procurement by the Nippon Telegraph and Telephone Company (NTT), and the announcement of non-application was withdrawn.

[48] For an explanation of the origin and meaning of SDRs, see Ch. 16, Sect. 16.8.

of the code and periodically thereafter, 'with a view to broadening and improving the Agreement . . . [and exploring] the possibilities of expanding the coverage . . . to include service contracts'. The Committee established by the Code did conduct negotiations to broaden and improve the agreement, and an amended version of the Code was completed in 1986 and put into effect in 1988.[49] More important, the Committee agreed to continue the negotiations, technically not a part of the main negotiations, but gradually building on the momentum (and the deadlines) of the Uruguay Round.

A major innovation in the Agreement as it emerged from these negotiations is that it applies to procurement by any contractual means, including purchase or lease, and including any combination of products and services (Art. I(2)).[50] A second innovation was to provide an Appendix of covered entities divided, for each state party, into five Annexes. Annex 1 lists central government entities; Annex 2 lists sub-central government entities;[51] Annex 3 lists other entities that procure in accordance with the agreement;[52] Annex 4 specifies services, whether listed positively or negatively, covered by the Agreement; and Annex 5 specifies construction services. The Parties to the Agreement are free, in their respective annexes, to set separate thresholds of coverage for the various categories, subject to bilateral negotiations.[53] Once an entity or a service is covered, national treatment and MFN treatment, as well as the various rules concerning publicity, forms of tenders, rules of origin, and offsets[54] are applicable, but only, as mentioned above, to products, services, and suppliers of other state Parties to the Agreement. Parties are permitted to announce classes of exclusions, and to some extent they did so, as they had done under the 1979 Code, both unilaterally and by negotiation on the basis of reciprocity.[55] The GATT Secretariat estimated that opportunities

[49] The principal amendments concerned extension of the Code to leasing as well as purchase contracts, and lowering the threshold of coverage to SDR130,000.

[50] The 1979 Code had covered services only when they were incidental to the supply of goods and constituted less than half the contract price.

[51] The United States, for instance, listed 37 states, some for all branches of government, some for specified agencies. Canada offered to cover entities in all ten provinces on the basis of commitments obtained from provincial governments; Switzerland listed all of its cantons; Israel listed its three principal cities; Japan listed 62 prefectures.

[52] This list includes state-owned corporations or authorities, such as the St. Lawrence Seaway Corporation (USA), the Japan National Oil Corporation, and the Israel Airports Authority. The EEC lists its entities by reference to *Council Directive 93/36/EEC of 14 June 1993 Coordinating Procedures for the Award of Public Supply Contracts*, 1993 EC O.J. L/199 (9 Aug. 1993).

[53] For instance, the Agreement provides that covered purchases by government-owned entities (list 3) have a threshold of SDR400,000 ($560,000), but the United States will apply a threshold of $250,000 for federally-owned utilities. The threshold for construction services is SDR5,000,000 ($7,000,000), except for Japan and Korea, which will apply a threshold of SDR15,000,000 ($21,000,0000).

[54] Offsets are defined as requirements by the contracting agency that the supplier engage in sub-procurement in the contracting country. Generally, offsets are prohibited, except for developing countries, and for these are subject to detailed restrictions.

[55] In the first case brought to the Dispute Settlement Body under the Government Procurement Agreement, the United States alleged that practices by the Korean Airport Construction Authority, including qualification for bidding as a prime contractor, domestic partnering, and absence of
.

for international trade in government procurement would increase tenfold over the coverage under the earlier code. Whether this estimate will stand up may depend in part on the pace of privatization among parties to the Agreement, as well as on which parties (particularly among developing countries) will eventually join.

5.4   THE AGREEMENT ON SAFEGUARDS

(a)   Background of the Agreement

As discussed in Chapter 3, the drafters of the original GATT had understood that in order to persuade states to accept a regime of binding commitments to reduce trade barriers, they would have to provide some kind of safety valve.[56] If a reduction in a tariff or other trade barrier resulted in an unexpected surge of imports and caused serious injury to a domestic industry, there should be a way for the importing country to reverse the concession or otherwise to protect its industry. The availability of an escape clause would be a necessary element both in securing commitment to the GATT overall and in securing concessions in the negotiating rounds.

Accordingly, Article XIX of the GATT, modeled on 'escape clauses' contained in several bilateral trade agreements negotiated by the United States, provided that a contracting party shall be free to suspend obligations incurred under the General Agreement, including tariff concessions if 'as a result of unforeseen developments and of the effect of [these] obligations' any product is being imported into its territory in such increased quantities and under such conditions as to cause or threaten serious injury to domestic producers of like or competitive products.[57] Unlike Article VI, which provides for anti-dumping and anti-subsidy duties, Article XIX, entitled 'Emergency Action on Imports of Particular Products' is not premised on any unfair or improper conduct by exporters or exporting nations. Article XIX was designed simply to provide temporary relief for an industry on which the burden of adjustment falls too fast or too unevenly.

Though Article XIX called for consultations and held out the potential for suspension of equivalent concessions by exporting countries, it had become clear by the mid-1970s that no adequate international scrutiny existed to prevent the use of escape clause relief to undo the benefits that implementation

---

access to challenge procedures, constituted breaches of the GPA. A dispute panel heard the complaint, but held that the entities conducting procurement for the project at issue were not covered entities under Korea's designation. *Korea—Measures Affecting Government Procurement*, Complaint by the United States, GATT Doc. WT/DS163/1, adopted June 19, 2000.

[56] See Ch. 3, Sect. 3.5(a).

[57] The text of Article XIX(1)(a) was taken almost verbatim from Article XI of the Agreement on Reciprocal Trade between the United States and Mexico of December 23, 1942, 57 Stat. 833, 845.

of the GATT system was supposed to produce. In particular, nothing in Article XIX gave a definition of 'emergency', or of 'serious injury', and the article made no provision for a limit of time for which import relief could be granted. Also, though the initial expectation seems to have been that invocation of the escape clause would lead to suspension of tariff concessions previously granted by the importing country, increasingly importing states had granted relief in the form of quotas. Moreover, in many instances, beginning with textile and apparel imports and over time including steel, automobiles, chemicals, and a variety of manufactured products, import relief had been granted through restraint agreements, more or less voluntarily entered into.

In some instances, the restraints had been embodied in formal agreements between countries; in other instances, the arrangements had been in form between industry associations on one or both sides, with at least tacit consent of the governments concerned.[58] In still other instances, the arrangements had in form been unilateral measures on the part of the exporting countries, but generally, there was at least an implied undertaking by the importing country that more restrictive measures that had been under consideration would not be put into place.[59] Since measures of this kind—whether called Orderly Marketing Agreements (OMAs), Voluntary Export Restraints (VERs), Voluntary Restraint Arrangements (VRAs), or something else—were typically concluded with the consent, express or implied, of the exporting country, there was usually no contracting party that could bring a complaint to the GATT.

In their own explanations of trade policy, contracting parties, notably including Canada, the European Community, and the United States, argued that these arrangements—often referred to as 'grey area measures'—were not subject to GATT because (i) they were voluntary; or (ii) they contained an express release of GATT obligations; or (iii) they were focused on exports, not imports.[60] But as the Director-General of GATT pointed out, such arrangements covered close to ten percent of world trade (counting textiles but not agriculture), and undermined the whole system of market-driven, as contrasted with managed, trade that was the essence of the GATT. While it was unlikely that contracting states would wholly abandon arrangements of this kind, it would be important to establish some ground rules to distinguish between emergency relief and protection against the effects of comparative advantage.

---

[58] See Ch. 4, Sect. 4.3(c), n. 46.

[59] See e.g. *Japan's Measures of Restraint on Car Exports to the United States: Statement by the Ministry of International Trade*, Tokyo 1 May 1981, reproduced in English in BNA, *Import-Export Reporter*, 6 May 1981, p. A2, discussed in A. Lowenfeld, *Public Controls on International Trade*, 399–419 (2nd edn. 1983).

[60] Professor Hudec wrote: 'The cynical defense was taken for what it was—a declaration of independence from GATT in these matters'. Robert E. Hudec, *The GATT Legal System and World Trade Diplomacy*, 231 (1975, 2nd edn. 1993).

As described in Chapter 4, an extended effort to address the problem of market disruption or escape clause relief had been undertaken in the Tokyo Round, but had not resulted in agreement.[61] When the Ministerial Declaration launching the Uruguay Round was drafted, a 'comprehensive agreements on safeguards' was high on the list of objectives, with a view to completing the effort begun in the Tokyo Round but left unfinished. This time the effort succeeded, with tough substantive standards, strict procedural requirements, an interesting compromise on the issue of selectivity, and a breakthrough on the issue of grey areas.

(b) The Basic Commitments

The Agreement recognizes in its preamble 'the need . . . to re-establish multilateral control over safeguards and [to] eliminate measures that escape such control.' Further, the Preamble recognizes 'the importance of structural adjustment', that is a need to preclude the protracted use of protection justified initially as emergency measures, thereby sheltering non-competitive industries in importing countries from adjustment to the global market.

According to Article XIX(1)(a) of the GATT, escape clause relief must be linked to 'unforeseen developments' and the effect of obligations incurred by a contracting party under the Agreement, including tariff concessions. Over time, this requirement was increasingly disregarded, and it is not recited in the Agreement on Safeguards as it emerged from the Uruguay Round.[62] Many observers, including the present author, believed that this omission was intentional, reflecting at least a tacit consensus that any industry that could make a persuasive case that the burden of adjustment fell on it too severely could apply for import relief, whether imports had increased as a result of reduction in tariffs, lower prices or more attractive products made abroad, or inefficiencies and management errors at home, subject only to the particular substantive and procedural standards set out in the Agreement, as summarized below.[63] However, in two cases decided in December 1999, involving imports

---

[61] See Ch. 4, Sect. 4.3(c).

[62] In the United States, which had the most detailed trade legislation, the required link was included in §301(b)(1) of the Trade Expansion Act of 1962, but was omitted in the successor statute, §201(b)(1) of the Trade Act of 1974 and subsequent legislation.

The European Community's law, embodied in 5 February 1982 on Common Rules for Imports 1982 *OJ L* 35/1 (9 Feb. 1982) recites in the Preamble and Article 15 the words 'imported into [the Community] in such increased quantities . . . as to cause or threaten to cause substantial injury' as in GATT Article XIX, but also omits the words 'as a result of . . . the effect of the obligations incurred by a contracting party under this Agreement including tariff concessions.'

[63] See e.g. Janet Nazum, 'The Agreement on Safeguards: U.S. Law Leads Revitalization of the Escape Clause', in Terence P. Stewart (ed.), *The World Trade Organization: The Multilateral Trade Framework for the 21st Century and U.S. Implementing Legislation*, 407 at 413–14 (1996); M. Trebilcock and R. Howse, *The Regulation of International Trade*, 228 (2nd edn., 1999); M. Bronckers, 'Voluntary Export Restraints and the GATT 1944 Agreement on Safeguards', in J. H. J. Bourgeois, F. Berrod, E. Fournier (eds.), *The Uruguay Round Results: A European Lawyers' Perspective* 275 (1995).

of footwear to Argentina and dairy products to Korea, the Appellate Body rejected that interpretation.[64] Two separate divisions of the Appellate Body held that a member state imposing a safeguard measure must comply with the provisions of *both* the Agreement on Safeguards *and* GATT Article XIX. Accordingly, in addition to the specific findings of causation and injury linked to increased imports, the importing state must satisfy the requirements of unforeseen developments and of the effect of obligations incurred under the GATT, including trade agreement concessions. In reversing the Panel's decision on this issue in the *Argentina/Footwear* case, the Appellate Body wrote:

> [W]e do not agree with the Panel that any safeguard investigations conducted or safe-guard measures imposed after the entry into force of the *WTO Agreement* 'which meet the requirements of the new Safeguards Agreement *satisfy* the requirements of Article XIX of GATT.' Therefore, we reverse the Panel's conclusion . . . that safe-guard measures imposed after entry into force of the WTO Agreement which meet the requirements of the Agreement on Safeguards necessarily 'satisfy' the require-ments of Article XIX of the GATT 1994, as well as the Panel's finding that the Uruguay negotiators 'expressly omitted' . . . [the unforeseen developments clause] from Article 2 of the Agreement on Safeguards.[65]

The Agreement provides that member states—i.e. all members of the GATT/WTO system—may impose safeguard measures only upon a deter-mination that increased imports have caused or threaten to cause serious injury to the domestic industry that produces like or directly competitive/products (Art. 2(1)). The increased imports may be either absolute or relative to domes-tic production.

The determination must be based on previously established and published procedures following an investigation of all relevant factors (Arts. 3(1), 4(2)(a)).[66] The determination shall not be made unless the investigation demonstrates, on the basis of objective evidence, the existence of a causal link between the increased imports and the serious injury or threat of seri-ous injury (Art. 4(3)(b)). Thus, for instance, a strike or a materials shortage

---

[64] *Safeguard Measures on Imports of Footwear (European Communities v. Argentina)*, WT/DS121/AB/R (14 Dec. 1999); *Definitive Safeguard Measures on Imports of Certain Dairy Products (European Communities v. Korea)*, WT/DS98/AB/R (14 Dec. 1999).

[65] *Argentina, Imports on Footwear*, n. 64 supra, para. 97. To the same effect, *Korea, Imports of Certain Dairy Products*, n. 64, para. 90:

> [W]e do not agree with the Panel that the clause—'as a result of unforeseen developments and of the effect of the obligations incurred by a Member under this Agreement, including tariff concessions . . .'—'does not specify anything additional as to the conditions under which measures pursuant to Article XIX may be applied.'

[66] Article 4(2)(a), which states the requirement that the competent authorities of the import-ing state shall evaluate all relevant factors, lists a number of such factors, apparently by way of illustration. In the *Argentina Footwear* case, n. 64 supra, however, the Appellate Body held that at least all those factors must be considered, and found fault with the investigation by the Argentine authorities, *inter alia*, because it had not considered productivity of the domestic industry or its capacity utilization, as affected by the challenged imports.

in the importing country might leave the domestic industry injured and the demand for the product might be filled by increased imports, but according to Article 4 of the Agreement, safeguard measures would not be justified.

Safeguard measures may include either increased tariffs or quotas (Art. 5), but the kinds of measures that had been used to bypass Article XIX of the GATT, such as VERs, OMAs, and similar 'grey area' measures are explicitly prohibited, with provision for phasing out of existing measures of this kind within four years (Art. 11).[67] If an import quota is imposed, it may not (absent 'clear justification') reduce the level of imports below the level of a recent representative period, generally the last three years for which statistics are available prior to the increase in imports that gave rise to the safeguard measure (Art. 5(1)).

Finally, even if all of the above requirements, substantive and procedural, are met, a member state is to apply safeguard measures 'only to the extent necessary to prevent or remedy serious injury and to facilitate adjustment' (Art. 5(1)).[68]

(c)   The Requirement of Notification

Under Article XIX of the GATT, most states did not give notice of imposition of import relief or grey area measures.[69] The Safeguards Agreement seeks to change this, by requiring immediate notification to the Committee on Safeguards at three stages: (a) upon initiating an investigation of serious injury or threat of serious injury; (b) upon making a finding of injury caused by increased imports; and (c) upon taking a decision to apply or extend a safeguard measure (Art. 12(1)). In making the notification, the Member is required to provide the Committee with 'all pertinent information'. In the *Korean Dairy Products* case cited above, the Appellate Body stated that the quoted words constitute 'an objective standard independent of the subjective assessment of the notifying member',[70] the idea being that other member states should be sufficiently informed to decide whether to request

---

[67] Each member was permitted to designate one existing measure which could be extended by agreement between the exporting and the importing member until December 31, 1999—in effect a one-year extension. One such extension was recognized in the Agreement itself, concerning export of passenger cars from Japan to the European Community.

[68] In the *Korean Dairy Products* case, n. 64, supra, the panel held that a Member applying a safeguard measure has an obligation to ensure that the measure in question is not more restrictive than necessary, and the Appellate Body upheld that statement. But the Appellate Body reversed the further statement by the panel that the Member was obligated to *explain* that its measure is necessary to remedy serious injury and facilitate adjustment. The obligation to make such an explanation applies only to the second sentence of Article 5(1), which calls for clear justification if a quota is imposed limiting imports to less than the average of the last three representative years. Id. paras. 93–103.

[69] See Ch. 4, Sect. 4.3(c) at n. 47.

[70] *Korean Dairy Products* case (n. 64 supra), para. 108.

consultations, and the Committee should be enabled to carry out effectively its function of surveillance.[71]

(d)   The Question of Selectivity

Selectivity, which had stumped the Tokyo Round negotiators, troubled the Uruguay Round negotiations as well. The developing countries, which saw themselves as likely targets, resisted selectivity strongly; the opposite view, espoused by the European Community, was that a narrower, more focused response to the principal cause of serious injury would be less disruptive of trade flows, and would also reduce the compensation required to be given by the country implementing the import relief measure.[72] The issue was eventually resolved—generally in favour of non-discrimination, but with some flexibility, and a partial exemption for the developing countries. Article 2(2) states that safeguard measures shall be applied to a product being imported 'irrespective of its source', i.e. on an MFN and not a selective basis. Further, if an import quota is allocated among exporting countries, the allocation (absent agreement) is to be made in proportion to their market share during a previous representative period (Art. 5(2)(a)). The importing member may, however, apply to the Committee on Safeguards established by the Code for permission to depart from allocation of quotas under a historical formula upon a 'clear demonstration' that imports from a particular member increased disproportionately during the representative period (Art. 5(2)(b)).

The developing countries sought both to oppose selective application of safeguard measures and to obtain a degree of preference, and largely prevailed under the Agreement. Safeguards are not to be applied against products originating in a developing country member unless that member's share of imports of the product in question by the member imposing the safeguard exceeds 3 percent, or the share of imports from all developing countries with an individual share of less than 3 percent is greater than 9 percent.[73]

(e)   Adjustment in Place of Protection

Perhaps the most important feature of the Safeguards Agreement, at least in concept, is the link between the objective of preventing or remedying serious injury and the objective of facilitating adjustment by the domestic industry. The Agreement states that a member shall apply safeguard measures only for such period of time as may be necessary to accomplish these two objectives,

[71] In addition to the factors required to be considered in the determination by the state seeking to impose a safeguards measure under Article 4(2), Article 12(2) calls for specification of the proposed introduction of the measure in question, expected duration and timetable for progressive liberalization, and in the case of an extension, evidence that the industry is adjusting.

[72] See e.g. Nazum (n. 63 supra), at pp. 410–11.

[73] Also, developing countries as importers may maintain safeguards somewhat longer, and reinstate them somewhat sooner than developed countries, as set forth in n. 74, infra.

and provides that this period shall not exceed four years (Art. 7(1)). The period may be extended only on the basis of a new investigation, but to a maximum of eight years, and upon a determination that the safeguard measures continue to be necessary and that there is *evidence that the industry is adjusting* (Art. 7(2) and (3)). Further, the Agreement prescribes that safeguard measures shall be progressively liberalized, that is if a protective tariff is imposed it shall be reduced in stages, and if a quota is imposed, the share of estimated domestic consumption available for imports shall be increased in stages (Art. 7(4)). If a measure is to be in effect for more than three years, there is to be a mid-term review. If a safeguard measure has expired, a new safeguard with respect to the product in question may not be imposed for at least two years or for the time equal to the time that the prior measure was in effect, whichever is longer (Art. 7 (5)).[74]

(f) Incentives to Compliance

The Agreement contains an interesting incentive for compliance with its various requirements—procedural and substantive. It retains the principle, set out in GATT Article XIX, that when an importing country suspends an obligation on the basis of unforeseen developments causing serious injury, it is supposed to negotiate with interested exporting countries for compensation, and that if these negotiations fail to result in agreement, the exporting countries are free to withdraw substantially equivalent concessions. Article 8(3) provides, however, that the right of the exporting members to suspend equivalent concessions shall not be exercised for the first three years of the safeguard measure *if the measure was taken as a result of an absolute increase in imports,* and *if the measure conforms to the provisions of the Agreement.* Thus long-term safeguard measures, or measures taken without adequate notice and investigations may draw retaliation; measures of three years' duration or less meeting all the procedural requirements are safe from retaliation.

As this volume went to press, it was too early to assess the effect of the Agreement on Safeguards.[75] It is fair to say, however, that the text, reflecting

---

[74] For developing countries imposing safeguards, the maximum time of a safeguard measure can be ten instead of eight years, and the interval between safeguard measures on a given product need only be half of the time that the prior measure was in effect.

[75] The Committee on Safeguards reported that in the period November 2000–October 2001, 92 Members had notified it of their domestic safeguards legislation, and 35 had not made the required notifications. The Committee received 20 notifications from eight states reporting decisions to apply safeguard measures; 14 notifications from seven states reporting application of provisional measures; 17 notifications from eight states reporting findings of serious injury or threat of injury; and 7 notifications from six states reporting termination of an investigations without imposition of a safeguard measure. *Report (2001) of the Committee on Safeguards to the Council on Trade in Goods*, 31 Oct. 2001, G/L/494. The only safeguards cases to come before the Disputes Settlement Body were the *Argentine Footwear* and *Korean Dairy Products* cases cited in this chapter.

negotiations over a period of more than twenty years, constitutes a striking affirmation of the philosophy underlying the GATT. Safety valves are to remain safety valves and not become walls; every safeguard action is to be subject to a time limit and to international scrutiny; and the response to change in international market conditions is to be adjustment, not protection.

5.5   TRADE-RELATED INVESTMENT MEASURES

With the demise of the Havana Charter and the ITO,[76] it became clear that the GATT was not concerned with international investment, or more precisely that the jurisdiction of the GATT did not extend to the conditions imposed by host states on investment from abroad. In many ways the separation between international trade and international investment, though not wholly persuasive in terms of economic behaviour, was beneficial to the always fragile GATT. The GATT was able to stay out of many of the most fundamental controversies between East and West, and between North and South—the responsibility of host states to foreign investors, the legal consequences of expropriation, the 'New International Economic Order', and the effort over many years to draft a Code of Conduct for Transnational Corporations. These issues were debated in the UN General Assembly and its subordinate organs, and to some extent in the World Bank, the International Monetary Fund, and in various bilateral negotiations of Treaties of Friendship, Commerce and Navigation and Bilateral Investment Treaties,[77] but not in the GATT.

(a)   Background: The Canada–United States Dispute over the Foreign Investment Review Act

When an investment issue did come before the GATT in the early 1980s, it was not in the context of a North–South dispute, but in the context of a dispute between the United States and Canada. The perception was widespread in Canada that too much of that country's economy was made up of enterprises owned and controlled from abroad, for the most part from the United States. Even local content rules and comparatively high tariffs had not resulted in self-standing enterprises, as contrasted with branch plants or assembly operations dependent on inventions, brand names, trade marks, and senior management decisions originating in Detroit or Pittsburgh or New York, rather than Toronto, Montreal, or Vancouver.

In December 1973, after lengthy debate, the Canadian parliament adopted the Foreign Investment Review Act,[78] the thrust of which was to make new investments or acquisition of Canadian companies by foreign

---

[76] See Ch. 3, Sect. 3.2.   [77] See Chs. 13–15 infra.   [78] 21–2, Eliz.II c. 46, 1973.

persons[79] subject to approval on the basis of vaguely stated criteria defining 'significant benefit to Canada'. Companies that sought to establish or acquire subsidiaries in Canada were required to apply to a newly established Foreign Investment Review Agency (FIRA), which would investigate the proposal with a view to recommending approval or disapproval to the designated Minister. Typically, approval would be given only upon undertakings by the foreign investor to comply with stated (and negotiated) conditions.[80]

In some instances the conditions, though interventionist, could not be said to be relevant to the GATT—for example undertakings by the multinational enterprise to conduct a certain percentage of its research and development in Canada or to give employment to certain number of persons in Canada. Other conditions might well interfere with the flow of international trade, and hence would be inconsistent—at least arguably—with the GATT. If, say, an American-based manufacturing company seeking to establish a subsidiary in Canada were required, as a condition for an entry permit, to export a stated percentage of its output, such a requirement might interfere with the parent company's share of the American market or of markets in third countries. Perhaps more directly contrary to the concerns of the GATT, a requirement that the Canadian subsidiary undertake to procure its supplies—or a stated percentage of its supplies—in Canada might well restrict the flow of goods into Canada, and thus constitute a restraint on imports.[81]

In 1982, the United States brought a complaint against Canada under Article XXIII of the GATT, contending that implementation of the Foreign Investment Review Act violated Article III(4) (the national treatment clause) and Article XI(1) (the prohibition against quantitative restrictions). Notwithstanding reservations by a number of developing countries on the ground that in agreeing to hear this dispute the GATT would be entering into matters beyond its jurisdiction, the GATT Council did refer the complaint to a panel. The panel was careful to state that it was addressing only the rules applied to foreign investment by developed countries, and that it was not addressing requirements or undertakings to manufacture locally goods that might otherwise be imported. Further, the panel rejected the contention that export requirements imposed on prospective foreign investors violated GATT. But the panel upheld the basic claim of the United States, challenging the requirement to procure inputs locally.[82] Such a requirement,

---

[79] The Act used the term 'non-eligible persons', which were not really ineligible, but were subject to the review provided in the Act by virtue of their non-Canadianness, as defined.

[80] See e.g. Thomas Franck and Scott Gudgeon, 'Canada's Foreign Investment Control Experiment: The Law, the Context, and the Practice', 50 *N.Y.U.L. Rev.* 76 (1975); A. Lowenfeld, *International Private Investment*, 54–78 and Document Supp. DS 64–133 (2nd edn. 1982).

[81] For an example of the kind of undertaking required by FIRA to be given by foreign investors, see A. Lowenfeld, n. 80 supra, and DS 129–131, reproducing an agreement between the government of Canada and the Apple Computer Corporation.

[82] *Administration of the Foreign Investment Review Act* (*U.S.* v. *Canada*), GATT BISD, 30th Supp. 140 (7 Feb. 1984).

as the Panel held, violated the national treatment requirement of the GATT, because it distinguished between imported and domestic products, even when the regulation was adopted in the context of regulation of investment.[83] Subsequently, Canada informed the GATT Council that it had fully complied with the Panel's ruling, by notifying all investors to regard commitments to make purchases in Canada as requiring no more than giving Canadian suppliers a full and fair opportunity to compete.[84]

(b)   From the *FIRA* Case to the TRIMs Agreement

The Ministerial Declaration of 1986 launching the Uruguay Round mentioned trade-related investment measures, but without any commitment to seek agreement on a code regarding TRIMs. For the United States, however, TRIMs was high on the agenda, in significant part because the US negotiators believed that in order to secure approval by Congress of participation in an expanded GATT system, it would be necessary to have the support of the multinational enterprises whose headquarters were in the United States. An agreement on investment measures as part of a larger package, the American delegates believed, would be an incentive to gain such support.

The Agreement that came out of the Uruguay Round is far from a comprehensive code on transnational investment or even on trade-related measures used by host countries to regulate such investment. But it contains in its preamble a statement that would not have won universal agreement two decades earlier, reciting that Members desire

to facilitate investment across international frontiers so as to increase the economic growth of all trading partners, particularly developing country Members, while ensuring free competition.

The Agreement recognizes 'that certain investment measures can cause trade-restrictive and distorting effects', and states (in Article 2) that no Member shall apply any TRIM that is inconsistent with Article III, the national treatment article of the GATT that had been found to be violated in the *FIRA* case, or Article XI, the prohibition on quantitative restrictions that had been found not to be applicable in that case because there had been no explicit restriction on importation. The illustrative list annexed to the Agreement is not very specific: it simply restates that local source requirements violate Article III(4), and that restrictions on importation of products used in local production and restrictions on exportation of goods produced by the enterprise violate Article XI. Thus the TRIMs Agreement in a sense

---

[83] The Panel held, however, that Article XI was not violated, because the Canadian law and regulations did not directly affect the importation of products. See GATT BISD, 30th Supp. 162–3, para. 5.14 (1984).

[84] See Minutes of Meeting of GATT Council 5–6 Nov. 1985, pp. 39–40, GATT Doc. C/M 194 (1985). In 1987, the Foreign Investment Review Act was repealed and replaced by a far more investor-friendly statute, the Investment Canada Act, Canada Laws, 1985, c.20.

ratifies the panel decision in the *FIRA* case, without adding new substantive provisions.

The Annex to the TRIMs Agreement does make one significant advance, in that it addresses not only mandatory requirements and prohibitions enforceable under domestic law, but also regulations and rulings with which it is necessary to comply in order to obtain an advantage, i.e. incentives that may distort the movement of goods. The Agreement contains no illustration of such incentives, but it seems that any benefit, such as a tax holiday, or negotiated tax regime, waiver of zoning regulations, preferential freight rate, or subsidy that is conditioned on behaviour inconsistent with Article III(4) or Article XI(1) of the GATT would come within the prohibition of Article 2 of the TRIMs Agreement.

Existing trade related investment measures were to be notified to the WTO Council on Trade in Goods, and to be eliminated on a schedule tied to the stage of the member state's development—within two years from January 1, 1995 for developed countries, five years for developing countries, and seven years for least developed countries.[85]

Host states may well impose other measures, such as discriminatory taxes, arbitrary licensing requirements, expropriation without compensation, exclusion from stated activities, requirements for local partners, and so on, that may be inconsistent with bilateral treaties or with customary international law. If the measures are not trade-related within the meaning of Articles III or XI of the GATT, however, they do not come under the TRIMs Agreement. Thus the TRIMs Agreement is not comparable in scope to the Agreement on the Trade-Related Aspects of Intellectual Property Rights (TRIPs). But Article 9 of the TRIMs Agreement states that the Committee on Trade in Goods shall review the Agreement within five years of the entry into force of the WTO Agreement, and in the course of that review 'shall consider whether the Agreement should be complemented with provisions on investment policy and competition policy'. A review was begun by the Council on Trade in Goods in October 1999, and reference was made to the relationship between trade and investment in the Ministerial Declaration issued at the close of the Doha Conference in November 2001, but serious efforts to go further in the GATT/WTO system on the subject of investment seem unlikely.[86]

---

[85] The transition period for developing and least developed members may be extended upon application to the Council on Trade in Goods upon demonstration of particular difficulties.

[86] The Ministerial Declaration devotes three paragraphs to work on this topic prior to the Fifth Ministerial Session in 2005.

Paragraph 22 states:

... Any framework should reflect in a balanced manner the interests of home and host countries, and take due account of the development policies and objectives of host governments as well as their right to regulate in the public interest. ... Account should be taken, as appropriate, of existing bilateral and regional arrangements on investment. (Doha WTO Ministerial Declaration adopted 14 Nov. 2001, WT/MIN(01)1)

5.6 Trade-Related Aspects of Intellectual Property Rights

(a) Intellectual Property Before the Uruguay Round

As the GATT was originally conceived in the early post-war years, the purpose was to establish a legal framework for international trade in goods. The emphasis was on manufactured goods, but at least in theory, raw materials, including minerals and the products of agriculture, were also covered. Other aspects of economic exchange across national frontiers were simply not addressed. Monetary law was to be developed by the International Monetary Fund, whose charter preceded the GATT by more than three years; transnational investment was not addressed at all in a multilateral setting; and intellectual property was subject to a number of international treaties going back to the nineteenth century that seemed to be quite removed from the concerns of the architects of international trade law.

The nineteenth-century treaties—notably the Paris Union Convention of 1883 for the Protection of Industrial Property, and the Berne Convention of 1886 for the Protection of Literary and Artistic Works had been designed to afford authors and inventors the opportunity to protect their creative works in states other than the state where the creation or an application for protection was first made.[87] The conventions also replaced various bilateral regimes based on reciprocity, under which a given invention might be protected in country *A,* where the inventor resided, and country *B, A*'s treaty partner, but not country *C,* with which *A* had no applicable treaty. The conventions were amended several times to bring new types of what came to be known as intellectual property within their ambit—including motion pictures, phonograph records, and later tape recordings and similar inventions. In 1967 the various conventions were brought together within a new World International Property Organization (WIPO), which regularly conducts reviews of the conventions, debates and adopts amendments and supplements, and offers facilities for resolving international disputes concerning intellectual property rights.[88] Neither the Paris and Berne Conventions, nor WIPO, however, imposed obligations on states to protect particular types of creative works, or provided for sanctions against states that did not do so.

The GATT did take notice of intellectual property in two respects, both related to imports. Article IX prescribes non-discrimination with respect to marks of origin, and also provides that marking requirements shall not be

---

[87] Current versions of these conventions may be found in 828 U.N.T.S. 107 (Paris) and 221 (Berne). For a convenient collection of the updated texts of these and other conventions, see Marshall A. Leaffer (ed.), *International Treaties on Intellectual Property* (2nd edn. 1997).

[88] See Convention Establishing the World Intellectual Property Organization, July 14, 1967, 828 U.N.T.S. 3.

used to impose undue burdens on imported products. Article XX, the General Exceptions article,[89] states in paragraph (d) that the General Agreement does not prevent measures 'necessary to secure compliance' with laws or regulations relating to protection of patents, trademarks and copyrights.[90]

As intellectual property, including systems used to run computers and outputs generated by computers, became an increasing element in the world economy, and transmission and reproduction of improved technology became ever easier, a new constituency for protecting intellectual property came into prominence. The high value of high technology, on the one hand, and the growing ease of reproducing or counterfeiting and 'piracy' of anything from blue jeans and watches to computer programs and satellite communications led to an effort to bring intellectual property protection within the GATT/WTO system. The proponents hoped to create a common understanding, binding on all the member states of the GATT/WTO, so that member states could not, for example, decline to grant patent protection to pharmaceuticals or copyright protection to computer software. Further, as the GATT system was being strengthened, the proponents of including intellectual property within that system aimed to bring the arrangements for dispute settlement and trade-related sanctions and retaliation to bear on member states that did not carry out the obligations to be imposed. Other states, particularly among the developing countries, were staunchly opposed to bringing intellectual property rules under the GATT/WTO system. On a general level, they resented the suggestion that other people's laws, reflecting other values and contained in treaties developed without their input, would now be imposed on them. More specifically, many developing countries (and some others) regarded patent protection for pharmaceuticals and related products as depriving their citizens of affordable health care for the benefit of foreign multinational corporations. Finally, some other states, particularly states in the Far East whose industries had prospered by selling imitations of such famous brands as 'Gucci' handbags, 'Levi' jeans, 'Rolex' watches, and 'Chanel' accessories, as well as counterfeit auto parts, chemicals, and computer-operating systems, were not anxious to be required to close such operations or face trade sanctions.[91] Inevitably, debates about the obligations to be undertaken became intertwined with debates about the appropriate scope of jurisdiction of the GATT, and about the different treatment to be accorded to developed and developing countries. An unspoken

[89] See Ch.3, Sect. 3.4(e).

[90] For an important decision on what measures are 'necessary' to enforce patent laws, see *EEC v. United States: Section 337 of the Tariff Act of 1930*, GATT BISD, 36th Supp. 345 (adopted 7 Nov 1989), holding that Article XX(d) could not be used to justify procedures concerning infringement claims that put unequal and less favourable burdens on imported products.

[91] For an account of a massive effort, apparently centered in Taiwan, to counterfeit the MS-DOS software operating system that was running 80 percent of the world's personal computers, see 'Microsoft Nails Some Pirates', *New York Times*, 10 May 1992, §3, p. 7.

element of the 'package deal' that became the Uruguay Round was that greater access for goods of the developing countries in developed country markets must be accompanied by greater protection of intellectual property in the developing countries.[92]

(b)   Introducing Intellectual Property Protection into the GATT/WTO System

The initial effort to bring intellectual property under the rules of international trade came in the form of an International Anti-Counterfeiting Coalition formed in the late 1970s by the United States and the European Community, later joined by Canada and Japan.[93] The Coalition drew up a draft Agreement on Measures to Discourage the Importation of Counterfeit Goods, which would have called upon states to intercept and seize goods bearing unauthorized trademarks at the point of importation, but would not have addressed the sale of such goods in the country of manufacture, and would not have addressed the substantive law of intellectual property within member states. Building on this initiative, the 1982 Ministerial Meeting of the GATT called for examination of the trade aspects of commercial counterfeiting, 'with a view to determining the appropriateness of joint action'.[94] At Punta del Este in 1986, the United States sought to place all aspects of intellectual property protection on the agenda; other countries, particularly the developing countries, were reluctant to go beyond the issue of counterfeiting. The final version of the paragraph in the Ministerial Declaration on Trade-Related Aspects of Intellectual Property Rights stressed negotiations on the problem of counterfeiting, but added that these negotiations 'shall be without prejudice to other complementary initiatives that may be taken in the World Intellectual Property Organization and elsewhere to deal with these matters.'[95]

As it turned out, the United States negotiators succeeded in broadening the agenda, in part by amending and then applying section 301, the 'self-help' provision of United States trade law,[96] to threaten and in a few

[92] For a slightly different formulation of the same point, see J. H. Reichman, 'The Trips Component of the GATT's Uruguay Round: Competitive Prospects for Intellectual Property Owners in an Integrated World Market', 4 *Fordham Intellectual Property, Media and Entertainment Law Journal* 171 at 173 (1993).

[93] See Joseph A. Greenwald, 'The Protection of Intellectual Property Rights in the GATT and the Uruguay Round: The U.S. Viewpoint', in *Conflict and Resolution in US–EC Trade Relations* (S. Rubin and M. Jones (eds.), 1989), 227 at 233–4.

[94] Ministerial Declaration of November 29, 1982, GATT BISD, 29th Supp. 9 at 19 (1983).

[95] Ministerial Declaration on the Uruguay Round, 20 Sept. 1986, GATT BISD 33rd Supp 19 at 25–6.

[96] 19 U.S.C. §2411 *et seq.* In particular, so-called 'special §301', actually §182 of the Trade Act of 1974 as added by §1303 of the Omnibus Trade and Competitiveness Act of 1988, 19 U.S.C. §2242, which required the United States Trade Representative to report to Congress those foreign countries that 'deny adequate and effective protection of intellectual property rights' or 'deny fair and equitable market access to United States persons that rely upon intellectual property protection'. Further, the US Trade Representative was required to

instances actually to impose trade sanctions against countries that failed to grant protection to patents, trademarks or copyrights owned by United States firms.[97] When the negotiating structure for the Uruguay Round was established early in 1987, one of the negotiating groups was dedicated to Trade Related Aspects of Intellectual Property (TRIPs), and that group soon began to work on proposals for a TRIPs Agreement. By the time of the mid-term review of the Uruguay Round in Montreal in December 1988, substantial consensus appeared to have been reached, but with Brazil and India leading the opposition, intellectual property remained one of the four areas on which agreement had not been reached, along with agriculture, textiles, and safeguards.[98]

Negotiations continued in the succeeding years, not only about counterfeiting, but about such subjects as whether compulsory licensing of patents should be permitted or prohibited, whether MFN rules should apply to intellectual property rights or developing countries should be granted more favourable treatment, and if the latter what that meant. A continuing subject of debate was whether intellectual property was an aspect of private property or an instrument of public policy. Also, as was pointed out by the opponents of a comprehensive TRIPs agreement, in some sense patents, copyrights, and the like are restraints on trade, and thus inconsistent with the ideals and objectives of the GATT/WTO system. The answer of the proponents was that while intellectual property rights could be abused to stifle competition, the objectives of the GATT are to improve the conditions of *fair* trade, and protection of the rights of authors and inventors is an important element of fairness in international trade. Intellectual property rights, as a leading German scholar wrote, 'may be viewed as competitive restrictions which can actively serve the advancement of competition'.[99]

---

prepare a list of 'priority foreign countries', i.e. those countries deemed to be the gravest offenders, with respect to which a formal investigation was to be initiated under §301.

[97] In the event, the US Trade Representative initially placed 17 countries on a Watch List and 8 countries on a Priority Watch List. In 1991, China, India, and Thailand were identified as priority foreign countries. Generally such actions by the US government led to prompt negotiations, some successful, some not.

[98] See Ch. 4, Sect. 4.3(b).

[99] Michael Lehmann, 'The Theory of Property Rights and the Protection of Intellectual and Industrial Property', 16 *Int'l Rev. Industrial Property and Copyright Law* 525 at 537 (1985), quoted also by Paul Edward Geller, 'Intellectual Property in the Global Marketplace: Impact of TRIPs Dispute Settlements?', 29 *Int'l Lawyer* 99 at 105 (1995).

Some scholars have attempted to address intellectual property protection from the point of view of trade theory, seeking to determine whether a given country has comparative advantage in innovation (e.g. the United States) or in imitation (e.g. Japan). See e.g. Michael J. Trebilcock and Robert Howse, *The Regulation of International Trade*, 310–12 (2nd edn. 1999). There is no evidence that such calculations played a role in the Uruguay Round, though doubtless some developing countries believed that greater protection for the innovators would leave them disadvantaged.

(c)   The TRIPs Agreement: An Overview[100]

While many of the detailed provisions of the TRIPs Agreement are of concern only to specialists in the law of patents, trademarks, copyright, and related fields, an overview of the Agreement is important to an understanding of the development of the international law of international trade, and its coming together under the umbrella of the World Trade Organization in the last years of the twentieth century.

First, each member state of the WTO is required not only to be a party to the TRIPs Agreement, but it must give effect to the principal provisions of the Paris Convention (as revised through 1967), the Berne Convention (as revised through 1971), and the other conventions now included in the WIPO system,[101] whether or not it is a party to those conventions (Arts. 2, 9).

Second, all members are obligated (with a few stated exceptions) to accord both national treatment (Art. 3) and most-favoured-nation treatment (Art. 4) to the nationals of all other member states with regard to the protection of intellectual property.[102]

Third, the Agreement covers virtually all aspects of intellectual property—copyright (Arts. 9–14); trademarks (Arts. 15–21); geographical indications (i.e. the use of words such as champagne, cognac, Madeira)[103] (Arts. 22–4); industrial designs (Arts. 25–6); patents (Arts. 27–34); layout designs of integrated circuits (Arts. 35–8); and trade secrets (Art. 39). For each of these areas, members are required to provide protection, that is the right to prevent unauthorized persons from using the property.

Fourth, each member 'shall ensure' that enforcement procedures against infringement of intellectual property rights are available (Art. 41). The procedures depend on each country's administrative and judicial system, but

---

[100] For a more detailed and specialized treatment, see e.g. J. H. Reichman, 'Universal Minimum Standards of Intellectual Property Protection under the TRIPs Component of the WTO Agreement', 29 *Int'l Lawyer* 345 (1995); Daniel Gervais, *The TRIPs Agreement: Drafting History and Analysis* (1998); Carlos M. Correa and Abdulqawi A. Yusuf (eds.), *Intellectual Property and International Trade: The TRIPs Agreement* (1998).

[101] In particular, the Rome Convention for the Protection of Performers, Producers of Phonograms and Broadcasting Organizations of 1961, 496 U.N.T.S. 43, and the Treaty on Intellectual Property in Respect of Protection of Integrated Circuits of 1989, 28 *Int'l Leg. Mats.* 1477 (1989). At the insistence of the United States, the requirement to comply with the Berne Convention excludes Article 6*bis* of that convention, addressed to 'moral', as contrasted with 'economic' rights. The concept of moral rights includes the author's right to be known as the author even after he or she has transferred the economic rights, and the right to prevent others from making deforming changes that would be prejudicial to the author's honour or reputation.

[102] Under Article 4(d), preferential agreements concerning intellectual property in effect at the time of entry into force of the Agreement establishing the WTO are exempt from the MFN requirement, provided they do not constitute an 'arbitrary or unjustifiable discrimination' against nationals of other member states. Article 3, the national treatment article, contains no comparable grandfather clause.

[103] But probably not hamburger, frankfurter, port, sherry, Swiss cheese, or other terms that originated in the name of a region or city but have acquired secondary significance.

they are to be 'fair and equitable', not 'unnecessarily complicated or costly', and they shall not entail 'unreasonable time-limits or unwarranted delays'. Decisions in such cases are to be in writing, reasoned, and subject to judicial review (Arts. 41–9). Though the Agreement makes clear in its Preamble that intellectual property rights are private rights, it seems clear that failure by a member to comply with these procedural requirements (albeit stated in general terms) could be the subject of state-to-state dispute settlement. States must provide adequate remedies to rights holders, including injunctions against the sale or use of infringing products, monetary damages, and forfeiture of infringing goods (Arts. 44–6, 50).

In several respects, the TRIPs Agreement goes beyond the traditional GATT approach to avoid discrimination and reduce trade barriers. *In regard to patents*, for instance, the Agreement provides that protection shall be available

for any inventions, whether products or processes, in all fields of technology, provided that they are new, involve an inventive step and are capable of industrial application. Subject to [exceptions on various grounds and grace periods for developing countries], patents shall be available and patent rights enjoyable without discrimination as to the place of invention, the field of technology and whether products are imported or locally produced. (Art. 27(1))[104]

Moreover, the Agreement spells out the rights that member states are to confer in connection with a patent, both with respect to products and with respect to processes (Art. 28), and prescribes a minimum period of validity of patents of twenty years counted from the date of filing (Art. 33).[105] With respect to process patents, the Agreement provides that the judicial authorities of Member states may require an alleged infringer to prove that its product was made with a process different from the patented process, and

---

[104] Members are authorized, by Article 27(3), to exclude from patentability certain classes of creations, such as plants and animals other than micro-organisms; this topic, which was debated vigorously with the United States on one side and the European Community on the other, is made subject to a special review within four years of the effective date of the WTO Agreement. The review was in progress as this volume went to press.

[105] A number of countries previously had different terms, and were required to change their laws. The United States, which had provided for a term of 17 years from date of issue, adopted the twenty-years from filing term, but provided in its amended statute that for existing patents or pending applications, the term would be either 17 years from the date of issue or 20 years from the date of filing, whichever was longer, 35 U.S.C. §154(c)(1). Canada, which had also had a 17-year term but had amended its law in 1989 to adopt the 20-years from filing term, did not again amend its law to provide for a transition, with the effect that some patents applied for before October 1989 would expire before 20 years were up. The United States brought a complaint against Canada in the WTO for breach of Article 33, and the complaint was successful. *Canada: Patent Protection Term* (*U.S. v. Canada*), WT/DS/170/1 (5 May 2000). For a related dispute, concerning the opportunity for generic drug manufacturers (i.e. the producers waiting for expiration of patents) to gear up to compete with the patent holders, see *Canada: Patent Protection of Pharmaceutical Products* (*European Community v. Canada*), WT/DS114/1 (7 April 2000).

that in the absence of such proof, the challenged product shall be deemed to have been made by the patented process (Art. 34).

In regard to copyright, the Agreement recites the basic principle that protection extends to expression and not to ideas, procedures, methods of operation, or mathematical concepts (Art. 9(2)). The Agreement provides that computer programs, whether in source or object code, shall be protected as literary works under the Berne Convention (Art. 10(1)).[106] Also, it provides that copyright protection is to be available for compilations of data or other material which by reason of the selection or arrangement of their contents constitute intellectual creations (Art. 10(2)), and it contains a detailed set of protections for performers, producers of sound recordings, and broadcast organizations (Art. 14). When a copyright (other than for a photographic work or a work of applied art) is not linked to the life of a natural person— as when the creator is a corporation or comparable entity—the Agreement requires that the applicable term shall be a minimum of fifty years from publication (Art. 12).[107]

In regard to trademarks, the Agreement states that any sign or combination of signs capable of distinguishing the goods or services of one undertaking from those of other undertakings shall be capable of constituting a trademark, and shall be eligible for registration. Further, the Agreement expressly incorporates and elaborates on Article *6bis* of the Paris Convention, which calls for refusal by member states to register or permit the use or imitation of 'well-known marks'—e.g. Coca Cola or Mercedes-Benz—by persons other than the owner or licensee of the mark, even if the mark was not previously registered in the state in question (Art. 16).[108]

Registration of a trademark is to be for at least seven years, and registration shall be renewable indefinitely (Art. 18). In contrast to the provision regarding patents, compulsory licensing of trademarks is precluded in all cases (Art. 21). Cancellation for non-use is permitted after an uninterrupted period of at least three years, but the owner must be given an opportunity to explain the non-use by circumstances beyond its control, such as import restrictions or other government requirements (Art. 19).

Geographical indications which identify a product as originating in a member state, or a region within that state are to be given special protection, including legal means for interested parties to prevent any misleading designation or presentation of a competing product. Member states are required

---

[106] The effect of this provision, which was much debated, seems to be to prevent wholesale copying of computer software, but not to prevent independent achievement by 'second comers' of functionally equivalent software. See, generally Reichman (n. 92 supra), at 370–3 and sources there cited.

[107] Article 7 of the Berne Convention, which is in effect incorporated into the TRIPs Agreement, provides for life plus fifty years for works created by a natural person.

[108] For a hypothetical illustration of this provision, see Dreyfuss and Lowenfeld (n. 112 infra), Case IV, 317–24.

to refuse or invalidate the registration of any trademark that contains a misleading indication of the geographic origin of the product in question. Additional protection and provision for further negotiations are set out for wines and spirits (Arts. 22–4).

The problem of counterfeiting—the entering wedge by which intellectual property became part of the GATT/WTO system—is dealt with in the sections on enforcement. The Agreement requires member states to provide civil remedies, including injunctions and provisional measures (Arts. 41–50), and also authorizes measures on the part of customs officials to bar entry of counterfeited or pirated goods (Art. 51). Further, the Agreement states that Members '*shall* provide for criminal procedures and penalties to be applied at least in cases of wilful trademark counterfeiting or copyright piracy on a commercial scale', including imprisonment and/or monetary fines sufficient to provide a deterrent (Art. 61).

(d)   The TRIPs Agreement within the GATT/WTO System

If any member state fails, or is alleged to fail to carry out one of the obligations stated, another member state—presumably the state of nationality of the holder of intellectual property whose rights have been impaired—can make a claim under the WTO Understanding on Dispute Settlement. All of the provisions of that Understanding[109]—consultation, submission to a panel, binding decision, and provision for retaliation as a last resort are made applicable to the TRIPs Agreement, except that non-violation complaints were not to be brought for five years from the effective date of the WTO Agreement, i.e. before January 1, 2000 (Art. 64).[110] It seems that the expectation was that WTO dispute panels would hear complaints about member states' failure to accord protection to particular classes of intellectual property, such as pharmaceuticals or computer software, or about refusal to provide remedies to private litigants pursuing infringers and counterfeiters.[111] As can be seen from the preceding description, however, it is possible—especially with respect to the newer kinds of intellectual property—that a WTO panel might be called upon to interpret the Paris or Berne Convention (or one of the related conventions) which had previously been interpreted and applied only in private actions in national courts.[112]

---

[109] See Ch. 8.

[110] At the Doha Ministerial Conference in November 2001, the member states agreed to study this subject further, and in the mean time (i.e. before the next Ministerial Conference in 2005) not to intiate non-violation complaints under the TRIPs Agreement.

[111] The first such case was brought against India by the United States.

[112] For a discussion of how WTO dispute panels might fit into intellectual property law, see Rochelle Cooper Dreyfuss and Andreas F. Lowenfeld, 'Two Achievements of the Uruguay Round: Putting TRIPs and Dispute Settlement Together', 37 *Va. J. Int'l L.* 275 (1997), stating five hypothetical cases and suggesting suitable solutions.

(e)   TRIPs and the Developing Countries

As noted in subsection (a), the developing countries were reluctant from the time the Uruguay Round was first planned to accept intellectual property into the GATT/WTO system. Right or wrong, their representatives generally believed that the 'third industrial revolution'—based not on steam or electricity but on information and knowledge—would leave them further behind. They feared that an enhanced system of protection of intellectual property would extract 'technologial rent' and would make it harder to catch up than if they were free to take advantage of the innovations made in the developed world. For instance, Brazil's delegate to the TRIPs negotiations wrote in 1989:

One of the possible outcomes of this new 'multilateral framework' would be the imposition of all 'obligations' upon the states (which would become actionable for infringements by private parties), whereas all the 'rights' would rest with the proprietors and holders of the rights; as a consequence, the balance between economic costs and social interests linked to the exercise of monopoly rights would be in jeopardy. Another outcome would be the artificial uniformisation of norms and standards for IPRs protection, with disregard to the existing (and presumably, in the foreseeable future, to the remaining) differences in the level of development among national states.[113]

The leading developed countries and the multilateral enterprises based in those countries considered this attitude quite wrong. They contended that the best way the developing countries—at least those with an educated middle class, such as Brazil, Argentina, Chile, India, and Pakistan—could become part of the international technological community would be if they agreed to protect the innovations of others and benefited from licenses and technological exchanges. It is also true that various studies made on behalf of governments and trade associations in developed countries estimated millions—if not billions—of lost revenue due to 'piracy' and non-protection of intellectual property rights in developing countries.[114]

To some extent this North–South controversy was a reprise of the debates over transnational investment that had occupied much of the preceding two

[113] Paulo Roberto de Almeida, 'The "New" Intellectual Property Regime and Its Economic Impact on Developing Countries', in Giorgio Sacerdoti (ed.), *Liberalization of Services and Intellectual Property in the Uruguay Round of GATT*, 74 at 84 (1990).

See also C. A. Primo Braga, 'The Economics of Intellectual Property Rights and GATT: A View of the South', 22 *Vanderbilt J. Transnat'l L.* 243 at 256 (1989):

Because LDCs are typically net importers of technology, a usual consequence of a more strict regime of intellectual property laws would be an increase in royalty payments to foreigners. . . . Other social costs associated with the reform would be the opportunity cost of additional domestic R&D . . . and the eventual loss of consumer surplus . . . brought by higher prices that could result from the 'monopolization' process.

[114] See e.g. US International Trade Commission, *Foreign Protection of Intellectual Property Rights and the Effect on U.S. Industry and Trade*, Publ. 2065 (1988).

decades—about transnational corporations, host state obligations to foreign investors, and the role of the state in the economy—though by the closing stages of the Uruguay Round those debates had largely subsided.[115] In any event, as noted earlier, without agreement on enhanced protection of intellectual property, the developing countries could not have secured enhanced market access for their agricultural products and relaxed restraints on textile exports. The proponents of the Uruguay Round, particularly in the United States, understood that without agreement by the developing countries on protecting innovation, particularly for the pharmaceutical and so-called 'informatics' industries, support for the Uruguay Round might well be diminished to the point that the whole effort might be in jeopardy.

The eventual compromise essentially gave to the developed countries most of what they had sought on substance, but gave to the developing countries a series of postponements of the obligations. Under the Transitional Arrangements in the TRIPs Agreement (Arts. 65–6), all member states were given a grace period of one year before being required to comply with the Agreement. Developing countries and some countries in transition from centrally planned to market economies, were given an additional four-year grace period, except for the obligation to accord national and MFN treatment with respect to protection of intellectual property. Moreover, developing countries were permitted to avail themselves of an additional five-year period (i.e. a total of ten years of grace) with respect to the obligation to grant patent protection to products to which they did not previously grant protection, such as pharmaceutical and medical products (Art. 65(4)).[116] Least developed countries are not required to comply with any of the provisions of the TRIPs Agreement, other than the MFN and national treatment requirements, for eleven years from the effective date of the Agreement, i.e. until January 1, 2006 (Art. 66).

(f) TRIPs and Competition Law

A continuing problem in the field of intellectual property, viewed differently in different states, is how to reconcile protection for intellectual property—i.e. grant of a monopoly—with competition or antitrust law. The Uruguay Round, as mentioned elsewhere, did not address competition law, and no consensus was achieved by the negotiators of the TRIPs Agreement on the relation between competition law and intellectual property protection. The TRIPs Agreement does provide however that 'some licensing practices or conditions pertaining to intellectual property rights which restrain competition may have adverse effects on trade' (Art. 40(1)), and it states that nothing in the Agreement shall prevent Members from specifying in their

---

[115] See Ch. 13.

[116] Article 65(5) states that members may not increase the degree of inconsistency with the Agreement while availing themselves of a permitted grace period.

national legislation 'licensing practices or conditions that may in particular cases constitute abuse of intellectual property rights having an adverse effect on competition in the relevant market' (Art. 40(2)). The Agreement lists, by way of illustration, exclusive grantback conditions, conditions preventing challenges to validity, and coercive package licensing, and it provides for consultation, at the initiative of either party, between the state of the intellectual property holder and the state concerned about abuse. The Agreement permits states to impose non-exclusive compulsory licensing of patents, but only upon payment of adequate remuneration to the patent holder and only if a proposed user has made efforts to obtain a license from the patent holder on reasonable commercial terms and these efforts have been unsuccessful (Art. 31).[117] Interestingly, the article authorizing compulsory licensing states that 'such use shall be authorized predominantly for the supply of the domestic market' (Art. 31(f)), i.e. not for export in competition with the patent holder. If the WTO moves in the direction of a global competition law,[118] one can envision that the relation to intellectual property law will be a major subject of discussion and contention.

Overall, the TRIPs Agreement constitutes by far the greatest breakthrough among the new items on the Uruguay Round agenda, far more ambitious than the limited achievements in respect of services and investment, and far more extensive than could have been expected when the Uruguay Round began. Even as intellectual property has slipped its national or sovereign moorings in the age of instant communication, so a discipline and an organization built around the theme of custom duties on manufactured goods has grown to embrace international exchange of a very different kind. It is no longer possible for specialists in the law of international trade to maintain that intellectual property is a different field, or for specialists in intellectual property to maintain that international trade law is not their concern.

SUMMARY

Viewed as an eight-year legislative session, the Uruguay Round must be regarded as an enormous achievement. Not only was the fragile GATT enabled to evolve into an apparently strong and close to universal World Trade Organization; there was an enormous expansion in scope of economic activity brought under the principles set down in the late 1940s— national treatment, most-favoured-nation treatment, and periodic collective efforts to reduce barriers to exchange across frontiers.

All of the Tokyo Round codes were clarified, and in the subsidies area an innovative new set of criteria was developed. For all but the Government

---

[117] Compulsory licensing of trademarks is expressly prohibited (Art. 21).
[118] See Ch. 12, Sect. 12.8.

Procurement Code, the optional character of the Tokyo Round Codes was abandoned, so that the coexistence of conditional and unconditional most-favoured-nation treatment as had prevailed from 1979 to 1994 was largely put aside. The resort to 'market disruption' and 'grey area' safeguard measures was subjected for the first time to quite rigid discipline, linked in text and, it appears, in commitment, to the need for adjustment and recognition of the effect of comparative advantage.

Beyond these advances in a system focused on the exchange of goods, the architects of the Uruguay Round—for all their differences—arrived at a common understanding that the international economy could also benefit from legal rules concerning services, intellectual property, and investment. On intellectual property, they developed a significant code of conduct, built on the earlier international treaties but now applicable to all the members of the WTO and linked to state-to-state dispute settlement and enforcement. On the exchange of services, they erected a foundation that was incomplete when the Uruguay Round came to a formal end, but that has provided a basis for continuing growth.[119] As for investment, the achievement was rather modest, and it appears that the consensus for a genuine multilateral legal regime remains a distant prospect, even as a web of bilateral agreements grows ever denser.[120] But investment no longer seems 'off limits' for an organization addressed primarily to trade.

Finally—or perhaps primarily—the whole system is now bound together by an Understanding on Dispute Settlement, which at least in concept, subjects all the other obligations, commitments, and understandings to a compulsory process of consultation, arbitration, and appeal, followed by a system which if not literally 'enforcement,' is designed to eliminate cost-free defiance.[121]

Of course, achievement on paper does not guarantee success in action. The unsuccessful attempt at the close of 1999 to launch a new 'Millenium Round' demonstrated the continuing controversies surrounding both the institution and the legal codes that came out of the Uruguay Round and its predecessors. But while there was much unfinished business, and a good deal of disagreement concealed beneath the signed accords, after completion of the Uruguay Round it was more plausible to speak of a body of International Economic Law than had ever been the case before.

---

[119] See Ch. 6. [120] See Ch. 15. [121] See Ch. 8.

6

The International Exchange of Services and the Creation of GATS

6.1 INTRODUCTION

(a) Services in the World Economy

The interest in rules for trade in services comes largely as a result of two economic trends. First, many developed countries, and particularly the United States, came to recognize that, measured by percentage of gross domestic product, their economies produce more services than goods. Thus services viewed collectively have become the dominant sector of the major industrial—or rather post-industrial—economies. *The Economist* reported in 1994 that manufacturing firms employed only one worker in six in the United States, one in five in Britain, and one in three in Germany.[1] Well over half the gross domestic product of the OECD countries as a whole is made up of service industries,[2] and new job creation has been predominantly in service-related fields, particularly those that require high levels of education, such as telecommunications and health care.

Second, countries that have lost their comparative advantage in the production of some goods now believe their advantage lies in trading certain services. A trade surplus in services can make up for any deficit in the merchandise balance of trade that has traditionally been identified with the state of a nation's trading health. In many years when the United States was running a deficit in its merchandise trade, the deficit was made up by a surplus in trade in services. The situation in Japan has generally been the reverse.

Of course, not all services are tradeable. Waiters, teachers, and taxi drivers, provide services that are counted in gross domestic product, but are not suitable for international exchange. But engineering, insurance, banking, telecommunications, accounting, consulting, and the like may well be amenable to international exchange, whether by trade, investment, lease, or some combination. It is striking, therefore, that as of the mid-1990s, trade in services accounted for only about 25 percent of overall world trade—just under $1.2 trillion.[3] The inference was that trade in services was being inhibited by a variety of barriers, which the international community should endeavour to reduce.

(b) Services in the GATT/WTO System

Until the last years of the twentieth century, the exchange of services across national priorities did not figure prominently in international trade relations.

---

[1] 'The Manufacturing Myth', *The Economist* (London) 19 Mar. 1994, 91.

[2] In only three OECD countries—Greece, Portugal, and Turkey—were fewer than 50 percent of jobs in the service sector.

[3] See *The Economist*, 'Economic Indicators', 3 May 1997, 99, based on estimates of the World Trade Organization.

Services were not mentioned in the GATT, negotiated in the years following World War II.[4] The broader Havana Charter, of which the GATT was originally supposed to be one component,[5] noted as one of its purposes the encouragement of demand for services as well as for goods, but the Charter did not make substantive provision for exchange of services.

The Treaty of Rome establishing the European Economic Community, drafted in the late 1950s, appears to have been the first international agreement directed to freeing trade in services as well as goods, and the Community's efforts in the 1990s directed to achieving the Single Market were aimed largely at finally reducing the barriers to exchange of services. United States law defined international trade as including both goods and services as early as 1974,[6] but efforts to include services in the Tokyo Round were not intensively pursued. In the GATT Ministerial Meeting of 1982, after strenuous debate, the subject of services was for the first time placed on the agenda, and contracting parties were invited to consider whether any multilateral action in respect of services is 'appropriate and desirable'.[7] Generally the United States and the European Community were in favour of including services in the GATT system, the developing countries were opposed.

In some ways the GATT system seemed ill-suited to discussion of trade of services, in that the initial focus of the GATT was on tariffs, which virtually never apply to the supply of services. Even the non-tariff barriers that had become part of the currency of GATT—dumping and anti-dumping, subsidies and countervailing duties, safeguards and quantitative restrictions—did not seem applicable to the exchange of services. But clearly states do impose restraints on provision of services, often depending on the state of origin of the service or the provider. Thus the overall teaching of the GATT, that international rules could and should moderate governmental restrictions on transborder economic activity, and that these rules should be subject to periodic multilateral negotiation and liberalization, might well be applied or adapted to trade in services. When the Uruguay Round was launched in Punta del Este in 1986, a separate group on Negotiations on Services was created, 'with a view to expansion of such trade under conditions of transparency and progressive liberalization' subject, however, to 'respect [for] the policy objectives of national laws and regulations applying to services.'[8] The architects of the Uruguay Round could not be sure of the

---

[4] The Preamble to the GATT, drafted in 1947 and not changed thereafter, states the objective as 'the full use of the resources of the world and expanding the production and exchange of goods'. The Preamble to the Agreement Establishing the WTO, signed in 1994, largely tracks the 1947 text, but adds 'and services'. The note to paragraph 2 of Article XVII of the GATT states 'The term "goods" is limited to products as understood in commercial practice, and is not intended to include the purchase or sale of services.'

[5] Ch. 3, Sect. 3.2.   [6] USA: Trade Act of 1974, §102(g)(3), 19 U.S.C. 2112(g)(3).

[7] GATT: Ministerial Declaration, 19 Nov. 1982, GATT BISD, 29th Supp. 9 at 21–2 (1983).

[8] GATT: Ministerial Declaration on the Uruguay Round, 20 Sept. 1986, GATT BISD, 33rd Supp. 19 at 28 (1987).

outcome of the negotiations on services: in order to make sure that failure on this new topic would not bring down the whole Uruguay Round, it was understood from the outset that negotiations on services would be separate, looking to a General Agreement on Trade in Services (GATS), distinct from, though linked to, the GATT or, as it began to take shape, the WTO system.

The attempt in the Uruguay Round to impose the principles of non-discrimination and comparative advantage on exchange of services was only partly successful, as described hereafter. But the negotiations did achieve a General Agreement on Trade in Services (GATS), which provides a framework for sector-specific agreements. The two most significant of those agreements—both completed well after the close of the Uruguay Round—focused on Financial Services and on Telecommunications.[9]

6.2   APPROACHING THE BARRIERS TO TRADE IN SERVICES

In theory, the same principles of comparative advantage that apply to trade in goods ought to apply to trade in services. Assuming barriers to trade in services are low, countries with large amounts of unskilled labour will tend to export labour-intensive services such as construction or simple data processing, while countries with skilled labour will have a comparative advantage in other areas such as financial services or software design. Other factor endowments would be relevant, just as they are for trade in goods, to give a comparative advantage to countries with a particular geography, history or culture. Concepts such as economies of scale and the availability of capital should also apply to determine the competitiveness of certain service industries, as they do for certain goods.[10] In practice, however, even a framework agreement for trade in services proved difficult to achieve, and the major agreements could be concluded only with the the benefit of several extensions beyond the close of the Uruguay Round.[11] The rules and disciplines governing trade in services were not in place until the Dunkel Draft of December 1991, and negotiations about commitments did not begin in earnest until 1992.

Several reasons may be cited for the difficulty in negotiating about barriers to trade in services. *First*, the subject was a new one, not only in that it had not been on the agenda of prior rounds but that officials, economists, and lawyers had not thought of services as tradeable. Prior to the technological

[9] See Sects. 6.6 on financial services and 6.7 on telecommunications.

[10] See e.g. Richard H. Snape, 'Principles in Trade' in *Services in The Uruguay Round: Services in the World Economy*, 6 (Patrick A. Messerlin and Karl P. Sauvant (eds.), 1990).

[11] The chief negotiator for the United States on services wrote that 'services negotiators from all countries were privately relieved that the Uruguay Round did not conclude on schedule', i.e. at the end of 1990. Richard B. Self, 'General Agreement on Trade in Services', in Terence P. Stewart (ed.), *The World Trade Organization: The Multilateral Trade Framework for the 21st Century and U.S. Implementing Legislation*, 523 at 524 (1996).

revolutions in telecommunication and transportation, which dramatically lowered their cost (both in time and money), many services were in effect not tradeable except in border regions. As a result, services were regarded as warranting little attention in the negotiation of international trade regimes and liberalization.

Second, barriers to trade in services are not simple and obvious like tariffs on goods; they are difficult to identify, to clarify, and to negotiate on the traditional basis of reciprocity. In many instances, the barriers to trade are domestic regulations, which may be designed to protect local monopolies, to protect consumers, or to achieve some objective of monetary or fiscal policy, but will have the effect of excluding supply of services by outsiders.

Third, most regulation of services focuses on the provider rather than the product. Unlike producers of goods, which can alter the characteristics of a product or modify the price, providers of services will often find that the requirements of a foreign market 'are inconsistent with the requirements of the home market'. To take a familiar example, the United States for many years prohibited banks from participating in most aspects of the securities industry (and vice versa). This was not a regulation directed at foreign providers, but since it went to the characteristics of the provider, it effectively kept many foreign banks from participating fully in the American banking market.

Fourth, in many cases, such as banking, insurance, travel agencies, and professional services, supply of service by a Xandian supplier to Patrian users will involve investment and establishment in Patria, and also movement of Xandian persons to Patria permanently or for extended periods. Issues of foreign investment and immigration often touch raw nerves, particularly in developing countries.

Finally, in traditional trade negotiations, it has generally been possible to exchange concessions in different products, so that Patria might grant a concession on a product of export interest to Xandia, in return for a concession by Xandia on a product of export interest to Patria. Of course Tertia might benefit through MFN from both concessions, but it would be expected to grant concessions as well, whether to Xandia, to Patria, or to Quarta, from which Xandia and Patria could expect to benefit. On the whole, while everyone was somewhat concerned about giving more than it got and about the 'free riders', the pattern of multilateral negotiations had evolved to a stage where—agriculture and a few other sectors aside—a cross-sectoral multi-item negotiation was possible, with most participants roughly satisfied with the exchange, even when it would be hard to prove mathematical reciprocity.

With respect to services, it soon appeared that the traditional GATT approach would not work. A few general principles might be agreed to—transparency, consistency, possibly national treatment, possibly MFN treatment, with some concession to existing rights. It was not clear whether states should be able to *opt out* of the standard commitments for particular industries through a negative list, or whether the commitments should apply only to a positive list of sectors for which states could *opt in*. At any event, the main negotiations, it became clear, would be about market access. And Xandia could not make a deal providing that it would open up its banking sector to foreign participation if Patria would open up its tourism sector to admit a Xandian hotel chain. Particular negotiations, it turned out, would have to be conducted for the most part by sectors, and with somewhat different perceptions of the elusive concept of reciprocity.

The plan that began to emerge, principally from proposals of the United States, had two aspects. *First*, the General Agreement on Trade in Services would set out a few general principles—non-discrimination, national treatment, transparency for national rules and regulations, and dispute settlement; *second*, the proposed agreement would contain a list of particular service sectors to which states could subscribe, specifying which services they were prepared to submit to negotiations under the GATS principles.

6.3   THE GENERAL AGREEMENT ON TRADE IN SERVICES: AN OVERVIEW

(a)   The Scheme of the GATS

In general, the scheme of a permanent agreement that bound all members, and sector-specific annexes subject to separate negotiations was accepted in the Uruguay Round. Not only was this a compromise between universalism and the optional code system of the Tokyo Round;[12] it also permitted signature of GATS as part of the conclusion of the Uruguay Round while leaving open negotiations on specific subjects such as telecommunications, financial services, shipping, and other sectors that had not been completed (or in some instances not even started) when the rest of the Round was being wound up. Like the GATT, the GATS does not itself provide for liberalization of trade, but provides for commitments (concessions) negotiated under the framework of the Agreement, and bound in schedules or annexes.

Part I of the GATS defines trade in services in four modes, focused supply of the service across national frontiers (Art. I(2)):

Mode 1 from the territory of one Member into the territory of any other Member, e.g. international telecommunications or database services performed in Xandia for benefit of a user in Patria.

---

[12] An alternative considered for a time would have been a code on services similar to the codes developed in the Tokyo Round, which would not require adherence by all parties to the GATT/WTO system. As this departure from universalism accepted in the 1970s was rejected in the course of the Uruguay Round, the proposal for an optional code was abandoned. In effect, the general framework plus optional specific commitments is not as different from the code concept as appears from universal membership in the GATS.

Mode 2 in the territory of one Member to the service consumer from another country, e.g. Patrian tourists traveling to Xandia on holiday or Patrian patients receiving medical treatment in Xandian hospitals.

Mode 3 by a service supplier of one Member, through commercial presence in the territory of any other Member, e.g. insurance issued in Xandia but sold through a branch office or subsidiary in Patria.

Mode 4 by a service supplier of one Member, through presence of natural persons of a Member in the territory of any other Member, e.g. an architect or construction engineer from Xandia who travels to a building site in another country.[13]

Part II of the GATS then sets down the basic principles—MFN, transparency, avoidance of abuse of dominant position, but not, interestingly, national treatment. Part III then provides for specific commitments by sector for market access and national treatment. The remaining parts of the GATS, closely following the GATT model, provide for periodic negotiating rounds, binding and unbinding of schedules, dispute settlement by recourse to the Understanding on Dispute Settlement,[14] and creation of a Council on Trade In Services.

(b)   GATT and GATS Compared

The 'General Obligations and Disciplines' applicable to all services covered by the Agreement are modeled on the GATT, but with some significant departures. *Most-favoured nation treatment* (GATS Art. II) essentially follows GATT Article I—i.e. it requires each Member to accord immediately and unconditionally to services and service suppliers of any Member treatment no less favourable than it accords to services and service suppliers of any other country, but only 'with respect to any measure covered by this Agreement'. The GATS does not contain a provision guaranteeing national treatment comparable to Article III of the GATT; instead, Article VI of the GATS requires—again with regard to sectors where specific commitments are undertaken—that all measures of general application affecting trade in services be administered in a 'reasonable, objective and impartial manner'. This obligation is taken to include prompt and impartial review (judicial, arbitral, or administrative) of decisions affecting trade in services, and objective and transparent criteria for issuing licenses or technical qualifications.

---

[13] The italicized phrases are quotations from Article I(2) of the Agreement. Note that some services can be supplied in more that one mode; for instance, the services of a foreign lawyer or accountant might be supplied through a visit by the client, by mail or fax, through an office maintained by the law firm or accounting firm in the country of the client's residence, or by a visit to the client in his country. Other services, such a tourism or construction supervision, obviously do not provide corresponding alternatives.

[14] See Ch. 8.

The problem of regional arrangements is addressed by a provision (GATS Art. V) drawn from Article XXIV of the GATT, in that it seeks to distinguish between special (and therefore discriminatory) arrangements, and arrangements of a wider and more general character. GATS Article V adapts Article XXIV(5) of the GATT in stating that an agreement of economic integration liberalizing trade in services 'shall be designed to facilitate trade between the parties to the agreement', and 'shall not . . . raise the overall level of barriers to trade in services' with non-parties to the regional agreement. GATS also contains a general exceptions provision (GATS Art. XIV) modeled on Article XX of GATT, permitting Members to take non-discriminatory measures *necessary* to protect public morals, human, animal or plant life or health, and (different from GATT) necessary to prevent deceptive and fraudulent practices or to deal with effects of default, and necessary for the protection of privacy and confidentiality in connection with transmission of data.[15]

An issue important to trade in services—as in others of the new topics addressed in the Uruguay Round—is transparency. GATS Article III states that each Member shall publish all relevant measures of general application pertaining to trade in services, shall give notice of proposed changes to the Council on Trade in Services created in accordance with the Marrakesh Agreement Establishing the World Trade Organization.

6.4   The GATS: A Closer Look

(a)   Most-Favoured-Nation Treatment

As in the GATT, the first principle of the GATS is MFN. Article II(1) states that

[E]ach Member shall accord immediately and unconditionally to services and service suppliers of any other Member, treatment no less favourable than that it accords to like services and service suppliers of any other country.

However, it turned out that states were not really ready to commit themselves to MFN across the board. Many states had issued licenses and permits on the basis of reciprocity and were not willing to eliminate such arrangements. Furthermore, some states—notably the United States—asserted that they already granted liberal market access in most situations; if they were required to extend their liberal regimes on the basis of MFN, they would lose the leverage to pry open markets of those states with closed regimes. The United States insisted, therefore, on a paragraph 2 of Article II, which

---

[15] GATS also contains a provision (Art. XIV*bis*) concerning 'essential security interests', drawn from Article XXI of the GATT.

takes back—or to be precise permits the taking back—with respect to particular measures—the general commitment of paragraph 1:

A Member may maintain a measure inconsistent with paragraph 1, provided that such a measure is listed in, and meets the conditions of, the Annex on Article II Exemptions.

The right to a derogation from MFN treatment is unilateral, in the sense that it is not subject to approval by any committee or other potential supplier; but it must be specific to a particular existing measure, not to a whole sector or to a future measure. Further, the Annex on Article II Exemptions states that all exemptions from MFN are to have a termination date, and in principle should not exceed a period of ten years. If new agreements on market access under one of the sectoral agreements described below are negotiated between two countries—as took place, for instance on financial services between Japan and the United States—the resulting benefits granted by the two states to each other must be generalized to all member states under the MFN principle. Since the measures taken in implementation of such an agreement would not qualify as existing measures previously notified, the right to an exemption would not apply.

(b)   Transparency and Fair Procedures

Article III of the GATS requires prompt publication of 'all relevant measures of general application' which pertain to or affect trade in services, whether or not they pertain to sectors for which commitments have been made under Part III. The requirement extends also to international agreements affecting trade in services, and provides further that each Member State is to report promptly and at least annually any new laws or regulations, and any changes to existing laws or regulations, which significantly affect trade in services covered by its specific commitments under Part III.[16]

Barriers to the supply of services in many instances are not border controls, as in respect to trade in goods, but regulations, licensing requirements, red tape, and the like. For administrative decisions affecting all trade in services, whether or not an applicable schedule has been submitted, the GATS requires Member States to provide for prompt and impartial review of administrative decisions by judicial, arbitral, or administrative tribunals or comparable procedures (Art. VI(2)). For sectors in which a Member State has made a commitment, the GATS requires that all measures of general application be administered 'in a reasonable, objective and impartial manner' (Art. VI(1)), and a series of further provisions endeavour to spell this

---

[16] Article III*bis* states that the requirements of transparency do not apply if the information is confidential and disclosure would impede law enforcement, or 'prejudice legitimate commercial interests of particular enterprises.'

standard out with respect to applications for authorizations, licensing criteria, and consistency with international standards.

(c) Market Access

Access by service providers of one state to the markets of other states is the central focus of the Agreement on Services, but access is not granted automatically. The GATS adopts an 'opt-in' or positive list approach, whereby Members are bound only with respect to specific commitments by sector or subsector. In a sector for which it has made a market access commitment, a Member State is required to refrain from imposing any limitations on the number of service suppliers, whether in the form of numerical quotas, monopolies, exclusive service suppliers, or the requirement of an economic needs test (Art. XVI(2)(a)). Further, the Member State may not impose limitations on the total value, the total number, or the total ouput of service operations (Art. XVI(2)(b) and (c)); and the state may not restrict the number of persons that may be employed by a service supplier or in a particular service sector who are necessary for and directly related to the supply of a specific service (Art. XVI(2)(d)).[17] Finally, the state may not restrict or require specific types of legal entity or joint venture through which a service is supplied, or limit the participation of foreign capital by a maximum percentage of shareholding or total value of the investment.

The market access article of the GATS, thus, is a kind of foreign investment code—more extensive than any obligation thus far concluded in the GATT/WTO system, but it is applicable only to the extent a Member State agrees to be bound. As illustrated below with respect to financial services, a state may, for example, make a commitment that it will grant market access with respect to banking, but provide that certain subsectors must operate through joint ventures with a limit on foreign capital.

(d) National Treatment

National treatment, as noted above, is not a fundamental obligation, as under the GATT, but, like market access, is subject to a specific undertaking, dependent on submission of sectoral schedules. If a Member State submits a schedule containing a market access commitment, Article XVII(1) states that it 'shall accord to services and service suppliers of any other Member . . . treatment no less favourable than that it accords to its own like services and service suppliers'. It is understood that the meaning of national treatment is the same as under Article III of the GATT, and

---

[17] Most states, in their general headnotes to their service schedules, limit the number of foreign personnel to senior executives or managers, as seems to be permitted by the phrase 'necessary for . . . the supply of a specific service'.

that the precedents, including panel decisions interpreting Article III will be relevant, if not controlling.[18]

One might have expected that as to a sector for which a schedule of commitments had been submitted, national treatment would be mandatory. But Article XVII(1) too contains the phrase 'subject to any conditions and qualifications set out [in the Schedule]', and a number of states, particularly among the developing countries, have submitted schedules containing derogations from national treatment such as limits on foreign ownership and limits on expatriate employees. Like the qualifications to market access, it was understood that these derogations or exemptions would be subject to negotiation both in the sectoral negotiations that were not completed by the end of the Uruguay Round but were supposed to be continued thereafter, and in the successive rounds of negotiation called for in GATS Article XIX, modeled on Article XXVIII*bis* of the GATT.

(e) Summary

The Framework Agreement—i.e. the GATS proper—was a breakthrough in that for the first time it subjected services to an international set of rules, linked to the WTO and therefore to the Understanding on Dispute Settlement as well as to any future negotiating round. The principles are clear enough—MFN, national treatment, and market access. But the commitment to the principles was made subject to a mixture of opt-out and opt-in provisions. *MFN* is mandatory, but subject to opting out for specific sectors on the basis of existing preferences. The United States, for example, initially opted out of MFN for financial services and for telecommunications, with a view to offering full MFN when other countries came up with satisfactory offers in the sectoral negotiations due to begin soon after the close of the Uruguay Round.

Market access is not mandatory but requires opting in by sector; but even if a member state submits a 'positive list', i.e. it opts in, it may opt out of certain of the requirements for full market access set out in the General Agreement.

National treatment is supposed to attach to any sector on a country's positive list, but that list may itself provide for opting out of national treatment for particular sectors or subsectors. To make clear which country has made what commitments, the General Agreement provides in Article XX that each schedule submitted by a state shall not only set out the specific commitments undertaken by that state, but also

---

[18] This is made clear by Article XVII(3) of the GATS, which provides that formally identical or formally different treatment shall be considered less favourable if it modifies the conditions of competition in favour of services or service suppliers of the Member compared to those of any other member.

(a) terms, limitations and conditions on market access;

(b) conditions and qualifications on national treatment; and

(c) undertakings relating to additional commitments;

plus, where appropriate, the time frame for the commitments and their effective date. In order that Members' schedules can be compared with each other, the schedules are to be classified in twelve principal sectors, but each state need not submit a schedule for each sector.[19]

6.5 IMPLEMENTING THE GATS

Ninety-seven countries submitted schedules of specific commitments concerning services subject to the GATS. Among the sectors covered were professional services (accounting, architecture, engineering); business services (advertising, market research, consulting, computing); communications, including couriers, value-added telecommunications, and certain audio-visual services; construction; distribution (wholesale and retail trade and franchising); health services; tourism; and some financial services.

The first important sectoral negotiations in implementation of the General Agreement on Trade in Services almost ended in complete failure in June 1995. The United States, which had been an active participant and indeed proponent of negotiations on Financial Services, withdrew its offers and stated that it would not participate further, because it was dissatisfied with the offers of several Asian and Latin American countries. This meant that the United States would enter a reservation to the MFN provision, so that, as its spokesman said, 'we treat those countries who treat us well better than others'. The European Union, however, took the lead in securing a 30-day extension in the negotiations, and in putting together an interim agreement—the first agreement in the history of GATT/WTO concluded without participation by the United States.

---

[19] The 12 sectors are:

business (including professional and computer) services
communication services
construction and related engineering services
distribution services
educational services
environmental services
financial (including insurance and banking) services
health-related and social services
tourism and travel-related services
recreational, cultural, and sporting services
transport services
other services not included elsewhere.

Many of the schedules may in turn be subdivided, for instance financial services into banking and insurance, insurance into life insurance and property insurance; tourism into hotels, restaurants, and travel bureaux, and so on. See WTO Secretariat, Trade in Services Division, *An Introduction to the GATS*, p. 14 (1999).

On July 26, 1995, some thirty countries (counting the EU as one) committed themselves to specified increased market access in their countries for foreign insurance companies, banks, and securities houses on an MFN basis. Renato Ruggiero, the Director-General of the WTO, called the agreement a victory for multilateralism in trade, and 'a very good second best'.[20] The interim agreement was to remain in effect until December 31, 1997, the hope being that in the interval a permanent agreement could be negotiated that would include the United States. That goal was accomplished, as important developing countries, particularly India and Brazil, as well as Turkey, South Africa, and others, came up with offers that the United States regarded as meaningful. On December 12, 1997, 70 WTO members reached agreement on a Protocol on Financial Services, containing the improved schedules and exemptions of the participating countries. The United States now accepted that US-based financial entities would be assured adequate opportunities to enter foreign markets, and therefore the United States could join in the revised, and permanent agreement. The US Secretary of the Treasury, Robert Rubin, said 'This agreement levels the playing field in global financial markets.'[21]

6.6 GATS AND FINANCIAL SERVICES

(a) The Annex on Financial Services

The GATS itself does not contain any provision or definition for Financial Services, but an Annex concluded at the same time as the GATS, i.e. as part of the Uruguay Round, defines financial services (Annex Art. 5), and provides for prudential regulation, that is, regulation not used as a means for avoiding the commitments or obligations under the Agreement (Annex Art. 2). The definitions cover insurance of all kinds, as well as banking and related services including participation in issuance of securities, underwriting, and asset management.

The concept of prudential regulation acknowledges that different states may need to impose different kinds and different levels of scrutiny of financial transactions, and if they do so without the motive of denying national treatment or market access, they will not thereby be violating the GATS. Further, the Annex permits, but does not require, recognition of another country's prudential measures, so that for example, a stock prospectus passed by the Xandian Securities and Exchange Commission might entitle the issuer to sell the securities therein described in Patria without further

---

[20] *Financial Times*, 27 July 1995, p. 1.
[21] White House Press Release, 13 Dec. 1997. According to the Press Release, the Protocol covered 95 percent of the global financial services market as measured in revenue, including securities, banking, and insurance and related industries.

scrutiny, if Patria had made an agreement with Xandia or otherwise had recognized Xandian securities law. Of course such an agreement between Patria and Xandia might raise concerns under an MFN commitment. Unless, in the example, Patria had excluded securities regulation from its MFN commitment, it would be obligated to grant Tertia, Quarta, etc. the opportunity to make a similar arrangement, provided those countries could demonstrate a regulatory system equivalent to that of Xandia.

The GATS as a whole, as previously noted, is tied in to the WTO Dispute Settlement Understanding; the Annex adds that panels addressing prudential issues and other financial matters 'should have the necessary expertise relevant to the specific financial service under dispute'.[22]

(b)   The Commitments: Market Access and National Treatment

Part III of the GATS, devoted to Specific Commitments, calls for proceeding in two stages. First, Member States are to list the sectors for which they are committing themselves (i) to grant access to their markets (Art. XVI); and (ii) to grant national treatment (Art. XVII)—in both categories in accordance with schedules filed with and bound to the WTO. Second, Member States are to set out in their schedules the terms, limitations, and conditions on market access, and conditions and qualifications on national treatment. Thus, the first stage is a positive list—Member States announce the sectors to which their commitments will apply—e.g. insurance, banking, issuance of securities, etc.— generally divided into subsectors—for instance for insurance, life insurance, property insurance, liability insurance; for banking, acceptance of deposits, lending of all types, mortgage credit, foreign exchange, etc.

The second stage is a negative list, announcing limitations on the respective commitments, cross-referenced to the four modes of supply. For instance, with respect to market access for most kinds of insurance, Brazil grants market access upon local incorporation, but excludes a commitment on market access on transborder supply. For Germany, international transport insurance may be issued by foreign firms having a branch in that country but only through that branch.

With respect to national treatment for federally regulated financial institutions, Canada requires that a minimum of half the directors must be Canadian citizens or permanent residents, in either case ordinarily resident in Canada. For Indonesia, expatriates may assume only executive positions, but at least one such position per enterprise must be held by an Indonesian national. In the United States, foreign banks (including branches) cannot be members of the Federal Reserve System, but subsidiaries of foreign banks can be. Foreign banks acting as investment advisers are required to register under the Investment Advisers Act, which involves record maintenance, inspections, and reports not required of domestic banks.

---

[22] Annex on Financial Services, Art. 4.

(c)   The Commitments: Most-Favoured-Nation Treatment

As noted in Section 6.4(a) above, Article II(1) of the GATS, modeled on Article I of the GATT, calls for immediate and unconditional MFN treatment to services and service suppliers. Paragraph 2 of the same article, however, states that a Member may maintain a measure inconsistent with MFN if it lists such a measure in its MFN exemption schedule, subject to negotiation in subsequent trade liberalization rounds. Several of these exemptions were listed in the schedules to the Financial Services Agreement. For instance, the United States schedule stated that a broker-dealer with its principal place of business in Canada may maintain its required reserves in Canada, subject to supervision in Canada. Presumably, other states, e.g. the United Kingdom or Australia, might ask for similar treatment in a subsequent negotiating round, but the United States would not be required to grant the same preference to states in whose supervision of brokers it had less confidence.

Italy notified a preferential tax treatment for financial service suppliers from formerly communist countries in Eastern Europe and the Soviet Union for a ten-year period, on the basis of a need to aid the countries concerned in their transition to a market economy. France, Britain, and Portugal notified waivers of nationality requirements in several sectors for citizens of former colonies, dependencies, and protectorates. Indonesia prohibits joint venture banks with a foreign partner unless the home country of the partner permits participation by Indonesian banks on a reciprocal basis. All of these notifications are derogations from MFN, in that they extend benefits to firms from some countries not available to others.

(d)   'Horizontal Commitments'

The schedules as submitted by the Member States also contain so-called 'horizontal commitments', that is conditions imposed by Member States applicable across sectors or industries. These commitments (in truth reservations from commitments) need to be listed in each of the schedules submitted by Member States, so that someone looking at a particular schedule will not be misled. For instance, Indonesia provides that wherever new joint ventures between domestic and foreign partners are permitted, the foreign partner's share of capital is limited to 49 percent. Canada provides that (except where NAFTA applies) acquisition by a non-Canadian of control of a Canadian business worth over a stated amount is subject to government approval. Japan reserves the right to limit the entry of corporate officers, lawyers, accountants, scientists, and other professionals. Several Member States of the European Union maintain restrictions on acquisition by foreign nationals of shares in newly privatized companies that were previously state monopolies.

(e) The Understanding on Commitments in Financial Services

In addition to the methods of presenting commitments and reservations as described in the preceding sections, the negotiators of the Financial Services Agreement provided another method of expressing commitments. A group of countries, generally speaking the industrial states, including the United States, the European Community, Canada, and Japan, referred in their schedules to an Understanding on Commitments in Financial Services drafted and agreed during the Uruguay Round. The Understanding recorded agreement on a set of commitments that would become operative once an Agreement on Financial Services was concluded. To take the most significant commitments listed in the Understanding, countries that incorporated the Understanding into their schedules were to endeavour to eliminate monopoly rights; to grant MFN treatment in public procurement; to grant financial service providers of any other Member (whether or not it subscribed to the Understanding) the right to establish a commercial presence; and to permit existing foreign financial service suppliers to offer any new financial service. Also, whereas the GATS itself does not contain a standstill provision, the Understanding provides that non-conforming measures shall be only those existing at the time that the schedules entered into effect.

It was the exchange of these commitments and extensions that took three years of negotiations. When all the commitments and exclusions were on the table and had been agreed, the Agreement on Financial Services could be announced. A Protocol incorporating all the schedules was issued, subject to acceptance by member states on or before January 30, 1999.[23]

6.7 GATS AND TELECOMMUNICATIONS[24]

(a) The Revolution in Telecommunications

The other major service sector left open at the end of the Uruguay Round in which significant advances seemed possible[25] was telecommunications. In some way the revolution proposed—and in substantial part achieved—was even greater than in Finanical Services because at the outset the vast majority of telecom markets were run by monopolies, most of which were state-owned. Indeed, in a real sense the telecom negotiations can be traced back to the break-up in the United States of AT&T in 1984 and the beginning of privatization of British Telecom and creation of a duopoly in the United

---

[23] Fifth Protocol to the General Agreement on Trade in Services, 3 Dec. 1997.
[24] For a book-length description of the Telecoms Revolution, see, e.g. Heather E. Hudson, *Global Connections: International Telecommunications Infrastructure and Policy* (1997).
[25] i.e. excluding maritime transport and movement of persons.

Kingdom in the same year. The negotiations in the WTO were consistent with the general wave of privatization and deregulation, which in turn was consistent with opening up of at least some competition within states and across national frontiers.[26]

By the end of the negotiations in February 1997, 92 percent of major markets were covered by commitments embodied in 55 schedules submitted on behalf of 69 governments to remove restrictions on competition and foreign entry.[27] In 44 countries enterprises providing basic telecom services could be 100 percent owned by foreign nationals; another twelve countries permitted foreign ownership or control of certain basic telecom services, and thirteen allowed some foreign participation in their basic telecom markets.[28] The US administration estimated that the average cost of international telephone calls would drop by 80 percent over the first few years after the effective date of the Basic Telecom Agreement, from an average of one dollar per minute to 20 cents per minute.[29]

(b)   The Telecommunications Annexes

As in the financial services negotiations, the essential commitments sought were national treatment and market access, and the derogation to be avoided concerned MFN. But because the history of telecommunication services had been heavily based on monopolies—indeed many thought of telephone and related services as natural monopolies— major attention had to be paid to the rules of competition. However, the Annex on Telecommunications contemplated competition across frontiers, and access not just to the market in general but to interconnections and public telecommunications transport networks and terminals. The telecommunications services sector was seen both as a distinct sector of economic activity and as the underlying transport means for other economic activities.

When the Agreement establishing the WTO was signed in Marrakesh in April 1994, no agreement had been reached, and indeed few offers had been

[26] Previously, negotiations about telecommunications had been carried out under the auspices of the International Telecommunication Union. However, the ITU had focused primarily on technical and related regulatory issues regarding the provision of telecom services across borders, such as radio-frequency allocations, standards, numbering, and accounting rates. Moreover, the ITU was seen by the trade negotiators as the meeting place of the traditional PTTs or other monopoly service providers, and not a suitable forum for liberalization and deregulation.

[27] The discrepancy between the number of schedules and the number of governments bound resulted from the fact that the European Commission submitted a single schedule on behalf of the fifteen members of the European Union.

[28] See Laura B. Sherman, ' "Wildly Enthusiastic" about the First Multilateral Agreement on Trade in Telecommunications Services', 51 *Fed'l Communications L.J.* 61 at 63–4 (1998). For a more critical look, see William J. Drake and Eli M. Noam, 'Assessing the WTO Agreement on Basic Telecommunications', in Gary Clyde Hufbauer and Erika Wada, *Unfinished Business: Telecommunications after the Uruguay Round* (1997).

[29] See Sherman, n. 28 supra.

made, in respect of basic (as contrasted with enhanced) telecommunications.[30] One of the Ministerial Decisions made at Marrakesh, reflecting the incomplete negotiations during the Uruguay Round but determination not to abandon the subject, was to establish a Negotiating Group on Basic Telecommunications, with a final report due on April 30, 1996. The Ministerial Decision said that negotiations were to be entered into on a voluntary basis, and the Negotiating Group began with only seventeen members (counting the European Union as one). Also, as in Financial Services, the decision was made early on to rely on positive list or 'opt-in' commitments. But at the insistence of the United States, a separate Annex on Negotiations on Basic Telecommunications suspended the application of Article II of the GATS, the basic MFN provision, until completion of the telecom negotiations or a final report to the effect that the negotiations had not succeeded. It would not be correct to say that the technique used in the financial services negotiations was repeated, because the negotiations on the two sectors proceeded at the same time. But in both cases, the idea was to limit the 'free-rider' effect by requiring MFN treatment only when a sufficient number of states (the 'critical mass') had made market access offers to justify conclusion of a multilateral agreement.

As in the negotiations on financial services, the United States withdrew from the negotiations on telecommunications at one point because the 'critical mass' had not been reached. As a result, the deadline for the negotiations was moved up from April 30, 1996 to February 15, 1997, and that deadline was met, with full participation—indeed leadership—by the United States in producing what came to be known as the Fourth Protocol to the GATS.[31]

(c) The Conditions of Competition and the Reference Paper

Accounting Rates

Most international telecommunications traffic until recently was based on a system of accounting rates. For a call from Patria to Xandia the Patrian telecommunication operator would collect an agreed price (the accounting rate), and credit a portion of that price to the Xandian operator as compensation for its completing the call (the settlement price). Calls originating in Xandia and destined for Patria would be handled in the same way, and at

---

[30] Basic telecommunications refers to voice telephone, telex, and telegraph, in contrast to enhanced or value-added telecommunications such as electronic mail, voice mail, on-line and databased information retrieval and data processing. In fact, the lines are often blurred, and negotiations did take place in the Uruguay Round on some enhanced telecoms, while negotiations on basic telecommunications were put off. The technical aspects of radio and television broadcasting, whether over the air, by cable, or by satellite, have not generally been included in the WTO negotiations or agreements.

[31] For a brief account of the negotiations leading to the Fourth Protocol, see Marco C. E. J. Bronckers and Pierre Larouche, 'Telecommunications Services and the World Trade Organization', 31 *J. World Trade* No. 3, p. 5 (June 1997). See also Sherman, n. 28 supra.

the end of the accounting period the two operators would settle their accounts. Generally, if more calls originated in Patria, its operator would end up making a payment to the Xandian operator.[32]

This system, developed soon after the creation of national telephone systems early in the twentieth century, worked reasonably well so long as the operators were monopolies and rates were fixed. When Patria (read in the first instance USA) deregulated and international rates fell as a result of competition, while Xandia (read, say, Brazil) maintained a high price monopoly, the settlement rate that Patrian operators had to pay to the Xandian operator resulted in a brake on rate reduction in Patria and—at least arguably and in the view of the United States, as a subsidy from Patria to Xandia.[33] The developing countries disputed this contention, maintaining that the payment to them was justified by their need to upgrade their telecoms infrastructure. For a time the issue threatened the outcome of the negotiations, as the United States Federal Communications Commission considered making the award of licenses to foreign providers contingent on an acceptable level of accounting rates with the foreign country. Eventually, the issue of differential accounting rates was deferred for future negotiations, with an understanding that the application of accounting rates would not give rise to action by members under the WTO dispute resolution mechanism.[34]

The Potential for Discrimination and MFN

The United States was also concerned that foreign monopolies or dominant carriers could use the accounting rate system to obtain concessions from American carriers by discriminating among them on return traffic, or by creating an American subsidiary to carry traffic from their country to the United States, thus cutting out American carriers at the receiving end. The solution implemented by the US Federal Communications Commission was to require foreign carriers to treat US carriers without discrimination, by sending return traffic to the United States in proportion to the proportion of outgoing traffic received from each American carrier. This practice would inhibit competition if both the United States and Xandia were liberalized and had competing carriers, and accordingly the FCC modified the requirement of proportional use for countries deemed to be in fact competitive. Of course this solution again challenged the general principle of MFN, and made agreement difficult to achieve.

---

[32] Note that since the sending carrier pays the receiving carrier, in trade terms, contrary to one's instincts, the country or carrier terminating a call is functioning as exporter of a service, and the country or carrier sending the call is functioning as an importer.

[33] According to the United States Federal Communication Commissiion, the account rate system led to an annual outflow of more than $5 billion, of which three-quarters was a subsidy to foreign telecom operators. See Bronckers and Larouche (n. 31 supra), pp. 10–12, also Sherman (n. 28 supra), pp. 68–9, 94–6, and FCC decisions and reports there cited.

[34] See Report of the Group on Basic Telecommunications, 15 Feb. 1997, para. 7, 36 I.L.M. 369 at 370 (1997).

The Reference Paper

On the above and similar issues, it became apparent that the concept of market access set out in Article XVI of the GATS was not adequate when in so many countries for so long a time one telecom carrier had held a monopoly position, and in many countries still did. On initiative of the United States as early as December 1994, a group of delegates was convened informally to explore ways to preserve the opportunities for competition, and to separate regulatory authorities from operators, which was not the case in many countries where the PTT performed both functions. The result of these meetings, informally chaired by the chief Japanese delegate, was a so-called Reference Paper, not binding on any Member State but designed to be incorporated by reference in Member States' schedules.[35] The Reference Paper set down in a brief document some important definitions, including *major supplier*[36] and *essential facilities*,[37] followed by a statement on prevention of anti-competitive practices, committing states that adopt the Reference Paper in their schedules to maintain 'appropriate measures' for the purpose of preventing major suppliers, alone or together from engaging in or continuing anti-competitive practices. In particular, the Reference Paper commits states to ensure market access, by ensuring interconnection with a major supplier under non-discriminatory terms no less favourable than for its own like services or services of affiliates and on reasonable and transparent terms and conditions including cost-oriented rates. Further, the Reference Paper calls for subscribing states to maintain or establish a regulatory body separate from and not accountable to any supplier of basic telecommunication services, and to afford a service supplier requesting interconnection with a major supplier opportunity for dispute settlement 'within a reasonable period of time'.[38]

---

[35] The Reference Paper is conveniently reproduced in 36 I.L.M. 367 (1997).

[36] A major supplier is a supplier which has the ability to materially affect the terms of participation . . . in the relevant market for basic telecommunications services as a result of:
   (a) control over essential facilities; or
   (b) use of its position in the market.

[37] Essential facilities mean facilities of a public telecommunications transport network or service that:
   (a) are exclusively or predominantly provided by a single or limited number of suppliers; and
   (b) cannot feasibly be economically or technically substituted in order to provide a service.

[38] This provision was needed in addition to the requirement in GATS Article VI that each Member State must provide some kind of tribunal to review administrative decisions affecting service providers in sectors where commitments had been undertaken, because the critical decision on interconnection might not have been made by a governmental agency, but rather by a private, dominant carrier.

(d)   The Schedules of Commitments

The Reference Paper, as noted, is not itself law; it simply is a way that states can commit themselves in their schedules to agreed definitions and to safe-guards against anti-competitive practices. The schedules themselves contain the overall commitments and limitations on the commitments, both 'hori-zontal', i.e. applicable to all sectors, such as limitations on direct foreign ownership or requirements for joint ventures, and sector-specific, in this case applicable to supply of telecommunication services within the permissible opt-in and opt-out provisions in the GATS.[39]

6.8   PRELIMINARY REFLECTIONS ON SERVICES IN THE WTO SYSTEM

At a conference in the mid-1980s as the Uruguay Round was just getting under way, the present writer suggested that the GATT could be amended to insert 'and services' wherever the existing text spoke of 'goods', and that not much more would be needed to bring the remaining quarter of world trade under the prevailing international rules. Fifteen years later that sug-gestion appears naïve, though not wholly wrong.

- The basic principles—MFN and national treatment—and the basic techniques—schedules of bindings, periodic negotiations, and organ-ized dispute settlement—have been made applicable to the exchange of services. But negotiations across sectors—Patria making an offer on banking in return for Xandia's concession on travel bureaux—is out of the question, and the permission for opting out (for MFN), and opting in (for national treatment) is quite different from the GATT/WTO tra-dition in other areas. Market access, a term not used in the GATT or the associated agreements (though clearly relevant), becomes the main focus in the Services Agreement and associated Annexes and Protocols. Monopoly, privatization, and competition law, a subject thus far largely avoided by the makers of international law,[40] become a major subject for negotiation and legislation, particularly in the area of telecommunications.
- As this volume went to press, the General Agreement on Trade in Services was largely untested. A high number of commitments had been made in the tourism sector, particularly in Mode 2 (the consumer

---

[39] In particular, GATS Article XVI on market access and Article XVII on national treatment. Note that GATS Article XVIII provides that Members may negotiate commitments not subject to scheduling under Articles XVI or XVII, including those regarding qualifications, standards or licensing matters, and this provision avoided any argument about whether the commitments concerning anti-competitive behaviour were subject to binding under the principal articles.

[40] See Ch. 12.

traveling to the territory of the supplier). Fewer commitments have been made for data processing and software, still fewer for the construction sector and health services. Looked at from the point of view of the 4 modes (Section 6.3(a)), commitments have been easiest to secure in respect of Mode 1—cross-border supply of services and Mode 2—consumption abroad, most difficult in Mode 4—presence of natural persons, which is typically linked in 'horizontal commitments' to Mode 3—commercial presence, and limited to technical specialists and senior executives.

• While bilateral controversies had arisen in several services sectors, no major trade dispute, comparable to disputes concerning steel, textiles, agricultural products, or more recently intellectual property, had broken out under the GATS as of year-end 2001, and no case had come before the Dispute Settlement Body.[41]

• The growth in trade in services in the final years of the twentieth century has been roughly parallel with the growth in merchandise trade, with substantial variation in the different regions. How much of the increased trade in services is attributable to implementation of the GATS, as contrasted with developments in the world economy as a whole is difficult to judge. What can be said with some confidence is that privatization, deregulation, non-discrimination, and enhanced market access for foreign suppliers form part of a common trend, and that the international rules of international trade have moved to keep up with that trend in the area of services. If the negotiations and agreements display a continuing ambivalence, that could be said about the evolution of the GATT as well. The overall movement, however, remains in the direction of reducing restraints, and trade in services appears to have joined that movement.

---

[41] However, the United States had initiated the consultation process called for by the Understanding on Dispute Settlement in a controversy with Mexico over market access by US-based telephone companies.

PART III
Dispute Resolution

7

Dispute Resolution in the GATT, 1948–94[1]

7.1 INTRODUCTION: RESOLUTION OF LEGAL DISPUTES BETWEEN STATES

It is a commonplace that dispute resolution and remedies in international law are not as developed as the corpus of substantive rules designed to govern the behaviour of states, or as dispute resolution and remedies available in domestic law. In fact the comparison between domestic and internal legal systems is flawed at both ends; the system of civil remedies in virtually all countries is far from fully effective; and the system of dispute resolution and remedies in controversies between states (putting aside war/peace issues) is more developed than is commonly supposed. Indeed, as brought out in detail in this and the following chapter, dispute settlement under the GATT/WTO has evolved, after many ups and downs, into a quite formal and it seems effective system, more strict in its procedures than is the case in

---

[1] For two fine books on this subject, see Robert E. Hudec, *The GATT Legal System and World Trade Diplomacy* (1975, repr. 1990); Robert E. Hudec, *Enforcing International Trade Law: The Evolution of the Modern GATT Legal System* (1993). For analysis and extended extracts of decisions rendered in GATT dispute settlement cases, see Pierre Pescatore *et al.*, *Handbook of WTO/GATT Dispute Settlement* (1991 and annual updates) [hereafter Pescatore, *Handbook*].

any other field of intercourse among states.[2] Prior to addressing this system in detail, a brief description is in order of other available means for resolution of legal disputes between states, both by way of indicating sources on which the architects of the GATT/WTO system drew and by way of comparison with that system.

(a)   The World Court[3]

All members of the United Nations, as well as a few other States, notably Switzerland, are parties to the Statute of the International Court of Justice.[4] However, the jurisdiction of the court depends on consent of the parties, and being party to the Statute of the Court does not constitute consent to the jurisdiction of the Court. States may give their consent to the Court's jurisdiction in a treaty that provides for submission of disputes arising under that treaty; under the so-called optional clause, (ICJ Statute Art. 36(2)), states may also declare that they recognize the jurisdiction of the court *ipso facto* and without special agreement, in relation to any other state accepting the same obligation. Only some 50 states have made such a declaration (many subject to various conditions and exclusions), and of these France and the United States withdrew their declarations in response to decisions of the Court with which they were dissatisfied. The World Court will also hear disputes submitted to it by special *ad hoc* agreement of the parties, i.e. by mutual consent. Article 94(1) of the UN Charter states that 'each member of the United Nations undertakes to comply with the decision of the International Court of Justice in any case to which it is a party', and Article 94(2) authorizes the Security Council to make recommendations or decide upon measures to give effect to a judgment of the Court. As of year-end 2001, no such action had ever been taken.[5]

In some ways the International Court of Justice and its predecessor, the Permanent Court of International Justice (1921–38), have been the model for other international tribunals. Only states may be parties; the documents submitted are confidential until a judgment is issued; and the composition of

---

[2] This statement refers to states not linked by regional arrangements. It does not include litigation within the European Community/Union before the European Court of Justice, or the various procedures for dispute resolution under the Canada–United States Free Trade Agreement or the North American Free Trade Agreement.

[3] The literature concerning the World Court is vast, and for the most part well outside the forces of this book. For a brief description, see Shabtai Rosenne, *The World Court: What it is and how it works* (5th rev. edn., 1994); for a thorough description and history by the same author, see *The Law and Practice of the International Court 1920–1996*, 4 vols. (3rd edn., 1997).

[4] See United Nations Charter, Art. 93.

[5] Following refusal of the United States to recognize the jurisdiction of the ICJ in the *Case Concerning Military and Paramilitary Activities in and against Nicaragua (Nicaragua v. United States)*, [1986] *ICJ Rep.* 14, Nicaragua introduced a resolution in the UN Security Council calling for compliance with the judgment. The United States vetoed the resolution. UN Docs. S/18250 and S/PV 2704 (1986), repr. in 25 *I.L.M.* 1352–65 (1986).

the Court—15 elected judges plus an *ad hoc* judge nominated by any state party to a case which does not have one of its nationals sitting on the Court—is supposed to reflect the major legal systems as well as the principal geographic regions of the world. Many organizations, however, have preferred to establish their own tribunals—typically smaller in size and with emphasis on expertise in their field of activity. Very early in the negotiations of the GATT, the secretariat suggested a provision accepting the jurisdiction of the World Court, but the suggestion was quickly rejected.[6] The World Court has been involved in economic disputes only in the context of fishing or mining rights depending on delimitation of boundaries,[7] and in a few instances of controversies arising out of alleged expropriations.[8] The kind of controversies that involve the GATT/WTO system have not come before the World Court, and are unlikely to do so.

(b) Interstate Arbitration

Many international treaties have provided for resolution of disputes relating to interpretation or execution of the treaty by arbitration. In some instances the treaties contain detailed provision for the method of selection of arbitrators; in others only rudimentary provision for the arbitral procedures is set out. Typically agreements providing for state-to-state arbitration—whether contained in a treaty or in a submission agreement prepared after the controversy arises—call for each side to appoint an arbitrator and for the two arbitrators so chosen to appoint the third or presiding arbitrator. In some instances provision is made for appointment of the presiding arbitrator by an appointing authority, such as the President of the World Court, the Secretary General of the Permanent Court of Arbitration, or of the Secretary General of the United Nations or the Organization of American States. It is nearly always required or assumed that the presiding or 'neutral' arbitrator have a different nationality from that of the disputing states.[9]

Most interstate agreements to arbitrate provide (or assume) that a resulting award is to be binding on the parties. This is understood to mean that

[6] See Robert E. Hudec, *The GATT Legal System and World Trade Diplomacy*, 52–3 (1975, repr. 1990). The proposal was made in February 1947, but there is no record of any debate on it. In the Havana Charter that never entered into effect (see Ch. 3), provision was made (in Art. 96) for appeal of legal questions to the ICJ, but only in the form of a request for an advisory opinion on consent of the Plenary Conference.

[7] See e.g. *Declaration of the Marine Boundary in the Gulf of Maine Area (Canada/United States)* [1984] *ICJ Rep.* 246 (Chamber); *North Sea Continental Shelf Cases (Federal Republic of Germany/Denmark and The Netherlands)* [1969] *ICJ Rep.* 3.

[8] See e.g. *Case Concerning the Barcelona Traction, Light & Power Co. Ltd. (Belgium v. Spain),* [1970] *ICJ Rep.* 3; *Case Concerning Elettronica Sicula S.P.A. (United States/Italy)* [1989] *ICJ Rep.* 15. (Chamber) both discussed in Ch. 14, Sect. 14.2.

[9] The word 'neutral' is placed in quotation marks, because in theory all arbitrators are supposed to act as judges and not as representatives of the parties that appointed them. This expectation is not always shared in state-to-state arbitrations. For a discussion of this issue in the GATT/WTO context, see Ch. 8, Sect. 8.2.

failure to comply with the award is a violation of international law. Other agreements to arbitrate provide that any award shall be advisory, with the parties obligated only to use their best efforts to carry out the award. Either way, provision for enforcement of arbitral awards in state-to-state arbitration is virtually never made. There is no counterpart in state-to-state arbitration to the United Nations Convention on the Recognition and Enforcement of Foreign Arbitral Awards (the New York Convention),[10] which provides for enforcement of awards rendered in international commercial arbitrations.[11]

Both the World Court model and the arbitration model have in some sense been relevant to the changing attitude toward dispute settlement in the GATT/WTO system, but only by way of background. Nearly all the issues of interstate dispute resolution have been faced as the GATT system has evolved—permanent vs. ad hoc panels, compulsory vs. voluntary jurisdiction, enforcement vs. voluntary compliance, public vs. confidential procedures, the problems of fact-finding and proof, the possibilities of counterclaims and of intervention by third parties, the fashioning of appropriate remedies, and the role of precedent—in sum all the problems of dispute resolution generally plus the problems of dealing with sovereign parties.

7.2   GATT AND DISPUTE SETTLEMENT: THE ORIGINAL CONCEPTION

The founders of the GATT in the 1940s understood that they were drafting a code of conduct, and that disputes could arise between Contracting Parties about how to interpret the code and what to do about violations. They provided for consultations at the request of any contracting party 'with respect to any matter affecting the operation of [the] Agreement' (Art. XXII); and they provided for a reference to the CONTRACTING PARTIES (i.e. the organization)[12] of any controversy with respect to which no satisfactory adjustment is effected within a reasonable time (Art. XXIII).

---

[10]   330 U.N.T.S. 3, signed at New York, 10 June 1958.

[11]   However, arbitrations involving a dispute between a state or state agency on one side, and a private party on the other, are often conducted under the rules of commercial arbitration, and are subject to recognition and enforcement under the New York Convention. The Convention on the Settlement of Investment Disputes between States and Nationals of Other States, 1965, 575 U.N.T.S. 159, also provides for arbitration between private parties on one side and states on the other, and for a treaty-based enforcement system. See Ch. 15, Sect. 15.1.

The Iran–United States Claims Tribunal, created by the Algiers Accords of 1981 between the United States and Iran as part of the settlement of the detention of American hostages in Iran and seizure of Iranian assets in the United States is a hybrid institution, in that it provides for arbitration both of claims by citizens of the United States against Iran and citizens of Iran against the United States and of official claims between the two states. See Ch. 15, Sect. 15.2.

[12]   See Ch. 3, Sect. 3.3(a).

No specific provision was written into Article XXIII about how a controversy submitted to the CONTRACTING PARTIES was to be resolved, except that the CONTRACTING PARTIES 'shall promptly investigate', and 'shall make appropriate recommendations . . . or give a ruling on the matter, as appropriate'. It seems that some form of Committee or panel was contemplated to prepare the collective decision of the CONTRACTING PARTIES; whether the committee or panel was to function like an arbitral tribunal or a committee of conciliators was not clear, and was the subject of differing approaches in the first two decades of the GATT. The founders of the GATT made provision for one additional element, straddling the agenda of diplomacy and adjudication. Article XXIII is entitled 'Nullification or Impairment', and it is applicable not only to allegation by one contracting party of failure of another contracting party to carry out its obligations 'under the Agreement' (para. 1(a)), but also the application by another contracting party of 'any measure, *whether or not* it conflicts with the provisions of this Agreement' (para. 1(b)) and also 'the existence of *any other situation*'—for instance a serious financial collapse or major unemployment.

The emphasis in Article XXIII is on injury—i.e. the complaining party must assert and eventually establish that a benefit accruing to it under the General Agreement is being nullified or impaired. With some exceptions introduced in the Uruguay Round, the dominant analogy in GATT/WTO dispute settlement is to tort or breach of contract—*nullum damnum absque injuria*—not to crime or to overriding principles such as the prohibition against the use of force in the United Nations Charter. An injury to a contracting party might be subject to redress even if it was caused by a measure of another party that did not constitute a violation;[13] a breach of a provision of the General Agreement—and later of the specialized agreements—would not justify redress if it did not cause injury. No provision was made in the original GATT or later for a complaint procedure initiated by the organization itself.[14]

The expectation, not spelled out in Article XXIII, was that if the CONTRACTING PARTIES, on the basis of a report submitted to them, found a complaint justified, they would so state, with a recommendation—not an order—to the respondent state to terminate the measure or practice complained of. Article XXIII does contemplate retaliation by the complainant state if the respondent state fails to comply with such a recommendation, i.e. suspension of the application to the respondent party of a concession equivalent to the injury caused to the complainant party—but only 'if the

---

[13] This would result from a so-called 'non-violation complaint', discussed in Ch. 8, Sect. 8.7(b) infra.

[14] Compare the quite different approach taken in the Amended Articles of Agreement of the International Monetary Fund and the Decisions implementing Article IV, which authorize the Managing Director of the IMF to bring complaints against Member States but make no provision for complaints by one Member State against another. See Ch. 17, Sect. 17.4.

CONTRACTING PARTIES consider that the circumstances are serious enough to justify such action.'[15]

The overall objective of the GATT—the reduction of barriers to trade—would evidently not be furthered if Xandia, the respondent, imposed a trade barrier and thereafter Patria, the complainant, also imposed a trade barrier. Accordingly, the thrust of Article XXIII is to seek termination or phasing out of objectionable practices, and not to encourage or authorize retaliation.[16]

7.3   EVOLUTION OF THE GATT AS A FORUM FOR DISPUTES: ADJUDICATION AND ITS ALTERNATIVES

(a)   The First Phase (1948–60)

'Dispute settlement' is an ambiguous term, in that it may refer to settlement in the sense that the disputing parties agree to end their quarrel, possibly with the assistance of a third party, or alternatively, that it may refer to a mechanism for decision by a court, arbitral tribunal or comparable body. The original conception of the GATT did not distinguish clearly between these two approaches to disputes. As Professor Hudec points out,[17] the GATT began in 1948 with 23 parties and by 1960 had grown to only 37. The countries' representatives in Geneva in good part were the same persons who had negotiated and drafted the General Agreement and the Havana Charter, shared common experiences and outlook, and behaved in some ways like a club, dominated by the United States and the United Kingdom. The GATT secretariat did not have a legal division, and when disputes came before panels or working groups, it was the economists/diplomats, and not lawyers, who presented the positions of the parties.

The GATT did provide a forum, however, as well as a code—not always clear or explicit—by which to appraise (not to say judge) practices of one state challenged by another state. At first the complaints by contracting parties came in the form of requests for rulings by the Chairman of the CONTRACTING PARTIES. The first Chairman, Dana Wilgress of Canada, did issue rulings in four cases in 1948–9—simple statements without detailed analysis, for instance that consular taxes came within the MFN requirement of GATT Article I and that 'existing legislation' for purposes of the grand-

---

[15] To be precise, the requirement that the value of the concession to be withdrawn be equivalent to the injury suffered by the complaining party is not stated in the text of Article XXIII, which speaks only of suspension of 'such concessions or other obligations . . . as [the CONTRACTING PARTIES] determine to be appropriate in the circumstances.' It is clear, however that punishment or sanctions do not fit within the concept of Article XXIII.

[16] For a summary of the few instances in which the GATT Counsel considered requests to authorize retaliatory withdrawal of concessions, see *Analytical Index of the GATT*, Vol. 2, pp. 692–700 (6th edn. 1995).

[17] Robert E. Hudec, *Enforcing International Trade Law*, 11.

father clause of the Protocol of Provisional Application[18] referred to the date of signature of the Protocol, October 30, 1947.[19]

Subsequently the practice developed of appointment of working parties to consider requests for rulings and to report back to the CONTRACTING PARTIES. Representatives of the disputants would meet with representatives of countries not directly involved in the dispute, with the aim of reaching agreement on the relevant facts as well as on the legal question at issue. In some instances this technique was successful; in others the report of the working party simply set forth the views of the disputants plus the views of other members of the working party. Beginning with a complaint by Chile against Australia in 1949, the practice of working parties moved in the direction of third-party adjudication, in that the report, prepared by the GATT secretariat, reflected a unanimous view of the 'neutral' members that supported Chile's position and rejected that of Australia. On the basis of the report of the working party, the CONTRACTING PARTIES recommended that Australia end the objectionable practice and report back at the next session. Though the Australian representative wrote a dissent to the working party's report, Australia did follow the recommendation and abandon the challenged practice.[20]

In 1952, a new Chairman of the CONTRACTING PARTIES decided to establish a panel on complaints to consider several cases that had been submitted to him. A significant difference between a panel and a working party was that whereas a working party included the disputants, and all members would meet together throughout the proceeding, a panel was distinct from the disputants and its members would meet among themselves (with the secretariat) to prepare their report, after having received the oral and written submissions of the parties. The procedure was not quite like a judicial or arbitral proceeding, in that the panel members would meet with the parties to discuss the draft of their report; it became clear, however, that the panel was a decision-making body, subject, of course to acceptance of its report by the CONTRACTING PARTIES. Over time panel procedures tended to become more formal, and less like committee meetings. The panelists would be seated at a head table, with the parties at tables on either side and observers in the back, much like the practice in arbitrations. Written submissions were not quite legal briefs, but they did spell out arguments and refer to exhibits, and as the repertory increased, to rulings or decisions of previous panels.

Even as the procedures gradually became more formal, the reluctance to move beyond persuasion to command persisted. For instance, in a case

[18] See Ch. 3, Sect. 3.4(b).

[19] These rulings were published in the GATT, 2 *Basic Instruments and Selected Documents* [BISD] Vol II, p. 12 (1952). They are reproduced in 2 Pescatore, *Handbook*, DD 1/1.

[20] *Australia Subsidy on Ammonium Sulfate*, 2 BISD 188 (8 Apr. 1950), Pescatore, *Handbook*, DD 5/1. This case, discussed in Hudec, *The GATT Legal System and World Trade Diplomacy*, ch. 14, is noteworthy also in that it was the first application of the doctrine of nonviolation impairment. See Ch. 8, Sect. 8.7(b) at n. 57.

involving a challenge by Italy to administration by Sweden of its antidumping regulations with respect to ladies' stockings, a panel of seven persons recommended

(a)   that the Swedish government *consider ways and means of* improving the administration of the decree in question;

(b)   that the governments of Italy and Sweden *make the necessary arrangements to facilitate* enquiry by the Swedish authorities to clarify the various points of fact on which the two governments hold different views . . . ; and

(c)   that the two parties report to the CONTRACTING PARTIES at the next session[21] (italics added).

In the event, the Swedish regulation was repealed within a few months after the panel's report had been adopted by the CONTRACTING PARTIES. A similar result was not reached in every case, but on the whole the first phase of the 'diplomat's jurisprudence', to borrow Professor Hudec's phrase,[22] worked reasonably well, indeed very well when compared to other types of controversies between States. Hudec's survey of the 40 complaints filed during the period 1952–8 concludes that 30 resulted in a settlement satisfactory to the complainant, one ended with a ruling for the defendant, five ended in impasse, and four 'simply disappeared without a trace'. Of the 30 cases in which the complainant was satisfied, the challenged measures were completely eliminated or corrected in 21 of the cases, the rest somehow compromised. 'Probably the best measure of the overall attitude toward the procedure', Hudec concluded, 'is the fact that governments did use it, again and again.'[23]

(b)   A Pause in the Process (1963–70)

Several major changes affected the GATT—and GATT dispute settlement—in the 1960s. For one thing the membership of GATT doubled as numerous new states emerged from colonial rule, and the characterization of the organization as a club of congenial representatives of the developed countries became increasingly less accurate. For another, the European Economic Community emerged as a powerful participant in the international economy roughly equal in strength to the United States, with a determination to insulate some of its policies from the constraints of GATT, notably the Common Agricultural Policy and also some of the association agreements with former colonies. The United States at one point considered a challenge to the

---

[21] *Swedish Antidumping Duties (Italy v. Sweden)*, GATT BISD, 3d Supp. 81 (1955), Pescatore, *Handbook*, DD 14/1.

[22] See Robert E. Hudec, 'The GATT Legal System: A Diplomat's Jurisprudence', 4 *J. World Trade Law* 615 (1970).

[23] Hudec, *The GATT Legal System and World Trade Diplomacy*, 107–8.

Common Agricultural Policy on legal grounds,[24] but settled for a less contentious claim under Article XXIV(6) (the renegotiation provision of the Customs Union article) addressed to a decline in poultry exports to West Germany. The United States government thought this initiative, immediately called 'The Chicken War' might serve at least as a kind of symbolic combat concerning the Common Agricultural Policy. The Executive Secretary of the GATT, however, defused the controversy by focusing exclusively on the amount of compensation due to the United States, which a working party determined without either determining the rights and wrongs of the Community's Poultry Policy or establishing a methodology for measuring the trade loss.[25] Following the Chicken War, GATT dispute settlement went into disuse for the remainder of the decade. It was not that there were fewer disputes, but it seems that negotiations within and outside the context of the Kennedy Round, rather than the working party/panel procedures of the preceding decade, became the principal forum.[26]

(c)   Dispute Settlement Revived (1970–9)

Dispute settlement in GATT was revived in the early 1970s, along with other pressures looking to a more rule-oriented regime for international trade generally, as reflected in the efforts to develop a series of codes on dumping, subsidies, safeguards, technical standards, customs valuation, etc. in the context of the Tokyo Round.[27] In particular, United States policy changed from one of avoiding confrontation in the 1960s to a series of challenges to measures taken by the European Community and (before it became a member) by the United Kingdom, in each instance accompanied by request for a panel. But in each instance there was resistance in the GATT Council to establishment of a panel; when panels were established, they seemed to be willing to delay coming to a decision, with the hope that delay would contribute to settlement. What some viewed as a shortcoming of the process— no right to have a panel appointed and no timetable or deadlines for the panel's work—others viewed as an advantage—preservation of the diplomacy side of the GATT forum. The continuing pull in opposite directions was reflected in the actions concerning dispute settlement in the Tokyo

[24] See A. Lowenfeld, 'The USA, the EEC, and the GATT: The Road not Taken', 1 *U. Pa. J. Int'l Econ. Law* 533 (1996), repr. in A. Lowenfeld, *The Role of Government in International Trade: Essays over Three Decades* (2000).
[25] See A. Chayes, T. Ehrlich, and A. Lowenfeld, *International Legal Process* Vol. 1, pp. 249–306 (1968) for a full account of this episode, and for the epilogue, A. Lowenfeld, 'Doing unto Others . . . The Chicken War Ten Years After', 4 *Journal of Maritime Law and Commerce* 599 (1973).
[26] For speculation about the reasons for the decline in resort to dispute settlement in the period 1963–70, see Robert E. Hudec, *The GATT Legal System and World Trade Diplomacy*, 235–50 (2nd edn. 1990).
[27] See Ch. 4. Sect. 4.3.

Round at the end of the decade, and in many of the cases that came before the GATT in the run-up to the Uruguay Round as well.

In 1973, the European Community brought a major complaint against a United States statute designed to induce US-based companies to export more from the United States by granting a complex set of tax deferrals to 'Domestic International Sales Corporations' or DISCs.[28] The European Community took the position that the DISC law constituted an export subsidy inconsistent with Article XVI(4) of the GATT. The United States contended that the DISC law was merely a device to restore tax equity with other countries that did not tax transactions made through tax-haven states, and responded with counterclaims against French, Belgian, and Dutch tax laws. The details of the respective contentions have long since been overtaken, as discussed in the chapter on subsidies.[29] But the DISC case, in many ways a litigation nightmare, had a lasting effect on the evolution of dispute settlement in the GATT/WTO system.

It took two and a half years—July 1973–February 1976—to secure appointment of a panel, consisting of three GATT delegates from 'neutral' countries plus two tax experts. Following a series of hearings and meetings, the panel issued four reports in November 1976, holding the United States law, as well as the three European laws, to be inconsistent with the GATT.[30] But the issues were complex, the procedures were shown to be vague, and the reports, prepared without support of a legal staff of the GATT, were regarded as unpersuasive, particularly in respect to the European tax laws based on the territoriality principle. The European Community blocked the adoption by the GATT Council of the reports concerning its members; the United States, for its part, took the position that it would accept the report criticizing its tax law only if the European countries accepted the findings criticizing their laws. The reports remained blocked for more than four years, until a deal was struck whereby the United States agreed not to block the adverse finding concerning the DISC law if the European countries unblocked the reports concerning their laws, subject to an understanding that the Europeans' laws would not need to be changed.[31]

Reactions to the procedures in the DISC case were uniformly negative, but different lessons could be drawn from the experience. Some states pointed out that the DISC case demonstrated how panels could go wrong, and thus justified the practice that all reports had to be submitted to the GATT

---

[28] For a reasonably comprehensible explanation of the DISC law, and citations to the original 1971 statute and successive amendments, see Robert E. Hudec, *Enforcing International Trade Law*, 59–62 (1993). The entire DISC episode is told in id. 59–100.

[29] See Ch. 9, Sect. 9.5(d).

[30] GATT BISD 23d Supp. 98, 114, 127, 137, (1977); and Pescatore, *Handbook*, Cases 31, 32, 33, and 34. All the reports were dated 12 Nov. 1976, but were not adopted by the GATT Council until 1981, as described in the text.

[31] This understanding, adopted on December 8, 1981, appears in GATT BISD, 28th Supp. at 114 (1982) and Pescatore, *Handbook*, DD 31/6.

Council for approval by consensus. Others criticized the practice whereby a party could by itself block adoption of a report unfavourable to its position. Since the earliest days in the late 1940s, the GATT secretariat had sat with panels and had helped draft both the statements of fact and the conclusions of the panel. But the GATT had not had a legal division and few GATT delegates or members of the secretariat were law-trained. As several observers pointed out, the DISC case showed the consequence of the lack of expert legal analysis in the work of the panels, a result of the hostility to lawyers in the formative years of the GATT. In the event, a legal division was not established in the GATT until the early 1980s, after conclusion of the Tokyo Round and the adoption of the many Codes resulting from that Round.

Even as DISC, and several other contentious and complicated cases,[32] were making their way through the GATT, dispute settlement became a subject on the agenda of the Multinational Trade Negotiations (1973–9). When the MTN had been launched in Tokyo in September 1973, dispute settlement was not expressly listed as an agenda item, but the Ministerial Declaration did call for 'more effective international discipline', and for 'improvements in the international framework for the conduct of world trade.'[33] In 1976, a Framework Group was established in the Tokyo Round on the initiative of Brazil. That group, while primarily focused on establishing 'special and differential treatment' for developing countries, negotiatied the first written set of procedures governing—or rather describing—the practices that had grown up over the preceding three decades without any written guidance.

The document that emerged at the end of the Tokyo Round was an Understanding Regarding Notification, Consultation, Dispute Settlement and Surveillance, including as an Annex an 'Agreed Description of the Customary Practice of the GATT in the Field of Dispute Settlement (Art. XXIII:2).'[34] In negotiation of the Understanding, the United States urged, and the European Community opposed, provision for an automatic right to appointment of a panel when a contracting party submitted a complaint. The outcome was another typical compromise: in the Understanding, there is no statement of a right to a panel; the Agreed Description, however, contains a statement (para. 4) that 'Before bringing a case, contracting parties

---

[32] Including, for instance, the so-called MIPS Case, referring to a Minimum Import Price regime imposed by the European Community on tomato concentrates, which began with protests by the United States that the Community had acted in bad faith in delaying appointment of a panel, and continued through lengthy argument about the contents of the terms of reference and about the composition of the panel. The MIPS case is summarized in Hudec, *Enforcing International Trade Law*, 47–50 and 462–5. The Report of the Panel, which is less important for the present discussion than the procedural wrangles that preceded it, appears in GATT BISD, 25th Supp. 68 (1979) and Pescatore, *Handbook*, Case 38.

[33] GATT Ministerial Declaration of September 14, 1973, GATT BISD, 20th Supp. 19, at paras. 3(b), 9 (1974). For a discussion of the progress of the Tokyo Round, see Ch. 4. Sect. 4.3.

[34] GATT BISD, 26th Supp. 210 (1980). For a detailed analysis, see Robert E. Hudec, 'GATT Dispute Settlement after the Tokyo Round: An Unfinished Business', 13 *Cornell Int'l L.J.* 145 (1980).

have exercised their judgment as to whether action under Article XXIII(2) would be fruitful.' The inference was that not all disputes could be fruitfully submitted to adjudication, and that the CONTRACTING PARTIES might exercise some discretion if respondents sought to block establishment of a panel. In the various Codes, and particularly the Subsidies Code, by contrast, provision was made for a right to establishment of a panel, and a short deadline for the panel to report to the Committee in charge of the particular code.[35] The Understanding stated that the CONTRACTING PARTIES 'should take appropriate action on reports of panels and working parties within a reasonable period of time', but set no timetable and made no change in the expectation that such action should be taken by consensus—i.e. that it was possible for a determined losing party to block adoption of the report.

All of these issues came back in the Uruguay Round and were resolved, to the surprise of many of the participants, in a far more rigorous manner.

7.4   DISPUTE SETTLEMENT IN THE 1980s AND THE URUGUAY ROUND

(a)   More Law, More Disputes, More Dispute Settlement

Disputes submitted to GATT panels intensified in the period between the close of the Tokyo Round, 1979, and conclusion of the Uruguay Round 1994. The caseload of contentious cases more than doubled, whether measured by number of complaints brought, panel reports completed, or rulings approved by the GATT Council.[36] The subject matter of the complaints also embraced not only significant economic injuries but also points of principle where the dispute mechanism could be used to establish or promote rules not laid down in the existing agreements. For instance, the United States successfully challenged performance requirements imposed on foreign investors under Canada's Foreign Investment Review Act, and, as described in Chapter 5, the result led to placing Trade-Related Investment Measures (TRIMs) on

[35] See e.g. Tokyo Round Subsidies Code Article 13, which provided for a panel to be established if consultations have failed to reach a solution within 30 days in case of an alleged export subsidy, and 60 days in case of any other subsidy. Article 18 then set up a time schedule for establishment of a panel (30 days), acceptance of nominees to the panel (seven working days), and delivery of the panel's findings (60 days). The Tokyo Round Anti-Dumping Code had a somewhat longer period for conciliation, but also stated 'the Committee shall, at the request of any party to the dispute, establish a panel to examine the matter' (Article 15 (5)).

[36] Different surveys reach slightly different conclusions, depending on how to count cases begun or concluded at a given time. Hudec reports that 115 formal complaints were filed by governments in the period 1980–9 (including both complaints under the GATT itself and under one of the Tokyo Round codes) compared with 37 in the 1970s and a total of 97 in the three decades 1948–79. *Enforcing International Trade Law* and Appendix, 395–608. Petersmann, who takes the count through 1993, writes that there were more than 250 legal complaints. Ernst-Ulrich Petersmann, *The GATT/WTO Dispute Settlement System: International Law, International Organizations, and Dispute Settlement*, 87 (1997).

the agenda of the Uruguay Round.[37] The European Community successfully challenged the so-called Manufacturing Clause in the United States Copyright Law, which had barred the importation of books by American authors printed abroad but had previously been defended under the 'existing legislation' provision of the Protocol of Provisional Application.[38] Again, a challenge by the European Community of a US law that enabled patent holders to bring an infringement proceeding against foreign products before an administrative agency at the point of importation led to a ruling spelling out the meaning of national treatment in Article III of the GATT and about the burdens of the exception provisions of Article XX.[39]

The United States, which had presented the results of the Tokyo Round to the United States Congress as a major achievement in protecting the rights of US exporters, continued as the principal user of the GATT complaint process, 39 in all in the 1980s, with half of those complaints brought against the European Community. The Community, for its part, changed its strategy from that of a defendant trying to deflect and slow down the legalization of the GATT to that of a litigant using the procedures as plaintiff as well. In the decade of the 1980s, the Community filed 26 complaints—as compared with only 4 complaints filed in the two previous decades.[40] Inevitably the GATT dispute process became a forum for US–EC controversy, in parallel and often overlapping the negotiations in the Uruguay Round.

The increased resort to litigation in the GATT—for litigation is what it had become in the 1980s—brought with it a notable increase in blockage of panel reports by the losing party, and non-compliance with reports whose adoption by the Contracting Parties had not been blocked. In the period 1980–2, the United States brought nine complaints against the European Community, of which five resulted in rulings by panels, four in favour of the United States, one in favour of the Community. But not one of the reports was approved by the CONTRACTING PARTIES, because in each instance the losing party blocked adoption of the report.[41] Not only did this pattern threaten the dispute settlement mechanism, as described, if not quite codified in the Tokyo Round; the Tokyo Round itself, and in particular the Subsidies Code, which was the focus of the United States' continuing campaign against the Community's Common Agricultural Policy, appeared to be much less useful than advertised. Moreover, as the Uruguay Round negotiations got underway, the pendency of these negotiations themselves served

---

[37] See *Administration of the Foreign Investment Review Act (FIRA) (US v. Canada)*, GATT BISD, 30th Supp. 140 (1984); Pescatore, *Handbook*, Case 54, discussed in Ch. 5, Sect. 5.5(a).
[38] *United States 'Manufacturing Clause' (EC v. US)*, GATT BISD, 31st Supp. 74 (1985); Pescatore, *Handbook*, Case 56.
[39] *European Community v. United States, Section 337 of the Tariff Act of 1930*, GATT BISD, 36th Supp. 345 (1990); Pescatore, *Handbook*, Case 74.
[40] Hudec, *Enforcing International Trade Law*, 300.   [41] See ibid. 145–64.

as a rationale—or an excuse—for postponing adoption of panel reports or deferring implementation of reports that had made it past the GATT Council.[42]

(b)   Dispute Settlement in the Uruguay Round

A possible consequence of the failures in the mechanism of dispute resolution might have been a general turning away from the GATT system, on the ground that there was little point in drafting rules if other states would not adhere to them or the rules were incapable of being enforced. To be sure, the instances of failed dispute resolution gave a distorted picture; most rules were followed by most states most of the time.[43] Moreover, the record of success of GATT dispute settlement overall was much better than the result of the cases brought under the Subsidies, Anti-Dumping, and Procurement Codes adopted in the Tokyo Round.[44]

But even as rethinking of dispute settlement got underway in earnest in the Uruguay Round in the second half of the 1980s, a policy of 'aggressive unilateralism', in Professor Bhagwati's phrase,[45] had gained favour in the United States, pursuant to a series of amendments to US trade legislation known collectively as section 301.[46] The premise of section 301 was that if other states would not respect the rights secured to the United States by international agreement, and if assurance of prompt and effective relief could not be assured in the GATT, then the United States would withdraw concessions or adopt discriminatory restrictions against the offending countries. In fact, the threat of section 301 action—i.e. an announcement that stated sanctions would be implemented in 30 or 60 days—more often than not brought the target states to the negotiating table, so that the unilateral trade restrictions authorized (under domestic law) by section 301 were actually not enforced very often.[47] No doubt, however, the prospect of unilateralism, which could

[42] See e.g. *Focus*: GATT Newsletter No. 81, May–June 1991. 'GATT Dispute Settlement stymied by non-implementation of reports', reporting on the statement by the Chairman of the GATT Council that 'The situation is serious and could get worse', in that the United States, the European Community, Japan, and Canada had all stalled in implementing panel decisions.

[43] Compare Louis Henkin, *How Nations Behave*, 47 (2nd edn. 1979): 'It is probably the case that almost all nations observe almost all principles of international law and almost all of their obligations almost all of the time.'

[44] This point is made, among others, by Ernst-Ulrich Petersmann, *The GATT/WTO Dispute Settlement System*, 192–5; see also Hudec, *Enforcing International Trade Law*, 352–5.

[45] See Jagdish Bhagwati, 'Aggressive Unilateralism', in *The World Trading System at Risk*, ch. 4 (1991).

[46] Sect. 301 *et seq.* of the Trade Act of 1974, in particular as amended by the Omnibus Trade and Competitiveness Act of 1988, 19 U.S.C. §§2411–20 and 2242.

[47] It should also be pointed out that while §301 was unilateral in the sense that international agreements and obligations were interpreted without participation of neutral decision-makers, the legislation provided for investigation and determination on the record by the US Trade Representative following an investigation, with submissions on behalf of the foreign country and in some instance by foreign industries as well as by US petitioners.

For more on section 301 in relation to the current GATT/WTO system, see Ch. 8, Sect. 8.8 infra.

of course be adopted by others as well, contributed to a renewed search for a way to preserve the advances made over the years in the GATT dispute mechanism while eliminating its evident shortcomings.[48]

An improved and strengthened dispute settlement process had been among the subjects for negotiation set out in the Ministerial Declaration that launched the Uruguay Round, including 'development of adequate arrangements for overseeing and monitoring of the procedures that would facilitate compliance with adopted recommendations.'[49] A negotiating group on dispute settlement worked for more than four years debating the issues that had come up since the inception of the GATT—automaticity or discretion in the establishment of panels, criteria for selection of panelists, timetables for panels, procedures for adoption or delay of panel reports, schedules for implementation of panel reports, and authorization of retaliation if reports were not complied with. In the Midterm Meeting in Montreal in December 1988, agreement was reached on a number of issues related to dispute settlement, which was issued as a Decision of the Contracting Parties on Improvements to the GATT Dispute Settlement Rules and Procedures in April 1989.[50] The 1989 Understanding made a number of advances that made it more difficult to delay establishment of panels or completion of panel reports, but did not depart from the practice that both establishment of panels and adoption of reports required decisions of the Contracting Parties by consensus, with full participation by the losing party.

Some time in the late summer or early fall of 1990, a new approach found favour in the negotiating group. In return for curbing unilateral action by the United States, the contracting states would agree to a system under which (i) there would be an absolute right to establishment of a panel, and (ii) adoption of a panel report within a finite period could not be blocked, except by consensus. 'Correction' of panel reports would not, thus, be a political process that the losing party could control. Instead, a review mechanism would be created, analogous to a court of appeal, insulated from the political process and also subject to a strict, short timetable. Furthermore, (iii) conditions would be set down for retaliation by a prevailing party if reports were not complied with within a reasonable period, again without the possibility of a veto by a non-complying party.

The main elements of the new Understanding on Dispute Settlement were contained in a Chairman's Text of October 1990.[51] They were further

---

[48] The Director-General of the GATT, referring to the 1988 amendments to Section 301, said they were 'the single trade policy intitiative which had most galvanized the attention of the international trading community'. Minutes of Meeting held on 22 Sept. 1988, GATT Doc. No. C/M224 (17 Oct. 1988) at p. 28, as quoted in Terence P. Stewart, (ed.) *The GATT Uruguay Round: A Negotiating History*, Vol. II, p. 2761–2 (1993).

[49] Ministerial Declaration on the Uruguay Round 20 Sept. 1986, GATT BISD, 33d Supp. p. 19 at 25 (1987).

[50] GATT BISD, 36th Supp. p. 61 (1990).

[51] GATT Doc. No. MTN GNG/NG13/23 (24 Oct. 1990).

developed in the Dunkel Draft of December 1991, and were made applicable (with some exceptions) not only to the GATT itself but to the many other agreements being negotiated as part of the Uruguay Round. By the time of the completion of the Uruguay Round in December 1993, agreement had been reached on the most complete system of international dispute resolution in history. It would be an exaggeration—at both ends—to say that the Understanding on Dispute Settlement had transformed the GATT/WTO system from a political to a legal system. The GATT had always been in substantial part based on rules, and inevitably there is no reason to believe that political/economic elements will cease to play a major role in trade relations among the Member States of the World Trade Organization. But there can be no doubt that in constructing and adopting the *Understanding on Rules and Procedures Governing the Settlement of Disputes*, the members of the WTO committed themselves to a system in which the rights and obligations were to be matched by an equally comprehensive system of remedies. The details of this system are spelled out in the next Chapter.

8

Dispute Settlement in the WTO

8.1   An Overview of the System

Inevitably, the WTO system of dispute settlement builds on the practices in the GATT as they had evolved over five decades. But whereas those practices had grown up largely in a series of informal or 'pragmatic' arrangements based on two articles of the General Agreement that gave little guidance—indeed did not even mention the idea of panels—the Understanding on Dispute Settlement is set out in an elaborate treaty of 27 articles and four appendices subscribed to by all member states of the World Trade Organization and applicable to virtually all of the WTO agreements. Moreover, the WTO system of dispute settlement contains two major innovations—provision for appellate review of panel decisions by a standing Appellate Body, and provision for compensation or retaliation if a respondent party found to be out of compliance does not repeal or modify its objectionable practice.

(a)   From Complaint to Final Report

1. *The Complaint.* If a member state considers that a measure adopted by another member state has deprived it of a benefit accruing to it under the GATT or under one of the other covered agreements, it may call for consultations with the other member state. The second state is to reply within 10 days and to enter into consultations within 30 days of receiving the request. If the second state does not respond within these deadlines, the complainant state may proceed directly to step 2, (Art. 4(3)).

2. *Request for a Panel.* If consultations fail to resolve the dispute within 60 days after receipt of the request for consultations, the complainant state may request the establishment of a panel (Art. 4(7)). Alternatively, the two states may make a joint request that a panel be established if they consider that consultations will not resolve the disputes.[1] The request must identify the specific measures at issue (Art. 6(2)); measures not specifically identified (or so closely related to an identified measure that the respondent can reasonably be found to have received adequate notice) will be excluded from consideration by the panel.[2]

3. *Establishment of a Panel.* If the complainant state so requests, an ad hoc panel shall be established at the latest at the meeting of the Dispute

---

[1] In cases of urgency, such as those involving perishable goods, the periods may be shortened to 10 days to enter into consultations and 20 days to request establishment of a panel (Art. 4(8)).

[2] See *Measures Affecting Consumer Photographic Film and Paper (United States v. Japan)*, Panel Report WT/DS44/R para. 10.1–.21 (31 Mar. 1998, adopted by DSB 22 Apr. 1998), in which three measures not specifically identified by the United States in its request were admitted, and five others were excluded as not being closely enough related to the measures that had been identified.

Settlement Body following the meeting where the request is first placed on the agenda, unless the DSB (i.e. the membership of the WTO as a whole, functioning under a separate chairman and with its own rules of procedure) by consensus decides otherwise at that meeting[3] (Art. 6(1)). Thus it is not possible for the respondent state to prevent or delay establishment of a panel, even if its position could command a majority of other member States.

4. *Proceedings before the Panel.* The panel, normally consisting of three persons appointed ad hoc by the Secretariat, sits to receive written and oral submissions of the parties, on the basis of which it is expected to make findings and conclusions for presentation to the DSB (Art. 11). Generally the complainant state will make the first written submission, the respondent state will make the second written submission, and thereafter a hearing (referred to as a meeting) will be held at which both parties will present their positions orally and answer questions put by the panel. Following the meeting, the parties may make further written submissions, and a second meeting with the parties may be convened—all within a timetable set out in advance in accordance with guidelines contained in an Appendix to the Understanding (Art. 12 and Appendix 3). The proceedings are confidential, and even when private parties are directly concerned, they are not permitted to attend or make submissions separate from those of the state in question.

5. *The Panel Report.* Following the second substantive meeting with the parties, the panel will issue to the parties for comment the descriptive part of its report, containing the relevant facts, a summary of the positions of the parties and any third parties,[4] but no indication of how the panel will come out. The idea of this practice, followed by some GATT panels in the 1980s, is to avoid mistakes that could have been corrected, and that should not be permitted later on to undermine the value of the final report. Within two to four weeks of receipt by the panel of comments on the descriptive part, the panel is to issue its complete report—first in an interim version for review by the parties, and subsequently in a final version (Art. 15). The final version is distributed first to the parties—a last chance for settlement—and two weeks later it is circulated to all members of the WTO. The Understanding provides that the period from the date of composition of the panel to issuance of the final report shall as a general rule not exceed six months (Art. 12(8)).[5]

---

[3] A footnote explains that the DSB shall be deemed to have decided by consensus on a matter submitted for its consideration, if no Member, present at the meeting of the DSB when the decision is taken, formally objects to the proposed decision (Art. 2, n. 1). Some writers have referred to this as 'negative consensus', in contrast to the situation in which an affirmative vote is taken and passed without dissent.

[4] For the place of third parties, see Sect. 8.5(b) infra.

[5] Again, in case of urgency, all the deadlines are shortened, and the panel is to aim to issue its report within three months (Art. 12(8)). If the panel considers that it cannot issue its report within six months, it may seek an extension from the DSB, but '[i]n no case should the period from the establishment of the panel to the circulation of the report to the Members exceed nine months' (Art. 12(9)). In practice, the nine-month period for the panel has become common.

6. *Adoption of the Panel Report.* As in prior GATT practice, the report of the panel is in form a recommendation to the full membership, sitting as the Dispute Settlement Body. But in sharp contrast with prior practice, the report *shall be adopted* at a meeting of the DSB within 60 days of circulation of the report unless the DSB by consensus decides not to adopt the report or a party to the dispute gives notice of its intention to appeal (Art. 16(4)). The parties and other states may give their views on the report, but (apart from appeal) they cannot block its adoption, even if the opponents command a majority of the DSB.

7. *Appeal.* A party may appeal a panel report to a standing Appellate Body, but only on issues of law and legal interpretations developed by the panel (Art. 17(6)). The Appellate Body will receive written and oral submissions of the parties, and it may uphold, modify, or reverse the legal findings and conclusions of the panel (Art. 17(13)). The drafters saw institution of the Appellate Body as a necessary safety valve to prevent erroneous panel decisions from being automatically adopted by the DSB, and also as a source for consistent development of a body of trade law embracing the many agreements subject to its review. They were careful, however, to see to it that appeals not serve as an instrument of delay, and wrote into the Understanding that as a general rule the proceedings before the Appellate Body shall not exceed 60 days from the notice of appeal to issuance of its report (Art. 17(5)). Remand of the case to the panel for further proceedings is not authorized.[6]

8. *Adoption of the Appellate Body Report.* Members may express their views on the report of the Appellate Body, but they cannot derail it. The Understanding states unequivocally that an Appellate Body report *shall be adopted* by the DSB and unconditionally accepted by the parties, unless the DSB decides by consensus within 30 days of its circulation not to adopt the report (Art. 17(14)).

Article 20 of the Understanding sums up the procedure: Unless otherwise agreed by the parties to the dispute, the period from establishment of the panel (step 3 above) to consideration (and presumably adoption) of the report by the DSB shall as a general rule not exceed 9 months if there is no appeal, and 12 months if there is an appeal.

(b)   The Effect of a Decision and the Issue of Sovereignty

1. *Finding in Favour of Respondent.* If the report of a panel, or of the Appellate Body, exonerates the challenged measure or practice, the losing party may not thereafter say 'We tried this process and it did not work, so

---

[6] This omission, which must have been deliberate, was evidently consistent with the desire to avoid delays, but it can be awkward when the Appellate Body holds that a particular fact should have been but was not investigated by the panel.

we will take retaliatory measures on our own.' Doubtless with an eye on section 301 of the United States Trade Act, which authorizes retaliatory action *inter alia* if the US Trade Representative determines that the rights of the United States under any trade agreement are being denied,[7] Article 23 of the Understanding on Dispute Settlement states:

When Members seek the redress of a violation of obligations or other nullification or impairment of benefits under the covered agreements . . ., they shall
(a)   not make a determination to the effect that a violation has occurred, that benefits have been nullified or impaired or that the attainment of any objective of the covered agreements has been impeded, except through recourse to dispute settlement in accordance with the rules and procedures of this Understanding.

In fact, the United States law is not necessarily inconsistent with that provision, as explored in Section 8.8(c) below, and of course the quoted provision applies to all member states. The point, however, is that the judicialization of dispute settlement in the WTO and the requirement of compliance with the result operates not only if a decision is rendered in favour of the complainant, but also if the decision favours the defendant. Either way, though the phrase is nowhere found in the Understanding, the issue becomes *res judicata*.

   2. *Finding in Favour of Complainant.* Article 19, consistent with prior practice, states what dispute settlement is supposed to accomplish:

Where a panel or the Appellate Body concludes that a measure is inconsistent with a covered agreement, it shall recommend that the Member concerned bring the measure into conformity with that agreement.

This rather mild statement reflects a decision, made nearly half a century earlier, to avoid any expression in Article XXIII of the GATT sounding like a command to 'cease and desist'.[8] In response to the age-old concerns in many countries about 'judicial activism' and its analogues, Article 19 goes on to reiterate that the panel or Appellate Body 'cannot add to or diminish the rights and obligations provided in the covered agreements.'[9] In contrast to the prior practice, however, the Uruguay Round Understanding makes elaborate provision for what may happen if the recommendations are not carried out, as described in the following subsections.

   As the results of the Uruguay Round were presented to legislatures around the world, the issue inevitably arose whether some 'unelected bureaucrats' could tell a sovereign state what laws to adopt or repeal. The proponents of

---

   [7] United States: §301(a)(1) of the Trade Act of 1974 as amended. For more on §301, see Sect. 8.8 infra.
   [8] For the drafting history of the corresponding provisions of the Havana Charter and its relation to the text of Article XXIII of the GATT, see Robert E. Hudec, 'Retaliation Against "Unreasonable" Foreign Trade Practices: The New Section 301 and GATT Nullification and Impairment', 59 *Minnesota L. Rev.* 461 at 467–70 (1975).
   [9] The same phrase appears is Article 3(2) of the Understanding, under 'General Provisions'.

the WTO system, and in particular of the new, stricter dispute settlement mechanism, were at pains to point out that only the Xandian legislature makes law for Xandia; whereas a panel or the Appellate Body might issue a *ruling* that a particular law or regulation was inconsistent with a covered agreement, it could issue only a *recommendation* that the law or regulation in question be repealed or modified in order to make it consistent with the pertinent international law.[10] That left open the question whether there is an obligation to comply with a recommendation consequent upon a ruling, or whether, as Justice Oliver Wendell Holmes wrote in a famous essay (before he became a Supreme Court Justice), 'The duty to keep a contract . . . means a prediction that you must pay damages if you do not keep it—and nothing else.'[11]

The drafters of the WTO system did not insist on an explicit answer to this question, since it would have unnecessarily raised political problems that might well have impeded passage of the Uruguay Round agreements in several national legislatures.[12] But it is clear that the GATT/WTO system prefers removal of trade barriers found to be inconsistent with covered agreements rather than imposition of a second trade barrier in retaliation for continuation of the first one. This preference suggests strongly that the attitude reflected in the quotation from Holmes—whatever its soundness in the field of private contract law—does not express the philosophy of the Agreement Establishing the WTO and the agreements thereunder.

Both as a matter of legal philosophy and as a matter of interpretation of the WTO Understanding on Dispute Settlement, this writer agrees with Professor Jackson:

[A]n adopted dispute settlement report establishes an international law obligation upon the member in question to change its practice to make it consistent with the rules of the WTO Agreement and its annexes. In this view, the 'compensation' (or retaliation) approach is only a fallback in the event of noncompliance.[13]

---

[10] See e.g. Judith Hippler Bello, 'The WTO Dispute Settlement Understanding: Less is More', 90 *Am. J. Int'l L.* 416 at 418 (1986):

> [T]he good news is that the United States is not required to comply with a WTO dispute settlement ruling adverse to the United States. (The correspondingly bad news is that neither is any other member.) Instead, the United States (or any other member) may choose to comply, to compensate, or to stonewall and suffer retaliation against its exports.

[11] Oliver Wendell Holmes, Jr., 'The Path of the Law', first published in 10 *Harvard L. Rev.* 457 (1897) and reprinted in many collections since that time e.g. 110 *Harv. L. Rev.* 991 at 995 (1997).

[12] See e.g. sect. 102(a) of the United States Uruguay Round Agreements Act, 19 U.S.C. §3512:

> No provision of any of the Uruguay Round Agreements, nor the application of any such provision to any person or circumstance, that is inconsistent with any law of the United States shall have effect.

[13] John H. Jackson, 'The WTO Dispute Settlement Understanding—Misunderstandings on the Nature of Legal Obligation' [Editorial Comment replying to Bello, n. 10 supra], 91 *Am. J. Int'l L.* 60 (1997).

> A perhaps useful analogy may be drawn from the field of international commercial law, as embodied in the Vienna Convention on the International Sale of Goods, 1980, 1489

(c) The Question of Compliance

The dispute resolution mechanism under the GATT rarely focused on compliance, though from time to time, particularly in the later stages of the Uruguay Round, failure to implement panel recommendations had become a serious issue.[14] GATT Article XXIII(2) does provide:

If the CONTRACTING PARTIES consider that the circumstances are serious enough to justify such action, they may authorize a contracting party or parties to suspend the application to any other contracting party or parties of such concessions or other obligations under this Agreement as they determine to be appropriate in the circumstances.

But this provision had been invoked only a few times in the 45-year history of the GATT, and retaliation in the form of withdrawal of a concession had been authorized only once, in a 1952 case permitting the Netherlands to place a limit on imports of wheat flour from the United States in response to the failure by the United States to remove restraints on the importation of dairy products that had been found to be in violation of the GATT.[15] The WTO Understanding on Dispute Settlement addresses the question of compliance and retaliation in unprecedented strictness and thoroughness, unprecedented not only for the GATT but for international relations generally. Article 21(1) states the general imperative:

Prompt compliance with recommendations or rulings of the DSB is essential in order to ensure effective resolution of disputes to the benefit of all Members.

The subsequent paragraphs of Article 21 set out a complicated sequence, designed to impose discipline on the process of compliance.

1. *The Intent to Comply.* At a meeting of the DSB held within 30 days of the adoption of the Report, the Member concerned is to inform the DSB of its intentions in respect of implementation of the recommendations and rulings.

2. *Time for Compliance.* If the Member explains that it is impracticable to comply immediately with the recommendations and rulings, for instance if compliance would require action by the legislature, the Member is to have a 'reasonable period of time' in which to comply.

> U.N.T.S. 59. Under the Anglo-American tradition, as reflected in the quotation from Justice Holmes, the normal remedy for breach of contract is award of damages, with specific performance reserved for transactions in unique goods or services. Under the CISG, reflecting the effort to bridge the civil and common law systems, the preferred remedy is an order to carry out an international contract—Article 46 if seller has failed to perform, Article 62 if buyer has failed to perform—with the award of damages only as a permitted alternative.

[14] See the statement of the Chairman of the GATT Council in May 1991, quoted in Ch. 7, Sect. 7.4(a), n. 42.

[15] See Robert E. Hudec, *The GATT Legal System and World Trade Diplomacy*, 181–200 (2nd edn., 1990); *Analytical Index of the GATT*, Art. XXIII, Vol 2. pp. 692–3 (6th edn., revd. 1995).

3. *The 'Reasonable Period' for Compliance.* The Understanding states that the reasonable period shall be the time proposed by the Member concerned, *if the DSB approves.* If the DSB does not approve, the reasonable period shall be a period agreed by the parties to the dispute within 45 days after adoption of the report (Art. 21(3)(b)).

4. *Disagreement about the Reasonable Period for Compliance.* If no agreement is reached about the reasonable period for compliance, that issue— and only that issue—is to be the subject of binding arbitration by a single arbitrator, subject to a guideline that the time should not exceed 15 months from the date of adoption of the report. The arbitrator is to be appointed by agreement of the parties, but if they cannot do so within 10 days, the Director-General is to appoint the arbitrator within another 10 days, after consulting the parties (Art. 21(3)(c)).[16]

5. *Judging Compliance.* If there is disagreement as to the satisfactory nature of the measures adopted by the respondent state to comply with the report, that disagreement is to be decided not by the arbitrator, but by a panel, if possible by the same panel that heard the original dispute, but apparently without the possibility of appeal from its decision (Art. 21(5)).[17]

6. *Surveillance.* The Understanding provides that even if the Respondent asserts that it has complied with the recommendation in a report, and even if the complainant party or the panel accepts that assertion, the DSB is supposed to keep the implementation of the recommendations under surveillance. Any member can bring up the subject at a meeting of the DSB, and even if no member state requests it, the subject is to be placed on the agenda of the DSB meeting after six months following the determination of the reasonable period and member concerned—i.e. the Respondent in the original proceeding—is to provide a written status report of its progress in implementation of the recommendations or rulings. The matter is supposed to remain on the agenda thereafter until the issue is resolved (Art. 21(6)).

(d) Compensation and Retaliation

If all else fails, two more possibilities are set out in the DSU. Article 22 provides that if a member fails within the 'reasonable period' as determined under Article 21 to carry out the recommendations and rulings, it may negotiate with the complaining state for mutually acceptable compensation. Compensation is not defined, but may be expected to consist of the grant of a concession by the respondent state on a product or service of interest to the complainant state. Though there is no explicit statement, it seems clear

---

[16] Typically, the arbitrator has been chosen by the parties or the Director-General from among the members of the Appellate Body.

[17] For the relation between the Articles 21(3) and 21(5) proceedings, and both of these proceedings with authorization for retaliation under Article 22, see the discussion of the *Bananas* case in Sect. 8.8(d) infra.

that compensation in this context must be on an MFN basis—i.e. so that any supplier of the product to the respondent state can bring the product in to the respondent state at the same reduced rate and no new discrimination is created as a way of paying for an existing violation.

If no agreement on compensation is reached within twenty days of the expiry of the 'reasonable period', the prevailing party may request authorization from the DSB to suspend application to the Member concerned (i.e. in a departure from MFN) of concessions or other obligations under the covered agreements (Art. 22(2)). The DSU makes clear that retaliation is not favoured (Art. 22(1)); nevertheless, Article 22(3) and (4) spell out, in detail, the principles and procedures for retaliation: (i) Suspension of concessions is to be in the same sector as the measure condemned by a panel or Appellate Body report; if that is not practicable, then the suspension is to be in other sectors governed by the same agreement—i.e. goods for goods, intellectual property for intellectual property, service for service, and only if that too is not practicable, may there be retaliation by suspension of an obligation under another agreement;[18] (ii) a retaliatory measure may not be inconsistent with a covered agreement; and (iii) as had been the tradition under Article XXIII (though not previously spelled out), the level of suspension of concessions or other obligation shall be equivalent to the level of nullification or impairment, without any element of punishment.

In sharp contrast to prior GATT practice, authorization to suspend concessions in this context is semi-automatic, in that the DSB '*shall grant the authorization* . . .within thirty days of the expiry of the reasonable period', unless it decides by consensus to reject the request (Art. 22(6)). But if the respondent state objects to the level of suspension proposed or to the consistency of the proposed suspension with the principles set out above, still another arbitration is provided for, if possible by the original panel members or by an arbitrator or arbitrators appointed by the Director-General, to be completed within 60 days from expiration of the reasonable period.

Any suspension of a concession or other obligation is to be temporary. As soon as the inconsistent measure has been eliminated by the respondent state, the suspension must be eliminated as well (Art. 22(8)). Whether or not the complainant has taken a measure of retaliation, surveillance by the DSB is to continue, to see whether the recommendations of the panel or the Appellate Body have been implemented (Art. 22(8)).[19]

---

[18] An example of cross-agreement retaliation occurred in the *Bananas* case discussed below, when Ecuador sought, and received, authorization to retaliate against the European Community's restriction on its banana exports by suspending obligations under the TRIPs Agreement. See Sect. 8.8(d), at nn. 114–15.

[19] For more on retaliation and how the respective tactics worked out in one major dispute between the United States and the European Community, see Sect. 8.8(d) infra.

(e)   The System in Context

Several more aspects of the system of dispute settlement in the WTO need to be set out to complete this introduction. *First,* Article 3 of the Understanding states that Members 'affirm their adherence to the principles for the management of disputes heretofore applied under Articles XXII and XXIII of GATT 1947.' This provision restates, with specific focus on dispute settlement, the principles set out in Article XVI of the Marrakesh Agreement Establishing the World Trade Organization, that except as otherwise provided in the various agreements making up the results of the Uruguay Round, 'the WTO shall be guided by the decisions, procedures and customary practices followed by the CONTRACTING PARTIES to GATT 1947 and the bodies established in the framework of GATT 1947.' Thus while reports of panels were technically binding only on the parties to a particular dispute—i.e. there is no principle of *stare decisis,* it is clear that the corpus of GATT law and practice, unless expressly modified in subsequent agreements, will have a continuing influence on future resolutions of disputes within the WTO. The radical departures of the new dispute settlement regime are not accompanied, in other words, by departures in the substantive traditions of the GATT. GATT 1947 is still a source document, and the corpus of law, practice, and tradition developed in the period 1948–93 retain their position in the new World Trade Organization as guidelines for the new generation of decision-makers. Of course, as the corpus of WTO panel reports, and particularly reports of the Appellate Body, mounts up, it is to those documents that panelists, other chambers of the Appellate Body, and litigants increasingly look for guidance.

Second, in addition to the procedures for litigation described in this section and hereafter, the Understanding on Dispute Settlement makes provision for less coercive techniques of dispute resolution as well—good offices (by the Director-General or one of his associates), conciliation, and mediation (Art. 5). The Understanding makes clear that opting for one of these paths is without prejudice to resort to the panel procedure, and indeed may be used, if both parties agree, in the interval between a request for a panel and establishment of the panel, and even while the panel process proceeds.

Moreover, while the innovations, notably elimination of the veto at the three crucial points—request for panel, adoption of panel report, and authorization of retaliation—all point to disciplined adjudication, the Understanding retains some of the ambivalence about law vs. diplomacy from earlier texts. Article 3(3), for instance, speaks of the need to maintain 'a proper balance between the rights and obligations of Members'; Article 3(4) speaks of the aim of 'achieving a satisfactory settlement of the matter'; and Article 3(7) states: 'A solution mutually acceptable to the parties to a dispute and consistent with the covered agreements is clearly to be preferred.'[20]

---

[20] This point is made by Judge Pescatore in his essay on 'Drafting and Analyzing Decisions on Dispute Settlement', in Pescatore, *Handbook,* Vol. I, pt. II, p. 31.

Finally, the emphasis on litigation, compliance, and enforceable deadlines should not be taken as a total transformation of the regime of adjustment of trade controversies. Not only has the Uruguay Round Understanding retained the text from the earlier agreements on dispute settlement to the effect that before bringing a case, 'a Member shall exercise its judgment as to whether action under these procedures would be fruitful' (Art. 3(7)). More generally, the overall aim of the World Trade Organization is to serve as a forum for oversight, administration, and development of the multilateral trading system, through negotiations, conferences, research, technical assistance, and comparable activities. The Understanding accepts (in Article 3(2)) that the dispute settlement system is 'a central element in providing security and predictability to the multilateral trading system'. It is not the only element.

8.2 A CLOSER LOOK AT THE PANELS

In devising the system of dispute settlement for the WTO, its architects had to choose between a standing body and a system for ad hoc selection of decision-makers. The more fixed and unambiguous the substantive rules were, the less critical it would be who made the decisions. Given the often ambiguous texts and the vast new body of law generated by the Uruguay Round, the selection of the decision-makers at both levels takes on great importance. The solution devised by the drafters of the DSU was to opt for ad hoc panels as the forum of first instance, but with review by an Appellate Body (no more elegant name emerged) that would have a continuing existence.

(a)   Selection of Panelists

Unlike most international arbitration—commercial as well as state-to-state—in which each party typically chooses one arbitrator and either the two so chosen or an appointing authority selects the presiding arbitrator or chairman, panelists under the WTO system are all to be chosen by the Secretariat, if possible with agreement of the parties. Disputing states do not nominate panel members; they can object to a proposed panel member, but only for 'compelling reasons' (Art. 8(6)). If there is no agreement on the panelists, the Director-General of the WTO, in consultation with the Chairman of the DSB, is to appoint the members of the panel within 10 days after receipt of a request by either party to do so (Art. 8(7)). Clearly the effort, which has not been wholly successful, is to avoid some of the delaying tactics through objection to panelists that plagued the GATT disputes process in the 1970s and 1980s.[21]

---

[21] See e.g. the discussion of the *Disc* case, Ch. 7, Sect. 7.3(c) at nn. 28–31. As to what may be compelling reasons, see below.

The tradition in GATT, as seen in the preceding chapter, had been to constitute panels from government officials, often from the GATT representatives stationed in Geneva. While that saved in expenses and made scheduling of meetings easier than coordinating programs of persons coming from abroad, it tended to perpetuate the club-like atmosphere that was coming under increasing criticism as the system became more rule-oriented. Moreover, having government officials on panels, even when serving in their individual capacities and without instructions from their governments, tended to emphasize the political, rather than the legal aspect of the disputes presented to panels. In the 1980s, the tradition was modified, and the GATT secretariat developed its own roster of panelists, including ex-government officials, retired judges, and academic experts in economics and law. The WTO Understanding provides that both government officials and others may serve on panels, provided they are 'well qualified' (Art. 8(1)). In fact, most panelists have continued to be present or former government officials.

Qualification to be a panel member may come through previous service on or presentation of a case to a panel; acting as a representative of a Member of the WTO or of a contracting party to the GATT; service as member of a Committee of any covered agreement or the GATT or WTO Council; previous service in the Secretariat; teaching and writing on international trade law or policy; or sevice as a senior trade policy official of a member state. The Secretariat maintains a roster of potential panelists, on the basis of suggestions of governments as well as its own lists. The Understanding continues the presumption that citizens of parties to a given dispute are not to serve on a panel concerned with that dispute, but makes provision for the parties to otherwise agree (Art. 8(3)).[22] But if a developing country is a party to a dispute, at least one member of the panel shall, if the developing country so requests, come from another developing country (Art. 8(10)).

The pay for serving on a WTO panel is modest, compared for example to the pay of members of tribunals in international commercial arbitration, but it is clear that panelists are not expected to donate their services. The Understanding makes clear that the expenses for panelists are to be met from the WTO budget (Art. 8(11)).

(b)   Conflicts of Interest and the Question of Bias

Whenever persons are asked to serve as part-time panelists, arbitrators, committee members or similar decision-makers without giving up all other professional or personal activities, the question of possible bias or conflict of

---

[22] The parties may well so agree, if the legal regime of the respondent country is an issue. This was the case, for example in the §337 case discussed in Ch. 7, Sect. 7.4(a), n. 39 supra, which involved some intricate questions of United States administrative law. The European Community, as Complaining Party, asked that an American familiar with US procedure and administrative law be named to the panel, as well as a citizen of a Community country. Of course, when citizens of disputing parties are panelists, present governmental officials are excluded.

interest arises.[23] For this reason, among others, the Understanding on Dispute Settlement, as mentioned above, rejects the idea of party-appointed panelists, and also rejects the idea of peremptory challenges. Only 'compelling reasons' may justify a challenge. A compelling reason would plainly include a financial connection, such as counsel and client or significant shareholder, between a potential nominee and a firm or industry that would stand to gain or lose from the outcome of a case. A more difficult question would arise if a challenge were brought on the basis of a potential panelist's past writing, or past service on a panel that dealt with a similar question. Such information should be disclosed, and the DSB quickly issued its Rules of Conduct calling for 'self-disclosure' by all persons requested to serve on a panel, on the Appellate Body, or as an arbitrator of 'any information . . . that is likely to affect or give rise to justifiable doubts as to their independence or impartiality', accompanied by an illustrative list of information to be disclosed.[24] But the criteria for selection of panelists, which emphasize experience and expertise in international trade law or policy, are bound to produce persons who have gone on record in books, articles, prior decisions, even political campaigns, on issues that may come before WTO dispute panels.

> Suppose, for instance, a challenge is brought by Patria under the Agreement on Anti-Dumping against the imposition of an anti-dumping duty by Xandia on a given product. Patria claims that the required findings of causation and injury were improperly made, or that the price comparisons contained errors. The Secretariat suggests a panelist from Tertia who is an expert on dumping, and who, in his writings, has warned against the use of anti-dumping laws as disguised protectionism. Does Xandia have a 'compelling reason' to object to appointment of this expert to the panel?
> Again, suppose Xandia has excluded a product of Patria on the ground that it was produced in an environmentally harmful factory, using techniques outlawed in Xandia. Patria brings a complaint to the WTO, and the Secretariat suggests as panelist an expert on the environment who has written about the 'necessary accommodation' between environmental controls and international trade rules. Should either Patria or Xandia be deemed to have 'compelling reasons' to object to this person's appointment?

A potential panelist, arbitrator, or expert should be forthcoming at the level of disclosure, listing, for instance, his or her relevant publications or membership in organizations. One may hope that disclosure is not equated with disqualification, and that questions such as those suggested above are

[23] For a thoughtful discussion of the problem of qualification, disqualification, disclosure, and recusal in international dispute settlement, see Detlev F. Vagts, 'The International Legal Profession: A Need for More Governance?', 90 *Am. J. Int'l Law* 250 (1996).

[24] WTO Doc. WT/DSB/RC/1 (11 Dec. 1996).

answered in such a way as to maintain a high standard of expertise on panels, and not to confuse experience and points of view with bias. There have in fact been complaints and objections, and contrary to the design of the DSU, the Director-General was obliged to appoint the panel in close to half the cases, as authorized (though not preferred) by Article 8(7).

(c)   Confidentiality

In the course of deliberations during the Uruguay Round and about its result, a number of critics, particularly in the United States, expressed the desire for more openness in the proceedings. Whether from the 'free trade' or the 'protectionist' wing (as well as from environmental, labour, or human rights organizations), critics had the fear that their government would not adequately represent their views, and that solutions or decisions crafted behind closed doors would undermine their interests. The opposite view, which had long been accepted in the GATT, was that to open the dispute settlement proceedings to press and public would politicize the process, increase lobbying and even demonstrations, and impair the opportunity for objective decision-making based on the facts and the law. The latter view prevailed in the Uruguay Round. Panel proceedings are confidential, with only the representatives of the parties permitted to be present at the hearings, and with deliberations limited to the panelists, plus a small number of members of the Secretariat assigned to the case.[25] If third parties ask to participate in a dispute before a panel, their representatives can be heard before the panel and make written submissions to the panel, but they receive only the first round of submissions of the parties, and they are not entitled to attend the proceedings apart from their own appearance (Art. 10 and Appendix 3).

The names of panelists are now published. But if members of the panel are divided over an issue, the report may state 'a majority of the panel concluded . . .'; no dissenting opinions are issued, and the opinions of individual members of the panel are not disclosed. The panel reports themselves are published—and displayed on the Internet—within a few days of their circulation to the parties.

(d)   Information for the Panel

Some judicial and arbitral tribunals proceed on the principle that they are limited by whatever the parties choose to submit to them. The WTO

---

[25] But Appendix 3 to the DSU states that 'Nothing in this Understanding shall preclude a party to a dispute from disclosing statements of its own positions to the public', and the Office of United States Trade Representative, for one, has regularly published its written submissions to panels or to the Appellate Body, as required by US law adopted in the Uruguay Round Agreements Act, 19 U.S.C. §3537.

Understanding on Dispute Settlement takes the opposite view. Article 13, entitled 'Right to Seek Information', makes clear that each panel shall have the right to seek information and technical advice from any individual or body which it deems appropriate. Further, Article 13 states that any Member of the WTO—whether or not a party to a given proceeding—should respond promptly and fully to any request by a panel for information. The fact that the information requested may be confidential is not a ground for withholding it from the panel; the panel is required to maintain the confidentiality of any information supplied on a confidential basis, and the Rules of Conduct obligate each panelist, arbitrator, and member of the Appellate Body to uphold this requirement.

(e)   The Use of Experts

Some issues that have come before GATT panels in the past—or would have come before panels if one side or the other had not blocked the process[26]—involve scientific questions that panel members cannot be expected to be familiar with. An example is the long-running dispute within the European Community and between the Community and the United States about whether use of growth hormones in animal feed for cattle poses a health threat to consumers of beef, as the European Community concluded, or poses no such threat, as the United States maintained.[27] The DSU states that a panel may seek information from any relevant source, and may consult experts (Art. 13(2)). With respect to a factual issue concerning a scientific or technical matter raised by a party, a panel may request an advisory report from an 'expert review group'; an appendix to the DSU sets out, in almost

[26] See the discussion of the *Beef Hormones* controversy, n. 27 infra.

[27] After lengthy negotiation and litigation before the European Court of Justice, the European Community issued a regulation forbidding the importation or sale of beef raised with food containing specified hormone additives. The United States regarded the regulation unjustified on health grounds. It filed a complaint in GATT in 1987, and requested a determination under the Federal Standards Code adopted in the Tokyo Round. The Community rejected submission of the issue to a technical panel, and the United States refused to submit the issue first to a legal panel. In November 1987 President Reagan announced a measure designed to retaliate for imposition of the EC ban on beef, to be put into effect in January 1988, but suspended application of the retaliation when the Community postponed its directive. In January 1989, the Community regulation did enter into effect, as did the United States retaliation—tariff increases on $100 million of imports from the Community. The EC requested a GATT panel to rule on the legality of the US retaliation, but the United States blocked this request, citing the Community's refusal to submit the hormone regulation to a technical panel. Consultations continued on and off between the two sides (as well as Australia, Canada, and New Zealand). In May 1996 the United States requested appointment of a panel under the WTO rules. The Community blocked appointment of a panel for one meeting, as the Understanding permits (see Sect. 8.1(a), step 3), but a panel was established at the next meeting. In July 1996, the Community in turn requested establishment of a panel to investigate the retaliatory action by the United States in 1989 and still in effect. For details of the controversy through 1989, see Werner P. Meng, 'The Hormone Conflict between the EEC and the United States within the Context of GATT', 11 *Michigan J. Int'l Law* 819 (1990); for a discussion of the merits as they came before the WTO system, see Ch. 11, Sect. 11.7.

the same terms as an appendix to the Agreement or Technical Barriers to Trade, rules for formation of such groups, including the avoidance (except in exceptional circumstances) of citizens of parties to the dispute. The expert review groups in turn may consult and seek information and technical advice from any source they deem appropriate. The report of an expert review group is advisory only, but it is to be submitted to the parties for their comments before being submitted in final form to the panel.

(f)   The Suggestion for Permanent Panelists

As more and more disputes have come before the DSU, and as the disputes have become more complicated and technical, the suggestion has been made that in place of the ad hoc selection of panel members, a permanent cadre of panelists be appointed—say twenty to twenty-five well-paid professionals, who might serve full-time, or be regularly on call and be expected to serve half-time.[28]

The thought is that availability of such a group of panelists would avoid the delays in organizing the actual proceedings that have characterized the process in a number of instances, and avoid the complaints about panel performance that have sometimes surfaced and sometimes simmered beneath the surface. On the other hand, if panels were selected from a standing body, it might make it more difficult to select experts—for instance in the environment, in financial services, or in patent law—as contrasted with international trade experts who could be expected to be the permanent members. Furthermore, if a standing body of panelists were established, the current de facto preference for government-affiliated panelists would probably have to be changed, which some states would favour, others not. As of year-end 2001, none of these suggestions had been acted on, and while there was some criticism, there was not such general dissatisfaction as to make amendment of panel selection a priority as the DSU evolves.[29]

8.3   THE APPELLATE BODY

The provision for a standing Appellate Body, as pointed out in Section 8.1, is the most innovative aspect of the Understanding on Dispute Settlement. On the one hand, the Appellate Body is a necessary complement to a process whereby reports of ad hoc panels are practically immune from blockage or veto. On the other hand, the Appellate Body is expected to provide continuity and

---

[28] See e.g. Robert E. Hudec, 'The New WTO Dispute Settlement Procedure: An Overview of the First Three Years', 8 *Minn. J. Global Trade* 1 at 35–9 (1999); William J. Davey, 'The WTO Dispute Settlement', 3 *J. Int'l Econ. L.* 15 at 17 (2000).

[29] The more urgent reform of the process, it would seem, has to do with the sequence of post-panel or post-Appellate Body proceedings, as discussed in Sect. 8.9 infra.

consistency not only for interpretation of a given agreement, but also—so far as the texts permit—among the more than twenty agreements, understandings, and decisions that comprise the WTO system. Several provisions of the Understanding on Dispute Settlement, and in the Working Procedures adopted by the Appellate Body shortly after its constitution, emphasize this second, less obvious but important, aspect of the dispute settlement system as 'a central element in providing security and predictability to the multilateral trading system' (Art. 3(2)). There is no filtering device, such as provision for leave to appeal. The right of a party to have recourse to the Appellate Body is guaranteed, not subject to any conditions except that a question of law must be at issue (Art. 17).

(a)   The Membership of the Appellate Body

The Understanding on Dispute Settlement provides for an Appellate Body consisting of seven persons appointed for staggered four-year terms, except that the terms of three of the first seven persons appointed (drawn by lot) had only two-year terms, so that there will never be a complete turnover of the membership. Members of the Appellate Body are eligible for reappointment once only.

Since there was no way to tell how many disputes would be brought under the new system, and how many of these would be appealed, there was some question about whether service on the Appellate Body should call for a full-time commitment or simply a commitment to be on call. The Understanding provides that the persons serving on the Appellate Body shall be available at all times and on short notice, but they need not reside in Geneva or give up other professional employment, so long as no conflict of interests is involved. The initial estimate, and the corresponding salary, assumed one-quarter of the members' professional activity. In the event, more cases have been filed than could have been expected, and more final decisions have been appealed, so that service on the Appellate Body has become close to a full-time job.

Selecting the members of the Appellate Body proved to be a more complicated task than anticipated, and in fact was not completed until the end of November 1995, eleven months after the WTO agreements entered into force. The Understanding states (Art. 17(3)) that the Appellate Body shall comprise persons of recognized authority, 'with demonstrated expertise in law, international trade, and the subject matter of the covered agreements generally.' Some, but not all the members of the Appellate Body were trade experts before they were selected. Greater emphasis has been placed on the statement in the same paragraph that the membership shall be 'broadly representative of the membership in the WTO', which was understood to comprehend geography, stages of economic development, legal traditions, and importance in the world economy. Both the European Community and the

United States insisted at first on two places each on the Appellate Body, and in retrospect it might have been preferable to have provided for nine members overall. But the Understanding called for only seven members, and reserving four places for the Big Two would have made it impossible to even approach the goal of broad representation of the membership of the WTO.

Eventually, a committee headed by the Director-General of the WTO and including the chairmen of four of the WTO councils plus the DSB selected seven persons as the initial members of the Appellate Body.[30] Of these, all had studied law, but two had been career diplomats, one from New Zealand, the other from Uruguay, one a senior official of the European Community; one a Supreme Court judge in the Philippines; two professors with substantial government service, one from Egypt and one from Japan; and one a practicing lawyer who had served two terms in the United States Congress. Classified differently, every continent was represented, there were four persons from developed and three from developing countries; only Eastern Europe was not represented.[31] The members of the Appellate Body elected as its first Chairman an 'old GATT-hand', Julio Lacarte-Muró of Uruguay, a long-time delegate to and official of the GATT, who had served as chairman of the negotiating group on dispute settlement in the Uruguay Round.

(b)   Functioning of the Appellate Body

Three members of the Appellate Body chosen at random sit as a 'division' to consider a given appeal, but there are no permanent chambers that would put the same members together repeatedly or would specialize in any particular class of cases. The Understanding does not specify whether or not a member of the Appellate Body should be disqualified from hearing an appeal in which the country of which he is a national is a party; when the Appellate Body issued its Working Procedures, effective February 15, 1996, it made clear that nationality would not be taken into account. The Chairman said:

> The Appellate Body is of the view that to deal with the issue of nationality in any other way would be unnecessary and undesirable. . . . unnecessary in view of the qualifications required for membership in the Appellate Body; undesirable as casting doubts on the capacity of members of the Appellate Body for independence and impartiality in decision-making.[32]

---

[30] A total of 32 candidates from 23 countries were nominated for membership in the Appellate Body, including 13 from the European Community, and two each from Japan and the United States.

[31] Of course neither Russia nor China was a member of the WTO as of 1995.

[32] Letter from Chairman Lacarte-Muró of the Appellate Body to Celso Lafer, Chairman of the WTO Dispute Settlement Body, quoted in BNA, *Int'l Trade Reporter*, 6 Mar. 1996, 379.
The Working Procedures for Appellate Review, WT/AB/WP/3, 28 Feb. 1997, state, in ¶ 6(2):

> The Members constituting a division shall be selected on the basis of rotation, while taking into account the principles of random selection, unpredictability and opportunity for all Members to serve regardless of their national origin.

The Working Procedures adopted by the Appellate Body contain a section on collegiality, which not only provides that the members shall meet regularly, but that each member, whether or not sitting on a given appeal, shall receive all documents filed in the appeal, and that the division responsible for deciding each appeal shall exchange views with the other Members before the division finalizes the appellate report (para. 4).[33]

(c) The Appeal Process and the Scope of Review

The most striking aspect of the appeal process is that it is expected to be completed within 60 days from the notice of appeal to circulation of the report by the Appellate Body (DSU Art. 17(5)). There are no page restrictions on submissions by the parties, but the appellant is required to make its written submission within ten days of filing the notice of appeal, and the appellee (as well as any third party) has 15 days thereafter to submit its written response (paras 21 and 22). The rules provide that an oral hearing is to be held, as a general rule, 30 days after the date of filing of the notice of appeal, i.e. within 5 days of receipt of the appellee's submission.[34] The division may, at the oral hearing, request additional memoranda from any participant,[35] but there is no routine second round of written submissions.

As noted in Section 8.1, the Understanding on Dispute Settlement states:

An appeal shall be limited to issues of law covered in the panel report and legal interpretations developed by the panel (Art. 17(6)).

Many domestic legal systems have needed to cope with similar injunctions, sometimes phrased in terms of the distinction between findings of fact and conclusions of law, sometimes in terms of the exercise of discretion by the court of first instance to which the upper court should defer, as contrasted with a legal interpretation which the upper court is free to overrule. In the context of the GATT and the related agreements that come before the WTO dispute settlement system, it may well prove impossible to draw a sharp line between unreviewable determinations of fact and reviewable determinations of law.

(i) Suppose, for instance, Xandia imposes a requirement for sale of a given product under standards that are met more easily by domestic than by foreign producers. Patria brings a complaint before the WTO asserting that its producers have been shut out of the Xandian market by Xandia's discriminatory regulation, in violation of the national treatment requirement of GATT Article III(4).[36] Xandia defends the

---

[33] If a member of the Appellate Body is recused under the conflict of interest rules—which are the same as for panelists,—or would be recused if he had been chosen for the division hearing the case, he or she would not take part in the exchange of views on the draft report. Id. ¶ 4(3).

[34] Working Procedures ¶ 27 and Annex I.   [35] Working Procedures ¶ 28.

[36] The example is suggested by the first case to come before a panel under the WTO dispute system, *United States—Standards for Reformulated and Conventional Gasoline* (*Venezuela and Brazil v. United States*), Report of panel, WT/DS2/R., 29 Jan. 1996, Report of Appellate Body, WT/DS2/AB/R, 29 Apr. 1996.

regulation under Article XX(b), on the basis that the regulation is necessary to protect human health. Patria contends that the defense must fail because alternative non-discriminatory means are available to achieve the same result; Xandia contends that the alternative proposal is infeasible. The panel, after written and oral submissions, issues a ruling on the Article XX(b) defense, and the losing party—either Xandia or Patria—seeks review before the Appellate Body. Does the appeal raise a legal question, or a factual one?

(ii) To take another example, Patria provides a subsidy on certain kinds of animal feed. Xandia, claiming that the subsidy gives a price advantage to Patrian exporters of pork, imposes a countervailing duty on pork imported from Patria.[37] Patria defends on the basis that the subsidy is available to all raisers of livestock, including cattle, sheep, and horses, as well as hogs, thus does not pass the specificity test of Article 2 of the Subsidies Agreement,[38] and therefore may not be subject of a countervailing duty. Xandia replies that while de jure the Patrian subsidy may be open to all, de facto it is primarily availed of by growers of hogs, and therefore comes under the 'notwithstanding any appearance of non-specificity' clause of Article 2.1(c) of the Agreement on Subsidies, thus justifying the imposition of the countervailing duty.

Again, the panel makes a determination, and the losing party, either Xandia or Patria, seeks review before the Appellate Body. Does the appeal raise a legal question, or a factual one?

It is difficult, in the abstract, to elaborate on the statement in Article 17(6) quoted above. The overriding principle ought to be the concern of the architects of the dispute settlement system that the decisions of ad hoc panels do not become automatically effective without the possibility of a second look. It would follow that the kinds of mixed fact/law questions illustrated in the above examples should be regarded as legal interpretations, and thus the Appellate Body should not deny its own competence. To pursue the examples further, the Appellate Body should not take new evidence in case (i) on the costs of an alternative environmental regulation or in case (ii) about the number of raisers of livestock who benefited from the subsidy on animal feed. But the conclusion from the pure facts—i.e. whether the challenged regulation was *necessary* or whether the challenged subsidy was *specific*— should be reviewable by the Appellate Body. Similar findings containing elements of both law and fact and often critical in determinations of trade

---

[37] This example is suggested by a case that arose under the Canada–United States Free Trade Agreement *Fresh, Chilled or Frozen Pork from Canada* (1989–91), described in detail in A. Lowenfeld, 'The Free Trade Agreement Meets its First Challenge: Dispute Settlement and the Pork Case', 37 *McGill L.J.* 597 (1992). A related case came before a GATT in 1989, *United States-Countervailing Duties on Fresh, Chilled and Frozen Pork from Canada*, (*Canada* v. *United States*), 11 July 1991 GATT BISD, 30th Supp. 30 (1992); Pescatore, *Handbook*, Case 83.

[38] See Ch. 9, Sect. 9.6(d).

disputes—such as *injury, causation,* and *like product*—should be treated in the same way, that is the conclusions and the sufficiency of the data on which the panel based its findings should be reviewable by the Appellate Body. Appeals should be granted or denied on the merits, but not rejected for want of jurisdiction. As of year-end 2001, that view has essentially been sustained by the Appellate Body.[39]

Like the European Court of Justice, and like the US Supreme Court in its early years, the Appellate Body has seen its mission in part as a teaching mission, and thus rarely has said 'issue *b* need not be decided because issue *a* is sufficient to decide the case.' Issue *b* may well come up again, and the Appellate Body's guidance now will be useful to the parties and to future panels. Correspondingly, even if a party has prevailed before the panel, it may appeal certain rulings or legal reasoning, and the Appellate Body will rule on that appeal. For instance, in the *Argentine Footwear* case discussed in connection with the Agreeement on Safeguards,[40] the European Community had prevailed before the panel in its challenge to the imposition by Argentina of an emergency duty on certain footwear. But the panel had ruled, contrary to the position of the Community (but consistent with the position of the United States as Third Participant) that a measure that satisfied the Agreement on Safeguards satisfied the requirements of GATT Article XIX. The Community appealed that ruling, and the Appellate Body, while upholding the 'bottom line' ruling of the panel, reversed on the issue of the relation of the Safeguards Agreement to Article XIX, and gave a ruling on that issue that may well be important in future practice of states and future cases under the DSU. The Appellate Body has often identified what it regarded as legal errors on the part of panels, but hardly ever reversed the decision of a panel. If the panel recommends that a challenged practice should be discontinued, that recommendation has almost always been upheld.

8.4   THE ROLE OF THE SECRETARIAT

From the earliest days of dispute settlement in GATT, professional members of the GATT secretariat participated in proceedings before panels, performing research, supplying an institutional memory, and often drafting substantial sections of panel reports. As mentioned in Chapter 7, until the 1980s there was no legal component of the GATT secretariat, but from 1983 on a member of the legal staff as well as a member of the secretariat section most closely familiar with the subject matter of the controversy would usually sit with the panels and assist in research, analysis, and drafting.

[39] For an approach similar to what is here proposed, see, e.g. the *Beef Hormones* case discussed in Ch. 11, Sect. 11.7, WT/DS26/AB/R/USA, para. 132.
[40] Ch. 5, Sect. 5.4 at nn. 64–5.

Article 27.1 of the Understanding expressly provides that the Secretariat shall have the responsibility of assisting panels 'especially on the legal, historical and procedural aspects of the matters dealt with'. With the greatly enlarged scope of dispute settlement, covering more that twenty agreements from textiles to intellectual property and a variety of services, the scope of expert assistance of the Secretariat continues to be important. But as Professor Hudec has pointed out, the existence of the Appellate Body as a continuing body with the last word on legal issues has brought about a pronounced shift in the center of power away from the Secretariat.[41]

In the past, while the professionals on the staff of the GATT were useful in imposing discipline on panels and in making their experience and expertise available, the Secretariat in some instances tended to urge panel members to express themselves in such a way as to make the least waves, for fear that a report might be blocked or endlessly debated. Under the dispute settlement system as it emerged from the Uruguay Round, with veto of panel reports no longer possible and strict timetables in place, these concerns have become less compelling.[42]

8.5   EXPANDING THE CONTROVERSY—COUNTERCLAIMS AND THIRD PARTY PARTICIPANTS

(a)   Counterclaims

In the experience of dispute settlement in the GATT, most notably in the *DISC* case in the period 1973–85,[43] counterclaims (or counter-complaints) had been used as a way to extend controversies and often to frustrate the dispute settlement process. The approach of 'look who's talking' was hardly a way to promote non-discriminatory and open markets that are the goal of the international law of international trade. The Tokyo Round Framework stated that 'it is . . . understood that complaints and counter-complaints in regard to distinct matters should not be linked', and that sentence is repeated verbatim in the Uruguay Round Understanding (Art. 3(10)). Nothing in the Understanding defines the word 'distinct', however, and consolidation of two aspects of a single controversy should not *a priori* be rejected.

---

[41]   Robert E. Hudec, 'The New WTO Dispute Settlement Procedure: An Overview of the First Three Years', 8 *Minn. J. Global Trade* 1 at 27 (1999).

[42]   The DSU says nothing about assistance by the Secretariat to the Appellate Body. There was some concern that the same persons who had assisted a panel might be called on to assist the Appellate Body when the panel's decision was appealed. In the event, the WTO established a separate office, headed by a senior legal officer, to assist the Appellate Body, so that there could be no suggestion that those who had worked on a panel report might have a role in defending the report on appeal.

[43]   See Ch. 7, Sect. 7.3(c) at nn. 28–31.

(i) For instance, suppose Xandia imposes a countervailing duty on product *X* imported from Patria, on the basis that Patria has bestowed an illegal or 'actionable' subsidy on the production or export of that product. Patria brings a complaint before a WTO panel challenging the imposition of the duty by Xandia, contending that the subsidy is not actionable, because it qualifies for the exemption stated in Article 8.2 of the Agreement on subsidies for assistance to comply with environmental regulations.[44] Xandia should be permitted to bring a counter-complaint before the same panel seeking a declaration that the Patrian subsidy for product *X* does not qualify for the environmental exception or exceeds the amount immunized by Article 8.2

The advantages of consolidation, including avoidance of the possibility of inconsistent outcomes, outweigh the dangers of delay inherent in permitting counter-complaints.

(ii) Alternatively, suppose Patria brings a complaint before a WTO panel challenging imposition of a countervailing duty on product *X* as in case (i); now Xandia wants to put before the same panel the assertion that Patria has imposed a countervailing duty on product *Y* under similar circumstances, contending that the pot should not be permitted to call the kettle black. In this case Xandia's complaint should be required to stand on its own (or not at all).

Case (ii) involves different factual situations, and it should be no defense to Patria's complaint that Patria has adopted a similar measure or even that 'everybody does it'.

(b) Participation by Third Parties

Third parties may have two kinds of interests in a dispute between Patria and Xandia brought to the WTO. A restriction by Xandia challenged by Patria may also impair the opportunity of producers in Tertia to compete in the Xandian market. If Tertia now brings a complaint challenging the same restriction, that complaint may be joined to the complaint of Patria in a single proceeding. Article 9 of the Understanding states that a single panel should be established to examine such complaints whenever possible, as in fact was done in the first case to come before the WTO.[45] Venezuela challenged as discriminatory a United States regulation on reformulated gasoline, Brazil brought a similar complaint three months later, and the two complaints were consolidated by the Dispute Settlement Body with the agreement of the parties. The consolidation of the two complaints and separate submissions on behalf of Brazil led to a delay of some three months in

---

[44] See Ch. 9, Sect. 9.6(b).
[45] *United States—Standards for Reformulated and Conventional Gasoline*, Sect. 8.3 n. 36 supra.

the issuance of the final report of the panel, but otherwise did not unduly complicate the proceeding.

A different situation is presented when Tertia has an interest in an issue presented in a case brought by Patria against Xandia, but does not have a major trade interest in the subject of the complaint. Tertia may want to add its voice and arguments to the challenge to the measures being implemented by Xandia. Alternatively, Tertia may have legislation or regulations in effect similar to those being challenged, and may wish either to present its own defense to the challenge or to put on record why its regulation is distinguishable from the restriction being challenged. Article 10 of the Understanding provides that in both cases a non-party shall have an opportunity to be heard by the panel and to make written submissions at the first meeting with the panel. Generally third parties will not participate in subsequent exchanges of written submissions or hearings, but their interests are to be 'fully taken into account' during the panel process. Third parties cannot appeal a panel report, but if they participated as third parties in the panel proceeding, they may make written submissions to the Appellate Body and be given the opportunity to make an oral presentation as well.[46]

8.6   DISPUTE SETTLEMENT AND THE DEVELOPING COUNTRIES[47]

Like most of the agreements adopted in the Uruguay Round—and indeed in the GATT from the mid-1960s on—the Understanding on Dispute Settlement contains several provisions directed to developing countries. Emphasis on the interests of the developing countries was important for the architects of the Uruguay Round not only in the context of achieving support for the large package of agreements, but also in the context of an effort to bring the developing countries to believe that the WTO is indeed a universal organization, not merely a forum for the United States and the European Community to air out their disputes.[48]

---

[46] In the *Reformulated Gasoline* case, n. 45 supra, the European Community and Norway took advantage of Article 10, and made presentations both to the panel and to the Appellate Body, generally in support of the position of Venezuela and Brazil, but with some differences in approach. Thus in that case, the first to be completed under the WTO dispute system, five separate submissions were made to the panel and to the Appellate Body.

[47] For a summary as of spring 2000 of the participation of the developing countries in appeals under the DSU by the first chairman of the Appellate Body, see Julio Lacarte-Muró and Petina Gapah, 'Developing Countries and the WTO Legal and Dispute Settlement System: A View from the Bench', 3 *J. Int'l Econ. L.* 395 (2000). The article reports that of 28 appeals heard by the Appellate Body up to April 2000, 18 involved a developing country as appellant or appellee, and 25 different developing countries had appeared as third participants. Brazil and India had each participated in five appeals, and Argentina, Guatemala, Korea, and Mexico had participated in two appeals each.

[48] Professor Hudec, in surveying the use of dispute settlement in GATT in the period 1948–89 found that 73 percent of all complaints were filed by the United States, the European Community and its members, Canada, and Australia. Adding in Japan the Scandinavian countries, Austria,

The Understanding takes special notice of the interests of developing countries in several articles. The provision on consultations states that Members should give 'special attention' to the problems and interests of developing country Members (Art. 4(10)). The provision on composition of panels states that if one party to a dispute is a developing country, that country is entitled to have at least one panelist who comes from a developing country (Art. 8(10)). Further, if a complaint is brought against a developing country, the time for consultations (i.e. before a panel is convened) may be extended, and if the dispute goes before a panel, the deadlines for the developing country to make its submissions may be relaxed (Art. 12(10)). Also, the Secretariat is authorized to make a qualified legal expert available to any developing country on request. Formal complaints against least developed countries are discouraged, and if consultations fail, the Director-General and the Chairman of the DSB stand ready to offer their good offices before a formal request for a panel is made (Art. 24). In the *Bananas* case discussed in Section 8.8(d), the issue was raised whether a member state could employ outside counsel to represent it before the WTO. The panel had declined to admit private counsel because the disputes were state to state disputes and no provision for outside counsel appeared in the DSU, but the Appellate Body reversed, on the basis that some developing states could not afford to retain full-time trade experts, and would be aided by the assistance of private counsel.[49]

As to substance, the Understanding provides that the report of panels shall 'explicitly indicate' how account has been taken of the 'differential and more favourable treatment' provisions of the agreement under which the complaint is brought (Art. 12(11)). Whether or not a developing country is a party to a particular proceeding, 'particular attention' is to be paid to the interests of developing countries in the course of implementing recommendations and rulings of panels. It is not clear how this injunction would be carried out if a panel recommended elimination of a preference from which some developing countries were beneficiaries and others claimed injury. An illustration of this problem is the continuing controversy over the European Community's policy on import of bananas, which granted preferential treatment to former colonies in Africa and the Caribbean, at the expense of Central American countries, supported by the United States, as described in Section 8.8(d). But at a minimum, the inference is that, as in other areas of the WTO system, MFN treatment is not the only consideration when developing country interests are at stake.

and South Africa would bring the total to over 80 percent. Focusing on defendants, the United States, European Community and is members, Canada, and Japan accounted for 83 percent of the cases filed, and adding in other developed countries would bring the figure to over 90 percent. Over 90 percent of the cases involved either the United States or the European Community and its members as at least one party. See Robert E. Hudec, *Enforcing International Trade Law*, 295–300.

[49] *European Communities—Regime for the Importation, Sale and Distribution of Bananas*, WT/DS27/AB/R, 9 Sept. 1997, paras. 10–12.

8.7   Nullification and Impairment

As pointed out throughout this Part, the dispute system elaborated in the Understanding on Dispute Settlement is founded on Articles XXII and XXIII of the GATT. According to Article XXIII(1), entitled 'Nullification or Impairment', the dispute settlement process may be invoked if any party should consider that any benefit accruing to it under the General Agreement [and now by extension under any covered agreement] (i) 'is being nullified or impaired,' or (ii) that 'any objective of the Agreement is being impeded as the result of

(a)   the failure of another contracting party to carry out its obligations under this Agreement, or

(b)   the application by another contracting party of any measure, *whether or not it conflicts with the provisions of this Agreement,* or

(c)   *the existence of any other situation.*' (italics added)

Category (c)—'any other situation' appears to have been included in the disputes article of the GATT as a kind of macroeconomic safety valve, in case a state was overwhelmed by massive unemployment or depression. While references to Article XXIII(1)(c) were raised from time to time in the course of controversies brought to the GATT,[50] no panel ever issued a decision based on that provision, and it would seem to have no place in the much more rule-oriented system of the World Trade Organization than existed when the GATT was being drafted in the 1940s.[51]

(a)   Violation Complaints

The great majority of complaints brought to GATT dispute settlement in the past have been complaints coming under Article XXIII(1)(a), that is, complaints alleging failure by the respondent state (or group of states) to carry out an obligation in the GATT or one of the associated agreements.

The GATT, and most of the other agreements within the WTO system, as previously noted, are based on redress of injury and restoration of the balance presumed to be achieved in the various negotiating rounds. But the Agreed Description of the Customary Practice of the GATT in the Field of Dispute Settlement that came out of the Tokyo Round in 1979 confirmed that a breach of the applicable rules by the respondent state will be presumed to have an adverse impact on the complainant state,[52] and in slightly modified

---

[50] See *Analytical Index of the GATT*, Art. XXIII, Vol. 2, pp. 668–71 (6th edn. revd. 1995).

[51] This point is made also by Ernst-Ulrich Petersmann, 'Violation Complaints and Non-Violation Complaints in Public International Trade Law', 34 *German YB Int'l Law* 175 at 227 (1991).

[52] GATT, BISD, 26th Supp. 210 at 216, Annex para. 5. See Ch. 7, Sect. 7.3(c) at n. 34.

form this presumption is stated in Article 3(8) of the Understanding on Dispute Settlement as a governing norm:

In cases where there is an infringement of the obligations assumed under a covered agreement, the action is considered *prima facie* to constitute a case of nullification or impairment. This means that there is normally a presumption that a breach of the rules has an adverse impact on other Members parties to that covered agreement, and in such cases, it shall be up to the Member against whom the complaint has been brought to rebut the charge.

Read literally, this statement suggests that a party found to have been in breach may still contend that the challenged trade restriction did not adversely affect the complainant state, or did so only to an insignificant extent. But GATT panels have not been prepared to condone measures found to be inconsistent with the General Agreement. The issue of the trade effect would become relevant in connection with establishing the level of compensation due if the offending member did not withdraw the challenged measure or practice. In a Report issued in 1987 on *United States Taxes on Petroleum and Certain Imported Substances*, the Panel reviewed prior cases in which the defendant state contended that it should be able to avoid condemnation if it could establish that no significant harm had occurred to the complainant:

The Panel noted that such claims had been made in a number of cases but that there was no case in the history of the GATT in which a contracting party had successfully rebutted the presumption that a measure infringing obligations causes nullification or impairment . . .
[W]hile the CONTRACTING PARTIES had not explicitly decided whether the presumption that illegal measures cause nullification or impairment could be rebutted, the presumption had in practice operated as an irrefutable presumption.[53]

(b) Non-Violation Complaints

In addition to complaints based on measures asserted to be inconsistent with a covered agreement, the WTO dispute system recognizes a kind of no-fault complaint based on GATT Article XXIII(1)(b) quoted above. The draft of Article XXIII(1)(b), as Professor Hudec has pointed out, was 'essentially a stop-action photograph of a provision still very much in flux',[54] reflecting, imperfectly, some of the same concerns, in 1947–8, as resulted in the escape clause, Article XIX, and the open season clause, Article XXVIII(1). 'You never can tell what might happen', and it would be wise not to foreclose relief from unforeseen events. The idea was that if Patria and Xandia agree

---

[53] GATT BISD, 34th Supp. p. 136 at 155, paras. 5.1.6, 5.1.7 (1988); Pescatore, *Handbook*, Case 62.
[54] Robert E. Hudec, 'Retaliation against "Unreasonable" Foreign Trade Practices: The New Section 301 and GATT Nullification and Impairment', 59 *Minnesota L. Rev.* (1975) 461 at 479. The negotiating history is told at 466–81. See also Ernst-Ulrich Petersmann, *The GATT/WTO Dispute Settlement System*, 142–7 (1996).

on an exchange of concessions—typically (but not necessarily) tariff bindings—and then Patria adopts a measure that changes the market conditions for Xandia's products in Patria that Xandia was justified in counting on, Xandia could apply to the CONTRACTING PARTIES—now to a WTO Dispute Settlement panel—for authorization to restore the expected balance of concessions. If Xandia proves that a benefit accruing to it under a covered agreement is being nullified or impaired by a measure of Patria but that measure is not itself a violation of the GATT or a covered agreement, there is no obligation on Patria to withdraw the challenged measure, but Article 26 of the Understanding states that the panel or the Appellate Body 'shall recommend that the Member concerned make a mutually satisfactory adjustment.'

The jurisprudence of non-violation complaints is sparse—only 14 such complaints were brought in the period 1948–94, and of these only four led to adoption by the CONTRACTING PARTIES of panel reports finding that benefits that the complainant could reasonably expect to accrue to it under agreed tariff concessions had been nullified or impaired by unforeseen trade measures that did not themselves violate the GATT.[55] The 'leading case' of non-violation complaint was the *Australian Subsidy* case,[56] brought early in the history of the GATT by Chile against Australia:

During World War II, Australia had granted a subsidy to distributors of nitrate fertilizers, to make up for wartime price controls on sales to Australian farmers. The subsidy supported purchases both of sodium nitrate fertilizers produced in Chile, and of ammonium sulphate fertilizers produced primarily in Australia. In 1947 Australia granted a tariff concession on sodium nitrate fertilizer to Chile, while the subsidy on purchase of both fertilizers remained in effect. In 1949 Australia repealed the subsidy on purchase of sodium nitrate fertilizer, but retained the subsidy on purchase of ammonium sulphate fertilizer. There was no breach of the concession, because the duty on the imported product had not been changed, but the effect of the repeal of the subsidy was a 25 percent price advantage for the local as compared to the Chilean product.

Chile contended that this change in the competitive conditions of the two products nullified or impaired the benefit of the concession that had previously been granted to it, and the working party agreed. Though Australia had no obligation to subsidize either type of fertilizer, and thus had not breached a GATT obligation, Chile could not reasonably have anticipated the action by the Australian government upsetting the competitive relationship between the two products. Accordingly, the Working Party recommended, and the Contracting Parties agreed, that Australia should correct the competitive inequality resulting from removal of its subsidy on one product but not on the other.[57]

---

[55] See Petersmann (n. 54 supra), 150–70.

[56] *Australian Subsidy on Ammonium Sulphate*, GATT BISD, Vol. 2, p. 188 (1952), Report of working party adopted 3 Apr. 1950; Pestcatore, *Handbook*, Case 5. The case is discussed in detail in Hudec, *The GATT Legal System and World Trade Diplomacy*, ch. 14 (2nd edn., 1990).

[57] This was the same case as discussed in Ch. 7, Sect. 7(3)(a), at n. 20, in which the working party practice evolved into third party adjudication. The report was prepared by the three neutral members of the working party—representatives of the United States, the United Kingdom, and Norway.

A more recent case that had a major impact on negotiations in the Uruguay Round[58] was the *Oilseeds* case brought by the United States against the European Community in the late 1980s, stimulated initially by a Section 301 proceeding initiated by American growers of soybeans.[59]

The European Community had given a zero-tariff binding on soybeans in 1962 in the closing days of the Dillon Round, as the EEC Common Agricultural Policy was just beginning to be implemented. The Community did not reinstate a tariff, but it introduced a system of payments to crushing mills within the Common Market when they used oil seeds of EC origin, but not when they used imported oil seeds. The United States raised a violation complaint—i.e., that these payments violated GATT Article III(4), the national treatment provision, and also a non-violation complaint, asserting that when the concession was negotiated, the United States could not have anticipated the introduction of a subsidy that protected the Community producers from the movement of prices for imports, and therefore nullified the benefits accruing to the United States in respect of the tariff binding. The panel found for the United States on both grounds, holding that even if the subsidy itself were not GATT-illegal, it would still constitute a nonviolation nullification and impairment of the tariff binding.

The focus on reasonable anticipation established in the *Australian Subsidy* case and confirmed in the *Oilseeds* case does not appear in the text of Article XXIII and it does not appear in Article 26 of the Understanding on Dispute Settlement. But it is generally understood—and has been stated in most of the other non-violation cases—that reasonable anticipation, justifiable expectation, or unforeseen circumstances must be shown before a non-violation complaint can be successfully pursued. In contrast to a violation complaint where once an infringement of a covered agreement is shown, the action is considered prima facie to constitute a case of nullification or impairment (Understanding Art. 3(8)), a case in which no infringement of an obligation is shown requires the complaining party to present a *detailed justification*, which generally would require demonstration not only of a loss in trade but of a justified reliance on the non-occurrence of an event that did in fact occur by decision of the defendant government.[60]

---

[58] See Ch. 4, Sect. 4.4(b), n. 60, describing what were expected to be the concluding negotiations about agriculture between the United States and the European Community.

[59] *EEC—Payments and Subsidies Paid to Processors and Producers of Oilseeds and Related Animal-Feed Proteins (United States v. EEC)* (adopted January 25, 1990), GATT BISD, 37th Supp. 86 (1991). The background and follow-up of the case, including a second panel report, are discussed in Robert E. Hudec, *Enforcing Trade Law*, 245–9 and appendix 558–61 (1993). See also GATT *Analytical Index*, Art. XXIII, vol. 2 pp. 659–60 (6th edn. rev. 1995).

[60] As described in Sect. 8.8(b) infra, in June 1996, the US government filed a massive complaint in the WTO against Japan, as the result of an investigation under section 301 of the U.S. Trade Act initiated by Eastman Kodak. In part, the complaint against Japan alleged infringement of obligations under covered agreements, notably the requirement of national treatment under Article III(4) of the GATT. The complaint also alleged nullification and impairment as a result of various alleged anticompetitive practices on the part of Fujifilm tolerated or encouraged, according to the United States, by the government of Japan. Absent an international agreement on competition law, the acts or omissions by the Japanese government could not be

8.8 THE UNDERSTANDING ON DISPUTE SETTLEMENT AND
UNILATERAL ACTION: HEREIN OF SECTION 301 AND THE
BANANAS DISPUTE

(a) The Uruguay Round Bargain

As noted in the preceding chapter,[61] a major impetus to the WTO dispute system as it emerged from the Uruguay Round was the use, or threat of use, by the United States of trade sanctions designed to persuade other countries to abandon practices that the United States regarded as (a) denials of its rights under trade agreements, including the GATT; or (b) other unjustifiable acts, policies or practices that 'burden or restrict United States commerce'. What came to be known as the §301 remedy actually consisted of a number of sections of US trade legislation, originally adopted in 1974 and expanded several times thereafter.[62] Section 301 had (and continues to have) two aspects. (1) An interested person—typically an exporter that asserts its opportunities in Patria have been impaired[63]—may submit a petition to the US Trade Representative calling for an investigation and eventually, if the problem is not satisfactorily resolved, for implementation of a sanction or other trade remedy against Patria;[64] (2) the Trade Representative is author-ized, after an investigation and subject to various conditions, to suspend or withdraw the application of trade agreement concessions to the foreign coun-try in question; impose duties or other import restrictions on that country; enter into agreements to eliminate or phase out the offending practice; or submit the issue to international dispute settlement.

The argument made in the United States in support of §301 had two parts. On the one hand, the proponents of §301—always a controversial statute—contended that the requirements of the GATT (as well as of bilateral agree-ments) were not being effectively enforced, even when dispute panels had

said to infringe a covered agreement, and thus could be considered only in the context of a non-violation complaint. To some extent, such practices, referred to generally as *keiretsu*, have been common in Japan for many years. To prevail on this aspect of the complaint, the United States would have had to show not only injury as a result of the anti-competitive practices but that it was justified in expecting, when it negotiated a tariff binding on photographic film, that these practices would not be applied (or would be phased out) in connection with marketing of film. In the event, the claim was dismissed by the panel and the case was not appealed.

[61] See Ch. 7, Sect. 7.4(b).

[62] Trade Act of 1974 §§301–10, 19 U.S.C. §§2411–20, amended in 1979, 1984, and 1988. Further amendments were adopted in 1994 as part of the Uruguay Round Agreements Act, 103 Pub. L. 465, §314, 108 Stat. 4809, 4939 (8 Dec. 1994), and again in 1996 and 2000.

[63] Section 301 applications are not limited to exporters; domestic producers claiming injury from an unjustified foreign practice such as 'export targeting' or employment of child labour also have standing to bring a §301 petition, as do persons asserting impairment of rights to intellectual property.

[64] §302(a), 19 U.S.C. §2412(a). §302(b) provides that the Trade Representative may also initiate an investigation without a petition, upon consultation with the relevant private sector advisory committee.

rendered reports condemning practices challenged by the United States, and even when those reports had been approved by the GATT Council. On the other hand, as the proponents contended, numerous aspects of fair conduct of international trade—notably in the field of protection of intellectual property—were not covered by the GATT at all, and these gaps in the international law of international trade permitted and justified action by the United States on its own. In the Uruguay Round, as seen throughout this and the preceding chapters, both concerns were mitigated to a considerable extent: (i) The dispute system was made much tighter, with short timetables, elimination of vetoes at the critical stages, and provisions for enforcement; (ii) The scope of the international legal system within the orbit of the WTO was greatly expanded, to include intellectual property, services, trade-related aspects of international investment, and other subjects, and to require all member states to adhere to almost all of the agreements. In return, as pointed out in Section 8.1(e), Article 23 of the Understanding on Dispute Settlement commits Members that seek redress of violations of obligations or of impairment of benefits under the covered agreements to have recourse to and abide by the rules and procedures of the Understanding. Thus, although Section 301 remains on the books, the adoption of the Uruguay Round agreements and establishment of the WTO reduce substantially the justification for unilateral trade remedies, and also increase the downside risk for the United States (or other countries considering emulation of Section 301) from imposing an unauthorized sanction which would itself violate a covered agreement.

(b) Section 301 after the Uruguay Round[65]

The provision of Section 301[66] that gives standing to private interested persons to initiate formal investigations into trade practices or policies of a foreign country was not directly affected by the Uruguay Round agreements.[67]

---

[65] For a useful discussion by the former General Counsel to the US Trade Representative and the former Deputy US Trade Representative, written before the Uruguay Round was completed but after issuance of the 'Dunkel Draft' of December 1991 which contained an almost final version of the Understanding on Dispute Settlement, see Judith H. Bello and Alan F. Holmer, 'GATT Dispute Settlement Agreement: Internationalization or Elimination of Section 301?', 26 *Int'l Lawyer* 795 (1992).

[66] Actually §302 of the Trade Act of 1974 as amended, 19 U.S.C. §2412.

[67] The European Community adopted a comparable regulation in 1984, enabling 'any natural or legal person . . . acting on behalf of a Community industry which considers that it has suffered injury' to petition the European Commission to undertake an examination looking to respond to illicit commercial practices of other States and to insure 'full exercise of the Community's rights', including consultations or initiation of dispute settlement procedures. EC Council Regulation (EEC) 2641/84 of 17 Sept. 1984 on the *Strengthening of the Common Commercial Policy with Regard in Particular to Protection against Illicit Commercial Practices*, O.J. L/252/1 (20 Sept. 1984). It was pursuant to a proceeding brought under this regulation that, for instance, the EC brought the complaint against §337 of the United States Tariff Act, s. 7.4(a), n. 4. In implementation of the Uruguay Round, the Community adopted a revised regulation, EC Council Regulation 3286/94 of 22 Dec. 1994, O.J. L 349/71 (31 Dec. 1994) as the vehicle to initiate dispute settlement in the WTO.

How a government relates to non-governmental persons within its own territory is generally not the subject of international concern. The US Trade Representative is still required to decide within 45 days of receipt of the petition whether to launch an investigation;[68] if an investigation is initiated, the Trade Representative is required to hold consultations with the foreign country concerned, and if appropriate, to initiate dispute settlement proceedings, all within specific deadlines. If the Trade Representative determines that a foreign government has violated a trade agreement, he/she must take responsive action unless a statutory exception applies. The most important exception *requires* the Trade Representative to initiate a dispute settlement proceeding if one is available,[69] and provides that the Trade Representative *is not required* to take retaliatory action (a) if the DSB has determined that the challenged measure did not violate the GATT or another agreement, or (b) if the Trade Representative finds that the foreign country is taking satisfactory measures to comply with the recommendation and rulings of the DSB.[70] Section 301 does not preclude retaliatory sanctions even if a WTO panel has exonerated the practice or policy of the foreign country. In fact, however, no foreign measure has ever been declared by the US Trade Representative to be unfair within the meaning of section 301 when a panel determined it to be fair, and it is highly unlikely that such a finding would ever be made, since it would put the United States in direct violation of the Understanding on Dispute Settlement and expose it to an adverse finding in a dispute settlement proceeding initiated by the other country in question.[71]

The effect of the DSU on response by the United States government to complaints from a major American industry was illustrated in a highly publicized dispute with Japan, concerning sale of consumer photographic products in Japan:

In May 1995, one of the United States' largest companies, Eastman Kodak, submitted a petition under section 301 asserting that its rights in the Japanese market to sell photographic film were being impaired by *inter alia*, toleration (and perhaps encouragement) by the Japanese government of anti-competitive practices on the part of the dominant supplier, Fujifilm. Kodak's petition requested direct action by the United States on the basis that available international remedies were unlikely to provide the necessary relief.

The US Trade Representative did launch an intensive investigation,[72] and determined that certain acts of the Government of Japan with respect to the sale of consumer

---

[68] If the answer is 'no', the Trade Representative must follow various requirements for notification of the parties, publication in the Federal Register, and public hearings.

[69] Trade Act of 1974 as amended, §303(a)(2), 19 U.S.C. §2413(a)(2).

[70] Id. §301(a)(2), 19 U.S.C. §2411(a)(2).

[71] See the excerpt from the US Government Statement of Administrative Action quoted in Sect. 8.8(c) at n. 91.

[72] USTR: *Initiation of Investigation pursuant to Section 302 Concerning Barriers to Access to the Japanese Market for Consumer Photographic Film and Paper*, 60 Fed. Reg. 35447 (7 July 1995).

photographic film are 'unreasonable and burden or restrict US commerce'. But rather than implementing sanctions as requested by Kodak, i.e., taking unilateral action, the United States government announced that it would invoke the dispute settlement procedures of the WTO with respect to the challenged measures of the government of Japan making both violation and non-violation complaints.[73] A panel was duly convened, and after lengthy hearings and voluminous submissions, it prepared a report of almost 500 pages plus various annexes.

From the point of view of Kodak, the case was a failure, as the panel eventually concluded that the United States had established neither its violation nor its non-violation claims.[74] From the point of view of development of dispute settlement of economic issues, however, the *Kodak–Fuji* case illustrates the success of the DSU in inducing the state parties—and particularly the United States—to move away from a unilateral to a multilateral approach to resolution of trade controversies. If the United States government had acted on its own to impose sanctions against Japan, as its domestic law arguably authorized, it would have severely undermined the Uruguay Round bargain concerning dispute settlement, and Japan, doubtless supported by a large number of other member states, could have brought a proceeding against the United States, asserting not only violation of whatever articles might have been violated by the sanctions imposed—e.g. Article I (non-discrimination), Article II (tariff binding), Article III (national treatment), Article XI (quantitative restrictions)—but also violation of Article 3 and Article 23 of the Understanding on Dispute Settlement.

(c)   Section 301 on Trial

The United States was not required by the Uruguay Round agreements to repeal §301, and, as noted, it did not do so.[75] Not only could its mechanism, including unilateral retaliation, continue to be employed vis-à-vis any nonmember of the WTO.[76] Section 301 would also provide the domestic authority to take retaliatory measures in the situations contemplated by the DSU, in case a Respondent failed to comply with the recommendations and rulings of a panel or the DSU within a reasonable period.[77]

Section 304 directs the US Trade Representative to make the determination whether any rights to which the United States is entitled under any trade

---

[73] USTR: *Section 304 Determinations: Barriers to Access to the Japanese Market for Consumer Photographic Film and Paper*, 61 Fed. Reg. 30929 (18 June 1996).

[74] *Japan—Measures Affecting Consumer Photographic Film and Paper (United States v. Japan)*, Panel Report WT/DS44/R (31 Mar. 1998, adopted by DSB 22 Apr. 1998).

[75] Section 314 of the Uruguay Round Agreements Act, 103 Pub. L. 465, 8 Dec. 1994, did make some conforming amendments to section 301, primarily directed to adoption in the WTO system of the Agreement on Trade Related Intellectual Property Rights (TRIPs).

[76] Notably, at the time the Uruguay Round Agreements Act was before the US Congress, Russia, China, and Taiwan, also Saudi Arabia, Iran, and Iraq.

[77] See Sect. 8.1(d) supra.

agreement are being denied, and if so, what action if any to take by way of retaliation. Further, §304 directs the Trade Representative to make the required determination by a date 30 days after the date in which dispute settlement procedure is concluded, or 18 months after the domestic investigation was initiated, whichever is earlier.[78] It seems that the deadlines established in the DSU were set with the US calendar in mind[79]—(i) two months for consultation (Art. 5(4)); (ii) six months for proceedings before the panel (Art. 12(9)); (iii) two months for review by the Appellate Body (Art. 17(5)); (iv) one month for adoption of the Report (Art 17(14));[80] one month for the Respondent to announce its intentions concerning implementation of the recommendations in the Report (Art. 21(3))—total 12 months, plus whatever time was taken by the Trade Representative in his/her investigation before resorting to the DSU—say another three months. If everything went according to schedule and there were no extensions, it would be a tight fit, but the US Trade Representative might be authorized to wait for conclusion of the dispute settlement process before making a decision on retaliation. But step (ii) could be extended by three months, step (iii) by one month, and already the deadline for action—unilateral action—would have been passed, without any of the post-adjudication steps having been taken: (v) decision of what is a reasonable period for compliance—arbitration within 90 days (Art. 21(3)(c)); (vi) a 'reasonable period' for compliance—up to 15 months from adoption of the Report (Art. 21(4)); (vii) referral to arbitration of disagreement about consistency of a proposal for compliance with the WTO agreements and the Report—three months from referral (Art. 21(5)); and arbitration of a dispute about the level of compensation or retaliation—60 days after expiry of the reasonable period (Art. 22(6)).

Did this mean that the United States law was on its face contrary to the Understanding on Disputes Settlement, and a sword hanging over any state considering how to respond to an unfavourable report in a case brought by the United States? The European Community thought so, and in February 1999, even as the *Bananas* case described below was becoming increasingly acrimonious, it brought a complaint before the DSU, claiming that sections 301–10, and particularly §304(a) and §306(b),[81] are inconsistent with Article 23(2)(a) of the DSU, in that they require the US Trade Representative

---

[78] Trade Act of 1974 as amended, §304(a)(2), 19 U.S.C. §3414(a)(2).

[79] See Terence P. Stewart (ed.), *The GATT Uruguay Round: A Negotiating History*, Vol. II, pp. 2761–2, 2795 (1993); Pieter-Jan Kuyper, 'The New WTO Dispute Settlement System: The Impact on the Community', in Bourgeois, Berrod, and Fournier (eds.), *The Uruguay Round Results: A European Lawyers' Perspective*, p. 87 at 89–90 (1995).

[80] Assuming there has been an appeal. If no appeal is taken, two months are saved, but one month is added to the period for adoption of the Report by the DSB.

[81] §306(b) provides for determination by the US Trade Representative within 30 days of the expiry of the 'reasonable period' whether a country that has entered into an agreement to provide satisfactory resolution to a dispute settlement proceeding is implementing the agreement, and what further action the Trade Representative should take by way of retaliation.

to take retaliatory action irrespective of whether the procedures set forth in the DSU have been completed.[82]

Article 23, entitled 'Strengthening the Multilateral System,' reads:

1. When Members seek the redress of a violation of obligations or other nullification or impairment of benefits under the covered agreements or an impediment to the attainment of any objective of the covered agreements, they shall have recourse to, and abide by, the rules and procedures of this Understanding.
2. In such cases, Members shall:
   (a) not make a determination to the effect that a violation has occurred, that benefits have been nullified or impaired or that the attainment of any objective of the covered agreements has been impeded, except through recourse to dispute settlement in accordance with the rules and procedures of this Understanding, and shall make any such determination consistent with the findings contained in the panel or Appellate Body report adopted by the DSB or an arbitration award rendered under this Understanding;
   (b) follow the procedures set forth in Article 21 to determine the reasonable period of time for the Member concerned to implement the recommendations and rulings; and
   (c) follow the procedures set forth in Article 22 to determine the level of suspension of concessions or other obligations and obtain DSB authorization in accordance with those procedures before suspending concessions or other obligations under the covered agreements in response to the failure of the Member concerned to implement the recommendations and rulings within that reasonable period of time.

Without referring to any specific case, the European Community contended that the scheme of section 301, and in particular the sections mentioned, were inconsistent with Article 23. Even if no specific instance of inconsistent behaviour had yet taken place, and even if sections 301–10 could be interpreted as leaving discretion in the US Trade Representative to comply with the WTO obligations of the United States, they cannot be regarded, the EC asserted, as a "sound legal basis" for the implementation of the US obligations. 'The lack of this "sound legal basis" produces a situation of threat and legal uncertainty against other WTO Members and their economic operators that fundamentally undermines the "security and predictability" of the multilateral trading system.'[83]

---

[82] *United States—Sections 301–310 of the Trade Act of 1974, (The European Communities v. United States)*, WTO/DS152/R, decided 22 Dec. 1999 [hereafter *Section 301* case].

[83] *Section 301* case, para. 4.35(b). The corresponding provision in the regulation of the European Community, n. 67 supra, reads:

> Where the Community's international obligations require the prior discharge of an international procedure for consultation or for the settlement of disputes, the measures [of retaliation] shall only be decided on after that procedure has been terminated, and taking account of the results of the procedure. In particular, where the Community has requested an international dispute settlement body to indicate and authorize the measures which are appropriate for the implementation of the results of an international dispute settlement

The United States, in reply, pointed out that §304 required the Trade Representative to determine *whether*—not *that*—the rights to which the United States is entitled . . . are being denied, which left open the possibility that the determination might be that these rights had not been violated, or that the issue remained open pending completion of the DSB procedures.

The complaint raised an interesting legal issue, and also a delicate political one, since the US Congress had been assured, when considering the Uruguay Round agreements, that there would be no diminution of the section 301 mechanism.[84] The panel itself wrote 'The political sensitivity of this case is self-evident,' pointing out that twelve of the sixteen third parties had expressed highly critical views of the legislation.[85] For its part, the United States said 'the EC has brought a political case that is in search of a legal argument.'[86] But the panel wrote that its function was judicial, 'to make an objective assessment of the facts of the case and the applicability of and conformity with the covered agreements' (quoting DSU Article 11).[87]

The panel came out with an interesting solution that seems to have left all sides satisfied, at least for a time. First, the panel said, §304 constitutes a prima facie violation of DSU rules and procedures, in that it explicitly allows the US administration to breach the mutual promise embodied in Article 23 not to make unilateral determinations of inconsistency with a covered agreement prior to exhaustion of DSU proceedings.[88] To the US defense that §304 merely *authorizes*, and does not *mandate* action inconsistent with WTO obligations, the panel replied:

[T]he very discretion granted under Section 304, which under the US argument absolves the legislation, is what, in our eyes, creates the presumptive violation. The statutory language which gives the USTR this discretion on its face precludes the US from abiding by its obligations under the WTO. In each and every case when a determination is made whilst DSU proceedings are not yet exhausted, Members locked in a dispute with the US will be subject to a mandatory determination by the USTR under a statute which explicitly puts them in that very danger which Article 23 was intended to remove.[89]

procedure, the Community commercial policy measures which may be needed in consequence of such authorization shall be in accordance with the recommendation of such international dispute settlement body. (EC Reg. 3286/94 Art. 12(2))

[84] §102(a)(2)(B) of the Uruguay Round Agreements Act, 19 U.S.C. §3512(a)(2)(B), states:

Nothing in this Act shall be construed . . . to limit any authority conferred under any law of the United States, including section 301 of the Trade Act of 1974.

The Statement of Administrative Action prepared by the Administration in connection with consideration of the Uruguay Round Agreements by the Congress, added:

The Administration expects that as a result of the Uruguay Round agreements in general, and the Dispute Settlement Understanding in particular, section 301 will be even more effective than it has been in the past in addressing foreign unfair trade barriers. (House Doc. 103–316, 364, 103d Cong., 2d Sess., 27 Sept. 1994)

[85] *Section 301* case, para. 7.11.   [86] Id. para. 7.9.   [87] Id. para. 7.12.
[88] Id. paras. 7.56–7.63.   [89] Id. para 7.61.

Having made this point, however, the panel changed course, on the basis that the prima facie violation had in fact been removed by the Statement of Administrative Action (SAA) that accompanied the submission to Congress of the legislation approving and implementing the Uruguay Round Agreements.[90] The panel quoted the following excerpt from the SAA, and accepted the assurance by the US representatives that this reflected official United States policy:

Although it will enhance the effectiveness of section 301, the DSU does not require any significant change in section 301 *for investigations that involve an alleged violation of a Uruguay Round agreement or the impairment of US benefits under such an agreement.* In such cases, *the Trade Representative will:*

- invoke DSU dispute settlement procedures, as required under current law;
- base any section 301 determination that there has been a violation or denial of U.S. rights under the relevant agreement on the panel or Appellate Body findings adopted by the DSB;
- following adoption of a favorable panel or Appellate Body report, allow the defending party a reasonable period of time to implement the report's recommendations; and
- if the matter cannot be resolved during that period, seek authority from the DSB to retaliate (emphasis added [by the panel]).[91]

The panel wrote that '[i]n response to our very insistent questions, the US explicitly, officially, repeatedly and unconditionally confirmed the commitment expressed in the SAA namely that the USTR would "base any section 301 determination that there has been a violation or denial of US rights under the relevant agreement on the panel or Appellate Body findings adopted by the DSB."' Accordingly, the panel concluded:

[W]e find that these statements by the US express the unambiguous and official position of the US representing, in a manner that can be relied upon by all Members, an undertaking that the discretion of the USTR has been limited so as to prevent a determination of inconsistency before exhaustion of DSU proceedings. Although this representation does not create a new international legal obligation for the US—after all the US was already bound by Article 23 in becoming a WTO Member—it clarifies and gives an undertaking, at an international level, concerning aspects of domestic US law, in particular, the way the US has implemented its obligations under Article 23.2(a) of the DSU.

The aggregate effect of the SAA and the US statements made to us is to provide the guarantees, both direct to other Members and indirect to the market place, that Article 23 is intended to secure. . . . [I]t is now clear that under Section 304 . . . the US is precluded from making a determination of inconsistency contrary to Article 23.2(a). As a matter of international law, the effect of the US undertakings is to anticipate, or discharge, any would-be State responsibility that could have arisen had the national law under consideration in this case consisted of nothing more than the

---

[90] See n. 84 supra.
[91] *Section 301* case, para. 7.112, quoting from SAA 365–6, n. 84 supra.

statutory language. It of course follows that should the US repudiate or remove in any way these undertakings, the US would incur State responsibility since its law would be rendered inconsistent with the obligations under Article 23.[92]

Both sides asserted that they had won, and the panel report was adopted without recourse to the Appellate Body. When the report was adopted, the US Trade Representative said 'Today's action by the WTO closes the door on the EU's unfounded claims regarding the legitimacy of section 301. Section 301 has been and will remain essential to our efforts to enforce our international trade rights.' The EU's ambassador to the WTO said 'section 301 has become an empty shell, as this panel report does not only impose on the US the clear obligation to follow [WTO] rules and procedures when using section 301, but it also impedes the use of Section 301 as a threatening tool.'[93]

Looking at the outcome of the *Section 301* case dispassionately, it appears that establishment of the quoted passage from the US Statement of Administrative Action[94] as a firm commitment does reduce the threat of unilateral action while dispute resolution is pending or in progress. But section 301 not only continues to offer the opportunity to American industry to engage the government in its concerns; it also continues to confer domestic authority on the US Trade Representative to submit disputes to the WTO and to suspend concessions or take other retaliatory action when authorized by the DSB. But as the *Bananas* case described below demonstrates, the sequence of steps set out in the Understanding on Dispute Settlement described in Section 8.1 turned out not to be as smooth as anticipated, and section 301 turned out to be more than an empty shell.

(d) The *Bananas* Dispute

From Complaint to Final Report

The underlying dispute about the regime of regulating the importation of bananas into the European Community, going back at least to 1993, is well beyond the scope of this chapter. In brief, the Community had long maintained a complicated system of import licenses, tariff quotas, and discriminatory tariffs for bananas, designed to favour the so-called ACP States, many previously former colonies in Africa and the Caribbean, as well as a few outlying areas considered parts of Europe, such as Madeira, Crete, Canary Islands, Guadaloupe, and Martinique. The regime was repeatedly

---

[92] Id. paras. 7.125–7.126.
[93] Statements of US Trade Representative Charlene Barshevsky, EU Ambassador Roderick Abbott, both reported in 17 *BNA Int'l Trade Rptr.* 189 (3 Feb. 2000).
[94] Text at n. 91 supra.

criticized and litigated, within the Community itself and (prior to establishment of the WTO) in the GATT.[95]

In the spring of 1996, Ecuador, Guatemala, Honduras, Mexico, and the United States brought complaints about the regime before the DSB, alleging violations of various articles of the GATT, GATS, the Import Licensing Agreement, and the TRIMs Agreement.[96] On May 22, 1997, the panel issued its reports, in large part upholding the complaints, and on September 9, 1997, the panel reports were upheld by the Appellate Body, which recommended that the Community's banana import regime be brought into conformity with its WTO obligations. The Report of the Appellate Body was adopted by the DSB on September 27, 1997.[97] The events on which this account focuses begin thereafter.[98]

Compliance, Enforcement, and Impasse

Article 21(3) of the DSU calls for the respondent state to inform the DSB at a meeting held within 30 days of adoption of the Report of its intentions in respect of implementation; if it is impracticable to comply immediately with the recommendations and rulings, 'the Member concerned shall have a reasonable period of time' in which to do so. The parties are supposed to agree within 45 days of adoption of the report on a reasonable period. Since they could not agree, an arbitrator was appointed pursuant to Article 21(3) to make the necessary determination within 90 days. On December 23, 1997 the arbitrator did so, setting the expiry of the reasonable period at January 1, 1999.[99]

In spring 1998, the EC announced the principal features of a new banana import regime. The United States and the other complainants asserted that the new proposals were still WTO-inconsistent, and began to publicly consider measures of retaliation. The US ambassador to the WTO said 'I think it's time the Commission started working with the [six complainant countries] on a solution that complies with the WTO commitments instead of finding ways to delay.'[100] In November, after the EC had formally adopted the proposed revised banana regime and implementing regulations to be

---

[95] For earlier phases of the controversy, see e.g. Zsolt K. Besskó, 'Going Bananas Over EEC Preferences: A Look at the Banana Trade War and the WTO's Understanding on Rules and Procedures Governing Settlement of Disputes', 28 *Case Western Reserve J. Int'l L.* 265 (1996); Nancy L. Perkins, Introductory Note, 34 *I.L.M.* 154 (1995), followed by Judgment of the European Court of Justice 5 Oct. 1994 and Report of GATT Panel (not adopted), *EEC Import Regime for Bananas*, 18 Jan. 1994.

[96] The scheme subject to challenge in the WTO proceeding was set out in EEC Council Reg. 404/93 of 13 Feb. 1993, on the *Common Organisation of the Market in Bananas*, 1993 OJ L47/1 (25 Feb. 1993), amended several times thereafter.

[97] *European Communities—Regime for the Importation, Sale and Distribution of Bananas*, WT/DS27/AB/R, 9 Sept. 1997.

[98] See also Cherise M. Valles and Brendan P. McGivern, 'The Right to Retaliate under the WTO Agreement: The Sequencing Problem', 34 *J. World Trade* No. 2, p. 63 at 71–8 (2000).

[99] Award of the Arbitrator under DSU Art. 21.3, WT/DS/15 (7 Jan. 1998).

[100] Reported by European Information Service, 25 Apr. 1998.

effective on January 1, 1999, Sir Leon Brittan, one of the architects of the Uruguay Round and vice-president of the European Commission, said, 'My message to the United States is a simple one: use the WTO system, but do not expect us to bend it to suit a timetable that you are seeking to impose by means of illegal unilateral action.'[101]

There was a timetable, however—in fact there were two timetables, one under US law, the other in the DSU. The reasonable period for compliance, as mentioned above, would be up on January 1, 1999. Article 22(6) of the DSU provides that if the respondent fails to bring the measure found to be inconsistent into compliance within the reasonable period (referring to Article 22(2)), the DSB shall, upon request, grant authorization to the complainant to suspend concessions or other obligations within 30 days after expiry of the reasonable period; under US law, as discussed above, even if the 18 months deadline is regarded as subject to interpretation, the US Trade Representative is supposed to undertake retaliation within 30 days after conclusion of the dispute settlement process if US rights continue to be denied.[102]

On December 21, 1998, the US Trade Representative published a list of products of the EC which would be subject to 100 percent duties upon authorization by the DSB.[103] The announcement said that the US government intended to request such authorization on or before January 21, 1999—20 days after expiry of the 'reasonable period', and to implement those punitive duties on or after February 1, 1999—30 days after the expiry of the reasonable period.[104] If the EC requested arbitration of the level of proposed suspension of concessions, the increased duties would go into effect on or after March 3, 1999—60 days after expiry of the reasonable period, in accordance with the timetable for arbitration under Article 22(6). In the US interpretation of Article 22, it had a 10-day window of opportunity, between the 20-day period for reaching agreement on compensation under Article 22(2) and the 30-day period for authorization to retaliate under Article 22(6), both measured from the end of the reasonable period. On January 14, 1999, the United States submitted its request for authorization to suspend concessions to the EC, equivalent to $520 million in annual trade.

[101] European Commission Press Release, IP 98/1012, 20 Nov. 1998.

[102] US Trade Act of 1974, §304(a)(2)(A)(i), 19 U.S.C. §2414(a)(2)(A)(i). In the event, and consistently with the representations made by the United States before the *Section 301* panel as described in the preceding section, the US Trade Representative determined in February 1998 that the EC's undertaking to implement all of the recommendations and rulings of the WTO reports by January 1, 1999 constituted the taking of satisfactory measures to grant the rights of the United States, and thus the original investigation pursuant to section 301 which had led to the US complaint was terminated, subject to monitoring in accordance with section 306. When the revised EC regime came out in January 1999, the US process began to run again, and as shown in the text hereafter, the United States immediately invoked Article 22.

[103] USTR Press Release 98–113, 21 Dec. 1998.

[104] 63 Fed. Reg. 71665, (29 Dec. 1998), referring to earlier announcements and requests for comments, 63 Fed. Reg. 56687 (22 Oct. 1998) and 63 Fed. Reg. 63099 (10 Nov. 1998).

The European Community, for its part, disagreed that its revised banana import regime was inconsistent with its WTO obligations, and under Article 21(5) it was entitled to have that disagreement arbitrated. The EC contended that retaliation by the United States and the other complainants under Article 22(6) must await the outcome of arbitration under Article 21(5)—a 90-day period from the date of referral. The memorandum on behalf of the EC said authorizing retaliation at this point would be, 'as if, in a criminal case, the punishment would already be pronounced while the jury was still deliberating on whether the defendant was guilty.'[105]

Searching for a 'Pragmatic Solution'

The DSB was not sure what to do at this stage. In the event, on January 12, 1999, the DSB established two panels under Article 21(5) to judge compliance by the EC, one at the request of Ecuador, one of the complainants, the other at the request of the European Community itself. The EC succeeded, to the 'dismay' of the United States and contrary to the design of the DSU, in blocking adoption of the agenda of the DSB meeting of January 25, 1999 at which the US request for authorization to suspend concessions was to come up.[106] On January 29, the EC made a request for arbitration under Article 22(6) concerning the level of the proposed suspensions of concessions announced by the United States, as well as the consistency of those measures with DSU Article 22(3).

Thus two proceedings concerned with the *Bananas* dispute were going on at the same time—the Article 22(6) arbitration on the proposed suspension of concessions—scheduled to be completed by March 2, (60 days from expiry of the reasonable period), and the two Article 21(5) panels on the EC's revised Banana regime scheduled to be completed by April 12, 1999 (90 days from date of referral). The 'pragmatic solution' turned out to submit all three matters to the same three persons who had composed the original *Bananas* panel that had completed its reports nearly two years earlier. It would have seemed odd to have the decision on the quantum of retaliation issued before the decision on whether retaliation was justified at all, but the panelists found a solution. They issued their 'initial decision' on the level of retaliation as required on the sixtieth day, but asked for additional information, so that their final decisions, both as arbitrators under Article 22(6) and as panelists under Article 21(5) all came out on the same day, April 6, 1999.

---

[105] EC Bananas Memorandum, 14 Dec. 1998, quoted by Valles and McGivern (n. 98 supra), at p. 74, n. 13.

[106] Ambassador Barshefsky, the US Trade Representative issued a statement saying,

I am extremely dismayed that the EU would jeopardize the operations of the WTO in this way. The EU has prevented the WTO from holding a meeting, prevented the United States from exercising its WTO rights, and prevented any other dispute settlement business from going forward. (USTR Press Release 99–08, 25 Jan. 1999)

The panelists/arbitrators decided under Article 21(5) that the new EC Banana regime was not fully compatible with the EC's WTO obligations,[107] but under Article 22(6) that the level of nullification and impairment suffered by the United States as a result of the incompatibility of the new Bananas regime with WTO obligations was $191.4 million per year, slightly more than a third of the amount requested.[108] That amount of suspension was authorized by the DSB on April 19, 1999, and promptly implemented by the United States.[109]

Back to Unilateralism?

On March 3, 1999, while the several panels were still deliberating, the United States had suspended liquidation on the targeted products and required a bond against future duties, on the theory that that was the date (60 days after expiry of the 'reasonable period') on which the suspension of obligations should have gone into effect. When the DSB authorized suspension of concessions in the amount fixed by the panel, the United States announced that the 100 percent duties would be collected retroactive to the date of suspension of liquidation, i.e. to March 3.

This step provoked still another proceeding. On May 11, 1999 the European Community requested establishment of a panel under Article XXIII of GATT and Articles 4 and 6 of the DSU, alleging 'flagrant breach' of four articles of the DSU plus four articles of the GATT, including Articles I and II. A panel was established in June, but selection of panelists was not completed until October 1999. Eventually, the panel found that the United States had violated DSU Article 23(1) by acting unilaterally on March 3, 1999, in effect interrupting trade in EC products before the proceedings under the DSU had been completed.[110] The United States argued in this proceeding that the EC had frustrated and delayed various DSU proceedings, with the consequence that the Article 22(6) panel had not been able to issue its final decision when it should have done so 60 days after expiry of the reasonable period. The panel, while not disagreeing that the EC had engaged in delaying tactics, rejected the US defense:

---

[107] *European Communities—Regime for the Importation, Sale and Distribution of Bananas, Recourse to Article 21.5 by Ecuador*, WT/DS27/RW/ECU, 12 Apr. 1999; *Recourse to Article 21.5 by the European Communities*, WT/DS27/RW/EEC, 12 Apr. 1999, both adopted 6 May 1999.

[108] *European Communities—Regime for the Importation, Sale and Distribution of Bananas, Recourse to Arbitration by the European Communities under Article 22.6 of the DSU*, WT/DS27/ARB, 9 Apr. 1999, adopted 19 Apr. 1999.

[109] United States Trade Representative, Notice of US Suspension of Tariff Concessions, 19 Apr. 1999, 64 Fed. Reg. 19209. Duties of 100 percent *ad valorem* were imposed on some nine different products from 13 of the 15 member states of the EC, ranging from bath preparations and handbags to electric coffee makers, lead-acid storage batteries, and folding cartons. Products of Denmark and the Netherlands were not included, because those states had voted against adoption of the EC's revised banana import scheme in the Council of Ministers.

[110] *United States—Import Measures on Certain Products from the European Communities*, WT/DS165/R, 17 July 2000.

First, **no** WTO violation can justify a unilateral retaliatory measure by another Member; this is the object of the prohibitions contained in Article 23.1 of the DSU. If Members disagree as to whether a WTO violation has occurred, the only remedy available is to initiate a DSU/WTO dispute process and obtain a WTO determination that such a WTO violation has occurred. . . . The fundamental obligation of Article 23 of the DSU would be a farce if every time there is a delay in a panel or arbitration process, the unsatisfied Member could simply unilaterally determine that a violation has occurred and unilaterally impose any remedy.[111]

Meanwhile, Ecuador

With all the legal skirmishing and acrimony between the European Community and the United States, one could easily lose sight of the underlying economic controversy. But for Ecuador, the banana question was very real indeed. Exports of bananas made up more than 30 percent of its total foreign exchange earnings, and its capacity to retaliate by raising tariffs against the European Community was obviously limited. Though Ecuador had been the lead party in the Article 21(5) proceeding on compliance,[112] it did not immediately seek authorization for retaliation, preferring to negotiate with the EC for increased market access or reduced tariffs. The negotiations did not succeed, however, and in November 1999, Ecuador requested authorization from the DSB to retaliate. Since Ecuador's imports were primarily capital goods or raw materials, withdrawal of tariff concessions would have hurt Ecuador more than the Community. Accordingly, Ecuador sought authorization to suspend obligations under the TRIPs Agreement and GATS, as well as GATT 1994, in an amount of $450 million. The EC requested arbitration of the level of suspension, and also challenged the proposed cross-sectoral and cross-agreement suspension of concession. The EC's request was once more referred to the same panel, and the DSB deferred authorization to Ecuador until the panel made its report under Article 22(6) and (7). Eventually, on March 2, 2000, that determination was issued. The panel authorized suspension in an amount of $201.6 million annual value, of which $60 million was to be in trade in goods, the remainder in withdrawal of protection for geographical indications for beverages, copyright protection on recorded music, and authorization to engage in wholesale distribution services.[113] On May 18,

---

[111] Id. para. 6.135. Still another dispute broke out between the European Community and the United States in the spring of 2000 provoked by the *Bananas* case as well as the *Beef-Hormones* case (n. 116 infra), when the United States announced that it was rotating the list of products subject to retaliatory tariffs, pursuant to a 'carousel approach', designed to keep exporters to the United States off balance, in order to maximize the effect of the sanctions. The European Community immediately cried 'foul', and requested consultations under Article 4 of the DSU with a view to bringing a formal complaint.

[112] See n. 107 supra.

[113] An Ecuadorian trade official said:

Of course Ecuador is not going to start producing wine and labeling it Bordeaux. But [the authorization we seek] will give a strong signal that this kind of protection valued by EU firms could disappear, not just in Ecuador but in other countries. Quoted in 16 BNA *Int'l Trade Reporter*, 1881, 17 Nov. 1999.

2000, more than four years after the original complaint had been filed and two and a half years after adoption of the Appellate Body report, the DSB authorized suspension by Ecuador in that amount, the first time that retaliation by a developing country against a developed Member had been authorized, and the first time also for cross-sectoral retaliation.[114]

Article 22(1) of the Understanding on Dispute Settlement, consistent with the tradition of the GATT, states:

[N]either compensation nor the suspension of concessions or other obligations is preferred to full implementation of a recommendation to bring a measure into conformity with the covered agreements.

On April 11, 2001, more than eight years after the start of the dispute, the European Union and the United States announced a settlement. The EU would immediately implement a new licensing system based on historical market share that would give greater opportunity to Latin American growers to export bananas to the Community; by January 1, 2006, the EU would move to a tariff-only system for bananas.[115] To the extent the new system required a GATT waiver, the United States would support the waiver application. The new regime went into effect on July 1, 2001, and on the following day the United States removed its retaliatory sanctions.[116]

8.9   A LOOK AHEAD AND SOME REFLECTIONS

The European Community issued a 'non-paper' in July 1999 repeating in a proposal to the WTO review group on the DSU some of the positions it had taken and continued to take in the *Bananas* dispute:[117]

(i) Disagreements over compliance by the respondent with a panel or Appellate Body ruling should be decided first by a compliance panel within a prescribed time limit before any member could request authorization to suspend concessions or otherwise commence retaliation. (ii) There should be a presumption that a Member

---

[114] See Minutes of Meeting of WTO Dispute Settlement Board in May 2000, Doc. WT/DSB/M/80.

[115] Ecuador at first opposed the agreement, but withdrew its opposition after receiving assurances from the EU that its growers would receive increased access to the European market.

[116] A comparable illustration, also pitting the United States (as well as Canada) against the European Community, concerned the so-called *Beef-Hormones* case, *EC—Measures Concerning Meat and Meat Products (Hormones)*, (*United States and Canada* v. *European Communities*), WT/DS26/AB/R, WT/DS48/AB/R (adopted 19 Feb. 1998), plus five subsequent decisions between April 1998 and July 1999, followed eventually by US implementation of sanctions as of 27 July 1999. As of year-end 2001, this dispute had not been settled, and the sanctions remained in effect. The merits of this case are discussed in Ch. 11, Sect. 11.7.

[117] European Communities, *Discussion Paper on Guiding Principles for the Clarification and Elaboration of Articles 21, 22, and 23 of the WTO DSU*, 23 July, 1999.

implementing a Report was acting in conformity with the Report and the covered agreements, with the burden of proof on the party alleging nonconformity. (iii) Time frames regarding compensation and suspension of concessions should begin to run from the end of the 'reasonable period' for implementation of a DSB Report or adoption of a finding of non-conformity with the Report, whichever is later. (iv) Suspension of concessions should not enter into force or be applied to imports that have taken place at any time before the authorization of suspension of concessions by the DSB.

Whether such a proposal could gain support of the WTO membership was doubtful as of year-end 2001.[118] Certainly the United States, as well as the other complainants in the *Bananas* controversy, would not accept the second proposal, that there was a presumption in favour of compliance with a DSB report by the losing party. But there can be no doubt that the relation between Article 21 on compliance and Article 22 on compensation and retaliation needs some repair. One might consider a proposal whereby if a Member were allowed 15 months for compliance with a Report, it would be required to announce its proposals for compliance within, say, seven months, so that objections to the proposals could be put before a panel under Article 21(5) that would finish its work by end of the 'reasonable period', and retaliation or compensation could begin at the close of that period or shortly thereafter.

Professor Hudec, perhaps the wisest observer of trade disputes, wrote in 1998:

If it is true that the key ingredient of international legal systems is the political will of member governments to comply with them, and if it is also true that the WTO legal reforms do not signal a sudden improvement in the less-than-perfect political will that caused the GATT legal system to suffer occasional failures, it follows that the new WTO legal system cannot expect to have one hundred percent compliance, even with its new and more rigorous procedures. To the contrary, it must be anticipated that there will be defeats when governments cannot, or will not, comply with some legal rulings—just as they did under GATT.

What this means is that, after celebrating its considerable initial success during its first three years or so, the new WTO legal system will have to learn to cope with legal failure. Just as the GATT did, it will have to learn how to get up off the floor, brush off its soiled authority, and move on to the next piece of business with the same high

---

[118] No substantive discussion of dispute settlement took place, as far as is known, at the Doha Ministerial Conference in November 2001, but in its Ministerial Declaration, the conference adopted a paragraph drafted by the Secretariat, stating:

We agree to negotiations on improvements and clarifications of the Dispute Settlement Understanding. The negotiations should be based on the work done thus far as well as any additional proposals by Members, and aim to agree on improvements and clarifications not later than May 2003, at which time we will take steps to ensure that the results enter into force as soon as possible thereafter. (WTO Ministerial Declaration adopted 14 Nov. 2001, para. 30, WT/MIN (01)/DEC/1 (20 Nov. 2001))

expectation of achieving compliance. In the meanwhile, it will have to learn to treat the failed legal ruling with persistence, patience and practicality—the *persistence* of keeping the matter on its agenda, the *patience* of doing so for what may be a long period of time, and the *practicality* of fashioning eventual accommodations that produce a result that can be said to be consistent with long-term respect for GATT/WTO law.[119]

Discussion of the disputes between the United States and the European Community about Section 301 and about the import of bananas is necessary to a realistic appraisal of the WTO dispute settlement system, but in the end neither dispute destroyed the system. As of year-end 2001, more than 200 disputes had come before the DSB, and about half of these had been referred to panels. To quote Professor Henkin again,[120] 'almost all nations observe almost all principles of international law and almost all of their obligations almost all of the time.' That has been true in the WTO, and the Understanding on Dispute Settlement has contributed greatly both to defining the obligations and to compliance with those obligations.

---

[119] Robert E. Hudec, 'The New WTO Dispute Settlement Procedure: An Overview of the First Three Years', Lecture delivered at the University of Geneva, 8 June 1998, repr. in 8 *Minnesota J. Global Trade* 1 at 14–15 (1999).

[120] See Ch. 7, Sect. 7.3, n. 43.

PART IV
The Rules of International Trade in Detail

9

The Question of Subsidies

9.1 INTRODUCTION

No question in international trade law is as contentious, and as complicated, as the question of subsidies. In part, the question is political. Subsidies are transfers of wealth from the general treasury to a particular group of beneficiaries, who, it is believed, could not survive, or at least could not maintain their standing, on the basis of market forces alone.[1] Though most such transfers take place within a given state, they may have adverse impact on the economies—or on particular sectors—of other states, because they distort the flow of goods that would take place without government intervention. At the most general level, the questions for international law are to what extent states may make, or should be restrained from making such transfers, and on the other hand, to what extent other states may take measures to counteract such transfers. Beyond that definition and measurement of subsidies turns out to be extraordinarily difficult.

Subsidies can distort the flow of international trade in three, sometimes overlapping ways: If State *A* subsidizes the production or export of product *x*,

(1) *A*'s producers may be able to sell the product in State *B*, which they could not do without the subsidy.

(2) But for the subsidy, State *B*'s producers might have been able to sell product *x* (or more of product *x*) in State *A*.

(3) State *A*'s producers may sell product *x* in States *C*, *D*, and *E*, in competition with (or to the exclusion of) producers in State *B*: the subsidy to *A*'s producers distorts the competition in the third country markets.

State *B* can defend against situation (1) by imposing a tariff corresponding to the subsidy: the international community, as well as State *A* and the advocates of competition in State *B*, will want to see to it that defense against the subsidy does not hide a measure of protection. One of the aims of the architects of an international law of subsidies, only imperfectly achieved, has been to provide remedies to State *B* in situations (2) and (3). The more basic

---

[1] The issue goes back a long way. Adam Smith devoted a whole chapter in his great treatise to 'bounties', of which, as one might expect, he was no friend, concluding that

> The effect of bounties, like that of all the other expedients of the mercantile system, can only be to force the trade of a country into a channel much less advantageous than that in which it would naturally run of its own accord. (Adam Smith, *An Inquiry into the Nature and Causes of the Wealth of Nations*, Bk. IV, ch. V (1776), repr. Modern Library, New York, 472, 473 (New York 1937))

In contrast, Alexander Hamilton, who believed in protection, at least for infant industries, proposed in effect a countervailing duty for commodities exported to the United States, with the revenue to be used to subsidize domestic production of the same commodities, including production for export. See Alexander Hamilton, *Report on Manufactures* (1791), pp. 50, 57, repr. in *National State Papers of the United States*, Part II, Vol. 10, No. 65 (1985) at pp. 57, 64.

questions, to what extent subsidies distort international trade and to what extent those that do are to be prohibited, have proved to be elusive.

The framers of the GATT addressed the issue of subsidies, but not very firmly. Section 4 of Article XVI, added to the GATT in the mid-1950s,[2] introduced a prohibition on export subsidies, but the prohibition did not apply to primary products, and even for non-primary products was applicable only if the challenged subsidy resulted in a difference between the home market price and the price at which the product in question was offered for export.

Subsidies and what to do about them became a major subject in the Tokyo Round of trade negotiations (1973–9), resulting in an Agreement (Code) on Subsidies and Countervailing Duties (see Section 9.4). In practice the 1979 Subsidies Code proved disappointing, both because adherence was optional and only a few developing states agreed to participate, and because it did not address, or at least did not restrict, many of the state aids that in fact distorted international trade. Subsidies once again became an important subject in the Uruguay Round of trade negotiations (1986–94). Building on the 1979 Code, the negotiators came up with a significantly revised agreement, this time, like the other Uruguay Round codes, required of all members of the new World Trade Organization (Section 9.6). No change was made in the underlying provisions of the GATT relevant to subsidies—Articles XVI and VI, but in fact the international law relating to subsidies looks very different at the turn of the century—more rigid, less ambivalent, and more legalistic—than it did when the GATT was established in the late 1940s.

9.2   GATT AND THE SUBSIDIES QUESTION: ARTICLE XVI

As discussed in Chapter 3, the drafters of the General Agreement believed that the measure of choice for intervention by governments in the international movement of goods was the customs tariff, and that other measures should be discouraged or prohibited. Quantitative restrictions on imports and exports were expressly prohibited in Article XI of the GATT (albeit with exceptions); subsidies were discouraged by the founders of GATT, but not prohibited.[3]

---

[2] See Sect. 9.2, nn. 8 and 9 infra.

[3] The Proposals for the Expansion of World Trade and Employment published by the United States in November 1945, which purported to represent a consensus resulting from consultations between the United States and Great Britain over the preceding two years, and which gave impetus to the negotiations that resulted in the GATT as well as the Havana Charter, were quite modest:

[M]embers granting any subsidy which operates to increase exports or to reduce imports should undertake to keep the [proposed International Trade Organization] informed as to the extent and nature of the subsidy, as to the reason therefor and as to the probable effects on trade. They should also be prepared, in cases where . . . it is agreed that serious injury

In its original version, Article XVI of the General Agreement (present Article XVI(1)) simply provided that 'if any contracting party grants or maintains any subsidy [which meets certain conditions discussed hereafter] it shall *notify* the contracting parties.' If upon such notification 'it is determined'—the Article did not say by whom[4]—'that serious prejudice to the interests of any other contracting party is caused or threatened by any such subsidization,' the state granting the subsidy shall upon request, '*discuss* with the other contracting party or parties concerned . . . the possibility of limiting the subsidization.'

When one contrasts this provision with the obligations contained in Articles I (MFN), II (tariff bindings), III (national treatment), XI (quantitative restrictions), or XXVIII (negotiation of modifications), one can see that there was not only no prohibition in the original version of Article XVI, but even the discouragement was quite weak, 'discussion' being clearly a lesser obligation than 'negotiation'. Nevertheless, Article XVI(1) was not useless, and much of the original thinking—including the ambivalence—remains at the center of the GATT law today.[5] On the one hand, subsidy is defined to include 'any form of income or price support'; on the other hand, the subsidy with which the GATT is concerned is one 'which operates directly or indirectly to increase exports of any product from, or to reduce imports of any product into, its territory.' To anticipate a policy debate that continued over more than four decades, Article XVI(1) thus indicates that the GATT is concerned not only with subsidies on exports, but with production subsidies as well.[6]

---

to international trade threatens to result from the operation of the subsidy, to discuss with other members or with the Organization possible limitations on the quantity of the domestic product subsidized. (US Dep't. of State Publication 2411, Commercial Policy Ser. No. 79, at 15–16 (1945))

[4] In practice, there was no requirement for a determination by the Contracting Parties or a GATT panel: if a state believed its interests were or would be prejudiced, it could request consultations with the state giving the subsidy. See John H. Jackson, *World Trade and the Law of GATT*, 391 (1969).

[5] For the origins of Article XVI of GATT in the exchanges between the United States and the United Kingdom during World War II, in which the British delegates opposed any restrictions on production subsidies and the Americans introduced the idea that the proposed rules not apply to agricultural commodities in surplus, see Seamus O'Cleireacain, 'Towards a Code on Subsidies and Countervailing Duties', 1 *The Word Economy* 437 (Oct. 1978).

[6] A working party concerned with Article XVI stated in 1955:

So far as domestic subsidies are concerned, it was agreed that a contracting party which has negotiated a concession under Article II may be assumed . . . to have a reasonable expectation . . . that the value of the concession will not be nullified or impaired by the contracting party which granted the concession by the subsequent introduction or increase of a domestic subsidy on the product concerned. (GATT, BISD, 3d Supp., 222, 224, para. 13 (1955))

The example, which so far as is known is not taken from an actual case, is Situation (2) in the introductory section, modified only to the extent that it is limited to a product on which State B had secured a concession from State A.

It was evident that Article XVI in its original version was insufficient if the contracting parties were serious about imposing some international discipline on subsidies. The subject was discussed at length at the Review Session of the GATT in 1954–5, and eventually new paragraphs (2)–(5) of Article XVI, plus interpretive notes to the original as well as the new provisions, were adopted by the Contracting Parties effective for the countries that accepted them.[7]

The new provisions, denominated Section B of Article XVI, applied only to export subsidies.[8] The contracting parties that accepted the amendments—essentially the industrialized but not the developing countries—now recognized that the granting by a contracting party of a subsidy on the export of any product may have harmful effects for other contracting parties, 'both importing and exporting'. Further, they agreed that such subsidies 'may cause undue disturbance' to the normal commercial interests of other contracting parties, and 'may hinder the achievement of the objectives' of the General Agreement.

One might have thought that recognition of these facts would lead to a prohibition on export subsidies. The actual commitment was a good deal less firm. *First*, the amended Article distinguished between primary products—notably products of agriculture but also minerals and fishery products[9]—and other products. *Second*, the prohibitions or admonitions were now tied for primary products to the effect of a subsidy on share of world export trade, and for non-primary products on a comparison between the price at which a product benefiting from a subsidy is exported and the price at which the same product is sold for domestic consumption. The standard introduced in Article XVI(4) with respect to non-primary products suggests the influence of thinking about dumping, though in many ways the considerations are quite different.[10] Article XVI(4) seems to say that, absent a difference between the home

---

[7] Protocol Amending the Preamble and Parts II and III of the General Agreement, Done at Geneva 10 Mar. 1955, GATT BISD, 3d Supp. 222, 224–7 (1955), entered into force 7 Oct. 1957, 8 U.S.T. 1767, 278 U.N.T.S. 168. Actually, the prohibition contained in Article XVI(4), discussed below, was stated to come into effect 'as from January 1, 1958 or the earliest practicable date thereafter'. The contracting parties did not agree on a Declaration Giving Effect to the Provisions of Article XVI(4) until November 1960, and that declaration became effective only two years later. GATT BISD, 9th Supp. 32 (1961), 13 U.S.T. 2605, 445 U.N.T.S. 294, entered into force 14 Nov. 1962. In the interval, successive declarations kept the standstill agreement in the second sentence of Article XVI(4) in effect.

[8] The 'Additional Provisions on Export Subsidies' were drawn, with some modification, from Article 26 of the Havana Charter, which had not been incorporated into the original version of the GATT. That article contained the substance of what became Article XVI(4) of GATT, including a two-year deadline for implementation of the prohibition; emphasis on price discrimination; a complicated provision on Special Treatment of Primary Commodities; and the concept of 'equitable share of world trade' discussed below.

[9] See Interpretive Note 2 ad Art. XVI, Section B.

[10] The theory behind a price discrimination standard in respect to dumping is that high home-market prices should not be used to 'subsidize' unfairly low prices for exports, and that if home-market prices were lowered, the producer in question could not afford over time to charge the low prices it charges on export sales. However persuasive that theory is with respect

market price and the export price, subsidies that affect exports as well as domestic sales are not covered by the prohibition even when, without benefit of the subsidy, the product in question could not be sold at all in the world market by producers from State *A* or indeed in State *A* itself.

Suppose for example that (putting aside transport and other transaction costs) product *x* costs 80 dollars (or marks, pounds, etc.) to produce in State *A* but costs 70 dollars to produce in States *B* and *C*:

(i) If there were no trade barriers, the market for the product in State *A* would be supplied by producers in *B* and *C*.

(ii) If State *A* maintained a tariff of about 12 percent ad valorem, there would probably be competition in State *A* among producers from *A*, *B*, and *C*.

(iii) If State A maintained a tariff in excess of 15 percent, producers in *A* would probably supply the bulk of the market in *A* to the exclusion of any imports. *A*'s producers, thus far, would have no share in the markets of *B* and *C*.

(iv) Suppose now State *A* introduces a subsidy of 10 dollars *per unit exported*, which should allow *A*'s producers, despite their higher costs, to compete with producers of *B* and *C* in those countries as well as in *D*, *E*, and *F*. If State *A* grants no comparable subsidy on products sold domestically, it is in violation of Article XVI(4).

(v) If the subsidy paid by State *A*, in contrast, is 10 dollars *per unit produced*, whether sold for export or for domestic consumption, and if therefore the price in *A* comes down to 70 dollars per unit, there is no violation, though the effect on the market in *B* and *C* (as well as *D*, *E*, and *F*) is same as in case (iv), and the effect on the sales by producers from *B* and *C* in *A* (i.e. under cases (i) or (ii)) is substantially greater.

For states whose industries export a large portion of their production—Canada, for instance, and also the Benelux countries—the example given is not far-fetched, though a domestic subsidy is more likely to be granted in the form of a tax exemption or deferral, a below-market loan, special terms for supply of raw materials or carriage of freight, or provision of infrastructure, than in the form of a direct payment of cash per unit of output. To convert such benefits into per/unit subsidy requires an extra step which in practice is very difficult and contentious, though in theory it is not problematical.[11] At all events, the contracting parties were not prepared in the early 1960s—and

to the conduct of individual enterprises (see Ch. 5), it is not self-evident that it is suitable in assessing the acceptability of state aids.

[11] Generally, the technique involves taking the value of the benefit, dividing by the number of units produced, and where relevant allocating the result to exported and home-market output. In practice, a benefit may be spread out over a number of years which needs to be determined, the difference between a commercial and a preferential rate may not be self-evident, and the benefit may be only partly specific (and therefore within the definition of subsidy) and partly general (and therefore excluded).

indeed for many years thereafter—to go beyond Article XVI(1) to address measures of this kind, for the very understandable—if not wholly persuasive—reason that an international commitment with respect to such measures would add a substantial additional component to major issues of internal politics and priorities.

For primary products, the GATT consensus in the early 1960s was still weaker. Article XVI(3) says only that contracting parties 'should seek to avoid' the use of subsidies on the export of primary products, quite different from the words 'shall cease to grant' in Article XVI(4) with respect to non-primary products. The next sentence of Article XVI(3) is baffling by any standard, reflecting the lack of consensus and multiple ambivalence that have characterized the discourse of the GATT contracting parties on this subject for close to half a century:

If, however, a contracting party grants directly or indirectly [a] any form of subsidy which [b] operates to increase the export of any primary product from its territory, [c] such subsidy shall not be applied in a manner which results in that contracting party having [d] more than an equitable share of world export trade in that product, account being taken [e] of the shares of the contracting parties in such trade in the product during a previous representative period, and [f] any special factors which may have affected or may be affecting such trade in the product.[12]

It seems that [a] goes beyond export subsidy, to include, for instance, price supports, crop loans, subsidized storage or shipping, and the like; [b] could mean 'increase from a prior period', but probably means 'increase over the level that would prevail without the subsidy'; [c] for the first time introduces the word 'shall', apparently meaning that if a more than equitable share results, the subsidy is prohibited; but what [d] means in the context of changes in productivity (or indeed of exchange rates) is only partly helped by [e] and [f].[13]

Some notable battles have been fought under the banner of Article XVI—including the so-called pasta war or *guerre des pâtes* involving Article XVI(3) (1981–6),[14] and the notorious *Disc* case (1971–81) involving Article

---

[12] The letters in brackets have been added for purposes of explication.

[13] Professor Jackson points out that the mention of 'representative period' and 'any special factors' is drawn from Article XIII(4). That article, it will be recalled, deals with rules for quantitative restrictions imposed notwithstanding the prohibition of Article XI(1), and is itself far from a model of clarity.

[14] For an account of the 'pasta war', see Robert E. Hudec, *Enforcing International Trade Law*, 151–4 (1993). The dispute centered around the contention by the European Community that it could take advantage of the permission (or rather the exclusion from the prohibition) concerning subsidies on exports of primary products in subsidizing export of pasta, a processed form of wheat. The eventual solution, after a panel report rejecting this argument had been blocked by the European Community, was an undertaking by the EC to limit the subsidy on pasta to the difference between the home-market price and the world price of the primary product contained in the processed product. The principle of this settlement was later restated as Article 11 of the Agreement on Agriculture negotiated in the Uruguay Round.

XVI (4).[15] Not surprisingly the outcomes have not been based on legal rulings alone.

9.3   GATT AND THE SUBSIDIES QUESTION: ARTICLE VI

As pointed out in the introduction to the chapter, one form of defense for State *B* against a subsidy granted by State *A*—situation (1) on page 200—is a special tariff imposed on the subsidized product, generally known as a countervailing duty. Such a tariff is exempt from the obligation to accord most-favoured-nation treatment to the products of all contracting parties (Art. I), as well as from the obligation (where applicable) not to impose tariffs in excess of the bound schedule (Art. II).[16] The conditions for countervailing duties are set out not in Article XVI but in Article VI, otherwise devoted to dumping and anti-dumping duties.[17]

One might have thought that a countervailing duty would be permitted only to the extent the subsidy against which it was imposed was prohibited. Given the lack of consensus on what is and what is not permitted by way of subsidy, however, the development of countervailing duty law has been quite different. Both under the GATT itself and under the later Codes on Subsidies and Countervailing Measures, the scope of countervailing duties permitted to State *B* is substantially wider than the restrictions as to

---

[15] The DISC (Domestic International Sales Corporation) was a device adopted by the US Congress in 1971 which had the effect (and purpose) of reducing and deferring income taxes payable by American exporters. The European Community challenged DISC as a violation of Article XVI(4), and the United States said, in effect, 'Look who's talking', by filing three counter-complaints against France, Belgium, and the Netherlands. Eventually several panel reports were issued, but they were either blocked or effectively countermanded in the GATT Council after which a kind of 'out-of-court settlement' was reached between the United States and the EC. See Ch. 7, Sect. 7.3(c) supra. Professor Hudec, who devotes more than forty pages to the DISC case, writes:

> The DISC case is considered by many to be the largest and most conspicuous failure in the history of GATT litigation. As often happens with dramatic failures, however, the DISC case has also exerted a strong influence on almost every aspect of modern GATT dispute settlement practice. . . . [O]n the institutional side, the DISC case presented the first of several demonstrations that a stronger dispute settlement procedure would need a stronger and more reliable source of legal expertise. It introduced the idea that lawyers as well as diplomats have a role to play in these cases. The eventual consequence of this lesson, and one of the DISC case's most important contributions, was the GATT legal office that came into being about six years later. (Robert E. Hudec, *Enforcing International Trade Law*, pp. 59, 100 (1993))

The controversy was revived in 1998–2000, when the European Community challenged the United States revised 'Foreign Sales Corporation' program [FSC]. See Sect. 9.7 at n. 112.

[16] The first point is clearly understood, though not expressly stated; the second is confirmed by GATT Article II(2)(b). It is also noteworthy that remedies against subsidization (as well as against dumping) may be imposed unilaterally, in contrast to remedies against other actions, such as impositions of quotas or raising of bound tariffs, which require permission of the organization as a whole, generally following consultation and dispute settlement proceedings.

[17] See Ch. 10.

subsidies that may be granted by State *A*. Putting the same point another way, a subsidy granted by State *A* may well be GATT-legal, in that it is not an export subsidy or does not result in two-tier pricing, but State *B* may nevertheless be entitled to impose a countervailing duty in response. Article VI(3) expressly speaks of countervailing duties against a 'bounty or subsidy . . . granted, directly or indirectly, on the manufacture, production or export' of the product in question, thus tracking the United States countervailing duty statute in force at the time the GATT was being drafted,[18] and going well beyond the provisions of Article XVI. When the issue of subsidies came to be negotiated and reformulated during the Tokyo Round in 1974–9 (Sect. 9.4 infra), the discrepancy between what was permitted to State *B* and what was prohibited to State *A* was retained in almost the same terms, and when the 1979 Code was substantially revised in the Uruguay Round (Sect. 9.6 infra), no change was made in this respect.

Article VI imposes two important conditions on countervailing duties: Paragraph 3 says that no countervailing duty may be imposed in excess of the estimated subsidy determined to be granted. This condition is often difficult to carry out with precision—the GATT itself speaks of an estimate—but in theory it is not controversial. A countervailing duty is not supposed to impose penalties or multiple damages, just to offset the distortion caused by the subsidy.

Paragraph 6, which applies equally to anti-dumping and to countervailing duties, introduces a new element. Even if State *A* has granted a subsidy on a product exported to State *B* and *B*'s authorities have correctly determined the amount of the subsidy, no countervailing duty may be imposed unless there has been a determination—by *B*—that the effect of the subsidy 'is such as to cause or threaten material injury to an established domestic industry, or is such as to retard materially the establishment of a domestic industry.' As we shall see, several of the quoted words have given rise to substantial controversy, particularly 'cause' and 'material'. Before exploring these issues of detail, however, it is worth asking why, if subsidies—at least some subsidies—are improper in that they distort the conditions of trade based on relative efficiency, there should be an injury requirement at all. Indeed, United States law from 1897 to 1979 made no provision for inquiry into injury as a condition for imposition of a countervailing duty, although it did (from 1921 on) have such a provision for anti-dumping duties.[19] Some writers

---

[18] Section 303 of the Tariff Act of 1930, formerly 19 U.S.C. §1303, first adopted with respect to sugar in the McKinley Tariff Act of 1890 and generalized in the Tariff Act of 1897. It is interesting to note that §303 and its forebears until 1974 applied only to dutiable products, the idea evidently being that if a product was not subject to an ordinary customs duty it either was not produced at all in the United States or else did not need the protection of a countervailing duty.

[19] When the United States changed its law in 1979 to conform to the new Subsidies Code, it did so only with respect to products originating in states that had accepted the Code, or that had assumed substantially equivalent obligations to the United States. The reason that the United States was able to avoid an injury requirement without being out of compliance with

have suggested that the injury requirement misses the point of anti-subsidy law, which is not to protect domestic industries, but to protect the conditions of trade and rational allocation of resources overall.[20] The drafters of the GATT, however, seem to have wanted to make sure that imposition of countervailing duties not be made too easy, remembering that such a duty represents a frustration by State *B* of a policy decision made, for what it regarded as good and sufficient reasons, by State *A*. Professor Jackson has referred to the injury requirement as an important 'mediating principle', to help balance the clash of policy goals on the subject of subsidies, especially domestic subsidies.[21] On the whole, the international community has agreed. However, it is worth pointing out that until the completion of the Subsidies Code discussed in the next section, only the United States imposed countervailing duties in any systematic way. Thus Professor Gilbert Winham, a Canadian, in describing the background of the Subsidies Code, wrote that at the start of the Tokyo Round GATT law on countervailing duties was strong but irrelevant—because the only state regularly imposing such duties was exempt under the Protocol of Provisional Application— while GATT law on subsidies was relevant—in that it bore on commonplace practices of the states that accepted it—but weak, because the definitions were fuzzy and the sanctions fuzzier still.[22] It was with this background that the effort to negotiate a Subsidies/Countervailing Duties Code became a centerpiece of the Tokyo Round.

9.4   THE SUBSIDIES AND COUNTERVAILING DUTIES CODE OF 1979

(a)   The Basic Compromise

As in many aspects of the Tokyo Round, the principal protagonists in negotiation of an Agreement on Subsidies and Countervailing Duties were the United States and the European Community. For the United States, emphasis on the subsidies question stemmed in large part from the disappearance of its trade surplus, and from pressure—particularly in Congress—brought by industries such as steel, consumer electronics (and later automobiles) that had seen their share of the domestic market declining but asserted that they

---

GATT from 1948 to 1979 was that the Protocol of Provisional Application—GATT's grandfather clause—applied with respect to Part II (which includes Article VI) only 'to the fullest extent not inconsistent with existing legislation', and as noted, the countervailing duty law predated GATT by 50 years.

[20] See e.g. John J. Barcelo, 'Subsidies and Countervailing Duties—Analysis and a Proposal', 9 *Law & Policy Int'l Business* 779 at 801 (1977).

[21] John H. Jackson, *The World Trading System: Law and Policy of International Economic Relations*, 263–4, 271 (1989).

[22] Gilbert R. Winham, *International Trade and the Tokyo Round Negotiation*, 169–70 (1986).

could compete on even terms with imports 'if only the playing field were level'. In addition, agricultural interests in the United States increasingly felt the impact of the European Community's Common Agricultural Policy, not only in declining market shares within the Common Market but in competition for third-country markets. Among particular complaints by United States interests, reflected in negotiating instructions contained in the Trade Act of 1974,[23] was the practice by members of the European Community, as well as Japan and other states, to forgive or rebate value-added or consumption taxes on goods destined for export, and to impose border adjustment taxes on imported goods to make up for value-added or similar taxes paid in respect of domestically produced goods. An Interpretive Note to Article XVI, adopted at the time of the 1962 amendments, had said exemption of an exported product from taxes borne by the like product when destined for domestic consumption, or remission of such taxes as have been paid through a cascade or value-added system 'shall not be deemed to be a subsidy'. The United States, at least at the outset, sought to secure a revision of this rule. Further, the United States sought to strengthen the prohibition on export subsidies by eliminating the price comparison test, and it sought to place some international restraints on domestic or production subsidies with adverse impact on international trade.

The European Community, for its part, sought to avoid all discussion of the Common Agricultural Policy in the subsidy context; it was concerned about the increasing resort to countervailing duty proceedings in the United States, and in particular about the fact that under US law then prevailing, countervailing duties could be imposed merely upon determination of a subsidy, without any inquiry concerning injury. The Community wanted a commitment from the United States that it would fall into line with the GATT rules that it had itself drafted and impose countervailing duties only upon determination of a causal link between a subsidy and 'material injury' to a domestic industry; the United States, at least initially, took the position that agreement on discipline on the use of subsidies should precede any discussion of countervailing duties. For several years, the two sides remained at an impasse, with other participants, and particularly the developing countries, on the sidelines.[24]

Eventually the United States and the Community achieved a compromise, or to be precise two compromises: *First*, in return for a prohibition on export subsidies and at least some comfort on domestic subsidies, the United States agreed to commit itself to an injury standard as called for by GATT Article

---

[23] Trade Act of 1974, §121(a)(5).

[24] For an account of the negotiations by the American negotiators of the 1979 Subsidies Code, see Richard R. Rivers and John D. Greenwald, 'The Negotiation of a Code on Subsidies and Countervailing Measures: Bridging Fundamental Policy Differences', 11 *Law & Policy in Int'l Business* 1447 (1979). See also Gilbert R. Winham, *International Trade and the Tokyo Round Negotiation* (1986).

VI and already applied in dumping cases, but only for goods originating in states that adhered to the Code or a comparable agreement.[25] *Second*, in return for a more permissive attitude on subsidies other than export subsidies, the determination relevant to imposition of countervailing duties was left, as before, to the authorities of the importing country. On this basis, it proved possible to reach agreement on a Subsidies and Countervailing Duties Code, formally known as an 'Agreement on Interpretation and Application of Articles VI, XVI, and XXIII of the GATT'.[26] The deficiencies and ambiguities in the Code, as discussed below, formed a major portion of the agenda of the Uruguay Round, a decade later.

Once the United States and the Community had reached substantial agreement, other states were brought in, and all the industrial member states of GATT joined the Code. Adherence to the Code however, was made optional, and a major effort to induce the developing states to join in the proposed Code, albeit with 'special and differential treatment', did not succeed. When 23 industrialized states signed the *procès-verbal* ending the Tokyo Round and accepting the six codes and three sectoral agreements achieved in the Multilateral Trade Negotiations of 1973–9, only one developing country was among the signatories, and it reserved on the Subsidies Code. Subsequently, about a dozen developing countries did adhere to the Subsidies Code, including Brazil, Chile, Colombia, India, Indonesia, Pakistan, and the Philippines.

(b)   Procedural Aspects: Countervailing Duties and Required Determinations

In filling out GATT Article VI, the Code adopted a largely procedural approach. Under Article 2 of the Code, countervailing duties could be imposed only pursuant to a formal investigation by authorities of the importing country, which, absent special circumstances, was to be completed within a year. A countervailing duty could be imposed only upon an affirmative determination (a) that the challenged imports had benefited from a subsidy; (b) that the domestic industry injury had suffered or was suffering injury (defined in a footnote to mean 'material injury'), and (c) that there was a causal link between the subsidized imports and the injury.

During the period of investigation, signatory states were to be given the opportunity to consult with the state conducting the investigation.[27] The

---

[25] See Sect. 9.3, n. 19, supra.

[26] The reason that Article XXIII of the GATT was included in the title is that, as discussed below, Articles 13, 14, 17, and 18 created a consultation and dispute settlement regime that in several ways went beyond the dispute settlement mechanism of Article XXIII.

[27] 1979 Subsidies Code, Art. 3. Another provision of the Subsidies Code, adapted from the 1967 Anti-Dumping Code but unusual in international relations generally, provided that the authorities of the state conducting the countervailing duty proceeding could carry out investigations in the territory of other signatories unless the other country objected; if the other state

decision on whether or not to impose a countervailing duty, however, remained as before with the importing state (Art. 4), with no definition or classification of government aids as countervailable or not, and no distinction for purposes of countervailing between export and domestic subsidies.

The Code provided that countervailing duties shall not be in excess of the amount of the subsidy.[28] It urged, but did not require, that the countervailing duty 'be less than the total amount of the subsidy if such lesser duty would be adequate to remove the injury to the domestic injury.'[29] The United States, in modifying its law to comply with the Subsidies Code, rejected the suggestion: its statute provides that if findings of subsidy and injury have been made, 'there shall be imposed upon such merchandise a countervailing duty . . . equal to the amount of the net subsidy.'[30] The European Community, in contrast, provides in Basic Regulation on Dumping and Subsidies, that 'The amount of [countervailing] duties shall not exceed . . . the amount of the subsidy . . . established; it should be less if such lesser duty would be adequate to remove the injury.'[31]

> Thus suppose the domestic price in the importing country is 90, the cost (including reasonable profit) to the exporter in Country *A* is 100, and the net subsidy granted by *A* is 15, so that the landed price in the importing country is 85. The United States as importing country would impose a countervailing duty of 15, bringing the price back to 100 and presumably eliminating all imports from country *A*. The European Community might impose a countervailing duty of 10 or 11, particularly if the injury is defined in terms of depressing effect on prices.[32]

Many exporters to the United States had complained that even when they eventually prevailed in an anti-dumping or countervailing duty case, provisional measures plus the threat of heavy duties chilled their opportunity to enter the United States market. For their part, domestic producers in the United States had argued that unless provisional measures were imposed—typically 'suspension of liquidation' of duties on imported merchandise[33]—

did object or otherwise failed to provide necessary information within a reasonable period, the determination 'may be made on the basis of the facts available,' which might well mean the information supplied by the complainant. See Art. 2, paras. 8 and 9.

[28] Art. 4(2).   [29] Art. 4(1).

[30] Trade Agreements Act of 1979, §701(a), 19 U.S.C. §1671(a), not changed in subsequent amendments to US trade legislation. 'Net subsidy' means the subsidy granted less: any application fee, deposit, or similar payment made as a condition for receiving the subsidy; the cost of deferred receipt of the subsidy; and any export taxes or similar charges specifically intended to offset the subsidy. Trade Agreements Act of 1979 §771(6), 19 U.S.C. §1677(6).

[31] Council Regulation (EEC) No. 2176/84 of 23 July 1984, 27 O.J. L 201/1, Art. 13(3) (1984) carried forward in Council Regulation (EC) No. 2026/97 of 6 Oct. 1997, 40 O.J. L 288/1, Art. 15(1) (1997).

[32] The pertinent provisions in the 1979 Code are replicated in the Uruguay Round Code in Article 19.2.

[33] Until a duty is finally determined and 'liquidated', merchandise can enter only against a bond, which of course not only adds to the cost but introduces uncertainty into any transaction.

they might prevail in their 'unfair trade' action but in the mean time be put out of business.

The Code (in Article 5) took a middle position: provisional measures were permitted, but only after a preliminary finding both of the existence of a subsidy and of evidence of injury. Moreover, the Code provided that provisional measures 'shall be limited to as short a period as possible, not exceeding four months.' If the final determination resulted in a finding of injury, countervailing duties could be imposed retroactively for the period for which provisional measures had been applied.[34] In the case of a surge of imports, i.e. massive imports in a short time before provisional measures could be imposed, the Code permitted a retroactive finding of injury for up to 90 days prior to the imposition of provisional measures.[35]

(c)   The Question of Injury

One of the most critical subjects of connection with the Subsidies Code was the effort to define the criteria for a determination of injury. An effort to write into the Code that the subsidy was 'demonstrably the principal cause' of the injury—the phrase used in 1967 International Anti-Dumping Code— was opposed by the United States and also Canada on the ground that such a standard would be impossible to meet. On the other hand, if injury were too easy to establish, the basic concession made by the United States in agreeing to an injury requirement would lose much of its value. Eventually agreement was reached on a simple statement in Article 9.4 that

[i]t must be demonstrated that the subsidized imports are through the effects of the subsidy, causing injury within the meaning of this Agreement

plus the statement that

[t]here may be other factors which at the same time are injuring the domestic industry, and the injuries caused by other factors must not be attributed to the subsidized imports.[36]

---

[34] If the final duty was higher than the amount guaranteed by the bond, the difference could not be collected; if the final duty was less than the provisional duty—the more common occurrence—the difference was to be reimbursed. If the final determination was affirmative only as to a threat of injury, the countervailing duty could not be collected, unless the effect of the subsidized imports would have led to a finding of injury in the absence of the provisional measures (Art. 5(6)-(8)).

[35] Art. 5(9). For the implementing legislation in the United States, see Trade Agreements Act of 1979 §703(e), 19 U.S.C. §167. For corresponding rule in the European Community, see EEC Council Regulation No. 2176/84, n. 31 supra, Art. 13(4)(b)(ii).

[36] A footnote said such factors can include *inter alia*, the volume and price of non-subsidized imports, contraction in demand or changes in the pattern of consumption, trade restrictive practices and competition between the foreign and domestic producers, developments in technology, and the export performance and productivity of the domestic industry. In the 1994 Code, this statement is reproduced in main text.

This formula was then adapted to the revised Anti-Dumping Code so that the tests of causation and injury in the 1979 Codes were substantially the same, and the formula was retained in the revised codes on Subsidies and Dumping negotiated in the Uruguay Round.[37]

Article 6 of the Code, devoted to Determination of Injury, contained nine paragraphs and five footnotes, and quoting any portion without the whole is bound to give an incomplete picture. It is noteworthy, however, that while moving away from a price comparison in the exporting country, the 1979 Subsidies Code placed emphasis on price movements in the importing country.[38] Article 6(2) of the Code, retained without substantive change in the Uruguay Round read:

With regard to volume of subsidized imports the investigating authorities shall consider whether there has been a significant increase in subsidized imports, either in absolute terms or relative to production or consumption in the importing signatory. With regard to the effect of the subsidized imports on prices, the investigating authorities shall consider whether there has been a significant price undercutting by the subsidized imports as compared with the price of a like product of the importing signatory, or whether the effect of such imports is otherwise to depress prices to a significant degree or prevent price increases, which otherwise would have occurred, to a significant degree. No one or several of these factors can necessarily give decisive guidance.[39]

Though the investigating authorities are instructed to look at several factors, it is clear that the focus is on direct, and not indirect effects of the subsidized imports. In *Canadian Countervailing Duties on Grain Corn from the United States*,[40] Canada had imposed a countervailing duty on grain corn from the United States, on the ground that a US subsidy had had the effect of depressing world prices, thus forcing Canadian producers to lower their prices as well. The United States contended that the Canadian Import Tribunal had not made an 'objective examination of the volume of subsidized imports', and hence was inconsistent with the Code. The Panel agreed, and its finding was accepted by the Committee:

[W]hereas the CIT equated the world market price decline with the decline and depression of the price for corn in the Canadian market, the CIT did not attempt to

[37] Uruguay Round Agreement on Subsidies and Countervailing Measures, Art. 15.5; Anti-Dumping Code, Art. 3.5.

[38] As noted above, the Anti-Dumping Code negotiated in the Kennedy Round was revised to track the Subsidies Code wherever possible, and the text of Article 3 of the 1979 Anti-Dumping Code is substantially the same as the text of Article 6 of the Subsidies Code. For dumping, this means that price comparisons are required for both the exporting and importing countries. See Ch. 10. In the Uruguay Anti-Dumping Code, the corresponding text appears in Article 3 as well.

[39] The corresponding provision in the Uruguay Round Subsidies Code appears in Article 15(2).

[40] *(United States v. Canada), Report of the Panel adopted by Committee on Subsidies and Countervailing Measures March 26, 1992*, GATT BISD, 39th Supp. 411 (1993); Pescatore, *Handbook*, Case 85.

make a link between subsidized imports and the price decline and depression in the Canadian market. No positive evidence was adduced on this point. . . . The Panel accordingly found that the CIT did not consider the price effects of subsidized imports, as required by Article 6.2.[41]

In sum, unilateral determination of countervailing duties by the authorities of the importing state remained in the 1979 Code, and no distinction for this purpose was introduced between prohibited, tolerated, and exempt practices by exporting countries. That step, discussed but not acted upon in the Tokyo Round, was to be the major achievement in the regulation of subsidies in the Uruguay Round, as discussed hereafter. One significant effect of the detailed procedural provisions of the 1979 Subsidies Code was that numerous countries that had not previously imposed countervailing duties or had done so on an ad hoc basis now established formal administrative procedures resembling those of the United States. As between countervailing duties and anti-dumping duties, the standard for determination of injury ended up substantially the same; by implication, if not by express text, that standard was easier to meet than in the context of an escape clause or safeguards case.[42]

(d)   Regulation of Subsidies

The Code maintained the distinction in Article XVI of the GATT between subsidies on exports and other subsidies. Export subsidies on products other than 'certain primary products'[43] were prohibited, without any reference to comparison between domestic and export prices (Art. 9). Subsidy was not defined, but an Annex provided a list of illustrations of what is meant by export subsidies. The provision in Article XVI(4) of the GATT that export prices of subsidized goods must be compared with home-market prices was not repeated in the Code. With respect to exports on 'certain primary products,' the Code did repeat the text of GATT Article XVI(3) concerning equitable share of world export markets, except that where the GATT says 'the parties should seek to avoid', the Code said 'signatories agree not to grant.'[44]

The key issue, however, remained unresolved. 'Signatories recognize that subsidies other than export subsidies are widely used as important instruments for the promotion of social and economic policy objectives' (Art. 11(1)). The paragraph went on to list six such objectives. Further, '[s]ignatories recognize that [these] objectives . . .may be achieved, *inter alia*, by means of subsidies granted with the aim of giving an advantage to certain enterprises', followed by another list of such measures, including govern-

---

[41] *United States* v. *Canada*, para. 5.2.6.   [42] See Ch. 5, Sect. 5.4

[43] Insertion of the work 'certain' is explained in a footnote that excludes minerals from the exemption, leaving only products of farm, forest or fishery.

[44] 'More than an equitable share of world export trade' was explained in Article 10(2) of the Code, but not made more precise, except that 'a previous representative period' was defined as 'normally . . . the three most recent calendar years in which normal market conditions existed.'

ment grants, loans or guarantees, government financing of research and development, and government provision of equity capital (Art. 11(3)). The signatories recognized that subsidies other than export subsidies 'may cause or threaten to cause injury to a domestic industry of another signatory' (Art. 11(2)), but provided that 'nothing in [Article 11] and in particular the enumeration of forms of subsidies creates, in itself, any basis for action under the General Agreement, as interpreted by [the Code]' (Art. 11(4)).

(e) The Second Track

The drafters of the Subsidies Code realized that countervailing duties provided a remedy—and not always the best one—for only one of the three situations in which subsidies granted by one state could harm another state (Sect. 9.1 at p. 200). Accordingly, they provided that in all three situations, a state that believed it (or its industry) had been injured—whether by an export subsidy (Arts. 12(1), 12(2), and 13(1)), or by 'any subsidy' (Arts. 12(3), 12(4) and 13(2))—could initiate an elaborate sequence of consultations, conciliation, and dispute system by a panel, all according to a tight time schedule and presided over by a Committee on Subsidies and Countervailing Measures, made up of representatives from each signatory to the Code. The panel, as with other GATT panels (Chapter 7), would submit a report to the Committee, which like the GATT Council in cases brought under Article XXIII, 'shall make such recommendations to the parties as may be appropriate to resolve the issue. . . .' (Art. 13(4)). If all else failed, the Committee could authorize 'appropriate countermeasures,' including withdrawal of GATT concessions or obligations. Many of the cases brought to the Subsidies Code dispute settlement process arose out of challenges by the exporting country to the findings made by the importing country in countervailing duty cases.[45] One important case brought directly under the second track was a challenge by the United States to a complicated system of subsidies paid by the European Community to processors of oil seeds which in part benefited producers of soy beans within the Community, with the effect of impairing, as the United States contended, the value of a zero tariff binding on oil seeds negotiated at the close of the Dillon Round in 1962, in that it reduced the market opportunities for American exporters within the Community (situation 2 on page 200 supra). The United States prevailed before the panel, and its decision was upheld by the GATT Council.[46]

[45] See e.g. the *Grain Corn* case, n. 40 supra; also e.g. *United States—Imposition of Countervailing Duties on Imports of Fresh and Chilled Atlantic Salmon from Norway,* (*Norway* v. *United States*) (28 Apr. 1994), GATT BISD, 41st Supp. ii, 576 (1994), Pescatore, *Handbook,* Case 93.

[46] *EEC—Payments and Subsidies on Oilseeds and Related Animal-Feed Proteins (United States* v. *European Economic Community)*, Panel Report Gatt Doc. L/6627 (14 Dec. 1989), adopted by GATT Council 25 Jan. 1990, GATT BISD, 37th Supp. 86 (1991). Pescatore, *Handbook,* Case 77; Hudec, *Enforcing International Trade Law,* Case 179.

However, the controversy remained active throughout the Uruguay Round, and almost led to breakdown in the negotiations before being resolved in the so-called Blair House agreement of November 1992.

(f) Subsidies and the Developing Countries

According to Article 14(1) of the Code, '[s]ignatories recognize that subsidies are an integral part of economic development programmes.' That would not be what the International Monetary Fund would say,[47] and subsidies by developing country A, with a deeper pocket, might well harm developing country B, particularly in situation (3) (p. 200 supra) in which A and B compete for exports in developed country C.[48] It was also true that developed countries, particularly the United States, were concerned about the penetration of their markets by subsidized exports from partially industrialized countries such as Brazil, and they were not prepared to accede to the demand that exports of developing countries be exempt from countervailing duties imposed by importing states. Again the resolution—fashioned after the basic bargain between the European Community and the United States had been tentatively concluded—was one of compromise and ambiguity.

On one side, the flat prohibition on export subsidies (other than on certain primary products) contained in Article 9 of the Code was made inapplicable to the developing countries (Art. 14(1));[49] on the other side the Code recites that 'developing country signatories agree that export subsidies on their industrial products shall not be used in a manner which causes serious prejudice to the trade or production of another signatory' (Art. 14(3)). Moreover, developing country signatories were encouraged to 'endeavour to enter into a commitment to reduce or eliminate export subsidies when the use of such export subsidies is inconsistent with its competitive and development needs,' an early codification of the concept of graduation applicable particularly to the East Asian countries but also, at least in part, to Mexico, Brazil, and several other countries of Latin America.[50]

Coming back to the first side, the consultation and dispute settlement provisions of the Code were made inapplicable to complaints against non-export subsidies of developing countries, except on a claim of nullification or impairment of a GATT concession in situation (2) (p. 200 supra), i.e. if

---

[47] See Ch. 17, Sect. 17.5(b).

[48] Rivers and Greenwald, the US negotiators of the Subsidies Code (n. 24 supra), at p. 1480, n. 140, report being told by LDC representatives from time to time of just such effects. But such conversations were always off the record. Formally, the developing countries stood together in the Tokyo Round behind the leadership of Brazil and India in demanding 'special and differential treatment' on this as on other issues.

[49] Recall (Sect. 9.2, at n. 8) that the developing countries had not signed the 1960 Declaration or adopted the 1962 Amendments to GATT Article XVI restricting subsidies on exports.

[50] According to Rivers and Greenwald, n. 24 supra at 1482, this was 'the heart of the deal' with the developing countries on export subsidies on industrial products.

the complainant showed that its exports to the developing country in question for which it negotiated a tariff binding were displaced as the result of the subsidy (Art. 14(7)). The same paragraph stated that the practices listed in Article 11(3) as illustrative of subsidies that may give an advantage to certain enterprises shall not, *per se*, be considered subsidies when they originate in developing countries. On the other side, nothing in the Code prevented an importing country from undertaking a countervailing duty proceeding against goods benefiting from such practices. Perhaps most important, the obligations (such as they were) with respect to 'certain primary products' were to apply equally to developed and developing countries (Art. 14(10)).

(g) Summary

In all, the Subsidies Code that emerged from the Tokyo Round introduced more law into the question of subsidies than had existed before. In normative terms, the rules seemed to be clear in prohibiting export subsidies by industrial countries on non-primary products, whether or not they caused injury. Any other signatory to the Code could request consultations, and could initiate dispute settlement, even if it did not assert that it had been injured.[51] But importing states were permitted to impose countervailing duties, provided they established in a formal investigation the existence of a subsidy, material injury to their industry, and a causal link between the subsidization and the injury.

The Code left many questions unanswered—how to measure a subsidy, how to allocate grants or loans over various products and over time, how to define and measure injury to an industry, and how to sort out the multiple causes of injury, given that in times of prosperity subsidy cases are rarely brought. All of these questions came up in disputes in the years following conclusion of the Tokyo Round. A fair number of these questions were resolved in the Uruguay Round fifteen years later. The next section sets out some of the questions in more detail. The section on the Uruguay Round ties up some of the loose ends.

9.5 SUBSIDY LAW: SOME ILLUSTRATIONS

Most 'case law' on subsidies has come in countervailing duty cases before national authorities; most of those cases have been brought in the United

---

[51] Such an initiative would be highly unusual, given the GATT's emphasis on injury as a condition precedent to dispute settlement. Evidently in order to emphasize the distinction between subsidies on exports and other subsidies, however, Article 13 required a showing of injury but Article 12 contained no such requirement. The distinction is maintained and developed in the Uruguay Round Subsidies Agreement, which, as described hereafter, classifies subsidies as prohibited (i.e. export subsidies), actionable (most other subsidies), and non-actionable (subsidies whose benefits are regarded as outweighing their possible adverse trade effects).

States, which, as noted earlier, has had a countervailing duty law for over a century.[52] Discussion of these cases can serve both to explain the issues and to provide source material (not to say precedent) in future controversies, at national as well as international level. The cases may also serve to explain, at least in part, the origin and significance of the Illustrative List of [Forbidden] Export subsidies annexed to the 1979 Subsidies Code, and restated without change in the Uruguay Round Code.

(a)   Direct Export Subsidies

Sometimes export subsidies are easy to identify. For instance in 1959, the US Treasury found that the Spanish government was paying eight pesetas per kilo to exporters of almonds. Accordingly, the United States imposed an equivalent countervailing duty until the subsidy was terminated.[53] Clearly such a subsidy would violate the Subsidies Code.

If a subsidy is general, i.e. not limited to a particular product, it may not be clear how to measure it. For instance, in the wake of a general strike in the 'Days of May' of 1968, the French government introduced a payment of 6 percent of labour costs to exporters, to make up for the 10 percent across-the-board wage increase it had been compelled to grant in order to end the strike. In response, the United States imposed a surcharge of 2.5 percent *ad valorem* on all dutiable goods covered by the French subsidy.[54] That France was paying an export subsidy was evident. But it was equally evident that not all products benefited from the subsidy to the same extent, since the labour content of the exported products was not uniform. Not long after the initial order, the countervailing surcharge was reduced to 1.25 percent.[55] Under the Subsidies Code of 1979, the subsidy granted by France would violate Article 9; the imposition by the United States of countervailing duties without a detailed investigation would violate Article 2.[56]

---

[52] Apart from having a countervailing duty law, the United States has also, for most of the time in question, had a system of on-the-record decisions in countervailing duty cases, at least when the decision was affirmative. In other countries, prior to adoption of the Subsidies Code in 1979, decisions on subsidy matters were often lacking in transparency, and thus could be understood only by the immediate participants.

[53] Treasury Decision (T.D.) 54792, 24 Fed. Reg. 1117 (17 Feb. 1959) revoked in T.D. 55184, 25 Fed. Reg. 7099 (27 July 1960).

[54] T.D. 68-192, 33 Fed. Reg. 11543 (10 Aug. 1968), republished with translation of French decree in 33 Fed. Reg. 11661 (6 Aug. 1968).

[55] T.D. 68-270, 33 Fed. Reg. 16056 (1 Nov. 1968). The duty was revoked as of February 1, 1969, T.D. 69-41, 34 Fed. Reg. 1377 (29 Jan. 1969). The episode is interesting because it illustrates the sometimes perverse effect of countervailing duty law. At the same time as the US Treasury Department was countervailing exports from France, the Federal Reserve Bank was taking the lead in arranging a $1.3 billion stand-by credit for France. See 20 *Int'l Financial News Survey* (IMF) 207, 221–2, 230–1 (21 June, 9 July, 12 July 1968).

[56] Corresponding to Articles 3 and 15 of the Uruguay Round Subsidies Agreement.

(b) Export Incentive Schemes

Subsidy schemes in the period following World War II only rarely consisted of direct payments per item exported. More commonly, they have involved complicated programs for remission of taxes previously paid or payable, favoured treatment in connection with exchange controls, loans and grants of various kinds, or other governmental interventions in the economy that may be said (fairly or unfairly) to be on preferential as opposed to commercial terms. When such schemes have been focused on exports, they have sometimes been met by diplomatic protests, and sometimes by countervailing duty proceedings. Important cases of this kind have found their way into the Illustrative List of [forbidden] Export Subsidies annexed to the Subsidies Code.

A notable example, which became the subject of a major international controversy, was a scheme adopted by Canada in October 1963 whereby import duties payable by Canadian motor vehicle manufacturers on vehicles and parts used for original equipment would be remitted to the extent that the Canadian content value of exports of those manufacturers exceeded the Canadian content value of their exports in the base period.[57] The Canadian vehicle manufacturers eligible for the rebate were all subsidiaries of the major American manufacturers and the object of the program, which was quickly achieved, was to allocate a greater portion of their production and procurement to Canada:

> Suppose, for example, Ford of Canada, a wholly-owned Canadian subsidiary of the Ford Motor Company (USA), needed an automobile transmission that cost 100 dollars and was not made in Canada. It would have to pay a 25 percent Canadian duty on that part, so that its total cost would be $125. Engine blocks, however, were made in both countries—for $85 in the United States, and $100 in Canada. In the base year before the rebate plan, Canadian-made engines were used for vehicles assembled in Canada, US-made engines for vehicles assembled in the United States. Under the plan, if Ford made more engines in Canada than it needed and exported them to the United States, (i.e. the engines were 'excess value' for purposes of the Plan), it would receive a $25 rebate from the Canadian government per engine. The cost of the Canadian-made engine used in assembling a vehicle in the United States would be $100+8.5 percent US duty or $108.50, compared to the cost of the locally produced engine of $85.

---

[57] See Canada: Order in Council Establishing Rebate Plan, P.C. 1963-1/1544. This and other documents connected with the Rebate Plan are collected in US Congress: Hearings on H.R. 6960 (a Bill to Implement the Automotive Products Agreement between the United States and Canada, signed to resolve the controversy here described) before House Comm. on Ways and Means, 89th Cong., 1st Sess. (1965). See also A. Chayes, T. Ehrlich, and A. Lowenfeld, *International Legal Process*, Vol. I, Ch. V (1968).

But the result of producing the engines in Canada would be a gain of $25 rebate on the Canadian import duty on transmissions minus $23.50 additional cost for the engine, for a net gain for Ford of $1.50.[58]

One could argue (and in fact it was argued) that the Canadian Rebate Plan did not constitute a 'bounty or grant upon the . . . *export of any article*'. Moreover, the US government understood that the Rebate Plan was an important element in the platform of the recently elected government of Canada to reduce American dominance of Canada's automotive and other industries, and it had no desire to provoke a confrontation with its northern neighbour by frustrating the plan through a countervailing duty. But as the example shows, the object of the plan was to divert procurement of auto parts from the United States to Canada and to stimulate Canada's exports of auto parts. When an American manufacturer of auto radiators petitioned for imposition of countervailing duties on the ground that increased imports were flowing to the United States with benefit of a subsidy, the US government tried to delay consideration of the petition, but eventually concluded that it had no alternative under US law as it then read (i.e. without a requirement to investigate injury) but to impose a countervailing duty on all exports of automotive parts from Canada. The US government never reached the stage of actually calculating the duty, because the impasse was broken by a decision to negotiate the Canada–United States Automotive Products Agreement of 1965,[59] which eliminated all duties on vehicles and original use auto parts in trade between the two countries.[60] Under the Subsidies Code, it seems clear that the Canadian Automotive Rebate Plan would come within paragraph (i) of the Illustrative List of Export Subsidies, in that it was a

remission . . . of import charges in excess of those levied on imported goods that are physically incorporated . . . in the exported product.

More generally, the Canadian rebate plan was a charge on the public account—i.e. a reduction of revenue from import duties—linked directly to an increase of exports by the beneficiary. If Canada had simply reduced or eliminated the duty on imports of auto parts (as it later did), without a direct

---

[58] The example is adapted from Chayes, Ehrlich, and Lowenfeld, *International Legal Process* (n. 57 supra), at 315. The rates of duty in the example were correct as of the early 1960s, before the reductions of 1968–72 resulting from the Kennedy Round of trade negotiations. The figures for the prices of the transmission and engine do not purport to be exact.

[59] 17 U.S.T. 1372, T.I.A.S. No. 6093, signed at Johnson City, Texas, 16 Jan. 1965. That Agreement created problems of its own, because it violated the most-favoured-nation provision of Article I of the GATT.

[60] Presumably the duty could have been calculated for each company by multiplying the increase in exports of auto parts from Canada in a given period over the base period by the average rate of duty payable on imports of auto parts by that company into Canada in the same period. Of course this technique would work only where the exporters and importers were the same, and where matching the subsidy to the countervailing duty by product was not needed. Also, of course, this calculation takes no account of any showing of injury, which might be possible for independent parts makers, but not for example, for Ford in the illustration on page 219.

link to export performance, there would have been no violation and no occasion for a countervailing duty, although the effect might have been similar, in that it would have reduced the cost of producing vehicles in Canada and thus might well have stimulated exports.

One might suggest that the US–Canada Automotive Pact was itself in part an export subsidy scheme, in that forgiveness of Canadian import duties was contingent *inter alia* on export performance. This challenge was in fact brought a generation later on behalf of Japanese and European automobile manufacturers who had not made the investments in Canada necessary to qualify for the exemption from duties.[61]

(c)   Export Credits and the OECD Arrangement

Many States have public or quasi-public agencies that promote exports by providing credits (or guarantees of credits) to finance export transactions, such as the Export Credits Guarantee Department (ECGD) in Great Britain, the Export-Import Bank in the United States, and the Compagnie Française d'Assurance pour le Commerce Exterieur [COFACE] in France. Such transactions may involve machinery and other capital goods, ships and aircraft, or grains and other products of agriculture. The credits, when generally available (i.e. not limited to a particular industry or sector) are ordinarily not considered to be subsidies, but rather are considered comparable to trade and tourism offices attached to embassies abroad, government support of trade fairs, and government-sponsored market research. Well before agreement was reached on the 1979 Subsidies Code, however, it was recognized that government credits or credit guarantees at more favourable terms than those available commercially could be used as a form of subsidy, with the effect of distorting competition that ought to be based only on price, quality, delivery schedules, and so on.

The effort to solve the problem through coordinated policies was centered not in the GATT, but in the Organization for Economic Cooperation and Development, where representatives of finance ministries and export credit agencies of the industrial states, rather than trade officials of all states, were accustomed to discuss problems of common interest.

The OECD Export Credit Arrangement

Discussion of competition in export credits among the industrial states began in the period of rising interest rates and heightened export competition in the aftermath of the massive rise in oil prices in the fall of 1973. The aim was to reach agreement on minimum interest rates, maximum periods of repayment, and minimum down payments for most officially supported

---

[61] See *Canada—Certain Measures Affecting the Automotive Industry, (Japan and European Communities v. Canada)*, WT/DS/139/AB/R and WT/DS/142/AB/R, 31 May 2000, discussed in Sect. 9.7, nn. 113–14 infra.

export credits of two-years or more, and to exchange information among the industrial states offering export credits. By 1976 the discussions had led to a 'Consensus' by all the members of the OECD's Group on Export Credits and Credit Guarantees.

It proved difficult to translate the 'consensus' into an agreement, both because there were differences on appropriate terms and rates for particular products—e.g. airplanes as contrasted with wheat—and because the respective export credit agencies were also in differing degree engaged in foreign assistance to developing countries that were seeking to purchase goods from the OECD countries.[62] In 1978, even as the Tokyo Round was reaching its climax, the Consensus was converted into a 'gentleman's agreement', known as the *Arrangement on Guidelines for Officially Supported Export Credits*, which with numerous amendments and modifications has remained in effect through the remainder of the Twentieth Century and beyond.[63]

The Arrangement seeks to restrain subsidized trade in three ways, referred to as the discipline, automaticity, and transparency functions.[64] The *discipline* function is designed to limit official support for direct credits and financing, refinancing, interest rate support, aid financing, and export credit insurance and guarantees. The *automaticity* function is designed to reflect changes in the domestic capital markets and international exchange rates, in order to maintain the permissible margin of government support without breach of the Guidelines. The *transparency* function is designed to promote exchange of information among participating states, so that derogations from the Guidelines will be kept to a minimum, and, in some instances, to permit a second state to match a first state's offers of export support.[65]

In 1978, the Participants adopted minimum interest rates of 7–8 percent, a minimum down payment of 15 percent, standardized repayment schedules, and maximum terms of repayment of 8½ years in credits for exports to

[62] See Rolf Geberth, 'The Genesis of the Consensus', in OECD, *The Export Credit Arrangement: Achievements and Challenges, 1978–1998* (OECD 1998).

[63] The Arrangement looks like a formal international agreement, with five chapters, 88 articles, and seven annexes, except that it bears no signatures, that the states subscribing to the Arrangement are referred to as 'Participants', not 'parties', and that it lacks 'final clauses' specifying its entry into effect, period of notice for withdrawal, termination, accession, etc. The text of the Arrangement is available on the OECD web site, www.OECD.org.

[64] See Andrew M. Moravcsik, 'Disciplining Trade Finance: the OECD Export Credit Arrangement', 43 *Int'l Organization* 173 at 178 (1989).

[65] Professor Moravcsik reports the following example of the importance of exchange of information among the exporting states as the borrowers seek to play the lenders off against each other:

> In a recent case, Canada offered a subsidized credit to a major African nation and called for a face-to-face consultation with the Netherlands, claiming that the Dutch had already offered a tied-aid credit to Kenya in violation of the Arrangement, a charge denied by the Dutch. When pressed to substantiate their accusation, the Canadians produced a letter from the Dutch ambassador which indeed proposed an illegal credit. It was later discovered, however, that the letter was a clever forgery, pasted together by the buyer government from previous (and legitimate) Dutch offers and designed to provoke the Canadian credit agency into extending an illegal credit. (Moravcsik (n. 64 supra) at p. 204)

other OECD states and 10 years in credits for exports to developing countries. In response to changes in international interest rates, in 1981 the Participants increased the minimum interest rates to 11.25 percent for medium-term loan rates to OECD members, with a floor of ten-year loan rates to Lesser Developed Countries at 10 percent. The minimum interest rates were again raised in 1983, to reflect worldwide interest rates increases. In the same year, the Participants attempted to address the problem of fluctuations in domestic interest rates by amending the Arrangement to provide for automatic semi-annual interest rate adjustments dependent on a weighted average of interest rates of currencies constituting the IMF's special drawing rights. Subsequently, the link to SDRs was replaced by 'Commercial Interest Reference Rates' (CIRRs) in 12 currencies, set at a fixed margin of 100 basis points (one percentage point) above the respective base rates of three-, five-, or seven-year government bond yields depending on the length of the repayment period, with a five-year government bond yield for all other maturities. The CIRRs are adjusted monthly to reflect current commercial rates. In all, by year-end 1999, the Arrangement had been subject to no less than seven revisions, in addition to modifications to reflect changing economic conditions.[66]

Apart from direct export credits, experts from export credit agencies of the participating states also wrestled with the question of how to set premiums for credit insurance, taking into account various country risk methodologies. To guard against participants providing favourable insurance premiums as an indirect export subsidy, the Arrangement was modified in the mid-1990s to include country-risk guidelines, minimum premium benchmarks, and review procedures.

The Arrangement also attempts to deal with the problem of credits linked to tied aid, i.e. credits to developing countries that are usable only for purchases in the donor country. The Arrangement sets down the following General Principle, followed by a series of detailed definitions and criteria of eligibility:

The Participants have agreed to the general principle that they should have complementary policies for export credits and tied aid. Export credit policies should be based on open competition and the free play of market forces. Tied aid policies should provide needed external resources to countries, sectors or projects with little or no access to market financing. Tied aid policies should ensure best value for money, minimise trade distortion, and contribute to developmentally effective use of these resources.[67]

If a tied loan to a developing country Patria nominally at, say, 9 percent—within the Guidelines—requires the borrower/purchaser to pay back only 65 percent of the cost of the product to be exported—the other 35 percent being

---

[66] See OECD, *The Export Credit Arrangement, Achievement and Challenges* (n. 62, supra), esp. ch. 2.
[67] OECD Arrangement (n. 63, supra), Art. 30(a).

a grant—then (depending on the length of the loan), Patria has effectively received a credit at approximately 6 percent, well below the Guidelines. Accordingly, the Arrangement limits the grant element in such combined grant and loan deals—provided the project in question is otherwise eligible—to a stated percentage of the cost of the product, say an irrigation system or an electric power plant. Initially (1983), the percentage was 20 percent; later it was raised to 35 percent for most developing countries and 50 percent for the least developed countries. Furthermore, in 1991, the Participants agreed to prohibit tied aid both for countries whose per capita GNP is above a threshold established by the World Bank, and for projects that normally should be commercially viable.[68]

Export Credits and the GATT Subsidies Codes

The Illustrative List of prohibited export subsidies annexed to the 1979 Subsidies Code and repeated without change in the 1994 Agreement on Subsidies and Countervailing Measures (Sect. 9.6 infra) includes export credits if they are granted at rates of interest below those at which the government borrows (or could borrow) on international capital markets in the same currency as the credits given.[69] The Annexes go on to say that if a state is a party to an international undertaking on official export credits to which at least twelve original parties to the Code (Agreement) are parties—i.e. the OECD Arrangement—or if in practice a state applies the interest rate provisions of the undertaking, an export credit practice in conformity with those provisions shall not be considered a prohibited export subsidy.

The inference of the reverse, i.e. that an export credit not satisfying the OECD Arrangement is a prohibited subsidy, was drawn in two cases decided at the same time by WTO disputes panels, both involving subsidies on the sale of so-called regional aircraft by the only two manufacturers of such aircraft, in one case by the Canadian firm Bombardier, in the other by the Brazilian firm Embraer. In the first round, two different panels and the Appellate Body ruled that Canada's export credit programs in respect of Bombardier's regional aircraft were inconsistent with Article 3 of the Subsidies Agreement,[70] and that Brazil's subsidy of the competing Embraer regional aircraft also violated the Subsidies Agreement.[71] Thereafter,

---

[68] OECD Arrangement Art. 34 (Country eligibility), Art. 35 (Project eligibility). The Arrangement expressly excludes agriculture. Negotiations were initiated in 1996 to apply the principles of the Arrangement to that sector, with some changes to reflect the different characteristics of trade in agricultural products. As of year-end 2001 the negotiations continued, but agreement had not been reached.

[69] 1979 Subsidies Code Annex, para. k; Uruguay Round Agreement Annex I, para. k. Note that the other conditions of the OECD Guidelines, such as maximum repayment periods and minimum down payments, are not mentioned in the respective Annexes.

[70] *Canada—Measures Affecting the Export of Civilian Aircraft, (Brazil v. Canada)* WT/DS70/AB/R (2 Aug. 1999).

[71] *Brazil—Export Financing Programme for Aircraft (Canada v. Brazil)*, WT/DS46/AB/R (2 Aug. 1999).

Canada modified its subsidy programs to bring them into line, as it contended, with the Agreement on Subsidies. Brazil challenged the revisions to the Canadian programs, and Canada defended on the ground that, as revised, its programs complied with the OECD Arrangement. The panel accepted that if the programs complied with the interest rate provisions of the OECD Arrangement, they would not violate the Agreement on Subsidies.[72] As to Brazil's subsidy program, the Panel hearing Canada's challenge considered that compliance with the reference rates set under the OECD Arrangement would satisfy Brazil's obligations under the Subsidies Agreement, even though Brazil was not a party to the OECD or the Arrangement on Export Credits. The Panel concluded, however, that Brazil's measures to comply with the Panel's original recommendation 'either do not exist or are not consistent with the SCM Agreement'.[73] Taking these two cases together, one may say that at least de facto, the WTO Agreement combined with the Dispute Settlement mechanism, renders the 'gentlemen's agreement' negotiated under the auspices of the OECD an enforceable agreement, if a competing state chooses to initiate the process.

(d) Defining a Subsidy: Charge on the Public Account or Benefit to the Recipient

One recurring issue in the law of subsidies has been whether a subsidy should be defined by the cost to government or by the benefit to the recipient. The American position generally was that if a governmental measure confers a benefit on the exporter, it constitutes a subsidy and (assuming injury and causation) is countervailable. Prior to the conclusion of the Uruguay Round, and in particular in the course of the *Steel Subsidies* cases discussed in the next section, the position of the European Community was that if a measure did not require a net expenditure of public funds, it was not to be regarded as a subsidy, and thus could not justify imposition of a countervailing duty.

> Thus suppose the Patria Steel Co. (PATSCO) seeks to export steel girders in a competitive market, say to the United States. The Patrian Export Credit Agency (PECA) offers to finance the transaction by a 36-month credit at 9 percent per annum.[74] Commercial banks would not finance this transaction at less than 12 percent, but PECA, backed by the full faith and credit of Patria, is able to sell bonds at 9 percent.

---

[72] *Canada—Measures Affecting the Export of Civilian Aircraft, (Brazil* v. *Canada)*, Panel Report on Compliance, WT/DS70/RW (9 May 2000). In the actual case, however, the Panel was not fully satisfied that Canada had complied with the OECD Arrangment sufficiently to get out from the prohibition of Article 3 of the Subsidies Agreement.

[73] *Brazil—Export Financing Programme for Aircraft—Recourse by Canada to Article 21.5 of the DSU (Canada* v. *Brazil)*, WT/DS46/RW para. 7.1 (9 May 2000).

[74] For purposes of the illustration, it does not matter whether the PECA makes a loan to the purchaser, discounts the purchaser's note, or lends the funds to the seller to be repaid over the agreed period.

The prior position of the European Community would have been that no subsidy had been given in connection with this transaction. But if it turns out that the favourable financing induced the purchase from PATSCO rather than from a domestic American steel company, the position now shared by both the Community and the United States and accepted by the 1994 SCM Agreement would be that a subsidy has been granted, equal to 3 percent of the purchase price per year, and that a countervailing duty in the same amount was appropriate.[75]

The issue of benefit to the recipient versus public charge came up in a series of cases decided by the European Court of Justice under the EEC law implementing the 1979 Subsidies Code.

> The controversy arose from a complaint by a European producers' association (FEDIOL) against the European Commission for failure to impose a countervailing duty against imports of soya products from Argentina. The facts underlying the complaint were that Argentina levied an export tax of 10 percent on soya meal and oil, but a 25 percent export tax on soya beans. Thus through intervention of the state, it became more profitable to export soya in processed form rather than in raw state. From the point of view of the developing countries, efforts to increase the value added to raw materials by engaging in processing or fabrication are encouraged. The complainants argued, however, that the Argentine seed processing industry was subsidized, in that it was able to procure supplies of beans below the world market price, and that as a result Argentine and Brazilian producers had taken over nearly half of the European market of soya meal. The European Commission had rejected the argument, *first* because holding such a practice to be a subsidy would be to blur the distinction made in GATT between subsidies and other measures which may have an impact on international trade, and *second*, because the challenged practice did not involve a charge on the public account.[76]

The Court of Justice did not directly pass on the first point, but it accepted the second one.[77] The Court pointed out that the last paragraph of the Illustrative List annexed to the EC regulation, corresponding to paragraph (l)

---

[75] If the goods are delivered in a shorter period than the maturity of the loan, the countervailing duty would be calculated by the difference between the present value of a 9 percent and a 12 percent obligation. For a celebrated instance implementing the American view, at least at preliminary state, see the so-called *Bombardier* case, involving cars for the New York City subway to be manufactured in Canada with official credits at 9.7 percent (47 Fed. Reg. 53760).

[76] Commission Decision 85/239/EEC of 18 Apr. 1985, L 108/2 at pt. 7.

[77] *EEC Seed Crushers' and Oil Processors' Federation (FEDIOL)* v. *Commission*, Case 187/85 (*FEDIOL II*), [1988] E.C.R. 4155 (14 July 1988). A companion case, 188/85 (*FEDIOL III*), [1988] E.C.R. 4193 (14 July 1988) involved a similar complaint concerning soya products from Brazil. In an earlier case, *FEDIOL I*, Case 191/82, [1983] E.C.R. 2913 (5 Oct. 1983), the Court of Justice had held that the Commission's refusal to initiate countervailing duty proceedings was judicially reviewable. Thereupon the Commission did initiate a proceeding on FEDIOL's complaint, but ultimately declined to impose a countervailing duty.

of the Annex to the Subsidies Code,[78] reads 'any *other* charge on the public account', and concluded that 'the Commission was not wrong or arbitrary in concluding that the concept of subsidy . . . presupposes the grant of an economic advantage through a charge on the public account.' [79]

As a rule of thumb for distinguishing practices of exporting countries that will and will not be subjected to countervailing duties, the focus on whether a given practice does or does not constitute a charge on the public account is often useful.[80] It does not follow as a general proposition, however, that any measure that does not result in a direct transfer from the public treasury to the beneficiary is thereby excluded from the definition of subsidy. Indeed, after lenthy debate during the Uruguay Round,[81] the opposite argument was accepted in Article 14 of the Uruguay Round Agreement on Subsidies, which sets out at length the methods of calculating the amount of a subsidy in terms of the benefit to the recipient.[82] In its post-Uruguay Round regulation, the European Community adopted this position as well, consistent with the general principle that the amount of a countervailable subsidy is to be calculated in terms of the benefit conferred on the recipient, rather than in terms of the charge on the public account.[83]

(e) United States Countervailing Duties against European Steel in the 1980s

Perhaps the most remarkable series of countervailing duty proceedings and certainly the one that stimulated the most discussion of approach and

---

[78] Para. (l) of Annex I of the 1994 Subsidies Agreement.

[79] For a strong critique of the FEDIOL cases and of the focus on the charge on the public account, see Bronckers and Quick, 'What is a Countervailable Subsidy Under EEC Trade Law?' 23 *J. World Trade Law* No. 6, p. 5 (1989).

[80] It is worth noting that the United States government, in a so-called section 301 proceeding, declined to investigate a complaint against the same practices challenged in the FEDIOL cases brought by the American counterpart of FEDIOL. *National Soybean Processor Association, Initiation of Investigation*, 48 Fed. Reg. 23947 (27 May 1983). The petition did not seek imposition of a countervailing duty, apparently because the petitioners did not believe they could meet the statutory requirement of a bounty or grant on an item of export; instead the petition sought a remedy for violation by Brazil, Argentina, and others of the Subsidies Code. The Section 301 Committee of the US Trade Representative held that the differential taxes did not constitute an export subsidy.

[81] See Terence P. Stewart (ed.), *The GATT Uruguay Round: A Negotiating History*, Vol. I, pp. 934–43 and documents there cited (1993).

[82] 1994 Agreement on Subsidies and Countervailing Measures, Article 14(b) (loans) and (c) (guarantees). The relevant passage states:

> a loan by a government shall not be considered as conferring a benefit, unless there is a difference between the amount that the firm receiving the loan pays on the government loan and the amount the firm would pay on a comparable commercial loan which the firm could actually obtain on the market.

The same wording, with appropriate changes, is repeated with respect to government guarantees.

[83] Council Regulation (EC) 2026/97 of 6 Oct. 1997, 40 O.J. L 288/1 (1997) Art. 5 (the general principle of benefit to the recipient); Art. 6(b) and (c) measuring the benefit from loans and loan guarantees.

method, concerned complaints filed by the American steel industry in the early 1980s against imports of steel, primarily from member countries of the European Community. In the course of the proceeding, which went through detailed preliminary and final determinations of subsidization and to the brink of actual imposition of massive countervailing duties,[84] the United States executive branch undertook a detailed explanation of how to identify and how to measure a variety of interventions by governments in industry.[85] Some of the explanations were accepted by the European Community; many were challenged in two major memoranda to the GATT,[86] as well as in numerous submissions by the individual exporters to the US authorities. Overall, the European Community maintained the position, discussed earlier, that only benefits that represented a charge on public account could be regarded as subsidies; the United States maintained its position that the crucial element is the benefit to the recipient, whether or not that benefit comes directly out of the public treasury. Both sides understood that the *Steel Subsidy* cases illustrated the compromise achieved at the close of the Tokyo Round, in that nearly all of the challenged practices fell outside the class of prohibited export subsidies (Art. 9 and Illustrative List), but many of the practices could be regarded as other subsidies 'widely used as important instruments for the promotion of social and economic policy objectives' (Art. 11(1)) which might nevertheless cause or threaten injury to a domestic industry of an importing country (Art. 11(2)) and could be subject to countervailing duties under Articles 1–6 of the Code. Moreover, the issues raised by the *Steel Subsidies* cases illustrate how much of the law of subsidies remained uncharted. Only a few of the many issues are discussed here, together with some comments reflecting the author's views, but not necessarily an international consensus.

(i)   *Allocation of government grants.* It was clear that the steel industry of several member states of the European Community, notably Belgium,

---

[84] *Certain Steel Products from Belgium, Brazil, France, Federal Republic of Germany, Italy, Luxembourg, Netherlands, South Africa, and United Kingdom*, 47 Fed. Reg. 26,300–48 (17 June 1982) (Preliminary Determination); Id. 47 Fed. Reg. 39,304–95 (7 Sept. 1982) (Final Determination).

At the last moment before duties were to be imposed, the United States and the European Community reached an 'out of court settlement', in effect adopting a complicated quota agreement in place of unilaterally imposed duties. For a brief discussion of the circumstances of the conclusion of the *Arrangements Concerning Trade in Certain Steel Products and Steel Pipes and Tubes between The European Communities and the United States of America*, as well as reproduction of the principal texts, see A. Lowenfeld, *Public Controls on International Trade*, 427–36 (2nd edn. 1983). For a full length article analyzing the *Steel Subsidy Cases*, see Barshefsky, Mattice, and Martin, 'Government Equity Participation in State-Owned Enterprises: An Analysis of the Carbon Steel Countervailing Duty Cases', 14 *Law & Policy in Int'l Bus.* 1101 (1983).

[85] In particular in detailed appendices on methodology to the preliminary and final determinations, 47 Fed. Reg. 26307–10 (Preliminary Determination); 47 Fed. Reg. 39,316–31 (Final Determination).

[86] EEC Memoranda of 9 July 1982 and 5 Oct. 1982.

France, Great Britain, and Italy, was in dire straits in the late 1970s and early 1980s, and that member governments had bestowed substantial grants on firms in their countries in order to keep depressed plants operating and also to help with needed modernization. Many beneficiaries of such grants had continued to export to the United States, even as restraints were placed on imports into the Community and on price cutting within it. One recurring question was whether to regard a government grant as received in a given year and therefore attributable solely to that year, or to spread out the effect over some period of time. The US Department of Commerce concluded that in so far as capital grants were to be used to acquire capital equipment, the benefit should be allocated, for countervailing duty purposes, over the average life of capital assets in the steel industry, determined to be fifteen years. But rather than simply dividing the amount of such a grant by fifteen, which would have ignored the time value of money, the Department treated the grant like a 15-year mortgage, with equal annual instalments of interest and principal, at an interest rate derived for each country from the secondary market rate for long-term government debt.[87] The amount thus calculated as hypothetically payable by the recipient firm for each year was then divided by the total output of the firm, and the result would be the amount of the subsidy per ton (or other unit) in a given year attributable to the grant.

> Thus suppose Patria Steel Company (PATSCO) received in year I a grant usable for purchase of capital equipment in the amount of $100,000, and suppose the interest rate determined as above was 12 percent per annum. The subsidy, based on a calculation of level quarterly payments over 15 years, would be $14,453.18 per annum.

Note that this approach makes no distinction between domestic and export subsidies; whether it increases or decreases the amount of countervailing duty in a given year depends on whether that year is a year of grant or a later year.[88] If a grant was given for a specific purpose other than acquisition of capital assets, for instance for current operations or to cover losses at year-end, the Department would not allocate the grant over time, but would attribute the whole amount to the year in which the funds were received. The approach of the US Department of Commerce does not seem a priori unsound or unfair, though it evidently uses a 'rule of thumb' to counter trade distortions, and may well create distortions of its own. One

---

[87] The Department explained that this rate was chosen to eliminate all risk factors from the interest rate and to count only the actual value of the use of funds.

[88] For instance, in a case brought before a binational panel under the Canada–United States Free Trade Agreement, the Canadian exporter argued that it was being penalized in the year under review for grants received many years earlier; the Panel, upholding the US Department of Commerce, recognized the continuing benefit of the use of assets acquired with an earlier grant (*New Steel Rail Except Light Rail from Canada*, Case USA-89-1904-07, Opinion of Panel 8 June 1990).

unresolved problem is how to treat a grant for an asset allocated over 15 years, when the asset is discarded in an earlier year.[89]

(ii)   *Government-supported loans.* The US Department of Commerce took as its point of departure that any long-term loan or credit on terms more favourable than terms available commercially was a countervailable subsidy, even if the terms were not more onerous than the cost of funds to the government agency. The subsidy was computed by comparing what a company would pay in principal and interest in any given year on a normal commercial loan with what the company actually paid on the preferential loan in that year. This too seems sound, provided one accepts the value-to-the-beneficiary rather than the cost-to-government theory, as discussed above.[90]

The more difficult issue was how to treat loans to enterprises—which included a number of steel companies in the countries concerned—that could not borrow in the commercial market at all, because they had a long history of losses or defaults. In the actual cases, there were a number of disputes concerning the time when a given firm, without the benefit of hindsight, could fairly be deemed to have become uncreditworthy, as contrasted to being merely unprofitable. Putting that issue aside,[91] the US Department of Commerce treated government loans to uncreditworthy enterprises as if they were contributions of capital, measured in each year by the difference between the company's rate of return on equity and the average rate of return on equity for the country as a whole, multiplied by outstanding principal; if a payment on the loan was made in the year in question, the amount of subsidy so calculated would be reduced by the amount of the payment.[92]

This approach seems questionable, as can be seen from the following example:

> Suppose Patria Steel Company (Patsco) has incurred losses in five of the last six years and has no more access to commercial long-term credits.[93] The Industrial Bank of Patria, a state-owned agency, makes available a ten-year loan of $20,000,000 at 9 percent per annum, with no requirement of repayment of principal until maturity. Suppose further

[89] Another problem, largely ignored by the US Department of Commerce, would be how to allocate a grant to an enterprise that made both products subject of the subsidy investigation and other products, not involved in the investigation. For still another problem, resulting from privatization of state-owned enterprises, see Subsect. (f) infra.

[90] See Subsect. (d) supra.

[91] In the actual cases, it resulted in substantial reduction in the proposed countervailing duty from the preliminary to the final determination.

[92] The Department realized that, in some cases, this method of calculation might result in determination of a subsidy greater than if the loan were treated as an outright grant, for instance if a firm had a negative rate of return; accordingly it announced a 'grant cap' on calculation of subsidies consisting of loans to uncreditworthy enterprises, based on calculations as under (i) above.

[93] Even such a finding may be questionable, since a firm with access to government credits might well not make an exhaustive exploration of the availability of commercial loans.

that the average rate of return on equity for all industries in Patria is determined by the US government to be 18 percent.[94] Commercial loans to firms that have access to the market are available at 12 percent.

In year III of the loan, PATSCO meets its interest obligations on the loan, paying $1.8 million. If PATSCO were deemed creditworthy, the subsidy would be deemed to be $600,000 for the year, i.e. the difference between the commercial and the preferential rate. But under Commerce's methodology, the subsidy would be 18 percent × $20 million, or $3.6 million, minus $1.8 million interest paid, or a total subsidy of $1.8 million, spread over the output of the firm.

The Department of Commerce in the *Steel Subsidies* cases justified its approach 'by the great risk, very junior status, and low probability of repayment of these loans absent government intervention or direction.'[95] In subsequent proceedings, the Department appears to have reconsidered this approach in favour of a comparison between the preferential interest rate and the highest commercial interest rate commonly available in the country in question, increased by a risk premium.[96] The risk premium, in turn was calculated as the difference between the interest rate paid by the most and least creditworthy company operating in the country in question.[97] The revised approach seems sounder. Of course an infusion of capital with no expectation of repayment does not gain by being denominated 'loan'. But for loans that cannot fairly be characterized as non-performing, it seems doubtful that the notional conversion of a loan to a grant meets the requirement in Article 4(2) of the Tokyo Round Subsidies Code (Article 19.4 of the Uruguay Round Code) that 'no countervailing duty shall be levied on any imported product in excess of the amount of the subsidy found to exist.'

(iii) *Government purchase of corporate shares.* Article 11(3) of the Subsidies Code lists government subscription to or provision of capital as a possible (but not a forbidden) form of subsidy. If the government (or a government agency) purchases shares of a company at market prices, or from the public, there is no subsidy. For example, the nationalization of five major industrial groups by the French government in 1981 raised questions of fair compensation to shareholders, but not of subsidization, even though the price paid exceeded the book value or the share price on the Paris stock exchange. But when government pays substantially more than market price to the company for treasury shares or newly issued stock, or acquires stock in return for cancellation of debt held by the government in circumstances

---

[94] This was the figure used by the US government for France in 1981.

[95] 47 Fed. Reg. 39304 at 39318.

[96] *Certain Carbon Steel Products from Mexico, Preliminary Affirmative Countervailing Duty Determination,* 49 Fed. Reg. 5142 at 5148 (10 Feb. 1984).

[97] *Cold-Rolled Carbon Steel Flat-Rolled Products from Argentina: Final Affirmative Countervailing duty Determination and Countervailing Duty Order,* 49 Fed. Reg. 18006, 18016, 18019–20 (26 Apr. 1984).

where such exchange is not consistent with commercial considerations, the view of the US Department of Commerce has been that a subsidy has been paid, measured for each year by the 'rate of return shortfall', i.e. by the difference between the rate of return on equity of the company in question and the average rate of return on equity in the country as a whole, multiplied by the amount of the purchase or contribution of capital. The European Community, in response to the *Steel Subsidies* cases, pointed out that there are occasions when payment of a premium over market price for shares is justified, for example if the investor expects that infusion of new capital (perhaps accompanied by new management) will lead to better prospects for the shares than the market expects. However, if there is no reasonable prospect for rapid recovery, or if, as for instance in the purchase of newly issued shares in British Steel in the period 1977/8–1981/2, purchase of stock is made in the absence of any public market, it seems not unreasonable to regard the equity infusion as a subsidy.[98]

(iv)   *Support for research and development.* The prevailing view, shared by the United States and the EEC in the *Steel Subsidies* cases, is to distinguish between support for research that has general application—such as funding scientific institutions—which is not regarded as countervailable, and specific product development, which is regarded as countervailable, measured according to the form of the subsidy—i.e. as grant or preferential loan. In the Uruguay Round Subsidies Agreement, this topic was developed further, as discussed in the next section.

(v)   *State aids to industrial rationalization.* Even as the US Government was conducting its subsidies investigations against steel imports from the European Community, the Community itself was endeavouring, pursuant to the so-called Davignon Plan, to rationalize the steel industry through closing down of inefficient and obsolete facilities, dismissal or retirement of redundant employees, and installation of new, more productive facilities. The United States administration took the position that if a firm laid off workers pursuant to a restructuring program and the government (or the Community) relieved the firm of the obligation to make severance payments, that constituted a subsidy. This approach seems unsound. Even if a program of subvention of severance pay is industry-specific, it is not product-specific and not trade distorting, and should not be regarded as constituting a countervailable subsidy. On the other hand, a government loan at preferential

---

[98] The basic *Steel Subsidies* cases, as noted, were settled at the last moment by agreement between the United States and the European Community. A very similar case, involving specialty steel, was decided on essentially the same basis by the US Department of Commerce, and was appealed to the Court of International Trade. In two lengthy opinions, the court generally upheld the Department's methodology, except that for instances when the subsidy was not used to acquire capital assets, it rejected the use of a 15-year allocation period and required instead an inquiry into the actual benefits of the subsidies in question (*British Steel Corporation* v. *United States*, 605 F. Supp. 286 (Ct. Int'l Trade 1985); 632 F. Supp. 59 (Ct. Int'l Trade 1986)).

rates to replace an obsolete plant by a modern plant might well be regarded as a subsidy, even if the result was a smaller output produced at lower cost.

(f) Benefit versus Public Charge Revisited: Subsidies and Privatization

As noted in subsection (e) above, in administering its anti-subsidy program, the US Department of Commerce generally allocated countervailing duties responding to equity infusions and loans to uncreditworthy enterprises over the useful life of assets presumed to have been purchased with the grant or loan. In the steel industry, this meant that a countervailing duty might be spread out over 15 to 18 years, subject to periodic reviews. This practice applied both to privately-owned and to state-owned enterprises. But what if a state-owned enterprise that had received massive equity infusions and loans from the government in the past, such as the British Steel Corporation, were sold to the public for fair market value?[99]

The US government took the position that change in ownership did not change the fact that British Steel (now 'plc') was producing steel using capital assets acquired with the help of subsidies, and therefore that the countervailing duties assessed when BSC was state-owned should continue to be collected. The European Community challenged this practice before the WTO, on the ground that the new owners of British Steel had acquired the assets and liabilities of the enterprise in arm's length transactions and were thus not recipients of any 'benefit' as required by Article 1.1.(b) of the Agreement on Subsidies and Countervailing Measures. In reply, the United States pointed to Article VI(3) of the GATT, which speaks of 'subsidy determined to have been granted . . . on the manufacture, production or export of such product in the country of origin.' Thus the controversy was in some sense the reverse of the issue raised in Section 9.5(d). In the cases there discussed, the argument was made (and later rejected) that even if the exporter received a benefit, there could not be an actionable subsidy if there had been no net charge on public account; in the *British Steel* case that came before the WTO in 2000, the argument was that even if public funds had been expended that were not fully countervailed there could not be an actionable subsidy if the current owners, i.e. the successors to British Steel Corporation, had not received a benefit.

Both the Panel and the Appellate Body upheld the position of the European Community and found the continued imposition of countervailing duties by the United States to be inconsistent with the GATT and the Agreement on Subsidies.[100] The Appellate Body wrote:

---

[99] In the case of British Steel Corporation, the government of Prime Minister Thatcher created a corporation in 1988 to assume the assets and liabilities of BSC, and then sold the shares of that corporation through a public underwriting on the London Stock Exchange.

[100] *United States—Imposition of Countervailing Duties on Certain Hot-Rolled Lead and Bismuth Carbon Steel Products Originating in the United Kingdom, (EC v. United States)*, WT/DS/138/R (23 Dec. 1999); WT/DS138/AB/R (10 May 2000).

The existence of a 'financial contribution' is not at issue in this appeal. The principal issue in this appeal concerns the interpretation of the term 'benefit' in Article 1.1 [of the SCM Agreement].

. . .

It is true, as the United States emphasizes, that footnote 36 to Article 10 of the *SCM Agreement* . . . refer to subsidies . . . 'upon the manufacture, production or export of any merchandise'. In our view, however, it does not necessarily follow from this wording that the 'benefit' referred to in Article 1.1.(b) of the *SCM Agreement* is a benefit to *productive operations*.

. . .

We, therefore, agree with the Panel's findings that benefit as used in Article 1.1(b) is concerned with the 'benefit to the recipient', that such recipient must be a natural or legal person, and that in the present case . . . 'it is necessary to determine whether there was any "benefit" to UES and BSplc respectively (i.e. the producers of the imported leaded bars at issue)'. [quoting the Panel Report]. (para. 55–6, 58).

Since it was conceded that creation of the successor corporations to BSC and sale of their shares had been conducted under fair market conditions, the conclusion was that no benefit had been conferred on the corporations and hence no countervailable subsidy had been granted within the meaning of the SCM Agreement.

One might argue, contrary to the holding in this case, that the assets acquired in the course of privatization were more valuable than they would have been absent the earlier government grants, because no debt needed to be retired in respect to some of those assets. It could well be that the resulting savings enable the privatized enterprise to reduce its prices, and thus that the effect of the subsidies continued. As privatization of state-owned enterprises becomes more and more widespread, it seems likely that the *British Steel* case here summarized will not be the last word on the subject.

9.6 THE URUGUAY ROUND AGREEMENT ON SUBSIDIES AND COUNTERVAILING MEASURES

Though at the conclusion of the Tokyo Round the Subsidies Code of 1979 was viewed as a major achievement, in practice the Code proved disappointing. The outcome of complaints under the dispute settlement procedure had been inconclusive.[101] Moreover, the subsidies that caused the most controversy, including the major confrontation between the European Coal and Steel Community and the United States discussed in Section 9.5(e), were not covered in the Code at all, and consisted in large part of governmental measures that many states regarded as not only justifiable but indeed desirable.

The Uruguay Round SCM Agreement is a revision of the Tokyo Round Code, but a substantial one. It carries forward the two-track approach for

---

[101] See Robert E. Hudec, *Enforcing International Trade Laws*, pp. 145–64 (1993).

disputes, and the procedural requirements for imposition of countervailing duties. It also restates, with minor changes, the provisions of the 1979 Code with respect to determination of injury and causation, except that it expressly authorizes cumulation of imports from more than one country, provided that each country whose imports are cumulated is granting more than *de minimis* subsidies (Art. 15(3)). But the 1994 Agreement departs from the sharp distinction between export and domestic subsidies, and instead defines subsidies in terms of financial contribution by a government conferring a benefit on the recipient (Art. 1). Further, the SCM Agreement divides subsidies as defined into three categories—*prohibited* (known as the 'red light' category), *non-actionable* (known as the 'green light' category), and in-between or *actionable* (known as the 'yellow light' category). Moreover, whereas the Tokyo Round Subsidies Code had essentially exempted developing countries from the discipline of the Code, the 1994 Agreement exempts only the least developed countries from the prohibition on subsidies contingent on export performance (Art. 27.2), and makes most of its other provisions (with some modifications and grace periods) applicable to all developing countries. Perhaps the key to reaching agreement, trade in agriculture was essentially written out of the 1994 SCM Agreement, to be dealt with on rather different principles in a separate Agreement on Agriculture.

(a)   Defining subsidy

The drafters of the Tokyo Round Subsidies Code had not been able to agree on a definition of subsidy, and had contented themselves with an 'Illustrative List of Export Subsidies' plus the statement that 'subsidies other than export subsidies are widely used as important instruments for the promotion of social and economic policy objectives' but 'may cause or threaten injury to a domestic industry of another signatory' (Art. 11). In the Uruguay Round Subsidies Agreement, the Illustrative List of Export Subsidies remains almost unchanged, but a comprehensive definition of a subsidy was agreed on. Article 1.1 of the Code states:

For the purposes of this Agreement, a subsidy shall be deemed to exist if:
  (a)   (1)   there is a financial contribution by a government or any public body within the territory of a Member . . ., i.e. where:
              (i) a government practice involves a direct transfer of funds (e.g. grants, loans, and equity infusion), potential direct transfers of funds or liabilities (e.g. loan guarantees);
              (ii) government revenue that is otherwise due is foregone or not collected (e.g. fiscal incentives such as tax credits);[102]

---

[102] A footnote in the text reproduces the Note ad Article XVI of the GATT to the effect that exemption of an exported product from duties or taxes borne by the like product when destined for domestic consumption, or the remission of such duties or taxes in amounts not in excess of those which have accrued, shall not be deemed to be a subsidy.

(iii) a government provides goods or services other than general infrastructure, or purchases goods;

(iv) a government makes payments to a funding mechanism, or entrusts
or directs a private body to carry out one or more of the type of functions
illustrated in (i) to (iii) above which would normally be vested in the government and the practice, in no real sense, differs from practices normally
followed by governments;

or

(a)   (2)   there is any form of income or price support in the sense of Article XVI
of GATT 1994.

and

(b)   a benefit is thereby conferred.

In earlier drafts, this definition would have applied only to actionable subsidies; eventually, however, the parties agreed to the comprehensive definition, followed by division of subsidies into the three categories of prohibited,
actionable, and non-actionable.

(b)   Red and Green Light Subsidies

Red light or prohibited subsidies include the previously condemned subsidies contingent on export performance (Art. 3.1(a)), but also import substitution subsidies, i.e. subsidies contingent upon the use of domestic over
imported goods (Art. 3.1(b)). Red light subsidies may be challenged by
member states either in countervailing duty proceedings (including a determination of injury) (Arts. 10–23), or in an expedited dispute settlement proceeding (Art. 4), where injury to the complainant state need not be shown,
once it is established that the challenged measure is prohibited. The remedy,
if a challenged subsidy is found to fall into the prohibited category, is withdrawal of the subsidy 'without delay'.[103] If a challenge to a red light subsidy
is taken to a dispute panel, the applicable time-periods are to be one half of
the periods provided under the Understanding on Dispute Settlement, so
that the entire proceeding can be completed within six months (Art. 4).[104]

Green light or protected subsidies—the major innovation in the 1994
Subsidies Code—are subsidies that may not be challenged in the WTO dispute settlement mechanism or be subjected to countervailing duties under
national law. The introduction of the concept of green light subsidies, borrowed from a similar regulation of the European Community, reflects a
recognition that many governments undertake certain kinds of expenditures
that have a relation to the production of goods—some more direct than others—but are not viewed as unfair trade practices. The agreement (in Article

---

[103] See the *Australian Leather Subsidy* Case, discussed in Sect. 9.7.

[104] If the recommendation to withdraw a prohibited subsidy is not followed within the time-
period specified by the panel, Article 4.10 provides for retaliation by the complaining state, according to the model laid out in the Understanding on Dispute Settlement. See DSU Article 21.5,
resorted to by both sides in the *Bombardier-Embraer* dispute described in Sect. 9.5, nn. 70–3 supra.

8) spells the criteria out quite carefully for three classes of subsidies—government assistance for research and development in the basic science or pre-competitive phase (Art. 8(2)(a)); government assistance for regional development to defined territories whose unemployment rate exceeds the national average by 10 percent or whose per capita income or product is no more than 85 percent of the national average (Art. 8(2)(b)); and one-time government assistance to firms of up to 20 percent of the cost of adaptation of existing facilities to new environmental requirements (Art. 8(2)(c)). Green light subsidies are supposed to be notified in advance to the Subsidies Committee and may then be subjected to scrutiny (Art. 8(3)), but it appears that if a given measure is not notified but is subsequently challenged, the government whose measure is challenged may still be able to attempt to establish that the measure in question fits into the green light category.

(c)   Yellow Light Subsidies

Yellow light or actionable subsidies are not expressly defined, except that they must meet a test of specificity—de jure or de facto, and that they do not come within the other two categories. The Agreement states that '[n]o Member *should cause*, through the use of any subsidy . . ., *adverse effects* to the interests of other Members . . . (Art. 5)) (emphasis added), and provides both for international challenge under the strengthened dispute settlement mechanism (Art. 7) and for countervailing duty proceedings under national law meeting the criteria of Article VI of GATT as elaborated in the Agreement—i.e. determination of subsidization and injury, and a causal link between them (Arts. 10–23). In another innovation compared to the prior code, the revised Agreement on Subsidies divides 'adverse effects' into three classes—traditional injury to the domestic industry of another member which is up to the complainant to establish; nullification or impairment of benefits accruing to other Members, also with the burden on the complainant; and what some observers have called 'dark amber' subsidies, i.e. four kinds of subsidies *presumed to cause serious prejudice*, with the burden shifted to the respondent state to show that no adverse effects were caused by the challenged measure (Art. 5). Among the 'dark amber' subsidies are total subsidization of a product exceeding 5 percent *ad valorem*; subsidies to cover operating losses sustained by an industry or an enterprise, and direct forgiveness of a debt (Art. 6.1). The continuing controversies, for the most part, may be expected to involve the yellow light subsidies.

(d)   The Question of Specificity

To a domestic producer in Patria faced with competition from abroad, it is little comfort that the government benefit that his Xandian competitor receives is available to a large number of enterprises or industries, rather than only to the particular competitor. But the law on subsidies well before the 1994 SCM Agreement had distinguished between generalized government benefits and state aids directed to a particular enterprise or industry, and the United States law defining domestic subsidy for purposes of countervailing had been qualified by the phrase 'if provided or required by government action to a specific enterprise or industry, or group of enterprises or industry.'[105]

The Uruguay Round Agreement leaves no doubt on the issue of specificity. Article 1.2 states that a subsidy as defined (in Article 1.1 quoted above) shall be subject to the provisions relating to actionable subsidies and countervailing measures 'only if such a subsidy is specific in accordance with the provisions of Article 2', and that article spells out the criteria of specificity in detail, covering not only de jure but also de facto limits to the beneficiaries of a challenged subsidy. Export subsidies are by definition considered to be specific.

(e)   Measuring a Subsidy

As mentioned previously,[106] the Uruguay Round SCM Agreement accepts the approach advocated by the United States, focusing on the benefit conferred on the recipient, rather than on the cost to the government providing the assistance. Once this decision had been made, the answers to several of the questions raised in the preceding section fell into place.

On *export credits*, Article 14(b) provides:

a loan by a government shall not be considered as conferring a benefit, unless there is a difference between the amount that the firm receiving the loan pays on the government loan and the amount the firm would pay on a comparable commercial loan which the firm could actually obtain on the market. In this case the benefit shall be the difference between these two amounts;

The same principle is applied in Article 14(c) to loan guarantees.

On *government grants*, Article 14(a) provides:

government provision of equity capital shall not be considered as conferring a benefit, unless the investment decision can be regarded as inconsistent with the usual investment practice (including for the provision of risk capital) of private investors in the territory of that Member;

---

[105] Trade Agreements Act of 1979 §771(5)(B). The successor provision, spelling out the result of the Uruguay Round Code, appears in 19 U.S.C. §1677(5A)(A)–(D). In the Steel Subsidies cases (Sect. 9.5(e) supra), the Department of Commerce had written:

All governments operate programs of benefit to all industries, such as internal transportation facilities or generally applicable tax rules. We do not believe that the Congress intended us to countervail such programs. (47 Fed. Reg. at 39328)

[106] See Sect. 9.5(d) supra.

On *provision of goods or services*, Article 14(d) provides:

the provision of goods or services or purchase of goods by a government shall not be considered as conferring a benefit unless the provision is made for less than adequate remuneration, or the purchase is made for more than adequate remuneration. The adequacy of remuneration shall be determined in relation to prevailing market conditions for the good or service in question in the country of provision or purchase (including price, quality, availability, marketability, transportation and other conditions of purchase or sale).

Each of these provisions is termed a guideline, applicable to Part V, the part of the Code directed to countervailing measures, but there would seem to be no reason why the same criteria should not be applied in the context of actionable subsidies submitted to dispute settlement by a panel. The Code also requires that the relevant legislation or regulation implementing the guidelines shall be transparent and adequately explained.[107]

(f) Subsidies and the Developing Countries

The statement in the Tokyo Round Code that subsidies may play an important role in economic development programs of developing country Members is repeated, but the exemptions from the discipline of the SCM Agreement are much narrower. Only the least developed countries are exempt from the prohibition on export subsidies; the others are supposed to phase out their export subsidies within eight years from the effective date of the WTO Agreement (January 1, 1995), preferably in a progressive manner (Art. 27(2) and (4)).[108] Most developing countries were given a five-year grace period with respect to the prohibition on subsidies contingent on the use of domestic goods; for the least developed countries, the grace period was set at eight years.

Building on the concept of 'graduation' mildly suggested in the Tokyo Round Code,[109] the 1994 Agreement provides for phasing out in two years of export subsidies for any given product in which the country in question has reached 'export competitiveness', defined as having attained a market share of at least 3.25 percent of world trade in that product for two consecutive calendar years (Art. 27.5–27.6).

Several of the presumptions with respect to 'red light subsidies' and 'dark amber subsidies' are made inapplicable to proceedings against developing countries, and other proceedings, both before panels and before investigating authorities in countervailing duty cases, are made subject to greater hurdles

---

[107] The European Community does this by restating the guidelines in Council Regulation No. 2026/97 Art. 6, 6 Oct. 1997 40 O.J. L 288/1; the United States legislation re-states the guidelines in 19 U.S.C. §1677(5)(E).

[108] Provision is made in Article 27(4) for extension of this deadline, but only upon application to and determination by the Committee on Subsidies, and subject to annual consultations.

[109] See Sect. 9.4(f), at n. 50 supra.

(Art. 27.7–27.10). Overall, however, the Uruguay Round Agreement on Subsidies and Countervailing Measures binding on all members of the WTO reflects an effort to bring the developing countries—with some leeway—into the global subsidies regime.

CONCLUSION

A footnote to Article 4 of the 1979 Subsidies Code said: 'An understanding among signatories should be developed setting out the criteria for the calculation of the amount of the subsidy.' Essentially, that understanding has been reached, generally along the lines advocated by the United States. A comprehensive definition of subsidy, which eluded the Tokyo Round, was achieved in the Uruguay Round, in combination with consensus on the kinds of governmental measures that, within appropriate limits, ought not to be opposed.

In addition to the Canadian and Brazilian regional aircraft cases discussed in Section 9.5(c), three other cases were decided by Dispute Panels in the first five years of the SCM Agreement. In each case the decision was that the challenged program violated the prohibition on export subsidies of the Agreement.

- The Australian government was held to have given grants to a manufacturer of automotive leather, de facto, in violation of the SCM Agreement because it was clear that the expanded production to be supported by the grant greatly exceeded the demand for the product in Australia.[110]
- The United States government was held to have violated the Agreement in its Foreign Sales Corporation [FSC] program,[111] which was designed to enable US manufacturers to reduce income taxes on exports by selling through a foreign subsidiary.[112]
- Perhaps the most interesting case was the holding that in implementing the Canada–United States Auto Pact of 1965,[113] Canada had acted inconsistently (*inter alia*) with the SCM Agreement, in that exemptions for manufacturers in Canada from import duties were contingent on export performance.[114]

---

[110] *Australia—Subsidies Provided to Producers and Exporters of Automotive Leather, (United States* v. *Australia)*, WT/DS/126/R (25 May 1999).

[111] US Internal Revenue Code §§ 921–7, adopted in 1984, in the aftermath of the DISC cases, Sect. 9.2, n. 15 supra.

[112] *United States—Tax Treatment for 'Foreign Sales Corporations', (European Communities* v. *United States)*, WT/DS/108/AB/R (24 Feb. 2000).

[113] See Sect. 9.5(b) n. 61 supra.

[114] *Canada—Certain Measures Affecting the Automotive Industry, (Japan and European Communities* v. *Canada)*, WT/DS/139/AB/R and WT/DS/142/AB/R, (31 May 2000).

At the risk of oversimplification of an inherently intricate subject not yet fully worked out, one may summarize the state of the law at the turn of the century as follows (agriculture excepted):

- State aids generally available without targeting particular industries or particular performance will not be treated in the regulation of international trade as subsidies. Better schools, lower taxes, easier availability of raw materials, devalued currency, may all help the producers and exporters of Patria, and may in some sense constitute transfers from the taxpayers or consumers of Patria to its producers, but they will not be regarded in the law and practice of international trade as 'unfair trade practices'.
- Benefits of government intervention linked explicitly to export performance (or to import substitution) are presumed to be specific, and will be treated as prohibited subsidies, even when they represent no net cost to the public fisc. Domestic subsidies are not automatically condemned, but if they are specific and cause injury, they are vulnerable to anti-subsidy remedies, national and international.
- Manipulation of internal taxes to benefit a country's exports is suspect, but forgiveness of excise taxes on exports is not generally regarded as a subsidy, and neither is differential taxation so as to favour export of processed products rather than of raw materials.
- Special and differential treatment for developing countries still plays a role in the law of subsidies, but that role is declining except for the least developed countries, and may be different for different products.

10

Dumping and Anti-Dumping

10.1   INTRODUCTION AND OVERVIEW

Dumping as a technical term in the law of international trade is quite different from the lay person's understanding of the term. The popular definition of dumping embraces any sales by a producer or merchant at low prices to dispose of surplus—if possible after costs of production of the entire line have been recovered. In the language and law of international trade, the definition of dumping is more limited and technical. Article VI of the GATT, modeled roughly but not precisely on the United States Anti-Dumping Act of 1921,[1] defines dumping as an export of a product by a producer or seller in Patria to importers in Xandia 'at less than its normal value', i.e. at less than the price at which the product in question is sold when destined for consumption in Patria. If there are no such sales, that is if a comparable domestic price in Patria cannot be established, normal value is to be determined by reference to the highest price in sales to a third country, or by reference to cost of production in Patria plus a reasonable addition for selling cost and profit.[2] In three successive Anti-Dumping Codes or agreements, concluded in the Kennedy, Tokyo, and Uruguay Rounds, the basic definition has been refined and elaborated somewhat, as discussed hereafter, but not essentially altered. Dumping in international trade law always depends on a comparison—between the price at which the product is offered in the importing country and the home-market price or a surrogate for that price. Thus a producer that lowers its year-end prices on its entire line may be dumping in the eyes of the public, but if there is no discrepancy between domestic and export prices, (making allowances for cost of packing, shipping, insurance, etc.), there is no dumping in the technical sense.

One may well ask what is wrong with dumping as so defined—a question that will recur throughout this chapter. The definition does not involve conduct by the government of Patria—it is thus quite different from the grant of subsidies, though the two subjects are often discussed together.[3] Moreover, dumping does not—at least not necessarily—involve predatory pricing, i.e.

---

[1] *U.S.*: 42 Stat. 11 (1921). In fact, Canada had adopted anti-dumping legislation as early as 1904, though without a requirement of injury. An Act to amend the Customs Tariff, 1897, 4 Edw. VII (Canada Statutes 111 (1904)). See K. G. MacKenzie, 'Anti-Dumping Duties in Canada', 21 *Canadian YB Int'l Law* 131 (1966). New Zealand, Australia, and South Africa also adopted anti-dumping legislation in the years before World War I. For a convenient summary of these early laws, see Terence P. Stewart (ed.), *The GATT Uruguay Round: A Negotiating History 1986–92*, Vol. II, pp. 1390–1401 (1993).

[2] GATT Art. VI(1).

[3] Indeed, a proposal to add a clause to the GATT providing 'Contracting Parties shall refrain from any action that might cause or encourage dumping of this kind' failed to be adopted. See John H. Jackson, *World Trade and the Law of GATT*, p. 402 (1969).

pricing with a view to destroying a competitor and thereafter raising prices. Nothing about motive appears in the GATT definition of dumping or in the corresponding definitions in the law of member states.

Dumping, according to the GATT, 'is to be condemned'—but only if it causes or threatens material injury to an established industry in the territory of a member state, or materially retards the establishment of a domestic industry in that state. Much of the law of dumping and anti-dumping is devoted to the meaning of 'injury' in this context, and to the procedures for making the determination of injury. The proponents of anti-dumping legislation—international and domestic—regard dumping as unfair trade, and view anti-dumping proceedings as a way to restore fairness to the export–import system. Opponents view anti-dumping legislation, or at least anti-dumping proceedings, as a form of disguised protectionism. The interest of consumers in lower prices—an important, and perhaps dominant concern in antitrust or competition law—rarely enters into the discussion or implementation of anti-dumping law.

While the GATT speaks of condemnation, it does not provide for punishment. The traditional remedy when both dumping and injury have been found is an anti-dumping duty, designed to bring the price paid by the importer up to the 'normal value'. In technical terms, an anti-dumping duty added to the challenged price is supposed to be equal to the 'margin of dumping'. Thus suppose the 'normal value' of a product of Patria is determined to be 100 dollars, but it is sold in Xandia (after the various adjustments have been taken into consideration)[4] for 80 dollars. The margin of dumping is 20 dollars, and assuming injury has been found, the anti-dumping duty should be set at 20/80 or 25 percent *ad valorem*, in order to bring the price to the importer in Xandia back to 100 dollars.

As developed below, the details of dumping and anti-dumping law are complicated and not always consistent with the underlying theory. In fitting this subject into the GATT/WTO system as a whole, it is important to note that anti-dumping measures (as well as anti-subsidy measures) consistent with Article VI of GATT are among the few instances in the GATT/WTO system where departure from most-favoured-nation treatment is permitted—indeed required, and where duties bound under Article II may be *pro tanto* unbound. States are not themselves liable in case of dumping by firms established in their territory.[5] But if Patria considers that Xandia has improperly imposed anti-dumping remedies on Patrian exports, it has the right to invoke the WTO dispute settlement process against Xandia.[6]

---

[4] Sect. 10.4(b) infra.
[5] Putting aside state-owned enterprises, discussed in Sect. 10.4(d) infra.
[6] Anti-Dumping Code 1994, Art. 17, discussed further in Sect. 10.11 infra.

10.2   ECONOMIC ARGUMENTS: PRO AND CON

Jacob Viner, the American economist who first developed the rationale for anti-dumping legislation, defined dumping as 'price discrimination between national markets'.[7] In fact, if a Patrian firm charges more for its product in Xandia than in its home market (because there is less competition in Xandia or the demand is higher or less elastic), no international wrong is committed, no breach of GATT or of the domestic law of either Xandia or Patria has taken place. The result that Xandian consumers may have paid too much does not by itself (i.e. absent abuse of monopoly power or concerted price fixing) engage the international community. It is only when the Patrian firm sells at higher price at home than in Xandia that the classical definition of dumping is met. Yet it is not Patria but Xandia that is deemed to have grounds to complain, and the complaint can be cured if the Patrian firm lowers its home market price as well as if it raises the price at which the product is sold in Xandia.[8]

This simple analysis has led many observers to view the dumping/anti-dumping law as a special kind of protectionism, dispensing with the constraints of most-favoured nation treatment and of bound duties generally applicable.[9] The emphasis on injury as a condition to imposition of anti-dumping measures, while mitigating the effect of 'condemnation' of price discrimination, supports the view that anti-dumping laws are essentially protectionist, made more important as the traditional barriers to trade come down.

The defenders of anti-dumping legislation, national and international, respond that dumping is basically unfair, because it distorts or masks the elements of comparative advantage that ought to determine movement of goods and services across international frontiers. In a market not segmented by national boundaries, such as the United States or (largely) the European Union, dumping could not long occur, because if, say, a French producer sells its product in Spain to an independent importer for less than it sells the

---

[7] Jacob Viner, *Dumping: A Problem in International Trade*, 3 (1923; repr. 1966). The 1966 reprint also contains Viner's Memorandum on Dumping submitted to the League of Nations in 1926, in response to a request from the Preparatory Committee for the International Economic Conference, as well as his article on Dumping for the *Encyclopedia of Social Sciences*.

[8] We speak here for the sake of clarity of Patria, the state of the exporter, and Xandia, the state of the importer. In fact until about 1990 four jurisdictions were the principal users of anti-dumping laws—in the posture of Xandia—Australia, Canada, the EC, and the United States. More recently over 50 states notified the WTO that they had or were soon to have anti-dumping laws in force, including Argentina, Brazil, Chile, Colombia, India, Japan, Korea, Mexico, Thailand, and Turkey. The states most frequently in the posture of Patria have been China, the EC, and Korea. See the WTO *Focus* No. 7, pp 10–11 (Dec. 1995).

[9] See e.g. most of the papers in Richard Boltuck and Robert E. Litan (eds.), *Down in the Dumps: Administration of the Unfair Trade Laws* (1991), which contains a vigorous rebuttal by Terence P. Stewart.

like product in France, the lower-priced product sold in Spain will find its way back to France to undercut the higher home-market price. Thus in the long run there is no possibility for the sales by the producer in France to 'subsidize' the sales in Spain. The same is not true, however, if say, a Japanese producer sells its product for less in Spain than in its home country, because (quite apart from transportation costs) import barriers in Japan preclude the Spanish importer or arbitrageur from penetrating the Japanese market. Accordingly, the proponents of anti-dumping measures contend, it is possible, and indeed likely, that some of the higher yield in the home market is used to support (not to say 'subsidize') increased production designed to be sold at lower price in the export market, leading to higher market share for the foreign producer not justified by lower costs or greater efficiency.[10]

Recently, the proponents of anti-dumping measures have shifted the argument—and to some extent the rules—to emphasize cost, rather than price in the home market. It may well constitute rational decision-making for the producer in Patria to keep its mill or factory at full production in times of falling prices or decreased demand and to sell abroad at reduced prices that cover its variable costs but not all of its fully allocated costs. To proponents of anti-dumping legislation, however, such conduct is unfair trade, an attempt to export recession and to pass on the burdens of adjustment. The argument is strengthened when there is a substantial difference in the way certain costs are treated in different countries. Suppose, for instance, that in Patria, workers are essentially lifetime employees who cannot be laid off, so that labour is a fixed cost. In Xandia, in contrast, workers are taken on and laid off in response to current market conditions. Also, suppose in Patria, as in Japan, capital is largely raised by loans, while in Xandia, as in the United States, capital consists equally of loans and shares of stock. Interest on loans cannot be skipped, and thus is a fixed cost, whereas dividends can be reduced or shipped, and are thus a variable cost. The argument is illustrated by the following stylized example (opposite), adapted from Professor Jackson.[11]

At the outset, the two firms have precisely equal costs. But suppose demand declines. The Patrian producer could rationally decide to continue production as long as its price remains over $250. The Xandian producer cannot afford to lower its price below $530. If the Patrian producer now sells its excess output in Xandia at, say, $280, it can expect to achieve a growing share of the Xandian market, injuring producers in Xandia, that are already, by hypothesis, suffering injury as a result of decreased demand. Even if the Patrian producer reduces its home-market prices by the same

[10] See e.g. Greg Mastel, *Anti-Dumping Laws and the U.S. Economy*, esp. ch. 4 'The Economic Case for Antidumping Laws' (1998).
[11] John H. Jackson, *The World Trading System: Law and Policy of International Economic Relations*, 220 (1989); also Jackson, Davey and Sykes, *International Economic Relations*, p. 669–70 (3rd edn. 1995).

		Costs per unit of production ($)	
		Patrian producer	Xandian producer
1	Plant maintenance	20 (fixed cost)	20 (fixed cost)
2	Interest on loans	90 (fixed cost)	50 (fixed cost)
3	Dividends	10 (variable cost)	50 (variable cost)
4	Labour	240 (fixed cost)	240 (variable cost)
5	Materials	240 (variable cost)	240 (variable cost)
6	Total Costs	600	600
7	Fixed Cost	350	70
8	Variable Cost	250	530

amount as its export price, so that the classic definition of dumping as price discrimination is not met, has the Patrian producer engaged in unfair trade?

Proponents of anti-dumping measures answer this question 'yes'. They argue that a regime of fair trade requires the producer to cover *all* its costs, not just over the long run but over a reasonable period of time, such as three months. Different assignment of certain costs as fixed or variable should not alter the underlying conditions of competition, which in the example given started out even.

The opposite argument is that selling below average cost is rational economic behaviour that both Patrian and Xandian firms can be expected to engage in. Indeed the Xandian firm has benefited from the ability to safely leave the market well before the Patrian firm can do so. Different attitudes concerning the tenure of workers are related to issues such as unemployment compensation, pensions, and social security that cannot be factored into the relatively mechanical calculations called for by anti-dumping law.

One other argument is relevant to the debate about dumping and anti-dumping. Predatory pricing, in the sense that the foreign producer lowers its prices in the importing country with the motive of putting the domestic firms out of business and thereafter exacting monopoly prices, can hardly ever be shown, and even if the motive could be demonstrated, the objective would be very difficult to achieve in most countries. However, the proponents of anti-dumping measure contend, a form of dumping is possible in which the Patrian producer, without aiming to put its Xandian competitors out of business, aims to achieve a foothold in the Xandian market and thereafter to expand its market share, without attention initially to profits. The foreign producer may well believe that over time superior quality or more imaginative merchandising will gain a significant market share at a price that will cover all costs and yield satisfactory profits. But the way to break into the market is through initially offering a price that does not cover fully allocated costs. The question is at what stage aggressive competition, which may occur in national markets as well as in international trade, becomes unfair competition, to be met with anti-dumping measures if carried out in trade between countries.

Overall, many economists and legal academics have remained unconvinced by the arguments in favour of anti-dumping laws. The officials and politicians charged with drafting and implementing the law of international trade, however, have viewed prevention of 'unfair trade' and preservation of the 'level playing field' as necessary to gain public support for the more general provisions of a liberal trading system. Neither the original negotiations in Geneva and Havana that led to the GATT nor the three legislative rounds—the Kennedy Round, the Tokyo Round, and the Uruguay Round— seem to have questioned the basic proposition that states should be entitled to defend against dumping by imposing anti-dumping duties. All the negotiations of three successive Anti-Dumping Codes (1967), (1979), and (1994) have revolved around elaborating and fine-tuning the issues discussed in the following sections, both as to the substantive standards and to the procedures to be employed by the respective national authorities.

10.3   Legislating the International Law of Dumping and Anti-Dumping (1947–94)

Article VI of the GATT established the framework for the law of dumping and anti-dumping, which has remained unchanged for decades. Article VI accepts the proposition that dumping is unfair trade, it defines the term, and it commits the determination of dumping to the authorities of the importing state. Further, Article VI states that the remedy against dumping is an anti-dumping duty, which is to be imposed only upon a finding of injury caused by the dumped imports. Beyond these bare bones, however, Article VI left a great deal to interpretation by individual states.

In 1959 the GATT Contracting Parties appointed a Group of Experts on Anti-Dumping and Countervailing Duties, and the reports of that group set the stage for placing dumping on the agenda of the Kennedy Round of trade negotiations (1964–7). As it turned out, the work of the Group on Anti-Dumping Policies produced the first of the codes negotiated under the auspices of GATT. The Code contained provisions concerning the determination of dumping, determination of injury, definition of industry, initiation and conduct of investigations, evidence, price undertakings, duration of anti-dumping duties, and provisional measures, plus a general article obligating each party to the Agreement to ensure the conformity of its laws, regulations, and administrative procedures with the provisions of the Code. Further, the Code provided for establishment of a Committee on Anti-Dumping Practices to which parties to the Code could complain about implementation of anti-dumping laws by other parties. Like all of the 'codes' produced by the Kennedy and Tokyo Rounds, the Anti-Dumping Code 1967 was optional. All of the industrial countries and a few East European states, but none of the developing States, became parties.

As the next round of multinational trade negotiations progressed in the period 1973–9, the Committee on Anti-Dumping Practices became a forum for amending the Code, by modifying provisions that had proven unclear and by making provision for issues not dealt with in the 1967 Code.[12] At the same time negotiations were under way in the Tokyo Round to develop a Subsidies Code,[13] and the Anti-Dumping Code was revised to make it parallel (but not identical) to the Subsidies Code. In particular, the provision in the 1967 Code that 'a determination of injury shall be made only when the authorities concerned are satisfied that the dumped imports are *demonstrably the principal cause of material injury*'[14] was replaced by a provision reading:

It must be demonstrated that the dumped imports are, through the effects of dumping, causing injury within the meaning of this Code. There may be other factors which at the same time are injuring the industry, and the injuries caused by other factors must not be attributed to the dumped imports.[15]

Presumably the change would make it somewhat easier for a domestic petitioner to establish its case in favour of imposition of an anti-dumping duty.

The 1979 Anti-Dumping Code remained, for the most part, an agreement among the industrial countries, but India and Brazil, the States that have been the leaders among developing states in the GATT/WTO system, both became original parties to the 1979 Anti- Dumping Code, and Egypt, Korea, Mexico, Pakistan, and Singapore signed on subsequently.

When the Uruguay Round was launched in 1986, dumping was not mentioned in the agenda set out in the Ministerial Declaration. In the later stages of the Uruguay Round, however, dumping and anti-dumping became seriously contested, with the European Community and the United States determined to plug 'loopholes', and the target countries, notably Japan, Hong Kong, and Korea, seeking both to revisit the basic concepts embodied in the 1967 and 1979 codes and to eliminate practices that seemed to tilt the required price

---

[12] See *Analytical Inventory of Problems and Issues arising under the Anti-Dumping Code*, GATT Doc. No. COM AD/W/68 (8 Mar. 1977), *List of Priority Issues in the Anti-dumping Field: Note by the Chairman*, GATT Doc. No. COM AD/W/77 (10 Apr. 1978). For a description of the priority issues and the position of the principal parties, EC, Australia, Canada, United States, and Japan, see Stewart (Sect. 10.10, n. 1 supra), Vol. II, pp. 1435–61.

[13] See Ch. 9, Sect. 9.4.   [14] 1967 Anti-Dumping Code Art. 3(1).

[15] 1979 Anti-Dumping Code Art. 3(4) (footnotes omitted). The corresponding provision in the 1979 Subsidies Code was Art. 6(4). The 1979 versions are repeated in Article 3.5 of the 1994 Anti-Dumping Agreement and Article 15.5 of the 1994 Agreement on Subsidies, with the footnotes from the 1979 codes moved into text.

comparisons against imports. By the closing days of the Uruguay Round, intricate issues of dumping law comprehensible only to the experts had become subjects of major contention among the principals, threatening at times the overall success of the Uruguay Round.[16] The outcome of the negotiations, as set down in the 1994 Agreement, reflects not so much a coherent philosophy as a package of compromises—some favouring imports, some domestic producers. Unlike the earlier codes, but like almost all the other Uruguay Round codes, the Agreement on Implementation of Article VI of GATT 1994 is binding on all members of the WTO.

10.4 ESTABLISHING THE FACT AND THE MARGIN OF DUMPING

The critical task in determining sales below normal value is, to make an accurate comparison of data that are inherently hard to compare. Article 2.4 of the Uruguay Round Anti-Dumping Agreement repeats the requirement stated in the prior codes that a 'fair comparison' be made between the export price and the normal value. To that end, the comparison is to be made at the same level of trade—normally ex-factory, and in respect of sales made as nearly as possible at the same time. The Agreement recognizes however, that adjustments need to be made at both ends.

(a) The Export Price

The *export price* is supposed to be the price actually paid by an unrelated purchaser in the importing country for the product being challenged. But if, for instance, the purchase price includes insurance and freight, as in a c.i.f. transaction, the costs of these items are deducted for purposes of the comparison.[17] So are duties paid by the importer, including anti-dumping and countervailing duties previously assessed. If the imported product has features or costs not included in the product as sold in the home market—for instance superior warranties or after-sales service, superior packing, or cost of credit extended to the purchaser—these costs will be deducted from the actual purchase price. In practice, such adjustments are often complicated and give rise to controversy; in principle, however, adjustments along these lines are generally accepted as necessary to establish a reasonably accurate basis for comparison with the home-market value or its surrogate.

---

[16] See e.g. Gary N. Horlick and Eleanor C. Shea, 'The World Trade Organization Anti-dumping Agreement', 29 J. *World Trade*, No. 1 p. 5 (1995).

[17] As Professor Jackson points out, transport costs from Patria are considered part of the comparative disadvantage of goods imported into Xandia, and therefore it is considered unfair to include such costs in the comparison with the home-market price in Patria. See John H. Jackson, *The World Trading System*, 232 (1989).

A more difficult problem is raised by the common practice of selling through intermediaries. Generally the solution depends on the relation between the intermediary and the producer/exporter. If the intermediary is an independent concern—for instance a Japanese trading company not related to the producer or exporter—the export price is generally derived from the effective price paid by that intermediary.[18] But if the trading company or other intermediary is a subsidiary or affiliate of the producer/exporter, the export price is derived from the first sale to an independent purchaser in the country of import.

Quite apart from intermediaries, it is common for major producers to have subsidiaries in the countries of their principal markets that act as importers and distributors. The 1994 Anti-Dumping Agreement recognizes that in transactions between parents and subsidiaries or other affiliates,[19] the export price as described above may well be unreliable. Accordingly Article 2.3 of the Agreement provides for a *constructed export price*, defined as the price at which the imported product is first resold to an independent buyer. If there is no resale to an independent buyer, for instance because the affiliated importer engages in further processing or uses the imported product as a component, Article 2.3 provides that the export price may be constructed 'on such reasonable basis as the authorities may determine'.

Again, implementing the rule is more difficult than stating the principle. First, there is occasionally controversy about whether the distributor in Xandia is really an affiliate of the producer in Patria. In general the test is looser than in determining 'ownership or control' for other purposes, such as taxation, securities regulation, judicial jurisdiction, or imposition of trade embargoes.[20] The distributor/importer will of course itself incur costs—of selling, carrying inventory, and general overhead, and it may have paid for some of the other costs discussed above, such as transport, insurance and handling, as well as import duties and taxes. The importer will also presumably, have made some profit.[21] All these costs are deducted from the price paid by the independent purchaser in arriving at the constructed

[18] Effective price in this context means the revenue received by the producer. Thus, for instance, if the producer charges the trading company $100 per unit but pays a commission of 5 percent, the effective price is $95 and this amount will be used (subject to other adjustments) to determine the export price. See Edwin Vermulst and Paul Waer, *E.C. Anti-Dumping Law and Practice*, p. 171 (1996).

[19] For instance the manufacturer in Patria and the importer in Xandia may both belong to the same corporate group, but not be in a parent–subsidiary relationship.

[20] See e.g. for the United States, 19 U.S.C. §1667(33) including ownership of as little as 5 percent of an entity in the definition of affiliate. For the European Community, see Vermulst and Waer, n. 18 supra, pp. 172–4 and the many cases there cited.

[21] Since the price paid by the affiliated importer is regarded as unreliable, so is the profit attributable to the resale. The European Commission disregards the profits shown in the importer's accounts and imputes a 'reasonable profit' allocable to the transactions in question. See Vermulst and Waer, n. 18 supra, 175–7. Under United States law, a special formula applies to allocation of profits to expenses incurred in the United States, based on the ratio of expenses in the United States to total expenses in producing the product in question (19 U.S.C. §1677a (d) and (f)).

export price, to be compared with the 'normal value' for purposes of establishing the fact and margin of dumping.

(b)   Normal Value

The Basic Rule

The primary focus of the dumping inquiry, as we have seen, is the comparison between the export price, as above described, with the price at which the product in question is sold in the producer's home market. If a 'like product' is sold in the ordinary course of trade in commercial quantities for consumption in the country of export, the price at which it is sold (or the average of such prices) in the period under investigation is the benchmark with which the export price is to be compared.[22] The difference between the two prices, after all the adjustments have been made, is the margin of dumping.

As with the export price, certain adjustments must be made. Postponing the question of currencies and shifting exchange rates,[23] costs not incurred in domestic sales, such as special packing or containers and freight from factory to port, should be added to the domestic sales price. Excise or consumption taxes collected on domestic sales but not collected (or rebated) on export sales should be deducted.

All of the above is based on the premise that there is a representative domestic market with which to compare the price at which the product is offered in the importing country. But what if there is no home market?[24] Or if the home market is insignificant in comparison with the export market? Or if the home-market price does not fully cover the costs of production? The anti-dumping laws of the major users, and the three generations of anti-dumping codes, have provided for two surrogate benchmarks—sales to third countries, and 'constructed value'.

Inadequate Home-Market Sales

Article 2.2 of the Anti-Dumping Agreement provides that when there are no sales of the product in question in the ordinary course of trade in the domestic market of the exporting country or the low volume of sales does not permit a proper comparison, the margin of dumping is to be determined by comparison with the price of exports to an appropriate third country, or with the cost of production in the country of origin plus a reasonable

[22] It is worth remarking that in the context of dumping investigations, the United States regards home market as referring only to the country of origin of the product, not to the customs territory. Thus, for anti-dumping purpose, the United States would look to sales by a French producer only in France, not in the European Community as a whole.

[23] See Sect. 10.4(e) infra.

[24] The famous case involved electric golf carts manufactured in Poland which did not, at the time of the investigation, have any golf courses. See e.g. Note: 'Dumping by State Controlled Economy Countries: The Polish Golf Cart Case and the New Treasury Regulations', 128 *U. Penn. L. Rev.* 216 at 227 (1979).

amount for general expenses and profits. A footnote states that if domestic sales amount to at least 5 percent by volume of the sales of the product to the importing country, domestic sales will normally be considered sufficient for purposes of the comparison with export price.[25]

GATT Article VI(1)(b) lists third country sales and cost of production in the country of origin as equally acceptable points of reference when home-market sales are not adequate to provide a fair comparison, and this is restated in Article 2.2 of the Code. In United States practice, third-country sales are the preferred point of comparison if the volume of such sales is sufficient (i.e. at least 5 percent of sales to the United States) and the market conditions in the third country are comparable. The European Community and most other countries prefer constructed value, apparently on the theory that it cannot be easily determined whether sales to the third country have not themselves been dumped.

Sales Below Cost

As seen above, the home-market value with which the export price is to be compared is the price in the home market 'in the ordinary course of trade'. The principal users of anti-dumping laws have long taken the position that sales made at a loss in substantial quantities over a significant period of time are not sales in the ordinary course, and therefore are to be disregarded in determination of home market price. But as discussed in Section 10.2, defining loss depends on defining costs—fixed and variable, and on defining the relevant time-period, which may vary depending on the industry involved. A number of states proposed a provision in the new Agreement to the effect that sales at a loss, even over extended periods, should not be deemed to be outside the ordinary course of trade if such sales result from market assessment and business strategies. Japan pointed out that high-tech products often required large initial investments, so that a pricing strategy geared to the long term might well show losses in the first year or even two, yet make economic sense over the long term when unit costs came down and a market was established. This proposal was rejected by the major users of anti-dumping law—the European Community and the United States.[26]

The eventual version in Article 2.2.1 accepts the principle that sales below cost may be disregarded in determining normal value, but 'only if the authorities determine that such sales are made [i] within an extended period of time [ii] in substantial quantities and [iii] are at prices which do not provide for the recovery of all costs within a reasonable period of time.' A footnote says that the 'extended period of time' shall normally be one year but in no case less than six months. Thus a sale below unit costs at time of sale

---

[25] The 1994 Anti-Dumping Agreement here follows the European Community practice. Until 1994, the United States also used a 5 percent figure, but applied it to the volume of sales to third countries.

[26] See Stewart (ed.), *The GATT Uruguay Round* (Sect. 10.1, n. 1 supra) at pp. 1543–53.

but above weighted average costs for the period of investigation will not be regarded as a sale below cost.[27] Another footnote says that 'substantial quantities' means either that the weighted average selling price of all the transactions under consideration is below the weighted average per unit cost—in which case the home-market sales may be disregarded completely, or that the selling price of at least 20 percent of the volume of transactions under consideration is below per unit costs, in which case those sales will be disregarded in establishing normal value.

The effect of this provision as implemented by the United States and the European Community is a 20-80-20 rule:

- Where profitable sales are greater than 80 percent by volume of total domestic sales of a product, normal value is calculated on the basis of the weighted average of all sales, even those made at a loss.
- Where profitable sales amount to 20 to 80 percent by volume of all domestic sales, normal value is calculated on the basis of the weighted average of those sales, disregarding the sales made at a loss.
- Where profitable sales are less than 20 percent of domestic sales, all domestic sales will be disregarded, and normal value will be based on constructed value.[28]

Constructed Value

Constructed value, for purposes of the law of dumping, is made up of three elements—(a) cost of production; (b) general administrative and selling expenses; and (c) profits—all in the country of origin of the product in question. The object is to determine the price at which the product would have been sold in the domestic market of the producer/exporter had normal conditions prevailed. It is possible that the actual sales price in the exporter's domestic market and in the importing country were the same and yet dumping is found, because calculation of the constructed value, reflecting fully allocated costs and reasonable profits yields a substantially higher amount than the prices actually charged. As we saw in Section 10.2, one might question why profit enters into the calculation in a period of declining demand, or whether fully allocated costs, should be used when it may well make sense for a producer to sell—at home and abroad—as long as its revenue exceeds its variable costs. The architects of the international anti-dumping law insisted, however, that lack of demand in Patria not be made up for in low prices in Xandia.

Cost of production is typically the subject of detailed questionnaires by the investigating authorities in the importing country. Conceptually, it is the easiest component of constructed value, though even if all data are available,

---

[27] Accord: *U.S.* law: 19 U.S.C. §1677b(b)(2)(D); *E.C. Reg.* Art. 2(4).

[28] See *E.C.*: Council Reg. No. 384/96, Art. 2(4) para. 3. *U.S.*: 19 U.S.C. §1667b(b). Prior to the Uruguay Round, the United States Department of Commerce generally applied a 10–90–10 formula.

it can give rise to numerous accounting controversies. Clearly manufacturing cost includes labour (wages, salaries, and associated benefits), cost of raw materials and purchased components, manufacturing overhead such as electric power, fuel, amortization of buildings, and import duties for imported components. Research and development expenses may be included, but views may differ about how much should be allocated to any given period or product. The Anti-Dumping Code contains a choice of law clause (Art. 2.2.1.1), which states that costs shall normally be calculated on the basis of records kept by the exporter or producer under investigation, 'provided that such records are in accordance with the generally accepted accounting standards [GAAP] of the exporting country' and reasonably reflect the costs associated with the production and sale of the product under consideration.

Until the entry into effect of the Uruguay Round code, United States laws provided that a formula be used for calculating minimum amounts for general expenses and profits.[29] The Code does not permit such a formula, but provides (in Article 2.2.2) that the amounts for administrative, selling, and general costs and for profits 'shall be based on actual data'. If such data are not available, three alternatives are presented for comparison—costs and profits in home-market operations, average costs and profits for other producers in the same category, and 'any other reasonable method', so long as the amount calculated does not exceed profits generally realized by other producers or exporters or sales of the same general category of profits.

(c) Averaging

The first reference point in making the price comparison called for by the dumping rules—the 'normal value' in terms of Article VI(1) of the GATT—is the 'comparable price, in the ordinary course of trade, for the like product when destined for consumption in the exporting country' (GATT Art. VI(1), also 1994 Agreement Art. 2.1). There is no reason to assume that either the home-market price or the export price remains constant. The practice of authorities in importing states when there is a genuine home market has been to use an average price over a given period of time—a year or a selling season—to arrive at the home-market price with which to compare the challenged export sale price. But in determining the export sale price, both the United States and the European Community formerly compared normal value with export prices on a transaction-by-transaction basis. This practice often tended to exaggerate the overall margin of dumping because sales for export at prices above normal value were disregarded. Thus if half of the sales from a given producer or country were made below normal value and

---

[29] Under the formula that prevailed until 1994, where *a* was cost of production, *b* was general expenses, and *c* was profit,

$b = 10\% \times a$, $c = 8\% \times (a + b)$, and constructed value = $a + b + c$.

half above, an anti-dumping duty could be imposed on those sales made below normal value, even if the overall average of all sales would not qualify as being dumped. The United States and the EC argued that their method was justified to counter 'targeted dumping', i.e. isolated instances of dumping that might otherwise go unpunished.[30] The 1994 Anti-Dumping Agreement prohibits this practice. Article 2.4.2 provides that the existence of margins of dumping shall normally be established 'on the basis of a weighted average normal value with a weighted average of all export transactions' or 'by a comparison of normal value and export prices on a transaction-to-transaction basis.'[31]

Subsequently, the European Communities, supported by the United States, adopted the method of 'zeroing', whereby all export sales of the product under investigation at prices less than home market or normal value were averaged to establish a margin of dumping, but export sales at prices greater than normal value were assigned a value of zero, and were thus excluded from the calculation of the margin of dumping on which the anti-dumping duty was based. In 2001, at the behest of India, supported by Japan and others, this practice was found by a Panel and by the Appellate Body to be inconsistent with Article 2.4.2.[32]

(d) Non-market Economies

The law of dumping and anti-dumping, as we have seen, is based on a comparison of prices in two markets, one in the exporter's market, the other the price offered by the exporter in the importing country. But what if in the exporter's country there is no real market at all, in the sense of supply, demand, and competition, but prices and supply are simply aspects of state planning?

When the GATT was drafted in the early post-war years, the Soviet Union was a major power, and many of the states of Eastern Europe were being brought into the Soviet orbit. In that context, Note ad Article VI stated:

It is recognized that, in the case of imports from a country which has a complete or substantially complete monopoly of its trade and where all domestic prices are fixed by the State, special difficulties may exist in determining price comparability for the

[30] The United States argued that the critics' position was analogous to arguing that a driver should not be found guilty of speeding if, along other portions of the road, he was driving under the speed limit. See Stewart (ed.), *The GATT Uruguay Round* (Sect. 10.1, n. 1 supra), Vol. II, p. 1540, quoting from a submission by the United States to the Negotiating Group (1989).

[31] The United States changed its law in compliance, present 19 U.S.C. §1677f-1. The EU did so in Council Reg. EC No. 384/96 of 22 Dec. 1995 in Art. 2(11). The Agreement provides an exception if there is a pattern of export prices which differ significantly among different purchasers, regions or time periods and if an explanation is provided why the prescribed mode of comparison cannot be used.

[32] *European Communities—Anti-Dumping Duties on Imports of Cotton-Type Bed Linen from India (India v. EC)*, WT/DS141/AB/R (1 Mar. 2001).

purposes of paragraph 1 [of Article VI] and in such cases importing contracting parties may find it necessary to take into account the possibility that a strict comparison with domestic prices in such a country may not always be appropriate.

In recent years, complaints of dumping from the Soviet Union and its successor states, as well as from China and from the 'countries in transition'— i.e. the former COMECON states—have made up about half of all anti-dumping cases in the European Community.[33] In the United States, China has been the most frequent target of anti-dumping complaints. Both of the major users of anti-dumping measures have responded to imports from non-market economies by looking for surrogate countries to establish a price to be compared with the export price, but they have gone about the process somewhat differently.

Under the European Community regulation,[34] the Commission chooses a surrogate country, the first choice being a market economy whose producers are subject to the same investigation, otherwise another country in which the product under investigation (or a similar product) is being manufactured. Unlike the United States, the Community does not attempt to find a country at the comparable level of development on the basis of gross national product per capita or other macroeconomic criteria. If the Commission finds a suitable surrogate country, the domestic price in that country for the product in question will be the price attributed to the non-market-economy country for purposes of the dumping inquiry. If the domestic price is inappropriate because there are insufficient profitable domestic sales, the comparison will be made with third-country sales or constructed value in the surrogate country. The choice of the surrogate country is within the discretion of the Commission, but the respondent has ten days to object, and the European Court of Justice has held that the discretion is not excluded from judicial review, since it was 'necessary to ensure that the matter had been examined with the care required to establish that the normal value had been fixed in an appropriate and reasonable manner.'[35]

Some importers have argued, with respect to China and also some East European countries, that the inquiry should be directed to individual firms that have become privatized or built up by private investment. Unless foreign ownership of the producer is established, the European Community has usually taken the position that 'it is in practice extremely difficult to establish in the case of a country such as the People's Republic of China whether

---

[33] See Vermulst and Waer, n. 18 supra, 199 at n. 269, reporting that of the 539 anti-dumping determinations published by the Community between 1980 and 1995, 207 involved imports from non-market economy states.

[34] Present Council Reg. No. 384/96 Art. 2(7).

[35] *Nölle* v. *Hauptzollamt Bremen-Freihafen* [1991-1] E.C.R. 5163, paras. 12–13 (22 Oct. 1991). Accordingly the Court held invalid a decision based on the use of Sri Lanka as a surrogate for China in a case involving the sale of paint brushes, rather than Taiwan, as the importer had urged.

a company really enjoys both legally and in fact, independence from the State.[36]

The United States approach to imports from non-market economies is similar in some respects, different in others.[37] It also uses a surrogate market economy country to establish the normal value, and its choice of surrogate has also been surprising in some cases.[38] Surrogates for the Soviet Union have included Canada, the United Kingdom, and West Germany; Romania and Hungary have been compared with Argentina, Brazil, Mexico, Spain, Portugal, Yugoslavia, and South Korea, and so on.[39] As in the European Community,[40] United States authorities have generally rejected claims that separate manufacturers in China should be treated separately for purposes of establishing dumping margins, and have placed the burden on exporters to demonstrate not only de jure but de facto absence of control by the central government.[41]

Rather than choosing the surrogate country and then looking to the domestic price of the product in question in that country, however, the US Department of Commerce aims at a constructed value by inquiring into individual factor inputs in the non-market country—so many hours of labour, x tons of steel, y kw of electricity, etc.—and then establishing the cost of these factors in the surrogate country. To the sum of costs thus established, the Department adds general expenses and profits. There is no need under this method for the surrogate country to produce or export the product in question. All that is needed is a comparison of costs of the factors of production, from which a constructed 'normal value' can then be imputed to the exports from the non-market country.

Under both the American and the European approach, an exporter from a non-market country can never plan its prices with security, because it cannot predict with which country its prices (in the (Community) or its costs (in the United States) will be compared. Moreover, both methods imply that the non-market country can never have a competitive advantage—for instance from lower labour costs or more efficient production techniques—greater than the market country chosen as surrogate. One may predict that as privatization spreads even in the still centrally-planned economies, distinctions

---

[36] *Photo Albums from China*, [1993] O.J. L/228/17, para. 15 (9 Sept. 1993).

[37] For an account of the evolution of the American approach, see Gary N. Horlick and Shannon S. Shuman, 'Nonmarket Economy Trade and U.S. Anti-Dumping/Countervailing Duty Laws', 18 *Int'l Lawyer* 807 (1984).

[38] See William Alford, 'When is China Paraguay? An Examination of the Application of Anti-dumping and Countervailing Duty Laws of the United States to China and other "Nonmarket Economy" Nations', 61 *S. Cal. L. Rev.* 79 (1987).

[39] For more of these comparisons, see Charlene Barshefsky, 'Non-Market Economies in Transition and the US Antidumping Law: Remarks on the Need for Reevaluation', 8 *Boston U. Int'l L.J.* 373 (1990).

[40] See the *Photo Album* case, n. 36 supra.

[41] See *Signa Corp.* v. *United States*, 117 F.3d 1401 (Fed. Cir. 1997), applying 19 U.S.C. §1677(18)B(iv) and (v).

will be drawn by importing countries among different suppliers, some state-owned and operated according to the state's priorities, some state-owned but responsive to market forces, some privately owned within the country, and some owned by foreign private investors or in joint ventures.[42] Whether the WTO will take up the subject in an amendment to the Anti-Dumping Agreement or in a separate understanding may well depend on the attitude and influence of China, now that it is a member of the organization.

(e) The Question of Exchange Rates

After all of the complicated calculations and adjustments looking to establish the difference between normal value and export price, one problem remains. In export transactions between Patria and Xandia, home-market price and its surrogates will generally be expressed in Patrian pesos, while export price will be expressed in Xandian crowns, or in some third currency commonly used in the trade in question, such as the US dollar. If the object of the dumping inquiry were to determine whether a given sale was an exercise of fair or unfair trade, the rate of exchange prevailing on the date of sale should be dispositive. That is in fact what is stated in Article 2.4.1 of the Anti-Dumping Agreement. But whether the date of sale refers to the date of the contract, or of the purchase order, order confirmation, or invoice is not clear, and a footnote to Article 2.4.1 states that any of these dates may define the date of sale. The aim is to look to the time when the price terms of the transaction were determined, which may well be long after a contract is signed.

> Suppose a Patrian firm undertakes to supply a Xandian firm with quarterly shipments of product x for a year at a fixed price. The product is sold for consumption in Patria for 200 pesos/unit, and at the time of contracting in January, 2 Patrian pesos = 1 Xandian crown. The contract price for sale to Xandia (omitting shipping and handling) is 100 crowns. There is no price discrimination and no dumping. In August, however, the exchange rate has moved so that 1.80 Patrian pesos = 1 Xandian crown and 200 Patrian pesos equals 111 crowns. If the price of product x remains the same in both countries, i.e. 100 crowns per unit in Xandia and 200 pesos in Patria, is this now dumping?

If the contract had called for price adjustment every month, the Patrian seller should have raised its prices at the latest for the August shipment. That is supposed to be the consequence of fluctuating exchange rates—as Patria's currency rises in value, its exports become more expensive and less competitive in Xandia and comparable markets and, so the theory goes, over time

---

[42] Indeed in some instances the US Department of Commerce has accepted that some inputs of Chinese products were based on market principles because these were imported from market economies while others needed to be constructed on the basis of data from surrogate countries. See e.g. *Lasko Metal Products, Inc. v. United States*, 43 F.3d 1442 (Fed. Cir. 1994).

equilibrium will be achieved.[43] But in our example, the Patrian seller took the exchange risk by agreeing to be paid in Xandian crowns. As the movement in currencies worked out, seller's profit is down, and perhaps the contract has resulted in a loss. Still, it is hard to assert that the Patrian seller has engaged in unfair trade and deserves to be assessed with an anti-dumping duty.

Consider the reverse case:

> Product y is made in Xandia and is sold there for 500 crowns/unit. The exchange rate in January, as in the first case, is 2 pesos = 1 crown. However, Xandian exporters sell Product y in Patria for 900 pesos—clearly a sale below normal value. Seven months later, the price in each country, expressed in its own currency, is unchanged, but since the crown has fallen relative to the peso so that 1.8 pesos = 1 crown, the 900 pesos price in Patria is now equal to the home-market price in Xandia.

No one has come up with a perfect answer to these examples. Article 2.4.1 of the Anti-Dumping Agreement does say, however, 'Fluctuations in exchange rates shall be ignored', and in any investigation the authorities 'shall allow exporters at least 60 days to have adjusted their export prices to reflect sustained movement in exchange rates during the period of investigation.'[44] Since the presumed purpose of dumping is to achieve a larger market share in the importing country, the kind of 'accidental dumping' illustrated in the first example should not lead to a finding of dumping. The contract price was not set with a significant change in the exchange rate in mind.[45]

A harder case may be presented in a variation of the first case, where there is no contractual commitment to a fixed price in crowns, but simply as a marketing strategy the exporter chooses not to raise its prices expressed in crowns. Over time, one can predict that exports from Patria will bear higher prices expressed in crowns. It does not seem that the dumping that is to be condemned can be derived merely from changes in exchange rates not followed by immediate rises in price. On the other hand, when dumping and injury have been established on other grounds,

---

[43] See Ch. 2, Sect. 2.2(c) for discussion of floating exchange rates in theory and practice.

[44] The Agreement also states that when a sale of foreign currency on forward markets is directly linked to the export sale involved, the rate in the forward sale shall be used. Thus if in the first case seller, knowing it was to receive 100,000 crowns in August for 1,000 units of product x, had hedged his exchange risk by selling 100,000 crowns for August delivery, he could not be found to have engaged in dumping in August.

[45] Compare the following statement by the United States Court of Appeals in a case that arose out of a sharp rise of the German mark against the dollar, followed by a somewhat smaller fall. *Melamine Chemicals Inc.* v. *United States* 721 F.2d 924 at 933 (Fed. Cir. 1984):

> The purpose of the anti-dumping law . . . would be ill-served by application of a mechanized formula to find [Less than Fair Value] sales and thus a violation of the anti-dumping laws, where none existed. A finding of LTFV sales based on a margin resulting solely from a factor beyond the control of the exporter would be unreal, unreasonable, and unfair.

with the margin of dumping typically determined on the basis of a period of investigation of six months to a year, movements in the exchange rate in one direction (as contrasted with fluctuations) should be used to make the most accurate determinations.

10.5   DETERMINATION OF INJURY

As pointed out in the introductory section of this chapter, the condemnation of dumping in Article VI of GATT is mitigated by the provision (stated twice) that the standard remedy—anti-dumping duties—may be imposed only upon a finding that dumped imports cause or threaten material injury to the domestic industry of the importing country (GATT Art. VI(1) and VI(6)(a)). In contrast to the prescriptions on determination of dumping, which have been spelled out with considerable precision in the successive anti-dumping codes and are supposed to result in a specific number—the margin of dumping, the prescriptions concerning injury and causation consist only of lists of factors and (if a *de minimis* threshold is passed) require only a yes or no decision.

(a)   The Elements of Injury

The Anti-Dumping Agreement does not define injury, except to provide in a footnote to the heading of Article 3 that the term 'injury' shall, unless otherwise specified, be taken to mean material injury to a domestic industry, threat of material injury to a domestic industry, or material retardation to the establishment of such an industry.'[46] But Article 3.1 states that a determination of injury shall be based on positive evidence and involve an objective examination of (a) the volume of dumped imports and the effect of the dumped imports on prices in the domestic market of like products, and (b) the consequent impact of *these imports* on domestic producers of such products. Thus, at least formally, the practice by authorities in several jurisdictions to take into account all imports of a given product once dumping has been found is impermissible; but since the dumped imports need not be the only cause of injury, it may well happen that imports from countries other than those under challenge, or imports not sold at dumping prices, enter into the overall finding of injury.[47]

---

[46] The placement of this text, repeated in Article 15 of the 1994 Agreement on Subsidies, goes back to the 1967 Anti-Dumping Code, as an effort to placate the European Community without excessively irritating the US Congress. The European Community Regulation places the same wording in text—Article 3.1. The US legislation provides 'In general, the term "material injury" means harm which is not inconsequential, immaterial, or unimportant' (19 U.S.C. §1677(7)(A)).

[47] See the discussion of the *Atlantic Salmon* case, Subsect. (b) infra.

Article 3 of the 1994 Agreement, tracked in the implementing legislation of most of the states with developed anti-dumping laws,[48] contains several lists of relevant factors to be considered, evaluated, or examined, accompanied by the statement that no one or several of the factors can necessarily give decisive guidance. Examination of the impact of the dumped imports on the domestic industry is to include actual and potential decline in sales, profits, output, market share, productivity, return on investment, or utilization of capacity; factors affecting domestic prices; actual and potential negative effects on cash flow, inventories, employment, wages, growth, and ability to raise capital or investments (Art. 3.4).

One other factor, not mentioned in the earlier codes, and not replicated in the (otherwise parallel) Subsidies Agreement 1994, is the magnitude of the margin of dumping. Previously, a Korean importer, Hyundai Pipe Co., had challenged before the US Court of International Trade a determination of injury by the International Trade Commission following a finding that certain steel pipes and tubes were being sold in the United States at prices of 0.90 percent and 1.47 percent below the home-market price, i.e. with a very small margin of dumping. The Commission had based its determination on sales in the United States of 30 percent and 19 percent below the prices charged by the domestic industry, accompanied by increased volume of imports and market penetration, but had rejected consideration of the size of the dumping margin. The Court held that the ITC was authorized but not required to engage in margins analysis, and that failure to do so would not invalidate an injury determination.[49] Following adoption of the Uruguay Round Agreement and corresponding statutory amendments,[50] the investigating authorities are required to take the margin of dumping into account, and if those margins are less than 2 percent, as in the *Hyundai* case, to dismiss the case at the outset.[51]

As to the volume of the dumped imports, the Agreement requires the investigating authorities to consider whether there has been a significant increase in dumped imports, either in absolute terms or relative to production or consumption in the importing state. Again, the Agreement gives no specific guidance as to what is a 'significant' increase, but states in Article 5.8 that dumped imports from a given country shall normally be regarded as negligible if their volume accounts for less than 3 percent of imports of the product by the importing state.[52] In *New Zealand—Imports of Electrical Transformers from*

---

[48] See e.g. Keith Steele (ed.), *Anti-Dumping under the WTO: A Comparative Review* (1996).

[49] *Hyundai Pipe Co. Ltd* v. *US International Trade Commission*, 670 F. Supp. 357 (Ct. Int'l Trade 1987).

[50] See *U.S.*: 19 U.S.C. §1673b(b)(3); §1673d(a)(4).

[51] See 1994 Anti-Dumping Code Art. 5.8. The corresponding *de minimis* rule under the Subsidies Code is 1 percent. Subsidies Code Art. 11.9.

[52] Article 5.8 adds that this rule does not apply if countries that individually account for less than 3 percent of the imports collectively account for more than 7 percent of the imports of the product in question by the importing state.

Finland,[53] a GATT panel in 1985 (i) rejected a contention by New Zealand that the finding of injury was to be made by the importing country alone, without international scrutiny; and (ii) held that imports found to be dumped but amounting to only 1.5 percent of domestic production plus imports or 2.4 percent of total imports of the product in question could not support imposition of anti-dumping duties under Article VI(6)(a) of the GATT, even though the domestic industry had been in poor economic condition due to lack of new orders, declining profitability, and a large increase in imports, among other factors constituting injury.

In a more recent case, decided after the WTO entered into effect but under the prior code, Brazil challenged imposition of an anti-dumping duty by the European Community on imports of cotton yarn on the ground, *inter alia*, that the volume of imports from Brazil had decreased both in absolute and in relative terms, and that the export price expressed in US dollars had actually increased.[54] Emphasizing the recitals in the Agreement that no one or several of the factors listed can necessarily give decisive guidance, the panel rejected the challenge. Even though the volume and market share of dumped imports from Brazil had decreased in the relevant period, dumped imports from all countries had increased, and the EC authorities were entitled to make a finding that the dumped imports from Brazil had caused material injury to the domestic industry, whether or not Brazilian imports had increased in volume or had the lowest level of price effects.[55]

In sum, both national courts and international panels allow substantial discretion to the investigating authorities to choose among the factors used to demonstrate injury. The 1994 Agreement tightened up the criteria in rejecting findings of injury where either the margin of dumping or the volume of imports is negligible as defined. Generally, if the complaining industry was operating at a profit in the relevant period, injury will not be found; but if profits have fallen sharply, the complaint may support a finding of threat of injury.[56]

(b) The Link between Imports and Injury

Under the 1967 Anti-Dumping Code, the determination of injury was to be made only upon a finding that the dumped imports are 'demonstrably *the principal cause* of material injury.'[57] As noted in Section 10.3, this standard

<hr />

[53] GATT BISD, 32d Supp. 55, 66, (1985), Pescatore, *Handbook*, Case 60.

[54] *EC—Imposition of Anti-Dumping Duties on Imports of Cotton Yarn from Brazil* (*Brazil v. EC*), Report of Panel adopted by Committee on Anti-Dumping Practices, 30 Oct. 1995. GATT BISD, 42nd Supp. 17 (1995); Pescatore, *Handbook*, Case 97.

[55] Id. paras. 517–31. On the issue of cumulation of dumped imports from several countries, see Subsect. (d) infra.

[56] See Subsect. (e) infra.

[57] 1967 Anti-Dumping Code Article 3(a). The omitted text refers to threat of material injury and material retardation of the establishment of an industry.

was replaced by a less demanding standard in the 1979 Code, and that standard was retained in the 1994 Agreement, so that it is sufficient that the dumped imports be *a cause* of the injury. However, the 1994 Agreement requires that the demonstration of a causal relationship between the dumped imports and the injury to the domestic industry be based on an examination of 'all relevant evidence', and states that the authorities shall also examine any known factors other than the dumped imports which are injuring the domestic industry (Art. 3.5).

For many years there was a debate in the United States among members of the International Trade Commission (the agency charged with making the determination) whether the process of finding injury by reason of dumping should be bifurcated or unitary.[58] Under a *bifurcated approach*, the agency charged with the determination would *first* determine whether the domestic industry was injured, and *second* (if the first determination was positive) whether imports of the unfairly traded goods (i.e. goods found to have been dumped or subsidized) had caused or contributed to the injury. There is a good deal of evidence, both in the United States and in Europe, that under this approach, once the industry has been found to be injured, all imports of the product in question, and not just the unfairly traded imports, tended to enter into the determination of causation. Under the *unitary* or *'but for'* approach, injury and causation would be examined together, so that the focus would be more directly on the link between the unfair practice as the cause of the injury. The unitary approach seems more in keeping with the provision in Article 3.5 of the 1994 Agreement that injuries caused by other factors than dumped imports must not be attributed to the dumped imports, followed by an illustrative list of such other factors, including the volume and prices of imports not sold at dumping prices, contraction in demand or changes in the patterns of consumption, etc.[59] However, as of year-end 2001 this conclusion was not reflected in the jurisprudence of the GATT/WTO dispute settlement mechanism.

In 1992, a GATT panel established pursuant to the 1979 Anti-Dumping Code was faced with a challenge to a finding of injury by the US International Trade Commission by reason of dumped and subsidized imports of Atlantic salmon from Norway. The respondents in the American proceeding contended, *inter alia*, that factors other than the dumped and

---

[58] For a proceeding in which the several commissioners lay out their approaches at length, see *New Steel Rails from Canada*, USITC Pub. 2217 (Sept. 1989) and cases cited therein. For an extended analysis, raising the question whether one approach or the other is likely to lead to more positive findings of injury, see Alan O. Sykes, 'The Economics of Injury in Antidumping and Countervailing Duty Cases', and Ronald A. Cass and Michael S. Knoll, 'The Economics of "Injury" in Antidumping and Countervailing Duty Cases: A Reply to Professor Sykes', both in Jagdeep S. Bhandar and Alan O. Sykes (eds.), *Economic Dimensions in International Law* (1997).

[59] The other examples given are trade restrictive practices of and competition between the foreign and domestic producers, developments in technology and the export performance and productivity of the domestic industry.

subsidized imports from Norway were the cause of the injury experienced by the American industry. Norway pointed to imports from other countries, to falling prices, to marketing and production difficulties in the US industry, and to the effects of entry of Pacific salmon into the market.

The USITC replied:

The Commission may consider whether causes other than the subject imports are responsible for injury, but it is not to weigh causes. The Commission need not determine that imports are the principal or a substantial cause of material injury in order to reach an affirmative determination. 'Any such requirement has the undesirable result of making relief more difficult to obtain for industries facing difficulties from a variety of sources, industries that are often the most vulnerable to less-than-fair value imports' [quoting from a US Senate Report]. Instead the Commission must determine whether imports are a cause of material injury.

Having first found that the US industry was experiencing material injury, the Commission concluded:

Although some of [the other factors mentioned] may have adversely affected the US industry, we determine that an industry in the United States is materially injured by reason of subsidized and [less than fair value] imports of fresh and chilled salmon from Norway.[60]

Norway challenged the result under the 1979 Anti-Dumping Code, which in the present context was substantially similar to the 1994 Agreement,[61] but the challenge was rejected:[62]

In light of [the ITC's statement as quoted], the Panel found that as a matter of fact, the USITC had not 'disregarded' possible other causes of injury. The USITC had expressly recognized that some of these factors might have 'adversely affected' the domestic industry but that this did not detract from the fact that material injury was (also) caused by the imports from Norway subject to the investigation

. . .

Given that . . . the USITC had not ignored the impact of factors other than the imports under investigation, the Panel considered that the basic question before it was whether the manner in which the USITC had treated those other factors was inconsistent with the obligations of the United States under Article 3.4 of the Agreement. . . . The basic question of interpretation was whether . . . the investigating authorities were required to carry out a thorough examination of all possible causes of injury and 'isolate' or 'exclude' injury caused by such other factors from the effects of the imports subject to investigation.[63]

---

[60] *Fresh and Chilled Atlantic Salmon from Norway*, USITC Pub. 2371 (Apr. 1991), pp. 16–17, 22.

[61] See 1979 Code Art. 3.4 and footnotes thereto; 1994 Code Art. 3.5.

[62] *United States—Imposition of Anti-Dumping Duties on Imports of Fresh and Chilled Atlantic Salmon from Norway*, Panel Dec. of 30 Nov 1992, adopted by Committee on Anti-Dumping Practices, 27 Apr. 1994, BISD 41st Supp. 229 (1994); Pescatore, *Handbook*, Vol. II, Case 92.

[63] Id. paras. 547, 548, 549.

The Panel's answer was no.

[T]he Panel considered that the focus of the requirement . . . of a causal relationship between the imports under investigation and material injury to a domestic industry was on the analysis of the factors set forth in Articles 3.2 and 3.3[64]—i.e., the volume and price effects of the imports, and their consequent impact on the domestic industry. . . . [T]his did not mean that . . . the USITC should somehow have identified the extent of injury caused by [the] other factors.[65]

The *Atlantic Salmon* case is not necessarily the last word on the issue of linking dumping with injury,[66] though it suggests a disposition to allow substantial discretion in the manner in which national investigating authorities approach the question of the causal link between dumping and injury to the domestic industry. The 1994 Agreement does call expressly for examination of any known factors other than the dumped imports, but it seems that the level of inquiry conducted by the USITC in *Atlantic Salmon* is sufficient.

(c)   Margin of Dumping or Margin of Injury

In some jurisdictions, notably the United States, once dumping and injury (and a causal link between them) have been found, an anti-dumping duty must be imposed equal to the margin of dumping, without regard to volume of imports or the margin of the injury.[67] In other jurisdictions, including Australia and the European Community, the anti-dumping duty is to be imposed in a lesser amount if such amount would be adequate to remove the injury to the industry of the importing country.[68] The Uruguay Round Anti-Dumping Agreement leaves the choice between the two approaches up to the authorities of the importing state.[69]

Thus suppose the normal value in Patria for a given product is 200, the export price of the Patrian product in Xandia (after the relevant adjustments) is 160 and the domestic price in Xandia is 180. Under United States law, the anti-dumping duty would be set to offset the margin of dumping—i.e. at 40/160 or 25 percent *ad valorem*; under EC law the anti-dumping duty could be set to offset only the injury margin—i.e. at 20/160 or 12.5 percent. If the normal value in Patria was

[64] Arts. 3.2 and 3.4 in the 1994 Agreement.

[65] *Fresh and Chilled Atlantic Salmon from Norway*, n. 62 supra, para. 555.

[66] See e.g. N. David Palmeter, 'Report on the United States', in Keith Steele (ed.), *Anti-Dumping under the WTO: A Comparative Review* (1996), suggesting (at p. 272) that the so-called 'minimal cause' doctrine might well be tested under the WTO's dispute settlement procedures.

[67] *U.S.*: 19 U.S.C. §1673.

[68] *E.C.*: Basic Anti-Dumping Regulation (Art. 9.4); *Australia*: Customs Tariff (Anti-Dumping) Act 1975, sect. 8(5)(A).

[69] Anti-Dumping Agreement 1994, Art. 9.1. However, the text states that it is 'desirable' that the duty be less than the margin of dumping, if such lesser duty would be adequate to remove the injury to the domestic industry.

180 and the export price in Xandia remained at 160, the injury margin and the dumping margin would be the same. But if the domestic price in Xandia was 205, the anti-dumping duty under either approach would be limited to the margin of dumping, i.e. to 25 percent.[70]

(d) Cumulation

In the prototype dumping or subsidies case before national investigating authorities, anti-dumping or countervailing duties are sought against one or more exporters from a given country. In many instances, however, complaints are brought and investigations are conducted at the same time in respect of imports from different countries. In such a proceeding, imports from any given country might well be viewed as not causing injury, in that they may have come in at the prevailing price, and if they were met by an anti-dumping or countervailing duty, their place would simply be taken up by imports from another country. If imports from Patria to Xandia are dumped while imports from Tertia and Quarta, etc. are not sold below their respective normal value, Patria probably has a good defense, unless its imports standing alone make up a major portion of imports or consumption in Xandia. But if imports from Patria, Tertia, and Quarta are all sold below their normal value, authorities in the United States, the European Community, Canada, Australia and other jurisdictions often added up all the imports found to be dumped, and if the total reached the level of injury, assessed anti-dumping duties against all such imports.[71]

A number of countries argued to the Anti-Dumping Committee and in the course of the Uruguay Round that this practice, known as cumulation, was inconsistent with the 1979 Anti-Dumping Code, in that, as discussed in the preceding section, 'it must be demonstrated that the *dumped imports* are, through the effects of dumping, causing injury . . . and the injuries caused by other factors [such as imports from other countries] must not be attributed to the dumped imports.'[72] In the United States, on the other hand, the practice of cumulation, which had been optional, was made mandatory by Congress in 1984, and a court challenge to that amendment as being contrary to the Anti-Dumping Code was rejected.[73]

Both sides proposed inclusion of the issue in the Uruguay Round Agreement.[74] In the semi-final Dunkel draft (1991), the subject was omitted, but it came back in the final version, supported both by the European

---

[70] For more detailed analysis of this issue, including citations to decided cases, see Edwin Vermulst and Paul Waer, *E.C. Anti-Dumping Law and Practice*, ch. 8, 'Injury Margins' (1996).

[71] Note that dumping margins and therefore the anti-dumping duties might well be different in respect of the imports from the different countries.

[72] 1979 Anti-Dumping Code, Art. 3.4.

[73] *Fundição Tupy S.A.* v. *United States*, 859 F.2d 915 (Fed. Cir. 1987).

[74] See Terence E. Stewart (ed.), *The GATT Uruguay Round: A Negotiating History 1986–1992*, Vol II, pp. 1592–1601 (1993).

Community and by the United States. Under Article 3.3 of the 1994 Anti-Dumping Agreement, the investigating authorities may cumulatively assess the effects of dumped imports from more than one country for the purpose of an injury determination, but only (i) if the investigations have been initiated simultaneously; and (ii) if (a) the margin of dumping in relation to imports from each country is more than *de minimis* (i.e. at least 2 percent) and (b) the volume of imports from each country is not negligible (i.e. at least 3 percent of imports of the product in question by the importing state).[75] It is clear than an existing anti-dumping order against Patria cannot be cumulated with injurious effects found in a later proceeding to have been caused by imports from Tertia. However, cumulation can be carried out as a result of separate proceedings, provided they were begun on the same day.

Article 3.3 of the Anti-Dumping Agreement is replicated in Article 15.3 of the Subsidies Agreement, permitting cumulation of subsidized imports from more than one country for purposes of determination of material injury. Prior to the 1994 Agreements, 'cross-cumulation'—i.e. adding the effect of dumped and subsidized products together—was regularly practised by the US International Trade Commission, and indeed was held to be required by the US statute.[76] Nothing is said about cross-cumulation in the Uruguay Round Agreements, and it would seem that the practice is inconsistent with the respective texts. The issue is not clear however, and may need to be decided in a panel proceeding.

(e)   Threat of Injury

One complaint by the proponents of anti-dumping laws is that the proceeding typically takes place after the damage is done, and even if the petition is granted and anti-dumping duties are imposed, compensation for past losses is not available and the market may already have been permanently altered.[77] On the other side, opponents of anti-dumping measures assert that giving relief for threats or likelihood of injury involves speculation, not hard facts, and should not be available as a second resort when the effort to prove actual injury has been unsuccessful.

Article VI of the GATT seems to draw no distinction between actual and threatened injury.[78] However, petitions looking to anti-dumping duties are rarely if ever brought alleging only threat of injury. The Group of Experts on Anti-Dumping and Countervailing Duties[79] recommended as early as

---

[75] The latter condition is not applicable if countries that individually account for less than 3 percent of imports collectively account for more than 7 percent of the imports of the product in question.

[76] *Bingham & Taylor Division, Virginia Industries Inc.* v. *United States*, 815 F.2d 1482 (Fed. Cir. 1987).

[77] In part, this argument is met by provisional measures, as discussed in Sect. 10.8(c) infra.

[78] See e.g. Article VI(1): '[D]umping . . . is to be condemned if it causes or threatens material injury to an established industry'; to the same effect Article VI(6)(a).

[79] See Sect. 10.3 supra.

1961 that in cases in which a threat of material injury was asserted 'the application of anti-dumping measures had to be studied and decided with particular care,'[80] and that phrase was included in the 1967 Anti-Dumping Code, along with the following provision, both repeated without change in the 1979 Code:

A determination of threat of material injury shall be based on facts and not merely on allegation, conjecture or remote possibility. The change in circumstances which would create a situation in which dumping would cause material injury must be clearly foreseen and imminent.[81]

The Uruguay Round Anti-Dumping Agreement repeats the text of the earlier codes, and adds a series of factors to be considered by the authorities in reaching the conclusion that further dumped exports are imminent and that, unless protective action is taken, material injury would occur.[82]

The jurisprudence of threat of injury is not great, but some anomalies emerge, suggesting that findings of threat of injury sometimes reflect a compromise among decision-makers and that the cautions set out in the codes are justified.

For instance, in the *New Steel Rails from Canada* case cited previously for the debate about bifurcated vs. unitary approach to causation,[83] the 'plurality' of the US International Trade Commission[84] found (i) there was material injury to the steel rail industry in the United States; (ii) there was insufficient causal relation between the challenged imports and the actual injury to meet the legal requirement; but (iii) there was also a *threat* of material injury and that threat was linked to the imports in question.[85] On appeal to a binational panel pursuant to the Canada–United States Free

---

[80] *Anti-Dumping and Countervailing Duties*, Report of the Group of Experts GATT/ 1961–2 at p. 10.

[81] 1967 Anti-Dumping Code Art. 3(e) and (f); 1979 Code Arts. 3.6 and 3.7. A footnote gives the example that there is a convincing reason to believe that there will be, in the immediate future, substantially increased importations of the product at dumped prices.

[82] 1994 Agreement Art. 3.7. The factors listed are:

(i) a significant rate of increase of dumped imports into the domestic market indicating the likelihood of substantially increased importation;

(ii) sufficient freely disposable, or an imminent, substantial increase in, capacity of the exporter indicating the likelihood of substantially increased exports to the importing Member's market, taking into account the availability of other export markets to absorb any additional exports;

(iii) whether imports are entering at prices that will have a significant depressing or suppressing effect on domestic prices, and would likely increase demand for further imports; and

(iv) inventories of the product being investigated.

A substantially similar list of factors appears in Article 15.7 of the Subsidies 1994 Code.

[83] See n. 58 supra.

[84] Actually three of the six members of the Commission, whose decision was dispositive pursuant to a provision in US trade law that an evenly divided vote is deemed to be an affirmative determination. 19 U.S.C. §1677(11).

[85] *New Steel Rails from Canada*, USITC Pub. 2217, pp. 11–14, 14–15.

Trade Agreement, the Canadian importers argued that 'threat' of injury presupposes that actual injury has not yet occurred, and thus that the Commission's finding of a threat of injury was inconsistent with the first finding, that injury already existed. The panel, required by the Free Trade Agreement to apply the importing country's law as the courts of that country would apply it,[86] did not accept the argument.[87] On reflection, if the missing element to justify an anti-dumping duty is the link of causation, it seems unpersuasive that that element would be sufficient to support a threat of injury finding but not a finding of actual injury.

In another case that came before a binational panel under the Canada–United States Free Trade Agreement, *Fresh, Chilled and Frozen Pork from Canada*,[88] the US International Trade Commission made the more usual finding—no present injury but a threat of injury attributable to the challenged (in that case subsidized) imports.[89] Among the facts adduced by the Commission to support the finding was evidence that Canada had recently increased exports of hogs to Japan, because of quality problems with supplies of hogs to Japan from Taiwan. Once Taiwan had corrected its problem, the Commission surmised, Canada's exports to Japan would decline, and the products not sent to Japan would find their way to the United States in the form of pork. The review panel, properly, found this kind of analysis unpersuasive.[90]

In a similar case in the European Community,[91] the Council had found a threat of injury on the basis that high anti-dumping duties imposed by the United States on ball-bearings from Japan would lead to diversion of exports to the European Community. The Court of First Instance, which since 1994 hears appeals in anti-dumping cases, rejected this finding. '[T]he fear expressed by the Council regarding diversion of Japanese exports to the Community', the court wrote, 'is mere hypothesis and is not sufficient to justify a finding of threat of injury within the meaning of Article 4(1) of the basic regulation, a term which must in any event be interpreted in the light

---

[86] Canada–United States Free Trade Agreement 1 Jan. 1988, Art. 1904.3. The same rule is stated in the North American Free Trade Agreement, 1 Jan. 1993, Art 1904.3.

[87] *In the Matter of New Steel Rails from Canada*, Case Nos. USA-89-1904-09, 1904–10 (10 Aug. 1990). One member of the Panel dissented, arguing that 'in order for the Commission to make a threat of injury finding, some "new element" of a significant nature must be identified which caused "non-injurious activities" to become "injurious" in a "likely" or "threatening" way.' The criteria for threat of injury in the US statute, 19 U.S.C. §1677(7)(F) were similar to but somewhat more extensive than the factors now incorporated in the 1994 agreements, as quoted in n. 82 supra.

[88] Case No. USA 89-1904-11 (24 Aug. 1990) (Round I); 22 Jan. 1991 (Round II).

[89] *Fresh, Chilled or Frozen Pork from Canada*, USITC Pub. No. 2218 (Sept. 1989); USITC Pub. 2230 (Oct. 1990).

[90] For a detailed account of this proceeding, see A. Lowenfeld, 'The Free Trade Agreement Meets Its First Challenge', 37 *McGill L.J.* 597 (1992).

[91] *NTN Corporation and Koyo Seiko Co. Ltd.* v. *Comm.* [1995–II] E.C.R 1381 (Court of First Instance, 2 May 1995).

of the 1979 Anti-Dumping Code and in particular Article 3(6) thereof [Article 3(7) in the 1994 Code], not merely on allegation, conjecture or remote possibility.'[92]

The possibility of diversion of exports from another market is apparently contemplated by Article 3.7 of the 1994 Code,[93] but the warning against conjecture or hypothesis seems especially pertinent in this context.[94]

In sum, a finding of threat of injury in the face of a negative finding of injury is rarely made and is difficult to justify. When a petition seeking anti-dumping or anti-subsidy duties alleges both injury and threat of injury, the authorities may well make an affirmative finding on both counts, without distinguishing sharply between the two. This seems to be true particularly in sunset review proceedings.[95] Of course, actual injury without a change in the importers' practices will often be a predictor of future injury as well.

(f) Material Retardation

The third, and least used leg of the injury requirement in Article VI(1) and VI(6)(a) of the GATT is material retardation of the establishment of a domestic industry. There are few such cases, because it generally takes an established industry with substantial resources to mount an anti-dumping or anti-subsidy case, and if there are several firms in the domestic industry, at least some will already be established and thus claim actual or threatened injury, rather than impediments to getting started. In perhaps the most important material retardation case, involving dynamic random access memories or DRAMs, major companies established in other industries were successful in persuading the European Commission that their entry into a new field was materially retarded by dumping.

> Major manufacturing firms in Europe, including Siemens, Thomson, Motorola and others, alleged that massive dumping by eight Japanese producers of Dynamic Random Access Memory chips had impeded efforts by the European companies to enter the market for DRAMs. The European Commission, after lengthy investigation, concluded that several of the European companies had made serious commitments to this market but had been delayed or prevented by a worldwide fall in price attributable to deliberate dumping by the Japanese companies, with margins over 200 percent. The Commission found that the

[92] Id. at para. 106. [93] See n. 82 supra, item (ii).

[94] On remand in the *Pork* case, n. 88 supra, the USITC came up with another theory—product shifting. The idea was that higher Canadian subsidies on hogs would lead to higher US countervailing duties on live swine, which in turn would lead to reduction of exports of live swine and higher exports of pork, thus creating threat of injury to the US pork industry. Once again, the binational panel rejected the decision of the Commission, finding it unsupported by substantial evidence.

[95] See Edwin Vermulst and Paul Waer, *EC Anti-Dumping Law and Practice*, pp. 313–14 (1996), summarizing EC practice from 1980 to 1996.

DRAM industry in the Community had either suffered material injury or injury in the form of material retardation, and that factors other than the imports of low-priced Japanese DRAMs had not contributed in any significant manner to the injury. Eventually, the controversy was resolved by price undertakings by all eight of the Japanese manufacturers at a level of 9.5 percent over cost of goods sold, backed up by a 60 percent anti-dumping duty.[96]

In one of the few American cases based on material retardation, the US International Trade Commission phrased the issue as 'whether the level of activities of [the complainant] reflect merely the normal start-up conditions of a company entering an admittedly difficult market or whether the performance is worse than what could reasonably be expected and thus be deemed materially retarded.' The complainants must show that the project is viable, i.e. that they had a serious business plan and the commitment of finances and personnel to make it succeed, absent unfair trade.[97]

Both the Agreement on Anti-Dumping (in Article 3) and the Agreement on Subsidies (in Article 15) mention material retardation of the establishment of a domestic industry in a footnote to the Article on Determination of Injury, but as of year-end 2001 no case raising this subject had come before the GATT/WTO dispute settlement mechanism. In the Ministerial Declaration

---

[96] *Dynamic Random Access Memories from Japan*, [1990] O.J. L20/5 (25 Jan. 1990). Under Article 21 of the EC Anti-Dumping Regulation, the Commission had to consider the 'Community Interest'—in this case whether higher prices for DRAMs would disadvantage industries that used DRAMs in their products. The Commission answered as follows:

The Commission is of the view that a viable Community DRAM industry will contribute to a strong Community electronics industry overall. This is because DRAMs serve as a technology driver for other more complex semiconductor devices and because the semiconductor industry, of which the DRAM industry is a part, is a strategic industry in that semiconductors are key components for the data processing, telecommunications and automotive industries. The use of the most advanced technology in DRAM production not only improves the competitiveness of this industry but also that of the downstream electronics industry. Furthermore a viable Community DRAM industry will provide an alternative source of supply to the Community electronics industry, thus reducing dependence on the dominant Japanese DRAM producers. This latter aspect is considered essential given the fact that Japanese producers are generally vertically integrated and also manufacture the end products which compete with those produced by the Community electronics industry.

[97] *Certain Dried Salted Codfish from Canada*, USITC Pub. 1571 (Sept. 1984) (Preliminary); USITC Pub. 1711 (July 1985) (Final), aff'd sub. nom. *BMT Commodity Corp. v. United States*, 667 F. Supp. 880 (Ct. Int'l Trade 1987). In the *Codfish* case, the petitioner had been the only firm in the domestic industry before filing for bankruptcy, and the Commission found that it never reached its projected break-even level of sales. The respondent Canadian producers and importers argued that petitioner's operation was inherently unviable because it sought to dry fish in the hot and humid climate of Puerto Rico. The Commission was not persuaded, and faced with evidence of repeated reduction in prices by the Canadian firms, made one of the few affirmative findings in the United States based on material retardation alone.

The Court of International Trade affirmed the decision on the basis that the complainant's viability absent unfair trade had been established, while stressing that it would be counterproductive for the unfair trade laws to provide relief to domestic industries that cannot compete (667 F. Supp. at 882).

adopted at the close of the Doha Conference in November 2001, the Member states agreed to negotiations aimed at clarifying and simplifying disputes under these two agreements, and the issue of retardation may well be among the topics to be discussed.

10.6   ANTI-DUMPING, ANTITRUST AND PUBLIC INTEREST

(a)   Could Antitrust Replace Anti-Dumping Laws?

Numerous critics of anti-dumping laws have suggested that the persuasive aspect of anti-dumping law—to prevent predatory pricing[98]—can be taken care of by antitrust or competition law, and that therefore there is no strong reason to preserve anti-dumping laws. Defenders of anti-dumping laws respond that the anti-dumping laws are not aimed primarily at predatory pricing, but rather at distortion of fair trade through 'subsidization' of lower prices in the importing country by higher prices in the home market than would prevail if that market were open and all prices were equalized. Further, the defenders of anti-dumping law fear that reliance on antitrust law and dismantling of the anti-dumping machinery would in practice leave little or no defense against what they regard as unfair trade.

A more subtle form of the argument against anti-dumping laws focuses on the alternatives available to the domestic industry, when met by competition from abroad at prices lower than charged by the foreign producer/exporter in its home market. Absent an anti-dumping law, the argument goes, the domestic industry in the importing countries would have an incentive to attempt to enter the home market of the foreign supplier, thereby regaining some of its lost sales volume and over time tending to equalize prices at home and abroad. With anti-dumping laws in place, the incentives work the other way and the domestic industry will use the anti-dumping law to discourage imports and to maintain higher prices in its own market.

Finally, the use of antitrust law as a substitute for anti-dumping law would—it seems inevitably—require more extensive application extra-territorially of the importing country's law, both on substance and on discovery of information. In both respects, as is well known, the practice of the United States courts and administrative agencies has given rise to continuing controversy. In contrast, the rules on anti-dumping—including fact-finding[99]—are by now internationally agreed and codified, so that to the extent the application of the laws produces controversy, it is about substance, not about jurisdiction or sovereignty.

---

[98] i.e. the practice whereby a supplier lowers its prices until the competitors are forced from the market, with a view to thereafter achieving monopoly or close to monopoly, and raising prices well above those previously prevailing.

[99] See Sect. 10.8(d) infra.

If competition law comes under the WTO system or some comparable multilateral regime that goes beyond consultation and affords remedies to private parties,[100] the anti-dumping regime that has prevailed since the founding of the GATT might be subject to re-examination. Until then it seems unlikely for antitrust to replace anti-dumping except for trade within economies that are truly unified or aiming to become unified, such as the European Community.[101]

(b) Anti-Dumping, Competition, and the Public Interest

The concerns of antitrust have relevance in another context, particularly in jurisdictions such as the European Community, whose Anti-Dumping Regulation contains an explicit provision on public (or 'Community') interest.[102] The tension between antitrust and anti-dumping was illustrated in the well known *Extramet* case that came before the European Court of Justice.[103]

> The case concerned the market for calcium metal. Only one firm, Pechiney, produced calcium metal within the Common Market, and it was also the complainant in the proceeding charging dumping from the Soviet Union and China. Extramet, a French firm, was the largest importer, and the principal competitor of Pechiney in purifying and processing the metal for industrial use. The Council imposed heavy anti-dumping duties against the imports from China and the Soviet Union, and Extramet appealed to the Court of Justice, contending (i) that Pechiney had refused to sell it the unprocessed metal; and (ii) that if the anti-dumping orders issued by the Council were permitted to stand, Pechiney would be the sole source of the product within the Common Market. Extramet argued that Community interest required rejecting intervention by anti-dumping procedures, in order to preserve

[100] See Ch. 12, Sect. 12.8.

[101] It is notable that when Canada and the United States were negotiating what became the Canada–United States Free Trade Agreement, 1989, Canada sought elimination of application of anti-dumping and anti-subsidy laws between the two countries. The United States negotiators responded that an FTA without preservation of these laws could not be submitted to the Congress, let alone be approved. The issue almost derailed the negotiations, but was finally composed by a procedural solution whereby each country would apply its own laws to the imports from the other country, but in place of national judicial review the decisions of each country's administrative agencies could be appealed to binational panels. This solution was preserved in the North American Free Trade Agreement, 1993 (NAFTA).

[102] Article 21 of the EC Basic Anti-Dumping Regulation Council Reg. E.C. No. 384/96 of 22 Dec. 1995 contains seven paragraphs. Para. 1 reads, in pertinent part:

A determination as to whether the Community interest calls for intervention shall be based on an appreciation of all the various interests taken as a whole, including the interests of the domestic industry and users and consumers. . . . In such an examination, the need to eliminate the trade distorting effects of injurious dumping and to restore effective competition shall be given special consideration.

[103] *Extramet Industrie S.A.* v. *Council*, [1991-I] E.C.R. 2501, [1992-I] E.C.R. 3183 (16 May 1991), (11 June 1992).

a competitive European industry. Pechiney and the Commission/ Council argued, on the contrary that without the anti-dumping duty, the viability of the sole domestic producer would be jeopardized. The Advocate-General argued *inter alia* that the effect of the duty on competition within the Common Market should have been examined, to ensure that the Community's intervention did not result in conferring or preserving an unjustified advantage by which Pechiney could abuse its dominant position within the meaning of Article 86 of the Treaty of Rome. The Court of Justice annulled the imposition of the anti-dumping duties on the ground that the competition issues had not been adequately considered.

Not many cases like *Extramet* have been reported, and in the end that case did not result in triumph of competition law over dumping law.[104] Still the tension between anti-dumping and competition law is now recognized in the European Community and is at least discussed in the context of Community interest. For instance, in a case imposing anti-dumping duties on imports of ferro-silicon from eight countries, the Council wrote:

It has also been argued that anti-dumping measures would reduce the number of competitors on the market. However, the Commission considers that the number of competitors on the Community market will not be reduced by the adoption of anti-dumping measures. On the contrary, the removal of the unfair advantages gained by the dumping practices is designed to arrest the decline of the Community industry and thus to help to maintain the availability of a wide choice of ferro-silicon producers.[105]

The Canadian Special Import Measures Act (SIMA)[106] has a comparable provision (Sect. 45) authorizing the Canadian International Trade Tribunal (CITT), which investigates injury, to recommend to the Minister charged with imposing anti-dumping duties of its opinion 'that the imposition of an anti-dumping or countervailing duty or the imposition of such a duty in the full amount. . . . would not or might not be in the public interest.' The

---

[104] Two years after the decision of the Court of Justice, and after a renewed investigation looking at Pechiney's conduct and at the effect on the market, the Council once again imposed a definitive anti-dumping duty on imports from China and Russia. Council Reg. (EC) No. 2557/94 of 19 Oct. 1994, [1994] O.J. L 270/27 (21 Oct. 1994).

[105] Council Reg. EC No. 3359/93 of 2 Dec. 1993 on *Imports of Ferro Silicon from Russia Kazakhstan, etc.,* [1994] O.J. L 302/1 at para. 83 (9 Dec. 1993). Compare also the DRAM case, Sect. 10.5 n. 96 supra.

For other attempts to bring competition law into the consideration of anti-dumping duties in the European Community, see Gabrielle Marceau, *Anti-Dumping and Anti-Trust Issues in Free Trade Areas,* 138–46 (1994); John Temple Lang 'Reconciling European Community Antitrust and Anti-dumping Transport and Trade Safeguard Policies—Procedural Problems', in Barry Hawk (ed.), [1988] *Annual Proceedings of the Fordham Corporate Law Institute,* ch. 7 (1989).

[106] R.S.C. 1985 c. S-15 as amended.

provision has not been used frequently, but representations on the anti-competitive character of the domestic injury may be made.[107]

No comparable provision exists in the American anti-dumping or countervailing duty law, and efforts by respondents to raise antitrust concerns before the respective agencies have generally been unsuccessful. It is understood, however, that those concerns exist, and from time to time agencies other than those charged with administering the anti-dumping laws—i.e. the Federal Trade Commission and the Department of Justice—have intervened in anti-dumping proceedings, to argue that anti-dumping duties should not be imposed to protect an industry that was already concentrated or where the imports came in at— not under—the US price. Generally these interventions have been unsuccessful, as the agencies charged with implementation of the anti-dumping laws have regarded the points raised as going beyond their mandate.[108]

10.7   ANTI-CIRCUMVENTION MEASURES

The traditional discussion of dumping, from pre-war national legislation to drafting the GATT in the 1940s to negotiation of the 1967 and 1979 Anti-Dumping codes, focused on the supply of a given product, made in Patria, to an importer in Xandia. Since the mid-1980s, as corporations located production of components and assembly of complex products in many countries, attention, particularly in the European Community and the United States, has been trained on various ways to avoid or get around anti-dumping orders by shifting production or assembly to another country not covered by the order. One way is so-called *screwdriver* assembly: a firm in Patria (read Japan) against which an anti-dumping order had been entered in Xandia (read the European Community or the United States) could open or acquire a subsidiary in Xandia that would import components not subject to the anti-dumping order, assemble them into the finished product which could not now be said to be imported, and market that product at what it regarded as a strategic price, which might well be below the 'normal value' in Patria. Another way is so-called *diversionary dumping*. The firm in Patria sells parts and components to a firm in Tertia (read Taiwan, Korea, Malaysia) which may be owned by the Patrian firm or may be independent, and that firm assembles the product in question and exports it to Xandia. There is no anti-dumping order outstanding against the Tertian firm; and

---

[107] See e.g. J.-G. Castel, A.L.C. de Mestral and W. C. Graham, *The Canadian Law and Practice of International Trade*, 369–70 (1991); also CITT: *Report on Public Interest: Grain Corn*, 20 Oct. 1987; CITT Opinion: *Public Interest: Beer*, 25 Nov. 1991.

[108] See Harvey Applebaum and David R. Grace, 'U.S. Antitrust Law and Antidumping Action under Title VII of the Trade Agreements Act of 1979', 56 *Antitrust L.J.* 497 at 515–17 (1987).

anyhow, the sale to Xandia is not made below 'normal value' in Tertia, and the export price is not below the cost of materials imported from Patria plus local labour and overhead.

In 1987, the European Community amended its anti-dumping regulations to deal with screwdriver assembly.[109] The regulation authorized imposition of anti-dumping duties on products assembled within the Community by enterprises affiliated with any foreign manufacturer whose products were subject to an anti-dumping order, if (i) the assembly or production is carried out by an organization affiliated with that importer, (ii) assembly or production in the Community was started or significantly increased after initiation of an anti-dumping investigation; and (iii) the value of parts or materials used in the assembly or production originating in the country of exportation of the product in question exceeds by at least 50 percent the value of all other parts used in the finished product. The duty was to be at the same rate as the anti-dumping duty on the imported product, but only on the value of the imported parts or materials.

In the following year the United States adopted a similar provision, directed both to assembly of a product in the United States from imported components, and to merchandise assembled in a third country from components originating in the country to which the anti-dumping order or question applies.[110] Subsequently the EC also made its anti-circumvention regulation applicable to imports from third countries.[111]

Seven cases were brought in the European Community in the first three years of the anti-circumvention regulation (1987–9) all against Japanese firms with facilities in the Community. In four of the cases the result was extension of the primary anti-dumping duties to the imported parts and components; in the others the respondent firms gave undertakings to use stated percentages of locally made components.[112]

Japan brought a complaint under the dispute mechanism of the GATT in what became known as the *Screwdriver Assembly* case.[113] Japan asserted that nothing in GATT or the 1979 Anti-Dumping Code authorized application of anti-dumping duties to products made in the importing country, and that the duties were either (i) violations of Article II(1)(b) of GATT because

---

[109] EC: Council Reg. No. 1761/87 of 22 June 1987, [1987] O.J. L 167/9 (26 June 1987), amending Council Reg. No. 2176/84 of 23 July 1984, 1984 O.J. L 201 (30 July 1984).

[110] 19 USC §1677j, as enacted in the Omnibus Trade and Competitiveness Act of 1988, Pub. L. No. 100-418, §1321(a)a.

[111] EC: Council Reg. 3283/94 of 22 Dec. 1994, [1994] O.J. L 349/1 (31 Dec. 1994), Art. 13, amended by Council Reg. 384/96, n. 122 infra.

[112] The products in question were electronic typewriters, electronic scales, hydraulic excavators, photocopiers, ball-bearings, and dot matrix printers. For citation of these cases, involving many of Japan's leading multinational corporations, see Vermulst and Waer, *E.C. Anti-Dumping Law and Practice*, n. 18 supra, at 415, n. 22 (1996).

[113] *EEC—Regulation on Imports of Parts and Components (Japan v. EEC)* Report of Panel 22 Mar. 1990, GATT Doc. L/6657, BISD, 37th Supp. 132 (1991); Pescatore, *Handbook*, Case 79.

they were 'other duties or charges on imports', or (ii) violations of Article III(2) in that they were internal charges on the assembled products in excess of those imposed or like domestic products. The panel appointed pursuant to Article XXIII of the GATT accepted the second argument, and rejected the Community's defense that anti-circumvention measures were justified under Article XX(d) of GATT as 'necessary to secure compliance with laws or regulations which are not inconsistent with the Agreement.'[114] Further, a number of firms hit with anti-circumvention duties had accepted the EC's offer to enter into undertakings to limit the use of imported parts as a way to avoid or secure suspension of the anti-dumping duties. The panel ruled that since the underlying duties were inconsistent with the GATT, the fact that acceptance of the conditions for their removal was voluntary[115] did not justify the program of undertakings, which was in effect a local content provision inconsistent with the national treatment provision of GATT Article III(4).[116] Interestingly enough, the EC did not assert GATT Article VI itself as a justification for the anti-circumvention regulations.

After some protest by the European Community, the panel report in the *Screwdriver Assembly* case was adopted, subject to an understanding that the subject would be taken up in the Uruguay Round, and an announcement by the Community that it would comply with the ruling only when the negotiations on anti-dumping were completed.[117] The topic was taken up in the negotiation of the new Anti-Dumping Code, and drafts that would authorize anti-circumvention measures were supported by the EC, the United States, Australia, and Canada. Japan, Korea, Singapore, Hong Kong, as well as the Nordic countries were opposed, arguing that if parts from Patria were used in a product in Tertia, the proper comparison by Xandia, the importing country, should be with the price of the product in Tertia, not in Patria.[118] The Dunkel Draft, prepared by the secretariat in December 1991 in an effort to preserve the momentum of the Uruguay Round,[119] contained a detailed provision authorizing application of anti-dumping duties to parts imported by a party related to the foreign producer subject to the order and assembled to produce a 'like product'.[120] However, the draft on anti-circumvention did not gain support either from the countries that were the

---

[114] The Panel's reasoning under Article XX(d) was that that provision related to law enforcement, such as measures against breach of anti-monopoly law, customs law, or patent law, etc., not to reinforcement of the objectives of lawful regulations, such as the anti-dumping laws. Id. at paras. 5.12–5.18.

[115] Compare discussion of the *Fira* case, *United States* v. *Canada*, Ch. 5, Sect. 5.5(a) supra.

[116] *EC Regulation on Imports of Parts and Components* (n. 113 supra), paras. 5.19–5.22.

[117] Professor Hudec, writing about the case from the point of view of dispute settlement, called it 'another black mark on the GATT's record', in that the recommendation of the panel was not carried out. Robert E. Hudec, *Enforcing International Trade Law*, 256–8 (1993).

[118] See Terence P. Stewart (ed.), *The GATT Uruguay Round*, pp. 1624–5.

[119] See Ch. 4, Sect. 4.4(b) at nn. 59–62.

[120] A convenient parallel chart of the various versions of an anti-circumvention article appears in Stewart (n. 1 supra), at pp. 1626–38.

common targets of anti-dumping measures or from the United States, which considered the draft inadequate because it did not deal with third country parts or with small variations in the finished products (such as consumer electronics) that might not qualify as a 'like product'. Japan, on the other hand, took the position that further discussion of the issue would be acceptable only when the European Community complied with the GATT panel's ruling. In the end, agreement on anti-circumvention could not be reached, and the 1994 Anti-Dumping Code makes no mention of the subject. All that was agreed in the Uruguay Round on this subject was a Ministerial Decision accompanying the Final Act that notes the inability of the negotiators to agree on the problem and refers the matter to the Committee on Anti-Dumping established by the new Code.[121]

Both the United States and the European Community revised their anti-circumvention rules somewhat after conclusion of the Uruguay Round,[122] but both took the position that their laws were WTO-consistent. The contention that the Ministerial Decision confers legitimacy on anti-circumvention measures is difficult to justify.[123] The inference remains that an anti-circumvention measure is subject to challenge in the WTO.

At a minimum, the petitioner must be required to show (i) that the challenged activity (whether in the importing country or in a third country) began after initiation of the principal anti-dumping investigation; (ii) that the imported parts or components originated in the country subject to the original anti-dumping order; and (iii) that the value added in the course of assembly is an insignificant portion of the value of the finished product.[124] In addition, (iv) the respondent should be given an opportunity to provide economic justification for the investment in assembly plants other than trying to circumvent the anti-dumping orders; (v) the investigating authorities should consider the relationship between the assembler and the primary manufacturer; and (vi) the investigating authorities should make a finding about the remedial effect of the original dumping order, i.e. whether the rise in price effected by the anti-dumping duty has been undermined by the challenged operation, or the reduction in the exporter's market share resulting from the anti-dumping duty has been made up by the market share gained by the product challenged in the anti-circumvention proceeding.

---

121 Decision on Anti-Circumvention Final Act, at 401 (1994).

122 See *US*: 19 U.S.C. §1677j; *EC*: Council Reg. No. 384/96 of 22 Dec. 1995, [1996] O.J. L/56/1 (6 Mar. 1996), Art. 13.

123 Note that Article 18.1 of the 1994 Anti-Dumping Code states 'No specific action against dumping of exports from another Member can be taken except in accordance with the provisions of GATT 1994, as interpreted by this Agreement.'

124 The EC regulation requires that the challenged parts constitute at least 60 percent of the total value of the parts of the finished product except if the value added to the imported parts exceeds 25 percent of the manufacturing cost. The US law contains no specified percentage, but requires a finding that the process of assembly or completion in the United States [or in the third country] is minor or insignificant, and that the value of the parts or components is a significant portion of the total value of the merchandise.

Whether or not the holding at the 1990 GATT panel remains the law,[125] a basic flaw in the anti-circumvention laws of both the United States and the European Community is that even when all the steps outlined in the preceding paragraph have been taken, there has been no new finding of injury as required by GATT Article VI and by Article 3 of the Anti-Dumping Code. The US statute provides that the administering authority (i.e. the Department of Commerce) is to notify the International Trade Commission before making any anti-circumvention determination, and the Commission may advise the Department whether the inclusion of merchandise assembled in the United States or a third country would be inconsistent with the Commission's prior affirmative injury determination.[126] The EC regulation has no comparable provision.

10.8   The Anti-Dumping Proceeding

By the time of the first GATT Anti-Dumping Code of 1967, it had become apparent that an anti-dumping proceeding could itself become a non-tariff barrier, even if at the end of investigation into comparative pricing, injury, and causation, no anti-dumping duty was imposed. Once an anti-dumping investigation was under way, neither exporters nor importers could make confident calculations about the future of the market. The chilling effect on trade was exacerbated when—as frequently happened—the authorities in the importing country withheld appraisement of the incoming merchandise under challenge, i.e. they did not clear the merchandise through customs without security against anti-dumping duties that might be imposed and made retroactive. Thus a petitioner with a plausible but not airtight case might well prevail in the market against its foreign competitor even if it lost in the actual proceeding.

The basic decision that anti-dumping (and anti-subsidy) determinations would be left to national authorities in the importing state was maintained in the successive codes of 1967, 1979, and 1994. But along with the various substantive clarifications, elaborations, and compromises discussed throughout this chapter, the codes imposed a number of procedural conditions designed not quite to achieve uniformity of administration, but to achieve a roughly uniform balance between efficiency and fairness, and to diminish the protectionist effect of the proceeding itself.

---

[125] Since the United States imposes anti-circumventing measures as duties at the point of import, the panel's finding under GATT Article III(2) would not be directly applicable as it was to the European measures.

[126] 19 U.S.C. §1677j(e).

(a)   Standing

Article VI(1) and VI(6) of the GATT, as we have seen, condition imposition of an anti-dumping duty on injury (or threat of injury) to an *industry*, not merely to a particular firm or group of firms. One of the first implementing provisions, introduced in the 1967 Code and maintained (with small changes) in the subsequent Codes, was the provision that investigations— not just ultimate findings—require application by or on behalf of the industry affected.[127] Domestic industry, in turn, was defined as 'referring to the domestic producers as a whole of the like products or to those of them whose collective output of the products constitutes *a major proportion* of the total domestic production of those products . . .'[128]

In practice, anti-dumping petitions are typically filed by individual firms, or by a group of firms in the same industry. Other firms may not wish to join the petition for a variety of reasons. In the age of multinationals, it is not uncommon for some members of the domestic industry to be subsidiaries of the foreign target firms, or for the foreign target firms to be subsidiaries of the domestic firms; some members of the domestic industry may themselves be importers of the product in question. The Code authorizes interpreting 'domestic industry' to refer to the rest of the industry in these situations. But there may be other reasons for some members of the industry not to support an anti-dumping petition. For instance, some members of the industry may be concerned that consulting about or participating in an anti-dumping case—which after all is about raising prices—may invite an antitrust investigation.[129] Or members of the industry may be parties to or beneficiaries of an international agreement contingent on refraining from anti-dumping or countervailing duty cases.[130] And some firms may be reluctant to furnish the data and make the disclosures required in an anti-dumping proceeding.

The US practice, prior to completion of the Uruguay Round, was generally to presume that a petition was supported by the domestic industry, unless an affirmative showing was made to the contrary.[131] On complaint

---

[127] 1967 Code Art. 5(a). The 1994 Code (in Article 5.1) speaks simply of 'the domestic industry'.

[128] 1967 Code Art. 4(a); 1979 Code Art. 4(1); 1994 Code Art. 4.1. The ellipses refer to exceptions as discussed below.

[129] For an elaboration of this thought, see Terry Calvani and Randolph W. Tritell, 'Invocation of United States Import Relief Laws as an Antitrust Violation', 31 *Antitrust Bulletin* 527 (1986).

[130] This was the situation in the *Gilmore Steel* case discussed in n. 131 infra, which arose from an anti-dumping petition brought shortly after the US–EC Steel Arrangements of October 1982 designed to settle massive antidumping and countervailing duty cases.

[131] The US Commerce Department did rule in one case that it was up to petitioner to show that its application was supported by the industry, and that ruling was upheld by the Court of International Trade. *Gilmore Steel Corp.* v. *United States*, 585 F. Supp. 670 (Ct. Int'l Trade 1984). However, the Department did not place any burden on petitioners in other cases. For confirmation of this practice by the Department of Commerce, see e.g. *Aleaciones Laminadas, C.A.* v. *United States*, 746 F. Supp. 139 (Ct. Int'l Trade 1990), reversed 966 F.2d 660 (Fed. Cir. 1992). In that case, the Court of International Trade reversed the Department's determination,

of Sweden with support of many other states, a GATT panel ruled that such a presumption without verification was contrary to the Code,[132] but the United States blocked enforcement of the Report and did not change its practice. The eventual outcome in the 1994 Code rejects the American position and provides (in Article 5.4) that an anti-dumping investigation shall not be initiated 'unless the authorities have determined, on the basis of an examination of the degree of support for, or opposition to, the application expressed by domestic producers of the like product, that the application has been made by or on behalf of the domestic industry.'

The typical targets of anti-dumping (and countervailing duty) proceedings—Japan, Korea, the South-east Asian countries, and the Nordics—urged in the Uruguay Round that 'a major proportion' of the domestic industry meant more than 50 percent in terms of production. The United States, for its part, urged that if its authorities were required to send out questionnaires to verify support for an anti-dumping petition, silence or 'no comment' (which it had previously construed as affirmative) at least not be construed as lack of support, that majority support be understood as a majority of firms responding, and further, that 'a major proportion' be construed as including something less than 50 percent. The outcome was a compromise with the American position. Under Article 5.4 an investigation may go forward only if it is supported by more than 50 percent of the total production of firms taking a position, provided that producers of at least 25 percent of the total domestic production of the product support the petition. Thus if total domestic production is 100,000 tons, responses are received on behalf of producers of 60,000 tons, of which producers of 32,000 tons (i.e. 53 percent) signify their support, the investigation can go forward; if producers of only 40,000 tons respond, producers of at least 25,000 tons (62.5 percent of those responding) must signify their support for the investigation to be continued.

(b)   Preliminary Injury Finding

In the United States and Canada, the determination of sales below normal value and the determination of injury are assigned to separate agencies. In other states and the European Community, the same agency makes both determinations.[133] Until the 1967 Code, the dumping investigation could go

but the Court of Appeals reversed again, thus deferring to and sustaining the practice by the Department.

[132] *Sweden* v. *United States: Anti-dumping Duties on Stainless Seamless Papers and Tubes from Sweden*, reported in Robert E. Hudec, *Enforcing International Trade Law*, Case 191, p. 572 (1991), and in Ernst-Ulrich Petersmann and Günther Jaenicke, *Adjudication of International Trade Disputes in International and National Economic Law*, pp. 112–17 (1992).

[133] However, in the European Community, two separate Directorates within the European Commission's Directorate-General I (External Relations) are charged with developing the facts in dumping cases, and the investigation generally proceeds with teams made up with officials from both directorates, one concentrating on dumping, the other on injury and Community interest. Final determinations are made not by the Commission, but by the EC Council.

forward and appraisement could be withheld prior to any consideration of injury and causation. The 1967 Code required that upon initiation of an investigation, the evidence of both dumping and injury be considered simultaneously in the decision whether or not to initiate an investigation. If either preliminary investigation resulted in a negative determination (including a determination that the volume of dumped imports or injury was negligible), the investigation should immediately be terminated. Furthermore, provisional measures could not be taken until there had been both a preliminary finding of dumping and a preliminary indication of injury. Essentially, the reforms inaugurated in 1967 were retained in the subsequent Codes, but Article 5 of the 1994 Agreement specifies in detail the information to be filed with the anti-dumping petition, and provides that simple assertion, unsubstantiated by relevant evidence, cannot be considered sufficient. Also, the Agreement now states (in Article 7.3) that provisional measures may not be imposed unless respondents have been given the opportunity to make a submission. In any event provisional measures may not be instituted before 60 days from initiation of the investigation, i.e. 60 days after the decision following the preliminary affirmative determination of dumping and injury, as well as support by the domestic industry.

Altogether, the thrust of the Anti-Dumping Agreement 1994 is to make it more difficult to initiate an anti-dumping petition, and less likely that a proceeding will actually go forward with inadequate showing of injury and industry support.

(c)   Provisional Measures

If the preliminary investigations of both sales below normal value and injury to the domestic industry result in affirmative findings, the importing country may withhold appraisement or suspend liquidation of the merchandise in question, and assess a provisional anti-dumping duty based on the estimated weighted average margin of dumping.[134] This step has two consequences. *First*, the merchandise in question may be cleared through customs and delivered to the importer only against a bond or other security guaranteeing, for each entry, the payment of an anti-dumping duty if there is a final affirmative determination. As noted in the introduction to this section, withholding of appraisement is likely to have a chilling effect on trade, particularly if the authorities' estimate of dumping margin is made before the respondents have been able to collect all the information required.[135]

---

[134] Article 7.1 of the European Community regulation contains an additional requirement—that Community interest calls for intervention to prevent injury pending completion of the investigation. Also, it is of interest that, in contrast to definitive anti-dumping duties, which are imposed by the Council acting by a simple majority, provisional duties are imposed by the Commission without reference to the Council.

[135] See the discussion of 'Best Information Available' in subsection (d) below.

Second, if the final determinations of dumping and injury are affirmative, the anti-dumping duty may be imposed as of the date of the preliminary determination and withholding of appraisement. If the final determination is negative, no anti-dumping duty will be assessed and the security will be refunded, but the damage to trade may have been done. It is for this reason that Article 7.4 of the Anti-Dumping Agreement states that the application of provisional measures shall be limited to 'as short a period as possible', not exceeding four months unless the exporters ask for an extension, presumably to complete their submission in opposition to the anti-dumping duties.

(d) Assembling the Facts

Given the need in dumping cases to compare prices in the importing country Xandia, with home-market prices or costs in the exporting country, Patria, and in some instances in other foreign markets, i.e. Tertia, administration of an anti-dumping program inevitably requires information gathering in or from foreign countries. To an outsider familiar with the fierce controversies concerning transnational discovery, particularly originating in the United States,[136] it is remarkable how wide-ranging the fact-gathering across national borders has been in the anti-dumping context.

The typical pattern in an anti-dumping investigation is that shortly after the initial petition and supporting documents are received by the Xandian authorities, they send out a detailed questionnaire both to exporters in Patria and to importers and domestic producers in Xandia, usually asking for response within 30 days. In theory, reply to the questionnaire is voluntary; it is not a subpoena, and no sheriff or marshal stands behind it. However, as the EU regulation states, 'If an interested party does not cooperate, or only cooperates partially, and thus relevant information is being withheld, the result could be less favourable to the party than if it had cooperated.'[137] The risk is that the Xandian authorities will make their determination on the basis of 'best information available' (BIA), which may well be the information supplied by the complainants.

Following submission of the replies to the questionnaires, and in some instances supplemental questionnaires, the investigating authorities typically undertake to verify the information furnished, not only by reference to published statistics, but also by on-site audits.[138]

---

[136] See, generally, A. Lowenfeld, *International Litigation and Arbitration* ch. VII (2nd edn. 2002); also *Restatement (Third) of the Foreign Relations Law of the United States* §442 (1987) and materials there cited.

[137] *EC*: Council Reg. 384/96, Art. 18(6).

[138] For instance, in another phase of the *New Steel Rails* Case from Canada discussed at n. 87 supra, a Canadian steel producer had responded to the questionnaire sent by the US Department of Commerce concerning its costs of production; thereafter the Department sent accountants to the producer's offices and plant in Canada and concluded that the costs of production had been significantly understated. Accordingly the Department disregarded the

Blocking statutes such as the British Protection of Trading Interests Act[139] or the French Law Relating to the Communication of Economic, Commercial, Industrial, Financial or Technical Documents or Information to Foreign Natural or Legal Persons[140] have no application in anti-dumping and countervailing duty cases, because the parties to the Agreements (i.e. all member states of the WTO) have accepted Article 6.7 of the 1994 Agreement, which provides:

In order to verify information provided or to obtain further details, the authorities may carry out investigations in the territory of other Members as required provided they obtain the agreement of the firms concerned and notify the representatives of the government of the Member in question, and unless that Member objects to the investigation.[141]

In individual cases, both the firms involved and the government of Patria can object to verification carried on in Patria, with the risk that the Xandian authorities will disregard the information furnished by the Patrian firms and rely on the facts available (i.e. BIA). Article 6.8 of the Agreement confirms that:

In cases in which any interested party refuses access to, or otherwise does not provide, necessary information within a reasonable period or significantly impedes the investigation, preliminary and final determinations, affirmative or negative, may be made on the basis of the facts available.

There has been some controversy and litigation over how to apply BIA when there are multiple defendants—whether in the same country or in different countries covered in the same investigation. For example, in one case before the European Commission involving exports from Taiwan and Korea, the Korean industry had refused to cooperate while the Taiwanese industry did cooperate. In its preliminary determination, the Commission thereupon calculated the dumping margin for the Korean exports on the basis of information supplied by the complainants, which yielded a lower duty than the duty imposed on the cooperating Taiwanese producer. In the definitive determination, the Council decided to impose the duty that had been imposed on the Taiwanese producer on the exports from Korea as well, lest non-cooperation be encouraged.[142]

company's submission and relied on 'best information available', which turned out to the US petitioner's costs. On appeal, the binational panel sustained the Department, with one dissenter, who thought the producer should have been given an opportunity to correct its previous submission. *In the Matter of New Steel Rails Except Light Rail from Canada*, FTA Panel USA 89-1904-08 (30 Aug. 1990).

[139] *UK*: L. 1980, c. 11. See also *Australia*: Foreign Proceedings (Excess of Jurisdiction) Act, 1984 Acts No. 3; *Canada*: Foreign Extraterritorial Measures Act, Stat. Can. 1984, c. 49.

[140] Law No. 80–538 of 16 July 1980, repr. in English in 75 *Am. J. Int'l L.* 382 (1981).

[141] Annex I to the Anti-Dumping Code sets out procedures to be followed in carrying out on-the-spot investigations, including advance notice, explicit agreement of the firms concerned, and preservation of confidentiality.

[142] *Oxalic Acid from Korea and Taiwan*, Commission Reg. (EEC) No. 699/88 of 15 Mar. 1988, [1988] O.J. L 72/12 (18 Mar. 1988); Council Reg. (EEC) No. 2089/88 of 11 July 1988, [1988] O.J. L 184/1 (15 July 1988).

(e) Transparency and the Right to be Heard

Over the years, there had been much criticism of the procedures in anti-dumping and countervailing proceedings—part adjudication, part bureaucratic decision-making.[143] The 1994 Anti-Dumping Agreement (in Article 6) requires that all interested parties be given notice of information required in the investigation, and that (subject to confidentiality) any evidence presented in writing by one interested party be made available promptly to other interested parties participating in the investigation, with the opportunity to reply.[144] 'Interested parties' includes at least (i) the exporters or foreign producers or a relevant trade association; (ii) the government of the exporter's state; and (iii) producers of the like product in the importing state or a trade association of these producers. There was debate in the Uruguay Round about whether others, such as associations of consumers or workers, and also users of the product in question, should be included as interested parties. The compromise was to permit states to designate others as interested parties, but not to require them to do so. But it is clear that the government of the target of the proceedings must be notified and may participate in the proceeding. Hearings are not required by the Agreement, but are required by regulation in the European Community, the United States, Canada, and many other states.

(f) Price Undertakings

Under the law of several jurisdictions, most notably the European Community,[145] it is possible to suspend anti-dumping proceedings, on the basis of an undertaking by the exporters to raise their prices to an agreed level, designed to eliminate the dumping or the injury. Article 8 of the Anti-Dumping Agreement makes provision for such undertakings, on condition that they are voluntary, and that the authorities of the importing state have at least concluded their preliminary investigations and have made preliminary affirmative determinations of dumping and injury caused by the dumping. The negotiation of an undertaking may be suggested either by the exporters or by the authorities, but the Agreement states (in Article 8.5) that no exporter shall be forced to enter into such undertakings, and that the fact

---

[143] See e.g. John H. Jackson and William J. Davey, 'Reform of the Administrative Procedures Used in U.S. Anti-dumping and Countervailing Duty Cases', Report to the Administrative Conference of the United States, repr. in 6 *Admin. L.J. Am.U* 399 (1992) and abridged in Jackson, Davey, and Sykes, *International Economic Relations*, 692–97 (1995); also e.g. the judgment of the European Court of Justice, as well as the Opinion of the Advocate General in *Al-Jubail Fertilizer Co. et al.* v. *Council*, [1991-I] E.C.R. 3187, 3219–35 (Adv. Gen.), 3240–43 (judgment).

[144] Interested parties supplying confidential information are to be required to submit non-confidential summaries.

[145] See EC Council Reg. 384/96, Art. 8, also Vermulst and Waer, n. 18 supra, Sect. 3.1.

that exporters do not offer undertakings or do not accept an invitation to do so 'shall in no way prejudice consideration of the case.'

The advantage of undertakings is that they terminate expensive and time-consuming proceedings.[146] The down side is on the one hand that undertakings are difficult to police, especially if a large number of exporters and importers are involved, and if the proceeding concerns many frequently changing products, such as is the case, for instance, with consumer electronics. On the other hand, price undertakings are government-approved cartels, and in a real sense are inconsistent with the disapproval in the Agreement on Safeguards of voluntary restraint agreements and similar interferences with market movements.[147]

(g) Judicial Review

Under United States law until the 1970s, judicial review was not available for injury findings by the Tariff Commission (later the International Trade Commission), and was in doubt about negative determinations in regard to sales at less than fair value or subsidization. Only imposition of an anti-dumping or countervailing duty was clearly reviewable by the Customs Court like the imposition of any other duty. Beginning in the 1970s the US Congress step-by-step provided for judicial review for both anti-dumping and countervailing duties, on the theory that judicial review would compel the agencies to enforce the law more strictly, i.e. more for the benefit of domestic complainants. Not only affirmative but also negative determinations were made reviewable, and not only final but in some instances preliminary determinations, and injury determinations as well as determinations of dumping and subsidization.[148] Indeed the Congress changed the name and character of the former Customs Court into a new Court of International Trade, in recognition that its principal role had changed, and was now to focus in major part on the cases involving allegations of 'unfair trade'. Nothing was said in either the 1967 or the 1979 Codes about judicial review.

The successive European Community Anti-Dumping regulations do not mention judicial review, and for many years there was doubt whether anti-dumping orders could be appealed, since the decisions are made formally by Council regulations, which are in theory of general application. In a series of decisions beginning in 1979,[149] the European Court of Justice affirmed its

---

[146] Recall the DRAMs case, n. 96 supra.

[147] See Ch. 5, Sect. 5.4. The Anti-Dumping Agreement says nothing about quantitative restrictions associated with an undertaking to terminate an anti-dumping proceeding. In the past the European Community has frequently imposed such requirements, notably in connection with the so-called Davignon plans concerning steel in the late 1970s and early 1980s. See A. Lowenfeld, *Public Controls on International Trade*, pp. 275–302 (1983).

[148] For the present law collecting the various stages of judicial review, see 19 U.S.C. § 1516a.

[149] *NTN Toyo Bearing Co. v. Council (The Ball Bearings case)* [1979] E.C.R. 1185, and related cases. See e.g. Trevor Hartley, 'Judicial Review, Locus Standi Under Article 173: The Japanese Ball Bearings Case', 4 *European L. Rev.* 265 (1979).

jurisdiction on the basis that while in form a regulation applied to all imports of a given product from a stated country, in fact it was a decision following proceedings contested by and directed to particular parties.[150] Gradually, the scope of review expanded not only to procedural irregularities but also to the conformity of a particular regulation to the basic regulation and eventually to the GATT Anti-Dumping Code of 1979.[151] Eventually, appeal from dumping cases became burdensome for the Court of Justice, and after a debate that lasted some five years, jurisdiction of dumping cases was shifted in 1994 to the Court of First Instance that had been established in 1989.[152]

The 1994 Anti-Dumping Agreement provides (in Article 13) that each member state of the WTO that has anti-dumping laws 'shall maintain judicial, arbitral or administrative tribunals or procedures for the purpose, *inter alia*, of the prompt review of administrative actions relating to final determinations and reviews.' Nothing is stated about the scope of review—i.e. facts as well as law, or compliance with the Agreement—but the principle is firmly set out that whether the reviewing authority is a court or some other kind of tribunal, it must be independent of the authorities responsible for the determination subject to review.

10.9   ACTION ON BEHALF OF THIRD COUNTRIES

All of the dumping and anti-dumping law here discussed proceeds from the assumption that Patrian goods are being sold in Xandia at a price alleged to be unfair and to be causing injury to the Xandian industry. It is also possible, however, that when Patrian goods are sold in Xandia below normal value, producers and exporters in Tertia are injured. In the analogous situation involving subsidies granted in Patria, Tertia is entitled under the Subsidies Agreement to initiate consultation and dispute settlement in the WTO against Patria.[153] Article 14 of the Anti-Dumping Agreement, in contrast, provides that in such a case the authorities of Tertia may request the Xandian authorities to initiate an anti-dumping proceeding against the imports from Patria. The decision to do so is up to the Xandian authorities, subject to consultation with the WTO Council for Trade in Goods. The

---

[150] For a brief summary of this development, see Vermulst and Waer, *E.C. Anti-Dumping Law and Practice*, n. 18 supra, ch. 5 (1996).

[151] *Nakajima All Precision Co.* v. *Council* [1993-I] E.C.R. 2069. The Court of Justice reiterated its prior holdings that the GATT does not have direct effect in the Community, but pointed out that the Community was bound by both the GATT and the Anti-Dumping Code, and that the basic EC anti-dumping regulation purported to implement the Code. In the *Nakajima* case itself, the Court accepted review but held that the challenged regulation was not inconsistent with the Code.

[152] EC Council Decision 7 Mar. 1994; [1994] O.J. L66/29 (15 Mar. 1994).

[153] Agreement on Subsidies, Arts. 4 and 7.

Code provides that in considering such a request, the Xandian authorities shall consider the effects of the alleged dumping on the Tertian industry as a whole, not just on its exporters to Xandia or even on all exports of the product from Tertia.[154]

10.10   REVIEW AND SUNSET

One of the criticisms of anti-dumping law is that anti-dumping measures tend to grow into quasi-permanent protectionism. As early as 1967, the Anti-Dumping Code stated that anti-dumping duties shall remain in force only as long as necessary, but different States interpreted that requirement in different ways. Australia, Canada, and the European Community provided that anti-dumping orders would expire within a stated period—two years in the case of Australia, five years in the case of Canada and the EC—unless renewed upon positive determinations. United States law made provision for annual review of an anti-dumping order if requested, with a view to keeping dumping margins (and therefore the level of duties) current, and it provided for review upon showing of changed circumstances. There was no provision, however, for automatic termination of anti-dumping (or countervailing) duty orders.[155] The Uruguay Round Anti-Dumping Agreement contemplates periodic reviews such as the United States conducted (Art. 11.4). It also states that any definitive anti-dumping duty *shall be terminated* not later than five years from its imposition, or from the latest review if that review covered both dumping and injury (Art. 11.3), unless the national authorities make a positive determination that the expiry of the duty 'would be likely to lead to continuation or recurrence of dumping and injury.' The duty may remain in force pending the outcome of such a review.

It seems clear (as it did not previously) that in a 'sunset review', the domestic industry seeking continuation of a five-year-old order has the burden of persuasion and proof. Under the European Community practice,[156] if no substantial request is received by the Commission, the order will expire without need for any determination by the Commission. Under US practice, initiation of a five-year review by the agencies is required both as to dumping and as to injury, but if no request is received after 90 days,[157] a final determination revoking or terminating the order will be issued.[158] The

---

[154] No cases of this type have been reported. For the United States legislation in implementation of Article 14 of the Code, see 19 U.S.C. §1677k (petition by US industry to US Trade Representative urging action against Patrian dumping in Xandia); 19 U.S.C. §1677n (authorizing investigation at the request of Tertia concerning dumping by Patrian exporters in the United States.)

[155] Similarly, such a review would examine the current level of subsidies, and if appropriate, adjust the prevailing countervailing duty.

[156] See EC Council Reg. No. 384/96, Art. 11(2).

[157] Or no adequate request is received after 120 days.   [158] 19 U.S.C. §1675(c).

United States law also provides that foreign parties (i.e. the exporters or their government) may waive their right to participate in the sunset review, but if they do so, 'the administering authority shall conclude that revocation of the order or termination of the investigation would be likely to lead to continuation or recurrence of dumping or a countervailable subsidy . . . with respect to that interested party.'[159]

It is not clear what 'likelihood' means in this context, though the standard required is the same as for the initial determinations under the Anti-Dumping Agreement and implementing laws. Since the question is, as to injury, what will happen (is likely to happen) if the special protection afforded by the existing anti-dumping order is removed, there is no requirement of finding present injury in the domestic industry. The statement by the US administration accompanying the submission to Congress of the Uruguay Agreement Act says, on this point:

The [International Trade] Commission should not determine that there is no likelihood of continuation or recurrence of injury simply because the industry has recovered after the imposition of an [anti-dumping] order. . . . Moreover, an improvement in the state of the industry related to an [anti-dumping] order . . . may suggest that the state of the industry is likely to deteriorate if the order is revoked.[160]

While this suggests less than complete sympathy on the part of the US government with the introduction of a sunset provision into the Anti-Dumping Agreement, it is nevertheless true that the parties to the Uruguay Round committed themselves to the conclusion that anti-dumping (and countervailing) duties are short- or medium-term remedies against specific practices, not acceptable long-term devices contrary to the overall principles of the GATT/WTO system.

10.11   DISPUTE SETTLEMENT

The basic decision concerning the subject of dumping, made at the inception of the GATT in the 1940s, was that importing states would administer and apply the rules. States were not required to adopt anti-dumping regulations, and many did not. Those that did were required to follow an increasingly detailed set of conditions on standing, on measuring price discrimination, on injury and causation, on procedural fairness including judicial review. But what relief was available if the authorities in Xandia, an importing state, did not follow the rules in imposing anti-dumping duties on products of Patria, or if the government of Patria believed that Xandia had broken the rules? Clearly there is a possibility that importing states may exceed the boundaries

---

[159] 19 U.S.C. §1675(c)(4).

[160] See *Message from the President of the United States Transmitting the Uruguay Round Trade Agreements*, H. Doc. 103-316, 103d Cong., 2d Sess., Vol. I, at p. 884 (23 Sept. 1994).

set out in the GATT and in the Anti-Dumping Agreement—both in their general regulations, as for instance the European Community was held to have done in its anti-circumvention regulations,[161] and in application of the regulations in a particular proceeding.

Each of the Anti-Dumping Codes established a Committee on Anti-Dumping Practices, to receive reports and keep track of anti-dumping practices and offer a forum for consultations. The Tokyo Round code provided for formal dispute settlement including consultation, conciliation, and panels that functioned like other GATT dispute panels but reported to the Committee rather than to the CONTRACTING PARTIES as a whole. The Uruguay Round Agreement does not charge the Anti-Dumping Committee with dispute settlement, but refers disputing members directly to the Understanding on Dispute Settlement.[162] The procedures set out in the Understanding of Dispute Settlement—consultation, establishment of panels, procedures for the panels, time limits, appeals, and decisions—all are applicable to dispute settlement under the Anti-Dumping Agreement, with one significant difference.

Under Article 11 of the DSU, the function of a panel is to 'make an objective assessment of the matter before it, including an objective examination of the case and the applicability of and conformity with the relevant covered agreements.' Article 17.6 of the Anti-Dumping Agreement, insisted upon by the United States and accepted reluctantly as the Uruguay Round was coming to a make-or-break close, provides a special standard of review of both factual and legal determinations by national authorities, not applicable to any other agreement, not even the Agreement on Subsidies and Countervailing Measures, which in most other procedural matters is parallel to the Anti-Dumping Agreement:

17.5 The DSB shall, at the request of the complaining party, establish a panel to examine the matter based upon:
  (i) a written statement of the Member making the request indicating how a benefit accruing to it, directly or indirectly, under this Agreement has been nullified or impaired, or that the achieving of the objectives of the Agreement is being impeded, and
  (ii) the facts made available in conformity with appropriate domestic procedures to the authorities of the importing Member.

17.6 In examining the matter referred to in paragraph 5:
  (i) in its assessment of the facts of the matter, the panel shall determine whether the authorities' establishment of the facts was proper and whether their evaluation of those facts was unbiased and objective. If the establishment of the facts was proper and the evaluation was unbiased and objective, even though the panel might have reached a different conclusion, the evaluation shall not be overturned;
  (ii) the panel shall interpret the relevant provisions of the Agreement in accordance with customary rules of interpretation of public international law. Where the

---

[161] See Sect. 10.7 at nn. 113–17 supra.   [162] See Ch. 8.

panel finds that a relevant provision of the Agreement admits of more than one permissible interpretation, the panel shall find the authorities' measure to be in conformity with the Agreement if it rests upon one of those permissible interpretations.

The standard of review appears to be based on a rule of deference gradually developed in United States administrative law,[163] though as has been pointed out, the analogy is not correct, because in US administrative law the agency whose decision is challenged in court is implementing and interpreting the same law as the reviewing court, whereas WTO panels are charged with reviewing conformity of application of national law with an international agreement.[164]

Whether, as has been suggested, Article 17.6(i) actually requires a complaining party to establish bias or lack of objectivity on the part of respondents' authorities before challenging a factual determination may be doubted.[165] Particularly if the investigating authorities use so-called Best Information Available, on the ground that the respondent's information was incomplete or not verified (see Article 6.8 and Annex II), Article 17.6 should not stand in the way of a hard look by the WTO panel.

As to legal interpretation, the first sentence of Article 17.6(ii) is understood to be a reference to Article 31(1) of the Vienna Convention on the Law of Treaties,[166] which provides that

A treaty shall be interpreted in good faith in accordance with the ordinary meaning to be given to the terms of the treaty in their context and in the light of its object and purpose.

The American proponents of Article 17.6 claim that the second sentence of paragraph (ii) is a recognition that the Anti-Dumping Agreement contains passages permitting of more than one interpretation,[167] which is surely true with regard to such terms as '*causal relationship* between the dumped imports and injury' (Art. 3.5), 'comparison with comparable price of the like product when exported to an *appropriate third country*' (Art. 2.2), or 'domestic industry . . . as referring to the domestic producers. . . . whose output . . . constitutes a *major proportion* of the total domestic production' (Art. 4.1). It is not clear that reference (by implication) to the Vienna Convention adds much to solution of the problem of interpretation, except

---

[163] The leading case is *Chevron U.S.A.* v. *National Resources Defense Council*, 467 U.S. 837 (1984).

[164] See David Palmeter, 'United States Implementation of the Uruguay Round Antidumping Code', 29 *J. World Trade* No. 3, p. 39 at 76–7 (1995).

[165] Vermulst and Waer, n. 18 supra, suggest that '. . . since the measures likely to be challenged in WTO panels are measures taken by importing countries favouring their domestic industries, WTO panels may well find bias and subjectivity inherent in any unconvincing evaluation of the facts which *de facto* results in favouring importing countries' domestic industries.'

[166] 1155 U.N.T.S. 331 (23 May 1969).

[167] See Gary N. Horlick and Eleanor C. Shea, 'The World Trade Organization Antidumping Agreement', 29 *J. World Trade*, No. 1, p. 5 at 30 (1995).

that the remainder of Article 31 gives some illustrations of context (e.g. contemporaneous documents) and invites consideration of subsequent agreement, practice, or evidence of intent.[168] It is clear, however, that the intent of Article 17.6 is to call for greater deference to the decisions of national authorities than prevails in other parts of the WTO system.

CONCLUSION

The law of dumping and anti-dumping turns out to be a blend of restraints on private activity and restraints on states in taking measures against that activity. The condemnation of dumping contained in Article VI of the GATT is tempered by the rule that anti-dumping measures are permissible only when injury is shown. The suggestion that anti-dumping is the last protectionism is probably overdrawn. But it is not too strong to say that anti-dumping is a price paid by the proponents of trade liberalization for the almost universal acceptance of the GATT/WTO system, and the vast expansion of subjects embraced by that system.

Dumping and anti-dumping are clearly more important in the work of lawyers and officials than in the overall conduct of international trade. But in the mixture of rules and discretion, of national and international law, and of conflicting values, the law of dumping and anti-dumping may fairly be said to reflect the ambivalence—currents and counter-currents—present throughout the international law of international trade.

---

[168] The Vienna Convention refers (in Article 32) to *travaux préparatoires* as supplementary means of interpretation when application of Article 31 leaves the meaning ambiguous or obscure or would lead to an unreasonable result. In practice, international tribunals, including panels established under the GATT/WTO system, generally accept drafting and negotiating history as aids to interpretation of texts and do not give them the subordinate place implied by the Vienna Convention.

PART V
Beyond the
World Trade Organization

11

The Environment and International Economic Law

11.1 INTRODUCTION

International concern for the environment, except in particular areas such as marine pollution and aircraft noise, is of relatively recent origin. Not a word is said about the environment in the Charter of the United Nations (1945), nor in the General Agreement on Tariffs and Trade (1947), nor in the Treaty of Rome establishing the European Economic Community (1957). Beginning in the 1950s, a number of widely read books and films, notably by Rachel Carson and Jacques-Yves Cousteau, stimulated a worldwide movement dedicated to preservation of the environment.[1]

Initially, the movement was propelled by non-governmental organizations, but they in turn pressured governments to become involved in the subject. It was not until a Conference on the Human Environment held under United Nations auspices in Stockholm in 1972 that attention was directed to government-sponsored efforts to restrain the despoliation of the atmosphere and the oceans, and to the concept of a global commons, i.e. the understanding that national frontiers do not fully define the interests of states, and that some aspects of environmental change, including the polar regions, outer space, and the oceans, concern all states. Further, the international concern for the environment embraces the goal of preservation of species of plants and animals, and warns of the consequences of deforestation and over-fishing, in principle regardless of territorial or sovereign boundaries.

It has long been understood as a general principle of international law that a state is obligated to prevent use of its territory in such a way as to be injurious to the inhabitants of the neighbouring state.[2] The principle *sic utere tuo ut alienum non laedas* (use your own property so as not to injure the property of another) applies to states as well as to individuals.[3] A leading case applying this principle was the *Trail Smelter Arbitration*, in which a binational

---

[1] See Rachel Carson, *The Sea Around Us*, (1951 and later editions), *Silent Shores* (1962); Jacques-Yves Cousteau, *The Silent World* (1953), *The Living Sea* (1963), *The Sea in Danger* (1974).

[2] See Oppenheim, *International Law*, Vol. I, pp. 408–9 (9th edn. Jennings & Watts (1992).

[3] Compare American Law Institute, *Restatement (Third) of the Foreign Relations Law of the United States International Law*, Part VI. Introduction to Law of the Environment (1987).

arbitral tribunal held that Canada was responsible for damage caused by emissions of sulphur dioxide from a privately owned smelter plant in British Columbia, Canada, to persons or property in the state of Washington in the United States. The responsibility is absolute, in the sense that it does not depend on a finding of negligence or intent to harm, and in the sense that it imputes to the state the consequence of conduct of a private party. But the teaching of *Trail Smelter* is limited, in that it requires a showing of direct harm across a frontier, analogous to the firing of a cannon across a river.[4]

The law of the environment has moved well beyond this fundamental principle, in developing a series of standards—some through treaties, others through resolutions and international conferences, and in many instances through regulation by individual states. Inevitably, establishment and implementation of such standards, from limits on fishing to control on use of pesticides to control of waste has aroused major controversy, often reflecting conflicting priorities between economy and ecology.

In addition to the effort to prohibit the importation of harmful *products*, the environmental movement has increasingly—and controversially—focused on the *process* by which internationally traded products are made or harvested—sometimes referred to as the 'PPM [process and production method] issue'. The most prominent of such cases have involved restrictions by the United States on importation of tuna caught by nets that may imperil dolphins, and on importation of shrimp harvested without the use of devices to protect sea turtles. Both of these efforts came before GATT/WTO dispute panels, and are discussed hereafter.[5] More generally, some proponents of environmental protection have urged that importing states such as the United States, Canada, and members of the European Community apply their (presumably stricter) standards to products made in states with looser environmental standards, or looser enforcement of comparable standards.

The argument in support of this effort is that environmental preservation will be discouraged in importing countries if domestic producers, for instance steel manufacturers, can claim to be unfairly saddled with higher costs than their foreign competitors. Conversely, enviromental preservation, it is argued, will be enhanced if foreign producers are required to adhere to stricter standards adopted by the major importing countries. In the effort to fit such proposals into the GATT/WTO system, which traditionally focuses on 'like products' and not the process by which the products are made,[6] it has been suggested that countervailing duties be imposed on products manufactured by industrial processes that do not meet the environmental standards of the importing country, on the ground that the less stringent standards of the exporting country constitute an export subsidy. A variation of this suggestion would impose anti-dumping duties on the imported product on the

---

[4] See Read, 'The Trail Smelter Dispute', 1 *Canadian Y.B. Int'l L.* 211 (1963) and sources cited in *Restatement of Foreign Relations Law* (n. 3 supra), §601, Reporters' n. 1.
[5] See Sects. 11.5, 11.6 infra.   [6] See e.g. GATT Arts. I(1) and III(4).

basis that the total social costs in the producing country, including pollution as well as ordinary product costs, are greater than the price charged in the importing state.[7]

None of these proposals has thus far been accepted in the GATT/WTO system or in regional arrangements such as the North American Free Trade Agreement (NAFTA). Segments of the international environmental community, spurred on by a growing number of non-governmental organizations, regard rejection of these suggestions as evidence of indifference of the GATT/WTO system to concerns about the environment and justification for the increasing demonstrations and protests against that system. For its part, the international trade community rejects differences in the cost of production as a justification for import restrictions, whether the differences stem from discrepancies in wage rates, tax burdens, availability of natural resources, level of education, or other elements of comparative advantage, and is traditionally suspicious of protectionism disguised as concern for health, safety, or the environment.

The effort here is not to present a comprehensive survey of the international law of the environment, a fast-growing field whose dimensions already greatly exceed the limits of this volume, as well as the expertise of the author. The effort, rather, is to present to readers focused on international economic law an idea of the growth of the environmental movement in the last quarter of the Twentieth Century, and to discuss in some detail a few of the cases in which the clash between economy and ecology has come before the GATT/WTO dispute system, a clash for which, it seems fair to say, neither constituency was well prepared.[8]

As of year-end 2001, no formal changes had taken place in the law administered by the World Trade Organization, but a change in perceptions seemed to be developing. The possible consequences of such a change are suggested in the concluding section of this chapter.

11.2   ENVIRONMENTAL REGULATION DEFINED

In the pathbreaking Declaration adopted in 1972 by the Stockholm

[7] For a discussion, but not advocacy of these suggestion, see e.g. Richard B. Stewart, 'International Trade and Environment: Lessons from the Federal Experience', 49 *Washington & Lee L. Rev.* 1329 at 1353–57 (1992).

[8] Controversies about environmental regulation and trade are not, of course confined to the WTO. They have arisen in every industrial country as well as in a number of developing countries, within the European Community, and in connection with regional agreements such as the North American Free Trade Agreement (NAFTA). In the NAFTA context, interestingly enough, the litigated controversies have not, for the most part, been state-to-state, but rather investor–state disputes, as foreign investors have asserted that measures taken by host states ostensibly for environmental purposes are 'tantamount to expropriation', or violate national treatment guarantees. Some of these cases are addressed in Ch. 15.

[9] See Report of the United Nations Conference on the Environment, Stockholm, 5–15 June 1972, U.N. Doc. A/CONF. 48/14/ Rev. 1, (1972); 11 *I.L.M.* 1416 (1972).

Conference on the Human Environment,[9] the environment was defined to include a variety of subjects that are relevant to the human condition, but have largely remained outside the definition of the environment in the context here relevant. Thus colonialism and apartheid are not usually considered in the context of environmental regulation, though they appear in Principle 1 of the Stockholm Declaration; nor are the calls for the transfer of substantial financial and technical assistance to the developing countries (Principles 9 and 10), or the calls for central planning (Principles 11–15); or other subjects recited in the Declaration related to the enthusiasm for the New International Economic Order popular in the early 1970s but largely forgotten by the end of the Twentieth Century. The principles set down in the Stockholm Declaration linked to science or nature, however, have remained as a framework, within which concern for the environment has been converted into law, hard and soft.[10]

Principle 2 of the Stockholm Declaration recites the need to safeguard the natural resources of the earth 'including the air, water, land, flora and fauna . . . for the benefit of present and future generations.' Further, the Declaration calls for maintenance of the capacity of the earth to produce vital renewable resources (Principle 3); conservation of the heritage of wildlife and its habitat (Principle 4); halt in the discharge of toxic substances in such quantities or concentrations as to exceed the capacity of the environment to render them harmless (Principle 6); and prevention of pollution of the seas (Principle 7). These and analogous goals constitute the objectives of environmental regulation as such regulation comes into conflict with economic market forces and the laws designed to minimize interference by states with such forces. The most debated, and most often quoted of the Stockholm principles, was Principle 21:

States have, in accordance with the Charter of the United Nations and the principles of international law, the sovereign right to exploit their own resources pursuant to their own environmental policies, and the responsibility to ensure that activities within their jurisdiction or control do not cause damage to the environment of other States or of areas beyond the limits of national jurisdiction.

Of course reciting desirable goals does not resolve specific controversies. Is a given substance toxic, for instance, and if so, at what level? What is a sustainable yield for a given species? How should the burdens of conservation be shared? If a particular material is asserted to be harmful, should its production or trade be halted while further investigation continues— the precautionary principle? Or on the contrary, is there something like a

---

[10] By soft law is meant the kind of resolution that authorizes conduct by states that might otherwise be questioned, for instance as extending beyond a nation's territory, but does not require states to take particular steps. See e.g. Ignaz Seidl-Hohenveldern, 'International Economic Soft Law', 163 *Recueil des Cours, Hague Acad. Int'l L.* 169 (1979); Pierre-Marie Dupuy, 'Soft Law and the International Law of the Environment', 12 *Mich. J. Int'l L.* 420 (1991).

presumption of innocence, so that useful economic activity should not be halted until evidence of harm is conclusive? To what extent should scientific studies in Patria be recognized in Xandia, or vice versa? What degree of international consensus rises to the level of international law, so that non-participants may be bound? These and comparable questions make up the agenda as concern over the environment moves from science to economics, politics, and law.

11.3   The Growth of the Environmental Movement

(a)   The Environment as a Popular Cause

While cooperative efforts to control river beds, reduce marine dumping, and protect particular species such as fur seals and whales had been undertaken since the beginning of the twentieth century and even earlier,[11] the worldwide environmental movement got underway only in the 1960s—well after the establishment of the post-war international organizations such as the IMF and the GATT. As political activism grew throughout Western Europe and the United States, environmental issues frequently became the focus, along with issues such as the Vietnam War, apartheid, and overcrowded universities. As the other issues faded, focus on the environment—clean air, clean water, preservation of forests, safeguarding of animals threatened with extinction—became perhaps the most popular cause worldwide, cutting across generations, political parties, and nationalities. A National Environmental Policy Act (NEPA) was adopted by the United States Congress in 1969,[12] followed by an expanded Clean Air Act directed *inter alia* to reduction of pollution from motor vehicles,[13] a Clean Water Act,[14] and a Resource Conservation and Recovery Act, regulating disposal of hazardous waste.[15] Similar legislation was adopted in the late 1960s and early 1970s by all member states of the European Community, first individually and soon thereafter in a series of Directives and Regulations from the EC Council.[16] Even as a worldwide trend was growing in favour of economic deregulation, an opposite trend was developing in favour of regulation on environmental grounds.

[11] See e.g. Ved P. Nanda, 'The Establishment of International Standards for Transnational Environmental Injury', 60 *Iowa L. Rev.* 1089 (1975).

[12] Pub. L. 91–190, 83 Stat. 852 (1 Jan. 1970) presently 42 U.S.C. §4321 *et seq.* In signing the Act on New Year's Day 1970, President Nixon said:

[T]he 1970s absolutely must be the years when America pays its debt to the past by reclaiming the purity of its air, its waters and our living environment. It is literally now or never. (Public Papers of the Presidents: Richard M. Nixon 1970, 2)

[13] Pub. L. 91–604, 84 Stat. 1676 (31 Dec. 1970), presently 42 U.S.C. §7401 *et seq.*
[14] Pub. L. 92–500, 86 Stat. 816, presently 33 U.S.C. §1251 *et. seq.*
[15] 42 U.S.C. §6901 *et seq.*
[16] For a convenient collection of the EC Council Directives, see e.g. Damien Geradin, *Trade and the Environment: A Comparative Study of EC and US Law*, esp. ch. 5 (1997).

(b)   The Stockholm Conference (1972)

In 1968, the government of Sweden, concerned particularly about the problem of acid rain,[17] proposed an international conference on the global environment. This call led four years later to the United Nations Conference on the Human Environment, attended by representatives of 114 states—virtually all states except the Soviet Union and its satellites.[18] The conference produced the Stockholm Declaration quoted in the preceding section, as well as proposals for the establishment of a United Nations Environmental Program (UNEP) and a related Environment Fund, and an Action Plan, which in turn led to a series of conventions on specific environmental subjects and major emphasis on the environment in the UN Law of the Sea Conference (1974–82).

Maurice Strong, the Canadian Chairman of the Stockholm Conference, described the Stockholm Declaration as:

[T]he first acknowledgement by the Community of Nations of new principles of behaviour and responsibility which must govern their relationship in the environmental era. And it provides an indispensable basis for the establishment and elaboration of new codes of international law and conduct which will be required to give effect to the principles set out in the Declaration.

Though many of the developing countries considered that the emphasis on the environment did not deal adequately with their priorities for economic growth, the UN General Assembly adopted without dissent a resolution 'noting with satisfaction' the report of the Stockholm Conference.[19] From that time on, conservation and improvement of the environment formally became the concern of governments, generally, though not always, under the auspices of the United Nations. There was no connection with the GATT, and apparently no discussion of how the projects contemplated in the Stockholm Action Plan might fit in with the law of international trade. Indeed, in most countries the departments and agencies concerned with the environment were quite separate from the departments and agencies concerned with trade and the economy.

(c)   A Flood of Treaties

Throughout the two decades following Stockholm, a series of treaties dealing with the environment were negotiated and adopted, some at regional

---

[17] The phenomenon of excess acidity in rainwater is caused primarily by emissions of sulphur dioxide (SO_2) and nitrous oxides (NO_x), both produced by emissions from industrial sources such as power plants and also from motor vehicles. Acid rain causes smog, respiratory illnesses, as well as adverse effects on fish, forests, and crops.

[18] The Soviet Union and members of the Soviet bloc did not oppose the aims of the Stockholm Conference, but stayed away in a dispute about the seating of East Germany.

[19] UNGA Res. 2994. 27 G.A.O.R. Supp. 30 (15 Dec. 1972). For a description of the debates at Stockholm and in the UN, see Louis B. Sohn, 'The Stockholm Declaration on the Human Environment', 14 *Harv. Int'l L.J.* 423 at 431 (1973).

level, most open to all states, and many designed not only to create obligations among the treaty partners, but to deal with non-parties as well. The best known of the multilateral treaties negotiated at this time were the Convention on the International Trade in Endangered Species (CITES) (1973),[20] the Vienna Convention for the Protection of the Ozone Layer (1985)[21] and the Montreal Protocol thereto (1987),[22] and the Basel Convention on the Control of Transboundary Movements of Hazardous Wastes and their Disposal (1989).[23] Among other conventions concluded in this period were treaties on marine pollution (1973, 1974, 1976, 1978), on conservation of wild life (1979); on Long-Range Transboundary Air Pollution (LRTRAP) (1979, 1994); on Environmental Protection for Antarctica (1980, 1988, 1992); and on Climate Change (1992, 1997).

(d)   The Rio Conference (1992)

In 1983, the United Nations General Assembly created a World Commission on Environment and Development, which in turn produced an influential document entitled *Our Common Future*, generally known as the Brundtland Report after its chairperson, the Prime Minister of Norway, Gro Harlem Brundtland. The Brundtland Report, published in 1987, urged that 'sustainable development' become the foundation for all human economic activity, and thus that concern for the environment and concern for lifting the standards of the world's poor were inextricably linked. In a frequently quoted definition, the Report stated:

Sustainable development is development that meets the needs of the present without compromising the ability of future generations to meet their own needs.[24]

Two years later the United Nations General Assembly adopted a resolution calling for a UN Conference on Environment and Development (UNCED), and after two years of contentious planning, the Conference was held in Rio de Janeiro in June 1992, the twentieth anniversary of the Stockholm Conference. Some 7,000 delegates representing 178 countries attended the Conference, including 115 heads of state or government, as well as the Secretary-General of the United Nations. In addition, some 1,400 non-governmental organizations (NGOs) were represented, and 9,000 journalists covered the conference and related meetings.[25]

---

[20]   27 U.S.T. 1087, 993 U.N.T.S. 243 (entered into force 1 July 1975).
[21]   26 *I.L.M.* 1529 (1987) (entered into force 22 Sept. 1988).
[22]   26 *I.L.M.* 1529 (1987) (entered into force 1 Jan. 1989).
[23]   28 I.L.M. 657 (1989) (entered into force 5 May 1992). The texts of these and other conventions concerning the environment are conveniently collected in James Cameron, Paul Demaret and Damien Geradin (eds.), *Trade & the Environment: The Search for Balance*, Vol. II (1994).
[24]   World Commission on Environment and Development, *Our Common Future*, 43 (1987).
[25]   For a book-length account, see Phillip Shabecoff, *A New Name for Peace: International Environmentalism, Sustainable Development and Democracy* (1996).

Clearly, concerted concern for the environment had by 1992 become a media event. But while that concern was broadcast around the world, major divisions between the developed and the developing countries (as well as within each of these groups) also became apparent. The developing countries were anxious to prevent protection of the environment from impeding their 'rights' to economic development, and they sought specific commitments to economic assistance from the industrial countries as the price for cooperating on environmental and conservationist issues.[26]

Eventually, the Rio Conference did reach agreement on a previously drafted Declaration on the Environment and Development,[27] plus two proposed conventions on Biodiversity and Climate Change, as well as 'Agenda 21'—an 800-page blueprint for sustainable development in the twenty-first century. In part, the Rio Declaration reflects the 'grand bargain' between North and South—cooperation on the environment by the South, commitment to development by the North.[28] In part it was a redeclaration of the principles first set out in Stockholm, but with some significant differences.

'[T]he sovereign right to exploit their own resources pursuant to their own environmental priorities.' (Principle 21 of Stockholm, p. 301 supra) was rewritten as Principle 2 of Rio to read 'pursuant to their own environmental *and development* policies.' Principle 15 of Rio states that 'the precautionary approach [not principle] shall be widely applied by States according to their capabilities', and that where there are threats of serious or irreversible damage, 'lack of full scientific certainty shall not be used as a reason for postponing cost-effective measures to prevent environmental degradation.'

Principle 16 calls for internalization of environmental costs, 'taking into account the approach that the polluter should, in principle, bear the cost of pollution, with due regard to the public interest and without distorting international trade and investment.' Principle 17 calls for environmental impact assessment as a national instrument, 'for proposed activities that are likely to have a significant adverse impact on the environment and are subject to a decision of a competent national authority.'

---

[26] For a detailed description of the fourth meeting of the preparatory committee, which lasted five weeks in the spring of 1992, see 15 *BNA Int'l Environment Reporter*, Vol.15, No 10, p. 311 (20 May 1992). Among the many controversies, the article reports an exchange between the American ambassador to UNCED, who said that the United States preferred a brief text for the Declaration that could be printed on a poster and used by children in their bedroom. The reply from the negotiator for the G-77 was 'many children in the developing countries don't have bedrooms.'

[27] Reproduced in 31 *I.L.M.* 874 (1992). Early drafts of what became the Rio Declaration were entitled 'Earth Charter', designed to parallel the 1948 Universal Declaration of Human Rights as a forerunner to binding conventions. The title was changed, however, because the developing countries regarded the original title as giving too much emphasis to the environment and insufficient emphasis to development.

[28] But the position of the developing countries that developed countries should commit to foreign assistance of 0.7 percent of GDP was not accepted.

The one principle expressly directed to international trade, tracks the cha-peau of GATT Article XX,[29] but also reflects a response to the *Tuna/Dolphin* case,[30] issued shortly before the Rio Conference. Principle 12 reads:

States should cooperate to promote a supportive and open international economic system that would lead to economic growth and sustainable development in all coun-tries, to better address the problems of environmental degradation. Trade policy measures for environmental purposes should not constitute a means of arbitrary or unjustifiable discrimination or a disguised restriction on international trade. Unilateral actions to deal with environmental challenges outside the jurisdiction of the importing country should be avoided. Environmental measures addressing trans-boundary or global environmental problems should, as far as possible, be based on an international consensus.[31]

Like the Stockholm Declaration, the Rio Declaration was 'soft law', in that it pointed countries in stated directions, without a system of obliga-tions, let alone remedies for breach. But notwithstanding the evident tension between the priorities of North and South, and between protection of the environment and economic development, the Earth Summit and the Rio Declaration (as well as accompanying documents) confirmed, and it seems intensified, the worldwide attention to environmental issues. Translation of the negotiated consensus at Rio de Janeiro into action, or into 'hard law', has been mixed, and has only intermittently come into contact or conflict with the law of international trade.

11.4   Translating the Environmental Movement into Positive International Law: Two Illustrations

A perception for the outsider of the international environmental movement, and of how that movement intersects with the law of international trade, may be gained from an account of the world's response first to the discov-ery that a common household and industrial product posed a serious threat to the health of new life, animals, and plants everywhere on earth, and sec-ond, how the international community attempts to deal with the problem of hazardous waste.

---

[29] See p. 316 infra.   [30] Sect. 11.5 infra.
[31] For a commentary on the Rio Declaration by an American participant in its drafting, see, Jeffrey D. Kovar, 'A Short Guide to the Rio Declaration', 4 *Colo. J. Int'l Envt'l Law & Policy* 119 (1993). See also Ved. P. Nanda, *International Environmental Law & Policy*, ch. VII (1995).

The Montreal Protocol

(a) CFCs and the Ozone Layer: The Road to the Montreal Protocol

Chlorofluorocarbons (CFCs) are a family of chemical compounds developed in the late 1920s and early 1930s, initially to serve as a coolant in electric refrigerators. For many years, virtually all household refrigerators used CFCs, generally marketed under the name Freon. As air-conditioning spread throughout the United States and more slowly elsewhere after World War II, freon or slight modifications became the universal refrigerant in houses, offices, theaters, shopping malls, and automobiles. A third use of CFCs was in aerosol spray cans, for insecticides, hairsprays, deodorants, shaving cream, and a host of similar applications. Four decades after their introduction, CFCs seemed to be everywhere, the most versatile and benign of industrial compounds, with no known danger to human beings or to the environment.

In 1974, two scientists working at the University of California at Irvine, Sherwood Rowland and Mario Molina, published a paper asserting that CFCs, while essentially stable in the atmosphere and the oceans, eventually shift into the stratosphere,[32] where they are broken down by ultraviolet light, releasing a free chlorine atom.[33] Further, the chlorine atoms freed from CFCs react with the ozone molecules (O_3) in the stratosphere to produce oxygen (O_2) and chlorine monoxide (ClO) which in turn breaks down, freeing the chlorine atom, which finds another ozone molecule, and the process is repeated in a chain reaction. Rowland and Molina predicted that over time the use of CFCs would significantly deplete the so-called ozone layer, which serves to filter out a certain portion of ultraviolet rays emanating from the sun. If the ozone layer were destroyed or significantly impaired, a substantial measure in ultraviolet light would reach the earth, leading to a variety of diseases, including skin cancers, cataracts, and sunburns.[34] Moreover, there would be major interruptions in the food chain, beginning with plankton, then krill which feed on plankton, then squid, shrimp, whales, seals, and so on.

In the United States the Rowland/Molina article and various follow-up studies led to a vigorous struggle between the chemical industry on one side, and a growing group of scientists and environmental organizations on the

---

[32] The stratosphere is the region of the upper atmosphere extending upward from the troposphere, from approximately 12 km. to about 50 km. above the surface of the earth.

[33] F. Sherwood Rowland and Mario Molina 'Stratospheric Sink for Chlorofluoromethanes: Chlorine Atom-Catalyzed Destruction of Ozone', 239 *Nature* 810 (28 June 1974). Twenty-one years later, Rowland and Molina, as well as a Dutch meteorologist working on the same problem, were awarded the Nobel Prize in chemistry for their work on CFCs and the ozone layer.

[34] More recently, other serious consequences of ozone depletion have been identified, notably suppression of the immune systems in human beings with respect to certain infectious diseases, and reduction in photosynthesis of certain plants including rice, corn, and soybeans.

other.[35] Early in 1975, the US government established an inter-agency task force on Inadvertent Modification of the Stratosphere (IMOS), and in September 1976 IMOS recommended a phased prohibition of CFCs on aerosols. A regulation to this effect was issued first by the Food and Drug Administration,[36] subsequently by the Environmental Protection Agency and the Consumer Products Safety Commission.[37] By year-end 1978 manufacture and sale of spray cans containing CFCs were virtually prohibited in the United States.[38] In the event, notwithstanding earlier dire predictions, manufacturers of aerosol spray cans were able to come up with alternative propellants, and the buying public hardly noticed the transition. That left the CFCs used in refrigerators and air-conditioners, which were not released directly into the air, but would also eventually find their way into the atmosphere, and (if Rowland and Molina, plus a growing though not unanimous group of other scientists were right), eventually into the stratosphere. It also left the rest of the world outside the United States, except for Canada, Norway, and Sweden, which had followed the latest United States lead in banning aerosols containing CFCs.

Activists from the United States persuaded the United Nations Environmental Program (UNEP) to organize and coordinate international research on CFCs and the problem of ozone depletion, and an Ad Hoc Working Group met regularly under UNEP's auspices. Though the ad hoc group did not make much progress in regulating CFCs, it did agree to convene a conference in Vienna in 1985, which in turn produced a 'Framework Convention' for the Protection of the Ozone Layer.[39] Framework meant that parties to the convention committed themselves to further research and to harmonization of 'appropriate policies' to protect human health and the environment against adverse effects of depletion of the ozone layer. Also, the Convention provided that the parties retained the right 'in accordance with international law', to adopt domestic measures to protect human health and the environment against the effects of ozone-depleting activities. The executive director of UNEP called it 'the first global convention to address an issue that for the time being seems far in the future and is of unknown proportions.'[40] But as a result of a dispute between the countries that sought a worldwide ban—United States, Canada, and the Nordic countries—and the European Community, no actual restriction on production of CFCs was written into the Convention. The conferees did agree, however, to establish

---

[35] For a detailed layman's account of this struggle, emphasizing in particular the role of one of the important American non-governmental organizations, the National Resources Defense Council (NRDC), see Seth Cagin and Philip Dray, *Between Earth and Sky: How CFCs Changed Our World and Endangered the Ozone Layer* (1993).

[36] 42 Fed. Reg. 22018–034 (1977).   [37] 43 Fed. Reg. 11301, 11318 (1978)

[38] Some medical uses, e.g. for asthma patients, and some military uses, were exempt from the prohibition.

[39] T.I.A.S. No. 11,097, 26 *I.L.M.* 1516 (1987).

[40] Mostafa K. Tolba, 'The Significance of the Convention', *Environment*, June 1985.

continuing cooperation among scientists, and to schedule a meeting in two years' time to create a protocol, which might contain actual restrictions.[41]

Just after the end of the Vienna Conference, a British observer of the atmosphere published his findings of a large hole in the ozone layer over Antarctica.[42] The depletion in the ozone of 30–40 percent compared to levels in the 1960s became the topic of intense discussion and concern, though it was not evident that the Antarctic ozone hole was linked to the use of CFCs, largely in the northern hemisphere.[43] Meanwhile representatives of some sixty countries assembled in Montreal in September 1987 to work out a protocol that would contain actual restrictions on production, consumption, and trade of ozone-depleting substances.

(b) The Montreal Protocol and its Amendments

In some ways the negotiations at Montreal were like a trade negotiation, with each party concerned that it not give up more than the other parties. But whereas negotiations in the GATT/WTO system generally focus on reducing or eliminating restrictions on trade, here the focus was the reverse—how much nations would be prepared to restrict production and consumption of CFCs, and over what period of time.[44] Eventually, the negotiators agreed on a five-year freeze on the calculated level of consumption and production of ozone-depleting substances at the 1986 calculated level for each party to the Protocol; from July 1993 to July 1998 consumption and production were to be limited to 80 percent of the 1986 level; and after July 1998 to 50 percent of the 1986 level.[45] In subsequent meetings, attended by representatives of more and more states, the permitted levels of consumption and production were revised downward. At London in 1990 it was agreed that from July 1991 the limit would be set at 50 percent of the

[41] For a detailed description of the negotiations of the Vienna Convention and the Montreal Protocol discussed below, see Richard E. Benedick, *Ozone Diplomacy: New Directions in Safeguarding the Planet* (2nd edn. 1998).

[42] J. C. Farman, B. G. Gardiner, and J. D. Shanklin, 'Large Losses of Total Ozone in Antarctica Reveal Seasonal ClO_x/NO_x Interaction', *Nature*, 16 May 1985.

[43] Two major Antarctic expeditions organized by the US National Aeronautics and Space Administration (NASA) in 1986 and 1987, including high-altitude airplane and balloon flights, did establish the link between the use of CFCs in the industrial nations of the north and the ozone hole over Antarctica, as well as the chemical explanation involving the effect on chlorine atoms of ice droplets in polar stratospheric clouds. See Cagin and Dray (n. 35 supra), 277–302, 339–54.

[44] See Benedick (n. 41 supra), pp. 77–82, 83–88.

[45] Montreal Protocol on Substances that Deplete the Ozone Layer 10 Sept. 1987, repr. in 26 *I.L.M.* 1541, 1550 (1987). Since not all of the substances to be controlled had the same ozone-depleting potential, each substance was assigned a coefficient set out in an Annex to the Protocol, and the sum of the weight of each substance times the pertinent coefficient became the 'calculated level' for purposes of the limitations set out in the Protocol. The basic CFCs, $CFCl_3$, and CF_2Cl^2 (also known as CFC-11 and CFC-12) had a coefficient of 1. All of the coefficients were stated to be derived from estimates based on existing knowledge and subject to revision in the light of subsequent findings.

1986 calculated level, from January 1997 at 15 percent, and from January 2000 at zero;[46] and at Copenhagen in 1992, the total ban on CFCs was moved forward to 1996 and phased bans were instituted on other substances found to be harmful to the ozone layers.[47]

(c)   The Montreal Protocol and GATT

Once the parties to the Montreal Protocol had agreed to limit production of CFCs and related substances, the question inevitably arose what to do about trade. Interestingly enough, trade in CFCs among parties to Montreal was not prohibited. The drafters seem to have thought that since the goal was a global reduction of the hazardous substances, if one treaty partner reduced its consumption of CFCs more than its production and another reduced its production more than its consumption, trade between the two member states was not harmful, so long as both parties operated within the overall limits set by the Protocol. But especially in the early years when it was not clear how many states would join the Protocol, it would be important to ban the import of CFCs from any state not party to the Protocol, and Article 4(1) of the Protocol so provided. Such a prohibition would, of course, conflict with Article XI of the GATT, which (with a few exceptions) prohibits quantitative restrictions on imports and exports,[48] and also with the MFN provision of Article I. To the extent that the participants in the Montreal Conference thought about the GATT, they would probably have been reassured that a ban on import of CFCs came within Article XX(b) of the GATT, i.e. the exemption from the obligations set out in the GATT for measures 'necessary to protect human, animal or plant life or health', and possibly also within Article XX(g) 'relating to the conservation of exhaustible natural resources if such measures are made effective in conjunction with restrictions on domestic production or consumption'. Thus even with respect to important non-parties to Montreal that were members of GATT—India for a number of years, for example—it seems that the GATT would not conflict directly with the controls on CFCs.

The architects of the Montreal Protocol, however, sought to go further. To discourage construction of plants producing CFCs and to induce states undecided about joining Montreal to come in, the Montreal Protocol contemplated, and the subsequent amendments implemented (i) a prohibition on imports from non-parties of products containing controlled substances, for example an automobile containing an air-conditioning unit using CFCs

[46] These limits were set out in the London Adjustments and Amendments to the Montreal Protocol on Substances that Deplete the Ozone Layer 29 June 1990, repr. in 30 *I.L.M.* 537 (1991).

[47] Amendments to Montreal Protocol adopted at Copenhagen 23–25 Nov. 1992, 32 *I.L.M.* 874 (1993).

[48] See Ch. 3, Sect. 3.3(b).

as a coolant;[49] and (ii) a prohibition on imports from non-parties of products produced with, though not containing, controlled substances—for example, electronic items whose producers had used CFCs to clean their microchips. These prohibitions would raise at least two major concerns under GATT if challenged by parties to GATT that were not parties to the Montreal Protocol and its amendments.

First, as noted in the Introduction, the articles of GATT all focus on trade in *products*, not on the process by which a product is produced. *Second*, the most-favoured-nation clause, Article I, as well as the national treatment clause, Article III, refer to 'like products'. The tradition in the GATT, motivated by concern that the exemptions in Article XX might be used as disguised protectionism, has been to construe Article XX narrowly, with emphasis on the chapeau of that article—'Subject to the requirement that [the measures for which an exemption is claimed] are not applied in a manner which would constitute a means of arbitrary or unjustifiable discrimination . . . or a disguised restriction on international trade.'[50]

In the event, no challenges have been brought in the GATT/WTO system against the trade practices mandated by the Montreal Protocol and its amendments, and as the scientific evidence became increasingly persuasive, nearly all states that participate in the international economy joined the agreement designed to protect the ozone layer. But the issues of trade vs. environment, process vs. product, and MFN vs. distinction according to participation in an international environmental program, remain. Some suggestions for approaching these problems are offered at the close of this section, following exploration of the Basel Convention dealing with the disposal of hazardous wastes.

The Basel Convention

(d) Background: The Problem of Waste Disposal

Trade is more directly involved in the Basel Convention of 1989 on the Control of Transboundary Movements of Hazardous Waste and their Disposal, which was also negotiated under the auspices of the United Nations Environmental Program.[51] In contrast to the Montreal Protocol,

---

[49] Montreal Protocol Art. 4(3); London Adjustments Art. 4(3*bis*); Copenhagen Adjustments and Amendments Art. 4 (3*ter*).

[50] The United States also urged an outright prohibition on exports of CFCs to non-parties, but this proposal was resisted by the European Community, which was not sure that its customers would join the Protocol. The eventual compromise was that in the formula for consumption levels—production plus imports minus exports—exports to non-parties could not be counted after January 1, 1993.

[51] Signed on 22 Mar. 1989, entered into force 5 May 1992, U.N.E.P. Doc. 1G. 80/3 (1989), 28 *I.L.M.* 657 (1989).

which called for gradual suppression of all production of ozone-depleting substances and provided for controls on trade only as an ancillary rule, the Basel Convention is expressly focused on international trade. But whereas in the normal conditions of international trade the exporter has goods or services to sell and the importer is expected to pay for the goods or services, in the context of waste disposal the exporter is prepared to pay an importer (or importing country) to take the waste products, and particularly hazardous waste. As environmental restrictions have grown more and more comprehensive in the industrial countries while the production of wastes has increased geometrically,[52] the pressure has grown to dispose of wastes in less developed countries.

In the 1970s both the United States and the European Community adopted laws or directives governing the storage, treatment, and disposal of hazardous wastes. In 1984, the Organization for Economic Cooperation and Development adopted a Decision and Recommendation on Transfrontier Movements of Hazardous Waste,[53] calling for regulation by member states of waste disposal, and including the principle that prior consent from importing countries should be obtained before waste could be exported to such countries. The OECD Decision and Recommendations were followed by the 'Cairo Guidelines' adopted by the governing council of the UN Environmental Program, with a reach beyond the OECD countries, and after two more years of negotiations, a binding international convention.

(e)   The Basel Convention

The details of the Basel Convention, including definitions of different classes of waste and categories of hazardous conditions are well beyond scope of this volume. But the basic obligations set out in the Basel Convention are pertinent to an exploration of the intersection of the law of international trade and the developing international law of the environment. *First*, Parties are generally prohibited from exporting covered wastes to non-Parties, or importing covered wastes from non-Parties (Art. 4(5)). *Second*, parties are committed to prevent export or import of hazardous wastes if they have reason to believe that the wastes in question 'will not be managed in an environmentally sound manner' (Arts. 4(2)(e), 4(2)(g), and 8). *Third*, parties may not initiate the export of hazardous or other wastes without detailed written confirmation that the importing country and any transit states have consented to the transaction, and have provided for environmentally sound management of the wastes in question (Art. 6 and Annex V A). If a transboundary

---

[52] One writer reports that worldwide generation of hazardous waste increased from approximately 5 million metric tons in 1945 to 300 million metric tons in 1988. See David M. Hackett, 'An Assessment of the Basel Convention on the Control of Transboundary Movements of Hazardous Wastes and Their Disposal', 5 *Am. U. J. Int'l L. & Pol.* 291 (1990).

[53] OECD Doc. C(83) 180 (13 Feb. 1984), 23 *I.L.M.* 214 (1984).

movement cannot be completed in accordance with the terms of a contract included in accordance with the Convention, the state of export is required to take back the exports if alternative arrangements for their disposal cannot be made within 90 days or other agreed time (Art. 8).

(f) The Basel Convention and GATT

To the extent the Basel Convention prohibits trade among Parties, there is no conflict with the GATT. It is clear that the parties to GATT/WTO may limit their rights by special agreements, bilateral or multilateral. But if Patria, a non-party to Basel, seeks to export waste to Xandia, which is a party to Basel (assuming that both Patria and Xandia are members of the GATT/WTO system), Xandia is faced with conflicting obligations. Article 4(5) of Basel requires Xandia to prohibit the shipment, GATT Article XI prohibits restraints on imports, and GATT Article I prohibits discrimination, which exists because Xandia may import waste from other parties to Basel.

As of year-end 2001 no such case had yet come before a GATT or WTO dispute panel. One may nevertheless venture some tentative judgments, based—at least by analogy—on the cases that have come before GATT and WTO panels.[54]

If the import prohibition imposed by Xandia is consistent with a finding that Patria has disregarded environmentally sound practices for waste arrangement and has declined to enter into a bilateral or regional agreement such as is contemplated in Article 11 of the Basel Convention, the exemption in Article XX(b) of GATT for measures necessary to protect human, animal, or plant life or health ought to be applicable. This conclusion is subject, however to the proviso contained in the chapeau of GATT Article XX that the restriction not be applied (i) in an arbitrary or discriminatory manner, or (ii) constitute a disguised restriction on international trade.[55] For instance (i) if Xandia prohibits imports of wastes from Patria but permits such imports from Tertia, also non-Party to Basel, the preamble (or chapeau) to Article XX would not be complied with and the prohibition should be ruled illegal; again, (ii) if the motivation for Xandia's import prohibition is to raise the fees paid Xandian proprietors of waste-disposal facilities, the prohibition should be ruled illegal.

(g) Conclusion

While particular cases may still call for inquiry into facts and on occasion into motives, the principle seems clear. Notwithstanding the fact that trade

---

[54] See Sect. 11.5–11.6 infra.
[55] The relevant provisions of Article XX are reproduced at Sect. 11.5(b) infra.

regimes and environmental regimes reflect different authors, different cultures, and different priorities, it is not impossible to reconcile the rules of the GATT in favour of open trade with widely accepted multilateral regulations designed to protect the environment.[56] Generally, an environmental measure taken in implementation of a multilateral convention is unlikely to be challenged, and if a challenge were brought, it would be likely to fail.

The more difficult problems, illustrated in the litigated cases discussed in the following sections, arise when individual members of the international community seek to implement environmental regulations not internationally agreed, or going beyond the requirements of international agreements. Two such celebrated cases, involving dolphins and sea turtles, came before GATT and WTO panels, and are discussed hereafter.

11.5   TRADE VERSUS ENVIRONMENT: THE *TUNA/DOLPHIN* CASE

Until the late 1980s, even as the environmental movement was growing in all the industrial countries, it was only sporadically suggested that the concerns of environmentalists and conservationists were in conflict with the objectives of the GATT and related movements to reduce trade barriers. It was occasionally suggested that trade contributes to economic growth, that increased economic activity leads to increased pollution, and therefore that trade is bad and so are rules discouraging or forbidding restraints on trade.[57] But on the whole these suggestions did not win favour. It was not until what came to be called the *Tuna/Dolphin* case was decided by a GATT panel in 1991[58] that the world's attention was captured by the perceived tension between the concerns of the environment and the law of international trade. Indeed the *Tuna/Dolphin* case became a kind of spark for a variety of different interest groups that were or became hostile to the GATT and the rules of international trade generally.

(a)   The Factual Background

In contrast to many trade cases in which the facts are controversial and complicated, the facts in the *Tuna/Dolphin* case were not in dispute and were easy for the public to grasp. Commercial tuna fishing had been carried on through the use of purse seine nets, which are large nets that are maneuvered around a school of fish and then drawn tight, so that the tuna remain

---

[56] Compare e.g. John H. Jackson, 'World Trade Rules and Environmental Policies: Consequence or Conflict', 49 *Washington & Lee L. Rev.* 1227 (1992).

[57] For a serious discussion of this line of thought see e.g. Daniel C. Esty, *Greening the GATT: Trade, Environment, and the Future* (1994).

[58] *United States Restrictions on Imports of Tuna* (Mexico v. United States), GATT Doc. DS21/R (3 Sept. 1991), 30 *I.L.M.* 1594 (1991).

trapped inside the nets and can be easily harvested. The problem was that tuna are frequently found together with dolphins; indeed the tuna boats often look for dolphins, which come up for air and often leap out of the water, in order to locate tuna swimming beneath the surface. Unless special protective measures are used, the dolphins become trapped in the purse seines along with the tuna, and many are fatally wounded or drowned. Some dolphin species are threatened with extinction or depletion; all dolphins are among the public's favourite animals.

(b)   The Restriction and Challenge

As early as 1972, the United States Congress adopted a Marine Mammal Protection Act,[59] designed to prohibit 'setting on dolphins', and to permit incidental killing by tuna boats only within strict limits. The American Tunaboat Association was granted a general permit for its members, subject to a stated ceiling on the number of dolphins killed, and subject to the requirement that a certified observer be placed on board of each tuna boat operating in the Eastern Tropical Pacific. In 1984, Congress amended the Act to provide that tuna caught in foreign vessels could be imported only upon a finding by the US Secretary of Commerce that the government of any nation from which yellowfin tuna were to be imported into the United States (i) has in place a regulatory program comparable to that of the United States; and (ii) has an average incidental marine mammal taking rate comparable to that of the United States fleet.

Following allegations by the proponents of the legislation that the US Government was not zealous enough in enforcing the import law against foreign fishing fleets, and litigation bought by environmental groups seeking improvement of the law,[60] the US Government imposed an embargo on imports of tuna from Mexico and several other countries, on the grounds that they had not met the comparability requirements of the US law. Mexico requested consultations in the GATT; in a move that later came to be regretted, when consultations failed to resolve the issues, Mexico initiated a dispute settlement proceeding under Article XXIII of the GATT. Mexico's contention that the US restriction on imports violated Article XI of the GATT was fairly evident, though a technical defense by the United States was met by an equally technical response by the panel.[61] The more general issue, and the one that captured the attention of the public, was the defense

---

[59]   16 U.S.C. §1361 et seq., amended numerous times.

[60]   *Earth Island Institute* v. *Mosbacher*, 746 F. Supp. 964 (N.D. Cal. 1990); 929 F.2d 1449 (9th Cir. 1991).

[61]   The United States argued that the restrictions regarding production of imported tuna were no less favourable than the restrictions regarding production of tuna by US vessels, and therefore were within the protection of a Note ad Article III that assimilated a border restriction to a similar restriction enforced with respect to domestic/products. *Tuna/Dolphin* case, paras. 5.8–5.13. The panel concluded that the Marine Mammal Protection Act and regulations

of the United States under Article XX, the General Exceptions article of the GATT. Article XX contains a so-called chapeau, designed to avoid discrimination or disguised protection, and a series of specific defenses, including two that were involved in the *Tuna/Dolphin* case and might well be relevant in other controversies concerning environmental measures affecting trade:

Subject to the requirement that such measures are not applied in a manner which would constitute a means of arbitrary or unjustifiable discrimination between countries where the same conditions prevail, or a disguised restriction on international trade, nothing in this Agreement shall be construed to prevent the adoption or enforcement by any contracting party of measures:

. . .

(b)   necessary to protect human, animal or plant life or health;

. . .

(g)   relating to the conservation of exhaustible natural resources if such measures are made effective in conjunction with restrictions on domestic production or consumption.

(c)   The Panel Findings

The panel held, first, that defenses under Article XX should be construed narrowly, with the burden on the defendant. Prior panels had taken differing views of Article XX. The panel in *Tuna/Dolphin* followed the decision on this issue of the so-called §337 case,[62] which had had to pass on a challenge to differential treatment by the United States of domestic and imported products alleged to infringe US patents, met with a defense under Article XX(d), addressed to measures 'necessary to secure compliance with laws or regulations . . . relating to . . . protection of patents, trade marks and copyrights.'[63] It had been held in the §337 case that a panel hearing a charge of violation of the GATT met with a defense under Article XX should first inquire whether an affirmative obligation of the General Agreement had been breached, with the burden on the complainant; if the answer was affirmative, the panel should then consider whether one of the exceptions stated in Article XX was applicable, with the burden on the responding party.[64] Moreover, the §337 *panel* had emphasized the word 'necessary' in Article

thereunder were focused on the taking of dolphin, not on the tuna products as such, and were therefore not governed by Article III and the note thereto.

Another argument concerned the extraterritorial aspect of the United States regulation, in that the United States sought to affect the conduct of non-nationals outside its territory (or rather outside its territorial waters). Again this argument was not without substance, but was not what caught the attention of the public.

[62]   See Ch. 7, sect. 7.4(a), n. 39.

[63]   *Section 337 of the Tariff Act of 1930 (European Community v. United States)*, GATT Doc. L/6439, Report adopted 7 Nov. 1989, *BISD*, 36th Supp. 345 (1990). The writer was a member of the three-person panel, along with a former judge of the European Court of Justice and as chairman the delegate to the GATT from New Zealand.

[64]   Id., para. 5.8.

XX(d), holding that if other, less trade restrictive measures were available, the challenged measure could not be found to be necessary.[65] Based on this approach, the panel in *Tuna/Dolphin* found that the United States embargo on imports of tuna from Mexico could not pass muster, since as the panel found, other measures, such as negotiation of an international agreement, might have been undertaken in place of the unilateral measure imposed by the United States.[66]

Accordingly, the panel concluded that the prohibition of imports by the United States of certain yellowfin tuna and products thereof pursuant to the Marine Mammal Protection Act was contrary to Article XI(l) of the GATT and unjustified by Article (XX)(b) or (g).

(d) Aftermath of the *Tuna/Dolphin* Case

The panel decision was discussed at several meetings of the GATT Council, but never formally presented for adoption. By the time the decision came out, negotiations concerning the North American Free Trade Agreement were nearing their conclusion, and neither the US government nor the Mexican government wished the growing controversy over the *Tuna/Dolphin* case to impede completion and approval of NAFTA. Nevertheless, the *Tuna/Dolphin* case became and continues as a focus, and a symbol, of the clash between the trade and environment constituencies.

The environmentalist community rejected—and continues to reject—the pro-trade bias reflected in the *Tuna/Dolphin* panel's interpretation of Article XX as applied to measures designed to protect the environment or to conserve threatened species. In part, the criticism is a textual one. Professor Thomas Schoenbaum, for instance, in a thoughtful article, argued that if the 'least degree of inconsistency' requirement that the *Tuna/Dolphin* panel took from the §337 case had been intended to be part of Article XX, it would have been easy to include such a phase in the appropriate exceptions in the chapeau.[67] A more compelling criticism, also raised by Schoenbaum and others, is that 'necessary' as interpreted by the *Tuna/Dolphin* panel is too great a constraint on the priorities and values of member states:

An international organization such as the WTO should employ a deferential standard of review with respect to certain national decisions and policy choices. Thus in

---

[65] Id., paras. 5.26–5.27.

[66] *Tuna/Dolphin* case, para. 5.28. In fact, following the GATT panel decision, the United States adopted an International Dolphin Conservation Act, and thereafter an International Agreement for Reduction of Dolphin Mortality (1992) was signed by 12 states, including the United States and Mexico. 33 *I.L.M.* 936 (1994).

[67] Thomas J. Shoenbaum, 'International Trade and Protection of the Environment: The Continuing Search for Reconciliation', 91 *Am. J. Int'l L.* 268 at 276 (1997). An answer to this point might well be that the issues of environmental legislation were only dimly perceived in the 1940s and that GATT, perhaps even more than other constitutive documents, has grown and developed in its half century of existence.

deciding what is 'necessary', WTO panels should employ a 'rule of reason' approach that allows some freedom of motion to member states.[68]

The argument is that such an approach would make it easier to invoke the exception in Article XX(b), and that the danger that environmentalists could team up with protectionists to threaten the basic tenets of the GATT/WTO system can be prevented by application of the chapeau of Article XX, i.e. by focusing on 'arbitrary or unjustifiable discrimination' or disguised protectionism.

11.6   FROM TUNA TO SHRIMP, FROM DOLPHINS TO TURTLES

(a)   *Tuna/Dolphin II*

Apparently because no request was submitted for adoption of the panel report in the *Tuna/Dolphin* case, a second complaint was brought by the European Community and the Netherlands, challenging the same regulation as in *Tuna/Dolphin I*. This time the complaining parties focused on the 'intermediary nation embargo', that is on the provision in the United States statute prohibiting imports of yellowfin tuna or products thereof from any nation that could not certify that it had not in the preceding six months imported such products from a state subject to the direct embargo in the preceding six months.[69] Thus, for instance, Dutch fishermen might well not use purse seines or even operate in the Eastern Tropical Pacific Ocean, but if tuna or tuna products had been imported from Mexico to the Netherlands, tuna harvested by Dutch fishermen would be embargoed. This secondary boycott, directed at what its proponents called 'tuna laundering', provoked once again the longstanding resentment against American exercise of extraterritorial jurisdiction, previously seen in connection with application by the United States of its controls in East–West trade, trade with Cuba, etc. to subsidiaries or licensees of United States-based companies.[70]

A second GATT panel was convened, and it came out substantially like the first panel, except that it did not suggest that the human, animal, or plant life or health to be protected by a challenged measure had to be located in the regulating state, as had been stated by the panel in *Tuna/Dolphin I*. Also, the second panel focused more on Article XX(g), addressed to conservation of exhaustible natural resources.[71] The outcome, however, was the same. The United States import prohibitions—both direct and intermediary—did

[68] Id. at 277.
[69] US Marine Mammal Act, 16 U.S.C. §1371(a)(2)(C). See *Earth Island Institute* v. *Mosbacher*, 785 F. Supp. 826 (N.D. Cal. 1992).
[70] See, generally, A. Lowenfeld, *Trade Controls for Political Ends* (2nd edn. 1983).
[71] Note that the word 'necessary' which appears in Article XX(b) (as well as (a) and (d)) does not appear in Article XX(g).

not meet the requirements of Article III and the Note thereto, were contrary to Article XI(1), and were not covered by any of the exceptions in Article XX.[72] As in *Tuna/Dolphin I*, the majority of GATT members supported the decision, but it was not formally adopted by the GATT Council. For the environmental community, *Tuna/Dolphin II* was confirmation that the first case was not an aberration, but that the trade community, and the laws that governed international trade, had a persistent bias against the values of conservation and environmental controls.

(b) The *Shrimp/Turtle* Case

Three years after *Tuna/Dolphin II*, another strikingly similar complaint was brought against the United States, which once again had been pressed by American environmental groups to enact legislation banning the importation of commercial seafood in order to protect against incidental killing of another species. In the meantime, however, the Uruguay Round had been completed and the World Trade Organization had come into being. Not only did these events strengthen the dispute settlement mechanism; they gave hope to some that the rationale of the *Tuna/Dolphin* cases might be reconsidered and that the new organization might make a new start on the trade vs. environment issues.[73]

Once again the imported product—this time shrimp—was not a scarce or endangered or beloved species, but modern techniques of harvesting shrimp by use of large nets let out by trawlers tended to catch sea turtles, which are classified as endangered species in an international treaty with more than 130 adherents, the Convention on International Trade on Endangered Species of Wild Fauna and Flora (CITES).[74] In 1987, the US Secretary of Commerce, acting pursuant to the US Endangered Species Act of 1973,[75] issued a regulation requiring all US flag shrimp trawlers in the Gulf of Mexico and in the Atlantic Ocean off the South-eastern United States to use

---

[72] *United States Restrictions on Imports of Tuna (European Economic Community and The Netherlands v. United States)*, GATT Doc. DS29/R (16 Jan. 1994), 33 *I.L.M.* 839 (1994).

[73] As unadopted reports, the two panel decisions in the *Tuna/Dolphin* controversy had no legal status in the GATT/WTO system. But both a WTO panel and a subsequent Appellate Body Report had said 'a panel could nevertheless find useful guidance in the reasoning of an unadopted panel report that it considered to be relevant.' Japan—*Taxes on Alcoholic Beverages (European Community v. Japan)*, WTO Doc. WT/DS8, 10, and 11/R (11 July 1996), para. 610 (Panel); affirmed, WTO Doc. WT/DS8, 10 and 11/AB/R/ 4 Oct. 1996 Section E. Pescatore, *Handbook*, Cases 99 and 99A.

[74] 993 U.N.T.S. 243, signed in Washington 3 Mar. 1973, entered into force 1 July 1975. Sea turtles are ancient reptiles that have roamed the Earth's oceans for 150 million years, 'long enough', as a pamphlet of the Sea Turtle Restoration Project said, 'to have watched the age of dinosaurs come and go.' Sea turtles are the longest-lived vertebrates, some living over 100 years. They hatch their eggs on beaches, but spend virtually all their lives at sea. There are seven or eight species of sea turtles, all of which are classified as endangered species.

[75] 16 U.S.C. §1531 et seq.

'turtle excluder devices' (TEDs) approved in accordance with standards set by US government agencies.[76]

In 1989 the US Congress adopted an amendment calling on the Secretary of State to negotiate agreements with other nations for the protection and conservation of sea turtles, and providing that as of May 1991 importation of shrimp harvested with technology that did not meet US standards was prohibited. Some nine states adopted regulatory programs meeting US standards, and were granted certificates permitting importation into the United States of shrimp harvested by their ships. Imports of shrimp from vessels registered in other states were subject to embargo.

Four states—India, Pakistan, Malaysia, and Thailand—which did not comply with the US regulations, brought a complaint under the WTO Understanding on Dispute Settlement, alleging violation by the United States of Article XI of the GATT, the same provision that had been invoked in the *Tuna/Dolphin* cases. The United States defended its restrictions on the basis that it was carrying out the intent of CITES, that its legislation and regulations were consistent with both the MFN and the national treatment requirements of GATT, and that they were in any event within the exceptions of Article XX(b) and (g). The complaining parties replied that CITES prohibited trade in sea turtles, but did not authorize, let alone require, restraints on imports of shrimp, which were not an endangered species but were a significant source of revenue for the complaining states.

The panel concluded that the US import ban on shrimp and shrimp products was not consistent with Article XI of GATT, and not justified by any of the provisions of Article XX.[77] This time, by virtue of establishment of the DSU, it was possible to appeal, and the United States did so, principally on the ground of Article XX(g) relating to the conservation of exhaustible natural resources. Though its program discriminated between states that had, and states that had not entered into a program to equip their shrimp boats with TEDs consistent with US standards, the United States argued that this was not *unjustifiable* discrimination within the meaning of the chapeau of Article XX. Moreover, the United States argued that 'it is legal error to jump from the observation that the GATT 1994 is a trade agreement to the conclusion that trade concerns must prevail over all other concerns in all structures arising under GATT rules.'[78] The response of the appellees was that the United States had abused Article XX by unilaterally developing a trade policy instead of proceeding down the multilateral path. 'If every WTO Member were free to pursue its own trade policy solutions to what it

---

[76] US 52 Fed. Reg. 24244, 29 June 1987. TEDs are trap doors placed in shrimp nets, which allow air-breathing turtles to escape without drowning. TEDs have been shown to reduce mortality of sea turtles by more than 90 percent. They cost between $50 and $400 per net.

[77] *United States—Import Prohibition of Certain Shrimp and Shrimp Products (India, Malaysia, Pakistan, Thailand v. United States)*. Report of the Panel WTO Doc. WT/DS58/R 15 May 1998, 37 *I.L.M.* 832 (1998).

[78] As quoted in the decision of the Appellate Body (n. 80 infra), para. 16.

perceives to be environmental concerns,' the complaining parties argued, 'the multilateral trade system would cease to exist.'[79]

The Appellate Body upheld the finding that the United States import ban was incompatible with GATT, but significantly altered the rationale.[80] The panel had held that the chapeau of Article XX only allows Members to derogate from GATT provisions so long as, in doing so, they do not undermine the GATT/WTO trading system.[81] The Appellate Body held that the chapeau of Article XX addressed not the challenged measure itself, but rather the manner in which it was applied. The proper way to look at environmental or comparable measures, as the Appellate Body held, is to look first to the specific provisions of Article XX(a) to (j); if a challenged measure is found to fit under one of the exceptions—for instance because it relates to the conservation of exhaustible natural resources (para. (g)), it must then be tested under the chapeau i.e. whether the measure is applied in a manner that would constitute unjustifiable discrimination or a disguised restriction on international trade.[82]

It seems that in emphasizing that the specific provisions of Article XX must be examined first, the Appellate Body has sought to make it easier than under the *Tuna/Dolphin* cases to defend measures taken by states without multilateral consensus. The fact that a measure is adopted unilaterally does not immediately lead to the conclusion that it is a threat to the multilateral trading system; the fear that the system could be disrupted if every member state applied its own environmental standards, as expressed by the panel, is to be tempered by examination of the measure itself.

One might have expected that after reversing the panel's decision on the approach to Article XX, the Appellate Body would remand the case to the panel for an examination of the United States restriction under Article XX(g), which the panel had not found necessary to undertake because it had found a breach of the chapeau. However, the Understanding on Dispute Settlement does not make provision for remands, evidently because of concerns about the kinds of delays that had weakened the pre-Uruguay Round dispute settlement mechanism.[83] The Appellate Body in *Shrimp/Turtles* accordingly concluded that it was 'our duty and our responsibility to complete the legal analysis, and make a finding under Article XX(g), on the basis of the thorough presentations of the parties to the panel.'[84]

---

[79] Id. para. 35.

[80] *United States Import Prohibition of Certain Shrimp and Shrimp Products (India, Malaysia, Pakistan, Thailand v. United States)*, Report on the Appellate Body, WTO Doc. WT/DS58/AB/R, 12 Oct. 1998; 38 *I.L.M.* 118 (1999).

[81] Panel Report, para. 7.44, cited in the Appellate Body Report, para. 116.

[82] Appellate Body Report, paras. 119–22.   [83] See Ch. 7, esp. Sect. 7.3(c).

[84] Appellate Body Report, paras. 123–4. The decision continues, 'In doing this, we are fully aware of our jurisdiction and mandate under Article 17 of the DSU.' Article 17 provides in pertinent part:

> 6. An appeal shall be limited of issues of law covered in the panel report and legal interpretations developed by the panel.
> . . .

cont./

The complaining parties argued that 'exhaustible natural resources' referred to finite resources such as minerals, not to living creatures. The Appellate Body rejected that view, holding that modern biological science had shown that living species, though in principle capable of reproduction, are in certain circumstances susceptible of depletion, exhaustion, and even extinction, frequently because of human activities. 'Living resources', the Appellate body wrote, 'are just as "finite" as petroleum, iron ore, and other non-living resources.'[85] While the words of Article XX had been drafted more than 50 years ago and had not been modified in the Uruguay Round, they must, the Appellate Body wrote, be read by a treaty interpreter in the light of contemporary concerns of the community of nations about the protection and conservation of the environment, citing the Preamble of the WTO Agreement and other texts stressing the objective of sustainable development.[86] Further, the United States measure was related to the objective of preserving the endangered species, and was in principle, enforced in an even-handed way as between domestic and foreign shrimp. Nevertheless, as the United States conceded, its regulation discriminated between states that did and did not adopt regulatory programs comparable to its own, i.e. requiring the use of TEDs. To the Appellate Body, 'comparable' in practice meant 'essentially the same'. This was too rigid for the Appellate Body. The United States should have been prepared to consider other measures to protect the sea turtles, and should have been more forthcoming in negotiating with other countries, including the complaining parties.

In contrast to the two *Tuna/Dolphin* panels half a decade earlier, the Appellate Body in the *Shrimp/Turtle* case was careful to quote from the Rio Declaration on Environment and Development, from Agenda 21, from the Convention on Biological Diversity, as well as from the Report of the Committee on Trade and the Environment of the WTO. The Appellate Body, in short, was anxious to dispel, to the extent possible, the perception that the GATT/WTO system was indifferent to the concerns of the environment. But all of the passages quoted looked to multilateral solutions, international consensus, and similar expressions, as opposed to the exercise of unilateral restraints. Here, the United States had negotiated with some, but not with other member states, including the complaining parties. The effect was plainly discriminatory and in the view of the Appellate Body, unjustifiable within the meaning of the chapeau of Article XX.

Thus in the end, the United States lost the case. But as the American Ambassador to the WTO pointed out:

---

13. The Appellate Body may uphold, modify or reverse the legal findings and conclusions of the panel.

[85] Appellate Body Report, para. 128, citing the report of the World Commission on Environment, *Our Common Future* (1987), see Sect. 11.3(d) supra at n. 24.

[86] Appellate Body Report, para. 129.

[T]he Appellate Body found no inconsistency between the U.S. legislation [as opposed to its application] and [the United States'] obligations under the WTO . . . [and] the Appellate Body made a number of important and positive findings that help clarify the critical relationship between the WTO rules and measures to protect the environment.'[87]

It is clear that the Appellate Body has sought to dampen down the conflict between the trade and environment communities—but, as one would expect, not to everyone's satisfaction.[88] The Appellate Body wrote:

In reaching these conclusions, we wish to underscore what we have not decided in this appeal. We have *not* decided that the protection and preservation of the environment is of no significance to the Members of the WTO. Clearly, it is. We have *not* decided that the sovereign nations that are Members of the WTO cannot adopt effective measures to protect endangered species, such as sea turtles. Clearly, they can and should. And we have *not* decided that sovereign states should not act together bilaterally, plurilaterally or multilaterally, either within the WTO or in other international fora, to protect endangered species or to otherwise protect the environment. Clearly, they should and do.[89]

11.7   THE SANITARY AND PHYTOSANITARY AGREEMENT AND THE BEEF HORMONES CASE

(a)   The SPS Agreement

The one area in which the GATT/WTO system explicitly undertook to address the intersection of health and trade concerns was in respect to so-called sanitary and phytosanitary measures.[90] Among the agreements to come out of the Uruguay Round was the Agreement on the Application of Sanitary and Phytosanitary Measures, and one of the early tests both of the underlying issues and of the dispute settlement mechanism turned on the application of the SPS Agreement to the long-running dispute between the United States and Canada on one side, the European Community on the other, with regard to hormone additives administered to cattle.

---

[87] Statement of US Ambassador Rita Derrick Hayes, Permanent US Trade Representative to the WTO, 15 Nov. 1998, quoted in 38 *I.L.M.* at p. 1. For elaboration of this position and announcement about how the US government was implementing the decision, see *US Implementation of WTO Shrimp/Turtle Decision*, in 'Contemporary Practice of the United States Relating to International Law', 94 *Am. J. Int'l L.* 348 at 361 (2000).

[88] For example, the Appellate Body in *Shrimp/Turtles*, reversing the panel, held that panels have the authority to receive submission from non-governmental organizations, when appended to submissions by a party. At the next meeting of the Dispute Settlement Body, several delegations protested this holding, both on the basis that it was not for the Appellate Body to rule, and on the basis that NGOs had no place in government-to-government disputes.

[89] Appellate Body Report, para. 193.

[90] Phytosanitary measures are regulations designed to protect the health of plants, from the greek *phyton* = plant.

The SPS Agreement essentially seeks to spell out in a limited area the principle of Article XX(b) of the GATT. On the one hand, member states should be free to make their own decisions about health and safety measures (Art. 2(1)); on the other hand, regulatory measures having the effect of excluding or limiting imports should be permitted only if they are backed up by scientific findings (Art. 2(2)) and should not become disguised efforts at protectionism or discrimination (Art. 2(3)). If the scientific findings on which an import restriction is based are incorporated into a widely accepted international standard, and the importing State's regulations conform to that standard, the import restraint should be deemed to be necessary to protect human, animal, or plant life or health, and presumed to be consistent with the relevant provisions of the SPS Agreement and the GATT (Art. 3(2)). If the restriction is stricter that an international standard, it is not *a priori* a violation, but it must be justified. For instance, suppose an international ceiling has been established for a given ingredient in a food product at 5 mg. per 1000 kg., but Xandia prohibits the ingredient altogether. Xandia is not forbidden to impose its prohibition on imports, but if the prohibition is challenged, Xandia is required to provide scientific justification, or to show that the prohibition is based on a risk assessment meeting criteria set out in the Agreement (Arts. 3(3) and 5). One might think that if the importing country acts without reference to an international standard or imposes a greater restraint than is internationally agreed, the burden of proof should be on the importing country. The SPS Agreement does not clearly so state, however, and this became one of the hotly contested issues in the *Beef Hormones* case.

(b)   The *Beef Hormones* Case: Round I

The dispute between the United States and the European Community over hormones given to cattle had its origin in the early 1980s, when the European Community issued the first of a series of proposed directives for forbidding the sale or importation of meat and meat products derived from farm animals to which any of a number of specified hormones had been administered.[91] The EC regulations were issued as a result of pressure from consumer groups in several European countries based on the suspicion that the hormones administered to cattle might be carcinogenic.[92] The United

[91]   See e.g. Michael B. Froman, 'The United States European Hormone Treated Beef Conflict', 30 *Harv. Int'l. L.J.* 549 (1989); *The Economist*, 24 Dec. 1988, 78, 'Beefing about the Bush'; *Time*, 16 Jan. 1989, p. 44. 'Why the Beef over Hormones?' Under practices approved by the US Food and Drug Administration, the hormones are given in small time-release capsules implanted in the animals under the skin behind the ears. The practice eliminates as many as 21 days of feeding time before reaching the target weight, thus saving the cattleman about $20 per head. Also, producers claim that hormone-treated cattle yield the leaner meat preferred by consumers.

[92]   In the early 1980s, a synthetic hormone DES (which had been linked to cancer and birth defects) had been detected several times in baby food made with veal. In the United States, DES had been banned since 1979. In the European Community, four countries and subsequently the EC as a whole, banned the use of all hormones in cattle.

States took the position that the prohibitions were unjustified on health grounds and if implemented, would unlawfully burden US exports.

The United States filed a GATT complaint in March 1987, and asked for appointment of technical panel under the Standards Code created in the Tokyo Round. The European Community contended that the Standards Code did not apply, and declined to submit the question to a technical panel. The United States, for its part, refused a mixed panel whose first task would be to consider the applicability of the Standards Code, and only thereafter to consider the regulation itself. After four meetings failed to resolve the question of establishment of a panel, the European Community announced that the regulation would go into effect with respect to imports as of January 1, 1989.[93] The United States, which had previously proclaimed retaliatory tariffs but suspended them pending negotiations, immediately put its retaliation into effect, with 100 percent duties on $100 million of imports from the EC.[94] Thereupon the European Community filed a complaint with the GATT against the United States retaliation, but the United States blocked appointment of a dispute panel except under the Standards Code. Both the European import ban and the American retaliatory duties remained in effect.[95] The dispute over hormone additives was one of the prime examples of the weakness of dispute resolution mechanism in the GATT, which led to the establishment of the much more disciplined system created by the Uruguay Round.

(c)   The *Beef Hormones* Case: Round II

The Community reissued its directive banning import of hormone-fed beef in April 1996.[96] In the meantime, the Uruguay Round had been completed, including both the Understanding on Dispute Settlement and the Agreement on the Application of Sanitary and Phytosanitary Measures. First the United States, and then Canada, filed a complaint with the DSU, asserting violation of several provisions of the SPS Agreement. The panel found for the complaining parties on almost all the issues.[97] The Appellate Body, though in the

---

[93]   EC Council Directive 85/358 of 16 July 1985, 1985 O.J. L191/45, 23 July 1985, postponed as to imports several times, brought into effect as of 1 Jan. 1989 for 'certain third countries', including the United States and Canada, by Commission Decision of 89/15/EEC of 15 Dec. 1988, 1989 O.J. L 8/11 (11 Jan. 1989).

[94]   Office of the US Trade Representative, *Determination to Impose Increased Duties on Certain Products of the European Community*, 53 Fed. Reg. 53115, (30 Dec. 1988).

[95]   The details of the two failed efforts to place the dispute before GATT panels are given in Robert E. Hudec, *Enforcing International Trade Law*, pp. 225–6, 229–30, and Appendix, Complaints 159 and 193 (1993).

[96]   EC Council Directive 96/23/EC of 29 Apr. 1996, 1996 O.J. L 125/10 (5 May 1996).

[97]   EC Measures Concerning Meat and Meat Products (Hormones) Complaint by United States, WT/DS26/R/USA; Complaint by Canada WT/DS 48/4/CAN (18 Aug. 1997). The same panel considered both complaints, and the two Reports are substantially similar, though not identical. The Appellate Body considered the two cases together and issued a single report.

end it affirmed the decision of the panel, differed in a number of respects with the panel, and drew a number of conclusions of general application under the SPS Agreement.[98]

(d)   Burden of Proof

The SPS Agreement makes reference in an Annex to an international standard-setting body concerned with food safety,[99] but it was clear that the prohibition by the European Community had not been based on standards or recommendations of that body or on any other internationally agreed standard. The United States and Canada contended, therefore, that a prima-facie case had been made out against the EC measure, and that the Community had not met the burden of proof of scientific justification set out in Article 3(3) of the SPS Agreement. The Community resisted this contention, arguing that Article 3(3) authorizes member states to maintain higher levels of protection than called for by international standards, and that the burden should fall on the states challenging such a measure.

The panel agreed with the American/Canadian contention, but the Appellate Body did not. It wrote:

It does not appear to us that there is any necessary (i.e. logical) or other connection between the undertaking of Members to ensure, for example, that SPS measures are 'applied only to the extent necessary to protect human, animal or plant life or health'.[100]

The Panel had reasoned that the presumption of consistency with the Agreement if international standards were followed (Art. 3(2)) implied the opposite if the measure in question was not based on international standards. The Appellate Body replied:

The converse or *a contrario* presumption created by the Panel does not arise. The presumption of consistency with relevant provisions of the SPS Agreement that arises under Article 3.2 in respect to measures that conform to international standards may well be an *incentive* for Members so to conform their SPS measures with such standards. It is clear, however, that a decision of a Member not to conform a particular

---

[98] *EC Measures Concerning Meat and Meat Products (Hormones). Report of the Appellate Body, (United States v. EC); Canada v. EC*, WT/DS26/AB/R, WT/DS48/AB/R, 16 Jan. 1998.

[99] SPS Agreement Annex A(3)(a), referring to the Codex Alimentarius Commission. The Codex Commission prescribes acceptable daily intakes for certain kinds of chemicals in food, and makes recommendations concerning maximum residue levels. See Vern R. Walker, 'Keeping the WTO from Becoming the "World Trans-Science Organization": Scientific Uncertainty, Science Policy, and Factfinding in the Growth Hormones Dispute', 31 *Cornell Int'l. L.J.* 251 at 273 and n. 107, plus sources there cited. See also Terence P. Stewart and David S. Johnson, 'The SPS Agreement of the World Trade Organization and International Organizations: The Roles of the Codex Alimentarius Commission, The International Plant Protection Convention, and the International Office of Epizootics,' 26 *Syracuse J. Int'l L. & Com.* 27 (1998).

[100] *Beef Hormones* case, para. 102.

measure with an international standard does not authorize imposition of a special or generalized burden of proof upon that Member which may, more often than not, amount to a *penalty*.[101]

(e) The Precautionary Principle

If, absent a clear showing of discrimination or arbitrary action, it is incorrect to place the burden of proof on the defendant party even after a prima-facie case is made out by the complaining party, does it follow that the opposite principle should be applied to environmental or health-related regulation, on the theory that 'one never can tell' or 'why take chances'? In the *Beef Hormones* case, the European Communities contended that the precautionary principle had become a general customary rule of international law.[102] The United States and Canada rejected that argument, contending that precautionary approach could be characterized at most as an emerging principle that may in the future crystallize into one of the 'general principles of law recognized by civilized nations'.[103]

In the *Beef Hormones* case concerning application of the SPS Agreement, the argument could be more focused than debate about emerging principles, because Articles 5.1 and 5.2 expressly call for risk assessment based on scientific evidence, and Article 5.7 permits provisional measures on the basis of available pertinent information, coupled with an obligation to obtain additional information 'necessary for a more objective assessment of risk within a reasonable time'. The restrictions enforced by the European Community on hormones in beef had been in effect in one form or another for close to two decades, and could hardly be considered provisional measures. Thus it was relatively easy for the Appellate Body to decline to apply the precautionary principle in the *Beef Hormones* case, without making a general pronouncement on the issue: The Appellate Body wrote:

We consider . . . that it is unnecessary, and probably imprudent, for the Appellate Body in this appeal to take a position on this important but abstract question. We note that the Panel itself did not make any definitive finding with regard to the status of the precautionary principle in international law and that the precautionary principle, at least outside the field of international environmental law, still awaits authoritative formulation.[104]

---

[101] Id. For criticism of this position and of the procedures in the WTO in science disputes generally by one of the Legal Advisers of the European Community, see Theophanis Christoforou, 'Settlement of Science-Based Trade Disputes in the WTO: Developing Case Law in the Face of Scientific Uncertainty', 8 *N.Y.U. Envtl L.J.* 622 (2000).

[102] Compare e.g. Philippe Sands, *Principles of International Environmental Law*, Vol. I p. 212 (1995).

[103] See Article 38(1)(c) of the Statute of the International Court of Justice. For discussion by the International Court of Justice on how a customary principle of international law is created, see the *North Sea Continental Shelf* Cases (*Federal Republic of Germany* v. *Denmark*; *Federal Republic of Germany* v. *Netherlands*), [1969] I.C.J. Rep. 4.

[104] *Beef Hormones* decision, para. 123.

It added, however, that

a panel charged with determining, for instance, whether 'sufficient scientific evidence' exists to warrant the maintenance by a member of a particular SPS measure may, of course, and should, bear in mind that responsible, representative governments commonly act from perspectives of prudence and precaution where risks of irreversible, e.g. life-terminating, damage to human health are concerned.[105]

We accordingly agree with the finding of the Panel that the precautionary principle does not override the provisions of Article 5.1 and 5.2 of the SPS Agreement.[106]

(f)   Risk Assessment

The elements of risk assessment, a new term in the vocabulary of international trade but known to science policy-makers for at least a decade previously, are spelled out in the SPS Agreement, somewhat along the lines of cost-benefit analysis. Members are to take account of available scientific evidence (Art. 5(2)); relevant economic factors (Art. 5(3)); and the objective of minimizing negative trade effects (Art. 5(4)). Further, Members are to avoid arbitrary or unjustifiable distinctions in the levels of protection (Art. 5(5)), and they shall assure that their SPS measures are not more trade-restrictive than required to achieve their appropriate sanitary and phytosanitary level of protection, 'taking into account technical and economic feasibility' (Art. 5(6)).

The Appellate Body in *Beef Hormones* viewed risk assessment as an affirmative obligation of the state imposing a protective measure not based on a recognized international standard. Drawing on the definition in the SPS Agreement,[107] the Appellate Body pointed out that risk assessment is at least a two-step process—first *identifying the adverse effects*, if any, on human, animal, or plant life or health from use of the challenged product, and second *evaluating the probability* of occurrence of such effects. The more dangerous the potential adverse effect is, the lower the threshold of probability required to justify a restraint.

The evaluation is to be made on the basis of scientific evidence, but as the Appellate Body noted, such evaluation cannot be limited to the kinds of experiments made in a controlled laboratory setting; nor does an acceptable risk assessment have to follow mainstream scientific opinion. Indeed, divergence of qualified opinions may indicate the kind of scientific uncertainty that would justify a restraint. But there must be an express connection

---

[105] *Beef Hormones* decision, para. 124.   [106] Id. para. 125.

[107] Annex A of the SPS Agreement defines risk assessment as follows:

The evaluation of the likelihood of entry, establishment or spread of a pest or disease within the territory of an importing Member according to the sanitary or phytosanitary measures which might be applied, and of the associated potential biological and economic consequences; or the evaluation of the potential for adverse effects on human or animal health arising from the presence of additives, contaminants, toxins or disease causing organisms in food, beverages or feed stuffs.

between a scientific report and the risk on which restraint is based.[108] A scientific report stating 'no adverse effects have been found.' will not support a restraint, even if the report continues 'but research is continuing'. In *Beef Hormones*, the European Communities presented one expert who estimated that approximately one out of every million women would develop cancer as a result of consuming meat treated with hormones. He had not, however, studied hormones as found in meat or meat products, and so his estimate could not be a valid risk assessment or element of a risk assessment, 'reasonably sufficient' to overturn the contrary conclusions reached in other studies submitted to the panel. It was on this ground, and apparently on this ground alone, that the Appellate Body upheld the conclusion of the Panel that the European Community's prohibition of imports of hormone-treated beef was contrary to the SPS Agreement.

(g) Discrimination

The SPS Agreement provides (in Art. 5(5)) that each member shall avoid arbitrary or unjustifiable distinctions, 'if such distinctions result in discrimination or a disguised restriction on international trade.' The text is almost (though not quite) a verbatim quotation from the chapeau of Article XX of the GATT, and so it seems reasonable to look beyond the SPS Agreement in reading the Appellate Body's judgment—at least in the context of environmental and health regulation (GATT Article XX(b)), and perhaps in respect to all the defenses listed in Article XX but subject to the chapeau.[109] The Appellate Body in *Beef Hormones* pointed out that Article 5.5 of the SPS Agreement contained three elements, and held that it was necessary to explore all three.[110] *First*, whether there is a difference in the level of protection imposed by the state in different situations; *second*, whether the differences in level of protection exhibit arbitrary or unjustifiable distinctions; and *third*, whether these distinctions result in discrimination or disguised restriction of international trade. One might have thought from the text that failing any one of these criteria could lead to a finding of violation. The Appellate Body in *Beef Hormones*, however, thought the elements were cumulative:

---

[108] Vern R. Walker, n. 99 above, writes, at 363:

Whenever scientific uncertainty is present in risk assessment, each member should be entitled to choose betwen scentifically plausible options and should be able to follow its own science policies.

[109] Not everyone shares this view. A panel report in *Measures Affecting Asbestos and Asbestos Containing Products, (Canada* v. *European Communities)*, WT/DS135/R, 18 Sept. 2000, at para. 8.180, stresses the differences between Article XX(b) and (g) of the GATT and the more detailed provisions in the SPS Agreement.

[110] *Beef Hormones* case, paras. 214–15.

The presence of the second element . . . may in practical effect operate as a 'warning' signal that the implementing *measure* in its application *might* be a discriminatory measure or *might* be a restriction on international trade disguised as an SPS measure for the protection of human life or health. Nevertheless the measure itself needs to be examined and appraised, and, in the context of the differing levels of protection, shown to result in discrimination or a disguised restriction on international trade (emphasis added).[111]

Thus it might be possible for a given measure to be based on an arbitrary or unjustifiable distinction, yet not be a violation. The Appellate Body realized that this statement was inconsistent—or at least potentially inconsistent—with the statement of the Appellate Body in the *Reformulated and Conventional Gasoline Case*[112] that the terms 'arbitrary discrimination', 'unjustifiable discrimination', and 'disguised restriction on international trade' in the chapeau of GATT Article XX may be read side by side and import meaning to one another.[113] The inconsistency was justified, however, as the Appellate Body believed, by the difference in wording between the chapeau of Article XX, which speaks of measures which would constitute a means of arbitrary or unjustifiable discrimination *or* a disguised restriction on international trade, and the SPS Agreement, which states in Article 5(5) that members 'shall avoid arbitrary or unjustifiable distinctions in the levels of protection *if* such distinctions result in discrimination or a disguised restriction on international trade.' The Appellate Body rejected the panel's conclusion that Article 5(5) had been violated, because it did not find discrimination or disguised restriction on international trade.[114]

If this is the lesson of the *Beef Hormones* case, i.e. if it must be determined in each case whether an 'arbitrary or unjustifiable distinction' rises to the level of a violation, the decision, it would seem, is a quite uncertain guide to other cases in which environmental or safety regulations come in conflict with international trade. To the present author it is difficult to understand how a measure can be unjustifiable, yet not constitute a violation. Perhaps this is only a word play, and what is meant is that some distinctions—here between restrictions on naturally occurring hormones and artificially added hormones—are not so arbitrary as to be unjustifiable. The inference that injury to the complaining party (or to international trade) must be shown even when unjustifiable distinctions in the application of protective actions

---

[111] *Beef Hormones* case, para. 215 (italics in original).

[112] *United States—Standard for Reformulated and Conventional Gasoline*, WTO Doc. WT/DS2/A13/R, adopted 20 May 1996.

[113] Id. Part IV. In this case, the Panel had found that the United States measures failed to qualify for the exemption in GATT Article XX(g) concerned with conservation of exhaustible natural resources. Accordingly the panel did not have to go into the application of the chapeau of Article XX. The Appellate Body reversed the panel on Article XX(g), then turned to the chapeau and held that the United States measures did not pass the test there set out, because they constituted 'unjustifiable discrimination' compared to regulations applied to domestic refiners, and also were a disguised restriction on international trade.

[114] *Beef Hormones* case, paras. 238–40, 246.

have been established seems unpersuasive. There is no reason to believe that actions challenged under the SPS Agreement—or by analogy other actions challenged under GATT and defended under Article XX including the chapeau—are exempt from the presumption set out in Article 3(8) of the Understanding on Dispute Settlement.[115] Article 3(8) of the DSU states:

In cases where there is an infringement of the obligations assumed under a covered agreement, the action is considered *prima facie* to constitute a case of nullification or impairment. This means that there is normally a presumption that a breach of the rules has an adverse impact on other Member parties to that covered agreement, and in such cases, it shall be up to the Member against whom the complaint has been brought to rebut the charge.

(h)   Lessons from the *Beef Hormones* Case: Some Tentative Conclusions[116]

The proposition here advanced is that the teaching of the *Beef Hormones* case (whether or not one agrees with all aspects of the decision) can be instructive in other cases of intersection between environmental regulation and the law of international trade. Indeed if the analysis in *Beef Hormones* had been applied in the *Tuna/Dolphin* or *Shrimp/Turtle* cases,[117] the outcomes—and the public's reaction—might well have been different. Certainly the concept of risk assessment makes sense beyond the SPS Agreement, and may well be a useful compromise between acceptance and rejection of the precautionary principle. In the context of environmental or health-related regulations, the opportunity to justify some types of apparent discrimination would remove some of the perceived rigidities of the traditional GATT/WTO system, without a real threat to that system.[118]

While burdens of proof and presumptions are never a wholly satisfactory way to approach a fact-intensive controversy, this writer comes away from the *Beef Hormones* case with the following suggestions about how a case brought by Patria against Xandia challenging an environmental or health-related regulation should proceed:[119]

> (1)   Patria asserts that an environmental regulation imposed by Xandia is an unlawful impediment to its exports to Xandia;
>
> (2)   Xandia defends the regulation as justified by known danger to human, animal or plant health, or as supported by a scientific risk assessment;

---

[115] See Ch. 8 Sect. 8.7(a).

[116] For the avoidance of doubt, it bears repeating that this conclusion, though informed by detailed consideration of the *Beef Hormones* case, does not purport to reproduce the conclusion of the Appellate Body, and may indeed differ from it, though that is not clear.

[117] See Sects. 11.5–11.6 supra.

[118] Note that this writer rejects the holding in *Beef Hormones*, at n. 111 supra, that an *un*justifiable discrimination may nevertheless not constitute a violation.

[119] The discussion here concerns the way a panel (and therefore the parties) should think about the case, not necessarily about the pleadings or procedure before the panel.

(3)   Patria asserts that the challenged regulation does not conform to international standards, is not scientifically justified, and is not supported by an appropriate risk assessment;

(4)   Patria asserts that the challenged regulation is discriminatory in intent or effect; Xandia denies that the regulation is discriminatory, or seeks to justify distinctions in its application.

Under (1), Patria has an initial burden to make a prima-facie case i.e. that if everything it asserts is true and is not controverted by Xandia, Patria is entitled to relief. Xandia does not bear the burden under (2), which may well depend on the adequacy of risk assessment, as discussed previously, or on resolution of scientific conflict. If Patria meets its burden under (3), it is entitled to prevail; Patria need not establish discrimination if the other elements are established. Under (4), if discrimination is necessary to the complaint and Patria has made the required showing, the burden shifts to Xandia to establish that the distinctions in application of the regulation are justifiable, i.e. not arbitrary, and do not constitute a disguised restriction on international trade. Step (5), assessment of injury to Patria or to international trade, should not be necessary, unless the controversy continues to the enforcement stage.[120]

11.8   SOME CLOSING THOUGHTS AND A LOOK AHEAD

As noted in the Introduction to this Chapter, neither the GATT, nor the agenda for the Uruguay Round contained any reference to protection of the environment. By the time the Uruguay Round was concluded, however, the relation between trade and the environment had become a major concern worldwide, and it was clear that the new WTO could no longer stand aside.

(a)   Further Thoughts on the Precautionary Principle

A recurring issue, inevitably, is the precautionary principle, which holds not only that uncertainty regarding the adverse environmental effects of an

---

[120] In the event, the *Beef Hormones* case unfolded similarly to, and roughly at the same time, as the *Bananas* case described in detail in Ch. 8 at Sect. 8.8(d). First, there was an arbitration under Article 21(3) of the Understanding on Dispute Settlement to determine the 'reasonable period' for compliance. That period was set at 15 months, to expire on May 13, 1999. Shortly before that date, the EC stated that it would not comply with the recommendations in the Report, but would consider compensation. On June 3, 1999, the United States and Canada requested authorization under DSU Article 22(2) to suspend concessions in the amount of US $202 million, and C$75 million respectively. The EC requested arbitration under DSU Article 22(6) of the level of suspension, and the arbitrators (the original panel) determined the level of nullification suffered by the United States to be US$116.8 million and by Canada C$11.3 million. WT/DS24/ARB, Decision of 12 July 1999. At its meeting of July 26, 1999, the Dispute Settlement Body authorized suspension of concessions by the United States and Canada in these amounts, and both countries promptly did so.

activity should not be a bar to adoption of measures to prohibit or otherwise regulate the activity, but that such uncertainty provides an affirmative justification for adopting such measures.[121] The issue comes up in connection with additives to food sources, such as in the *Beef Hormones* case; with genetic modification of plants or animals; with new pharmaceutical products; with construction or drilling in sites where particular species of plants or animals dwell; and with decisions on whether to invest in costly remedial measures that may or may not accomplish their tasks and may or may not create unwanted side effects.

Not all of these decision points involve international trade, but some do, and it is likely that decision-makers in different countries will come to different conclusions in the face of uncertainty. In the *Beef Hormones* case, the Appellate Body held that the precautionary principle had not become customary law—at least not yet—but that it made sense to weigh the asserted severity of the danger against the degree of likelihood that the danger would be enhanced by the challenged activity. The Appellate Body was not willing, at least in that case, to proceed on the basis of the 'worst case scenario', as seemed to be called for by the precautionary principle.

The European Community Treaty, as amended by the Maastricht Treaty of 1992, provides (in Article 174(2)):

Community policy on the environment shall . . . be based on the precautionary principle and on the principles that preventive action should be taken, that environmental damage should as a priority be rectified at source and that the polluter should pay.

Article 174(3) states further that

In preparing its policy on the environment, the Community shall take account of:
—available scientific data . . . [and]
—the potential benefits and costs of action or lack of action.

It seems clear that this policy, though focused in the Treaty only on the environment, applies also in comparable contexts, such as health and safety measures, and the European Court of Justice has so held.[122] However, neither the EC Treaty nor case law contains a definition of the precautionary principle. In April 1999, the EC Council adopted a resolution urging the Commission to prepare 'clear and effective guidelines for the application of the principle', and in February 2000, the Commission issued a Communication of 22 pages plus appendices undertaking to do so.[123] The Communication looks not only to a common understanding among regulatory authorities within the Community but also to a 'harmonized approach' within the WTO.

---

[121] I have borrowed this definition from a forthcoming paper by Prof. Richard B. Stewart, 'Environmental Decisionmaking Under Uncertainty', 20 *Research in Law and Economics* (2002).

[122] See *United Kingdom* v. *Commission*, Case C-180/96 [the 'Mad Cow Disease' case], [1998] E.C.R. 2211, 5 May 1998, at para. 100.

[123] *Communication on the Precautionary Principle*, EC COM(2000), 2 Feb. 2000.

In many ways, the Communication is consistent with the approach of the United States and other states. Most people in and out of government who have thought about the problem of innovation versus risk would agree that the approach to new products or processes should involve proportionality, non-discrimination, consistency, examination of the benefits and costs of action or lack of action, and examination of scientific developments.[124] But the Communication also states that for certain products, such as drugs, pesticides, or food additives, the burden of proof should be shifted to the proponents, so that the substance would be deemed hazardous until proven safe.[125] Further, the Communication concludes that the decision whether to act or not to act is of an 'eminently political nature', which has an element of truth, but is inconsistent with the stated attitude of the United States.[126]

To the present author, writing from an economic law perspective, the precautionary principle as formulated by the European Community seems too harsh. On the one hand, it is susceptible to misuse for purposes of competition and protection; on the other, it seems both to overestimate and underestimate science. The approach that uncertainty justifies inaction or prohibition overestimates science, in that the suggestion is that science can in a finite period achieve certainty, as contrasted with a high—and acceptable—degree of probability. It underestimates science in that the 'what if . . .?' question, stirred up by political considerations, is given—or may be given—too much weight.

It is evident that Article XX of the GATT, and particularly XX(b) and (g), needs some refinement, along the lines of the SPS Agreement but applicable more generally.[127] The case-by-case approach, depending on *ad hoc* panels plus an overworked Appellate Body, is probably not the best way to achieve such refinement.[128] However, if the underlying differences among the

---

[124] Commission Communication, para. 6.3.   [125] Id. para. 6.4.

[126] For instance, one of the US Special Trade Negotiators said in a speech to the New York Academy of Science:

> To find political solutions to these issues is to run significant risks—and not only of trade disputes. It is, in fact, to risk the public health. The political approach inherently moves away from decisions based on science, and towards decisions guided by ignorance, fear, or material gain. This approach resulted in the 'mad-cow' fiasco in Britain, the tainted-blood scandal in France, and the recent dioxin debacle in Belgium.
>
> . . .
>
> We do not insist that the EU—or any other country—adopt the US standard for these products. All we are asking for are clear, transparent, timely, science-based and predictable regulations. (Ambassador Peter Scher, 'Trade Policy and the Scientific Revolution: The Case of Agricultural Biotechnology', 19 Nov. 1999)

[127] Another model might be the TBT Agreement. See Ch. 5, Sect. 5.3(b).

[128] Note, in this connection, the express warning against 'activist judges' in the Understanding on Dispute Settlement, Art. 3(2), which states:

> Recommendations and rulings of the DSB cannot add to or diminish the rights and obligations provided in the covered agreements.

This statement, repeated almost verbatim in DSU Article 19(2), is cited also by Christophorou, Sect. 11.7, n. 101 in his criticism of how the dispute settlement process worked in *Beef Hormones* and other cases involving issues of science.

European Community, the United States, and the developing countries persist, it may be the only way, at least in the short run.

Whether legislative reform should be undertaken within the WTO, for instance in a new Framework Agreement on Environmental Issues, as is suggested in the excerpts from Sir Leon Brittan reproduced below, or in a new organization with both legislative and umpiring authorities, is taken up briefly in the next section.

(b) Beyond the World Trade Organization?

The Marrakesh Agreement Establishing the WTO recites concerns for the environment in the first preambular clause,[129] and a Ministerial Decision accompanying the Final Act of the Uruguay Round expressly referred to the Rio Declaration and Agenda 21[130] as a basis for establishing a Committee on Trade and Environment open to all members of the WTO.[131] At the first Biennial Ministerial Conference of the WTO in December 1996, the Committee reported that it had been examining and 'will continue to examine, *inter alia*, the scope of the complementarities between trade liberalization, economic development and environmental protection', but the Ministers said only that further work needs to be undertaken.[132]

In March 1999, the WTO organized a High Level Symposium on Trade and the Environment, bringing not only delegates from almost all member states of the WTO, but for the first time 26 inter-governmental organizations and 130 non-governmental organizations, from farm and fishing lobbies to Greenpeace, animal lovers, labour unions, chambers of commerce, and so on. The outgoing Director-General, Renato Ruggiero, urged an institutional and legal counterpart to the WTO, a World Environment Organization that would bring together developed, developing, and least developed countries under one dispute settlement mechanism.[133] That proposal did not catch on, and indeed was viewed by some as an effort to divert responsibility away from his organization.

Klaus Töpfer, the Executive Director of the United Nations Environment Program (UNEP)[134] said it was neither fair nor reasonable to expect the

---

[129] The first preambular clause reads, in pertinent part:

Recognizing that their relations in the field of trade and economic endeavour should be conducted with a view to raising standards of living . . . and expanding the production of and trade in goods and services, while allowing for the optimal use of the world's resources in accordance with the objective of sustainable development, seeking both to protect and preserve the environment and to enhance the means for doing so in a manner consistent with their respective needs and concerns at different levels of economic development.

[130] See Sect. 11.3(d) supra.

[131] Ministerial Decision of 14 Apr. 1994 on Trade and the Environment, 33 *I.L.M.* 1267 (1994).

[132] WTO *Singapore Ministerial Declaration*, 13 Dec. 1996, para. 16.

[133] WTO *Opening Remarks to the High Level Symposium on Trade and the Environment by Renato Ruggiero*, 15 Mar. 1999.

[134] See Sect. 11.3(a) supra.

WTO to shoulder all the responsibility, and urged that his organization be given a greater role on the relation between trade and the environment. The developing countries urged differentiation between their responsibilities and those of the industrial countries. The NGO's, supported on this issue by the United States, urged more 'transparency', including open hearings in dispute settlement proceedings and opportunity to make *amicus curiae* submissions. Some participants in the symposium urged review of Article XX, particularly by eliminating or reinterpreting the word 'necessary' in paragraph b.

Perhaps the most interesting proposals came in the keynote address by Sir Leon Brittan, who had been the chief negotiator for the European Community throughout the Uruguay Round and who had made the proposal that led to the Symposium on Trade and the Environment:

The reason for my original suggestion was that I felt that the debate on the relationship between trade and environment had got bogged down in technicalities and that underlying all the genuine complexities there were a limited number of issues which could be resolved by elevating the level of the debate and opening it out to a wider public. The reason why I allowed myself the optimistic belief these issues were not incapable of resolution was because I had the impression that while there were extremists on both sides of the argument, a broad consensus could be achieved between traditional free-traders, such as myself, who nonetheless saw the importance in today's world of accommodating environmental concerns in trade policy, and environmentalists who saw that their objectives could best be achieved by incorporating them in the system in a reasonable way, rather than pursuing policies which would, however unfairly, be interpreted as being protectionist in effect, if not in intention.

. . .

Multilateral Environmental Agreements
First, Multilateral Environmental Agreements (MEAs). It is in my view important to foster effective MEAs so as to have a common base, agreed among as many states as is feasible, for tackling particular environmental problems. These include animal welfare.

Such MEAs are clearly preferable to unilateral action, which will often rightly fall foul of WTO rules. The problem is that even multilateral agreements are not necessarily proof against a WTO challenge by non-members of such agreements.

I strongly believe that what we need here is a framework to help ensure compatibility between MEAs and WTO rules. Where an MEA commands wide support among WTO members, we need to be more confident than at present that WTO trade rules do accommodate the aims of the parties to the MEA, and therefore allow the necessary trade measures to be taken under such an MEA. If, to achieve that confidence, we need a new interpretation of, or even a textual amendment to, WTO rules, I believe we should go down that route.

We must of course be cautious about the scope for the use of trade measures against non-members of MEAs. I believe there should be a series of agreed principles for such cases.

Before taking trade measures against non-members, MEA members should exercise all possible efforts to persuade non-members to cooperate with the environmental objectives of the MEA, and should offer non-members the possibility of joining the MEA. Trade measures should only be considered as a last resort, and should be no more restrictive to trade than is necessary to ensure the effectiveness of the goals agreed by MEA members.

I believe it is important that WTO members should resolve this conundrum as soon as possible. Early agreement, whether formal or informal, that they will not take dispute settlement against action taken under MEAs which meet the kind of criteria I have outlined would seem a highly desirable course of action.

Process and production methods

There has also been discussion of the extent to which process and production methods can legitimately be taken into account in framing trade rules.

It is clearly undesirable for each WTO member to take whatever trade measures it sees fit, based on its view of the acceptability of the way in which products are made in third countries. Such an approach is subjective and therefore arbitrary. It risks damaging one of the great virtues of the GATT system, namely its transparency and predictability. It is one thing for there to be an agreed international standard on a particular production method or use of a particular substance, such as CFCs. It is quite another for each WTO member to decide, purely unilaterally, that it disapproves of some practice elsewhere in the world, and for it to ban imports on that basis.

Labelling

It is clear that in a few cases, a multilaterally agreed ban is justified. In many more cases a labelling solution may be the best way to tackle the problem.

It seems to me perfectly legitimate to inform the consumer that particular goods have been produced in third countries in a way which meets certain defined standards or is, at least, more environmentally friendly than other methods.

The consumer is then in a strong position to make an informed choice based on the importance they attach to the overall environmental impact of production methods, even among apparently identical products.

Process and production methods are, therefore, closely linked to the very important area of eco-labelling. In that context I think it is important to agree on and adopt a clear and workable approach to the compatibility of labelling schemes with WTO rules.

First, I do not see a need to make an artificial distinction between the product itself and the way it is made. It seems to me legitimate for the label to describe the environmental impact of production methods as well as the content of the product provided the criteria for granting that label are objective.

I think that we should seek a clear understanding that voluntary labelling schemes are compatible with GATT rules provided they conform to certain agreed requirements.

Clearly, such schemes need to be transparent in that producers need to know how to apply for recognition, and consumers should have proper information about what the label actually indicates. But on that basis, I think that should be facilitated and indeed encouraged.

Compulsory labelling schemes obviously raise greater questions since they force producers to create separate production arrangements for those markets which require labelling. They therefore need to meet tighter requirements for WTO approval. Further work is urgently needed on what those requirements should be. In the first place they should be no more trade restrictive than necessary. Secondly, there should be some basis for claiming that the environmental objective that is sought to be achieved is a substantial one that cannot be achieved by less restrictive means. I believe, however, that provided we can create a clear set of principles which avoids the abuse of such schemes for protectionism purposes, they too should be available as part of the environmental policy tool-kit.

Precautionary Principle
There is of course a dilemma for policy-makers when partial but not complete evidence becomes available that products may be harmful to the consumer, or damaging to the environment, or both.

I accept the legitimacy of the concept of precaution in the field of environment and health. However, there are dangers in allowing a general, open-ended precautionary principle without defining what it means and in what circumstances it might be used.

It is clear also that using such a principle as the basis for action designed to reduce risks to zero would be unjustified. Indeed, it is difficult to think of any aspect of life where risk can be eliminated altogether. In a sense, we need to ensure that the costs and benefits of precautionary action are looked at in a coordinated way, taking into account sustainable development principles, so as to have reassurance that such action is not excessive in relation to the objective.

The best way forward is, to my mind, to ensure the right balance between prompt action where justified and the avoidance of overkill. The precautionary principle has already been recognised in international agreements but not explicitly in the WTO, although several key provisions explicitly allow for precautionary action.

We should together reflect on how, at the same time, to give it greater definition and prevent it from being invoked in an abusive way.

Of course, these are merely suggestions, and may not even reflect the thinking of the European Community, let alone the rest of the world. They do, however, reflect to a considerable extent the experience illustrated in the preceding sections of this chapter. The idea of linking restrictions by importing countries to widely accepted multilateral agreements has been raised several times in this chapter. Sir Leon Brittan's suggestion that a *framework agreement* that might establish a threshold for applying an MEA to non-members may well by pursued, at least to the extent of permitting trade restraints by members against non-members. The reluctance to fully embrace the *precautionary principle* is consistent with the view of the Appellate Body in the *Beef Hormones* case.[135]

The *'PPM' issue*, i.e. the assertion that an imported product may not be a 'like product' for purposes of the national treatment or MFN provisions of the GATT because the imported product is made by different processes or production methods came up in the first *Tuna/Dolphin* case,[136] though the panel ultimately rejected the US position that tuna not caught by dolphin-safe methods was a different product from tuna caught with a dolphin-safe

---

[135] See Sect. 11.7 supra.   [136] See Sect. 11.5 supra.

net. Again, Brittan accepts the prevailing decision, but suggests that labelling—e.g. 'dolphin-safe' tuna—can to some extent take the place of the PPM approach, but may be subject to abuse if suitable rules are not adopted and implemented.

In the Ministerial Declaration adopted at the Doha Conference in November 2001, Member States agreed to negotiations 'without prejudging their outcome' on the relationship between existing WTO rules and specific trade obligations set out in multilateral environmental agreements.[137] No mention is made in the Declaration or in the accompanying Decision on Implementation-Related Issues and Concerns[138] of the precautionary principle. News Reports indicated that in return for agreement by the United States to support new negotiations on the link between trade and the environment, the European Union had assured the United States in writing that it would not promote the use of the precautionary principle to justify the imposition of illegitimate trade barriers.[139]

---

[137] Ministerial Declaration adopted 14 Nov. 2001, para. 31, WT/MIN(01)/DEC/1 (20 Nov. 2001).

[138] WT/MIN(01)/17 (20 Nov. 2001).

[139] Letter from Pascal Lamy, EU Commissioner for Trade, to Robert B. Zoellick, US Trade Representative, as quoted in BNA 18 *Int'l Trade Reporter* No. 47, p. 1894 (29 Nov. 2001).

12

Competition Law

BY ELEANOR M. FOX*

* Walter J. Derenberg Professor of Trade Regulation, New York University School of Law. I am deeply grateful to my valued colleague and friend Professor Fox for agreeing to contribute this chapter, without which she and I both believe that a volume on International Economic Law would be incomplete.

12.1 INTRODUCTION: THE PLACE OF COMPETITION LAW IN INTERNATIONAL ECONOMIC LAW

Competition law regulates business practices and transactions that create or abuse market power and interfere with the free play of market forces. In the United States, this body of law is called antitrust law. The law was enacted at the end of the nineteenth century in response to the formation of trusts by Rockefeller, Morgan, and others to control major sectors of the American economy, such as railroads, steel, oil, farm machinery, and sugar. Until the end of World War II, the United States alone was a prominent enforcer of antitrust law. At the end of the war, in connection with US assistance programs, Germany and Japan adopted antitrust policy as an antidote to political authoritarianism. In the 1950s the states of Western Europe created a common market designed to eliminate government-imposed barriers to trade, and the blueprint included a common competition policy to facilitate the creation of a common market and, in particular, to prevent a redivision of markets by commercial actors.

In the late 1980s Communism fell in the Soviet Union and Central and Eastern Europe, and the newly democratic states adopted market systems. The economic reforms included adoption of competition laws in order to check abuse of private power, to limit privilege, and to open markets to trade and competition.

The end of the Uruguay Round, with yet lower barriers to world trade, increased the visibility of remaining trade barriers and fueled the demand for open markets free from private as well as public restraints. More than 80 countries now have competition laws, most of which were adopted since 1990. These include South Korea, South Africa, Indonesia, Brazil, Mexico, Bulgaria, Croatia, and most other countries in Eastern Europe and South America.

Competition policy has taken a prominent place among international economic concerns. Markets commonly transcend national borders, and there is often a poor fit between national law and international market problems. Globalization raises the question whether there is a need for a supranational framework or at least for multinational networks to bring coherence to market problems of global dimension.

This chapter explores, first, the origins and evolution of competition law, second, the reach of national law to foreign actors and transactions, and third, substantive and procedural rules of the American and European systems. The last two sections of the chapter explore bilateral and multilateral initiatives to improve the competition process in a global economy.

12.2   THE ORIGINS AND EVOLUTION OF ANTITRUST LAW IN THE UNITED STATES

The basic and principal United States antitrust law, the Sherman Act, was adopted in 1890.[1] The principal merger law, the Clayton Act, was adopted in 1914,[2] with a major amendment in 1950.[3] The language of these statutes is short and general, and the antitrust law as applied has developed largely through judicial decisions in a common law tradition. Development of the law is influenced by guidelines and perspectives of the antitrust agencies. Since the 1980s, the antitrust law has increasingly reflected the view that the law should serve efficiency and consumer welfare, and no other goals.

The Sherman Act was adopted in response to the power and predations of the large trusts that were formed in the wake of the Industrial Revolution. The trust was a form of business organization developed by the leaders of American business in the late nineteenth century. A small control group acquired and held the stock of competitors, and ran the businesses in the interests of the combined firms. The trusts were usually secret, so that neither buyers nor suppliers of the apparent competitors knew of the common control. The trusts controlled many of the necessities of life.

The Sherman Act is a simple statute. Section 1 prohibits contracts, combinations, and conspiracies in restraint of trade in the form of trust or otherwise. Section 2 prohibits monopolization and attempts and conspiracies to monopolize. Both sections apply to trade and commerce among the several states and with foreign nations.

Congress left to the courts the task of construing the vague words of the Act. Nearly from the start, the Supreme Court held that Section 1 prohibited agreements among competitors to fix prices, rig bids, or divide markets.[4] Other agreements were held to come within the prohibitory category, 'restraint of trade', if they were 'unreasonable' in view of their purpose and

---

[1] 26 Stat. 209 (1890), codified as amended as 15 U.S.C. §1 et seq. The same Congress that adopted the Sherman Act adopted the McKinley Tariff Act of 1890, 26 Stat. 567 (1890). Adoption a tariff law fueled the need for an antitrust law. See Hans B. Thorelli, *The Federal Antitrust Policy*, 166–8 (1955); William L. Letwin, 'Congress and the Sherman Antitrust Law: 1887–1890', 23 *U. Chi. L. Rev.* 221 (1956).

[2] 38 Stat. 730 (1914). The antimerger provision, §7, is codified as amended, as 15 U.S.C. §18.

[3] Celler–Kefauver Amendment, 64 Stat. 1125 (1950).

[4] *United States* v. *Trans-Missouri Freight Association*, 166 U.S. 290, 340–2 (1897).

market effect.[5] 'Unreasonableness,' however, soon proved to be an elastic concept. Its meaning has changed over time.

Section 2's prohibition of 'monopolization' is likewise in need of definition. Does it prohibit growth to monopoly, or only bad acts of firms with power? What is a 'bad act' that the law condemns? Courts have given different answers at different times. In the early years of the twentieth century the Supreme Court prohibited the big railroad combinations as restraints of trade,[6] but it upheld US Steel's acquisition of 140 competitors because the big steel company had committed no 'brutalities' against its competitors.[7]

Perceptions that the Sherman Act had no teeth, that it failed to protect small and middle-sized businesses against exclusionary acts, and that it failed to protect the people against the growth of power and privilege, led to passage of the Clayton Act in 1914.[8] The Clayton Act contains restrictions against tying, exclusive dealing, price discrimination, interlocking directors, and mergers of competitors if the effect of such conduct 'may be substantially to lessen competition or tend to create a monopoly.' In 1936 the Robinson–Patman Act[9] extended the Clayton Act's prohibition of certain price discrimination to protect small businesses from favouritism granted to their more powerful competitors.

In the 1940s, in the midst of the war, there was a great merger wave. Observing the giant firms in Germany working hand-in-hand with Hitler, Americans were deeply concerned by the rise of industrial concentration in the United States. Mergers were viewed as the principal vehicle for increased concentration. In 1950 Congress passed the Celler–Kefauver Amendment to the Clayton Act, strengthening government controls over mergers that 'may' lessen competition.[10]

Huge networks of international cartels operated during the war years. Many had been organized by dominant German firms, such as Krupp and General Aniline. Some of the German cartels co-opted American competitors, suppressing output and undermining US war production efforts.[11] Under the leadership of Assistant Attorney General Thurman Arnold, the US Justice Department tried to root out the international cartels by prosecuting them under the Sherman Act.

World cartels have never abated; or perhaps they have reappeared to capture the gains of globalization. International cartel enforcement forms a backbone of modern antitrust.

Since the early twentieth century the US antitrust laws have been subject to both public and private enforcement. The federal government can bring

[5] *Standard Oil Co. of New Jersey* v. *United States*, 221 U.S. 1, 43 (1911).

[6] See *United States* v. *Union Pacific R.R. Co.*, 226 U.S. 61 (1912); *United States* v. *Reading Co.*, 253 U.S. 26 (1920); *United States* v. *Southern Pacific Co.*, 259 U.S. 214 (1922).

[7] *United States* v. *United States Steel Corp.*, 251 U.S. 417 (1920).   [8] n. 2 supra.

[9] 49 Stat. 1526 (1936), codified as 15 U.S.C. §13a–13b.   [10] n. 3 supra.

[11] See Thurman Arnold, *Fair Fights and Foul: A Dissenting Lawyer's Life*, 145 (1965).

civil or criminal actions in court against suspected violators, seeking injunctions, fines, divestitures, and even jail terms. Private persons with standing can bring civil actions seeking injunctions and damages in the amount of three times their actual injury. Private antitrust complaints can be brought as class actions. Private persons can rely on findings of fact contained in litigated judgments in government actions. These and other procedures are discussed in greater detail in Section 12.6.

12.3   THE ADOPTION OF COMPETITION LAW IN EUROPE AND JAPAN

At the end of World War II, antitrust law was widely perceived as an important check against both governmental power and private corporate power. Antitrust took root in West Germany, both because of the persistence by the US occupation authorities under the aegis of the Marshall Plan, and because of the appeal of the ordo-liberal philosophy underpinning the Freiburg School.[12]

The American occupation forces sought to introduce antitrust law into Japan, also, but the Japanese Antimonopoly Law (1947)[13] did not take easy root.[14] The history of cooperative business networks through the zaibatsu, and the tradition of government-business collaboration, made it difficult for Japan to achieve a consensus on competition policy comparable to that in the other developed world economies.[15]

In 1957, six European nations signed the Treaty of Rome, creating the European Economic Community.[16] Articles 85 and 86 (later renumbered

---

[12] For an account of the efforts to eliminate the cartels in Germany and later Western Europe, especially the coal and steel cartels, see Volker R. Berghahn, *The Americanisation of West German Industry 1945–1973*, 84–145 (1986). For a conflicting view that attributes more importance to the Freiburg School than to American influences, see David J. Gerber, *Law and Competition in Twentieth Century Europe: Protecting Prometheus*, 232–65 (1998).

[13] *Japan*: Law Relating to Prohibition of Private Monopoly and Methods of Preserving Fair Trade, 12 Apr. 1947 (the Japan Antimonopoly Law).

[14] For the development of this law and the debates between Japanese and American authorities in the immediate post-war period, see Harry First, 'Antitrust in Japan: The Original Intent', 9 *Pac. Rim L. & Policy J.* 1 (2000).

[15] See Eleanor M. Hadley, *Antitrust in Japan*, 11–16 (1970). See also Hiroshi Iyori & Akinori Uesugi, *The Antimonopoly Laws of Japan*, vi–vii (1983). The regime of the zaibatsu was succeeded by a loose system of reciprocity known as keiretsu. Japanese industrial policy tended to preserve Japanese business for the Japanese firms. Even at the close of the twentieth century, despite many reforms in Japan and a much increased profile of Japanese Antimonopoly Law enforcement, outsiders struggled to develop business footholds in Japanese markets. See Jiro Tamura, 'Foreign Firm Access to Japanese Distribution Systems: Trends in Japanese Antitrust Enforcement', 4 *Pac. Rim L. & Policy J.* 267, 269 (1995). But see Shogo Itoda, 'Japan Fair Trade Commission Barks', remarks at Chatham House, London, 22 Feb. 2001, available at www.jftc.admix.go.jp/e.

[16] The first European economic community was the European Coal and Steel Community, established by the Treaty of Paris in 1951.

Articles 81 and 82) contained the Community's basic competition policy.[17] These articles were deeply influenced by the German competition law and were influenced also by US law. Related Treaty provisions prohibit Member States from restraining trade in the European internal market,[18] control Member State subsidies that distort competition in the internal market,[19] and bring state-owned enterprises under the discipline of the competition law.[20]

Administration of the competition law of the European Community was centralized in the European Commission pursuant to enabling legislation, Regulation 17.[21] By the late 1960s, the EC competition system began to assume a significant role in the world competition community. Indeed, EC competition law has become a major model for the world. While the United States today extends the purview of its law principally by extraterritorial applications, the European Union 'exports' EC competition law through free trade agreements with most of its trading partners; the agreements require the partner to apply European Community law to restraints in the free trade area,[22] and they require nations that have applied for membership in the EU to revise their own national laws to approximate European competition law.[23]

Much of the substance and doctrine of US antitrust law was adopted or adapted by the European Community, although with some important differences. Procedurally, US antitrust law entails important features that are not widely shared; e.g., criminal actions, jail terms, private treble damage actions, jury trials, extensive pretrial discovery, class actions, and contingent fees. These US procedural vehicles, especially in combination, are often considered draconian by other nations and by firms abroad, and have led to tensions sometimes erupting in debates on extraterritoriality.

12.4   THE REACH OF NATIONAL LAW AND THE EFFECTS DOCTRINE

Generous reach of national law has stirred controversy throughout the history of antitrust. Although an early US opinion held that the Sherman Act stops at US shores,[24] this rule was short-lived. The substantial impact of offshore acts on the domestic market led American courts to develop the 'effects

---

[17] The Treaty of Amsterdam of 1997 renumbered most of the articles of the Treaty of Rome.
[18] Arts. 28–31 (ex 30–7).   [19] Art. 87 (ex 92).   [20] Art. 86 (ex 90).
[21] First Regulation implementing Arts. 85 and 86 of the Treaty, Regulation 17/62, 1962 O.J. 204, effective 13 Mar. 1962, amended as of 15 June 1999. Regulation 17 is expected to be replaced by 2002.
[22] See E. Fox, 'Antitrust and Regulatory Federalism: Races Up, Down and Sideways', 75 *N.Y.U.L. Rev.* 1781 (2000).
[23] See Thinam Jakob, 'EEA and Eastern European Agreements with the European Community', Ch. 18, 1992 *Fordham Corp. L. Inst.* 403 (1993).
[24] *American Banana Co.* v. *United Fruit Co.* 213 U.S. 347, 357 (1909).

doctrine'.[25] This development offended US trading partners, especially Great Britain, which considered extraterritorial application of economic regulation an affront to its sovereignty.

(a) Protecting Competition in Domestic Markets

The early defining case for the effects doctrine was *United States* v. *Aluminum Co. of America (Alcoa)*.[26] *Alcoa* concerned an international cartel formed in Switzerland by a group of aluminum producers designed to restrict the production of aluminum. There was no proof that Alcoa, the only US producer, was a member of the cartel. Each member was required to pay a royalty, to be allocated among all members, for sales in excess of the assigned quota of each. Exports to the United States were included in the quotas. The United States sued Aluminum Ltd, the Canadian member of the cartel and a sister corporation of Alcoa, as well as Alcoa. Subject matter jurisdiction over the international cartel was asserted under the language of the Sherman Act, which prohibits 'restraint of trade or commerce among the several states or with foreign nations'. The court noted that there are limits to jurisdiction, but found jurisdiction to exist in the case. In a now famous opinion by Judge Learned Hand, the court wrote:

We should not impute to Congress an intent to punish all whom its courts can catch, for conduct which has no consequences within the United States. On the other hand, it is settled law . . . that any state may impose liabilities, even upon persons not within its allegiance, for conduct outside its borders that has consequences within its borders which the state reprehends.[27]

Judge Hand distinguished mere ripple effects of foreign conduct, which he thought were not caught by the Sherman Act, from substantial intended effects, which, he said, Congress had the right to reach, and did. The court found that the aluminum cartel was intended to restrict imports into the United States, and once the government established intent, the burden shifted to defendant to show that there was no actual effect on the US market. The defendant did not meet this burden.

After *Alcoa* the US courts liberally and expansively applied the effects doctrine. Usually the doctrine was applied to offshore acts that directly and substantially impacted competition in the United States.[28] Sometimes, however, the law was applied against US firms doing business abroad even when the anticompetitive effect was abroad.[29]

---

[25] *United States* v. *Sisal Sales Corp.*, 247 U.S. 268, 276 (1927); *United States* v. *Aluminum Co. of America (Alcoa)*, 148 F.2d 416 (2d Cir. 1945).

[26] Note 25 supra. The Court of Appeals sat as a court of last resort because the Supreme Court was unable to muster a quorum.

[27] 148 F.2d at 443.

[28] See e.g. *In re Uranium Antitrust Litigation*, 617 F.2d 1248 (7th Cir. 1980).

[29] *Continental Ore Co.* v. *Union Carbide and Carbon Corp.* 370 U.S. 690, 704 (1962); *Industria Siciliana Asfalti* v. *Exxon Research & Engineering Co.*, 1977–1 (CCH) Trade Cas. ¶61,256 (S.D.N.Y. 1977).

Early controversial assertions of American regulatory jurisdiction involved discovery requests concerning international shipping consortia and the overproduction and orderly marketing of uranium. In the wake of these controversies, a number of countries, including the United Kingdom, Germany, France, Norway, Sweden, Canada, and Australia, enacted statutes to block discovery of documents and other information needed to prosecute cases against foreign defendants. Some of the statutes were limited to shipping or atomic energy; some were general in application.[30]

The best known of the retaliatory statutes is the British Protection of Trading Interests Act of 1980. This act authorizes the relevant minister to direct persons in the United Kingdom to refuse to comply with any law or order issued under the law of 'any overseas country' for regulating or controlling international trade upon a finding that such measures 'in so far as they apply or would apply to things done or to be done outside the territorial jurisdiction of that country by persons carrying on business in the United Kingdom[,] are damaging or threaten to damage the trading interests of the United Kingdom.' Also it restricts enforcement in the United Kingdom of judgments for multiple damages, and allows UK firms forced to pay more than compensatory damages to sue in the UK to 'claw back' the penal portion of the foreign judgment.

From at least the mid 1970s, pressure was applied to the United States to curb judicial 'excesses' in exercising jurisdiction over foreign firms acting abroad. US jurists reacted by retreating (at least rhetorically) from the simple *Alcoa* formulation. Courts began to require not only that foreign defendants' conduct taken abroad have a direct, substantial, and reasonably foreseeable effect on US commerce, but also that account be taken of other factors, including the actors' nationalities, their intent to affect US competition, conflicts with foreign law and policy, and the practical ability to enforce a judgment.[31]

---

[30] Among these statutes are *UK*: Shipping and Commercial Documents Act, 1964 c.87; *France*: Law No. 68–678 of 26 July 1968 Relating to the Transmission of Documents and Information to Foreign Authorities in the Area of Maritime Trade, 1968 Jour. Off. 7267; *Australia*: Foreign Proceedings (Prohibition of Certain Evidence) Act, 1976, Austr. Acts No. 121. For a more complete list of these acts and their amendments, see American Law Institute, *Restatement (Third) of the Foreign Relations Law of the United States*, §442, Reporters' Note 4 (1987). For a collection of English texts of blocking statutes, see A. V. Lowe, *Extraterritorial Jurisdiction, An Annotated Collection of Legal Materials*, 79–143 (1983).

[31] The leading cases were *Timberlane Lumber Co.* v. *Bank of America*, 549 F.2d 597 (9th Cir. 1976) and *Mannington Mills, Inc.* v. *Congoleum Corp.*, 595 F.2d 1287 (3d Cir. 1979). See also Kingman Brewster, *Antitrust and American Business Abroad* (1958) (original edn.); A. Lowenfeld, 'Public Law in the International Arena: Conflict of Laws, International Law, and Some Suggestions for their Interaction', Hague Academy Int'l Law, 163 *Rec. des Cours* 311, 373 (1979); *Restatement (Third) of the Foreign Relations of the United States*, §§403, 415 (1987); E. Fox, 'Extraterritoriality, Antitrust, and the New Restatement: Is Reasonableness the Answer?' 19 *N.Y.U.J. Int'l L. & Pol.* 565 (1987).

Many courts believed that they were obligated to balance foreign contacts and interests against US contacts and interests.[32]

But complaints against the reach of US antitrust law continued. On the one hand, US trading partners complained that their firms were caught by the excessive reach of the US law. On the other hand, American firms complained that application of US law to their international transactions handicapped them in their foreign trade and investment.

In the early 1980s, the two streams converged. In response to American firms' complaints of handicap, Congress, in 1982, adopted the Export Trading Company Act, providing a procedure whereby firms that propose to export may seek an export certificate of review, which, if granted, would protect them from treble (but not single) damages if they were later sued for harming US competition.[33] The Foreign Trade Antitrust Improvements Act of 1982 (FTAIA) addressed both the Americans' claims and its trading partners' claims. For the American business community, the new law cut back the reach of the Sherman and Federal Trade Commission Acts so as not to apply to conduct causing competitive harm only in foreign markets. The FTAIA clarified that, as far as the US antitrust laws are concerned, US-based firms may form export cartels and firms may engage in other anticompetitive conduct in and directed at foreign markets as long as the activity does not have a spill-back effect on competition in the United States. To mollify trading partners, the FTAIA decreed non-applicability of US law unless the conduct has a direct, substantial, and reasonably foreseeable effect on interstate or import commerce.[34]

Meanwhile, Europe, too, began to complain of harm from offshore acts, and Europeans rose to the challenge of regulating those acts. The German Law against Restraints on Competition is expressly applicable 'to all restraints on competition that have effect within the territory where this law is in force, even if they are caused outside of said territory.'[35] Moreover, EC Treaty Article 85 (now 81) prohibits competition-distorting 'agreements . . . and concerted practices which may affect trade between Member States.' In the 1972 *Dyestuffs* case,[36] the European Commission alleged price-fixing by several

---

[32] See n. 31 supra. But see *Laker Airways Ltd.* v. *Sabena, Belgian World Airlines*, 731 F.2d 909, 949–50 (D.C. Cir. 1984), and *In re Uranium Antitrust Litigation*, 480 F. Supp. 1138 (N.D. Ill. 1979), doubting the ability of courts to balance incommensurables.

[33] Pub. L. 97–290, Title 1, 8 Oct. 1982, 96 Stat. 1233, codified at 15 U.S.C. §§4001–3.

[34] There are two exceptions to the last clause. Harm to US-financed exports is still cognizable harm to US commerce, see *Pacific Seafarers, Inc.* v. *Pacific Far East Line, Inc.*, 404 F.2d 804 (D.C. Cir. 1968), cert. denied, 393 U.S. 1093 (1969), and 'a domestic exporter . . . [injured] by unlawful conduct of a competing United States exporter' retains the rights it would have in the absence of the act. Report to Accompany H.R. 5235, 10–11, 2 Aug. 1982.

Some authorities have, in this writer's view, misinterpreted FTAIA §1(B) to give a right under the Sherman Act to US exporters to sue foreign firms that use anticompetitive means to block their home markets.

[35] German Law against Restraints on Competition, Art. 98(2).

[36] *Imperial Chemical Industries Ltd.* v. *Commission*, Cases 48, 49, 51–7/69, [1972] ECR 619.

firms including ICI, a British firm, before the UK joined the Community. ICI challenged the action of the Commission on grounds, among others, 'that the Commission is not competent to impose fines on it for actions that it took outside the Community solely because the actions had effects within the Community.' The Court of Justice affirmed the applicability of the Treaty to ICI's acts, but sidestepped the effects doctrine. Wholly owned subsidiaries of ICI were located in the Community. The Court treated the parent and its subsidiaries as one economic entity, and found it sufficient that the entity had acted within the Community.

In 1988, in the *Woodpulp* case,[37] the European Court again faced the issue, and this time could not use the single entity doctrine. The Commission had found that United States, Canadian, and Finnish firms fixed prices of wood pulp bound for the European Community, and it applied the effects doctrine to reach the offshore acts of these foreign firms. The Court of Justice did not endorse the language of 'effects', but it upheld the Commission's jurisdictional finding on the basis that the alleged offshore price-fixing conspiracy was 'implemented' in the Community. Such conduct, the Court said, 'is covered by the territoriality principle as universally recognized in public international law.'[38] An American trade association, KEA, however, which was merely a forum for the competitors' meetings, did not implement any price agreements in the EU and its conduct was held not to fall within the scope of Article 85.

A few years later, in the *Hartford Fire Insurance* case,[39] the US Supreme Court reaffirmed and simplified the American effects doctrine in the context of inbound restraints on competition. It held the Sherman Act applicable to combinations of and boycotts by American and British (Lloyds of London) reinsurers targeted at the American insurance market, despite a British statutory scheme placing self regulation of reinsurance in the hands of Lloyds of London. The British defendants had argued that the British insurers were acting in England and their acts were permitted by English law; therefore, they said, a conflict resulted and application of US law was inappropriate. The Court rejected the defense, in a split decision (5 to 4). It held that, where offshore collaborators intend to affect and significantly affect the US market, only a direct conflict, such as an order from the British government requiring the firms to do the challenged acts, could provide a defense to application of US law.[40]

---

[37] *Åhlström Osakeyhtiö v. Commission*, Case 89/85, [1988] ECR 5193.
[38] Id., para. 18.   [39] *Hartford Fire Ins. Co. v. California*, 509 U.S. 764, 798–99 (1993).
[40] *Hartford* thus put into question the continued viability of a jurisdictional rule of reason, such as set forth in *Timberlane*, n. 31 supra. Nonetheless, some lower courts continue to apply comity principles. For a critique of the *Hartford* decision for failure to balance contacts and interests, see A. Lowenfeld, 'Conflict, Balancing of Interests, and the Exercise of Jurisdiction to Prescribe: Reflections on the *Insurance Antitrust Case*', 89 Am. J. Int'l Law 42 (1995). For a defense of *Hartford* as applied to a targeted offshore conspiracy, and its holding that a home-country's grant of self-regulatory powers does not create a conflict that shields the competitors

Jurisdiction over offshore acts that directly harm a regulating state, once the center of controversy, is now well accepted in the world. The official commentary to the 2000 revision of the OECD Guidelines for Multinational Enterprises[41] makes the following statement:

Enterprises should be aware that competition laws are being enacted in a rapidly increasing number of jurisdictions, and that it is increasingly common for those laws to prohibit anti-competitive activities that occur abroad if they have harmful impact on domestic consumers. Moreover, the growth of cross-border trade and investment makes it more likely that anti-competitive conduct taking place in one jurisdiction will have harmful effects in other jurisdictions. As a result, anti-competitive unilateral or concerted conduct that is or may be legal where it occurs is increasingly likely to be illegal in another jurisdiction. Enterprises should therefore take into account both the law of the country in which they are operating and the laws of all countries in which the effects of their conduct are likely to be felt.[42]

(b)   Opening Foreign Markets

The *Hartford* case involved an alleged offshore cartel that targeted Americans. A different type of foreign restraint was to attract the attention of the trade and competition community at the end of the twentieth century: market access restraints by private firms closing their markets to foreign goods and services.

The US position on this issue evolved in the 1980s. As background, in the 1960s to the mid-1970s, the substantive scope of the US antitrust law had been continually expanding. In the early 1980s, the Department of Justice sought to rein in the law by providing a consumer welfare (output limiting) focus.[43] Consistent with the newly constricted scope for antitrust, in 1988,

---

from enforcement by the targeted state, see E. Fox, 'National Law, Global Markets, and *Hartford*: Eyes Wide Shut', 68 *Antitrust L.J.* 73 (2000).

The principal question in contemporary cases is whether the challenged acts plausibly cause an anticompetitive effect in the United States or on US commerce, and whether that effect is sufficiently direct and substantial. A number of contemporary cases have taken a narrow view of what constitutes a sufficiently direct effect. See e.g. *Den Norske Stats Oljeselskap AS* v. *Heeremac*, 241 F.3d 420 (5th Cir. 2001) (Sherman Act does not reach conspiracy of providers of heavy-lift barge services dividing Gulf of Mexico and North Sea markets, which caused plaintiff Norwegian oil company to pay inflated prices for barge services in the North Sea and thereby inflated prices plaintiff had to charge for crude oil exported to United States). If defendants' conduct causes direct anticompetitive effects in the United States, subject matter jurisdiction lies and is not defeated merely because plaintiff is harmed by conduct directed at a foreign market. *Kruman* v. *Christie's Int'l PLC*, 284 F. 3d 384 ((2d Cir.) 2002).

[41] See Sect. 12.7(b) infra.

[42] OECD, *Guidelines for Multinational Enterprises*, 27 June 2000, Commentary, ¶ 58.

[43] E. Fox and L. Sullivan, 'Antitrust—Retrospective and Prospective: Where Are We Coming From? Where Are We Going?', 62 *N.Y.U.L. Rev.* 936 (1987). Beginning in the early 1980s, the Department of Justice urged no antitrust intervention even against domestic conduct unless the conduct artificially limited market output in the relevant product and thus raised its price to consumers.

the Department of Justice issued Antitrust Enforcement Guidelines for International Operations[44] and, in footnote 159, stated:

[T]he Department is concerned only with adverse effects on competition that would harm US consumers by reducing output or raising prices.

The US government came to regret this limitation. By the start of the 1990s, the United States had serious market access claims against Japan, and the United States and Japan were engaged in negotiations known as the Structural Impediments Initiative in an effort to break down trade barriers to Japanese markets. American officials claimed that Japanese markets were artificially closed, and that if the barriers were not the reflection of government restraints, they must be the reflection of private restraints. The American officials suggested that if Japanese firms protected their markets by restraints that excluded American competitors, the Justice Department would seek enforcement by the Japanese Fair Trade Commission under the Japanese Antimonopoly Law; and if the Japanese authorities did nothing to eliminate the restraints, the Justice Department would sue the offending Japanese firms in the United States under the Sherman Act, as long as US courts could obtain personal jurisdiction and comity did not counsel restraint. This initiative was, of course, contrary to footnote 159, and, in 1992, the Attorney General withdrew footnote 159 from the 1988 international guidelines.[45]

In 1995 the Department of Justice and the Federal Trade Commission issued superseding *Antitrust Guidelines for International Operations* that reinforced the policy of the US antitrust authorities to sue foreign firms under the Sherman Act if they anticompetitively closed their market to US exporters.[46] The 1995 Guidelines give the following hypothetical example:

Companies E and F are the only producers of product Q in country Epsilon, one of the biggest markets for sales of Q in the world. In order to prevent a competing US producer from entering the market in Epsilon, E and F agree that neither one of them will purchase or distribute the US product, and that they will take 'all feasible' measures to keep the US company out of their market. Without specifically discussing what other measures they will take to carry out this plan, E and F meet with their distributors and, through a variety of threats and inducements, obtain agreement of all of the distributors not to carry the US product. There are no commercially feasible substitute distribution channels available to the US producer. Because of the actions of E and F, the US producer cannot find any distributors to carry its product and is unable to make any sales in Epsilon.[47]

---

[44] 4 *Trade Reg. Rep.* (CCH) ¶ 13,109.

[45] Foreign Restraints and Consumer Injury—US Policy, Trade Reg. Reports (CCH) ¶ 50,084 (3 Apr. 1992).

[46] US Department of Justice and Federal Trade Commission *Antitrust Enforcement Guidelines for International Operations*, printed at 4 *Trade Reg. Rep.* (CCH) ¶ 13,107 (1995).

[47] 1995 *International Guidelines*, Illustrative Example D.

The Guidelines state that the agreement between E and F 'would clearly have a direct and reasonably foreseeable effect on US export commerce'; the effect 'would almost certainly qualify as a substantial effect'; and the agreement would thus come within the reach of US law.

Since the 1982 cutback of the Sherman Act by the FTAIA[48] and the counterpuntal deletion of footnote 159 from the 1988 Guidelines,[49] there has been no litigated case applying the Sherman Act to foreign acts on foreign soil that close foreign markets to US exports and do not also harm US consumers buying in the US market.[50] Nonetheless, enforcers' threats to apply the Sherman Act to foreign firms that close foreign markets have fueled a new-generation critique of American extraterritoriality. Foreign market closure, it is said, is a world problem that requires a world solution; not an American problem that allows a unilateral solution.[51]

(c)   Regulating Multijurisdictional Mergers

A third problem—neither inbound nor outbound—is the problem of mergers of firms whose sales cross the borders of countries, often the borders of numerous countries. The merger problem involves both jurisdiction to require filing and clearance by national authorities, and jurisdiction to prohibit the merger or impose conditions on the merged firm.

Jurisdiction to require premerger notification of offshore mergers has apparently never been challenged in court, even where only a small stream of sales flows into the regulating nation.

Jurisdiction to prevent or condition a merger of firms where both are located abroad and an anticompetitive effect is likely to occur within the regulating jurisdiction has received only a slightly higher level of scrutiny. The United States pioneered the extension of the effects doctrine to this situation in connection with the merger of Institut Mérieux of France and Connaught of Canada. The Federal Trade Commission procured a consent

---

[48] See Sect. 12.4(a) supra.   [49] See text at nn. 44–5.

[50] See *Continental Ore*, supra n. 29, decided before the 1982 cutback. See consent decree in *Pilkington*, a case that involved defendants' reciprocal covenants to stay out of the markets of one another. Pilkington had blocked Americans from the UK market and the rest of the world other than the United States, and Pilkington agreed to stay out of the US market. *United States v. Pilkington PLC*, No. CV-94-345, 1994 WL 750645, at *2–6 (D. Ariz. 1994).

Despite the cutback by the FTAIA, a new-generation claim has been launched in antitrust consumer class actions. The claim is: In view of the increasing acceptance of the anti-cartel principle by nations around the world, and the recognition that private cartels violate the individual rights of consumers, there is now a customary international anti-cartel law. The claim continues: Even if the Sherman Act is inapplicable because of the limits imposed by the FTAIA, the US courts have jurisdiction, under the Alien Tort Claims Act, to adjudicate antitrust wrongs to foreigners harmed in foreign markets. Thus far, these claims have not been successful. See e.g. *Kruman* v. *Christie's Int'l*, 2001–1 Trade Cas. (CCH) ¶ 73,149 (S.D.N.Y. 2001) rev'd on other grounds, 284 F. 3d 384 ((2d Cir.) 2002). *In re Microsoft Corp. Antitrust Litigation*, 2001–1 Trade Cas. (CCH) ¶ 73,140 (D. Md. 2001).

[51] See Karel van Miert, 'International Cooperation in the Field of Competition: A View From the EC', ch. 2 in B. Hawk (ed.), 1997 *Fordham Corp. L. Inst.* (1998).

decree imposing conditions on the merger.[52] A decade later, the Gencor-Lonrho merger combined two South African platinum mining firms, which hold most of the world's platinum mining assets. The parent of one of the two, Lonrho, was a British firm, and its principal sales subsidiary was in Belgium. The European Commission prohibited the merger, contrary to the wishes of the South African authorities, after finding that, by reason of sales in the EU, the merger would be 'implemented' in the EU.[53] Also, in 2001, the European Commission prohibited the merger of General Electric and Honeywell, two American firms operating in world markets, after the merger had been cleared by authorities in the United States.[54]

Mergers of firms in world markets, which may or may not be anti-competitive, are clearly an international problem, not merely a national one. The traditional perspective that mergers of a nation's firms are a matter for that nation's industrial policy seems to be losing its hold in favour of a more cosmopolitan view that would take account of externalities.

Multination intervention into multinational mergers at both levels—pre-merger notification and substantive action—is treated today largely as a matter of practical politics and antitrust agency coordination, rather than jurisdictional limits on application of national law. These problems are treated further in Section 12.5(e) below.

12.5   Modern Competition Law: Substantive Rules and Principles

(a)   Overview

Most competition laws contain rules that prohibit cartels[55] and prohibit or control certain conduct of dominant firms, refusals to deal, horizontal and vertical contractual restraints, and mergers.

From the point of view of the United States, cartels are the major concern and target of antitrust law, because cartels—if they work—unambiguously harm competition, raise prices, and lower output, and they have no pro-competitive or efficiency justifications. Other antitrust systems reserve equal concern for abuses of dominance because of their potential to harm market

---

[52] *In re Institut Mérieux S.A.*, Docket No. C-3301, 113 F.T.C. 742 (FTC Consent Order, 23 Aug. 1990).

[53] *Gencor Ltd.* v. *Commission*, Case T-102/96, [1999] 5 C.M.L.R. 1076.

[54] *General Electric/Honeywell*, Case Comp/M. 2220 Commission Decision 3 July 2001, discussed further in Sect. 12.5(e) infra.

[55] As defined herein, cartels are agreements among competitors to lessen the competition among them. This is typically done by price-fixing, bid-rigging, allocating customers or territories, assigning quotas, or a combination of these devices. Such collaborations are also called hard-core cartels. In Europe, the word 'cartel' is sometimes used more broadly for all private firm collaborations.

actors unfairly. The European Community system and the many countries that follow its model share this concern.

Competition may also be harmed by acts of monopolization and attempts to monopolize (a category that may include abuses of dominance); by agreements among competitors or potential competitors that are not cartels but that create or facilitate the use of market power; by mergers, acquisitions, alliances, and other joint ventures that create or facilitate the use of market power; and, more rarely, by agreements between a buyer and a supplier, which are classified as vertical restraints.

The word 'competition' has different meanings in the competition laws of different jurisdictions, and states have different conceptions about what constitutes 'harm to competition', or 'lessening of competition'. In the United States, lessening of, or harm to, competition is found when the conduct or transaction creates, will probably create, or increase economic power in a relevant market to the detriment of buyers.[56] The harm normally reveals itself in lower output and in higher prices to buyers and ultimate consumers. It may also reveal itself in lessened innovation in highly concentrated, high-barrier markets to the detriment of buyers and ultimate consumers; but there is no consensus on this point and there is uncertainty as to analytical guideposts.

Historically, US antitrust law had defined harm to competition much more broadly than consumer harm though price rises. For example, mergers of significant competitors that tended to concentrate fragmented markets were regarded as anticompetitive; and exclusive distribution agreements or uses of leverage that foreclosed competitors from opportunities to compete were for that reason regarded as anticompetitive. In the early 1980s, the 'consumer welfare' paradigm was introduced to confine the scope of the US antitrust laws.[57]

Other systems for the protection of competition have somewhat different points of focus. In the European Union, for example, the case law on abuse of dominance often has reference to behaviour that 'unlevels the playing field', and to acts by dominant firms that exclude, coerce, or exploit weaker firms or create market hurdles for the flow of goods or investment across national borders. Law and policy statements refer to protecting market actors as well as consumers, and preserving the freedom to trade across state lines.

(b) Cartels and Boycotts

Cartels are agreements among competitors to lessen the competition among them. In the United States, the most common form of cartel is the price-fixing

---

[56] Conversely, the harm could be to suppliers where buyers exert economic power against suppliers, as in a buyers' cartel.

[57] See E. Fox, 'Chairman Miller, The Federal Trade Commission, Economics, and Rashomon', 50 *Law & Contemp. Probs.* 33, 37 (1987); E. Fox and L. Sullivan, 'Antitrust—Retrospective and Prospective: Where Are We Coming From? Where Are We Going?', 62 *N.Y.U.L. Rev.* 936, 946–7 (1987).

agreement. In the early days of the European Community as the Member States were removing the border restraints in the internal market, the most common form of cartel was market-division—re-erecting barriers at Member State borders. Enterprises did not welcome the flow of foreign goods into 'their' territories. Early cartels re-established national markets for quinine, dyestuffs, cement, and sugar, and the EC authorities undertook to end the agreements.[58] Similarly, liberalization in Japan may have triggered private restraints in glass, automobiles and auto parts, and photographic film.[59] This history holds lessons for the world: liberalization of trade tends to induce market actors to protect their markets by private restraints.

Private cartels are illegal, or illegal subject to defenses, in virtually every jurisdiction that has an antitrust law. Some jurisdictions allow, as justifications, the need to counteract a crisis or depression or serve some other public interest. All jurisdictions have exceptions and immunities; some more than others.

Under US law, cartels are illegal *per se*. That is, competitors who agree to fix prices or divide markets have no affirmative defense under law. They cannot escape the consequences by proof that they had no market power, that the cartel had no effect, that the cartel would ease a market crisis, depression, or other market failure, that the prices fixed were reasonable, or that government officials knew of and even encouraged their plan.[60] Moreover, the legal consequences of the cartel offense are severe, as described in Section 12.6(a).

In the European Union, cartels come within Article 81 of the Treaty of Rome, which declares that anticompetitive agreements are incompatible with the common market and void unless exempted. Regulation 17 gives the exempting power solely to the Commission. (Pending legislation to replace Regulation 17 would substantially revise the procedure.)[61] Exemptions are not normally granted to cartels, but the Commission has on rare occasions granted a limited exemption in cases of a crisis of structural overcapacity where the problem might be solved by cooperation to reduce excess capacity.[62] No price-fixing is allowed.

Cartels are often accompanied by boycotts to keep non-members from flooding the market with cheaper goods, thereby undermining the cartel.

[58] For excerpts from and analyses of these cases, see Bermann, Goebel, Davey, and Fox, *Cases and Materials on European Community Law*, 653–73 (1993).

[59] For the controversy about photographic film distribution in Japan, the governmental aspects of which were brought before a WTO dispute panel, see the *Kodak-Fuji* case, discussed in Ch. 8, Sect. 8.8(b). The private restraint (antitrust) aspects were never adjudicated. The law as presently constituted provides no forum for addressing as a whole an interrelated public and private restraint.

[60] *United States* v. *Socony-Vacuum Oil Co.*, 310 U.S. 150 (1940).

[61] A pending proposal for modernization would abolish the notification procedure and grant exemption powers to Member State competition authorities and courts.

[62] See e.g. *Stichting Baksteen* (Dutch brick-makers), Commission Dec. IV/34.456, [1994] 2 CEC 2051.

Boycotts by competitors against competitors or potential competitors to keep firms out of the market and thus to protect the incumbents are illegal under US and EC law and the law of almost all jurisdictions. If an underlying cartel is not found, the plaintiff may be required to prove, as a constituent part of a boycott violation, that the boycotting competitors have market power and that the concerted refusal to deal is not a mere by-product of a productive joint venture or other collaboration.[63]

Proving the existence of a cartel is often daunting, and especially so in a globalized world. While cartel members sometimes leave their footprints in the sand, and sister antitrust agencies sometimes cooperate to provide evidence from the scene of the offense,[64] at other times there are no footprints at all, key witnesses from abroad elude process,[65] and plaintiffs are forced to rely on whatever inferences can be drawn from circumstantial evidence. Circumstantial evidence often falls short.[66] Sometimes an industry is so highly concentrated and has such established patterns of interdependent behaviour that the few market participants can behave non-competitively without the need for an agreement, and the interdependent pricing behaviour can slip through an antitrust crack.[67]

Nonetheless, the United States Justice Department has been highly successful in proving world cartels and winning multimillion dollar fines and prison terms, as it has done in the cases of vitamins and animal feed.[68]

(c)   Monopolization and Abuse of Dominance

The monopolization offense under US law requires proof that the defendant has monopoly power and that it has wilfully acquired or maintained its monopoly by anticompetitive acts.

---

[63] See *Northwest Wholesale Stationers, Inc.* v. *Pacific Stationery and Printing Co.*, 472 U.S. 284 (1985) (*per se* boycott rule applies only if defendants have market power). Cf. *NYNEX Corp.* v. *Discon, Inc.*, 525 U.S. 128, 136 (1998) (*per se* boycott rule applies only to refusals to deal by combination of two or more competitors); *FTC* v. *Superior Court Trial Lawyers Assoc.*, 493 U.S. 411 (1990) (boycott in support of cartel is illegal *per se*).

[64] See e.g. *United States* v. *Nippon Paper Industries Co. Ltd.*, 109 F.3d 1 (1st Cir. 1997), cert. denied, 522 U.S. 1044 (1998).

[65] See e.g. *United States* v. *General Electric Co.* (industrial diamonds), 869 F. Supp. 1285 (S.D. Ohio 1994).

[66] See *Matsushita Electric Industrial Co.* v. *Zenith Radio Corp.*, 475 U.S. 574 (1986); Case C-89/85 etc., *Åhlström Osakeyhtiö* v. *Commission (Woodpulp)*, [1993] ECR I–1307.

[67] See e.g. *Woodpulp*, id.; *Blomkest Fertilizer, Inc.* v. *Potash Corp.*, 203 F.3d 1028 (8th Cir.), cert. denied, 531 U.S. 815 (2000); *Baby Food Antitrust Litigation*, 166 F.3d 112 (3d Cir. 1999).

[68] See e.g. *Wall Street Journal*, 21 May 1999, p. A3, 'Vitamin Firms to Pay U.S. $725 million' (settling US Justice Department price-fixing suit); id., 9 June 1999, p. B9D, 'Global Markets push Swiss Companies to Rework their Corporate Culture'; id., 4 Nov. 1999, p. A3, 'Vitamin-Firm Accord to Pay $1.17 billion' (seven of the world's largest vitamin makers settling class-action lawsuit in US); id. 8 May 2000, p. C32, 'Firms in Germany, US Plead Guilty in Vitamin Cases' (summarizing results of 24 prosecutions by US government against participants in international vitamin cartels).

It has sometimes been suggested that it may be illegal to achieve and maintain monopoly status, even without anticompetitive acts by the monopolist. That is not the case under current interpretations of law. Even monopoly firms are encouraged to compete and to engage in hard competition, even though that might mean the demise of smaller firms.

Challenges under the monopoly law have often involved claims of predatory pricing and exclusionary acts or agreements such as tying, exclusive dealing, and refusals to deal. Predatory pricing claims are seldom successful because the policy of the law favours low pricing and reflects the concern that price competition—even by a monopolist—not be chilled. Therefore the plaintiff in a predatory pricing case is required to prove that defendant priced below its costs (usually marginal or average variable costs) and if not restrained would be likely to destroy the competitors, raise prices without inviting new entry, and enjoy a higher monopoly price at least long enough to recoup its investment in predation, including interest on the profits foregone.

In challenging exclusive dealing that forecloses competitors from a part of the market, plaintiffs must normally show exclusion from critical inputs or outlets such that the competitors are deprived of efficiencies and prices to consumers will rise. The monopolist may defend that the exclusive dealing arrangement was efficient for it and its customers, and that the agreement or practice helped consumers rather than hurting them.

Tying involves conditioning the sale of a desired product on the purchase of another product; e.g. to buy my computer you must buy my software. Illegal tying by a dominant firm is somewhat easier to prove than illegal exclusive dealing because it is subject to a modified *per se* rule: plaintiffs prevail upon proof that defendant had significant market power over the tying product, that it used this power to force buyers to accept a separate tied product, and that the tie involves a not insignificant dollar amount of commerce. This modified *per se* rule dispenses with the need to prove that competition in the tied product market is harmed. The rule is under attack for exactly this reason; tie-ins do not necessarily harm competition in the price-raising sense, even though they may shift market share to a firm with power. Accordingly, some courts seem willing to hear and weigh defendants' arguments that the tie was efficient and that it did not raise or threaten to raise consumer prices, i.e. that it did not cause competitive harm. Willingness to adopt a rule more sympathetic to the tying defendant is especially evident in the case of technological ties, as in the case of bundling a browser with an operating system.[69]

---

[69] In the case of a technological tie, the bundled elements might be seen as one product. See *United States* v. *Microsoft Corp.*, 147 F.3d 935 (D.C. Cir. 1998) (interpreting 1995 consent decree). In the later plenary *Microsoft* case, the Court of Appeals held that packaging applications with platform software must be analysed under a rule of reason. *United States* v. *Microsoft Corp.*, 253 F.3d 34 (D.C. Cir.), cert. denied, 122 S.Ct. 350 (2001).

Normally, in the United States, a monopolist has no duty to deal[70] except in the rare case in which the monopolist controls an essential facility. A facility is essential if competitors cannot feasibly duplicate the facility and they need access to the facility in order to compete. For example, in telecommunications, access by long-distance service providers to the local service loop is essential. If the monopolist can give access without undermining its own business needs, then it has the duty to do so (for which it may charge a fee).

A monopoly case under Section 2 of the Sherman Act is most likely to succeed when the plaintiff is able to prove that the monopoly firm undertook a pattern of conduct that had no purpose or effect other than to raise rivals' costs and thereby hurt consumers. The challenge will fail if defendant shows that it was merely responding to the market and to consumers, trying to give consumers what they need or want, and doing so at a lower price.

Under US law, the attempt-to-monopolize violation requires anticompetitive conduct, a dangerous probability that conduct will produce monopoly, and specific intent to do so. Again, to qualify as anticompetitive, the conduct must threaten harm to consumers.

The European Union's equivalent to monopolization is abuse of dominance in violation of Article 82 of the Treaty of Rome. The EU perspective takes account of consumer harm but also takes account of the rights of excluded competitors. The Commission and Court tend to find abuses of dominance when competitors are foreclosed from significant segments of the market, excluded by a tie-in (even though the tied product market is competitive), or hurt by fidelity rebates or by a below-cost price (even if recoupment of lost profits through later monopoly overcharges is unlikely).[71] Moreover, dominance under EC law seems to require less market power than monopoly under US law, and the EC case law is less demanding of economic proof. A firm may be dominant at a 40 percent market share and upwards, as long as it can act without significant regard to competitors and customers.[72]

(d) Vertical Restraints

1. Vertical Restraints in General

Vertical restraints are restraints imposed in the course of the distribution of a product or service. They include restraints imposed by manufacturers on

[70] The right to refuse to deal may be reinforced by ownership of intellectual property that is the subject of the refusal. See *Independent Service Organizations Antitrust Litigation* (Xerox), 203 F.3d 1322 (Fed. Cir. 2000), cert. denied, 531 U.S. 1143 (2001); but compare *Image Technical Services* v. *Eastman Kodak Co.*, 125 F.3d 1195 (9th Cir. 1997), cert. denied, 523 U.S. 1094 (1998).

[71] See e.g. *Akzo Chemie BV* v. *Commission*, Case C-62/86, [1991] ECR I-3359, [1993] 5 C.M.L.R. 215.

[72] See e.g. *Hoffmann-La Roche* v. *Commission*, Case 85/76, [1979] ECR 461, 3 C.M.L.R. 211 (1978-9).

distributors that confine where, to whom, and at what price the distributor may resell. They include, also, exclusive dealing, requirements contracts, and tie-in contracts, which may have exclusionary effects on strangers to the contract.

In the 1960s and early 1970s, United States law broadly condemned vertical restraints on grounds that they lessened the autonomy of dealers and foreclosed firms from the economic opportunity to supply significant customers and market segments.[73] This aspect of the law was sympathetically received in developing countries, where firms protested against the practice of multinational enterprises to invest in domestic fabricators and distributors and to impose on them covenants not to export their product to countries in which the multinational enterprise had other fabricating and distribution affiliates.[74] Market actors in developing countries invoked US law against US multinationals, and sometimes were successful.

But by the middle to end of the 1970s, the US law began to shift away from protection of dealer autonomy and economic opportunity. In a watershed decision, *Continental T.V. Inc.* v. *GTE Sylvania*,[75] the Supreme Court reversed earlier precedent. It declared that the US antitrust law must be driven by economic, not social or political, concerns; and it observed that vertical restraints may be efficient and thereby enhance interbrand competition, which, it said, ought to be the concern of the law.[76]

Since *Sylvania*, decisions of the US Supreme Court have continued to narrow the universe of prohibited vertical restraints. In the area of vertical distribution restraints, only resale price maintenance (minimum vertical price-fixing) remains illegal *per se*. This is so because resale price maintenance may facilitate cartels of competitors and possibly because it may aid unilateral exploitation. All other restraints on wholesalers or retailers as to where, to whom, and at what price to sell are subject to a rule of reason, and they are rarely found to be unreasonable because they generally do not cause consumer prices to rise and they often create efficiencies such as preventing discounters from free-riding on full service providers.[77]

Exclusive dealing agreements are likewise presumptively lawful, because they are deemed likely to be a means to capture efficiencies. Tying agreements, as noted, are subject to a modified *per se* rule, but this rule may erode in favour of market- effect analysis. Tying and exclusive dealing can have net

---

[73] The leading case was *United States* v. *Arnold, Schwinn & Co.*, 388 U.S. 365 (1967), overruled by the *Sylvania* case cited below.

[74] See E. Fox, 'Harnessing the Multinational Corporation to Enhance Third World Development—The Rise and Fall and Future of Antitrust as Regulator', 10 *Cardozo L. Rev.* 1981 (1989).

[75] 433 U.S. 36 (1977).

[76] Efficiency can be stated in terms of firm efficiency (lower firm costs, better responsiveness of the firm to customers), or in terms of market efficiency (lower market prices for given quality levels, better responsiveness to all customers).

[77] This assumes that the agreement is purely vertical and does not reflect or include an agreement among competitors.

negative effects if they fence off so much of the market that not even a few efficient-sized competitors can survive or can bring their products to market efficiently. In such cases, consumer prices are likely to rise and the practice is likely to be found to be illegal under a market-based rule of reason.

European law on vertical distribution restraints is more complicated. Vertical minimum resale price-fixing is caught by Article 81(1) and is not likely to receive an exemption under Article 81(3). (Thus, on this point, US and EC law coincide.) Absolute territorial distribution restraints at Member States' borders are clear offenses of the law, and they are the worst kind of offense because they prevent the free flow of goods across state frontiers within the Community.[78] Other distribution restraints are forbidden or permitted under rules provided by block exemption regulations (see Section 12.6(b)). As for foreclosing restraints such as exclusive dealing and tying (when they are not placed in a safe harbour by the block exemption), EC law is concerned with unjustified impediments to market access. It condemns restraints, especially by dominant firms, with significant exclusionary effects, but exempts vertical restraints (other than hard-core restraints, i.e. minimum and fixed resale price agreements and territorial restraints that partition national markets) when the parties' share is not more than 30 percent of the market.[79]

2. *Licenses of Intellectual Property*

Many of the international cartels before and during World War II involved patent pools and networks of cross-licensing that were actually covers for the cartels. Beyond this clear misuse of intellectual property rights, there is a tension between free trade and open markets on the one hand, and exclusive rights to exploit an invention or other intellectual creation on the other.[80] Nearly all developed countries, including the United States and the Member States of the European Union, have concluded that protection of intellectual property provides desirable incentives to creativity and economic growth, but that care must be taken that the legal monopoly conferred by patents, trademarks, and similar rights are not used beyond the government grant of rights to stifle competition.

In the 1960s and 1970s in the United States, and the 1970s and 1980s in the European Community, the owner of intellectual property was characterized as a monopolist and faced significant constraints on its licensing activity. In the United States, prohibitory rules were summarized in a speech

---

[78] The early leading decision of the Court of Justice on this issue, upholding the European Commission, was *Consten and Grundig* v. *Commission*, Cases 56, 68/64, [1966] ECR 299, [1966] C.M.L.R. 418, prohibiting efforts by the French licensee of the German manufacturer to restrain parallel imports into France from Germany.

[79] Commission Regulation 2790/99 of 22 Dec. 1999, O.J. L 336/21 (29 Dec. 1999). See also the Commission's Guidelines on Vertical Restraints, OJ C 291, 13 Oct. 2000, 0001–0044.

[80] Compare the discussion of the place of the TRIPs Agreement in the Uruguay Round, Ch. 5, Sect. 5.6(b).

in 1970 entitled 'The Nine No-Nos'[81]—a phrase that became a symbol for the prohibitory nature of the law. An owner or licensor of a patent, for example, was categorically enjoined not to tie, not to require grant backs, and not to charge royalties after the patent expired.

Beginning in the 1980s, the presumptions that lay at the foundation of the categorical prohibitions were reversed. Intellectual property rights came to be regarded with deference rather than suspicion. Inventiveness was seen as the driving force that would make American business more competitive in the global economy. Antitrust policy shifted to give firms freer rein to exploit their intellectual property. In 1981 the Nine No-Nos were withdrawn.[82]

In 1995 the US Department of Justice and the Federal Trade Commission issued *Antitrust Guidelines for the Licensing of Intellectual Property*.[83] The *Guidelines*, state three general principles (§2):

(a) for the purpose of antitrust analysis, the Agencies regard intellectual property as being essentially comparable to any other form of property;

(b) the Agencies do not presume that intellectual property creates market power in the antitrust context; and

(c) the Agencies recognize that intellectual property licensing allows firms to combine complementary factors of production and is generally procompetitive.

Antitrust concerns might arise, the *Guidelines*, state, 'when a licensing arrangement harms competition among entities that would have been actual or likely potential competitors in a relevant market in the absence of the license'; for example, by dividing markets or combining the research and development activities of two of the only few entities that could possibly engage in the activity (§3.1).

In the European Union an additional element comes into play: free movement of goods across Member State lines. Intellectual property protection is often pitted against free movement and competition concerns and is often subordinated to those concerns. The practical consequences are complicated by the fact that patent protection in the Member States varies. For instance, in a much discussed case, the Court of Justice held that the holder of a Dutch patent on a pharmaceutical product could not prevent importation of the product into the Netherlands by someone who had purchased the product in Italy, where pharmaceuticals were not subject to patent protection.[84]

---

[81] See Bruce B. Wilson, 'Patent and Know-How License Agreements: Field of Use, Territorial, Price and Quantity Restrictions', Address before the Fourth New England Antitrust Conference (6 Nov. 1970).

[82] See remarks of Abbott Lipsky, *Antitrust and Trade Regulation Report*, No. (1039)A-9 (1981).

[83] US Department of Justice, 6 Apr. 1995. The guidelines are not law. They state the enforcement policy of the agencies that issue them. To a large extent they reflect what the law is, and they usually reflect what the agency believes the law, or mode of analysis, should be.

[84] *Merck & Co.* v. *Stephar BV*, Case 187/80, [1981] ECR 2063, [1981] 3 CMLR 417.

In 1984, the European Commission issued a regulation granting a group exemption from Article 85 (now 81) for qualifying patent licenses.[85] A regulation was issued in 1989 directed to know-how licensing agreements, and the regulations were consolidated and modified by a regulation issued in 1996.[86] The 1996 regulation applies only to agreements between two firms. It contains a 'white list' of permissible clauses, including clauses that bar the licensee from divulging know-how, from sublicensing, and from exploiting the patent after termination of the agreement, and that require non-exclusive grant-backs on improvements.[87] The regulation also contains a black list of prohibited clauses. The parties may not restrict price, quantity of goods that may be manufactured, competition between the licensee and the licensor, or division of customers if the licensor and the licensee were competitors prior to the license.[88] If an agreement contains a provision that is neither expressly permitted nor expressly prohibited, the parties may notify the agreement to the Commission. If the Commission does not oppose an exemption within four months, the agreement will be considered exempt. (We note, again, that the exemption procedure and the Commission's monopoly over it is expected to be substantially revised. A simplified technology block exemption is expected not to contain a white list or opposition procedure.)

Both the United States regulatory authorities and courts and the European Commission and courts continue to wrestle with the interface between intellectual property and antitrust. The European authorities have shown somewhat less reluctance than American authorities to privilege competition protection over intellectual property protection.[89]

(e) Mergers

In the 1960s and early 1970s, the US merger law was interpreted, faithfully to its spirit, to favour diversity and pluralism and to disfavour concentration of assets and power in the hands of few firms. In the 1980s the federal agencies adopted a new perspective, and the courts followed. The law was interpreted to favour mergers, or at least not to stand in their way, unless they could be proved likely to raise consumer prices. The underlying question became: does this merger create or enhance market power or facilitate its

---

[85] Commission Regulation 2349/84 of 23 July 1984 on the Application of Art. 85(3) of the Treaty to Certain Categories of Patent Licensing Agreements, O.J. L 219/15 (16 Aug. 1984).

[86] Commission Regulation (EC) No. 240/96 of 31 Jan. 1996 on the application of Art. 85(3) of the Treaty to Certain Categories of Technology Transfer Agreements, O.J. L 31/2 (9 Feb. 1996) (soon to be replaced).

[87] Id., Art. 2.   [88] Id., Art. 3.

[89] Compare *Radio Telefis Eireann* v. *Commission (Magill)*, Cases C-241/91P and C-242/91P, [1995] ECR I–743 with *Independent Service Organizations Antitrust Litigation (Xerox)*, 203 F.3d 1322 (Fed. Cir. 2000), cert. denied, 121 S.Ct. 1077 (2001); but as to US law, compare the *Xerox* case with *Image Technical Services* v. *Eastman Kodak Co.*, 125 F.3d 1195 (9th Cir. 1997), cert. denied, 523 U.S. 1094 (1998).

exercise? Higher consumer prices are the usual indicia of these effects.[90] For lack of evidence of price-raising effects, American authorities have cleared such huge mergers as Exxon–Mobil (oil), Bell Atlantic–NYNEX (telecoms), Daimler–Chrysler (motor vehicles), Boeing–McDonnell Douglas (commercial jet aircraft), General Electric–Honeywell (jet engines and avionics), and AOL–Time Warner (communications, media, and Internet).

As in all antitrust issues other than cartels and resale price maintenance agreements (the *per se* offenses), market definition is a critical element of merger analysis. In general, a market is the smallest product and geographic area capable of being monopolized. The market is capable of being monopolized where, if only one firm produced the relevant product in the relevant geographic area, it could profitably raise its price to a supracompetitive level and maintain that price without fear that competing sellers would enter or expand in the market, or fear that buyers would shift their purchases to other goods, beating back the price to a competitive (or the pre-merger) level.

As for Europe, in 1989 the Council finally adopted a Merger Regulation, after years of debate often involving national industrial policy. The Merger Regulation requires pre-merger notification of proposed mergers to the Commission if the combined turnover of the parties exceeds a stated threshold, and provides for possible prohibition by the Commission.[91] The Merger Regulation prohibits concentrations that create or enhance dominance as a result of which effective competition would be significantly impeded. For nearly the first decade of European merger control, the EU 'dominance' standard was significantly narrower than the US 'lessening of competition' standard. Recent European decisions, however, have construed the Merger Regulation to cover 'collective dominance' and thereby address the duopoly and oligopoly problem.[92] Even so, US and European analyses are not always uniform, with US courts requiring, and often being more demanding of, economic proof of the likelihood that the merger will cause a rise in prices.

Differences occur in part because the European merger law is not driven solely by a consumer welfare paradigm. The EC merger law, like the EC law on abuse of dominance, is designed in part to protect rights of access to markets.

---

[90] Eliminating a significant source of technological innovation in a highly concentrated market may be deemed anticompetitive.

[91] Council Regulation 4064/89, O.J. L 395 (30 Dec. 1989, corrected O.J. L 257/14 (21 Sept. 1990), amended by Council Regulation No. 1310/97 of 30 June 1997, O.J. L 180 (9 July 1997).

[92] Joined Cases C-68/94 & C-30/95, *French Republic Société Commerciale des Potasses et de L'Azote (SCPA)* and *Enterprise Minière et Chimique (EMC)* v. *Commission (Kali und Salz)*, [1998] ECR I 1375, 4 C.M.L.R. 829; Case T-102/96, *Gencor Limited* v. *Commission* (Germany intervening), [1999] 4 C.M.L.R. 971 (CFI); *Air Tours* v. *Commission*, case T-342/99 (6 June 2002 (CFI)).

Boeing/McDonnell Douglas is an example. Probably in connection with acquiring its jet aircraft competitor McDonnell Douglas, Boeing entered into contracts with three large American airlines to be their exclusive supplier of commercial jet airplanes for twenty years. The European Commission saw the exclusive contracts as an emanation of Boeing's increased dominance (its share of the commercial jet aircraft market would increase to about 70 percent upon purchase of McDonnell Douglas), and feared that the contracts would unfairly foreclose the European consortium, Airbus Industrie, Boeing's only remaining competitor, from access to a substantial part of the market. The US Federal Trade Commission closed its investigation of the merger on grounds that McDonnell Douglas was in a weak innovation position and could no longer compete in sales of future generation aircraft. The European Commission, while agreeing with this assessment, permitted the merger to proceed only on the condition that Boeing forego the exclusivity of the contracts and share technology of McDonnell Douglas that had been subsidized by the US government.[93]

In another high profile case, as noted above, General Electric sought in 2000–1 to acquire Honeywell, a transaction that would have combined two American companies, one a leading producer of jet aircraft engines, the other a leading producer of avionic products and navigation equipment, all purchased by aircraft makers or airlines. General Electric was also one of the world's largest purchasers of aircraft (it bought about ten percent), and one of the world's largest aircraft leasing companies. Also, General Electric was an important financer and launch customer for new models. The US Department of Justice cleared the merger upon the firms' undertaking to spin off overlapping assets. The European Commission, however, prohibited the merger on the grounds that it would lead to bundling of products and would steer business away from single-line competitors, eventually pressuring them to exit the market.[94]

Merger law presents two distinct problems in the international arena. One is the set of problems that results when two or more jurisdictions apply their sometimes different standards to the same transaction and produce different results. The second is the set of problems that results when numerous states (or the EU)—apply their varying premerger notification and clearance provisions to the same transaction, imposing high transaction costs.[95]

---

[93] For the suggestion that the European Union's opposition to the merger was driven by politics, not by competition policy, and a reply thereto by the present authors, see *Wall Street Journal* editorial 'A "Dangerous" Merger,' 21 July 1997, p. A22, and letter to the Editor 'Boeing Affair's Valuable Lessons', 5 Aug. 1997, p. A19. See also E. Fox, 'The United States of Boeing versus the European Union of Airbus', 16 *Brookings Rev.* 30 (Winter 1998).

[94] *General Electric/Honeywell*, Case Comp/M. 2220 (Commission Decision) 3 July 2001.

[95] The same problem can occur when jurisdictions applying the same standard reach different results. In *General Electric/Honeywell*, one ground of the prohibition by the EU was the prediction that the merger would raise prices. The United States authorities concluded that the merger did not threaten to raise prices.

The first set of problems may raise questions of jurisdiction to prescribe and the appropriate exercise of such jurisdiction, including remedies. In practice, it seems accepted today that any state whose citizens or domestic markets are threatened with significant antitrust harm has a proper interest in applying its merger law even to an offshore merger of firms with no assets in the forum state.[96] Challenges for policy-makers include coordinating merger analysis and enforcement, devising rules of priority in the case of clashes and limits to conflicting relief, and imposing limits on a substantive standard that allows 'national champion' interests to trump competition concerns.

Some experts propose rationalization of premerger clearance requirements.[97] For example, nations could agree to waive prior clearance rights where the potential impact of the merger within their market would be minor as compared with its potential impact in states vetting the merger, unless there is a separate, distinct market effect within the regulating nation.[98] Nations could agree to a common clearing house for multiple merger notifications, or to mutual recognition of merger notifications with rights to codicils for nation-specific problems.[99]

(f) Joint Ventures and Alliances

Joint ventures are agreements between firms to engage in a specific joint activity, often through the creation of a jointly owned and controlled subsidiary, to perform a task useful to both or to realize synergies from the parents' contributions. Joint ventures may, for example, produce commonly needed inputs, fabricate commonly produced outputs, or combine expertise for research and development.

Alliances are a form of joint venture. The term is often used for joint endeavours by firms in different geographic markets. The alliance helps each partner penetrate the market of the other. Many telecom and airline collaborations are alliances.

Joint venture analysis follows the usual analytical framework. Sometimes there are grounds for suspicion that the venture is a cover for a cartel, i.e. for price-fixing or market division. But if the collaboration is *bona fide*—i.e. to do a new job or to do an old one better—it has procompetitive aspects. The questions are whether the venture also creates or enhances market power and whether it entails overly restrictive ancillary agreements, and if so whether the benefits can be achieved by apparent less anticompetitive means.

[96] See E. Fox, 'Extraterritoriality and the Merger Law: Can All Nations Rule the World?', *Antitrust Report*, Dec. 1999, p. 2 (Matthew Bender).

[97] See e.g. *Policy Directions for Global Merger Review, A Special Report by the Global Forum for Competition and Trade Policy* (1999).

[98] See *Report of International Competition Policy Advisory Committee to the Attorney General and Assistant Attorney General for Antitrust* (ICPAC) (2000).

[99] See E. Fox, *Separate Statement*, ICPAC Report, Annex 1-A.

(g) Other Collaborations among Competitors

Competitors may collaborate loosely (i.e. not through merger or joint venture) in various ways. They may, for example, exchange information, participate in trade association decisions, agree on standards, and form buying or selling groups, including business-to-business platforms on the Internet. All of these practices could produce efficiencies that inure to the benefit of consumers; but all of them could be conspiracies against consumers or entail risks to them. If the collaborations are designed to exploit consumers and evidence a cartel, they are illegal. If there is no cartel, the analyst must define the market, assess the participants' market power, consider all power-creating and efficiency-enhancing aspects, and consider whether the behaviour is so likely to dampen rivalry that it should not be tolerated (e.g. competitors' sharing of proposed future prices or sensitive cost information). If the gravamen of the collaboration is better market performance (good business reasons), courts do not lightly second-guess the business decision; but still, if the anticompetitive effects ostensibly outbalance the procompetitive effects, the collaboration is likely to constitute an unreasonable restraint and fall afoul of the Sherman Act.[100]

(h) Government Action Defenses

Governments are, in theory, the keepers of the public interest, and may sometimes decide that competition is not in the public interest. When a government replaces competition within its borders with public or private regulation, it does so presumably because the political community as a whole gains more than it loses. Trade-restraining government action may, however, be a concession or pay-back to powerful interest groups.

A special problem arises when government exemptions or immunities cause harms to people outside of the electorate.

Under US law, the government action defenses are organized into the following categories:

(1) *State action defense.* Private conduct is shielded by the state action defense if (i) a state (of the United States), by clear articulation, replaces competition with regulation or with restraints that have foreseeably anticompetitive aspects, and (ii) the state actively supervises the private conduct.[101]

---

[100] See *California Dental Ass'n* v. *FTC*, 526 U.S. 756, 775 n.12, 776–8 (1999) (rejecting the claim that a court or agency may infer anticompetitive effects from professional associations' restrictions on discount advertising, and requiring a plaintiff to introduce empirical evidence of price-raising, output-limiting effects).

[101] e.g. *California Retail Liquor Dealers Ass'n* v. *Midcal Aluminum, Inc.*, 445 U.S. 97 (1980), which expresses the modern formulation of a doctrine that originated with *Parker* v. *Brown*, 317 U.S. 341 (1943).

(2) *Petitioning-government (Noerr-Pennington) defense.*[102] There is a right to petition and lobby for government action, even by competitors in combination with one another, even though the competitors' sole intent is to eliminate the competition, and even though the petitioning is carried out by fraudulent means. The defense does not apply if the petitioning activity is a mere sham to cover up a conspiracy; for example, a pattern of baseless lawsuits the mere pendency of which is designed to and likely to delay or abort would-be competitors' entry.

(3) *Act of State defense.*[103] This is a doctrine of judicial abstention based on separation of powers and considerations of comity. Pursuant to this doctrine courts generally decline to examine public acts of a foreign state taken within its territory on matters pertaining to its sovereignty. Primarily invoked in the context of expropriation, the act of state doctrine has also been invoked in the context of antitrust. In a 1981 decision in a lawsuit against the Organization of the Petroleum Exporting Countries (OPEC), the court invoked the act of state doctrine in refusing to adjudicate antitrust claims against the OPEC cartel, even though the OPEC countries made most of their agreements to limit production and fix prices outside of their territories and substantial purchases of oil were made in the United States.[104] When private defendants' conduct can be judged without exploring the motives of the foreign government or questioning the foreign sovereign act, the act of state doctrine has generally not provided a successful defense.[105]

(4) *Foreign Sovereign Immunity defense.* Foreign sovereigns taking action in their sovereign, not commercial, capacity are immune from suit.[106]

---

[102] The defense gets it name from two cases in which concerted activity seeking to influence government action was held not prohibited by the Sherman Act, on grounds that Congress did not intend to regulate political activity and presumably did not wish to undermine the constitutional right of petition. *Eastern Railroad President's Conference* v. *Noerr Motor Freight, Inc.*, 365 U.S. 127 (1961); *United Mine Workers of America* v. *Pennington*, 381 U.S. 657 (1965).

[103] For more on the Act of State doctrine, in the context of international investment and expropriation, see Ch. 14, Sect. 14.3(b).

[104] *International Association of Machinists and Aerospace Workers (IAM)* v. *Organization of the Petroleum Exporting Countries (OPEC)*, 649 F.2d 1354, 1361 (9th Cir.), cert. denied, 454 U.S. 1163 (1981). For a concise explanation of the act of state doctrine with sources, see *ALI Restatement of the Foreign Relations Law of the United States* §443 (1987). The antitrust cases are collected in id. Reporters' n. 7, and in *US Department of Justice and Federal Trade Commission Antitrust Enforcement Guidelines for International Operations* (1995), point 3.3, printed in 4 *Trade Reg. Rep.* (CCH) ¶13,107.

[105] See e.g. *Timberlane Lumber Co.* v. *Bank of America National Trust & Savings Association*, 549 F. 2d 597 (9th Cir. 1976). But see *Trugman-Nash, Inc.* v. *New Zealand Dairy Board*, 954 F. Supp. 733 (S.D.N.Y. 1997) (shielding dairy board's export cartel).

[106] The Foreign Sovereign Immunities Act was held to shield a state-owned enterprise (France Telecom) from antitrust liability for refusing to share with a French seller of marketing data the list of persons named in French telephone directories who disallow use of their names for marketing purposes. The challenged commercial activity did not have a substantial connection with or direct effect in the United States, as required for jurisdiction under the commercial activity exception to the FSIA. *Filetech S.A.* v. *France Telecom, S.A.*, 2002-2 CCH Trade Cas. ¶73,800, 2002 U.S. App. LEXIS 18627 (2d Cir. 2002).

(5) *Foreign sovereign compulsion defense.* Private action is protected from US antitrust scrutiny if it is compelled by a foreign sovereign and takes place in the foreign state. Attempts to rely on the foreign compulsion defense in antitrust actions in the United States have generally not been successful.[107]

These doctrines were developed for a more nationally contained world, and for a world in which competition was not a shared culture and was often a hostile one.[108] Deference to a cartel on a trading partner's territory was then an acceptable modus operandi. In a world of global market competition, freer trade, the shrinking sovereign state, and the continuous growth of the antitrust 'family of nations', some or all of these principles may be open to reconsideration.[109]

12.6   ENFORCEMENT OF COMPETITION LAW

(a)   The United States

1. *The Justice Department and the Federal Trade Commission*

The US federal antitrust laws may be enforced by the government and by private parties. Two arms of the federal government have responsibility for antitrust enforcement—the Department of Justice, an executive branch department headed by a member of the President's cabinet, and the Federal Trade Commission, an independent regulatory agency, not subject to instruction by the executive branch.

---

[107] But see *Trugman-Nash*, n. 105 supra. US courts have been careful not to order foreign defendants to perform acts in their own territory forbidden by the law of their state. See *ALI Restatement (Third) of the Foreign Relations Law of the United States* §441 (1987) and sources there cited.

[108] See for instance the different approaches to the Nylon Cartel taken by the United States and by the United Kingdom in the early 1950s. Cf. *United States* v. *Imperial Chemical Industries, Ltd.*, 100 F. Supp. 504 (S.D.N.Y. 1951) and 105 F. Supp. 215 (S.D.N.Y. 1952) (US court sought to break up the cartel and end territorial monopolies established through patent licenses and assignments) with *British Nylon Spinners, Ltd.* v. *Imperial Chemical Industries, Ltd.*, [1953] Ch. 19 (UK Court of Appeal) (upholding injunction against ICI ordering it not to comply with decree of US court), and [1955] 1 Ch. 37 (Chancery Division 1955) (upholding English contract concerning English patent, notwithstanding finding by US court that the patent assignments and licenses were part of an unlawful worldwide combination).

[109] For example, it is fair to ask: if a principal effect of one state's economic acts is to harm persons outside its borders, should national or world disciplines require non-parochial justifications? Should the same be true of private acts encouraged or tolerated by the state but not now caught by the GATT? Should cartelists who claim shelter by reason of their government's acts be required, at least, to disclose the official acts in advance in order to be entitled to sympathetic treatment by a regulating state (e.g. freedom from criminal enforcement and treble damage remedies)? Why is it necessary for the *Noerr-Pennington* doctrine to be expansive in order to protect democratic values of association and informed government? Why should the doctrine not be restricted to *individual* lobbying, and why should the exemption not be lost in the event of fraud?

The Department of Justice, through its Antitrust Division which is lead by an Assistant Attorney General, enforces the Sherman Act and the Clayton Act. The Sherman Act, as noted, is a criminal statute as well as a civil statute. The Justice Department chooses to sue criminally only in the event of hard-core violations, principally price-fixing. Individuals convicted of a Sherman Act violation may be imprisoned for up to three years and may be fined up to $350,000 or twice the victim's loss or defendant's gain, whichever is larger. Corporations may be fined up to ten million dollars. Criminal defendants have a constitutional right to a jury trial, and either party in a damage action may demand trial by jury. In cases which the Department of Justice brings civilly, it may seek injunctive and other equitable relief, including divestiture or break-up of a firm. It may sue for damages if, but only if, the government itself is a direct purchaser from the defendants, such as a purchaser of medical equipment for military hospitals.

The Federal Trade Commission is comprised of five commissioners, each of whom is appointed for a term of seven years. Within the agency is a Bureau of Competition. The Director of the Bureau recommends antitrust cases; the Commission must approve and issue complaints. The Federal Trade Commission may sue to enforce the Clayton Act and the Federal Trade Commission Act, which in effect incorporates the substantive standards of the Sherman Act. It has no criminal jurisdiction. If an FTC complaint proceeds to litigation, the staff tries the case before an Administrative Law Judge (ALJ). The decision of the ALJ may be appealed to the Commission, and a losing respondent may appeal the decision of the FTC to a federal appellate court. More commonly, FTC proceedings are disposed of informally by way of a cease and desist order negotiated between the parties and the FTC staff and formally entered by the FTC as a final order.

The Justice Department and the FTC share responsibility for merger enforcement. Planned mergers of a threshold size, including mergers involving a foreign firm (and in some instances involving only foreign firms) with sufficient assets in or sales into the United States, must be reported to the agencies pursuant to the Hart-Scott-Rodino Act, which was enacted in 1976 to permit analysis by the government agencies and possible suit or imposition of conditions before the merger occurs.[110] The parties must provide information and respect a specified waiting period before consummating the merger.[111]

2. *Private Enforcement of Federal Law*

The federal antitrust laws may be enforced also by private parties, provided they have antitrust standing,[112] as discussed below. To ease the burden of suit faced by victims of violations, the Clayton Act provides that a litigated

---

[110] 15 U.S.C. §18a.
[111] See B. Fox and E. Fox, *Corporate Acquisitions & Mergers*, ch. 19 (revised as of 2002), for the regulatory requirements.
[112] Clayton Act §4, codified as 15 U.S.C. §15.

judgment for the United States is prima-facie evidence of a violation based on the same facts in a later private suit against the same defendants.[113] Successful private plaintiffs are entitled to three times their losses, plus costs and attorneys' fees. Congress adopted the treble damage remedy in order to enlist private 'attorneys general' and thus to provide incentives to detect violations, to sue, and thereby to deter prohibited conduct.

Private plaintiffs must have standing to assert the antitrust claim. In cases that involve a chain of direct and indirect purchasers, the Clayton Act damage remedy is limited to direct purchasers. In *Illinois Brick*, the Supreme Court held that the State of Illinois could not sustain a claim against manufacturers who had allegedly fixed prices because the state had purchased concrete blocks not from the violators but from contractors who had purchased from the violators.[114] The Court reasoned that permitting indirect purchasers to recover overcharges would create the risk of duplicate damages for the same violation, and would diminish the effectiveness of the treble damage remedy by diminishing the incentives for direct purchasers to bring suit.

To recover, plaintiffs must show a sufficiently direct causal connection between the alleged violation and the harm,[115] and the harm must qualify as antitrust injury. The plaintiff must show that its injury is, or is reciprocal to, consumer injury; not in tension with it. The Supreme Court dismissed, for lack of antitrust injury, a competitor's suit against the merger of the plaintiff's two largest competitors.[116] Consumer injury could have occurred only if the merging firms raised their prices. If they did so directly, the plaintiff competitor would benefit under the price umbrella. While it was theoretically possible that a newly created dominant firm could charge prices below cost to eliminate the plaintiff and thereafter charge monopoly prices (predatory pricing en route to monopoly pricing), the plaintiff did not demonstrate that such a scenario was likely.[117] Rather, the Court thought, plaintiff was worried about competition itself.[118]

3. *Enforcement of Federal Law by State Attorneys General*

Since 1976, state attorneys general also may sue to enforce the federal antitrust laws.[119] As *parens patriae* on behalf of natural persons residing in

---

[113] Clayton Act §5, codified as 15 U.S.C. §16.

[114] *Illinois Brick Co.* v. *Illinois*, 431 U.S. 720 (1977). A narrow exception is made for indirect purchasers who are party to a pre-existing cost-plus contract or other arrangement that does not present the complex problems of tracing the overcharge. Id. at 733.

[115] *Associated General Contractors* v. *California State Council of Carpenters*, 459 U.S. 519 (1983).

[116] *Cargill, Inc.* v. *Monfort of Colorado*, 479 U.S. 104 (1986).　　　　[117] Id.

[118] See also *Atlantic Richfield Co.* v. *USA Petroleum Co.*, 495 U.S. 328 (1990), dismissing a case challenging a maximum price-fixing agreement between an oil company and its dealer, with whom plaintiff competed; even if the agreement was *per se* illegal, plaintiff could not show antitrust injury from the agreement.

[119] The statutory provisions authorizing such lawsuits, Sects. 4C to 4H of the Clayton Act, were added to the law by the Hart-Scott-Rodino Antitrust Improvements Act of 1976, codified at 15 U.S.C. §§15c–15h, 18a, 66.

its state, a state attorney general may seek treble damages, along with costs and attorneys fees. The law allows the use of statistical and sampling means to prove aggregate damages, and it authorizes the payment of damages into one fund, which would then be subject to the claims of the injured residents.

In the late 1980s when merger enforcement by the federal agencies was at a near standstill, state attorneys general embarked upon active merger enforcement under both federal and state law. They challenged mergers that had nationwide as well as state effects. Through the National Association of Attorneys General, they issued their own merger guidelines, effectively harmonizing the state laws and the states' interpretation of the federal laws.

In these early days there was a hostile relationship between the state attorneys general and the federal enforcers. This hostility largely dissolved in the 1990s. The federal and state enforcers normally work harmoniously, sometimes apportioning tasks, and sometimes, as in the *Microsoft* monopoly litigation, they sue in tandem, both pursuing the same cause of action.[120]

(b) The European Union

The European system is more regulatory than the US system, thus following the tradition of many European nations.

As of the time this book went to press, agreements that may affect competition must be notified to the European Commission, and in particular to the Competition Directorate. The Competition Directorate reviews the agreements and may give a negative clearance (finding that the agreement is not caught by EC Treaty Article 81(1)), or may grant or deny an exemption under Article 81(3). Only the Commission may grant an exemption. Exemptions are granted for a specified period of years and normally contain conditions.[121]

Alternatively, the Commission may give a comfort letter stating informally that the agreement appears to meet the standards for an exemption, but such a letter is not full protection because a comfort letter is not an exemption. An agreement is technically void if it is caught by Article 81(1) and is not formally exempted. The recipient of a comfort letter who wishes to enforce the agreement in a national court may find itself unable to do.[122]

---

[120] The cooperation, however, is not always smooth and seamless. In the *Microsoft* case the federal government and the 19 state attorneys general who were plaintiffs did not always agree. Indeed, the 19 attorneys general did not always agree among themselves. The disagreements affected strategy and may have been an obstacle to a settlement before entry of the district court's judgment. See Ken Auletta, *World War 3.0: Microsoft and Its Enemies*, ch. 21 (2000).

[121] A modernization proposal would eliminate the notification/authorization system and would devolve limited exemption powers to Member State competition authorities and courts.

[122] This effect will be eliminated by the proposed reform. A national court will be able to enforce a contract that meets the conditions of Article 81(3).

To simplify the process of review of common transactions, such as exclusive dealing contracts, the Commission has promulgated block exemptions.[123] Block exemption regulations specify clauses or conditions that are necessary to qualify and clauses that are prohibited. If an agreement fits within a block exemption, it automatically gets the benefits of an exemption, unless the Commission withdraws the agreement from the block exemption on grounds that the agreement, in its particular market context, harms competition. In view of the benefits, many firms steer their transactions into the confines of the block exemption.

A firm may also offend the EC competition law by violating Article 82, which prohibits abuse of a dominant position.

If a firm violates either Article 81 or Article 82, the Commission may impose large fines, up to 10 percent of the firm's worldwide turnover.[124] The Commission may also order parties to terminate infringements. For notified agreements, no fine may be imposed for the period from the date of notification to the date of denial of an exemption.

As described in the previous section, the Merger Regulation governs merger control.[125] The law requires the vetting of large mergers of Community dimension before they are consummated. After a merger successfully passes through this process, it is immune from challenge in the European Union or any Member State. This is unlike US law; Hart-Scott-Rodino clearance gives no immunity.

The person or firm to which a Commission decision is addressed and other persons individually and directly affected may bring proceedings before the Court of First Instance and seek to have a Commission decision annulled. An appeal on points of law lies to the highest court, the European Court of Justice.

Private parties may not directly challenge mergers embraced by the Merger Regulation, except that a complaining competitor or other individually affected person may seek to annul a Commission decision.

For Article 81 and 82 violations, private actions are theoretically available. A person or enterprise can sue to enforce Article 81 or 82 in a Member State court, using the procedures of the Member State.[126] In practice, this course is seldom taken. In contrast to the practice in the United States, there

---

[123] Valentine Korah, *An Introductory Guide to EC Competition Law and Practice*, 71 (7th edn. 2000). See e.g. the discussion of block exemptions in the intellectual property area, Sect. 12.5 supra.

[124] More commonly, the Commission uses the turnover of the offending company or division as the basis for imposition of the fine.

[125] See Sect. 12.5(e) at n. 91.

[126] See *Garden Cottage Foods Ltd.* v. *Milk Marketing Board*, [1984] A.C. 130, [1983] 3 CMLR 43 (UK House of Lords). Currently, only the European Commission can grant an exemption under Article 81(3), and if a defendant credibly claims entitlement to an exemption, the national court will normally stay proceedings until the Commission acts. If the proposed plan of modernization is implemented, national courts and authorities also will have power to approve agreements that satisfy the criteria of 81(3).

are few incentives, and there are serious disincentives, to private action. Class actions, contingent fees, and more than compensatory damages are not available; permissible discovery is minimal; and a losing plaintiff must normally pay the defendant's costs including attorneys' fees.

12.7 INTERNATIONAL COOPERATION AND COMITY

(a) Impairment of Foreign Market Access

World trading agreements normally aim to open markets to trading partners. If government barriers to a nation's markets recede but the markets are still not accessible to efficient outsiders, then there may be blockage by an illegal private restraint.

The three most obvious types of private (or hybrid public/private) restraint that may hinder market access are:

(1) Cartels with boycotts. If access to one of a few established dealers is critical to efficient market entry, a boycott may be carried out through dealers instructed by their cartelized suppliers not to handle foreign goods. This was the claim by US authorities against Japanese glass companies.

(2) Monopolistic exclusions. A single firm with dominant power may tie up the only available distributors or may use expired intellectual property rights to exclude competitors. These scenarios reflect Kodak's claim against Fuji Film and the US claim against the British float glass producer, Pilkington.[127]

(3) Exclusive dealing contracts and other vertical foreclosing restraints, in the absence of a concerted boycott or monopoly power. This is a version of the complaints against the Japanese glass companies. Each of the three Japanese glass companies may have had an exclusive arrangement with one of the only three available and effective distributors, with the effect that no potential entrant could penetrate the market.

As noted in Section 12.5, a cartel with a boycott is illegal in virtually every country that has antitrust laws. The challenge is to prove that the cartel and boycott existed.

Monopolistic exclusion is illegal if its purpose and effect is to keep competitors out, and perhaps also (even without proof of purpose) if exclusion and resulting consumer harm is the dominant effect.

Vertical contract restraints are more difficult to challenge successfully. Some jurisdictions prohibit such agreements if their effect is to foreclose the market to outsiders. US law, however, is sympathetic to vertical contracts, which are presumed to be justified by efficiencies and responsive to consumer interests. They are illegal if they are not efficiency-justified and their dominant effect is to keep competitors out of the market and to raise prices.

---

[127] See nn. 50 and 59 supra.

The problem of foreign market-access foreclosure by private or hybrid restraints lies at the intersection of trade and competition law. Such restraints are difficult to reach, practically, jurisdictionally, and substantively, by enforcement of the antitrust laws of the exporting nation. The problem is a major subject on the agenda for possible international antitrust disciplines.

(b) International Codes

Since at least the 1940s, some policy-makers have argued that a liberal world trading system implies rules against private as well as public restraints of trade. The Havana Charter, negotiated in 1947–8 as the blueprint for the International Trade Organization (ITO)[128] would have required nations to take appropriate measures against transnational restrictive business practices, including price-fixing, market division, and restraints limiting market access and fostering monopolistic control. The Charter would have authorized the ITO to request an offending member nation 'to take every possible remedial action'.[129] The US government withdrew its support for the ITO, however, and the Havana Charter was never adopted.[130]

In the decades that followed, many large corporations based in the United States and elsewhere expanded multinationally, and sentiment rose to control the behaviour of the multinational firms.[131] In 1976, the Organization for Economic Cooperation and Development, an organization of the industrialized countries, issued *Guidelines on Conduct for Multinational Enterprises*.[132] The *OECD Guidelines*, which principally concerned investment, contained a section on restrictive business practices, stating that enterprises should:

(1) refrain from actions which would adversely affect competition in the relevant market by abusing a dominant position of market power, by means of, for example, [anticompetitive acquisitions, predation toward competitors, unreasonable refusal to deal, anticompetitive abuse of intellectual property rights, and discriminatory pricing including transfer pricing];
(2) allow purchasers, distributors and licensees freedom to resell, export, purchase and develop their operations consistent with law, trade conditions, the need for specialisation and sound commercial practice;
(3) refrain from participating in or otherwise purposely strengthening the restrictive effects of international or domestic cartels or restrictive agreements which adversely affect or eliminate competition and which are not generally or specifically accepted under applicable national or international legislation;

---

[128] Havana Charter for an International Trade Organization, 24 Mar. 1948 (E-Conf.2/78). See Ch. 3, Sect. 3.2.
[129] Id. at Art. 48(7).   [130] See Ch. 3. Sect. 3.2.   [131] See Ch. 13, Sect. 13.4(b).
[132] 1976 OECD Declaration on International Investment and Multinational Enterprises, revised in *OECD Guidelines for Multinational Enterprises*, adopted 27 June 2000.

(4) be ready to consult and co-operate, including the provision of information, with competent authorities of countries whose interests are directly affected in regard to competition issues or investigations.[133]

Meanwhile the United Nations Conference on Trade and Development had become a forum for consideration of world antitrust principles, to be negotiated among the industrialized countries, the socialist bloc countries, and the less developed and developing countries (Group of 77). The resulting Set of Multilaterally Agreed Equitable Principles and Rules for the Control of Restrictive Business Practices (the 'RBP rules' or the 'UNCTAD Code') was presented to the UN General Assembly and accepted by consensus resolution as a non-binding recommendation in 1980.[134] The RBP rules state that they should be interpreted in favour of developing countries and that they are intended to provide fair and equitable control of business practices for the benefit of the trade and welfare of the developing countries.

Just after the adoption of this voluntary code, however, US antitrust law made a U-turn. US antitrust became rules in the interests of efficient allocation of resources, as seen through the eyes (and pocketbooks) of US consumers. If the United States had once desired or tolerated a world antitrust scheme sympathetic to distributional concerns of the less well off, it did not do so any more. At least in the United States, the UNCTAD Code became a non-document, although that part of the code that overlaps with allocatively efficient antitrust continues to be cited with approval.[135]

(c) Bilateral Cooperation

Even while the UNCTAD RBP code was being negotiated, jurisdictional clashes were occurring as a result of aggressive US antitrust enforcement against foreign actors. The antitrust clashes of the 1970s, and particularly the claim of trading partners that the US agencies and courts had exceeded jurisdictional bounds and were treading on their sovereignty, led to the adoption of three memoranda of understanding (MOUs). Agreements were signed by the United States and Germany (1976), the United States and Australia (1982), and the United States and Canada (1984, revised

---

[133] These guidelines on restrictive business practices were withdrawn as outdated (they would seem to prohibit some conduct that could be deemed efficient and procompetitive or competitively neutral by certain industrialized countries, particularly the United States). They were replaced by a more general statement in 2000. See Sect. 12.4(a) at n. 42. Similarly, a 1967 OECD competition recommendation against restrictive business practices was replaced in 1995 by a Revised Recommendation of the Council concerning Cooperation between Member Countries on Anticompetitive Practices affecting International Trade, 27 and 28 July 1995—C(95)130/FINAL.

[134] UN Doc. A/Res/35/63 (5 Dec. 1980).

[135] Negotiation of a code of conduct on the transfer of technology was in progress in 1980, but, given the US U-turn, it was never completed.

1995).[136] These agreements provide for notification by one authority of its actions that may affect the important interests of the other party, consultations if there is a conflict of interests, and cooperation in gathering and sharing information of mutual benefit. The major purpose of the MOUs was to resolve or modulate conflicts of interest by the exercise of restraint, e.g. by deciding not to challenge the neighbour's cartel.

A second generation of bilateral agreements came into being at the end of the 1980s and particularly in the 1990s when many nations adopted market systems and competition laws. The new agreements were designed principally to enhance positive measures, such as assistance in investigation and enforcement.

The United States has entered into a number of Mutual Legal Assistance Treaties (MLATs) whereby nations agree to assist one another in the enforcement of criminal law. The United States entered an MLAT with Canada in 1988 which expressly includes criminal antitrust enforcement.

The year 1991, however, marked a new stage: the foundation for 'positive comity'. The United States and the European Community signed a Cooperation Agreement Regarding the Application of their Competition Laws.[137] The most innovative article (Article V) lays the groundwork for one party to take action to protect market access for the firms of the other: if one party believes that anticompetitive acts taken on the territory of the other are adversely affecting its important interests, it may request the other to initiate enforcement activities. The notified party will consider the request and advise the notifying party of its decision, and of developments.

The 1991 Cooperation Agreement also provides for notification of enforcement activities that may affect the other's important interests. It contemplates that notification would be given far enough in advance of a complaint or settlement for the enforcing party to take the views of the other party into account. The parties agree to exchange information in order to promote understanding, to assist enforcement and coordination of parallel enforcement, and, based on comity factors, to avoid conflicts.

In 1998, the United States and the EU strengthened Article V.[138] The scope-and-purpose clause of the 1998 agreement explains:

---

[136] Agreement between the Government of the United States of America and the Government of the Federal Republic of Germany, 23 June 1976, repr. in 4 *Trade Reg. Rep.* (CCH) ¶13,501; Agreement between the Government of the United States and the Government of Australia Relating to Cooperation on Antitrust Matters, 27 Apr. 1999, US–Australia, repr. in 4 *Trade Reg. Rep.* (CCH) ¶13,502; Agreement between the Government of the United States of America and the Government of Canada Regarding the Application of their Competition and Deceptive Marketing Practices Laws, 3 Aug. 1995, US–Can., repr. in 4 *Trade Reg. Rep.* (CCH) ¶13,503.

[137] Agreement between the Government of the United States of America and the European Communities Regarding the Application of Their Competition Laws, 23 Sept. 1991, repr. in 4 *Trade Reg. Rep.* (CCH) ¶13,504.

[138] Agreement between the Government of the United States of America and the European Communities on the Application of Positive Comity Principles in the Enforcement of their Competition Laws, 4 June 1998, repr. in 4 *Trade Reg. Rep.* (CCH) ¶13,504A.

6. This Agreement applies where a Party satisfies the other that there is reason to believe that the following circumstances are present:

(a) Anticompetitive activities are occurring in whole or in substantial part in the territory of one of the Parties and are adversely affecting the interests of the other Party; and

(b) The activities in question are impermissible under the competition laws of the Party in the territory of which the activities are occurring.

7. The purposes of this Agreement are to:

(a) Help ensure that trade and investment flows between the Parties and competition and consumer welfare within the territories of the Parties are not impeded by anticompetitive activities for which the competition laws of one or both Parties can provide a remedy, and

(b) Establish cooperative procedures to achieve the most effective and efficient enforcement of competition law, whereby the competition authorities of each Party will normally avoid allocating enforcement resources to dealing with anticompetitive activities that occur principally in and are directed principally towards the other Party's territory, where the competition authorities of the other Party are able and prepared to examine and take effective sanctions under their law to deal with those activities.

The problem addressed is thus the same problem addressed by the US withdrawal of footnote 159 of the 1988 US *International Guidelines*[139]—to open foreign markets to each party's exports. An implicit purpose of the 1998 agreement, on the part of the EU, is precisely to forestall US extraterritorial enforcement of US antitrust laws to pry open the Community market when it is closed by private restraints.

Under the 1998 agreement, a party may request enforcement, and the two parties may then agree that the requesting party will suspend its contemplated enforcement. The agreement states that the requesting party will normally suspend its enforcement if:

(a) the challenged acts 'do not have a direct, substantial and reasonably foreseeable impact on consumers in the Requesting Party's territory', or the acts 'occur principally in and are directed principally towards the other Party's territory,' and

(b) the adverse effects on the Requesting Party are likely to be adequately remedied in the Requested Party's jurisdiction, and

(c) the Requested Party agrees to devote adequate resources, use best efforts, and notify the Requesting Party of intentions and status and take into account its views.[140]

The United States made one referral to the European Commission in anticipation of the 1998 agreement: the claim that SABRE, a US-based airline computer reservation system, was blocked from effective competition in the French, German, and Spanish markets for airline computer reservation

---

[139] See Sect. 12.4(b) at n. 45.

[140] Mergers are excluded from the 1998 agreement, apparently in response to the concerns of US business about the sharing and leakage of confidential information.

services by anticompetitive refusals to provide it with accurate up-to-date scheduling information by the French, German, and Spanish airlines that owned the competing (and dominant) computer reservation system, Amadeus. After two years and much pressure from US political sources, the European Competition Directorate opened an investigation and subsequently entered into a settlement with Air France.[141]

The United States has entered into similar bilateral agreements with Canada, Japan, Australia, Brazil, Mexico, and Israel, and the European Community, Canada, Australia, and Japan are developing similar networks of bilateral agreements.

(d) Regional Cooperation

In addition to the various cooperation agreements noted above, nations in a number of regions of the world have formed free trade areas, and their commitments often contemplate increasing economic integration of the area and in some cases coordination of competition policies.

The European Union is by far the most tightly integrated community of nations short of a federation; it has a common competition policy, discussed at length above. There are numerous looser variations. In the North American Free Trade Agreement, Canada, Mexico, and the United States have committed themselves to adopt or maintain measures to proscribe anticompetitive conduct, take appropriate action, and consult.[142] Canada has a free trade agreement with Chile with a similar provision, and which, unlike NAFTA, precludes use of anti-dumping laws in the free trade area.[143] Australia and New Zealand have created the Australia New Zealand Closer Economic Relations Trade Agreement (CER),[144] which establishes a common abuse-of-dominance law and abolishes application of anti-dumping laws in the free trade area. In South America, nations have joined together in the Andean Pact and MERCOSUR.[145] In Africa, they have joined together in COMESA (Common Market for Eastern and Southern Africa) and in separate agreements for southern, western, and eastern Africa. In the Carribean, nations have formed CARICOM. Asian Pacific countries maintain a loose cooperation forum (APEC), at which members discuss competition principles. Europe itself has concentric circles of free trade agreements, including EFTA

---

[141] See *Report of the International Competition Policy Advisory Committee to the Attorney General and Assistant Attorney General for Antitrust* (ICPAC Report), 232–4 (2000).

[142] See North American Free Trade Agreement signed at Mexico City, Ottawa, and Washington Dec. 1992, entered into force 1 Jan. 1994 ch. 15.

[143] Canadian–Chile Free Trade Agreement entered into force 1997, Chapter J.

[144] Adopted in 1983. See Allan Fels, 'Administrative/ Prosecutorial Discretion of Antitrust Authorities', in 1999 *Fordham Corp. Law Inst.*, ch. 27 (B. Hawk (ed.), 2000), describing common competition policy in Australia and New Zealand.

[145] See Treaty Establishing the Southern Common Market, signed at Asuncion, 26 Mar. 1991, 30 I.L.M. 1041.

(most of whose members have now joined the European Union, but which still maintains a separate court), and the EEA (the European Economic Area), which includes the EU Member States and, like EFTA, provides for application of EC competition law in the area.

These regions vary in their consideration and treatment of competition principles. Only in Europe and to a lesser extent in Australia/New Zealand is competition law one of the organizing and central policies of the free trade area.

(e) The Problem of Evidence

Despite bilateral and other agreements, the US Department of Justice has sometimes been frustrated in its enforcement against international cartels because of the difficulty of obtaining evidence located abroad. To facilitate obtaining foreign-located evidence, it proposed and Congress enacted the International Antitrust Enforcement Assistance Act of 1994.[146] The Act authorizes the Attorney General of the United States and the Federal Trade Commission to conduct investigations and provide antitrust evidence to foreign authorities regarding a possible violation of the foreign antitrust laws if these authorities are confident that their foreign counterparts can and will reciprocate in providing information to the US authorities and that the foreign counterparts will safeguard the confidence of the confidential information provided. The act contemplates that reciprocating countries will enter into mutual assistance agreements pursuant to the act. In 1999, Australia became the first nation to enter into such an agreement with the United States. As this book goes to press, it is the only other country or region to do so.

12.8 COMPETITION POLICY AND WORLD ECONOMIC INTEGRATION—A LOOK AHEAD

In 1992 Sir Leon Brittan, European Commissioner in Charge of External Relations for the European Union and previously European Commissioner in Charge of Competition, gave a speech at the Davos World Economic Forum observing the globalization of markets and noting that, as public restraints recede, private restraints tend to emerge. He called for an internationalization of competition law and integration of competition issues with those of the world trading system.

Thereafter the European Commissioner in Charge of Competition, Karel van Miert, appointed a Group of Experts to study the issues. The Experts' Report, submitted in 1995, concluded that an international initiative is needed; that it should be built upon a foundation of agency-to-agency

---

[146] 15 U.S.C. §§6201–6212.

cooperation, including bilateral agreements with positive comity; that rules should require transparency and non-discrimination; and that, at a later stage, states should proceed to adopt common minimum rules for trans-actions and conduct of international dimension, with a system for dispute resolution.

The Report of the Group of Experts and the many related proposals that followed were not well received in the United States. American antitrust authorities maintained that US national tools for enforcement combined with bilateral cooperation are generally adequate to deal with international competition problems that face Americans, and that a multilateral initiative would lead to the corruption of antitrust principles (which aid consumers) by trade bargains (which protect competitors). Further, US officials expressed the fear that a multilateral competition agreement would result in 'lowest common denominator' rules; in a distant, expanding faceless bureaucracy; and in inept and unprincipled dispute resolution by unknown and untrusted decision-makers.[147]

On the other side of the ocean, the European Union vetted the Experts' ideas through the various directorates general of the Commission and through the Commission and Council, and proposed at the Singapore Ministerial Meeting of the WTO in December 1996 that an initiative on trade and competition should be launched. The United States at first opposed the initiative, but eventually accepted a recommendation—which was adopted—that a Working Group on the Interaction between Trade and Competition Policy be created, on condition that the group be authorized only to discuss the issues and enhance mutual knowledge, and on the under-standing that formation of the group did not imply a next step, i.e. negotia-tion of competition rules or disciplines in the WTO.

As the WTO Working Group began its meetings, the United States antitrust authorities proposed an initiative within the Organization for Economic Cooperation and Development. The United States preferred the OECD as a forum because its members are 'like' (industrialized) nations and because the OECD has no dispute resolution mechanism and is not a rule-making body. There are no OECD rules, only recommendations. The United States proposed a Recommendation Concerning Effective Action against Hard Core Cartels, which was adopted at the OECD ministerial meeting in Paris in April 1998.[148] The document recommends to member countries that they ensure that their competition laws effectively halt and deter hard core cartels. The recommendation is subject to all exceptions authorized in the member countries' laws, but it states that those derogations should be

---

[147] See Joel Klein, 'Anticipating the Millennium: International Antitrust Enforcement at the End of the Twentieth Century', in 1998 *Fordham Corp. Law Institute* 9, 9–10 (B. Hawk (ed.), 1999).
[148] OECD Doc. C(98)35/Final.

transparent and should be reviewed periodically to assess whether they are necessary and whether they are tailored to overriding policy objectives.

Also, the United States proposed,[149] and with the European Union, Canada, and others facilitated, the formation of the International Competition Network. Launched in October 2001, this network of antitrust agencies around the world is designed to work towards consensus on procedural and substantive convergence, and to find practical solutions to soluble problems.

In anticipation of the WTO Ministerial Conference at Doha in November 2001, the European Union, Canada, Japan, and others proposed that competition issues be included on the agenda for the next round of trade negotiations. Their efforts appear to have been successful. The Ministerial Declaration provides that the member states will undertake negotiations on competition policy after the Fifth Session of the Ministerial Conference (to be held in 2005), subject to explicit consensus on the modalities of negotiations. In the interim, the Working Group is to focus on clarification of 'core principles, including transparency, non-discrimination and procedural fairness, and provisions on hardcore cartels; modalities for voluntary cooperation; and support for progressive reinforcement of competition institutions in developing countries through capacity building.'[150]

Meanwhile, there is a growing literature on internationalization of antitrust. Proposals span the continuum from the status quo to a complete international antitrust code.[151] More generally, there is a growing literature on globalization, market integration, the limits of national law, and the challenges posed by supra-national agreement.[152] Lawrence Summers, when US Secretary of the Treasury, characterized the problem as the 'economic integration trilemma'.[153] World economic integration is critical to world peace and economic welfare, he said. But more economic integration requires more government and more constraints on national sovereignty, and there are reasons to prefer less government and more reservation of national sovereignty. The 'profoundly important' question, he posited, is how to reconcile the three legs of the dilemma—economic integration, management, and national sovereignty. This, indeed, is the challenge.

---

[149] See Joel Klein, 'Time for a Global Competition Initiative?' Speech at the EC Merger Control Tenth Anniversary Conference, Brussels (14 Sept. 2000). Klein endorsed the proposal of the International Competition Policy Advisory Committee, as presented in the ICPAC Report, ch. 6 (2000). See proposal for a free-standing World Competition Forum for competition issues not tightly related to trade, in E. Fox, 'Competition Law and the Millennium Round', 2 *J. Int'l Econ. L.* 665 (1999).

[150] WTO Ministerial Declaration 14 Nov. 2001, para. 23–5, WT/MIN (01)/DEC/1 (20 Nov. 2001).

[151] See D. Tarullo, 'Norms and Institutions in Global Competition Policy', 94 *Am. J. Int'l L.* 478 (2000); E. Fox, 'Toward Antitrust and Market Access', 91 *Am. J. Int'l L.* 1 (1997).

[152] See J. Braithwaite and P. Drahos, *Global Business Regulation* (2000).

[153] Lawrence H. Summers, 'Reflections on Managing Global Integration', *J. Econ. Perspectives* (Spring 1999), 3, 7, 9–10, 17.

There is a logical starting point: the point at which private restraints undermine existing state obligations already embodied in the WTO, and where state measures facilitate just such private restraints. This approach suggests reforms in three areas.

First, private restraints not infrequently block outsiders from access to markets. For example, a cartel of domestic producers may tie up essential distributors and require them to reject foreign goods. While states have WTO obligations not to block their markets by state restraints, they have no meaningful obligation to keep their markets free of private restraints. This is a gap that allows states to blink at their open-market obligations. WTO provisions could usefully require members to keep their markets free of commercial restraints that unreasonably block their markets. An obvious way—but not the only way—for nations to fulfil this obligation would be to adopt and enforce national competition laws.[154] To avoid the problem of indeterminate legal standards,[155] the law of the country in which the exclusionary restraint operates could be designated as the applicable law, as long as it is a credible law that prohibits unreasonable market blocking restraints. As under the TRIPs Agreement,[156] states could be authorized to complain through dispute settlement procedures if a state fails to carry out its obligations.

Second, WTO rules could usefully expand the obligations of member states to prohibit transborder cartels or at least to aid in discovery and enforcement against their own nationals when requested to do so by states that have been injured by cartels. This is a small and logical next step, since, under the Safeguards Agreement, states have the obligation to refrain from ordering or encouraging import or export cartels.[157] It is a fair step. Industrialized countries normally have the tools, resources and power to protect themselves from offshore cartels by extraterritorial enforcement of their antitrust laws and through bilateral cooperation. Developing countries, however, do not have comparable resources, and, given their vulnerability, they are often the special targets of world cartel activity emanating from the industrialized world.

Third, governmental measures often facilitate cartels and market access restraints. Many of the resulting restraints are hybrid, i.e. both public and private. The WTO could usefully prohibit such state action unless the measure is transparent, nondiscriminatory to non-nationals, and justified by the need to meet objectives consistent with WTO obligations.

Progress in many other areas may be made. For example:

---

[154] The obligation need not be limited to restraints that discriminate against outsiders. Nor need it be defeasible by an absence of reasonable expectations. Thus, the *Kodak/Fuji-Film* loophole should be closed. On *Kodak-Fuji*, see Ch. 8, Sect. 8.8(b).

[155] Countries differ on what is an anticompetitive market-blocking strategy.

[156] See E. Fox, 'Trade, Competition, and Intellectual Property—TRIPs and its Antitrust Counterparts', 29 *Vand. J. Transnat'l L.* 481 (1996). See also Ch. 5, Sect. 5.6.

[157] Agreement on Safeguards, Art. 11. See Ch. 5, Sect. 5.4(b).

- Pre-merger notification systems might be rationalized by obligations of mutual recognition or use of a common clearing house;
- Systems clashes could be alleviated by an agreed framework for modulating disputes; e.g. choice of law;
- States could be required to count costs outside of as well as within their borders in assessing alleged anticompetitive conduct, at least in the case of clashes of jurisdiction;
- In general, states could be encouraged to analyse competition problems in view of the total market impact, not merely their own national interest;
- GATT principles of non-discrimination against non-nationals and transparency could usefully apply to competition rules and their enforcement;
- Bilateral cooperation agreements could be multilateralized.

In short, competition law can be globalized so that national blinders are removed and the analyst takes a comprehensive world view; not a nationalistic perspective. These incremental steps could help to bring antitrust law into the twenty-first century.

PART VI
International Investment

INTRODUCTION

The United States Supreme Court, writing in 1964, said 'There are few if any issues in international law today on which opinion seems to be so divided as the limitations on a state's power to expropriate the property of aliens.'[1] That statement made in the context of declining to review the actions of the government of Cuba in taking over properties owned by US-based corporations, upset a great many people in the international investment community, in the United States and elsewhere. Justice White, dissenting wrote:

I am dismayed that the Court has, with one broad stroke, declared the ascertainment and application of international law beyond the competence of the United States in a large and important category of cases. . . .[2]

Of course there are many unsettled areas of international law, as there are with domestic law, and these areas present sensitive problems of accommodating the interests of nations that subscribe to divergent economic and political systems. It may be that certain nationalizations of property for a public purpose fall within this area . . .

But none of these considerations relieve a court of the obligation to make an inquiry into the validity of the foreign act, none of them warrant a flat rule of no inquiry, at all.[3]

Justice Harlan, writing for the 8–1 majority, explained that the Supreme Court was reluctant to place the interests of the United States as home base for many multinational enterprises before its view of the state of the law.

[Respondents'] basic contention is that United States courts could make a significant contribution to the growth of international law, a contribution whose importance, it is said, would be magnified by the relative paucity of decisional law by international bodies. But given the fluidity of present world conditions, the effectiveness of such a patchwork approach toward the formulation of an acceptable body of law concerning state responsibility for expropriations is, to say the least, highly conjectural. Moreover, it rests upon the sanguine presupposition that the decisions of the courts of the world's major capital exporting country and principal exponent of the free enterprise system would be accepted as disinterested expressions of sound legal principle by those adhering to widely different ideologies.[4]

In the mid-1960s the Supreme Court's characterization of the law of international investment was essentially accurate. However much writers and a few arbitral and judicial decisions in the United States and Europe proclaimed their adherence to the so-called 'Hull rule',[5] calling for prompt, adequate, and effective compensation in case of expropriation of alien-owned properties, large sections of the world regarded the Hull rule and its analogues as law

---

[1] *Banco Nacional de Cuba* v. *Sabbatino*, 376 U.S. 398, at 428 (1964).
[2] 376 U.S. at 439. [3] Id., at 458–9. [4] Id. 434–5.
[5] See Sect. 13.3(b) infra.

made in other times by and for the imperialist powers. Not only in the Soviet Union and China and the states within their orbit, but in large parts of what came to be known as the 'Third World' and among not a few Western scholars,[6] other values, such as the 'social function of property' and redistribution of wealth competed with the traditional Western concepts of private property and protection of aliens.

In the 1980s, the fundamentals began to change. It became evident that countries dedicated to state ownership of productive assets and hostile or ambivalent to foreign investment were being left behind in economic growth, while countries engaged in privatization and attraction of foreign investment prospered. The Soviet Union crumbled economically for several years before it finally collapsed in 1991. Reliance on public funds to stimulate economic development of less developed countries, as had been stressed in the 1960s and 1970s,[7] turned out to be disappointing on two levels. For one thing the funds made available through the World Bank, the regional development banks, and national foreign aid programs were inadequate; for another, public assistance was generally not accompanied by the kind of transfer of technology, as well as of management and marketing skills, that came along with investment in the private sector. In short, the assumptions of the 1960s and 1970s that informed much of the world's attitude towards direct foreign investment, and therefore to the law governing such investment, proved to be erroneous. That realization, not universal and not arrived at everywhere at the same time, in turn led to a changed understanding of the applicable law—in part to a return to older principles, in part to creation of new devices, such as bilateral investment treaties, investment guarantees, various facilities for dispute settlement, and a new set of common criteria for the treatment of foreign investment.

The mix of pragmatism and shifts in ideology is impossible to disentangle. But there can be no doubt that at the close of the twentieth century, the conditions for transnational private investment, including 'investment climate' and including the legal foundations, are significantly different from what they were in the 1960s. If there is not yet worldwide consensus, and no widely accepted treaty comparable to the GATT/WTO system, there is nevertheless a network of institutions, treaties, and decisions that together may be said to constitute the state of international law on transnational private investment as of year-end 2001.

---

[6] For a representative selection, see Oscar Schachter, 'Compensation for Expropriation', 78 *Am. J. Int'l L.* 121 (1984) and sources there cited.

[7] See e.g. *Partners in Development*, Report of the Commission on International Development (the Pearson Report), chaired by the former Prime Minister of Canada (1969); *North-South, A Program for Survival*, Report of the Independent Commission on International Development Issues (the Brandt Report), chaired by the former Chancellor of the German Federal Republic (1980).

Chapter 13 reviews the divergent sources of the customary law of state responsibility to foreign investors, and Chapter 14 presents some of the applications of that law in international arbitrations, international adjudication, and domestic litigation. Chapter 15 then explores the shifts in the relevant international law, as well as some of the newer issues—for instance regulation vs. expropriation, the acceptance of limits on performance requirements, and investor–state dispute mechanisms.

13

The Responsibility of Host States to Foreign Investors: Customary International Law

13.1 Before the First World War[1]

Prior to 1917, it appears to have been accepted among the principal nations—without a great deal of discussion—that a state that took an alien's property was obligated to make prompt and adequate compensation. It was not clear whether this understanding was derived from a general principle of law—for instance the Declaration of the Rights of Man and the Citizen of

---

[1] For a somewhat fuller account with sources, which has served as a guide for this section, see Rudolf Dolzer, *Eigentum, Enteignung and Entschädigung im geltenden Völkerrecht*, 13–23 (1985).

1789[2]—or was unique to international law, and the principle tended to coalesce with the principle that aliens are entitled, with respect to their property, to at least equality of treatment with nationals of the taking state. Since virtually every nation recognized the right of private property and the duty of the state to compensate an owner of property taken for public use, the property of foreign investors generally would be protected by a national treatment standard. The actual incidence of state taking in peacetime was rare, and the legal literature sparse. A later commentator wrote, 'It is probable that text-writers have given little attention to the status of the private property of aliens in time of peace because the inviolability of such property was so generally recognized.'[3]

Elihu Root, the leading American international lawyer in the first quarter of the twentieth century (as well as former Secretary of War and Secretary of State), wrote in 1910:

There is a standard of justice, very simple, very fundamental, and of such general acceptance by all civilized countries as to form a part of the international law of the world. The condition upon which any country is entitled to measure the justice due from it to an alien by the justice which it accords to its own citizens is that its system of law and administration shall conform to this general standard. If any country's system of law does not conform to that standard, although the people of the country may be content or compelled to live under it, no other country can be compelled to accept it as furnishing a satisfactory measure of treatment to its citizens.[4]

Thus Root, in his opening presidential address to the annual meeting of the American Society of International Law, laid down the principle of national treatment and its relation to a minimum treatment standard, but not focused particularly on protection of property.

13.2   Breakdown of the Consensus

(a)   The Russian Revolution and Repudiation of Private Property

In October 1917 (by the old Russian calendar), the Communist Party took control of the government of Russia, and over the next few years consolidated its hold in what became the Soviet Union, stretching from Poland on the west to the Pacific Ocean in the Far East. By Decree of October 26, 1917,

---

[2] Art. 17 of the Declaration states:

Property being an inviolable and sacred right, no one may be deprived of his property except when public necessity, lawfully established, so requires, and on condition of just and prior compensation.

[3] John P. Bullington, 'Problems of International Law in the Mexican Constitution of 1917', 21 *Am. J. Int'l L.* 685 at 695 (1927).

[4] Elihu Root, 'The Basis of Protection to Citizens Residing Abroad', 4 *Am. J. Int'l L.* 517 at 521–2 (1910), quoted also by Dolzer (n. 1 supra), 17.

private ownership in land was abolished—without any provision for compensation. A few months later, all banks were nationalized and their assets and liabilities consolidated in a new State Bank. Within the following two years, ownership of mines, factories, the oil industry, and eventually all industry was transferred to the state, and the public debt was repudiated. No compensation was provided in any of the measures of nationalization, and no distinction was made between property owned by Russian nationals and foreign-owned property.[5]

The Western Powers protested, asserting in a formal declaration 'that they view the decrees relating to the repudiation of Russian State loans, the confiscation of property and other similar measures as null and void in so far as their nationals are concerned.'[6] Over the next several years, discussions and conferences were held from time to time with the Western Powers concerning claims against Russia and counterclaims by Russia resulting from intervention in the civil war, essentially without result.[7]

The Western nations never formally accepted the Soviet position as legal, but gradually came to terms with the 'facts on the ground'. Even the United States, which had refused to extend recognition to the Soviet Union until 1933, made a kind of claims settlement with the USSR in that year—the so-called Litvinov Assignment.[8]

(b) The Mexican Revolution, the Social Function of Property, and the Calvo Doctrine

Until 1910, Mexico was governed under constitutions and civil codes emphasizing individualism and the right to own property. Under the Civil Code of 1884, issued during the reign of Porfirio Díaz (1876–1911), a landowner owned not only the surface, but the subsoil as well, including oil and mineral deposits. The revolution against Díaz, sparked by a combination of landless peasants and liberal intellectuals, continued for a decade, with a succession of leaders and on-and-off intervention by the United States. In 1917, a new Constitution was promulgated, containing a new, revolutionary approach to property. Article 27 of the Constitution of 1917 (still in effect) reads:

Ownership of the lands and materials included within the boundaries of national territory belongs originally to the Nation, which has had and continues to have the right to transmit ownership thereof to private parties, thereby constituting private property.

[5] For a detailed recital of the successive decrees, see S. Friedman, *Expropriation in International Law*, 176–23 (1953, repr. 1981).

[6] Declaration of the US Ambassador to Russia, 13 Feb. 1918 on behalf of the 14 Allied Powers and 6 neutrals, quoted in Friedman (n. 5 supra), 18.

[7] See Friedman (n. 5 supra), 18–23.

[8] See *Establishment of Diplomatic Relations with the Union of Soviet Socialist Republics*, Dept. of State, East European Series No. 1 (1933). The text of the actual Assignment, in the form of a letter to the President of the United States from Litvinov, People's Commissar for Foreign Affairs, is reproduced in *United States* v. *Pink*, 315 U.S. 203 at 212 (1942).

Expropriations may only be made for reasons of public utility and by means of compensation.

The Nation shall have at all times the right to impose on private property the modalities required by the public interest, as well as the right to regulate the exploitation of natural resources capable of appropriation in order to conserve them and to make an equitable distribution of public wealth.

One of the draftsmen of the Constitution explained that the fundamental purpose of the delegates at the Constitution Assembly was to interpret a unanimous feeling born of the Revolution 'that Mexican law establish fully as a basic, solid, and unalterable principle that above the rights of individuals to property there were superior rights of society represented by the state to regulate its distribution as well as its use and conservation.'[9]

The Mexican Supreme Court has said:

[Article 27] sought to eliminate the classical concept which defined the right of property as an absolute untouchable right, and to replace it with a concept which recognizes private property as a social function. Thus, private property would not be the exclusive right of one individual, but a right subordinated to the common welfare.[10]

For Mexico, and other countries of Latin America, the social function of property did not mean expropriation without compensation. But it meant distinctions between state-taking of a private home where a school or highway was to be built, and state ownership (or acquisition of ownership) of a major industry, such as electric power generation, petroleum exploration, or railroads.[11] For the former, compensation, generally prior and more or less in full value, was contemplated, if not always implemented. For the latter, as well as for redistribution of land pursuant to agrarian reform programs, compensation was not excluded, but it need not be prior or prompt, and the state's ability to pay was an important factor in determining what level of compensation was appropriate.[12] As for the rights of foreign investors, many of the

---

[9] Pastor Rouaix, *Genesis de los Articulos 27 y 123 de la Constitución politica de 1917*, 135 (1945), quoted by Julio C. Treviño in A. Lowenfeld (ed.), *Expropriation in the Americas: A Comparative Law Study*, 113 at 120. (1971).

[10] *Castellanos Vda. de Zapata*, Amparo Administrativo en Revision 605/1932, Sec. 1A (8 Dec. 1936), 50 *Semanario Judicial de la Federación* (5th Epoca) 2568, p. 2950, quoted in Treviño (n. 9 supra), at p. 120.

[11] For a survey of Argentina, Brazil, Chile, Mexico, Peru, and Venezuela, differing in detail but all consistent, as of 1970, with the above statement, see *Expropriation in the Americas*, n. 9 supra.

[12] In Chile, a corresponding constitutional amendment was not adopted until 1967, in contemplation of a major program of agrarian reform. The title of Article 10(10) of the Constitution of 1925 was changed from 'The inviolability of all property without any distinction' to 'The Right of Property in its Diverse Aspects'. The amended article, six paragraphs in all, stated, in part:

No one may be deprived of his property except by virtue of a general or special law which authorizes expropriation for reasons of public utility or social interest determined by the legislature. The expropriated party shall always have the right to compensation, the amount and payment of which are to be equitably determined, taking into consideration the interests of the collectivity and of the expropriated parties. The law shall determine the norms for fixing

Latin American countries, including Mexico, invoked the writings of the nineteenth-century Argentine jurist Carlos Calvo, who had taken the position that under international law aliens had no rights greater than citizens of the host country. Some states carried the Calvo doctrine further, requiring owners of land or commercial property to be incorporated in the host country, and to renounce all forms of protection of their home country.[13]

13.3 THE CLASSICAL WESTERN VIEW

(a) Judicial Sources

Evidently the reliance by the capital-exporting states and their corporations on an understanding concerning national treatment, as had on the whole proved adequate prior to World War I, could not survive the changed attitudes toward private property coming from the Soviet Union and Latin America. A few international decisions, and a famous exchange between the United States and Mexico served to reassert the classical approach of state responsibility to foreign investors.

One influential case involved a dispute between Norwegian owners of ships being constructed in American shipyards at the time that the United States entered World War I. The US government requisitioned the ships for

compensation, the tribunal which shall hear claims concerning the amount of compensation according to law, the form of satisfying the obligation to compensate, and the opportunities and manner in which the expropriating agency shall take material possession of the expropriated property.

For the full text, with analysis, see *Expropriation in the Americas* (n. 9 supra), 90. When Salvador Allende was elected President of Chile three years later, Article 10(10) of the Constitution was again substantially revised, not eliminating compensation completely, but providing for a special tribunal in place of the regular courts, and providing for an unreviewable power in the President to deduct 'excess profits' from the compensation due, with the intent and effect that the major foreign-owned copper companies received no compensation at all.

See A. Lowenfeld, *International Private Investment*, 140–61 and for the relevant documents, DS–162–78 (2nd edn. 1982).

[13] For a full discussion of the teachings of Calvo, published both in Spanish and in French in several editions between 1863 and 1896, see Donald R. Shea, *The Calvo Clause* (1955). One may get an idea of the Calvo doctrine from the following excerpts, as translated and quoted by Shea, 17–19:

It is certain that aliens who establish themselves in a country have the same right to protection as nationals, but they ought not to lay claim to a protection more extended. If they suffer any wrong, they ought to count on the government of the country prosecuting the delinquents, and not claim from the state to which the authors of the violence belong any pecuniary indemnity.

. . .

The rule that in more than one case it has been attempted to impose on American states is that foreigners merit more regard and privileges more marked and extended than those accorded even to the nationals of the country where they reside.

The principle is intrinsically contrary to the law of equality of nations.

use in its war effort, and after the war tendered only the value of the materials actually taken, some $2.6 million, while the Norwegian shipowners claimed the full value of the ships, about $18 million, including interest. Norway took up the claim of its nationals, and eventually the controversy was submitted to an arbitral tribunal under the Permanent Court of Arbitration.[14]

The Tribunal found essentially for Norway, stating:

> Whether the action of the United States was lawful or not, just compensation is due to the claimants under the municipal law of the United States, as well as under the international law, based on the respect for private property.[15]

Similarly, a claims commission between the United States and Panama held in favour of an American who had lost part of her estate in Panama as a result of grants by the government of Panama to other persons, saying:

> It is axiomatic that acts of a government in depriving an alien of his property without compensation impose international responsibility.[16]

By far the best known and most often quoted case on state responsibility to foreign investors was the so-called *Chorzow Factory* case, which came several times before the Permanent Court of International Justice.[17] The case grew out of the change in frontiers between Germany and the newly re-established Poland at the close of World War I, and turned principally on taking by the government of Poland of a nitrogen factory erected when the territory was part of the German Reich. A Geneva Convention in implementation of the Treaty of Versailles had authorized the government of Poland to take property in Silesia previously owned by the German government, crediting the value of the property against Germany's obligation to make reparations. Privately owned German property, however, could be taken only under provisions governing expropriation, including compensation to prior owners. Poland took the position that the factory at Chorzow had been owned by the German government, or that transfer of ownership to private parties had been fraudulent. Eventually the World Court decided these issues in favour of Germany, and concluded that the seizure of the factory by the Polish government had been unlawful:

---

[14] *United States Norway Arbitration Award*, 13 Oct. 1922 1 *U.N. Rep. Int'l Arbitral Awards* [R.I.I.A.] 307 (1918).

[15] Id., at 334. The United States paid the amount awarded, but Secretary of State Hughes (later Chief Justice of the United States) wrote that 'the award cannot be deemed by this Government to possess an authoritative character as precedent.' See 17 *Am.J. Int'l L.* 287 at 289 plus comment thereto by James Brown Scott (1923).

[16] *DeSabla Claim* (*United States* v. *Panama*) (29 June 1933), *Annual Digest and Reports of Public Int'l Law Cases 1933–34*, 241 at 243 (1940); 28 *Am. J. Int'l L.* 602 at 611 (1934).

[17] *Case concerning German interests in Upper Silesia*, P.C.I.J. Series A, Nos. 7, 9, 17, 19 (1926–9).

It follows that the compensation due to the German Government is not necessarily limited to the value of the undertaking at the moment of dispossession, plus interest to the day of payment . . .

The essential principle contained in the actual notion of an illegal act—a principle which seems to be established by international practice and in particular by the decisions of arbitral tribunals—is that reparation must, as far as possible, wipe out all the consequences of the illegal act and re-establish the situation which would, in all probability, have existed if that act had not been committed. Restitution in kind, or, if this is not possible, payment of a sum corresponding to the value which a restitution in kind would bear.[18]

Some writers and tribunals have taken this statement as an enunciation by the highest international judicial body of the basic principle of compensation in case of expropriation by a state of foreign-owned property; others have cited the same passage for the proposition that unlawful expropriation—for instance a taking that violates an express treaty provision or concession or is based on discrimination—calls for a higher measure of compensation than an expropriation carried out in lawful exercise of a state's right to take private property for public use, where the only violation is failure to pay compensation. Also, some writers have stressed that the claims involved in the *Chorzow Factory* case were brought pursuant to the Peace Treaties and the Geneva Convention of 1922, and should not be taken as expression of general customary law.[19] Nevertheless, the *Chorzow Factory* case has become one of the principal sources cited in support of the obligation of just compensation, particularly the phrase 'reparation must, as far as possible, wipe out all the consequences of the illegal act and re-establish the situation which would have existed if that act had not been committed.'

(b) The Hull Formula

Even before the Mexican Constitution of 1917 had been promulgated,[20] agrarian expropriations were carried out in Mexico, including properties owned by American citizens. A binational claims commission was established by agreement of the two countries in 1927, but by 1938 not a single claim had been adjusted or paid. In July of that year, the United States Secretary of State began a series of diplomatic exchanges with the government of Mexico which together came to be known as the Hull formula, expressing the American view, and perhaps the Western view generally, of the rights and obligations of host states vis-à-vis foreign investors and their home states.[21] As the

---

[18] P.C.I.J. Series A, No. 17, at p. 47.   [19] See, esp. Friedman (n. 5 supra), at pp. 75–81.

[20] See Sect. 13.2(b) supra.

[21] For a more complete text, from which the excerpts here presented are taken, see G. Hackworth, *Digest of International Law*, Vol. III, 655–61 (Dept. of State 1942). The complete correspondence, in English and Spanish, was published by the Dept. of State under the title 'Compensation for American-Owned Lands Expropriated in Mexico', (Dept. of State Publ. 1288, *InterAmerican Series* 16, 1939). See also 32 *Am. J. Int'l L.*, Supp. 181–207 (1938).

correspondence shows, Mexico did not accept the American position, and did not accept the suggestions for arbitration, but did eventually negotiate. Ultimately, the two countries reached agreement on compensation, but not on the law.

Hull's first note laid out the basic American position:

The taking of property without compensation is not expropriation. It is confiscation. It is no less confiscation because there may be an expressed intent to pay at some time in the future.

If it were permissible for a government to take the private property of the citizens of other countries and pay for it as and when, in the judgment of that government, its economic circumstances and its local legislation may perhaps permit, the safeguards which the constitutions of most countries and established international law have sought to provide would be illusory. Governments would be free to take property far beyond their ability or willingness to pay, and the owners thereof would be without recourse. We cannot question the right of a foreign government to treat its own nationals in this fashion if it so desires. This is a matter of domestic concern. But we cannot admit that a foreign government may take the property of American nationals in disregard of the rule of compensation under international law. Nor can we admit that any government unilaterally and through its municipal legislation can, as in this instant case, nullify this universally accepted principle of international law, based as it is on reason, equity and justice.

The representations which this Government has made to the Government of Mexico have been undertaken with entire friendliness and good will, and the Mexican Government has recognized that fact. We are entirely sympathetic to the desires of the Mexican Government for the social betterment of its people. We cannot accept the idea, however, that these plans can be carried forward at the expense of our citizens, any more than we would feel justified in carrying forward our plans for our own social betterment at the expense of citizens of Mexico.

The whole structure of friendly intercourse, of international trade and commerce, and many other vital and mutually desirable relations between nations indispensable to their progress rest upon the single and hitherto solid foundation of respect on the part of governments and of peoples for each other's rights under international justice. The right of prompt and just compensation for expropriated property is a part of this structure. It is a principle to which the Government of the United States and most governments of the world have emphatically subscribed and which they have practiced and which must be maintained. It is not a principle which freezes the status quo and denies changes in property rights but a principle that permits any country to expropriate private property within its borders in furtherance of public purposes. It enables orderly change without violating the legitimately acquired interests of citizens of other countries.[22]

The Secretary proposed that the question 'whether there has been compliance by the Government of Mexico with the rule of compensation as prescribed by international law' be submitted to arbitration. The Mexican Minister of Foreign Affairs replied as follows, clearly illustrating the divergence of views of the applicable international law:

[22] US Secretary of State to Mexican Ambassador to the United States, 21 July 1938.

My Government maintains . . . that there is in international law no rule universally accepted in theory nor carried out in practice, which makes obligatory the payment of immediate compensation nor even of deferred compensation, for expropriations of a general and impersonal character like those which Mexico has carried out for the purpose of redistribution of the land.

The expropriations made in the course of our agrarian reform, do, in fact, have this double character, which ought to be taken very much into account in order to understand the position of Mexico, and rightly appraise her apparent failure to meet her obligations.

Without attempting to refute the point of view of the American Government, I wish to draw your attention very specially to the fact that the agrarian reform is not only one of the aspects of a program of social betterment attempted by a government or a political group for the purpose of trying out new doctrines, but also constitutes the fulfilling of most important of the demands of the Mexican people, who, in the revolutionary struggle, for the purpose of obtaining it, sacrificed the very lives of their sons. The political, social, and economic stability and the peace of Mexico depend on the land being placed anew in the hands of the country people who work it; a transformation of the country, that is to say, the future of the nation, could not be halted by the impossibility of paying immediately the value of the properties belonging to a small number of foreigners who seek only a lucrative end.

. . .

As has been stated above, there does not exist in international law any principle universally accepted by countries, nor by the writers of treatises on this subject, that would render obligatory the giving of adequate compensation for expropriations of a general and impersonal character. Nevertheless, Mexico admits, in obedience to her own laws, that she is indeed under obligation to indemnify in an adequate manner; but the doctrine which she maintains on the subject, which is based on the most authoritative opinions of writers of treatises on international law, is that the time and manner of such payment must be determined by her own laws.[23]

The government of Mexico declined the American offer of arbitration, but suggested that the two governments each appoint one representative to 'fix within a brief period of time the value of the properties affected and the manner of payment.'[24]

Secretary Hull responded:

The fundamental issues raised by this communication from the Mexican Government are therefore, first, whether or not universally recognized principles of the law of nations require, in the exercise of the admitted right of all sovereign nations to expropriate private property, that such expropriation be accompanied by provision on the part of such government for adequate, effective, and prompt payment for the properties seized; second, whether any government may nullify principles of international law through contradictory municipal legislation of its own; or, third, whether such Government is relieved of its obligations under universally recognized principles of international law merely because its financial or economic situation makes compliance therewith difficult.

---

[23] Mexican Minister of Foreign Affairs to US Ambassador, 3 Aug. 1938.   [24] Id.

The Government of the United States merely adverts to a self-evident fact when it notes that the applicable precedents and recognized authorities on international law support its declaration that, under every rule of law and equity, no government is entitled to expropriate private property, for whatever purpose, without provision for prompt, adequate, and effective payment therefor. In addition, clauses appearing in the constitutions of almost all nations today, and in particular in the constitutions of the American republics, embody the principle of just compensation. These, in themselves, are declaratory of the like principle in the law of nations.

The universal acceptance of this rule of the law of nations, which, in truth, is merely a statement of common justice and fair-dealing, does not in the view of this Government admit of any divergence of opinion.

. . .

The Mexican Government refers to the fact that, when it undertook suspension of the payment of its agrarian debt, the measure affected equally Mexicans and foreigners. It suggests that if Mexico had paid only the latter to the exclusion of its nationals, she would have violated a rule of equity. In that connection, the Mexican Government refers to Article 9 of the Convention signed at the Seventh Pan American Conference, which says: 'The jurisdiction of states within the limits of national territory applies to all the inhabitants. Nationals and foreigners are under the same protection of the law and the national authorities and the foreigners may not claim rights other or more extensive than those of the nationals.'

Your Excellency's Government intimates that a demand for unequal treatment is implicit in the note of the Government of the United States, since my Government is aware that Mexico is unable to pay indemnity immediately to all of those affected by her agrarian reform and yet it demands payment to expropriated landowners who are nationals of the United States. This, it is suggested, is a claim of special privilege which no one is receiving in Mexico.

I must definitely dissent from the opinions thus expressed by the Government of Mexico. The Government of the United States requests no privileged treatment for its nationals residing in Mexico. The present Government of the United States has on repeated occasions made it clear that it would under no circumstances request special or privileged treatment for its nationals in the other American republics, nor support any claim of such nationals for treatment other than that which was just, reasonable, and strictly in harmony with the generally recognized principles of international law.

The doctrine of equality of treatment, like that of just compensation, is of ancient origin. It appears in many constitutions, bills of rights and documents of international validity. The word has invariably referred to equality in lawful rights of the person and to protection in exercising such lawful rights. There is now announced by your Government the astonishing theory that this treasured and cherished principle of equality, designed to protect both human and property rights, is to be invoked, not in the protection of personal rights and liberties, but as a chief ground of depriving and stripping individuals of their conceded rights. It is contended, in a word, that it is wholly justifiable to deprive an individual of his rights if all other persons are equally deprived, and if no victim is allowed to escape. In the instant case it is contended that confiscation is so justified. The proposition scarcely requires answer.

. . .

. . . The statement in your Government's note to the effect that foreigners who voluntarily move to a country not their own assume, along with the advantages which they may seek to enjoy, the risks to which they may be exposed and are not entitled to better treatment than nationals of the country, presupposes the maintenance of law and order consistent with principles of international law; that is to say, when aliens are admitted into a country the country is obligated to accord them that degree of protection of life and property consistent with the standards of justice recognized by the law of nations. Actually, the question at issue raises no possible problem of special privilege. The plain question is whether American citizens owning property in Mexico shall be deprived of their properties and, in many instances, their very livelihood, in clear disregard of their just rights. It is far from legitimate for the Mexican Government to attempt to justify a policy which in essence constitutes bald confiscation by raising the issue of the wholly inapplicable doctrine of equality.[25]

The Mexican Government replied in a long note, including the following passage:

This attitude of Mexico is not, as Your Excellency's Government affirms, either unusual or subversive. Numerous nations, in reorganizing their economy, have been under the necessity of modifying their legislation in such manner that the expropriation of individual interests nevertheless does not call for immediate compensation and, in many cases, not even subsequent compensation; because such acts were inspired by legitimate causes and the aspirations of social justice, they have not been considered unusual or contrary to international law. As my Government stated to that of Your Excellency in my note of August 3, it is indispensable, in speaking of expropriation, to distinguish between those which are the result of a modification of the juridical organization and which affect equally all the inhabitants of the country, and those others decreed in specific cases and which affect interests known in advance and individually determined.[26]

Just before World War II spread to the Western Hemisphere, an agreement was reached between the United States and Mexico for a commission to determine the compensation for agrarian properties expropriated after August 30, 1927. Mexico agreed to pay $40 million in instalments to settle these and other claims, and the United States agreed to set up a $40 million fund to stabilize the peso, to grant a $30 million credit to finance road construction in Mexico, and to purchase large quantities of Mexican silver at agreed prices.[27]

In March 1938, the Mexican government had issued a decree expropriating British and American-owned oil companies, following a year of labour strife and litigation.[28] As in respect to the agrarian properties, the United

[25] US Secretary of State to Mexican Ambassador, 22 Aug. 1938.

[26] Mexican Minister of Foreign Affairs to US Ambassador, 1 Sept. 1938.

[27] See 5 *US Dept. of State Bull.* 399–403 (22 Nov. 1941); also Henry J. Steiner and Detlev Vagts, *Transnational Legal Problems*, 405–6 (3rd edn. 1986).

[28] For a contemporary account by an American law professor, see Josef L. Kunz, 'The Mexican Expropriations', 17 *N.Y.U. L. Q. Rev.* 327, esp. 359–84 (1940). For the relevant decisions of the Mexican Supreme Court, see *Expropriation in the Americas*. Sect. 13.2(b) (n. 9 supra), 134–6 and notes thereto, and in particular *Cia Mexicana de Petroleo 'El Aguilar' S.A.*, Amparo

States and Mexico exchanged diplomatic correspondence for several years.[29] President Cárdenas wrote to the US Ambassador in Mexico that his government would 'know how to honor its obligations of today and its obligations of yesterday.' Secretary Hull wrote:

The Government of the United States readily recognizes the right of a sovereign state to expropriate property for public purposes. This view has been stated in a number of communications addressed to your Government during the past two years and in conversations had with you during that same period regarding the expropriation by your Government of property belonging to American nationals. On each occasion, however, it has been stated with equal emphasis that the right to expropriate property is coupled with and conditioned on the obligation to make adequate, effective and prompt compensation. The legality of an expropriation is in fact dependent upon the observance of this requirement.[30]

The Mexican Foreign Minister responded:

Your Excellency's Government insists, as on other occasions, in maintaining the opinion that to expropriate, without a just and prompt compensation, is confiscation and does not cease to be so because there may be the express desire to pay at some time in the future. Mexico considers that it is not in such a situation, since it not only has manifested its desire to pay, but also has expressed unequivocally its readiness to do so, having done everything that it should in accordance with its own laws, in order that ultimately the total amount may be fixed that is to be paid.[31]

In the same agreement of November 1941 in which Mexico undertook to settle the agrarian claims of American former owners,[32] the two countries agreed to each appoint an expert to establish just compensation to be paid to the American owners of the nationalized petroleum properties 'on the basis of common rules of justice and equity'.[33] The experts were appointed, and agreed on an evaluation of the properties at about $24 million, less than 10 percent of what the companies had demanded, plus interest at 3 percent from the date of the 1938 Decree of Expropriation.[34] Mexico agreed to make the required payments in annual instalments through October 1947,[35] and complied in full with this undertaking.[36] The Report of the two experts to President Roosevelt and President Avila Camacho stated:

Administrativo en Revision 2902/1939, Sec. 2a (12/2/39), 62 Semanario (5th Epoca) 3201, summarized in English in 34 *Am. J. Int'l L.* 297 (1940).

[29] See Hackworth (n. 21 supra) pp. 661–5.
[30] Secretary Hull to Mexican Ambassador, 3 Apr. 1940.
[31] Mexican Minister of Foreign Affairs to US Ambassador, 1 May 1940.
[32] See n. 27 supra.   [33] Exchange of Notes, para. 9.
[34] See 6 *US Dept. of State Bull.* 351 (18 Apr. 1942).
[35] 9 *US Dept. of State Bull.* 230 (2 Oct. 1943).
[36] See 17 *US Dept. of State Bull.* 747 (12 Oct. 1947).

Expropriation, and the exercise of the right of eminent domain, under the respective constitutions and laws of Mexico and the United States, are a recognized feature of the sovereignty of all modern States.[37]

13.4 THE DISCONNECT BETWEEN THEORY AND PRACTICE

Even as the United States and Mexico were debating publicly about the obligations of host states to foreign investors, doubts began to grow among scholars in the Western tradition—not so much about the basic principle as about the extent of its application. For example, in its 1928 edition, Oppenheim's treatise on international law had barely mentioned expropriation of alien property in a footnote to a section on international delinquencies.[38] The 1937 edition, by Lauterpacht, stated in text that 'The rule is clearly established that a State is bound to respect the property of aliens.'[39] The text went on to say, however:

This rule is qualified, but not abolished, by two factors: the first is that the law of most States permits far-reaching interference with private property in connection with taxation, measures of police, public health, and the administration of public utilities. The second modification must be recognized in cases in which fundamental changes in the political system and economic structure of the State or far-reaching social reforms entail interference, on a large scale, with private property. In such cases neither the principle of absolute respect for alien private property nor rigid equality with the dispossessed nationals offers a satisfactory solution of the difficulty. It is probable that, consistently with legal principle, such solution must be sought in the granting of partial compensation.[40]

World War II, of course, led to a general decline in respect for international law, only partly reversed by the creation of the United Nations, the OAS, the Bretton Woods agencies, and the GATT, among others. The multilateral agencies were the product of treaties that not only served as organic charters but established codes of conduct for the member states. However vague and ambiguous they were, and however much they lacked in enforcement, the

---

[37] Settlement with Great Britain, whose companies had held 65 per cent of the oil properties taken, proved much more difficult, and was not completed until 1947. The total amount of compensation was fixed at $130 million, plus interest at 3 percent from the date of expropriation, to be effected over a 15-year period. According to British estimates, the compensation amounted to about one-third of the value of the expropriated properties. See S. Friedman, *Expropriation in International Law* (n. 5 supra), p. 29 and sources there cited.

[38] L. Oppenheim, *International Law*, i,§ 155, n. 2 (4th edn., McNair 1928). The thrust of the footnote was to point to many authorities discussing the defence of equal treatment of nationals and aliens of the taking state.

[39] L. Oppenheim, *International Law* Vol, I, §155, n. 2 (5th edn. H. Lauterpacht, 1937).

[40] Id. The quoted text remained unchanged through the eighth edition (1955), the last edition edited by Lauterpacht. The ninth edition devotes 15 pages to the topics, about two-thirds in footnotes. L. Oppenheim, *International Law*, Vol. I, §407 (9th edn., Jennings and Watt 1992).

codes constituted international legislation. The law of host states' obligation to foreign investment, meanwhile, remained unwritten—customary international law in the age of treaties.

(a)   The Havana Charter

In the first draft of the Havana Charter for the International Trade Organization, submitted by the United States in 1946, no provision at all was included concerning international investment. As the principal American negotiator wrote, 'It was feared . . . that investment provisions negotiated at a multilateral conference might express the lowest common denominator of protection to which any of the participants would be willing to agree.'[41]

When a chapter on economic development was added to the American proposals, the subject of international investment could no longer be avoided, but the draft that eventually emerged seems to have pleased no one. As signed in March 1948 on behalf of 53 countries, the Havana Charter provided (in Article 11(1)(b))

no Member shall take unreasonable or unjustifiable action within its territory injurious to the rights or interests of nationals of other Members in the enterprise, skills, capital, arts or technology which they have supplied.

Article 12, entitled 'International Investment for Economic Development and Reconstruction', stated that Members recognize that

international investment, both public and private, can be of great value in promoting economic development and reconstruction and consequent social progress;

and further, that

the international flow of capital will be stimulated to the extent that Members afford nationals of other countries opportunities for investment and security for existing and future investments.

But the draft went on to say

a Member has the right to determine whether and to what extent and upon what terms it will allow future foreign investment; to prescribe and give effect on just terms to requirements as to the ownership of existing and future investments;

and finally:

Members therefore undertake:

. . .

to give due regard to the desirability of avoiding discrimination as between foreign investments.

---

[41] Clair Wilcox, *A Charter for World Trade*, 145–6 (1949, repr. 1972).

A provision requiring member states to make just compensation for property taken into public ownership, subject to various exceptions, was dropped from the final version as adopted at Havana. The Charter itself was abandoned by the United States in 1950, and thereafter by all the other signatories, mostly for reasons unrelated to the investment articles.[42] It is fair to say, however, that even without participation of the Soviet Union, or of the many states that gained their independence only in the 1960s, no real consensus had developed around the subject of international investment, and no disposition to craft legal rules, as contrasted with phrases such as 'Members undertake . . . to give due regard.'

(b)   The Wave of Expropriations (1945–70)

In the quarter-century following the end of World War II, expropriations and nationalizations of all kinds took place, in Eastern Europe, in former colonies, and in newly invigorated countries of Latin America. All the countries that had come under Communist rule following World War II—all of the states of Eastern Europe (except Greece), as well as China and later Cuba—nationalized land and private industrial property, including the property of aliens.[43] Utilities, mines, and other major enterprises were subject to state-takings in Bolivia, Brazil, Argentina, Peru, and Guatemala, among other states of Latin America (but not, in this period Mexico).[44] The most widely known instances of state take-overs were the expropriation of Dutch properties in Indonesia (1958–9), in the nationalization of the Anglo-Iranian Oil Company's properties in Iran (1951), and Egypt's nationalization of the Suez Canal Company (1956).[45] In the early 1970s, nearly all the Arab states from Algeria to Saudi Arabia and Iraq nationalized or abrogated the concessions of the major Western oil companies, with surprisingly little outcry.

Typically the expropriations were followed eventually by negotiations—in some instances government-to-government, in others between the government of the taking state and the former owners directly, in still other cases with the help of intermediaries, notably the World Bank's 'good

---

[42] See Ch. 3, Sect. 3.2.

[43] For an account of the events in the first post-war years, see Nicholas Doman, 'Postwar Nationalization of Foreign Property in Europe', 48 *Columbia L. Rev.* 1125 (1948).

[44] In an effort—not wholly convincing—to study and classify the determinants of what he called 'forced divestment', Professor Kobrin came up with 1,535 firms forced to divest in 511 acts by 76 less developed countries over the years 1960–76. See Stephen J. Kobrin, 'Foreign Enterprise and Forced Divestment in LDCs', 34 *Int'l Organization* 65 at 73 (1980).

[45] For a detailed survey of state-takings of properties in which US nationals or corporations, see *Expropriations of American-Owned Property by Foreign Governments in the Twentieth Century*, Committee Print of House Comm. on Foreign Affairs, 88th Cong., 1st Sess. (1963), repr. in 2 *I.L.M.* 1066 (1963); updated in US Dept. of State. *Nationalization, Expropriation, and other Takings of United States and Certain Foreign Property since 1960* (1971), repr. in 11 *I.L.M.* 84 (1972).

offices' in negotiations between Egypt and the Universal Suez Company. In the case of the nationalizations in Eastern Europe, for example, the United States negotiated so-called 'lump-sum agreements' with each state, between 1948 (Yugoslavia) and 1982 (Czechoslovakia), under which the taking state kept the property but agreed to payment of stated sums over an extended period, and the United States agreed to adjudicate the claims of eligible former owners and make pro rata payments to them out of the funds recovered.[46] In most cases the United States held some 'bargaining chips', such as frozen assets or promise of economic assistance. The United Kingdom also negotiated lump-sum agreements with the East European states as well as Egypt but, with fewer bargaining chips (and less willingness to jeopardize its position as a financial center by blocking bank accounts), settled sooner than the United States and generally for lesser amounts relative to the value of the properties in question.[47]

Wholly uncompensated expropriation of the property of aliens was rarely seen in the years following World War II.[48] But the property was virtually never returned, and the amounts of compensation tendered could rarely be fitted into the Hull formula or anything close to it, either in the relation of the payments to the value of the property in question, or in the period between the taking and the beginning—let alone the completion—of the compensation.

Thus none of the potential sources of international law on the obligation of host states to alien investors—not Hull, not Calvo, and not the Soviet model—turned out to be a reliable guide to practice, and none was wholly irrelevant. Moreover, the search for customary law in the practice of states was also unsatisfactory, because the formation of customary international law through the practice of states requires not only consistency in the practice but evidence that the practice followed from a sense of legal obligation (*opinio juris*).[49]

---

[46] See Richard B. Lillich and Burns H. Weston, *International Claims: Their Settlement by Lump Sum Agreements* (1975). A sequel to this book by the same authors and David J. Bederman for the period 1975–95 was published in 1999. For a description of the methods of adjudication and distribution of the claims, see Edward D. Re, 'The Foreign Claims Settlement Commission and the Adjudication of International Claims', 56 *Am. J. Int'l L.* 728 (1962).

[47] See Richard B. Lillich, *International Claims: Postwar British Practice* (1967).

[48] Accord, Rudolf Dolzer, 'New Foundations of the Law of Expropriation of Alien Property", 75 *Am. J. Int'l L.* 553 at 560 (1981). A significant exception was the expropriation by Cuba of the property of US nationals and companies. Pointing out that Cuba had eventually settled with foreign property owners other than American, Dolzer wrote in 1981, 'It requires no gift of prophesy to predict that even Cuba will pay some compensation in a political arrangement with the United States at some date in the future.' As of year-end 2001, this had not occurred and seemed unlikely so long as Fidel Castro remained alive and in power in Cuba.

[49] For a discussion of the formation of customary international law, including the conundrum in the assertion that law is built by state practice based on a sense of legal obligation, which in turn depends on the practice of states, see e.g. American Law Institute, *Restatement (Third) of the Foreign Relations Law of the United States*, §102 and comments *b* and *c* and Reporters' Note 2 (1987). The *Restatement* suggests:

> perhaps the sense of legal obligation came originally from principles of natural law or common morality, often already reflected in principles of law common to national legal systems . . . ; practice built on that sense of obligation then matured into customary law.   *cont./*

Clearly law played a part—a not insignificant part—in the decisions of states to take or not to take particular properties, to negotiate settlements, and to pay—and accept or reject—compensation. But equally clearly, the lump-sum agreements, as well as the individual agreements with such firms as ITT in Brazil,[50] Marcona in Peru,[51] and the Western oil companies operating in the Middle East,[52] were driven by political and economic considerations, generally without even an attempt to fit them into international legal doctrine.

13.5   THE UN'S ATTEMPTS TO DECLARE CUSTOMARY LAW

(a)   Permanent Sovereignty over Natural Resources (1962)[53]

After ten years of debate in the UN Human Rights Commission, the Economic and Social Council, and a Special Commission on Permanent Sovereignty over Natural Resources, the UN General Assembly came in the fall of 1962 to consider a proposed Declaration on Permanent Sovereignty over Natural Resources. Though a resolution of the General Assembly, even in the form of a Declaration, is not positive law and does not come before parliaments for ratification, the proposed Declaration was seen at the time as an attempt to record—and perhaps to shape—the customary law then prevailing. The debate reflected much of the world's division on the question of foreign investment, and the outcome remained ambiguous.[54]

As the draft was introduced upon recommendation of the Special Commission, it contained a series of recitals of sovereign rights, and only

Alternatively

Perhaps the definition reflects a later stage in the history of international law when governments found practice and sense of obligation already in place, and accepted them without inquiring as to the original basis of that sense of legal obligation.

Neither of these explanations quite fits the search for customary law on international investment in the years following World War II.

[50] For a brief account which ends with the sale of all of ITT's telephone properties but an agreement for compensation which is to be reinvested by ITT in manufacturing in Brazil, see Henry J. Steiner and Detlev F. Vagts, *Transnational Legal Problems*, 440–3 (2nd edn. 1976).

[51] See David Gantz, 'The Marcona Settlement: New Forms of Negotiation and Compensation for Nationalized Property', 71 *Am. J. Int'l L.* 474 (1977).

[52] See Ahmed S. El-Kosheri 'Le Régime Juridique Créé par les Accords de Participation dans le Domaine Petrolier', 147 *Recueil des Cours* 219 (Hague Acad. Int'l Law 1975–IV).

[53] This section relies principally on Stephen M. Schwebel, 'The Story of the UN's Declaration on Permanent Sovereignty over Natural Resources', 49 *ABA Journal* 463 (1963); see also Karol N. Gess, 'Permanent Sovereignty over Natural Resources', 13 *Int'l & Comp. L.Q.* 398 (1964), which reproduces the final text along with two earlier drafts. Mr. Schwebel was at the time the legal adviser to the US delegation; he later became a judge and President of the World Court. Mr. Gess was a member of the Office of Legal Affairs of the United Nations, and in that capacity a member of the UN secretariat monitoring the debate.

[54] The final text of what became General Assembly Resolution 1803, 14 Dec. 1962, is reproduced in both the Schwebel and Gess articles cited at id., as well as in many textbooks and collections of documents on international law. The official citation is G.A. Res. 1803, 17 U.N. G.A.O.R. Annexes, Vol. I, Agenda Item No. 39 at p. 59.

vague references to international law. The United States, supported by the United Kingdom, sought to balance the draft with statements concerning the *obligations* of states under international law. The draft resolution did speak of compensation for nationalization or expropriation, but said only that

the owner shall be paid appropriate compensation, in accordance with the rules in force in the state taking such measures in the exercise of its sovereignty and in accordance with international law.

The United States proposed an amendment to the effect that 'appropriate compensation in accordance with international law' means 'prompt, adequate and effective compensation'. But this amendment, in various versions, did not win favour, and was eventually withdrawn so that the quoted sentence remained as introduced. For the record, the American Ambassador stated that his delegation

was confident that the expression 'appropriate compensation' in operative paragraph 4 of the draft resolution would be interpreted as meaning, under international law, prompt, adequate and effective compensation.

Not everyone agreed with this interpretation, but a Soviet amendment that would have read:

The question of compensation to the owners shall in such cases be decided in accordance with the national law of the country taking these measures in the exercise of its sovereignty.

was defeated by 39 votes against, 28 in favour, with 21 abstentions. Further, the draft resolution provided that

in cases where capital is imported pursuant to authorization by the host state, the capital imported and the earnings on that capital shall be governed by the terms thereof, by national legislation in force, and by international law.

The United States proposed an amendment that would expressly state that foreign investment agreements shall be faithfully observed. That amendment was not approved, but came back in a modified form, as set out below. Meanwhile the United States and other home countries of investors could draw comfort from rejection of an amendment sponsored by Afghanistan and the United Arab Republic to the effect that

the owner shall be paid adequate compensation, when and where appropriate.

In any event, the resolution as proposed, and as adopted, read 'the Owner *shall* be paid appropriate compensation' making it plain, in the United States view, that the payment of appropriate compensation was a matter not of discretion but of obligation.[55]

---

[55] See Schwebel (n. 53 supra) at p. 466.

On the question of dispute settlement, the draft as proposed by the Special Commission provided that

In any case where the question of compensation gives rise to a controversy, national jurisdiction should be resorted to. Upon agreement by the parties concerned, settlement of the dispute *may* be made through arbitration or international adjudication (italics added).

The United States sought an amendment that would preclude an interpretation that resort to national jurisdiction could be avoided only by an agreement entered into after the dispute had arisen. That amendment also failed, but 'may' was changed to 'should', and the sentence beginning with 'upon agreement' was changed in the final version to read

upon agreement by sovereign states and other parties concerned.

Considering developments not much later in another forum,[56] it is interesting to recall the debate on the US-UK amendment to add

Agreements freely entered into shall be faithfully observed.

The American ambassador said that this 'generally accepted principle' applies 'alike to agreements between states, states and international organizations and states and private foreign investors.' Other states took the position that agreements between a government and a company, whether foreign or domestic, could not be equated with agreements between governments, and were subject only to national law. On this issue the US-UK position prevailed, though not by mentioning foreign investors expressly, but by providing (in a new Article 8) that 'Foreign Investment Agreements freely entered into *by or between* sovereign States shall be observed in good faith.'

The American ambassador sought to nail down the point:

My delegation is especially gratified that this Committee has affirmed the binding character of foreign investment agreements, whether these agreements are for arbitration of disputes or are of a more comprehensive character, and whether these agreements are concluded between states, or between states and international organizations, or states and private foreign investors.

One might have wondered, at the end, whether the United States would vote for or against Resolution 1803. In the event, after some debate within the US government, the United States joined 86 other states in voting in favour.[57] The US delegation concluded that the United States gained from the provision that foreign capital shall be governed by the terms of its importation and by international law, meaning as it believed that the resolution incorporated by reference the requirement of international law that foreign capital shall not be subjected to discriminatory treatment.[58] Also, it

---

[56] See the discussion of the World Bank or ICSID Convention in Ch. 15, Sect. 15.1 infra.

[57] France and South Africa voted no; 12 states abstained—the Communist bloc (including Cuba) plus Ghana and Burma.

[58] See Schwebel (n. 53 supra), 469.

appreciated the provisions in the resolution as adopted that taking of private property must be for a public purpose,[59] and that profits derived from the investment 'must be shared in the proportions freely agreed upon between the investor and the recipient State.'

There is no question that Resolution 1803 was ambiguous, and that different interests could cite different provisions for their own purposes. President Allende of Chile, for instance, addressing the United Nations in 1972 shortly after his government had expropriated the interests of US-owned copper companies, essentially without compensation, quoted only from the first preambular clause of the Declaration, concerning the 'inalienable right of all states freely to dispose of their natural wealth and resources in accordance with their national interests.'

Nevertheless, the Resolution on Permanent Sovereignty did constitute a consensus of sorts between developed and less developed countries, around four basic principles:[60]

— that compensation must be paid in the event of taking of alien property;
— that such compensation must be paid in accordance with international law;
— that investment agreements between states and private parties have a binding effect; and
— that arbitration agreements between states and private parties have a binding effect.

(b)   From Permanent Sovereignty to the New International Economic Order

The consensus (or apparent consensus) cobbled together in the context of Resolution 1803 did not last long, though the 1962 Declaration on Permanent Sovereignty has continued to be studied and quoted. But the idea that resolutions of the UN General Assembly—especially if labelled 'Declaration'—could make law caught on in the UN community, even as the many newly independent states were gaining ever larger majorities in the one nation-one vote bodies.

Of course, technically the UN General Assembly has no power to make law.[61] But if an existing norm—for instance that expropriation of the prop-

---

[59] Actually, the text of Article 4 reads 'on grounds or reasons of public utility', a translation from the Spanish as introduced by Chile. See Gess (n. 53 supra), at p. 420. The text continues:

... public utility, security or the national interest which are recognized as overriding purely individual or private interests, both domestic and foreign.

[60] This summary is adapted from Gess (n. 53 supra), at p. 448.

[61] Article 13 of the UN Charter reads in pertinent part as follows:

1. The General Assembly shall *initiate studies* and *make recommendations* for the purpose of: *cont./*

erty of aliens calls for compensation—is based on customary law, it is at least arguable that a resolution denying the existence of that norm impairs its continuing validity.[62] Soon after the 'consensus' of 1962, a coalition of Second and Third World representatives to the United Nations set out to pursue this course.

In November 1966, the General Assembly adopted another resolution entitled Permanent Sovereignty over Natural Resources, but with several tilts to the balance of Resolution 1803.[63] Resolution 2158 recognized (in paragraph 5)

the right of all countries, and in particular of the developing countries, to secure and increase their share in the administration of enterprises which are fully or partly operated by foreign capital and to have a greater share in the advantages and profits derived therefrom on an equitable basis, with due regard to development needs and objectives of the peoples concerned and to mutually acceptable contractual practices.

104 countries voted in favour of the resolution, six countries, including the United States, abstained.

The US ambassador said that paragraph 5

does not state with sufficient clarity the fact that no country can escape the obligations arising out of international law and economic cooperation and out of contractual arrangements which have been mutually accepted.[64]

If the 1966 resolution lacked clarity, as the American delegate asserted, this could not be said about the next major Resolution on Permanent Sovereignty. In Resolution 3171, adopted in December 1973, the General Assembly affirmed

that the application of the principle of nationalization carried out by States, as an expression of their sovereignty in order to safeguard their natural resources, implies that each State is entitled to determine the amount of possible compensation and the mode of payment, and that any disputes which might arise should be settled in accordance with the national legislation of each State carrying out such measures.[65]

   (a) promoting international cooperation in the political field and encouraging the progressive development of international law and its codification;
   (b) promoting international cooperation in the economic, social, cultural, educational, and health fields, and assisting in the realization of human rights and fundamental freedoms for all without distinction as to race, sex, language, or religion.

[62] For elaboration of this point and discussion of the significance of 'non-binding' or 'non-legal' international documents, see Oscar Schachter, *International Law in Theory and Practice*, ch. VI, 'Resolutions and Political Texts', 178 *Recueil des Cours*, 9. esp. at 120 (Hague Acad. Int'l Law (1982-V). See also ALI, *Restatement (Third) of the Foreign Relations Law of the United States*, §103, comment c and Reporters' note 2 (1987).

[63] G.A. Res. 2158, 21 U.N. G.A.O.R. Supp. (No. 16), 29 (25 Nov. 1966).

[64] Statement of Ambassador James Roosevelt published in Press Release No. 4987 of US Delegation to the United Nations, 25 Nov. 1986, repr. in Steiner, Vagts, and Koh, *Transnational Legal Problems*, 486–7 (4th edn., 1994).

[65] G.A. Res. 3171, 28 U.N. G.A.O.R. Supp. (No. 30) p. 52 (17 Dec. 1973), UN Doc. A/9030, repr. in 68 *Am.J. Int'l L* 381 (1974), also 13 *I.L.M.* 238 (1974).

Nothing was stated about international law, and nothing was stated about international adjudication or arbitration. As for 'possible' compensation, it would be up to each state to determine the amount and mode of payment. The resolution carried by 108 to 1, but this time with 16 abstentions, including ten Western European countries and the United States.[66]

In the following year the reign of the 'Group of 77'[67] reached its high point, with the adoption of a Charter of Economic Rights and Duties of States,[68] designed to describe (or bring about) a 'New International Economic Order'. Article 2 of the Charter shows the extent of departure from the traditional international law:

1. Every State has and shall freely exercise full permanent sovereignty, including possession, use and disposal, over all its wealth, natural resources and economic activities.

2. Each State has the right:

(a) To regulate and exercise authority over foreign investment within its national jurisdiction in accordance with its laws and regulations and in conformity with its national objectives and priorities. No State shall be compelled to grant preferential treatment to foreign investment;

(b) To regulate and supervise the activities of transnational corporations within its national jurisdiction and take measures to ensure that such activities comply with its laws, rules and regulations and conform with its economic and social policies. Transnational corporations shall not intervene in the internal affairs of a host State. Every State should, with full regard for its sovereign rights, co-operate with other States in the exercise of the right set forth in this subparagraph;

(c) To nationalize, expropriate or transfer ownership of foreign property in which case appropriate compensation should be paid by the State adopting such measures, taking into account its relevant laws and regulations and all circumstances that the State considers pertinent. In any case where the question of compensation gives rise to a controversy, it shall be settled under the domestic law of the nationalizing State and by its tribunals, unless it is freely and mutually agreed by all States concerned that other peaceful means be sought on the basis of the sovereign equality of States and in accordance with the principle of free choice of means.

If this were really a statement of prevailing law—*lex lata* in the language of international law—most of what had come before would be gone. Not only would no state be compelled to grant preferential treatment to foreign investment—a principle never incorporated as such into international law—

---

[66] For the 'legislative history' of Resolution 3171, as well as of the Charter of Economic Rights and Duties of States, see F.V. García-Amador, 'The Proposed New International Economic Order: A New Approach to the Law Governing Nationalization and Compensation', 12 *Lawyer of the Americas* 1 (1980).

[67] i.e., the non-aligned countries, by now containing well over a hundred states.

[68] G.A. Res. 3281, 29 U.N. G.A.O.R. Supp. (No. 31) 50, UN Doc. A/9631, repr. in 69 *Am. J. Int'l L.* 484 (1975), also 14 *I.L.M.* 251 (1975). For discussion of the Charter in the context of expropriation, see García-Amador, (n. 66 supra); Burns H. Weston, 'The Charter of Economic Rights and Duties of States and the Deprivation of Foreign-Owned Wealth', 75 *Am. J. Int'l L.* 437 (1981).

there seemed to be no right for foreign investment to equal treatment, i.e. no prohibition of arbitrary or discriminatory treatment of foreign investments or investors. The right to nationalize or expropriate foreign-owned property—long recognized—was restated, but without any requirement of public purpose or public utility.[69] And while 'appropriate compensation' was mentioned, as in Resolution 1803 twelve years earlier,[70] 'shall' was changed to 'should,' and 'in accordance with international law' was omitted altogether.

At minimum, the Charter on the Rights and Duties of States was a concerted effort by the developing countries to repudiate a system of law in whose creation they had played little or no part. Some writers, notably García-Amador, who was the Reporter on State Responsibility to the International Law Commission and later Legal Adviser to the Organization of American States, thought that the Charter went further: 'The Third World attitude,' Garcia-Amador wrote, 'at least insofar as measures affecting foreign-owned property are concerned, is to place State responsibility outside the realm of international law.'[71]

Viewed more than a quarter century later, the Charter of the Rights and Duties of States seems less significant than it appeared at the time. If there was indeed an effort to divorce international investment from international law, that effort did not succeed, though appeals to 'sovereignty' and other echoes of the debates of the 1960s and 1970s continued to be heard in the United Nations and other international fora.[72] Nearly all the capital-exporting states either voted against the Charter or abstained, so that the consensus attributed to Resolution 1803 of 1962, and with decreasing persuasiveness to the intervening resolutions, could not be attributed to the Charter.[73] Notwithstanding the statements of several of its proponents designed to endow the New

---

[69] Generally, the requirement of public purpose or public utility has not been significant in nationalization or expropriation cases, because the policy of the taking state has been presumed to be in its national interest as seen by that state. The issue was raised however, in connection with the nationalization of foreign petroleum concessions by Libya in the period 1971–4, because the Libyan government expressly stated that its actions were in response to the policies of the British and American governments regarding the Persian Gulf and Israel. See Ch. 14, Sect. 14.1(a) infra.

[70] See p. 408 supra.   [71] García-Amador (n. 66 supra), 10 and 57.

[72] For instance, one initiative that occupied the United Nations for a decade was creation of a Commission and Centre on Transnational Corporations, which in turn undertook to draft a Code of Conduct. The Code was never completed, and the debates, while vigorous, did not command public attention in the way the resolutions on Permanent Sovereignty and the New International Economic Order had done in the period 1962–74. For a brief description of the Commission, as well as a draft of the proposed code (with the controversial points in brackets signifying disagreement) see A. Lowenfeld, *International Private Investment*, 197–8 and DS–333–55 (2nd edn. 1982).

[73] The final vote on the Charter was 120 states in favour, 6 against, and 10 abstentions. Negative votes were cast by the United States, the United Kingdom, the Federal Republic of Germany, plus Belgium, Denmark, and Luxembourg. Austria, Canada, France, Ireland, Israel, Italy, Japan, the Netherlands, Norway, and Spain abstained. All other states that participated in the vote, including Australia, New Zealand, and Sweden, voted for the Charter.

International Economic Order with the characteristics of law and to equate the resolutions with legislation,[74] the challenge appeared essentially political.

The United States and other home countries of multinational corporations rejected the challenge by the developing states, refused to agree to any change in the traditional principles, and denied that they had been replaced or modified in customary law by state practice (as contrasted with resolutions in the United Nations). The capital-exporting states took the position that the traditional requirements are solidly based both on the moral rights of property owners and on the needs of an effective international system. Moreover, they argued, whatever objections might be made to the traditional rules as applied to investments established in the colonial era, the traditional rules should clearly apply to arrangements made between investors and independent governments negotiated on a commercial basis.[75]

The response to the debate in international dispute settlement is illustrated in the following chapter. The response in state practice, in the form of bilateral and multilateral agreements, as well as in a marked change in the attitude of most developing countries to international investment generally, is the subject of Chapter 15.

Summary

The 'traditional consensus' based on nineteenth-century attitudes concerning private property and on the practice of relatively few states, was drawn into question after World War I, particularly in the context of the Russian and Mexican revolutions. As national treatment no longer satisfied the defenders of private property and transnational investment, the basic principle was reformulated. The right of a state to nationalize or expropriate foreign-owned property was generally recognized, subject to the condition that the former owners receive compensation.

The 'Hull formula' calling for prompt, adequate, and effective compensation was not applied literally, even in the context where the formula was first enunciated. 'Prompt' did not exclude payments over time; 'adequate' was often not the equivalent of full value (putting aside how that term should be defined); 'effective' meant that the taking state could not subject the compensation to taxation or exchange controls, but did not exclude

---

[74] See e.g. Weston (n. 68 supra), at pp. 451–5; Hans Joerg Geiser, 'A New International Economic Order, Its Impact on the Evolution of International Law', 9 *Annals of International Studies* 89 (1978); *contra*, Charles N. Brower and John B. Tepe, Jr., 'The Charter of Economic Rights and Duties of States: A Reflection or Rejection of International Law?', 9 *Int'l Lawyer* 295 (1975).

[75] This paragraph is adapted from a paragraph in ALI, *Restatement (Third) of the Foreign Relations Law of the United States*, §712, Reporters' Note 1, entitled 'Status of International Law on Expropriation' (1987). The present author was one of the Reporters of the *Restatement*, but not the drafter of the note here borrowed.

more or less voluntary agreement by the former owner to reinvest some or all of the compensation in the taking state in sectors not designated for nationalization. Later formulations looked to 'just compensation' or 'appropriate compensation', taking account in some instances of the taking state's ability to pay.[76]

The views of the law of international investment were inevitably shaped by varied, and often ambivalent, attitudes to private investment generally, to sovereignty, to multinational enterprises, and to the role of the state in the economy. Efforts to reach international agreements on the law of international investment—in GATT, in the United Nations and its organs, or elsewhere—foundered, except for the 1962 Resolution on Permanent Sovereignty that contained something for everyone and reflected consensus, if at all, for a short time only.

The next chapter provides some illustrations of how courts and arbitral tribunals coped with the several kinds of ambiguities described in this chapter.

---

[76] See e.g. ALI, *Restatement (Third) of the Foreign Relations Law of the United States*, §712, esp. comment *d* (1987).

14

Dispute Settlement and International Investment

As the preceding chapter has shown, by the mid-1970s the customary international law of the protection of international investment was made up of numerous ingredients and influences. States often preached one thing in the United Nations and practised another in bilateral and multilateral agreements, as described in the next chapter. Scholarly support could be found all along the spectrum between complete denial that international law applied to protection of international investment to contining prevalence of the Hull formula and its antecedents.[1] One useful way to explore the state of the

---

[1] For comprehensive bibliographies as of the 1980s, see e.g. Rosalyn Higgins, 'The Taking of Property by the State: Recent Developments in International Law', 176 *Recueil des Cours*, 259 at 390–911 (Hague Acad. Int'l Law 1982-III); Rudolf Dolzer, *Eigentum, Enteignung und Entschädigung im geltenden Völkerrecht*, 306–28 (1987). See also ALI *Restatement (Third) of the Foreign Relations Law of the United States*, §§711–13 and Reporters' Notes thereto (1987).

customary law of international investment is to examine the results of international adjudication and arbitration.

Section 14.1 presents excerpts from three roughly contemporaneous arbitrations arising out of the termination of petroleum concessions granted to western oil companies by King Idris of Libya and repudiated by the revolutionary government of Col. Muammar Qaddafi, followed by excerpts from an influential arbitral award arising out of termination of a petroleum concession by the (continuing) government of Kuwait. Section 14.2 explores the rather limited contribution to the law of international investment by the World Court. Section 14.3 explores the role of national courts, first in selected European courts, and then in more detail the changing position of the courts of the United States in formulation of the act of state doctrine and variations thereon.

14.1   International Arbitral Tribunals

(a)   The *Libyan Nationalization* Cases

Oil was discovered in Libya in 1959, and soon thereafter Western oil companies negotiated concession agreements with the government, pursuant to a Petroleum Law of 1955, adopted during the reign of King Idris. In 1969, a military coup led by Col. Muammar Qaddafi overthrew the monarchy and established a Socialist People's Arab Republic. In the period 1971–4 the Libyan government carried out the nationalization of all the interests and properties of the Western oil companies, including in particular, subsidiaries of British Petroleum (BP Libya), Texaco and Standard Oil of California (Topco/Calasiatic) and Atlantic Ridgefield (Libyan American Oil Company or Liamco). Each of these companies had been operating in defined areas of Libya pursuant to concessions issued in accordance with the Petroleum Law. No compensation was tendered or paid in any instance. The reasons given in press releases by the Libyan government had to do with failure by the British government to protect some islands in the Persian Gulf from seizure by Iran and support by the United States for Israel.[2]

Each of the concessions contained a so-called 'stabilization clause', stating

The contractual rights expressly created by this concession shall not be altered except by mutual consent of the parties.

and further

Any amendment to or repeal of [the Regulations in force on the date of execution of the agreement] . . . shall not affect the rights of the Company without its consent.

[2] For a thorough discussion by counsel for Topco, see Robert B. von Mehren and P. Nicholas Kourides, 'International Arbitrations between States and Foreign Private Parties: The Libyan Nationalization Cases', 75 *Am. J. Int'l L.* 476 (1981).

Each of the concessions also contained an elaborate arbitration clause, providing for each party to appoint one arbitrator and for the two arbitrators so chosen to appoint an Umpire, but if one party failed to appoint an arbitrator then for a Sole Arbitrator to be appointed by the President of the International Court of Justice. The arbitration clauses also contained the following provision on the applicable law:

This concession shall be governed by and interpreted in accordance with the principles of law of Libya common to the principles of international law and in the absence of such common principles then by and in accordance with the general principles of law, including such of those principles as may have been applied by international tribunals.[3]

BP, Topco/Calasiatic, and Liamco each initiated an arbitration claiming breach of its concession agreement. In each case Libya refused to name an arbitrator or otherwise participate in the arbitration,[4] and the President of the World Court appointed a Sole Arbitrator. Thus each case went forward on the basis of submissions to the Sole Arbitrator by the Claimants alone.

Each of the arbitrators wrote a lengthy award; while the awards differed from one another on a number of points, including construction of the governing law clause and the available remedies, each of the arbitrators concluded that the actions of the Libyan government constituted breach of its obligations to the claimants under the concession agreements.[5]

The most elaborate award, and the one most pertinent to the focus of this chapter, was rendered by Professor René-Jean Dupuy in the Topco/Calasiatic case. Not having two adverse parties before him, Prof. Dupuy addressed every argument that he imagined might have been made on behalf of Libya if it had participated in the arbitration.

Dupuy construed the governing law clause to call for analysis of both Libyan and international law:

On the one hand, as regards the principles of Libyan law [including both Islamic Law (quoting the Koran 'O ye believers, perform your contracts') and the Libyan Civil Code], Art. 148 of which reads 'A contract must be performed in accordance with its contents and in compliance with the requirements of good faith,' . . .

On the other hand, as regards the principles of international law, . . . it is unquestionable . . . that the maxim *pacta sunt servanda* is a general principle of law; it is an essential principle of international law. . . .

---

[3] Note the resemblance (but not identity) of the governing law clause in the Libyan concession agreements to Article 42 of the ICSID Convention, reproduced and discussed in Chapter 15, Sect. 15. 1(c).

[4] In the Topco/Calasiatic case, the Libyan government wrote a memorandum to the President of the World Court urging him to decline to appoint a Sole Arbitrator, on the ground that the disputes were not subject to arbitration because the nationalizations were acts of sovereignty. In the other two cases, Libya did not respond at all.

[5] The BP Award, dated 1 Aug. 1974, is published in 53 *Int'l Law Reports*, at 297 (1979); the original French text of the Topco/Calasiatic award, dated 19 Jan. 1977, is published (in part) in 104 *J. du Droit Int'l* 350 (1977) and complete in English trans. in 53 *Int'l Law Reports*, 389. The Liamco Award, dated 12 Apr. 1977, is published in 20 *I.L.M.*, 1 (1981).

The conformity, on this essential point, of the principles of Libyan law with the principles of international law relieves the Tribunal from discussing the matter further—in particular from going to the second part provided for subsidiarily in [the governing law clause] of the Deeds of Concession—and enables it to conclude that the Deeds of Concession in dispute have binding force.[6]

But what about the concept of sovereignty, and the recently adopted New International Economic Order? A few excerpts from a discussion that ranges over 27 printed pages may serve to convey the sense of the award, and its perception of the state of international law in the mid-1970s.

[T]he right of a State to nationalize is unquestionable today. It results from international customary law, established as the result of general practices considered by the international community as being the law. . . . It is an essential prerogative of sovereignty for the constitutionally authorized authorities of the State to choose and build freely an economic and social system. International law recognizes that a State has this prerogative just as it has the prerogative to determine freely its political regime and its constitutional institutions. . . .[7]

Even though, for a State, the decision of nationalizing is an expression of its sovereignty, which this Tribunal fully recognizes, does not the exercise of the right to nationalize know some limits in the international order? In particular, does the act of sovereignty which constitutes the nationalization authorize a State to disregard its international commitments assumed by it within the framework of its sovereignty?

It is clear from an international point of view that it is not possible to criticize a nationalization measure concerning nationals of the State concerned, or any measure affecting aliens in respect to whom the State concerned has made no particular commitment to guarantee and maintain their position. . . .

But the case is totally different when the State has concluded with a foreign contracting party an internationalized agreement, either because the contract has been subjected to the municipal law of the host country, viewed as a mere law of reference, applicable as of the effective date and 'stabilized' on that same date by specific clauses, or because it has been placed directly under the aegis of international law. Under these two assumptions, the State has placed itself within the international legal order in order to guarantee vis-à-vis its foreign contracting party a certain legal and economic status over a certain period of time. In consideration for this commitment, the partner is under an obligation to make a certain amount of investments in the country concerned and to explore and exploit at its own risks the petroleum resources which have been conceded to it.

Thus, the decision of a State to take nationalizing measures constitutes the exercise of an internal legal jurisdiction, but carries international consequences when such measures affect international legal relationships in which the nationalizing State is involved.[8]

. . .

---

[6] *Topco/Calasiatic* Award, paras. 51–2.   [7] Id., para. 59.

[8] Id., paras. 61–2. Dupuy adds, in para. 68—'without prejudice to anything which may be added later as to the legal value of the Resolutions of the General Assembly of the United Nations'—a reference to the paragraph in Resolution 1803 that 'foreign investment agreements freely entered into by or between sovereign States shall be observed in good faith.' See Ch. 13, Sect. 13.5(a).

Such is the present state of international positive laws. The fact that various nationalization measures in disregard of previously concluded agreements have been accepted in fact by those who were affected, either [by] private companies or by the State of which they were nationals, cannot be interpreted as recognition by international practice of such a rule; the amicable settlements which have taken place having been inspired basically by considerations of expediency and not of legality.[9]

As for the resolutions of the United Nations General Assembly, 'it is impossible to deny that the United Nations' activities have had a significant influence on the content of contemporary international law.'[10] But while Resolution 1803 reflected a balanced view, and the support of several Western countries depended on the reference in that resolution to international law, 'it appears to this Tribunal that the conditions under which Resolutions 3171, 3201, and 3281 (Charter of the Economic Rights and Duties of States) were notably different.'[11] The award traces the voting pattern not only on the resolutions as a whole, but even of specific paragraphs and on the question of the binding character of the Charter:

With respect to . . . the appraisal of the legal value on the basis of the principles stated, it appears essential to this Tribunal to distinguish between those provisions stating the existence of a right on which the generality of the States has expressed agreement and those provisions introducing new principles which were rejected by certain representative groups of States and having nothing more than a *de lege ferenda* value only in the eyes of the States which have adopted them. . . .

On the basis of the circumstances of adoption mentioned above and by expressing an *opinio juris communis*, Resolution 1803 seems to this Tribunal to reflect the state of customary law existing in this field. . . .

While Resolution 1803 appears to a large extent as the expression of a real general will, this is not at all the case with respect to the other Resolutions mentioned above. . . .

The absence of any connection between the procedure of compensation and international law and the subjection of this procedure solely to municipal law cannot be regarded by this Tribunal except as a *de lege ferenda* formulation, which even appears *contra legem* in the eyes of many developed countries.[12]

One should conclude that a sovereign State which nationalizes cannot disregard the commitments undertaken by the contracting State: to decide otherwise would in fact recognize that all contractual commitments undertaken by a State have been undertaken under a purely permissive condition on its part and are therefore lacking of any legal force and any binding effect. From the point of view of its advisability, such a solution would gravely harm the credibility of States since it would mean that contracts signed by them would not bind them; it would introduce in such contracts a fundamental imbalance because in these contracts only one party—the party contracting with the State—would be bound. In law, such an outcome would go directly against the most elementary principles of good faith and for this reason it cannot be accepted.[13]

---

[9] *Topco/Calasiatic* Award, para. 69.   [10] Id., para. 83.   [11] Id., para. 85.
[12] Id., paras. 87–8.   [13] Id., para. 91.

The arbitrators in the other two cases did not write comparable essays on international law, but apart from the remedy came to roughly the same conclusions. Judge Lagergren in *BP* found without much difficulty that Libya had committed a fundamental breach of the concession, and 'on the basis of rules of applicable systems of law too elementary and too voluminous to require or permit citation, the Tribunal so holds.'[14]

Further the taking by the Respondent of the property, rights and interests of the Claimant clearly violates public international laws as it was made for purely extraneous political reasons and was arbitrary and discriminating in character. Nearly two years have now passed [October 1973] since the nationalization, and the fact that no offer of compensation has been made indicates that the taking was also confiscatory.[15]

Judge Lagergren discussed international law in some detail on the question of damages, but (possibly because the arbitration was conducted before the New International Economic Order was proclaimed) made no reference to the UN resolutions on Permanent Sovereignty.

Arbitrator Mahmassani in *LIAMCO* did invite the Claimant to comment on the UN Resolutions, and concluded (in 1977) that 'the said Resolutions, if not a unanimous source of law, are evidence of the recent dominant trend of international opinion concerning the sovereign right of States over their natural resources, and that the said right is always subject to the respect for contractual agreements and to the obligation of compensation.'[16]

However, Arbitrator Mahmassani wrote that 'the right to conclude contracts is one of the primordial civil rights acknowledged since olden times.' The contract is the law of the parties—under Libyan, Islamic, and International Law.[17]

Unlike Judge Lagergren, Mahmassani did not find discrimination (because by the time of his award all the concessions in Libya had been cancelled). As to the contention that the measures of nationalization were politically motivated and not in pursuance of a legitimate public purpose, Mahmassani wrote:

[I]t is the general opinion in international theory that the public utility principle is not a necessary requisite for the legality of a nationalization. This principle was mentioned by Grotius and other later publicists, but now there is no international authority, from a judicial or any other source, to support its application to nationalization. Motives are indifferent to international law, each State being free 'to judge for itself what it considers useful or necessary for the public good . . . The object pursued by it is of no concern to third parties.'[18]

---

[14] 53 *Int'l Law Reports*, 329.   [15] Ibid.   [16] *LIAMCO* Award, 20 *I.L.M.* 53.
[17] Id., 54.
[18] Id., 20 *I.L.M.* 58. The text in quotes comes from S. Friedman, *Expropriation in International Law* (1953), cited (in a different context) in Ch. 13, Sect. 13.2, n. 5.

Thus for Arbitrator Mahmassani, the question came down to a simple set of propositions, drawn, as he said, both from municipal and from international law.

(a) The right of property, including the incorporeal property of concession rights, is inviolable in principle, subject to the requirements of its social function and public well-being.

(b) Contracts, including concession agreements, constitute the law of the parties, by which they are mutually bound.

(c) The right of a State to nationalize its wealth and natural resources is sovereign, subject to the obligation of indemnification for premature termination of concession agreements.

(d) Nationalization of concession rights, if not discriminatory and not accompanied by a wrongful act or conduct, is not unlawful as such, and constitutes not a tort, but a source of liability to compensate the concessionnaire for said premature termination of the concession agreements.

Examined in the light of the above propositions, LIAMCO's Concession Agreements are binding, and cannot validly be terminated except on one of the following grounds:

[Expiry of the contractual period; mutual consent of the contracting parties; revocation by the Libyan government for non-fulfillment by LIAMCO of its contractual obligations, with the latter's right of recourse to arbitration; or non-discriminatory nationalization coupled with the required compensation.] Therefore, the nationalization measures complained of constitute a source of obligation, for which LIAMCO is entitled to request remedy by way of arbitration.[19]

Since for Mahmassani the only thing wrong with the nationalization of LIAMCO's concession was the failure to pay compensation, the remainder of his award was directed to the subject of damages. He briefly considered *restitutio in integrum*, i.e. re-establishment of the situation that would have existed but for the challenged act,[20] quoting the general common principles that 'obligations are to be performed, principally, in kind, if such performance is possible.'[21] But here restitution is impossible, because it would be 'an intolerable interference in the internal sovereignty of States'. Accordingly, Mahmassani awarded the value of the nationalized physical plant and equipment—*damnum emergens*; as to the value of the nationalized concession rights—i.e. the loss of profits or *lucrum cessans*—he concluded that it is 'just and reasonable' to adopt the formula of equitable compensation, with the classical formula of 'prior, adequate and effective compensation' remaining as a maximum and a practical guide for such assessment.'[22]

Judge Lagergren, in *BP*, spent a good part of his award on the issue of *restitutio in integrum*. He took up the *Chorzow Factory* case, but held that

---

[19] 20 *I.L.M.* 61–2.
[20] Compare the statement in the *Chorzow Factory* case, Ch. 13, Sect. 13.3(a), at n. 18, where the requirement of restitution or its equivalent is linked to an *illegal* act, which Mahmassani does not find.
[21] LIAMCO Award, sect. VI(2).   [22] LIAMCO Award Conclusions, 20 *I.L.M.* 86.

it was not applicable to the present case.[23] Under general principles of law, including international law, Lagergren concluded:

Taking a broad view of State practice over the past decades, there is reason to believe that the sovereignty actually claimed and exercised by modern nations over their natural wealth and resources (with the tacit or explicit acquiescence of other States) constitutes weak support for the contentions of the Claimant in this case as to the remedies available to a concessionaire in circumstances such as the present. The trend of practice has gone the other way, and may have become a custom and acquired the force of law.[24]

In contrast to the LIAMCO and *BP* awards, Professor Dupuy in TOPCO/CALASIATIC found that restitution is the primary form of reparation—'both under the principles of Libyan law and under the principles of international law, the normal sanction for non-performance of contractual obligations . . . inapplicable only to the extent that restoration of the *status quo ante* is impossible.[25]

Dupuy also took up the *Chorzow Factory* case, and indirectly replied to Judge Lagergren's point that the famous quotation about wiping out 'all the consequences of the illegal act' was an *obiter dictum*. 'The fact remains,' he wrote, 'that the principle was expressed in such general terms that it is difficult not to view it as a principle of reasoning having the value of a precedent.'[26]

Of course, if *restitutio* were absolutely impossible, it should not be awarded. But Dupuy did not think this was the case here.

[S]o far as the Tribunal can determine, the performance of its obligations by the defendant seems to depend on the defendant itself, and it should, in all likelihood, be possible for the Libyan Government to take the necessary measures to restore the situation as postulated by the application of legal principles. If, for reasons which would not have been brought to its knowledge, a situation irreversible and beyond the will of the parties has been created, this Tribunal can only regret that this has not been brought to its knowledge. The Tribunal must note that only the defendant could have been in a position to bring forward information tending to establish that there was an absolute impossibility beyond its control, that eliminated the possibility of restoring things to the previous state, and the Tribunal can only regret . . . the default in which the defendant seems to have thought it necessary to take shelter.[27]

Though Prof. Dupuy did not spell out how the restitution is to be carried out, his award 'pronounces and decides that the Libyan Government, the defendant, is legally bound to perform these contracts and to give them full effect' and grants the Libyan government five months to comply with and implement the award.[28]

---

[23] *BP* Award, 53 *Int'l Law Rep.* 337–40.

[24] Id., 348. For strong criticism of this part of the award in *BP*, see von Mehren and Kourides (n. 2 supra), 533–9.

[25] TOPCO/CALASIATIC Award, para. 109.　　　[26] Id., para. 98.　　　[27] Id., para. 112.

[28] Id., Operative Part, 53 *Int'l Law Rep.* 511.

The Claimants were able—within eight months, not five, to negotiate a settlement providing for $152 million worth of crude oil. BP settled for a cash payment; LIAMCO sought to enforce its award of about $80 million in courts in France, Switzerland, Sweden, and the United States, and some four years after the award, reached a settlement in an amount not disclosed.[29]

(b)   AMINOIL v. *Kuwait*

This case also grew out of termination of an oil concession, but both sides fully participated in the arbitration, and the government party fully carried out the award. As in the Libyan cases, the sums claimed were very large, and the arbitrators men of great prestige.

Background

In 1948, the Ruler of Kuwait had granted to the American Independent Oil Company (AMINOIL) a concession for 60 years to explore and exploit oil and gas resources in Kuwait's half of the so-called 'neutral zone' between Kuwait and Saudi Arabia.[30] The Agreement contained a stabilization clause similar to the clause in the Libyan concessions, as well as a termination clause and an arbitration clause.[31]

The 1948 Agreement was amended in 1961, essentially to conform to the fifty–fifty profit-sharing pattern that had become common in the Middle East since the time of the original concession. As OPEC became more powerful throughout the Middle East, pressure mounted on AMINOIL to agree to greater participation by the government as well as to imposition of higher taxes. Step by step AMINOIL accepted the required changes. Because of the quadrupling of oil prices by OPEC following the October War of 1973, AMINOIL's profits after the increased payment of taxes and royalties to Kuwait still remained higher than originally anticipated—up to a point. As negotiations under threat of shut-down of AMINOIL's operations continued in the years 1975–7, AMINOIL proposed a revised arrangement whereby its profits would amount to about 70 cents per barrel or $18–20 million per year. The government of Kuwait, which had meanwhile taken over—by

---

[29] For details of the settlements, see von Mehren and Kourides (n. 2 supra), 545–9 and sources there cited. The litigation in the United States between LIAMCO and Libya is discussed in Sect. 14.3(b)(2), at n. 125 infra in connection with the act of state doctrine.

[30] AMINOIL was truly an independent oil company, owned by a group of American investors, but not related to any of the 'Seven Sisters' or other major oil companies.

[31] The original stabilization clause read:

The Sheikh shall not by general or special legislation or by administrative measures or by any other act whatever annul this Agreement except as provided in [the Termination Clause]. No alteration shall be made in the terms of this Agreement by either the Sheikh or the Company except in the event of the Sheikh and the Company jointly agreeing that it is desirable in the interest of both parties to make certain alterations, deletions or additions to this Agreement.

The Termination Clause provided three specific defaults by the Company which would authorize the Ruler to terminate the concession before the expiry of the 60-year period.

agreement—all but one of the other oil concessions in the country, offered a plan that would result in profits to AMINOIL of about 25 cents per barrel or about $7.5 million per year. For a brief period the parties negotiated about the price of a take-over of the concession by the government, but they failed to reach agreement. Finally, in September 1977, the government issued a decree-law terminating the concession and providing that all property should revert to the state. Kuwait did not deny the obligation to pay compensation: the decree-law established a Compensation Committee 'whose task it will be to assess the fair compensation due to the Company as well as the Company's outstanding obligations to the State or other parties.' AMINOIL declined to appear before the Compensation Committee and demanded arbitration in London pursuant to the 1948 agreement.

The Arbitration and the Governing Law

Eventually the two sides entered into an agreement to arbitrate in Paris. Neither side would be designated as claimant or defendant, and the claims would be limited to monetary compensation or damages, thus excluding the issue of *restitutio in integrum* that had occupied so much of the attention of the arbitrators in the Libyan cases.[32] The tribunal consisted of Sir Gerald Fitzmaurice, a former judge of the World Court, Prof. Hamed Sultan of Cairo University, and as chairman, Prof. Paul Reuter, the dean of French professors of international law.

The agreement to arbitrate provided (in Article III(2)):

The law governing the substantive issues between the Parties shall be determined by the Tribunal, having regard to the quality of the Parties, the transnational character of their relations and the principles of law and practice prevailing in the modern world.

The arbitrators interpreted this clause as follows:

Article III(2), with good reason, makes clear that Kuwait is a sovereign State entrusted with the interests of a national community, the law of which constitutes an essential part of intracommunity relations within the State. At the same time, by referring to the transnational character of relations with the concessionaire, and to the general principles of law, this Article brings out the wealth and fertility of the set of legal rules that the Tribunal is called upon to apply.

The different sources of the law thus to be applied are not—at least in the present case—in contradiction with one another. Indeed if, as recalled above, international law constitutes an integral part of the law of Kuwait, the general principles of law correspondingly recognize the rights of the State in its capacity of supreme protector of the general interest. If the different legal elements involved do not always and

---

[32] The arbitral award in *Kuwait v. American Independent Oil Company (AMINOIL)*, dated March 24, 1982, is published in 21 *I.L.M.* 976 (1982). For detailed discussion of the case, see Pierre-Yves Tschanz, 'The Contributions of the Aminoil Award to the Law of State Contracts', 18 *Int'l Lawyer* 245 (1984); Philippe Kahn, 'Contrats d'Etat et Nationalisation—Les Apports de la Sentence Arbitrale du 24 Mars, 1982', 109 *J. Droit Int'l* 844 (1982).

everywhere blend as successfully as in the present case, it is nevertheless on taking advantage of their resources, and encouraging their trend towards unification, that the future of a truly international economic order in the investment field will depend.[33]

As in the Libyan cases (and in Article 42 of the ICSID Convention),[34] the governing principles seem to be a blend of the law of the host state, traditional international law, and general principles of law.[35]

Kuwait's Defenses

Several of the issues in *Kuwait-AMINOIL* were the same as the issues raised in the Libyan cases. The Tribunal did not find the decree-law terminating the Aminoil concession to be discriminatory, because it was consistent with the government's overall policy of nationalizing the oil industry and no evidence had been produced suggesting that the decree was motivated by AMINOIL's US nationality.[36] Kuwait argued that the Resolutions on Permanent Sovereignty over National Resources had become an imperative rule of *jus cogens* prohibiting states from affording guarantees of any kind against the exercise of public authority in regard to all matters regarding natural resources. The Tribunal said, 'This contention lacks all foundation.' Even if Resolution 1803 could be regarded as reflecting the state of international law at the time of its adoption, this could not be said about the subsequent resolutions:

Even if some of their provisions can be regarded as codifying rules that reflect international practice, it would not be possible from this to deduce the existence of a rule of international law prohibiting a State from undertaking not to proceed to a nationalisation during a limited period of time. It may indeed well be eminently useful that 'host' States should, if they so desire, be able to pledge themselves not to nationalise given foreign undertakings within a limited period; and no rule of international law prevents them from doing so.[37]

The Tribunal considered the argument that the concession agreement was an 'administrative contract', a type of state contract that confers greater authority on the state with respect to requiring changes, or even termination, than ordinary commercial contracts. Even if the AMINOIL contract fell in this category, however, the State could never go so far as to disturb the general equilibrium of the rights and obligations of the parties.

The Stabilization Clause

The most controversial issue for the arbitrators was the effect of the stabilization clause and of modifications that AMINOIL had agreed to in the period 1961–73. In particular, Article 9 of the 1961 Supplemental

---

[33] *Kuwait-AMINOIL* Award, paras. 9–10.   [34] See Ch. 15, Sect. 15.1(c).
[35] This point is developed by Tschanz (n. 32 supra), 262–4.
[36] *Kuwait-AMINOIL* award paras. 85–7.   [37] Id., para. 90.

Agreement had called for consultations with the Ruler concerning increased benefits to Kuwait in line with the terms of oil concessions in other states in the Middle East. Such consultations had in fact been held several times, and as mentioned previously, the terms of the concession had been significantly altered by agreement—the company had really had no choice.[38] Did the Supplemental Agreement and subsequent negotiations in effect overtake the stabilization clause?[39]

This question might well be critical to the arbitration, because if the stabilization clause had been violated, the nationalization decree would have been unlawful, calling (at least under one view) for higher level of compensation than if the nationalization had been lawful. The Tribunal conceded that 'a straightforward and direct reading of [the stabilization clauses] can lead to the conclusion that they prohibit any nationalisation.'[40] But Kuwait pointed out that nationalization is not mentioned in the stabilization clause,[41] and argued that therefore it did not apply to the nationalization decree. The Tribunal did not entirely accept this argument, but it carried substantial weight:

The case of nationalisation is certainly not expressly provided against by the stabilization clauses of the Concession. But it is contended by Aminoil that notwithstanding this lacuna, the stabilization clauses of the Concession . . . are cast in such absolute and all-embracing terms as to suffice in themselves—unconditionally and in all circumstances—for prohibiting nationalisation. This is a possible interpretation on the purely formal plane; but, for the following reasons, it is not the one adopted by the Tribunal.

No doubt contractual limitations on the State's right to nationalise are juridically possible, but what that would involve would be a particularly serious undertaking which would have to be expressly stipulated for, and be within the regulations governing the conclusion of State contracts; and it is to be expected that it should cover only a relatively limited period. In the present case however, the existence of such a stipulation would have to be presumed as being covered by the general language of the stabilization clauses, and over the whole period of an especially long concession since it extended to 60 years. A limitation on the sovereign rights of the State is all the less to be presumed where the concessionaire is in any event in possession of important guarantees regarding its essential interests in the shape of a legal right to eventual compensation.

Such is the case here,—for if the Tribunal thus holds that it cannot interpret [the stabilization clauses] as absolutely forbidding nationalisation, it is nevertheless the fact that these provisions are far from having lost all their value and efficacy on that account since, by impliedly requiring that nationalisation shall not have any

---

[38] On the subject of such negotiations, see Detlev F. Vagts, 'Coercion and Foreign Investment Rearrangements', 72 *Am. J. Int'l L.* 17 (1978).

[39] Article 11 of the Supplemental Agreement provided that it was to be construed as an amendment and supplement to the Principal Agreement, and 'all the provisions of the Principal Agreement shall continue in full force and effect except in so far as they are inconsistent with or modified by this [supplemental] Agreement.'

[40] *Kuwait-*AMINOIL Award, para. 88.   [41] See n. 31 supra.

confiscatory character, they reinforce the necessity for a proper indemnification as a condition of it.

There is another aspect of the matter which has weighed with the Tribunal. While attributing its full value to the fundamental principle of *pacta sunt servanda*, the Tribunal has felt obliged to recognize that the contract of Concession has undergone great changes since 1948: changes conceded—often unwillingly, but conceded nevertheless—by the Company. These changes have not been the consequence of accidental or special factors, but rather of a profound and general transformation in the terms of oil concessions that occurred in the Middle-East, and later throughout the world. These changes took place progressively, with an increasing acceleration, as from 1973. They were introduced into the contractual relations between the Government and Aminoil through the play of Article 9, or else as the result of at least tacit acceptances by the Company, which entered neither objections nor reservations in respect of them. These changes must not simply be viewed piece-meal, but on the basis of their total effect,—and they brought about a metamorphosis in the whole character of the Concession.

. . .

The Tribunal thus arrives at the conclusion that the 'take-over' of Aminoil's enterprise was not, in 1977, inconsistent with the contract of concession, provided always that the nationalisation did not possess any confiscatory character.[42]

In other words, as Judge Fitzmaurice spelled out in his separate opinion, the danger that the stabilization clauses were really intended to protect against were that of a confiscatory termination and take-over. If the take-over was not confiscatory, it would not be contrary to the stabilization clauses. Since the Government had made an offer of monetary compensation, it was not confiscatory.[43]

Fitzmaurice disagreed:

It is an illusion to suppose that monetary compensation alone, even on a generous scale, necessarily removes the confiscatory element from a take-over, whether called nationalization or something else. It is like paying compensation to a man who has lost his leg. Unfortunately, it does not restore the leg. When a Company such as Aminoil procures the insertion in its Concession of a clause like Article 17, its aim is not to obtain money if the Article is breached, but to guarantee if possible that it is not breached. . . . Nationalization, or any other form of take-over, is necessarily confiscatory in the sense that, irrespective of the wishes of the legal owner, it dispossesses him of his property and transfers it elsewhere. Nationalizations may be lawful or unlawful, but the test can never be whether they are confiscatory or not; because by virtue of their inherent character, they always are.[44]

As to the argument that the process of change was brought about by mutual consent, even if AMINOIL's consents were voluntary rather than due to the force of circumstances, Fitzmaurice does not accept the majority's conclusion. 'It was change, not termination, that Aminoil agreed to.' To Fitzmaurice,

---

[42] *Kuwait-*AMINOIL *Award*, paras. 94–7, 102.
[43] See Separate Opinion of Judge Fitzmaurice, 21 *I.L.M.* 1043, para. 21.
[44] Id., para. 26.

good faith and my professional conscience compel me to conclude that although the nationalization of Aminoil's undertaking may otherwise have been perfectly lawful, considered simply in its aspect of being an act of State, it was nevertheless irreconcilable with the stabilization clauses of a Concession that was still in force at the moment of the take-over.[45]

Compensation

With Kuwait found not to have violated either the concession agreement or international law—provided it paid appropriate compensation to AMINOIL, that left open the question of how the amount of compensation was to be determined. For the Tribunal, the starting point was 'legitimate expectations', based on 'the weighing-up of rights and obligations, of chances and risks; constituting the contractual equilibrium.'[46] To assess that equilibrium, the tribunal would start with the text of the contract—but not only the original text. 'There are also the amendments, the interpretations, and the behaviour manifested along the course of the existence, that indicate (often fortuitously) how the legitimate expectations of the Parties are to be seen, and sometimes seen as becoming modified according to the circumstances.'[47]

AMINOIL sought an amount calculated on its anticipated revenues through 2008 (the expiration date of the concession), based on its projections of the amount of oil produced, the price of the oil, and the cost of production, all discounted to present value. The Tribunal rejected this approach on several grounds. AMINOIL's projections were not only speculative—all evaluations include speculative elements—but the dealings between the parties since 1961 showed that what AMINOIL was really interested in was a reasonable rate of return.

Kuwait, for its part, sought to base the amount due to AMINOIL for termination of its concession on the amounts paid to other oil companies operating in the Middle East whose concessions had been taken over by agreement in the 1970s. The Tribunal rejected this approach as well, both on grounds of fact and on grounds of law. As to fact, in many instances the cash paid for termination of the concession often did not reflect the real value of the

---

[45] Id., paras. 28, 30. Professor Rosalyn Higgins (as she then was) criticized the majority interpretation of the Stabilization clause in her Hague Lectures:

While this perhaps represents an imaginative method of reconciling the right to nationalize with stabilization provisions freely entered into (and subsequently reaffirmed), the present writer confesses to finding it implausible as a matter of construction and unpersuasive as a matter of reasoning.

Nor did she find persuasive the statement that by impliedly requiring that nationalization shall not have any confiscatory character, stabilization clauses reinforce the necessity for a proper indemnification. Higgins responded:

But the obligations of non-confiscatory nature and of compensation are surely provided for by the requirements of international law itself. (Rosalyn Higgins, 'The Taking of Property by the State: Recent Developments in International Law', 176 *Recueil des Cours* 259 at 304 (Hague Acad. Int'l Law 1982-III)).

[46] *Kuwait-AMINOIL* award, para. 148.   [47] Id., para. 149.

new arrangements to the integrated companies, which might well include service contracts, preferential access to the oil, and anticipation of down-stream profits. As to law, it would be 'somewhat rash', the Tribunal said, to accept the suggestion that the negotiations had been inspired by juridical considerations: 'The *opinio juris* seems a stranger to consents of that type.'[48]

At the end, after discussion of the change in the value of the US dollar, the volatility of interest rates, inflation, and the price of oil, including the depre-ciated replacement value of the fixed assets and the legitimate expectations of AMINOIL over the thirty years of the concession remaining at the time of its termination, the arbitrators came to a figure of $206 million due to AMINOIL. From this amount $123 million were to be deducted for payments due to Kuwait, leaving a net amount of $83 million, as of September 19, 1977, the date of the decree-law. To this sum, the Tribunal added interest at 7.5 percent per annum and inflation at 10 percent per annum, compounded annually from the date of the decree to the date of the award—about 4½ years. The result of compounding at 17.5 percent was that the base amount of the award was more than doubled, to a final sum of $179 million. Kuwait, anxious to remain in good standing in the international community, (and not cash-poor) promptly made full payment.

Summary

The four awards here presented have been discussed and excerpted at length to illustrate some of the different strands and the variety of issues that together made up the corpus of the international law of international invest-ment and that are inevitably lost in summaries. One finds agreement (though not unanimity) that the termination of a concession is subject to inter-national law, and that that law calls for compensation to the foreign investor. One finds agreement that proceeding by a state against a foreign investor in a discriminatory way is unlawful, but disagreement about what constitutes discrimination in this context. Public utility or public purpose is still relevant but is rarely questioned, unless the taking state expressly recites retaliation against the home state of the investor as its motive.

Classical international law, domestic law of the host country, and general principles of law come together, but each decision-maker interprets the blend somewhat differently. The 1962 Resolution on Permanent Sovereignty has continuing appeal—particularly the balance between the right to nationalize for a public purpose and the obligation to pay compen-sation and to carry out investment agreements. The later UN resolutions, notwithstanding their adoption by large majorities, have not achieved acceptance as declarations of existing law, and are questioned as well as expressing desirable goals.

---

[48] *Kuwait-AMINOIL* Award, paras. 156–7.

Compensation is to be 'appropriate,' but there is no clear consensus on what this means, and each arbitrator adopts a somewhat different approach. Nor is it clear that an unlawful expropriation commands greater compensation—*restitutio in integrum*—than a lawful one, though that is the inference drawn from the TOPCO/CALASIATIC award and perhaps also from the sharp difference on interpretation of the stabilization clause between the majority and Judge Fitzmaurice in AMINOIL.[49] Stabilization clauses generally, once considered the brilliant invention of western investors or their counsel, turn out to give some protection, but not to overcome the truth that nothing is permanent except change.[50]

Finally, a striking feature of the four cases here presented is the emphasis on contract, as contrasted with property. Of course, without a concession or other long-term agreement, it is unlikely that any of the controversies would have been submitted to international arbitration. That said, nothing in these cases or similar decisions addresses the claim of investors as property owners, along the lines, for instance, of the correspondence between Secretary of State Hull and the Mexican foreign minister four decades earlier.

14.2 THE INTERNATIONAL COURT OF JUSTICE

The role of the post-war World Court in developing the international law of international investment has been quite modest. For one thing, the Court has jurisdiction only over state-to-state disputes, reflecting the traditional—and largely overtaken—view that international law is applicable only to conduct of states vis-à-vis other states. Thus the jurisdiction of the World Court in investment disputes depends on the 'espousal' by states of the claims of their nationals or corporations, and states have not often been willing in the post-War period, to undertake such espousal before the court. Indeed the rise of arbitration between private enterprises and states, such as in the arbitrations described in the preceding section and institutionalized in the ICSID Convention and the NAFTA as described in Chapter 15, is to a significant extent a response to the limited role of the World Court in the field of investment disputes. For its part, the World Court has been reluctant, in this as in other areas, to move beyond positive law, i.e. to set out norms of behaviour in the absence of treaties or comparable evidence of universal consensus. Finally (or perhaps first), the jurisdiction of the World Court depends on consent. States have been reluctant to give their consent to adjudication of economic controversies by

---

[49] It has been suggested that the high rate of compound interest in *Kuwait-AMINOIL* was a way to induce Judge Fitzmaurice to concur in the award, rather than turning his disagreement into a dissent.

[50] Compare Heraclitus: 'Everything flows and nothing stays.'

the World Court, and the Court has been careful to construe such consents as have been given quite narrowly.[51]

Three cases involving claims of expropriation of foreign investment have come before the post-War International Court of Justice. In each case the claim was dismissed, but in each case the Court has avoided pronouncing on the underlying question of the responsibility of the host state to the foreign investors. None of the cases resulted in a pronouncement comparable to the decision of the pre-War Permanent Court of International Justice in the *Chorzow Factory* case.[52]

(a)   The *Anglo-Iranian* Case (1952)[53]

The Anglo-Iranian Oil Company, a company incorporated in the United Kingdom (later British Petroleum) held a concession in Iran, originally nego- tiated in 1933. In March 1951, the Iranian parliament adopted a law nation- alizing the oil industry and creating a state-owned National Iranian Oil Company (NIOC). Anglo-Iranian first invoked an arbitration clause, which Iran rejected. The British government then took up the case, first seeking interim measures of protection, and subsequently relief on the merits.

The Court 'indicated' interim measures without prejudice to the question of its jurisdiction. In the plenary phase, Britain invoked a Declaration made by Iran in 1930 accepting, on conditions of reciprocity, the jurisdiction of the Court 'in any disputes arising after the satisfaction of the present decla- ration with regard to situations or facts relating directly or indirectly to the application of treaties or conventions accepted by Persia and subsequent to the ratification of this declaration.' The Court had to decide whether 'sub- sequent' referred to 'situations or facts' as Britain contended, or to 'treaties or conventions' as Iran contended. This was significant because Britain sought to rely on treaties between Iran and Denmark and between Iran and Turkey in both of which Iran had undertaken to treat the nationals of those countries in accordance with the principles and practice of ordinary inter- national laws. Though both of those treaties had been concluded in the 1930s, i.e. subsequent to Iran's acceptance of the jurisdiction of the Court, Britain claimed the benefit of those treaties by virtue of most-favoured- nation clauses in treaties with Iran (Persia) of 1857 and 1903. The Court held (by 9 to 5) that the text of Iran's Declaration referred to treaties con- cluded after its ratification. Accordingly, the United Kingdom could not

---

[51] States can consent to jurisdiction of the World Court in three ways—by special agreement concerning a particular dispute; by a treaty providing for submission to the Court of a category of disputes including the dispute in question; or by a declaration accepting the jurisdiction of the Court generally or in respect of a category of disputes that includes the dispute in question. See Introduction to Part III supra.

[52] See Ch. 13, Sect. 13(a) at notes 17–18.

[53] *Anglo-Iranian Oil Co.* case (*United Kingdom v. Iran*), [1952] I.C.J. Rep. 93.

invoke the MFN provisions of its earlier treaties with Iran, which formed the sole connection with the treaties between Iran and Denmark and Turkey.

Thus the Court arrived at the conclusion that it lacked jurisdiction. Case dismissed.

(b)   The *Barcelona Traction* Case (1970)[54]

Barcelona Traction, Light and Power Company Limited was a holding company incorporated in Toronto, Canada in 1911 to develop a system to produce and distribute electric power in Catalonia (Spain). According to the government of Belgium, the shares of the company came to be very largely held by Belgian nationals—both natural and juristic persons. Barcelona Traction issued a series of bonds payable in British pounds and Spanish pesetas, secured by mortgages on assets of various subsidiaries in Spain. In 1948 three Spanish holders of bonds of Barcelona Traction petitioned a Spanish Court for a declaration of bankruptcy for Barcelona Traction. A judgment of bankruptcy was entered several days later, and the Court ordered seizure of the assets of Barcelona Traction. The Spanish court appointed a receiver, and the Traction Company lost the capacity to administer any of its properties.[55] The principal managers of the company were dismissed, new directors were appointed, new shares were issued of the Spanish subsidiaries of Barcelona Traction, and these shares were sold by public auction to a newly founded Spanish company.

Following several years of diplomatic representations on behalf of Barcelona Traction, also by Canada, Great Britain, and the United States, Belgium initiated proceedings against Spain in the World Court, alleging essentially 'creeping expropriation' and claiming some $90 million in reparations, or 88 percent of this sum representing the Belgian share interest in the company. Belgium asserted jurisdiction on the basis of a 1927 Treaty of Conciliation, Judicial Settlement and Arbitration between Spain and Belgium. Spain objected to the Court's jurisdiction, on the basis that the Barcelona Traction Company was not a Belgian company, and that Belgium had no right to exercise diplomatic protection, including standing in the World Court, on behalf of mere shareholders. The Court began its analysis by distinguishing among the obligations of host states:

When a State admits into its territory foreign investments or foreign nationals, whether natural or juristic persons, it is bound to extend to them the protection of

---

[54] *Case concerning the Barcelona Traction, Light and Power Company Limited* (New Application: 1962) (*Belgium* v. *Spain*) Second Phase, [1970] *I.C.J. Rep.* 3. For a summary of the decision and the arguments made to the Court, see Herbert W. Briggs, 'Barcelona Traction: The *Jus Standi* of Belgium', 65 *Am. J. Int'l L.* 327 (1971).

[55] For a discussion of the significance of the bankruptcy proceedings, which the Court did not address, see F. A. Mann, 'The Protection of Shareholders' Interests in the Light of the Barcelona Traction Case', 67 *Am. J. Int'l L.* 259 (1973).

the law and assumes obligations concerning the treatment to be afforded them. These obligations, however, are neither absolute nor unqualified. In particular, an essential distinction should be drawn between the obligations of a State towards the international community as a whole, and those arising vis-à-vis another State in the field of diplomatic protection. By their very nature the former are the concern of all states. In view of the importance of the rights involved, all States can be held to have a legal interest in their protection; they are obligations *erga omnes*.

Such obligations derive, for example, in contemporary international law, from the outlawing of acts of aggression, and of genocide, as also from the principles and rules concerning the basic rights of the human person, including protection from slavery and racial discrimination . . .

Obligations the performance of which is the subject of diplomatic protection are not of the same category. It cannot be held, when one such obligation in particular is in question, in a specific case, that all States have a legal interest in its observance. In order to bring a claim in respect of the breach of such an obligation, a State must first establish the right to do so. . . . In the present case it is therefore essential to establish whether . . . a right of Belgium [has] been violated on account of its nationals having suffered infringements of their rights as shareholders of a company not of Belgian nationality.[56]

The Court sought the answer to its question in corporate law:

Seen in historical perspective, the corporate personality represents a development brought about by new and expanding requirements in the economic field, an entity which in particular allows of operation in circumstances which exceed the normal capacity of individuals.

. . .

It is a basic characteristic of the corporate structure that the company above, through its directors or management acting in its name, can take action in respect of matters that are of a corporate character. . . . Ordinarily, no individual shareholder can take legal steps, either in the name of the company or in his own name.[57]

If the shareholders had no rights independent from the company, it followed, as the Court saw it, that a state with links only to the shareholders had no rights of diplomatic protection, and therefore no standing before the International Court. The Court conceded that the measures complained of, although taken with respect to Barcelona Traction and causing it direct damage, also caused damage to the Belgian shareholders.

But, as the Court has indicated, evidence that damage was suffered does not *ipso facto* justify a diplomatic claim. Persons suffer damage or harm in most varied circumstances. This in itself does not involve the obligation to make reparation.[58]

Canada, of course, could have exercised diplomatic protection on behalf of Barcelona Traction, and as the Court pointed out, it had done so for several years. The fact that no link of compulsory jurisdiction existed between Canada and Spain did not confer standing on Belgium.

---

[56] *Barcelona Traction* Judgment, paras. 33–5.   [57] Id., paras. 39, 42.
[58] Id., para. 46.

It follows from what has already been stated above that where it is a question of an unlawful act committed against a company representing foreign capital, the general rule of international law authorizes the national State of the company alone to make a claim.[59]

One might have thought that the Court would stop there, having found that the claimant lacked standing. But the Court seems to have felt that something more should be said about the substance of protection for foreign investments, in view of the wide attention given to the *Barcelona Traction* case in twelve years of litigation.

What the Court said could hardly have pleased those who were looking for an affirmative pronouncement from the World Court about protection of foreign investment.

Considering the important developments of the last half century, the growth of foreign investments and the expansion of the international activities of corporations, in particular of holding companies, which are often multinational, and considering the way in which the economic interests of States have proliferated, it may at first sight appear surprising that the evolution of law has not gone further and that no generally accepted rules in the matter have crystallized on the international plane. Nevertheless, a more thorough examination of the facts shows that the law on the subject has been formed in a period characterized by an intense conflict of systems and interests . . .

[I]n the present state of the law, the protection of shareholders requires that recourse be had to treaty stipulations or special agreements directly concluded between the private investor and the State in which the investment is placed. States ever more frequently provide for protection, in both bilateral and multilateral relations, either by means of special instruments or within the framework of wider economic arrangements . . . . No such instrument is in force between the Parties to the present case.[60]

In other words, special agreements could provide substantive protections or avenues for dispute settlement. But customary law would not be built from these arrangements, or at least had not been built. Like the United States Supreme Court six years earlier,[61] the International Court of Justice saw 'an intense conflict of systems and interests' and decided to get out of the way.

(c)   The *Elsi* Case[62]

Elettronica Sicula S.p.A.(Elsi) was an Italian company engaged in manufacturing sophisticated electronic equipment in its plant in Palermo, Sicily. Elsi

---

[59] Id., para. 88.   [60] Id., paras. 89–90.

[61] See Introduction to this Part VI, pp. 387–9 supra.

[62] *Case concerning Elettronica Sicula S.p.A (Elsi) (United States v. Italy)*, 1989 I.C.J. Rep. 15, repr. in 28 I.L.M. 1109 (1989). For a detailed statement of the facts as well as the arguments of the parties and the analysis of the judgment of the Court, see Sean D. Murphy, 'The Elsi Case: An Investment Dispute at the International Court of Justice', 16 *Yale J. Int'l L.* 391 (1991).

was owned by the Raytheon Manufacturing Company, a major American manufacturer of electronic equipment, and ELSI's business depended largely on patents, licenses, and technical assistance from Raytheon. ELSI never became economically self-sufficient, and never paid any dividends. In March 1968, after more than fifteen years of investment in ELSI, Raytheon decided not to invest any more capital in its Italian subsidiary. ELSI developed a plan for the orderly shutdown of its operations; existing orders would be completed, efforts would be made to sell the plant, and employees not needed during the liquidation were sent notices of dismissal. Two days after the dismissal letters were sent out, the mayor of Palermo 'requisitioned' the plant, pursuant, as he said, to an 1865 law that authorized disposal of private property for reasons of 'grave public necessity'.

ELSI's management surrendered control of the plant, but petitioned the mayor to lift his order. The mayor did not respond, and ELSI appealed to the Prefect of Palermo, contending that the order of requisition was illegal, arbitrary, and *ultra vires*. The Prefect ultimately allowed the appeal, but only sixteen months later. Three weeks after giving up control of the plant, ELSI's directors voted to file for bankruptcy, and three weeks later the court in Palermo adjudged ELSI bankrupt and appointed a trustee.

For six years ELSI sought before various Italian courts and officials to recover its plant or secure compensation.[63] Eventually, Raytheon, the parent company, sought help from the US government. In February 1974, the State Department submitted a diplomatic note to Italy espousing Raytheon's claim, alleging illegal actions and interferences by Italian authorities with ELSI's management, contrary to treaty provisions, Italian law, and international law. It took four years for Italy to give its answer, denying the claim on the ground that even if unlawful, the seizure of the ELSI plant did not cause damage to the shareholders. After close to a further decade of diplomatic exchanges, the two countries agreed to submit the dispute to a chamber of the World Court. Following two rounds of written pleadings and three weeks of oral hearings, a five-member Chamber presided over by the President of the World Court and including both the Italian and the American judge of the Court, issued its judgment on July 20, 1989, 21 years after the events giving rise to the dispute.[64]

The Chamber ultimately rejected the claim, essentially on the ground that the United States had not proven that the ELSI plant had substantial value before the action of the mayor, and that the shareholder (i.e. Raytheon) had been damaged by the requisition. But while the finding of facts went against

---

[63] For the details, see *ELSI* case judgment, paras. 27–45; Murphy (n. 62, supra), pp. 401–5.

[64] One may wonder why the United States brought just this case to the World Court, so long after the event and involving a relatively small amount of money—$6–8 million before interest. A clue may be that the United States wanted to demonstrate its continued support for the Court, on the same day that it announced that it was terminating its acceptance of the compulsory jurisdiction of the Court, following its withdrawal from participation in the Nicaragua case. The possible connection is pointed out by Murphy (n. 62, supra), pp. 448–9.

the United States, several legal rulings, some explicit, others by implication, went in favour of the United States, and added to the picture of the World Court as a source of the international law of international investment.

First, Italy pleaded failure by ELSI to exhaust its local remedies. This had been a successful defense by the United States in the *Interhandel* case on the ground that the controversy was still in active litigation in the United States.[65] In *ELSI*, the Chamber rejected the defense. While it was true that the FCN Treaty on which the United States founded its international claim had not been litigated in Italy, the Chamber, having reviewed the proceedings in Italy, concluded:

> With such a deal of litigation in the municipal courts about what is in substance the claim now before the Chamber, it was for Italy to demonstrate that there was nevertheless some local remedy that had not been tried; or at least exhausted. . . .
>
> . . .
>
> It is never easy to decide, in a case where there has in fact been much resort to the municipal courts, whether local remedies have been truly 'exhausted'. But in this case Italy has not been able to satisfy the Chamber that there clearly remained some remedy which Raytheon . . . independently of ELSI, and of ELSI's trustee in bankruptcy, ought to have pursued and exhausted. Accordingly, the Chamber will now proceed to consider the merits of the case.[66]

Second, what about the holding in *Barcelona Traction* that shareholders had no rights cognizable in international law independent of the corporation? Here ELSI was an Italian corporation, and the United States was bringing a claim on behalf of ELSI's shareholder Raytheon. To Judge Oda, writing separately, *Barcelona Traction* and the fundamental distinction between the rights of a corporation (here ELSI) and its shareholders (here Raytheon) were fatal to the claim of the United States. In not adopting Judge Oda's view and addressing the claim on the merits, it seems fair to say that the Chamber retreated from that position, as Judge Schwebel pointed out in his dissent. The closest the Chamber's judgment comes to going beyond inference on this point is in discussing the provision of the FCN Treaty calling for protection for nationals and corporations of either High Contracting Party in respect to 'acquisition, ownership . . . or disposition of property or interests therein' in the territory of the other High Contracting Party. Italy argued that the property affected belonged to ELSI, not to Raytheon, and hence was not subject to the treaty; the United States said that 'interests therein . . .' covered indirect ownership, including rights held through a subsidiary. The Chamber wrote that it had 'some sympathy with the contention of the United States, as being more in accord with the general purpose of the FCN

---

[65] See *Interhandel* Case (*Switzerland* v. *United States*) (Preliminary Objections), Judgment of 21 Mar. 1959, [1959] *I.C.J. Rep.* 6, esp. 26–30. For the sequence of the litigation in the United States and the World Court, see A. Lowenfeld, *International Litigation and Arbitration*, 695–6 (1993).

[66] *ELSI* case judgment, paras. 59, 63.

Treaty.'[67] But it did not have to decide the matter, because it had found that the facts did not support the claim of the United States.

Third, as in *Barcelona Traction*, the claim was not for an overt taking, as in the Libyan and Kuwait cases, but for a disguised or 'creeping' expropriation. Italy contended that the FCN Treaty and Protocol did not cover the claim because the term used in the Italian version of the treaty, *espropriazione*, was narrower than the term *taking* in the English version, both texts being equally authentic. The Chamber wrote

neither this question of interpretation of the two texts of the Protocol, nor the questions raised as to the possibilities of disguised expropriation or of a 'taking' amounting ultimately to expropriation have to be resolved in the present case, because it is simply not possible to say that the ultimate result was the consequence of the acts or omissions of the Italian authorities, yet at the same time to ignore the most important factor, namely ELSI's financial situation, and the consequent decision of its shareholders to close the plant and put an end to its activities.[68]

One may regard this statement as an acknowledgement of creeping expropriation, which has figured in a number of more recent controversies, as described in the next chapter.[69]

Altogether, the judgment of the Chamber of the World Court did not add much to the international law of international investment.[70] Its opinion can, however, be a resource for advocates and judges in other fora. Along with the other cases discussed in this chapter, the *Elsi* case helps to explain the search for such other fora, which permit companies to bring claims on their own without waiting for governments to espouse their claims, and which avoid for the most part, the doctrine of exhaustion of local remedies, as described in Chapter 15.

14.3   International Law in National Courts

(a)   Litigation around the World

1. *The Classic English View*

In a leading case in the aftermath of the Russian revolution, *A. M. Luther* v. *James Sagor and Co.*,[71] the former owner of a woodworking mill in Russia that had been nationalized sought to gain possession of a quantity of plywood marked with an identifying mark that had been sold by the Soviet government to an American company and imported into England. The plaintiff charged that the decree of the Soviet government, nationalizing the wood,

---

[67] *Elsi* case judgment, para. 132.   [68] Id., para. 119.

[69] See e.g. Ch. 15, Sects. 15.2(c)(3) and 15.3(b)(4).

[70] Accord, F. A. Mann, 'Foreign Investment in the International Court of Justice: The *ELSI* Case', 86 *Am. J. Int'l L.* 92 at 99.

[71] [1921] 3 K.B. 532 (C.A.).

was 'in its nature so immoral, and so contrary to the principles of justice as recognized by this country, that the Courts of this country ought not to pay any attention to it.' The Court of Appeal, reversing the lower court, rejected the claim. The Court recited the rule that English courts will not enforce a right otherwise duly acquired under the law of a foreign country where the enforcement of such right is inconsistent with the policy of English law, or with the moral rules upheld by English law.[72]

> But it appears a serious breach of international comity, if a state is recognized as a sovereign independent state, to postulate that its legislation is 'contrary to essential principles of justice and morality.' Such an allegation . . . should in my view be the action of the Sovereign through his ministers, and not of the judges. . . . I do not feel able to come to the conclusion that the legislation of a state recognized by my Sovereign as an independent sovereign state is so contrary to moral principles that the judges ought not to recognize it.[73]

2. *The* Anglo-Iranian *Cases in National Courts*

At the same time as the British government was attempting to place the nationalization of Anglo-Iranian's concession before the World Court,[74] the Anglo-Iranian Oil Company itself, with the cooperation of the other major international oil companies, undertook to deny to the newly formed National Iranian Oil Company any markets in Europe and North America. A significant aspect of this campaign was a series of lawsuits seeking to repossess shipments of oil from Iran as they arrived in foreign ports, on the ground that the nationalization that had vested title in NIOC had been confiscatory and in violation of international law.

The first case was brought in Aden, the port at the entrance to the Red Sea that at the time was a British colony. *Anglo-Iranian Oil Co. Ltd.* v. *Jaffrate and Others (The Rose Mary).*[75] The captain, Jaffrate, defended on the ground, *inter alia*, that he had been forced to put in to the port of Aden in distress by a Royal Air Force plane that threatened to bomb his vessel. The captain and the charterers (purchasers of the cargo) also denied that Anglo-Iranian owned the cargo. The court found for Anglo-Iranian.

The judge did not believe the defense that the ship had come into Aden in distress, and that its cargo was therefore arguably immune from seizure:

> As to [the captain's] fear of the aeroplane, it seems to me very unlikely that this really existed. No reasonable man could think it likely that Her Majesty's Government in

---

[72] As slightly reformulated, this rule, cited in *Luther* v. *Sagor* to the second edition of *Dicey on the Conflict of Laws* (1908), appears as Rule 2 in the 13th edition of *Dicey and Morris on the Conflict of Laws*, Vol. 1, p. 81 (L. Collins (ed.), 2000).

[73] [1921] 3 K.B. at 558–9 (per Scrutton, L.J.). For a more recent decision of the House of Lords, to the effect that expropriation of the shares of a Spanish company by the Government of Spain was entitled to recognition in a dispute concerning subsidiaries and trademarks in the UK, see *Williams & Humbert, Ltd.* v. *W. & H. Trade Marks (Jersey) Ltd.*, [1986] A.C. 368.

[74] See Sect. 14.2(a).

[75] [1953] 1 W.L.R. 246, [1953] *Int'l Law Repts.* 316 (Aden, Sup. Ct., 9 Jan. 1953).

the year 1952 would try to resolve a commercial dispute by what would be little short of an act of war.[76]

As to the defense based on the nationalization, the judge could find nothing more than a suggestion that at some future time the matter of compensation might be considered:

The question of adequacy [of compensation] may often be difficult for a court to decide and no doubt this has caused and will cause considerable trouble in other cases dealing with the extraterritorial effect of foreign nationalization. But here I can only find to be true the plaintiff's contention that expropriation has taken place without any compensation and that this is confiscation.[77]

The judge held that *Luther* v. *Sagor* was applicable only when the property nationalized had belonged to nationals of the taking state, describing the more expansive statements of Scrutton, L.J.[78] as dicta. He concluded that expropriation without compensation was violative of international law and therefore ineffective to pass title.

Another vessel put in to Venice with a cargo of oil from Iran, and Anglo-Iranian applied to the local court to have the oil sequestered. *Anglo-Iranian Oil Co. Ltd.* v. *Società Unione Petrolifera Orientale (S.U.P.O.R.) (The Miriella).*[79] Defendant, which had purchased the oil from NIOC, argued that the court was without power to examine the nationalization, because the oil had been in Iran at the time that the government of Iran adopted the nationalization law. The Venice court rejected that contention, on the basis that it needed to examine the nationalization to determine whether it came within the limits of the rule of private international law that prevented application in Italy of foreign laws or acts that are contrary to public order.[80] On the merits, however, the court held that the Iranian Oil Nationalization Law was not contrary to Italy's public policy (*ordine pubblico*), and therefore that Anglo-Iranian had no right to possession of the oil in question. The court said that the Nationalization Law did not exclude the payment of compensation. Even though no compensation had yet been paid, the provision in the Iranian law for executive and legislative review of Anglo-Iranian's rights was a recognition of the principle of compensation sufficient to comply with Italian concepts of public order, since under Italian law private property may be nationalized for the public good, provided compensation is paid.

Following failure to prevail on its possessory action in Venice, Anglo-Iranian brought an action in Rome for restitution for oil imported by the

---

[76] [1953] *Int'l Law Repts.* at 319–20. (This passage is not reproduced in the *Weekly Law Reports.*)

[77] [1953] W.L.R. at 253, [1953] *Int'l L. Repts.* at 322.   [78] Note 73 supra.

[79] Court of Venice, 11 Mar. 1953, 76 *Il Foro Italiano* (I) 719, [1955] *Int'l Law Repts.* 19.

[80] Preliminary Rules of the Italian Civil Code, Art. 31, (now replaced). Note that this holding is the reverse of the American act of state doctrine, discussed in subsection 14.3(b) infra.

same defendant on four ships, including the one that had offloaded its cargo in Venice. *Anglo-Iranian Oil Company, Ltd.* v. *S.U.P.O.R.*[81] The result was essentially the same:

In order to establish whether the acquisition of any movable property has been validly effected and whether the transfer of ownership rights has taken place by way of a valid transaction, the law applicable at the place where the property was situated . . . must be taken into consideration, whilst the transport of the movable property to another place subsequent to the transfer does not alter the legal ralations once they are validly established by virtue of the *lex rei sitae* . . .

. . .

[T]he provisions of the foreign law governing the substance of the case are incorporated in our legal system so that the Court, in respect of such provisions, as in respect of provisions of Italian law, has the right and the duty to examine their constitutional validity.[82]

As in the case in Venice, the Rome court found that since the Iranian law made some mention of compensation, it did not violate the fundamentals of Italian law.

[I]t is not required either by our law or by the generally accepted provisions of international law that the *quantum* of the compensation must appear actually equivalent to the value of the property forming the subject of the expropriation, that is to say, it is enough that there is some compensation for the expropriation to be lawful.[83]

Thus the result of the *Anglo-Iranian* cases was that in the British colony, the court examined the foreign law and held it unenforceable as contrary to international law; in Italy (as well as in a similar case in Japan)[84] the courts did not decline to examine the foreign law, but accorded it every benefit of the doubt. The threat of litigation by Anglo-Iranian made oil from Iran hard to sell in the industrial states in the early 1950s, except in Italy and Japan, but no court other than the one in Aden actually held the nationalization unlawful.

3. *The* Indonesian Tobacco *Cases*[85]

In 1958, the government of Indonesia issued a decree nationalizing all Dutch-owned enterprises in the Republic of Indonesia, including several tobacco plantations. The decree stated that it was Indonesia's response to the refusal of the Netherlands government to transfer sovereignty over a disputed territory of the former Netherlands East Indies. Compensation was to be determined by a committee appointed by the government, subject to further legislation.

---

[81] Civil Court of Rome, 13 Sept. 1954, 78 *Il Foro Italiano* (I) 256 (1955), [1955] *Int'l L. Repts.* 23.

[82] [1955] *Int'l Law Repts.* at 26–7, 33.   [83] Id., at 36.

[84] *Anglo-Iranian Oil Company* v. *Idemitsu Kosan Kabushiki Kaisha*, Dist. Ct. Tokyo (1953), aff'd, Higher Ct. of Tokyo (1953), [1953], *Int'l Law Repts.* 305, 312.

[85] This section is based on Martin Domke, 'Indonesian Nationalization Measures before Foreign Courts', 54 *Am. J. Int'l L.* 305 (1960) and sources there cited.

Indonesia shipped the bulk of the 1958 harvest to Bremen, West Germany, for the account of a newly established company in which the Indonesian administrator of nationalized tobacco companies held a participation. Two Dutch companies brought suit in Bremen, claiming property rights in the 1958 tobacco harvest, including several cargoes shipped to Bremen on specified vessels. Claimants asserted that recognition of the nationalization by German courts would be contrary to established principles of international law, contrary to German law, and contrary to German public policy. The claim failed.[86]

First, since the Dutch companies were no longer in possession of the plantations at the time of the harvest, they could not prove their property rights in the tobacco sought to be attached.

Second, the court had no jurisdiction to review the internal validity of the Indonesian Nationalization Act.[87]

Third, even if the nationalization was contrary to international law, this would not mean that the defendant's title derived from the nationalization decree was invalid, but only that a claim for damages might be raised by the state of the investor against the nationalizing state:

[E]ven assuming that the Indonesian nationalization law violates in various regards generally valid principles of international law, it still cannot be said that according to the state of present-day doctrine of international law and case law, the Indonesian Act No. 86 can be treated on that ground as void from its inception by the judge of the forum, and that, as the petitioners assert, the national judge, by recognizing nationalization law which is contrary to international law, and by referring petitioner to diplomatic channels for damages, if any, would commit himself a violation of international law.

. . .

[P]ursuant to the common opinion of writers and courts, national courts should recognize even those acts of state which infringe on international law, and the petitioners did not prove that . . . the hitherto existing principle of international law has already been replaced by a new rule which would oblige the national courts under international law to treat an Act of State which is contrary to international law as null and void from its inception.[88]

As to the charge of discrimination, the Bremen court had little difficulty. The principle of non-discrimination meant that equals must be treated equally, and that different treatment of unequals is admissible. Clearly the Dutch estate owners had been dominant in Indonesia and in the worldwide

---

[86] *Verenigde Deli-Maatschapijen* v. *Deutsch-Indonesische Tabak-Handelgesellschaft m.b.H*, Decision of the Oberlandesgericht Bremen of 21 Aug. 1959, translated and excerpted by Domke, n. 85 supra.

[87] The Court of Appeals (Oberlandesgericht) added that even if such review were permissible under principles of conflict of laws, it could not be exercised in this case because judicial review would have to be carried out under the *lex rei sitae*, and under the Indonesian constitution, 'Laws are inviolate', i.e. there is no provision for judicial review.

[88] Decision of 21 Aug. 1959 (n. 86 supra), Domke, n. 85 supra at 313, 314.

distribution of Indonesian products; thus a law directed particularly to them did not violate the principle of equality.[89]

Finally, as to compensation, for one thing the Dutch plaintiffs had not proven that Indonesia was in fact unwilling to pay compensation. That no compensation had been paid at the time of nationalization or even provided for might in case of an individual expropriation be contrary to international law.

> Here, however, the expropriation of the Dutch companies constitutes at the same time a shifting of proprietary relations (Umschichtung der Besitzverhältnisse) which was effected by a former colony after its independence in order to change the social structure. The opinion has often been advanced recently and not without reason, that by the nature of the matter alone, the same principles cannot prevail for such overall expropriations and for individual expropriations of the conventional type. Compensations could not be paid in full and promptly out of the substance, but only out of the proceeds of the nationalized enterprises. Compensation as to time and amount must therefore be made in accordance with the conditions in the expropriating state. Thus the long-standing principle of strong protection of private property clashes here with the modern concept that underdeveloped countries must be given the possibility of using their own natural resources.[90]

Meanwhile, a similar controversy was being litigated in The Netherlands, with the opposite outcome.[91] As to competence of the Dutch courts to review acts of a foreign state, the Amsterdam Court of Appeals wrote:

One cannot speak of a universally accepted rule of international law; the judge generally refrains and should refrain from determining the legal validity of acts *jure imperii* of a foreign sovereign; an exception, however, must be made if the respective sovereign acts are to be considered a flagrant contradiction to international law.[92]

As to discrimination, the Amsterdam court wrote that the nationalization decree was

a manifestly discriminatory measure which in a very sharp manner attacks the rights and interests exclusively of nationals of the State of the Netherlands, though a state of war does not exist between Indonesia and the country.[93]

As to compensation, whereas the German courts said the issue had not been tested, the Dutch courts had no doubt. The Nationalization Act allowed many avenues of evasion and in any case such compensation as might be awarded would come, according to Indonesian officials, only after surrender of West New Guinea.

---

[89] Id., p. 315. [90] Id., p. 317.

[91] *Senembah Maatschappij N.V. v. Republiek Indonesie Bank Indonesia and De Twentsche Bank, N.V.*, Decision of 4 June 1959, *1959 Nederlandse Jurisprudentie* 850, 855.

[92] Id., as quoted by Domke, n. 85 supra at 315. [93] Id., p. 316.

All these considerations, as the Netherlands courts saw it, added up to violation of the public policy of the forum:

[I]t cannot be presumed that Dutch public policy should permit recognition in this country of any legal consequence of a measure [Indonesian] which obviously discriminates against the rights and interests of Netherlanders, seriously affecting in its consequences the Dutch economy in general and in particular the property of numerous Dutch nationals, and which moreover serves political claims—the latter being rejected by the Netherlands government.[94]

Cynics might conclude that the stark difference in the views of the courts of neighbouring states with a common legal tradition may be explained in that the courts of each state were defending their national interests—the Germans to promote a new market, the Dutch to uphold the rights of the former colonial proprietors. In the writer's view, such a conclusion would be unfair and unsound. Rather, it is submitted, the *Indonesian Tobacco* cases, like others not here set out,[95] illustrate the disarray of the international law of international investment, the hazards of commingling international law and public policy, and the wisdom of the United States Supreme Court, despite strong pressure, to find a way to avoid the controversy, as described in the following section.

(b) The Act of State Doctrine in the United States

In a number of decisions going back to the nineteenth century, the United States Supreme Court had set down the rule—not based on any statute or constitutional precept—that courts in the United States would not review actions of foreign governments taken within their own territory. In *Underhill* v. *Hernandez*, decided in 1897,[96] the Supreme Court had written:

Every sovereign State is bound to respect the independence of every other sovereign State, and the courts of one country will not sit in judgment on the acts of the government of another done within its own territory. Redress of grievances by reason of such acts must be obtained through the means open to be availed of by sovereign powers as between themselves.

---

[94] Decision of 21 Aug. 1959 (n. 86 supra), Domke, n. 85 supra at 320. Subsequently, the Netherlands proposed that dispute between the Netherlands and Indonesia concerning the nationalizations of Dutch-owned properties be submitted to the International Court of Justice. So far as is known, no response was received to this proposal. The full text of the Netherlands note of December 18, 1959, including extensive quotations from earlier Indonesian diplomatic notes, was published in 54 *Am. J. Int'l L.* 484 (1960).

[95] See e.g. Bernard Audit, *Droit International Privé*, Sects. 771–3 (2nd edn. 1997), and sources there cited, summarizing decisions of French courts based generally on the territoriality principle, with varying outcomes.

[96] 168 U.S. 250, 252 (1897). The case involved an action for assault and false imprisonment against the commander of a revolutionary army in Venezuela whose government the United States subsequently recognized.

The rationale of what became known as the act of state doctrine seemed to be part judicial restraint, part respect for foreign states, and part separation of powers, i.e. a desire not to interfere with the conduct of foreign relations by the executive branch. Though the rationale was not made explicit, the thrust of the doctrine was repeated in several decisions of the Supreme Court,[97] as well as in decisions of other state and federal courts.

Spurred by the large volume of expropriations of American-owned property in Cuba, a substantial initiative was launched in the United States in the early 1960s to repudiate the act of state doctrine, or more likely, to revise the formulation in *Underhill* to add at the end of the first sentence 'except when such acts violate international law'. The proponents of a 'new look' at the act of state doctrine argued that while it was improper on grounds both of conflict of laws and of respect for independent states to subject the acts of foreign governments to challenge under the laws or constitutions of those states, it was not improper, and indeed highly desirable, to subject foreign governments to the restraints of international law, which was by definition applicable to all states with no possibility of opting out. The issue came to the Supreme Court in *Banco Nacional de Cuba* v. *Sabbatino*, heard in 1963 and decided in 1964.[98]

1. *The* Sabbatino *Case*

Facts of the Case

The case was in many ways an odd one, and the actual amount involved was small, but it set the tone for many other cases that followed. A Cuban company, C.A.V., whose shareholders were American, had owned a sugar plantation included in a decree of nationalization issued by the Cuban government. Prior to the expropriation, C.A.V. had sold a cargo of sugar through a New York broker to a purchaser in Morocco, with payment in New York against the bill of lading and accompanying documents. When the nationalization decree was issued, the broker had concluded a second contract with an agent for the Cuban govenment covering the same shipment on the same terms.

While the cargo was on its way to Morocco, Banco Nacional, as assignee of the Cuban government, tendered the bill of lading and other documents to the broker in New York. The broker took up the documents and negotiated them to its customer, but did not pay Banco Nacional, because in the interval C.A.V., the former owner, had procured the appointment of a receiver (Mr. Sabbatino) who claimed the proceeds of the shipment. Accordingly, Banco

---

[97] In particular, *Oetjen* v. *Central Leather Co.*, 246 U.S. 297 (1918) and *Ricaud* v. *American Metal Co.*, 246 U.S. 304 (1918), both arising out of events during the Mexican Revolution. See also *American Banana Co.* v. *United Fruit Co.*, 213 U.S. 347 (1907), an attempt to apply US antitrust laws to an alleged conspiracy with a foreign government, discussed in Ch. 12, Sect. 12.4, at n. 24.

[98] 376 U.S. 398 (1964). The present writer was of counsel to the US government as *amicus curiae*, as described hereafter.

Nacional had a simple claim for conversion of documents of title, and it brought suit in federal court in New York. The receiver, acting on behalf of the former owners, asserted, however, that the claim must fail, because Banco Nacional had acquired its title pursuant to an invalid act, i.e. the nationalization. The receiver asserted that the nationalization had been discriminatory, in that it was directed only against US interests; retaliatory, in that it was a response to elimination by the United States of Cuba's sugar quota; not for a public purpose, in that it was politically motivated; and in any event confiscatory, in that the provision for compensation was illusory.

In the Lower Courts

The District Court agreed with the Receiver on all counts. As to the act of state doctrine, the judge wrote:

The basis for [the act of state doctrine] vanishes . . . when the act of a foreign state violates not what may be our provincial notions of policy, but rather the standards imposed by international law. There is an end to the right of national sovereignty when the sovereign's acts impinge on international law.[99]

The Court of Appeals was less certain than the District Court about the asserted violations of international law. After surveying various decisions and writings, it wrote:

Since it is unnecessary for this Court in the present case to decide whether a government's failure, in and of itself, to pay adequate compensation for the property it takes is a breach of international responsibility, we decline at this time to attempt a resolution of that difficult question.[100]

Instead, the court focused on the combination of discrimination and retaliation plus failure to provide compensation, and concluded that taken together these elements rendered the decree violative of international law.

The argument was made to the Court of Appeals that international tribunals had never granted restitution for property taken, and that therefore Banco Nacional should be regarded as owner of the bill of lading, with C.A.V. entitled to damages from the Cuban state. The Court of Appeals responded:

[I]nternational tribunals are not the sole custodians of international law. . . . Municipal courts also play a part in the development of that body of law. Furthermore, municipal courts are competent to give a restitutory remedy. . . . We need not at present go into the question whether the granting of this type of remedy is a feature of international law or of domestic law. But we do suggest that the failure of an international tribunal to give a remedy of this type results from the inability of that kind of court to enforce its awards and is not a result of the dictates of substantive international law principles.[101]

---

[99] *Banco Nacional de Cuba* v. *Sabbatino*, 193 F. Supp. 375 at 381 (S.D.N.Y. 1961).
[100] *Banco Nacional de Cuba* v. *Sabbatino*, 307 F.2d 845 at 864 (2d Cir. 1962).
[101] Id., at 368.

As to the act of state doctrine, the Court of Appeals was made to under-stand—wrongly—that the State Department had no objection to adjudication of the case and that therefore the doctrine need not be applied.[102]

In the Supreme Court[103]

When the case came to the Supreme Court, the US government appeared as *amicus curiae*, (i) to correct the misapprehension that a 'no comment' letter to a private party had meant that the State Department had in some way waived the act of state doctrine; and (ii) to urge that the doctrine be applied. The parties, and several organizations concerned with international law, sought a pronouncement by the Supreme Court on the substantive issues. For its part, the US government took no position on the many questions raised in the lower courts concerning the contours of state responsibility to foreign investors, or the consequences of a state' failure to comply with international law, on the ground that under the act of state doctrine the court should not be reviewing the actions of the Cuban government taken within its own territory.

The Court accepted the proposal to re-examine the continued vitality of the act of state doctrine—'an issue concerned with a basic choice regarding the competence and function of the Judiciary and the National Executive in ordering our relationships with other members of the international community,' as the Court put it.[104] 'It should be apparent,' the Court wrote,

that the greater the degree of codification or consensus concerning a particular area of international law, the more appropriate it is for the judiciary to render decisions regarding it, since the courts can then focus on the application of an agreed principle to circumstances of fact rather than on the sensitive task of establishing a principle not inconsistent with the national interest or with international justice. It is also evident that some aspects of international law touch much more sharply on national nerves than do others; the less important the implications of an issue are for our foreign relations, the weaker the justification for exclusivity in the political branches.[105]

As quoted at the beginning of this Part,[106] the Court found the opposite of consensus. 'There are few if any issues', the Court wrote, 'in which opinion seems so divided'.

When we consider the prospect of the courts characterizing foreign expropriations, however justifiably, as invalid under international law and ineffective to pass title, the wisdom of the precedents is confirmed. While each of the leading cases in this Court may be argued to be distinguishable on its facts from this one [citing *Underhill, Oetjen and Ricaud*], the plain implication of all these opinions . . . is that the act of state doctrine is applicable even if international law has been violated.[107]

Counsel for C.A.V. argued that even if there was no agreement regarding general standards for determining the validity of expropriations, the

---

102 Id., 858–9.   103 *Banco Nacional de Cuba* v. *Sabbatino*, 376 U.S. 398 (1964).
104 Id., at 425.   105 Id., at 428.   106 p. 387 supra.   107 Id., at 430–1.

combination of retaliation, discrimination, and inadequate compensation made it 'patently clear' that this particular expropriation was in violation of international law. The Court rejected the argument:

If this view is accurate, it would still be unwise for the courts so to determine. Such a decision now would require the drawing of more difficult lines in subsequent cases and these would involve the possibility of conflict with the Executive view. Even if the courts avoided this course, either by presuming the validity of an act of state whenever the international law standard was thought unclear or by following the State Department declaration in such a situation, the very expression of judicial uncertainty might provide embarrassment to the Executive Branch.[108]

The holding of the Court, subject to several reservations, was as follows:

[R]ather than laying down or reaffirming an inflexible and all-encompassing rule in this case, we decide only that the Judicial Branch will not examine the validity of a taking of property within its own territory by a foreign sovereign government, extant and recognized by this country at the time of suit, in the absence of a treaty or other unambiguous agreement regarding controlling legal principles, even if the complaint alleges that the taking violates customary international law.[109]

Since a court in the United States could not sit in judgment of the expropriation decree of the government of Cuba, Banco Nacional would remain the title holder, and C.A.V.'s challenge would fail.

2. Limiting the Act of State Doctrine

The *Sabbatino* decision provoked an outcry in the United States, the more so in that it had been rendered by 8 to 1 in an opinion by Justice John Marshall Harlan, who had been a pillar of the Wall Street bar prior to becoming a judge, and was considered one of the conservative members of the Supreme Court.

The Hickenlooper Amendment[110]

The Congress almost immediately adopted the so-called Hickenlooper or Sabbatino Amendment, which began

---

[108] Id. at 433. The Court added in a footnote that even if it accepted the argument about the combination of breaches, it would have to decide as well that for the purpose of judging the expropriation under international law, C.A.V. was not to be regarded as Cuban, and that international law provides other remedies for breaches of international standards of expropriation than suits for damages before international tribunals.

[109] 376 U.S. at 426.

[110] §620(e)(2) of the Foreign Assistance Act of 1961, as amended, 22 U.S.C. §2370(e)(2). Actually the amendment here described was the second Hickenlooper Amendment. §620(e)(1), adopted in 1962, required the President to suspend all foreign assistance to the government of any country that had nationalized or expropriated or seized ownership of control of property owned by any United States citizen or by any corporation at least 50 percent owned by United States citizens, and had not within six months after such action taken appropriate steps, which may include arbitration, to discharge its obligations under international law, including speedy compensation for such property equivalent to the full value thereof, 'as required by international law'. That amendment, mandatory when adopted, was made subject to a waiver by the President on national interest grounds in 1973. See Richard D. Lillich, 'Requiem for Hickenlooper', 69 *Am. J. Int'l L.* 97 (1975).

no court in the United States shall decline on the ground of the federal act of state doctrine to make a determination on the merits giving effect to the principles of international law. . . .

But American banks that had operated in Cuba were concerned that without more, such an amendment would subject them to liability on letters of credit issued prior to nationalization, and the Administration was concerned that litigation initiated by the owner of expropriated property might at some time interfere with delicate negotiations—with Cuba or with another country. Accordingly, two reservations were introduced into the legislation, one to exempt letters of credit, the other to permit the President to invoke the act of state doctrine if he determined that this was required in a particular case by the foreign policy interests of the United States. Most important, after protracted debate the final version of the amendment limited its application to

a case in which a claim of title or other right *to property* is asserted by any party . . . based upon a . . . confiscation or other taking after January 1, 1959, by an act of that state in violation of the principles of international law. (italics added)

The effect of the addition of the italicized words, as construed by the courts,[111] was that if a ship flying the Patrian flag, or a cargo of copper from an identified mine arrived in the United States, a possessory action could be brought by a former owner, and the act of state doctrine would not be a defense unless the President expressly invoked it.[112] But plaintiffs whose claims were not directly related to property before the court—whether for an expropriation, breach of an investment agreement, or challenge to an excessive tax—would still be met by the act of state doctrine and not covered by the Hickenlooper Amendment.[113]

The Role of the Executive Branch
One of the arguments made in *Sabbatino* was that if the executive branch advised the court that it had no objection to adjudication of a claim arising out of an expropriation, the court should not thereafter refrain from hearing the claim. It seems that this argument was rejected in *Sabbatino*, but the argument came back in *First National City Bank* v. *Banco Nacional de Cuba*,[114] a case in which the Banco Nacional brought suit to recover excess

---

[111] See *First National City Bank of New York* v. *Banco Nacional de Cuba*, 431 F.2d 394, 399–402 (2d. Cir. 1970), rev'd on other grounds, 406 U.S. 759 (1972); A. Lowenfeld, 'Act of State and Department of State: *First National City Bank* v. *Banco Nacional de Cuba*', 66 Am. J. Int'l L. 795, 801 (1972).

[112] Of course the court would still have to consider the substantive issues of whether the taking had violated international law, what remedies were available, and whether the state or its successor in interest had any counterclaim.

[113] For more on the Hickenlooper Amendment and its implementation, see American Law Institute, *Restatement (Third) of the Foreign Relations of the United States*, §444 and the comments and Reporters' Notes thereto (1987).

[114] 406 U.S. 759 (1972), discussed in detail in Lowenfeld, 'Act of State and Department of State', n. 111 supra.

of collateral deposited with Citibank, and Citibank counterclaimed for the loss of its branches in Cuba. When the case reached the Supreme Court, the Legal Adviser of the State Department wrote to the Court that 'the foreign policy interests of the United States do not require application of the [act of state] doctrine.' A plurality opinion of the Supreme Court written by Justice Rehnquist, who had replaced Justice Harlan, held that since the act of state doctrine was justified primarily on the basis of potential embarrassment of the conduct of foreign relations by the executive branch, the letter from the State Department removed the reason to refrain from adjudicating Citibank's (counter-)claim. Accordingly, the Court reinstated the finding of the district court that the expropriation of Citibank's branches in Cuba had violated international law. While it was not clear that the State Department would write such a letter in each case, and the actual letter was limited to counterclaims, the message to litigants appeared to be 'try the Department first'.

International Law without the Act of State Doctrine
In a companion case to *First National City Bank*, Banco Nacional also claimed for return of excess collateral from the Chase Manhattan Bank, and Chase counterclaimed for expropriation of four branches that it had maintained in Cuba.[115] Chase presented letters from the State Department confirming that the views expressed in the *First National City Bank* case applied to it as well, and accordingly the Court of Appeals undertook to adjudicate the merits of the counterclaim:

Finally, we find no merit in Banco Nacional's argument that even if the counterclaim is justiciable, the damage issue is nonjusticiable because there is insufficient international consensus as to standards of required compensation. Although we agree that it is difficult to state precisely what international law requires regarding damages for expropriation, and we note that this was a consideration of the majority in *Sabbatino* in deciding to apply the act of state doctrine, . . . we conclude that in cases such as the present one any argument as to the justiciability of damages has been foreclosed by the *Citibank I* decision as to the justiciability of the counterclaim in which those damages are sought. Thus, the opinion of Justice Rehnquist in *Citibank I* indicated that where, as here, the act of state doctrine is inapplicable, a court of the United States 'will decide cases before it by choosing the rules appropriate for decision from among various sources of law including international law.'[116]

This conclusion required the court to face the question of what compensation was required by international law.[117]

The Court of Appeals saw the range of choices before it as including (1) no compensation; (2) partial compensation; (3) appropriate compensation;

---

[115] *Banco Nacional de Cuba* v. *Chase Manhattan Bank*, 658 F.2d 875 (2d. Cir. 1981).
[116] Id. at 885.
[117] Banco Nacional had prevailed on its claim for return of its collateral in the amount of about $9.8 million. The lower court had awarded about $6.9 million on Chase's counterclaim, and this sum was contested by Banco Nacional.

and (4) full compensation. It rejected (1) and (2) as not reflecting international law.

As for the Hull Doctrine and the theory that full compensation is required, we are mindful that it has long been under attack by many commentators as not accurately reflecting international law. . . .

It may well be the consensus of nations that full compensation need not be paid 'in all circumstances,' and that requiring an expropriating state to pay 'appropriate compensation,' even considering the lack of precise definition of that term, would come closest to reflecting what international law requires. But the adoption of an 'appropriate compensation' requirement would not exclude the possibility that in some cases full compensation would be appropriate. We see no reason why the two standards may not overlap, and indeed on the facts of the present case we conclude that we need not choose between a standard of full compensation and that of appropriate compensation. Although the award we approve for Chase is less than it seeks and more than Banco Nacional would wish, we nevertheless view it as full compensation for Chase's loss, and neither more nor less than is appropriate in the circumstances.[118]

The main dispute concerned the claim by Chase not only for the net asset value of its branches, but also for their value as a going concern. Banco Nacional argued that an award for going concern value would be inappropriate, and the court agreed. The transformation of Cuba's economy and the emigration of many of Chase's actual and potential customers made the prospect for future earnings highly speculative and therefore an inappropriate basis for an award of damages. Accordingly, Chase's claim was reduced from $6.9 million to about $5.5 million based only on confirmed net assets.[119]

A Treaty Exception

Many of the variations in cases raising the act of state doctrine in the United States are beyond the scope of the present chapter, in that they focus on acts of states not directly related to expropriation of foreign-owned property.[120] One qualification to the holding of the *Sabbatino* case requires mention, however. The Supreme Court wrote (p. 448 supra) that the Judicial Branch would not examine the validity of a taking of property within its own territory by a foreign sovereign government 'in the absence of a treaty or other unambiguous agreement regarding controlling legal principles.' What if there were such a treaty?

---

[118] 658 F.2d at 892–3.   [119] Id., at 894.

[120] For explanation of the act of state doctrine including private antitrust actions, allegations of corrupt practices, and claims on banks, see A. Lowenfeld, *International Litigation and Arbitration*, ch. VI (1993). See also *Restatement* (n. 113 supra), §443 and comments and Reporters' Notes thereto.

In *Kalamazoo Spice Extraction Co. v. Government of Ethiopia*,[121] the state-controlled successor to an Ethiopian company that had been 80 percent owned by an American company brought suit in a US court for non-payment for goods sold and delivered, and the American company counterclaimed for expropriation of its controlling interest in the Ethiopian company. The American company argued that the act of state doctrine had no application, because a Treaty of Amity and Economic Relations was in force between the United States and Ethiopia which contained a provision that 'property of nationals and companies of either High Contracting Party shall not be taken without prompt payment of just and effective compensation.'

The district court dismissed the counterclaim on the basis of the act of state doctrine, on the ground that the quoted provision did not constitute an 'unambiguous agreement'. The Court of Appeals, fortified by strong support from the State Department, reversed, holding that the standard clause of the FCN treaty did provide a controlling legal standard in the area of international law.[122] The Court of Appeals remanded the case to the district court for inquiry into the actions of the (new) government of Ethiopia, but eventually the case was settled as part of a lump-sum settlement. Thus the Supreme Court has not had occasion to confirm that there is a treaty exception. As seen in the next chapter, FCN treaties have been largely replaced by so-called BITs (Bilateral Investment Treaties) which make express provision for dispute settlement, and are thus not likely to engage the act of state doctrine.[123]

Consent of the Acting State

Finally, it is necessary to point out that the act of state doctrine is based in significant part on the premise that the government of Patria has not consented to have its conduct judged by a foreign court under rules to which it has not submitted. If that premise is not applicable, for instance because Patria has agreed to arbitration in a stated forum—as in the cases in Section 14.1—or has agreed that disputes concerning a particular transaction—for instance a sovereign loan[124]—shall be subject to adjudication in a specified court, the act of state doctrine is not applicable.[125]

---

[121] 729 F.2d 422 (6th Cir. 1984), reversing 543 F. Supp. 1224 (W.D. Mich. 1982).

[122] Id. at 425–6.

[123] See also *Callejo* v. *Bancomer S.A.*, 764 F.2d 1101, 1116–21 (5th Cir. 1985), holding that application of the treaty exception to the act of state doctrine 'depends on pragmatic considerations, including both the clarity of the relevant principles of international law and the potential implications of a decision on our foreign policy.'

[124] See e.g. *Allied Bank International* v. *Banco Credito Agricola de Cartago*, 757 F.2d 516 (2d Cir. 1985).

[125] One United States district court held the award in the *LIAMCO* arbitration, Sect. 14.1(a), not enforceable, because as the court said, the underlying dispute was not arbitrable under US law by virtue of the act of state doctrine. *Libyan-American Oil Co.* v. *Socialist People's Libyan Arab Jamahiriya*, 482 F. Supp. 1175 (D.D.C. 1980). On appeal the State and Justice Departments, as well as the American Arbitration Association, urged reversal. The case was settled prior to decision by the Court of Appeals, and the judgment of the district court was vacated. 684 F.2d 1032 (D.C. Cir. 1981).

Summary

Like much of this chapter, the outcome of domestic challenges to foreign expropriations remains ambiguous. Some courts simply consider that it would be wrong for them to judge the acts of foreign states within their own territories. Other courts consider that they should subject such acts of foreign states to review, but often find no violation, or at least no breach that entitles the claimant to relief in their court. The United States Supreme Court in 1964 reconsidered and reaffirmed the act of state doctrine to preclude judicial review of foreign expropriations, but subsequent legislation and judicial decisions introduced various exceptions to application of the doctrine. Thus some expropriations are subject to judicial challenge in the United States on international law grounds, but as of year-end 2001 no clear signal had emerged from the Supreme Court as to how it interprets the international law of international investment.

SUMMARY

Faced with the lack of consensus, ambiguous precedents, and conflicts of ideology, many courts either avoided the issues altogether, as the World Court did, or relied on the teachings of conflict of laws or the act of state doctrine to avoid general declarations on the applicable international law. Arbitral tribunals had fewer means to avoid deciding. They generally upheld the principle that foreign investors whose property was taken by a host state were entitled to compensation, but differed on how the compensation was to be measured.

Much was made of the decision of the inter-War World Court in the *Chorzow Factory* case that reparation for an illegal act must, as far as possible, re-establish the situation which would have existed if the act had not been committed. But once the right of a state to expropriate foreign-owned property subject to payment of compensation was recognized, it was difficult—even in the face of an express concession or investment agreement—to determine illegality for the purpose of assessing compensation. If the illegality consisted primarily in the failure to pay compensation, could or should an arbitral tribunal adopt the *Chorzow* formula, including award of future profits or *restitutio in integrum*? Some arbitral tribunals thought so, others were reluctant.

Discrimination was generally viewed as illegal, but unless an invidious motive on the part of the taking state was unequivocally expressed, it was not often found. Taking the property of all foreigners in a given period, or of all holders of oil concessions, was often regarded as not amounting to discrimination, as contrasted with implementation of the taking state's social or economic objectives.

The decisions described in this chapter, as well as the trends and countertrends traced in the preceding chapter, remain relevant as precedents, models, and warnings. While the deconstruction of the old order was never complete, neither was the effort at reconstructing a new law of international investment, made up of the practice of states, decisions of courts and arbitrators, and agreements among states. That effort, and the results as of the turn of the century, are addressed in the following chapter.

15

Evolving Standards of International Law on International Investment

Several developments came together in the latter part of the twentieth century to change the perceptions concerning international investment, the investment climate in developing countries, and the prevailing international law. *First*, even as some of the premises of classical international law came under attack, as shown in the two preceding chapters, the World Bank launched a major effort to provide ground rules for international arbitration of investment disputes between foreign private investors and host states. *Second*, following the revolution in Iran, the reversal of the previous Iranian policy of attracting foreign investment, the seizure of American hostages, and the freezing of Iranian assets by the United States, a settlement was reached between the United States and Iran establishing a Claims Tribunal that heard hundreds of investor–state claims over a period of about 15 years and made major contributions to the corpus of international law. *Third*, more than a thousand Bilateral Investment Treaties were concluded between developed and developing countries (and some between developing countries *inter se*), closely similar in content, all providing for security of foreign investments, and all providing for international arbitration of investor–state disputes. *Fourth*, in another initiative by the World Bank, a Multilateral Investment Guarantee Agency was created, dedicated to encouragement of international private investment as a way to advance economic growth in less developed countries, in part by providing for security of investments and agreement on basic principles of law.

Each of these developments is taken up hereafter, on the theory that taken together, they have shaped, or reshaped, the prevailing principles of the international law of international investment.

15.1 THE ICSID CONVENTION

(a) Origins and Purpose of the Convention

By the early 1960s, following the wave of decolonization in Africa and parts of Asia, and a wave of take-overs of foreign investments throughout the Third World, it had become apparent that it would be very difficult to achieve consensus on the obligations of host countries toward alien investors (read multinational corporations). The leading international aid institution, the World Bank,[1] began to consider how, on the one hand, it could avoid becoming embroiled in controversies between home and host states concerning expropriation, and on the other hand, how it could assist the resolution of such controversies so as to further its overall purpose of promoting economic development in the world's poor countries.[2]

---

[1] For more on the World Bank, see Ch. 19, Sect. 19.1.

[2] The President of the World Bank had previously been involved as mediator in certain major investment disputes, most notably the seizure in 1956 by the government of Egypt of the Suez Canal, and had brought the General Counsel of the Bank into these efforts. One of the objectives of the convention discussed hereafter was to regularize this function.

Of course, every dispute between an investor and a host state does not involve expropriation, nor is right always on one side. The World Bank came up with a plan for settlement of disputes not between states, but between private parties on one side, host states on the other, under the auspices of an institution to which almost every state outside the Soviet bloc belonged, and which could be seen as a neutral umpire. The result, which took several years of negotiations to achieve, was the Convention on the Settlement of Investment Disputes between States and Nationals of other States.[3] The Convention established the International Centre for Settlement of Investment Disputes (ICSID) within the World Bank, and the Convention became known generally as the ICSID Convention. In contrast to the MIGA Convention also sponsored by the World Bank but two decades later,[4] the ICSID Convention says nothing directly about encouraging the flow of foreign investment to developing countries. Its preamble speaks only of 'the possibility that from time to time disputes may arise in connection with [private international] investment between Contracting States and nationals of other Contracting States' and of recognition that 'international methods of settlement may be appropriate in certain cases.'

(b)   The Scheme of the Convention and the Question of Consent

The scheme of the ICSID Convention is quite simple. First, both the home country of the investor—say the United States or France—and the host state—say Morocco—must have been parties to the Convention.[5] Second, in order for the Convention to be applicable, a given investment dispute must be the subject of a consent to arbitrate under the auspices of ICSID, which may be given in an investment agreement at the time the project in question is undertaken, or in an ad hoc agreement after the dispute arises.[6] A consent once given is not subject to revocation (Art. 25(1)).

To avoid the problems with the Calvo doctrine in its various versions,[7] as well as requirements in many states that a corporation be established under the law of the state where it operates, Article 25(2)(b) defines 'National of Another Contracting State' to include not only a foreign corporation or

---

[3] 17 U.S.T. 1270, 575 U.N.T.S. 159, entered into force 16 Oct. 1966.

[4] See Sect. 15.4 infra.

[5] The Convention is open to all member states of the World Bank, and with approval of the Administrative Council by a two thirds vote, to any other State party to the Statute of the International Court of Justice. See Article 67. The reason for the complicated formula is that at the time of presenting the draft to the Bank's Board of Governors (1965), the United States wanted to do nothing to imply recognition of the People's Republic of China.

[6] The Preamble confirms:

That no Contracting State shall by the mere fact of its ratification, acceptance or approval of this Convention and without its consent be deemed to be under any obligation to submit any particular dispute to conciliation or arbitration.

[7] See Ch. 13, Sect. 13.2, at n. 13.

other juridical entity but also 'any juridical person, which, because of foreign control, the parties have agreed should be treated as a national of
another Contracting State for the purposes of the Convention.' Article 26
provides that, unless otherwise stated, consent of the parties to arbitration
under the Convention shall be deemed to exclude any other remedy. A
Contracting State may make a reservation to require the exhaustion of local
administrative or judicial remedies, but typically host states have not done
so. Correspondingly, home states of an investor are precluded from giving
diplomatic protection or bringing an international claim in connection with
a dispute subject to the Convention (Art. 27(1)).[8]

Normally, an arbitral tribunal under the ICSID Convention consists of
three persons, one selected by each party to the dispute, (i.e. the host state
and the investor) and the presiding arbitrator selected either by the parties
or, if they cannot agree, by the Chairman of ICSID, who is *ex officio* the
President of the World Bank.[9] Thus the pattern of choosing an arbitral tribunal follows the pattern of other international arbitration—commercial or
state-to-state—except that Article 39 provides that the majority of arbitrators shall be nationals of States other than the host state or of the home state
of the investor.

The details of arbitration under the ICSID Convention are beyond the
scope of this volume.[10] The focus here is on the law to be applied under the
Convention, and on the role of the Convention itself in the modern evolution of the law of international investment.

(c)   The Convention and International Law

The Convention is addressed to *investment disputes*. That term was deliberately not defined, but efforts to limit the scope of the Convention, for
instance to claims of denial of justice or discrimination, or to claims of violation of investment promotion laws, were rejected.[11] The key question in
drafting the Convention was what law an arbitral tribunal should apply

---

[8] Article 27(2) adds that diplomatic protection in this context does not include informal
diplomatic exchanges for the sole purpose of facilitating a settlement of the dispute.

[9] The active head of ICSID is the Secretary-General, who has always been the General
Counsel of the World Bank, and one of whose deputies devotes full time to administrating
ICSID, together with a small staff. When the Chairman or his delegate selects the Presiding
Arbitrator, he usually appoints from a standing list of potential arbitrators nominated by each
Contracting State, subject to consultation with the parties.

[10] In particular, the Convention provides a complicated system of interpretation, revision,
and annulment of the award of a tribunal (Arts. 50–2), and for direct enforcement of an ICSID
award as if it were a final judgment of the State where enforcement is sought (Arts. 54–5).

[11] See Aron Broches, 'The Convention on the Settlement of Investment Disputes', 136
Recueil des Cours 331 at p. 363, n. 21 (Hague Acad. Int'l Law 1972-II); repr. in Aron Broches,
Selected Essays, ch. 8, 208, n. 43; IBRD, *The Convention on the Settlement of Investment
Disputes, Documents Concerning the Origin and the Formulation of the Convention (ICSID
History)*, Vol. II, pp. 564–7 (1970).

when it had an investment dispute before it.[12] The resolution adopted in the Convention, was to avoid all attempts to define the substantive obligations between host state and foreign investor, but to provide the following in Article 42(1):

The Tribunal shall decide a dispute in accordance with such rules of law as may be agreed by the parties. In the absence of such agreement, the Tribunal shall apply the law of the Contracting State party to the dispute (including its rules on the conflict of laws) and such rules of international law as may be applicable.

Aron Broches, who as General Counsel of the World Bank and first Secretary-General of ICSID may be said to be the founding father of the Convention, explained the provision as follows:

The Tribunal will first look at the law of the host State and that law will in the first instance be applied to the merits of the dispute. Then the result will be tested against international law. That process will not involve the confirmation or denial of the host State's law, but may result in not applying it where that law, or action taken under that law, violates international law. In that sense . . . , international law is hierarchically superior to national law under Article 42(1).[13]

Broches explains further that four situations may be envisioned in which an ICSID Tribunal will have occasion to apply international law.

(i)   where the parties have so agreed;
(ii) where the law of the host state calls for the application of international law, including customary international law;
(iii) where the subject-matter or issue is directly regulated by international law, for instance a treaty between the host state and the home state of the investor;
(iv) where the law of the host state or action taken under that law violates international law. In this instance, international law could operate as a corrective to national law.

In the event, category (iii) has been the most useful category, as hundreds of Bilateral Investment Treaties have set out substantive provisions concerning the obligations of host states, and have provided for adjudication pursuant to the ICSID Convention as at least one available option for resolution of disputes.[14]

Category (iv) may be said to beg the question. It gives no clue as to the content of that law; evidently in 1964 no useful clue could have achieved approval from the World Bank's Board of Governors, let alone widespread ratification from both developed and developing countries.[15] But at a

---

[12] The Convention was drafted following four regional meetings of experts, each chaired by the General Counsel of the Bank, in Addis Ababa, Santiago de Chile, Geneva, and Bangkok. The present writer was one of two US representatives at the Santiago meeting in February 1964.

[13] Aron Broches, n. 11 supra, 136 *Recueil des Cours* 331 at 392; *Selected Essays* at 229.

[14] See Sect. 15.3 infra.

[15] This statement is based not only on the ICSID History, n. 11 supra, but from the present writer's own experience as one of the delegates to the regional conference in Santiago de Chile in 1964, and as an official of the US Department of State.

minimum, it represented an understanding, widely subscribed, that international law did have something to say about the obligation of host states to foreign investors.

(d) Gradual Acceptance of the Convention

Notwithstanding the fact that joining the ICSID Convention did not constitute consent to arbitration of any given investment dispute, present or future,[16] there was a widespread perception, particularly among the states of Latin America, that the ICSID Convention was an intrusion on host country sovereignty, and that if states did sign and ratify the Convention, they would be under pressure to consent to arbitration in particular investment agreements or investment disputes. When the report of the regional meetings on the proposed convention came before the Board of Governors of the World Bank (i.e. the full membership) at the Annual Meeting of the Bank in Tokyo in 1964, all Latin American member states voted 'no'—the first time in the Bank's history that a major resolution had met with substantial opposition on a final vote—'El No de Tokyo', as it became known in the Latin American press.[17] By 1972, 68 states, including 51 developing countries, had either completed or were in the process of ratification of the Convention, primarily from Africa, and not including India, Iran, Iraq, Philippines, or Saudi Arabia, and not including a single state from Latin America.[18] A significant measure of the change in attitude toward international investment, consistent with other developments described in this chapter, is the change of heart among the countries of Latin America. Ecuador, El Salvador, and Honduras joined the Convention in the mid-1980s, and Argentina, Chile, Colombia, Costa Rica, Grenada, Nicaragua, Peru, Uruguay, and Venezuela jointed in the last decade of the century.[19]

---

[16] See n. 6, supra.

[17] For a discussion of the reasons for the negative attitude toward the Convention in Latin America, see Paul C. Szasz, 'The Investment Disputes Convention and Latin America', 11 *Va. J. Int'l L.* 256 (1971).

[18] Among developed states, Australia, Canada, Portugal, and Spain were conspicuous by their absence, though all had voted in favour of the Convention at the Tokyo meeting. As of year-end 2001, Australia, Portugal, and Spain had become parties to the ICSID Convention, but Canada had not.

[19] In 1978, ICSID opened a so-called Additional Facility, to administer arbitrations and conciliation in disputes between host states and investors, when jurisdiction would not be available under the Convention, because either the host state or the home state of the investor was not a party to the Convention. The rules for conduct of the arbitration or conciliation are substantially similar to the rules set out in the Convention, except that no provision is made for interpretation and revision of an award or for direct enforcement of the award (compare n. 10 supra). The condition for resort to the Additional Facility is that either the host country or the home country of the investor is a party to the ICSID Convention. Thus, for example, the Investment Chapter of the North American Free Trade Agreement (NAFTA) provides for arbitration under the ICSID Additional Facility as one of the available options for settlement of disputes between investors and host states. The United States is a party to the ICSID Convention, Mexico and Canada are not. A Mexican–American and an American–Canadian dispute may

As of year-end 2001, 149 states had signed the ICSID Convention and of these 134 had completed the process of ratification. Only Brazil and Mexico among the Latin American countries, as well as India, which has been ambivalent about international arbitration generally, remained outside the ICSID family.[20] About 80 investment disputes had been submitted to ICSID for arbitration or conciliation; 30 cases were in progress, and 51 cases had been concluded, either by final award or by settlement in the course of the proceeding.

15.2 THE IRAN–UNITED STATES CLAIMS TRIBUNAL

The concept of international arbitration of disputes between foreign investors and host states received a major and unexpected boost in the 1980s, when through a curious combination of circumstances the United States and Iran agreed to create an international tribunal at The Hague to adjudicate claims between United States nationals and companies on one side and the government of Iran and its state-owned entities on the other. For fifteen years and more the Tribunal heard hundreds of cases, large and small, growing out of the sharp change of direction in Iran brought about by the fall of the Shah Reza Pahlavi and the arrival of the Islamic Revolution led by the Ayatollah Ruholla Khomeini.[21] Not all of the cases concerned expropriation; many cases involved commercial disputes about payments for goods and services not made, contracts terminated or not performed, and letters of credit dishonoured or wrongfully drawn on. A substantial number of cases, however, concerned the responsibility of the state to foreign investors for takings and arguably comparable acts.

(a) Background

For present purposes the origins of the Iran-United States Claims Tribunal may be summarized very briefly. Following the ten-fold rise in the price of oil in 1973–4, the Shah of Iran embarked on a massive program of industrialization and modernization, principally through soliciting private investment and long-term contracts from firms in the United States. In 1979, the Islamic Revolution, led by the Ayatollah Khomeini, took over Iran, and reversed the policies of the Shah in virtually all respects, including foreign

be submitted for arbitration under the Additional Facility; a dispute between a Canadian investor and Mexico (or vice versa) could not come before the Additional Facility.

[20] Iran and Iraq were also not parties, and neither was Cuba, which was not, as of year-end 2001 a member of the IMF or the World Bank. Mexico, though not a party to ICSID, is committed to arbitration under ICSID auspices through the North American Free Trade Agreement (NAFTA) and the ICSID Additional Facility.

[21] As of year-end 2001, the Tribunal was still in operation, but the remaining controversies were the so-called 'B cases' involving claims by the government of Iran against the government of the United States.

investment and contracts with Americans. Most enterprises owned or managed by American firms were 'intervened', expropriated, or abandoned under threat, and payments for goods supplied or services performed were withheld. In November 1979, the US Embassy in Tehran was invaded by Iranian 'students'. Fifty-two Americans present at the embassy were taken hostage, and the hostages were detained for more than 14 months.

Iranian banks held large dollar deposits in the United States (as well as in European branches of American banks)—predominantly proceeds of sales of oil—and these deposits, along with other Iranian assets in the United States were frozen by the United States Government.[22] Meanwhile, American claimants sought to bring claims against Iran in United States courts and to attach Iranian assets both for jurisdictional and for security purposes.[23] Negotiations proceeded on and off throughout 1980, primarily through the intermediation of the government of Algeria. Eventually, on the last day of the administration of President Jimmy Carter, a settlement was concluded— the Algiers Accords: (i) the hostages were released; (ii) a major part of the frozen Iranian assets was released and returned to Iran; (iii) all litigation against Iran or Iranian entities in the United States was terminated by executive order;[24] (iv) a Claims Tribunal was established at The Hague to hear claims by US nationals and companies against Iran (and vice versa); and (v) a $1 billion fund from the previously frozen assets was placed in a Security Account in The Netherlands, out of which claims against Iran recognized by the Tribunal would be satisfied, with provision that whenever the balance in the Security Account fell below $500 million, Iran was to make new deposits sufficient to maintain a minimum balance of $500 million, until the Tribunal announced that all arbitral awards had been satisfied.[25]

The irony that from a series of unlawful acts there emerged a tribunal that was to make a major contribution to international law has been often commented on. It is only this contribution that is here addressed.

(b) Constitution and Mandate of the Tribunal

According to the Algiers Accords—in particular the Claims Settlement Declaration[26]—an international arbitral tribunal was to be established con-

---

[22] For discussion of the legal authority and consequences of the freeze, pursuant to the US International Emergency Economic Powers Act, see A. Lowenfeld, *Trade Controls for Political Ends*, 537–63 and Documentary Annex (2nd. edn. 1983).

[23] See id., at pp. 579–87.

[24] For a discussion of the authority for this action, see id. 598–604. The action was subsequently upheld by the US Supreme Court in *Dames & Moore* v. *Regan*, 453 U.S. 654 (1981).

[25] For a more detailed account and recollections of many of the participants in the Iran Hostage Crisis and the creation of the Claims Tribunal, see A. Lowenfeld *et al.*, (ed.), *Revolutionary Days: The Iran Hostage Crisis and the Hague Claims Tribunal, A Look Back* (1999).

[26] Formally the *Declaration of the Government of the Democratic and Popular Republic of Algeria concerning the Settlement of Claims by the Government of the United States of America and the Government of the Islamic Republic of Iran*, 19 Jan. 1981.

sisting of nine members, three appointed by Iran, three by the United States, and three by agreement of the two parties. To the surprise of many skeptics; each side did appoint three members, and agreement was reached on the three neutral members—at first two Swedish judges and a former Chief Judge of the French Cour de Cassation.[27]

For most cases, the Tribunal sat in chambers, each with an Iranian, an American, and a neutral chairman; in some instances, all nine members of the Tribunal sat together, with the President of the Tribunal presiding. The Algiers Claims Settlement Declaration provided that the UNCITRAL Arbitration Rules would govern the proceedings, except to the extent modified by the parties or by the Tribunal. The Tribunal did modify the rules to some extent, but on the whole the conduct of the arbitrations resembled, if they did not quite replicate commercial arbitrations, except that Iran was always a party and the US government was represented by an agent who could intervene, generally to discuss the application of the rules, only rarely on the merits of the claims.[28]

Article II of the Claims Declaration provided that the jurisdiction of the Tribunal shall extend to claims existing on the date of the Algiers Accords that arise out of 'debts, contracts . . . expropriations or other measures affecting property rights' by nationals of the United States against Iran and claims by nationals of Iran against the United States. Article V provided:

The Tribunal shall decide all cases on the basis of respect for law, applying such choice of law rules and principles of commercial and international law as the Tribunal determines to be applicable, taking into account relevant usages of the trade, contract provisions and changed circumstances.

(c) The Claims Tribunal and the Expropriation Cases

Evidently, one section of one chapter cannot do justice to the massive case law of Iran–United States Claims Tribunal.[29] Several topics pertinent to the

[27] As neutral members of the Tribunal stepped down for various reasons, they were replaced in part by agreement, in part by the Appointing Authority, the Chief Judge of the Supreme Court of the Netherlands, who had been designated by the Secretary-General of the Permanent Court of International Arbitration, in accordance with Articles 6 and 7 of the UNCITRAL Arbitral Rules. Without exception, the neutral members of the Tribunal had been well-known members of the international law community who had held important positions as judges, practitioners, diplomats, or academics prior to their appointment to the Tribunal. All but one of the judges were European; the one non-European was an Argentine citizen who had been President of the International Court of Justice.

[28] For accounts of the establishment of the Tribunal, by the first president, Judge Lagergren, and the first US Agent, Arthur Rovine, see *Revolutionary Days*, n. 25 supra. pp. 116–35; for explanation of the changes in rules by US Judge Howard Holtzmann, see id. 137–46. Two commentaries on the UNCITRAL Rules in the light of the Tribunals have been published. Jacomijn J. van Hof, *Commentary on the UNCITRAL Arbitration Rules: Their Application by the Iran–U.S. Claims Tribunal* (1991); Stewart A. Baker and Mark D. Davis, *The UNCITRAL Arbitration Rules in Practice: The Experience of the Iran–United States Claims Tribunal* (1992).

[29] In addition to 29 volumes of the *Iran–United States Claims Tribunal Reports* (1981/2–1993) [hereafter Iran–U.S. C.T.R.], more than a dozen books and close to 70 articles have been published about aspects of the Tribunal, including several by Iranian writers. I have

present inquiry were taken up repeatedly by the Tribunal, and though no principle of *stare decisis* prevailed and the chambers occasionally viewed similar issues differently from one another, there was an effort on the part of most of the neutral arbitrators to achieve consistency.[30]

1. Eligible Claimants

The Claims Declaration (in Article VII(2)) defined nationals of the United States (and of Iran) to the same effect as the ICSID Convention,[31] the Bilateral Investment Treaties,[32] and the Multilateral Investment Guarantee Agency,[33] i.e. to include a corporation or other legal entity organized in the host country if nationals of the home country hold directly or indirectly a controlling interest in the corporation or other entity equivalent to 50 percent or more of its capital stock. The Tribunal in several cases confirmed the right of US corporations to bring claims for taking of Iranian corporation that they had controlled—not just 100 percent-owned subsidiaries but joint venture companies in which the American interest exercised effective managerial control.[34]

2. Availability of the Forum

The Tribunal, again construing the Algiers Accords,[35] held early on that its jurisdiction did not depend on exhaustion of local remedies and could not

found most useful two books by American members of the Tribunal, George H. Aldrich, *The Jurisprudence of the Iran–United States Claims Tribunal* (1996) and Charles N. Brower and Jason D. Brueschke, *The Iran–United States Claims Tribunal* (1998), as well as John R. Crook, 'Applicable Law in International Arbitration: The Iran–US Claims Tribunal Experience', 83 *Am. J. Int'l L.* 278 (1989).

[30] In a review of Judge Aldrich's book, the present author wrote that from the point of view of the institution of international arbitration, the Iran–US Claims Tribunal presents a distorted picture, because the Iranian judges never voted against the Iranian party, and the American judges rarely voted against the American claimants. Book Review, 92 *Am. J. Int'l L.* 149 (Jan. 1998). Judge Richard C. Allison, a member of the Tribunal for a decade, responded that while I was right about the Iranian judges, the American judges often voted against the American claimants, in some instances on the case as a whole, in others on certain claims or in respect of the quantum of damages. Allison wrote:

> [T]he American judges have endeavored to reach just decisions based on objective analysis. This was seen as both an ethical imperative and, as a practical matter, the surest way to preserve the judge's credibility with his (third country) chairman. (Letter, 92 *Am. J. Int'l L.* 488, July 1998).

I take Allison's point. As I wrote in my review, if the Claims Tribunal is not the ideal prototype for international arbitration, its decisions nevertheless make a significant contribution to the development of international law. Thus, the jurisprudence of the Tribunal is a significant element in the evolution of the international law of investment to which this chapter is addressed.

[31] See Sect. 15.1.   [32] See Sect. 15.3.   [33] See Sect. 15.4.

[34] See e.g. *Sedco, Inc. et al v. National Iranian Oil Co.* 9 Iran–U.S. C.T.R. 248 at 258–64 (28 Oct. 1985).

[35] General Principle B of the General Declaration, stating that 'It is the purpose of both parties . . . to terminate all litigation as between the government of each party and the nationals of the other, and to bring about the settlement and termination of all such claims through binding arbitration.'

be defeated by the availability of national remedies.[36] An agreement for settlement of all disputes implies that there are no conditions or impediments to resort to the agreed forum.[37]

3. What is a Taking?

The Tribunal was repeatedly confronted with the fact that the revolutionary government of Iran did not, for the most part (banks and insurance companies excepted) adopt laws or decrees nationalizing foreign-owned property. In many instances, the government appointed managers, intervenors, or members of a reconstituted board of directors. In other instances workers' councils took control of foreign-owned enterprises and the government did nothing to protect the owners. The Tribunal generally accepted the definition of 'taking' in the 1961 Sohn and Baxter Draft Convention on State Responsibility:[38]

(a) A 'taking of property' includes not only an outright taking of property but also any such unreasonable interference, use, enjoyment, or disposal of property as to justify an inference that the owner thereof will not be able to use, enjoy, or dispose of the property within a reasonable period of time after the inception of such interference.

(b) A 'taking of the use of property' includes not only an outright taking of property but also any unreasonable interference with the use or enjoyment of property for a limited period of time.[39]

For instance, in *Tippetts, Abbett, McCarthy, Stratton* v. *TAMS-AFFA Consulting Engineers' of Iran*,[40] an American engineering firm, TAMS had been engaged in a joint venture with an Iranian engineering firm, AFFA. The government appointed a temporary manager of AFFA, who began signing cheques and making decisions for the joint enterprise without consulting TAMS. Following the seizure of the American embassy, the TAMS employees left Iran, and TAMS-AFFA broke off all communications. The Tribunal upheld TAMS' claim:

In light of these facts, the Tribunal concludes that the Claimant has been subjected to 'measures affecting property rights' by being deprived of its property interests in

---

[36] See e.g. *Phillips Petroleum Co. Iran* v. *The Islamic Republic of Iran*, 1 Iran–U.S. C.T.R. 487 (30 Dec. 1982).

[37] Compare Art. 26 of the ICSID Convention:

Consent of the parties to arbitration under the Convention shall, unless otherwise stated, be deemed consent to such arbitration to the exclusion of any other remedy.

[38] Louis Sohn and Richard Baxter, *Draft Convention on the International Responsibility of States for Injury to Aliens*, Art. 10(3), sometimes referred to as the Harvard Draft, repr. in 55 *Am. J. Int'l L.* 545 (1961).

[39] Quoted by Judge Aldrich in a Concurring Opinion published after a last minute settlement of *ITT Industries* v. *Islamic Republic of Iran*, 2 Iran–U.S. C.T.R. 348 (26 May 1983) and reproduced in Aldrich, *The Jurisprudence of the Iran–United States Claims Tribunal* (n. 29 supra) at pp. 175–6.

[40] 6 Iran–U.S. C.T.R. 219 (29 June 1984).

TAMS-AFFA since at least 1 March 1980 and that the Government of Iran is responsible, by virtue of its acts and omissions, for that deprivation. The Claimant is entitled under international law and general principles of law to compensation for the full value of the property of which it was deprived. The Tribunal prefers the term 'deprivation' to the term 'taking', although they are largely synonymous, because the latter may be understood to imply that the Government has acquired something of value, which is not required.

A deprivation or taking of property may occur under international law through interference by a state in the use of that property or with the enjoyment of its benefits, even where legal title to the property is not affected.

While assumption of control over property by a government does not automatically and immediately justify a conclusion that the property has been taken by the government, thus requiring compensation under international law, such a conclusion is warranted whenever events demonstrate that the owner was deprived of fundamental rights of ownership and it appears that this deprivation is not merely ephemeral. The intent of the government is less important than the effects of the measures on the owner, and the form of the measures of control or interference is less important than the reality of their impact.

In the present case, the Claimant and the Government-appointed manager of TAMS-AFFA managed to cooperate sufficiently well in mid-1979 so that such appointment could not by itself in this case be considered an act depriving the Claimant of its property. However, the developments of late 1979 and early 1980, particularly the complete absence of answers to letters and telexes and of any communication from TAMS-AFFA to the Claimant, effectively ended such cooperation and deprived the Claimant of its property interests in TAMS-AFFA. If any doubt remained about this question in early 1980, it has been removed by the absence of new developments and the passage of time.[41]

Other awards confirmed that the emphasis in finding a compensable taking is not on acquisition by the State but on deprivation of the prior owner.[42]

4. *Standard of Compensation*

The issue of the applicable standard of compensation was confused by doubts about whether the 1955 Treaty of Amity between Iran and the United States[43] remained in force, as claimants and the US government asserted, or had been overtaken by events, as Iran asserted. The Treaty of

---

[41] Id. at 225–6. Citations, *inter alia*, to the *Chorzow Factory* case and to Whiteman, *Digest of International Law*, omitted.

[42] See Aldrich (n. 29 supra), 176–88, quoting from *Sedco*, 9 Iran–U.S. C.T.R. 248 (28 Oct. 1985); *Phelps-Dodge*, 10 Iran–U.S. C.T.R. 121 (19 Mar. 1986); *Foremost—Teheran*, 10 Iran–U.S. C.T.R. 228 (11 Apr. 1986), and other cases. In some instances, the Tribunal declined to find a taking but awarded damages for 'other measures affecting property rights'. For a somewhat different treatment of the awards on this issue but reaching the same general conclusion, see Brower and Brueschke (n. 29, supra), ch. 12, 'Actions Engaging State Responsibility for Takings', 369–441.

[43] Treaty of Amity, Economic Relations, and Consular Rights, signed at Tehran 15 Aug. 1955, 8 U.S.T. 899, T.I.A.S. 3853, 284 U.N.T.S. 93.

Amity—a typical American FCN Treaty—called essentially for application of the Hull formula,[44] while Iran contended for something like 'appropriate compensation', on the assumption that this would lead to lower awards.

The Tribunal did not expressly hold until 1985 that the Treaty of Amity was applicable.[45] In earlier cases it suggested that the standard under customary international law and under the Treaty were the same. *In American International Group, Inc.* v. *Iran*,[46] for example, Chamber Three wrote:

The Claimants advance their claims both under the Treaty of Amity and under customary international laws. They maintain that in either case they are now entitled to the pay of 'just' compensation equal to the 'full' value of their interest in Iran America as of the date of nationalization.

The Respondents, who contend that the Treaty of Amity is no longer in force, argue that there is no legal entitlement to compensation equal to the 'full' value of the property nationalized. They maintain that the traditionally accepted standard of 'prompt, adequate and effective' compensation has been repudiated by modern developments in international law. They refer, inter alia, to the United Nations Charter of Economic Rights and Duties of States, Resolution 3281 (XXIX) of 1974 which uses the expression 'appropriate' compensation. They also cite the practice of States in arriving at settlements of nationalization claims. These developments, they argue, require that only 'partial' compensation be paid.

As previously stated, the parties disagree as to the method of valuation to be used. The Claimants maintain that Iran America should be valued as a going concern, including such elements as good will and prospects of future profit. The respondents contend that the assessment should be made exclusively on the basis of the 'net book' or 'break up' value of the company.[47]

The Tribunal did not decide between the arguments of the parties, but found simply that whether the Treaty or customary law was applicable, either way the appropriate method is to value the company as a going concern, 'taking into account not only the net book value of its assets but also such elements as good will and likely future profits.'[48] Similarly, in TAMS, as quoted above,[49] Chamber Two wrote 'The Claimant is entitled under international law and general principles of law to compensation for the full value of the property of which it was deprived.'

When the issue came before Chamber One in *INA Corporation* v. *Iran*,[50] it turned out that the Iranian party did not contest the applicability of the

---

[44] Art. IV(2) of the Treaty of Amity reads as follows:

Property of nationals and companies of either High Contracting Party, including interests in property, shall receive the most constant protection and security within the territories of the other High Contracting Party, in no case less than that required by international law. Such property shall not be taken except for a public purpose, nor shall it be taken without the prompt payment of just compensation. Such compensation shall be in an effectively realizable form and shall represent the full equivalent of the property taken; and adequate provision shall have been made at or prior to the time of taking for the determination and payment thereof.

[45] *INA Corporation* v. *Iran*, 8 Iran–U.S. C.T.R. 373 (13 Aug. 1985).
[46] 4 Iran–U.S. C.T.R. 96 (19 Dec. 1983).   [47] Id., at pp. 105–6.
[48] Id., at p. 109.   [49] See text at n. 41 supra.   [50] n. 45 supra.

Treaty of Amity, and so the Tribunal assumed that for the purpose of that case the Treaty remained binding. For the actual case, it awarded full compensation. But the Tribunal added that

international law [unless not governed by a *lex specialis*, i.e. the Treaty of Amity] has undergone a gradual reappraisal, the effect of which may be to undermine the doctrinal value of any 'full' or 'adequate' (when used as identical to 'full') compensation standard as proposed in this case.[51]

Thereafter each of the three arbitrators filed a separate opinion. Judge Lagergren, the Swedish President of the Tribunal, argued that in some cases of large-scale nationalization principles of international law no longer require full compensation equivalent to the fair market value of the property taken; Judge Holtzmann, the American member of Chamber One, argued essentially for the continued validity of the Hull formula; and Judge Ameli, the Iranian member of the Chamber, though dissenting on the award, supported Judge Lagergren's view on the current status of international law on nationalization and compensation.

A few months after the award in *INA Corporation*, the Tribunal held in *Phelps Dodge Corporation* v. *Iran*[52] that whether or not the Treaty of Amity remained in effect at the time of the award, it was clearly applicable to the investment at issue at the time the claim arose, and thus was a 'relevant source of law on which the Tribunal is justified in drawing in reaching its decision.'[53] Later decisions of the Tribunal consistently applied the Treaty of Amity and the standard of 'just compensation' representing the 'full equivalent of the property taken'.[54] Most, though not all of the cases also stated that the standard of full compensation is the same under the Treaty of Amity and under customary law, i.e. that the *lex specialis* and the *lex generalis* apply equally and with the same outcome.[55] In *Amoco International Finance Corporation* v. *Iran*,[56] Chamber Three wrote:

As a *lex specialis* in the relations between the two countries, the Treaty supersedes the *lex generalis*, namely customary international law. This does not mean, however, that the latter is irrelevant in the instant case. On the contrary, the rules of customary law may be useful in order to fill in possible *lacunae* of the Treaty, to ascertain the meaning of undefined terms in its text or, more generally, to aid interpretation and implementation of its provisions.[57]

---

[51] 4 Iran–U.S. C.T.R. 96 at 378 (19 Dec. 1983).
[52] 10 Iran–U.S. C.T.R. 121 at 132 (19 Mar. 1986).   [53] Id., at 132.
[54] See Crook (n. 29, supra) at pp. 301–2; Aldrich (n. 29 supra) 221. Judge Aldrich writes:

The holding by Chamber Two in *Phelps Dodge* was gratefully followed in virtually all subsequent Awards, although it did not always stop the Tribunal from stating its views on the meaning of customary international law.

[55] Accord also Brower and Bruescke (n. 29 supra), 485–8, citing, as does Aldrich, *Sedco*, 10 Iran–U.S. C.T.R. 180 (27 Mar. 1986); *Sola Tiles, Inc.*, 14 Iran–U.S. C.T.R. 223 (22 Apr. 1987); and *Petrolane, Inc.*, 27 Iran–U.S. C.T.R. 64 (14 Aug. 1991).
[56] 15 Iran–U.S. C.T.R. 189 (14 July 1987).   [57] Id., at 222.

5. The Quantum of Compensation

The most difficult issue for the Iran–US Claims Tribunal, as it has been for other courts and tribunals, was how to establish full value or fair market value. In other contexts, as seen, for instance, in the Bilateral Investment Treaties discussed in the next section, the aim has been to look to the value unaffected by the taking or by the knowledge that the taking was about to occur, as well as by events between the time of taking and the time of the arbitration. In principle, the Claims Tribunal agreed with that aim. In *INA Corporation*,[58] for example, Chamber One defined fair market value as

the amount which a willing buyer would have paid to a willing seller for the shares of a going concern, disregarding any diminution of value due to the nationalization itself or the anticipation thereof, and excluding consideration of events thereafter that might have increased or decreased the value of the shares.[59]

Applying the principle to particular cases amid the turmoil in Iran in the early years of the Revolution, as well as the turmoil in the world market for oil, inevitably produced contradictory outcomes. In *Phillips Petroleum Co v. Iran*,[60] the Tribunal was faced with the task of placing a value on the loss to the American company of its right to produce and export oil pursuant to a 'Joint Structure Agreement' with the National Iranian Oil Company and others. The taking was found by the Tribunal to have occurred in September 1979, at the peak of international oil prices, a decade before the Tribunal's award. The Tribunal sought to place itself in the position of the investor at that time:

In order to estimate what revenue could have reasonably been expected in September 1979 to be received from the sales of the oil to be produced under the JSA, an assessment has to be made of what oil prices would have been foreseen in September 1979 to prevail on world markets during the remaining years of the JSA. While experience shows that forecasting future crude oil prices is difficult and open to high risk of being proved wrong by the subsequent realities of the actual market, the Tribunal's objective here is to determine the range of expectations that seemed reasonable in September 1979, not the accuracy of those expectations in fact. The actual course of prices since 1979 to the date of this Award, while relevant to the present value of the property, is irrelevant to the value of the property in 1979, and it is the 1979 value which the Claimant seeks and to which it is entitled. Having determined the range of those expectations, the risk that world oil prices from 1979 to 1999 would prove to fall outside that foreseeable range will be discussed in the assessment of the risk factors affecting the value of the Claimant's . . . interests.

In this connection, it should clearly be understood that the Tribunal is not determining price levels and oil production quantities in order to award anticipated profits lost through breach of contract, but rather to determine what was the value of the property interests taken from the Claimant in September 1979. Those property

---

[58] See n. 45 supra.   [59] 8 Iran–U.S. C.T.R. at 380.
[60] 21 Iran–U.S. C.T.R. 79 at 128–9 (29 June 1989).

interests constituted part of an income-producing going concern, the value of which at the time of taking . . . cannot be determined without taking fully into account its future income-producing prospects as they would have been perceived at that time by a buyer of those interests. History, to date, has shown that the price expectations generally held in 1979 were grossly inflated, but that does not make it wrong or unfair to use those expected price levels in the determination of the value of the property in 1979. *A state that takes property assumes the risk of its subsequent decline in value, just as it assumes the benefits if the value appreciates.*[61] (italics added).

However, one could not simply ignore the events of the Iranian Revolution, which in many cases reduced the expectations and value of prior investment. An early example of the Tribunal's thinking was the decision of Chamber Three in *American International Group Inc. v. Iran*,[62] which arose out of nationalization in June 1979 of the Iranian insurance industry. AIG owned a substantial share of an Iranian insurance company, and the Tribunal determined that it was entitled to its share of the going-concern value of the company. In presenting its claim and the relevant accounts, AIG urged omission of the most recent data, on the ground that the revenues for the last fiscal year reflected abnormal conditions related to the Revolution itself. The Tribunal rejected this approach. The Tribunal wrote:

It is necessary to exclude the effects of actions taken by the nationalizing State in relation to the enterprise which actions may have depressed its value. . . .

On the other hand, prior changes in the general political, social and economic conditions which might have affected the enterprise's business prospects as of the date the enterprise was taken should be considered. Whether such changes are ephemeral or long-term will determine their overall impact upon the value of the enterpise's future prospects. Thus, financial data available for the [last fiscal year of the company] should not be ignored.[63]

Judge Mosk, the American member of Chamber Three, wrote in a separate concurrence that he would have attributed the abnormal conditions that caused a decline in the insurance company's revenues in the last year of operation to actions of the Government of Iran. The prevailing view on this issue was published by Judge Aldrich as a concurring opinion, but actually represented the view of Chamber Two in a case settled just before the award was to be issued:

That Iran might experience revolution was a risk assumed by investors in Iran, as in any country; and any reduction in value of investments as a result of revolution cannot be ignored by the Tribunal. The Islamic Revolution in Iran was not a 'wrong' for which investors are entitled to compensation under international law. In computing compensation for expropriated property, the Tribunal must find as best it can the

---

[61] 21 Iran–U.S. C.T.R. 79 at pp. 128–9 (29 June 1989).

[62] 4 Iran–U.S. C.T.R. at 96 (19 Dec. 1983).

[63] Id., pp. 106–7. The Tribunal pointed out, for example, that during the period autumn 1978–June 1979 many Iranians belonging to the wealthier part of the population—who might be expected to purchase insurance—left the country.

real value at the moment of taking, excluding only any decline in value resulting from the threat of taking or other acts attributable to the government itself.[64]

It followed that firms marketing Western music, or imported electronics equipment in Iran, could not justify their claims on the basis of pre-Revolution earnings.[65]

Apart from these views on the effect of past and future events, the use of accounting techniques such as *net book value, replacement cost, discounted cash flow*, to go beyond the agreed terms such as 'fair market value' and 'going concern value' seems to have followed no consistent pattern. Each case was examined in detail, with accountants and industry experts, in some instances presented by the parties, in others called by the Tribunal itself. The awards rarely accepted the experts' detailed submissions, but reflected also the judgments of the Chamber hearing the case.

Judge Brower, in his book, summarized the consensus, as far at it went:

[T]he Tribunal's taking practice establishes that in valuing expropriated property, the best evidence is the actual market value of the property. In the majority of cases, where such actual market pricing is unavailable, the Tribunal will consider all relevant factors in determining a fair market value for the property or business entity. With regard to these relevant factors, the Tribunal generally (i) will exclude the effects of the taking itself, and any acts related to it; as well as (ii) the effect of all events occurring after the date of the taking not reasonably foreseeable; but (iii) will include the general effects, both economic and social, of the Revolution on the value of the enterprise, but not specific policies within the State's control that depress the value of the property.[66]

(d) The Iran–US Claims Tribunal and International Law

There can be no doubt that in the number of cases, the large sums involved, the availability of the Security Account from which awards to the American claimants would be paid, the continuity of the Tribunal and the high caliber of its members, and the many issues raised in actual hard-fought controversy, the Iran–US Claims Tribunal has been a milestone in the evolution of the international law of investment, as well as of dispute settlement. The arguments about whether the Tribunal administered *a lex specialis*, i.e. the Treaty of Amity, or a *lex generalis*, i.e. customary international law, gradually became irrelevant, as the two sources blended together. The questions about the unique circumstances of the creation of the Tribunal and the composition of its members, while not irrelevant, lose significance beside the twenty-nine volumes of reports of thoughtful decisions, concurrences, and dissents.

---

[64] *ITT Industries, Inc.* v. *Iran*, 2 Iran–U.S. C.T.R. 111 at 120 (30 Dec. 1983).

[65] See *CBS Inc.* v. *Iran*, 25 Iran–U.S. C.T.R. 131 at 148–9 (28 June 1990) (music); *Thomas Earl Payne* v. *Iran*, 12 Iran–U.S. C.T.R. 3 at 15 (8 Aug. 1986) and *Motorola, Inc.* v. *Iranian National Airlines Corp.*, 19 Iran–U.S. C.T.R. 73 at 90–1 (28 June 1989) (electronics).

[66] Charles N. Brower and Jason D. Brueschke, *The Iran–United States Claims Tribunal*, 556 (1998).

Overall, the Iran-U.S. Claims Tribunal confirmed the principle that property rights of foreign investors are to be respected, and that compensation is to be paid when the owner is deprived of these rights by acts attributable to the State.[67] A clear teaching of the Claims Tribunal, consistent with the developments described in the other sections of this chapter, is that international law applies directly between states and foreign parties, not merely between states.

Further, again consistently with other developments as described in this chapter, the liability of the state is engaged in respect of the deprivation or loss to the prior owner, not in respect of the gain to the state.

Third, a revolution or other social upheaval does not itself create liability, but does not provide justification for a state to avoid the duty to compensate a foreign investor for acts attributable to the state.

Fourth, not thus far discussed, the Tribunal consistently awarded interest as damages for delay in payment, measured from the date of taking to the date of the award or date of payment. The chambers agreed, consistently with most international arbitral tribunals, that the awards would include simple interest only, but they did not agree on a common rate.[68]

Finally, the most difficult subject, as discussed above, has concerned the quantum of compensation. Given the availability of the Security Account, the suggestion that 'appropriate compensation' called for something less than full compensation was not accepted. In a revolution by a poor country with no substantial assets, 'exceptional circumstances' might call for something less than full compensation or for stretched out payments.[69] That was not the case here. Just compensation seems to call for full value. For a going concern, i.e. a business that has a known market and a record of performance, full value is determined not by historical cost or replacement cost of physical assets, but on the basis of reasonable expectation of future earnings at the time of taking. There appears to be agreement with the goal stated in the *Chorzow Factory* case,[70] to place the prior owner in the position it

---

[67] Portions of this and the next two paragraphs are adapted from Aldrich, *The Jurisprudence of the Iran–United States Claims Tribunal* (n. 29, supra), 217.

[68] Iran challenged the authority of the Tribunal to award interest, which was not mentioned in the Algiers Declaration. In a decision in 1987 in a state-to-state case, the full Tribunal held:

> The Tribunal is required by Article V of the Claims Settlement Declaration to decide claims on the basis of respect for law. In doing so, it has regularly treated interest, where sought, as forming an integral part of the 'claim' which it has the duty to decide.

The Islamic Republic of Iran v. The United States of America, DEC 65-A19-FT, 16 Iran–U.S. C.T.R. 289 (30 Sept. 1987).

Compare the different treatment in *AMINOIL v. Kuwait*, Ch. 14, Sect. 14.1(b), where the tribunal not only awarded interest but made allowance for inflation and then compounded annually from the date of termination of the concession to the date of the award.

[69] See the discussion in the *Chase Manhattan* case, Ch. 14, Sect. 14.3(b)(2), at n. 115; also the discussions throughout Ch. 13, esp. in Sect. 13.5 concerning the various resolution of the UN General Assembly.

[70] See Ch. 13, Sect. 13.3(a), at nn. 17–19.

would have been in had the taking not occurred, but there is skepticism about such methods as Discounted Cash Flow Analysis, i.e. the effort to establish present value on the basis of future earnings, because it requires speculation both about future earnings and about the interest or discount rate used.[71]

15.3 BILATERAL INVESTMENT TREATIES

(a) Introduction: The Spread of BITs

A striking illustration of the changing perception of the rules of international investment has been the growth—one could almost say explosion—of bilateral investment treaties or BITs. The first such treaty was concluded between the Federal Republic of Germany and Pakistan in 1959. Since then Germany has entered into over 90 BITs; France and Switzerland soon followed with similar programs, and all the Western European states as well as the United States have made BITs an element of their foreign economic policy.[72] As of year-end 2001, more than 1100 bilateral investment treaties were in effect, most between developed and developing countries but a substantial number between developing countries *inter se*.[73] Of the 1100 treaties; more than 800 were concluded since 1987. Overall 155 countries were parties to BITs, covering every continent.[74] Just as the Latin American countries were slow to accept the ICSID Convention,[75] so they were slow to accept bilateral investment treaties. As of year-end 2001, however, nearly all the states of Latin America, including Cuba, have concluded one or more BITs.[76] Moreover, the investment chapter of the North American Free Trade Agreement (NAFTA) is in many ways modeled on the BITs, and is here discussed along with those treaties.

[71] See, in particular *Amoco International Finance Corporation* v. *Iran*, 15 Iran–U.S. C.T.R. 189, esp. at 258–60 (14 July 1987). In that case, concerning claimants rights to exploit natural gas resources, the Tribunal wrote:

One of the best settled rules of the law of international responsibility of States is that no reparation for speculative or uncertain damages can be awarded.

Note the contrast between this decision by Chamber Three, with the statement by Chamber Two two years later in *Phillips Petroleum*, at n. 48 supra.

[72] For a book-length study of BITs, including a history of their development, see Rudolf Dolzer and Margrete Stevens, *Bilateral Investment Treaties* (1995).

[73] For present purposes, the investment chapter of the North American Free Trade Agreement may be discussed together with BITS, though it has three parties, two developed and one developing. The provisions of NAFTA Chapter 11 closely track the typical BITs.

[74] The figures are based on the collection of BITS by the International Centre for the Settlement of Investment Disputes, (ICSID), as set out in the ICSID annual report and on the ICSID website.

[75] See Sect. 15.1(d), supra.

[76] It worth noting that as of year-end 2001 China had entered into 71 bilateral investment treaties, but not with the United States. India had signed 11 BITs, but only three were in force, with the United Kingdom, the Netherlands, and South Korea.

(b)   The Content of BITs

Considering the large number of BITs in force, they are remarkably similar. BITs generally start with a preamble that recites the desire to promote greater economic cooperation between the parties, and to encourage the flow of private capital and create conditions conducive to such flow. The definitions article typically contains a broad definition of investment or covered investment, and makes clear, as in the ICSID treaty and also in the MIGA Convention,[77] that whether or not the investment is held by an entity incorporated in the host country, if it is owned or controlled by nationals of the other party, it is entitled to the protections afforded by the treaty.

1. *Admission of the Investment*

All the BITs appear to cover admission or entry into the host country. Some treaties, including all those entered into by the United States, require national treatment on conditions for entry, with the possibility of reserving certain sectors, such as airlines, telecommunications, and financial institutions from the national treatment undertaking. Those treaties that do not contain a national treatment requirement for entry typically provide that investments of the other contracting party will be admitted in accordance with each party's legislation, rules, and regulations.[78]

Some BITs, notably the recent treaties concluded by the United States, including the NAFTA, have introduced a new element into the international law of investment—a prohibition, or partial prohibition, of so-called performance requirements. The recent US BITs provide that neither Party shall mandate, as a condition for the establishment, acquisition, expansion, or operation of a covered investment any of six performance requirements:

- (a) to achieve a particular level or percentage of local content or to give a preference to products of services of domestic content or source;
- (b) to limit imports in relation to a particular volume of production, exports, or foreign exchange earnings;
- (c) to export a particular level or percentage of products or services;
- (d) to limit sales in the Party's territory in relation to a particular volume or value of production, exports, or foreign exchange earnings;
- (e) to transfer technology to a national company in the Party's territory; or
- (f) to carry out a particular type, level or percentage of research and development in the party's territory.[79]

The standard American BITs provide that the prohibition on these performance requirements does not extend to conditions for receipt (or continued

---

[77] See Sect. 15.4, infra.

[78] See e.g. the model Netherlands BIT Article 2; the model Swiss BIT, Article 2(1); the model British BIT, Article 24(1), all reproduced in Annex I of Dolzer and Stevens, n. 72 supra.

[79] Compare the limited steps on this subject taken in the Uruguay Round of Trade Negotiations, stimulated by the dispute about performance requirements between the United

receipt) of an advantage, such as a subsidy, tax deferral, land grant, or similar benefit from the government. The North American Free Trade Agreement prohibits substantially the same performance requirements, but except for the requirement to export a given level or percentage of goods and the requirement to transfer technology, the prohibition applies whether or not it is a condition for an advantage.

2. Fair and Equitable Treatment

Whether or not the entry requires special permission once an investment is admitted, it is entitled under virtually all the treaties to 'fair and equitable treatment' and 'full protection and security'. The United States BITs, including the Investment Chapter of the North American Free Trade Agreement, add 'as required by [or no less favourable than required by] international law.'[80] At a minimum, 'fair and equitable treatment' means no discrimination by nationality or origin, in respect to such matters as access to local courts and administrative bodies, applicable taxes, and administration of governmental regulations. But the reason for the clause, separate from the MFN and national treatment requirements, is to make clear that a minimum international standard of behaviour applies to treatment of foreign investment even if no discrimination can be shown. For instance, in an arbitration under the North American Free Trade Agreement between a US-based firm and Mexico, the investor had received a permit from the national government to construct a facility for disposal of hazardous waste, and had spent 13 months and 20 million dollars constructing the plant when the local authorities announced that their permission was required and would not be forthcoming. The arbitral tribunal concluded:

Mexico failed to assure a transparent and predictable framework for [the investor's] business planning and investment. The totality of these circumstances demonstrates a lack of orderly process and timely disposition in relation to an investor of a party acting in the expectation that it would be treated fairly and justly in accordance with the NAFTA.[81]

States and Canada, which led to the Agreement on Trade-Related Investment Measures (the TRIMs Agreement), Ch. 5, Sect. 5.5.

[80] One of the participants in the United States program of drafting and negotiating BITs, pointed out that some of the earlier treaties of Friendship Commerce and Navigation had avoided reference to international law standards, apparently from fear on the part of the treaty drafters that, given the contemporary controversy over the content of international investment law, specific reference to international standards might undercut superior treaty language.

The incorporation of international law in the BITs, [he continued] reflects a more optimistic view of its current state of health. The framers of the model BIT believed that reference to international law would add to, rather than detract from, the bundle of rights set forth in the treaty. (K. Scott Gudgeon, 'United States Bilateral Investment Treaties: Comments on their Origin, Purposes, and General Treatment Standards', 4 *Int'l Tax & Business Law* 105 at 124–5 (1986))

[81] *Metalclad Corporation* v. *United Mexican States*, Final Award, 30 Aug. 2000, para. 99 ICSID Case No. ARB(AF)/97/1.

Accordingly, the Tribunal held that Mexico had violated the requirement of fair and equitable treatment in Article 1105 of the NAFTA.[82]

3. 'Full protection and security'

BITs seem to require the government of the host state not only not to attack the facilities or personnel of the investor, but to defend the investor or investment against others, including, for instance, rebel forces. In an ICSID arbitration initiated under the BIT between the United Kingdom and Sri Lanka, claimant asserted that its shrimp farm was destroyed during a military operation conducted by the security forces of Sri Lanka against installations reported to be used by local rebels. Following an evidentiary hearing, the tribunal was unable to conclude that the government security forces were themselves the actors of the destruction. But a majority of the tribunal did conclude that the governmental authorities failed to take the appropriate precautionary measures in view of fighting in the area.

Therefore, and faced with the impossibility of obtaining conclusive evidence about what effectively caused the destruction of the farm premises during the period in which the entire area was out of bounds under the exclusive control of the government security force, the Tribunal considers the State's responsibility established . . . under international law.[83]

4. Expropriation

All of the Bilateral Investment Treaties (including as previously noted, Chapter Eleven of the NAFTA) contain provisions on expropriation, in closely parallel, if not identical wording. Expropriation is lawful and not inconsistent with the BITs if it (i) is carried out for a public purpose; (ii) is non-discriminatory; (iii) is carried out in accordance with due process, and (iv) is accompanied by payment of compensation—in some treaties qualified by the word 'just', in most other recent treaties by the traditional 'Hull formula'[84]—'prompt, adequate and effective'. Many of the treaties speak also of 'expropriation or nationalization', of 'expropriation direct or indirect', or 'expropriation through measures tantamount to expropriation' or variations of these terms.[85]

The reason for including 'direct or indirect', 'similar to', or 'tantamount to expropriation' is to confirm or establish that so-called 'creeping expropriation' is included within the provisions on expropriation. The use of these terms, however, has caused major controversy, particularly in disputes brought under the investment chapter of NAFTA, in which investors cite the

---

[82] The tribunal in the *Metalclad* case also found the actions to constitute an indirect expropriation, as discussed in Sect. 15.3 (b)(4) infra. The award was subsequently set aside in part by a court in British Columbia on the ground of excess of jurisdiction, after which the parties reached a settlement. (*United Mexican States* v. *Metalclad Corp.*, 2001 BCSC 664 (2 May 2001).

[83] *Asian Agricultural Products Ltd.* v. *Republic of Sri Lanka*, Award of 27 June 1990, paras. 85–6, 30 *I.L.M.* 577 (1991), 4 *ICSID Rep.* 246 (1997)).

[84] See Ch. 13, Sect. 13.3(b).

[85] For samples of the variations, see Dolzer and Stevens (n. 72 supra), 99–101.

expropriation text 'No Party [i.e. no host state] may directly or indirectly . . . take a measure tantamount to nationalization or expropriation' to challenge what the host state regards as an exercise of regulatory or police powers. Investors have argued, in effect, that they are not challenging the state's power to regulate, but if the regulation results in closing down or significantly impairing the investor's business, then compensation is required. The state Parties have replied that while they committed themselves not to expropriate except under the conditions set out in the treaty, they have not agreed to place their regulatory authorities—particularly in connection with management of the environment—under the treaty regime.

In the *Metalclad* case described in Sect. 15.3(b)(2), the NAFTA tribunal concluded that the deprivation of the right to operate the investor's hazardous waste disposal facility after it had been built constituted not only a failure to accord fair and equitable treatment under NAFTA Article 1105, but also expropriation under Article 1110. The Tribunal wrote:

[E]xpropriation under NAFTA includes not only open, deliberate and acknowledged takings of property, such as outright seizure or formal or obligatory transfer of title in favour of the host State, but also covert or incidental interference with the use of property which has the effect of depriving the owner, in whole or in significant part, of the use or reasonably-to-be-expected economic benefit of property even if not necessarily to the obvious benefit of the host State.

By permitting or tolerating the conduct of [the local authority] in relation to Metalclad which the Tribunal has already held amounts to unfair and inequitable treatment breaching Article 1105 and by thus participating or acquiescing in the denial to Metalclad of the right to operate the landfill, notwithstanding the fact that the project was fully approved and endorsed by the federal government, Mexico must be held to have taken a measure tantamount to expropriation in violation of NAFTA Article 1110(1).[86]

In contrast, in the *Pope & Talbot* case,[87] another NAFTA panel hearing a claim by a US investor alleging unfair administration by the Canadian Government of an export control regime in implementation of a trade agreement with the United States, rejected the assertion that the allegations stated a claim under the expropriation article:

[T]he Tribunal concludes that the Investment's access to the U.S. market is a property interest subject to protection under Article 1110 and that the scope of that article does cover nondiscriminatory regulation that might be said to fall within an exercise of a state's so-called police powers. However, the Tribunal does not believe that those regulatory measures constitute an interference with the Investment's business activities substantial enough to be characterized as expropriation under international law. Finally, the Tribunal does not believe that the phrase 'measure tantamount to nationalization or expropriation' in Article 1110 broadens the ordinary

---

[86] *Metalclad Corporation* v. *United Mexican States*, (n. 81 supra), paras. 103–4.
[87] *Pope & Talbot Inc.* v. *Government of Canada*, Interim Award, 26 June 2000.

concept of expropriation under international law to require compensation for measures affecting property interests without regard to the magnitude or severity of that effect.

. . .

The next question is whether the Export Control Regime has caused an expropriation of the Investor's investment, creeping or otherwise. Using the ordinary meaning of those terms under international law, the answer must be negative. First of all, there is no allegation that the investment has been nationalized or that the Regime is confiscatory. The Investor's (and the Investment's) Operations Controller testified at the hearing that the Investor remains in control of the investment, it directs the day-to-day operations of the investment, and no officers or employees of the investment have been detained by virtue of the Regime. Canada does not supervise the work of the officers or employees of the Investment, does not take any of the proceeds of company sales (apart from taxation), does not interfere with management or shareholders' activities, does not prevent the Investment from paying dividends to its shareholders, does not interfere with the appointment of directors or management and does not take any other actions ousting the Investor from full ownership and control of the Investment.

. . .

Even accepting (for the purpose of this analysis) the allegations of the Investor concerning diminished profits, the Tribunal concludes that the degree of interference with the Investment's operations due to the Export Control Regime does not rise to an expropriation (creeping or otherwise) within the meaning of Article 1110. While it may sometimes be uncertain whether a particular interference with business activities amounts to an expropriation, the test is whether that interference is sufficiently restrictive to support a conclusion that the property has been 'taken' from the owner. Thus, the *Harvard Draft* defines the standard as requiring interference that would 'justify an inference that the owner . . . will not be able to use, enjoy, or dispose of the property. . . .' The *Restatement* in addressing the question whether regulation may be considered expropriation, speaks of 'action that is confiscatory, or that prevents, unreasonably interferes with, or unduly delays, effective enjoyment of an alien's property.'[88] Indeed, at the hearing, the Investor's Counsel conceded, correctly, that under international law, expropriation requires a 'substantial deprivation'. The Export Control Regime has not restricted the Investment in ways that meet these standards.

As noted, the Investor expressly agreed that 'the Export Control Regime is a measure not covered by customary international law definitions or interpretations of the term expropriation.' It contends that NAFTA goes beyond those customary definitions and interpretations to adopt broader requirements that include under the purview of Article 1110 'measures of general application which have the effect of substantially interfering with the investments of investors of NAFTA Parties.' The Investor discerns this additional requirement because of the use of the phrase 'measure tantamount to . . . expropriation' in Article 1110.

---

[88] Citing *Restatement (Third) of the Foreign Relations Law of the United States*, §712, comment *g*.

The Tribunal is unable to accept the Investor's reading of Article 1110. 'Tantamount' means nothing more than equivalent. Something that is equivalent to something else cannot logically encompass more. No authority cited by the Investor supports a contrary conclusion.[89]

Again, in *S.D. Myers* v. *Canada*,[90] another NAFTA Tribunal followed the *Pope & Talbot* decision in a case arising out of an alleged wrongful closure by the government of Canada of the border with the United States for disposal by the US investor of hazardous waste generated in Canada. The Tribunal found for the investor on its claim of failure to accord fair and equitable treatment and national treatment, but rejected the claim of expropriation.

The Tribunal accepts that, in legal theory, rights other than property rights may be 'expropriated' and that international law makes it appropriate for tribunals to examine the purpose and effect of governmental measures. The Interim Order and the Final Order were regulatory acts that imposed restrictions on [the Investor]. The general body of precedent usually does not treat regulatory action as amounting to expropriation. Regulatory conduct by public authorities is unlikely to be the subject of legitimate complaint under Article 1110 of the NAFTA, although the Tribunal does not rule out that possibility.

Expropriations tend to involve the deprivation of ownership rights; regulations a lesser interference. The distinction between expropriation and regulation screens out most potential cases of complaints concerning economic intervention by a state and reduces the risk that governments will be subject to claims as they go about their business of managing public affairs.

[The Investor] relied on the use of the word 'tantamount' in Article 1110(1) to extend the meaning of the expression 'tantamount to expropriation' beyond the customary scope of the term 'expropriation' under international law. The primary meaning of the word 'tantamount' given by the Oxford English Dictionary is 'equivalent'. Both words require a tribunal to look at the substance of what has occurred and not only at form. A tribunal should not be deterred by technical or facial considerations from reaching a conclusion that an expropriation or conduct tantamount to an expropriation has occurred. It must look at the real interests involved and the purpose and effect of the government measure.

The Tribunal agrees with the conclusion in the Interim Award of the *Pope & Talbot* Arbitral Tribunal that something that is 'equivalent' to something else cannot logically encompass more. In common with the *Pope & Talbot* Tribunal, this Tribunal considers that the drafters of the NAFTA intended the word 'tantamount' to embrace the concept of so-called 'creeping expropriation,' rather than to expand the internationally accepted scope of the term expropriation.[91]

It seems clear from the cases here excerpted and others that expropriation as governed by the BITs is defined by the deprivation to the investor, not by the gain to the host state. Thus destruction of the investor's property may

[89] *Pope & Talbot* (n. 87 supra), paras. 99–104.
[90] *S. D. Myers, Inc.* v. *Government of Canada*, Partial Award, 13 Nov. 2000.
[91] Id., paras. 281–2, 285–6.

come within the definition of expropriation if the actions are attributable to the host state, even if the state does not acquire the property in question.[92] Further, intangible rights, such as the right to import or export a given product or to participate in a given industry, may be subject to the constraints on expropriation set out in the BITs. However, a regulation of temporary duration, or a regulation that reduces the profitability of an investment but does not shut it down completely and leaves the investor in control, will generally not be seen as an expropriation, even when it gives rise to liability on the part of the host state for violation of the national treatment and fair and equitable treatment clauses.

5. Compensation

The subject of compensation, as discussed in Chapters 13 and 14, has been at the center of the debate about the rights and responsibilities related to foreign direct investment. Since virtually all statements of the law recognize the right of host states to expropriate or nationalize, subject to stated conditions, and since the requirement of public purpose is generally a tautology because it is the state that has acted for what it considers its benefit, the critical question has been whether compensation is due to the investor, and if so, how much, in what form, and in what period of time.[93]

Most, though not all BITs adopt the 'Hull formula' for compensation for takings; many of the BITs—notably the German and the American treaties—elaborate at least somewhat on the meaning of 'prompt', 'effective', and 'adequate'. *Adequacy* is typically defined as 'market value' or 'fair market value' before the expropriation took place, and is supposed to exclude any change in value occurring because the plan to expropriate had become known before the actual taking. The object is spelled out most clearly in the BIT between Japan and China of 1988.[94] Article 5(3) states:

---

[92] For a recent decision of an ICSID tribunal, not under a BIT but under the ICSID Convention, declining to attribute to the government destruction of the claimant's property by local populations, see *Tradex Hellas S.A.* v. *Republic of Albania*, Award of 29 Apr. 1999, 14 *ICSID Rev.-FILJ* 197 (1999).

[93] The statement in the text leaves out the issue of non-discrimination, which is generally stated to be a requirement of 'lawful' expropriation. In fact, while discrimination is often an element in claims brought under Bilateral Investment Treaties, it seems that if compensation is paid equal to the economic loss of the claimant, determined as discussed hereafter, the issue of discrimination does not call for additional compensation.

As for 'public purpose', it might not be met if the dictator of a host state expropriated a mansion for his own use; so long as the stated object of an expropriation or other violation is to benefit the national interest, no other nation, and no court or arbitral tribunal, would undertake to examine a taking on this ground. Accordingly, public purpose has not figured prominently in international claims.

Accord: *Restatement (Third) of the Foreign Relations Law of the United States*, §712, comment *e*.

[94] *Agreement Concerning the Encouragement and Reciprocal Protection of Investment*, done at Beijing 27 Aug. 1998, repr. in English in 28 *I.L.M.* 575 (1989).

The compensation . . . shall be such as to place the nationals and companies [of the other Contracting Party] in the same financial position as that in which the nationals and companies would have been if expropriation, nationalization or any other measures the effects of which would be similar to expropriation or nationalization . . . had not been taken. Such compensation shall be paid without delay. It shall be effectively realizable and freely transferable at the exchange rate in effect on the date used for the determination of the amount of compensation.

Prompt need not mean immediate. Indeed it is generally contemplated in the BITs that there may be disputes about the amount of compensation, and provision is made for resolution of those disputes, as described below.[95] But 'prompt' means that interest shall accrue from the date of the expropriation and shall be included in any agreement, or any arbitral award, concerning the amount of compensation. Some agreements, including the United States model agreement, state that interest shall be paid at a 'commercially reasonable rate' for the currency (assuming it is freely usable) in which the compensation is paid. Some other BITs refer expressly to the London Interbank rate (LIBOR). Still other BITs say nothing about interest or provide for interest but say nothing about the rate.[96]

The question has arisen whether bonds of the taking state calling for payment over time meet the requirement of prompt compensation. None of the BITs expressly addresses this question, and no case is known that addresses it in connection with a BIT. The answer should be that if the bonds are marketable and bear interest realistically related to market rates, they meet the requirements of the Hull formula. This was the answer given by the French Conseil Constitutionnel in upholding the compensation through negotiable interest-bearing 15-year bonds offered by the French government as compensation (otherwise just) for nationalizing several major French companies.[97] The challenge by the former owners was not brought under international law, but under Article 17 of the Declaration of the Rights of Man and the Citizen of 1789, incorporated by reference into the French Constitution of 1958, which provides that property can be taken only 'on condition of a just and prior indemnification'.[98] In this context 'prior' and 'prompt' would seem to be be call for the same interpretation.

---

[95] An Agreed Minute of the Japan–China treaty reads:

The term 'without delay' referred to in the provisions of paragraph 3 of Article 5 of the Agreement shall not exclude a reasonable period of time necessary for deciding the amount, way of payment and so on.

[96] For various provisions concerning interest, see Dolzer and Stevens (n. 72 supra), 113–14. Whether the interest is to be simple or compound is not stated in any of the treaties. Arbitral tribunals generally award simple interest only, unless the delay in payment is exceptionally long.

[97] Conseil Constitutionnel, Decision No. 81–132 DC of 16 Jan. 1982, *Journal Officiel*, 17 Jan. 1982, 299. For a summary of the other challenges to the nationalizations by the newly elected government of President Mitterand, none of which involved foreign-owned companies, see A. Lowenfeld, *International Private Investment*, 203–5 (2nd edn. 1982).

[98] For the complete text of Article 17, see Ch. 13, Sect. 13.1, n. 2.

Effective means in a form usable by the investor. The currency of payment must be freely usable or convertible into a freely usable currency, without restrictions on transfer. As discussed above, marketable bonds are acceptable, provided their actual value, as contrasted with their nominal value, is equal to the compensation determined to be payable. Thus if ten-year bonds issued by Patria are selling in the market at a 10 percent discount and compensation for SUNATCO's property is set at 5 million dollars equal to 20 million pesos, adequate and effective compensation would be 22.2 million pesos face value of Patria's bonds.

The most difficult problem—with or without BITs—is how to establish 'market value', 'fair market value', or 'genuine value' all of which are essentially synonymous, or even 'just compensation,' which usually is as well.[99] If the value of the investment can be defined—for instance if the shares of the entity in question have been traded on a stock exchange, the price of the shares on the relevant date may be used to determine the market value of the investment. If the investment is unique—for instance a mine or a large manufacturing entity—it may be hard to find comparable assets or a hypothetical willing buyer, and thus establishment of market value may be difficult. The BITs generally do not give guidance for such cases, but if the enterprise has a record of earnings over a representative period, negotiators or a disputes panel may attempt to establish *going concern value*, i.e. the present value of the expected future earnings.[100] When an investment is expropriated or destroyed before it has been able to establish an earnings experience, or when it has failed to make a profit in the period prior to the expropriation or destruction, arbitral tribunals tend to be skeptical about claims of prospective earnings, and to found their awards rather on the actual funds invested in the enterprise. In the *Metalclad* case previously discussed,[101] the Tribunal, drawing on various precedents from arbitrations in ICSID and elsewhere as well as in the Iran–United States Claims Tribunal, awarded the amount actually invested by the investor, less certain costs allocated by the

---

[99] 'Just compensation' is the term used in the Fifth Amendment to the United States Constitution, and in decisions of the US Supreme Court. In *United States* v. *Cors*, 337 U.S. 325 at 332 (1949), the Supreme Court wrote:

The Court in its construction of the constitutional provision has been careful not to reduce the concept of just compensation to a formula. The political ethics reflected in the Fifth Amendment reject confiscation as a measure of justice. But the Amendment does not contain any definite standard by which the measure of 'just compensation is to be determined'.

In *United States* v. *Commodities Trading Corp.*, 339 U.S. 121 at 123 (1950) the Court wrote:

Fair market value has normally been accepted as a just standard. But when market value has been too difficult to find, or when its application would result in manifest injustice to owner or public, courts have fashioned or applied other standards.

[100] For a discussion of this method, often termed 'discounted cash flow analysis,' see e.g. Charles L. Brower and Jason D. Brueschke, *The Iran–United States Claims Tribunal*, n. 29 supra, 575–83 (1998) and sources there cited.

[101] See Sect. 15.3(b)(2) at n. 81 supra.

investor in part to the waste disposal facility in question but disallowed by the Tribunal.[102]

It is worth noting that the BITs set out the criteria for compensation only in respect to expropriation or measures tantamount to expropriation. No comparable criteria are set out in any of the treaties for breach of the obligations to accord national treatment, most-favoured-nation treatment, full protection and security, or fair and equitable treatment. Arbitral tribunals that have found a violation of one or more of these provisions have in effect borrowed from the provisions and precedents concerned with appropriations.

In *American Agricultural Products Ltd.* v. *Republic of Sri Lanka*,[103] in which the claim concerned damages for breach of the obligation to provide full protection and security to an enterprise that had not yet had a record of earnings, the Tribunal based its award solely on the investor's tangible assets, rejecting claims for intangible assets, loss of crops to be harvested in the future, or expected profits.[104]

In *Metalclad*, where both denial of fair and equitable treatment and expropriation were found, the Tribunal held that compensation under both provisions would be the same, since both violations involved the complete frustration of the operation and loss of the investment.[105]

In *S.D. Myers*, where the claim of expropriation was rejected but breach of the national treatment and fair and equitable treatment was established, the Tribunal wrote:

By not identifying any particular methodology for the assessment of compensation in cases not involving expropriation, the Tribunal considers that the drafters of the NAFTA intended to leave it open to tribunals to determine a measure of compensation appropriate to the specific circumstances of the case, taking into account the principles of both international law and the provisions of the NAFTA. In some non-expropriation cases a tribunal might think it appropriate to adopt the 'fair market value' standard; in other cases it might not. In this case the Tribunal considers that the application of the fair market value standard is not a logical, appropriate or practicable measure of the compensation to be awarded.

There being no relevant provisions of the NAFTA other than those contained in Article 1110, the Tribunal turned for guidance to international law, [specifically the *Chorzow Factory* case].[106]

In sum, the Bilateral Investment Treaties reflect a turn away from the search for 'appropriate compensation', and a return to the earlier standards

---

[102] *Metalclad Corporation* v. *United Mexican States*, n. 81 supra, Award of 30 Aug. 2000, paras. 113–26.

[103] See Sect. 15.3(b)(3).   [104] *AAPL* v. *Sri Lanka* (n. 83 supra), paras. 88–108.

[105] *Metalclad Corporation* v. *United Mexican States*, n. 81 supra, para. 113.

[106] *S.D. Myers* v. *Canada*, Partial Award (n. 90 supra), paras. 309–11 (13 Nov. 2000). As of the date this book went to press, the Tribunal had not completed the proceedings to establish the quantum of damages, but stated that it would assess the compensation on the basis of the economic harm that claimant could establish. Id., para. 317.

reflected in the Hull formula. In principle, that formula is easy to understand—an effort to put the investor in the position in which it would have been had the expropriation or other breach not taken place. Working out the details has never been easy, either under classical international law or under the regime of the BITs.

6. Dispute Settlement

As shown in Chapter 13, one of the prime goals of the New International Economic Order was to establish the principle, previously advocated by Calvo and others, that disputes between a foreign investor and a host state be submitted exclusively to the courts or administrative tribunals of the host state. The ICSID Convention negotiated in the early 1960s offered an alternative to this principle; the Bilateral Investment Treaties reject this principle completely and explicitly. Every modern BIT makes provision for settlement of disputes between the investor and the host state.[107] The ICSID Convention, it will be recalled, requires consent by the parties to arbitration under a particular investment agreement or in respect to a particular dispute, but provides that the consent once given may not be withdrawn.[108] The BITs go a significant step further, by providing in nearly all of the treaties that the host state gives its consent to arbitration of any investment dispute subject of the treaty, generally by reference to the rules or arbitral institutions provided for in the treaty. If the treaty provides for arbitration pursuant to the ICSID Convention, the consent given in the BIT satisfies the requirement of Article 25(1) of that Convention; if the treaty provides for arbitration under the UNCITRAL rules or under some other set of rules, the consent by the state satisfies those rules as well as the requirements of the United Nations Convention on the Recognition and Enforcement of Foreign Arbitral Awards (the New York Convention).[109]

The most common reference in the BITs is to arbitration under the auspices of International Centre for the Settlement of Investment Disputes (ICSID), provided both the host state and the home state of the investor are parties.[110] Many recent BITs provide also for alternatives to ICSID arbitration, in particular for arbitration pursuant to the UNCITRAL rules, but in some treaties also for arbitration under the auspices of the International Chamber of Commerce or under purely ad hoc arbitration if agreed by the parties to the dispute. The recent American treaties, as well as the NAFTA, provide for

---

[107] Dolzer and Stevens (n. 72 supra), 129, write '*Virtually* all modern treaties provide for the arbitral settlement of investment disputes', but they do not mention any treaty that does not so provide and the present author has not found any.

[108] See Sect. 15.1, n. 6, discussing Article 25(1) of the ICSID Convention.

[109] The United States model BIT recites the above explicitly; it is clearly implied in most other BITs. For various versions of the consent, see Dolzer and Stevens, n. 72 supra, pp. 131–6.

[110] Nearly all developed states, with the exception of Canada, are parties to the ICSID. If the host is not a party to the ICSID Convention or has signed but not yet ratified the Convention, some of the BITs provide for arbitration under the ICSID Additional Facility. See Sect. 15.1, n. 19.

a choice by the investor between arbitration under UNCITRAL rules and under ICSID (or the Additional Facility); the British model treaty also provides options, but subject to agreement of the disputing parties, with UNCITRAL arbitration called for in the absence of agreement.[111]

It may be asked on what basis the choice is made among the various options for dispute settlement, either by the claimant (investor) alone or by the two disputing parties jointly. Some parties or their counsel prefer the discipline and fixed fee schedule of institutional arbitration. Others prefer the greater freedom of ad hoc arbitration without scrutiny by an institution. No jurisprudential answer can be given, and no prediction that one forum for arbitration is advantageous for one side or the other. The present writer's experience is that differences among different arbitral rules and institutions are significant at the initial stage, concerning fees, deposits, schedules, and appointment of arbitrators, and at the enforcement stage if that becomes necessary.[112] The process of determining facts, ruling on evidence, choosing the applicable law and construing that law depends on the arbitrators and counsel, not on differences in the rules.

As of year-end 2001, arbitral proceedings under BITs and the NAFTA have been confidential, and no participation by non-governmental organizations or other *amici curiae* have been permitted.[113] ICSID awards are published in the *ICSID Review* and are made available on ICSID's website. Most other awards based on disputes under BITs have also been published, and arbitral tribunals hearing investment disputes have freely considered other awards made under treaties similar to the one before them. Thus a substantial body of decisions on investor–state disputes under BITs has been building up. Arbitral tribunals have also relied on awards and judgments not arising from BITs but involving disputes between investors or their governments and host states. It may fairly be said that dispute resolution under BITs both draws on and contributes to the corpus of international law.

---

[111] UNCITRAL arbitration proceeds without supervision by an institution such as ICSID, the ICC, the London Court of International Arbitration, or the American Arbitration Association. Each of these institutions may be designated as appointing authority to choose the presiding arbitrator (or sole arbitrator) in the absence of agreement by the parties. In the NAFTA, the Secretary-General of ICSID is designated as the appointing authority. When no appointing authority is designated in an agreement, the UNCITRAL rules provide that the Secretary-General of the Permanent Court of Arbitration at The Hague may be requested to designate the appointing authority.

[112] Under Article 54 of the ICSID Convention (but not under the Additional Facility) awards are directly enforceable in all Contracting States as if they were a final judgment of a court of the state where enforcement is sought. Other awards, whether under UNCITRAL rules or under the rules of an arbitral institution, are generally entitled to enforcement under the New York Convention, i.e. under the same conditions as a domestic arbitral award, subject to a limited number of defenses.

[113] However, under Article 1128 of the NAFTA, any Party, i.e. the government of a state not directly involved in the dispute, may make written submissions to a Tribunal on a question of interpretation of the Agreement, and all three Parties have taken advantage of this opportunity.

(c)   BITs and International Law

Given the large web of BITs covering every continent and countries from the First, the Second, and the Third World, a fair inference might be drawn that, taken together, the Bilateral Investment Treaties are now evidence of customary international law, applicable even when a given situation or controversy is not explicitly governed by a treaty.[114] Some writers strongly resist such an inference, arguing that the BITs merely constitute a *lex specialis* between the parties.[115] The argument is that to create or evidence customary law, states not only need to follow a certain practice, but need to do so from a sense of legal obligation (*opinio juris*).[116] Professor Guzman, for instance, writes:

[S]igning a BIT offers an LDC an advantage in the competition for foreign investment. That BITs have been signed in large numbers merely demonstrates the magnitude of the perceived benefits associated with the dynamic inconsistency problem. Thus, if countries have signed BITs out of economic motives, the treaties should not be interpreted as evidence of customary international law. It is equally plausible that BITs represent a permissible derogation from the existing rules of customary law and that countries have pursued the treaties because it is in their economic interest to do so. This means that BITs offer no evidence concerning the rules of customary international law that govern compensation for appropriations.[117]

---

[114] The word 'situation' is used to indicate that the issue need not arise only in the context of a dispute, but may, for instance, be raised if the government of Patria is considering a measure that might be inconsistent with international law, but not with any given treaty to which Patria is a party.

[115] See e.g. Bernard Kishoiyian, 'The Utility of Bilateral Investment Treaties in the Formulation of Customary International Law', 14 *Northwestern Int'l Law & Business* 327 (1994).

[116] Compare *Restatement (Third) of the Foreign Relations Law of the United States*, §102(2):

Customary international law results from a general and consistent practice of states followed by them from a sense of legal obligation.

Comment *c*, on *opinio juris*, adds:

For a practice of states to become a rule of customary international law it must appear that the states follow the practice from a sense of legal obligation (*opinio juris sive necessitatis*); a practice that is generally followed but which states feel legally free to disregard does not contribute to customary law. A practice initially followed by states as a matter of courtesy or habit may become law when states generally come to believe that they are under a legal obligation to comply with it. It is often difficult to determine when that transformation into law has taken place. Explicit evidence of a sense of legal obligation (e.g. by official statements) is not necessary; *opinio juris* may be inferred from acts or omissions.

See also the discussion of customary law in Ch. 13, Sect. 13.4 (b) at n. 49.

[117] Andrew T. Guzman, 'Why LDCs Sign Treaties that Hurt Them: Explaining the Popularity of Bilateral Investment Treaties', 38 *Va. J. Int'l Law* 639 at 686–7 (1998). By 'dynamic inconsistency' the author means a situation in which a preferred course of action cannot be undertaken without the establishment of some commitment mechanism; since contracts between a developing country host state and a foreign investor do not give a sufficient assurance to the investor, the host state is led to agree to a BIT. Id., at 658–60.

F. A. Mann, in contrast, writing well before the BITs had reached the level of acceptance that they reached in the last decade of the twentieth century, argued that by concluding BITs in large numbers, the developing countries that in the 1960s and 1970s had rejected the classical view of international law must have had a change of view:

Is it possible for a State to reject the rule according to which alien property may be expropriated only on certain terms long believed to be required by customary international law, yet to accept it for the purpose of these treaties?[118]

To this writer, the debate need not be answered conclusively. There can be no doubt that bilateral investment treaties are relevant to the development of the international law of international investment.

— If Patria, a host country, is considering a given investment, existing or proposed, it should take its own and others' BITs into account, even if the investor in question is not from a contracting state with which Patria has concluded a BIT.
— Courts and arbitral tribunals, whether national or international, may rely on the common principles in the bilateral investment treaties.
— In adjudicating under a given BIT, courts and arbitral tribunals may, and indeed will be expected to, take into account decisions of other courts and tribunals that have heard disputes under comparable treaties.

Suppose Patria has entered into BITs with Xandia, Tertia, and Quarta, but not with Quinta. However, Patria has joined the ICSID Convention, and has consented to ICSID arbitration of disputes that may arise in connection with an investment agreement with Supranational Corporation [SUNATCO], a corporation organized and existing under the laws of Quinta. A dispute arises and is submitted to an ICSID Tribunal. In the present writer's view, the arbitrators should take into account all the obligations undertaken by Patria in its BITs with Xandia *et al.*, as evidence of Patria's understanding of international law, for the purpose of applying Article 42 of the ICSID Convention.[119] Patria should be given the opportunity to explain why

[118] F. A. Mann, 'British Treaties for the Promotion and Protection of Investment', 52 *Brit. Y.B. Int'l Law* 241 at 249 (1981).
Dr. Mann answered his question as follows:

The paramount duty of States imposed by international law is to observe and act in accordance with the requirements of good faith. From this point of view it follows that, where these treaties express a duty which customary international law imposes or is widely believed to impose, they give very strong support to the existence of such a duty and preclude the Contracting States from denying its existence. (Id., 249–50)

[119] Article 42, as discussed in Sect. 15.1(c) reads in the pertinent part:

The Tribunal shall decide a dispute in accordance with such rules of law as may be agreed by the parties. In the absence of such agreement, the Tribunal shall apply the law of the
cont./

it had not concluded a treaty with Quinta, but unless the explanation is compelling that a different standard of treatment of investors from Quinta was contemplated and communicated to the government of Quinta and to SUNATCO, the failure to conclude an agreement with Quinta applicable to the dispute should not be decisive. In contrast, if Patria has consistently declined to conclude a BIT with any country, the argument in favour of applying the principle set out in the BITs, while not excluded, is significantly weaker.[120]

It is important in this discussion to distinguish between the *common principles* that may be said to have ripened into customary international law, and *particular provisions* of BITs that even if widely utilized are applicable only between the treaty partners or investors entitled to the benefits of the treaty in question. For example, an agreement to arbitrate under a particular set of rules, or a prohibition of specified performance requirements would not be regarded as general principles, but would depend on the applicability and text of a given treaty. But the understanding that international law is applicable to the relation between host states and foreign investors, that expropriation must be for a public purpose and must be accompanied by just compensation, and that disputes between foreign investors and host states should be subjected to impartial adjudication or arbitration are general principles, and do not depend on the wording or indeed on the existence of an given treaty.

15.4   THE MULTILATERAL INVESTMENT GUARANTEE AGENCY (MIGA)

(a)   Introduction

In the early 1980s, the staff of the World Bank, urged by its new President, A. W. Clausen of the United States, launched a project for a Bank-sponsored multinational agency that would 'enhance the flow of developing countries of capital and technology for productive purposes' by improving the conditions for direct foreign investment and reducing—and insuring against—the political risks of such investment.[121] The promoters of MIGA had two purposes in mind. One, of course, was to create a multilateral

Contracting State party to the dispute (including its rules on the conflict of laws) and such rules of international law as may be applicable.

[120] Not many countries fit into the category of states that have not entered into any modern bilateral investment treaties. Libya, Mozambique, Myanmar (Burma), and Surinam had concluded no BITs as of year-end 2001. Among developed countries, Ireland appears to be the only one that has not concluded a BIT. It is, however, a party to several treaties of Friendship, Commerce and Navigation, which contain some of the same guarantees in less detail.

[121] For a detailed history of the often difficult negotiations that led to the creation of MIGA, see Ibrahim Shihata, *MIGA and Foreign Investment: Origins, Operations, Policies and Basic Documents of the Multilateral Investment Guarantee Agency* (1988).

investment guarantee agency linked in some way to the World Bank. Beyond this, by involving all member states of the World Bank in serious debate and information exchange, the sponsors of MIGA sought to change the 'investment climate' in developing countries.

The 1970s had been the decade of the New International Economic Order.[122] In the five years preceding the first consideration of MIGA in 1983 by the Executive Directors of the World Bank, i.e. 1978–82, 42 expropriations had taken place in 24 countries of Africa, Latin America, and Asia.[123] At the same time, the debt crisis of many developing countries had severely slowed down commercial bank lending, and had further undermined confidence among potential investors in the developing world.[124] MIGA would be a vehicle, it was hoped, for turning these trends around. This could be achieved by a combination of technical assistance to developing countries that sought to attract foreign investment—what kind of laws, infrastructure, and attitudes would be useful—and by establishing an institution whose common purpose would be clear, but where the developing countries, i.e. the potential host countries, would have an equal say with the developed countries.

Thus MIGA could serve as an honest broker, 'guiding all concerned parties', as its brochure stated,[125] 'toward a common definition of fairness and equitable treatment.' In addition to investment guarantees and insurance, MIGA's Legal and Claims Department could provide legal advice and guidance to parties involved in investment disputes, not necessarily covered by an investment guarantee issued by MIGA.[126]

The World Bank's Board of Governors approved the MIGA Convention in the fall of 1985, but it took two and a half more years before the minimum number of states in each category—five from Category One, the developed states, and fifteen from Category Two, the developing states—had deposited their instruments of ratification.[127] As of year-end 2001 MIGA had 22 industrial and 132 developing country members.

(b)   Covered Risks

Eligible investors can purchase insurance against risks of inconvertibility of local currency; expropriation; breach of contract; and war and civil

---

[122] See Ch. 13, Sect. 13.5(b).

[123] See Multinational Investment Guarantee Agency, *The First Ten Years*, 3 (1998).

[124] See Ch. 18, Sects. 18.1–18.4.

[125] MIGA, *The First Ten Years* (n. 123 supra), at p. 6.

[126] See MIGA Convention Article 23(b), which under the heading 'Investment Promotion' provides that the Agency shall 'encourage the amicable settlement of disputes between investors and host countries', without reference to MIGA insurance.

[127] *Convention Establishing the Multilateral Investment Guarantee Conventions*, done at Seoul 11 Oct. 1985, entered into force 12 Apr. 1988. T.I.A.S. 12089, 1508 U.N.T.S. 99. The requirements for entry into force appear in Article 61.

disturbance, including politically motivated acts of sabotage or terrorism.[128] To be an eligible investor, a person must be a national of a member country other than the host country, a corporation organized or established in such a country, or, if it is incorporated in the host country, a corporation the majority of whose capital is owned by nationals of member countries.[129] Two interesting additional classes of investors are stated to be eligible for coverage by MIGA. *First*, state-owned enterprises are eligible if they operate on a commercial basis. Thus, for instance, the Norwegian Statoil, the Mexican Pemex, and numerous enterprises of the People's Republic of China, would qualify as investors if they undertook a project in another eligible country. *Second*, upon agreement of the host country and the investor, the MIGA Board may extend eligibility to an investor (natural or juridical) from the host country that seeks to engage in so-called 'round-tripping',— i.e. to invest assets left abroad back to the host country, thus reversing prior capital flight.[130]

Eligible projects can include new investments as well as expansion, modernization, restructuring, and privatization of existing investments, and in some circumstances loans made or guaranteed by holders of equity in the enterprise in question.[131]

(c) MIGA and International Law

If the practice of states and international organizations is evidence of prevailing thinking about international law, the MIGA Convention—adhered to by more than 150 states—developed and developing—makes several contributions to international law and to the receptivity of foreign direct investment loosely referred to as investment climate. Not only does it state explicitly the objective 'to encourage the flow of investment for productive purposes among member countries, and in particular to developing member countries' (Art. 2).[132] Article 12 concerning investments eligible for a MIGA guarantee states, in paragraph (d):

In guaranteeing an investment, the Agency shall satisfy itself as to

...

(iv) the investment conditions in the host country, including the availability of fair and equitable treatment and legal protection for the investment.

---

[128] MIGA Convention, Art. 11.

[129] This provision, which acknowledges the requirement in many states that corporations must be locally incorporated but then looks to ownership and control, is similar to Article 25(2)(b) of the ICSID Convention, Sect. 15.1(b).

[130] MIGA Convention, Art. 13.   [131] Id., Art. 12.

[132] Contrast this commitment of 1988 with the very different tone and substance of the excerpt from the Charter of Economic Rights and Duties of States of 1974, reproduced in Ch. 13, Sect. 13.5(b) at n. 68 supra.

A promise of the host country addressed only to the particular investment is not sufficient. The Agency must be satisfied with the 'investment conditions'.[133] Turning the sentence around, if Patria fails to accord fair and equitable treatment for one investment, it cannot count on approval of a MIGA investment guarantee for another investment.

Further, Article 23, which is directed to Investment Promotion, i.e. not explicitly to issuance of investment guarantees, states in section (b).

The Agency also shall:

(i) encourage the amicable settlement of disputes between investors and host countries;

(ii) endeavor to conclude agreements with developing member countries, and in particular with prospective host countries, which will assure that the Agency, with respect to investment guaranteed by it, has treatment at least as favorable as that agreed by the member concerned for the most favored investment guarantee agency or State in an agreement relating to investment, such agreements to be approved by special majority of the Board; and

(iii) promote and facilitate the conclusion of agreements, among its members, on the promotion and protection of investments.

Thus, far from maintaining the traditional neutrality of international agencies toward investment in developing countries, the MIGA Convention requires the agency to encourage developing countries to enter into Bilateral Investment Treaties; to join the ICSID Convention, or adopt other indicia of an investor-friendly legal regime. The official Commentary to the MIGA Convention confirms that in case no protection is assured under the laws of a host country or a BIT, the Agency will issue a guarantee only after it reaches agreement with the host country pursuant to Article 23(b)(ii), in which investments guaranteed by the host country will receive MFN treatment.[134]

Finally, as pointed out in the preceding section, there has been and continues to be a debate about the contours of *expropriation*, which requires compensation (and almost always triggers an investment guarantee if one is applicable), and regulation, which does not call for compensation and generally does not engage international law unless it is discriminatory or violates fair and equitable treatment. The MIGA Convention adopts a fairly broad definition of 'expropriation and similar measures', and makes clear that the focus is on the loss to the investor, not on the gain to the host government:

any legislative action or administrative action or omission attributable to the host government which has the effect of depriving the holder of a guarantee of his ownership

---

[133] See Ibrahim Shihata, *MIGA and Foreign Investment* (n. 121, supra), at pp. 222–3.

[134] *Commentary on the Convention Establishing Multilateral Investment Guarantee Agency*, republished in Shihata (n. 121, supra) at Appendix 3 and on MIGA's web page, ¶¶21 and 44, Article 44. Agreements under Article 23(b)(ii) require approval of the MIGA board by a special majority.

or control of, or a substantial benefit from, his investment, with the exception of non-discriminatory measures of general application which the governments normally take for the purpose of regulating economic activity in their territories.[135]

Breach of contract is in some ways more difficult, because it is clear that neither MIGA nor traditional international law is concerned with commercial risks, and it is not always clear whether a contract with a government or governmental agency is repudiated for commercial or 'sovereign' purposes. MIGA's solution is not to attempt to distinguish among the motives of the host government, but to link the scope of its coverage to the remedies available to the holder of a guarantee. Thus MIGA will cover

any repudiation or breach by the host government of a contract with the holder of a guarantee, when (a) the holder of a guarantee does not have recourse to a judicial or arbitral forum to determine the claim of repudiation or breach, or (b) a decision by such forum is not rendered within such reasonable period of time as shall be prescribed in the contracts of guarantee pursuant to the Agency's regulations, or (c) such a decision cannot be enforced;[136]

The regulations define the reasonable period as not less than two years, and define judicial or arbitral forum as 'any competent court or arbitral tribunal which is independent from the executive branch of the host government, acts judicially, and is authorized to make a final and binding decision.'[137]

There can be little doubt that these various provisions, and their broad acceptance by countries all around the globe, reflect and contribute to a relatively warm investment climate. The more difficult and controversial question is whether these provisions, along with similar provisions in a great many BITs, and in regional agreements such as the NAFTA, reflect and contribute to the international *law* of international investment. One could take the position that MIGA clauses, like provisions of specific bilateral investment treaties, bind only the parties to those arrangements, and that states subscribe to them do so on the basis of a particular calculation of advantage, not from any sense of obligation.[138] A more sophisticated understanding, in the view of the present author, would regard the MIGA Convention, even more than the web of bilateral (and in the case of NAFTA trilateral) agreements as evidence of state practice and of a growing consensus that may well be regarded, not just by writers, but by courts, arbitral tribunals, and governments as laws. It is fair to add that if one regards these commitments as

---

[135] MIGA Convention, Art. 11(a)(ii). The Commentary adds in ¶14 that the definition would encompass measures attributable to the host government such as nationalization, confiscation, sequestration, seizure, attachment, and freezing of assets. It would include measures by the executive, but not measures taken by judicial bodies in exercise of their functions.

[136] MIGA Convention Art. 11(a)(iii).

[137] MIGA Operational Regulations, §§1.42, 1.43.

[138] This is the position, for example, of Prof. Andrew Guzman, Sect. 15.3 at n. 117, writing specifically about BITs but more generally about the growing mass of instruments setting down definitions and guides to behaviour concerning investments.

law, very little breach occurred in the last two decades of the twentieth century, as compared with the preceding three decades.

SUMMARY

The corpus of international law concerning international investment, and in particular the relation between host countries and foreign investors greatly expanded in the last quarter of the twentieth century. Two major treaties sponsored by the World Bank have endeavoured—with considerable success—to improve the investment climate and to encourage transborder investment as a vehicle for economic growth. Over a thousand bilateral investment treaties have provided specific protections and guarantees for foreign investors, and—one may fairly say—have contributed to prevailing customary international law. The pace and content of international arbitration of investment disputes has vastly increased, notably in the hundreds of decisions rendered over more than a decade by the Iran–United States Claims Tribunal, but also in arbitrations under ICSID, BITs, and NAFTA. The resolution of disputes under international law directly between foreign investors and host states has become firmly established.

The law that emerges from this rich load of sources—treaties, statutes, scholarly writing, and arbitral awards—is not wholly uniform. No body of law is monolithic, and certainly one would not expect complete consensus on the subject of international investment, inevitably intertwined with history, economics, and politics, local and international. But there has been a substantial shift from the time when the United States Supreme Court issued the famous statement quoted at the beginning of this Part. In 1964, the Supreme Court could fairly write of the law concerning expropriation 'There are few if any issues on which opinions are so divided.' That statement, it is submitted, could not be made at the beginning of the third millennium.

PART VII
The International Monetary System

Introduction

The subject of international monetary law may be conveniently divided into three periods—before Bretton Woods (i.e. prior to the end of World War II; the Bretton Woods regime (1946–71 or 1973); and the post-Bretton Woods Regime (1973). It is useful to describe the first period briefly to understand the changes brought about by the Articles of Agreement of the International Monetary Fund; and it is useful to describe to regime of the original Articles of Agreement, both for the substantial body of law developed thereunder that remains in effect, and to understand the significance of the changes brought about by the Second Amendment (1976) which gave de jure recognition to the demise of much of the original Agreement in the early 1970s.

The line between 'hard law' and 'soft law' in respect to the international monetary system is not always clear, and discussion of the rules, practices, and institutions here described is sometimes carried on without any mention of law—let alone international law—in a way that would be unthinkable in a comparable discussion of international trade.[1] Though its institutions—the International Monetary Fund and its sister organization, the World Bank—were much stronger than the GATT, as sources of law their constitutive documents—in particular the IMF Articles of Agreement—have stood the test of time less well. Nevertheless, no discussion of international economic law would be complete without a careful exploration of those constraints on action in the monetary area that states have been willing to assume, and on those constraints that states have declined to assume or to continue to assume.

---

[1] See e.g. Paul Volcker and Toyoo Gyohten, *Changing Fortunes, The World's Money and the Threat to American Leadership* (1992).

16

The Bretton Woods System

16.1   Before Bretton Woods: Good and Bad Memories

It would not be accurate to say that before 1945 there was no international monetary system. States and their enterprises traded with one another, currencies were exchanged, and states held monetary reserves—in gold, in silver, and in foreign currencies. It would be accurate, however, to say that prior to the close of World War II no international legal regime governed the conduct of states with respect to monetary affairs.[1]

For about 35 years prior to the outbreak of World War I, the major western countries—the United Kingdom, France, Germany, and the United States—all tied their currencies to gold, so that the rates of exchange among the franc, the mark, the pound, and the dollar were essentially fixed. Many other states in effect tied into what was known as the gold standard by linking their currencies to one of the key currencies and keeping their reserves either in gold or in one of those currencies. No international legal obligation required adherence to the gold standard, and it collapsed almost overnight at the start of World War I. But though the era of the gold standard was neither as long nor as smooth as it seemed in retrospect,[2] the period before World War I brought to the minds of the planners of the post-World War II economy memories of fixed exchange rates, great expansion of trade, and the growth of transnational investment on a scale the world had not previously seen.[3]

By contrast, the period between World War I and Word War II seemed like a nightmare. The pound floated against the dollar from 1919 to 1925, while the dollar remained tied to gold. Then Britain returned to gold as well, pretty clearly at an overvalued rate. The French franc floated—generally down—for most of the 1920s, then was linked to gold, first de facto and then de jure, accompanied by a variety of exchange controls. Both the franc and the pound, it seems, were sustained by large capital exports from the United States; when these ceased at the close of the decade, Great Britain suspended gold payments, France did not. The United States abandoned the gold standard as one of the first acts of the Roosevelt presidency, and rejected a proposed dollar–franc–pound stabilization proposal at the London International and Monetary Conference of 1933, which broke up in disarray.[4] As trade contracted sharply and unemployment increased

---

[1] In contrast, states had for many centuries entered into trade agreements, some providing for most-favoured nation treatment, others for preferential arrangements, customs unions, and other efforts to influence the movement of goods through governmental regulation.

[2] For a concise demonstration of this point, see Kenneth W. Dam, *The Rules of the Game: Reform and Evaluation in the International Monetary System*, 13–40 (1982).

[3] See Dam (n. 2 supra), 38.

[4] For an account of the London Conference as seen through American eyes, see A. M. Schlesinger, Jr., *The Age of Roosevelt*, Vol. II, *The Coming of the New Deal*, 201–32 (1959).

worldwide, each of the major countries tried to use competitive devaluations, multiple exchange rates, trade restrictions, subsidies, and controls of various kinds to divert economic distress abroad.

Seen from the 1940s, the 1930s were a period of 'beggar thy neighbour', every nation for itself, with disastrous results. That Nazi Germany seems to have been particularly adept at the various manipulative devices confirmed the determination that the pattern of the interwar years must not be repeated. In the post-war world there would be an international regime of monetary *law*, established by treaty and overseen by a permanent international organization. The regime would be founded on principles of non-discrimination, fixed exchange rates, and so far as possible, avoidance of exchange controls and other devices that distorted the flow of goods, services, and credits. The American Secretary of the Treasury, in his closing statement as Chairman of the Bretton Woods Conference, summed up:

I take it as an axiom that after this war is ended no people and therefore no government of the people—will again tolerate prolonged and widespread unemployment. A revival of international trade is indispensable if full employment is to be achieved in a peaceful world and with standards of living which will permit the realization of men's reasonable hopes.

What are the fundamental conditions under which commerce among the nations can once more flourish?

First, there must be a reasonably stable standard of international exchange to which all countries can adhere without sacrificing the freedom of action necessary to meet their internal economic problems.

This is the alternative to the desperate tactics of the past—competitive currency depreciation, excessive tariff barriers, uneconomic barter deals, multiple currency practices and unnecessary exchange restrictions—by which governments vainly sought to maintain employment and uphold living standards. In the final analysis, these tactics only succeeded in contributing to world-wide depression and even war. The International Fund agreed upon at Bretton Woods will help remedy this situation.[5]

---

[5] *Proceedings and Documents of United Nations Monetary and Financial Conference*, Bretton Woods, N.H., 1–22 July 1947, Vol. I, pp. 1117–18 (1947). See also the following excerpt from Secretary Morgenthau's article, 'Bretton Woods and International Cooperation', 23 *Foreign Affairs* 182, 185 (1945):

The decade of the 1930s was almost unique in the multiplicity of ingenious schemes that were devised by some countries, notably Germany, to exploit their creditors, their customers, and their competitors in their international trade and financial relations. It is necessary only to recall the use of exchange controls, competitive currency depreciation, multiple currency practices, blocked balances, bilateral clearing arrangements and the host of other restrictive and discriminatory devices to find the causes for the inadequate recovery in international trade in the decade before the war. These monetary devices were measures of international economic aggression, and they were the logical concomitant of a policy directed toward war and conquest.

16.2   THE BRETTON WOODS CONFERENCE

The history of the negotiations of what became the Bretton Woods Agreement has often been told, and need not be repeated here.[6] What is remarkable in retrospect two generations later is that planning and negotiations began in the United Kingdom and the United States in 1942, at a time when the outcome of World War II was far from clear, and that in July 1944, nine months before signing of the United Nations Charter, ten months before the end of the war in Europe, and more than a year before the end of the war in the Pacific, representatives of 44 nations were able to agree on a plan for the post-war international economy that endured largely intact for a quarter of a century, and that even in a much changed world continues to have significant importance.[7] Lord Keynes wrote in 1942 that only a 'Single act of creation, made possible by the unity of purpose and energy of hope for better things to come' brought about by the war would bring about an international monetary institution.[8] That unity of purpose and energy of hope has not been replicated since the 1940s.

The Bretton Woods Conference created two permanent financial organizations, the International Monetary Fund and the International Bank for Reconstruction and Development (the World Bank), both designed to have universal membership, based on contribution of resources by all members. The World Bank would be devoted to long-term economic development, first to reconstruction of countries ravaged by the war, then to development of countries not yet in the economic mainstream. The International Monetary Fund would enable states to achieve financial stability with growth, by making its resources available to them for purposes consistent with the Articles of Agreement.[9]

---

[6] See Richard N. Gardner, *Sterling-Dollar Diplomacy* (revd. edn. 1969); Roy F. Harrod, *The Life of John Maynard Keynes*, 525–85 (1951, repr. 1963, 1969); J. Keith Horsefield and Margaret Garritson de Vries, *The International Fund, 1945–1965*; *Twenty Years of International Monetary Cooperation* (hereafter *IMF History 1945–65*), Vol. I, p. 3–113 (1969).

[7] The 45th nation represented at Bretton Woods—the USSR—did not sign the Final Act, and never joined the IMF or the World Bank. See Sect. 16.3, n. 30 infra.

[8] Quoted in Harrod, n. 6 supra, 551.

[9] It is useful to recall the stated purposes of the International Monetary Fund, as set forth in Art. I of the Articles of Agreement. The italicized words were added in the First Amendment to the Articles, effective 1969:

The purposes of the International Monetary Fund are:

(i) To promote international monetary cooperation through a permanent institution which provides the machinery for consultation and collaboration on international monetary problems.

(ii) To facilitate the expansion and balanced growth of international trade, and to contribute thereby to the promotion and maintenance of high levels of employment and real income and to the development of the productive resources of all members as primary objectives of economic policy.   *cont./*

Calls for a 'new Bretton Woods Conference' are heard from time to time; as of year-end 2001, however, no serious plan for such a conference had come to light, and the organizational structure of the IMF remains substantially as it was agreed at Bretton Woods, with a strong Managing Director and Staff, an Executive Board chosen on a regional basis, and weighted voting.[10] Portions of the code of conduct incorporated in the Articles of Agreement and elaborated in early interpretations of the Articles also remain in effect—in particular the provisions concerning exchange controls (Section 16.5) and the provisions concerning drawing by member states on the resources of the Fund (Section 16.7). The provisions concerning fixed exchange rates were abandoned in 1971 and have been replaced by a much looser regime of flexible exchange rates, first created by unforeseen events, and subsequently codified in substantially Amended Articles of Agreement.[11] The overriding concept of the founders of the post-war monetary system, however, remains in effect: the value of a nation's currency, while clearly an important subject of each nation's concern, and indeed an aspect of its sovereignty, is also a matter of international concern—and of international law.

16.3 THE IMF AS AN ORGANIZATION

Article XII of the Articles of Agreement of the IMF established a three-tiered organization, consisting of a Board of Governors, an Executive Board, and a Managing Director, who presides over the staff and also functions as non-voting chairman of the Executive Board.

The *Managing Director* and the staff owe their duty entirely to the Fund and to no other authority (Art. XII(4)(c)); on the whole this mandate has been complied with—certainly more fully that in the secretariat of the United Nations and many other organizations. In many instances the non-political character of the IMF staff has stood it in good stead, in making

(iii) To promote exchange stability, to maintain orderly exchange arrangements among members, and to avoid competitive exchange depreciation.

(iv) To assist in the establishment of a multilateral system of payments in respect of current transactions between members and in the elimination of foreign exchange restrictions which hamper the growth of world trade.

(v) To give confidence to members by making the Fund's resources *temporarily* available to them under adequate safeguards, thus providing them with opportunity to correct maladjustments in their balance of payments without resorting to measures destructive of national or international prosperity.

(vi) In accordance with the above, to shorten the duration and lessen the degree of disequilibrium in the international balances of payments of members.

The Fund shall be guided in all its *policies and* decisions by the purposes set forth in this Article.

[10] The same formula is used in governance of the International Bank for Reconstruction and Development, the other institution created at Bretton Woods.

[11] See Ch. 17, Sect. 17.3.

unpopular recommendations or prescriptions to member states; on the other hand some critics in and outside of the governments of member states have regarded the staff as inflexible, insensitive to 'political realities', and too much tied to a standard remedy for economic difficulties.[12]

The *Board of Governors* consists of one governor (and one alternate) appointed by each member state—typically the Minister of Finance or the President of the member's central bank. The Board of Governors meets at least once a year or when called into special session;[13] it may also take decisions by postal or telegraphic ballot in specified circumstances.[14] All powers of the Fund not otherwise delegated are vested in the Board of Governors, but unlike the United Nations, the WTO, and most other international organizations, voting at meetings of the Board of Governors, as in the Executive Board, depends on a complicated formula, designed to reflect (with some adjustments) the economic importance of the member state, as described below. In practice the Board of Governors delegates to the Executive Board all powers that are not expressly made non-delegable.[15]

The *Executive Board* consists in principle of five appointed directors and a number of elected directors that may not be less than fifteen.[16] The five appointed directors represent the five member states having the largest quotas—as of year-end 2001 the United States, Japan, Germany, France, United Kingdom. In addition, each of two member states whose currencies have been drawn from the General Resources Account in the largest amount in the two years preceding an election is entitled to appoint a director as well. For a number of years, Saudi Arabia appointed an Executive Director under this provision.[17]

Under the original Articles of Agreement two places on the Executive Board were reserved for 'American Republics not entitled to appoint directors', i.e. for states from Latin America;[18] this provision was dropped when the Articles of Agreement were amended effective 1978. In practice, the Executive Directors—24 as of year-end 2001—do represent regional and (in so far as practical) politically compatible groupings of states.

---

[12] As of year-end 2001, the Managing Director of the IMF has always been a national of a European state; by some kind of unwritten understanding, the President of the World Bank has always been a national of the United States.

[13] See Art. XII(2)(c).

[14] Art. XII(2)(f); By-Laws of the IMF, sect. 13. In fact this procedure was used in the course of both of the general amendments to the Articles of Agreement.

[15] See By-Laws of the IMF, sect. 15.

[16] Art. XII(3)(b). Under the original Articles of Agreement there were five appointed and twelve elected directors.

[17] The Board of Governors decided in 1980 to expand the number of elected directors from 15 to 16, and the number has been increased several times since then. As of year end 2001 the Executive Board consists of 5 appointed and 19 elected directors, representing a total of 182 member states.

[18] Articles of Agreement, original version, Art. XII(3)(b)–(iv).

The Executive Directors have a position somewhere in between the staff, who are wholly independent and committed to the organization, and the Governors, who are political (or central bank) officials of the member states. Executive Directors are supposed to seek and take instructions from the states that appoint or elect them. But the Executive Directors reside in Washington, draw their salaries from the Fund, and have tended to be viewed as Fund professionals.

Since the mid-1970s, when fundamental problems with the international monetary system became apparent,[19] the perception has grown up that the Executive Directors are not sufficiently close to the governments they represent to provide the kind of high-level interchanges necessary for major decisions. An *Interim Committee* chosen along the same voting lines as the Executive Directors but consisting of senior government officials was created in 1975, and functioned until 1999.[20] A 'Council', a more permanent body with similar objective—closer to the political process in member states—was provided for in the Amended Articles, but only upon approval of 85 percent of the total voting power.[21] An intiative to bring the Council into being was considered in 1999 but failed to pass. However, at the Annual Meeting in 1999, the Board of Governors approved a proposal to transform the Interim Committee into the *International Monetary and Financial Committee*, with similar functions of consultation among senior financial officials, including representatives of states not included in the various informal groups of the major powers—the G–5, G–7, G–10, etc.[22]

The formula for voting power, in the Executive Board as well as in the Board of Governors is, as already noted, designed to reflect economic importance as shown in quotas in the Fund, adjusted to give each member state a minimum voting power. Under the original Articles of Agreement, each member state had 250 basic votes plus one additional vote for each 100,000 US dollars of its quota. Under the amended Articles, the formula remains the same, except that Special Drawing Rights[23] are substituted for US dollars as the unit in which quotas, and therefore voting power is measured.

In practice, it is rare for the Fund to actually vote; typically the Managing Director will not bring a matter to the Executive Board unless there is a consensus.[24] However, a few matters, for instance adjustment of quotas, have always been subject to decision by super-majorities, and under the amended Articles, a substantially increased number of decisions require

---

[19] See Ch. 17, Sect. 17.1.   [20] See Ch. 17, Sect. 17.1(c) at n. 11.

[21] See Article XII(1) and Schedule D of the Amended Articles.

[22] The Development Committee, which did not have a name suggesting temporary status, remained as it was.

[23] See Sect. 16.8 infra.

[24] See IMF Rules and Regulations, Rule C–10F (Executive Board); By-Laws, sect. II (Board of Governors).

super-majorities—in some instances 70 percent of total voting power,[25] in others 85 percent,[26] thus on the one hand preserving a veto power for the United States, and for the European Community if it votes as a bloc, on the other hand approaching formally the tradition of acting by consensus.[27] The fact that it is the Managing Director and his principal advisers who decide what proposals should be submitted to the Board and when a proposal is ready for decision tends to enhance the role of the staff, which has a greater role in the work of the IMF (as well of the World Bank, which operates under a similar formula) than in most public international organizations. That effect was consistent with the original understanding at Bretton Woods. The effect is particularly apparent in the Fund's relation to developing countries, less so in dealings with the major economic powers.[28]

One more institutional feature of the IMF is important in understanding its role in shaping international monetary law. According to Article VIII(5), the IMF acts 'as a centre for the collection and exchange of information on monetary and financial problems', and member states are obligated to furnish detailed information on their economic situation. In a world where statistics were often negotiated or distorted, the Fund has been a source of useful and generally reliable statistics and technical studies.[29] It seems that the requirements of detailed disclosure of economic data figured in the decision of the Soviet Union not to join the International Monetary Fund, though it had participated actively in the Bretton Woods Conference and had secured adoption of several provisions of special concern to it.[30]

---

[25] See e.g. Art. V(7)(g) (Postponement of Repurchase Obligations); V(8) (Determination of charges); XV (Determination of method of valuation of Special Drawing Rights).

[26] See e.g. Art. III(2)(c) (Adjustment of quotas); IV(4) (Introduction of fixed exchange rate system); XVIII (Allocation, cancellation, and determination of conditions of use of Special Drawing Rights); XXIX(b) (Overruling Decision of Committee on Interpretation). For a complete list of Special Majorities under Amended Articles, see *Report by Exec. Directors to Board of Governors on Proposed Second Amendment to Articles of Agreement*, 79–84 (Washington: IMF 1976), repr. in Gold, *Effects of the Second Amendment*, n. 27 infra.

[27] See Joseph Gold, *Voting and Decisions in the International Monetary Fund* (1972); supplemented by Joseph Gold, *Voting Majorities in the Fund: Effects of the Second Amendment of the Articles* (IMF Pamphlet Series No. 20, 1977).

[28] Paul Volcker, the former US Under-Secretary of the Treasury and Chairman of the Board of Governors of the Federal Reserve System, quotes a 'distinguished finance minister' of a large developing country, 'cynically but not entirely inaccurately':

When the Fund consults with a poor and weak country, the country gets in line. When it consults with a big and strong country, the Fund gets in line. When the big countries are in conflict, the Fund gets out of the line of fire. (Paul Volcker and Toyoo Gyohten, *Changing Fortunes*, 143 (1992)).

[29] See, however, Ch. 18 on recent regional crises in Latin America and South-east Asia, which suggests that the information given to the IMF was often incomplete and in some instances simply false.

[30] e.g. the last sentence of Art. XII(8) reading:

The Fund shall not publish a report involving changes in the fundamental structure of the economic organization of members.

It seems also that the Soviet Union demanded a quota of more than $1 billion, as compared to the $800 million proposed in the Agreement; moreover, the Soviet Union objected to paying

16.4   THE FUND AGREEMENT AS A CODE OF CONDUCT

As noted in Section 16.1, one of the principal purposes of the Articles of Agreement of the International Monetary Fund was to impose legal obligations on member states not to engage in the kinds of practices that had contributed, it was believed, to the Great Depression and the outbreak of World War II. Pursuant to Article XX(2)(a) of the original Articles (Article XXXI(2) of the amended Articles), each state, upon joining the Fund, certifies that 'it has accepted this Agreement in accordance with its law and has taken all steps necessary to enable it to carry out all of its obligations under this Agreement.' Thus it is no defense to a charge of conduct inconsistent with the Agreement that a required action would be contrary to the member state's domestic law, or that a forbidden action is required by that law.[31] Member states were supposed to adopt implementing or authorizing legislation prior to deposit of the instrument of ratification and they generally did so, though in some instances with strings attached.[32] For states such as the United States, under whose law a conflict between a statute and a treaty is resolved in favour of the instrument last adopted, an inconsistent action taken pursuant to a domestic law would not relieve the state of the obligation undertaken in the Articles of Agreement.[33]

The overriding obligation undertaken by member states in the original Articles of Agreement and stated in Article IV(4)(a):

Each member undertakes to collaborate with the fund to promote exchange stability, to maintain orderly exchange arrangements with other members, and to avoid exchange alteration.

The principal way in which this obligation was to be carried out was to be by maintenance of par values, as set out in Article IV(3), which is no longer in force.[34] The general obligation to collaborate with the Fund to promote a stable system of exchange rates remains in effect under the Amended Articles,[35] and many of the obligations under the original Articles designed to support the overall objective remain in effect as well.

---

one-quarter of its quota in gold. The delegates were prepared to raise the Soviet quota but not to make a concession on the requirement for payment in gold. See Edward Bernstein, 'USSR took "Costly Detour" to IMF Association', 20 *IMF Survey* 337, (18 Nov. 1991).

[31] See also the Vienna Convention on the Law of Treaties, 1969, Article 46; American Law Institute, *Restatement (Third) of the Foreign Relations Law of the United States*, §311(3) (1987).

[32] See e.g. the United States Bretton Woods Agreement Act, 59 Stat. 512, approved July 31, 1945, which required specific authorization by Congress for consent to any change in the US quota in the Fund or the par value of the US dollar or any amendment to the Articles of Agreement. The United Kingdom Bretton Woods Agreement Act (9 & 10, Geo. VI, ch. 19) did not contain a similar constraint.

[33] See *Restatement (Third) of the Foreign Relations Law of the United States* (n. 31 supra), §115(1)(b).

[34] See Sect. 16.9 infra.

[35] See Amended Articles Art. IV(1), discussed in Ch. 17 at Sect. 17.3.

16.5   THE IMF AND EXCHANGE CONTROLS

(a)   Current Transactions

A principal feature of the original Articles of Agreement was Article VIII(2)(a), which provided:

[N]o member shall, without the approval of the Fund, impose restrictions on the making of payments and transfers for current international transactions.

Further Article VIII(3) provided that:

No member shall engage in . . . any discriminatory currency arrangements or mult-iple currency practices except as . . . approved by the Fund.

Despite fundamental change in the exchange rate system from the Bretton Woods era and major amendments to the Articles of Agreement, the provisions of Article VIII remain unchanged in substance. Second, however, the disfavour of exchange controls was much weakened by Article XIV(2) the Articles of Agreements, which provided that

In the post-war transitional period members may, notwithstanding the provisions [of Article VIII], maintain and adapt to changing circumstances . . . restrictions on payments and transactions for current international transactions.[36] (italics added).

'Payments for current international transactions' was defined in the Articles of Agreement;[37] 'post-war transitional period', however, was not, and the Fund never declared that period to have ended.[38] When the Articles of Agreement were amended in 1976, the reference to 'post-war' was dropped, but the (undefined) concept of transitional arrangements remained, and many member states retained their rights under Article XIV for decades.

A state's undertaking to accept the obligations of Article VIII is, in theory, equivalent to maintaining convertibility of the state's currency.[39]

Thus if a Patrian importer seeks to purchase machinery from a Xandian exporter, the government of Patria (an Article VIII country), may not impose restrictions on the importer's expenditures of Patrian pesos to make the purchase, whether directly or by purchasing, say, dollars with

---

[36] Emphasis added.   [37] See text at n. 45 infra.

[38] The question of declaring the transitional period at an end was debated within the Fund in 1959–60, following achievement of de facto convertibility by 15 European states. However, the Legal Department advised the Executive Board that the Board had no authority to termin-ate the transitional period: 'the most it could do would be to express the opinion that condi-tions were favorable for the withdrawal of restrictions on the ground that, in its opinion, post-war transitional conditions had disappeared.' See *IMF History 1945–65*, Vol. I pp. 477–81.

[39] But a number of states declared that their currency was convertible into other currencies without restriction, without making the commitment under Article VIII not to reimpose exchange controls without the Fund's approval.

which to make payment for the machines. Further, if the purchase is made for Patrian pesos, and the Xandian exporter brings its pesos to Xandia's central bank, the central bank is entitled under Article VIII(4) to require Patria to redeem its pesos for Xandian crowns or for usable reserve assets.[40] If the exporter in Xandia seeks to use its pesos to make a purchase from Tertia, neither Patria nor Xandia (also an Article VIII country) may restrict that transaction, and Patria is required to convert the pesos in the possession of the central bank of Tertia as well.

Once a state notifies the Fund that it is prepared to assume the obligations of Article VIII, i.e. not to impose restrictions on payments and transfers for current transactions, there is no going back. States can move from Article XIV to Article VIII, as all the members of the European Community (as well as the United Kingdom and Ireland) did on the same day in 1961 and Japan did in 1964, but they are not permitted to move the other way. As of the early 1990s, just over half the member states of the IMF remained under Article XIV—all developing or former communist bloc countries. By the end of the decade, 150 out of 182 member states had accepted the obligations of Article VIII, and thus had become bound to adopt only those restrictions on current transactions that are approved by the Fund.[41] Failure to abide by this prohibition carries no immediate sanction, but may be held against a member if it applies to use the Fund's resources, as discussed below.[42]

(b) Capital Transactions

It is important to note that the prohibition on exchange controls does not include controls on capital transfers, and indeed Article VI(3) of the Articles of Agreement expressly provides that 'Members may exercise such controls as are necessary to regulate international capital movements.' The reason for the distinction appears to have been British fear that without some form of capital controls at the close of World War II, excessive sums would be transferred out of the United Kingdom. In later years, as the role of capital movements became more pronounced, states have been unwilling to forego the right to impose restraints, and several of the leading states, including the United States, have from time to time done so.[43]

It was realized that at the margin capital and current transactions blend into one another, and the characterization of a given transaction as one or

[40] In the original version of Article VIII(4), Xandia would have been entitled to redeem the pesos for gold. In fact reliance on Article VIII(4) is rarely necessary if an exchange market exists where pesos and crowns are traded.

[41] India became an Article VIII member in 1994, Russia and China in 1996. Brazil became the last major country to accept the obligations of Article VIII, effective November 1999.

[42] See Sect. 16.6 infra.

[43] See e.g. the Foreign Direct Investment Regulations adopted by the United States in 1968 and kept in effect (with various modifications) until 1974. A brief account appears in A. Lowenfeld, *The International Monetary System*, 80–9 (2nd edn. 1984).

the other may be different for purposes of corporate accounting, taxation, or exchange controls.

For instance amortization of a loan may be regarded for tax purposes as a capital transaction, if the loan had as its purpose the acquisition of a capital good. For purposes of limiting exchange controls, payments for amortization of such a loan would come within the definition of current payments, meaning that Article VIII countries could not restrict them without the Fund's approval.[44]

The Articles of Agreement do not define capital transactions, except to say that no member may exercise capital controls in a manner which will restrict payments for current transactions. Payments for current transactions are defined as

(1)   All payments due in connection with foreign trade, other current business, including services, and normal short-term banking and credit facilities;
(2)   Payments due as interest on loans and as net income from other investments;
(3)   Payments of moderate amount for amortization of loans or for depreciation of direct investments;
(4)   Moderate remittance for family living expenses.[45]

(c)   The Question of Discrimination

As noted in Section 16.1, the drafters of the IMF Articles were very much aware of discriminatory currency arrangements such as had been perfected by Nazi Germany in the years prior to the war, and Article VIII(3) expressly prohibits such arrangements. At a minimum, this means that Patria, being an Article VIII country, may not, without permission of the Fund, apply different exchange rates for different current transactions—say one rate for tourists and another for export–import trade, or one rate for 'essential' imports, another for luxury items. Moreover, states may not discriminate against payments in a particular currency, such as the dollar. It was the reluctance to give up such discrimination in the 1950s that delayed the move to Article VIII by Great Britain and other European countries, because the staff of the Fund made clear that it preferred that states wait in assuming Article VIII status until such time as they would be in position not to immediately ask the Fund's permission to retain controls inconsistent with Article VIII.[46]

The question arose early in the history of the Fund whether the prohibition on discriminatory measures applies to capital controls. The Executive Board, after debate and advice from the Legal Department, held that

---

[44] For more complex examples, see Richard W. Edwards, Jr., *International Monetary Collaboration*, 394–6 (1985) and sources there cited.
[45] Art. XIX(i) in the original Articles, retained without challenge as Art. XXX(d) of the Amended Articles.
[46] See *IMF History 1945–65*, Vol. I, pp. 400–2, 477–82.

'Members are free to adopt a policy of regulating capital movements for any reason',[47] which was understood to mean even for a discriminatory purpose. Thus there appears to be no legal impediment to controls that distinguish between long-term and short-term capital, or to controls that permit investments within certain economic blocs but not elsewhere. The 1956 decision has been criticized, both on technical grounds[48] and on the basis of possible inconsistency of the position with the overall objectives of the IMF.[49] But when the Fund Articles were amended in 1976, no effort was made to change Article VI(3), and the Executive Board decision remains in effect.

16.6 THE FUND AS A POOL OF RESOURCES

(a) Member States' Quotas

A major purpose of the International Monetary Fund, reflected in its title, was to create a pool of resources based on mandatory contributions from member states, which could be drawn on by member states when needed for balance of payments purposes. Member states entered the organization with a quota designed, roughly, to reflect their importance in the world economy, but subject to negotiation of both economic and political considerations.[50] The larger a state's quota, the greater its contribution of resources to the Fund would have to be; on the other hand, the larger its quota, the greater its entitlement to draw on the resources of the Fund, as well as its voting power in the Fund.[51]

From the outset, contributions to the Fund have been payable one-quarter in hard assets (gold in the original articles,[52] SDRs under the Amended Articles), and three-quarters in the member's own currency (Art. III(3)). As the overall quotas of the Fund were increased following periodic reviews

---

[47] Ex. Bd. Dec. No. 541-(56/39), 25 July 1956, *Selected Decisions of the International Monetary Fund* [hereafter *Selected Decisions*], 365 (25th issue 2000). See *IMF History 1945–65*, Vol. I, pp. 403–4.

[48] Note that while Article VIII(2) is expressly directed to current payments, Article VIII(3) on 'Avoidance of discriminatory currency practices' is not in terms limited to current payments and might thus have been construed to cover controls on capital movements as well.

[49] See Edwards (n. 44 supra), 455–8; Joseph Gold, *International Capital Movements under the Law of the International Monetary Fund*, 16–17, 43–5 (IMF Pamphlet Series No. 21, 1977).

[50] Both prior to and at the Bretton Woods Conference, the United States proposed several formulas based on national economic data, which served as a point of departure from the negotiations that ensued, but not for precise allocation of quotas, either at Bretton Woods or as additional member states applied for membership. See *IMF History 1945–65* Vol. I, pp. 94–8, 149–50.

[51] The USSR urged that it be allocated a larger quota than the Quota Committee had originally assigned, but at the same time urged that it be partly exempt from the obligation to pay one quarter of its subscription in gold. See Sect. 16.3 (n. 30, supra).

[52] States with very small holdings of gold or monetary reserves could pay in the 10 percent of their net official holdings of gold and US dollars. Act. III(b)(ii).

under Article III(2), members were required to make additional payments following the same formula.

In concept, all of the resources contributed by way of quota subscriptions were to be available for drawing by member states. In fact, only those currencies generally accepted for settlement of international accounts, i.e. 'freely usable currencies', were useful for drawings by states. This is one— though not the only—reason that the IMF has had to call regularly for increases in the total quota.[53]

(b) Drawing on the Fund

In effect, member states drawing on the Fund's resources borrow from the Fund, subject to an obligation to pay interest while the loan is outstanding and to repay the principal within a specified period. In form, however, Article V of the original Articles provided for a purchase by a member state of dollars (or other freely usable currency) in exchange for its own currency, subject to an obligation to repurchase its own currency within a given time, and subject to stated charges payable by the purchaser based on the amount of its own currency held at any given time by the Fund.

> Thus suppose at the outset Patria had a quota in the Fund of 200 million dollars, of which 50 million was paid in in gold, and an amount equivalent to 150 million dollars was contributed in Patrian pesos. When Patria draws 50 million dollars (the 'gold tranche'), it must pay in an equivalent amount in pesos, and the Fund's holdings of pesos will be equal to 200 million dollars, or 100 percent of Patria's quota. If Patria draws another 50 million dollars, the Fund's holdings of pesos will stand at the equivalent of 250 million dollars, or 125 percent of Patria's quota, and so on. The charges (comparable to interest) payable to the Fund are measured by the Fund's holdings of pesos, and the rate increases in proportion to the percentage of Patria's quota held by the Fund in Patrian pesos.
>
> If another member state, say Xandia, now draws Patrian pesos from the Fund, that reduces the amount of pesos held by the Fund, and therefore reduces the obligation on Patria to repurchase its currency, and *pro tanto* the charges payable to the Fund. This reflects the reality that Patria has a creditor position vis-à-vis Xandia (or Xandia's creditor), with the Fund acting as intermediary.

The unwritten premise is that Patria will always have sufficient amounts of its own currency with which to make purchases (drawings). By the time the 'repurchase obligation' comes due, Patria is supposed to have overcome

---

[53] In January 1999, the Eleventh General Review of Quotas was completed, bringing total quotas in the Fund to SDR212 billion (*ca.* US$280 billion), up from the previous amount of SDR146 billion and original quota of US$8.8 billion.

the problems that led it to make the purchase in the first place, and to have acquired amounts of dollars (or whatever currency it drew) to effect the repurchase.

(c) Conditions for Drawing

The most critical legal question to arise under the original Articles of Agreement concerned the conditions, if any, under which a member state could draw on the resources of the Fund. In the debates preceding the Bretton Woods Conference, Lord Keynes, on behalf of the United Kingdom, which expected to be a debtor or deficit country, had urged that member states have an automatic entitlement to draw on the resources of the Fund. Harry Dexter White, the chief negotiator on behalf of the United States, which expected to be a creditor or surplus country, urged that the pool be available only upon an undertaking by the state to which resources were to be made available that it would comply with conditions to be set down by the Fund. The original Articles of agreement did not resolve the controversy. Article V(3) stated that a member '*shall be entitled* to buy the currency of another member [if]

(i)   The member desiring to purchase the currency represents that it is presently needed for making in that currency payments which are consistent with the provisions of this Agreement.

Article V(5), however, provided that, subject to procedural safeguards,

Whenever the Fund is of the opinion that any member is using the resources of the Fund contrary to the purposes of the Fund,[54] . . . the Fund may limit the use of its resources by the member . . . or may, after giving reasonable notice to the member, declare it ineligible to use the resources of the Fund.

As early as 1946, the first year of the Fund's operation, the Executive Directors, on request of the United States, issued a decision interpreting the Articles of Agreement to mean

that authority to use the resources of the Fund is limited to use in accordance with its purposes to give temporary assistance in financing balance of payments deficits on current account for monetary stabilization operations.[55]

In 1947 and again in 1948 Executive Directors issued a further interpretation, holding that a member state representing, in accordance with Article V(3)(a)(i), that the currency it sought to purchase 'is presently needed for making payments in that currency which are consistent with the provisions of the Agreement' had fulfilled the condition mentioned in Article V(3)(i), i.e. the requirement to so represent.

---

[54] See Sect. 16.2 n. 9 supra.
[55] Ex. Bd. Dec. No. 71–2, 26 Sept. 1946, *Selected Decisions*, 128 (25th issue 2000).

But [the decision went on] the Fund may, for good reasons, challenge the correctness of this declaration, on the grounds that the currency is not 'presently needed' or because the currency is not needed for payment 'in that currency', or because the payments will not be 'consistent with the provisions of the Agreement.' If the Fund concludes that a particular declaration is not correct, the Fund may postpone or reject the request, or accept it subject to conditions.[56]

Thus was born the practice of *conditionality*, which has been the most important, and most controversial aspect of the relation between the IMF and member states.

In 1952, the IMF's position on conditionality was further set out in a statement by the Managing Director, accepted by the Executive Board as a formal decision:

I think it must be clear that access to the Fund should not be denied because a member is in difficulty. On the contrary, the task of the Fund is to help members that need temporary help, and requests should be expected from members that are in trouble in greater or lesser degree. The Fund's attitude toward the position of each member should turn on whether the problem to be met is of a temporary nature and whether the policies the member will pursue will be adequate to overcome the problem within such a period. The policies, above all, should determine the Fund's attitude.

In addition, the Fund should pay attention to a member's general creditworthiness, particularly its record with the Fund. In this respect, the member's record of prudence in drawing, its willingness to offer voluntary repayment when its situation permitted, and its promptness in fulfilling the obligation to transmit monetary reserves data and in discharging repurchase obligations would be important. I would expect that in the years to come, with extended activities of the Fund, we shall be able more and more to rely on the Fund's own experience, thus providing a further link between Fund drawings and repurchases.[57]

Conditionality is explored further in the next chapter.[58] Suffice it to say here that conditionality has been the principal means by which the IMF has endeavoured to impose discipline on member states in respect to their monetary and fiscal policies. For member states in need of resources from the Fund, conditionality has meant a kind of rule of law, extending not only to the terms of a drawing from the Fund but, as the Managing Director wrote, to the economic policies of those members generally.

[56] Ex. Bd. Dec. No. 284–4, 10 Mar. 1948, *IMF History 1945–65*, Vol. III, p. 272; *Selected Decisions*, 129 (25th issue 2000).

[57] Ex. Bd. Dec. No. 102-(52/11), 13 Feb. 1952, *Selected Decisions*, p. 100 (24th issue 1999). Joseph Gold, writing in the official history, called this decision, 'the Mount Everest that towers over all other decisions on the use of the Fund's resources', *IMF History 1945–65*, Vol. II, pp. 523–24.

[58] See Ch. 17, Sect. 17.5.

16.7   DRAWING RIGHTS AND STAND-BY ARRANGEMENTS

(a)   **Limitations on Drawing Rights**

In the same statement of 1952 quoted in the preceding section,[59] the Managing Director said

In view of the Executive Board's interpretation of September 26, 1946, concerning the use of the Fund's resources,[60] and considering especially the necessity for ensuring the revolving character of the Fund's resources, exchange purchased from the Fund should not remain outstanding beyond the period reasonably related to the payments problem for which it was purchased from the Fund. The period should fall within an outside range of three to five years. Members will be expected not to request the purchase of exchange from the Fund in circumstances where the reduction of the Fund's holdings of their currencies by an equivalent amount within that time cannot reasonably be envisaged.

. . .

When unforeseen circumstances beyond the member's control would make unreasonable the application of the principles set forth in paragraph 2 above, the Fund will consider extensions of time.

When requesting use of the resources of the Fund in accordance with the arrangements described above, a member will be expected to include in its authenticated request a statement, that it will comply with the above principles.

These principles will be an essential element in any determination by the Fund as to whether a member is using the resources of the Fund in accordance with the purposes of the Fund.

Each member can count on receiving the overwhelming benefit of any doubt respecting drawings which would raise the Fund's holdings of its currency to not more than its quota.

Thus on the one hand, the Executive Board, in ratifying the Managing Director's statement, defined the normal period of a drawing—three to five years, and on the other hand established the principle that a drawing equal to the first 25 percent of a member state's quota—the so-called gold tranche (later renamed the reserve tranche)—would be virtually automatically available, on the ground that it was fully collateralized. The clear implication, borne out by subsequent practice, was that additional purchases—so-called credit tranches—would be subject to increasing scrutiny and perhaps more stringent conditions. The greater the (cumulative) drawing in terms of the member state's quota, the greater the demands by the Fund for commitments to measures that the Fund would regard, in the Managing Director's words as 'adequate to overcome the problem within [the period of the drawing].'

---

[59] Sect. 16.6, at n. 57 supra.   [60] Sect., 16.6 at n. 55 supra.

(b) The Origins of Stand-by Arrangements

In subsequent years the policies announced in the 1952 decision were spelled out in more formal ways, and in fact both the time period and the size of the credit tranches were enlarged.[61] But the basic principle was confirmed that a drawing beyond the gold or reserve tranche depended on an undertaking by the member state satisfactory to the Fund, with the expectation that before the undertaking could be accepted the Fund itself would conduct an examination of the relevant economic data, which might take several weeks or even longer.

There was thus no assurance that if a member state ran into a balance of payments difficulty it could have speedy access to the resources of the Fund, beyond the gold tranche. Negotiations between a member state and the Fund concerning a prospective drawing might themselves undermine confidence in the ability of the State to cope with its economic difficulties; moreover, the important function of drawing rights as a confidence builder might well be undermined by the process of implementing conditionality. Put another way, drawing rights subject to conditionality did not have the quality of reserves.

The idea soon grew up that the examination and negotiations looking to the Fund's approval of a state's economic commitments could take place in advance of an actual need for a drawing. In June 1952, Belgium became the first state to benefit from what became known as a *stand-by arrangement*, whereby the Fund gave a formal commitment (for a small fee) that if Belgium should request a drawing from the Fund within the next six months up to a stated amount, that request would be immediately approved.[62] Later in the same year the practice of stand-by arrangements was generalized and formalized in a decision of the Executive Board.[63] Thereafter, stand-by arrangements became—and continue to be—the principal device through which the resources of the IMF are made available to member states.[64]

---

[61] In part the Fund's practices with regard to drawings were set down in the First Amendment to the Articles of Agreement, effective July 28, 1969; and further developments of the practice were set down in Article V of the Amended Articles, effective April 1, 1978. See Ch. 17, Sect. 17.5 infra.

[62] See *IMF History 1945–65*, Vol. I, pp. 328–30. The stand-by arrangement was regularly renewed until April 1957, when Belgium finally drew the amount specified.

[63] Ex. Bd. Dec. No. 155-(52/57), 1 Oct. 1952, *IMF History 1945–65*, Vol. III, p. 230. Several subsequent decisions spelled out the practice in more detail, generally in the direction of greater flexibility and longer duration. See e.g. *IMF History 1945–65*, Vol. II, ch. 23 (Joseph Gold).

[64] Stand-by arrangements, which were not mentioned, or apparently contemplated, in the original Articles of Agreement as drafted and adopted at Bretton Woods, were specifically authorized in Article V(3) of the Amended Articles. Article XXX(b) of the Amended Articles defines a stand-by arrangement as

a decision of the Fund by which a member is assured that it will be able to make purchases from the General Resources Account in accordance with the terms of the decision during a specified period and up to a specified amount.

(c) Stand-by Arrangements and Letters of Intent

Typically when a member applies for a stand-by, negotiations are initiated between the staff of the Fund and financial officials of the member state. Usually a mission is dispatched from Fund headquarters, both to gather information and to discuss the undertakings that the Fund will require in return for, in effect, making a line of credit available to the State for six months, a year or—under so-called *Extended Arrangements*, for longer periods.[65] The end-product is a Letter of Intent to the Managing Director of the Fund signed by the Minister of Finance or Governor of the Central Bank of the applicant state (often by both), in consideration of which the Executive Board approves the stand-by. For many years the Fund did not, as a matter of policy, make the documents public, though it generally issued a press release stating that a stand-by had been concluded with the state in question, specifying the amount in question and the period of the stand-by, and usually supplying some information about the purpose of the stand-by.[66] It was not uncommon, however, for the text of stand-by arrangements to come out, in some instances by leaks to the press, in other instances by decision of the government itself designed to put to rest rumours of undertakings more drastic than were in fact made. More recently, stand-by arrangements as well as the Letters of Intent and accompanying memoranda have been made public and put on the Internet as soon as they are concluded and appoved by the Executive Board.

(d) The Legal Status of Stand-by Arrangements

There has been a good deal of discussion in the literature about whether a Letter of Intent and an announcement by the Fund that a stand-by arrangement has been approved together constitute a legally binding agreement. The Fund, and in particular its long-time General Counsel, Sir Joseph Gold, have been at pains since the early 1960s to maintain that a stand-by is an 'arrangement', not an 'agreement', and does not create obligations at law.[67] Early versions of the standard form of stand-by, which began:

In consideration of the policies and intentions set forth in the annexed letter, the *International Monetary Fund agrees* to a stand-by arrangement for the support of those policies and intentions.

---

[65] See Ex Bd. Dec. No. 4377–(74/114) 13 Sept. 1974, amended numerous times, *Selected Decisions*, p. 165 (25th issue 2000).

[66] For a sample of a Letter of Intent and Stand-by Arrangement, see Joseph Gold, 'The Stand-by Arrangements of the International Monetary Fund', p. 57, repr. in Lowenfeld, *The International Monetary System*, p. DS–246 (2nd edn. 1984). See also Richard W. Edwards, Jr., *International Monetary Collaboration*, 251–62 (1985) reproducing an Extended Arrangement of 1981 for India. A standard form of stand-by arrangement was approved by the Executive Board in 1993, and is reproduced in *Selected Decisions*, at pp. 173–85 (25th issue 2000).

[67] See esp. Joseph Gold, *The Legal Character of the Fund's Stand-by Arrangements and Why It Matters* (IMF Pamphlet Services, No. 35, 1980).

have been replaced by a statement deliberately omitting the italicized words:

> Attached hereto is a letter [with annexed memorandum] dated____
> from the Minister of Finance [and/or the Governor of the Central Bank]
> of Patria requesting a stand-by arrangement and setting forth:
>
> (a) the objectives and policies that the authorities of Patria intend
> to pursue for the period of this stand-by arrangement;
>
> (b) the policies and measures that the authorities of Patria intend
> to pursue in the [period] [first year] of this stand-by arrange-
> ment;
>
> (c) understandings of Patria with the Fund regarding reviews that
> will be made of progress in realizing the objectives of the pro-
> gram and of the policies and measures that the authorities of
> Patria will pursue for the remaining period of this stand-by
> arrangement.
>
> To support these objectives and policies the International Monetary
> Fund grants this stand-by arrangement in accordance with the follow-
> ing provisions.[68]

The comprehensive decision on the Use of the Fund's General Resources and
Stand-by Arrangements of 1979 contains an express statement that 'Stand-
by arrangements are not international agreements and therefore language
having a contractual connotation will be avoided in stand-by arrangements
and letters of intent.'[69] Governments of states entering into stand-by
arrangements have generally taken the position that no approval from the
legislative branch was required for the commitments made, as would be
required in a treaty or other formal agreement.

Nevertheless, as stand-by arrangements have grown beyond the original
six- or twelve-month commitment, the Fund has provided for performance
targets on such matters as budgetary deficits, tax collection, removal of subsidies, and rates of inflation, with disbursements or drawing at intervals
linked to conformance with the targets. If a state is out of compliance with
the performance targets, the Fund will not automatically cut off disbursement under a stand-by, but the stand-by arrangement itself usually requires
immediate consultation, and if the consultation does not result in agreement
to modify the performance targets, the Fund has from time to time suspended disbursement under stand-by arrangements, on the basis that failure
to meet the performance criteria has created a new situation not provided
for in the stand-by.[70]

[68] Adapted from the form cited at n. 66 supra.
[69] Ex. Bd. Dec. No. 6056-(79/38) 2 Mar. 1979, ¶3, *Selected Decisions*, 149 (25th issue
2000). A substantially similar provision was contained in an earlier decision with the same title,
Ex. Bd. Dec. No. 2603-(68/132), 20 Sept. 1968, ¶7, *Selected Decisions*, 47 at 49 (8th issue
1976).
[70] See Edwards (n. 66 supra), 268 and nn. 179–182; for one well-known instance involving
Brazil in 1982–3, see Lowenfeld (n. 66 supra), 299–304.

More generally, an unjustified failure to live up to a stand-by arrangement may be a basis for non-renewal of a stand-by or for limitations on future drawings. Thus while failure to fulfill a commitment under a stand-by is not regarded as a breach of the Articles of Agreement carrying specified penalties,[71] it is not unfair to regard a stand-by arrangement as constituting an obligation of a state on whose behalf a Letter of Intent is signed and to which a stand-by has been granted.[72] It is not open to a government that takes office after a prior administration has signed a letter of intent to repudiate it as contrary to the program on which the new administration was elected. A Letter of Intent signed by an authorized official on behalf of a member state commits the state.

16.8   CREATION OF RESERVES: SPECIAL DRAWING RIGHTS IN THE IMF

(a)   The Problem of the Supply of Reserves

The Bretton Woods regime contemplated a system in which all member states strive for equilibrium in the balance of payments, using reserves, i.e. convertible foreign currencies and gold, to redeem balances of their currencies held by other states.[73] If Patria's reserves were temporarily insufficient, the Fund was available to sell 'fully usable currencies' to Patria, subject to the conditions described in the preceding sections of this chapter, including the requirement to repurchase its own currency with reserves acquired from other sources within the period prescribed, usually three to five years. Nothing in the Articles of Agreement addressed the total supply of or demand for reserves.

During the first two decades of the IMF, member states' reserves consisted primarily of US dollars and gold (plus to a declining degree British pounds). In the mid-1960s, the perception grew that the supply of reserves was not— or might not be—adequate to the ever-growing level of international economic activity. The supply of gold was limited and arbitrary,[74] and increase in foreign holdings of US dollars and British pounds depended on continuing balance of payments deficits of the United States and the United Kingdom, which were neither certain to continue nor in the long run desirable. Moreover, if member states were to lose confidence in the dollar and

---

[71] See e.g. Arts. V(5), VI(1), XXVI(2)(a) of the Amended Articles.

[72] Cf. American Law Institute, *Restatement (Third) of the Foreign Relations Law of the United States*, §821, comment *e* (1987).

[73] See original Articles of Agreement, Article VIII(4), modified in the Amended Articles for reasons explained herein, but not changed for purposes of the present discussion.

[74] And much of the world's gold did not go into official holdings.

present their holdings to the United States for conversion into gold, there could be an actual shrinkage in world reserves.[75]

(b) Creating Reserves by Conscious Decision: The First Amendment to the IMF Articles

After several years of negotiation and debate, primarily among the Group of Ten and their Deputies, the IMF in 1968 adopted an amendment to the Articles of Agreement authorizing creation by the Fund itself of a reserve asset, in the form of rights by member state holders to draw on a new Special Drawing Account of the Fund for purposes of clearing outstanding balances.[76]

Special Drawing Rights (SDRs) may be created only by deliberate decision of the Board of Governors, approved by a vote of 85 percent of the total voting power in the Fund, on the basis of proposals of the Managing Director concurred in by the Executive Directors. In fact agreement on an allocation of SDRs has been difficult to achieve. In the first twelve years (1969–81), a total of SDR $21.4 billion was authorized, in two series of allocations (1970–2 and 1979–81); as of year-end 2001 no further allocations of SDRs had been made, and SDRs constituted no more than about one percent of total world reserves.

When a decision to allocate SDRs is taken, the amount agreed on is to be allocated to all participating member states in proportion to their quota in the Fund, with no questions asked and without any conditionality. Member states are supposed to use SDRs only in case of need (i.e. not just to get rid of them), but their use is not subject to challenge.[77] When a participating state wishes to use its SDRs to acquire foreign currency for balance of payments purposes, it notifies the Fund, which will designate the member state that must accept the SDRs in return for other reserves.[78] The idea behind the provision for designation was to assure, as far as possible, a balanced distribution of SDRs, with no country being obliged to take an excessive share.[79]

---

[75] Thus suppose Germany presented $100 million to the US gold window in accordance with the US understanding to convert official holdings of dollars into gold. The total reserves of Germany would not change, only their composition; the total reserves of the United States would be reduced by the amount of gold paid out, because by definition, holdings of one's own currency do not constitute international reserves.

[76] The First Amendment to the Articles of Agreement was approved by the Board of Governors of the Fund by mail vote on May 31, 1968. The Amendment took effect on July 28, 1969, upon acceptance by three-fifths of the members of the Fund representing four-fifths of the total voting power. The Special Drawing Account was opened on August 6, 1969, with the participation of 50 members of the Fund having 75 percent of the total quota. 21 *Int'l Financial News Survey* 254 (15 Aug. 1969). The provisions of the First Amendment relating to SDRs appear in the current version of the Articles of Agreement (somewhat modified) in Articles XV–XXV.

[77] First Amendment, Art. XXV(3), current version Art. XIX(3).

[78] First Amendment, Art. XXV(5), current version Art. XIX (5).

[79] Also, at the time when the SDR scheme was first developed, it contained a provision for partial reconstitution of SDR holdings (see subsection (c) below); designation could be used to

Under the Amended Articles of Agreement, countries may also engage in transactions involving SDRs by agreement,[80] and in recent years transfer by agreement have comprised the majority of transfers of SDRs with the Fund acting as an informal broker.[81]

(c) Special Drawing Rights, Reconstitution, and Links to Development

In their original version as adopted in 1969, the amendments creating the Special Drawing Account contained a requirement for partial reconstitution of SDR holdings by each participating State. A member that used its allocation to finance a balance of payments deficit was required to replenish its supply so that at the end of the first five years, and thereafter on a quarterly basis, the moving average of its holdings of SDRs would be equal to 30 percent of its net cumulative allocation over the same period.[82] Presumably a country would meet this requirement by achieving a balance of payments surplus or otherwise acquiring reserves usable to redeem SDRs from other states. The requirement for reconstitution was reduced to 15 percent of net cumulative allocation in 1979, and eliminated entirely in 1981, apparently in the belief that elimination of the reconstitution requirement would contribute to greater use of SDRs.[83]

Developing countries and a number of academic commentators have often urged that allocation of SDRs be linked to development assistance, so that for instance eligible member states might share in an allocation of SDRs in a proportion equal to twice their quota (or some other multiple), rather than in proportion only to their actual quota. As of year-end 2001, all suggestions along these lines had been rejected, principally on the ground that any such link would destroy or impair the character of SDRs as money, and on the related ground that if developing countries transferred extra SDRs to industrial countries to clear balance of payments deficits, the industrial

---

assist member states in meeting the requirements for reconstitution. As of year-end 2001, no reconstitution requirements are in effect, though the Fund is authorized to reintroduce a restoration requirement by a qualified majority vote.

[80] Amended Articles of Agreement, Art. XIX(2)(b).

[81] See *IMF Annual Report 2000*, 74–7 and accompanying tables.

[82] First Amendment, Art. XXV(6) and sched. G.

[83] Exec. Bd. Dec. No. 6832-(81/65)S (22 Apr. 1981) *Selected Decisions*, 413 (17th issue 1992). Prof. Edwards regards this decision as a mistake, because if some members spent all of their SDR allocations while holdings of SDRs were concentrated in a few member states, the usefulness of SDRs as a reserve asset would be impaired, if not destroyed. Richard W. Edwards Jr., n. 66 supra, 211–12, 220 (1985). In fact, as of the end of FY2000, holdings of SDRs by all non-industrial countries as a group stood at 54.6 percent of their net cumulative allocations and holdings of SDRs by industrial countries stood at 96 percent. The volume of SDR transactions peaked in FY1999 at SDR49.1 billion, largely because many states used SDRs in connection with the increased payments required under the Eleventh General Quota Review (see Sect. 16.6, n. 53 supra). In FY2000 the volume of SDR transactions fell to SDR22.9 billion, and in FY2001 it fell further to SDR18.7 billion.

countries would in effect be making foreign assistance grants without having voted for them or having established conditions for their use. The Amended Articles of Agreement do not authorize allocation of SDRs except in accordance with a recipient's quota, so that any attempt to revive the idea of linkage of SDRs to development aid would require an amendment to the Articles of Agreement.[84]

(d)   Valuation of Special Drawing Rights

Initially the value of Special Drawing Rights was defined in terms of gold, with one SDR being equal precisely to the value of the US dollar at its official rate of $35 per ounce. As early as 1972, the Fund began to use the SDR as the unit in which it stated its own accounts, including not only allocations of SDRs, but contributions to quotas, drawings under stand-by arrangements, and all other official transactions. When the dollar was devalued in terms of gold in 1973 (Section 16.9 infra), the value of the SDR was not changed in terms of gold, so that for a time one SDR was equal to approximately US$1.20. In 1974, as most major currencies (as well as gold) were floating, the Executive Board of the Fund adopted an interim system of valuation of SDRs on the basis of a composite basket of 16 currencies, weighted roughly in accordance with the issuing countries' shares of world trade and finance.[85] The Second Amendment to the Articles of Agreement (Ch. 17. Sect. 17.2) simply contains an enabling clause authorizing the Fund to establish the method of valuation of SDRs by a 70 percent majority of the total voting power. From 1981 to 1998, the value of the SDR was calculated on the basis of a basket of five currencies—the US dollar, the British pound, the French franc, the German mark, and the Japanese yen, weighted according to their relative share of world trade and finance; since the introduction of the euro in January 1999, the franc and the mark have been replaced by the euro, so that the basket now consists of four currencies.[86] The SDR has been used as a unit of account in some private long-term transactions, and in numerous international treaties, particularly those establishing limits of

[84] See Amended Articles, Art. XVIII(b). At the 1997 Annual Meeting of the Fund, the Board of Governors adopted a resolution proposing an amendment to the Articles of Agreement to equalize the cumulative allocation of SDRs as a percentage of the member states' quota, designed to allow the 38 member states that had never received an SDR allocation to participate in the SDR system If ratified by three-fifths of the member states having 85 percent of the total voting power, the amendment would authorize a one-time allocation of SDR21.4 billion, thus doubling the total amount of SDRs allocated. As of August 2001, the Amendment had received assent by members holding 72.18 percent of the voting power. It would go into effect if the United States, with 17.16 percent of the voting power, would give its approval.

[85] Exec. Bd. Dec. No. 4233-(74/67S (13 June 1974), amended by Dec. No. 4261-(74/78S (1 July 1974). See 1974 *IMF Annual Report*, 116–17.

[86] The weights in the basket have varied from time to time, but effective January 1, 2001 for a period of 5 years, the basket consists of 45 percent US dollar, 29 percent euro, 15 percent yen, and 11 percent pound sterling. As of August 14, 2001, SDR1 = US$1.269 and US$1 = SDR0.788.

liability for accidents, including the proposed Montreal Convention to amend the Warsaw Convention concerning International Carriage by Air.[87]

(e) Interest and Charges

The Fund imposes charges on net cumulative allocations of SDRs, and pays interest at the same rate on holdings of SDRs.[88] Thus if a member state neither uses its SDRs nor takes in SDRs from other states, the charges and interest cancel each other out. States holding SDRs in excess of their allocation receive interest on the excess, and states that have used their SDRs pay charges on the net amount used. The appropriate rate of interest for SDRs has long been a subject of debate. In principle, it should be set high enough to compensate a country for holding SDRs rather than foreign currency, but not so high as to discourage member states from using their SDRs for their intended purpose. Initially the interest rate was set at 1.5 percent, in 1974 the rate was increased to 5 percent, and since 1981 the rate has been set at a market rate based on the short-term interest rate of the currencies used in valuation of the SDR.

(f) Special Drawing Rights in the International Monetary System

The original version of the amendments concerning SDRs stated that 'each participant undertakes to collaborate with the Fund and with other participants in order to facilitate the effective functioning of the Special Drawing Account.'[89] In the Second Amendment, this provision was augmented by the statement of 'the objective of making the special drawing right the principal reserve asset in the international monetary system.'[90] In the three decades since the creation of SDRs, that objective has not been achieved, and indeed it is no longer seriously seen as a goal of international monetary system.

The shortage of international liquidity anticipated in the 1960s did not occur, and as noted above, the required consensus to create new SDRs was achieved only twice. The idea of creation and allocation of reserves by decision of the Fund remains on the books, however, and it might again come to be viewed as a significant policy instrument.

---

[87] For a list with explanation of the treaties and proposed treaties using SDRs rather than gold or particular currencies, see Joseph Gold, *Floating Currencies, Gold and SDRs, Some Recent Legal Developments* (IMF Pamphlet Series, 19 Nov. 1976); *Floating Currencies, Gold and SDRs, Further Legal Developments* (IMF Pamphlet Series, No. 22 (1977); and further pamphlets in the series, No. 33 (1980); No. 36 (1980); No. 40 (1983), and No. 44 (1987).

[88] Original version Art. XXVI; Amended Articles, Art. XX.

[89] First Amendment, Art. XXVIII.

[90] Amended Articles, Art. XXII. The same statement appears also in Article VIII(7).

16.9   THE FIXED EXCHANGE REGIME (1945–71)

As noted in the Introduction to this Part, one of the principal decisions taken by the architects of the Bretton Woods agreements was a commitment to fixed exchange rates. The organizing idea was that the many changes in exchange rates in the inter-war period had produced instability, introduced extra risk to international trade, encouraged manipulation, and generally contributed to the depression and war that were on the minds of all those who planned the post-war world.

(a)   The Par Value System

Under Article IV of the original Articles of Agreement, each member state was required to adopt a par value for its currency, expressed in terms of gold or of the US dollar, it being understood that the value of the dollar in terms of gold had been fixed in 1934 at $35 per ounce and would not be changed, i.e. that the United States Treasury would continue to buy and sell gold in transactions with monetary authorities at that price.[91] For original parties to the IMF whose territory had not been under enemy occupation, the par value was required to be based on the rate of exchange prevailing on the sixtieth day before the Agreement entered into force, which turned out to be December 27, 1945, subject to negotiation between the Fund and the member state within 90 days.[92] Other states could set their own par values, but they were required to do so and to notify the Fund.[93]

All member states were required by Article IV(3) to maintain that value—by governmental intervention in the market if necessary—so that spot transactions within their territory did not differ from the stated par value by more than one percent.[94] Typically member states carried out this obligation by buying their own currency with US dollars or selling their currency for dollars, but other currencies convertible into dollars, such as the British pound or the German mark, could also be used.[95] One purpose of drawings from

---

[91] The US policy was announced in a statement of the US Secretary of the Treasury on January 31, 1934, 20 *Fed. Reserve Bulletin* 69 (1934). Fifteen years later, well after entry into force of the IMF Agreement, the policy was confirmed by a letter from the Secretary of the Treasury to the Managing Director of the Fund on May 20, 1949. The letter, together with the Fund's acknowledgement that 'the policy of the United States has not changed in this respect since prior to the signing and entry into force of the Articles of Agreement', are reproduced in *The Balance of Payments Mess*, Hearings before Subcomm. on International Exchange and Payments of Joint Economic Committee at 417, 92d Cong. 1st Sess. (1971).

[92] Original Articles, Art. XX(4)(a).   [93] Art. IV(1).

[94] Art. IV(3)(i). Article IV(3)(ii) obligated members to maintain the value of their currency in other transactions, such as forward contracts, within margins that the Fund could prescribe.

[95] The United States did not intervene in exchange markets, but complied with its obligation under Article IV by freely buying and selling gold at the stated rate, as was permitted by the second sentence of Article IV(4)(b); no other state availed itself of this option.

the Fund, as described in section 16.6, was to obtain reserves to carry out the obligation imposed by Article IV(3).

Par values were not expected to last forever, but Article IV(5) prohibited a change (whether up or down) except to correct 'fundamental disequilibrium'—a term not defined but understood, it seems, to mean a situation not correctable within the time for which resources of the Fund would be made available to members under drawings.[96] The Fund could not itself initiate a change in the par value of a member state's currency, but if a member state wanted to change the par value of its currency it was required to consult with the Fund in advance, and (except for an initial 10 percent change from its original value) to secure approval by the Fund (Art. IV(5)). The theory was that the Fund needed to be satisfied that the proposed change (presumably a devaluation) was neither too small, so that it would not stick, nor too large, so that the state's exports would gain unfair competitive advantage. If a state violated the injunction of Article IV(5) and changed its par value despite the objection of the Fund, then according to Article IV(6) the member would (unless the Fund otherwise determined) be ineligible for drawings from the Fund, and might even be expelled from the organization.

In fact, the idea that in a currency crisis—that is at a time when more persons were seeking to sell the currency than were offering to buy it—a state could wait for the Fund to satisfy itself of the correctness of a proposed change proved unattainable for major currencies.[97]

(b) Demise of the Par Value System

In the event, the par value system as described above was only partially adhered to. France made an unauthorized change in par value in 1948, Canada permitted its dollar to float in the 1950s, i.e. it did not intervene in the market to maintain a given par value, and many of the developing countries did not establish par values for their currencies at all. No punishment was meted out by the Fund. But until the late 1960s a rough approximation of the Bretton

---

[96] The principal American author of the Bretton Woods system, Harry Dexter White, explained the absence of a definition of fundamental disequilibrium as follows:

> In the drafting of the Articles of Agreement no attempt was made to define fundamental disequilibrium. This, as we know, was not an oversight. It was generally agreed that a satisfactory definition would be difficult to formulate. A too rigid or narrow interpretation would be dangerous; one too loose or general would be useless in providing a criterion for changes in currency parities. It was felt too that the subject matter was so important, and the necessity for a crystallization of a harmonious view so essential that it were best left for discussion and formulation by the Fund. Because of the key position of the term and the importance attached to its precise meaning, it would be desirable, if possible, to reach agreement on a tentative formulation before any definitive position be taken by any of the officials of the Fund. (Unpublished memorandum of Aug. 1946, reproduced in Joseph Gold, 'The Legal Structure of the Par Value System', 5 *Law & Pol'y Int'l Bus.* 155 at 161 (1973)

[97] See e.g. Lowenfeld, n. 66 supra, *The International Monetary System* pp. 47–67 (2nd edn. 1984), describing the devaluation of the British pound in November 1967.

Woods goal was maintained, dependent on the 'fixed star', i.e. the US dollar and the undertaking by the United States to convert dollars to gold and vice versa at the rate in effect incorporated into the Articles of Agreement.

Eventually, following many years of current account deficits, the pressure on the US dollar became too great to sustain. The causes were manifold and cumulative—the war in Vietnam; the massive rise in imports from Japan, which maintained its exchange rate of ¥360 = US$1 from 1949 on; continuing direct foreign investment by corporations based in the United States; and overall a very changed economic environment from the early post-war years, when only the United States had economic strength. In the spring of 1971, the Managing Director of the Fund suggested devaluation of the dollar, but the United States rejected the idea. In May 1971 the German mark and the Netherlands guilder were permitted to float, and they floated upward against the dollar. The yen was not permitted to float, but the Bank of Japan was forced to acquire several billions of US dollars in order to maintain the par value of the yen.

Finally on August 15, 1971, after the United States gold stocks were approaching the symbolic level of $10 billion, as contrasted with $13 billion in 1967 and $25 billion in 1949, and as even the Bank of England sought to convert its dollar holdings into gold, the United States acted. In a dramatic Sunday night broadcast, President Nixon announced that the United States would no longer convert foreign-held dollars into gold or other reserve assets, 'except in amounts and conditions determined to be in the interest of monetary stability and in the best interests of the United States.'[98] Moreover the United States would not intervene in exchange markets to maintain the par value of the dollar against other currencies.

There was some discussion, at the time and later, about whether the United States action was in breach of its international obligations. The maintenance by the United States of the gold window could not be said to be an absolute requirement—it was an option permitted by the second sentence of Article IV(4)(b) that had been designed for the United States and that no other country had taken up.[99] On the other hand, many countries, large and small, had held their reserves in dollars in reliance on the undertaking of the United States around which the par value system had been built. It was also true that once the United States had renounced the option of buying and selling gold at a fixed rate, it became subject to the requirement in Article IV(3) to maintaining the exchange rate for its currency within the prescribed margins, and it did not honour that requirement.[100] For the time being,

---

[98] Address of President Richard Nixon of August 15, 1971. Public Papers of the Presidents: Richard Nixon 1971, 263.

[99] See n. 95 supra.

[100] Further, the United States action made clear that it was not prepared, for the time being, to comply with the provision in Article VIII(4) concerning conversion of foreign acquired balances held as a result of current transactions.

however, neither did any of the other major states. The United States did formally communicate to the IMF its commitment to 'collaborate with the Fund to promote exchange stability, to maintain orderly exchange arrangements with other members, and to avoid competitive exchange alterations' (tracking Art. IV(4) of the original Articles).[101]

(c) Attempt at Repair: The Smithsonian Agreement

Throughout the fall of 1971 the United States, the major European states, and Japan engaged in negotiations about realigning exchange rates. In December 1971 in a conference at the Smithsonian Museum in Washington, they reached agreement on what were called 'central rates',—a ratio of major currencies to each other with a wider margin within which they were permitted to fluctuate, and with several options available to member states as to how these rates would be maintained.[102] The link of the dollar to gold was maintained (or rather reestablished) at a new price of $38 per ounce, representing a devaluation from pre-August 15 of 8.5 percent; the yen was revalued to ¥308 = US$1, up 16.88 percent against the pre-August 15 dollar, the German mark was revalued by 13.58 percent, and the British pound and French franc remained unchanged, i.e. they appreciated against the dollar only by the amount of the dollar's devaluation. Never before had so many countries agreed on a set of exchange rates at one time. From the point of view of the IMF, while the technical rules of changes in par value had been put aside and a system of wider margins had been reintroduced, it seemed that the fixed exchange rate system overall had been preserved or restored.

In the event, the Smithsonian Agreement lasted about six months. Great Britain announced in June 1972 that it would no longer maintain the agreed rate of exchange for the pound. The remainder of the Smithsonian Agreement held for another half year, and in February 1973 the United States negotiated another realignment of currencies, in effect a further devaluation of the dollar against the yen and the major European currencies.[103] This realignment, however, lasted only a few weeks; another effort was made in March, but it too failed to achieve stability. By July 1973, all the major currencies were floating, i.e. central banks were not intervening in markets at all, or at any event were not intervening to maintain any particular exchange

---

[101] See Memorandum from Secretary of the Treasury Connolly to Managing Director, IMF, summarized in 23 *International Financial News Survey* 261 (25 Aug. 1971).

[102] See Decision of the Executive Board ratifying the agreement made by the Group of Ten Ministers, Ex. Bd. Dec. No. 3463–(71/126); 18 Dec. 1971, 23 *Int'l Financial News Survey* 419 (22–30 Dec. 1971). The same issue also contains the G–10 Communiqué and a table of value of all the currencies. Id., at 417–18, 421–2. For a description by the present author of the negotiations and analysis of the result, see Lowenfeld, *The International Monetary System*, 144–60, (2nd edn. 1984), reproducing the relevant documents. For eyewitness accounts of the negotiations see Paul Volcker and Toyoo Gyohten, *Changing Fortunes*, (n. 28 supra), 81–90, 95–100 (1992).

[103] See Volcker and Gyohten (n. 102 supra), 105–12, 129–31.

rate. It had become clear that it was no longer possible to design a fixed exchange system with sufficient accuracy to withstand global volatility—not only in exchange markets, but in interest rates, rates of inflation, capital movements, trade flows, and political expectations.

Even as consensus was building around this conclusion, the Arab–Israel War of October 1973 broke out. Though the War soon ended, it provided the opportunity for fourfold increase in the price of oil, carried out by the members of the Organization of Petroleum Exporting Countries—resulting in the largest shift in real resources ever seen in peacetime.[104] Notwithstanding the shock of the OPEC coup, the world economy did not plunge into depression, as many had feared, and as might well have occurred had the member states of the IMF regarded themselves as bound to intervene to maintain fixed exchange rates. The *de facto* regime of floating exchange rates, not tied to any legal agreement, seemed to enable the major internationally traded currencies to 'roll with the punch', and as it turned out, even enabled the non-oil-producing developing countries to secure financing for their continued development.[105]

The press, as well as academic economists concluded unanimously that the Bretton Woods regime was finished. In fact, not only the IMF itself but much of the law and practice described in the preceding sections of this chapter remain in place, and remain relevant, a full generation after the collapse of the par value system. In particular, the rules and practice of resort to the resources of the Fund, through purchase of currencies with obligation to repurchase (Section 16.6), and the practice of stand-by agreements, including conditionality (Section 16.7) were not rendered obsolete by the events of 1971–3. Only the exchange rate regime established at Bretton Woods, based on the US dollar and its fixed relationship to gold, has become obsolete. What took its place is the subject of the next chapter.

---

[104] See *IMF Annual Report 1975*, 12, reporting a collective surplus on current account for the major oil exporters for 1974 of $70 billion, compared with less than $6 billion in 1973.
[105] See Ch. 17, Sect. 17.6(c).

17

The International Monetary Fund as Amended

17.1   THE IMF IN TRANSITION

From August 15, 1971 on, it was clear that fundamental changes were needed in the rules of international monetary law. The system had been unable, from the mid-1960s onward, to achieve anything like sustained equilibrium, and when its main anchor, the United States, acted contrary to the rules, the other states had been neither able nor willing to uphold the rules themselves.[1] It was the rules that had to change.

Three tracks were followed in the aftermath of August 15. The first track aimed at restoring the fixed exchange rate system, but with wider margins, i.e. with more flexibility for market movements around a target or central rate, but with a continued (or renewed) obligation on states to maintain the agreed rates. That effort resulted in the Smithsonian Agreement of December 1971.[2] Though the measures approved in the Smithsonian Agreement were not technically legal under the Original Articles, they were recommended by the IMF on the basis of consensus, and had the Agreement stood up, it would not have been difficult to draft amendments to the Articles to reflect the new practices, under a regime of 'stable but adjustable par values'. This effort, however, soon broke down, as described in the preceding chapter.

A second effort aimed at more fundamental reform of international monetary law, looking to symmetry in the international monetary system. The central idea, based on a presentation first made by the United States,[3] was that the goal of a sound monetary system was equilibrium, and that persistent surplus and persistent deficit in a country's balance of payments were both wrong, and equally so. Proposals largely based on this idea were considered over a two-year period by a Committee of the Board of Governors of the Fund on Reform of the International Monetary System and Related Issues established by the Fund in the summer of 1972, generally known as the Committee of Twenty.[4]

---

[1] The General Counsel of the IMF, in an interesting footnote to an analysis of August 15, wrote:

Other members were released from the obligation to maintain the effectiveness of the parties of their currencies with the U.S. dollar, but were they released from the obligation to maintain parities among their own currencies? The answer probably is that they were not, but the next question is whether there was any practicable way of performing this obligation, given the dominance of the dollar as a reserve and intervention currency. (Joseph Gold, 'Developments in the International Monetary System, The International Monetary Fund, and International Monetary Law since 1971', 174 *Recueil des Cours* 107, 194, and n. 216, p. 347 (Hague Acad. Int'l Law 1982-I) (hereafter Gold, *Hague Lectures*))

[2] See Ch. 16, Sect. 16.9(c).

[3] See in particular the address of George P. Shultz, US Secretary of the Treasury, to the 1972 Annual Meeting of the Fund and World Bank, 67 *Dep't of State Bull.* 460, 463–4 (23 Oct. 1972); 1 *IMF Survey* 70 (9 Sept. 1972); Summary Proceedings of 1972 Annual Meeting of IMF, 153.

[4] The popular name of the Committee reflected the fact that its membership corresponded to the constituencies represented in the Executive Board of the Fund, but at the level of finance minister or principal deputy.

(a) The Outline of Reform

The proponents of reform pointed out that while some discipline had been imposed on states in deficit, through conditionality accompanying drawings from the Fund and conditions imposed by other creditors, no comparable discipline had been imposed on states in persistent surplus, such as Germany and in particular Japan. Just as states in deficit had regularly been pressured to reduce government spending, raise interest rates, tighten credit, improve investment opportunities, and in some circumstances devalue their currency, so comparable 'remedies' were available for countries in surplus—increased imports, greater foreign assistance or long-term loans, lower domestic interest rates or other stimuli to domestic demand, or revaluation of their currency. If states in persistent surplus did not adopt these measures on their own, the international community should have the means to compel them to do so.

The Committee of Twenty and its Committee of Deputies seriously considered proposals designed to turn the idea of symmetry into positive law.[5] A number of techniques were suggested based on 'objective indicators', generally related to growth or decline in reserves over stated periods. If a state departed from equilibrium targets and declined to take corrective measures, a series of graduated sanctions, labelled 'pressures', would be imposed by the Fund, either automatically unless the Fund voted otherwise, or upon affirmative vote by the Fund. The pressures on surplus controls could include a charge on excessive reserve accumulation, a requirement that excess reserves be deposited with the Fund without interest, suspension of entitlement to future allocations of SDRs,[6] an unfavourable report by the Fund, and even authorization to other states to apply discriminatory trade or currency restrictions against the offending states.[7]

As an intellectual effort, the product of the Committee of Twenty, published in June 1974 under the title of *Outline of Reform* with Annexes,[8] was an impressive achievement, and it did have some lasting effect on the way the international community viewed the monetary system. As a project for amendment of the legal regime governing the obligations of states, the *Outline of Reform* was a failure, one of the great might-have-beens of history.

(b) Acceptance of Floating Exchange Rates

As the Committee of Twenty was completing its work in the fall of 1973, the world's attention was diverted from long-term reform to the massive rise

---

[5] See IMF, *Outline of Reform: Documents of the Committee of Twenty* (IMF 1974).
[6] See Ch. 16, Sect. 16.8.
[7] See *Outline of Reform*, Annex 1 and 2, pp. 22–30; see also Paul Volcker and Toyoo Gyohten, *Changing Fortunes*, 188–20 (1992).
[8] See n. 5 supra.

in oil prices, followed initially by sharp rise in unemployment as demand dropped both in the industrialized and in the non-oil developing countries, and thereafter by a realization that the economic crisis was not as grave as had been feared at first. The *Outline of Reform* had proceeded on the assumption that there would be a return to 'stable but adjustable par values'.[9] The OPEC coup and the world's adjustment thereto, as mentioned in the preceding chapter, led to the general (though not universal) perception that this was not the time to return to fixed exchange rates. Consensus on that point would probably not alone have doomed the movement toward symmetrical adjustment built into a new legal regime. But the oil shock—the unforeseen circumstance—gave a convenient excuse to governments that were in any event uneasy about the degree of scrutiny, and of obligation, that the reform plans would have imposed on member states.

At all events, no agreement could be reached on the proposals for long-term reform discussed in the Committee of Twenty. By the time the Committee's final report came out in June 1974, it was already clear that the political will to move in the direction pointed by the *Outline of Reform* was simply not there. On the other hand, opposition within the Fund and among member states to a regime of floating exchange rates for the long term—as contrasted with a stop-gap at a time of crisis—seemed to be dissolving.

(c)   Amending the Articles of Agreement

Since many states, as well as the staff of the Fund, were anxious for a 'return to legality', that left open a third track—in effect a plan to amend the Articles of Agreement to reflect actual behaviour, i.e. floating exchange rates, while establishing some discipline, i.e. rules of law, governing the conduct of States.[10] One recommendation of the Committee of Twenty that did win general acceptance was for establishment of an Interim Committee, which would continue to bring together senior officials of the relevant constituencies to plan the future even as they negotiated about the present.[11] Much of the negotiation of the Amended Articles was carried out in the Interim Committee.

By this time the United States government had become fully converted to a regime of floating exchange rates; some other governments of member

---

[9] See *Outline of Reform*, 11–12, 30–3.

[10] As the General Counsel of the Fund wrote several years later, just as the Fund was in the midst of its transition with respect to its charter—1974–5—the Fund was also in the middle of a general increase in quotas, the sixth in the Fund's history, and that this call for additional resources from all the member states was meeting considerable resistance. It would have been embarrassing, to say the least, to ask legislatures to appropriate additional funds to an organization in which member states were failing to perform fundamental obligations. Gold, *Hague Lectures* (n. 1 supra), 207–8. In this context, it seemed easier to change the obligations than the performance of states.

[11] See Ch. 16, Sect. 16.3. A companion Development Committee was created at the same time, and usually met in the same city on the same or following day as the Interim Committee.

states, led by France, still sought a return to par values, either immediately or after an interim period. Moreover, the United States, as well as the staff of the Fund, sought to reduce the role of gold as a reserve asset, now that its price fluctuated like that of other commodities. France, again the principal protagonist of a different view, sought for a time to retain the role of gold in the system.

Eventually a deal—or rather two deals—were struck between the United States and France, the first on gold in August 1975, the second on exchange rates in secret bilateral negotiations throughout the fall.[12] In November 1975 the first 'economic summit' of presidents and prime ministers of the leading countries was held at the Chateau de Rambouillet, 30 miles south-west of Paris. The communiqué from that conference, 'welcom[ing] the rapprochement, reached at the request of many other countries, between the views of the United States and France on the need for stability that the reform of the international monetary system must promote', set the course for the formal amendment process.[13] The amendments themselves, drafted over a two-year period by the legal staff of the Fund, were submitted to a meeting of the Interim Committee in Kingston, Jamaica in January of 1976.

Some further amendments, in particular to meet the concerns of the developing countries, were agreed on at Jamaica, and the final version of the proposed amendments was approved by the Executive Directors on March 31, 1976.[14] Thereafter the Board of Governors approved the Amended Articles by postal ballots, subject to submission to member states for acceptance in accordance with their respective constitutional procedures. The Amended Articles of Agreement entered into force on April 1, 1978, when 78 member states (three-fifths of the membership of 130), having four-fifths of the total voting power, had notified the Fund of their acceptance of the amendments.

17.2   SCOPE OF THE AMENDMENTS

The document submitted to the Board of Governors and thereafter to member states of the IMF was a complete version of the Articles of Agreement as they would read upon approval of the amendments. Certain provisions, notably Article I on the purposes of the Fund and Articles VIII and XIV

[12] For an interesting play-by-play description of the negotiations, in which the United States prevailed on the principal issue—floating rates with no legal or even moral commitment to return to par values, while France succeeded in introducing the concept of 'firm surveillance' over exchange rate policies by the Fund, see Margaret G. de Vries, *The International Monetary Fund 1972–78*, Vol. II, pp. 743–50 (1985) (Hereafter *IMF History 1972–78*). See also George P. Shultz and Kenneth W. Dam, *Economic Policy Beyond the Headlines*, 126–31 (2nd edn. 1977).

[13] Joint Declaration issued at Rambouillet 17 Nov. 1975, ¶11, 4 *IMF Survey*, 350 (24 Nov. 1975). This meeting also marked the beginning of what came to be known as the Group of Seven or G-7, which has met annually at the level of heads of state or government since that time.

[14] See 5 *IMF Survey*, 113 (19 Apr. 1976).

concerned with exchange restrictions, were not changed.[15] Other provisions, notably Article V concerning stand-by arrangements, extended arrangements and conditionality, were amended to codify practices that had been developed in the three decades of the Fund's existence,[16] and to eliminate reference to gold and the 'gold tranche' wherever they existed.[17] Also, the unit of account for use in the Articles of Agreement became the Special Drawing Right (SDR), in place of either dollars or gold, and the provisions on issuance of SDRs were modified.[18] Finally, the special majorities required to implement various authorities contained in the Articles of Agreement were raised from 80 to 85 percent of total voting power, with a view to retaining a veto for the United States (as well as for the European Community when voting as a bloc), despite reduction in their voting power in recognition of the greater economic strength of the oil-producing developing countries.[19] The key amendment was an entirely recast Article IV, designed to replace the par value system that had broken down, and to establish (or reestablish) a legal regime concerning the role of governments in respect to exchange rates and to some extent in respect to international economic relations generally.

17.3   NEW ARTICLE IV AND THE LAW OF EXCHANGE ARRANGEMENTS

(a)   Freedom to Choose

Article IV(2)(b) of the Amended Articles of Agreement provides that exchange arrangements of member states may include

(i)   the maintenance by a member of a value for its currency in terms of the special drawing right or another denominator, other than gold, selected by the member; or

(ii)   cooperative arrangements by which members maintain the value of their currencies in relation to the value of the currency or currencies of other members; or

(iii)   other exchange arrangements of a member's choice.

---

[15] Article 1 had been slightly changed in the First Amendment to the Articles, effective 1969, as shown in Ch. 16, Sect. 16.2, n. 9.

[16] See Ch. 16, Sect. 16.6.

[17] See e.g. Amended Articles, Art. III(3) concerning payments to the Fund when quotas are changed; Art. IV(2) concerning permissible exchange arrangements; and Art. V(3) concerning use of the Fund's general resources.

[18] See Amended Articles, Arts. XV–XX.

[19] See e.g. Amended Articles, Art. III(2)(c) concerning changes in quotas; Art. IV(4) concerning return to an exchange rate system based of 'stable but adjustable' par values; Art. XVIII(2) and (4) concerning allocation or cancellation of Special Drawing Rights; and Art. XXVIII(a) concerning acceptance of proposed amendments.

A number of critics have suggested that this outcome of the amendment process provided for no rule at all, just full freedom of choice.[20] In the event some states elected to maintain the value of their currency in terms of the SDR, whose value is determined by a basket of currencies, and thus tends to vary less than any given individual currency.[21] Other states have maintained the value of their currency in terms of 'another denominator', principally the US dollar, but also the French franc, the pound sterling, and other currencies. Still other states have linked their currencies to each other, while floating together against non-participating currencies. This was the system in effect on and off since 1972 among the members of the European Community, known at first as the 'snake', as it became more precise and formal, as the European Monetary System, and since 1999 as the European Economic and Monetary Union, based on a single currency, the *euro*.[22] Finally, a number of countries, including the United States, Japan, Canada, and (on and off) the United Kingdom, have adopted 'other exchange arrangements', i.e. they have permitted the value of their currency to be set by the market, with occasional intervention by the central bank but with no commitment to any given target rate.[23]

Each of these policies is permitted by Article IV, and member states can change their policies at any time, provided the Fund is promptly notified. There is no requirement of *prior* notification, however.[24]

(b) Obligations under Article IV

Notwithstanding the broad range of options permitted to member states, a number of constraints do apply with respect to exchange arrangements. According to Article IV(1), taken over in part from Article IV(4) of the Original Articles, each member undertakes to 'collaborate with the Fund and other members to assure orderly exchange arrangements and to promote *a*

---

[20] See e.g. Tom de Vries, 'Jamaica, or the Non-Reform of the International Monetary System', 54 *Foreign Affairs* 577 (1976); Alexandre Kafka, 'The International Monetary Fund: Reform Without Reconstruction', *Essays in Int'l Finance* No. 118 (Princeton Univ. Press 1976); Fritz Machlup, 'Between Outline and Outcome Reform Was Lost', and Robert Triffin, 'Jamaica: "Major Revision" or Fiasco', in Edward M. Bernstein *et al.* 'Reflections on Jamaica', *Essays in Int'l Finance*, No. 115, 30, 45 (Princeton Univ. Press 1976).

[21] See Ch. 16, Sect. 16.8.   [22] See Ch. 20.

[23] Still other variations on the above include pegging to another currency within wide margins (5 percent plus or minus) or changing the exchange rate against another currency frequently (the 'crawling peg') as for instance Brazil has often done vis-à-vis the US dollar. See, generally, Richard W. Edwards, *International Monetary Cooperation*, 521–6 (1985).

[24] Notification is required not only for a change from one option to another, but for a significant change within a given option, for instance with regard to policies related to floating or to calculating a basket of currencies against which a given currency is pegged. See Ex. Bd. No. 5712-(78/41), 23 Mar. 1978 and Attachment thereto, *Selected Decisions*, 8 (25th issue 2000); Edwards (n. 23 supra), 529–30.

stable system of exchange rates' (italics added).[25] In particular, each member shall

(i)   endeavor to direct its economic and financial policies toward the objective of fostering orderly economic growth with reasonable price stability, with due regard to its circumstances;

(ii)   seek to promote stability by fostering orderly underlying economic and financial conditions and a monetary system that does not tend to produce erratic disruptions;

(iii) avoid manipulating exchange rates of the international monetary system in order to prevent effective balance of payments adjustment or to gain an unfair competitive advantage over other members; and

(iv)   follow exchange policies compatible with the undertakings under this Section.

The first two obligations, evidently, are 'soft law'—'shall endeavor' and 'shall seek'—but they must be read together with the Fund's new authority to conduct surveillance over member states' exchange arrangements, as described below.

The third obligation is more specific—'shall . . . avoid manipulating'. Not many instances of direct breach of Article IV(1)(iii) are known, but one instance received substantial publicity and may be regarded as a 'leading case'.[26]

> In the early 1980s, Sweden pegged its currency to a trade-weighted basket of currencies centered on the German mark. On September 19, 1982, Olof Palme, after six years out of office, won re-election as prime minister. On October 8, his first full day back in office, Palme announced a devaluation of the Swedish krona of 16 percent. Palme said that the devaluation was intended to restore confidence in the krona and improve conditions for Swedish industry. The other Nordic countries, each of which had recently made small devaluations in their currencies, complained both publicly and to the IMF that Sweden had sought an unfair advantage by its large devaluation, which far exceeded what would have been necessary to restore the competitiveness of its industry.
>
> The Fund's Executive Board met in formal session within the week to consider Sweden's action, and thereafter the Managing Director held a 'special consultation' with Sweden pursuant to the Supplemental Surveillance Procedure.[27] There was no formal decision or sanction,

---

[25] The italicized words were the subject of a major controversy in the course of the negotiations over Article IV (Sect. 17.1 supra). At a dinner meeting of the Interim Committee in June 1975, the French Foreign Minister, working in English, thought agreement had been reached on 'a system of stable exchange rates'. When the text was made available next morning reading 'a stable system of exchange rates', the agreement fell apart and was not concluded for another half-year. The episode is described in *IMF History 1972–78*, 740.

[26] The episode is described in *The Times* (London), 9 Oct., p. 5; 12 Oct., p. 15; 18 Oct., p. 14 (1982).

[27] See Sect. 17.4 infra.

but it was generally understood within the Fund and the international financial community that Sweden had acted contrary to Article IV(1)(iii).[28] The practical effect was that while Finland followed the Swedish krona down, Denmark and Norway did not.

(c) Overseeing the International Monetary System

Article IV(3)(a) of the Amended Articles states the principle that the Fund 'shall oversee the international monetary system', and that it 'shall oversee the compliance of *each member* with its obligations' under Article IV(1). This statement, and in particular the emphasis on 'each member', is in some sense a survival of the much more ambitious proposals of the Committee of Twenty, though without any of the sanctions and pressures there contemplated. Article IV(3) goes on to provide, in paragraph (b) that in order to fulfill its oversight functions under paragraph (a), the Fund 'shall exercise firm surveillance over the exchange rate policies of members,' and 'shall adopt specific principles for the guidance of all members with regard to those policies.'

Critics of the Amended Articles have pointed out that these provisions contain no real obligations;[29] but Article IV(3) may be seen as enabling legislation, authorizing the international community as represented by the IMF to carry out surveillance over exchange rate policies of all member states, whether or not they apply for drawings or stand-by arrangements, and whether or not they maintain exchange restrictions that require approval by or consultation with the Fund. At a minimum no member state may refuse, without violating Article IV(3), to supply information when requested by the Fund, and no member state may decline to enter into consultation with the Fund about its exchange rate policies. Whether there is more to Article IV(3), for instance whether Patria can complain to the Fund about Xandia's exchange rate policies and require Patria to defend and justify those policies, is not clear, except perhaps in the case of manipulation, as in the episode concerning devaluation of the Swedish krona in 1982.[30] In the trade field, governments, parliaments, courts, and international panels often debate whether a particular measure is 'GATT-illegal'; no comparable complaint system, and no comparable jurisprudence has arisen, classifying practices of member states as 'IMF-illegal'.

For instance, in the first half of 1992, the US Federal Reserve System several times lowered interest rates, in an effort to stimulate the

---

[28] See *IMF Annual Report 1983*, 62–3, 65, and 104.
[29] See e.g. Triffin (n. 20 supra), 47:

Frankly, I find this text more worthy of a slapstick comedy than of a solemn treaty defining a new international monetary system. The only obligations I can find [in Article IV] . . . are so general and obvious as to appear largely superfluous.

[30] See text at n. 26 supra.

American economy, which seemed to be coming out of recession more slowly than expected. At the same time the German Bundesbank raised interest rates, in an effort to curb the threat of inflation believed to inhere in the consequences of the unification of East and West Germany. One result of these divergent policies was to drive the exchange rate of the US dollar down against the German mark (and the European Monetary System as a whole) by more than would be justified by underlying facts such as relative productivity or domestic prices. It is not known what went on in individual consultations between the IMF and the United States and Germany; no formal complaint mechanism, however, was available under the IMF Articles relevant to this situation, and it could not be said that either Germany or the United States was failing to carry out an obligation undertaken in the Amended Articles of Agreement.[31]

17.4   SURVEILLANCE BY THE IMF

Even before the Amended Articles entered into effect, the Executive Directors issued a decision in implementation of the requirement of Article IV(3) that the Fund 'shall adopt specific principles for the guidance of all members.'[32] The jurisdiction of the Fund, it seemed, had been expanded in the Amended Articles, at the same time as the specific rules for member states' actions with respect to exchange rates had nearly disappeared.

(a)   The Decision on Surveillance

In their Decision on Surveillance of April 29, 1977, the Executive Directors set out a number of developments that might indicate the need for discussion with a member, i.e. developments that might indicate policies inconsistent with the overall commitment to assure orderly exchange arrangements and to propose a stable system of exchange rates:

(i)   protracted large-scale intervention in one direction in the exchange market;

(ii)   an unsustainable level of official or quasi-official borrowing, or excessive and prolonged short-term official or quasi-official lending, for balance of payments purposes;

---

[31] In its *1992 Annual Report*, reflecting consultations pursuant to Article IV, the IMF criticized the United States for not raising interest rates and reducing its deficit, but did not criticize Germany's interest rate policy. *IMF Annual Report 1992*, 16–18, 19–29.

[32] Ex. Bd. Dec. No. 5392-(77/63) 29 Apr. 1977, reproduced as amended in *Selected Decisions*, 10 (25th issue 2000). The decision was regarded as so important, and had been subject to so much debate, that it was adopted in tentative form by the Executive Directors, subject to approval by the Interim Committee. See *IMF History 1972–78*, Vol. II pp. 846–7. The decision entered into force definitively on April 1, 1978, at the same time as the entry into force of the Amended Articles of Agreement.

(iii)   (a)   the introduction, substantial intensification, or prolonged maintenance, for balance of payments purposes of restrictions on, or incentives for, current transactions or payments, or

      (b)   the introduction or substantial modification for balance of payments purposes of restrictions on, or incentives for, the inflow or outflow of capital;

(iv)   the pursuit, for balance of payments purposes, of monetary and other domestic financial policies that provide abnormal encouragement or discouragement to capital flows; and

(v)   behaviour of the exchange rate that appears to be unrelated to underlying economic and financial conditions including factors affecting competitiveness and long-term capital movements.[33]

The existence of one or more of these conditions does not demonstrate conclusively that the state in question is out of compliance with its obligations under the Amended Articles. It does, however, place the onus on the member state to offer an explanation or justification, and to listen to—if not necessarily to obey—the advice of the Fund.

As Professor Edwards has pointed out, taken literally items (ii), (iii)(a), (iii)(b), and (iv) seem to be limited to actions taken for balance of payments *purposes*, whereas what should concern the international community, and therefore the Fund in its surveillance and consultation practice, is the *effect* on the balance of payments of the state in question or other states.[34] In practice it seems unlikely that a state can resist an inquiry from the Fund on the basis that a given policy had an unintended effect on the balance of payments. For instance, a state's change in interest rates may have been made for domestic purposes only, but—particularly if the state is the issuer of a currency held by foreigners, such as the dollar, the mark, the pound, or the yen—the action may well have significant impact not only on that state's balance of payments but on the balance of payments of numerous other states. The clear impact of Article IV of the Amended Articles and the Decision on Surveillance is that no narrow fence is to be drawn around the scope of scrutiny by the Fund over the economic policies of member states at a macroeconomic level.

(b)   The Reach of the Fund's Jurisdiction

Paragraph 3 of the Principles of Fund Surveillance contained in the Decision, moving beyond focus on exchange rate policies, calls for comprehensive analysis of the *general economic situation* and *economic policy strategy* of

---

[33] See also Decision No. 6026-(79/13), 22 Jan. 1979, *Selected Decisions*, 10 (25th issue 2000), authorizing the Managing Director to initiate a discussion, and thereafter, if he considers that the matter is of importance, an ad hoc consultation whenever he considers that the behaviour of a member's exchange arrangement may be important or may have important effects on other members.

[34] See Edwards, *International Monetary Collaboration*, 559–60 (1985).

the member state. Further, it provides that the Fund 'shall recognize that domestic as well as external policies can contribute to timely adjustment of the balance of payments.' Though the Decision was deliberately worded more vaguely than some inhouse drafts had proposed, it seems fair to summarize the Principles as authorizing the Managing Director to raise with a member state, at least on a confidential basis, almost any matter of the member's economic policy that has effect on the member's exchange rate or the international economy.

The last sentence of Article IV(3) of the Amended Articles, which is the authority for the Principles on Fund Surveillance, states that the principles

shall respect the domestic social and political policies of members, and in applying these principles the Fund shall pay due regard to the circumstances of members.

This suggests that there is a line between matters within the advisory jurisdiction of the Fund and matters 'essentially within the domestic jurisdiction' of member states, though where to draw the line is not easy.[35] Indeed in later developments, particularly in connection with major financial crises in Latin America, South-east Asia, and Russia in the 1980s and 1990s, the scope of inquiry and even instruction by the Fund moved considerably beyond the understanding reflected in the amended Articles of Agreement as drafted and adopted in the 1970s. However, these always controversial developments took place in the context of massive infusion of funds, both from the IMF itself and in programs linked to approval by the IMF.[36] Thus technically the intrusiveness and (as some viewed it) impingement on sovereignty involved conditionality under Article V on Use of the Fund's Resources rather than surveillance under Article IV on Obligations Regarding Exchange Arrangements. More generally, however, the question of the reach of the Fund's jurisdiction is related to the question of symmetry raised in the *Outline of Reform* but not resolved. It also became apparent in the regional crises in Latin America and South-east Asia that Fund surveillance did not accomplish the objectives envisioned when the Articles of Agreement were amended in the 1970s, and that surveillance has not meant—at least has not achieved—the degree of transparency needed to carry out the mandate of Article IV(3)(a)—'The Fund shall oversee the international monetary system in order to ensure its effective operation.'

Viewing the Principles of Surveillance from a legal perspective, one may suggest the following formulation: *The basic monetary and fiscal policies of a member state are appropriate for inquiry and comment by the international community represented by the IMF, but detailed choices of policy come within the restriction stated in the last sentence of Article IV(3).*

---

[35] The quoted phrase comes, of course, from Article 2(7) of the United Nations Charter.
[36] See Ch. 18.

For instance, it is acceptable for the Fund to urge that Patria's budgetary deficit be reduced, and further that government subsidies make up an excessive component of that deficit. It may even be appropriate to set out specific targets for achieving the desired reduction within a stated period of time, as is done in connection with stand-by arrangements under Article V. But it would not be within the mandate of the Fund to suggest that the national health service should impose charges for filling prescriptions, that veterans' benefits should be reduced, or that farm subsidies should be phased out. If any one of these measures could cure Patria's deficit, it would not be within the authority of the Fund to choose among them. However, if the Fund concludes that one of the measures alone would not suffice, it would not be out of bounds for the Fund to say so, in a Report submitted to, and approved by the Executive Directors.[37]

(c) Surveillance in Practice

Typically, a team of four economists and a secretary from the IMF travels to Patria—in principle once a year—and stays for two to three weeks of research and meetings with officials of Patria's ministry of finance, central bank, and other agencies, and sometimes also non-governmental groups such as trade unions and business organizations. The visits are designed both to gather information and to convey to the relevant Patrian officials the thinking of the IMF about its problems and proposed solutions.

Before traveling to Patria, the country team will have prepared a briefing paper raising questions of both fact and policy, focused on Patria's exchange rate arrangements, its balance of payments position, and its adjustment needs. The briefing paper will have been cleared with the relevant area department at the IMF, the Fund's Policy Development and Review Department, and the Managing Director or one the Deputy Managing Directors.

Following the visit of the country team, a report is prepared—generally about twenty pages long (plus a more detailed back-up report)—for review by the various departments, as well as by the Executive Director responsible for Patria. Thereafter, about three months after initiation of the process, a discussion of Patria will be held by the Executive Board, followed by a summing up by the chairman, the Managing Director or one of his deputies. The summing up will form the basis of a Public Information Notice, as well as publication in the Annual Report of the Fund or the semi-annual World Economic Outlook.[38]

---

[37] For development of this approach, see Lowenfeld, Review of Kenneth Dam, 'The Rules of the Game: Reform and Evaluation in the International Monetary System', 50 *U. Chi. L. Rev.* 380, 397–8 (1983).

[38] See Edward H. Brau, 'The Consultation Process of the Fund', 18 *Finance and Development* No. 4, p. 13 (Dec. 1981); also *External Evaluation of IMF Surveillance*: Report by a Group of Independent Experts, 24–8 (IMF 1999).

Judging by the published reports, the practice of IMF consultations pursuant to Article IV has been consistent with the suggestions made in the preceding section concerning the reach of the Fund's jurisdiction. In some instances, however, the consultations have come rather close to the line, as may be illustrated by excerpts from the *IMF Annual Reports 1991* and *1992.*

France [1991]: . . . The Board agreed that the overall tax burden in France was too high. The Government needed to redouble its efforts to curb nonpriority spending. Particular concern in this respect was expressed about the social security funds; prospects for spending on pensions and health care were especially worrisome. The Board commended the authorities plans to broaden the base of social security contributions to include non-wage income, as this would lower the opportunity cost of hiring labor. . . . Directors were concerned about possible actions that would hinder labor market adjustment by raising the relative cost of unskilled labor; they were also concerned that measures to index minimum wages to average wages would undermine efforts to sustain wage moderation and reduce unemployment. They urged the authorities to address labor market imbalances, mainly through manpower training programs, and not to add to rigidities in the labor market. . . .

United Kingdom [1991] . . . While deepening recession was a matter of concern, Directors believed that the key policy challenge facing the authorities was to reduce inflation to the level of the United Kingdom's low-inflation partners in the ERM;[39] in this connection, they warmly welcomed the Chancellor of the Exchequer's statement that bearing down on inflation is and will remain the Government's top priority. . . .

Italy [1992]: Directors welcomed the adoption of structural measures aimed at improving tax administration and broadening the tax base. At the same time, they urged rapid implementation of fundamental structural reforms in the area of health services, pensions, and public sector employment. The progress made toward privatization was welcomed, but the sale of public assets was to be seen as a means of reducing public debt and not as a substitute for fiscal adjustment over the long run. . . .

United States [1992]: . . . A number of concerns clouded the medium-term outlook, in the Board's view. These included low national savings, with adverse implications for domestic investment, productivity growth, international trade, and the external current account; underlying inflation; and problems facing depositary institutions. Also requiring attention, in the view of some Directors, was the state of the health-care sector. . . .

As for measures that might help achieve the medium-term fiscal goal, the Board favored an emphasis on spending cuts, but felt that additional revenue measures would also be required. Possible revenue measures could include, in the view of many Directors, elimination of certain tax expenditures . . . and further excise taxes on gasoline or, more generally, on energy use, which would also address environmental concerns. A few Directors preferred revenue increases that relied on more broadly based taxes.

If the summaries here quoted do seem to have something of an intrusive quality, it is important to stress that the consultations do not reflect 'decisions',

---

[39] Exchange Rate Mechanism of the European Monetary System.

whether phrased in terms of 'the Board', 'Directors', 'some directors', or 'many directors.' The suggestion, made among others by the IMF's long-time general counsel,[40] that 'conclusions' be made more formal, for instance that they be characterized as 'decisions', has never been adopted.

The continuing tensions concerning the reach of surveillance by the Fund may be illustrated by the report in 1999 of a group of independent experts commissioned by the IMF to evaluate Fund surveillance, and by the reaction to the report on the part of the Fund's directors and staff.[41]

The outside experts wrote:

We recommend that surveillance focus, above all, on the core issues of exchange rate policy and directly associated macroeconomic policies, in particular the international implications of such policies. Other analysis should only be underaken if directly relevant.[42]

The Managing Director, Mr. Camdessus, responded on behalf of the Fund staff:

This recommendation runs counter to most of the pressure on us from the Board and the membership, who have given increasing emphasis to the interactions between macroeconomic and structural policies, ranging even beyond the financial sector. The evaluators base their recommendation in part on evidence that Fund advice outside the core areas is not regarded by the authorities as commanding the same authority as that on macroeconomic issues. The staff presents a careful response to the recommendation for more focus; we conclude, as they do, that while the core issues should continue to be at the center of the surveillance process, other areas will—depending on the country—have also to be included in the surveillance process. At a minimum, social sector issues and poverty will have to be discussed in most Article IV reports. In order to make surveillance in these areas more effective, the Fund will have to further strengthen its cooperation with other institutions, primarily of course the World Bank.[43]

The issue was debated by the Executive Directors, and the Managing Director summed up:

Directors underlined the substantial common ground between the evaluators' report and the Fund's own internal evaluations. They noted, in particular, the need to (i) revisit the definition of the core areas; (ii) give more explicit attention to international aspects of a country's macroeconomic policies and spillover issues; (iii) focus more on cross-country comparisons and regional developments; (iv) devote substantially more attention to vulnerability analysis; and (v) give more emphasis to financial sector and capital account issues. . . .

Nevertheless, Directors expressed a range of views on which issues should be considered generally as noncore issues in the context of Fund surveillance. Most

---

[40] Joseph Gold, 'Strengthening the Soft International Law of Exchange Arrangements', 77 *Am. J. Int'l L.* 443, at 483 (1983); see also Edwards (n. 34 supra), 577–80.

[41] *External Evaluation of IMF Surveillance* (n. 38 supra).

[42] Id., Appendix IV—Recommendations, p. 90, para. 4.

[43] Id., Statement by the Managing Director, 96, para. 6.

Directors thought that one of the main recommendations of the report—that surveillance should focus only on the core areas of exchange rate policy and directly associated macroeconomic policies—ran counter to the demands of the membership and the international community for increasing emphasis on the interactions between macroeconomic, structural, and social policies. They viewed the broader focus of surveillance as appropriate in light of global developments and the need for a surveillance process that remains relevant to the policy challenges faced by Fund members . . . Other Directors, however, felt that Fund surveillance had moved inappropriately beyond the original core issues, including into areas such as labor markets, pension reform, social policy, and governance. . . .

Directors supported increased attention to the international and regional aspects of surveillance. They saw the need for increased cross-country comparisons—in which the Fund has a unique advantage—in the context of greater emphasis on regional and international developments. . . . However, Directors agreed that, while the Article IV process should be enriched through the integration of global and regional dimensions, it should remain clearly focused on a country's own policies.

The issue remains, as does much of this area, a mixture of politics, economics, and law.

(d) Summary

The evident truth that the actions of the major states have effect on one another and on the international economy as a whole is now written into positive law in the Articles of Agreement and the Decision on Surveillance. The scope of review by the international community of actions of sovereign states has widened, covering not only exchange rates, but interest rates, monetary policy, fiscal policy, trade policy, and even some countries' social agenda and priorities.

The international community has not been prepared, however, to turn scrutiny into judgment, or the search for equilibrium into obligation. In some instances, of course, the advice of the IMF is persuasive from its own force of analysis; in other instances, what the IMF says becomes an ingredient in domestic policy debates. But the idea that the IMF could prescribe conduct under amended Article IV comparable to what the Fund prescribes as a condition for stand-by arrangements under Article V has not proved viable, if indeed it was ever seriously held. As the major industrial countries have essentially withdrawn from the practice of applying for stand-by arrangements, this has meant that the Fund's economic prescriptions have fallen predominantly on the developing nations as well as its newer members from the former Soviet bloc.[44]

The IMF remains an important forum for discussion of the international economy, and an essential participant in certain types of multilateral operations, such as the provision of debt relief and restructuring in the early 1980s (see Chapter 18). But such coordination of economic policies as does go on

---

[44] See Sect. 17.5 at n. 53 infra.

among the major industrial countries, loosely organized as the Group of Seven[45] or the Group of Five,[46] or the Basle Club,[47] is conducted largely without legal constraint or major input on the part of the IMF.

17.5   CONDITIONALITY UNDER THE AMENDED ARTICLES OF AGREEMENT

(a)   Conditionality Codified

The practice of stand-by arrangements entitling member states to draw on the resources of the Fund had, as described in the preceding chapter grown up without any express provision in the original Articles of Agreement.[48] In the Amended Articles, the term 'stand-by arrangement' is expressly defined,[49] and the concept of conditionality which underlies stand-by arrangements is spelled out in Article V(3).

Article V(3)(b) sets out the conditions for purchase from the Fund of currencies of other members in exchange for the members' own currencies, which are understood to be applicable to stand-by arrangements as well. Indeed, though in theory, and in prior practice among the developed states, stand-by arrangements were often used as insurance and not drawn upon, the more recent practice is that all drawings are based on a stand-by arrangement or comparable facility, and usually the first drawing is made as soon as the stand-by is approved.

In order to be entitled to make a purchase (drawing), the member state must meet four conditions:

(i)   The purpose for which it intends to use the resources of the Fund must be in accordance with the Articles of Agreement *and the Fund's policies* (emphasis added);

(ii)   The member must represent that it has a need to make the purchase because of its balance of payments or reserve position or developments in its reserves;

(iii)   The proposed purchase would be a reserve tranche purchase [i.e. secured by gold or other convertible assets held by the Fund][50] or would not cause the Fund's holding of the member's currency to exceed 200 percent of its quota;

(iv)   The Fund has not previously declared . . . that the member desiring to purchase is ineligible to use the general resources of the Fund.

---

[45] United States, United Kingdom, France, Germany, Japan, Italy, and Canada.

[46] All the above except Italy and Canada.

[47] The members of the Bank for International Settlements, the central bankers' bank, whose officials meet at the headquarters of the BIS in Basle once a month.

[48] See Ch. 16, Sect. 16.7.

[49] Article XXX (b) reads:

Stand-by arrangement means a decision of the Fund by which a member is assured that it will be able to make purchases from the General Resources Account in accordance with the terms of the decision during a specified period and up to a specified amount.

[50] Compare the gold tranche under the Original Articles, Ch. 16, Sect. 16.6.

Article V(4) provides that conditions (iii) and (iv) may be waived, and indeed the limit on drawings to 200 percent of quota has regularly been waived.[51] The first two conditions may not be waived, however, and Article V(3)(c) confirms that except for drawings under the reserve tranche, 'the Fund *shall examine* a request for a purchase to determine whether it would be consistent with the provisions of the Fund Agreement and the policies adopted under them.' Thus conditionality is firmly established in the Amended Articles of Agreement, and the protracted debate about conditionality described below really could not be about whether drawings should be made subject to conditions, but about how strict the conditions should be, and whether the conditions should contain specific targets and performance criteria.

(b)   Conditionality and the Changed Clientele of the IMF

For a number of reasons, but chiefly because the need to maintain a par value, as under the Original Articles, no longer prevails, developed countries have not drawn on the general resources of the Fund since Italy and the United Kingdom made massive drawings in 1977.[52] For developing countries, which typically are able to pay for imports or service their debts only with foreign exchange, stand-by arrangements have become fairly common, and for some countries, the IMF has become the only source of external finance.[53] As the IMF has thus gradually changed its role from serving the same states that supplied its usable currencies to serving as a source of finance for developing countries, the controversy about conditionality has become largely a north–south debate. The official historian of the IMF writes that 'by 1978 attacks on the Fund's conditionality had become vitriolic.'[54]

Sir Joseph Gold wrote that:

The word conditionality refers . . . to the policies that the Fund wishes to see a member follow in order that it can use the Fund's resources in accordance with the purposes and provisions of the Articles.[55]

Applicants for drawings or stand-by arrangements might well say that 'wishes' is too weak a term, and that 'insists' would be more accurate. In fact the conditions set out in the letter of intent (and sometimes in side letters as

---

[51] See Sect. 17.6 concerning Extended Arrangements as well as a variety of special facilities established by the Fund.

[52] See Margaret Garritson de Vries, *The International Monetary Fund 1972–1978*, vol. I chs. 23–24 (1985).

[53] In the financial year ending April 30, 2001, 25 stand-by arrangements and 12 extended arrangements were in effect, in favour of 33 member states. Of these, 12 were formerly communist states (or components of communist states) and 21 were developing countries. See *IMF Annual Report 2001*, tables II.3, II.4. In addition, 44 arrangments were in effect under the so-called Poverty Reduction and Growth Facility (see Sect. 17.6(f)), in favour of 40 least developed countries.

[54] *International Monetary Fund 1972–1978* (n. 52 supra), vol. I, p. 489.

[55] Joseph Gold, *Conditionality*, 2 (IMF Pamphlet Series, No. 31 (1979)).

well) are negotiated, typically between an IMF staff mission to the country concerned and the country's ministry of finance and central bank.

In principle, the conditions sought by the Fund, in implementation of stand-by or extended arrangements under Article V, like the questions raised in implementation of the surveillance functions under Article IV, concern macroeconomic targets—the money supply, budget deficits, trade balances, government credit, bank credit, and so on. In practice, the targets and performance criteria often became quite detailed, particularly when stand-by or extended arrangements entitled the applicant country to draw for three years or even longer. Inevitably the critics asserted that the Fund was intervening in the internal affairs of the applicant country.

Criticism of Fund conditionality has been partly about independence and sovereignty, and partly about specific prescriptions by the Fund.[56] Typically these prescriptions have called for reduced government borrowing, 'fiscal responsibility', reduction in domestic subsidies, especially for food, and generally emphasis on a policy that balance of payments deficits should not just be financed, but that the underlying conditions must be addressed within a finite time period. When developing countries have maintained an exchange rate pegged to another currency,[57] Fund missions have often recommended devaluation, and have discouraged restraints on imports and exchange controls. The critics' repeated charge was that the Fund ignored or neglected political and social factors, from increases in unemployment attributed to the Fund's prescriptions to riots following a rise in the price of basic foodstuffs or housing when the Fund 'ordered' an end to subsidies.[58] The defenders, from the staff of the Fund including successive Managing Directors to academic and government observers from the developed countries, argued on the contrary, that conditionality was the key contribution that the Fund could make, in contrast to commercial and even individual governmental lenders, and that the Fund's prescriptions called for doing what borrowing countries should be doing whether or not they were committed to the Fund.

(c)   The Guidelines on Conditionality

As the debate about conditionality was carried out within the IMF and in the capitals of developed and developing countries,[59] the IMF decided to

---

[56] It is worth noting that the Fund generally avoids discussion of military expenditures on the ground that this is too sensitive, though of course the subject is far from irrelevant to a discussion of overall government expenditures, as well as of imports and exports.

[57] Compare Sect. 17.3.

[58] For a thorough inquiry into the impact of Fund conditionality, particularly on social welfare in developing countries, see, *IMF Conditionality 1980–1991*, a research report by the IMF Assessment Project, Alexis de Tocqueville Institution (1992). See esp. Part 3: 'Social Welfare Policy and Fund Conditionality'.

[59] See *International Monetary Fund 1972–1978*, vol. 2, ch. 25, 'Conditionality: A Disputed Issue Arises'; ch. 26, 'Conditionality: the Fund Answers.'

conduct a formal review of its practices. The review proceeded for eight months in 1978–9, and resulted in a new Decision of the Executive Board, generally referred to as the *Guidelines on Conditionality*.[60] For over two decades, the *Guidelines* have remained the basic outline setting forth the techniques and requirements for stand-by and extended arrangements by which the Fund provides financial assistance to member states.

In Guideline 1, the Fund seeks to link regular consultations under Article IV with stand-by arrangements under Article V, the point being that consultations under the surveillance practice may serve to begin necessary adjustment at an early stage, 'including corrective measures that would enable the Fund to approve a stand-by arrangement.'[61]

The most important new feature was the emphasis on performance criteria, accompanied by a policy of staged entitlement to draw. Guideline 6 provides:

Phasing and performance clauses will be omitted in stand-by arrangements that do not go beyond the first credit tranche. They will be included in all other stand-by arrangements but these clauses will be applicable only to purchases beyond the first credit tranche.

Since the late 1970s, provision for phasing, i.e. drawing on the Fund's resources at regular intervals, and for performance clauses, looking to specified targets concerning rates of inflation, loss of reserves, money supply, and other objective criteria, have come to be the normal practice for stand-by arrangements beyond the first credit tranche.[62] The inference is that if a country does not live up to the performance targets, the right to continue to draw in the next stated phase may be suspended, either automatically if the stand-by arrangement says 'Patria will not draw . . .', or upon decision of the Executive Directors. Drawing rights under stand-by arrangements have in fact been suspended more often than is made public.[63] More commonly, an emergency consultation will be held, the targets will be adjusted somewhat, and a supplemental or amended Letter of Intent will be submitted to the Fund, or a short-term waiver will be granted.

---

[60] *Use of Fund's General Resources and Stand-By Arrangements*, Decision No. 6056-(79/38) of 2 Mar. 1979, *Selected Decisions*, 149 (25th issue 2000).

[61] The experience in the early 1980s leading up to the debt crises in Mexico, Brazil, and other countries that had not resorted to borrowing from the Fund, and again in the 1990s with respect to South-east Asia, suggests that this link has not been effective, at least where other sources of credit were available. See Ch. 18.

[62] Initially, drawings were scheduled at quarterly or semi-annual intervals. In 1985, in a further Decision setting out 'operational guidelines', the Fund provided that:

There would be no fewer than four purchases during a 12-month period of the arrangement, five being the preferred course of action. The purchase dates would also be distributed as evenly as possible throughout the arrangement. (Decision No. 7925–(85/38), 8 Mar. 1985 as amended, ¶(4), *Selected Decisions*, 149 (25th issue 2000))

[63] See e.g. Edwards, *International Monetary Collaboration*, p. 268, n. 179 and sources there cited.

Inevitably, the use of performance criteria raises again the question of the reach of the Fund's jurisdiction. Guideline 4 provides:

In helping members to devise adjustment programs, the Fund will pay due regard to the domestic social and political objectives, the economic priorities, and the circumstances of members, including the causes of their balance of payments problems.

Guideline 9, however, while reciting the normal emphasis on macroeconomic variables, is careful not to confine performance criteria, if more specific criteria are necessary:

The number and content of performance criteria may vary because of the diversity of problems and institutional arrangements of members. Performance criteria will be limited to those that are necessary to evaluate implementation of the program with a view to ensuring the achievement of its objectives. Performance criteria will normally be confined to (i) macroeconomic variables, and (ii) those necessary to implement specific provisions of the Articles or policies adopted under them. Performance criteria may relate to other variables only in exceptional cases when they are essential for the effectiveness of the member's program because of their macroeconomic impact.

Once a case-by-case approach is suggested, the question of discrimination is bound to be raised. Guideline 8 provides:

The Managing Director will ensure adequate coordination in the application of policies relating to the use of the Fund's general resources with a view to maintaining the nondiscriminatory treatment of members.

Thus the African, Western Hemisphere and Asian departments of the Fund are not, a priori, supposed to have different priorities, as critics had sometimes complained. Guideline 10 adds that—again 'in exceptional circumstances'—it is possible that new performance criteria will be set out in the course of consultations during the period of the stand-by that were not contained in the original arrangement, especially when the stand-by extends over two or more years, or the period of the stand-by is different from the country's fiscal year or planning period.

All of the *Guidelines* were put to the test—and to a considerable extent stretched—in the crises in Latin America, South-east Asia, and Russia described in Chapter 18.

17.6   SPECIAL FACILITIES OF THE FUND: RESOURCES BEYOND
THE FORMAL LIMITS

Over the more than half century of its existence, the IMF has in many ways changed its character, and expanded the programs under which it grants assistance, essentially to developing countries, and more recently to so-called 'economies in transition', i.e. former members of the Soviet Union or the Soviet bloc. Thus the original rules, as codified in Article V of the

Amended Articles (Section 17.5(a)) have come to serve more as a model than as a limitation on the Fund's activities.

All of the programs and facilities have been designed to increase the scope of available financial assistance; all of the programs carry some form of conditionality. On the one hand the scope and volume of the Fund's lending has been greatly expanded, with the help of increased quotas and substantial borrowing by the Fund (see Section 17.7). On the other hand the law administered by the Fund—in the sense of constraints on the actions of the beneficiaries—is vastly expanded.

A selection of the programs is described in this Section, not with the aim of providing a complete menu of the available facilities but with the aim of illustrating the progression and the approach of the IMF and its member states in the changing international monetary system.

(a)   The Extended Fund Facility

As the Fund was moving closer to becoming more involved with developing countries, it concluded that in many instances provision should be made for longer-term assistance than would be available under the time and quota limits applicable to the typical stand-by arrangements that had been made since the 1950s. Accordingly, in 1974 the Fund established an Extended Fund Facility, pursuant to which member states could enter into so-called *Extended Arrangements*.[64] Essentially, an extended arrangement is similar to a traditional stand-by arrangement, except that the assistance is granted for longer periods, and in amounts larger in relation to quotas than for ordinary stand-by arrangements.[65] The repayment period may run between four and a half to as long as ten years.

(b)   The Compensatory Financing Facility

As early as the 1960s, the IMF established a Compensatory Financing Facility, designed to tide member states dependent on export of particular commodities—coffee, copper, cocoa, etc.—over temporary difficulties caused by a fall in the world price likely to be reversed, or by a shortfall in the country's output caused by a non-recurring event such as a flood or drought or frost.[66] The idea was that the Fund would lend (i.e. permit the

---

[64] Decision No. 4377–(74/114), 13 Sept. 1974, reproduced as amended several times in *Selected Decisions*, p. 169 (25th issue, 2000).

[65] Accordingly, the Decision states (in ¶4(b)) that when necessary and if the other conditions are met, the Fund will be prepared to grant a waiver of the limits in Article V(3)(a)(iii) concerning the maximum holding by the Fund of the purchasing member's currency.

[66] *Compensatory Financing of Export Fluctuations*, Ex. Bd. Dec. No. 1477 (63/8) adopted 27 Feb. 1963, *Selected Decisions*, 62 (8th issue, 1976). A much expanded facility, entitled Compensatory and Contingency Financing Facility, reflecting consolidation of numerous decisions and amended more than 20 times, is reproduced as Decision 8955-(88/126), 23 Aug. 1988, *Selected Decisions,* 220–30 (25th issue, 2000).

member to purchase) fully usable currencies up to a stated portion of the member's shortfall, whether or not the limits measured by the amount of the member's currency already held by the Fund had been reached. Thus the Compensatory Financing Facility enabled a member state that could demonstrate the kind of shortfall contemplated to draw on the Fund without impairing its other drawing rights, and usually without conditionality other than being required to make a reasonable estimate regarding future trends of the export in question.

(c) The Oil Facility

The pattern of a Fund facility to aid members trapped by an unforeseen exogenous event was adapted to the sudden rise in oil prices in the 1970s.[67] Member states were required to prove that their needs were attributable to increased cost of petroleum imports, and also that they had not engaged in restrictions on current payments, competitive depreciation of exchange rates, or other practices disapproved by the Fund. If these conditions were met, the resources would be available without reference to the applicant's eligibility for further drawings under the general account, i.e. without the stricter conditionality that a drawing in the upper credit tranches might otherwise call for. For its part, the Fund obtained the resources used for the Oil Facility by borrowing, primarily from the newly rich oil-producing states.[68]

(d) Other Facilities for Unforeseen Contingencies

More recently, similar facilities have been created from time to time in response to other unexpected external shocks not deemed to be fundamental. Not only exports and imports of merchandise, but also shortfalls in receipts from worker remittances and from tourism have been added.[69] Many of these facilities were consolidated into a single Compensatory and Contingency Financing Facility.[70] Conditionality, as noted, was not totally absent: in order to be eligible to draw under the CCFF, member states must have cooperated adequately with the Fund 'in an effort to fund where required, appropriate solutions for its balance of payments difficulties.' If the Fund considered that the record of the applicant state's cooperation with the Fund had not been satisfactory, the state was not deprived completely of

---

[67] The first decision to create the Oil Facility was adopted as Ex. Bd. Dec. No. 4241-(74/67) of 13 June 1974, *Selected Decisions*, No. 70 (8th Issue 1976). In fact the Managing Director had proposed the Oil Facility on January 3, 1974, only 11 days after the oil exporting countries announced that crude oil prices would be quadrupled. See *IMF History 1972–1978* (n. 12 supra), 308.

[68] See Sect. 17.7(c) infra.

[69] Also, compensatory financing has been available since 1981 for imports of cereals when sharp price rises occur.

[70] See n. 66 supra.

access to the CCFF, but its entitlement to draw was reduced. The drawing did not however, count against the limits on ordinary drawings in the credit tranches, and the member state was usually not required to take measures unrelated to the purpose of the drawing under the CCFF. In February 2000, the 'contingency' element of the CCFF was eliminated by decision of the Executive Board, and the 'compensatory' element was linked more closely to upper credit tranche stand-by or extended arrangements.

(e)   Supplementary Financing and Related Facilities

As efforts to enlarge the quotas in the Fund encountered difficulty in the mid-1970s, while drawings under the Oil Facility and the Compensatory Financing Facility (as well as large regular drawings by the United Kingdom and Italy) were straining the resources of the Fund, the Managing Director, H. Johannes Witteveen, proposed that the IMF borrow from member states with surplus reserves, in order to supplement the funds that the IMF could make available to member states in need. The idea behind what came to be known as the Witteveen Facility was that the Fund would take on the role of financial intermediary, as it had already done in the Oil Facility, borrowing from states with excess reserves, such as Kuwait and Saudi Arabia, for relending to member states, subject to charges (i.e. interest rates) sufficient to cover the Fund's interest obligations to the lenders, plus a small service charge. Not only would this Supplementary Financing Facility serve to recycle funds to states with growing deficits from states with huge payments surpluses—primarily the sparsely populated oil-producing states that had benefited from the quadrupling of oil prices in 1973–4—by making more funds available for drawings, the Fund would be able to make its often unpopular programs of austerity more worth while for countries in need of genuine reform, because greater resources would accompany the Fund's prescriptions.[71]

Since drawings under the Supplementary Financing Facility were more expensive than ordinary drawings, the Fund established a policy that drawings in the first credit tranche would come entirely from the ordinary resources of the Fund; for upper credit tranches, a member state could draw on a combination of ordinary and supplementary resources. Drawings beyond the upper credit tranches would be made entirely under the Supplementary Facility, i.e. subject to the interest rates at which the Fund borrowed.[72]

---

[71] The Supplementary Financing Facility was agreed on by Ex. Bd. Dec. No. 5508–(77/127) of 29 Aug. 1977, *Selected Decisions*, 154 (17th issue 1992). For various reasons the facility did not actually enter into effect until February 1979. See *IMF History 1972–1978* vol. I, ch. 28.

[72] To relieve the burden of the near-market interest rates charged by the Fund on drawings against borrowed resources, the Fund established a special Subsidy Account. See Sect. 17.7(c) at n. 104 infra.

The Supplementary Financing Facility was phased out in the mid-1980s, but the idea of lending beyond the normal tranche limits on the basis of resources borrowed by the Fund has remained a significant element in the Fund's program of making resources available to developing countries in balance of payments difficulties, notably through the Policy on Enlarged Access, in effect between 1981 and 1992.[73] The details of the various facilities created by the IMF to supplement ordinary drawings under Article V differ in respect to the amounts available, the mix of ordinary and borrowed resources, the charges levied, the source of the funds borrowed, and the time period for repurchase. As noted in the introduction to this Section, what they have in common is that the resources made available exceed the limits under the ordinary tranche policies, but in general preserve the Funds's policies of conditionality, i.e. they require a detailed statement of the economic and financial policies that the member will follow and the Fund's determination that these policies, spelled out in a Letter of Intent, will be adequate for solution of the member's problems.

(f) The Poverty Reduction Facilities

Two more facilities are worth mentioning in this list of the assistance menu of the IMF, as they further illustrate the evolution (not to say metamorphosis) of the International Monetary Fund, and a variation on, though not abandonment, of the theme of conditionality.

The Heavily Indebted Poor Countries Initiative

In the mid-1990s the Fund and the World Bank, reacting to wide concern about the inability of a number of very poor countries to both service their accumulated debt and engage in economic growth, announced an initiative for debt relief for heavily indebted poor countries. The HIPC Initiative was intended to help with the debt problems of the most heavily indebted poor countries—originally 41 countries, nearly all in Africa, with total population of 600 million and combined accumulated debt of about $200 billion. In many instances, the debt service obligations—interest and amortization—were consuming up to half, and sometimes even more, of the countries' export earnings. The typical IMF stand-by arrangements were generally not suitable for these countries, or else the maximum available through the traditional facilities had long been exhausted and the countries were in arrears in keeping up their payments to the Fund as well as to other lenders. On the other hand, simple charity, i.e. debt forgiveness without conditions, seemed wrong on several grounds, including reports of massive corruption, civil strife, human rights abuses, and unsound economic policies. The Fund and

---

[73] *Policy on Enlarged Access*, Ex. Bd. Dec. No. 6783–81/40 of 11 Mar. 1981, as amended, *Selected Decisions*, p. 207 (24th issue 1999).

the World Bank were determined to ensure that the money freed by debt relief would be used for sustainable development, so that the beneficiaries would not again face unmanageable debts and that their people could begin to escape from extreme poverty. Further, the Fund and the World Bank did not want to duplicate debt relief that might be available from individual creditors operating through the Paris Club (for official lenders) and the London Club (for commercial lenders), which had worked since the 1980s to reschedule debts of middle income developing on a shared basis.[74] But for the first time the IMF and the World Bank (as well as the regional development banks), which had historically viewed their loans as preferred credits not subject to restructuring, were prepared to participate directly in writing down, or even canceling their own loans, as well as assisting in debt relief of other credits.

Under the original HIPC initiative as inaugurated in 1996,[75] a country seeking debt relief was required to complete a two-stage qualification period. During the first stage—at first three years but later shortened—the country was supposed to work with the Fund and the World Bank to establish a track record of sound economic and social policies. If Patria passed this test at the 'First Decision Point', a determination would be made whether its debt service burden was or was not 'unsustainable', i.e. whether concessions available to it through the Paris and London Clubs or otherwise could enable its debt service burden to be reduced to tolerable levels. If so, Patria was remitted to those sources of relief, without benefit of the HIPC initiative. If Patria's debt burden was deemed to be unsustainable, generally meaning that the accumulated debt exceeded 200–250 percent of export earnings and debt service exceeded 20–25 percent of export earnings, the IMF and World Bank boards would make an assessment of needed assistance and appropriate relief, including a reduction in Patria's stock of debt, to be implemented at a 'Completion Point' following a further period of sound economic policies—generally at the end of another three years.

In the first three years, twelve countries applied for assistance under the HIPC initiative, seven qualified, and as of April 1999 funds had been released to two of the seven.[76] In June 1999 the Group of Eight countries recommended relaxing the criteria to provide faster and deeper debt relief, and in September of 1999 the World Bank and the Fund adopted an Enhanced HIPC Initiative and created a new Poverty and Growth Facility.[77] Under the improved HIPC initiative, interim relief would be available between the Decision Point and the Completion Point, and instead of a fixed timetable for the second evaluation, the HIPC facility would now focus on a 'Floating Completion Point' to be reached as soon as Patria implemented

---

[74] See Ch. 19, Sect. 19.3.
[75] See Ex. Bd. Dec. No. 11436–(97/10) of 7 Feb. 1997 as amended, *Selected Decisions*, 80 (25th issue 2000).
[76] *IMF Annual Report 1999*, p. 83.   [77] See 28 *IMF Survey*, p. 326 (11 Oct. 1999).

a set of predetermined reforms, framed around a 'Poverty Reduction Strategy Paper' prepared by the borrowing country with the help of the World Bank and the IMF. The effect, as expected, was that more countries were ruled eligible for debt relief, and the amounts disbursed were substantially greater than in the first three years. As of November 2001, 24 countries (20 in Africa) had reached their decision points, and one country, Uganda, had reached its completion point, so that debt relief could be delivered unconditionally.[78]

The Poverty Reduction and Growth Facility

A second facility was also decided on in September 1999, further involving the Fund in aid to least developed countries, known as the Poverty Reduction and Growth Facility or PRGF, replacing the Enhanced Structural Adjustment Facility established a decade earlier. Aid under the PRGF is not necessarily linked to debt service burden, though some countries may be eligible for both programs. As under the HIPC Initiative, the PRGF calls for borrowing countries to prepare a Poverty Reduction Strategy Paper, covering structural reforms aimed at reduction of poverty, transparent budgets, accountability of government, and strategy for growth. There is still some conditionality, determined jointly by the World Bank and the Fund, but, it seems more attention than previously is paid to the social impact of proposed reforms. As of April 2001, 77 low-income countries were eligible for assistance under the PRGF, on the basis of per capita income criteria reflecting eligibility under the World Bank's concessional lending facility, set at per capita income in 2000 of less than $885, and 37 countries had entered into arrangements with the Fund under the PGRF.[79] Loans under the PRGF carried an annual interest rate of 0.5 percent, with repayments to begin five and a half years after disbursement and ending ten years after disbursement. Some governments of highly indebted countries are apparently still reluctant to apply for relief under the HIPC or PRGF facilities, because it means subjecting their finances to external audit.

Funds for loans under the Poverty Reduction and Growth Facility are handled under a PRGF Trust, which borrows at market-related interest from official sources, receives contributions from donor countries, and from profits from off-market sales of gold held by the Fund.[80] It was under the PRGF that the IMF Executive Board approved a $1.3 billion credit to Pakistan in December 2001, at least in part in return for that country's assistance in the efforts to root out terrorism in Afghanistan and elsewhere. Like other beneficiaries of the Poverty Reduction and Growth Facility, the Government of Pakistan was required to prepare an Interim Poverty

---

[78] See *IMF Annual Report 2001*, pp. 47–52; also Fact Sheet on Debt Relief for Poor Countries, available on IMF Web Site, www.imf.org.

[79] *IMF Annual Report 2001*, pp. 64–6.

[80] See Ex. Bd. Dec. No. 11436 (n. 75 supra), para. 3.

Reduction Strategy Paper, which was submitted to and approved by the executive boards of both the IMF and the World Bank.[81]

17.7   BORROWING BY THE FUND

In principle, the IMF was supposed to provide facilities enabling member states to draw on the pool of currencies contributed by other members pursuant to their quota subscriptions. As the needs of member states grew faster than increases in quota, and as the subscriptions of many members of 75 percent of their quota in their own currencies did not add to the pool of 'freely usable currencies' that other members would wish to purchase, the IMF has assumed the role of financial intermediary, borrowing from some countries and lending to others. The authority for this step, not seriously challenged, is Article VII(1) of the Articles of Agreement 'Measures to replenish the Fund's holdings of currencies'.[82]

The Fund had not, as of year-end 2001, sought to borrow money from the private sector, as its sister agency, the World Bank, has long done, but there would seem to be no impediment in the Articles of Agreement to doing so.[83] It has however, borrowed from a variety of public sources, with a view to making the resources so borrowed available for drawing by member states in a number of instances subject to specific terms.

(a)   The General Arrangements to Borrow

In 1961, midway through the Bretton Woods regime, it became apparent that the resources of the IMF might not be adequate if one or more of the major industrial nations—and particularly the United States and the United Kingdom—needed to make a large drawing to support its currency. At that time the aggregate of all quotas in Fund stood at the equivalent of about 16 billion dollars, but only about half of that amount consisted of freely usable currencies and gold. If, say, the United Kingdom sought to exercise

---

[81] See *IMF Press Release* No. 01/51, 7 Dec. 2001.

[82] In the Original Articles, the corresponding provision was Article VII(2), and included the work 'scarce' before 'currencies'. The point of the change was to make clear that the criterion for replenishment is not scarcity of the currency to be replenished but the need of the Fund for additional resources. See *Report by Executive Directors on Proposed Second Amendment to the Articles of Agreement of the International Monetary Fund*, 50 (1976).

[83] See Article VII(1)(i), authorizing the Fund to borrow 'from some other source'. The suggestion that the Fund borrow from private sources has been made a number of times; while there is no impediment under the Articles of Agreement to a decision by the Fund to go into the market for funds, such a step would raise a number of legal questions, such as the probable necessity of waiver by the Fund of immunity from suit, the law to be applied to disputes, possibly a chosen forum, and if securities were to be issued, compliance with the rules of the US Securities and Exchange Commission and comparable agencies in other states where the securities might be offered.

its drawing rights in full—125 percent of its quota or about $2.4 billion, the Fund's holdings of pounds would have to be subtracted from the usable total. Given the requirement that the IMF keeps funds in reserve against gold tranche drawings, a request by the United Kingdom—and even more by the United States—would severely strain the resources of the IMF.

The solution for this problem, adopted largely at United States initiative, was to negotiate in advance among ten major states (or their central banks) the terms and conditions under which they would lend their currencies to the IMF, to be re-lent by the Fund to one of them in connection with a drawing from the Fund. The result was the General Arrangements to Borrow, in effect a stand-by arrangement among ten member states of the IMF and the Fund.[84] Each participant agreed, tentatively, to make its currencies available upon a call by the Fund's Managing Director, in response to a request by one of the other participants in the GAB. Generally the calls by the Managing Director on the participants would be in proportion to their commitments of funds, except for the participant state requesting the drawing, and for any other participant that notified the Fund that it was not for the time being in position to honour a call.[85]

A proposal for a drawing under the GAB requires a two-thirds majority of the number of participants, plus a three-fifths majority of the votes of the participants weighted in proportion to their subscription to the GAB. In contrast to the voting rules of the Articles of Agreement of the IMF, the prospective drawer under the GAB is not permitted to vote on its own application.[86]

> In the original version of the GAB, the equivalent of $6 billion was committed by the ten participants—$2 billion by the United States, $1 billion each (in pounds and marks) by the United Kingdom and Germany, $550 million each (in francs and lire) by France and Italy, and $900 million in smaller amounts by Japan, Canada, the Netherlands, Belgium and Sweden. Thus if the United Kingdom sought to draw on the GAB, as it did several times in the 1960s and 1970s, six of the other nine participants accounting for the equivalent of 3 billion dollars in subscriptions, would have had to vote in favour of the request.

Since the form of a drawing under the GAB is applicant to Fund, Fund to GAB, a drawing making use of the GAB would be subject to the normal terms of Fund drawings, with a Letter of Intent and a stand-by negotiated

---

[84] The decision to create the General Arrangements to Borrow was adopted by the Executive Directors of the Fund on January 5, 1962 and entered into force on October 24, 1962. Exec. Bd. Dec. No. 1289–(62/1), reproduced, as amended many times, in *Selected Decisions*, 366 (25th issue 2000).

[85] General Arrangements to Borrow (n. 84 supra), para. 7(d).

[86] Because the voting arrangements under the GAB are different from those under the Fund's Articles of Agreement, they were set out in a separate letter from the Minister of Finance of France to the United States Secretary of the Treasury and the other ministers of finance. The Letter, dated December 15, 1961 is reproduced in *Selected Decisions*, at 379 (n. 84 supra); it is regarded as an integral part of the GAB.

among the applicant state, the Fund, and those participants in the GAB that were to supply funds, all approved by the IMF Executive Board. In the event, most drawings by participants in the GAB consisted in part of use of the Fund's own resources, and in part of resources lent by other participants under the GAB.

Apart from the commitment of funds as described above, the General Arrangements to Borrow had an important institutional impact. It led to establishment of the participating states as a semi-official body, the Group of Ten, as described in Chapter 19;[87] and it marked the first time that Japan was invited to become a member of the group of states that had assumed a special responsibility for the international monetary system.[88] Switzerland, though not then a member of the IMF, became associated with the General Arrangements to Borrow in 1964.[89]

The General Arrangements to Borrow was activated for the first time in November 1964, to support a drawing under a $1 billion stand-by previously granted by the Fund to the United Kingdom.[90] Subsequently, drawings on the Fund by France, Italy, the United Kingdom, and the United States have in fact been met by calls under the GAB.[91] In 1983, the GAB was expanded from its original pool of $6 billion to a total of SDR17 billion, including a subscription of just over SDR1 billion from the Swiss National Bank, plus an associated arrangement with Saudi Arabia for an additional SDR 1.5 billion.[92] At the same time the Arrangements were amended to permit the Fund to make calls under the GAB for non-participants if the Managing Director considers

that the Fund faces an inadequacy of resources to meet actual and expected requests for financing that reflect the existence of an exceptional situation associated with balance of payments problems of members of a character or size that could threaten the stability of the international monetary system.[93]

---

[87] See Ch. 19, Sect. 19.4.

[88] See Paul A. Volcker and Toyoo Gyohten, *Changing Fortunes*, 28 (1992). It is interesting to note, as Volcker does, that Japan's initial commitment to the GAB was the equivalent of $250 million, compared to $1 billion for the United Kingdom and $2 billion for the United States. In the 1983 revision of the GAB, Japan's portion was raised to 12.5 percent of the total, in third place just under that of Germany, and well in excess of the commitment of the United Kingdom and France.

[89] Switzerland became a member of the IMF in 1993; the Swiss National Bank has remained a participant in the GAB, as well as in the New Arrangements to Borrow described below.

[90] See J. Keith Horsefield, *The International Monetary Fund, 1945–1965*, Vol. I, pp. 568–9 (1969).

[91] For details of these drawings, see Richard W. Edwards, Jr., *International Monetary Collaboration*, 290, n. 278 and sources there cited (1985).

[92] For the exchange of documents consituting the borrowing agreement with Saudi Arabia, see *Selected Decisions*, pp. 386–96, (25th issue 2000).

[93] Exec. Bd. Dec. No. 7337–(83–37), 24 Feb. 1983, 12 *IMF Survey*, 26 (7 Mar. 1983) adding para. 21, 'Use of Credit Arrangements for Non-participants'. The same resolution also provided that the Board decided that the Swiss National Bank would become a full participant, rather than merely being associated with the GAB, id., para. 22.

This authority was used for the first time to support a massive drawing by Russia during its crisis in the summer of 1998.[94]

(b) The New Arrangements to Borrow

Following the second Mexican financial crisis in 1994–5,[95] the international financial community became concerned that some day substantially more resources might be needed than were available from the Fund's General Account plus the GAB. The June 1995 Summit of the G–7 countries, meeting in Halifax, called for an additional contingency plan that would double the amounts available under the General Arrrangements,[96] and after some delay and negotiation, the Fund adopted a decision in January 1997 to establish the New Arrangements to Borrow, with 25 participants and a total commitment of twice the amount committed under the GAB, i.e. SDR34 billion.[97]

The scheme of the NAB is essentially the same as under the amended GAB, in particular that it depends on an application for a stand-by and Letter of Intent by the country making a request for a drawing, and that it is usable in the case of proposed drawings by non-participants. All the participants in the GAB became participants in the new undertaking, but the NAB includes not only the smaller developed countries such as Denmark, Finland, and Austria that do not belong to the G–10, but also a number of developing countries, such as Korea, Malaysia, and Thailand, plus the Hong Kong Monetary Authority.[98] As under the GAB, calls under the NAB are to be made by the Managing Director of the Fund upon consultation with the participants and the Fund's Executive Directors, and in proportion to the amount of each participant's credit arrangement with the Fund. The New Arrangements did not replace the General Arrangements, but the Decision states that the New Arrangements to Borrow shall be the facility of first and principal recourse, except if the country making a request for a drawing is a participant in both the GAB and the NAB, in which case either facility may be used.[99] The NAB entered into effect in November 1998, and was promptly activated to finance an extended arrangement for Brazil of SDR9.1 billion (approximately $12.7 billion) of which SDR2.9 billion was actually drawn. That activation, like the one for Russia under the GAB, was canceled on March 11, 1999, when the General Account of the Fund was replenished pursuant to the Eleventh

---

[94] See Ch. 18, Sect. 18.14. The activation of the GAB for Russia was canceled in March 1999, when the Fund repaid the outstanding amount following the effectiveness of the Eleventh General Review of Quotas and payment of the bulk of the quota increases.

[95] See Ch. 18, Sect. 18.6.   [96] See 24 *IMF Survey*, 201, (3 July 1995).

[97] Ex. Bd. Dec. No. 11428–(97/60) of 27 Jan. 1997, *Selected Decisions*, 397 (25th issue 2000).

[98] The other new participants are Australia, Kuwait, Luxembourg, Norway, Saudi Arabia, and Singapore.

[99] Decision establishing the New Arrangements to Borrow (n. 97 supra), para. 21.

General Quota Increase, and the Fund repaid the members of the NAB. As of year-end 2001, the NAB has not been used again, but it remains available as as an important facility, and as a symbol of commitment to the international monetary system as a whole.

(c)   Borrowing for Special Facilities

As mentioned in the preceding section, in 1974 and again in 1975 the IMF sought and obtained loans from oil-producing countries to support the Oil Facility, permitting drawing outside of the normal limits by non-oil developing countries (as well as some developed countries) affected by the sudden sharp rise in the price for oil. The loans to the Fund were different from the General Arrangements to Borrow in that once a state agreed to lend funds to the Oil Facility, there was no provision for further voting or imposition of conditions, except that the funds borrowed could only be used for the Oil Facility. Also, in a number of instances, the Fund made arrangements to borrow the currencies of the lending states, rather than US dollars, which meant that the lenders had to stand ready to convert their currencies into a reserve currency, even though many of the lender states were still formally Article XIV states.[100]

Most important, the Oil Facility established a practice that was controversial when instituted but became common later on, that when the Fund borrowed at or close to commercial rates, drawings based on the resources so borrowed would be charged the same rate plus a small service charge. Article V(8)(c) of the Original Articles of Agreement stated that the Fund shall levy charges 'uniform for all members' on balances of the member states' currency held by the Fund in excess of quota. The Legal Department of the Fund construed this provision to mean that different charges for use of the same facility could not be levied for different categories of member states, such as developed and developing states. However, it was permissible to impose a separate schedule applicable to a facility that existed independently of other resources of the Fund.[101] Since the charges for the Oil Facility averaged about 7 percent, the Fund subsequently established a subsidy account to assist the least developing countries in meeting charges under the Oil Facility, financed principally by donations.[102] When the Supplementary Financing Facility was created shortly after the Oil Facility,[103] the same techniques were adopted.

---

[100]   See Ch.16, Sect. 16.5(a).

[101]   See *IMF History 1972–1978*, Vol. I, p. 328. The requirement of uniform changes for all members was not retained in Article V(8) of the Amended Articles of Agreement.

[102]   Ex. Bd. Dec. No. 4773–(75/136) of 1 Aug. 1975, *Selected Decisions*, p. 455 (as amended) (17th issue 1992). The list of least developed countries was borrowed from a list drawn up by the United Nations of countries with per capita incomes of $400 or less in 1971. Eventually some 25 countries contributed to the Subsidy Account, including most of the industrial democracies plus Venezuela and Yugoslavia, but not the United States.

[103]   See Sect. 17.6(e) supra.

The Fund borrowed at negotiated rates comparable to market rates of interest, placed the resources thus obtained in a separate account, and charged member states drawing on that account the same rate that it was obligated to pay plus a small service charge. Again, a Subsidy Account was created to reduce the cost to the least developed countries of the charges levied for drawing on the facility.[104]

From the point of view of the lenders, claims on the Fund growing out of Fund borrowings—whether under one of the special programs or under the General/New Arrangements to Borrow—can be counted as reserve assets, because they are callable on demand by the lending state if it represents that it has a balance of payments need, and because the claims may be transferred to any other official lender or agency (but not to private entities) at a price agreed between the original lender and the transferee.[105]

17.8   ENFORCEMENT OF OBLIGATIONS TO THE INTERNATIONAL MONETARY FUND

As noted in Chapter 16 and repeated in paragraph 7 of the *Guidelines on Conditionality* (Sect. 17.5(c) supra), the IMF has been careful not to make the undertakings in Letters of Intent and related documents bear the character of legally binding obligations. If a member state fails to follow through on an economic program set out in a Letter of Intent, or fails to meet performance targets established in a stand-by arrangement, the consequence may be suspension of the right to draw under the stand-by, or reluctance by the Fund to renew a stand-by when it expires. The Fund is careful, however, not to characterize such consequences as sanctions or punishment, let alone enforcement.

In contrast, drawings from the Fund are made in the form of a purchase with the drawer's own currency, subject to an obligation to repurchase for SDRs or freely usable currencies;[106] failure to meet the repurchase obligation within the period stated is regarded as a breach of a legal obligation, and sanctions for such default may be imposed.

---

[104] Supplementary Financing Facility: Subsidy Account Instrument, Ex. Bd. Dec. No. 6683–80/185 G/TR, 17 Dec. 1980, *Selected Decisions*, p. 578 (25th issue 2000). The account was put together from donations plus transfers from a Special Disbursement Account of proceeds from the sale of the Fund's gold in excess of the use made of those proceeds for other purposes.

[105] See e.g. *General Arrangements to Borrow*, Ex. Bd. Dec. No. 1289-(62/1) as amended, para. 11(e) (repayment), para. 13 (transferability), *Selected Decisions*, pp. 372, 373 (25th issue 2000); *New Arrangements to Borrow*, para. 11(e) (repayment), para. 13 (transferability), *Selected Decisions*, pp. 406, 409, 415; *Replenishment in Connection with Supplementary Financing Facility*: Annex, para. 5(c) (repayment), para. 8 (transferability), *Selected Decisions*, p. 479 (24th issue 1999).

[106] See Ch. 16, Sect. 16.6.

The Fund has worked out an elaborate procedure for putting pressure on a member state for overdue financial obligations.[107] The first step is a cable to the member state as soon as a due date is missed; after two weeks a communication is sent to the Governor for the member in arrears stressing the seriousness of the failure to meet the member's obligations and urging full and prompt settlement; thereafter a formal communication is submitted to the Executive Board; and finally a formal notification of the default is sent to all Governors of the Fund. When the longest obligation has been outstanding for six weeks, the Managing Director informs the member state that a formal complaint will be issued to the Executive Board in two weeks' time, with a view to a decision by the Board to limit the member state's use of the General Resources of the Fund. If the member persists in its failure to settle its overdue obligations to the Fund, the Executive Board may, under Article XXVI(2)(a) of the Articles of Agreement, declare the member ineligible to use the general resources of the Fund. Normally such a declaration would be sent to all Fund Governors and to the heads of other international financial institutions such as the World Bank and the relevant regional development bank.

The procedures of the IMF contemplate a declaration of non-cooperation if the member in question has not only failed to pay its arrearages to the Fund, but has failed to cooperate with the Fund in working out its default and has made payments to other creditors, 'thus ignoring the preferred creditor status that members are expected to give the Fund.'[108] As many as eleven states were declared ineligible to use the resources of the Fund in 1989, of which eight returned to the Fund's good graces in the decade of the 1990s. As of 30 April 2000, seven states were in arrears to the Fund by six months or more, and four of these had been declared ineligible to use the Fund's resources.

In November 1992, a Third Amendment to the Articles of Agreement of the IMF entered into force, designed to provide an intermediate sanction between ineligibility to use the resources of the Fund and compulsory withdrawal. Under new Article XXVI(2)(b), the Fund may, by a 70 percent majority of the total voting power, suspend the voting rights of a member that persists in failure to fulfill its obligations to the Fund, and this sanction was applied to Sudan and Congo (Kinshasa) in the 1990s.[109] The ultimate sanction of compulsory withdrawal was recommended by the Executive Directors for Sudan for several years, but the recommendation was lifted in

---

[107] See *Overdue Obligations to the Fund, Selected Decisions*, pp. 549–67, including timetables, at pp. 566–67 (25th issue 2000).

[108] See *Draft Declaration on Censure or Noncooperation, Selected Decisions*, p. 561 (25th issue 2000).

[109] The Third Amendment also added a new Schedule L, which spells out what suspension of voting rights means, including the loss of the right to appoint a Governor or Alternate Governor and the requirement of a new election of an Executive Director in place of the Director in whose election the suspended member participated.

February 2000. As of year-end 2001, no state had been required to withdraw from the Fund for failure to pay its obligations.[110] The preferred resolution is a so-called 'rights approach', something like a stand-by arrangement, whereby the member in arrears adopts a program of adjustment and reform monitored by the Fund, which must include efforts to reduce its arrearages to the Fund and probably some solicitation of outside support. If the program is completed, the member has accumulated 'rights' to the first disbursement under a new stand-by or extended arrangement with the Fund.[111]

SUMMARY

In the three decades following the demise of the par value system established at Bretton Woods,[112] the international monetary system and particularly the International Monetary Fund changed substantially. The discipline of fixed exchange rates has gone,[113] and with it the requirement of balance of payments equilibrium for those countries—notably the United States—whose currency is willingly held or used by other states and private entities. For this reason, as well as others, the IMF has been little used since the 1970s as a source of funds for the industrial democracies. For those states—primarily the developing countries—whose currencies are not freely usable and not willingly held by others, the constraints of the balance of payments continue to be significant, and the IMF continues to be a major source of assistance and impetus for adjustment, as discussed in Chapter 16. A new role for the IMF developed in the 1990s as a source of funds plus economic discipline for the countries of Eastern Europe and the former Soviet Union attempting to make the transition from centrally planned to market economies.[114]

The IMF's program of surveillance of the economic policies of all member states under Article IV of the Amended Articles of Agreement has not been successful in achieving coordination in economic policy among the major financial powers, which have in many instances looked to other fora.

---

[110] Czechoslovakia was subjected to compulsory withdrawal from the IMF in 1954 pursuant to Article XV(2) of the Original Articles (corresponding to Article XXVI(2) of the Amended Articles), but the reason was failure to provide required information under Article VIII(5) following a complicated controversy about exchange rate changes, not default on a repurchase obligation. See Joseph Gold, *Membership in the International Monetary Fund*, pp. 345–72. (1974). The Czech and Slovak Federal Republic was readmitted to the Fund in September 1990, and when the Czech Republic and the Slovak Republic separated in 1993, each was admitted to the Fund.

[111] See the description of the 'rights approach' by the Managing Director, reproduced in *Selected Decisions*, pp. 140–6 (25th issue 2000).

[112] See Ch. 16, Sect. 16.9(b).

[113] Except where member States of regional groups such as the European Community have attempted to establish more or less fixed relationships among their currencies. See Ch. 20, Sect. 20.3.

[114] See Ch. 18, Sect. 18.10–18.14.

The IMF's program of conditionality for member states seeking to draw on the resources of the Fund has remained controversial, but has to some extent led to increased attention to reduction of subsidies, liberalization of trade, and attention to fiscal and monetary discipline. Unlike private financial intermediaries, the IMF has to some extent been able to impose conditionality in recycling funds from countries in balance of payments surplus, a value more appreciated in the late 1980s and 1990s than it was prior to the debt crisis of the early 1980s.

In all, the IMF remains a major forum for discussion of international financial issues, and the Articles of Agreement remain a major source of international economic law. One could not fairly state, however, that the prescription in Article IV(3)(a) of the Amended Articles has been fulfilled, to the effect that the Fund 'shall oversee the international monetary system in order to ensure its effective operation.'

18

The International Monetary System and Regional Crises

INTRODUCTION

In the early 1980s, Mexico, then Brazil, and then a number of other states, principally in Latin America, became unable to pay their external debts—and even interest on their debts—as they came due. In the early 1990s, as the states of Eastern Europe and the former Soviet Union turned away from communism, they found themselves without the resources needed to join the international economy and the international monetary system that had grown up largely without their participation. In the late 1990s, a series of countries in South-east Asia, each with a rather different economic and political situation, found themselves in financial distress, brought on at least in part by the perception of the outside world—investors and creditors—that there were parallels among the countries.

The international financial community responded unevenly to these developments, and it would be an exaggeration to say that rules were either followed or made. Nevertheless a certain pattern of international joint endeavour developed that may fairly be said to constitute a body of precedent, and thus part of the law of international monetary affairs. The foundations were the Articles of Agreement of the International Monetary Fund, and the acceptance by member states that the IMF had the authority—legal and political—to impose requirements on the behaviour of states seeking its assistance, i.e. to apply conditionality. The new element, however, was intensive cooperation among the IMF, the central banks of the major industrial countries, the 'money-center' commercial banks, and the World Bank as well as the debtor countries, as each participant in the international monetary system came to realize that it needed all the others.

The events in this chapter are presented in narrative form, not for the sake of completeness or historical record, but to demonstrate how the international monetary system brought its rules to bear on the debtor countries, in large part with the IMF as catalyst, coordinator, and scapegoat. Viewed as history, this chapter is inevitably selective and incomplete; viewed as 'law through cases', the chapter aims to be accurate and illustrative.

A.   LATIN AMERICA, 1982–95

18.1   ORIGINS OF THE CRISIS

The details of the origin of the crisis of developing country debt are beyond the scope of this volume, and indeed vary from state to state.[2] In broad brush, however, it may be said that in the 1970s, following the first sharp rise in oil prices, many developing countries, particularly in Latin America, undertook massive borrowing from commercial banks in the United States, Western Europe, and Japan. The banks, which were bidding, through high interest rates, for deposits from the newly super-rich oil-producing states and sheikdoms of the Middle East, were more than willing to re-lend the funds thus acquired to developing countries as long as the interest rate was high enough, without, as it turned out, conducting searching inquiries into the ability of the borrowers to service their debt or to repay the loans. The governments of the creditor countries, as well as the international financial institutions, seemed pleased with the successful recycling process, which smoothed the transfer of real resources to OPEC countries. Regulators in the developed countries, for their part, were less than fully attentive to the exposure of borrowing countries to debts nominally incurred by different entities, but ultimately dependent on the same source of foreign exchange; moreover commercial banks, particularly those based in the United States, found that regulation and examination could in large part be avoided by operating offshore, through the Eurodollar market centered in London but with outlets in many parts of the world. At the same time, the character of bank lending changed. In place of traditional types of private finance to public entities such as bonds, suppliers' credits, and direct investment, the pattern of the 1970s shifted to syndicated loans without link to any particular

---

[1] An astonishing number of books addressed the crisis of developing country debt. Among those most useful for the issues raised here, see e.g. Ralph Reisner, Emilio J. Cardenas, and Antonio Mendes (eds.), *Latin American Sovereign Debt Management: Legal and Regulatory Aspects* (Inter-American Development Bank 1990); Catherine Gwin and Richard E. Feinberg (eds.), *Pulling Together: The International Monetary Fund in a Multipolar World* (1989); Ishrat Husain and Ishac Diwan (eds.), *Dealing with the Crisis: A World Bank Symposium* (World Bank 1989).

[2] See, generally, Karin Lissakers, *Banks, Borrowers and the Establishment* (1991); Benjamin J. Cohen, *In Whose Interests: International Banking and American Foreign Policy* (1986), reviewed in Lowenfeld, 'Political Economy for the 1980s; Global and National Governments', 101 *Harv. L. Rev.* 1061 (1988); Margaret Garritson de Vries, *Balance of Payments Adjustment 1945 to 1986: The IMF Experience*, ch. 10 (1987); William N. Eskridge, Jr., 'Les Jeux Sont Faits: Structural Origins of the International Debt Problem', 25 *Va. J. Int'l L.* 281 (1989).

project or transaction, i.e. to what in many instances became loans for balance of payment purposes.[3]

On the other side, the developing countries, uncomfortable with conditionality administered by the IMF and to some extent by the World Bank, found that commercial banks had neither the will nor the political legitimacy to enforce conditions on sovereign decision-making by the borrowers.[4] And as Mexico's Finance Minister later conceded, the debtor countries did not always devote the resources obtained from abroad to the most economically and socially productive uses.[5]

While the commercial banks did not, as noted, evaluate credit risk as carefully as they should have done, they did, for the most apart, understand and make provision for interest rate risk, i.e. that they were taking short-term deposits from the oil-producing states, and lending on long term to the developing countries and state entities. The typical response of the banks was to subject the loans to developing countries to 'floating' interest rates, usually a stated margin over the London Interbank Offered Rate (LIBOR). As interest rates, including LIBOR, rose to the 15–17 percent range in the early 1980s but large borrowing continued, the debt service obligation of the developing countries became unbearable.

The crisis was not entirely unforeseen or unforeseeable. Arthur Burns, then Chairman of the US Federal Reserve System, had warned of excess bank lending to developing countries as early as February 1977, pointing out that the practice by countries of borrowing from commercial banks 'circumvented the rule of law that only the IMF can impose.'[6] Paul Volcker, Burns's successor as Chairman of the Federal Reserve, relates that in the spring of 1982, he repeatedly urged Mexico's financial officials to apply to the IMF for a stand-by, and to use the conditions attached to the stand-by as a way to introduce an effective program to reform Mexico's domestic economy and to stanch the flight of Mexican capital to the United States. The reply always was that Mexico had freed itself from a tough and unpopular IMF program in the mid-1970s, and that the President of the country could never accept submitting to another such program.[7] Surveillance teams from the IMF must have known of the situation in Mexico and the other major borrowers, but the Fund made no public statement, and without requests for use of the Fund's resources, the IMF was unable to influence

[3] See Margaret G. de Vries, *Balance of Payments Adjustment 1945 to 1986*, (n. 2 supra) 212.

[4] At the end of 1974, foreign loans of all banks to developing countries totalled $44 billion, about one-third made by American banks. By the end of 1979, as the second oil crisis broke out in the wake of the revolution in Iran, bank loans to developing countries stood at $233 billion. See Paul A. Volcker and Toyoo Gyohten, *Changing Fortunes*, (n. 4 supra) 190–1 (1992).

[5] Jesus Silva-Herzog F. 'External Debt and Other Problems of Latin America', in *International Monetary Cooperation; Essays in Honor of Henry C. Wallich* (*Princeton Essays in Int'l Finance* No. 169), p. 44 at 46 (1987).

[6] Testimony of Chairman Arthur Burns in *1977 Economic Report of the President*, Hearings before Joint Economic Committee, 95th Cong., 1st Sess., Part III, p. 415 (23 Feb. 1977).

[7] Volcker and Gyohten, *Changing Fortunes*, n. 4 supra at p. 199.

either the external or the internal policies of the borrowing states. As for the lenders, they did reduce maturities as loans came due, but to decline to roll loans over, or to make additional loans so that interest payments would remain current would have subjected their balance sheets to huge charges for 'non-performing loans', and to painful instructions from bank examiners. All these elements came together in August 1982.

18.2   THE CRISIS ERUPTS: THE CASE OF MEXICO

More than a dozen developing countries in nearly every continent fell into the debtors' crisis of 1982–3, each with a slightly different story, but all affected by the same overall factors—excessive public sector borrowing, unexpectedly high interest rates, recession in the developed countries, and a loss of confidence on the part of the private lending institutions which spread from one country to another as the crises widened. The first, and most watched case, involved Mexico.

In many ways Mexico was in a favourable economic position in the 1970s, because major discoveries of oil in 1978 promised to turn it into a large exporter of petroleum and petroleum-based products. The discoveries of oil were translated into marketable production with astonishing speed as pipelines, terminals, and other facilities grew up in the jungles of Tabasco and Chiapas. Aided by massive loans, Mexico's production of oil doubled in four years, and the state-owned oil company PEMEX reached Number 24 on the Fortune list of the world's largest industrial corporations.

Overall, Mexico's economy grew by more than 8 percent per year in the period 1977–81, and employment increased by more than half a million jobs per year. But by the end of 1981, price inflation had reached an annual rate of 28.7 percent, compared with 5.4 percent in the years 1950–73; the current account deficit which had stood at US$7.5 billion in 1980, grew to $12.9 billion in 1981, equal to 15 percent of gross domestic product. Even as both the price and the demand for oil were falling, the figure for Mexico's foreign debt—public and private—stood at some $70 billion, with about $18 billion due to be repaid in 1982 unless it could be rescheduled or refinanced.

As inflation in Mexico exceeded that of the United States and other developed states, its currency, pegged to the dollar, became increasingly overvalued. Mexico maintained no exchange controls, and conversion of pesos into dollars, i.e. capital flight, took place on a massive scale. When the Bank of Mexico ceased to support the peso in February 1982, the peso dropped by more than 40 percent in a few days. The government ordered wage increases to compensate for the de facto devaluation of the peso, which did nothing to slow up the flight of capital, but contributed to the nervousness of the lending banks. It was in this context that Chairman Volcker gave the advice—and received the answer—quoted above.[8]

In April the government of Mexico announced a 17-point program to adjust the Mexican economy, including reduction in the budget deficit, reduced imports, and reduced public sector borrowing from abroad. The program was only partially carried out, however. The proposed reduction in public sector spending proved politically unattainable, and targets for external borrowing—though reduced from prior periods—could not be met as the banks grew nervous about Mexico, as well as about sovereign borrowers in general.

On August 1, 1982, the government of Mexico announced major price increases for electricity and gasoline, as well as for bread and tortillas. On August 5, as capital flight intensified, the government imposed exchange controls. On August 12, it ordered all dollar-denominated bank deposits to be converted to pesos at a rate about 20 percent below the market rate. On Friday, August 13, 1982, the Mexican Minister of Finance announced to the world that Mexico would not be able to meet the payments on its debt due on August 15.

Notwithstanding some distant early warnings, Mexico's announcement came as a shock to the international financial community. Not only was Mexico in trouble, but so was the international monetary system as a whole, linked through a web of reciprocal deposits, guarantees, and participation loans that might well unravel if Mexico's debts had to be charged off on the books of money-center banks in the major industrial countries, as well as on the books of many smaller and regional banks that had taken part in lending syndicates in the preceding years. Moreover, Mexico was far from alone among overextended developing countries that had counted on roll-overs and extensions which now were unlikely to be forthcoming. Both in the developing and in developed countries, financial authorities recalled the crises of the 1930s, when widespread repudiation of debts had been caused by global depression and had in turn prolonged the depression. This time, of course, the Bretton Woods institutions were in place, as well as a more informal network of central bankers and finance ministers, shaped over several decades of cooperation in time of crisis and otherwise.[9]

---

[8] See Sect. 18.1, n. 7.

[9] For details on the exposure of commercial banks to developing country debt, broken down by debtor country, creditor country, and major banks see Harry Huizinga, 'The Commercial Bank Claims on Developing Countries: How Have Bank Claims Been Affected', in Husain and Diwan, *Dealing with the Crisis* (n. 1 supra), 129–43.

18.3   THE RESPONSE OF THE INTERNATIONAL SYSTEM: THE MEXICAN CASE CONTINUED

(a)   The First Quick Fix

In the long run, it was clear to all concerned that any program of assistance to Mexico would require both the resources and the discipline of the International Monetary Fund. But the Fund would not permit a drawing without a stand-by agreement, and negotiation of a stand-by would take time. The first priority was to keep the international payments system in operation while longer-term programs of adjustment and financing were being developed. Over a five-day period including a weekend, August 12–17, 1982, the US government came up with a $1 billion advance payment on purchases of oil from Mexico for the US Strategic Petroleum Reserve; a $1 billion line of credit from the Commodity Corporation for purchases by Mexico of agricultural products from the United States, and $700 million under an existing swap arrangement with the Federal Reserve Bank of New York. In addition, the Bank for International Settlements put together a bridging credit of $1.85 billion, half on behalf of the United States, half on behalf of the central banks of ten other states[10] designed to be repaid as soon as a more permanent credit could be arranged with the IMF.

On August 19, Mexico's Secretary of the Treasury met in New York with representatives of more than 100 of Mexico's commercial bank creditors from around the world, to ask for a 'standstill' on debts coming due for at least 90 days.[11] The banks had little choice but to acquiesce (subject to interest payments being continued), but they too were given to understand that in the interim Mexico would seek credits from the IMF, and that it was committed to negotiating the kind of program of economic reform that the Fund would require.

No Mexican loans were charged off on the balance sheets of commercial banks, no banks became insolvent, and export–import transactions between Mexico and the rest of the world continued.[12]

---

[10] The Group of Ten states (except for Belgium) plus Switzerland and, because of its traditional relationship with Mexico, the Bank of Spain.

[11] Paul Volcker, the Chairman of the Board of Governors of the Federal Reserve System and one of the principal architects of the rescue operation, writes that 'standstill' was a less frightening or aggressive term than 'moratorium' or 'default', which might well have triggered legal action forcing banks to foreclose on the loans. Volcker and Gyohten, *Changing Fortunes*, (n. 4 supra) 202.

[12] But the government of Mexico, in an action not suggested or approved by the international financial community, nationalized all the privately owned banks in Mexico, on the basis that they had not been vigilant against capital flight.

(b)   Managing the Medium Term

Both the short-term credits offered by the United States and the Bank for International Settlements, and the acquiescence (without formal agreement) by the commercial banks in deferral of repayment of principal were based on the understanding that Mexico would apply to the IMF for a stand-by supported by a long-term program of economic reform and adjustment. Though resort to the Fund was a bitter pill for Mexico to swallow and indeed produced charges of betrayal and surrender of independence in the Mexican press, it was clear that Mexico had no alternative. Neither the commercial banks nor the central banks and treasuries of the developed countries would proceed beyond short-term bridging credits unless a serious and detailed economic plan was in place for Mexico, subject to the kind of discipline that only the IMF could provide. From the point of view of international economic law, it could fairly be said that the decade of avoidance was being replaced (first for Mexico, and subsequently for other debtor states) by a regime in which IMF conditionality was to play a dominant, if not exclusive role.

For its part, the IMF saw its role not only as supervising reform and adjustment in Mexico (and the other states similarly situated), but as the coordinator of an effort to mobilize all those involved in the crisis of developing-country debt. Jacques de Larosière, the Managing Director of the Fund since 1978, made clear early on that the Fund would not grant a stand-by to Mexico (and thus release funds to replace the bridge credits) unless the commercial banks as well as the central banks of the creditor countries committed themselves to supply new funds on their own, roughly in proportion to the amount of credits that they had previously extended. As de Larosière later explained:

It is simply not possible for borrowing countries to go from a situation in which they were absorbing $50 billion a year of net new lending from commercial banks to one where inflows are zero or negative without disastrous consequences for both current welfare and future development prospects. It is certainly true that too much was borrowed in the past in too short a time with too little consideration of the consequences. But the correct solution is not to cease all lending and let the chips fall where they may. That would provoke disproportionate economic hardship that might well lead to political instability the consequences of which could not fail to rebound on economic and financial structures in industrial countries. The task, therefore, is to achieve a smooth transition in which sufficient external financing is available to indebted countries to enable them to scale back their dependence on foreign savings in an orderly fashion, while preserving their ability to invest and grow in the medium term.[13]

---

[13] Jacques de Larosière, Remarks to American Enterprise Institute, Washington, 5 Dec. 1983, 12 *IMF Survey*, 379 at 382 (5 Dec. 1983), quoted also in Margaret G. de Vries, *Balance of Payments Adjustment 1945 to 1986*, (n. 2 supra) p. 22.

The 'cooperative' strategy, as it came to be known, involved the governments of the debtor countries, the governments of the developed countries, the Bank for International Settlements, the World Bank, the IMF, and the private creditors—large and small. The strategy had two main elements, adjustment by the debtors, and financing by the creditors; neither could proceed without the other. In a real sense, as a senior official of the Fund later put it, the strategy amounted to extending the principle of conditionality to creditors.[14] Only if they committed a 'critical mass' of new lending would the Fund and the other public institutions offer their own funds and undertake to supervise the painful reforms that could enable the debtor countries to resume their status as reliable borrowers. In return, the Fund undertook a close monitoring of the debtor countries' performance under the criteria set out in the stand-by arrangement, and to make the information gained from its monitoring activity available to the creditor banks as they were engaged in negotiating restructuring and refinancing agreements with the debtor countries.

The negotiations between the Fund and the government of Mexico are summarized hereafter, not with a view to giving a detailed account of a non-recurring event, but with a view to illustrating how the IMF's techniques of granting a stand-by[15] were adapted to a situation that all the participants understood had far wider implications than the typical situation of a particular country in balance of payments difficulties.[16]

The Fund pressed, as one might expect, for reduced public spending, further devaluation of the peso and elimination of exchange controls, and reduced external borrowing; the Mexican government preparing the transition from one administration to another, sought to protect its standing with the people of Mexico as much as it could, particularly with respect to public sector employment and the level of real income. The Fund initially sought to reduce Mexico's budget deficit, which was running at an annual rate of 17 percent of gross domestic product to 6.7 percent; the government held out for a target of 10 percent of GDP. The final figures set out in the Letter of Intent signed on behalf of Mexico set a deficit target of 8.5 percent of GDP for 1983, 5.5 percent for 1984, and 3.5 percent for 1985. The public sector external debt, which had risen by $19 billion in 1981 and by some $6 billion in the

[14] Manuel Guitan, Assoc. Director, Central Banking Dept. IMF, in Volcker and Gyohten, *Changing Fortunes*, n. 4 supra, Appendix, p. 318 at 320.

[15] See Ch. 16, Sect. 16.7; Ch. 17, Sect. 17.5.

[16] Amid various rumours of 'sell-out' the government of Mexico made the Letter of Intent of November 10, 1982 public as soon as it was signed. In addition, the Mexican press published a 'Technical Memorandum of Understanding' attached to the Letter of Intent which contained detailed dates for performance and disbursement of funds. The formal Statement by the IMF, more detailed than usual, was released on December 23, 1982, and published in 12 *IMF Survey*, p. 1 (10 Jan. 1982).

first half of 1982 was to rise by no more than $5 billion net new borrowing in 1983. (Later this figure was changed to $7 billion, precisely the amount the commercial banks plus foreign governments were supposed to furnish.) A dual exchange control system was permitted to remain in effect, subject to consultation with the Fund, but Mexico was required to provide for an orderly system of counterpart deposits in pesos whereby both private and public sector debts could gradually be brought current. Inflation, which had been running at 90–100 percent in 1982 was to be reduced to about 55 percent in 1983 and further in succeeding years; the IMF press release reporting the stand-by stated 'Incomes policy is of central importance in the adjustment program, as it affects not only the chances of curtailing the public sector deficit but is also crucial to the goals of price, balance of payments, and exchange rate stability.'

In return, the IMF agreed to permit Mexico to draw SDR3.6 billion (just under US$4 billion) equivalent to 450 percent of Mexico's quota, to be disbursed over a three-year period under a so-called Extended Arrangement.[17] In addition, as noted above, conclusion of the stand-by was a condition precedent to commitment by Mexico's commercial bank creditors of a new package of loans of about $5 billion, adding about 7 percent to the banks' exposure and to commitment of an additional package of official loans, primarily from the United States, of about $2 billion. Correspondingly, commitment by the commercial and official creditors (or at least 'sufficient assurance' of such a commitment)[18] was a condition precedent for the commitments by Mexico and by the IMF.

Thus by year-end 1982 (or a little after)[19] the pattern had been set for Phase I of a rescue operation in the case of inability of a major debtor country to meet its international financial obligations. No one was completely satisfied, but all of the necessary parties participated and there was no meltdown, no chain reaction of failure of money-center commercial banks, nothing to remind the general public (as contrasted with senior financial officials) of the 1930s. The International Monetary Fund, spurned in many instances in the preceding decade, turned out to play an essential part—far greater than the volume of its own resources made available would indicate—as umpire, organizer, cajoler, and lawgiver.

[17] See Ch. 17, Sect. 17.6(a). To be precise, Mexico's quota in the Fund stood at SDR802.5, and the full amount to be drawn under the Extended Arrangement was SDR3,611.25 million. SDR200.625 million, constituting Mexico's first credit tranche (i.e. 25 percent of its quota) was available for immediate drawing.

[18] This was the phrase used in the official press release of December 23, 1982 (n.16 supra); by that time the official lenders and the major money-center banks had signed on to the Volcker-de Larosière plan, but not all of the 1400 smaller participants in syndicated loans had done so. Final arrangements for the new private credits were not concluded until late February, 1983.

[19] See n. 18 supra.

18.4   PRECEDENT BECOMES PATTERN: A BRIEFER LOOK AT THE BRAZILIAN CASE

On November 10, 1982, the same day that Mexico signed its Letter of Intent with the IMF, Brazil announced that it, too, could not meet its foreign exchange obligations as they came due. Brazil's announcement did not cause quite the same shock as had Mexico's announcement two and a half months earlier. It was clear, however, that many of the same parties involved in the Mexican crisis had another major problem before them, somewhat different in origin but comparable in dimension and in potential threat to the international financial system.

In a number of ways Brazil was different from Mexico. For one thing, Brazil was a huge importer of oil, and its development had been set back after the second oil price rise in 1979. For another, Brazil had been experiencing (and living with) inflation averaging 50 percent per year for nearly 20 years. Also, from 1964 on, Brazil had been governed by a military junta, and was just beginning a transition to democracy. But Brazil's economy had been growing at an average of 9 percent per year in the period 1964–73, and (after the first oil shock) at about 6½ percent per year in the period 1973–82.

Brazil had broken off relations with the IMF as early as 1958, on the ground that the Fund's conditions were humiliating. But as it built the world's largest dam, five major steel mills and supporting networks, a new highway system, huge mining projects, and two nuclear power stations, Brazil had no difficulty in finding sources of funds from the commercial banks in the industrial countries. Most of Brazil's new industry was owned and operated by huge 'parastatal enterprises'—Petrobras (oil and gas), Sidebras (steel), Electrobras (electric power), Nuclebras (nuclear power), etc.

In 1981–2, as the market for Brazil's industrial products shrank, commodity prices fell, and interest rates rose, Brazil was forced to draw down its reserves. Once the Mexican crisis erupted in August 1982, Brazil found it impossible to roll over or refinance its existing loans or to secure new ones. When its cash ran out in late 1982, Brazil's external debt stood at $84–90 billion, approximately one-quarter of its gross domestic product. About 70 percent of Brazil's external debt was owed to commercial banks. Its debt service obligations came to $10 billion per year, equal to more than 90 percent of its foreign exchange earnings on goods and services.

(a)   Again a First Quick Fix

Brazil first sought short-term loans from the big five New York banks, and secured a commitment of $600 million, not quite enough to meet current interest obligations. The Exchange Stabilization Fund of the US Treasury provided $1.23 billion in bridging credits and the Federal Reserve added $400 million. Once Brazilian officials made known that they were seeking an agreement with the IMF, the Bank for International Settlements offered a bridging credit of $1.2 billion, subsequently raised to $1.45 billion when the Saudi Arabian Monetary Agency added its support.

Each of these credits was designed not to provide new funds, but to prevent default, pending conclusion of a longer-term arrangement with the IMF. The Fund dispatched a mission to Brazil as soon as practical (i.e. just after Brazil's first election in 18 years), and at the same time Brazilian officials and its principal creditors began negotiations in New York, looking both to maintaining existing lines of credit and interbank deposits, and to a supply of new loans amounting to $4.4 billion. By December 15, the IMF team had reached a tentative agreement on a drawing of SDR4.5 billion under the Fund's Enlarged Access Facility, subject to a variety of conditions and subject to approval by the Fund's Executive Board, which, as in the Mexican case, would come only upon assurance of commitment of new funds by the commercial bank creditors. On January 6, 1983, Brazil submitted its Letter of Intent—actually the first of seven letters, but as in the Mexican case reaching agreement from the private banking sector proved to be the most difficult and time-consuming part of the package.[20] Despite considerable arm-twisting by the IMF, the Federal Reserve, the leading money-center banks, and by the Brazilian government itself, de Larosière did not have 'sufficient assurance' to submit the stand-by to the Executive Board for approval until the last day of February 1983.[21] By that time Brazil had submitted a second Letter of Intent, to take account of a 'maxi-devaluation' of the cruzeiro undertaken on February 18. The total amount covered in the stand-by was SDR4.955 billion—equal, as in the Mexican case, to 450 percent of quota—to be drawn over a three-year period.[22] Again, the performance criteria were tough—a halving of the financing requirement of the public sector from 1982 to 1983 and a further halving by 1985; a reduction in the current account deficit from 4.5 percent of GDP in 1982 to 2 percent in 1983 and eventually to 1 percent in 1985. Most difficult—practically and politically—Brazil committed itself to bring down the rate of inflation from

[20] In the meantime, Brazil was permitted to draw SDR498 million under the Compensatory Financing Facility, Ch. 17, Sect. 17.6(b) supra, for a shortfall in Brazil's earnings from sale of commodities in 1982.

[21] IMF Press Release No. 83/16, 18 Feb. 1983; 12 *IMF Survey*, 65, 7 Mar. 1983.

[22] Again, also, about 30 percent would be available from the general resources of the fund, the remainder, at higher interest rates, from borrowed resources.

100 percent in 1982 to 87 percent in 1983, 40 percent in 1984 and 20 percent in 1985, to be accomplished by interrupting the cycle of wage and price increases reflected in, and at least partly caused by, Brazil's practice of indexation.

One important additional factor came out in the Brazilian case that had only been hinted at in the case of Mexico. What if Brazil did not adhere to its Letter of Intent? Would the IMF, which had laboured so hard in the belief that a Brazilian default could pose a major threat to the world's financial system, actually declare a default and cut off additional disbursements?

(b)   The Tap Turned Off, and On Again

By May 1983, when figures for the first quarter of the year came out, it was evident that Brazil was not in compliance with the Fund's performance criteria. The Fund sent another mission to Brazil, and let it be known that the second tranche under the extended arrangement, totalling about $400 million, would not be disbursed on June 1, as scheduled. The commercial banks announced that they too would postpone the next instalment of $634 million, due June 1. This meant that Brazil would not have the funds to repay the bridging loan to the Bank for International Settlements. The BIS extended the due date, first to the end of June, then to July 15, but on July 11, it announced that there would be no further extension. However, the BIS did not formally declare a default, and did not invoke the guarantees of the supporting central banks. As the Annual Report of the BIS for 1983–4 stated:

In reaching this decision account was taken of encouraging reports from the Fund about the progress of its negotiations. By the end of November, however, which was the time at which the last instalment [on the bridge loan] was originally due, the negotiations had been completed, and the IMF was able to resume disbursements to Brazil. The Central Bank of Brazil was thus able to complete the repayment of the BIS bridging loan on the final maturity date despite the difficulties encountered during the life of the facility in meeting the maturity dates of individual instalments.[23]

The negotiations involved a Decree-Law issued by the president of Brazil providing that wage increases would be limited to 80 percent of price increases, and relaxation by the IMF of the targets for reducing the public sector deficit, plus agreement to set inflation targets on a monthly, rather than an annual basis. A third Letter of Intent was prepared and the Managing Director was able to announce to the Annual Meeting of the Fund and the World Bank that an agreement in principle had been reached on financing of the Brazilian adjustment program for the remainder of 1983 and 1984 and that disbursements under the stand-by would be resumed.[24] The Chairman of the Advisory Committee of the commercial banks also

[23] Bank for Int'l Settlements, *54th Annual Report*, 151–2 (1984).
[24] Statement of Managing Director, 26 Sept. 1983, 12 *IMF Survey*, 293 (10 Oct. 1983).

announced that, subject to details being worked out later, the private credit-ors had agreed on a $6.5 billion package of new funds. Further, foreign gov-ernments agreed to postponement of repayment of $2 billion in official credits through the Paris Club,[25] and also agreed to extend $2.5 billion in export credits. Thus the pressure of the IMF, plus the BIS and the commer-cial creditors had substantial effect, and though the President of Brazil's Central Bank resigned because he would not sign the revised Letter of Intent, a combination of increased commitment to compliance plus somewhat relaxed conditionality led not only to resumption of the IMF credits, but to a package of some $11 billion of other credits, public and private, that would not have been available if the Fund had continued to treat Brazil as out of compliance with the stand-by.[26]

18.5   RESCHEDULING, RESTRUCTURING, AND THE BAKER AND BRADY PLANS

As is true with all the subjects addressed in this chapter, it is not always evi-dent how to distinguish non-recurring events from precedents of enduring value. There can be no doubt, however, that taken together, the events of the 1980s concerning the debt of the developing countries were a significant for-mative element in the evolution of the international monetary system, including its legal and institutional as well as financial aspects.

(a)   The First Assessment (1982–5)

Virtually all the loans made by commercial banks to developing countries in the 1970s became the object of some kind of renegotiation in the 1980s, with the complementary objectives of restoring the borrowing countries to credit-worthiness and of saving the creditor banks from having to take major charges against earnings because of non-performing loans.[27] The 'cooperative strategy' among the IMF, the central banks and treasuries of the principal

---

[25] See Ch. 19, Sect. 19.3.

[26] The story did not end there. In fact, the Brazilian Congress subsequently rejected the Decree-Law, and two more presidential decrees and several more revisions of the Letter of Intent, were issued. The purpose here, evidently, is not to tell the complete story of Brazil's rela-tions with the IMF or the international financial community, but to illustrate the force, and the limitations, of conditionality in the context of linkage between the public and private sector creditors.

[27] Altogether, 39 countries rescheduled some $140 billion in commercial bank debt in the 1980s, several more than once:

Argentina, Bolivia, Brazil, Chile, Congo (Brazzaville), Costa Rica, Dominican Republic, Ecuador, Gabon, Gambia, Guinea, Guyana, Honduras, Ivory Coast, Jamaica, Madagascar, Malawi, Mexico, Morocco, Mozambique, Nicaragua, Niger, Nigeria, Panama, Peru, Philippines, Poland, Romania, Senegal, Sierra Leone, South Africa, Sudan, Togo, Trinidad and Tobago, Uruguay, Venezuela, Yugoslavia, Zaire, and Zambia.

industrial countries, the commercial banks and the debtor countries succeeded in the short run in averting a breakdown of the global payments system, and none of the debtor countries literally ran out of funds so as to be denied even short-term trade credits. From mid-1982 to mid-1986, the IMF provided about $34 billion in balance of payments financing to developing countries, and from the beginning of 1983 to mid-1986, the commercial banks provided about $27 billion in new money through concerted (i.e. involuntary) lending to indebted countries that had restructured or rescheduled their debts.[28]

Crisis management, however, was not the same as long-term solution, and by the mid-1980s, it had become clear both that the debt problem remained—rescheduling of debt did not mean reduction—and that spontaneous capital flow to the debtor countries—voluntary lending and direct investment—had virtually ceased. Moreover, the adjustment programs prescribed by the Fund, while solving the immediate crises and improving the current account balance of the countries concerned, had in many instances slowed down economic growth even as population growth continued unabated, thus leading to decline in real per capita income.[29]

(b) The Baker Initiative (1985–8)

At the Annual Meeting of the IMF and the World Bank in Seoul, Korea in October 1985, the American Secretary of the Treasury, James Baker, laid out the agenda for the next phase, which he identified as a 'Program for Sustained Growth'.[30] The Baker Initiative, developed over several months and discussed in advance with the staff of the IMF and with representatives of the G–7, started from the proposition that the best long-term means for overcoming the effects of the debt crisis was concentration on economic growth, rather than on the programs of austerity that had been required in the preceding three years.

Baker's strategy had three related elements:

First, adoption by the principal debtor countries of comprehensive macroeconomic policies, designed to promote growth and balance of payments adjustment, to reduce inflation, and generally to emphasize the role of

---

[28] Margaret Garrison de Vries, *Balance of Payments Adjustment 1945 to 1986*, pp. 232–4.

[29] For instance, Mexico, which accounted for about one-fourth of the debt of the Baker 15 (n. 31 infra) moved from a $4 billion trade deficit with the United States in 1981 to surpluses in 1982–4 that totalled $18 billion; real wages, however, declined by an estimated 40 percent. Brazil reduced its imports from the United States by one-half, while doubling its exports to the United States, achieving a bilateral trade surplus of $5.8 billion with the United States in 1984, and an overall trade surplus of about $12 billion.

[30] Statement of James A. Baker III before Joint Annual Meetings of IMF and World Bank, 8 Oct. 1985, *IMF Summary Proceedings of 40th Annual Meeting of Board of Governors*, 50–8. For an account of the development of Secretary Baker's thinking, see the account by the Chairman of the Federal Reserve System, Paul A. Volcker, in Volcker and Gyohten, *Changing Fortunes*, pp. 211–14 (1992).

the private sector. Baker spoke of such measures as better mobilization of domestic savings through tax reform, labour market reform, development of financial markets, encouragement of foreign investment, and liberalization of trade, all supported by the international financial institutions.

Second, a continued central role for the IMF, in conjunction with increased and more effective structural adjustment lending by the World Bank and the regional development banks.

Third, increased lending by the commercial banks in support of the adoption by the debtor countries of the reform proposals. Baker indicated a range of net new lending (i.e. in addition to any roll-over of existing debt) of $20 billion over three years to fifteen heavily indebted countries, which immediately became known as the 'Baker Fifteen'.[31]

The IMF, the World Bank, and the governments of the industrial countries reacted favourably to the Baker initiative, and so, initially, did the commercial banks. But, as Paul Volcker put it, 'when it came to moving beyond moral support to making actual commitments, the latter [i.e. the commercial banks] were not so eager.'[32] The flaw in the Baker initiative, it soon became clear, was that it made no provision for coercion, or even strong incentives for the commercial banks to fulfill their assigned role as suppliers of new capital. In fact, the financing contribution from the private sector turned negative from 1985 on: for the Baker Fifteen, debt to commercial countries was reduced by more than $15 billion between 1985 and 1988.[33] Only the Japanese banks, which held some 15 percent of Latin American private debt, widened their lending.[34] Put another way, as official lenders, the IMF, the World Bank, and the regional development banks were increasing their contribution of funds to the debtor countries (though not as much

---

[31] Ten of the countries were in Latin America: Argentina, Bolivia, Brazil, Chile, Colombia, Ecuador, Mexico, Peru, Uruguay and Venezuela. The others were Ivory Coast, Morocco, Nigeria, Philippines and Yugoslavia.

[32] Volcker and Gyohten, *Changing Fortunes* (n. 4 supra), p. 214.

[33] See *IMF World Economic Outlook*, April 1989, 51–2 and table 12. In fact after long and painful negotiations, Mexico succeeded in October 1986 in concluding a deal in line with the Baker initiative:

First, the IMF gave conditional approval of a stand-by credit of SDR1.4 billion, subject to availability of financing from other official sources and from the creditor banks. Eventually $43.7 billion of previously rescheduled debt was stretched out to 20 years, with 7 years interest-free. The principal commercial creditors agreed to advance an additional $6 billion to be repaid over 12 years with 5 years' grace, and the official lenders, including the IMF, the World Bank, and the US Government, agreed to advance an additional $6.5 billion. Mexico sought an interest rate of 3/4 percent over LIBOR, the banks held out for 7/8, and eventually agreement was reached on a rate 13/16 percent over LIBOR. The commercial banks agreed to provide further credit up to $1.2 billion if the price of oil fell below $9 per barrel for three months, and up to $500 million if Mexico failed to reach its growth targets, with these contingent credits guaranteed by the World Bank.

[34] See Volcker and Gyohten, *Changing Fortunes*, (n. 4 supra) 222–3. Of course, as Gyohten points out, the appreciation of the yen against the dollar at this time inflated the dollar amount of the credits offered by the Japanese banks, which in any case were highly liquid as the result of Japan's massive trade surpluses.

as envisaged in the Baker Initiative), the commercial banks were withdrawing funds. At the same time the anticipated revival of direct investment in the developing countries as a function of gross domestic product did not take place.

In focusing the world's attention on the need to move from emergency relief to growth as the way to address the debt problem, the Baker initiative was a success. In terms of achievement by mobilizing new private as well as public funds, the Baker initiative clearly fell short.

(c)   The Brady Initiative (1989–)

In the spring of 1989, James Baker's successor as American Secretary of the Treasury, Nicholas F. Brady, came out with a new initiative, designed to combine the structural reforms advocated by Baker and supported by the World Bank and the IMF with actual debt relief, i.e. either reduction in principal or reduction in interest rates.[35] Debt relief was to be voluntary—negotiated with the commercial lenders country-by-country, but with incentives provided by the governments of the industrial countries and the international financial institutions. If the private creditors could come to an agreement with the debtor country, the public institutions would provide not only stand-by arrangements geared to programs of adjustment, but also collateral to be relied on by the private creditors.

Two major elements of the Brady initiative merit discussion from a legal perspective. *First*, whereas in 1982–3, as well as under the Baker plan, the Fund stand-by arrangements, bilateral official credits, and agreements by the commercial banks were strictly linked, so that nothing was agreed until everything was agreed, under the Brady initiative as interpreted and implemented by the Fund's Executive Board (with the concurrence of the United States), the IMF would approve a stand-by arrangement *before* conclusion of a financing package where negotiations with the banks have begun and 'where it is expected that an appropriate financing package will be concluded in a reasonable period of time.'[36]

Second, the idea that the value of a loan to the creditor was measured solely by contract was modified to a more property-based, market-oriented approach. In the time between the Baker and the Brady initiatives, a significant secondary market in developing country debt had grown up. One measure of the value of a developing country loan was what price it would bring in the secondary market. The discount varied from country to country

---

[35] Secretary Brady first made his proposal public at a conference sponsored by the Brookings Institution in Washington in March 1989. The text of Brady's address as well as comments thereon, are reproduced in Edward R. Fried and Philip H. Trezise (eds.), *Third World Debt: The Next Phase* (Brookings 1989). The details summarized here emerged later, but not in any single document.

[36] 'Guidelines for Debt Strategy', approved by IMF Ex. Bd. (23 May 1989), 18 *IMF Survey*, 161 (29 May 1989). See also *IMF Annual Report 1989*, 23–8.

depending on its overall economic performance and prospects, its punctuality in servicing existing debt, and its performance under Fund adjustment programs. But even for Mexico, the most conscientious performer under Fund programs, the discount grew from 37 percent (63 cents on the dollar) in early 1986 to around 60 percent (40 cents on the dollar) at the end of 1989.[37] Since both borrower and lender could be said to be responsible for the debt problem, the idea behind the Brady plan was that the loss in market value reflected in the discount from face value could be shared by the parties.

Furthermore, following the lead of Citibank, which in 1987 took a one-time charge against earnings of $3 billion against outstanding loans of $14.9 billion, many creditor banks had 'provisioned', i.e. created reserves of 30–50 percent against losses on loans to developing countries, reflecting the uncertainty of collecting 100 cents on the dollar on these loans.

The Brady initiative, building on earlier efforts by Mexico to auction off some of its debt in conjunction with offers of increased security,[38] proposed a menu of options for debt relief. As under the Baker initiative, there would be no coercion, but there would be pressure for concerted action, and assurance of support from the international financial institutions and the Paris Club creditors if the private creditors acting together, exercised one of the options.

Once again Mexico was the test case:

> 1. In May 1989, the IMF approved a three-year Extended Arrangement for SDR2,797.2 million, equal to about $3.5 billion (240 percent of quota) to support Mexico's medium-term growth-oriented adjustment program. A new feature in Fund programs, consistent with the Brady proposals,[39] was that 30 percent of each drawing under the extended arrangement could be set aside for debt reduction. Further, the Fund announced that it would consider augmenting the stand-by by up to 40 percent of Mexico's quota (i.e. up to SDR466.2 million or about $590 million) if financing arrangements were concluded with the private creditors for debt service reduction and the Fund determined that such arrangements would be consistent with Mexico's adjustment program 'and would represent an efficient use of set-aside resources.'[40]

[37] See Claudio Loser and Eliot Kalter, *Mexico: The Strategy to Achieve Sustained Economic Growth*, p. 53 (IMF Occasional Paper No. 99 (Sept. 1992)).

[38] In late 1987 Mexico and J. P. Morgan announced a debt conversion program involving the exchange of bank debt for 20-year bonds, guaranteed by the US Treasury. The goal of the program had been to exchange $10 billion in debt; in the event, only $3.7 billion in debt was exchanged with 95 banks, primarily from Japan, collateralized by $500 million in purchases of US Treasury zero coupon bonds.

[39] See Brady's address, in Fried and Trezise, *Third World Debt* (n. 35 supra), 73–4.

[40] See 18 *IMF Survey*, 210 (10 July 1989). The Letter of Intent submitted by Mexico to which the Extended Arrangement responds was released by the Mexican government, and is summarized in 18 *IMF Survey*, pp. 114–15 (17 Apr. 1989). It summarized a number of major economic reforms undertaken by Mexico including joining GATT, rationalizing its tariff schedules, reforming its tax system, and devaluing the peso.

2. Also in May, the Paris Club creditors signed an agreement with Mexico to reschedule debts of some $2.5 billion, representing 100 percent of principal due in the years 1987–9.

3. In mid-June, the World Bank approved three 'structural adjustment' loans, each for $500 million, to support further reforms in finance, industry, and public enterprise management, designed to encourage private investment and to increase efficiency in several sectors. Like the Fund, the World Bank announced that up to 25 percent of the funds made available could be used for debt reduction over a three-year period, and another 15 percent could be made available for this purpose if needed.

4. The most difficult part of the package, but the most critical, involved the private banks, which together held more than $48 billion of medium- and long-term Mexican sovereign debt. In July 1989, after direct intervention of Presidents Salinas de Gortari and Bush, and apparently a decision by Mexico to suspend all its foreign debt payments if agreement could not be reached,[41] it was announced that an agreement in principle had been reached between the Government of Mexico and members of the 'Bank Advisory Committee' negotiating on behalf of close to 500 banks. As long as all, or nearly all banks concurred, each bank would have the choice of three options:[42]

(a) A bank could exchange its existing debt for 30-year *Debt Reduction Bonds*, having a face value of 65 percent of the debt being exchanged with interest continuing at the existing rate of 13/16 percent over Libor (at the time about 10 percent).

(b) A bank could exchange its existing debt for 30-year *Debt Service Reduction Bonds*, in the same face value as the existing debt but with a fixed interest rate of 6.25 percent;

(c) A bank could retain its debt under the original terms without conversion into bonds on condition that it provided new credits equal to 25 percent of the bank's existing exposure, repayable at market interest rates over 15 years including seven years' grace.

After the experiences of the past decade, the menu of options would not have been acceptable to the banks without substantial security. Supplying that security involved not only the United States government, but the government of Japan, the IMF, and the World Bank. Repayment of the principal of the 30-year 'Brady Bonds', as they came to be known, was secured by 30-year zero coupon bonds sold to

[41] The decision to suspend was confirmed by President Salinas some months later. See *New York Times*, 2 Mar. 1990, p. D–16.

[42] For an account of the last-minute negotiations at the US Treasury, see 'How the Mexican Debt Pact was Achieved', *New York Times*, 31 July 1989, §IV, p. 1. In the final sessions, the American banks were represented by the chairmen of Citibank and Bank of America, which had the largest exposure, and a representative of Swiss Bank Corporation on behalf of all non-American bank creditors.

Mexico by the US Treasury.[43] In addition, Mexico established a revolving 18-month interest guarantee account at the Federal Reserve Bank of New York. These collaterals, in turn, were financed by the IMF, the World Bank, and the Export-Import Bank of Japan.

The original expectation had been that 20 percent of the outstanding debt would be covered by debt reduction, 60 percent by interest rate reduction, and 20 percent by term loans. When all the returns were counted, banks holding 41 percent of the debt chose to reduce principal, banks holding 49 percent of the debt chose to reduce interest, and banks holding 10 percent of the debt chose the new credits option. Thus about $43 billion of new Brady Bonds in two classes were issued, and $4.4 billion of debt was allocated to the new credits option, implying about $1.1 billion in new credits.[44]

For the banks, the new bonds, being guaranteed, would not require creating special reserves. The reduction from prior face amount could be charged against existing reserves; if the reserves against Mexican loans exceeded the charges, regulators in the United States and elsewhere were encouraged to permit switching the reserves to cover other more troubled sovereign loans, such as those to Brazil and Argentina.

For Mexico, the Brady plan arrangements had two major effects. *First*, they extinguished about $7.1 billion of debt, and by reducing the interest rate on about half the total debt, saved the equivalent of another $7.9 billion, for a total saving of about 30 percent of its bank debt, and 15 percent of its total outstanding debt. *Second*, conclusion of the arrangements amid much publicity signalled to the world that Mexico was now a safe place for investors, whether in the form of debt or of equity.[45]

---

[43] A zero coupon bond is a bond that pays no interest, and is accordingly sold at a steep discount from its face value. In the actual case, the US Treasury proceeded (with some uncertainty) on the basis of a 7.925 percent annual yield; it sold $43.1 billion worth of zero coupon bonds to Mexico for $7.1 billion.

[44] The facts here summarized are presented in more detail in Mohammed A. El-Erian, 'Mexico's Commercial Bank Financing Package', 27 *Finance & Development* 3, 26 (Sept. 1990); Loser and Kalter, *Mexico: The Strategy to Achieve Sustained Economic Growth*, (n. 37 supra) 57–60; and *Third World Debt Strategy*, Hearing before Subcomm. on Int'l Finance and Monetary Policy of Senate Comm. on Banking, Housing and Urban Affairs, Testimony of David Mulford, Under-Secretary of the Treasury, and William R. Rhodes, principal co-chairman of the Bank Advisory Committee for Mexico (21 Mar. 1990).

[45] For confirmation of this fact, see e.g. the following excerpts from the appendix by Mexico's chief debt negotiator, Angel Gurría, Under-Secretary for International Financial Affairs, Mexican Finance Ministry, in Volcker and Gyothen, *Changing Fortunes*, (n. 4 supra) at pp. 317–18:

The importance of getting relief in the debt has proven, particularly in Mexico, a very big boost. Why? Because in Mexico we were ready to do the right thing in terms of economic policy but there was a perception that we had too much debt. We struck a deal with our commercial bank creditors that reduced the debt somewhat. . . . There followed an enormous surge in confidence in Mexico's economy from both foreigners and Mexicans.
. . .

Suddenly . . . the market brought its money back to invest. Even the banks started offering new loans to Mexico.   *cont./*

As several other countries sought to negotiate their own versions of Brady packages, the international financial community—public and private—looked to Mexico for 'demonstration effects'.[46]

18.6   A NEW MEXICAN CRISIS (1994–5)[47]

(a)   The Collapse of the Peso

For half a decade, Mexico continued to be a model, recovered from the ills of the 1980s, and, as its political leaders said, poised to graduate from the class of developing nations. Mexico not only finally joined the GATT, but even the Organization for Economic Cooperation and Development (OECD), the club of the developed industrial nations. Mexico had no exchange controls, inflation was low, the budget was in balance, the exchange rate stable, and the economy was less dependent than in the early 1980s on exports of oil. Mexico's current account deficit was down to 5.7 percent of GDP, which was more than covered by capital inflows, both port-folio and direct investment. Most significant, Mexico had joined with the United States and Canada in the North American Free Trade Agreement, which not only reduced trade barriers among the three countries but attracted substantial cross-border investments. Many observers, as well as the leaders of Mexico, spoke of the final take-off that would allow Mexico to graduate from a developing to a developed country. The IMF's Summary of the Article IV Consultation, concluded in February 1994, said:

For later developments in Mexico, see the following section.

[46] Costa Rica and the Philippines made arrangements with their creditors at about the same time as Mexico did, and Venezuela followed shortly thereafter. By the end of 1994, 17 other countries had reached some kind of agreement loosely modeled on the Brady/Mexico model. Argentina signed debt reduction agreements with the IMF, the World Bank, the Paris Club, the Inter-American Development Bank, and the private bank creditors at year-end 1992.

Brazil, the largest debtor, secured a stand-by agreement from the IMF in January 1992 which made provision for support of debt reduction in the event of an agreement with the private banks. Such an agreement (with six options for the banks) appeared to have been reached, at least in principle, in July 1992. However, Brazil failed to meet the targets set in the stand-by for the first two quarters of 1992, and negotiations on revision of the stand-by were canceled at year-end 1992, following the impeachment and resignation of President Collor. Brazil continued to negotiate both with the IMF and the private banks throughout 1993 and the first part of 1994, but agreement on an IMF stand-by was not reached. Nevertheless in April 1994 Brazil made a Brady-type agreement to restructure some $52 billion in debts to private banks, partially secured by US Treasury zero coupon bonds but not a formal agreement with the United States or the Fund.

[47] For a more detailed description, analysing both the 1982 and the 1994–5 crises, see Nora Lustig, 'Mexico in Crises, the US to the Rescue: The Financial Assistance Packages of 1982 and 1995', 2 *UCLA J. Int'l Law & For. Aff.* 25 (Spring/Summer 1997); and by the same author, *Mexico, The Remaking of an Economy*, esp. ch. 7, 'Rescue, Recession and Recovery' (2nd edn. 1998).

Directors expressed admiration for the dramatic transformation of Mexico's economy . . . [and] satisfaction with the narrowing of the external current account deficit in 1993.[48]

In fact, while the public budget was balanced, there were a great many off-budget expenditures, in particular loans by state-owned banks. Further, the peso, linked to the US dollar in a narrow band supported by the Bank of Mexico, became increasingly overvalued, as Mexico's rate of inflation exceeded that of the United States. In addition, several negative events occurred in Mexico in the course of the year, each diminishing the optimism that both Mexican and foreign observers had felt about the country's progress. In January 1994, an uprising broke out among the Indian population in the southern state of Chiapas, with which the government never fully coped. Two months later, the presidential candidate of the governing party, the PRI, was assassinated, and while a single gunman was arrested and convicted, the persons behind the assassination were never identified. In September 1994, the Secretary-General of the PRI was murdered and the links between the two assassinations, as well as with the administration of the outgoing President, Carlos Salinas de Gortari and his brother Raul, remained murky. Each of these events seems to have affected both foreign investors, with the result that capital inflow slowed down, and Mexican investors, who increasingly moved their capital to the United States or elsewhere.

When Mexico's new president, Ernesto Zedillo, took office on December 1, 1994, it was announced that there would be no change in Mexico's exchange policy. On December 20, however, the government allowed the peso to fall to about 4.0 to the US dollar, compared with about 3.46 the day before. Two days later, as the Mexican stock market plunged and interest rates rose, and the Bank of Mexico had spent $5 billion to support the new rate, the government announced that it was abandoning its policy of supporting the peso. The now freely floating peso closed at 4.80 to the dollar, a fall of about 30 percent. By the end of the following week, the peso fell another 10 percent, and by January 10, 1995, the peso had lost over half of its value compared with the day before the initial devaluation three weeks earlier. Mexico's finance minister, who had also been his country's chief negotiator of the NAFTA, resigned.

(b)   The Response of the International Community

Once again, the international financial community, led by the United States and the IMF, concluded that a rescue effort was required, lest Mexico default on the large volume of its short-term dollar-denominated (or dollar-tied) notes (known as *Tesobonos*) that were about to become due and could

---

[48] *IMF Annual Report 1994*, pp. 81–2.

probably not be renewed. The first effort was a short-term credit of some $18 billion furnished half by the United States, half by the European central banks acting through the Bank for International Settlements, plus Canada, and a group of commercial banks led by Citibank and J. P. Morgan. That credit proved insufficient to calm the market, even when accompanied by a formal austerity plan announced by President Zedillo, with the support of Mexican labour leaders.[49]

The Mexican government applied to the IMF for a new stand-by credit, though it had not yet repaid its last loan, taken out in 1989. President Clinton quickly announced that the United States would offer up to $40 billion in loan guarantees, on the assumption that if the full faith and credit of the United States stood behind it, Mexico could borrow in the market to pay off its short-term loans and could support the still sliding peso.[50] The expectation in the United States was that if the IMF approved a new stand-by with appropriate conditions, the US Congress could be persuaded to approve the loan guarantees.

The Fund did approve a stand-by of $7.8 billion—its largest loan up to that time, both in absolute amount and in terms of percentage of member states' quota;[51] the US Congress, however, balked. Senator Feinstein of California summed up the reaction of the American electorate: 'I know no one in the financial community who is against this. I know no one in my constituency who is for it.'[52]

If the US Congress had actually voted on the administration's loan guarantee plan and it had been defeated, the peso and Mexico's economy would almost certainly have fallen still further. President Clinton therefore withdrew the plan, and announced in its place a $20 billion program to support the Mexican economy, using the United States Exchange Stabilization Fund. Whether the use of this fund to support another country's currency came within the statutory authority that had created the ESF in the 1930s was doubtful;[53] but use of the fund made it possible for the administration to

---

[49] See e.g. *New York Times*, 4 Jan. 1995, p. 1 A–1. Investors seem to have calculated that about $50 billion in payments would come due in the course of 1995, counting tesobonos, certificates of deposit, and various other short- and long-term debts. Mexico's international reserves stood at about $6 billion, and thus even with the $18 billion rescue package, barely half of Mexico's foreign financial obligations would be covered. See Lustig, *Mexico, The Remaking of an Economy* (n. 47 supra), 177–8.

[50] See *Wall St. Journal* 13 Jan. 1995, p. 1.

[51] See IMF Press Release of 1 Feb. 1995, reproduced in 25 *IMF Survey*, p. 43, 6 Feb. 1995; *Wall St. Journal*, 27 Jan. 1995, p. A–6.

[52] *New York Times*, 30 Jan. 1995, p. A–1, reporting a hearing with the Secretary of State and the Secretary of the Treasury.

[53] In a 14-page opinion, the general counsel of the US Treasury Department sustained the President's authority, pointing out that while the original purpose of the 1934 legislation creating the Exchange Stabilization Fund was to stabilize the US dollar, as amended in 1976 the statute authorized the Fund to be utilized as the Secretary of the Treasury may deem necessary to and consistent with the United States obligations in the IMF. Those obligations were to maintain orderly exchange arrangements and a stable system of exchange rates rather than to

create a support program for Mexico that did not have to be submitted to Congress. For the most part, members of Congress were relieved that they did not have to vote, and did not challenge the President's authority or wisdom.[54] At the same time, in a coordinated action the IMF agreed to an additional 18-month stand-by credit of $10 billion on top of the $7.8 billion approved just a few days earlier, and the central banks of the leading industrial countries acting through the Bank for International Settlements agreed to issue short-term credits for another $10 billion.[55]

Thus the total package of cash, credits, and guarantees for Mexico, assembled in six weeks, came to $48.8 billion—$17.8 billion from the IMF, $10 billion via the BIS principally from Germany and Japan, $1 billion from Canada, and $20 billion from the United States. Looking back a few months later the Managing Director of the Fund said:

On January 31 of this year, this was the problem: either large-scale financial assistance was put in place together with the support of the U.S.—and the IMF was the only institution in a position to extend it without delay—or Mexico had no solution other than to resort to 'measures destructive of national or international prosperity', such as a moratorium on foreign debt or a reimposition of trade and exchange restrictions, with a major risk of the spread of such measures to a number of countries.[56]

There is no doubt that the coordinated response to the Mexican crisis could not have been achieved without approval by the IMF of Mexico's program of adjustment just negotiated. Without approval of the stand-by, neither the United States nor the central banks acting through the BIS would have gone forward. But in contrast to other programs of relief and rescue when only the IMF was in position to impose conditions, in this instance the United States insisted on conditions of its own, focused not only on Mexico's economic policies, but also on security for the American loans.

After several more weeks of negotiations, Mexico and the United States entered into a detailed Framework Agreement for Mexican Economic Stabilization plus several annexes, whereby the United States government formally undertook to make available to Mexico the short- and medium-term swap transactions and securities guarantees already announced. The Agreement recited that the Mexican government had made available to the

---

maintain any particular value of the dollar. Further, while the authority to use the Exchange Stabilization Fund is ordinarily limited to credits up to six months, the statute authorizes longer credits 'if the President gives Congress a written statement that unique or emergency circumstances require the loan or credit to be for more than six months', 31 U.S.C. §5402(b). The President did make the required statement, 31 *Weekly Comp. Pres. Docs.* 155 (31 Jan. 1995); id. 390 (9 Mar. 1995).

[54] See e.g. *New York Times*, 1 Feb. 1995, p. A–1.

[55] 24 *IMF Survey*, p. 33 (6 Feb. 1995).

[56] Michel Camdessus, 'Drawing Lessons from the Mexican Crisis: Preventing and Resolving Financial Crises—The Role of the IMF', Address to the Council of the Americas, Washington, DC, 22 May 1995. The quoted phrase comes from the purposes clause of the IMF's Articles of Agreement, Art. I(v).

US Treasury its 'comprehensive and detailed financial plan', which would be updated at least annually as long as loan funds or guarantees were outstanding, and which included a description of how the resources furnished by the United States would be used. In part, the plan restated the policies undertaken in connection with the IMF stand-by. But the Agreement also called for prompt and detailed information to be furnished to the US Treasury at its request, and contained default and acceleration clauses of the kind found in commercial bank loan documents, but never in the documents prepared by or for the IMF. The Agreement and various annexes recited that they were to be governed by the law of New York; further, Mexico and its central bank agreed to the exclusive jurisdiction of the US district court in New York for all purposes in connection with the Agreement, and waived irrevocably any defense of inconvenient forum.[57]

Most striking in the last years of the twentieth century, Mexico was required, as a condition for provision of funds or loan guarantees by the United States, to deposit receipts of virtually all export sales of petroleum or petroleum products by PEMEX, the state-owned oil company, to a special account maintained at the Federal Reserve Bank of New York by the Banco de Mexico.[58] As such deposits were received by the New York Fed, Banco de Mexico was to credit a corresponding amount on its books in favour of PEMEX, but the funds remained in New York, and the Federal Reserve Bank was authorized and instructed by Banco de Mexico to use the funds to repay the US Treasury all amounts due and payable under the Financing Arrangements.[59]

In the event, the security arrangements that the United States imposed did not have to be drawn on. Mexico drew $13.5 billion under the United States plan, but repaid the full amount with interest (actually a fee based on the risk element and amounts outstanding) at the end of 1996. Mexico drew $13 billion from the IMF under the February 1995 stand-by arrangement, and also made an advance repayment to the Fund. Mexico's trade balance turned positive in 1995 as imports declined sharply; the gross domestic

[57] Though the Framework Agreement and the Stabilization Plan as a whole were clearly a state-to-state matter, the Agreement stated:

The obligations to be performed by the parties . . . shall constitute commercial activities within the meaning of the [US Foreign Sovereign Immunities Act].

[58] PEMEX customers—new and existing—were to be instructed, according to a form made part of the Agreement, to make payments for crude oil or derivatives to an account of PEMEX at the Swiss Bank Corporation, which would in turn transfer the receipts to the Federal Reserve Bank for the account of PEMEX.

[59] Oil exports from Mexico had played a part in the 1982 rescue effort as well, but in a quite different form. In 1982, the United States government had made an advance payment of $1 billion for future purchases of the Strategic Petroleum Reserve, at a price that Mexico regarded as oppressive. See Roger S. Leeds and Gale Thompson, *The 1982 Mexican Debt Negotiations: Response to a Financial Crisis* at p. 29 (1987). This time there was no negotiation about price, since the United States was not the purchaser, but the proceeds would serve only a security function.

product declined by about 7 percent in 1995, but began to grow again in 1996. The peso continued to decline slowly as Mexico pursued a semi-floating exchange rate policy, trading at 7.7 to 7.9 pesos per US dollar in 1997.

(c)   Looking back at the Crisis: Success of the Rescue

From a financial point of view (if not from the point of view of the living standards of the Mexican population), the rescue package for Mexico may be considered a success. The austerity package to which the administration of President Zedillo had committed his nation was on the whole adhered to. Gross domestic product declined by almost 7 percent in 1995, but began to grow again in 1996. The fall in the value of the peso led to a rise in prices in Mexico of about 52 percent, far more than the rise in personal income. Indeed, real wages contracted by about 23 percent. The balance of trade, which had stood at a deficit of US$80 billion in 1994, turned around to a surplus of about $20 billion in 1995, and as the Mexican recession eased and imports increased, to a surplus of about $8.4 billion in 1996. The peso, after its rapid fall in 1994, continued to decline slowly as Mexico pursued a semi-floating exchange rate policy, trading at a range of 7.7–7.9 pesos per US dollar in 1997.[60]

In January 1997, President Clinton announced that Mexico had repaid all of the $13.5 billion that it had borrowed from the United States early in 1995.[61] Mexico also made an advance payment of US$1.5 billion to the IMF of the $13 billion actually drawn under the stand-by arrangement of February 1, 1995. President Zedillo said in a speech in Mexico City:

Some predicted that our country would collapse, that the foreign aid would be unpayable and infringe our sovereignty, and that in the short term we'd be in a worse crisis. But the early retirement of the debt to the United States Treasury demonstrates the coherence and responsibility the Mexican people and Government have shown in these tough times.[62]

By 2000, Foreign Direct Investment had tripled, inflation was down to single figures, and in August 2000, President Zedillo announced that Mexico would repay its $3 billion debt to the IMF, three years ahead of schedule.[63]

---

[60] As of year-end 2001, the Mexican peso stood at about 9.11 per US dollar.

[61] President Clinton said that the United States had made a profit of more the half a billion dollars from the rescue package for Mexico:

Some said that we should not get involved, that the money would never be repaid, that Mexico should fend for itself. They were wrong. (*New York Times*, 16 Jan. 1997, p. A-1)

[62] Ibid.

[63] Not everyone was happy with the outgoing president's decision to repay the IMF, rather than using the cash generated by the increase in oil prices to build highways or hospitals. The *Economist* (London) quotes a popular saying in Mexico about President Zedillo, 'He's not a president, he's a finance minister.'

Summary

The decision by the industrial countries in the 1970s to leave recycling of petrodollars to the private sector, and the efforts by many of the developing countries to look to the private banks for financing without discipline or adjustment, led to prolonged crisis in the 1980s. The International Monetary Fund regained a place of central importance in the international economy, and at least with respect to the heavily indebted developing countries the link between credit facilities and policy prescriptions central to the original conception of the Fund was to a large extent restored.

The Fund demonstrated that its role was critical to the mobilization of worldwide resources in an emergency. On the other hand the Fund demonstrated that it was prepared to stop disbursements under its stand-by arrangements when states were out of compliance with their negotiated undertakings, and that other sources of credits usually fell in line behind the Fund.

At the end of the decade of the 1980s, the international monetary system came together as it had not done since the early post-war years, with the IMF, the World Bank, the principal creditor states, and the private bankers joining in a concerted effort to move the problem of developing country debt from crisis to normality.

A second crisis, in 1994–5, was in some ways more threatening, because by that time the globalization of the international monetary system had intensified, with more capital—particularly short-term capital and portfolio investment—moving in and out of countries with the speed of light. Mexico, the showpiece of the crisis and recovery of the 1980s, became the showpiece of the crisis of the 1990s. Again, the international community came to the rescue, with cash, credits, and guarantees, and managed in a relatively short time to restore confidence in an economy that had confused promise with results. Conditionality, in the Mexican case, was imposed not only by the IMF, but in ways that would have been unthinkable a few years earlier, by the United States as well. The IMF remained the catalyst, and coordinator, of multilateral relief, but the traditional limits of Fund assistance, measured in terms of a member state's quota, became essentially irrelevant. Drawing on the broadly worded purpose clauses of the Articles of Agreement, i.e. the prevention of measures destructive of international prosperity, the Fund seemed increasingly to improvise solutions, substituting case-by-case responses for a rule-based system. This evolution, not articulated, let alone voted upon, was repeated in the South-east Asia crisis of the late 1990s, and in the case of Russia throughout the 1990s, both discussed in the following sections.

B.   SOUTH-EAST ASIA, 1997–8

18.7   THE FALLING DOMINOES

On July 2, 1997, the central bank of Thailand announced that it would let market forces determine the value of the Thai currency, the baht. Until then, the baht had been tied to a basket of currencies essentially based on the US dollar. The baht fell immediately by about 17 percent against the dollar, somewhat less against the yen. On July 11, the Central Bank of the Philippines announced that it, too, was abandoning the policy of defending its currency, and the peso quickly dropped by 11 percent. Malaysia followed three days later, and a month later, so did Indonesia. The South Korean won, which had not been pegged, slid steadily throughout the summer. Inevitably, the countries of South-east Asia turned to the IMF.

For the Philippines, the IMF acted quickly. Resorting for the first time to the Emergency Financing Mechanism created after the Mexican crisis of 1994–5,[64] the Fund's Executive Board, within one week, approved extension of an existing credit of about $652 million, plus an additional credit of $435 million, of which two-thirds was available for immediate drawing. The remainder would be available at the end of September, following a review of performance under the program linked to the drawing.[65]

Thailand, which was at first reluctant to approach the IMF, did so at the end of July. The Fund convened an emergency meeting in Tokyo, and by August 11 a rescue package of $16 billion was assembled—$4 billion from the Fund (more than five times Thailand's quota), $4 billion from Japan, the remainder from Australia, Hong Kong, Malaysia, Singapore, Indonesia, and South Korea, plus the Asian Development Bank and the World Bank—all in support of what the Fund called Thailand's 'bold adjustment measures'.[66] The Western industrial nations—United States, Germany, United Kingdom, France, and Canada participated in the meeting and helped draw up the conditions for the credits, but offered no funds of their own, on the theory, evidently, that Thailand's problem was a regional problem.

By October, Indonesia, whose currency had sunk by about 30 percent against the dollar since mid-July, was ready to look for support from the international community. Once again, the IMF was prepared to help, this time in combination with a $3 billion contribution from the United States as well.

---

[64] The Emergency Financing Mechanism is not yet another facility, but a procedure that in the event a member faced a crisis, would facilitate rapid approval of support from the Fund—within five to seven days rather than the normal two months—i.e. before conducting the full review of data and policy generally required for a stand-by arrangement. See Summing Up by the Managing Director 12 Sept. 1995, *Selected Decisions*, pp. 192–97 (25th issue 2000).

[65] See 26 *IMF Survey*, 250, 5 Aug. 1997, reproducing announcement of the Executive Board of 18 July 1997. See also *New York Times*, 21 July 1997, p. A–1.

[66] 26 *IMF Survey*, 259, 18 Aug. 1997; *New York Times*, 12 Aug. 1997, p. A–1.

Using the Emergency Financing Mechanism, and on the basis of what the Fund's Managing Director called 'an impressive program of macroeconomic adjustment and structural reform', the Fund approved a $10 billion stand-by, to be supplemented by another $8 billion from the Asian Development Bank and the World Bank.[67]

In late fall 1997, South Korea, by far the largest of the economies of South-east Asia, also found itself with large debts to foreign lenders, a declining gross domestic product, and a declining currency, and on November 21, it too turned to the IMF for assistance. The Fund's Managing Director responded:

I welcome today's announcement by the Korean authorities that they intend to initiate a financial arrangement with the IMF, and I have already assured the Korean authorities of our full support.[68]

An IMF mission was quickly dispatched to Seoul, with the assignment of negotiating a comprehensive package of reforms that could be supported by the Fund and the international community. On December 4, 1997, the Fund approved a $21 billion stand-by credit for Korea, the largest credit ever approved for a member of the IMF.[69]

Thus by year-end 1997 Thailand, the Philippines, Indonesia, and South Korea had received large credits from the IMF. In each case the credits were accompanied by linked credits from individual states and multilateral banks. In each case, also, the credits came with conditions—major programs of adjustment subject to negotiation and approval by the IMF. Only Malaysia of the wounded tigers resisted calling on the IMF. Malaysia announced its own program of austerity, modeled on the Fund-designed programs, but without intervention by the Fund or other external lenders.[70]

18.8   THE RESPONSE OF THE IMF: INTRODUCING STRUCTURAL REFORM

The adjustment programs for Thailand, Indonesia, and Korea, though different in detail from one another, all reflected a new stage in the development of international monetary law as administered by the IMF. Whereas previously the IMF had concentrated on macroeconomic targets—the balance of payments, rate of inflation, fiscal deficit or surplus, gain or loss of reserves—

---

[67] 26 *IMF Survey*, 353, 354, (17 Nov. 1997), reproducing announcements of 5 Nov. 1997.

[68] 26 *IMF Survey*, 371, (1 Dec. 1997), reproducing Mr. Camdessus' statement of 21 Nov. 1997.

[69] 26 *IMF Survey*, 385, (15 Dec. 1997), reproducing announcement of 4 Dec. 1997.

[70] See *Financial Times* (London) 6 Dec. 1997, p. 3. It was reported that Prime Minister Mahatir Mohamad complained that despite economic hardship, people were plunking more than one spoonful of sugar into their coffee. 'One spoonful a day', the *Financial Times* commented, 'keeps the IMF away'. *Financial Times*, 18 Dec. 1997, p. 11.

the inquiries were now much more detailed, focused on particular aspects of each country's economic activity. As the Managing Director put it,

The centerpiece of each program is not a set of austerity measures to restore macro-economic balance, but a set of forceful, far-reaching, structural reforms to strengthen financial systems, increase transparency, open markets,and, in so doing, restore market confidence.[71]

Moreover, the IMF urged, and the countries agreed, that their Letters of Intent, accompanied by elaborate Memoranda of Economic Programs, would be made public and posted on the Internet for all to see. For instance, Korea's Letter of Intent addressed not only the traditional macroeconomic factors, but contained commitments about regulation of merchant banks, indicating criteria regarding liquidity, asset quality, and management capability, and a statement that those banks that had not yet been closed would be promptly shut down if they did not pass their second evaluation in thirty days.[72] When two commercial banks were taken over by the new government, the equity of existing shareholders was written down and a privatization committee was to be created to find new owners.

Banks would be required to maintain capital adequacy standards consistent with the recommendations of the Basle Committee,[73] to adopt internationally accepted accounting standards including 'mark to market' requirements for holdings of securities, loan classification criteria based solely on commercial considerations, and global limits on combined spot and forward positions in foreign exchange.

The commitments to the IMF were not only financial. Korea was required to eliminate restrictions on foreign ownership of domestic corporations; to permit foreign banks and brokerage houses to establish subsidiaries in the country; and to eliminate a variety of quotas, subsidies, import certification requirements, and similar practices inconsistent with the rules of the GATT/WTO system.

Further, restrictions on lay-offs of employees would be clarified and unemployment benefits would be expanded, with specific commitments as to the ratio of benefits to the minimum wage and to their duration. As to corporate governance, the new commitments included the use of independent accountants and auditors; a requirement of at least one outside director for companies listed on the Korean stock exchange; provision for wider rights of minority shareholders, including even the right to file representative law suits; and permission of take-overs of non-strategic Korean corporations by foreign investors without government approval.

---

[71] Remarks of Michel Camdessus at the Council on Foreign Relations 6 Feb. 1998, 27 *IMF Survey*, 49 at 50, (23 Feb. 1998).

[72] This and the following statements are taken from South Korea's Letter of Intent and accompanying Memorandum of February 7, 1998, as posted on the IMF website, http://www.imf.org.

[73] See Ch. 21, Sect. 21.3(b).

Similar, but not identical commitments to the Fund were made by Thailand and Indonesia, covering not only strictly economic subjects such as accounting standards, modern bankruptcy codes, and transparent laws on foreign investment, but also improved medical and maternity benefits and HIV/AIDS facilities.[74]

Critics said that the IMF was risking its effectiveness by the way it now defined its role, emphasizing major structural and institutional reforms rather than, as before, limiting its focus on balance of payments adjustment.[75] The IMF, supported in particular by the United States government, responded that 'there is neither point nor excuse' for the international community to provide financial assistance to a country unless that country takes measures to prevent future such crises.[76]

The perception by the IMF, and by the principal countries that participated in the efforts to contain the Asian crisis, was that such factors as 'crony capitalism', corruption, reciprocal dealings not based on commercial considerations, and weakness in the kind of regulation that went along with capitalism in the major industrial countries, were major causes of the Asian crisis, and of its unexpectedly rapid spread from one country to another. Moreover, as the Fund's Deputy Managing Director wrote,

Although a Fund-supported program is often seen in the press as the international community's way of imposing changes on a country's economy, it is more often the international community's way of supporting a government or a group within the government that wants to bring about desirable economic reforms conducive to long-term growth.[77]

18.9 AN INTERIM APPRAISAL

From an economic point of view, the rescue package overseen by the IMF for South-east Asia seems to have succeeded, albeit unevenly. The 'Asian contagion' was contained, the dominoes did not keep falling around the world. By August 2000, Korea had repaid about two-thirds of the amounts it had drawn under the December 1997 rescue package, and announced that

[74] See e.g. Thailand, Letter of Intent and Memorandum on Economic Policies of 24 Feb. 1998; Indonesia, Memorandum of Economic and Financial Policies, 15 Jan. 1998, both posted on the IMF website, n. 72 supra.

[75] See e.g. Martin Feldstein, 'Refocusing the IMF', *Foreign Affairs* Vol. 77, No. 2, 20, Mar./Apr. 1998. Professor Feldstein had been Chairman of the Council of Economic Advisers in the administration of President Reagan, and was President of the National Bureau of Economic Research.

[76] Stanley Fischer, 'The IMF and the Asian Crisis', Forum Funds Lecture, Los Angeles, 20 Mar. 1998, reproduced on the IMF website and excerpted in 27 *IMF Survey*, 97, (6 Apr. 1998). Mr. Fischer, the First Deputy Managing Director of the IMF, replied directly to Feldstein, n. 75 supra. For the insistence of the United States on detailed commitments of the kind illustrated, see e.g. 'I.M.F.'s New Look: A Far Deeper Role in Lands in Crisis', *New York Times*, 8 Dec. 1997, p. A–1.

[77] Id.

it did not intend to draw the final installment of the stand-by credit. Thailand had not begun to repay its drawings, but it too did not draw its last installment, as its economic recovery, led by growth in its exports, seemed to be on track. Economic recovery was least pronounced in Indonesia, which underwent a major political transition from many decades of authoritarian rule to a lively democracy, and also experienced various sectarian and regional episodes of violence. But Indonesia's crisis appeared to have abated, inflation brought down to manageable levels, and the decline in output reversed.

From a legal point of view, the intrusive nature of the IMF intervention under the rubric of 'structural reform' seems to have been accepted, even as authoritarian governments were replaced in Thailand, Korea, and Indonesia—but not in Malaysia, which did not accept IMF intervention.[78] The biggest changes in organization of the economy appear to have been brought about in Korea, which may well have been ready for such changes in any event, but needed the external push from the outside world that could come about only in the context of a crisis, and probably only with the IMF as catalyst. In all three countries benefiting from IMF-led financial support, howver, at least some of the structural prescriptions of the international community led by the Fund had been initiated—particularly in regard to reform of their financial institutions. De facto, the jurisdiction of the IMF expanded further, into such areas as honest government, corporate governance including cross-holdings and cross-guarantees, greater disclosure requirements coupled with credible auditing and accounting standards, domestic bank lending, nepotism and cronyism, competition policy, and openness to foreign investment. 'Structural reform', it seems, has become a permanent element in the repertoire of the Fund, suggesting at least some reconsideration of the discussion of the reach of the Fund's jurisdiction in the preceding chapters.[79]

---

[78] Stanley Fischer, the Acting Managing Director of the Fund, was asked at his Spring Press Conference about dealing with democratically elected as contrasted with autocratic governments. He answered as follows:

There is a lot of evidence that growth is higher in democracies. That is, incidentally, something which is a change in view since the 1980s. There used to be the line that only under an autocratic government could you get growth going. That has gone by the wayside, particularly as Latin America became democratic.

. . .

I am continually concerned about the expansion of conditionality on IMF lending, and requiring various measures in favor of democracy to be put in place as a condition for lending would, I think, take us too far beyond our mandate. But everything has its limits. There are governments so repressive that we should not lend to them, and that is clear. And there are things we support which are inherently pro-democratic. All the emphasis on transparency the emphasis in the [Poverty Reduction and Growth Facility] on participatory processes, those are things, both of them, transparency and participatory processes, are pressures that would move in the direction of creating democracy. But I do not think we should have explicitly conditionality on that. (Press Conference by Stanley Fischer, Washington 13 Apr. 2000)

[79] Cf. esp. Sects. 16.7, 17.4, and 17.5.

C. RUSSIA, 1990–2000

18.10 THE COLLAPSE OF THE SOVIET UNION

Until the late 1980s, the Union of Soviet Socialist Republics had been known as an excellent credit risk. While estimates varied widely about the Soviet Union's gold reserves, and even its current export–import figures were subject to conflicting statistics, its payments were punctual and its financial obligations to western creditors, public and private, appeared well within its ability to service. As of the time Mikhail Gorbachev came to power in March 1985, the gross foreign debt of the Soviet Union stood at about $25 billion, and there were no arrearages. By 1991, the Soviet debt to the West had more than doubled.

Gorbachev had become a hero in the West, because of his tolerance of the fall of the Berlin Wall and the liberation of Eastern Europe from Soviet domination, and he was rewarded with an invitation, for the first time for a Soviet leader, to a summit meeting of the G–7 leaders of the major industrial states. When he arrived in London in July 1991 for the summit meeting, Gorbachev apparently had with him a proposal for rescheduling the Soviet debt, but he did not submit it.[80] Instead, he surprised the assembled leaders of the principal industrial states by letting it be known that the Soviet Union wished to join the IMF and the other international financial agencies.[81] The reply was that, for the time being, 'associate membership' was the best the Soviet Union could expect in the short run. Associate membership, a new concept for the Fund, would require the Soviet Union to furnish the same kind of information required of regular member states in connection with the Fund's surveillance function,[82] and would permit the Soviet Union to benefit from the Fund's technical assistance and advice, but would not permit drawing on the Fund's resources. In fact the Soviet Union did enter into a 'Special Association' with the Fund in October 1991, after the abortive coup against Gorbachev of August 1991 and as the disintegration of the Soviet Union was becoming evident.[83]

As of the fall of 1991, the hard currency debt of the Soviet Union stood at about $66 billion, comparable in amount to the debt of Mexico when it

---

[80] See *Wall Street Journal*, 7 Aug. 1991, p. A8, quoting the chief of the foreign currency and economic department of the USSR State Bank.

[81] Note that under Article II(1) of the Articles of Agreement of the World Bank, membership in the IMF is a prerequisite to membership in the Bank. There is no reciprocal requirement for membership in the Fund.

[82] See Ch. 17, Sect. 17.4.

[83] See 14 *IMF Survey*, 289, 293–6 (14 Oct. 1991), reporting on and reproducing the agreement reached between President Gorbachev and Michel Camdessus, the Managing Director of the IMF. Shortly thereafter the World Bank entered into a technical cooperation agreement with the USSR, financed by a $30 million interim grant.

declared default in August 1982. The Soviet Union did not declare default, but it stopped repaying principal, and representatives of Vnesheconombank, the Soviet bank in charge of foreign financial transactions, began to seek rescheduling. After a four-day meeting in Moscow in November with representatives of the USSR and its republics, the G–7 agreed to a deferral for a year of payments of principal to official creditors in respect of debt contracted before January 1, 1991. Eight of the republics in turn agreed to be jointly and severally liable for the existing external debt, and to put into place comprehensive macroeconomic adjustment programs in full consultation with the IMF. Yegor Gaidar, President Yeltsin's chief lieutenant for economic policy, said,

The stand of the Group of Seven was extremely tough. 'Either you accept our conditions without any reservations', they said, 'or we stop the negotiations and thus stop all credits, including food credits.'[84]

On December 4, 1991, following a referendum, Ukraine declared its independence. On the same day Vneshneconombank announced immediate suspension of payments of principal to commercial banks on medium- and long-term loans. On December 8, the leaders of the three Slavic Republics—Russia, Ukraine, and Belarus—declared that the USSR no longer existed, and announced formation of a Commonwealth of Independent States. On December 18, twelve Western banks from seven countries, meeting in Frankfurt under the leadership of the Deutsche Bank, agreed to a 120-day deferral of repayment of Soviet commercial debt falling due in December and a 90-day deferral of repayments of principal coming due in the first quarter of 1992, provided interest payments were kept current. On December 21, 1991, eleven of the twelve remaining Republics signed agreements creating the Commonwealth of Independent States. On December 25, 1991, Gorbachev resigned as President. The Union of Soviet Socialist Republics (1917/22–91) had ceased to exist.

The collapse of the Soviet Union was, of course, a monumental event from every point of view, many well beyond the scope of this volume. But it was true, and evident to the whole world—quite apart from any familiarity with economics, let alone with law—that it was the economic ideas and institutions of the West that had prevailed, and the very different ideas behind communism, however developed and distorted since the days of Karl Marx, that had failed.

---

[84] Quoted in *Los Angeles Times* dispatch from Moscow, 22 Nov. 1991, p. 1. The actual debt restructuring agreement, which involved ten other creditor countries in addition to the G–7, was signed in early January 1992 under the auspices of the Paris Club. Though by then the Soviet Union no longer existed, Vnesheconombank still did, and apparently acted for all of the republics that had agreed in November to be liable for the debt. Ukraine, which had not agreed to be liable for Soviet debt in excess of what it calculated was its share, signed on to 'joint and several liability' in March 1992, under pressure from the G–7, which indicated that failure to do so would jeopardize its chances to share in new grants or credit being prepared.

This left the task of integrating the member states of the now expired Soviet Union into the international economy, and of adapting the institutions that had developed without their participation.[85]

18.11 INTEGRATING RUSSIA INTO THE SYSTEM

(a) The First Steps

Russia, emerging from the Soviet Union, entered the world economy with several handicaps. For one thing, while goods in the Soviet Union—raw materials, intermediate goods, and end products—had all had prices attached to them, the prices had been set arbitrarily by a combination of central planning and negotiation among state enterprises, with no accurate relation either to cost or to demand, let alone to the world market.[86] For another, the Soviet Union had not had a real tax system, only transfers to and from state enterprises to and from the state budget. Still further, though the Soviet Union had a central bank with branches, it had made no provisions for credit or for cost of credit. Concepts such as interest rates, money supply, budget deficit, and fiscal policy—if not wholly alien—were not well understood by the people who would manage post-communist Russia. The absence of meaningful prices, interest rates, and genuine profit and loss often made it impossible to determine which enterprises were operating efficiently, which survived only on the basis of subsidies, direct or indirect, which made products that no one wanted, and which did or did not meet world quality standards. Money losing enterprises had generally not been shut down, and by the 1990s, the Soviet Union had become one of the most inefficient and wasteful users of such resources as energy, electricity, and labour. Moreover, while the Soviet Union had a legal system, including judges and prosecutors, the legal infrastructure of a market economy, including contract law, civil litigation, and enforcement of judgments, had not been well understood or practiced.

No one had ever attempted to transform an economy of the size of Russia from central planning to a system with decentralized decision-making based on supply, demand, and price. Moreover, in contrast to Hungary, Poland, and Czechoslovakia, no one was alive in Russia in the 1990s who had the experience of living in a market economy, let alone a democracy. Quite apart from political conflicts between reformers and anti-reformers, the unsteady leadership of President Boris Yeltsin, and a built-in tradition of

[85] The People's Republic of China became a member of the IMF in April 1980, replacing the Republic of China, which had been a member since Bretton Woods. The PRC was generally grouped with the developing countries; from 1981 on its quota was high enough to elect a director on its own.

[86] For instance, in 1992 the Russian price of oil was still one percent of the world market price.

corruption, the task of integrating Russia into the world economy presented an unprecedented, perhaps overwhelming challenge.[87]

In the event, prices were liberalized in Russia in January 1992, with the result on the one hand that after 30 years of grain shortages, enough grain became available to discontinue imports, but on the other hand that inflation went to 30 percent per month and the ruble fell from 120 to over 400 per US dollar. The government attempted to control credits and to use commercial banks as intermediaries. But as credits tended not to be repaid, but just rolled over, they worked in effect as subsidies and drains on the national budget. The budget deficit in Russia was essentially financed by printing money or issuing short-term government securities. Taxes were legislated intermittently, but not regularly collected. A new central bank was established, but the Duma (parliament) rejected the western idea of independence for the bank, which became one more object of lobbying and pressures, licit and illicit. Gross domestic product declined in 1992 by 15–20 percent.[88]

Into this situation came the IMF, as surrogate and intermediary of the G–7 nations, whose leaders were thrilled at the end of the Cold War and, it seems, were prepared to place all their hopes in Boris Yeltsin as the architect of both economic reform and democratic governance.

(b)   Enter the IMF: Phase I

In February 1992, even before the Russian Federation (and the other former republics of the USSR) had formally applied to the IMF for membership, the Fund adopted a 'shadow program' for Russia, i.e. a program of economic reforms negotiated between the Fund and Russia's economic authorities, including removal of price controls, reduction of state subsidies, privatization of numerous state-run enterprises, removal of import quotas and tariffs, improved tax collection, and similar objectives as they might be contained in a Letter of Intent leading to a stand-by agreement. None of the commitments was accompanied by any offer of funds, because Russia was not yet a member of the IMF. But the incentive for the commitments was that Russia would quickly be admitted to full membership, and in fact that did happen.

On March 31, 1992, after a meeting with representatives of the Russian government, the IMF Executive Board voted to endorse Russia's economic reform plan, and to recommend to the Board of Governors that Russia be admitted to the Fund. On the following day, President Bush in Washington

---

[87]   For details supporting this statement, see e.g. Augusto Lopez-Claros and Sergei V. Alexashenko, *Fiscal Policy Issues during the Transition in Russia*, IMF Occasional Paper 155 (Mar. 1998).

[88]   Different sources give different readings on the decline of GDP, which continued for every year of the 1990s except 1997. Given the distorted price system, as well as incentives to underreport private sector production, the official statistics were inevitably unreliable. The fact that GDP declined significantly in the period 1992–6 is not in doubt, however.

and Chancellor Kohl in Bonn made worldwide headlines by announcing a $24 billion package of assistance by the G–7 countries to Russia, consisting of $18 billion in credits, loan guarantees, and deferral of debt, plus $6 billion for a fund to stabilize the ruble. The German Chancellor, as chairman for the year of the G–7, spoke of a 'decisive signal of the political and economic support' for the reforms being introduced by President Yeltsin. In fact, except for deferral of debt coming due, all the pledges, including funds from the IMF, the World Bank, the European Bank for Reconstruction and Development, as well as from individual members of the G–7, were subject to agreement between the Russian government and the IMF, which was not yet in place.

The formalities moved along smoothly. But Russia had only partly implemented the 'shadow program' of February 1992, and agreement on the stand-by on which all the other commitments depended proved difficult. On May 4, 1992 Russia, along with thirteen other former constituent states of the Soviet Union, became a regular member of the IMF. Its quota was set at SDR2,876 million, equal to 3 percent of total quotas, just under the quota for Italy and Canada, but substantially higher than the quota for the People's Republic of China.[89] Simultaneously the World Bank approved the application of Russia and twelve other former Soviet republics for membership. The international monetary system, incomplete from 1945 on, was now, at least formally, virtually universal.

The G–7 Finance Ministers met in Washington with representatives of the Russian Federation, 'welcome[d] the reform already undertaken in Russia', and reaffirmed their commitment to a $24 billion multilateral assistance package 'within the context of an agreed IMF program'.[90] Just prior to President Yeltsin's visit to Washington, the United States Secretary of State, James Baker, said that while Russia should comply with the 'major elements' of an economic reform program being negotiated with the IMF, President Yeltsin's government shouldn't be judged by the crossing of each and every 't' and the dotting of each and every 'i'. 'That isn't the way it works',

---

[89] Altogether, the quota for the former states of the USSR came to SDR4,559 million, equal to 4.76 percent of total quotas. For the formula used to determine the new members' quotas, see *IMF Annual Report 1992*, 70. Under the Ninth General Review of Quotas, which entered into force on November 11, 1992, each member's quota was increased by 50 percent, putting Russia's quota at SDR4,313.1 million. As of August 2000, following a 45 percent increase in total quotas under the Eleventh General Review of quotas completed in 1999, Russia's quota stood at SDR5,945.4 million, equal to 2.84 percent of total quotas in the Fund. Ukraine's quota stood at 0.65 percent, and the quota of all of the former states of the USSR came to a total of 4.48 percent of total quotas. China's quota stood at SDR4,687.2 million, equal to 2.24 percent of total quotas. As of year-end 2001, Russia's quota stood at SDR5,945.4 million, equal to 2.80 percent of total quotas; China was granted an increase in quota outside the general review of quotas effective February 2001, to take account of its resumption of sovereignty over Hong Kong SAR, to SDR6,369.2 million, equal to 3.0 percent of total quotas.

[90] 21 *IMF Survey*, 150 (11 May 1992).

Mr. Baker said. 'That isn't the way it normally works with any country, and it shouldn't work that way with Russia.'[91]

In this case, however, that was the way it worked. Russia, in political as well as economic turmoil, did not comply with its undertakings, especially with respect to prices and the money supply. Despite almost non-stop negotiations in Moscow and Washington, agreement could not be reached on a stand-by, scheduled for completion first by June 1, and then by July 1, 1992.

Given the fragile political situation in Russia, the link with the various pledges and commitments of assistance, and pressure from the United States and other Western governments, the IMF did not wish to let Mr. Yeltsin down completely. Mr. Camdessus, the Managing Director, flew to Moscow just before the G–7 summit in July 1992 to attempt to find a compromise solution. President Yeltsin, it was reported, resisted the demands of the IMF, saying 'To force us to our knees for this loan; No! Russia is still a great power . . . We know the mood of the people and the IMF and Mr. Camdessus do not.'[92]

President Yeltsin and Mr. Camdessus did reach an agreement, providing for a drawing under the first credit tranche only, i.e. for SDR719 million (US$1.04 billion) equal to 25 percent of Russia's quota, to be drawn over a five-month period with an interest rate of 7.5 percent. The stand-by agreement, approved by the Executive Board of the IMF in August, was identified as the 'first stage of a phased process of collaboration with the IMF',[93] another way of saying that the contemplated longer-term stand-by arrangement providing for substantially greater resources had not been concluded. Mr. Camdessus described it as 'basically a damage control program.'[94] The arrangement called for Russia to reduce its budget deficit from 17 percent to 5 percent of gross domestic product, and its inflation rate from 15–20 percent to below 10 percent per month. The issues of debt servicing and energy prices remained unresolved, presumably to be discussed further in the context of the longer-term stand-by, to be concluded in the fall. Stabilization of the ruble would, apparently, be postponed to a third phase.

With at least a partial agreement with the IMF in place, the World Bank also approved its first loan to Russia for some $600 million, and the G–7 leaders, meeting in Munich at the 1992 Summit, were able to commit themselves somewhat further:

We encourage the new States to adopt sound economic policies, above all by bringing down budget deficits and inflation. Working with the IMF can bring experience to this task and lend credibility to the efforts being made. Macroeconomic stabilization should not be delayed. It will only succeed if at the same time the building blocks of a market economy are also put into place, through privatization, land reform,

---

[91] *Wall Street Journal*, 16 June 1992, p. A14.
[92] *Wall Street Journal*, 6 July 1992, p. 8.
[93] 21 *IMF Survey*, pp. 257, 267 (17 Aug. 1992).
[94] *Wall Street Journal*, 7 Aug. 1992, p. A4.

measures to promote investment and competition and appropriate social safeguards for the population.

. . .

We support the phased strategy of cooperation between the Russian government and the IMF. This will allow the IMF to disburse a first credit tranche in support of the most urgent stabilization measures within the next few weeks while continuing to negotiate a comprehensive reform programme with Russia. This will pave the way for the full utilization of the $24 billion support package announced in April. Out of this, $6 billion earmarked for a ruble stabilization fund will be released when the necessary macroeconomic conditions are in place.[95]

For the time being, this meant a decision, to be worked out within the Paris Club, to postpone for two years payment on Russia's official debt— saving some $2.5 billion in principal and interest.

18.12   CONDITIONALITY MAINTAINED

(a)   Conditionality, Russian Style

Completion of the second phase of negotiations between the Russian Federation and the IMF kept being postponed, as targets for privatization, stabilization of the ruble, and reduction of the rate of inflation proved impossible to achieve. Negotiations with the Paris Club agreed on in principle at the Munich Summit, also kept being postponed, with deferral of current payments agreed on 90 days at a time as arrearages built up, while capital flight continued unabated.

Many persons, including senior officials of Western governments anxious to assist President Yeltsin in his efforts at economic reform and political survival, were critical of the IMF, though their own commitments had been tied to conclusion of a stand-by arrangement between Russia and the Fund. Mr. Camdessus remained firm.

In February 1993, following a shuffle in the Russian government, and submission of a program calling for a reduction of the budget deficit from 17 percent to no more than 5 percent of GDP and reduction of inflation from 25 percent to 5 percent per month by the end of the year, the Managing Director of the Fund gave an unusually blunt interview to the Russian newspaper *Izvestia*:

You will certainly understand that, for the international community, and for the members of our Board here, it does not make great sense to utilize the very scarce resources the international community puts at our disposal to finance your country.

---

[95] Communiqué issued by the leaders of the Group of Seven, following the economic summit in Munich, 8 July 1992, paras. 32 and 40. Mr. Camdessus told a press conference in Munich, 'My job has been to say "Yes, with that you reach the basic threshold of credibility, and with that you get the first release of credits".' *Los Angeles Times*, 7 July 1992, p. A16.

We [want to be] certain that you have taken appropriate steps to strengthen the monetary and financial policy so that this money stays in Russia instead of going immediately to the credit of foreign bank accounts in Zurich, Paris, or London.

. . .

Already, a lot has been done. Already, a lot of enterprises are starting to function [better] in Russia, but if we want it to be sufficient for your economy to grow positively, this stabilization, these reforms have got to be confirmed.

. . .

We are hopeful that the setbacks in the monetary and financial field can be corrected and that . . . you will continue with your bold structural reforms. If this is done, I am certain that we will soon have the necessary conditions to restart our program for financial support to your country, and to go from the first credit tranche arrangement to a full-fledged stand-by program.[96]

Mr. Camdessus was asked by his Russian interviewer why he would be prepared to believe in a loan program submitted by the new Russian government, when it was clear that the promises of July 1992 were unrealistic to begin with and had not been fulfilled:

[The 1992] program was approved unanimously by the Executive Board of this institution representing the entire world. The problem is that immediately after the approval of this program, the monetary chapter of the program was abandoned. Instead of pursuing a strong, restrictive market-oriented monetary policy, the authorities implemented a totally different monetary policy, which was inflationary, whereas normally monetary policy is there to stop inflation or to reduce it to a more acceptable level.

. . .

What I would like for the image of your great country is that the next program be strictly implemented as pledged, as negotiated. The world wouldn't understand that twice consecutively your country made commitments which weren't respected. So we will work very carefully in making sure that the next program is well understood, well established on a common understanding of the situation.[97]

(b)   Conditionality Modified: The Systemic Transformation Facility

In April 1993, President Clinton called for a $4 billion package of aid to Russia, on the assumption that each of the G–7 countries would agree with the program and participate in proportion to their economic strength. It turned out, however, that the other G–7 countries did not agree, and in any event insisted on funneling the assistance through the IMF.[98] This in turn

[96] Interview with IMF Managing Director, Michel Camdessus, 2 Feb 1993, reproduced in 22 *IMF Survey*, 49–50 (22 Feb 1993).

[97] Id., 51.

[98] See e.g. 'Much Ado About Lending: Financial Considerations Alone No Longer Dictate Aid Strategy for Russia', *Financial Times*, 12 May 1993, p. 19. See also the following Q & A at Mr. Camdessus' press conference of June 30, 1993 announcing the loan discussed below:

Question: How direct was the US pressure to approve this credit before the G–7 meeting? Were you contacted by Secretary Bentsen or other people of the administration?   *cont./*

meant that the aid would be subject to the IMF conditions, which probably could not be met. The IMF response was a new 'Systemic Transformation Facility', designed to look beyond performance on Russia's previous commitments without creating a precedent that could be invoked by every other country straining under stand-by arrangements with strict performance criteria.[99] The Fund announced that it would be prepared to provide financial assistance to members that were experiencing balance of payments difficulties as a result of severe disruptions in the traditional trade and payments arrangements that are manifested by

(i) a sharp fall of total export receipts due to a shift from significant reliance on trading at non-market prices to multilateral, market-based trade,

(ii) a substantial and permanent increase in net import costs, due to a shift from significant reliance on trading at non-market prices toward world market pricing, particularly for energy products, or

(iii) a combination of both.[100]

Clearly, this characterization fit Russia. Even under the new facility, however, it took several more months for Russia and the IMF to reach an agreement.

On June 30, 1993, just a few days before another G–7 summit to which President Yeltsin would be invited, it was announced that the Fund had approved a credit for Russia under the new Systemic Transformation Facility. Though inflation was running between 20 and 25 percent per month, Russia would be permitted to immediately draw SDR1.078 billion (about

---

Camdessus: Well, I will tell you several things. I suspected the word 'pressure' would be pronounced this morning. But, please, don't allow what is anecdotal to blur what is essential. What is essential is the excellent cooperation we have with the most important members of the international community in support of a historic development in Russia.

Now, 'pressures'. The old Fund watchers here, and I see several of them, have heard me say that pressure is the most natural thing, the most ordinary thing in Fund life. It is like atmospheric pressure for human beings. So we have developed, I would say, a kind of very simple, good-sense philosophy about pressures in the IMF. I will give you the three basic tenets, even if there are more.

First, never yield to pressures.

Second, equally important, never be deterred from doing reasonable things, even if you are pressured to do them.

And third, possibly even more important, be sure that your sense of humor grows in proportion to the pressure. (22 *IMF Survey*, 209 at 215, 12 July 1993)

[99] See 22 *IMF Survey*, 129, 136 (3 May 1993). The Press Release emphasized that the STF was designed for former members of the Council for Mutual Economic Assistance (i.e. the East European states formerly in the Soviet sphere) plus the former states of the Soviet Union, and that the facility was designed to be a precursor to full-fledged stand-by arrangements with the IMF.

[100] Decision No. 10348-(93/61) STF, 23 Apr. 1993, *Selected Decisions*, 251, (25th issue 2000). The first use of the STF was by Kyrgyzstan in May 1993, 22 *IMF Survey*, p. 166 (31 May 1993), in conjunction with a regular stand-by. The credit to Russia was the second use of the facility, and was not accompanied by an ordinary stand-by.

US$1.506 billion), equal to 25 percent of Russia's current quota.[101] The objectives stated were essentially the same as those stated in February 1992 and July 1992—reducing the government deficit, elimination of subsidies, containing the monetary supply, deepening the privatization effort, but the deadlines were not as tight. The agreement stated that a second equal disbursement would be available to the Russian government under the STF 'provided that progress continues to be made in the implementation of the policy program.'

Once the arrangement with the IMF was in place, the G–7 leaders meeting in Tokyo announced a $3 billion package of other credits for Russia, including US$1.5 billion in loans from the World Bank and the European Bank for Reconstruction and Development, about $1 billion in export credits from individual countries, and $500 million in grants from the members of the G–7, all focused on Russia's efforts at privatization of industry.[102]

The decision establishing the Systemic Transformation Facility made an interesting modification in the Fund's policy. Whereas under the basic stand-by arrangement and most of the various longer-term or special facilities created by the Fund, the drawing was supposed to be repaid in the period of time necessary to implement the adjustment program on which the drawing was based, drawing under the STF required only that the Fund was satisfied that the member would cooperate with the Fund, on the basis of a declaration of its intention to reach understandings with the Fund as soon as possible on a comprehensive program that could be supported by a Fund arrangement, and describing the policies and measures that the member intended to pursue for the next 12 months consistent with that intention. Thus a drawing under the STF would be available before the conditions for a regular stand-by were met—as was the situation with regard to Russia in the spring and summer of 1993. The plan was that the second half of the drawing under the STF would be disbursed in October 1993, and a regular stand-by arrangement would be granted in spring 1994. As Russia did not implement its commitments under the first STF drawing—inflation, for instance, continued to run at an annual rate of 1000 percent—the second tranche under the STF was not released.[103]

---

[101] 22 *IMF Survey*, 209, 220 (12 July 1993). Note that in the interim between Russia's admission to the IMF and the 1993 drawing, all quotas in the Fund, including Russia's, had been increased by 50 percent. See Ch. 16, Sect. 16.6(a).

[102] See *Financial Times*, London, 9 July 1993, p. 1.

[103] Jeffrey Sachs, a well-known American professor and for a time adviser to President Yeltsin, wrote that the IMF was 'missing its big chance', and that 'When a drowning man is 10 metres from shore the IMF throws a 5 metre lifeline, content that it has met the drowning man half-way.' John Odling-Smee, the head of the Department of the IMF negotiating with Russia and the other 'countries in transition', replied:

The main industrial countries said publicly this year that if economic reform and stabilisation in Russia proceeded in line with agreed targets, the IMF could make available 13 billion dollars to Russia. But Russia did not implement its stabilisation plans. . . .

The disbursement of IMF Funds must be linked to actual performance and not merely . . . to hopes and promises. (*Financial Times*, London, 11 Nov. 1993, p. 3; Nov. 17, p. 24; Nov. 22, p. 14)

Further difficult negotiations took place in the first quarter of 1994, the Executive Directors extended the terms of the STF, and in March 1994 the second half of the $3 billion STF credit, which had been held up in the previous October, was released.[104] At the press conference announcing the agreement with the Russian government, the Fund's Managing Director said:

While I am aware of the many risks of the present situation, I must tell you I am confident that this program under the second tranche of the STF can be properly carried out.[105]

To a question whether the Fund had eased its standards to come to this conclusion, Mr. Camdessus replied:

No. The standards are the standards of the STF, which are a little bit more lenient than the standards of a stand-by arrangement. Our lengthy discussions with the Russian authorities on the proper solutions to their problems have made us all more knowledgeable about the issues. The Russians certainly now have a much better recognition of our purposes in assisting them. And at times this painful process has certainly contributed to strengthening the program itself.[106]

It was understood that if the Russian government could prepare a budget for 1995 acceptable both to its parliament (Duma) and to the Fund, and if the STF program were implemented as intended, a larger and longer stand-by arrangement would become available for 1995.[107]

Russia's economy continued to deteriorate throughout 1994, and on 'Black Tuesday'—October 11, 1994—the ruble fell by more than 20 percent. Inflation, which had fallen to 5 percent per month (within the IMF guidelines), was back up to 15 percent per month at year-end 1994. Nevertheless, in April 1995 the IMF approved a stand-by credit of about $6.6 billion on the basis of a program to reduce inflation from 17 percent to 1 percent per month by major tightening of monetary policy, to cut the federal government deficit from about 11 percent to 6 percent of GDP, and to liberalize the trade regime, in particular the restraints on oil and gas exports which had made a few persons very rich, but had done little to improve Russia's balance of payments. The stand-by was to be protected under 'especially strict conditionality', with monthly consultation and review in advance of drawings under the stand-by.[108]

---

[104] 23 *IMF Survey*, p. 148, (2 May 1994).

[105] Press Conference of Mr. Michel Camdessus, 24 Mar. 1994, 23 *IMF Survey*, p. 97 (4 Apr. 1994).

[106] Id. p. 98.

[107] Professor Sachs (n. 103 supra), wrote that the Fund's action was too little too late:

After withholding a $1.5 billion loan from the Russian reformers in the second half of 1993 on the grounds that the budget deficit was too high, it finally freed the loan, in spite of a vastly larger deficit today. IMF inaction in the past contributed to Russia's gathering storm. Its action last week was a desperate move to help head off Russia's descent into chaos. (*Financial Times*, London, 31 Mar. 1994, p. 21)

[108] 24 *IMF Survey*, pp. 114, 124 (17 Apr. 1995).

18.13   ECONOMICS AND POLITICS: BETTING ON YELTSIN (1996)

In part the 1995 program was successful. Inflation was reduced, not quite to the target rate, but to 3.5 percent per month by year-end 1995. The budget deficit, however, which had been running at less than 4 percent of GDP, rose again at year-end, suggesting that subsidies were being expanded in advance of the presidential election scheduled for summer 1996. In January 1996, however, Anatoly Chubais, who had been in and out of the government since the end of the Soviet Union and who had overseen compliance with the IMF program in 1995, was dismissed by President Yeltsin. To government workers and pensioners who had suffered from late payments, Chubais was a convenient scapegoat; to creditors and investors in the West, the dismissal of Chubais was a signal that the reformers had lost out, that the oligarchs and bureaucrats, and possibly the growing criminal element in Russia, would prevail. Nevertheless, the western countries encouraged the IMF to follow up the 12 month $6 billion stand-by with a credit of $10 billion under the IMF's Extended Fund Facility (EFF), equal to 160 percent of Russia's quota.[109] The credit was to be front-loaded, with 65 percent of the quota available in 1996 (the election year), 55 percent in the second year, and the remaining 40 percent in the third year. The press release announcing the credit said:

The program to be supported by the EFF is highly ambitious and its success will require bold efforts on the part of the Russian government. Such efforts deserve the support of the international community.[110]

The expectation was that the commitments made under the EFF would be followed by a comprehensive rescheduling of Russia's extended debt, both official and commercial, and that in fact happened.[111] The *Financial Times*, in an editorial as the credit was being negotiated, put the case as follows:

The best reason to continue to support the government is to keep the flame of stabilisation policy flickering, and provide the electorate with four more months' evidence of the benefits of falling inflation and rising demand. That in turn, would put pressure on the winner, whoever he may be, to keep with the program.[112]

In fact, as was eminently clear, the international community, led by President Clinton and Chancellor Kohl, was not at all indifferent about the winner of the coming election. The Fund's Managing Director, aware that his credibility and that of the IMF as a whole had been drawn into question, responded as follows:

---

[109] *25 IMF Survey*, p. 1, (14 Mar. 1966); p. 119, (1 Apr. 1996).
[110] *25 IMF Survey*, p. 119 at 121, (1 Apr. 1995).
[111] Agreement with the Paris Club concerning foreign sovereign debts inherited from the Soviet Union was reached on April 29, 1996.
[112] *Financial Times*, London, 20 Feb. 1996, p. 15.

Why embark on the program now? IMF cannot equivocate on the basis of the electoral time table. . . . To postpone a program simply because of the elections would be a 'political act' in itself. Worse,. . .it would invite policy drift during the pre-electoral period, and the inevitable renewal of adjustment would be all the more painful. The IMF does not support individuals, . . . it supports economic programs.[113]

Just in case someone other than Yeltsin should win,[114] for instance the Communist candidate who was leading in the public opinion polls at the time, Mr. Camdessus concluded:

As long as the duly constituted authorities continue to fulfill the requirements of the program agreed with the IMF, the IMF will continue to support that program.[115]

Like the 1995 program (but unlike other IMF programs), the new EFF credit was subject to monthly monitoring and monthly disbursement, with at least the implication that if the budgetary limits or other targets were breached, disbursements could be interrupted.

In the event, Yeltsin led in the first round of the election with 35 percent of the votes, and won a majority of votes in a run-off on July 3, 1996. A few weeks later, the IMF held up disbursement of the July installment of the EFF credit, on the ground that tax collection had not met the agreed targets.[116] If the IMF's reputation as an independent non-political body was drawn into question and conditionality was seen in new light, the central role of the Fund was preserved. It was still the one institution that could impose conditions on a sovereign government and request (though not always enforce) assurances of sound use of the resources it made available.

18.14   CONDITIONALITY, CRISIS, AND CORRUPTION (1997–2000)

(a)   Building Confidence

When the Managing Director of the IMF visited Russia in the spring of 1997, he could feel moderately satisfied with what he saw. Inflation had

---

[113] 25 *IMF Survey*, pp. 129, 130, (15 Apr. 1996), summarizing remarks of Mr. Camdessus in Washington, 1 Apr. 1996.

[114] It is worth recalling that by election time 1996, the bloody and unpopular war in Chechnya had been going on for a year and a half. Moreover, President Yeltsin had at least two heart attacks and various mysterious disappearances in the year leading up to the election.

[115] See n. 113 supra. The *Financial Times* reported that during his trip to negotiate the credit, Mr. Camdessus insisted he was not in Moscow 'to buy votes for President Yeltsin' and brushed off the Kremlin leader's boast of forcing the Fund to reach a deal with Russia by lobbying friendly western heads of state. 'I don't doubt that President Yeltsin had the conversations with his colleagues', Mr. Camdessus said. 'But I must tell you that the decision we took was not influenced by these telephone calls.' *Financial Times*, London, 24 Feb. 1996, p. 2.

[116] The disbursement was resumed in August 1996, following increased tax collection by the government; the Fund again suspended a disbursement in October, 1996 but released the suspended tranche of $336 million in December, on the basis of 'improved revenue performance'.

been slowed, the exchange rate of the ruble stabilized, two-thirds of the economy was in private hands, trade barriers had been reduced, and the ruble was now traded freely and could be readily converted into foreign exchange.[117] There were, as Mr. Camdessus pointed out, down sides to the Russian economic picture. There was a mass of unpaid wages and pensions, public services were in poor state, production was declining, and there seemed to be increasing lawlessness, both in the streets and in avoidance of taxes. These problems, as President Yeltsin had himself said, had to do with the role of the state. Addressing matters that in the past would have been regarded as well beyond the subjects addressed by an official of the IMF, Mr. Camdessus urged a simple and transparent regulatory system, an effective judicial and legal system that protected property rights, enforced contracts, and helped create an atmosphere of law, order, and personal security, plus a stable tax system based on fairly low and uniform rates and effective collection. An important element in the strategy of establishing an appropriate system of tax collection, was to fight corruption.

This is also the time [Mr. Camdessus told his Moscow audience] for the IMF, as part of the international community, to go ahead with our support for the completion of Russian reforms—by continuing our friendly and constructive dialogue on policies, by extending, when needed, our technical assistance; and by resuming our financing and risking our resources once again in support of your economic program.[118]

Throughout 1997, tax collection in Russia lagged, and a proposed new tax code failed to get through the parliament (the Duma). The IMF continued monthly monitoring, and several times held up disbursements under the EFF credit.[119] Meanwhile the financial crises had broken out in South-east Asia,[120] with consequences for Russia not yet clear.

In February 1998, Mr. Camdessus visited Moscow again. After some difficult bargaining, he reached agreement with the Russian prime minister to extend the EFF $10 billion credit for a fourth year, through early 2000. The 1998 program was designed, according to the joint communiqué, 'to take into account the recent international financial market turmoil', i.e. the Asia crisis, 'in which the Russian economy has not been entirely spared.'[121] The communiqué said:

---

[117] See summary of remarks of Michel Camdessus in Moscow, 2 Apr. 1997, 26 *IMF Survey*, p. 110, (7 Apr. 1997).

[118] Ibid.

[119] According to the US Secretary of the Treasury, monthly tranches were delayed eight times, and in the two-year period 1996–7 actual disbursements under the EFF program totalled 28 percent less than originally planned, because of Russia's failure to meet performance targets. Testimony of Treasury Secretary Lawrence H. Summers before House Comm. on Banking and Financial Services, 106th Cong., 1st. Sess, 21 Sept. 1999.

[120] See Sect. 18.7 supra.

[121] Joint IMF–Russia Communiqué, 19 Feb. 1998, 27 *IMF Survey*, p. 49, (23 Feb. 1998).

In concluding the negotiations, the Managing Director was confident that fulfillment of the policies under the program would result in Russia's successful transition to a dynamic market economy.[122]

Of course, even as the purpose of an IMF stand-by is to inspire confidence of investors and creditors in the member state in question, so the Managing Director may have felt it part of his duty to sound more optimistic than the cold record would support. Russian share prices had lost nearly 50 percent of their value, and interest rates had to be raised to 39 percent. President Yeltsin told Mr. Camdessus, 'I do not recall an occasion when after meeting you personally, we have left each other disappointed. . . . It is not without your assistance that the Russian economy is recovering.'[123]

(b) Losing Confidence

In the last week of May 1998, the ruble once again came under pressure, and as the Central Bank raised its interest rate on short-term notes to 150 percent, Russia sought further support from the IMF to shore up its reserves. Mr. Camdessus insisted there was no crisis,[124] but Russian share prices kept falling, in part as investors hurt in the Asia crisis sought to avoid all risky investment, in part as commodity prices, oil and gas in particular, dropped sharply.

The Fund released the monthly tranche under the EFF, and President Clinton said 'The United States endorses additional conditional financial support from the international institutions, as necessary, to promote stability, structural reforms, and growth in Russia.'[125] Initially, the IMF declined to create another stabilization loan. The opponents of a new safety net maintained that more funds now would create moral hazard, i.e. that it would encourage imprudent new foreign investment that would simply contribute to a new crisis later on, encouraged by the perception that the IMF and the US Treasury would always bail out the country 'too big to fail', as well as its creditors. On June 10, the Deputy Finance Ministers of the G–7 issued a public statement supporting 'growth promoting reforms' pledged by Russia, indicating that their Executive Directors would support the Fund program to strengthen investor confidence.[126] A few days later, however, the Fund suspended disbursement of the latest tranche under the EFF credit.

Meanwhile, as the IMF and the leaders of the industrial countries were debating whether to augment Russia's reserves in defense of the ruble, reports became more frequent of funds flowing out of Russia into a series of offshore havens—the Channel Islands, the Isle of Man, Antigua, the

---

122 Id.   123 *Financial Times*, London, 20 Feb. 1998, p. 2.
124 See *Financial Times*, 28 May 1998, p. 1.
125 34 *Weekly Comp. Pres. Docs.* 1006, 31 May 1998.
126 *Financial Times*, 11 June 1998, p. 2.

Cayman Islands, and other locations that freely accepted funds and asked no questions. Such reports had been circulating for years, but it began to appear now that the funds came not only from the 'crony capitalists' or 'oligarchs' who had grown rich and largely unaccountable as a result of the privatizations of state enterprises, but from the Russian Central Bank itself, possibly including funds made available by the IMF or the other credits supplied in conjunction with IMF arrangements.[127]

Though these reports disturbed the western creditors and the IMF,[128] on July 13, 1998 Mr. Camdessus recommended an immediate increase in the IMF's financial support for Russia of about $11.2 billion, half to be provided as soon as the Russian government had taken the actions it had agreed to take, the remainder during the course of the year.[129] A structural adjustment loan from the World Bank and a loan for balance of payments support from the government of Japan would be made available at the same time. On July 20, 1998, the Executive Directors of the IMF approved the recommendation.[130] The funds were to be drawn from the General Arrangements to Borrow[131]—the first time that that facility had been used in twenty years, and the first time it had been used to support a drawing by a non-participant.[132]

The next four weeks were chaotic, as Russia reeled towards crisis. First, the Duma rejected the government's revenue-raising program. Next, President Yeltsin attempted to implement the program anyway by decree; that effort failed either to raise significant revenue or to build investor confidence. Given the on-again, off-again disbursements by the IMF under prior credits, with each tranche dependent on the government's current performance, the new credit turned out not to be the confidence-builder anticipated. As in South-east Asia a year earlier, holders of short-term high-yield investments—both foreign and Russian—withdrew their funds, exchanged rubles for dollars, and sought to put their assets beyond the reach of the Russian authorities.

---

[127] It subsequently came out that a Financial Management Company (FIMACO) controlled by the Central Bank and incorporated in Jersey (Channel Islands) had received at least a billion US dollars for the account of the Russian Central Bank, not listed under Russia's reserves or reported to the IMF. Other large movements of funds went to or through banks not controlled by the Russian Central Bank, notably the Bank of New York.

[128] And indeed led to an audit by the accounting firm Price Waterhouse Coopers, nominally requested by the Russian Central Bank, but in fact required by the IMF and eventually posted on the IMF's Internet website.

[129] 27 *IMF Survey*, p. 221, (20 July 1998).   [130] 27 *IMF Survey*, p. 237, (3 Aug. 1998).

[131] See Ch. 17, Sect. 17.7(a).

[132] The use of the GAB for drawings by non-participants had been authorized by an amendment to the decision creating the GAB, Ex. Bd. Dec. No. 7337–(83/37) 24 Feb. 1983. See *Selected Decisions* of the IMF, 378 (25th issue 2000). Such use of the GAB requires a statement by the Managing Director 'that the Fund faces an inadequacy of resources to meet actual and expected requests for financing that reflect the existence of an exceptional situation . . . of a character or aggregate size that could threaten the stability of the international monetary system.' Id. ¶21.

On Thursday, August 13, the *Financial Times* published a letter by the financier George Soros, stating that the 'meltdown in Russian financial markets has reached the terminal phase', and urging devaluation of the ruble.[133] Shares on the Russian stock market fell by 15 percent until trading was suspended. President Yeltsin, speaking by telephone from his holiday home, instructed his prime minister to 'steadfastly fulfill the plan of action' agreed to with the IMF.[134] On the next day, Friday, August 14, President Yeltsin, still on his holiday, said 'There will not be a devaluation of the ruble . . . The situation is fully under control.'[135] The G–7 said that for the time being no additional financial assistance would be forthcoming.

(c)   Default

On Monday, August 17, Russia declared a 90-day moratorium on foreign commercial debt and a unilateral restructuring of its domestic debt (treasury bills or GKOs).[136] Further, the ruble would be permitted to be traded within so wide a band as to effectively be devalued by more than a third.[137] It seems that the IMF officials in Moscow were told about the government's decision, but the Fund's approval was neither sought nor given.

As a consequence of the moratorium and default, Russia overnight lost access to international capital markets. The Russian banking sector, which held most of the domestic debt, virtually collapsed. Everyone who had invested in the Russian economy—including the 'oligarchs' who had grown rich during the period of privatization—lost as the result of the default and devaluation of August 17.

Should the next tranche of the July loan now be disbursed, when what the loan was designed to prevent had in fact occurred? Mr. Camdessus issued a statement saying 'I hope that the government's economic program will continue to be implemented in full, so that the economic and financial situation will improve and the IMF can be in a position to disburse the second tranche . . . in September as scheduled.'[138] In the event, the IMF did not release the September tranche of the July support loan. If conditionality—the law of the IMF—was to retain any meaning, it could hardly do so. If the major industrial countries still considered it necessary to aid Russia, they would have to do so directly. But while it could be said that the geopolitical considerations in favour of supporting the Russian government had not changed, none of the western governments—in particular none of the parliaments—were

---

[133] *Financial Times*, 13 Aug. 1998, p. 18, picked up by wire services around the world.
[134] *Financial Times*, 14 Aug. 1998, p. 1   [135] *Financial Times*, 15 Aug. 1998, p.2.
[136] An English text of the announcement issued by the Russian government and central bank was published in 27 *IMF Survey*, p. 275, (31 Aug. 1998).
[137] Eventually the ruble depreciated by about 70 percent against the dollar in the last five months of 1998.
[138] 27 *IMF Survey*, p. 275, (31 Aug. 1998).

willing to proceed without the IMF and without the conditionality only the IMF could demand—if not enforce.

(d)   A Fresh Start?

Only 11 months later Russia was once again granted a credit by the IMF—nominally a 17-month stand-by credit of about $4.5 billion, in seven equal disbursements of $640 million.[139] Once again, the Russian government—several prime ministers later—undertook in a Letter of Intent to implement a fiscal program, structural reform, and a monetary policy agreed with the Fund.[140] The loan itself was provided in the form of SDRs credited to Russia's account at the IMF, which apparently could be used only to pay off prior drawings that were due to be repaid. Thus on the one hand the IMF would not be facing a default to it by Russia; on the other hand whatever was the truth concerning money laundering and diversion of western aid—the stories kept coming out in bits and pieces—the July 1999 loan would remain in Washington fully protected against unauthorized use.[141] Russia benefited from approval of the stand-by not only in keeping its obligations to the Fund from falling into arrears; once the IMF had accepted the Letter of Intent and accompanying assurances, the way was opened for the World Bank and the Japanese government to resume their programs of assistance, and for the Paris Club and the London Club to resume negotiations for rolling over outstanding debts going back to the Soviet era.

---

[139] 28 *IMF Survey*, p. 241, (2 Aug. 1999).

[140] The 16-page Letter of Intent, dated July 13, 1999 and released by the IMF on its Internet website, included the following passage:

> We readily acknowledge that the negative economic and social consequences of the economic crisis that arose in August, 1998 reflect, in part, the fact that implementation of the government's economic program, over the last several years, has been incomplete. Further in certain respects, weak implementation has served to worsen structural problems. In particular, the inability of the government to enforce cash payment of statutory tax liabilities and to pay its own bills in a timely fashion has played a significant role in the spread of the nonpayment problem. Moreover, potential benefits from reforms, most significantly privatization, have been diminished owing to the absence of transparency in the process and a failure to ensure that economic gains were broadly distributed among the population, and this has served to dampen public support for the reform process in general.

[141] In the Press Release announcing approval of the new loan, the IMF said:

> Directors expressed strong disapproval of the finding that the channeling by the Central Bank of domestic transactions through FIMACO and, in 1996, the transfer of assets in the books of the Central Bank to FIMACO meant that the balance sheet of the Central Bank had given a misleading impression of the true state of reserves and monetary and exchange rate policies. Without these indirect transactions and the inaccurate reporting of foreign reserves, it is possible that one or more of the disbursements of IMF funds to Russia in 1996 would have been delayed. Directors urged the Russian authorities to take immediate steps to prevent a recurrence of these problems. Directors took note of the findings that the July 1998 tranche from the Fund had not been misappropriated. (IMF Press Release No. 99/35 of 28 July 1999, repr. in 28 *IMF Survey*, p. 241 at 242, (2 Aug. 1999).

Summary

The break-up of the USSR was in many ways a new event for the international financial community, which had become accustomed to the mysterious east functioning largely (though of course not completely) outside the market system of the rest of the world. But the political gains from integrating the states of the former Soviet Union, and particularly Russia, into the international community were quickly appreciated. The risks of failure were assessed differently in different quarters—some worrying about renewal of the cold war, others about massive famine, new forms of dictatorship, or civil war with nuclear weapons. Western governments spoke of a 'peace dividend', i.e. a reduction in the amounts necessary to be spent on defense, but with budgetary constraints in all the major countries the translation of savings in defense costs into funds for assistance to the newly non-communist states was not easily carried out.

No country was prepared to give assistance (other than humanitarian aid) without some type of assurance that the resources made available would be used productively. But no country—and no private creditor or potential creditor—was willing or able to impose conditions or request assurances of sound use of the resources made available. As in the case of the debtor countries of Latin America and South-east Asia, the international community looked to the IMF to carry out this function, and the various pledges of assistance made at successive summit meetings of the G–7 and similar occasions were nearly always accompanied by a statement tying the offer of support to an IMF program. Thus the influence of the IMF greatly exceeded the amount of its own resources, including borrowed funds, that could be devoted to the former communist states. International monetary law in major part became IMF conditionality, and by releasing or suspending release of funds, the IMF became even more than in previous years the enforcement agency of the international monetary system.

The IMF itself changed in the course of a decade of preoccupation with Russia. The efforts of the IMF to remain non-political, as had been contemplated at Bretton Woods and largely followed in the Fund's early years, broke down in its dealings with Russia—on two levels. In resorting to monthly monitoring and frequent suspension of disbursements, the Fund became involved in internal decision-making to a far greater extent than before. Further, despite its protestations to the contrary, the Fund was drawn into the efforts of the G–7 not only in imposing conditions on the Russian government, but in taking sides in a domestic election.

Finally, the story of Russia in the 1990s illustrates both the limits of sovereignty and the limits of conditionality. The IMF lowered its requirements at several stages, but in the end could not impose its will—its law—on a government that was disorganized, ambivalent, in part incompetent, and in several respects corrupt. But if Russia could not live in the international economy according to the rules of the IMF, neither, it turned out, could it live without the IMF and its backers, as it contemplated the membership in the international community in the twenty-first century.

19

Other Institutions of the International Monetary System

While the International Monetary Fund is the centerpiece of international monetary law, it would be misleading to suggest that it is the only institution, or that its Articles of Agreement form the only code of conduct relevant to the many participants in the international financial arena. This chapter contains brief sketches of some of the other institutions, formal and informal, that together constitute the international monetary system.

19.1 THE WORLD BANK AND ITS AFFILIATES

(a) The World Bank

The International Bank for Reconstruction and Development, commonly known as the World Bank, was created in 1944 at Bretton Woods at the same time as the International Monetary Fund. Like the Fund, the World

Bank functions under a three-tier system of governance—a Board of Governors consisting of all member states' ministers of finance or central bank governors, a board of Executive Directors permanently in residence in Washington, DC, and an independent staff headed by a president chosen for a five-year term. As in the Fund, voting power in the Bank depends on quota but also as in the Fund, most decisions are taken by consensus, so that the prestige and preparation of executive directors often count for more than weighted votes. Unlike the Fund, in which members' quotas must be paid in full, the World Bank is organized in corporate form, and quotas in the World Bank reflect both paid-in capital and subscribed capital subject to call. Only about 10 percent of authorized capital is in fact paid in. The headquarters of the World Bank and Fund are housed in adjacent buildings and they always hold their annual meetings at the same time, two years in succession in Washington and one year in another city. In contrast to the Fund, whose Managing Director has always been a European, as of year-end 2001, the President of the World Bank has always been an American.[1]

Formally, the division of functions between the IMF and the World Bank is that the Fund is supposed to render short- and medium-term assistance to countries in balance of payments difficulties (Fund Articles of Agreement, Art. I and V(3)) while the Bank is supposed to render longer-term assistance to particular projects of reconstruction or development (Bank Articles of Agreement Art. I and III(l)).[2] In the early years of the two institutions, the distinctions between medium- and long-term lending on the one hand, and between balance of payments and project lending on the other were fairly carefully observed. The Fund, as described in the preceding chapters granted stand-by credits of three- to five-year duration tied to balance of payments adjustment, and the Bank made five- to fifteen-year loans to governments for electric power stations, harbours, railroads, and similar 'bankable' projects. More recently, as the World Bank has focused also on projects to improve human capital—education, health care, population control, and the like—while the Fund has addressed the longer-term nature of developing countries' adjustment problems through a variety of new facilities,[3] the separation of functions between the sister institutions has become somewhat blurred.

---

[1] No law requires this tradition, and suggestions have been made from time to time that a Japanese citizen might be given the leadership position in one of the Bretton Woods agencies.

[2] The inspiration for the World Bank came principally from the United States, whereas the British government at Bretton Woods, concerned about balance of payments problems after the war, focused on the Fund. The US representatives hoped that by establishing a Bank for Reconstruction, the Soviet Union could be induced to join in post-war economic cooperation. The Soviet Union, though represented at Bretton Woods, did not join either institution. The developing countries represented at Bretton Woods insisted on adding 'development' to the name and the functions of the Bank. See I. G. Patel, Foreward to Barend A. de Vries, *Remaking the World Bank*, p. ix (1987).

[3] See Ch. 17, esp. Sect. 17.6.

Both the World Bank and the IMF have understood that their functions include research, technical assistance, and overall economic analysis, and they have tried to harmonize their statistics and economic strategies. The suggestion that they send joint missions to recipient countries and prepare joint country reports has not been generally accepted.[4] In the 1980s, as described in the preceding chapter, the World Bank was brought in to programs coordinated by the IMF to supply new funds and refinance existing loans of developing countries caught up in the debt crises.[5]

Unlike the IMF, which draws all of its resources from governments, the World Bank is financed primarily through the sale of its bonds in the capital markets of the principal industrial countries, guaranteed by the callable capital of the Bank's shareholders, i.e. the member states. Under its Articles of Agreement, the Bank is required either to lend directly to member states or, if the borrower is a private enterprise or a subordinate unit of government, subject to a guarantee by the member state (Art. III(4)). The Articles of Agreement also provide that before making or guaranteeing a loan the Bank must be satisfied that 'in the prevailing market conditions the borrower would be unable otherwise to obtain the loan under conditions which in the opinion of the Bank are reasonable for the borrower' (Art. III(4)(ii)).[6] For the most part, the Bank grants loans on terms designed to cover its own cost of funds, and on condition that the project being financed (for instance an electric power station) be permitted to generate sufficient revenue to service the loan, as well as meeting the development needs of the beneficiary state.[7]

In many ways the documentation required by the World Bank in connection with a development loan is similar to what commercial banks require, i.e. a loan agreement, if the state or a state agency is the borrower; a guarantee agreement if the borrower is not the state itself; a project agreement if the entity in charge of the project is not itself the borrower; and related contractual agreements such as leases and mortgages. In addition, the World Bank generally requires evidence that the obligations undertaken by the borrowing country are consistent with its constitution and laws, and that where

---

[4] See e.g. Barend A. de Vries, *Remaking the World Bank*, 88–94 (1987); Margaret G. de Vries, *The International Monetary Fund 1972–1978*, Vol. II. pp. 955–6 (1985).

[5] See Ch. 17, Sect. 17.6 and Ch. 18, Sect. 18.5. For a legal and historical analysis of what he refers to as 'sibling rivalry' by the long-time General Counsel of the Fund, see Joseph Gold, 'The Relationship between the International Monetary Fund and the World Bank', 15 *Creighton L. Rev.* 499 (1982).

[6] In contrast to the IMF, which jealously guards its immunity from suit in national courts, the World Bank waives its immunity and includes choice of forum clauses in its offerings of bonds to the public. See Articles of Agreement of the Bank, Art. VIII(3). In most countries where its bonds are marketed, they are exempt by special legislation from local securities regulation. See e.g. (U.S.) 22 U.S.C. §286k–1 and §286k–2.

[7] Since 1980 interest costs on World Bank loans are based on a weighted average of all of its outstanding borrowings plus a 0.5 percent spread; committed but undisbursed loans carry a charge of 0.5 percent.

necessary they have been ratified by the appropriate organs of government. World Bank loan agreements generally contain negative covenants requiring the member state (or the project in question) not to incur additional debt without the Bank's approval, or *pari passu* clauses providing that if any lien is created on any governmental assets (or on the Project's assets), such lien shall equally and ratably secure payment of the World Bank loan. In some instances, where legislation will need to be enacted or amended, or where an existing project appears to be overstaffed or poorly managed, the Bank has negotiated Letters of Intent signed by the relevant officials of the beneficiary country similar to those required by the IMF for stand-by arrangements.[8]

(b)   The International Development Association

As early as the mid-1950s it was realized that the normal conditions of World Bank lending were inadequate to the problem of economic development for the weakest and poorest of the developing countries, which simply could not afford to service loans even on the favourable, though market-related terms offered by the World Bank. For those countries, a subsidiary organization of the World Bank was created in 1960, using the World Bank's staff and facilities but providing so-called 'soft loans'. IDA makes loans on terms as long as 50 years and interest rates as low as 0.75 percent per annum to eligible member states. To be eligible, a state must meet three criteria—(i) relative poverty, defined as Gross National Product below an established threshold; (ii) lack of creditworthiness to borrow on market terms; and (iii) good policy performance, defined as the implementation of economic and social policies that promote growth and poverty reduction. As of year-end 2001, the threshold of poverty stood at per capita income of less than $885 in 2000; 79 countries were listed as eligible, including a few 'blend countries' such as India and Indonesia, which were eligible in principle for IDA loans because of their low per capita income, but also were considered creditworthy for some World Bank loans.[9] Unlike the World Bank itself, which as noted raises its funds in the market, IDA relies on income from World Bank investments, and on contributions of cash ('replenishments') from the governments of the industrial nations, normally every three years, and in principle in proportion to the donor countries' initial subscription and voting power.

---

[8] Loan agreements of the World Bank are regularly published in the UN Treaty Series. For the Loan Regulations incorporated into loan agreements by reference, see 260 U.N.T.S. 376 (1956); 414 U.N.T.S. 268 (1961).

[9] China, long an IDA customer, graduated from IDA in fiscal year 1999; according to an official briefing to the World Bank Executive Directors, there was no lending to Pakistan in fiscal year 2000, previously a leading borrower from IDA, 'as a result of political instability and unresolved policy issues.'

(c)   The International Finance Corporation

Like the IMF, the World Bank has been subject to criticism from the left and the right. One group of critics has asserted that the World Bank is too intrusive into the affairs of foreign states, requiring a variety of commitments and reforms as a condition for development lending. The other group has complained that the Bank is too much involved with governments, thus encouraging central planning and bureaucracy at the expense of market forces and free enterprise.

Partly in response to the latter critique, the World Bank created a subsidiary in 1956 designed to link private enterprise with internationally encouraged economic development. The International Finance Corporation is separately organized but with the same membership and organizational structure as the Bank. The President of the World Bank is also president of IFC. IFC makes loans at market rates to private ventures in developing countries and invests in shares in such ventures, in either case usually without government guarantees. The fact that IFC is prepared to invest in a project tends to attract other private investors, both because it shows that IFC regards the project as economically sound and because it is thought less likely that the host country would expropriate or otherwise deal unfairly with a project in which the World Bank, through its subsidiary, has a substantial stake. Typically, IFC will assume no more than 25 percent of total cost of a project, counting both debt and equity; it may supply technical assistance to an enterprise in which it has an interest, but will not assume a management role, and will not be the largest shareholder. IFC's equity investments are funded out of its own assets, i.e. paid in capital and retained earnings; its lending operations are funded 80 percent from its bonds or other borrowing in international financial markets, and 20 percent from loans by the World Bank.

Two more units of the World Bank family may be briefly mentioned here, but are more appropriately discussed in connection with international private investment.[10] The International Centre for the Settlement of Investment Disputes (ICSID) administers a Convention on the Settlement Disputes between States and nationals of other States,[11] as well as serving as appointing authority for disputes between host states and foreign investors under Bilateral Investment Treaties and the North American Free Trade Agreement. The Multilateral Investment Guarantee Agency (MIGA) seeks to encourage foreign investment in developing countries by insuring approved investments against non-commercial risks. Both of these institutions, and their influence in the changing legal climate for transnational investment, are explored in Chapter 15.

---

[10] See Ch. 15, Sect. 15.1.   [11] Ch. 15, Sect. 15.4.

19.2   THE BANK FOR INTERNATIONAL SETTLEMENTS[12]

(a)   The Central Banks' Bank

The Bank for International Settlements was founded in 1930 in Basle, Switzerland to promote cooperation among central banks, to provide additional facilities for international operation, and to act as trustee or agent in connection with German reparations arising out of World War I. The Bretton Woods Conference that created the IMF and the World Bank adopted a resolution in its Final Act recommending the liquidation of the BIS 'at the earliest possible moment',[13] essentially on the ground that its functions would be assumed on a global scale by the IMF.[14] In fact the BIS remained in business and over time assumed an increasing role in the international monetary system. In connection with the Marshall Plan for the reconstruction of Europe after World War II, the BIS served as agent for the clearing operations under the Organization for European Economic Cooperation and for the European Payments Union. More recently, the BIS acted as clearing agent and keeper of accounts for the European Monetary System in connection with creation and use of the European Currency Unit (the 'ECU'), and it supplied bridge-financing in international financial crises such as those described in the preceding chapter while the IMF, the United States, and other creditor states were putting together their rescue packages and negotiating the necessary commitments.[15]

The Bank for International Settlements is a unique institution, both a functioning bank that takes deposits and makes loans and an international organization, with international legal personality and with the privileges and immunities customarily enjoyed by international organizations.[16] The members and shareholders of the BIS are central banks, not governments,

[12] For a more detailed description, see Mario Giovanoli, 'The Role of the Bank for International Settlements in International Monetary Cooperation and its Tasks Relating to the ECU' in Robert C. Effros (ed.), *Current Legal Issues Affecting Central Banks*, Vol. I, p. 39 (IMF 1992), also 23 *Int'l Lawyer* 841 (1989). See also *The Bank for International Settlements and the Basle Meetings*, published by the BIS on the occasion of its 50th Anniversary (Basle, May 1980).

[13] Resolution V of the Final Act of the Bretton Woods Conference, *Proceedings and Documents* of the United Nations Conference, Bretton Woods, N.H. 1–22 July 1944, p. 939. Though the Final Act adopted and urged ratification of the Articles of Agreement of IMF and the IBRD, it was not itself submitted to signatories for ratification or approval by parliaments, and thus Resolution V did not need to be, and was in fact not acted upon.

[14] Also, the BIS was seen as too closely identified with the interests of Germany in the interwar years and possibly even during the war. See *Bretton Woods Proceedings*, 915–16, 1166.

[15] See e.g. Ch. 18, Sect. 18.3(a) at n. 10 concerning the first Mexican crisis, and in particular, Sect. 18. 4(b) concerning the Brazilian crisis.

[16] See e.g. the Brussels Protocol regarding the Immunities of the Bank for International Settlements of 30 July 1936, and the Headquarters Agreement between the Swiss Federal Council and the Bank for International Settlements of February 10, 1987, *Recueil Officiel du Droit Federal* 0.192.122.971.3.

and its depositors are also almost entirely central banks, plus some other institutions such as the IMF, the European Monetary Cooperation Fund, and other public or quasi-public institutions. Unlike the IMF, the BIS administers no code of conduct applicable to its members, and it does not aim at universal membership. Originally, the membership of the BIS was primarily European, plus the United States in an ambiguous role.[17] More recently, the Bank has expanded its membership to include central banks from most parts of the world—50 as of June 2001, including the central banks of all of the Group of Ten states,[18] plus the central banks of Argentina, Australia, Brazil, China, Mexico, Russia, Saudi Arabia, South Africa, Turkey, and most of the countries of Europe not in the G–10, as well as the European Central Bank. It holds some 7 percent of global foreign exchange reserves on deposit from about 120 central banks, equal at the end of the Bank's fiscal year 2001 to about US$130 billion.

The BIS places its funds in the market, principally in the form of investments with top-quality commercial banks and purchases of short-term government securities. Thus when funds are needed on short notice, as in the various regional crises described in the preceding chapter, the BIS is able both on its own and on behalf of its member central banks to furnish short-term credits on short notice and generally without conditions. The BIS also intervenes in foreign exchange markets, in some instances on confidential instructions from central banks, in other instances on its own behalf, and it carries out swap arrangements in foreign currencies.

(b) A Forum for Regulators

In addition to its banking functions, the Bank for International Settlements has assumed an important function as an international forum for discussion of monetary and bank regulatory issues, in a smaller, less political, and more technically oriented format than is generally possible in the IMF. The central bank governors of the Group of Ten (including Switzerland) meet once

---

[17] The place of the United States in the BIS is difficult to understand or explain. The US Federal Reserve System was one of the founding institutions of the BIS, and American citizens served as chairmen of the BIS in 12 of its first 16 years, 1930–46. But the Federal Reserve Board did not accept its seat on the board of directors of the BIS or exercise its voting rights until September 1994, and the original subscription of shares allocated to the United States was taken up not by the Fed but by a consortium of three major American commercial banks. Nevertheless officials of the Fed regularly attended monthly meetings of the 'Basle Club', participated in the work of the committees of experts and regulatory authorities organized under the auspices of the BIS, and as shown in Chapter 18, worked closely with the BIS in response to crises in the international monetary system. For discussion of the ambivalence on the part of the United States authorities to the BIS in the decades following World War II by a senior official of the Federal Reserve Board, see Charles J. Siegman, 'The Bank for International Settlements and the Federal Reserve', 80 *Fed'l Reserve Bull.* No. 10, p. 900 (Oct. 1994).

[18] See Sect. 19.4.

a month at the BIS headquarters in Basle, and in the 1960s these meetings of the 'Basle Club' became the focus for a series of rapid mobilization of funds designed to support the pound sterling and the Italian lira.[19] In 1974 the central bank governors of the G–10 plus Switzerland created a Committee on Banking Regulation and Supervisory Practices (later renamed the Committee on Banking Supervision) which meets regularly at the BIS. The first major product of this committee was the so-called Basle Concordat (1975, revised 1983), designed to allocate regulatory responsibility for multinational banks among the authorities of the home country and the countries where branches, subsidiaries, or consortium banks were established.[20] Subsequently the Basle Committee on Banking Supervision has worked to develop coordinated standards governing the amount of capital (and the ways to measure the capital) of commercial banks operating in the international monetary system.[21] As the activities of banks, insurance companies, and securities firms have become increasingly intermingled, the Basle Committee, the International Organization of Securities Commissions (IOSCO), and the International Association of Insurance Supervisors (IAIS) established in 1996 a Joint Forum on Financial Conglomerates, not, at least at the outset, as a law-making organization but as a medium for coordinating approaches to cross-sectoral as well as cross-frontier supervisory issues.[22] In these and other committees, the BIS acts not only as host, but it collects and publishes data not otherwise available, and it performs secretarial and reporting functions for the European Community, for the Group of Ten, and for a variety of other official and semi-official institutions concerned with international economic affairs.

19.3   THE PARIS CLUB[23]

The Paris Club is an informal organization of creditor countries—without a charter and without permanent officers or staff—that meets to consider common problems of threatened or actual default by debtor countries on

---

[19] See the lively account by the American member of the Basle Club, Charles A. Coombs, *The Arena of International Finance* (1976), reviewed by Lowenfeld, 90 *Harv. L. Rev.* 1558 (1977).

[20] See *Principles for the Supervision of Banks' Foreign Establishments* (1983) and supplements thereto (1990 and 1992); also *Minimum Standards for the Supervision of International Banking Groups and Their Cross-Border Establishments*, and *The Supervision of Cross-Border Banking*. These and other documents are available on the website of the BIS.

[21] See *Core Principles for Effective Banking Supervision* (Basel Core Principles) (Sept. 1997).

[22] See e.g. Joseph J. Norton, 'A "New International Financial Architecture?"—Reflections on the Possible Law-Based Dimension', 33 *Int'l Lawyer* 891 (1999) and sources there cited.

[23] For more detailed accounts, from which this section is in large part drawn, see Alexis Rieffel, 'The Paris Club, 1978–1983', 23 *Colum. J. Transnat'l Law* 83 (1984), and Rieffel, 'The Role of the Paris Club in Managing Debt Problems', *Princeton Essays in International Finance* No. 161 (1985). Mr. Rieffel was the US Treasury Department's technical expert on official debt relief during the period described in the article.

government-to-government debt. When a country indebted to several creditor countries requests debt relief, a meeting of representatives of the creditor countries with representatives of the debtor is scheduled at a conference center in Paris, usually under the chairmanship of a senior official of the French Treasury.[24] Representatives of the IMF, the World Bank, the OECD, and UNCTAD also usually attend the sessions of the Paris Club, and a representative of the relevant regional development bank may do so as well. The ad hoc character of the Paris Club and the absence of a permanent secretariat are consistent with the point of view that debt rescheduling is an extraordinary event; if the Paris Club were viewed as a more formal institution, it would follow that official debt rescheduling is a normal transaction, thus to some degree undermining the sanctity of contracts and encouraging debtor countries to seek relief.[25] Nevertheless, negotiations under the auspices of the Paris Club have become sufficiently common so that they may fairly be regarded as an element of international monetary law.

Since its first meeting in 1956 in connection with a debt relief arrangement for Argentina after the fall of Peron, the Paris Club has focused on medium- and long-term debt owed by sovereign states to other sovereign states or their agencies; sovereign debt to private creditors such as banks, is handled elsewhere,[26] and so is debt to international organizations such as the IMF and the World Bank. The guiding principles of the Paris Club are on the one hand that debt relief should be granted where necessary while keeping the debtor country subject to a discipline of adjustment, and on the other hand that the burdens of debt relief should be shared fairly, with each creditor country providing relief commensurate with its loan exposure to the debtor country.

Thus a Paris Club agreement combines conditionality with assistance, but unlike an IMF stand-by which usually provides fresh resources, the assistance offered by a Paris Club agreement consists of postponement of obligations on existing debt. In most instances, the Paris Club does not itself propose a program of economic adjustment, but makes debt relief contingent on compliance with a stand-by arrangement with the IMF, usually involving borrowing in the upper credit tranches and thus subject to strict conditionality.[27] A problem may arise if a stand-by is not already in place, since a stand-by is supposed to take into account the country's ability to

[24] It is interesting to note that from 1978 to 1984 the Chairman of the Paris Club was Michel Camdessus, who, after a brief term as Governor of the Banque de France, became Managing Director of the IMF in 1987, a position he held until February 2000.

[25] Rieffel, n. 23 supra, makes this point at 23 *Colum. J. Transnat'l Law*, 91–2.

[26] See Chapter 13.

[27] In 1981 Poland, not then a member of the Fund, sought debt relief from the Paris Club. The creditor states attempted to negotiate policy reforms directly with Poland but the effort was unsuccessful. Poland applied for membership in the Fund in November 1981, but martial law was declared in the following month, and the application was not acted upon. Poland became a member of the Fund in 1986 and thereafter was able to reschedule its debts both with the Paris Club and with commercial bank creditors.

repay the drawing, and that may well depend on whether it can negotiate postponement of its obligations to the Paris Club creditor states. In some instances the Fund may grant conditional approval of a stand-by arrangement and the Paris Club may grant debt relief subject to final approval of the IMF stand-by.

The conclusion of a successful Paris Club negotiation is an agreement (in the form of an 'agreed minute') whereby the debtor country undertakes to implement specified reforms that will enable it to resume its payments, and the creditor countries agree to a stretched out schedule of repayments for a certain amount of obligations due in the so-called period of consolidation, normally one year. A typical Paris Club rescheduling agreement might provide that 75 percent of payments (other than on short-term credits) due from Patria to the participating states will be postponed for a three-year grace period, and that payments on the full amounts due will thereafter be resumed in semi-annual installments over a four-year repayment period. Once a Paris Club agreement is concluded between the debtor and all the creditor countries, the debtor country will negotiate implementing bilateral agreements with each participating creditor state, and in some instances with particular lending agencies of the creditor state.

Unlike commercial bank lending, which generally proceeds from a common commercial motive and at market-determined rates, government-to-government loans may be made from a variety of motives—from export promotion to development assistance to humanitarian relief to military support—and on a wide range of terms and 'reasonable expectation' of repayment.[28] Accordingly, no general formula has emerged for allocating the burden of relief, and a straight arithmetic solution, whereby for instance, each creditor country would agree to grant relief with respect to 75 percent of all the obligations due to it, has usually been difficult to achieve. More commonly, what emerges is a solution including some credits and excluding others, whether by purpose of the loan, or by the date of origin and maturity, by the extent of the creditor's exposure, or by some combination.[29]

The participants in a Paris Club negotiation generally require the debtor country to agree to a non-discrimination cause, to ensure that the debtor will not make more generous payments to non-participating creditor countries than it does to the signatories to the agreement. The Paris Club creditors will be entitled to demand larger payments as well. There is no requirement that

---

[28] Also, a significant portion of official credits began as commercial export financing, with some or all of the purchase price guaranteed by a governmental expert finance agency, such as the British Export Credit Guarantee Department, the French COFACE, the German Hermes, or the Export-Import Banks of Japan and the United States. When one of these agencies pays off the exporter or its commercial bank, the debt is assigned to the agency; if the purchaser was a government agency or the transaction was guaranteed by the purchaser's government, the debt is added to the debtor country's official debt.

[29] Interest rates on the rescheduled debt are left for bilateral negotiation in order to reflect the different terms and purposes of the debt subject to rescheduling.

the debtor country treat private creditors such as commercial banks in the same way that it treats official creditors, but only that the debtor country will seek 'comparable relief' from its private creditors.[30]

In 1988–91, the Paris Club countries introduced a series of exceptional measures designed first to help the severely indebted low-income, or 'IDA only' borrowers—the so-called 'Toronto Terms', and subsequently for lower middle-income countries—the 'Trinidad Terms'. In both cases the requirement of a comprehensive IMF adjustment program in place supported by upper-credit IMF resources remained, but the grace period became much longer and for official assistance debt maturities were extended to a maximum of 25 years (Toronto) and 20 years (Trinidad). The severely indebted countries were also granted the option of cancelling a portion of their debt not linked to official development assistance, or of reducing or postponing payment of interest.[31] Subsequently new terms were worked out—the 'London Terms' and the 'Naples Terms'—varying in the definition of eligible countries and the length of grace period and maturities, but consistent with the aim of treating all creditors similarly situated equally and renewing the commitment among the debtor countries to eventual repayment.

19.4 THE GROUP OF TEN

(a) The Rise and Decline of the Group of Ten

When the General Arrangements to Borrow was created in 1962,[32] there was some discontent among member states of the IMF about a rich countries' 'members only' club—a fund within the Fund to which the poorer states need not apply. The official IMF History quotes the Executive Director of The Netherlands as describing the GAB as a 'compromise between the ideology of the Fund as a global monetary institution and a newer ideology which sought solutions by closer cooperation between the main industrial countries.'[33]

In the 1960s and early 1970s, this prediction to a large extent came true. Having worked their way through the complex negotiations that resulted in

---

[30] A parallel informal institution known as the London Club has from time to time met to restructure sovereign debt to commercial lenders such as banks, generally after the debtor country has reached agreement with sovereign lenders through the Paris Club, and often also after, or in connection with, a stand-by arrangement with the IMF. Several East European countries, notably Poland, have gone through the London Club procedure, as have some Latin American countries. Negotiations to reschedule Russia's debt to some 500 commercial lenders were begun through the London Club just after the dissolution of the Soviet Union, and were completed in 1997, before the crisis described in Chapter 18.

[31] For a concise summary, see Thomas Klein, 'Innovations in Debt Relief, The Paris Club', 29 *Finance and Development*, p. 42 (Mar. 1992).

[32] See Ch. 17, Sect. 17.7.

[33] J. Keith, Horsefield, *The International Monetary Fund 1945–1965*, 514 (1969).

the General Arrangements to Borrow, the ministers of finance and central bank governors of the participating states, and more commonly, their deputies, began to meet regularly on other matters connected with the international monetary system. Both the ministers and governors themselves and the Deputies of what came to be known as the Group of Ten (or G–10) played a major role, for instance, in developing the plan for Special Drawing Rights in the 1960s.[34] The Central Bank Governors of the Group of Ten plus Switzerland made up the 'Basle Club' that meets monthly at the Bank for International Settlements.[35] It was also in the Group of Ten that the interim arrangement designed to preserve the par value system was negotiated in the fall of 1971, embodied in the so-called Smithsonian Agreement.[36]

When the reform program of the international monetary system was initiated, however, the perception among some members of the IMF was that as the G–10 consisted entirely of the prosperous industrial countries, it was insufficiently representative of the membership as a whole. The United States, for its part, felt that the G–10 was excessively weighted in favour of the European Community, but on the other hand that the reform task should not be entrusted to the Executive Directors of the Fund, because they were likely to be too close to the staff of the Fund, and, at least by inference, too dedicated to preserving the par value system.[37] Accordingly, the reform task was entrusted initially to the Committee of Twenty, a committee on which developing as well as developed countries were represented at a level between the Fund Governors (i.e. the finance ministers and central bank governors) and the Executive Directors. Since the mid-1970s, the Group of Ten has not played as important a role in international affairs as it did in the period 1961–72, but both the G–10 itself and the Deputies of the G–10 continue to exist. At the Fund itself, an Interim Committee, roughly reflecting the membership of the Committee of Twenty, but with different personnel, formally submitted the proposals that led to the amendments to the Articles of Agreement approved in Jamaica in 1976,[38] and thereafter met at least twice a year to initiate and pass on important new programs and facilities of the IMF, until it was transformed into the International Monetary and Financial Committee in 1999.[39] On the major issues of exchange rate man-

---

[34] See Ch. 16, Sect. 16.8. For a description of the meetings of the G–10 Deputies by a senior staff participant, see Robert Solomon, *The International Monetary System 1945–1981*, 65–9, 128–50 (expanded edn. 1982). Generally the meetings were held in Paris, but conducted in English with an American chairman.

[35] See Sect. 19.2 supra.   [36] See Ch. 16, Sect. 16.9(c).

[37] See Margaret G. de Vries, *International Monetary Fund 1972–1978*, Vol. I, pp. 142–5 (1989). See also George P. Shultz and Kenneth W. Dam, *Economic Policy Beyond the Headlines*, 121–2 (2nd edn., 1998).

[38] See Ch. 17, Sect. 17.1(c).

[39] See Ch. 16, Sect. 16.3. As there noted, when the Amended Articles of Agreement of the IMF were being drafted in the mid-1970s, it was assumed that a permanent Council would be created to take over the functions of the Interim Committee. However, opposition arose to such a body, and the final version of the Amended Articles provides, in Article XII(1) and Schedule D, for

agement, leadership has passed to the Group of Seven, i.e. the G–10 minus The Netherlands, Belgium, Sweden (and Switzerland), or the Group of Five, i.e. the G–7 minus Canada and Italy. The activities of the G–7 (G–5) are discussed in the next section.

(b) Working Party Three

The same group of countries, and sometimes the same persons who met in the Committee of Deputies of the Group of Ten, also met for years under the auspices of the Organization for Economic Cooperation and Development (OECD), which had been formed in 1960 as a successor agency to the Organization for European Economic Cooperation that had overseen coordination among the West European countries in the context of reconstructing Europe after World War II. The OECD never became a law-making or regulatory agency, but it became an important forum for fact-gathering and for consultation on a variety of subjects.[40] The Economic Policy Committee of the OECD, and particularly its Working Party Three, became an important forum in the 1960s for exchange of views and development of policies on monetary and balance of payments. Many of the professionals who later became principals in the Group of Ten or the Group of Seven got to know one another through the meetings of Working Party Three.

Working Party Three remains in existence, as a forum for exchange among financial officials of the Group of Ten. Like the Group of Ten itself, however, the influence of WP3 declined as economic policy coordination in the 1980s and 1990s took place more often in Summit Conferences, and tended to shrink from G–10 to G–7, G–5, and even G–2 (United States and Japan), as described in the next section. A number of persons—participants as well as observers—have urged a return to the less political and more intellectual exchanges within established institutions such as Working Party Three of the OECD,[41] but this had not taken place as of year-end 2001.

---

creation of the Council only upon vote of the Board of Governors by an 85 percent of the total voting power. The Council was never created, however, and with the elimination of the word 'interim' from the name of the Committee, it does not appear that there is continuing interest in creating a Council as a permanent institution. For reasons for doubt about a permanent Council in the organization of the IMF, see de Vries, *International Monetary Fund 1972–1978*, n. 37 supra, Vol. II, pp. 971–2.

[40] See e.g. the OECD *Arrangement on Export Credits*, discussed in Ch. 9, Sect. 9.5(c).

[41] See e.g. Emile van Lennep, 'Institutional Aspects of International Economic Policy Cooperation and Coordination', in H. J. Blommestein (ed.), *The Reality of International Economic Policy Cordination* (1991). Mr. van Lennep was for many years the Chairman of Working Party Three, and later Secretary-General of the OECD.

19.5   THE GROUP OF SEVEN AND RELATED GROUPS

(a)   Origin of the G–7

In November 1975, as the negotiations for reform of the international monetary system were reaching their climax, President Giscard d'Estaing of France invited the chiefs of state or government of the United States, the United Kingdom, the Federal Republic of Germany, Italy, and Japan to the Château de Rambouillet not far from Paris, where the essential breakthrough was reached that led to the amended Articles of Agreement of the International Monetary Fund.[42] Since that time, the leaders of the principal industrial states have met once a year 'at the summit', each time in a different country. The leader of the country where the next meeting is scheduled acts as informal chairman in the year preceding the meeting; committees of 'sherpas' (carrying on the metaphor)[43] meet in preparation for the summit meetings, and the Ministers of Finance and Central Bank Governors of the participating states meet from time to time between summit meetings. Canada was invited by President Ford to join the group in 1976 in Puerto Rico, and since that time the summit meetings and the participants in general have been known as the Group of Seven or G–7. While topics from airplane hijacking to Middle East peace negotiations and developments in the cold war have come up in the summit meetings, the focus of the G–7 has generally been on the international economy, and particularly on the macroeconomic issues with which the international monetary system is concerned. Together the G–7 states control more than half the votes in the IMF and the World Bank, (as well as three of the five permanent seats in the UN Security Council) and if the members of the European Community take a common position—not always the case—the fact that four of the seven members of the G–7 are members of the European Community strengthens their influence in both groups.[44] Mikhail Gorbachev, the last president of the Soviet

---

[42] See Ch. 17, Sect. 17.1(c). The idea seems to have sprung from meetings of finance ministers of Germany, France, Great Britain, United States, and later Japan that began informally in Washington in 1973. Giscard d'Estaing and Helmut Schmidt, the West German Chancellor in 1975, had participated in the earlier meetings as finance ministers. See George P. Schultz and Kenneth W. Dam, *Economic Policy beyond the Headlines*, 12–14 (2nd edn.1998).

[43] Sherpas are persons native to the Nepalese Himalayas who are often employed as guides or porters on expeditions to Mount Everest and other formidable peaks. In the usage of the G–7, the sherpas are senior officials of the ministry of finance or of the office of the president or prime minister who meet to establish the agenda, note disagreements, and prepare drafts of the final communiqué, often with bracketed items showing where agreement could not be reached except at the highest level.

[44] Indeed the suggestion has been made that one should more properly speak of the G–3— the European Community, Japan, and the United States. While this fairly accurately reflects the power structure in negotiations on trade in the GATT/WTO system, it would not be an accurate description of the annual summit meetings, nor of the negotiations and tensions concerning international monetary affairs. Since 1978, the President of the EC Commission has attended summit meetings, although not all sessions when non-economic subjects were being

Union, was invited to the G–7 summit in London in 1991, and since then the President of Russia usually attends parts of the summit meetings, though to call the group 'G–8', as the press has often done, is not really justified.

(b)   The G–7, the G–5, and Attempts to Manage Exchange Rates

A recurring theme for the Group of Seven has been discussion of coordinated policies of intervention in the foreign exchange market. At the 1982 summit conference in Versailles, the leaders of the G–7 pledged 'to intensify our economic and monetary cooperation', and added that they were ready 'if necessary, to use intervention in exchange markets to counter disorderly conditions, as provided for under Article IV of the IMF Articles of Agreement.'[45] The leaders of the G–7 commissioned a working group to examine the question further, but the result was a generally negative recommendation, on the ground that 'intervention, whether co-ordinated or not [has] been no substitute for necessary changes in economic policies.'[46] At the next summit meeting in Williamsburg, Virginia in May 1983, the G–7 announced that

[W]hile retaining our freedom to operate independently, [we] are willing to undertake coordinated intervention in instances where it is agreed such intervention could be helpful.[47]

In the following two years, the dollar kept rising in value, notwithstanding massive and growing US deficits on current account, as well as very large budget deficits. As the Reagan administration pursued a policy of benign neglect (i.e. non-intervention and non-coordination), both the yen and mark fell back close to their 1973 levels relative to the dollar.[48] It was believed that the dollar was overvalued in terms of purchasing power by 30–35 per cent, and that if the exchange rate at the beginning of 1985 continued, the

---

discussed. For changes in the representation of the European Community in the G–7 Finance Ministers' meetings since the introduction of the euro, see Ch. 20, Sect. 20.5(e) at n. 72.

[45] Joint Communiqué issued at close of summit conference, Versailles, 6 June 1982 and Joint Statement on Monetary Undertakings, 11 *IMF Survey*, 189 (21 June 1982).

[46] See Summary of Report of Working Group and Statement by Central Bank Governors and Finance Ministers of the Seven, 29 Apr. 1983, 12 *IMF Survey*, 137 (9 May 1983).

[47] 12 *IMF Survey*, 171 (13 June 1983).

[48] March 1973 was the last time that the United States attempted to maintain a fixed rate (then known as a central rate), linked to gold. At that time the dollar stood at US$1 = DM2.81 and ¥262. Selected later years (annual average) show the trend:

> 1974 US$1 = DM2.59 = ¥292
> 1978 US$1 = DM2.01 = ¥210
> 1980 US$1 = DM1.81 = ¥227
> 1982 US$1 = DM2.43 = ¥249
> 1983 US$1 = DM2.55 = ¥238
> 1984 US$1 = DM2.84 = ¥237
> 1985 US$1 = DM2.94 = ¥238

United States current account deficit could reach $300 billion by 1990.[49] In Washington, the pressures for protectionist trade legislation were becoming almost irresistible.[50]

Some time in 1985, the American administration changed its strategy. The new Secretary of the Treasury, James A. Baker, initiated a series of unannounced discussions, bilaterally with Japanese officials and also with his counterparts and their deputies from Germany, the United Kingdom, and France, looking to joint action to drive the dollar down (or the yen and the mark up). On Sunday, September 22, 1985, the finance ministers and central bank governors of the G–5 (i.e. without Italy or Canada)[51] met for five hours in the White and Gold Room of the Plaza Hotel in New York. Five hours later, with press and television cameras previously notified that an important announcement would be made, they were ready with their communiqué:

The Ministers and Governors agreed that exchange rates should play a role in adjusting external imbalances. In order to do this, exchange rates should better reflect fundamental economic conditions than has been the case. They believe that agreed policy actions must be implemented and reinforced to improve the fundamentals further, and that in view of the present and prospective changes in fundamentals, *some further orderly appreciation of the main non-dollar currencies against the dollar is desirable. They stand ready to cooperate more closely to encourage this when to do so would be helpful.*[52] (emphasis added).

Neither monetary policy (i.e. agreement on money supply and interest rates) nor fiscal policy (i.e. agreement on budgetary balances) were discussed at the Plaza. Nevertheless, the Plaza Accord, focusing on exchange rate policy, was the highwater mark in policy coordination among the G–5. Though the word 'intervention' did not appear in the communiqué, it was intervention in the foreign exchange markets that the five countries agreed to coordinate, and in considerable detail. The G–5 agreed about the time period for the coordinated interaction—about six weeks, about the total amount of resources to be committed—$18 billion, about the maximum daily operations in each participant market—$300–400 million, and

---

[49] It is worth pointing out that in the period 1979–84 the United States was pursuing a high-interest policy, so that US securities, particularly government securities, were very attractive to foreign investors for combining high yield with almost complete liquidity.

[50] One Congressman said later that 'Smoot-Hawley [the highly protectionist Tariff Act of 1930 that led to depression in the United States and abroad] would have been passed overwhelmingly in the fall of 1985', quoted in Funabashi, *Managing the Dollar: From the Plaza to the Louvre*, 4 (1988).

[51] And also without the presence of the IMF Managing Director or a representative of the EEC Commission or Council.

[52] Announcement of the Ministers of Finance and Central Bank Governors of France, Germany, Japan, the United Kingdom, and the United States, New York, 22 Sept. 1985, ¶18, 14 IMF Survey, 295 at 297 (7 Oct. 1985).

about the currencies that each participant would use—basically the dollar, the mark, and the yen.[53]

In the short run, coordinated intervention was a success. By the end of the first week after the Plaza Accord, the G–5 countries had sold 2.7 billion dollars; the yen had appreciated by 11.8 percent against the dollar, and the mark and the French franc just under 8 percent. At the end of the six weeks programmed for the operation, some 10.2 billion dollars had been sold. Overall, the dollar fell by about 8 percent in the two months following the Plaza meeting, for a total of 17 percent from its peak in February 1985, and the yen appreciated 24 percent from February 1985, of which 13.5 percent occurred in the period October–November 1985.[54] How much of the decline was directly due to the coordinated intervention in the foreign exchange markets, and how much was continuation of a trend already underway, is impossible to tell. Certainly the markets were impressed by the clear change in the policy of the United States, and by the confirmation of that change in the mutual commitments at the Plaza.

Meetings of the G–5 Finance Ministers and Central Bank Governors— ad hoc and in connection with other conferences—continued in the next 18 months, but while there was much talk of coordination of economic policies—interest rates, budget deficits, stimulus packages, tax reforms, even 'rules' or automaticity for governmental action, the most that came out was common surveillance, i.e. an exchange of information among the G–5 countries. At the Tokyo summit in May 1986, the Heads of State or Government formally agreed to create 'a new Group of Seven Finance Ministers',[55] dedicated, it was said, to coordination looking beyond exchange rates. Apart from bringing Italy and Canada into the discussions, the Tokyo Declaration had the effect of transforming the process from the confidential and informal meetings among men who knew each other very well into a more political negotiation, requiring the participants, particularly Japanese participants, to account for their statements and undertakings made to their peers from other states. The process legitimized proposals by the participating states with respect to other states' economic policies. Typically, the United States urged that Japan and Germany reduce taxes and interest rates in order to stimulate domestic demand; France sought to set limits on exchange rate movement; and Germany and Japan requested the United States to reduce its budget deficits as a step to

---

[53] Pounds and French francs could be used in certain circumstances; the United States made clear that it was not prepared to commit its resources to the defense of the European Monetary System (Ch. 20, Sect. 20.1 infra), by purchasing the weaker currencies of the EMS, such as the Italian lira. For these and other details, see Funabashi, *Managing the Dollar*, n. 50 supra, pp. 18–32.

[54] 14 *IMF Survey*, 374 (9 Dec. 1985).

[55] Tokyo Economic Declaration, 6 May 1986, 15 *IMF Survey*, 145 (19 May 1986).

reducing the trade deficit.[56] But while it was now accepted that giving such advice—whether in private or in public—was not an unfriendly act or interference in other countries' internal affairs, it was not clear that the finance ministers had the authority to act on the advice, nor that they agreed with each others' analyses.[57]

In February 1987, the G–7 Finance Ministers (minus Italy),[58] meeting in the offices of the French Ministry of Finance in the Palais du Louvre (across the courtyard from the museum), made a second major effort at exchange rate management, this time not to realign but rather to stabilize the relation between the dollar and the other principal currencies:

> The Ministers and Governors agreed that the substantial exchange rate changes since the Plaza Agreement will increasingly contribute to reducing external imbalances and have now brought their currencies within ranges broadly consistent with underlying economic fundamentals, given the policy commitments summarized in this statement. Further substantial exchange rate shifts among their currencies could damage growth and adjustment prospects in their countries. In current circumstances, therefore, they agreed to cooperate closely to foster stability of exchange rates around current levels.[59]

Each participating country's commitment to take certain policy steps was set out in the communiqué, including stimulation of domestic demand by Japan, reduction by the United States of its budget deficit to 2.3 percent of GNP in fiscal year 1988 from the 1987 estimate of 3.9 percent; 'prudent monetary policy' by the government of the United Kingdom and tax reduction and reform looking to 'sustained economic growth' by the Federal Republic of Germany. These statements were labeled 'undertakings', and a

---

[56] Whether reducing the US budget deficit would reduce the trade deficit or halt the depreciation of the dollar is not self-evident. The standard Keynesian analysis was that a reduced deficit would release more US savings for other needs, interest rates would fall, less capital would be attracted from abroad, and the United States would export more and import less. Paul Volcker reports that he once put the question to a group of highly respected economists: half said that a reduced US budgetary deficit would cause the dollar to rise, and half said it would cause the dollar to fall; Paul Volcker and Toyoo Gyohten, *Changing Fortunes*, pp. 182–3, 185 (1992).

[57] Moreover, there was often disagreement among the principal officials within a single country. For instance, in the period following the Plaza Accord, the US Treasury under James Baker seems to have sought a lower dollar in order to reduce the trade deficit and avoid protectionist trade legislation, while the Federal Reserve, under Paul Volcker, was concerned that a lower dollar would fuel renewed inflation. In Japan, Kiichi Miyazawa, as Finance Minister, was more willing to see the yen rise and to collaborate with the United States than either the Finance Ministry bureaucracy or the Bank of Japan. See generally, Volcker and Gyothen, *Changing Fortunes*, id., pp. 187–286; Funabashi, *Managing the Dollar*, (n. 50 supra) *passim*.

[58] The plan for the Louvre meeting was that the G–5 ministers would meet informally on Saturday, and would be joined by the ministers from Italy and Canada on Sunday. The Italian minister, realizing that the essential decisions would be made without him, returned home in protest on Sunday morning, and the communiqué could only be issued on behalf of six of the G–7 countries. In later meetings, to the regret of some of the veterans of the process, Italy was nearly always included, and G–7 and G–5 became locus of multilateral relationship among the finance ministers of the major industrial countries.

[59] Statement of Group of Seven, Paris, 22 Feb. 1987, 16 *IMF Survey*, 73 (9 Mar. 1987).

purely legal analysis might suggest that each such undertaking was made in consideration of all the others. In fact it was clear that the United States executive branch, even if fully united, could not commit the Congress on matters of spending and taxation. In theory, the ministers of countries operating under the Westminster model of parliamentary government, such as Japan, the United Kingdom, Germany, and Canada, could make firm commitments; in practice, the degree of authority of the finance ministers was limited, and in domestic debates promises made in the context of G–7 coordination have been one factor, but not the only one, in the formulation and implementation of policy. No government regarded the Louvre Agreement as a document to be submitted to its parliament for approval.[60]

The participants in the Louvre Agreement also agreed on a new mechanism of surveillance. They committed themselves to 'regularly examine' and exchange information on a stated list of economic indicators—growth, inflation, current account trade balances, budget performance, monetary conditions, and exchange rates.[61] The idea was that if a country's results were out of line with its medium-term projections, the G–7 would consult.

Potentially the most significant aspect of the Louvre Agreement was only hinted at in the phrase 'around current levels' in the last line of the excerpt from the communiqué quoted above, and never announced publicly. In fact the finance ministers and central bank governors agreed on a range or target zone in the exchange rate between the dollar and yen and the mark and the dollar, which would be defended by coordinated intervention in the market and possibly by other measures such as interest rate adjustments. The range was reminiscent of the early 1970s—2½ percent on either side of the rate prevailing as of the Louvre meeting—but the targets were never published, and in fact were soon overtaken by events, despite substantial intervention in the markets by the Federal Reserve, the Bank of Japan, and the Bundesbank. When the G–7 finance ministers and central bank governors met again in April 1987 in Washington, they 'noted the progress achieved in implementing the undertakings embodied in the Louvre Agreement', and 'reaffirmed the view that around current levels their currencies are within ranges broadly consistent with economic fundamentals.'[62] By then the yen had appreciated by 7 percent against the dollar over the rate prevailing at the time of the Louvre Agreement, breaking through not only the 2½ percent voluntary intervention range, but also a 5 percent obligatory consultation point.

The regular meetings among finance ministers of the G–7 have continued, and may fairly be said to have become a part of the intertwined monetary

---

[60] In the event, the US deficit for fiscal year 1988 was 3.2 percent of GNP, far above the Louvre understanding; in Germany, the GNP rose by only 1.6 percent. Only Japan accomplished a significant shift in the course of 1987 that could be linked to the Louvre Agreement. See Volcker and Gyothen, *Changing Fortunes*, n. 56 supra, pp. 282–3.

[61] Statement of Group of Seven, n. 59 supra, para. 9.

[62] Statement of the Group of Seven, 8 Apr. 1987, 16 *IMF Survey*, 137 (9 May 1987).

system. Indeed, the US Secretary of the Treasury, James Baker, who had been the driving force behind the Plaza accord and to a lesser extent behind the Louvre Agreement, said in 1988 that coordination of economic policies in the G–7 'is the new international monetary system'.[63] But concerted intervention in the foreign-exchange markets seems to have subsided after 1987. And multilateral surveillance as promised in the Louvre Agreement has not, on the whole meant coordinated action. In particular situations, however, such as the massive fall in share prices on the New York Stock Exchange on Black Monday, October 19, 1987, and the invasion of Kuwait by Iraq in August 1990, coordinated intervention by the G–7 appears to have prevented excessive swings in the exchange markets.[64]

(c) The Group of Seven in Other Contexts

Viewed as a substitute for the discipline of Bretton Woods concerning exchange arrangements, it is evident that the G–5/ G–7 mechanism was at best partially successful, essentially for the same reason that the Bretton Woods system broke down—movement in the fundamentals inconsistent with fixed bands, reference ranges and other devices to improve exchange rate stability on an unpredictable world in which the principal actors often had incompatible priorities. In terms of multilateral surveillance, the G–7 appears to have functioned somewhat better, in partial collaboration with the IMF. The existence of the Group of Seven, however, and in particular the annual summit meetings, have become the focus of collaboration and (often) commitment by the principal industrial nations in a variety of areas. G–7 ministers of trade, the environment and energy, as well as finance, have met regularly to attempt agreement among themselves and where possible to formulate joint or coordinated positions to be taken in larger conferences. In some instances, these efforts failed. For example, every G–7 summit conference from the mid-1980s through 1993 promised major progress or renewed dedication to the success of the Uruguay Round of GATT negotiations, without actual breakthrough.[65] In other instances, the G–7 forum has

---

[63] 'Economic Policy Coordination and International Monetary Reform', Address by Secretary of the Treasury James A. Baker, III, Paris, 20 May 1988, repr. in *1988 American Foreign Policy: Current Documents*, 19. For an interesting article by the former Chairman of the OECD Working Party Three deploring the development of the G–7 outside the treaty-based framework of the post-war economic arrangements, see Emile van Lennep, 'Institutional Aspects of International Economic Policy Cooperation and Coordination', in H. J. Blommestein (ed.), *The Reality of International Economic Policy Coordination*, n. 41 supra (1991).

[64] Toyoo Gyohten writes that after Black Monday the G–7 Finance Ministers dared not call a meeting for fear that if it failed to produce anything tangible, the market might collapse again. They did issue a 'Christmas Communiqué', 'reaffirm[ing]their commitment that the basic objectives and economic policies agreed in the Louvre Accord remain valid and provide for a positive development of the world economy': Statement of the Group of Seven, 22 Dec. 1987, 17 *IMF Survey*, 8 (11 Jan. 1988).

[65] See e.g. Ch. 4, Sect. 4.4(b), describing the 1990 Houston Summit, in particular the acrimony over agriculture.

enabled coordinated or parallel initiatives by the major industrial states. Illustrations of such joint efforts are described in Chapter 18, concerned with the debt of the developing countries and the efforts to integrate the countries of the former Soviet Union into the international economic community.

If the statement of the American Secretary of the Treasury quoted above was something of an exaggeration,[66] it was nevertheless true that the G–7, or the triad composed of the European Community, the United States, and Japan, had to a considerable extent replaced the United States as the anchor of the international monetary system, and to some extent had replaced the IMF as the principal forum for discussion of international monetary affairs.

[66] See text at n. 63 supra.

20

The European Monetary System and the Rise of the Euro

20.1   THE EUROPEAN MONETARY SYSTEM (1972–92)

(a)   The Origin of the EMS

Throughout the 1970s, the ups and downs of the US dollar described in the preceding chapter[1] were in significant part reflected in downs and ups of the West German mark, much more than in the other European currencies. Thus the exchange rates among the currencies of the member states of the European Common Market underwent frequent changes, often quite unrelated to any developments within the European Community. Changes in the relative value

[1] See Ch. 19, Sect. 19.5(b).

of the currencies made agreement on such inherently controversial matters as agricultural support payments and contributions to community projects even more difficult to achieve, and subject to frequent need for realignment and recalculation. Moreover, intra-Community trade was often distorted, as currency realignments took place much faster than internal price adjustments. The drafters of the Treaty of Rome had to some extent foreseen this problem,[2] but so long as the member states' currencies were linked through the par value system of the IMF, the problem was only rarely a serious one. Once the par value system collapsed in the early 1970s,[3] the problem became a serious one for the builders of the Community.

Efforts to link the European currencies were initiated as early as April 1972 in the so-called 'Snake', an arrangement under which each participating member's currency was assigned a bilateral central rate with each other participating member's currency, and the linked currencies were supposed to move together against the dollar and other non-participating currencies.[4] But the British pound left the Snake within a few weeks, and the French franc joined and dropped out twice. By year-end 1978, only the German mark, the Dutch guilder, the Danish krone, and the Belgian franc were still participating.[5] When France left the Snake for the first time in 1974, Valéry Giscard d'Estaing, then still the French Finance Minister, described the Snake as 'un animal de la préhistoire monétaire européenne.'[6]

In October 1977, Roy Jenkins, the former British Chancellor of the Exchequer who was in his first year as President of the European Commission, made a major speech in Florence renewing the idea of a European Monetary Union. The two former finance ministers now serving as chiefs of state or government, President Giscard d'Estaing of France and Chancellor Helmut Schmidt of the German Federal Republic, picked up the idea and formally launched the idea at the Copenhagen European summit in April 1978. In July 1978 the Council of Ministers meeting in Bremen adopted the basic principles of a European Monetary System:

[2] Treaty of Rome Arts. 104–9. Article 107 provided, in paragraph 1, that 'Each Member State shall treat its policy with regard to rates of exchange as a matter of common concern.' Paragraph 2 provided for consultation and if necessary counter-measures, if a Member State made an alteration in its rate of exchange inconsistent with the objectives of balance of payments equilibrium, a high level of employment, and a stable level of prices. These provisions were replaced by the Maastricht Treaty discussed hereafter.

[3] See Ch. 16, Sect. 16.9(b).

[4] The term 'Snake' came from the fluctuating lines or 'wriggles' of the participating currencies within a 2¼ percent band against each other superimposed on one another on a graph recording their value over time against an outside currency such as the dollar. During the time of the Smithsonian Agreement (Ch. 16, Sect. 16.9(c)), when reference rates were themselves restricted to a band of plus or minus 2¼ percent on either side of a central rate, the Snake was said to be moving inside a tunnel 4½ percent wide.

[5] For a careful explanation of the Snake, including a chronology of entry, exit and changes in the exchange rates 1972–8, see Richard W. Edwards, Jr., 'The European Exchange Arrangement Called the Snake', 10 *U. of Toledo L. Rev.*, p. 47 (1978).

[6] Quoted in Peter Ludlow, *The Making of the European Monetary System*, 3 (1982).

- exchange rate management would be at least as strict as the Snake;
- the obligation to intervene and adjust would be symmetrical, i.e. it would apply to both surplus and deficit countries;
- a reserve asset would be created for use in financing intervention and settlement of accounts; and
- member states would also be expected to coordinate their exchange policies vis-à-vis third countries.[7]

By December 1978 the Council of Ministers had adopted a resolution to create such a system,[8] and it entered into force on March 13, 1979. All nine of the member states of the Community—i.e. the original six plus Denmark, Ireland, and the United Kingdom—nominally joined the EMS, but for more than a decade the United Kingdom did not become a party to the Exchange Rate Mechanism that was at the heart of the system.

(b)   The Exchange Rate Mechanism in Operation (1979–92)[9]

In essence, the Exchange Rate Mechanism created by the EMS was designed to function like a mini-Bretton Woods par value system, but only among the participating countries.[10] In addition, by floating together against the dollar and the yen, the EMS could provide a counterweight against the movement of those two currencies, thereby, it was believed, also contributing to both exchange stability and growth.

Each participant in the Exchange Rate Mechanism was required to establish a central rate for its currency, denominated in terms of a European

---

[7] Annex to the Conclusions of the Presidency of the European Council, Bremen 6–7 July 1978, 7 *IMF Survey*, 221 (17 July 1978); 11 *EC Bull* No. 6 ¶1.5.1, pt. IV (1978); *Compendium on Community Monetary Texts*, 43 (EC 1989 edn.).

[8] Resolution of the European Council on the Establishment of the European Monetary System (EMS) and Related Matters, 5 Dec. 1978, *1978 Bull. European Communities* No. 12, 10; *Compendium of Community Monetary Texts*, 45 (EC 1989 edn.). An implementing agreement between the Central Banks of the Member States was adopted on March 13, 1979, *Compendium of Community Monetary Texts* (as amended), 50. A political analysis of the motivation of Messrs. Jenkins, Schmidt, Giscard d'Estaing and also James Callaghan, the British Prime Minister, is offered in Ludlow, *The Making of the European Monetary System*, n. 6 supra. See also, e.g. Daniel Gros and Niels Thygesen, *European Monetary Integration*, ch. 2, 'The Making of the European Monetary System' (1992).

[9] Many books and articles were written about the EMS, most concentrating on its political aspect in the context of European integration, or its effects on the economics of the member and non-member states. Perhaps the best technical explanation was written by the chairman of the European Monetary Committee and a principal architect of the 'Belgian Compromise', which combined an approach based on a parity grid with an approach based on central rates. See Jacques van Ypersele, *The European Monetary System* (EC 1985).

[10] Note that such a system is expressly permitted, when notified, by Article IV(2)(b)(ii) of the Amended Articles of Agreement of the IMF: '. . . cooperative arrangements by which members maintain the value of their currencies in relation to the value of the currency or currencies of other members.' See Ch. 17, Sect. 17.2. The word 'system' was apparently chosen deliberately to provide a contrast with the 'non-system' under the Amended Articles of the Fund. See Jean-Jacques Rey, 'The European Monetary System', 17 *Common Market. L. Rev.* 7 (1980).

Currency Unit (the ECU).[11] In collaboration with the other participating states, each participant was obligated to maintain that rate within a prescribed margin. When a currency reached the ceiling or the floor of the prescribed margin, the issuing country (or its central bank) was required to intervene. If a participating state needed funds to finance intervention, these would be available, on a short-term basis, from a central fund, the European Monetary Cooperation Fund (EMCF), to which all member states had contributed. One innovation, suggested in connection with the reform proposals of the Committee of Twenty in the early 1970s but never adopted,[12] was a 'divergence indicator' or 'threshold of divergence': when a currency reached 75 percent of its maximum permitted spread relative to the Community average represented by the ECU, there would be a presumption that the concerned authorities would correct the situation, not necessarily by intervention in the exchange market but also by other measures taken alone or in concert. If such measures were not taken, the country in question would be required to give reasons for its non-action to the appropriate Community organs.

The ECU, in some ways the forerunner of the euro created twenty years later, was both a unit of account, based like the SDR on a basket of currencies assigned different weights according to their economic importance, and an asset, which could be used for intervention and settlement among central banks of the Community. All the currencies of the EC member states were used in the valuation of the ECU, even if the countries that issued them did not participate in the Exchange Rate Mechanism. In particular, the pound sterling was a significant component of the basket, although, as mentioned above, the United Kingdom did not participate in the Exchange Rate Mechanism for over a decade. At the start of operations of the EMS, the mark weighed 32.98 percent in the basket, the French franc 19.83 percent, and the pound sterling 13.34 percent.[13] For most currencies, the maximum spread was 2¼ percent. For the Italian lira, which had not participated in the Snake, the maximum spread would be 6 percent.

The architects of the EMS aimed at 'stable but adjustable' exchange rates—the same phrase used by the Committee of Twenty during the effort to reform the international monetary system in the 1970s. The Snake had

[11] Not wholly by coincidence, the acronym ECU recalled an ancient French gold or silver coin, first issued in the reign of St. Louis (Louis IX) in the 13th century.

[12] See Ch. 17, Sect. 17.1(a).

[13] The weights were based on the GNP of the issuing country, its share in intra-Community trade, and its share in the EEC's short-term credit arrangements. The other initial weights were as follows:

Netherlands guilder	10.51 percent
Belgian franc	9.63 percent
Italian lira	9.5 percent
Danish krone	3.06 percent
Irish punt	1.15 percent

When the Spanish peseta and the Portuguese excudo were added to the calculation, the percentages were adjusted, but the German mark remained above 30 percent.

experienced nine realignments in six years (not counting withdrawals and re-entries), essentially carried out unilaterally. Under the resolution creating the EMS, adjustments of central rates were to be subject to 'mutual agreement by a common procedure which will confine all countries participating in the exchange rate mechanism and the [European] Commission.'[14]

It was understood from the outset that the European Monetary System depended not merely on the mechanism described in the preceding paragraphs but on the economic performance of the participating states. If growth rates, inflation rates, interest rates, and the balance of payments of the participating states moved roughly in parallel, the EMS could smooth over temporary fluctuations and promote economic activity. If economic performance diverged too much, however, the narrow bands and relative rigidity of the system could prove untenable for the weaker currencies, with results similar to the events of August 1971 that had brought down the Bretton Woods system. Put another way, the European Monetary System had two objectives: greater stability in exchange rates among the EMS currencies, and greater convergence among the economies of the participating countries.

Of course the EMS was not a closed system in the sense that it could avoid outside shocks. In its first decade, the EMS was confronted in late 1979–80 by the second oil shock, in 1982–5 by the sharp rise in the value of the US dollar, in 1986–9 by the fall of the dollar and the continuing rise of the yen, in October 1987 by the sharp drop in the value of shares in the US stock market and then in other markets, and in 1990–2 by the collapse of communism and in particular by the integration of East Germany into the Federal Republic.[15]

In the first four years of the EMS (1979–83), there were seven realignments of the central rates in the system, all essentially devaluations against the German mark.[16] All of the realignments were made after consultations among the EMS finance ministers on request of a country seeking a devaluation; in a number of instances the negotiations were difficult, and the requests were not always granted in full. From 1982 on, the state requesting a devaluation or realignment was expected to support its plea with a program of economic measures, such as a proposed rise in interest rates or a tightening of domestic credit.[17]

---

[14] Resolution of 5 Dec. 1978, Pt. A, Art. 3.2.

[15] Also, the EMS was constructed largely under the joint leadership of President Giscard d'Estaing of France and Chancellor Helmut Schmidt of the German Federal Republic. Their replacement, respectively, by François Mitterand (1981) and Helmut Kohl (1982) made coordination of the policies of the two largest members of the EMS substantially more difficult, as is reflected in the several realignments described hereafter.

[16] The three general realignments of October 5, 1981, June 14, 1982, and March 21, 1983 were nominally a combination of increase in the mark (revaluation) and decrease in the other currencies (devaluation). The Dutch guilder generally preserved its relation to the mark.

[17] For a description of the realignment and of the negotiating positions of the parties, see Gros and Thygesen, *European Monetary Integration* (n. 8 supra), pp. 67–97 (1992). For a somewhat different description of the same events for the first five years of the EMS, see van Ypersele, *The European Monetary System* (n. 9 supra), pp. 71–92.

From March 1983 to January 1990 there were two general realignments and three involving a single currency only, in one instance the Irish punt, in the other two the Italian lira. A major realignment between the mark and the French franc took place in April 1986, just after parliamentary elections in France had brought about for the first time 'cohabitation' between a Socialist President and a Center-Right Premier with a majority in parliament. The Louvre Agreement among the Group of Seven countries in February 1987[18] seems to have calmed movement in and out of the mark and therefore the demand for realignment in the EMS as well.

By the end of the decade, the EMS appeared to be working smoothly. Spain, which had become a member of the European Community in 1986, joined the EMS in June 1989; the United Kingdom, which had remained outside the Exchange Rate Mechanism for over a decade, joined in October 1990, shortly before Margaret Thatcher's ouster as party leader and Prime Minister, in significant part over her opposition to increased European integration.[19] The pound and the peseta each entered the ERM with a 6 percent margin, both at the time with an inflation rate well in excess of the EMS average. Until late summer 1992, however, both the pound and the peseta operated within their respective ranges—with each other and with the other seven currencies and the ECU.

In two respects the European Monetary System as it developed was different from the original plan. *First*, the Bremen Annex of July 1978 had promised that within two years of the start of the EMS, the existing arrangements and institutions would be consolidated in a European Monetary Fund.[20] That step was never taken, essentially because of disagreement about whether the EMF would function like a central bank, like a political regulatory agency, or—as the Bundesbank feared—as both.[21] *Second*, the founders of the EMS expected that the ECU would be at the center of the system.[22] The markets, however, never accepted the ECU as the anchor of the system. From the outset, the anchor of the system was the German mark. This meant that the burden of adjustment, as well of realignment, tended to fall on the weaker currencies, and that the goal of symmetrical obligation on surplus as well as deficit countries could not be achieved.[23] Critics in Europe

---

[18] See Ch. 19, Sect. 19.5(b).

[19] In her memoirs, Mrs. Thatcher writes that she was opposed to Britain's entry into the ERM, but '[t]here are limits to the ability of even the most determined democratic leader to stand out against what the Cabinet, the Parliamentary Party, the industrial lobby and the press demand', Margaret Thatcher, *The Downing Street Years*, 722 (1993).

[20] Annex to the Conclusions of the Presidency of the European Council, (n. 7 supra), para. 4. See also the Resolution of the European Council on the Establishment of the European Monetary System of 5 Dec. 1978 (the Brussels Resolution), *1978 Bull. European Communities* No. 12, para. 1.4.

[21] See Gros and Thygesen, *European Monetary Integrations* (n. 8 supra), pp. 54–6, 71.

[22] See Bremen Annex, para. 1; Brussels Resolution, para. 2.1.

[23] Recall the similar issue raised by the United States in the early 1970s in connection with the work of the Committee of Twenty, and also not achieved. See Ch. 17, Sect. 17.1.

argued that focus on the mark tended to emphasize stability at the expense of growth. On the other hand, as the German defenders of the system pointed out, use of the mark as the key currency brought discipline to all the participants, and reduced the danger of the scourge of inflation.[24]

In any event, the evolution of the European Monetary System seemed to be successful, and to pave the way for the next steps. The member states of the Community—or at least their governments—were ready to build on the EMS and to support the creation of an Economic and Monetary Union. In the Treaty of Maastricht, the twelve member states of the European Community committed themselves to form an Economic and Monetary Union (EMU) built around a common currency and a single European Central Bank.[25]

Before the European Economic and Monetary Union could be translated from a document to a working institution, however, the European Monetary System went through a convulsion that delayed ratification of the Maastricht Treaty and almost led to a change of direction.

20.2   COLLAPSE OF THE EMS: TWO CRISES

(a)   September 1992: The Pound and the Lira

The Maastricht Treaty calling for full monetary union—one currency, one central bank—in 1997 if possible, and in any event not later than 1999, was formally signed in February 1992, subject to ratification by all twelve member states of the European Community. By summer 1992, every state in the Community was in recession. Germany, now united politically but with the task of integrating the former German Democratic Republic into its economy proving much more difficult than expected, was experiencing inflation near an annual rate of 5 percent and unemployment over 5 percent—both high by German standards. In every state in the Community, opposition to Maastricht was stronger than anticipated; in Denmark, the treaty had narrowly lost in a referendum, but might be resubmitted with various 'opt-out' provisions. In the United Kingdom, the vote on the treaty kept being postponed; in France, a referendum on the treaty was set for September 20, with the polls showing an even split among the voters, and growing disenchantment with President Mitterand, a strong supporter of Maastricht.

On August 26, as the pound was falling toward its ERM floor, the Bank of England began to purchase pounds for marks. On Friday, August 28, the Community Finance Ministers issued a statement asserting that 'a change in

---

[24] See e.g. the interesting discussion by the President of the Bundesbank, Helmut Schlesinger, 'The Lessons of the EMS for International Policy Coordination', in H. J. Blommestein (ed.), *The Reality of International Economic Policy Coordination*, 177 (1991).
[25] Treaty on European Union signed at Maastricht, The Netherlands, 7 Feb. 1992, Art. A.

the present structure of central rates would not be the appropriate response to the current tensions in the EMS.' On the following Monday, activity in the foreign exchange markets turned into turmoil: despite obligatory intervention, the Italian lira closed at its ERM floor. On September 3, the United Kingdom announced that it had borrowed the equivalent of ECU 10 billion (£7.25 billion) to support the pound.

On September 5, the finance and economic ministers of the EEC (ECOFIN) met in Bath, England, but no announcement emerged concerning the German interest rates; if that rate were not lowered, it seemed clear, the United Kingdom could not lower its base rate and maintain the value of the pound in the ERM, which fell to within one pfennig of its ERM floor against the mark. On September 10, Prime Minister Major announced that there was to be no devaluation and no realignment. The attack on the pound, however, continued. On the morning of September 16, 1992, 'Black Wednesday', the British government authorized the Bank of England to raise its base interest rate from 10 to 12 percent; three hours later the rate was raised to 15 percent; at 7.30 p.m. the Chancellor of the Exchequer announced that 'in current circumstances' the UK was suspending its membership in the ERM immediately.[26]

Italy also announced that it would 'abstain temporarily from intervention', having, as was later made public, spent some $24 billion in defense of the lira in September alone. Ireland and Spain devalued their currencies, but remained in the system, as did Portugal, which had joined the ERM only a few months earlier.

On September 20, the French referendum resulted in a narrow victory for the Maastricht Treaty, and the French and German authorities made clear that they were determined to defend the parity between the French franc and the mark, and to preserve the ERM. Between them, the Bundesbank and the Banque de France spent about $32 billion on defense of the franc in the seven days up to September 23. For the time being the defense of the French franc held. The Exchange Rate Mechanism survived, minus Britain and Italy. The Bank for International Settlements, in its Annual Report, wrote:

It is probably no exaggeration to say that the period from late 1991 to early 1993 witnessed the most severe and widespread foreign exchange market crisis since the breakdown of the Bretton Woods system twenty years ago.[27]

(b) July–August 1993: The French Franc

In midsummer 1993, turmoil again broke out in the ERM. In the third week in July, the central banks of Belgium, France, Denmark, and Portugal had

---

[26] On the following day the base interest rate was reduced back to 10 percent, and by mid-November it had fallen to 7 percent. The pound settled at about DM2.40, down about 15 percent from its ERM floor of DM2.778 and about 20 percent lower than when it entered the ERM two years earlier.

[27] Bank for International Settlements, *63rd Annual Report* (Apr. 1992–Mar. 1993), 200.

all been forced to raise their interest rates in order to keep their currencies within the ERM band, although their domestic situation would have indicated a different policy. The Banque de France raised its short-term interest rate to 10 percent, notwithstanding unemployment of 11.6 percent and negative growth in GDP. On Thursday, July 29 (at the last session before its summer recess), the Council of the Bundesbank reduced its Lombard [money market] rate by a half a point, but left the more significant discount rate unchanged. On the following day, the French franc sank to its floor relative to the mark, despite massive intervention by the central banks of both countries. The Bundesbank alone, it was reported, spent more than $35 billion in purchases of French francs, as well as Belgian francs, pesetas, escudos, and krone.

Over the weekend of July 31–August 1, the finance ministers and central bank governors of the EMS met in emergency session in Brussels. One idea apparently discussed was to permit the mark (along with the Dutch guilder) to leave the ERM temporarily, to find its proper level by floating against the remaining currencies linked in the ERM. That idea was rejected, however. After a meeting that lasted until 2 a.m. of Monday, August 2, the ministers and governors announced that there would be no official intervention so long as the currencies linked in the ERM moved within a band of 15 percent.[28]

Nominally, the Exchange Rate Mechanism of the European Monetary System remained in existence. Practically, a band of 15 percent was very much like a floating system—very far from the system created in 1979, and hardly on the path to a single currency envisaged by the Maastricht Treaty. The founding fathers of the EMS, Helmut Schmidt and Valéry Giscard d'Estaing, both now out of office, issued a joint statement saying the solution arrived at by their successors was tantamount to suspending the EMS:

We ask that this suspension be provisional and that normal functioning of the EMS resume as rapidly as possible.[29]

(c)　Some Lessons from the Experience of the EMS (1979–93)

The European Monetary System was well conceived from a technical and legal point of view. The combination (compromise) of parity grid and divergency indicators imposed a kind of discipline on the member states, and a measure of how well coordination was progressing. But like Bretton Woods on a larger scale, the EMS had two built-in limitations.

First, the system depended on the essential stability of the currency of the anchor state—the United States dollar under Bretton Woods, the German

---

[28] The mark and the guilder, which had moved in parallel throughout the period of the EMS, retained the 2.25 percent margin inter se.

[29] Quoted in the *Financial Times*, 3 Aug. 1993, p. 1.

mark under the EMS. When the German Bundesbank felt compelled to maintain relatively high interest rates in order to finance the rehabilitation of its new Eastern Provinces without raising taxes and in order to restrain inflation that might have followed the increase in the supply of marks, the other states of the EMS were torn between raising their own interest rates even higher or following their domestic priorities. The effort both to follow the leader and to follow their domestic priorities could not succeed, and the foreign exchange markets dramatically demonstrated the inconsistency.

Second, the EMS was able, by a combination of realignments and fiscal discipline, to guide its member states into limited adjustments for some dozen years. But fundamental adjustment, as well as fundamental coordination of policies and priorities, were beyond the scope, and beyond the powers of the European Monetary System as it existed before the Maastricht Treaty.

While the ratification and implementation of the Maastricht Treaty took place with the events of 1992–3 fresh in mind, negotiation and drafting of the Treaty were completed before the demise of the EMS. Thus while the twenty years' experience with the Snake and the ERM clearly influenced the drafters of Maastricht, one could not say that the last years of the ERM did so. Of course the challenge of imposing uniformity of monetary policy on a dozen states with different starting points and different priorities remained.

20.3   ECONOMIC AND MONETARY UNION: THE TREATY OF MAASTRICHT[30]

(a)   The Vision of Economic Union

The model for the EMU, as for so many other aspects of European integration, was the United States. Just as only one currency, one interest rate (with minor variation), and one monetary policy prevails in California as in Maine, in Texas as in New York or Florida, the proponents of EMU looked to the day when only one currency, one monetary policy, one interest rate would prevail in all member states of the European Union. Monetary policy—that is interest rates and the supply of money—were to be set by a single European Central Bank (ECB), presiding over a European System of Central Banks (ESCB), modeled on the US Federal Reserve System, but wholly independent of national governments as well as of the institutions

---

[30] When the Treaty of Maastricht was signed and submitted for ratification by the Member States of the European Community (Union), some articles were given letters—A, B, C, etc.; others were given numbers followed by letters, e.g. 104, 104a, 104b, etc. In the Amsterdam Treaty of 1997, it was decided to renumber the entire Treaty of Rome, with its numerous amendments. In the citations to the Maastricht Treaty in this chapter, the original number is given first, and the revised number according to the Amsterdam Treaty is given in brackets.

of the EU, including the Commission, the Council of Ministers, and the European Parliament.[31]

Clearly EMU, if successful, would bring significant economic effects—savings on transaction costs in transborder trade and investment within the Community; exchange stability in place of the volatility that had characterized the preceding twenty years of the European Monetary System; possibly creation of a reserve currency to rival the US dollar. At least equally important, a successful EMU would have significant political meaning—a major further step in the integration of Western Europe, even as expanding membership might lead to a loosening of the Community bonds. On the down side, there was a risk that not all member states would go along, or would go along only partially, perhaps with the result that the Community would have two tiers, an inner fully integrated core, composed of most (if not all) of the original Six and anchored by the Franco-German axis, and an outer rim, within the customs union and the expanding field of Community legislation and regulation, but not joined by a common currency, interest rate, and monetary policy. The proponents of EMU were prepared to accept that risk—notably Jacques Delors, the long-time President of the European Commission whose Report in April 1989[32] set the movement to EMU into high gear, and Chancellor Helmut Kohl, who had presided over the unification of Germany and wanted to preside over the unification of Europe.

(b)   The Treaty of Maastricht

In December 1991, in Maastricht, The Netherlands, the members of the European Community, having previously committed themselves to achieving a barrier-free area for the movement of persons and goods by the end of 1992, agreed on a major amendment of the Treaty of Rome, covering common citizenship, implementation of a common defense and security policy, and economic and monetary union. On February 7, 1992, the foreign ministers of all twelve Member States signed the Treaty of Maastricht, subject to ratification by each Member State, in some cases through parliamentary action, in others by a popular referendum. To symbolize their renewed commitment, the Member States changed their collective name from European Community (or Communities) to the European Union.

Some critics, both in Europe and outside, regarded the EMU as too ambitious and insufficiently realistic.

---

[31] The role of the ECB compared with the role of the Council in setting exchange rates vis-à-vis non-member currencies such as the dollar and the yen was not clearly spelled out. For exploration of this question, see Sect. 20.5(c) infra.

[32] EC Committee for the Study of Economic and Monetary Union, *Report on Economic and Monetary Union in Europe*, published in April 1989 and accepted by the European Council in June 1989 as a basis for an Intergovernmental Conference. A summary appears in *EC Bull.* 4–1989, at p. 8

Consider, for instance two Member States of the European Union, Patria and Xandia, that have a large trading relationship with each other. A shift in the demand for Patria's goods in favour of those of Xandia creates unemployment in Patria, inflationary pressures in Xandia. If the European Central Bank adopts an expansionary monetary policy, unemployment in Patria might be relieved, but inflation in Xandia would be aggravated. Absent EMU, a possible outcome might be an adjustment in the exchange rate between Patrian pesos and Xandian crowns. This remedy is excluded by the single currency system of the EMU.

Proponents of EMU concede this criticism, but point out that the phenomenon of regional discrepancies in not unknown even in the United States.[33] Moreover, the plan was to move to convergence of some of the principal economic determinants, particularly government deficits and government cumulative debt. While fiscal policy would not be completely homogenized, with a single currency, a single central bank, and a single monetary policy, the opportunity for governments of member states to adopt widely different economic strategies would be gradually diminished. Clearly the goal could not be achieved all at once, and it would make no sense to provide for a 'one size fits all' monetary policy if the underlying economic conditions in the member states diverged significantly. If Xandia's chief concern was inflation, while Patria's concern was unemployment or stagnant growth, a single monetary policy set by a single European Central Bank could well be disastrous.

The drafters of the Maastricht Treaty addressed this problem by providing for the EMU to be created in several stages. In the first stage, beginning even before completion of the ratification process, each member state was to adopt internal legislation necessary to implement the subsequent stages, including, notably, removing the national central bank from the obligation to report to, or take instructions from the national government.[34] In the second stage, beginning on January 1, 1994, member states were obligated to regard their economic policies 'as a matter of common concern' to be coordinated within the European Council, with a view to achievement of the objectives of the Community, and subject to surveillance by the European Commission.[35] Surveillance was to be focused on two basic macroeconomic criteria:

[33] See e.g. Robert Mundell, 'The Case for the Euro', *Wall St. Journal*, 24 Mar. 1998, p. A22. Mundell, the 1999 Nobel laureate in economics, cited the situation in the middle 1980s when rising oil prices led to a boom in the oil-producing states of the South-western United States, while causing real hardship in the oil-importing states of New England. 'Doubtless', Mundell wrote, 'many Harvard or MIT Ph.D's wished at the time that New England had a separate currency so they could devalue it. But all that New England would have got out of it would have been a higher price level and higher interest rates associated with expectations of future devaluations. No new resources are brought to a region by devaluation.'

[34] Maastricht Treaty Art. 108[109].   [35] Maastricht Treaty Art. 103[99].

(a) the ratio of the government deficit to gross domestic product (i.e. an annual measure of performance); and

(b) the ratio of government debt to gross domestic product (i.e. a cumulative measure whose trendline is linked to current economic performance).

In each case performance of the country in question was to be measured by comparison to reference values set out in a Protocol to the Treaty.[36] The Protocol set the values as 3 percent for ratio (a), and as 60 percent for ratio (b). The Treaty contains 'unless' clauses based on coming close to the reference values and a favourable trend, but if a member state is out of compliance with one or both of the stated criteria, the Commission is to prepare a report, which would be discussed first in the Monetary Committee of the EU, and subsequently in the Commission and Council.[37] Thus the criteria were not an automatic test, but a point of reference, which recognized, implicitly, that not all the member states began from the same base.[38]

Both criteria evidenced a commitment to stability rather than growth, that is to fiscal conservatism and defense against inflation. Only member states that demonstrated adherence to this commitment would be eligible to advance to the third stage. That stage was supposed to be reached by the end of 1997 if the Council (i.e. the Heads of State or Government) so decided not later than December 31, 1996, but in any event not later January 1, 1999.[39]

During the transition, the Commission, and the European Monetary Institute (EMI) created by the Treaty[40] were to report on each member state's achievement of 'a high degree of sustainable convergence', based on four convergence criteria set out in the Treaty and a Protocol:[41]

a high degree of *price stability*,—i.e. a rate of inflation that does not exceed by more than 1½ percentage points, the rate of inflation of the three best performing Member States;

the sustainability of the *government financial position*, as measured by the ratios of governmental deficit and debt described above;

the observance of the normal *fluctuation margins* of the European Monetary System, with no devaluation for at least two years;

an average *long-term interest* rate that does not exceed by more than two percentage points the interest rate of the three best-performing Member States.

[36] Maastricht Art. 104c[104](2).

[37] Recall the sanction of a Report in the Outline of Reform of the Articles of Agreement of the IMF proposed by the Committee of Twenty in the early 1970s, Ch. 17, Sect. 17.1(a).

[38] Note also that the binding character of Article 104c[104](1): 'Member States *shall avoid* excessive government deficits' was softened for the second stage by Article 109e[116](4): 'Member States *shall endeavour to avoid* excessive government deficits.'

[39] Maastricht Art. 109j[121](3) and (4).   [40] Maastricht Art. 109f[117].

[41] Maastricht Art. 109j[121](1) and Protocol on the Convergence Criteria Referred to in Art. 109j.

Though the criteria were fairly specific, the Treaty recognized that in the end the decision as to which states satisfy the conditions for proceeding to the stage of a single currency is a political one, to be taken by the Council on a proposal from the Commission upon the vote of a qualified majority.[42] Upon the effective date of Stage Three, i.e. on January 1, 1999,

(i)   the European Central Bank as well as the European System of Central Banks (ESCB) were to come into being, succeeding the European Monetary Institute, and presiding over a single monetary policy;

(ii) the euro (called 'ECU' in the Treaty) was to become the currency of the EMU, for a few years in parallel with national currencies of participating Member States, but after January 1, 2002 as the sole currency;

(iii) conversion rates between the currencies of participating Member States and the euro were to be locked in place irrevocably;

(iv) the criteria for avoiding excessive budget deficits were to become mandatory, including provisions for sanctions.[43]

By year-end 2001, each of the listed events had taken place, and the Euro was ready to become the currency of everyday trade and commerce, with new 'European' notes and coins circulating in all the participating states in replacement of national currencies.

Ratification of the Treaty proved more difficult than anticipated—for instance the referendum in France on Maastricht resulted in just 51.05 percent of the votes in favour of ratification, and in Denmark it took a second referendum to approve the Treaty, and then only on the condition that Denmark would not be required to join the Economic and Monetary Union. Eventually however, all the member states gave their approval, and the Treaty formally entered into effect on November 1, 1993. EC became EU, just in time for the final negotiations on the Uruguay Round.

(c)   From Maastricht to E-Day

The second stage in the move toward EMU began on January 1, 1994, as provided in Article 109e[116](1) of the Maastricht Treaty. One aspect of

---

[42] Maastricht Art. 109k[122](2). Following the entry of Austria, Finland, and Sweden into the EU in 1995, the weighted votes in the EU added up to 87, and a 'qualified majority' requires 62 votes. Denmark and the United Kingdom, which were permitted to opt out of EMU, do not vote on many of the decisions to be taken under the Maastricht Treaty but do participate in the basic decision under Article 109k[122](2). As of year-end 2001 these numbers were again subject to revision, pending further enlargement of the EU. Admission of new states into the EU does not automatically mean admission into the EMU.

[43] Maastricht Treaty Art. 109l[123](1)–(5); also, with respect to sanctions Maastricht Art. 104c[104](3)–(11) and Protocol on the Excessive Deficit Procedure. Note that Maastricht Art. 104c[104](13) provides that in voting to impose sanctions for violation of the deficit criteria, the Council is to act by a two-thirds majority, excluding the votes of the Member State concerned. For more on the possibility of sanctions, see Sect. 20.4 infra.

this transition was that all restraints on the movement of capital between member states and between member states and third countries were henceforth prohibited. A second important step was the founding of the European Monetary Institute (EMI), with the task of preparing the transition to the European Central Bank and the European System of Central Banks at the beginning of Stage Three.[44]

Third, member states became committed to *endeavour* to avoid excessive government deficits, and to start the process leading to independence of the respective central banks.[45] While these commitments were not yet binding, the Commission was to monitor the progress of member states;[46] it was understood that this progress would determine the transition by member states and the EU as a whole to the third stage.

In December 1995, the European Council meeting in Madrid, confirmed the timetable set out in the Maastricht Treaty, and after much speculation and debate in the press, settled on the name *euro* for the single currency of the EMU.[47] The President of the European Commission said 'We are now irreversibly on track towards the Union's single currency.' 'The Council', he said, has given 'a strong signal which should discard remaining doubts and hesitations.'[48]

When the European Council met in Dublin in December 1996 in accordance with Article 109j[121](3), it noted that a majority of Member States did not meet the convergence criteria set out in Article 109j(1) and the corresponding Protocol. This meant that the first, discretionary starting date for Stage Three would not be utilized, and that the alternative date of January 1, 1999 would become mandatory, as provided in Article 109j[121](4). The Council was to decide by July 1998 which member states fulfilled the necessary conditions for adoption of the single currency.

On March 25, 1998, the European Commission submitted its recommendation in accordance with Maastricht Article 109j[121], concluding that eleven states should adopt the single currency regime of Stage Three, i.e. all the states of the European Union except Greece and the three states that had chosen not to join—Denmark, Sweden, and the United Kingdom. The European Monetary Institute, also required by Maastricht to give its recommendation, concurred with the Commission, though with some concern over the two countries whose ratio of debt to GDP remained near 120 percent—Italy and Belgium.[49]

---

[44] Art. 109f[117].   [45] Art. 109e[116] (4) and (5).   [46] Art. 104c[104].

[47] Though *euro* had the advantage of neutrality unlike eurofranc or euromark, the press enjoyed pointing out that term would have a different pronunciation in each of the EU's languages.

[48] The Portuguese Prime Minister, paraphrasing Christ's reference to St Peter, said 'The Euro is the rock on which we will build a United Europe.' See *The Guardian* (London) 16 Dec. 1995, p. 12.

[49] As of March 1998, Italy's public debt stood at 121.6 percent of GDP, compared with 123.8 percent in 1996 and 124.9 percent in 1994. Its budget deficit, thanks to a special 'Euro tax', stood at 2.7 percent in 1997, compared to about 8 percent in 1995, and 9.5 percent in 1993. As the

In its communiqué, the Commission pointed out that the founding members of the EMU constituted a zone of nearly 300 million inhabitants accounting for 19.4 percent of world GDP and 18.6 percent of world trade, compared with 19.6 percent of world GDP and 16.5 percent of world trade for the United States and 7.7 percent of world GDP and 8.2 percent of world trade for Japan.[50]

On May 2, 1998, the Heads of State and Government met in Brussels to confirm the recommendations of the Commission and to formally enact the creation of Stage Three of the European Economic and Monetary Union.[51]

20.4 THE CONSTRAINTS OF THE EURO REGIME: THE STABILITY AND GROWTH PACT

Even as the member states of the European Community were preparing to enter the third state of the EMU and with it the single currency regime, the Council of the European Union reached agreement on the main elements of a Stability and Growth Pact—not a new treaty but a combination of Council Regulations and Resolutions, reflecting a compromise between Germany's emphasis on monetary discipline and the desire of France and other states for more freedom of maneuver if economic conditions so indicated.[52]

The Stability and Growth Pact did not change the requirements for participation in Stage Three of the EMU, but was intended to reinforce the prevention and deterrence aspects of the rules concerning governmental deficits in excess of the Maastricht criteria by making credible the provisions for sanctions in the Treaty.

Sanctions would not quite be automatic if a Member State exceeded the limit, but would require a two-thirds vote of the Council (Article 104c[104](13)), following an overall assessment after having heard from the Member State in question (Article 104c[104](6)). But Maastricht had provided an escape valve if the excessive government deficit is considered 'exceptional and temporary' (see Article 104c[104](2)(a), para. 2), and the

Commission reported in the report accompanying its recommendations, 'the Italian government recently renewed its commitment to maintain the primary surplus at an appropriately high level over the medium term.' Thus the Commission was able to justify its conclusion with respect to Italy that the debt/GDP ratio 'is sufficiently diminishing and approaching the reference value at a satisfactory pace'. (Maastricht Article 104c[104](2)(b)). Italy met the criteria on price stability (i.e. the rate of inflation) and on convergence regarding long-term interest rates.

A similar analysis was presented with respect to Belgium, leading to the conclusion that Belgium had maintained a steady decline in the debt ratio, from a high of 135.2 percent in 1993 to 122.2 percent in 1997, and that a further decline was to be expected.

[50] European Commission Press Release IP/98/273, 25 Mar. 1998.

[51] See Council Decision of 3 May, 1998 in accordance with Art. 109j[121](4) of the Treaty (98/317/EC), EU O.J. L 139/30 (11 May 1998).

[52] The Stability and Growth Pact was formally set out in Council Regulations No. 1466/97 and 1467/97, both reproduced in EU O.J. L209 (2 Aug. 1997), and Resolution of the European Council on the Stability and Growth Pact, 17 June 1997, EU O.J. C236/01 (2 Aug. 1997).

Stability and Growth Pact says that 'exceptional and temporary' 'as a rule' meant that there had been an annual fall of real GDP of at least 2 percent.[53] There might be circumstances when the Council would not impose sanctions for an excessive budget deficit although the fall in the Member State's GDP had been less than 2 percent,[54] but the Member States committed themselves not to invoke the benefit of this escape valve unless they are in a severe recession, i.e. an annual fall in real GDP of at least 0.75 percent.[55]

Absent this somewhat ambiguous escape valve, the Pact restates the monetary sanctions to be imposed by the Council.

(i)   non-interest-bearing deposits;
(ii)   conversion of such deposits into a fine after two years unless the excessive deficit has been corrected.[56]

The Pact also puts into place an early warning system, pursuant to which the Council would alert a Member State of the need to take corrective action to prevent a government deficit from becoming excessive. Further, all Member States, whether or not they have adopted the single currency, are required to present a Stability and Convergence Programme by March 1, of each year beginning in 1999.[57]

For Member States that have moved to Stage Three, called 'participating Member States', the Stability Programme is to present the medium-term objective for a budget close to balance or in surplus and the adjustment path toward this objective, and the expected path of the general government debt ratio, as well as the main assumptions about expected economic developments and a description of budgetary and other economic policy measures being taken or proposed. For Member States not yet in Stage Three (known as 'pre-ins'), the Convergence Programme is to contain essentially the same information, but in particular information on variables related to convergence.[58] In both situations, the programmes are to be made public, and are to be used by the Council in carrying out the surveillance functions assigned to it by Article 103(3)[99] of the Maastricht Treaty. The Regulation on Stability and Growth .Programmes entered into force on July 1, 1998; the Regulation on Sanctions entered into force on January 1, 1999.

---

[53] Reg. 1467 (n. 52 supra), Art. 2(2).   [54] Id., Art. 2(3).

[55] See Council Resolution on the Stability and Growth Pact, (n. 52 supra), para. 7.

[56] Regulation 1467/97, Arts. 11–13. As with other provisions relating to EMU, the excessive deficit obligation and provisions for sanctions for breach do not apply to the United Kingdom unless it decides to join the third stage. The obligation under Article 109e[116](4) of Maastricht to *endeavour* to avoid excessive government deficits does continue to apply.

[57] To be precise, participating Member States, i.e. those that have moved to Stage Three are to present a *stability programme*, on the theory that convergence has already been established; non-participating Member States are to present a *convergence programme*. See Regulation 1466/97 (n. 52 supra), Arts. 3–6 (Stability Programmes); Arts. 7–10 (Convergency Programmes).

[58] Id., Art. 7(2).

20.5   PRELIMINARY REFLECTIONS ON THE EURO REGIME

As this book went to press at year-end 2001, it was too early to write with confidence about the regime of the euro. The United Kingdom, which had elected not to join the single currency, seemed generally pleased with that decision, though pro- and anti-Europe views continued to roil British politics, and another referendum was a possibility. Denmark, which had approved the Treaty of Maastricht only on the basis of an opt-out provision for the single currency, held a second referendum on the euro in September 2000, and again the negative votes prevailed. Greece, which had not qualified for the single currency regime in 1998, applied again in March 2000, and in June 2000 was found to have met the convergence criteria and accordingly was admitted into the single currency regime, effective January 1, 2001.[59] Sweden, which had not qualified in 1998 but could have done so by 2000, elected not to join. Thus as of 2001, twelve of the fifteen members of the European Union were participants in the single currency regime; three— Denmark, Sweden, and the United Kingdom—were not. All fifteen, however, were bound by other provisions of the Maastricht regime, notably the requirement of submitting a 'convergence programme' to the Council each year.[60] The Council can make recommendations to both groups of member states, but the sanctions authorized by Article 104c[104] are applicable only to participant states.[61]

(a)   The First Years of the Euro

The exchange value of the euro declined steadily from about US$1.18 when it was launched on January 1, 1999 to its low point of $0.85 in October 2000 before rising to about $0.92 at year-end 2000 and closing at about $0.89 at year-end 2001. The cause for the decline was difficult to explain. The most persuasive theory suggested that the exchange rate had more to do with the attraction of the United States as a place to invest, including several massive acquisitions by European companies of American enterprises, than with the management of the euro. Nevertheless the slide of the euro led to much criticism of the European Central Bank and its president, Wim Duisenberg.

Whether in the long run a lower euro is good or bad for Europe is hard to tell; one result of its generally unexpected decline in value was that the

---

[59] Council Decision of 19 June 2000 in accordance with Art. 122(2) of the Treaty, (2000/427/EC), O.J. L 167/19 (7 July 2000).

[60] See Council Regulation 1466/97 of 7 July 1997, Sect. 20.4 (n. 52 supra), in implementation of Maastricht Art. 103[99](5), which distinguishes between 'stability programmes' to be submitted to the Council by 'participating Member states' (Arts. 3–6), and 'convergence programmes' to be submitted by 'non-participating Member States' (Arts. 7–10).

[61] See Maastricht Treaty Art. 109k[122](3).

euro did not become—at least in the early years—either a universal trans-action currency or a reserve currency to rival the US dollar.[62]

Putting aside the fall of the euro in comparison with other currencies, in particular the US dollar, the euro largely accomplished the aims of the creators of the European Economic and Monetary Union. All of the euro area has been essentially free of inflation, and the countries that were required to make major changes in fiscal discipline—notably Italy and Greece—have benefited from the measures that probably could not have been undertaken without the pressure of monetary union. The capital market inside the Union has been essentially unified and made more liquid, sales of corporate bonds within the euro area quadrupled, and corporate managers have been forced to pay more attention to shareholder value. Tax rates are more easily compared, and a common trend toward lower rates is in evidence. Export and import transactions within the euro area are carried on without exchange risk, and cross-border investment and cross-border mergers have increased.

On January 1, 2002, the next stage in the development of the euro took place—the introduction euro bank notes and coins and the gradual elimination of francs, marks, guilders, etc.

(b)   The Mandate of the EMU

Article 105 of the Maastricht Treaty (the only article whose number did not change) sets out in clear terms that the primary objective of the European System of Central Banks 'shall be to maintain price stability'. Thus the traditional German preoccupation with prevention of inflation is spelled out explicitly, as well as in the emphasis throughout the provisions on EMU on curbing budget deficits. No other criterion, regarding unemployment, for instance, or sustainable economic growth, or encouraging competitiveness, is spelled out in the Treaty. Maastricht thus rejects the Keynesian belief that inflation (unless excessive) is a normal companion to economic growth.

The Treaty also accepts the theory that inflation is a function of the money supply, and that if the ECB/ESCB manages the money supply correctly, price stability will be maintained or achieved. Whether it is possible to accurately manage the relationship between demand and supply of money in as large and varied an area as the EU may well be doubted. In its first two years, however, inflation in the euro area was modest, rising to an annual rate of 2.9 percent in November 2000, less than the United States, Canada, or the United Kingdom.

---

[62] At year-end 2000, the US dollar accounted for 68 percent of official holdings of foreign currency reserves, and the euro for 13 percent. But Saddam Hussein insisted that Iraq be paid for its oil exports in euros instead of 'the devil's gold'. See 'Bouncing Back?', *The Economist*, 4 Nov. 2000, p. 79.

To those who worry that in order to maintain price stability, the ECB will have to maintain tight money and high interest rates, the proponents say that so long as the convergence factors are adhered to—low budget deficits or indeed budgets in surplus—it will not be necessary to raise interest rates. Not all the political leaders of the Member States agreed with these priorities, and as elections changed the composition of the respective governments in the decade of the 1990s, it is quite possible that the Member governments or their electorates would not have reached agreement on the Maastricht priorities had the negotiations been held at the close of the decade. It is clear that the emphasis on the independence from political pressures of the ECB as well as of the Member States' central banks is related to the emphasis on the priorities reflected in the Maastricht Treaty, and on the need to insulate the management of the money supply and interest rates from changes in the politics of Europe.

To some, the independence of the ECB and the ESCB illustrate the 'democracy deficit' of the European institutions; to the financial community, it provides assurance of the stability of the system. The ECB has consistently resisted calls to raise interest rates to support the falling euro.

(c)   The European Central Bank and the Politicians

The independence of the European Central Bank and the Member States' national central banks is set out in Article 107[108] of the Maastricht Treaty and restated in Article 7 of the Statute of the European System of Central Banks and of the European Central Bank:[63]

[N]either the ECB, nor a national central bank, nor any member of their decision-making bodies shall seek or take instructions from Community institutions or bodies, from any government of a member State or from any other body. The Community institutions and bodies and the governments of the Member States undertake to respect this principle.

This provision stands in some tension with Article 109[111](2) of the Maastricht Treaty, which states that the Council (i.e. the representatives of the Member States),

acting by a qualified majority *either* on a recommendation from the Commission and after consulting the ECB *or* on a recommendation from the ECB may formulate *general orientations* for exchange-rate policy in relation to [non-Community] currencies. These general orientations shall be without prejudice to the primary objective of the ESCB to maintain price stability. (italics added)

In the negotiation of the Treaty, some states, in particular France, wanted the words 'directives' or 'guidelines' in place of the word 'orientations', and

---

[63] Protocol No. 18 (formerly Protocol No. 3) of the Treaty Establishing the European Economic Community.

some earlier drafts did contain these words.[64] The German delegation, reflecting the tradition of the Bundesbank, insisted on the word 'orientations' together with the qualification 'general' to emphasize that the Council—typically the Council of Finance Ministers or ECOFIN Council— could not require the ECB to take a given action, and in particular to depart from its statutory task of maintaining price stability.

> Thus suppose the ECOFIN Council decides that the euro is overvalued, and that it should be devalued by 10 percent against the US dollar. Such a step would make Community products more competitive in world markets and therefore, in the view of the Council, decrease unemployment within the Community. The ECB, however, considers that a devaluation would be inflationary, and thus would be inconsistent with the objective of price stability.

It seems that the Council could urge or recommend a devaluation, but that the decision (as well as the amount of any devaluation) would be up to the European Central Bank. The word 'seems' is used here because an argument could be built not only on the unclear term 'orientations', but on the second sentence of Article 105(1), which, following definition of the primary objective of the ESCB to maintain price stability, states 'the ESCB shall support the general economic policies in the Community', and on the second indent of Article 105(2) which lists among the basic tasks of the ESCB 'to conduct foreign exchange *operations* consistent with the provisions of Article 109[111]' (italics added). On balance, the present writer agrees with Professor Hahn (see note 64) that while consultation is desirable and a direct confrontation is improbable, the power to decide rests with the European Central Bank, and the political organs should use caution in seeming to go beyond consultation on the matters committed to the ECB.[65]

The potential for conflict between the politicians and the 'faceless bankers' erupted within two weeks of the effective date of the euro. In May–June 1997, the center-right coalition that had governed France since 1993, had lost the parliamentary election, and had been replaced by a Socialist-led coalition headed by Lionel Jospin. In October 1998, the Federal Republic of Germany had held a national election, with the result that the 16-year reign of Chancellor Helmut Kohl and the Christian Democratic Party had come to an end. A new Social Democratic government had been elected, led by Gerhard Schroeder, with the head of the Party, Oskar Lafontaine as Finance Minister. Lafontaine, a long-time spokesman for the German labour movement, was concerned about the issues raised in the preceding paragraphs, and attempted to put pressure both on the European

---

[64] See Hugo J. Hahn, 'European Union Exchange Rate Policy?', in Mario Giovanoli (ed.), *International Monetary Law: Issues for the New Millennium*, 195 (2000).

[65] Accord, Groeben, Thiesing, Ehrlermann, Bardenhewer, *Kommentar zum EU-/EG Vertrag*, Vol. 3, Comment on Article 105, pp. 163–6 (5th edn. 1999).

Central Bank and on Chancellor Schroeder to lower interest rates in order to stimulate employment.

On January 14, 1999, Mr. Lafontaine and his French counterpart, Dominique Strauss-Kahn, published a 2000-word Memorandum in leading German and French newspapers, entitled (in the French version) 'Making the most out of the euro'.[66] The Memorandum began by pointing out that in thirteen of the fifteen members of the EU, socialists or social democrats now held office:

All are in agreement on the necessity of preserving the stability of prices and soundness of public finances, but all consider that the search for stability must not serve as a pretext for governments and central banks to neglect their role in management of the business cycle. . . . Given that 18 million persons are looking for work in Europe, there can be no doubt that we must devote all our efforts to eradicate unemployment.

Thus far, the Memorandum made the point made above that price stability is not everyone's top priority, particularly for those who owe their election in large part to workers. But the Memorandum went further, and arguably beyond the limits set in the Maastricht Treaty:

We must watch over the exchange rate developments within the Euro–11 group, and formulate a coherent position. We should also have the ability to jointly communicate this position to the markets, and if necessary, to make use of the treaty provisions which contemplate the possibility to issue general orientations [guidelines] for exchange rates. This is of particular importance in connection with the introduction of the euro. Participants in the market should know that we do not welcome an excessive appreciation of the euro.[67]

The European Central Bank did not directly take up the challenge of the ministers, but on the following day the President of the ECB told a meeting in Amsterdam that the ECB deliberately did not set a target zone for the euro, since the actions needed to maintain such a target might be inconsistent with the goal of price stability. 'It might be very painful', Mr. Duisenberg said, 'if interest rates had to be raised during a recession, in order to defend the exchange rate of the euro.'[68] Four weeks later, the same German newspaper that had published the Lafontaine/Strauss–Kahn Memorandum, published a reply from the man who had been President of the Bundesbank at the time the Maastricht Treaty was negotiated, concluding that it would be regrettable if the German government now adopted the French and German

[66] *Die Zeit* (Hamburg), 14 Jan. 1999, pp. 17–18; *Le Monde* (Paris), 15 Jan. 1999, p. 1. The German title read 'Europe—Social and Strong'.

[67] This passage is quoted also in Hahn, 'European Union Exchange Rate Policy?', n. 64, supra, p. 195 (2000). The reference to the Treaty is evidently to Article 109[111](2), quoted above (p. 657). As Hahn points out, the German version of the Memorandum uses the word *Leitlinien* (guidelines) in place of the word 'orientations' which appears in the French text, and is used in all versions of the Treaty.

[68] As quoted in the *Frankfurter Allgemeine Zeitung*, 16 Jan. 1999, p. 25.

finance ministers' incorrect interpretation of the Treaty, 'which concerns more than a dispute about words, namely the independence of the European Central Bank.'[69]

As it turned out, the overvaluation of the euro feared by the two ministers did not take place in the first two years of the euro. The ECB did not respond to the pressure to cut interest rates, but some observers believe that fear that it would do so led to the beginning of the slide in the value of the euro. Less than two months after publication of the Memorandum, Mr. Lafontaine resigned both from his post as Minister of Finance and from leadership of the Social Democratic Party. He gave no explanation for the unexpected move, but it doubtless had to do with his uneasy relationship with the Chancellor, and not with the controversy over the euro. Mr. Strauss-Kahn remained in his post as France's Minister of Finance until November 1999, when he was forced to resign in connection with a corruption inquiry predating his service as Minister. As of year-end 2001, the potential for controversy between the ECB and the Council, and the relation of Article 105 to Article 111[109](2) concerning the euro, though widely discussed both in the press and in academic writing, had not led to actual conflict.

(d)   The EMU and Member States

One question not answered in the first two years was what would be the responsibility of the European Union and its Member States if a sudden (or not so sudden) economic downturn hit one of the Member States only. That state could not, according to the Maastricht Treaty, run a large budget deficit to encourage employment or investment. Would the other member states, or the ECB, be obligated to help the state in trouble?

Article 104b[103](1) seems to say 'no'. 'The Community shall not be liable for or assume the commitments of central governments . . . or public undertakings of any Member State.' 'A member State shall not be liable . . . [except in the case of] mutual financial guarantees for the joint execution of a specific project.' But could the Member State in difficulty not ask the EMU for assistance? Article 103a[100](2) says the Council may under certain conditions grant financial assistance to the member state concerned, but only when acting unanimously on a proposal from the Commission, unless the difficulty is caused by a natural disaster, in which case a qualified majority will do. The Economic and Monetary Union, it seems, falls short of a mutual defense treaty on the economic front.

---

[69] Helmut Schlesinger in *Die Zeit*, 18 Feb. 1999, repr. in Deutsche Bundesbank, *Auszüge aus Presseartikeln* No. 11, 19 Feb. 1999, 4, as quoted by Hahn, 'European Union Exchange Rate Policy' (n. 64 supra), 196.

(e) The EMU and the International Monetary System

As of January 1, 1999, the IMF incorporated the euro into the basket used for valuation of Special Drawing Rights in place of the French franc and German mark, based on the fixed conversion rates announced by the European Council.[70] Thus the SDR now reflects the values of euros, yen, British pounds, and US dollars.[71] Whether euros may be used to pay quota increases, or for lines of credit issued by the Fund, had not been decided as of year-end 2001.

The question of voting and membership in the IMF was not as easy. One might have thought that the EU, or the EMU, should become members of the IMF with a quota corresponding to the economic strength of the members of the euro area, and that the states that no longer had a currency for which they were responsible would either withdraw from the Fund entirely or assume some kind of observer role. But Article II of the Articles of Agreement of the International Monetary Fund provides that membership shall be open to *countries*, and the European Union is not a country. Moreover, the member states of the EMU were not keen to yield their membership in the IMF.

The solution, adopted at a summit meeting of the European Council in Vienna in December 1998, was that participating states in the EMU would keep their membership in the IMF, and that the European Central Bank would request observer status in the Executive Board of the IMF.[72] The views of the EC/EMU would be presented at meetings of the Executive Board by the Director who represents the state that for the time being is chairman of the European Union, supported by a member of the European Commission.

One wonders whether this solution can last, since it seems to assume that there is an Executive Director of the Fund from each member of the EMU, and that the Director who represents a member state of the EMU has no

---

[70] See 28 *IMF Survey*, 1, 5 (11 Jan. 1999). The method of valuation of the SDR was reviewed in the fall of 2000, to be effective for a five-year period commencing January 1, 2001. See *IMF Annual Report 2001*, p. 68.

[71] The weights for the five-year period 2001–6, in percentages, are US dollar 45, euro 29, Japanese yen 15, and pound sterling 11. As of August 14, 2001, the resulting value of the SDR was SDR1 = US$1.269390.

[72] By decision of the Executive Board of the IMF, the ECB was granted observer status for meetings on Fund surveillance under Article IV over the common monetary and exchange rate policies of the euro-area; Fund surveillance under Article IV over the policies of individual euro-area members; the role of the euro in the international monetary system; World Economic Outlook; international capital markets reports; and world economic and market developments. In addition, the ECB is to be invited to send a representative to meeting on agenda items of mutual interest. As an observer, the representative of the ECB will be able to address the Board with the permission of the Chairman 'on matters within the responsibility of the ECB'.

Exec. Board Decision No. 11875–(99/1) 21 Dec. 1998, *Selected Decisions*, 478 (25th issue 2000), renewed 27 Dec. 2000.

other constituents. For instance, as of April 30, 2001, Spain belonged to the group of countries represented on the Executive Board by a Director from Venezuela, who also represents five small Central American countries; when Spain becomes President of the EU for six months, it seems improbable that the Mexican Director is expected to speak for the EU. Correspondingly, The Netherlands had a Director on the Executive Board, but he represented also eleven other countries, including Armenia, Bosnia, Cyprus, Israel, and Ukraine.[73]

A related question, though not encumbered by statute or treaty, concerned representation of the EMU in the G–7, in particular in meetings of finance ministers and central bank governors. Initially, the EMU participants who were also members of the G–7 wanted simply to continue their participation in G–7 meetings, with the addition of the President of the ECB and the President or other representative of the European Commission. The other G–7 participants, and especially the United States, rejected this arrangement, on the ground that it would make the G–7 even more top-heavy towards the EU than it already was. Eventually, the solution was that G–7 meetings (other than summit meetings) would be divided into two parts. One part would be devoted to the world economy and exchange rates, at which the EMU would be represented by the president of the European Central Bank and the chairman for the time being of the Euro–11 Finance Ministers, but not by the finance ministers or central bank governors for France, Germany, and Italy. A second part of the meeting could be devoted to all other issues—for instance how to deal with Russian debt or the least developed countries—which the finance ministers and central bank governors for the EMU member states could attend.[74]

Apart from the issues of representation, it seems appropriate to ask, without here venturing an answer, what the Economic and Monetary Union of the European states means for the international monetary system as a whole.

As mentioned above, the euro did not in its first two years display the strength and stability to propel it to true rivalry with the US dollar. It seems unlikely in the foreseeable future that the euro would displace the dollar, but if in subsequent years the value of the euro remained stable vis-à-vis the dollar and other hard currencies, and if the EMU gained further members, in particular the United Kingdom, the euro might well come to coexist with the

---

[73] See *IMF Annual Report 2001*, Appendix VII, pp. 168–71. The points made in the text are made also by Eric Denters, 'Representation of the EC in the IMF', in Mario Giovanoli (ed.), *International Monetary Law* (n. 64 supra), 211 (2000).

[74] See e.g. *Financial Times*, 14 June 1999, p. 5, 'Europe Bank Chiefs Reduce G7 Presence.' See also Denters (n. 73 supra), p. 212.

dollar as a transaction and reserve currency, possibly with a third, yen-based reserve currency.[75]

In the past, the world has known only one dominant currency at a time— the British pound in the nineteenth century and up to World War I, the US dollar in the period after World War II. As this volume went to press, it was far too early to venture a prediction about a new bipolar, or tripolar inter-national monetary system, and whether such a system could exist within the legal framework of the Bretton Woods Articles as revised at Jamaica. It seemed not too early, however, to begin to think about such a system.

---

[75] Some American commentators were worried about such a prospect just as the euro was being introduced. The 1999 Economic Report of the President responded as follows:

The emergence of the euro as an international currency should not be viewed with alarm, for a number of reasons. Even if the euro emerges as a strong international currency, the neg-ative effects on U.S. economic welfare are likely to be small and outweighed by the advan-tages of EMU to U.S. residents. . . . And in any case the euro is unlikely to rapidly displace the dollar as a major international currency, given that the foundations of the successful per-formance of the U.S. economy remain intact. International currency status does not auto-matically follow from a currency's possession of a large home base. (Economic Report of the President, Feb. 1999, 297–8)

21

International Monetary Law and Private Activity

Much of the discussion in the preceding chapters, while focused on states and international organizations, has inevitably involved the role of private parties. The creditors of the developing countries and the 'countries in transition' have been in significant part commercial banks (see Chapter 18); the holders of financial assets that make up much of a state's balance of payments are also to a large extent private parties, as are those who trade in goods and services or make transnational investments. Indeed, one way to view the demise of the Bretton Woods system (see Chapter 16) and the demise of the Exchange Rate Mechanism of the European Monetary System (see Chapter 20, Sect. 20.2) is as the triumph of individual decision-making over the will of governments. Still, the preceding chapters have on the whole been devoted to the public international law of monetary affairs. This chapter is addressed to selected subjects at the frontier between public and private international law.

21.1 EXCHANGE CONTROLS, EXCHANGE CONTRACTS, AND ARTICLE VIII(2)(B)

(a) The IMF and Exchange Controls

As described in Chapter 16,[1] the Articles of Agreement of the IMF contain contradictory provisions with respect to exchange controls. In principle, the Articles of Agreement prohibit restrictions by member states on payments and transfers in international transactions (Article VIII(2)(a)). The Articles of Agreement contain three major exceptions to the principle. *First*, the prohibition in Article VIII(2)(a) is limited to payments and transfers for *current international transactions*, and Article VI(3) expressly states that 'Members may exercise such controls as are necessary to regulate international capital movements.' *Second*, the prohibition on restrictions on current international transactions in Article VIII(2)(a) is qualified by the phrase 'without the approval of the Fund', and the Fund has frequently approved exchange controls, typically for limited periods of time. *Third*, the prohibition in Article VIII(2)(a) is subject to Article XIV, which permits member states to avail themselves of 'transitional arrangements' to maintain and adapt to changing circumstances the restrictions on current payments and transfers in effect when they became members of the IMF.

In its original version, Article XIV was focused on the 'post-war transitional period', but the Fund never announced the end of that period; in the Amended Articles the reference to the post-war period was eliminated while the thrust of the Article was retained, so that no time limit with respect to a

---

[1] See Ch. 16, Sect. 16.5.
[2] Article XIV (2) of the Articles of Agreement, both in the original and the amended version provides, however, that:

> Members shall . . . as soon as conditions permit . . . take all possible measures to develop such commercial and financial arrangements with other members as will facilitate international payments

and further:

> [M]embers shall withdraw restrictions maintained under this Section as soon as they are satisfied that they will be able, in the absence of such restrictions, to settle the balance of payments in a manner which will not unduly encumber their access to the general resources of the Fund.

transition is expressed or implied in Article XIV.[2] The United States (and also Mexico and Panama) accepted the obligations of Article VIII from 1946 on; the member states of the European Community became Article VIII countries in February 1961, and Japan did so in 1964, thereby undertaking not to impose exchange controls on current transactions except upon approval by the Fund. But at the time the Amended Articles entered into effect in 1978, only 46 of the 138 member states of the Fund had accepted the obligations of Article VIII, and a number of industrial countries, including Spain, Portugal, and New Zealand, had not done so. Gradually, most states—developed and developing—accepted Article VIII status; as of April 30, 2001, only about 30 of the 182 members of the Fund had still not done so.[3]

If a member state imposed exchange controls contrary to the provisions of the Articles of Agreement, the Fund did not directly take any action, but the issue could come up in consultations under Article IV,[4] and would certainly come up in connection with negotiation of a stand-by arrangement or a debt-rescheduling package.[5] If a member state maintained exchange controls not inconsistent with the Fund Articles on one of the three bases listed above, the question could arise whether other member states were obliged to cooperate in enforcing the regulations, or could ignore foreign 'public law', as had been the tradition of most states prior to conclusion of the Bretton Woods Agreement.

(b)   Exchange Contracts and the Fund Agreement

The Articles of Agreement of the IMF contain one cryptic sentence addressed to this question. Article VIII (2)(b) reads in its entirety, as follows:

(b)   Exchange contracts which involve the currency of any member and which are contrary to the exchange control regulations of that member maintained or imposed consistently with the Agreement shall be unenforceable in the territories of any member. In addition, members may, by mutual accord, cooperate in measures for the purpose of making the exchange control regulations of either member more effective, provided that such measures and regulations are consistent with this Agreement.

A large body of commentary,[6] and a substantial number of judicial decisions in numerous countries have attempted to construe Article VIII(2)(b).[7]

---

[3] Brazil became an Article VIII member state in November 1999; among the states still under Article XIV were Colombia, Egypt, Congo (Kinshasa), Iran, Iraq, Libya, Syria, Zambia, and Vietnam. See *IMF Annual Report 2001*, Appendix II, Table II.14.

[4] See Ch. 17, Sect. 17.4.   [5] See Ch. 18, Sect. 18.5.

[6] See e.g. Joseph Gold, *The Fund Agreement in the Courts*, Vol. I, 1962; Vol II (1982); Vol III, 1986; F. A. Mann, *The Legal Aspect of Money*, ch. XIII (5th edn. 1992); Francois Gianviti, 'Reflexions sur l'Article VIII, Section 2(b) des Status du Fonds Monétaire International', 62 *Rev. Critique de Droit Privé* 471 and 629 (1973); Stephen A. Silard, 'Money and Foreign Exchange' in *Int'l Encyclopedia of Comparative Law*, Vol. 17, ch. 20, sects. 86–93 (1975).

[7] For a detailed, though inconclusive history of the drafting of Article VIII(2)(b), see Joseph Gold, *The Fund Agreement in the Courts*, Vol. II, Appendix A, pp. 429–38 (1982).

Despite considerable variation in interpretation of Article VIII(2)(b), no serious effort was made to clarify the provision when the Articles of Agreement were amended in 1976.

1. 'Public Policy'

Some courts have thought that Article VIII(2)(b), in the context of the Bretton Woods Agreement as a whole, implied a collective reversal of the traditional so-called 'revenue rule' that currency control laws of other states are contrary to the public policy of the forum state and will not be enforced. This, for example, was the view of Chief Judge Desmond of the New York Court of Appeals, dissenting in *Banco do Brasil, S. A. v. A. C. Israel Commodity Co., Inc.*[8] Others have agreed with the view of the Solicitor General of the United States, in urging that review of the *Banco do Brasil* case not be granted by the US Supreme Court, that the 'bare acceptance' of the Bretton Woods Agreement, without conclusion of an accord such as is suggested but not required by Article VIII (2)(b), 'did not establish a national policy' requiring the courts of the state of New York to entertain an action in tort against an American alleged co-conspirator in a fraudulent scheme to deprive the Bank of Brazil of the foreign exchange proceeds of an export of coffee.[9] The American Law Institute's *Restatement of Foreign Relations Law* takes the position that the 'revenue rule' is obsolete at least with respect to action to enforce exchange contracts covered by Article VIII(2)(b), as discussed below.[10] When Article VIII(2)(b) does apply, it prevails over the 'proper law' of the contract, whether that law is specified in the contract itself or is derived from applicable principles of conflict of laws.

2. 'Exchange Contract'

Two principal views have been expressed about the meaning of 'exchange contract'. Some courts, including the New York Court of Appeals in the *Banco do Brasil* case cited above and the English Court of Appeal in a case involving an Italian seeking to avoid a margin call for trades on the London Metal exchange,[11] have taken the position first advocated by Professor Arthur Nussbaum[12] that exchange contract refers only to transactions which have as

---

[8] 12 N.Y.2d 371 at 377, 239 N.Y.S.2d 872 at 876, 190 N.E.2d 235 at 237 (1963), cert. denied, 376 U.S. 906 (1969).

[9] For a more detailed statement of the arguments on this issue and extended quotations, see Joseph Gold, *The Fund Agreement in the Courts*, n. 6 supra, Vol. II, pp. 22–30 (1982).

[10] American Law Institute, *Restatement (Third) of the Foreign Relations Law of the United States*, §822, comment *a* (1987). Accord: F. A. Mann, *The Legal Aspect of Money*, 368 (5th edn., 1992). But particular exchange controls may be contrary to the public policy of the forum. See *J. Zeevi & Sons Ltd.* v. *Grindlays Bank (Uganda) Ltd.*, 37 N.Y.2d 220, 371 N.Y.S.2d 892, 333 N.E.2d 168 (1975), in which the New York Court of Appeals declined to recognize an exchange control imposed by President Idi Amin of Uganda directed specifically against Israel and nationals of Israel.

[11] *Wilson, Smithett & Cope Ltd.* v. *Terruzzi*, [1976] Q.B. 683, 709 (UK Ct. App.).

[12] Nussbaum, 'Exchange Control and the International Monetary Fund', 59 *Yale L.J.* 421, 426 (1949).

their immediate object the exchange of one currency for another. In 1982, the House of Lords adopted the narrow view of an exchange contract, but divided a transaction that nominally was simply a contract for the purchase of goods into two parts, one for the fair price of a plant to be shipped from England to Peru which was permitted to go through, the other for excessive payments that were to be credited to buyer's account in the United States, which was deemed a disguised exchange transaction in violation of Peru's exchange controls and therefore disallowed under Article VIII(2)(b).[13] The better view, favoured by F. A. Mann, Sir Joseph Gold, and the staff of the IMF, is that an exchange contract for purposes of Article VIII(2)(b) is any contract that affects the exchange resources of the country imposing the exchange controls, including a contract for the purchase of goods, charter of a ship, payment of a commission, and deposit of funds.[14] Courts in Germany, Austria, France, and other civil law countries have generally taken this view, and accordingly have refused to enforce (or give damages for non-performance of) contracts inconsistent with the exchange controls of other states.[15]

3. '. . . *which involve the currency*'

Interpretation of the quoted phrase raises essentially the same issue as interpretation of 'exchange contract'. A narrow view would hold that a contract between a resident of Patria and a resident of, say, Germany would involve the currency of Patria only if it called for payment in Patrian pesos, but not if it called for payment in German marks or US dollars. A broader view, looking to the underlying economic effects of the transaction, would hold that if the Patrian buyer needs to purchase marks with pesos or to make use of existing supplies of marks or dollars that previously were includible in Patria's reserves, the transaction would equally 'involve the currency' of Patria.[16] Note that Article VIII(2)(b) will be applicable whether or not the

---

[13] *United City Merchants (Investments) Ltd.* v. *Royal Bank of Canada*, [1983] 1 A.C. 168, [1982] 2 W.L.R. 2039 (H.L. (E)).

[14] See F. A. Mann, *The Legal Aspect of Money*, n. 6 supra, 379–83; Joseph Gold, *The Fund Agreement in the Courts*, n. 6 supra, Vol. III, 787–9 and *passim*, and earlier volumes. The staff of the Fund rejects a test of exchange contract based on effect on the balance of payments as not being a sufficiently clear legal criterion. It would define an exchange contract as 'any contract that provides for payment in foreign exchange' or for a payment between a resident and a non-resident of the country imposing the control. Pierre Francotte, 'The Fund Agreement in the Courts: Comment', in Robert C. Effros (ed.), *Current Legal Issues Affecting Central Banks*, 15 at 19 (1992).

[15] See *Restatement* (n. 10 supra), §822, Reporter's Note 2; Mann, *The Legal Aspect of Money*, 381–3; and for extensive discussion, J. Gold, *The Fund Agreement in the Courts*, n. 6 supra, Vols. I, II, and III.

[16] Accord: F. A. Mann, *The Legal Aspect of Money*, n. 6 supra, 386 (5th edn. 1992), quoting, *inter alia*, *Moojen* v. *von Reichert*, 51 *Rev. Critique de Droit International Privé* 67 (1962) (Cour d'Appel, Paris, 20 June 1961), described at length in Joseph Gold, *The Fund Agreement in the Courts*, n. 6 supra, Vol. I, pp. 143–53 (1962). In that case, the French court refused under Article VIII(2)(b) to enforce a contract by which a resident of The Netherlands was to sell shares of a French company to a resident of Germany for French francs, on the ground that the transaction could affect Netherlands financial resources and would contravene Netherlands exchange controls.

effect of a given transaction on the currency of the member imposing exchange controls is adverse. If, for instance, in the preceding example the resident of Germany is the buyer and the resident of Patria is the seller, the transaction still affects the currency of Patria and thus may be subject to Patria's exchange controls, though it would add to the exchange resources of Patria.[17]

4. '... *Maintained or imposed consistently with this Agreement*'

Often the most difficult question in litigation concerning foreign exchange controls is whether a given regulation is consistent with the Articles of Agreement of the Fund. The Fund publishes an *Annual Report on Exchange Arrangements and Exchange Restrictions*, but the fact that a regulation is described in the *Report* does not mean that it is maintained or imposed consistently with the Fund Agreement.[18] There is no presumption that a particular control is maintained or imposed consistently with the Agreement, whether the country imposing the control is an Article VIII or an Article XIV country.[19]

As early as 1949, the Executive Board of the Fund issued a decision interpreting Article VIII(2)(b), which concluded:

The Fund will be pleased to lend its assistance in connection with any problem which may arise in relation to the foregoing interpretation or any other aspect of Article VIII, Section 2(b). In addition, the Fund is prepared to advise whether particular exchange regulations are maintained or imposed consistently with the Fund Agreement.[20]

If plaintiff demands payment of an obligation, defendant asserts that payment would contravene the exchange control regulations of a member state, and plaintiff challenges the consistency of the regulation with the Fund Agreement, either party or the court may seek the advice of the Fund in accordance with the decision quoted, but resort to the Fund's advice is not

---

[17] In *Weston Banking Corporation* v. *Turkiye Garanti Bankasi, A.S.*, 57 N.Y.2d 315, 326, 456 N.Y.S.2d 684, 689, 442 N.E. 2d 1195, 1200 (1982), the New York Court of Appeals suggested that Article VIII(2)(b) did not apply to a contract asserted to be contrary to Turkish exchange controls whereby a Turkish bank was obligated to repay in New York a loan denominated in Swiss francs, on the ground that the obligation did not involve the currency of Turkey. While the decision may have been correct on other grounds, this phase of the court's opinion seems wrong. Accord: Mann, n. 6 supra, at p. 388.

[18] Nor is the opposite inference appropriate. An exchange control regulation may not have been reported to the Fund, or may have been reported too late for inclusion in the *Report* and may nevertheless not be inconsistent with the Agreement.

[19] Contra, *Callejo* v. *Bancomer, S.A.*, 764 F.2d 1101, 1119, n. 25 (5th Cir. 1985). Sir Joseph Gold pointed out that the court in that case based its statement on a statement by the Legal Department of the IMF in 1948 and reproduced in J. Keith Horsefield, *The International Monetary Fund 1945–1965*, Vol. I, pp. 209–10 (1969) which has not represented the Fund's view for many years. See Joseph Gold, *The Fund Agreement in the Courts*, n. 6 supra, Vol. III, pp. 543, 547–48 (1986).

[20] Ex. Bd. Dec. No. 446–4, 10 June 1949, *Selected Decisions*, 420 (25th issue 2000).

required.[21] It seems that a statement by the Fund (normally by the head of the Legal Department) to the effect that a regulation is not maintained or imposed consistently with the Agreement—for example that approval by the Fund would be required and has not been granted—is conclusive; a statement that a control is maintained consistently with the Agreement is entitled to great weight, but the final determination is up to the court.[22] For instance, an exchange regulation may be imposed by Patria, which would be contrary to the Articles of Agreement unless approved by the Fund, but that approval may not be granted until three or four months after promulgation of the regulation. The Fund might well determine that the regulation was imposed consistently with the Agreement but a court would not be bound to accept that determination as applied to obligation entered into in the interim.[23] The court will in any event have to determine whether the particular obligation in suit is governed by the exchange control regulation relied on by the defendant.

21.2   REGULATION OF BANKS: INTERSECTION OF PUBLIC AND PRIVATE INTERNATIONAL LAW

More even than manufacturing and marketing firms, major banks have long been multinational enterprises. Not only have the major banks accepted deposits from overseas depositors and made loans to overseas borrowers, public and private; banks with headquarters in one of the principal financial centers—London, New York, Frankfurt, Tokyo, Hong Kong—generally are established in all the other financial centers, as well as in other cities and countries, including both important sources of economic activity, and banking havens such as the Bahamas, the Cayman Islands, and Luxembourg. Unlike other enterprises engaged in economic activity across national frontiers, multinational banks commonly operate through branches, i.e. through

---

[21] Professor Edwards contends that if neither party seeks the advice of the IMF, the court should do so on its own motion, and that if the judge makes an independent determination, he commits error. Richard W. Edwards, Jr., *International Monetary Collaboration*, 481–2 (1985). This seems to be the rule only in Germany. See Werner F. Ebke, 'Article VIII, Section 2(b), International Monetary Cooperation and the Courts', in *Festschrift in Honor of Sir Joseph Gold* (Ebke and Norton, (eds.)), 63 at 89–90 (1990).

[22] Accord: *Restatement (Third) of the Foreign Relations Law of the United States*, §822, Comment *c* and Reporters' Note 1 (1987). F. A. Mann (n. 6 supra) 391 regarded advice from the Fund as 'no more than a valuable piece of evidence'. Sir Joseph Gold, on the other hand, argued from Article XXIX of the Articles of Agreement, authorizing the Executive Board to make a *decision* on any question of interpretation of provisions of the Agreement, that the Fund's advice should be conclusive whatever it says, though he concedes that courts have often made their own decisions on the issue when the Fund's advice has not been sought. Gold (n. 6 supra), Vol. III, 700–3, 768–72.

[23] Ibid., 642–5, discussing *Callejo* v. *Bancomer, S. A.*, 764 F.2d 1101 (5th Cir. 1989) which involved the exchange controls imposed by Mexico after outbreak of the 1982 foreign debt crisis, Ch. 18, Sect. 18.2.

establishments not separately incorporated in the states in which they are established. Operation through branches rather than through subsidiaries has the advantage that it is usually not necessary to meet the capital requirements of each state where the bank has an establishment: the capital of the enterprise as a whole—in some instances supported by pledges to local authorities—is available to satisfy the requirements for operation of a branch in a particular jurisdiction.

Nearly every state maintains some form of licensing and supervision over banks organized within its territory. In many instances, however, this supervision has not in the past extended (or has extended only superficially) to foreign operations of banks organized within the state's territory, or to operations within the state's territory of banks organized abroad. Several developments in the 1970s and 1980s contributed to the perception that national regulation of banks was inadequate to an increasingly global (and interconnected) banking system.

— The collapse of the fixed exchange rate system created at Bretton Woods inevitably led not only to volatility in exchange rates and interest rates, but to a huge new source of revenue (and also of risk) for money-center banks.
— The massive transfer of resources to the oil-producing states after the 1973 Middle East War, oil embargo, and subsequent price increases, led to massive competition for deposits among the major money-center banks,[24] and also to a quantum jump in deposits of currencies in banks located in countries other than the issuers of the currencies, notably 'Eurodollars', both in branches of American banks located in London, Hong Kong, Frankfurt, etc., and in banks organized in countries whose banking authorities were concentrated on their own currencies—pounds, marks, etc.—rather than on obligations denominated in dollars.
— The contemporaneous revolution in computer technology and telecommunications fueled a blurring between domestic and international financial transactions, and as it turned out, risks.

(a)   The Basle Concordat

When several important banks failed within a few months of each other in 1974, in significant part because of uncovered foreign exchange transactions—Herstatt Bank in Germany, Franklin National Bank in New York and London, British-Israel Bank in Tel Aviv and London—the Central Bank Governors of the Group of Ten, who had been collaborating for a decade on macroeconomic matters,[25] decided to establish a Committee on Banking

---

[24] For the other side of this phenomenon, see the discussion of the origin of the crisis of developing country debt, Ch. 18, Sect. 18.1.

[25] See Ch. 16, Sect. 16.8, Ch. 19, Sect. 19.4.

Regulations and Supervisory Practices.[26] The Committee was to be based at the Bank for International Settlements in Basle, and soon became known as the Basle Committee. It held its first meeting in December 1974 under the chairmanship of an official of the Bank of England—a logical choice since most important multinational banks maintained branches, subsidiaries, or joint venture operations in London, and since London—no longer the home of a major reserve currency—had become the most important Eurocurrency and interbank market. By September 1975, the Committee was ready with a document of Principles for the Supervision of Banks' Foreign Establishments, generally known as the Basle Concordat.

Technically, the Basle Concordat is not an international agreement binding on states, but only a report of a committee made up of central bank and supervisory agency representatives of twelve states. In fact, the Basle Concordat does represent an assignment and allocation of responsibility among national authorities over transnational activity, and a recognition of jurisdiction to prescribe in a context where previously various claims of extraterritorial jurisdiction and limits thereon had been or might have been raised.[27]

The basic objective of the Concordat is to close gaps in the supervision of banks with international operations. In its first version the Concordat assigned primary responsibility for supervision of the *liquidity* of foreign banking establishments to the authorities of the country in which the foreign bank operated (i.e. the host country) whether that operation was by way of branches or subsidiaries. As to *solvency*, host countries were to have primary responsibility for joint ventures and subsidiaries, while supervision of branches was to be the primary responsibility of authorities from the parent country.[28] It was realized that this division was in many ways artificial, and was made more difficult by legal restraints on disclosure of information, as well as by differences in the ways accounts were kept by banks in different countries. Accordingly, the Basle Committee soon turned to developing standards for reporting the worldwide operations of banking groups on a consolidated basis. The purpose was to enable the parent bank's supervisors to understand the totality of a banking group's international business, with a view to intervention if the group seemed to be engaging through a subsidiary in risky practices not objected to where the subsidiary was established. In the course of the 1970s, authorities in Canada, The Netherlands, the United States, Japan, the United Kingdom, and Switzerland moved toward the system of consolidation and reporting recommended by the Basle Committee.

---

[26] In addition to the G–10, Switzerland and Luxembourg, both important banking centers, were represented on the Committee.

[27] See also n. 33 infra.

[28] The text of the original Basle Concordat was published only in 1981, as an annex to an IMF Occasional Paper, R.C. Williams and G. G. Johnson, *International Capital Markets, Recent Developments and Short Term Prospects* (IMF Occasional Paper, 7 Nov. 1981).

(b)   The Concordat Revised

Before the steps contemplated by the Concordat could be fully implemented, another major bank failure demonstrated the shortcomings of the initial version of the Basle Concordat. In July 1982, Italian authorities closed the Banco Ambrosiano, Italy's largest privately owned bank, after its Chairman, Roberto Calvi, was found hanging from a bridge in London, a victim either of murder or of suicide. It turned out that among the assets of the bank were more than $1 billion in overdue foreign loans, many booked through banking subsidiaries of a Luxembourg holding company, Banco Ambrosiano Holding (BAH). Italy's central bank acted quickly, in collaboration with Italy's major domestic banks, to provide full backing to depositors at Banco Ambrosiano's 107 branches in Italy, but not to creditors of BAH, which the Italian authorities did not regard as a bank, and whose activities in any event were not consolidated for reporting and supervisory purposes. The Luxembourg authorities, however, took the position that responsibility to BAH's creditors also lay with Italy; Luxembourg's banking commissioner wrote to the Bank of Italy that 'the way matters have been handled is not easy to understand.'[29]

In part as the result of the Banco Ambrosiano affair (as well as the growing problem of developing country debt),[30] and in part as a result of inconsistent interpretations of the original version of the Concordat,[31] the Basle Committee prepared a substantially revised Concordat, and (in contrast to the original version) distributed it widely to banks and others.[32]

The basic principles reflected in the revised Concordat are 'firstly, that no foreign banking establishment should escape supervision, and secondly, that the supervision should be adequate.'[33] What this means is that apart from the allocation of primary responsibility, as in the original Concordat, if parent authorities consider that supervision by host countries is inadequate, the parent authority should either extend its own authority to cover the foreign establishment, or should discourage (forbid?) the parent enterprise to continue operations at the foreign establishment, whether that establishment is

---

[29] See *Financial Times*, London, 9 Aug. 1982, p. 1; 10 Aug. 1982, p. 1; 12 Aug 1982, p. 1; Richard Dale, *The Regulation of International Banking*, 161–3, 175 (1986).

[30] See Ch. 18.   [31] See Dale (n. 29 supra), 173–4.

[32] The revised Concordat, dated May 1983 is published in 12 *IMF Survey*, 20 (11 July 1983), and in 22 *International Legal Materials*, p. 900 (1983). This and other documents of the Basle Committee are also now available on the web site of the Bank for International Settlements, www.bis.org/publ.

[33] Committee on Banking Regulations and Supervisory Procedures, *Principles for the Supervision of Banks' Foreign Establishments*, May 1983, Pt. III, 'General Principles'. The Introduction to the Revised Concordat states:

> The principles set out in the report are not necessarily embodied in the laws of the countries represented on the Committee. Rather they are recommended guidelines of best practices in this area, which all members have undertaken to work towards implementing according to the means available to them.

a branch, a subsidiary, or a joint venture. Correspondingly, the Concordat states that the host country authorities should discourage operation of local entities belonging to a banking group not adequately supervised by a parent bank or parent supervisory authorities, or that the host country should set specific conditions on the operations of foreign banks in their territory.

Specifically, since branches are not subject to separate limits of liability, solvency of branches is deemed to be indistinguishable from solvency of the parent bank, and thus remains the primary responsibility of the parent authority.[34] For subsidiaries, supervision of solvency is a joint responsibility of host and parent authorities. While subsidiaries are deemed to be separate entities from the point of view of corporate law and thus subject to supervision of the country of incorporation, the revised Concordat states that 'parental supervision' on a consolidated basis is needed, both because solvency of parent companies cannot be adequately judged without taking account of all their foreign establishments and because parent banks 'cannot be indifferent' to the situation of their foreign subsidiaries.[35]

For liquidity, the revised Concordat also prescribes overlapping authority, but provides that the initial presumption for supervising liquidity should lie with the host authority, for branches as well as for subsidiaries. But host authorities have a duty, according to the 1983 Concordat, to ensure that the parent authority is immediately informed of any serious inadequacy in liquidity in a parent bank's foreign establishment.

(c)   Another Disaster, Another Agreement: The BCCI Affair

In 1991, still another major bank disaster took place, much larger in dollar amounts and much more extensive in terms of the number of countries affected.

> The Bank for Credit and Commerce International had been established in 1972 by a group of bankers from Pakistan, with technical and financial support from the Bank of America and major investment by the ruler of Abu Dhabi and wealthy citizens of Saudi Arabia.[36] BCCI advertised itself as a Third World answer to the traditional banks based in the G–10

---

[34] This is so even when the host country imposes a requirement of minimum start-up capital (*donation de capital*), as is true, for instance, in Germany.

[35] In other words, even if a parent corporation is not technically liable for the obligations of its subsidiary, see e.g. *Liability of Multinational Corporations for Obligations of Subsidiaries*, Report to the Institute of International Law, 65 *Annuaire de l'Institut de Droit International*, 244–313 (1993), a bank or similar institution dependent on public trust cannot easily walk away from liabilities of an institution bearing its name without damaging its overall credit standing. For an analogous situation, involving the warehousing subsidiary of American Express victimized in the 'salad oil swindle' in the early 1960s, see Smedresman and Lowenfeld, 'Eurodollars, Multinational Banks, and National Laws', 64 *N.Y.U.L Rev.* 733, 789–90 (1989).

[36] Bank of America sold its holdings in BCCI in 1980 and withdrew most of its personnel who had been lent to BCCI for start-up purposes.

countries, and by 1990 it had become one of the biggest banks in the world, with branches or affiliates (in some instances with the connection concealed) in more than seventy countries, and assets, according to its balance sheets, in excess of $20 billion.

The organization of BCCI did not fit within the models on which the Basle Committee had focused—that is a parent bank subject to supervision in one country, and branches and subsidiaries subject to supervision in host countries. BCCI was managed through a parent holding company in Luxembourg, BCCI Holdings;[37] Holdings had two principal banking subsidiaries—BCCI S.A., incorporated in Luxembourg and BCCI (Overseas), incorporated in the Cayman Islands. These subsidiaries, in turn, controlled separate networks of branches and subsidiaries in Europe, the Middle East, the Far East, Africa, the Caribbean, and the United States. Banking operations were run out of London, but a given deposit or loan could be booked anywhere. In many instances, it later turned out, one entity would direct its sister or cousin to book a transaction that had never in fact taken place. Also, some of the branches and subsidiaries were real banks, accepting deposits and making loans, others were mere shells, without separate manager, working offices, or funds, but useful in obscuring the paper trail for anyone who cared to probe.

Until 1987 two different Big Eight accounting firms audited BCCI, so that neither firm had a complete picture of BCCI's operations, or an obligation to report to the same supervisory authority. Several of BCCI's customers, including the CIA, General Manuel Noriega of Panama, and the international arms dealer Adnan Kashoggi, appreciated the secrecy of BCCI's operations and the facility with which it was able to switch accounts or transfer funds between them.

In a general way, bank supervisors were aware of the shadowy dealings of BCCI. None of the major credit rating agencies would give a report on BCCI; the bank's affiliate in Florida pleaded guilty to money-laundering charges; and, apparently on orders from the Bank of England, a single firm, Price Waterhouse, had become the sole auditor for the BCCI group of banks.

Neither the Bank of England nor the Luxembourg Banking Commission was prepared to assume primary responsibility for supervising BCCI, though (or perhaps because) both had their doubts about its soundness and integrity. A 'college' of regulators from the United Kingdom, Switzerland, Spain, and Luxembourg was established in 1988 to exchange information about BCCI; in 1989, representatives of Hong Kong, Cayman Islands, and later France and the United Arab

---

[37] Recall that Luxembourg had taken the position in the Ambrosiano affair that bank holding companies were not subject to regulation by banking authorities. See text at n. 29 supra.

Emirates, were added to the college. Price Waterhouse, which initially had stated that BCCI's systems of control were adequate, reported in April 1990 that a number of false accounting transactions had been booked in the Caymans and elsewhere. The ruling family of Abu Dhabi injected new capital and bought out the Saudi Arabian investors. As further shortfalls in the accounts of BCCI were revealed—a mixture of sloppy accounting and outright fraud—the Bank of England (a host country authority) ordered Price Waterhouse to conduct a formal inquiry under the fraud section of the English Banking Act. The Report, received by the Bank of England on June 25, 1991, showed, as the Governor of the Bank of England put it, 'evidence of massive and widespread fraud, going back over a number of years.' Some 6,000 files, the Report stated, had been kept personally by the BCCI's chief executive, apparently in Pakistan or the United Arab Emirates, and withheld from the auditors. At 1 p.m. London time on July 5, 1991, regulators in England, Luxembourg, the United States, Spain, France, and the Cayman Islands acted to close the doors of BCCI, stating that BCCI had been engaged in massive fraud, that it was insolvent, and that its management was both incompetent and dishonest. Parliamentary inquiries, criminal actions, civil actions, and attempts at winding up followed in England, Luxembourg, the United States and elsewhere, looking to salvage some assets for BCCI's depositors. As of year-end 2001, this activity had not been completed, though the ultimate losses turned out to be less than at first feared.[38] The gaps in banking supervision, however, had been amply demonstrated.[39]

Until the BCCI disaster came to worldwide attention, the Basle Committee had been content to enunciate 'principles' for supervision of banks' foreign establishment.[40] After *BCCI*, the Basle Committee concluded that while the principles of the Concordat 'are still viewed as being sound', it was time to acknowledge that 'there needs to be a greater effort to ensure that these principles can be applied in practice.'

---

[38] See e.g. 'BCCI: Silver Lining', *Economist*, 27 June 1998; 'Dead and Buried', *Economist* 15 Apr. 2000.

[39] Several full-length books have been written about the BCCI affair. See e.g. James R. Adams, *A Full Service Bank: How BCCI Stole Billions around the World* (1992); Jonathan Beaty, *The Outlaw Bank: A Wild Ride into the Secret Heart of BCCI* (1993); Peter Truell, *False Profits: The Inside Story of the World's Most Corrupt Bank* (1992). The most authoritative source, focused on the supervision (or lack of supervision) by the Bank of England, is the Bingham Report, *Inquiry into the Supervision of the Bank of Credit and Commerce International* (London: Oct. 1992).

[40] In April 1990, the Basle Committee, renamed the Committee on Banking Supervision, issued a Supplement to the Concordat designed to ensure exchange of adequate information between banking supervisory authorities. Again, the introduction stated that the recommendations were not designed as minimum legal requirements, but rather as 'statements of best practice which all members have undertaken to work towards implementing, according to means available to them.'

The principles were still not embodied in a formal agreement submitted to parliamentary approval and ratification, but they were now denominated as 'minimum standards . . . which G–10 supervisory authorities expect each other to observe.' The minimum standards were published in a seven-page communiqué released in July 1992:[41]

1. *All international banking groups should be supervised by a home-country author-ity that capably performs consolidated supervision.*

Evidently, this had not been true with respect to BCCI. Whether Luxembourg or England or the Cayman Islands was the true 'home coun-try' authority, plainly none of these countries had had clear responsibility, and none of their banking supervisory authorities had striven (at least until 1990) to fill the supervisory and information gaps.

2. *The creation of a cross-border banking establishment should receive the prior consent of both the host-country supervisory authority and the bank's and, if differ-ent, banking group's home-country supervisory authority.*

Again, this was consistent with the Concordat, but the requirement (if that word can be applied to the word 'should') of double approval was new. In *BCCI*, the Luxembourg authorities had not been concerned with the Cayman subsidiary (and vice versa), and the English authorities had not, it seems, looked in either direction with sufficient care. With some delay, all of the G–10 countries amended their laws to provide for double approval.

3. *Supervising authorities should possess the right to gather information from the cross-border banking establishments of the banks or banking groups for which they are the home country supervisor.*

This principle supplements the concept of double approval: each author-ity should have full information before giving its approval, and the flow of information should continue as long as continuing double approval is required, as set out in Principle 4. Without a bilateral understanding or exchange of information, the objective of continuing supervision with respect to both liquidity and solvency may well not be achievable.

4. *If a host-country authority determines that any one of the foregoing minimum standards is not met to its satisfaction that authority could impose restrictive mea-sures necessary to satisfy its prudential concerns consistent with these minimum standards, including the prohibition of the creation of banking establishments.*

The commentary makes clear that the suggestion of restricting a foreign bank's operations or prohibiting its activity completely is not only accept-able, but is necessary to give force to the other conditions. The host country authority is supposed to determine (i) whether the bank or banking group in

[41] *Minimum Standards for the Supervision of International Banking Goups and their Cross-Border Establishments* (July 1992), available from the Bank for International Settlements and on its web site.

question is chartered in a country with which it has an understanding about gathering and exchange of information; (ii) whether the home country has given its approval to the foreign operation; and (iii) whether the bank and the banking group (i.e. including a holding company) are supervised in the home country not only *de jure*, but by an agency that has the practical capability of performing consolidated supervision. If the answer to any of these questions is no—as was certainly the case with respect to BCCI, the host country 'should prevent the creation in its jurisdiction of any cross-border establishment by that bank or banking group.' However, the Basle Committee provided an alternative: if the host-country authority itself accepts the responsibility to perform supervision of the local establishments of the bank or banking group consistent with the Minimum Standards, then, 'in its sole discretion', it may do so.

Though the Basle Committee could not speak for all countries, it could speak to them, and it expressly communicated the Standards to bank supervisory authorities throughout the world and urged them to join with the G–10 authorities in adhering to the Minimum Standards.

Summary
As of year-end 2001, no failure of a major international bank had again occurred, comparable to the *Herstatt, Banco Ambrosiano,* or *BCCI* cases. If one could not safely say that no such case would ever occur again, a number of conclusions could safely be drawn:

— the belief that the jurisdiction of national banking authorities is limited by national frontiers is no longer valid;
— whatever purposes banking secrecy laws serve in attracting or protecting depositors at particular banks or in particular countries, they no longer justify refusal of banking authorities to share information with authorities in other states;
— the information to be shared concerns at least liquidity, solvency, exposure to particular borrowers, and country risk, and may also cover the reputation of managers and principal investors;
— for purposes of banking supervision, the distinction between branches and subsidiaries has lost much of its significance;[42] and
— at least the principal financial states are united in understanding that though interest rates, inflation rates, and the money supply may move in different directions and at different speeds in different countries, the failure of any substantial bank affects—and in some instances threatens—the entire international banking systems.

---

[42] Note, however, that in the United States under the Foreign Bank Supervision Enhancement Act of 1991, §214(a), 12 U.S.C. §3604(c), only banks covered by Federal Deposit Insurance may accept retail deposits (less than $100,000), and (apart from branches previously permitted to take out Federal Deposit Insurance) only separately incorporated subsidiaries are eligible for such insurance.

21.3   MORE INTERNATIONAL COORDINATION: CAPITAL
REQUIREMENTS FOR BANKS

(a)   Development of Capital Adequacy Standards[43]

By the mid-1980s, three only loosely related phenomena came together to worry bank regulators, initially in the United States and subsequently in the Basle Committee. *First*, the crisis of developing country debt, explored in Chapter 18 with focus on the debtor countries and the IMF, had also exposed weakness among the major (and some not so major) banks. Generally banks listed their 'assets', i.e. primarily outstanding loans, without distinction between, say, claims on the US Treasury and claims on a developing country borrower or a speculative real estate venture.

Second, many banks had only very thin capital cushions between their liabilities—principally deposits but also a variety of other obligations—and their assets, which might well be overstated in light of the shakiness of their debtors. Moreover, as banks all over the world competed against one another and against non-bank financial institutions, a low capital to asset ratio was viewed by some banks (notably in Japan) as a competitive advantage.[44] From the point of view of the supervisory authorities, however, inadequate capital was seen as a sign of danger, made very real by the experience of Herstatt, Ambrosiano, and also Continental Illinois, the seventh largest bank in the United States in 1984, which lost some $6 billion in deposits (including $2.5 billion booked in London) in a two-week run, amid rumours of its imminent collapse,[45] and which had to be bailed out by a massive infusion of capital partly from a consortium of other money-center American

---

[43] For a more detailed description of the background here described, see Ethan B. Kapstein, 'Supervising International Banks: Origins and Implications of the Basle Accord', *Princeton Essays in International Finance* No. 185 (1991); Raymond Vernon, Debora L. Spar, and Glenn Tobin, *Iron Triangles and Revolving Doors*, ch. 6. 'The International Capital Adequacy Agreement' (1991).

[44] The element of competition is return on capital, which can be illustrated by a simple illustration. Suppose Bank A and Bank B each have $100 million in assets and $1 million in earnings in a given period. Assume the same operating costs, but Bank A has a capital:asset ratio of 8 percent and B has a capital:asset ratio of 4 percent. A's return on capital is 12.5 percent, while B's return on capital is 25 percent. The comparison is meaningful, however, only if both the definition of capital and the classification of assets are substantially the same.

A counter-consideration to the focus on return on capital is that a bank with high capital:asset ratio may have better standing in the credit market than one with a minimal ratio, and may therefore be able to borrow at more favourable rates. See e.g. *Proceedings of Symposium on Risk-Based Capital Adequacy Guidelines*, Brooklyn Law School, 8 Oct. 1988, I–59–61.

[45] This was not the classic phenomenon of nervous depositors lining up around the block to preserve their hard-earned savings. Rather, the withdrawals were effected by electronic transfer, largely by foreign depositors who had been attracted to Continental Illinois by high interest rates but who could shift their funds with the touch of a computer keyboard.

banks, partly by the US Federal Reserve and the Federal Deposit Insurance Corporation.[46]

Third, banks were not only linked more closely than ever before by the interbank market (i.e. short-term borrowing by Bank *A* from Bank *B* or *C* so that *A* could take advantage of a loan or investment opportunity and *B* or *C* could earn interest on temporarily idle funds); more and more banks had moved beyond their traditional role of taking deposits and making loans to dealing—for their own account as well as for their customers—in a variety of innovative 'financial products'. These deals produced substantial revenue—close to half of the profits of some banks—but also entailed risks not only to the individual parties, but possibly to the interconnected system as a whole.

When US government officials attempted to secure approval by Congress for the Eighth General Quota increase for the IMF due to go into effect in November 1983, they ran into substantial difficulty. Numerous influential members of Congress viewed the proposal to increase the resources of the IMF as in effect a 'bail-out' for the big banks that had made imprudent loans to Mexico, Brazil, and the other developing countries no longer able to meet their obligations.[47] In return for approving the American contribution to the Fund's quota increase, Congress demanded a program for improved supervision and regulation of international lending.[48] The US regulators came back with a five-point program for increased supervision of international activity of US-based banks.[49] The American banks responded that any new regulations unilaterally imposed by the US government would result in

[46] An important aspect of the Continental Illinois rescue effort was that while the shareholders were essentially wiped out, depositors were protected, without the $100,000 limit nominally placed on FDIC insurance, and without distinction between domestic and foreign deposits. The Continental Illinois case came to be viewed as confirmation of the 'Too Big to Fail' principle of US bank regulation. For detailed accounts of the Continental Illinois collapse and rescue, see Hilary Foulkes, 'The Federal Deposit Insurance Corporation; The Rescue of Continental Illinois National Bank and Trust Company', 1985 *Annual Survey of Amer. Law* 137; Irving H. Sprague, *Bailout: An Insider's Account of Bank Failures and Rescues*, 149–228 (1986). Mr. Sprague was for many years a member of the three-person board of the FDIC and for several years its chairman.

[47] For some flavour of the debates in Congress, see A. Lowenfeld, *The International Monetary System*, 157–61 (2nd edn. 1984).

[48] See e.g. the following remarks of Senator Garn, Chairman of the Senate Banking Committee, to the Chairman of the Federal Reserve, the Comptroller of the Currency and the Chairman of the Federal Deposit Insurance Corporation:

The price of $8.4 billion increase [in the U.S. quota in the IMF] in the Congress is going to be legislation . . . so [we] can go home and say we didn't bail out those big banks and we're helping international trade and all that, but we are asking that they don't do it again.

Proposed Solutions to International Debt Problems: Hearings before Sen. Comm. on Banking, Housing and Urban Affairs, 98th Cong., 1st Sess., 95 (11 Apr. 1983), cited also by Kapstein (n. 43 supra), 12.

[49] See *International Bank Lending*, Hearings before House Comm. on Banking, Finance and Urban Affairs, 98th Cong., 1st Sess., 233–61 (1983).

decreased international lending, and in a loss of competitiveness vis-à-vis foreign banks and non-bank financial institutions.[50]

Eventually Congress added a new chapter to the legislation to approve the Fund quota increase, entitled the International Lending Supervision Act of 1983.[51] In its Declaration of Policy, Congress called for 'strengthening the bank regulatory framework . . . and enhancing . . . international coordination among bank regulatory authorities.'[52] Further, it provided that:

The Federal banking agencies shall consult with the banking supervisory authorities of other countries to reach understandings aimed at achieving effective and consistent supervisory policies with respect to international lending.[53]

In particular, the banks were to be required to collect and report, at least quarterly, 'information regarding material foreign country exposure in relation to assets and to capital;'[54] and the federal agencies were authorized and directed to establish minimum levels of capital for each banking institution. If a bank failed to comply with minimum capital requirements set for it, that might be deemed by the appropriate federal agency to constitute 'an unsafe and unsound practice within the meaning of the Federal Deposit Insurance Act, subject to various measures of enforcement.'[55]

In accordance with the instructions from Congress, the United States presented a request for development of coordinated capital standards to the Basle Committee in 1984. Without committing itself to any coordinated strategy, the Basle Committee began by designing a 'framework' to enable the regulators to compare their national definitions, statistics, and requirements.

It turned out that the member countries of the Basle Committee had very different approaches to the problem of capital adequacy. In the United States, banks were supposed to maintain a capital:asset ratio of 5.50 percent, without any distinction as to the type or quality of assets, so long as they appeared on the balance sheet.[56] Off-balance sheet items were not counted at all. In Belgium, France, and Great Britain, by contrast, sophisticated capital adequacy standards had been developed, under which the riskier a bank's asset portfolio appeared, the more capital it was required to hold. In most instances, application of these standards was made on an ad hoc basis, i.e. bank by bank, a method of supervision evidently impossible for the United States, with 14,000 banks.

---

[50] Id., p. 183.
[51] Pub. L. 98–181, 97 Stat. 1153, Title IX (30 Nov. 1983), codified at 12 U.S.C. §3901–3913. The relevant sections are reproduced in A. Lowenfeld (n. 47 supra), DS–369–78.
[52] Id., §902(a)(2), 12 U.S.C. §3901(a)(2).
[53] Id., §902(b), 12 U.S.C. §3901(b). For an analysis of this legislation, see Cynthia C. Lichtenstein, 'The US Response to the International Lending Supervision Act of 1983', 25 *Va. J. Int'l Law* 401 (1985).
[54] Id., §907(b), 12 U.S.C. §3906(b).   [55] Id., §908(b), 12 U.S.C. §3907(b).
[56] Capital was defined as shareholders' equity plus loan loss reserves.

Early in 1986, the Federal Reserve Board and the other US bank regulators issued for public comment a proposal for evaluating bank assets according to riskiness.[57] American banks protested, arguing that implementing the proposal would further undermine their ability to compete in the international market.

One way to have met this argument would have been to seek agreement on common standards in the Basle Committee, a strategy eventually followed. First, however, the American regulators approached the Bank of England, which quickly accepted the idea of a bilateral agreement on the subject. By January 1987 a joint US–UK proposal was released for comment, containing an agreed definition of capital, a risk-weighted system for evaluating capital adequacy, and a method for including off-balance sheet commitments in the evaluation. No minimum level of capital was stated at this time, though it was understood that the foundation for such a requirement was being laid.[58] Again, American banks were dissatisfied, pointing out that the US-British accord had left out numerous other important financial centers, notably Japan, which was the home base of seven of the world's ten biggest banks, many of which were acquiring banks in the United States. On the other side, Britain was accused by the European Community of once again not living up to its commitments to Europe, and the Basle Committee, chaired by an Englishman, was concerned that it might lapse into irrelevance. The American and British negotiators responded first by negotiating an agreement with Japan.[59] Once the bilateral accord had become trilateral in the summer of 1987, it was essentially unstoppable. Negotiations resumed in the Basle Committee, and by year-end 1987 that group was ready to issue its Proposals for International Convergency of Capital Measurement and Capital Standards' in preliminary form, with a six-month deadline for comments. The final version of what came to be known as the Basle Accord was published in July 1988. Each member country would be responsible for adopting and enforcing the necessary legislation or regulations, subject to

[57] Federal Reserve Board, 'Capital Maintenance: Supplemental Adjusted Capital Measure', 51 Fed. Reg. 3976 (31 Jan. 1986); US Comptroller of the Currency, 'Minimum Capital Ratios: Risk-Based Capital for National Banks', 51 Fed. Reg. 10602 (27 Mar. 1986).

[58] See *Risk-Based Capital Requirements for Banks and Bank Holding Companies*, Hearing before Subcomm. on General Oversight and Investigations of Sen. Comm. on Banking, Finance and Urban Affairs, 100th Cong., 1st Sess. (30 Apr. 1987) with testimony by Chairman Paul Volcker of the Federal Reserve and the complete text of the US–UK Agreed Proposal. Volcker's prepared statement appears also in 73 *Fed. Reserve Bull.* 435 (June 1987).

[59] A particular problem for Japanese regulators was how to account for 'hidden reserves' held by Japanese banks, in the form of large unrealized capital gains on corporate securities and real estate. The banks contended that these holdings could be sold if the need arose, and thus performed the function of bank capital. The American and British regulators objected to permission to create 'revaluation reserves', because their banks were not permitted to count similar gains as capital under existing rules, and also because their banks held a far smaller proportion of their assets in equity investments. Eventually a compromise was worked out that permitted Japanese banks to count 45 percent of unrealized gains as part of capital for purposes of the capital adequacy rules.

phasing in the various requirements by the end of each bank's fiscal year 1992. Ultimately, over 100 countries adopted the approach of the Basle Accord.

(b) The Basle Capital Adequacy Accord (1988)

(i) *Defining Capital.* The Basle Accord proceeds on the assumption—not shared by everyone—that there is a direct relation between the soundness of banks and their capital base.[60] Bank capital provides assurance to depositors, and it serves to absorb unexpected losses. Just what constitutes capital, however, is not self-evident, and indeed this question, more than the issue of risk assessment, proved to be the most contentious issue between the regulators and the banks, and among the regulators, in the negotiations leading to the Accord. Shareholders' common stock is clearly capital, and so is paid-in capital surplus; but what about preferred stock, which has some aspects of equity, but also some aspects of fixed obligations? Should a bank's holdings of investments in subsidiaries—whether bank or non-bank—be characterized as capital, or as assets? And if the function of capital is to protect against unanticipated losses, do reserves meet the definition?

The solution, reached first in the bilateral agreement between the US Federal Reserve and the Bank of England and ultimately by the Basle Committee, was to split the definition of capital in two. Primary or Tier 1 capital, on which everyone could agree, must make up at least half of total capital; other accounts, on whose classification reasonable persons could differ, may make up the other half, or Tier 2 capital, with some subdivisions in the maximum components. Tier 2 capital is not permitted to exceed Tier 1 capital. Skipping over transitional targets, the Basle Accord stated that as of year-end 1992 each bank's capital:asset ratio must be at least 8 percent, of which at least half, i.e. 4 percent of assets, must be primary or Tier 1 capital.[61]

The fundamental component of primary or core capital is shareholders' equity in common stock in the bank (or bank holding company). In addition, disclosed (as contrasted to hidden) general reserves created or increased out of income or retained earnings may be included, but not

[60] The basic assumption seems persuasive, as it was to the regulators assembled in the Basle Committee. The doubt arises because not all bank failures were associated with low capital:asset ratios; Continental Illinois, for instance, had relatively high capital in comparison to stated assets, but its assets were of poor quality and its liabilities included an excessive amount of purchased deposits that were quickly withdrawn once adverse reports began to circulate. The Basle Accord, as discussed below, addresses the quality of assets; it does not address the quality of liabilities.

[61] In Septemeber 1993, a statement was issued confirming that all the banks in the G–10 countries with material intrnational banking business were meeting the minimum capital requirements of the 1988 Accord. It seems that as the result of the 'real estate bubble' and other credit problems in Japan in the 1990s, many Japanese banks may not have remained in compliance in subsequent years.

reserves created to meet special vulnerability in assets, for example special reserves for developing country debt, which are placed in Tier 2.[62] Perpetual non-cumulative preferred stock may be included, on the theory that dividends on such stock are subordinate to deposits and general debt obligations, and that such dividends may be omitted without constituting default. Cumulative preferred stock, which provides that dividends may be deferred but must be made up, does not meet the standards of core capital, and accordingly is assigned to Tier 2.[63]

Tier 2 or supplemental capital includes various accounts that had been counted as capital in some but not all the participating countries. In addition to the two items described above, Tier 2 capital may include such hybrids as perpetual debt, mandatory convertible securities, and similar instruments reflecting contributions to the funds of the bank but no security interest, and no rights to redemption at the initiative of the holder. These instruments are not core capital, because they carry an obligation to pay interest which may be deferred but not permanently reduced or waived, but they are supplementary capital because the holders have paid for them and the amounts received are available to cover losses without requiring the issuer to cease trading.[64]

One issue that was much debated was how to treat 'goodwill' resulting from acquisitions, i.e. amounts paid by the reporting bank in excess of the book value of an acquired bank. In the end it was decided that goodwill should be deducted from Tier 1 capital. Holding by banks of capital issued by other banks has the potential for spreading one institution's problem throughout the system, and serious consideration was given to requiring that such holdings be deducted from capital. However, because of the insistence of Japan, where cross-holdings are common, it was decided that individual country regulators would have discretion whether to order deduction of holdings in other banks from capital.[65]

(ii) *Defining Assets: The Balance Sheet.* The definition of capital, as described above, yields the numerator, i.e. the minimum 8 percent in the agreed capital:asset ratio. The denominator has two principal components:

---

[62] Such reserves, reflecting lower valuation of assets or losses not identified on the balance sheet, are limited to 1.25 percent of weighted assets.

[63] For bank holding companies (but not for banks), the US Federal Reserve permits such stock to be counted up to 25 percent of Tier 1 capital.

[64] A variety of hybrid instruments exists in different countries, including 'long-term preferred stock' in Canada, 'perpetual subordinated debt' in the United States and Great Britain, 'titres particips' and 'titres subordonnés à dureé indetermineé' in France, and 'Genussscheine' in Germany; see Basle Accord, Annex I, para. D (ii)(d).

[65] The US Federal Reserve and Comptroller of the Currency exercised their discretion to deduct cross-holdings from capital. See 12 C.F.R. Part 208 Appendix A para. II(B)(2) (state chartered banks); Part 225, Appendix A, para. II(B)(2) (bank holding companies); 12 C.F.R. Part 3, Appendix A, sect. 2(c)(3).

The Federal Reserve's thinking about this and other issues is set out at length in 'Final Risk-Based Capital Guidelines', 54 Fed. Reg. 4186–221 (27 Jan. 1989).

balance sheet assets, i.e. claims held by banks, classified according to their riskiness by major categories, and off-balance sheet items notionally converted to assets and also classified by riskiness. Wholly risk-free assets, such as cash, require no capital cushion, and accordingly are left out of the capital:asset standards. Other assets are assigned various weights, increasing according to the level of riskiness.

> For those not trained in banking or accounting, the analysis takes some getting used to. When a bank accepts a deposit, that becomes a liability; when it makes a loan, that is recorded as an asset. A loan of $1,000 to a wholly creditworthy borrower is worth $1,000; a loan of $1,000 to, say, an overburdened developing country is also listed as a $1,000 asset, but a special 30 percent reserve might have been credited against it, to leave a net asset of $700. A $1,000 loan on which interest (or amortization) was overdue might have been classified as non-performing, and written down on the asset side of the balance sheet, say to $500, with a corresponding debit to current income or retained earnings. The capital adequacy project that culminated in the Basle Accord focused on loans between these extremes, i.e. on loans that were not wholly risk-free but had not been subjected to a special reserve or written down as non-performing.

The Basle Accord uses five weights for purposes of establishing the asset total in the minimum capital:asset ratio of banks—0, 10 percent, 20 percent, 50 percent, and 100 percent. The face amount of each item on a bank's balance sheet is to be multiplied by one of these factors to determine its amount on the list of assets against which capital is to be maintained. In concept, only credit risk, i.e. default or failure of the counterparty, is supposed to be reflected in the weights or factors specified in the Basle Accord, not interest rate risk or exchange rate risk or other considerations that an individual investor might look at.[66] In fact, by making distinctions between OECD and non-OECD borrowers, transfer or exchange risk is addressed at least indirectly.

The Basle Committee came up with some twenty categories of balance sheet assets. Table 21.1 (following) illustrates a sample of the weights and the method of arriving at the asset total for purposes of the capital adequacy standards. As the table shows, at the same time as the nominal capital requirement (the numerator) was raised for most participating countries, the asset base against which capital must be held (the denominator) was reduced, to the extent that the bank in question holds cash, treasury bills, or other assets considered to bear no (or less than ordinary) risk.[67] However,

---

[66] Individual regulators in participating countries can, however, take other risks into account, for example by restricting the amounts to be lent to a single borrower or a single country.

[67] There was some discussion whether the relevant dates should be quarterly averages or end-of-period figures. The Basle Accord generally uses the latter, on the theory that averaging would add another burden to an already difficult process of measuring and reporting.

other items not previously included in the calculations were added to the asset side, as described below.

Table 21.1

Type of Asset	Face amount as shown on balance sheet	Risk weight %	Adjusted amount
(1) Cash (domestic or foreign)	1,000	0	0
(2) Claims on national central bank	1,600	0	0
(3) Claims on other OECD gov't or central bank	1,200	0	0
(4) Short-term claims on non-OECD banks	4,000	20	800
(5) General obligations of local governments of OECD countries	2,500	20	500
(6) Loans secured by residential mortgages owned by borrower or rented	5,000	50	2,500
(7) Claims on non-OECD banks with residual maturity over one year	20,000	100	20,000
(8) Claims on commercial firms owned by a gov't	12,000	100	12,000
(9) Loans to and other claims on private firms wherever located	15,000	100	15,000
(10) Real estate and other investments (including investments in other companies unless consolidated)	8,000	100	8,000
(11) Premises, plant, and equipment, other fixed assets	14,000	100	14,000
(12) All other assets	5,000	100	5,000
Total as shown on balance sheet	$89,300	Total to be used for capital adequacy purposes	$77,800

(iii) *Defining Assets: Items not on the Balance Sheet.* Perhaps the most difficult part of evaluating the risk exposure of banks is how to measure so-called off-balance sheet items. To one not accustomed to bank accounting, it may appear strange that a significant portion of banks' activities are not reflected on their balance sheet. In fact, however, a major—and increasing—share of the activity and revenue of banks has come not from the spread between interest paid on deposits and interest received on loans, but from fees received for undertaking contingent liabilities—guarantees of third-party obligations (including performance bonds, stand-by letters of credit, and sales of assets with recourse), plus dealing for their own account in new 'products' such as options and futures contracts on exchange rates, interest rates, and stock or commodity exchange indices, and 'swaps' of various kinds.[68]

Banks do, of course, keep records of these and similar transactions. What all these transactions have in common is that they usually do not involve acquisition by banks of the kinds of claims that appear on the asset side of balance sheets.[69] They also have in common that they involve some element of risk. Added together, the risks incurred in off-balance sheet activities can affect the soundness of a bank in the same way that a loan to an uncreditworthy borrower can. Both kinds of risks, as the regulators came to see, call for a cushion to absorb possible losses, i.e. for an appropriate amount of capital. After some years of discussion, the bank regulators constituting the Basle Committee concluded that they should analyse off-balance sheet risks separately, and convert them into assumed loan equivalents by use of stated credit conversion factors. The sums thus arrived at could be listed on the asset side of the capital:asset ratios, even though what is measured is really a series of contingent liabilities.

Direct credit substitutes, such as loan guarantees and stand-by letters of credit serving as financial guarantees for loans and securities, are to be converted at 100 percent; certain *transactions-related contingent obligations*, such as performance bonds, bid bonds, warranties, and stand-by letters of credit related to particular non-financial transactions, are to be converted at 50 percent; and *short-term self-liquidating trade-related contingencies*, such as documentary letters of credit in which the issuing bank takes a security interest in the goods being shipped, are converted at 20 percent. The thinking (and experience) is that counterparties give higher priorities to obligations of this type so that they can stay in business, and thus that the credit risk is lower than with respect to loans or loan guarantees. *Commitments* by banks, such as note issuance and revolving underwriting facilities, and undrawn lines of credit with a maturity of more than one year, are assigned a 50 percent credit conversion factor. Similar commitments of less than a year are given a zero conversion factor. After the conversion to credit equivalent is made, a further weighing is required according to the nature of the counterparty, as under the scheme for on-balance sheet assets.

[68] For a simplified explanation of swaps, see n. 70 infra.
[69] In many cases, the transaction appears as notes to financial statements, or in a separate listing of contingent obligations.

There was a good deal of disagreement among the regulators about how to treat foreign exchange and interest rate-related contingencies, such as those undertaken in the many varieties of futures contracts, options, and swaps, each of which involves both a market exposure and a risk of default of the counterparty.[70] The focus of the Basle Accord with respect to these contracts is not on their face amount, but generally on the cost of replacement of the cash flow if the counterparty defaults, plus an 'add-on' to reflect market risk. The regulators could not agree on a single method of translating the banks' experience, and accordingly two methods are permitted—a mark-to-market method adopted by most countries, including the United States and the United Kingdom, and an original exposure method, simpler to apply but requiring higher conversion factors. Since movement in exchange rates is more volatile than movement in interest rates, the conversion factors for exchange rates contracts are significantly higher—1 percent for contracts of one year or less, 5 percent for contracts of more than one year—than for interest rates contracts—zero and 1 percent respectively.[71] Thus translation of a bank's exposure for purposes of complying with the capital:asset requirements might look as shown in Table 21.2.

TABLE 21.2   Potential exposure

Type of contract	Notional principal	×	Conversion factor	=	Potential exposure	+	Replacement cost	=	Credit equivalent
(1) 120-day forward foreign exchange	$5,000,000		0.01		$50,000		$100,000		$150,000
(2) 3-year single currency fixed/floating interest rate swap	$10,000,000		0.005		$50,000		$200,000		$250,000

[70] Explanation of the many kinds of innovative financial products is well beyond the scope of this volume. A description of a simple interest rate swap (known in the trade as 'plain vanilla') may be useful, however, and may serve to illustrate the problems faced by banking regulators in trying to set down common standards for assessing the soundness of banks:

Bank A and Bank B arrange to exchange interest payments from two loans of equal face value and equal credit risk. The loan made by A and transferred to B is made at a fixed rate—say 8 percent; the loan made by B and transferred to A is made at a variable rate—say at 1.5 percent over the New York prime rate, which stands at 6.5 percent when the swap is entered into. If on the settlement date the prime rate has risen to 7 percent, A, which acquired the variable rate loan, has come out ahead; if the prime rate has fallen to 6 percent, B has come out ahead.

In fact, the loans would not actually be transferred; the transaction merely involved hypothetical transfer of the interest income, with settlement as above.

[71] These figures reflect the mark-to-market method; for the alternative original exposure method, the figures are as follows: *cont./*

The resulting sums—$150,000 in the first illustration, $250,000 in the second illustration—are then to be added to the asset total against which the capital requirement is computed.

In 1995 the Basle Committee issued an amendment to the 1988 Accord to take account of off-balance sheet activities of banks—in particular with respect to the issue of *'netting'* in connection with the options, futures, and swaps that keep burgeoning.[72]

(c) A Look Ahead

1. *Revising the Capital Adequacy Accord*[73]

In the first decade of its effectiveness, the Basle Capital Adequacy Accord of 1988 had worked fairly smoothly. The common standards for maintenance of capital had reduced the competitive advantages or disadvantages among banks based in the countries that were following the Basle Accord, and thus had reduced incentives for a 'race to the bottom'. Further, in each participating state, assessment of the risks undertaken by banks and classification of their capital are now made on a more sophisticated basis than was true previously. Also, by removing low-risk holdings from the requirement to hold corresponding capital, the Basle Accord and national implementing regulations removed prior disincentives to holding low-risk assets. However, in the interim changes in financial markets, including growth of secondary markets in which credit risk can be traded, to some extent overtook the basic credit risk measurement scheme on which the 1988 Accord was built.

For one thing, major international banks came to securitize their loan portfolios, by selling credit risk in the secondary market. A variety of credit derivatives were developed, under which third parties—neither lenders nor borrowers—can trade counterparty risks and enable banks to fine-tune credit exposure that they retain or lay off.

For another, the experience in crisis countries—South-east Asia, Brazil, and Russia among others[74]—showed that the indicative power of the capital

Maturity	Interest rate contracts (%)	Exchange rate contracts (%)
Less than one year	0.5	2.0
1—2 years	1.0	5.05
For each additional year	1.0	3.0

[72] Netting refers to the amalgamation and substitution of separate swap, foreign exchange, or other payments due on specified dates or on termination into a single obligation of a given counterparty. The problem would be faced most critically in the event that one counterparty might become insolvent and that under the bankruptcy or similar laws applicable to that party, netting might not be permitted, i.e. that 'in the money' or favourable contracts might be taken into the bankrupt estate but that other, unfavourable contracts would be disallowed or thrown into the category of unsecured claims.

[73] For a brief explanation on which this note draws heavily see Jan van der Vassen, 'Basel Committee presents proposals for new capital adequacy standards.' 30 *IMF Survey*, 37 (5 Feb. 2001).

[74] See Ch. 18.

adequacy ratio in those countries, as well as to some extent among outside lenders to those countries, was largely illusory. Banks could show adequate capital to asset ratios and, at the time of crisis, be in serious trouble.

Accordingly, in June 1999, the Basle Committee on Banking Supervision issued a set of proposals based on three 'pillars', designed to build on and eventually replace the 1988 Capital Accord.

Pillar I is intended to link capital requirements more closely to actual risks; Pillar II is designed to strengthen the supervision process for enforcing capital standards; and Pillar III is designed to enhance the effectiveness of market discipline through uniform requirements for disclosure by banks.

Pillar I moves from the relatively rigid categories of risk, as illustrated in Table 21.1 to more precisely evaluated risk categories and the corresponding capital requirements. The risk to capital requirement may be higher or lower as compared to the 1988 categories. For instance, whereas under the 1988 Accord the maximum credit risk capital requirement was 8 percent of the face amount of the loan, i.e. a 100 percent risk weight, under the new proposal a borrower with a poor credit standing might be assigned a risk weight of 12 percent, i.e. a risk weight of 150 percent, so that a loan of $5 million would call for capital in the lender's portfolio of $600,000. On the opposite end, a high-quality corporate borrower might be assigned a risk weight as low as 1.6 percent, so that the same $5 million loan would call for capital in the lender's portfolio of only $80,000.

The risk assessment could be made by standard third-party rating agencies, or by sophisticated banks themselves through an internal ratings based (IRB) risk management system, when approved by the bank supervisors. For sovereign borrowers, the new proposals abandon the distinction between OECD and non-OECD countries. Under the new proposals, sovereign borrowers would be assigned risk weights in the same way as other borrowers, so that some non-OECD borrowers—say Kuwait or Saudi Arabia—would be assigned low risk or no risk weights, while loans to weakly rated OECD members could call for higher capital requirements.[75] Banks themselves, as borrowers, would be assigned risk weights, which might be linked to the sovereign risk rating of the country in which they are based, so that, for instance a sound bank in a weak country, e.g. Thailand or Philippines, would be assigned a higher risk weight than a bank with a comparable balance sheet in a low-risk country.

Pillar II, as noted above, focuses on the supervisory process, and is thus directly linked to the Concordat and the Core Principles described in Section 21.2. Supervisors are to look out for the risk profiles of the banks under their care, and for the banks' strategies to maintain capital at the appropriate level. If they find weaknesses in a bank's capital plan, the supervisors are

---

[75] Note that Mexico joined the OECD in 1994, shortly before its peso crisis, and South Korea joined in 1996, shortly before it became caught up in the South-east Asia crisis.

supposed to take action. Moreover, supervisors are to be authorized to require capital levels above the internationally agreed minimum, and to intervene before capital falls below the minimum.

Pillar III focuses on disclosure by banks, including detailed information on controlling entities (e.g. group holding companies), minority interests, provisions for loan losses, and the composition of capital, as well as detailed information on credit exposures, including geographic breakdowns, sectoral breakdowns, volume of impaired loans by area and sector, credit risk techniques and strategies, and market risk management.

Since the new proposals call for a good deal of sophistication on the part both of bank managers and of regulators, many countries will need help in understanding the new accord, and the IMF is prepared to offer technical assistance.[76] Correspondingly, the information gathered concerning implementation of the new Basle Accord will be used by the IMF in its periodic consultations under Article IV as well in its broader 'Financial Sector Assessment Program' conducted jointly with the World Bank.[77]

The Basle Committee recceived more than 250 comments on its proposals for fundamental revision of the 1988 Capital Accord, and it postponed more than once its target for putting revised accord into effect. According to a year-end 2001 press release, a final draft was to be completed in 2002, with a view to implementation in 2005.[78]

2. *Beyond Banks*

In the closing decades of the twentieth century, the activities of banks and securities firms increasingly overlapped, and the 'wall of separation', as it was called in the United States, slowly crumbled, even in countries, such as the United States and Japan, which had long maintained strict distinctions between the permitted activities, as well as the regulatory framework, of the two types of financial institutions. In a variety of ways securities firms based in one country compete with securities firms based in another, and also compete with banks, foreign and domestic. The basic assets of securities firms, i.e. shares of stocks and bonds, are liquid and usually marked to market, whereas the basic assets of banks, i.e. loans, tend to be held to maturity and recorded at face value without reflecting market fluctuations. Both securities firms and banks, however, operate under minimum capital requirements in most countries.[79]

---

[76] See van der Vassen, n. 73 supra. The author is an officeer of the IMF in the Monetary and Exchange Affairs Department.

[77] See *IMF Annual Report 2001* pp. 24–5.

[78] *Progress towards Completion of the New Basel Capital Accord*, BIS Press Release 13 Dec. 2001.

[79] It is also true, as a first generalization, that in concept securities regulators see their primary mission as protecting investors, while banking supervisors focus primarily on the soundness of the banking system. This generalization also breaks down to some extent on closer scrutiny.

In 1989, shortly after issuance of the Basle Committee's Report on Capital Adequacy, the Technical Committee of the International Organization of Securities Commissions (IOSCO) issued an Initial Report on Capital Adequacy Standards for Securities Firms, looking to harmonize standards for capital maintenance, both within the securities industry around the world and, if possible, with the banking industry.[80] Two years later, as the members of IOSCO were approaching consensus among themselves but before an international understanding had been reached among them, the Technical Committee of IOSCO, chaired at the time by the chairman of the United States Securities and Exchange Commission, issued a Memorandum suggesting cooperation with the Basle Committee on Banking Supervision.[81] In January 1992 the IOSCO Technical Committee and the Basle Committee held a joint meeting of principals, reflecting, as the press release put it, 'both ongoing internationalization of global capital markets and the similarity of market risks undertaken by both banks and securities firms.'[82]

As of the turn of the century, discussions among securities regulators and between them and the banking regulators continued, but the anticipation of prompt agreement had not been fulfilled, at least in part because American securities regulators were concerned that such agreement would weaken the standards imposed on US-based securities houses. Over time, however, one may expect some kind of further international rule-making, reflecting consensus among securities regulators and between securities regulators and banking supervisors, even as the industries for which they are responsible overlap more and more.[83]

SUMMARY

Fully understanding all the details of the regulation of capital adequacy calls for a sub-subspecialty including knowledge of banking practice, accounting, mathematics, and law, plus experience not yet available as this volume went to press. In concept, however, the development of this new

---

[80] International Organization of Securities Commissions, *Capital Adequacy Standards for Securities Firms* (1989).

[81] Memorandum from IOSCO's Technical Basle Committee on Banking Supervision (Sept. 1991).

[82] Joint Statement by Richard C. Breeden, Chairman, Technical Committee, IOSCO, and E. Gerald Corrigan, Chairman Basle Committee on Banking Supervision, 29 Jan. 1992. For a detailed history and analysis, see Nancy Worth, 'Harmonizing Capital Adequacy Rules for International Banks and Securities Firms', 18 *N.C. Journal of Int'l Law and Commercial Regulation* 133 (1992).

In addition to the Basle Committee and IOSCO, the International Association of Insurance Supervisors (IAIS) has participated since 1996 in a Tripartite Joint Forum on Financial Conglomerates.

[83] See, for more details and source material, Klaus Peter Follak, 'International Harmonization of Regulatory and Supervisory Frameworks', in Mario Giovanoli (ed.), *International Monetary Law* (2000).

branch of international monetary law is comprehensible and significant, in several respects. Having decided in the Basle Concordat and its amendments and supplements to coordinate regulation of banks engaged in international activity, the Basle Committee on Banking Supervision has moved to creation of an analytical and apparently objective framework plus detailed criteria for measuring the soundness of banks, to be employed both by parent country and by host country supervisors in the twelve countries, as well as by other countries that may choose to emulate the criteria in order to gain full international acceptance for their banks. All covered banks must now hold capital equal at least to 8 percent of assets as defined; half of this capital must be primary or core capital—essentially shareholders' equity and close equivalents. Assets for the purpose of the capital:asset ratio on the one hand exclude the holdings deemed to bear no risk, such as cash, but on the other hand include items not previously recorded on the balance sheets, but which entail risk exposure on the part of banks, measured by complex but agreed conversion techniques.

Overall, there is broad consensus not only on the technique of measuring and classifying both elements in the capital:asset ratio, but on the purpose of maintaining an agreed ratio for banks based on operating in all the principal financial centers. As individual bank failures have had repercussions throughout the system, the regulatory consensus is directed to safeguarding the international banking system as a whole, by giving tools and mandates to national regulators to look after the banks for which they are responsible according to common standards.

While the Basle accords—the Concordat as well as the Capital Adequacy Accord—are not treaties in the sense that they are to be submitted to parliaments for ratification and that failure to comply with their provisions rises to the level of violation of international law, they clearly constitute coordinated law-making in the international arena. If a bank from one member country operates, or hopes to operate, in another member country, performance both by that bank and by the relevant supervisory authorities under the Capital Adequacy Accord will need to be disclosed and weighed under the Concordat. Thus the Basle accords are more than 'soft law'; they reflect mutual commitments made after intense negotiations, and taken together, they contain both incentives for compliance and at least the suggestion of meaningful sanctions for non-compliance.

PART VIII

Economic Controls for Political Ends

INTRODUCTION

Economic sanctions have had mixed acceptability in the international community. In the 1930s, the League of Nations sought to respond to Italy's attack against Ethiopia by imposing a partial trade embargo, but the embargo was so poorly observed that instead of restraining Italy or its Axis partners, the sanctions effort more than any other episode served to discredit the League itself.[1] Notwithstanding this experience, the drafters of the United Nations Charter made express provision for collective economic sanctions, when authorized by decision of the Security Council following a finding of existence of a threat or breach of international peace (Arts. 39–41).[2] The Inter-American Treaty of Reciprocal Assistance of 1947 (the Rio Treaty) contains a similar provision, authorizing measures short of force, including partial or complete interruption of economic relations (Arts. 6 and 8).[3] Thus mandatory sanctions imposed by an organization pursuant to specific findings involving danger to international peace and security are clearly authorized by international law, and indeed a decision to impose such sanctions is binding on all member states.[4] In fact, economic sanctions in the period since World War II have taken a variety of different forms— collective non-mandatory sanctions (for example against South Africa); sanctions imposed by groups of states against a non-member state and those who trade with that state (for example the boycott of Israel sponsored by the League of Arab States); and unilateral sanctions of various kinds, from total embargoes to selective controls on exports, blocking of assets, withdrawal of normal tariff rates, and withdrawal of special benefits such as trade preferences or foreign assistance—all undertaken at one time or another by the United States, and to a lesser extent by other states.

This Part sets out some norms with respect to economic sanctions, where possible on the basis of international agreements and common practice of states. However, in many ways economic sanctions have developed beyond the standard sources of international law, and the following chapters offer legal analysis, and to some extent normative conclusions, even where universal consensus cannot be demonstrated.

---

[1] The sanctions effort against Italy, led by Great Britain was from the outset ambivalent. Winston Churchill, who was not in the government at the time, wrote in the *Evening Standard*, 26 June 1936:

> First, the Prime Minister had declared that sanctions meant war; secondly, he was resolved that there must be no war; and thirdly, he decided upon sanctions. It was evidently impossible to comply with these three conditions.

Quoted in *International Sanctions*, A Report by a Group of Members of the Royal Institute of International Affairs, 204, n. 7 (1938). Churchill himself repeats this observation in *The Gathering Storm*, p. 175 (1948).

[2] See Sect. 22.1.   [3] See Sect. 22.8.

[4] See UN Charter Art. 25; also Sect. 22.4 infra.

THE QUESTION OF DEFINITION

The term 'economic sanction' is used here to define measures of an economic—as contrasted with diplomatic or military—character taken by states to express disapproval of the acts of the target state or to induce that state to change some policy or practice or even its governmental structure. While the line of demarcation is not always sharp and sometimes motives are mixed,[5] economic sanctions generally are measures taken not for economic gain, and often at commercial sacrifice on the part of the state engaged in a program of denial.[6] A measure of retaliation in a trade dispute—whether or not consistent with the GATT or other international economic agreement—is not within the definition of economic sanctions to which this Part is addressed. Withdrawal or suspension of drawing rights or voting rights in the International Monetary Fund is also excluded from this Part, on the ground that such actions, even though in some sense fit the present definition, are better discussed in Part VII. Denial of economic benefits in response to acts such as expropriation of foreign investments may be regarded as having characteristics both of economic sanctions as here defined and of trade disputes, but are more usefully discussed in connection with protection of foreign investment.[7]

The definition here adopted rejects the view that by depriving state *B* of something that *B* is not entitled to, state *A* is not imposing any kind of sanction.[8] It is clear, for instance, that no state is obligated to provide development assistance to another state.[9] Even if *A* is a developed and *B* a developing state, *A* has no duty to establish a foreign assistance program, or if it has such a program, to include *B* within it. Nevertheless, if state *A* terminates an existing program of assistance to state *B* because *B* has voted against *A* on an important issue in the United Nations, or has joined a cartel adverse to *A*'s interests, or has committed abuses of human rights against

---

[5] For instance, among the strongest proponents of continued sanctions by the United States against Iran in the 1980s were domestic growers of pistachios, one of Iran's important export crops.

[6] Compare A. Lowenfeld, *Trade Controls for Political Ends* (2nd edn. 1983), which deals not only with sanctions, but makes the point that certain types of economic relations, such as those between the United States and the Soviet Union in the period 1945–91, are different in character, and in their legal underpinnings, from relations among say, the United States and Canada, or Japan and the European Community.

[7] See Ch. 14, Sect. 14.3(b), n. 110, describing the United States Hickenlooper Amendment, calling for suspension of foreign aid to countries that expropriate US-owned property.

[8] For a contrary view, see e.g. Michael Malloy, *US Economic Sanctions*, §1.21 (1990). Malloy defines economic sanction as 'any country-specific economic or financial prohibition imposed on a target country or its nationals with the intended effect of creating dysfunction in commercial and financial transactions with respect to the specified target, in the service of specified foreign policy purposes.'

[9] Putting aside the transitory obligations of a departing colonial power toward a newly independent state.

its own citizens or those of *A*, or has expropriated investments belonging to companies based in *A*, *A*'s response should be considered an economic sanction, subject to the limitations on economic sanctions here set out.[10]

A priori, one would think that the more a sanction moves along the spectrum from failure to renew benefits to termination of existing benefits to denial of normal rights to imposition of penalties to selective boycott to full embargo and finally to seizure of assets, the more stringent should be the constraints on the state or group of states imposing the sanction, and the more blatant the conduct to which the sanction responds. Whether this is actually true is one of the themes running throughout this Part.

---

[10] Note that the reason for *A*'s action, which will usually be stated but if it is not may be fairly inferred, is important in making the judgment that *A*'s action is a sanction. For instance, termination of aid to *B* as part of a general reduction in *A*'s foreign assistance program due to a prolonged budget deficit in *A* would not be regarded as a sanction. Here, too, of course, there may be borderline cases, for instance if all foreign aid is reduced by *A*, but the reductions fall more heavily on state *B* than on states *C* and *D*.

A reduction in foreign aid to *B* based on a determination that *B* had not made efficient use of previous aid would not, under the definition here adopted, be regarded as a sanction, though it might be so perceived by the people or government of *B*.

22

United Nations and Other
Collective Sanctions

A.   UNITED NATIONS SANCTIONS

22.1   SANCTIONS BY ORDER OF THE SECURITY COUNCIL

The drafters of the United Nations Charter, as mentioned in the introduction to this Part, made provision for economic sanctions, along with other provisions not involving the use of force, in Articles 39 and 41 of the Charter.[1] But the decision on sanctions was to be taken only in the event of a threat to the peace, breach of the peace, or act of aggression, and both the determination of the existence of such a situation and the determination on what if any measures should be taken in response were committed to the Security Council. Thus sanctions under Articles 39 and 41 could only be required with the concurrence (or as it came to be understood, the abstention) of the five permanent members of the Security Council (Art. 27(3)).

From the creation of the United Nations to 1990, sanctions under Articles 39 and 41 were adopted only in one case, involving the Unilateral Declaration of Independence by the white settler regime in Rhodesia (1966–79) plus an arms embargo against South Africa (1977). Since the imposition of mandatory sanctions against Iraq following that state's invasion of Kuwait (as well as the end of the stalemate in the Security Council resulting from the Cold War), UN sanctions have become almost routine, with embargoes, asset freezes, restrictions on air or sea communications, and comparable measures imposed (as of year-end 2001) against some thirteen states and territories, plus sanctions against all persons who commit terrorist acts or facilitate such acts.

The formal sequence under the Charter is (i) a determination must be made by the Security Council of the existence of a threat to the peace, breach of the peace, or act of aggression (Art. 39); (ii) the Council must vote in favour of a *recommendation* or a *decision* on what measures not involving the use of armed force are to be employed in response (Arts. 39 and 41); (iii) if the Council *decides* on a measure or measures to be taken under Article 41 and calls on member states to apply such measure or measures, implementation of the measure or measures becomes mandatory under Article 25 of the Charter.[2] The three steps can be taken in a single resolution; reference to the specific articles of the Charter is not necessary, but some statement

---

[1] The provisions of Article 41 were contained in Chapter VIII, Section B(3) of the Dumbarton Oaks Proposals for Establishment of a General Organization, as tentatively agreed on in 1944 by the United States, the United Kingdom, the Soviet Union, and China. They were adopted at the San Francisco Conference with hardly any debate. See Ruth B. Russell, *A History of the United Nations Charter*, 675–6 (1958); *Documents of the United Nations Conference on International Organization, San Francisco, 1945* (UNCIO), Vol. XI, p. 20.

[2] Article 25 of the Charter reads:

The members of the United Nations agree to accept and carry out the decisions of the Security Council in accordance with the present Charter.

It is interesting to note that the corresponding provision of the Dumbarton Oaks Proposals, Chapter VI, Section B(4), called for members to obligate themselves to carry out the decisions of the Security Council 'in accordance with the provisions of the Charter'. These words were dropped in San Francisco after Belgium proposed an amendment that would have authorized a member state to ask the International Court of Justice whether a decision or recommendation of the Security Council infringed the essential rights of a member under international law. The amendment was withdrawn when it was pointed out that such a procedure could delay Council action necessary in circumstances of threat to or breach of the peace. See Russell (n. 1 supra), 664–5.

showing that the Security Council has determined that a threat to the peace or breach of peace or act of aggression exists is required to bring the enabling provisions of Article 41 into play.[3]

It is apparent from the above that, contrary to statements in the popular press, the Security Council cannot actually impose economic sanctions; rather it can call on member states to implement particular sanctions as set forth in its resolution, and it can require compliance pursuant to Article 25.[4] In each of the instances in which it has decided upon mandatory sanctions—beginning with respect to Rhodesia's 'Unilateral Declaration of Independence' (1966–79), the Security Council has created a committee to monitor implementation of sanctions through questionnaires to governments, public hearings, investigations, and reports to the Security Council, and to recommend suspension or repeal of the particular sanctions. The Sanctions Committees have always included the five Permanent Members of the Security Council, and they have functioned through consensus or unanimity. Typically the sanctions resolutions, in contrast to peace-keeping resolutions, have not included a sunset or termination clause, and thus each of the permanent members has had something like a veto over terminating or modifying sanctions.

Some member states of the United Nations have adopted ad hoc authorization to implement Security Council resolutions or have attempted to fit the call from the Security Council into other existing economic emergency legislation.[5] Other states have enacted permanent legislation authorizing the

---

[3] Note that this exposition is consistent also with Article 2 of the Charter, in particular with Article 2(7), which reads:

Nothing contained in the present Charter shall authorize the United Nations to intervene in matters which are essentially within the domestic jurisdiction of any state or shall require the Members to submit such matters to settlement under the present Charter; but this principle shall not prejudice the application of enforcement measures under Chapter VII.

A measure taken by member states pursuant to a decision under Article 41 is an enforcement measure within the meaning of Article 2(7), and thus the argument about intervention in matters essentially within the domestic jurisdiction of the target state is overcome.

[4] The word 'require' is perhaps too legalistic, though it carries through the meaning of Article 25 of the Charter. In theory, the Security Council could adopt a resolution calling for sanctions against a state that had failed to comply with a prior obligation to impose sanctions against another state, and indeed various African states urged such action against Portugal and South Africa when those states failed to implement mandatory sanctions against Rhodesia. In fact, the Security Council did no more than 'condemn' those countries, as well as the United States when it adopted the so-called Byrd Amendment authorizing the inspection of chrome from Rhodesia, Sect. 22.4 infra. See Security Council Resolutions 253 (29 May 1968); 277(18 May 1970); 288 (17 Nov. 1970); 314 (28 Feb. 1972); 318 (28 July 1972); 320 (29 Sept. 1972); 333 (22 May 1973); 411 (30 June 1977).

[5] For a comparative survey of member states' legislation and implementation of UN sanctions, see Vera Gowlland-Debbas (ed.), *The Implementation and Enforcement of Security Council Sanctions under Chapter VII of the United Nations Charter* (Grad. Inst. Int'l Studies, Geneva (2001)).

government to carry out decisions of the Security Council.[6] Typically such legislation is geared to the distinction between recommendation and decision: for instance, when the Security Council, shortly after Rhodesia's declaration of independence, adopted a resolution *calling upon* all states to break all economic relations with Southern Rhodesia,[7] that did not constitute a *decision*, thus was not mandatory under Article 25 of the Charter, and did not bring authority conferred by UN Participation Acts into effect. Some states, with substantial control over their economies, acted in accordance with the Security Council's recommendation; others, such as the United Kingdom, adopted special legislation to implement (and even go beyond) the recommendations;[8] those states, such as the United States and France, which had no general power over the economy, could not and did not fully implement the recommendation.[9] When the Security Council, a year later, adopted 'selective

---

[6] For instance, the United States United Nations Participation Act of 1945, 22 U.S.C. §§287a–287e provides in §5:

Notwithstanding the provisions of any other law, whenever the United States is called upon by the Security Council to apply measures which said Council has decided, pursuant to Article 41 of said Charter, are to be employed to give effect to its decisions under said Charter, the President may to the extent necessary to apply such measures, through any agency which he may designate, and under such orders, rules, and regulations as may be prescribed by him, investigate, regulate, or prohibit, in whole or in part, economic relations or rail, sea, air, postal, telegraphic, radio, and other means of communication between any foreign country or any national thereof or any person therein and the United States or any person subject to the jurisdiction thereof, or involving any property subject to the jurisdiction of the United States.

A similar provision is contained in United Kingdom: United Nations Act 1946, (9 & 10 Geo. 6, c. 45), 10 *Halsbury's Statutes* 554 (4th rev. edn. 1995). In introducing this legislation, the Lord Chancellor explained:

Assuming the Security Council takes . . . a decision [under Article 41] . . . there is an obligation on our Government to give effect to it. At present, the Government have no powers to impose upon its nationals the duty to comply with such a decision. Hence this Bill . . . provides that if under Article 41 of the Charter the Security Council call upon His Majesty's Government to take certain decisions, then His Majesty's Government may, by Order in Council, in their turn, impose upon their nationals the obligation and the duty to observe the provisions of the Order in Council. (*H. L. Debates*, Vol. 139, col. 375 (12 Feb. 1946))

[7] SC Res. 217 (20 Nov. 1965).

[8] Indeed, the United Kingdom enacted its legislation even before passage of Resolution 217, in exercise of its sovereignty over Southern Rhodesia. Southern Rhodesia Act 1965 (16 Nov. 1965), Laws 1965 c. 76.

[9] An illustration of the distinction between recommendation and decision, misunderstood by much of the press and public as evidence of hypocrisy on the part of the government, was the response of the United States to the 1965 resolution of the Security Council. Imports into the United States, including a general requirement of most-favoured-nation tariff treatment, were regulated by a detailed statute that could not be modified by the President, and therefore imports from Rhodesia into the United States continued unimpeded until mandatory sanctions were approved by the Security Council. Exports, in contrast, were subject to a very broad delegation under the Export Control Act of 1949, as amended, which vested wide discretion in the President. The President had the authority under domestic law to create a new 'country group' for Rhodesia and did so, with the consequence that a 'validated license' was required for virtually all exports to Rhodesia, and such licenses were for the most part denied.

mandatory sanctions,'[10] those states that depended on United Nations Participation Acts for their authority to impose sanctions, adopted prohibitions limited to the specific items listed in the Security Council's resolution.[11]

22.2   THE PREDICATE FOR MANDATORY SANCTIONS

As stated above, the condition precedent for a decision in favour of mandatory sanctions is the existence of a 'threat to the peace, breach of the peace, or act of aggression', as determined by the Security Council. The question arose in the context of responding to the Unilateral Declaration of Independence by the white minority regime of Rhodesia whether that situation existed. Some persons, at the United Nations and elsewhere, contended that whatever the legal relations had been between the United Kingdom and former Southern Rhodesia, and whatever one thought of a regime that disenfranchised the vast majority of its citizens, there was no evidence of any aggressive intent or act on the part of the Rhodesian government, and thus the predicate for action under Articles 39 and 41 did not exist. While some delegates argued that UDI constituted a threat to the stability of Africa and thus fit the terms of Article 39, the Security Council in 1966—13 months after UDI—simply recited its determination that 'the present situation in Southern Rhodesia constitutes a threat to international peace and security,'[12] and this phrase was reiterated and reaffirmed in the 1968 resolution imposing comprehensive mandatory sanctions,[13] and with slight variation in wording in nearly all of the subsequent resolutions of the Security Council on the Rhodesia question.

Similar determinations have been made by the Security Council as a predicate for sanctions in respect to Somalia, Haiti, Liberia, and other countries in which the crisis was real enough, but did not cross national frontiers and was not likely to do so. In some instances, the Security Council has explicitly stated that it determines the situation to constitute a 'threat to international peace and security'; in other instances, the Security Council has contented itself with stating that it was 'acting under Chapter VII of the Charter'.

[10]   SC Res. 232 (16 Dec. 1966).

[11]   For instance, paragraph 2(a) of Resolution 232 stated that all member states of the UN shall prevent import into their territory from Southern Rhodesia of nine primary commodities, including hides, skins, and leather. It seems that this resolution would not have served as authority for a state to prohibit importation of shoes made in South Africa from Rhodesian leather.

In the absence of a UN Participation Act or similar legislation, the High Court of Australia held unlawful an action by Australia's Postmaster General cutting off postal and telephone services for the Rhodesian Information Centre and a publication entitled *Rhodesian Commentary*, notwithstanding the mandatory character under international law of the decision of the Security Council. *Bradley* v. *Commonwealth of Australia*, [1973] 1 *Austr. L. Rep.* 241, 259–60.

[12]   SC Res. 232, para. 1 (16 Dec. 1966).   [13]   SC Res. 253, Preamble (29 May 1968).

It seems fair to conclude that while the determination of threat or breach of the peace is a legal prerequisite to a call for mandatory sanctions, the content of that determination is a political question, and a threat to the peace under Article 39 is whatever the Security Council determines to be a threat to the peace. Quite apart from the question whether there can ever be jurisdiction in a court to review actions of the Security Council,[14] the determination of the existence of a threat to international peace and security is uniquely assigned to the Security Council by the UN Charter, and seems immune to judicial challenge in either international or domestic courts.[15] Putting the point in a larger context, the restraint on action by the Security Council to require imposition of sanctions lies more in the requirement of nine votes including the affirmative vote (or abstention) of the five permanent members than in any particular factual assessment of actual or potential danger to international peace and security.[16]

22.3   The Scope of Sanctions

(a)   What Sanctions May Be Ordered

Article 41 of the UN Charter contains a list of possible measures 'to be employed to give effect to its decisions', and resolutions calling for mandatory sanctions have typically specified the measures to be applied. The list, developed at Dumbarton Oaks on the basis of proposals of the Soviet Union,[17] includes 'complete or partial interruption of economic relations and of rail, sea, air, postal, telegraphic, radio, and other means of communication, and the severance of diplomatic relations.' It is apparent from the introductory words, 'These may include . . .' that the list is not exhaustive. For instance, during the Iranian Hostage crisis of 1979–81, it was suggested that an appropriate sanction might have been to deny Iran access to INTELSAT, by means of which the hostage takers and a parade of Iranian political leaders were able to reach television audiences throughout the world. If the Security Council had found the existence of a threat to international peace

---

[14] See e.g. José E. Alvarez, 'Judging the Security Council,' 90 *Am. J. Int'l L.* 1 (1996) with elaborate citations to other sources; also John Dugard, 'Judicial Review of Sanctions', in Vera Gowlland-Debbas (ed.), *United Nations Sanctions and International Law* (2001).

[15] See Myres McDougal and W. Michael Reisman, 'Rhodesia and the United Nations: The Lawfulness of International Concern', 62 *Am. J. Int'l L.* 1, esp. at 5–7, 18–19 (1968).

[16] For the history of repeated failure of the attempt to define 'threat to international peace and security' or 'aggression,' from Dumbarton Oaks to San Francisco to various organs of the United Nations, including the International Law Commission, as well as of efforts to invoke Article 39 in the first two decades of the United Nations, see the commentary on Article 39 in Goodrich, Hambro, and Simons, *Charter of United Nations: Commentary and Documents*, 190–302 (3rd edn., 1969).

[17] See Dumbarton Oaks Proposals, Chapter VIII, Section B(3); Robert C. Hilderbrand, *Dumbarton Oaks: The Origins of the United Nations and the Search for Security*, 138–9 (1990).

and security—in fact a resolution to that effect was vetoed by the Soviet Union[18]—a call to Member States to cause access to INTELSAT to be denied to Iran would have been a permissible sanction. If the objection had been raised that such a measure conflicted with the agreements relating to INTELSAT,[19] it is clear that under Article 103 of the UN Charter, a decision of the Security Council pursuant to Articles 39 and 41 would prevail over the INTELSAT agreements or any other agreements that might be applicable.[20] Similarly, a sanction implemented pursuant to decision of the Security Council might well conflict with a bilateral trade or air services agreement,[21] or with the most-favoured-nation provision of the GATT.[22] Such conflict would not relieve a state from the obligation to comply with mandatory sanctions decided upon by the Security Council; likewise compliance with the mandate of the Security Council should be regarded as justification or excuse in the event the target of sanctions presented a claim under a bilateral or multilateral agreement against the state applying the sanctions.[23]

Some, but not all the economic sanctions mandated by the Security Council have contained provisions modeled on the comprehensive sanctions resolution in the Rhodesia case, *Deciding*

that all States Members of the United Nations shall give effect to the decisions set out in operative paragraphs [. . .] of this resolution *notwithstanding any contract entered into or licence granted before the date of this resolution.*[24] (italics added)

In a civil action in a state applying the sanctions brought by the target state or a national or resident of that state on the basis of a pre-existing contract, a regulation relying on the quoted passage or an analogous provision would almost certainly provide a good defense. As between two private parties in

---

[18] Draft Resolution proposed by the United States, UN Doc. S/13735, 35 UN SCOR Supp. 1st Qtr., 10 (10 Jan. 1980); 35 UN SCOR 2191st Meeting, 14 (11 and 13 Jan. 1980).

[19] Agreement Relating to the International Telecommunications Satellite Organization (INTELSAT) and Operating Agreement relating to the International Telecommunications Satellite Organization (INTELSAT), both done at Washington, 20 Aug. 1971, 23 UST 3812, 4091.

[20] Article 103 of the UN Charter provides:

In the event of a conflict between the obligations of the Members of the United Nations under the present Charter and their obligations under any other international agreement, their obligations under the present Charter shall prevail.

[21] For instance, the resolutions imposing a civil aviation embargo on Libya for failure to cooperate in investigation and extradition of persons involved in the downing of Pan American Flight 103 over Lockerbie, Scotland, SC Res. 748 (31 Mar. 1992), SC Res. 883 (11 Nov. 1993).

[22] For instance, the resolutions imposing embargoes on trade with Yugoslavia in reponse to continued use of force in violation of previous Security Council Resolutions, SC Res. 757 (30 May 1992), SC Res. 787 (16 Nov. 1992), and numerous follow-up resolutions.

[23] For confirmation of this statement in the context of sanctions against Iraq following the invasion of Kuwait in 1990, see Sect. 22.5, nn. 66–8 infra.

[24] Security Council Res. of 29 May 1968, para. 7. Similar provisions were included, e.g., in Security Council Res. 670 of 25 Sept. concerning Iraq; and Security Council Res. 917 of 6 May 1994 concerning Haiti; but not, for instance, in Security Council Res. 942 of 23 Sept. 1994 concerning Bosnian Serb forces in the Republic of Bosnia and Herzegovina, which orders States to prevent specified economic activities 'on or after adoption of this resolution'.

the sanctioning state, say a supplier and an exporter, the question of who should bear the loss is less clear, depending on the terms of the contract and the applicable law on frustration of contracts.[25] In its order to carry out the mandatory sanctions against Rhodesia in 1967, Canada authorized residents and citizens of Canada who suffered damage as a result of being prohibited from carrying out a contract or receiving a benefit to which he was entitled by law under an agreement entered into before the coming into force of the Regulations to apply to the Government for compensation.[26] Neither the United States nor the United Kingdom adopted a similar provision.

(b) The Increasing Use of Sanctions

As previously mentioned, the use of sanctions by the Security Council gained currency following the end of the Cold War and the continuing application of sanctions to Iraq following its invasion of Kuwait in 1990. Sanctions by order of the Security Council were imposed on the territory of the former Yugoslavia from 1991 on, including the Federal Republic of Yugoslavia (Serbia and Montenegro) (1992), the Bosnian Serb party (1993), and the Federal Republic of Yugoslavia again in connection with the Kosovo crisis (1998–9). Sanctions were also ordered with respect to Somalia (1992); the Khmer Rouge (Cambodia) (1992); Libya (1992–9); Liberia (1992–); Haiti (1993–4); UNITA (Angola) (1993–); Rwanda 1993–6); Sudan (1996–); Sierra Leone (1997–); and Afghanistan (1999–).[27] In the case of Libya, sanctions were imposed to induce the surrender for trial of the men charged with the bombing of Pan American Flight 103; in the case of Sudan, the object of the sanctions was to respond to the attempt on the life of the President of Egypt in Ethiopia by persons believed to be sheltered in Sudan. The other cases arose primarily out of crises within the target state's borders.

(c) The Pattern of Mandatory Sanctions

Mandatory economic sanctions pursuant to decision of the Security Council have focused on four main areas: prohibition of imports from the target country; prohibition of transfer of funds to or for the benefit of the target country; prohibition of transport in vessels or aircraft registered in member states of cargoes originating in or destined for the target country; and prohibition of exports to the target country, in some instances all exports, in

---

[25] For a discussion of this question, including reference to several decisions following sanctions against Iraq, see Geneviève Burdeau, 'Les Effets Juridiques des Résolutions du Conseil de Sécurité sur les Contrats Privés', in Vera Gowlland-Debbas (ed.), *United Nations Sanctions and International Law* (2001).

[26] *Canada*: United Nations Rhodesia Regulations, s. 11, P.C. 1967–323, [1967] 101 *Stat. Instr.* 324 (No. 5).

[27] For a case-by-case summary, see David Cortright and George A. Lopez, *The Sanctions Decade: Assessing UN Strategies in the 1990s* (2000).

others arms and munitions, or petroleum and its products, or both. In the Rhodesia case, the prohibitions on exports and imports were at first limited to specified products,[28] and later were expanded to cover all commodities and products.[29] In addition, the sanctions resolutions directed against Rhodesia, as well as the resolutions directed against Iraq, specifically called for prohibition against the export of arms, ammunition, and associated equipment. As the campaign against Iraq intensified in the fall of 1990 while Kuwait remained under occupation, the Security Council decided that all states shall deny permission to take off from their territory to all aircraft carrying cargo destined for Iraq or Kuwait, regardless of the state of registration of the aircraft, unless a given flight is expressly approved by the Security Council's sanctions committee, and also that all states shall deny overflight rights to any such aircraft unless it lands at a designated airfield to permit inspection.[30] Further, ships of Iraqi registry that had been used to carry cargoes to or from Iraq or Kuwait were to be denied entrance to the ports of member states.[31]

In response to Libya's failure to cooperate with the investigation of the downing of Pan American Flight 103 over Lockerbie in December 1988, the Security Council decided that all States shall deny permission to any aircraft to take off from, land in, or overfly their territory if it was destined to land in or took off from Libya.[32] In response to the continuing civil war in Angola, the Security Council decided to prohibit suppply of arms and petroleum products to UNITA, the rebel group fighting against the recognized government in that state.[33] In general, sanctions under Article 41 have not involved use of armed force; in connection with sanctions against the regime in Haiti that had overthrown the elected president, the Security Council went one step further, and called upon Member States

to use such measures . . . as may be necessary . . . under the authority of the Security Council to ensure strict implementation of the [prior sanctions resolutions], and in particular to halt outward as well as inward maritime shipping as necessary.[34]

This resolution did not impose an *obligation* on Member States, but served as an *authorization* for a naval blockade, which was, in fact carried out

---

[28] SC Res. 232 (16 Dec. 1966).   [29] SC Res. 253 (29 Nov. 1968).

[30] SC Res. 670 (25 Sept. 1990).

[31] Id. The resolution expressly recalled the provisions of Article 103, as discussed above, and prefaced the decision regarding aircraft by the statement 'notwithstanding the existence of any rights or obligations conferred or imposed by any international agreement or any contract entered into or any license or permit granted before the date of the present resolution.'

[32] Security Council Res. 748 of 31 Mar. 1992. A further resolution, SC Res. 883 of 11 Nov. 1993 required, *inter alia* the immediate closure of all Libyan Arab Airlines offices and prohibited the honouring of tickets issued by that airline, and provision of any engineering or maintenance servicing of any aircraft or components within Libya. The resolution stated that the measures would be suspended at such time as the two men charged with the bombing of Pan American Flight 103 were surrendered for trial, which in fact took place in April 1999. Most states thereupon resumed air services to Libya, but the United States did not.

[33] SC Res. 864 (15 Sept. 1993).   [34] SC Res. 917 (6 May 1994).

under the leadership of the United States, with cooperation from Argentina, Canada, France, and The Netherlands.

In short, the pattern of economic sanctions has remained similar—sometimes selective, i.e. focused on embargo of arms and petroleum products, sometimes comprehensive, and often escalating in coverage.

(d)   The Territorial Scope of Sanctions

In the course of the sanctions against Rhodesia, and particularly in the context of the quite unsuccessful effort to interdict the supply of petroleum and petroleum products, it became apparent that supplies were reaching Rhodesia through the participation of South African subsidiaries of the major oil companies—notably Shell, BP, Mobil, and Total—whose home bases were located in states committed to enforcing the sanctions.[35] The question was raised before the Sanctions Committee whether states implementing the resolutions of the Security Council were authorized, entitled, or obligated to control the actions of companies outside their national territories linked by ownership to parent companies organized in member states. Had the Security Council drafted its resolutions to call for states to impose prohibitions on 'any activities by their nationals or corporations and other associations organized under their laws *and any corporations owned or controlled by its nationals or by corporations organized under its laws*,' it seems clear that such a provision would be valid. Any claim by a state where a subsidiary was established of interference with its laws or policy would be overridden by the obligation under Articles 25 and 103 of the Charter to comply with decisions of the Security Council. However, a provision requiring or even authorizing such exercise of jurisdiction on the basis of corporate affiliation has never been approved by the Security Council. The Sanctions Committee under the Rhodesia Sanctions put the question to the Legal Counsel of the United Nations whether states could nevertheless enforce the sanctions extraterritorially, for instance by ordering parent companies or their officers to direct their subsidiaries, to cease to make shipments likely to violate the sanctions. The Legal Counsel was clear that activities carried on outside the territory of the state in question with the effect of circumventing the sanctions could be effectively prohibited:

---

[35]   See e.g. M. Bailey, *Oilgate: The Sanctions Scandal* (1979); Center for Social Action of the United Church of Christ (USA), *The Oil Conspiracy* (1976), reproduced in *South Africa—US Policy and the Role of US Corporations*, Hearings before Subcommittee on Africa of Senate Committee on Foreign Relations, 94th Cong., 2d Sess. (8–30 Sept. 1976); Foreign and Commonwealth Office (UK), *Report on the Supply of Petroleum and Petroleum Products to Rhodesia*, by T. H. Bingham, QC and S. M. Gray, FCA (1978) as well as various Reports of the Security Council Committee established in Pursuance of Resolution 253 (Sanctions Committee).

If those companies are organized under the law of the State concerned, have its nationality and are registered under its law, it would appear to be open to the competent authorities to decide whether or not to allow the companies to maintain whatever status they enjoy under local law.[36]

As for adopting legislation applying sanctions to conduct outside its borders,

it would be at variance with both law and precedent, to assert that public international law precludes a State from enacting laws having extraterritorial effect and providing for enforcement within the territory of the legislating state.[37]

In fact, while some states—notably the United States—have sought to enforce their own economic sanctions on the basis of jurisdiction based on control of corporate subsidiaries as well as on territoriality and nationality of individuals,[38] the practice of UN sanctions has been based on the view that each member state has an obligation to enforce the sanctions in its territory, and thus there is no need to provoke the controversy attendant on extraterritorial enforcement.

(e)   The Duration of Sanctions

Nothing in Article 41 of the UN Charter or in the resolutions initiating or extending mandatory sanctions makes provision for expiration of sanctions after a given period of time or the happening of a given event. It might be thought, therefore, that a program of mandatory sanctions in implementation of a resolution of the Security Council can be terminated only by another resolution adopted in accordance with the Security Council's normal voting procedures, including the possibility of veto. An alternative view would be to look to the original understanding of the post-war settlement, as embodied in the Charter, according to which enforcement action under Chapter VII would be undertaken only with the concurrence of the five permanent members of the Security Council: if one or more of the permanent members declared that it would no longer implement the sanctions, the required consensus would be destroyed and sanctions would cease to be mandatory.

The issue arose briefly just as Rhodesia's Unilateral Declaration of Independence was coming to a close, but it was overtaken by a political solution before becoming a major source of conflict:

In April 1979, in the context of a so-called 'internal settlement' in Rhodesia/Zimbabwe and an election open to blacks as well as whites but boycotted by the principal black guerrilla organization, the 'Patriotic Front,' the Security Council adopted a resolution in which it

---

[36] Opinion of Eric Suy, Legal Counsel, United Nations, reproduced in Sixth Report of Security Council Sanctions Committee, 29 UN S.C.O.R. Spec. Supp. No. 2, para. 138 (1974).
[37] Ibid.   [38] See Ch. 23, Sect. 23.4(b) infra.

'reiterate[d] its call to all States not to accord recognition to [the "so-called elections"] and to observe strictly the mandatory sanctions against Southern Rhodesia.'

In the fall of 1979, the British government convened a lengthy conference in London among all parties, looking to an orderly transfer of sovereignty to an elected black majority government. On December 3, 1979, before all the parties had signed the necessary documents, notably a cease-fire agreement, the British government announced that it was reasserting sovereignty over Southern Rhodesia for an interim period, until elections could be held under its supervision. On December 12, the British government declared the conference over, and announced that it would no longer enforce Security Council sanctions against Southern Rhodesia. On December 15, the United States announced that it was revoking its Rhodesian sanctions regulations, effective the following day. On December 18, the UN General Assembly passed a resolution 'deploring the moves by certain states to lift sanctions unilaterally' and declaring that 'Security Council Resolution 253 (1968) . . . can be revoked only by a decision of the Council and that any unilateral action in this regard would be a violation of the obligation assumed by Member States under Article 25 of the Charter.'[39] On December 21, the same day that the Patriotic Front signed the cease-fire in London, Britain introduced a resolution into the Security Council calling for the sanctions to be terminated, though it argued that the resolution was unnecessary, since the obligation to impose the sanctions fell away automatically with the return to legality of the colony.[40] The representative of Zambia, among others, disagreed, saying 'This sad precedent should have been avoided before the meeting and decision of the Council today.'[41] The Soviet Union agreed with Zambia and circulated a letter stating that the American and British decision to end their compliance with the sanctions prior to action by the Security Council 'represents a flagrant violation of the . . . Charter.'[42]

Eventually the resolution calling for termination of sanctions was adopted,[43] and the issue receded.[44]

In the case of Iraq, the original Security Council resolution of August 6, 1990 ordering the sanctions against Iraq had stated as its purpose 'to bring the invasion and occupation of Kuwait by Iraq to an end and to restore the

[39] G. A. Res. 192 (18 Dec. 1979).
[40] 34 UN SCOR 2181st Meeting p. 2 (21 Dec. 1979). The United States made a similar statement, id., at p. 8.
[41] Id., at p. 4.
[42] UN Doc. S/13702 of 21 Dec. 1979, 34 UN SCOR Supp. 4th Qtr. p. 138.
[43] SC Res. 460 (21 Dec. 1979).
[44] For a full-length discussion, see Kreczko, 'The Unilateral Termination of the UN Sanctions against Southern Rhodesia by the United Kingdom', 21 *Va. J. Int'l L.* 97 (1980).

sovereignty, independence, and territorial integrity of Kuwait.'[45] That objective was accomplished subsequently by military force, pursuant to later authorization by the Security Council.[46] Nevertheless, the sanctions were not terminated. By Resolution 687, adopted by the Security Council a month after hostilities ceased (plus several follow-up resolutions), an elaborate program of sanctions was created, including limitations on Iraq's ability to produce and sell oil, requirements that Iraq contribute to a UN Gulf War Compensation Fund, and UN supervision of the purchase and distribution of food and medicine in Iraq under an Oil for Food Program.[47] As these sanctions remained in place for close to a decade, critics, including at various times at least two member states of the Security Council (France and Russia), urged termination or substantial modification of the sanctions, on the ground that they had failed to bring down the government of Saddam Hussein but had caused massive damage to the civilian population in Iraq, particularly to children deprived of food and medicines. The United States, however, maintained the position that the civilian suffering was attributable to the Iraqi government, and that relaxing sanctions would be rewarding the cruel actions of that government.[48] Whatever the rights and wrongs of this controversy, as of year-end 2001 the consistent practice of the Security Council in connection with sanctions, as noted earlier, has been to adopt resolutions with no sunset or terminal date. Termination of UN sanctions, accordingly, remains a political issue, dependent primarily on the will of the permanent members of the Security Council.

22.4 COMPLIANCE WITH SANCTIONS

As pointed out in Section 22.1, compliance with a decision of the UN Security Council ordering sanctions pursuant to Articles 39 and 41 of the UN Charter is mandatory, and a failure to carry out the decision is a violation of Article 25 of the Charter.[49] The fact that enforcement of sanctions

---

[45] SC Res. 661 (6 Aug. 1990) (Preamble).   [46] SC Res. 678 (29 Nov. 1990).

[47] Security Council Res. 687 of 3 April 1991 was followed by SC Res. 689, 692, 705, 706, 707, 712 (all in 1991); 778 in 1992; 806 and 833 in 1993; 986 in 1995; 1060 in 1996; and 1115 and 1134 in 1997, all concerned in part with the implementation and to some extent modification of sanction, and incidents in which the government of Iraq impeded in some way the disarmament and inspection functions of UN missions operating in Iraq pursuant to the cease-fire conditions laid down in Res. 687.

[48] See e.g. F. Gregory Gause III, 'Getting It Backward on Iraq', 78 *Foreign Affairs* No. 3, p. 54 (May/June 1999). The article quotes, *inter alia*, the US Secretary of State, Madeleine K. Albright, saying in May 1998:

the fact that Iraqi children are dying is not the fault of the United States, but of Saddam Hussein. . . . [I]t is ridiculous for the United States to be blamed for the dictatorial and cruel, barbaric ways that Saddam Hussein treats his people.

[49] States 'confronted with special economic problems' arising from the imposition of sanctions have the right under Article 50 of the Charter to, in effect, get a dispensation to continue to

would conflict with a requirement of domestic law is not an excuse under international law for non-compliance with the orders of the Security Council, nor any relief from the obligation stated in Article 25.[50]

In theory, a state failing to follow a mandate from the Security Council to cut off trade (or air transport, supply of petroleum, etc.) with a target state could itself be subject to sanctions, though it might be difficult to determine that such a failure constituted a 'threat to the peace'. Still, failure by a state to observe mandatory sanctions may well not be cost-free. For instance, during the invasion of Kuwait in 1990–1, Jordan continued to maintain economic relations with Iraq notwithstanding the series of mandatory sanction resolutions adopted by the Security Council. No sanctions were imposed against Jordan, but when that country's leaders sought support under Article 50 of the UN Charter for the economic losses it had suffered as a result of the sanctions against Iraq, it received a cool reception and little assistance.

Whether the obligation to comply with a decision of the Security Council can be enforced against a government by national courts depends both on the jurisdiction of such courts to review actions of the government and on the hierarchy of domestic and international law in the particular state.[51]

The only known case in which an effort at such enforcement was attempted in the context of sanctions occurred in the United States, whose law, generally speaking, places international and domestic legislation on an equal plane, but holds that when conflict cannot fairly be avoided, the later authority prevails.[52]

In 1971, three years after the Security Council had adopted comprehensive mandatory sanctions against Rhodesia,[53] the US Congress adopted an amendment to an unrelated bill sponsored by Senator

do business with the target state of the sanctions, or to obtain outside economic assistance in case of hardship. Zambia, and after their independence Angola and Mozambique, were given benefits under Article 50 in the Rhodesia case.

[50] See Vienna Convention on the Law of Treaties, Art. 27:

A party may not invoke the provisions of its intenal law as justification for its failure to perform a treaty.

See also e.g. *Advisory Opinion on Treatment of Polish Nationals in Danzig*, P.C.I.J. ser. A/B, No. 44 at 22 (1932). For a holding by a US Court of Appeals that the obligation to observe a *decision* of the Security Council under Article 41 is equivalent to the obligation to observe a treaty, see *Diggs* v. *Shultz*, discussed hereafter.

[51] Thus, for instance, in the United Kingdom an Act of Parliament prevails over an international obligation; in The Netherlands and France, an international obligation, at least if contained in a treaty, prevails over internal law. In the United States the hierarchy is as stated in the text. For a survey covering these countries, as well as Belgium, Denmark, Germany, Italy, and the Euopean Communities, see Francis Jacobs and Shelley Roberts (eds.), *The Effect of Treaties in Domestic Law, United Kingdom National Committee of Comparative Law*, Vol. 7 (1987).

[52] See *Restatement (Third) of the Foreign Relations Law of the United States*, §§114, 115 (1987).

[53] SC Res. 253 (29 Nov. 1968); see Sect. 22.3(c), at n. 29.

Harry F. Byrd that denied to the President 'notwithstanding any other provision of law' (i.e. including the UN Participation Act) the authority to prohibit the importation of chrome from Rhodesia.[54]

As could be expected, the UN General Assembly adopted a resolution expressly condemning the United States policy as 'in open contravention' of Security Council resolutions and 'contrary to the specific obligations assumed . . . under Article 25 of the Charter'.[55] The Security Council adopted three resolutions declaring the United States action 'contrary to the obligations of states'.[56] The United States made no attempt to defend the Byrd Amendment, and abstained from voting on all three resolutions.

In April 1972, a group of 'concerned individuals and organizations,' led by a member of Congress, brought suit in a US federal court against the Secretary of State and other officers, seeking (i) a declaration that the Byrd Amendment was in violation of law, and (ii) a decree enjoining further importation into the United States of chrome and other minerals from Southern Rhodesia. The Court of Appeals, reversing the lower court, held (i) that the plaintiffs were entitled to bring the suit; and (ii) 'that there can be no blinking the purpose and effect of the Byrd Amendment . . . to detach this country from the UN boycott of Southern Rhodesia in blatant disregard of our treaty obligations.' However, (iii) 'Congress can denounce treaties if it sees fit to do so,' and therefore the complaint stated 'no tenable claim in law'.[57]

Thus the court specifically equated an obligation imposed by resolution of the Security Council to an obligation under the Charter itself, without any questioning of the legality of the sanctions.[58] On the other hand the court upheld the will of Congress, and declined to strike down the statute or to order the President to comply with the international obligation of the United States as superior to the statute.[59]

22.5 ENFORCEMENT OF SANCTIONS

Article 41 of the UN Charter contains no provision for enforcement of sanctions mandated by the Security Council. The original understanding of the

---

[54] Pub. L. 92–156, 85 Stat. 423 (17 Nov. 1971) adding a new section 10 to the Strategic and Critical Stock Piling Act. 50 U.S.C. §98–98h. To be precise, the provision applied to importation from any non-communist country of 'any material determined to be strategic and critical' if such material was at the time permitted to be imported from any communist country. The actual and intended effect was as stated in the text.

[55] G.A. Res. 2946, 7 Dec. 1972, 27 G.A.O.R. Supp. 30 at 78; see also G. A. Res. 2765, 17 Nov. 1971, 26 G.A.O.R. Supp. 29 at 97.

[56] SC Res. 314 (28 Feb. 1972); 318 (28 July 1972); and 320 (29 Sept. 1972).

[57] *Diggs* v. *Shultz*, 470 F.2d 461, 466–67 (D.C. Cir. 1972), cert. denied, 411 U.S. 931 (1972).

[58] Compare Sect. 22.2 supra, esp. text at n. 15.

[59] Congress repealed the Byrd Amendment as one of the first legislative acts in the Carter administration. Pub. L. 95–12, 91 Stat. 22 (18 Mar. 1977).

drafters of the Charter appears to have been that if in the view of the Security Council economic and diplomatic sanctions failed, military measures 'to maintain or restore international peace and security' might have to be undertaken by the Security Council pursuant to Article 42. The Security Council would call on member states to make forces available to it, in accordance with a special agreement or agreements contemplated in Articles 43 and 45. No such agreements have ever been made, and the idea of a standing or stand-by military force under the control of the Security Council has receded from the international legal system. Article 42, however, has also been read as entitling the Security Council to authorize individual member states to use force in order to maintain or restore international peace and security, including enforcing of economic sanctions approved by the Security Council.

> In the spring of 1966, prior to the decision by the Security Council on mandatory sanctions but after the decision to condemn Rhodesia's Unilateral Declaration of Independence and to urge economic sanctions,[60] two tankers laden with oil approached Beira, Mozambique, the ocean terminal of a new pipeline to Rhodesia. The United Kingdom, which had previously proclaimed an embargo on all shipment of petroleum products to Rhodesia, felt pressure to prevent the tankers from blatantly defying the embargo, but was reluctant to use force on its own to stop them. Accordingly, it introduced a resolution in the Security Council that would 'call upon the government of the United Kingdom . . . to prevent, *by the use of force if necessary*, the arrival at Beira of [the tankers].' After a day-long debate in which the African states accused the British government of hypocrisy (because the proposed resolution was limited to the two tankers), the Security Council adopted the resolution as proposed by the United Kingdom.[61] Thereupon the British navy intercepted one of the tankers and the other one turned back; the navy also established a patrol of the Mozambique Channel to prevent oil from reaching Rhodesia through the pipeline.

While the Resolution did not recite the authority under which it was adopted, the point was made by the British and American delegates that the use of force on the high seas by the United Kingdom without authorization of the Security Council would have been contrary to international law, but that an endorsement by the Security Council made the use of force, limited to the terms of the resolution, consistent with international law.[62]

The Security Council did not again authorize the use of force in the Rhodesian situation. Thus the resolution concerning the tankers was not, technically, enforcement of mandatory sanctions by the Council. It may, however, fairly be regarded as a precedent demonstrating that the Security

---

[60] SC Res. 217 (20 Nov. 1965).   [61] SC Res. 221 (9 Apr. 1966).
[62] See 21 UN SCOR 1276th Meeting (9 Apr. 1966).

Council may, under Article 42, authorize individual states to use force in support of an approved program of sanctions. Moreover, one may draw an inference from the episode of the tankers that without such authorization, states may not use force outside their own territory to enforce sanctions, even when such sanctions themselves are authorized, or even required to be implemented, by the respective states.

The precedent of authorization of force by individual states to implement sanctions was revived in the context of Iraq's invasion of Kuwait in 1990. Within five days of the invasion the Security Council had adopted a resolution deciding that all states (i.e. not just member states of the United Nations) shall impose a complete embargo on exports to and imports from Iraq and occupied Kuwait as well as a prohibition on carriage of goods to or from Iraq on vessels registered in member states, and complete restriction on the use of financial resources by or for the benefit of Iraq.[63] By the end of August the Security Council adopted a further resolution calling upon those Member States cooperating with the government of Kuwait which are deploying maritime forces to the area

to use such measures commensurate to the specific circumstances as may be necessary under the authority of the Security Council to halt all inward and outward maritime shipping in order to inspect and verify . . . strict implementation of [the earlier] resolution.[64]

Thereafter American and other naval vessels stopped and boarded numerous vessels in the Persian Gulf to check whether they were carrying cargo to or from Iraq. On September 14, American and Australian warships fired warning shots across the bow of an Iraqi tanker that had refused to stop for inspection.[65] President Bush said the naval action was taken 'in accordance with the United Nations resolutions, in accordance with the sanctions.'

In the ensuing weeks the question was raised at the United Nations whether the sanctions against Iraq should be tightened to include restrictions on civil aviation to and from Iraq and overflights by Iraqi aircraft of the territory of other states. Landing rights for commercial aircraft were in many instances governed by bilateral air service agreements between Iraq and other states, and Iraq as well as most members of the United Nations were parties to the so-called Transit Agreement, by which state parties grant overflight and non-traffic landing rights to all other state parties.[66] But under Article 103 of the UN Charter a decision of the Security Council under Chapter VII would prevail over any conflicting agreements, and the Security Council did adopt a resolution confirming that the basic sanctions resolution (SC Resolution 661) 'applies to all means of transport, including

---

[63] SC Res. 661 (6 Aug. 1990).   [64] SC Res. 665 (25 Aug. 1990).
[65] *New York Times*, 15 Sept. 1990, p. 1.
[66] International Air Services Transit Agreement signed at Chicago 7 Dec. 1944, 84 U.N.T.S. 389.

aircraft,' and requiring all states to deny permission to any aircraft to take off from their territory carrying cargo to Iraq, or to overfly their territory without stopping to permit inspection, 'notwithstanding the existence of any rights or obligations conferred or imposed by any international agreement or any contract entered into or any license or permit granted before the date of the present resolution.'[67]

In the course of the fall and early winter of 1990, as Iraq made no move to withdraw from Kuwait, a major debate took place, particularly in the United States, about whether to 'let sanctions work,' or to escalate the collective response to the invasion by direct use of force against Iraq. At the end of November 1990, the Security Council linked the success of sanctions to the use of force by allowing Iraq 'one final opportunity' to comply with the earlier resolutions demanding withdrawal from Kuwait, and at the same time authorizing Member States 'to use all necessary means' to uphold and implement the earlier resolutions and to restore international peace and security, unless Iraq withdraws from Kuwait on or before January 15, 1991.[68]

Iraq did not withdraw and a coalition of states led by the United States initiated an air and ground assault against Iraq on January 16, 1991 that drove Iraq out of Kuwait. Thus the debate about whether sanctions work was overtaken by events. In a sense Churchill's syllogism of 1935 in connection with collective sanctions against Italy for its invasion of Ethiopia[69] again became applicable. This time, however, the leading country and the world organization were prepared to move from economic sanctions to the use of force if necessary, as contemplated by the progression in Chapter VII of the UN Charter.

22.6   Common Exemptions from Mandatory Sanctions

Though Article 41 of the UN Charter places no limits on the sanctions that the Security Council may impose, it has become customary as the use of sanctions has multiplied to include certain exemptions. The most common exemptions are supplies strictly intended for medical purposes. Other common exemptions included educational equipment; publications and news materials; food, if its supply can be controlled by the Red Cross or similar organization to ensure that it does not go to groups favoured by the target government; and payments made for imports excluded from the sanctions.

---

[67] SC Res. 670 (25 Sept. 1990).

[68] SC Res. 678 (29 Nov. 1990). For the suggestion that Resolution 678 was adopted not only under Article 42 of the UN Charter but also under Article 51, the self-defense article, see Schachter, 'United Nations Law in the Gulf Conflict', 85 *Am. J. Int'l. L.* 452, 459–61 (1991). The resolution itself says only 'Acting under Chapter VII of the Charter', which includes both Article 42 and Article 51.

[69] See Introduction to this Part at n. 1.

Other exemptions have included, for instance, propane gas for cooking in Haiti, notwithstanding a ban on supply of petroleum products, and permission for flights to and from Iraq for persons making the pilgrimage to Mecca. Overall, as the UN has gained experience in the application of sanctions, it seems that particular prohibitions and exemptions are to some extent negotiable, within the framework of the evident contradiction between the desire to punish the target government and to protect the population of the country being oppressed.

22.7 Non-binding Sanctions under United Nations Auspices

Under Article 39 of the UN Charter, as discussed in Section 22.1, the Security Council can either *make recommendations* or *decide* on measures to be taken to maintain or restore international peace and security. On a number of occasions, particularly in connection with proposed sanctions against South Africa, a *recommendation* to states to impose specified sanctions has been adopted with the abstention of one or more of the permanent members, when a resolution *deciding* to impose the same sanctions and therefore binding on all member states would have been vetoed.[70]

The General Assembly, in contrast, has authority, under Article 11 of the Charter, only to *make recommendations* with respect to matters of international peace and security—either to member states directly or to the Security Council or to both.[71] The General Assembly has made frequent use of this authority, from its first recommendation in 1946 that member states should sever diplomatic relations with the Franco government of Spain because of that government's sympathies with the Axis powers during World War II,[72] to a resolution in 1951 recommending 'additional economic measures' against North Korea and the People's Republic of China during the Korean War,[73] to a series of resolutions in the 1960s calling for sanctions against Portugal because of its continued rule over Angola and Mozambique.[74] From 1962 to

---

[70] See e.g. SC Res. 566 (19 June 1985) and SC Res. 569 (26 July 1985), both adopted 13–0, with the United Kingdom and the United States abstaining.

[71] Article 12 of the Charter provides that while the Security Council is exercising its functions in respect of any dispute or situation, the General Assembly shall not make any recommendation with regard to that dispute or situation unless the Security Council so requests. In practice, this limitation on the General Assembly's powers, which was inserted in the UN Charter to avoid the overlap of jurisdiction that had prevailed under the League of Nations Covenant, has not restrained the General Assembly from taking up and voting on any matter it chooses. See Goodrich, Hambro, and Simons, *Charter of the United Nations: Commentary and Documents*, 129–33 (3rd edn. 1969) and the many resolutions concerning South Africa and Rhodesia, adopted while the Security Council was also 'seized' of the matter.

[72] GA Res. 39(I) (12 Dec. 1946) 1 U.N. GAOR Resolutions, pt. II, 63 (1947).

[73] GA Res. 500(V) (18 May 1951), 5 UN GAOR Supp. No. 20A.

[74] See e.g. GA Res. 2107(XX) (21 Dec. 1965), 20 U.N. GAOR Supp. 14, 62 (1965).

1991, an unrelenting series of resolutions of the General Assembly called for sanctions against South Africa, based on that country's occupation (until 1990) of South-West Africa (Namibia), on its support of Rhodesia (1965–79), and, more generally, on continuance of the system of apartheid and prevalence of racial violence.

The moral and political effect of UN recommendations for sanctions has been variously estimated. For example, the Western powers allied with Portugal through the North Atlantic Treaty and other formal and informal arrangements did not heed the call to impose sanctions on Portugal in the 1960s. On the other hand the passage of the Security Council's resolution in 1985 recommending a broad program of economic sanctions against South Africa[75] was followed shortly thereafter by adoption of substantially similar measures by the United States,[76] by all but one member of the European Economic Community,[77] and somewhat later by Japan. The legal effect of recommendations to impose sanctions may be divided in two. On the one hand, no breach is implied for any state that declines to comply with such a recommendation, whether from the Security Council or the General Assembly or both; on the other hand, when a state does act in accordance with such a recommendation, it cannot be held to be acting unlawfully.[78]

B. ECONOMIC SANCTIONS AND REGIONAL ARRANGEMENTS: COLLECTIVE ACTION IN THE OAS

22.8 THE COMPROMISE AT SAN FRANCISCO

One of the issues discussed at length both at the Dumbarton Oaks preparatory conference and at the San Francisco Conference where the final version of the UN Charter was drafted was the relation between the new universal organization and regional organizations, notably what became the Organization of American States.[79] The full scope of the compromise eventually worked out,

---

[75] SC Res. 569, n. 70 supra.

[76] Ex. Order No. 12,532 of 9 Sept. 1985, 50 Fed. Reg. 36,861 (10 Sept. 1985); adopted to pre-empt passage of legislation mandating a broad range of sanctions. In the following year, Congress nevertheless adopted the Comprehensive Anti-Apartheid Act of 1986 over President Reagan's veto. Pub. L. 99–440, 100 Stat. 1086, codified in 22 U.S.C. §§5001–5116.

[77] See *Washington Post*, 11 Sept. 1985, p. A1. Nine of the ten members of the EEC, plus Spain and Portugal, agreed on a 'common but limited' package of sanctions; the United Kingdom abstained pending further study.

[78] This proposition is prefaced by 'some States would argue that' in Bowett, 'Economic Coercion and Reprisals by States', 13 *Va. J. Int'l L.* 1 at 6 (1972). While Bowett does not refute the proposition, he is less comfortable with it than the present author, writing three decades later.

[79] The Inter-American system, described by Thomas and Thomas as 'a strange mixture of shadow and substance', (A. V. Thomas and A. J. Thomas, Jr., *Non-Intervention* 114 (1956) may be traced back to the efforts of Simon Bolívar in the early nineteenth century to create a league of newly independent American states. Throughout the nineteenth century a series of

which resulted in reference to regional arrangements in Article 33 of the UN Charter concerning peaceful settlement of disputes, a new Article 51 concerning the inherent right of individual *and collective* self-defense, and an expanded version of what became Chapter VIII of the UN Charter (Arts. 52–4) is beyond the scope of this volume.[80] In brief, the Charter preserved the primacy of the UN Security Council in matters of international peace and security, but said that nothing in the Charter precludes the existence of regional arrangements relating to international peace and security (Art. 52), except that only the Security Council could authorize 'enforcement action', a critical but undefined term in the UN Charter (Art. 53).[81]

22.9 THE OAS CHARTER AND THE RIO TREATY

In 1948, the members of the Inter-American system formally adopted the Charter of the Organization of American States;[82] even before adopting their charter, all the independent Latin American states plus the United States of America signed the Inter-American Treaty of Reciprocal Assistance of 1947, usually known as the Rio Treaty.[83] The Rio Treaty is essentially a mutual

Inter-American Conferences took place involving most of the former Spanish colonies, but not Brazil or the United States. In 1889, the United States became a part of the Pan American movement, and the Pan American Union was established the following year in Washington as a permanent secretariat. The permanent charters of the system were not drawn up until 1947 and 1948, as described in the text.

[80] See, generally Ruth B. Russell, *A History of the United Nations Charter*, ch. XXVII (1958); also Arthur H. Vandenberg, Jr. (ed.), *The Private Papers of Senator Vandenberg* 186–93 (1952). For excerpts of the debates, see Chayes, Ehrlich, and Lowenfeld, *International Legal Process*, Vol. II, 1077–82 (1969).

[81] Article 52 of the UN Charter reads, in pertinent part:

Nothing in the present Charter precludes the existence of regional arrangements or agencies for dealing with such matters relating to the maintenance of international peace and security as are appropriate for regional action, provided that such arrangements or agencies and their activities are consistent with the Purposes and Principles of the United Nations.

Article 53 reads, in pertinent part:

The Security Council shall, where appropriate, utilize such regional arrangements or agencies for enforcement action under its authority. But no enforcement action shall be taken under regional arrangements or by regional agencies without the authorization of the Security Council.

Article 54 reads, in full:

The Security Council shall at all times be kept fully informed of activities undertaken or in contemplation under regional arrangements or by regional agencies for the maintenance of international peace and security.

[82] 2 U.S.T. 2394; T.I.A.S. 2361; 119 U.N.T.S. 3, signed at Bogota, 30 Apr. 1948, amended effective 1970, 21 U.S.T. 607; T.I.A.S. 6847. All of the former Spanish and Portuguese states of the Western Hemisphere plus the United States became members of the OAS. Later eleven former British and Dutch possessions, including Jamaica, the Bahamas, and Trinidad, as well as Canada, became members of the OAS, but most did not join the Rio Treaty discussed hereafter.

[83] 68 Stat. 1681; T.I.A.S. 1838; 4 Bevans 559; 21 U.N.T.S. 77, signed at Rio de Janeiro, 2 Sept. 1947.

defense arrangement, similar to the North Atlantic Treaty of 1949. The basic purpose of the Rio Treaty, stated in Article 3, is that 'an attack by any State against an American State shall be considered as an attack against all the American States,' and that each of the Contracting Parties undertakes to assist in meeting the attack in the inherent right of individual or collective self-defense. Article 6 of the Rio Treaty, however, contemplates other situations and other responses, including economic sanctions collectively authorized:

If the inviolability or the integrity of the territory or the sovereignty or political independence of any American State should be affected by an aggression which is not an armed attack or by an extra-continental or intra-continental conflict, or by any other fact or situation that might endanger the peace of America, the Organ of Consultation [i.e. the foreign ministers of the member states] shall meet immediately in order to agree on the measures which must be taken in case of aggression to assist the victims of aggression or, in any case, the measures which should be taken for the common defense and for the maintenance of the peace and security of the Continent.

Article 8, loosely tracking the catalogue of measures contained in Articles 41 and 42 of the UN Charter, provides that

the measures on which the Organ of Consultation may agree will comprise one or more of the following: recall of chief of diplomatic missions; breaking of diplomatic relations; breaking of consular relations; partial or complete interruption of economic relations or of rail, sea, air, postal, telegraphic, telephonic, and radiotelephonic or radio-telegraphic communications; and use of armed force.

Decisions of the Organ of Consultation require an affirmative note of two-thirds of the parties to the Rio Treaty (Art. 17), and there is no provision for a veto. Article 20 of the Rio Treaty, similar but not identical to Article 25 of the UN Charter, provides:

Decisions which require the application of the measures specified in Article 8 shall be binding upon all the Signatory States which have ratified this Treaty, with the sole exception that no State shall be required to use armed forces without its consent.

However, it follows from the distinction in Article 6 between measures which *must* be taken in case of aggression and those which *should* be taken in response to 'any other fact or situation' that response to the latter may be authorized by the Organ of Consultation without being required, i.e. that the Organ of Consultation could adopt either mandatory or discretionary sanctions.[84]

---

[84] In 1975, the parties to the Rio Treaty adopted a Protocol of Amendment, which *inter alia* added a new Article 23 that makes explicit the point made in the text:

The measures mentioned in Article 8 may be adopted by the Organ of Consultation in the form of
   (a) Decisions whose application is binding on the States parties, or
   (b) Recommendations to the States Parties.

The Protocol had not entered into effect as of year-end 2001.

22.10 THE LEADING PRECEDENTS

(a) Sanctions against Dominican Republic (1960)

On June 24, 1960, President Betancourt of Venezuela was injured in an attempt on his life in Caracas. Venezuela charged that the attempted assassination had been the work of the Dominican Republic, then governed by Rafael Trujillo, and called for a meeting of the Organ of Consultation under the Rio Treaty. The Council of the OAS constituted itself a Provisional Organ of Consultation, and appointed a committee to investigate the charges. On the basis of the report of the Investigating Committee, the Meeting of Consultation concluded that the attempt on the life of President Benancourt had been part of a plot to overthrow the government of Venezuela, that it had been assisted by the government of the Dominican Republic, and that this assistance constituted acts of intervention against Venezuela. Accordingly, the Meeting of Consultation voted

(1) that all member states of the OAS should break diplomatic relations with the Dominican Republic; and
(2) that there should be partial interruption of economic relations with the Dominican Republic, beginning with immediate suspension of trade in arms, and extending later to suspension in trade in other items to be decided on by the Council of the OAS.[85]

Subsequently the OAS Council voted to extend the embargo to include trade in petroleum and petroleum products, as well as to trucks and spare parts.[86] The United States sought authority from Congress to suspend reallocation to the Dominican Republic of any part of the sugar quota that had previously been allocated to Cuba, and imposed a surcharge of two cents a pound on sugar imported from the Dominican Republic.[87]

The resolution of the Meeting of Consultation was formally transmitted to the UN Security Council in accordance with Article 54 of the UN Charter, and the Soviet Union promptly introduced a resolution in the Security Council to approve the resolution of the Organ of Consultation in accordance with Article 53 of the UN Charter. The United States opposed the Soviet initiative on the ground that resolution of approval would imply that the action under the Rio Treaty had been 'enforcement action' subject to veto in the Security Council. The United States position prevailed, and the Security Council merely 'took note' of the report from the Secretary General of the OAS.[88]

---

[85] OEA/Ser. F/11.6, Doc. 25, San José, 16 Aug. 1960, repr. in Pan American Union. *Inter-American Treaty of Reciprocal Assistance: Applications*, Vol. II, p. 8, hereinafter *Applications*; 43 *Dept. State Bull.* 358 (1960).
[86] *Applications*, Vol. II pp. 11–12 (4 Jan. 1961).
[87] See 43 *Dept. State Bull.* 412, 640 (12 Sept., 24 Oct. 1960).
[88] See 14 U.N. SCOR 893d–895th meeting (8–9 Sept. 1960); SC Res. 156 (9 Sept. 1960).

(b)   Sanctions against Cuba (1962–)

In January 1962, following various actions and counter-actions between the United States and the Castro government of Cuba, a Meeting of Foreign Ministers serving as Organ of Consultation under the Rio Treaty resolved that 'the present government of Cuba, which has officially identified itself as a Marxist-Leninist government is incompatible with the principles and objectives of the inter-American system.'[89] Further, the Ministers voted:

1. To suspend immediately trade with Cuba in arms and implements of war of every kind.
2. To charge the Council of the OAS, in accordance with the circumstances and with due consideration for the constitutional or legal limitations of each and every one of the member states, with studying the feasibility and desirability of extending the suspension of trade to other items, with special items of strategic import-ance.[90]

The United States had sought a stronger mandate for the sanctions it intended to impose,[91] but it treated the vote of the Organ of Consultation as sufficient to authorize a complete embargo on all trade and financial trans-actions with Cuba. In proclaiming the embargo on the day after the vote in Punta del Este, President Kennedy spoke of acting 'in accordance with [the United States'] international obligations.'[92]

Cuba requested a meeting of the UN Security Council, contending that the United States and the other American republics acting pursuant to the resolu-tion of the OAS had taken 'enforcement action' contrary to Article 53 of the UN Charter. Seeing that it could not prevail directly with this position in the Security Council, Cuba proposed submitting the question to the International Court of Justice for an advisory opinion. The Security Council debated this proposal at length, but eventually rejected it by 7–2.[93] Two years later, Venezuela charged that Cuba had initiated a campaign of 'terrorism sabotage, assault and guerilla warfare' designed to subvert Venezuela's institutions and overthrow the government of that country. The Organ of Consultation was again convened, and on receiving the report of its Investigating Committee substantially confirming the charges, the Ministers resolved that the govern-ments of the American states

---

[89]   Res. VI of Eighth Meeting of Consultation of Ministers of Foreign Affairs, Punto del Este, 31 Jan. 1962, OEA/Ser. F. II 8, Doc. 18, at 17–19, *Applications*, 75–6; 46 *Dept. State Bull.* 281 (1962).

[90]   Id., Res. VIII; *Applications*, Vol. II at 77–8; 46 *Dept. State Bull.* 282 (1962).

[91]   See A. Schlesinger, Jr., *A Thousand Days: John F. Kennedy in the White House*, 780–3 (1965).

[92]   Pres. Proclamation No. 3447, 3 Feb. 1962; 27 Fed. Reg. 1085 (1962). For more on the United States embargo on economic relations with Cuba, see Ch. 23, Sect. 23.2.

[93]   17 UN SCOR 992d–998th meetings (14–23 Mar. 1962).

(a) not maintain diplomatic or consular relations with the government of Cuba;
(b) suspend all their trade, whether direct or indirect with Cuba, except in food and medicine sent for humanitarian reasons; and
(c) suspend all sea transportation between their countries and Cuba.[94]

This resolution was unambiguously mandatory, and was so treated by member states for a period of over ten years.[95]

The Dominican and Cuban cases remain the leading precedents for the relation between economic sanctions imposed by regional organizations and the primacy of the UN Security Council.[96] While the text of Article 53 of the UN Charter would support the view that 'enforcement action' includes all measures enumerated in Articles 41 and 42 of the UN Charter and that only the Security Council may take—or authorize others to take—enforcement action, the practice as it developed in the first two decades after San Francisco suggests that if either (i) no force is used, or (ii) the regional organization's resolution is not mandatory, a resolution by a regional organization authorizing its member states to impose economic sanctions against another member state in accordance with the organization's charter or comparable document is not incompatible with the UN Charter and does not require approval of the Security Council.[97]

22.11   THE OAS, THE UN SECURITY COUNCIL, AND THE HAITI CASE (1991–4)

On September 29–30, 1991, a military coup led by General Raoul Cédras overthrew President Jean-Bertrand Aristide, who had been inaugurated in February of the same year following an election in which he had received 67 percent of the vote. Aristide was permitted to leave the country, and first from Venezuela and later from the United States he mobilized the international community in his favour and against the military and police leaders who had taken over the government.

---

[94] Resolution of Ninth Meeting of Consultation, Washington 26 July 1964, *Applications* Vol. II, pp. 181–6.

[95] On July 29, 1975, the Sixteenth Meeting of Consultation of Foreign Ministers voted to remove the mandatory character of the sanctions against Cuba, but left individual states free to maintain or discontinue the embargo. The United States supported the resolution, on the ground that a mandatory resolution no longer acceptable to the majority of members of the OAS was an anomaly, but it kept its own embargo in place.

[96] Supporting this view, see F. Garcia-Amador, *The Inter-American System*, Vol. I, part II, pp. 408–18 (1983).

[97] Accord. Goodrich, Hambro, and Simons, *Charter of the United Nations*, (n. 16 supra) 364–7 (3rd edn. 1969). For discussion by the International Court of Justice of 'enforcement action' in the context of military measures undertaken by authority of the UN General Council, see *Certain Expenses of the United Nations*, Advisory Opinion of 20 July 1962, [1962] I.C.J., 151, esp. 164–5.

Four months earlier, following a coup deposing the elected President of Surinam, the General Assembly of the OAS, meeting in Santiago, Chile had adopted a Declaration entitled 'Santiago Commitment to Democracy and the Renewal of the Inter-American System', designed to trigger a prompt collective response to

any occurrences giving rise to the sudden or irregular interruption of the democratic political institutional process or of the legitimate exercise of power by the democratically elected government in any of the Organization's member states.[98]

The Secretary-General was to call a meeting of the OAS General Assembly or Ministers of Foreign Affairs within ten days of a coup, to decide upon economic sanctions, interruption of diplomatic relations, or other joint measures, similar to those enumerated under the Rio Treaty but not linked to external aggression. The coup in Haiti was the first test of the Santiago Commitment.

On the day after the overthrow of President Aristide, September 30, the OAS Council convened an Ad Hoc Meeting of Ministers of Foreign Affairs, and on October 3, having heard Aristide in person, the Meeting adopted a resolution condemning the coup and calling for diplomatic isolation of the people who brought it about.[99] The Foreign Ministers sent a special mission to Haiti, and when that failed to change the situation, adopted a resolution on October 8, 1991 urging member states to proceed immediately to freeze the assets of the Haitian state, and to impose a complete trade embargo on Haiti, except for humanitarian aid.[100]

The OAS formally transmitted its resolution to the United Nations, with a request that its member states adopt the same measures agreed upon by the American states. This seems to have had the effect of persuading some reluctant members of the Security Council, in particular India and China, that the Haiti situation was indeed a matter of international concern. The President of the Council expressed support of the Security Council for 'the efforts of the OAS to bring about the restoration of legitimate authority in Haiti.'[101] But the Security Council did not take action on its own, on the theory, apparently, that the situation properly fell within the purview of the regional organization under Chapter VIII of the UN Charter.[102]

It turned out that only the United States could really carry out an embargo, and the US administration was ambivalent. In February 1992 the

---

[98] OAS-AG/Res. 1080 (XXI–0/91) (5 June 1991).

[99] OAS-MRE/Res.1/91 'Support for the Democratic Government of Haiti' (3 Oct. 1992).

[100] OAS-MRE Res. 2/91 (8 Oct. 1991). The United States, which had already frozen Haitian assets under its jurisdiction, immediately implemented the OAS resolution. President Bush issued a second Executive Order, No. 12779 of 28 Oct. 1991, 56 Fed. Reg. 55975 (1991) taking account of the action of the OAS, and adding a trade embargo to the sanctions previously ordered.

[101] See David M. Malone, *Decision-Making in the UN Security Council: The Case of Haiti*, 62–4 and sources there cited (1998).

[102] See Sect. 22.8.

United States announced that it would be prepared to grant licenses to assembly export plants in Haiti, on the ground that 'the sanctions on the assembly sector largely affect innocent Haitians only and have no serious impact on these behind the coup.'[103] However genuine the effort was to separate the innocent workers from the actual targets of the sanctions, the decision was that of the United States alone, not of the OAS, and it was perceived both in Haiti and elsewhere as a loosening of the embargo, and perhaps as a loss of will by those who could oust the '*de factos*'. The embargo, already leaky, leaked more; the border between the Dominican Republic and Haiti opened ever wider.

For another year and a half various diplomatic efforts were made on behalf of the OAS and the UN, often together. The Special Envoy of the UN Secretary-General, an Argentine diplomat, was also named Special Envoy of the OAS Secretary-General, which reduced, if it did not wholly eliminate, conflicts on the ground between the two organizations. However, until the United Nations adopted a worldwide oil embargo—'selective mandatory sanctions' under Chapter VII[104]—little changed.

The embargo decided on by the Security Council under Chapter VII brought the *de factos* to the negotiating table, and President Aristide and General Raoul Cédras entered into the so-called Governors Island Agreement, looking to the resignation of General Cédras and his confederates, the return of President Aristide, and the suspension of both the OAS and UN sanctions.[105] On August 27, 1993, the Security Council (as well as the OAS) called on member states to suspend but not terminate sanctions against Haiti.[106] The sanctions were suspended, but the generals did not leave, and the Governors Island Agreement fell apart.

On October 11, 1993, a UN Mission to Haiti consisting of 50 Canadian police and 30 American soldiers arrived in Haiti by ship, but was not permitted to land. President Clinton called for reimposition of sanctions, and on October 13, the Security Council adopted a resolution terminating the suspension and reinstating the sanctions.[107] Following the assassination of Haiti's minister of justice, first Canada and then the United States, withdrew their personnel from the UN mission in Haiti. But on American initiative, the Security Council adopted a resolution—under Chapters VII and VIII—calling upon Member States

acting nationally or through regional agencies or arrangements . . . to use such measures commensurate with the specific circumstances as may be necessary under the

---

[103] US State Department announcement, 4 Feb. 1992, as reported in BNA *Int'l Trade Reporter*, Vol. 9, No. 7, p. 254 (12 Feb. 1992). Assembly plants receive material made in the United States for assembly in Haiti and re-export to the United States. Most of these plants were US-owned.

[104] SC Res. 841 (16 June 1993).

[105] Agreement between President Jean-Bertrand Aristide and General Raoul Cédras signed at Governor's Island, New York, 3 July 1993, UN Doc. A/47/975 (1993).

[106] SC Res. 861 (27 Aug. 1993).   [107] SC Res. 873 (13 Oct. 1993).

authority of the Security Council to ensure strict implementation of the [prior sanctions resolutions] relating to the supply of petroleum or petroleum products or arms and related matériel of all types, and in particular to halt inward maritime shipping as necessary,

in other words, to impose a naval blockade.[108] Of course the main burden fell on the United States, but Argentina, Canada, France, and The Netherlands contributed to the blockade.

One more round of sanctions was effected in May 1994, after the octogenarian President of the Supreme Court of Haiti was installed by the military leaders as President of the Republic. The Security Council and the OAS condemned the action, and the Security Council now adopted Comprehensive Mandatory Sanctions, acting under Chapter VII alone.[109]

Eventually, in the fall of 1994 the Haitian crisis was resolved with the departure of the leaders of the coup, as a multinational force assembled by the United States was apparently ready to invade, while former President Carter was on the island negotiating with the *de facto* regime for a safe withdrawal from the island. On September 26, the United States suspended all unilateral sanctions against Haiti, and three days later, the Security Council terminated the sanctions set out in its sanctions resolutions of 1993 and 1994.[110] By this time the OAS, which had been in the lead in condemning and seeking to isolate the leaders of the coup, had taken on the role of follower. On October 14, 1994, President Aristide returned to Haiti. On the following day the Security Council adopted one more resolution, welcoming the lifting of sanctions now that President Aristide had returned to his country, and urging 'that cooperation continue between the Secretaries-General of the United Nations and of the Organization of American states.'[111]

A number of observers have pointed to the Haiti case as evidence of the inadequacy of economic sanctions, as contrasted with the threat or actual use of military force. It has also been suggested that the Haiti case demonstrates the weakness—even impotence—of the OAS. To this writer, while the Haiti case is instructive in several respects, such judgments are overdrawn. Without sanctions, the leaders of the military coup against the elected President might well have consolidated their hold on the country, which had no reserve of a democratic tradition. And while it was the threat of force by the United States that ultimately brought down the military regime in Haiti, the United States would probably not have moved—and certainly would have had no legal authority for moving—without support and endorsement from the United Nations Security Council acting under Chapter VII. The Security Council in turn—or so it seems—would not have become involved in Haiti, and would not have seen the situation as a threat

---

[108] SC Res. 875, (16 Oct. 1993).   [109] SC Res. 917 (6 May 1994).
[110] SC Res. 944 (29 Sept. 1994).   [111] SC Res. 948 (15 Oct. 1994).

to international peace and security, without the prodding, the diplomatic efforts, and the sanctions—diplomatic and economic—initiated by the OAS.

From a legal standpoint, the Haiti case illustrates a number of points:

(1) the expanded legal authority of the OAS pursuant to the Santiago Commitment, responding not only to external aggression or threat of aggression, but to interference with democracy;

(2) the collaboration, perhaps for the first time, between the OAS and the United Nations, including one of the critical resolutions of the Security Council reciting both Chapter VII and Chapter VIII;

(3) the threat of force at the end of a period when economic sanctions have not succeeded, which almost certainly could not have been authorized at the beginning of the period.

SUMMARY

United Nations sanctions pursuant to mandatory resolutions were rare until the 1990s. Beginning with the response of the international community to the invasion of Kuwait in 1990, which coincided roughly with the end of the Cold War, the Security Council has adopted mandatory economic sanctions with increasing frequency. The sanctions have ranged for complete embargo on exports and imports plus order to freeze the target state's assets in member states' territories to arms embargoes, restraints on supply of petroleum, prohibitions on financial transactions, and restrictions on air and sea transportation. Whatever limitations were placed on the predicate for action under Chapter VII by the framers of the UN Charter have clearly eroded, even as the world's conception of international law has expanded. Thus though sanctions are still seen as reponse to a crisis, a state's treatment of its own citizens, or of a minority group within its territory, is now regarded as a subject of international concern, and so is overthrow of an elected government. If the treatment of a minority group, or the interference with the political group rises to the level of a crisis, a response in the form of sanctions can often command a majority of the Security Council, including the affirmative vote (or abstention) of the five permanent members of the Council, even if the crisis is confined to a single state or territory.

The distinctions between jurisdiction of regional arrangements and the United Nations—never crisp—have become blurred when the objectives of the organizations coincide or overlap. While 'enforcement action' is still committed to the Security Council alone, sanctions designed to change the will of those in control of a state are permitted to the regional organization, and in the case of the OAS are provided for in the constitutive documents, at least if actual use of force is not contemplated. Sanctions remain unpopular, and often hurt the innocent populations more than the leaders at whom they are directed. But they remain the response of choice, when the alternatives are doing nothing—'business as usual'—or rushing in to apply military force, which is both unattractive and often unlawful.

Sanctions gain in legal authority from being decided upon collectively. The extent to which sanctions may be employed by one nation alone is the subject of the next chapter, with focus on the United States.

23

Economic Sanctions without Benefit of Treaty

23.1   INTRODUCTION

It was once contended that any measures taken by a state for purposes of foreign policy or national security were contrary to international law. Article 16 of the Charter of the Organization of American States of 1948[1] (Article 19 of the 1967 revision)[2] gives some support to this argument, in that it provides:

No State may use or encourage the use of coercive measures of an economic or political character in order to force the sovereign will of another State and obtain from it advantages of any kind.[3]

But this provision has not been observed, and as Prof. Barry Carter has written the frequent use of sanctions by the United States and many other countries constitutes persuasive evidence that no clear norm exists in customary law against the use of economic sanctions.[4] Even in ruling against the United States in the *Nicaragua* case on account of various military activities, the International Court of Justice said of the economic sanctions that the United States had imposed—cut-off of economic assistance, 90 percent reduction of the sugar quotas, and eventually a complete embargo on trade:

[T]he Court has merely to say that it is unable to regard such action on the economic plane as is here complained of as a breach of the customary-law principle of non-intervention.[5]

Nevertheless, legal considerations do play a significant role in regard to economic measures taken by states for political purposes and in the response of other states, private persons, and courts. These considerations make up the contents of this chapter.[6]

It is not surprising that most of the illustrations are taken from the practice of the United States, which has been the leading user of economic sanctions since World War II.[7] However, the effort here is to propose some

---

[1] 1119 U.N.T.S. 3.   [2] 21 U.S.T. 607, T.I.A.S. 6847.
[3] A similar statement appears in the Declaration of the UN General Assembly on Principles of International Law Concerning Friendly Relations and Cooperation among States in Accordance with the Charter of the United Nations, G.A. Res. 2625, 25 UN GAOR Supp. 8 at 121, 65 *Am. J. Int'l. L.* 243 (1970).
[4] See Barry E. Carter, *International Economic Sanctions*, 6, n. 6 (1988).
[5] *Military and Paramilitary Activities in and against Nicaragua* (*Nicaragua* v. *United States of America*), Merits Judgement, [1986] I.C.J. Rep. 14, para. 245.
For discussion of the US sanctions against Nicaragua in the context of GATT, see Sect. 23.5(e) infra.
[6] For extensive discussion of the legal issue, with elaborate sources, see Omer Yousif Elagab, *The Legality of Non-Forcible Counter-Measures in International Law* (1988).
[7] For a comprehensive summary of economic sanctions for foreign policy goals in the period 1914–84, see Gary Clyde Hufbauer and Jeffrey J. Schott, *Economic Sanctions Reconsidered: History and Current Policy* (1985).

general principles, not to reflect the views of the US government, nor to judge programs of sanctions as successful or unsuccessful.[8]

23.2   The Range of National Sanctions: The United States as Model

(a)   Total Embargo

The most severe form of economic sanction is a total embargo, i.e. a complete cut-off of exports, imports, financial transactions and travel. This was the regime imposed by the United States in 1950 against the People's Republic of China, North Korea, and later North Vietnam and Cambodia, pursuant to the US Trading with the Enemy Act and a Presidential Proclamation of National Emergency. As of year-end 2001, the controls thus initiated remain in effect with respect to North Korea pursuant to the so-called Foreign Assets Control Regulations administered by the Department of the Treasury.[9] Similar regulations, though with some differences, were imposed by the United States against Cuba in 1963, against Iran in 1979–80, and against a number of other states for shorter periods. In their most stringent forms the regulations, backed up by heavy fines and imprisonment for, violators prohibit

(i)   all transfers of credit and all payments by, to or through the designated foreign country or national of such country with respect to any property subject to the jurisdiction of the United States or by any person subject to the jurisdiction of the United States; and

(ii)   all dealings in property, including, sale, purchase, lease, export or import, again by any person subject to the jurisdiction of the United States or with respect to any property subject to the jurisdiction of the United States.

The effect is not only to stop all trade with the designated country or area, but to block or freeze (the terms are used interchangeably) all assets in the United States, and to some extent elsewhere, as discussed below. Generally, travel by residents or citizens of the United States to the designated country has come within the prohibition, but, especially with respect to Cuba, licenses have been granted for humanitarian purposes, such as seeing elderly family members.

In the mid-1970s, the US Congress concluded that use of the Trading with the Enemy Act by successive administrations had been excessive, and amended

---

[8]   Hufbauer and Schott employ a rating system to the many episodes in their collection, from 1 (failed) to 4 (success). If one views economic sanctions not just designed to achieve a stated goal but as a response to another state's conduct between 'business as usual' and resort to force, such a rating system seems unsuitable, and the tables derived from it misleading.

[9]   31 Code of Federal Regulations [C.F.R.] Pt. 500. The People's Republic of China was removed from the sanction in stages in the years 1969–72. For the details see A. Lowenfeld, *Trade Controls for Political Ends*, ch. II, §1.33 (2nd edn. 1983).

the Act to be applicable only in wartime. However, the administration persuaded Congress (a) to maintain in effect the controls promulgated under the Trading with the Enemy Act; and (b) to adopt a new statute, the International Emergency Economic Powers Act (IEEPA),[10] which essentially granted the same wide powers to the President, subject only to the requirement of a new Proclamation of National Emergency for each new program of sanctions. The national emergency proclamation may remain in effect for only one year, but the proclamation can be renewed, and successive presidents have done so, almost as a matter of routine.[11] The United States comprehensive embargoes have served as the model for the UN sanctions against Southern Rhodesia, Iraq, and other states. So far as appears, the model has not been followed in toto by other states in the absence of a United Nations mandate.

(b)   Assets Freeze and Financial Controls

Blocking or freezing of financial assets of a foreign state has been resorted to by a number of states. The United States froze Iranian assets subject to jurisdiction of the United States just after the seizure of the US Embassy in Teheran in November 1979, but did not impose an embargo on trade between Iran and the United States until several months later.[12] The Bank of England froze Argentine assets held in the United Kingdom and suspended official insurance cover on exports to Argentina in April 1982, in response to that country's invasion of the Falkland (Malvinas) Islands.[13]

A freeze of assets can be applied with different levels of intensity. In the case of the Bank of England regulations, the measure took immediate effect, so that, for instance, debts of Argentina or its nationals due to British lenders or suppliers of goods and services—or indeed to others that would have been paid with funds deposited in London—could not be paid without a license. Nor, correspondingly, could anyone in the United Kingdom make a loan or satisfy a debt to Argentina or an Argentine national or resident as defined. In contrast to the American freeze of Iranian assets in 1979 and Libyan assets in 1986, as discussed below,[14] the British order did not extend to overseas branches of British banks; it did apply, however, to British branches of foreign banks, and to assets in Britain of foreign branches of Argentine enterprises.

---

[10] 50 U.S.C. §1701 et seq.

[11] One other legislative change made by Congress in 1977 was to eliminate from the powers available to the President the power to *vest* 'enemy property', i.e. to actually transfer title to the United States, as contrasted with blocking or freezing such property pending some settlement. In fact, the power to vest had not been used in the United States since World War II, and might be subject to constitutional challenge that has not succeeded in respect to merely blocking assets.

[12] See, A. Lowenfeld *et al.* (eds.), *Revolutionary Days: The Iran Hostage Crisis and The Hague Claims Tribunal*, 16–19 (1998).

[13] See *Financial Times*, London, 5 Apr. 1982, 1; *UK*: Control of Gold, Securities, Payments and Credits (Argentine Republic) Directions 1982, 3 Apr. 1982, [1982] Stat. Instr. No. 512, 1296.

[14] See Sect. 23.4(c) infra.

Initially the Bank's notice stated that irrevocable letters of credit issued before April 3, 1982, the date of the order, in respect of exports to Argentina could be paid, and if a British bank made the payment it could apply to be reimbursed out of frozen Argentine assets. A few weeks later, as the British task force neared the Falkland Islands, the order was amended to prohibit honouring of letters of credit used to finance purchases of aircraft, ships, or arms and ammunition. For its part, the Argentine government froze British assets in Argentina, and suspended payments on debts to British banks.[15]

(c) Import Controls

Great Britain banned imports from Argentina just after it had imposed the financial controls described above, and a few days later Argentina banned imports from Great Britain. Sanctions are inevitably more powerful when they reflect the decisions of more than a single state, both in respect of the economic pain that they inflict and in respect of their symbolic value in characterizing the target state as an outcast. Prime Minister Thatcher describes in her Memoirs that she sought support from fellow members of the European Community, but did not ask for a complete import ban because she thought it would be bad tactics to press for too much at once.[16] In the event, the European Community announced in mid-April a one-month suspension of imports of all products originating in Argentina, subject to the proviso, however, that contract documents issued and contracts concluded prior to the entry into force of the regulation (except as to imports to the United Kingdom) would not be affected.[17] The suspension was to run for one month, and was extended twice before being repealed in the last week in June.[18]

New Zealand banned all trade with Argentina, and Australia and Canada suspended imports. For the United States, an embargo on imports was not an available option except under emergency powers that could be exercised only pursuant to a proclamation of national emergency or a mandatory order of the UN Security Council. In contrast to export controls as discussed below, imports are subject to detailed regulation set out in successive Trade

---

[15] *Argentina*: Decree No. 683 of 5 Apr. 1982, [1982] *Legislación Argentina 1982-A*, 142.

[16] Margaret Thatcher, *The Downing Street Years*, 190–1 (1993).

[17] Council Regulation (EEC) No. 877/82 of 16 Apr. 1982, 1982 OJ L 101/1 (16 Apr. 1982). For an interesting discussion of the place this decision had in the development of Community action under Article 113 (the commercial policy article) of the Treaty of Rome, rather than the consultation provisions of Article 224 concerning serious international tension, see Pieter Jan Kuyper, 'Community Sanctions against Argentina: Lawfulness under Community and International Law', in David O'Keefe and Henry G. Schermers (eds.), *Essays in European Law and Integration* (1982).

[18] Council Regulation (EEC) No. 1977/82 of 21 June 1982, 1982 OJ L 177/1 (20 June 1982). Parallel regulations were issued, extended and repealed by the European Coal and Steel Community.

Acts, including a provision for most-favoured-nation treatment for imports of all states other than certain communist states.[19]

(d) Export Controls

Export controls were a prime instrument of the Cold War (1948–89), led for the Western countries by the United States, with the Soviet Union and the communist states of Eastern Europe as the principal targets.[20] Export controls have not been used to impose total embargoes, but (with exceptions as described below) were used to restrict exports of weapons, as well as exports of products and technical data with 'dual-use' potential, i.e. with military as well as civilian uses, or designs and products incorporating advanced technology believed to be capable of contributing to the military and economic strength of the Soviet Union and its allies.

The United States has always taken the position that its jurisdiction applies to all goods and technical data of US origin, wherever they may be located, and thus that its controls cover both initial exports and re-exports.[21] Though they did not formally accept the extraterritorial aspect of re-export controls, most member states of the North Atlantic Treaty and Japan participated to varying degrees in a system of verification of destination control, and also in a joint program of determining which products should be kept away from the Soviet bloc.[22] As (1) the West European countries and Japan became less dependent on aid from the United States, (2) the technological gap between the United States and both Western Europe and the East narrowed, and (3) perceptions of the communist threat declined more quickly in Europe and Japan than in the United States, the effort at multilateral denial through export controls became gradually less significant and more subject to disagreement.[23] For the United

---

[19] See, 19 U.S.C. §2136 (Reciprocal Non-discriminatory Treatment). Most of the communist states, notably including the People's Republic of China, have been receiving annual waivers, entitling their goods to MFN treatment as well. See 19 U.S.C. §§2431–41 (Exceptions to non-discriminatory treatment and waiver authority). Upon China's entry into the WTO, which finally took place on 11 Dec. 2001 following the Doha Conference, it ceased to be subject to the annual waiver requirement. See Pres. Procl. of 27 Dec. 2001 Granting Permanent Normal Trade Relations to China, in implementation of Pub.L. 106–286 (10 Oct. 2000).

[20] Because they were subjects of almost total embargo under the Trading with the Enemy Act and its successor statute, the People's Republic of China, North Korea, North Vietnam, and Cambodia were not in practice targets of US export controls, though nominally they were placed in country groups, as described hereafter.

[21] The Commerce Department Regulations have been revised and renumbered a number of times. As of year-end 2001 the statement in the text is confirmed by 15 C.F.R. §§734.2 and 734.3.

[22] For an informative (though somewhat outdated) description of the US program of re-export controls and the participation in that program by other states, see Ruth L. Greenstein and Mitchel B. Wallerstein, 'Exports, Reexports, and Re-Reexports: An Endless Echo of Controls', in Moyer, Cassidy, Buckley, and Fraizier (eds.), *Law and Policy of Export Controls: Recent Essays on Key Export Issues* (ABA 1993).

[23] For a brief description of the multilateral efforts to coordinate export controls through a little-known organization called 'CoCom', see A. Lowenfeld, *Trade Controls for Political Ends*, ch. I, §1.3 (2nd edn. 1983). For a book-length, critical description of the process, see Gunnar

States, however, export controls have been a major tool of foreign policy, and it is useful to describe the American system in some detail before exploring the questions of international law raised in the succeeding sections of this chapter.

23.3   United States Export Controls: A Closer Look[24]

(a)   The System of Licenses

Under the Export Control Act of 1949 and successor statutes, all commercial exports from the United States—of technology as well as of goods—require a license as a condition for leaving the country.[25] Some products are restricted to all countries, i.e. any export requires a *validated license*, that is a license that is specifically applied for, and is granted only upon satisfaction by the authorities that it will be sent to reliable end-users for peaceful purposes, and will not be re-exported to a state or person under sanction. Most products may be exported under a general license, and require a validated license only for export to certain target countries. In principle, validated licenses are required for products that may have strategic uses, but many products have both strategic and peaceful uses;[26] moreover, the United States from time to time restricted exports of wheat, and even soccer balls to the Soviet Union.

(b)   Country Groups

Export controls have been applied by the United States through a system of country groups, which are declared eligible for different categories of licenses. Exports from the United States to Canada, for instance, have virtually always been permitted, provided that the purchaser could show that it was the end-user or would pledge not to re-export to specified countries or end-users. Exports to Latin America (Cuba excepted) and to Western Europe have been lightly controlled; other countries have been shifted between categories according to the current state of political relations. For

---

Adler-Karlsson, *Western Economic Warfare 1947–1967* (1968). Co-Com faded away in the 1990s, and was replaced by a somewhat different, more open organization known as the Wassenaar Arrangement on Export Controls for Conventional Arms and Technologies, formally approved by 33 nations (including Russia) on 11–12 July 1996. See e.g. 13 *BNA Int'l Trade Rep.* No. 29 p. 1162 (19 July 1996); also note: 'From Containment to Cooperation: Collective Action and the Wassenaar Arrangement', 19 *Cardozo L. Rev.* 1079 (1997). The Headquarters for the Wassenaar Arrangement is in Vienna.

[24] The description here pertains to civilian or dual-use items. Arms exports are subject to a different statutory scheme, not here discussed.

[25] 50 U.S.C. App. §§2031–2 (1949–69). The Export Control Act was never adopted as permanent legislation, and was replaced in 1969 by the Export Administration Act, 50 U.S.C. App. §§2401–20. On several occasions the Export Control or Export Administration Act expired before the renewal had been adopted, but each time the President continued the authorities and implementation by executive order, relying on the Twea or Ieepa.

[26] Premier Khrushchev of the Soviet Union once suggested that buttons should be controlled, since they could be used to hold up soldiers' trousers.

instance, in the period 1960–80 first Poland and later Hungary were moved from Country Group Y to Country Group W which was eligible for more classes of products under general license (or for which validated licenses were more readily granted). Subsequently Country Group Q was created for Romania, but Albania, Bulgaria, Czechoslovakia, East Germany, and the Soviet Union remained in Group Y. When Libya was placed under sanction for foreign policy reasons in 1982, a new Country Group S was created, which provided that a validated license or re-export authorization would be required for all US origin commodities or technical data, except for medicines, medical supplies and food; the regulation indicated that licenses would generally be denied, unless the proposed export had been under contract prior to the effective date of the regulation in circumstances where failure to obtain a license would not excuse performance under the contract.[27]

(c)   Multiple Objectives of Export Control

As of 2001, some fourteen countries or parts of countries were under some kind of complete or partial trade embargo.[28] In addition, the United States applied export controls to different countries for a number of stated purposes, including controls against terrorism; proliferation of chemical and biological weapons; nuclear proliferation; crime control; missile technology; national security; regional stability; and restrictions on instruments of torture.[29]

Further, validated licenses are required for certain high performance computers, communications interception devices and encryption items. Many of the specific controls have 'contract sanctity' provisions, i.e. licenses are available upon submission of documentation showing a contract was entered into before the date when the particular regulation entered into force. For some prohibitions, for instance those related to nuclear non-proliferation and national security (i.e. advanced weapons), contract sanctity provisions are not available. Many of the prohibitions contain a provision reading as follows:

Although the United States seeks cooperation from like-minded countries in maintaining [anti-terrorism controls] [controls on crime control and detection items] [regional stability controls] [. . .], at this time these controls are, maintained only by the United States.[30]

---

[27] 47 Fed. Reg. 112479 (16 Mar. 1982). The Country Groups are regularly in response to developments in international relations. As of 2001, the Commerce Department maintained Country Groups A to E (15 C.F.R., Part 740, Supp. 1–3) plus a partly overlapping list of embargoes and special controls (15 C.F.R., Part 746).

[28] 15 C.F.R. Part 746 and updates.

[29] Not all of these categories mean that licenses will be denied. But, for example, when both India and Pakistan detonated nuclear devices in May of 1998, a policy of denial was announced for exports (or re-exports) of items controlled for nuclear non-proliferation and missile technology reasons. See 15 C.F.R. §742.16.

[30] This statement does not appear with respect to nuclear non-proliferation, missile technology, chemical and biological weapons, high-performance computers, encryption, or national security, reflecting international agreements on these matters. It appears with respect to controls for regional stability, crime control, and anti-terrorism (Iran, Syria, Sudan). 15 C.F.R. Part 742.

(d)   Enforcement and the Blacklist

Though violation of US export controls may lead to criminal penalties, including fines, imprisonment, or both, the far more common means for enforcement of export controls is through administrative sanctions, and in particular through suspension or denial of 'export privileges'. If a person engaged in an export transaction from the United States—exporter, freight forwarder, carrier, warehouser, purchaser or end-user—is found in an administrative proceeding before the Department of Commerce to have violated the controls—for instance by exporting (or attempting to export) an item on the 'Commerce Control List' without a validated license, or to a country to which the license did not extend—that person (natural or juridical) will be subject to denial of export privileges.[31] The denial may be for all exports, or only for exports of controlled items, or only for petroleum products, etc.; the denial may be for a few months, or for a year, or even until the end of controls. Moreover, denial orders may cover persons not in the United States—even persons who have never been in the United States, so long as they engaged in an export transactions as defined.[32] Denial Orders are published in the *Federal Register*, and a Denied Persons List is published regularly in alphabetical order and by area in Department Bulletins and on electronic bulletin boards.

The effect is not only that persons on the list are prohibited from engaging in whatever activity is stated in the denial order, but that all other persons are prohibited from dealing with the person subject to the denial order in any export transaction from the United States or (with minor exceptions) in any transaction involving US-origin products or technology, on pain of being subject to a denial order themselves.[33] Thus a firm violating a

[31] Formerly the regulations referred to a 'Commodity Control List'. The name was changed to recognize that the controls cover not only commodities, but also software and technology. The CCL appears as Supplement No. 1 to 15 C.F.R., Part 774, covering about 180 pages double-column small print.

[32] It was reported that in 1988 four times as many foreign as domestic parties were subject to denial orders. See Werner Hein, 'The Denial List: A European Perspective', in Moyer, Cassidy, Buckley, and Fraizier (eds.), *Law and Policy of Export Controls: Recent Essays on Key Export Issues* (ABA 1993).

[33] 15 C.F.R., Part 764 and supplements thereto. For an early case involving the contagious black list, see e.g. *Cacermet S.A. and André Letiers*, 36 Fed. Reg. 13048 (13 July 1971), reproduced in A. Lowenfeld, *Trade Controls for Political Ends*, ch. I, §2.66 (2nd edn. 1983). In that case, LeCoq, a French firm, had been placed on a Denial List for the duration of export controls, for knowingly participating in the re-export of US-origin commodities from France to the USSR contrary to the terms of the relevant export license and accompanying documents. Cacermet, who had been made aware of LeCoq's place on the Denial List, engaged in France in transactions with LeCoq involving US-origin products, and was therefore also made subject to denial of export privileges for a period of 5 years, with the right to apply after 2 years for probation in place of the absolute denial.

For a more recent case involving the German subsidiary of a major American computer company charged with dealing with a company known, as the Commerce Department contended, to be controlled by a 'notorious diverter' of computer products, see Hein (n. 32 supra), 399–400.

US export prohibition risks being cut off from all opportunity to deal in US-origin products or technology, even if it is not engaged in business in the United States, and is therefore not subject to US judicial jurisdiction.

In practice the impact of the regulations is not quite as harsh as this brief description suggests: a respondent is entitled to a hearing, to be represented by counsel, to submit evidence, and to a (limited) appeal to the Under Secretary.[34] Nevertheless, the proceeding, little changed since it was instituted shortly after the end of World War II, raises questions of jurisdiction to prescribe and enforce under international law, as discussed in the following section.

23.4   ECONOMIC SANCTIONS AND THE JURISDICTION OF STATES

(a)   Jurisdiction to Prescribe and Jurisdiction to Enforce

Jurisdiction to prescribe, in the present context, refers to the authority of a state as a matter of international law to make its law applicable to the activities, relations, or status of persons or the interests of persons in things, whether by legislation, executive act, regulation, or determination of a court.[35] For example, suppose (as has occurred several times) the President of the United States issues an order blocking all assets of state X subject to the jurisdiction of the United States. Whether the President has the domestic authority to take this step is a matter of US law.[36] The question of which assets such an order reaches—for instance whether it reaches all dollar accounts, or deposits in foreign branches or subsidiaries of US banks—involves not only US law but the question of jurisdiction to prescribe.

Jurisdiction to enforce, in the present context, refers to the authority of a state to induce or compel compliance, or to punish non-compliance, with its laws or regulations, whether through its courts or by use of executive, administrative, police, or other non-judicial action.[37] To take the example mentioned in the preceding section,[38] may the United States government deprive a French corporation of the opportunity to engage in trade with the

---

[34] 15 C.F.R., Part 766. Since an amendment adopted in 1988, judicial review of civil penalties and denial orders is available, but not of the decision to place an item on a list of commodities requiring a validated license, or decision to place a country in a given country group. 50 U.S.C App. §2412(c)(3).

If a Respondent neither appears nor submits an answer within the time prescribed (normally 30 days from notice of issuance of a charging letter), a default will be entered, finding the facts as alleged. There is provision for a petition to set aside a default. 15 C.F.R. §766.7.

[35] The definition here offered is a slight abridgement of the definition in §401(a) of the *Restatement (Third) of the Foreign Relations Law of the United States* (1987).

[36] See Sect. 23.2(a) supra.

[37] Again, the definition here is taken from the *Restatement (Third) of the Foreign Relations Law of the United States*, §401(c).

[38] See Sect. 23.3(d), n. 33.

United States, on the ground that it re-exported a US-origin product in contravention to US regulations, though in compliance with the law of France? It is clear that a state does not have jurisdiction to enforce a law or regulation that it did not have jurisdiction to prescribe.[39] The example demonstrates, however, that on the one hand a state may have jurisdiction to enforce (i.e. punish or induce compliance) even when it does not have jurisdiction to adjudicate; on the other hand, even when it has jurisdiction to prescribe, different considerations (and different perceptions) may determine whether the state has jurisdiction to enforce.

(b)   International Law and the Jurisdiction of States

No treaty or convention governs jurisdiction to prescribe or enforce. It is generally agreed, however, that international law does set limits on the application by a state of its law.[40] It is also generally agreed that the principal bases of jurisdiction are territoriality and nationality.[41] In the context of antitrust and trade regulation, the principal controversy comes in the definition of, or analogy to, territoriality—in particular whether *effect* in the territory of Patria justifies Patria in exercising jurisdiction over *conduct* in Xandia (see Chapter 12, Section 12.4). In the context of economic sanctions, the principal controversy comes in the definition of, or analogy to, nationality—in particular whether the conduct of the Xandian branch or subsidiary of a corporation organized in Patria is subject to the regulation of Patria. To the general public, Coca Cola and Ford are American, Mitsubishi is Japanese, Volkswagen is German, and so on, regardless of where a given activity is centered. The government of Xandia may well have a different view, particularly when Patria (say the United States) seeks to prohibit or punish conduct that Xandia (say Canada or France) permits or encourages.

In its standard regulations imposing a complete embargo and freeze of assets, the United States applies its prohibitions to persons 'subject to the jurisdiction of the United States', defined as follows:

(1) Any person, wheresoever located, who is a citizen or resident of the United States;

(2) Any person actually within the United States;

---

[39] See *Restatement* §431(a).

[40] In *The S.S. Lotus (France v. Turkey)*, [1927] P.C.I.J. Ser. A. No. 10, the inter-War World Court declined to set down any limits on the exercise of jurisdiction outside a state's territory. The Court wrote:

> [T]he first and foremost restriction imposed by international law upon a State is that . . . it may not exercise its power in any form in the territory of another State. . . . It does not, however, follow that international law prohibits a State from exercising jurisdiction in its own territory, in respect of any case which relates to acts which have taken place abroad, and in which it cannot rely on some permissive rule of international law. ([1927] P.C.I.J. Ser. A. No. 10, at 18–19)

[41] See e.g. *Restatement* §402(i); *Oppenheim's International Law* (Jennings and Watts (eds.)), Sect. 136 (1992).

(3) Any corporation organized under the laws of the United States or of any State, territory, possession, or district of the United States; and

(4) Any partnership, association, corporation, or other organization, wheresoever organized or doing business, *which is owned or controlled by persons specified in subparagraph (1), (2), or (3) of this paragraph.*[42] (italics added)

This formula is based on the belief, generally (though not always) conforming to the facts, that fundamental decisions of multinational enterprises such as with which countries to do business, are made by the senior management or board of directors of the parent corporation—in the case of US-based enterprises in New York, Pittsburgh, Detroit, Chicago, not in Canada, France or England. While the US government would not direct a foreign affiliate of a US-based enterprise as to which side of the street its vehicles should drive on, or what wages and vacation benefits its workers should receive, the United States more often than not took the view that whether it was acceptable to trade with North Korea or Cuba or Iraq or Iran was up to the parent company board and therefore within the proper scope of the US emergency legislation and regulations.

The other side of this argument is that a company incorporated in Xandia ought not only to comply with the laws of Xandia, but also with its foreign economic policy, and that it is wrong—an invasion of sovereignty—to involve Xandia in a quarrel between the United States and Tertia, a state with which Xandia has no quarrel or at any rate has chosen not to cut off economic relations.

The country most affected by the United States policy, as could be expected, has been Canada. For instance, shortly after the United States imposed its embargo against the People's Republic of China in the early 1950s, Imperial Oil Company, a Canadian company at the time 70 percent owned by Standard Oil Company of New Jersey (now Exxon) was instructed not to sell oil produced in Canada to China, though such sale would not have been contrary to Canadian law. In 1958, Ford of Canada was required to turn down an order for 1000 vehicles to be produced in Canada, because the US Treasury ruled that the transaction would violate the US Foreign Asset Control Regulations. Since virtually all of Canada's automobile industry at the time was conducted by wholly owned subsidiaries of US-based companies, the result was that a proposed opening of trade between Canada and China was lost to Canada. This and similar cases led to strong protests within Canada, and to formal talks between the Prime Minister of Canada and the President of the United States, looking to 'full

---

[42] Foreign Assets Control Regulations, 31 C.F.R., §500.329 (1950–); Cuban Assets Control Regulations, 31 C.F.R., §515.329 (1963–); Iranian Assets Control Regulations, 31 C.F.R. §535.329 (1979–81). The italicized words did not appear in the US Rhodesian Transaction Regulation or the Rhodesian Sanctions Regulations, 31 C.F.R., §525.307 (1967); §530.307 (1968).

consultation between the governments' on a case-by-case basis.[43] The United States maintained its position on the right to restrict activities of US-controlled companies established abroad, but in some cases in which Canada's concern was clearly greater than that of the United States the prohibition was relaxed.

When the United States promulgated its Cuban Assets Control Regulations in 1963,[44] the assertion of jurisdiction over corporations owned or controlled by US persons was maintained,[45] but the potential for collision with Canada and other countries that continued to trade with Cuba was diminished by a general license to non-banking corporations organized under the laws of a foreign country to engage in transactions not involving US dollar accounts or US origin products.[46] Even that concession to Canada turned out not to solve the conflict, because the license did not extend to US individual nationals, many of whom were employed in managerial positions in Canadian subsidiaries of US-owned companies.

The United States government has taken the position—never fully articulated but implemented in practice—that in terms of jurisdiction to enforce, its actions as described above are not extraterritorial, because the orders, and the threat of punishment, are directed to the parent companies in the United States. The argument is unconvincing once the distinction set out in subsection (a) between jurisdiction to prescribe and jurisdiction to enforce is kept in mind. However enforcement is threatened or carried out, it is clear that the United States has sought in the context of economic sanctions to prescribe with respect to conduct abroad by foreign corporations linked to the United States through ownership or control, often through company names and trademarks as well.[47] It does not necessarily follow that all such efforts transgress the bounds of international law. At a minimum, it should not be regarded as unreasonable—and therefore unlawful—for the United States (or other governments in similar position) to prevent evasion of a prohibition by reincorporation across the border to carry out the same activity shut down in the home state.

The American Law Institute's *Restatement (Third) of Foreign Relations Law* sets out an intermediate position between the position of the US

---

[43] See *Joint Statement on Export Policies issued at Conclusion of Meeting between President Eisenhower and Prime Minister Diefenbaker*, 9 July 1958, 39 *Dept. State Bull.* (1958). For a detailed account of this and other cases, see J. I. W. Corcoran, 'The Trading with the Enemy Act and the Controlled Canadian Corporation', 14 *McGill L.J.* 174 (1968).

[44] 31 C.F.R., Part 515   [45] 31 C.F.R. §§ 515.329 and 515.330.

[46] 31 C.F.R. §515.341. Later the license for subsidiaries was revoked, reinstated, and again revoked.

[47] It is worth remarking that in other contexts efforts by home states of multinational enterprises to exercise jurisdiction to prescribe with respect to activities of foreign affiliates provoke little controversy. Consolidated financial reports, for instance, require disclosure to investors in the parent corporation, and tax returns reflecting worldwide activities of multinational enterprises are commonly required and rarely contested.

government and of those who regard any action by the parent country as an infringement of the sovereign rights of the host country of the subsidiary.

414. Jurisdiction with Respect to Activities of Foreign Branches and Subsidiaries

(1) [. . .][48]

(2) A state may not ordinarily regulate activities of corporations organized under the laws of a foreign state on the basis that they are owned or controlled by nationals of the regulating state. However, . . . it may not be unreasonable for a state to exercise jurisdiction for limited purposes with respect to activities of affiliated foreign entities

  (a) by direction to the parent corporation in respect of such matters as uniform accounting, disclosure to investors, or preparation of consolidated tax returns of multinational enterprises; or

  (b) by direction to either the parent or the subsidiary in exceptional cases, depending on all relevant factors, including the extent to which

   (i) the regulation is essential to implementation of a program to further a major national interest of the state exercising jurisdiction;

   (ii) the national program of which the regulation is a part can be carried out effectively only if it is applied also to foreign subsidiaries;

   (iii) the regulation conflicts or is likely to conflict with the law or policy of the state where the subsidiary is established.

  (c) In the exceptional cases referred to in paragraph (b), the burden of establishing reasonableness is heavier when the direction is issued to the foreign subsidiary than when it is issued to the parent corporation.

In the best-known cases testing these propositions, the United States sought in 1965 to require Fruehauf-France, a maker of truck trailers 70 percent owned by Fruehauf-USA, to cancel a contract to supply a French manufacturer of truck tractors, Berliet, in fulfillment of a contract to sell tractor-trailers to China. For France, the contract was to be the first concrete result of a trip by President de Gaulle to the People's Republic of China. For the United States, the contract appeared to be an attempt to breach the US embargo, just as the Vietnam War was escalating. The two states exchanged various communications about extraterritoriality and sovereign rights, but eventually the minority French shareholders, asserting possible large liability of Fruehauf-France to Berliet, secured the appointment by a French court of a temporary receiver, who took care that the contract was carried out.[49] The US government did not modify the regulation or grant a license, but took the view that under the court's order, the US parent company no longer controlled Fruehauf-France, and thus no violation needed to be prosecuted.[50] An

---

[48] Subsection (1) provides that with respect to foreign *branches*, as contrasted with subsidiaries, a state may exercise jurisdiction to prescribe for limited purposes.

[49] *Société Fruehauf Corporation* v. *Massardy*, [1968] D.S. Jur. 147, [1965] J.C.P. II 14274*bis*, [1965] Gaz. Pal. 86 (Cour d'Appel Paris, 22 May 1965).

[50] The fact that the French corporation was still 'owned' by the American parent within the meaning of the Foreign Assets Control Regulations was not mentioned.

informal understanding appears to have been reached however, that in the future Fruehauf-France would not again participate in deals involving Communist China.[51]

The teaching of the *Fruehauf* case seems to be that an absolute corporate veil can no longer be drawn around a member corporation of a multi-national enterprise to separate it from its corporate parent and the parent corporation's government, but that that government applies its regulations to foreign subsidiaries at considerable cost—legal and political. To illustrate that the issue is not as straightforward as many critics of the United Sates practice have written, it is instructive to recall the widespread anti-apartheid movement in the 1980s seeking by legislation, demonstrations, and con-sumer boycotts to induce major American and European companies to divest their holdings in South Africa. None of the companies targeted by the divestment movement said, or could have gotten away with saying, 'we are not doing business in South Africa, that is only Kodak South Africa, Pty., or General Motors South Africa, Pty., or Philips South Africa, Pty.' Clearly the public, including university students, pension funds, parliaments, and con-sumers, had no patience with distinctions based on place of incorporation or on the difference between branches and subsidiaries.[52]

(c)   Bank Deposits and the Freezing of Assets

The situs of intangibles, and in particular of bank deposits, is critical in con-nection with the reach of orders of freezing assets, such as those of the United States in response to seizure of the US embassy and the taking of hostages in Tehran in November 1979 and of the United Kingdom in response to Argentina's invasion of the Falkland Islands in March 1982. In many ways the issues are the same as those discussed in the preceding sec-tion. A significant difference, however, is that while major money-center banks, with home offices in London, New York, Frankfurt, or Tokyo, vir-tually all operate worldwide, they generally do business through branches, rather than through separately incorporated subsidiaries along the lines of most non-banking multinational enterprises.[53]

---

[51] See 'US–French Clash over Red China Case Dramatizes the Plight of Multinational Firms', *Business International* 249, 250 (6 Aug. 1965). The entire episode is described in more detail in A. Lowenfeld, *Trade Controls for Political Ends*, §§3.3–3.4 (2nd edn. 1983). See also W. L. Craig, 'Application of the Trading with the Enemy Act to Foreign Corporations Owned by Americans: Reflections on *Fruehauf* v. *Massardy*', 83 *Harv. L. Rev.* 579 (1970).

[52] These thoughts are developed further in A. Lowenfeld, *International Law and the Quest for Reasonableness*, ch. 5 'National Jurisdiction and Multinationals' (Oxford 1996; also 245 *Recueil des Cours*, (Hague Academy Int'l Law), 1994-I).

[53] An important reason for the difference is that, generally, by operating through branches banks can satisfy capital requirements of host states by reference to their worldwide capital; if they operate through subsidiaries, as is required in some states, the lending limits are more likely to be tied to capital held by the locally incorporated entity. For more on this topic, see Ch. 21, Sect. 21.2.

If a bank deposit is viewed as analogous to placing a jewel in a safe, it is located where the safe (or the branch) is located; if it is viewed as a debt owed by the bank to the depositor, a bank deposit has no real situs, and may well be sued on wherever the bank does business, or at any rate at the head office of the bank. That was indeed the outcome of a number of actions brought in US courts by persons who had made deposits in branches of American banks in Saigon before that city was taken over by North Vietnam.[54] Similar actions brought against French banks in French courts came out the other way, holding that the deposit contracts were subject to the law applicable where the deposit was made, i.e. to Vietnamese law.[55]

In the context of economic sanctions, the question is reversed: to what extent may the state of the home office freeze or otherwise control deposits made at branches in other countries?

When the Bank of England froze Argentine assets in 1982, it considered but rejected application of its order to deposits made in British banks outside the United Kingdom. When the United States froze Iranian assets in November 1979 it initially took an expansive position, then modified it slightly:

No property subject to the jurisdiction of the United States or which is in the possession of or control of persons subject to the jurisdiction of the United States in which on or after the effective date Iran has an interest of any nature whatsoever may be transferred, paid, or exported, withdrawn or otherwise dealt in except as authorized.[56]

'Persons subject to the jurisdiction' carried the same definition as in the Foreign Assets and Cuban Assets Control Regulations as quoted above.[57] Assuming, to simplify the illustration, that only Iranian accounts in New York and London were under consideration, the quoted definition could have included at least the following accounts:

	Denomination	*Depositary*	*Place of Account*
(1)	Dollar Account	US Bank	New York
(2)	Dollar Account	British Bank	New York Branch
(3)	Dollar Account	US Bank	London Branch
(4)	Sterling Account	US Bank	London Branch
(5)	Dollar Account	British Bank	London
(6)	Sterling Account	British Bank	London

Each of these accounts could be said to have some link to the United States, though for category (6) the link was only that the British bank had a New York branch and thus technically fit within the definition of persons

---

[54] See e.g. *Vishipco Line* v. *Chase Manhattan Bank, N.A.*, 660 F.2d 854 (2d Cir. 1981), cert. denied, 459 US 976 (1982); *Trinh* v. *Citibank, N.A.*, 850 F.2d 1164 (6th Cir. 1988).

[55] *Dame Ba Ta Thu Van* v. *Banque Nationale de Paris*, Trib. Grande Instance Paris, 8 Mar. 1985; *Dame Dang Thi To Tam* v. *Banque Française Commerciale*, Trib. Grande Instance Paris, 12 Mar. 1985, both reported in 1985 *D.S. Inf. Rapides* 346–7.

[56] 31 C.F.R., §535.201 (15 Nov. 1979).   [57] See text at n. 42 supra.

within the United States and therefore subject to the jurisdiction of the United States. It would not be reasonable for the United States to block sterling deposits in London, and one could expect that if jurisdiction on this basis were sought to be exercised, a court in London would reject it. On the other side, category (1) should not give rise to controversy, nor should category (2)—both based on territoriality. Category (5) was not covered by the US–Iranian Assets Regulations; an effort to define all US dollars wherever or by whomever held as 'property subject to the jurisdiction of the United States' would have been regarded as unreasonable, and therefore unlikely to withstand challenge. Category (4) would seem to be covered by the regulation, and the United States maintained the formal assertion of jurisdiction, but quickly issued a general license unblocking such accounts because foreign governments objected and the amounts were not large.[58]

That left Category (3), by far the most important category—dollars deposited by Iranian entities with foreign branches of US banks.[59] The United States government directed the US banks in London, Paris, Frankfurt, and elsewhere to refuse to honour payment or withdrawal orders. The Iranian banks brought suit, asserting that they had made deposits in London, Paris, etc. and that only the law applicable at the place of deposit could govern between the depositary and the account holder.[60]

None of the lawsuits brought in connection with the Iranian Hostage Crisis went to judgment, possibly because it was hoped that the crisis could be over and the assets would be unfrozen before the suits would have to be decided. Seven years later a similar situation arose, involving a freezing of Libyan assets by the United States, in response to a series of terrorist acts attributable, according to the US government, either directly or indirectly to Libya. Libya, like Iran an oil exporter, also had substantial dollar accounts in US banks, including their London branches. Demand was made on behalf of Libya to withdraw the funds deposited in London, and the US banks refused on the basis of order from the US government.[61] In the resulting lawsuits, the first English judge granted summary judgment on the ground, simply, that a bank account is located solely at the branch where it is kept, but this was reversed by the Court of Appeal, which considered that 'there were strongly arguable issues whose events could only be assessed at a full trial in

---

[58] 31 C.F.R., §535.566 (21 Nov. 1979). See Robert Carswell, 'Economic Sanctions and the Iran Experience', 60 *Foreign Affairs* 247 at 250–1 (Winter 1981/2).

[59] It was estimated that this category included about $6 billion, primarily reflecting revenue from oil exports by Iran.

[60] See e.g. *Bank Markazi, v. Citibank, N.A.*, 1979 B No. 5903, filed 30 Nov. 1979, Queen's Bench Division, Commercial Court. Excerpts from the pleadings are reproduced in A. Lowenfeld, *Trade Controls for Political Ends*, 557–61 (2nd edn. 1983).

[61] Exec. Order No. 12,544, 51 Fed. Reg. 1,235 (10 Jan. 1986). One interesting change from the Iranian sanctions was that this time the freeze applied only to 'US persons', thus excluding foreign subsidiaries of US banks, but not foreign branches.

the ordinary way.'[62] Following a full trial, a different judge in the High Court found for plaintiff Libyan bank in a 30-page opinion, based essentially on the conclusion that the case (i) involved performance of a contract; (ii) that performance would be excused if it had become illegal by the proper law of the contract; but (iii) though the deposit agreement contained no choice of law clause and was in fact managed from New York, the proper law of the contract was the law of the place where the account is kept.[63] Thus the issues of jurisdiction to prescribe and enforce, and the issue of how a second state should treat economic sanctions of a friendly foreign state, were scarcely touched upon. The US government, which had participated *amicus curiae* in the High Court, considered appealing against the judgment, but did not go ahead or urge the bank to go ahead with an appeal, and instead issued a license so that the bank would not be exposed in the United States to penalties for obeying the order of the English court.

(d)   Limits on Export Controls[64]

1. *Patrian Regulations in Tertian Courts*

It was once said—indeed is still often said—that no state will have regard to the penal, revenue, or political laws of another state.[65] In fact, though there is certainly resistance to other states' political trade controls and their extraterritorial enforcement, there is an opposite trend that takes as its point of departure that states and their courts ought not to lend themselves to evasion of the laws of friendly foreign states. For instance, in a famous English case in the 1950s, an Indian company had made a contract with a Swiss merchant to export 500,000 jute bags from India, destined, as both parties knew, to South Africa. The contract contained a clause providing for arbitration in London, and when the Indian company failed to ship, buyer initiated an arbitration that eventually reached the English courts all the way to the House of Lords.[66] The seller defended on the ground that the sale would have violated Indian export controls, which prohibited all trade with South Africa because of the latter's policies of apartheid. Buyer replied that an English Court must not recognize the trade control laws of a foreign state,

---

[62] *Libyan Arab Foreign Bank v. Bankers Trust Co.*, 1986 L. No. 1567, Slip. Op. at 3 (C.A. 19 Dec., 1986), available also on Lexis.

[63] *Libyan Arab Foreign Bank v. Bankers Trust Co.*, [1988] 1 Lloyd's Rep. 259, [1989] 1 Q.B. 728. For more on this litigation, see Peter S. Smedresman and Andreas F. Lowenfeld, 'Eurodollars, Multinational Banks, and National Laws', 64 *N.Y.U. L. Rev.* 733 at 754–61 (1989).

[64] For a group of essays by authors from ten countries discussing the issues raised in this section, see Karl M. Meessen (ed.), *International Law of Export Control: Jurisdictional Issues* (1992).

[65] The origin of the axiom goes back, it seems, to a famous one-line dictum by Lord Mansfield in *Holman* v. *Johnson*, 1 Cowp. 341 at 343, 98 Eng. Rep. 1120 at 1121 (K.B. 1775), 'for no country ever takes notice of the revenue laws of another.'

[66] *Regazzoni* v. *K.C. Sethia (1944) Ltd.*, 1958 A.C. 301.

and in any event the proper law of the contract was English. The House of Lords upheld the seller's defense. Viscount Simonds wrote:

[A]n English court will not enforce a penal law at the suit of a foreign State, yet it would be surprising if it would enforce a contract which required commission of a crime in that State.[67]

Lord Reid added:

It was argued that this prohibition of exports to South Africa was a hostile act against a Commonwealth country with which we have close relations, that such a prohibition is contrary to international usage, and that we cannot recognize it without taking sides in the dispute between India and South Africa.

My Lords, it is quite impossible for a court in this country to set itself up as a judge of the rights and wrongs of a controversy between two friendly countries, . . . and, if we tried to do so, the consequences might seriously prejudice international relations.[68]

The German Supreme Court, in two cases decided in the early 1960s arising out attempts to evade American restrictions on export or re-export of borax to the East bloc, also upheld the foreign restriction, but was not afraid to take sides.[69]

The court wrote:

Even if German laws that incorporate the American embargo regulations cannot be found, intentional evasion of those regulations is nevertheless an action contrary to good morals [*Sittenverstoss*]. . . . It is undisputed that the American embargo regulations are designed to uphold the peace and freedom of the West. The measures, therefore, were taken not only in the interest of the United States, but in the interest of the entire free Western World and therefore also in the interest of the Federal Republic of Germany.[70]

Whether the same view would be upheld in the post-Cold War context— say in connection with a scheme to re-export US-origin goods from Germany to Libya despite a prohibition under US law, is not clear.[71]

---

[67] 1958 A.C. at 322.   [68] 1958 A.C. at 325–6.

[69] *G.B. A.G. v. W.R.*, 34 BGHZ 169 (Sup. Ct. 21 Dec. 1960); Decision Sup. Ct. of 24 May 1962, 1962 *Neue Juristische Wochenschrift* [*NJW*], 1436.

[70] 34 BGHZ at 177. The second case cited in the preceding note repeats this passage, 1962 *NJW* at 1437.

[71] The drafters of the Rome Convention of 1980 on the Law Applicable to Contractual Obligations wrestled with this problem, and came up with a highly controversial provision, Article 7(1) which reads as follows:

When applying under this Convention the law of a country, effect may be given to the mandatory rules of another country with which the situation has a close connection, if and in so far as, under the law of the latter country, those rules must be applied whatever the law applicable to the contract. In considering whether to give effect to these mandatory rules regard shall be had to their nature and purpose and to the consequences of their application or non-application.

The Convention permitted contracting states to reserve the right not to apply Article 7(1), and the United Kingdom and Germany declared that they would not apply that provision.

2. *The* Siberian Pipeline *Case*[72]

A highly publicized episode in 1982 brought together the continuing resentment in Western Europe and Canada at the perceived exorbitant exercise by the United States of its jurisdiction—some said its 'muscle'—and a genuine difference of opinion about how the West should react to a political crisis in Poland.

Background

The background of the confrontation was twofold. On one side six countries in Western Europe had contracted in 1980–1 with the Soviet Union to build a large-diameter pipeline to carry natural gas from the Yamal Peninsula near the Arctic Circle in Western Siberia to a place in Germany from which the gas was to be distributed by smaller pipelines to utilities in the six countries. The West European countries would finance the project, estimated to cost between $10 and $15 billion, to be repaid with proceeds from the sale of the natural gas. The pipe, compressor stations, and pipelaying equipment were to be procured as far as possible in the states making the loans. For the Soviet Union, the project was a way to earn hard currency and to tap a huge, thus far unused resource base; for the West European countries, it was seen as a way to reduce their energy dependence on the unstable Middle East, and also as a way to employ unemployed steel workers in productive tasks.

The United States had no direct role in the project, but having recently completed the trans-Alaska pipeline, its companies had certain technical capabilities difficult to duplicate in Western Europe. Several European companies that had committed themselves to build portions of the pipeline had contracts to purchase components and equipment, and to use technology under licenses from American companies such as General Electric, Caterpillar Tractor, and others. Moreover, a number of European subsidiaries of American companies, such as Dresser-France, were engaged in portions of the project. The US government, though opposed to the project on policy grounds, had imposed no legal impediments to participation by American companies in supplying equipment or technology to the project.[73]

---

[72] A large amount of writing has focused on this affair, both in the United States and in Europe. A longer version by the present author of the account given here appears in A. Lowenfeld, *Trade Controls for Political Ends*, 267–306 (2nd edn. 1983). See also *Restatement (Third) of the Foreign Relations Law of the United States*, §414, Reporters' Note 8 and sources there cited (1987).

[73] In fact one case related to the pipeline had come before CoCom (Sect. 23.2, n. 23 supra), involving a proposed sale by a French company of computerized gas flow control equipment, and had been resolved by a change in the proposal to eliminate the most advanced technology. Caterpillar Tractor had secured a license from the Commerce Department on 9 Dec. 1981 to export 200 pipelayers for use on the pipeline. The parts for compressor turbines made by General Electric did not, until the events described hereafter, require validated licenses at all.

On the other side, communism was beginning to loosen in Eastern Europe, particularly in Poland. A labour union at a shipyard in Gdansk (formerly Danzig) had gone on strike in August 1980 and had seized the shipyard. The strike had spread throughout Poland, a new popular leader, Lech Walesa, had emerged, and a new movement had been born, *Solidarity*. For sixteen months freedom in Poland seemed to grow day by day. Close to 10 million persons joined Solidarity, a related movement arose among Poland's farmers, and even the Central Committee of the Communist Party held free elections by secret ballot, with the result that only one-tenth of the membership was re-elected.

At midnight, Saturday, December 12, 1981, everything changed. Warsaw was ringed by tanks, soldiers manned check points on all major roads, guards stood outside major buildings, bayonets fixed. At 6 a.m. Sunday, December 13, martial law and a national emergency were proclaimed. All public gatherings were forbidden, Solidarity's leaders were arrested, telephone lines were cut, and a total news blackout was imposed. The tanks and soldiers now running Poland were Polish, not Russian; in Washington, however, the perception was that the Soviet Union must be behind the crackdown.[74]

A Clash of Wills
In Western Europe, the political leaders deplored the situation in Poland, but (with minor exceptions) imposed no sanctions. President Reagan, in contrast, responded to martial law in Poland by saying, 'We're not going to let them get away with it.'[75]

Within two weeks the United States put in place a program of export controls and related economic sanctions, both against Poland and against the Soviet Union. The most important sanction concerned the pipeline:[76] all exports from the United States destined to be used for the pipeline, regardless of country of destination or level of technology, would henceforth require a license, and no licenses would be issued. As with other export controls, penalties for violation would include 'denial of export privileges' for

---

[74] Secretary of State Haig writes in his memoirs:

If there had been any question about Soviet responsibility for events in Poland, it was dispelled by reports that Moscow had informed the governments of every country in the Soviet bloc that martial law would be imposed in Poland *before the Russians told the Warsaw government.* (Alexander M. Haig, Jr. *Caveat: Realism, Reagan, and Foreign Policy*, 250 (1984)) (italics by Haig)

[75] News Conference of President Ronald Reagan, 17 Dec. 1981, 17 *Weekly Comp. Pres. Docs* 1379, 1381 (21 Dec. 1981).

[76] Other sanctions included suspension of landing rights in the United States for the Soviet airline, Aeroflot; closing of the Soviet Purchasing Commission in the United States; suspension or non-renewal of licenses for export of high-technology items to the Soviet Union; and suspension of negotiations looking to a long-term grain agreement, a maritime agreement and agreements on scientific and cultural exchanges.

the firm in question, regardless of its place of establishment or of its place in the chain of export.[77]

The announcement brought about some grumbling from Western Europe, especially from firms contractually obligated to deliver compressors to the Soviet Union that contained components built in the United States, and also from governments about lack of consultation. There were no vehement protests, however, and no assertion that the United States had transgressed international standards. As a matter of international law, the United States had exercised its territorial jurisdiction to control exports of products and technology originating in the United States.

By the spring of 1982, however, there was no sign that the situation in Poland had improved. Efforts by the United States to persuade the European states to join in sanctions against the Soviet Union and Poland had essentially come to naught. In June 1982, following an economic summit in Versailles, President Reagan decided to tighten the screws. New regulations were issued to include (1) equipment produced abroad by foreign subsidiaries of US companies; and (2) equipment produced abroad by foreign-owned companies under technology licenses issued by US companies.[78] The assertion of jurisdiction under (1) was not new; it had been asserted amid substantial protests in the *Fruehauf* case and other particular situations under the Trading with the Enemy Act and its successor statute, though not under export controls.[79] The assertion under (2) was unprecedented—a new link, based on private licenses between American and foreign companies.

The reaction in Europe was quick, and all negative. The foreign ministers of the European Community met within a few days, and declared:

This action, taken without consultation with the Community, implies an extraterritorial extension of US jurisdiction, which in the circumstances, is contrary to international law.[80]

[77]   The controls were announced by President Reagan in his Christmas address of 23 Dec. 1980 and in a follow-up statement a few days later, 17 *Weekly Comp. Pres. Docs.* 1404, 1429–30 (23 and 29 Dec. 1980). The actual regulations, 'Controls on Exports of Petroleum Transmission and Refining Equipment to the USSR' were issued by the Dept. of Commerce on 5 Jan. 1982, 47 Fed. Reg. 141 (1982). The Department made clear that the new regulations were not national security regulations, but that 'this rule is necessary to further significantly the foreign policy of the United States.' Commodities or technical data that were on dock for loading or in transit on December 30, 1981 were licensed for export up to January 14, 1982. Shipments thereafter would require licenses that presumably would not be granted.

[78]   Statement of the President on Extension of US Sanctions, 18 June 1982, 18 *Weekly Comp. Pres. Docs* 820 (21 June 1982), implemented by the Dept. of Commerce at 47 Fed. Reg. 27250 (24 June 1982).

[79]   When the regulations implementing the new sanctions were issued, the definition of 'person subject to the jurisdiction of the United States' was amended to replicate the definition under the Foreign Assets Control Regulations (Sect. 23.4(b) at n. 42 supra), but only for §385.2, the section applicable to exports of oil and gas equipment to the USSR.

[80]   Statement of the Foreign Ministers of the European Community, 23 June 1982; *N.Y. Times* 24 June 1982, p. 1, col. 5. Subsequently, the European Community submitted a longer Aide-Mémoire developing the arguments about violation by the United States of international law, reproduced in 21 *I.L.M.* 891 (1982). It is worth noting that the legal part of the Aide-Mémoire

More than that, the governments of Great Britain, France, and West Germany (but not Italy) ordered companies organized in their territories (locally owned as well as owned by American firms) to carry out their contractual obligations, notwithstanding the prohibition under the US regulations.

Even as the US Department of Commerce was issuing denial orders to firms that were continuing to work on the pipeline, other parts of the US government were coming to the conclusion that the June sanctions order was untenable. American diplomats seeking agreement on a variety of other issues,[81] found that every conversation came down to the Pipelines Sanctions, Phase II. Instead of focusing on East–West tensions and the bad things happening in Poland, the sanctions had become a major West–West issue, not only pitting the United States against its West European allies, but dividing the American business community, the legal community, and the Congress.[82]

One case was actually litigated in Europe. Sensor Nederland B.V., the Netherlands subsidiary of an American company, had a contract with a French firm to supply geological sensing equipment to be used in construction of the pipeline. On orders from the parent company, the subsidiary notified the French company that it would be unable to perform its obligations under the contract. The French company brought suit in The Netherlands for specific performance, and on September 17, 1982 the District Court in The Hague gave judgment for the plaintiff, ordering delivery of the equipment contracted for not later than October 18, on penalty of a 10,000 guilder fine per day of default after that date.[83] Though the court was careful not to exclude all extraterritorial jurisdiction, it stated the general principle that it is not permissible for a state to exercise jurisdiction over acts performed outside its borders, and held that none of the grounds for exceptions to the principle was applicable.

By the fall of 1982, the US government was looking for a graceful way out, possibly some kind of agreement whereby the European countries would reconsider their strategies on East–West trade, in return for withdrawal of

---

was based largely on American sources, including both the *Restatement (Second) of the Foreign Relations Law of the United States* (1965) and early drafts of what became the *Restatement (Third) of the Foreign Relations Law of the United States* (1987).

[81] See e.g. the Agreement of October 1982 between the United States and the European Economic Community on Restraint of Steel Imports , Ch. 9, Sect. 9.5(e), n. 84.

[82] In August 1982, the Foreign Affairs Committee of the House of Representatives approved a bill to terminate the export controls related to the pipeline. When the bill came to a vote in the full House, it failed by only three votes (206–203). An amended version of the bill, including a provision for waiver, was subsequently approved by the House, but did not come to vote in the Senate.

[83] *Compagnie Européenne des Petroles, S.A.* v. *Sensor Nederland, B.V.*, Distr. Ct. The Hague, 17 Sept. 1982, 36 *Rechtspraak van de Week-Kort Geding* 167, English transl. 22 *I.L.M.* 66 (Jan. 1983).

the offending regulations and cancellation of the denial orders that had been issued for violation of the regulations.

On November 13, 1982, President Reagan announced that the export controls of December 1981 and June 1982 directed against the Siberia–Western Europe natural gas pipeline would be revoked immediately, in the context of an agreement with the nations of Western Europe on an 'enduring realistic and security-minded economic policy toward the Soviet Union . . . a victory for all the allies.'[84] Two days earlier General Secretary Brezhnev had died. One day later the leader of Solidarity, Lech Walesa, was released from detention and permitted to return to his family in Gdansk.

Whether these three events were connected either in causation or timing is not known. Nor is it known to what extent, if any, the American sanctions affected Soviet actions vis-à-vis Poland or other East European states. What is clear is that exercise by the United States of jurisdiction over foreign unaffiliated enterprises on the basis of a commercial technology license was almost universally condemned and has not been repeated. Exercise by the United States of jurisdiction over foreign enterprises on the basis of affiliation with a parent corporation established in the United States, already strongly criticized, came under further attack, and has been resorted to more sparingly since that time.

(e)   Summary

The exercise of jurisdiction to prescribe and to enforce economic sanctions remains controversial, with the United States the most assertive, other states resistant to varying degrees. In some instances other industrial states, particularly in Europe but also in Canada and Japan, have been content to have the United States take the lead, but to cooperate in accepting, and even in enforcing, restraints on re-exports intended for states deemed dangerous, even when they have not imposed or enforced their own prohibitions. The more the perceptions concerning the merits of sanctions have differed, the more jurisdictional objections have been raised in formal protests, counter-orders, and litigation.

No absolute rule can be stated to the effect that a state may make economic sanctions effective only in its own territory. When a state attempts to apply its sanctions beyond its own territory however—whether to foreign branches of domestic enterprises, to foreign affiliates separately incorporated, to assets held in foreign branches or subsidiaries of domestic banks, or

---

[84] Radio address of President Reagan of 13 Nov. 1982, 18 *Weekly Comp. Pres. Docs.* 1475 (19 Nov. 1982). The regulations were formally revoked on November 16, effective November 13, 1982, 4 Fed. Reg. 51538 (18 Nov. 1982). The orders temporarily denying export privileges that had been issued against AEG-Kanis (Germany), Creusot-Loire (France), Dresser-France, John Brown Engineering (UK), Mannesmann (Germany), and Nuovo Pignone (Italy) were vacated on the same day on motion of the Commerce Department. No text of the agreement referred to by President Reagan was ever published.

to goods sold to foreign buyers and offered for resale—it risks challenge, in an arena where political, economic, and legal considerations interact and overlap.

23.5   ECONOMIC SANCTIONS AND THE GATT

(a)   Introduction

Economic sanctions, by definition, are inconsistent with the golden rule of the GATT—non-discrimination and most-favoured-nation treatment. Article I of the GATT, it is worth recalling, applies not only to restraints on imports, but to restraints an exports as well. Article XI, the prohibition on quantitative restrictions, also applies by its terms to exports and imports, and also would be inconsistent with any prohibition or embargo such as are typically the focus of economic sanctions. Nevertheless the GATT has had very little impact on economic sanctions, and the efforts by some contracting parties to use the GATT as a forum to protest or to secure relief from the imposition of sanctions have all been unsuccessful.

Quite apart from the details discussed hereafter, two principal reasons may be adduced for the relative insignificance of the GATT (and more recently the WTO) to the subject of sanctions. For one thing, many of the targets of sanctions applied by the Western industrial states were not contracting parties to the GATT—notably the Soviet Union and the People's Republic of China; also North Korea, Vietnam, and Cambodia; Libya, Iran, and Iraq; for many years Hungary, and Romania; and also East Germany and Bulgaria.

For another, the consensus among the officials and delegates has been that the GATT was always a quite fragile organization, with more than it could handle in disputes about steel and wheat and wine and motion pictures, about subsidies and dumping and safeguards, and about the many negotiating rounds: if it became embroiled in political controversies where it was apparent that the State imposing the sanctions was not acting to secure an illicit economic gain, the GATT would lose its focus, and might well see its most important member—notably the United States—turn its back on the organization.[85]

---

[85] For two thoughtful articles, both coming to somewhat different conclusions from the one here proposed, see Michael Hahn, 'Vital Interests and the Law of GATT: An Analysis of GATT's Security Exception', 12 *Mich. J. Int'l L* 558 (1991); Hannes L. Schloemann and Stefan Ohlhoff, ' "Constitutionalization" and Dispute Settlement in the WTO: National Security as an Issue of Competence', 93 *Am.J. Int'l L.* 424 (1999).

(b)   The Security Exception Article

Article XXI of the GATT, reads in pertinent part:

Nothing in this Agreement shall be construed

    . . .

(b)   to prevent any contracting party from taking any action which it considers
    necessary for the protection of its essential security interests

    . . .

    (iii) taken in time of war or other emergency in international relations. . . .

At the 1947 Geneva session of the Preparatory Committee that drafted
the GATT, the question was raised what was meant by 'essential security
interests'. One of the drafters of the original Draft Charter (not otherwise
identified) said:

We gave a good deal of thought to the question of the security exception which we
thought should be included in the Charter. We recognized that there was a great danger of having too wide an exception and we could not put it into the Charter, simply
by saying: 'by any Member of measures relating to a Member's security interests,'
because that would permit anything under the sun. Therefore we thought it well to
draft provisions which would take care of real security interests and, at the same
time, so far as we could, to limit the exception so as to prevent the adoption of protection for maintaining industries under every conceivable circumstance. . . . there
must be some latitude here for security measures. It is really a question of balance.
We have got to have some exceptions. We cannot make it too tight, because we cannot prohibit measures which are needed purely for security reasons. On the other
hand, we cannot make it so broad that, under the guise of security, countries will put
on measure which really have a commercial purpose.[86]

The Chairman of Commission A (the commission in charge of most of the
substantive provisions of the proposed charter) responded that the spirit in
which Members of the Organization would interpret these provisions was
the only guarantee against abuses of this kind.[87]

In the event, Article XXI was another of the provisions of the GATT that
might have eaten up the whole agreement, but did not do so.[88] With a few
exceptions, Article XXI was invoked only in the context of measures that fit
within the definition of sanctions, i.e. measures taken for reasons of foreign
policy, not to gain commercial advantage.[89] On the other hand, the suggestion that 'essential security interests' might be given an objective definition
or be subjected to some kind of collective decision-making, was never

---

[86] As quoted in the *Analytical Index of the GATT*, under Art. XXI, 600. (6th edn. 1995).
[87] Ibid.   [88] Cf. Ch. 3, Sect. 3.4(d).
[89] The United States Oil Import Program (1959–72) was stated to be a national security
measure but was primarily designed to protect the interests of independent oil producers in the
United States against the low prices then prevailing on oil from the Middle East and Venezuela.
See Kenneth W. Dam, 'Implementation of Import Quotas: The Case of Oil', 14 *J. Law &
Economics* 1 (1971). The oil import program never came before GATT, because the Middle
East oil producers, as well as Mexico and Venezuela, were not then contracting parties, and
Canada preferred to negotiate an 'overland exemption'.

adopted.[90] It is not excluded that at some time in the future measures defended on the basis of Article XXI will be subjected to international scrutiny, but as of year-end 2001, the quoted provision of Article XXI had remained—not without some grumbling—a self-judging provision.[91]

(c) Czechoslovakia and United States Sanctions (1948, 1951)

Czechoslovakia was a founding member of the GATT, having signed the Final Act of the 1947 Geneva Conference several months before the February 1948 coup that brought the country firmly into the communist orbit. In the following year, as the US export controls increasingly restricted exports to the Soviet bloc (as it came to be known), Czechoslovakia complained to the Third Session of the Contracting Parties that the American export restrictions violated articles XI(1) and XIII of the GATT. Czechoslovakia argued that the restrictions could not be justified as national security measures under Article XXI because the embargoed goods were of no military significance. The United States replied that the goods could have military significance—for example coal mining equipment could also mine uranium.[92]

The case came up before the practice of appointing panels had been introduced, and was discussed by the Contracting Parties in plenary session. During the discussion, it was stated that 'every country must be the judge in the last resort on questions relating to its own security. On the other hand, every contracting party should be cautious not to take any step which might have the effect of undermining the General Agreement.'[93] As Professor Hudec wrote, 'the infant GATT had neither the capacity nor the prestige to undertake a serious examination of US cold war measures.'[94] The complaint was rejected by a roll-call vote of 17–1 with 3 abstentions.[95]

---

[90] Professor Jackson, in his treatise of 1969, wrote:

The GATT security exception, as well as certain other GATT clauses . . . can reopen the door to arbitrary abuse. For this reason it might be wise to try to put Article XXI invocations on a more multilateral basis. For example, it might be made clear that although wide leeway will be granted an individual contracting party's decision to take measures under the Article XXI exceptions, whenever these come to the attention of GATT, they will be subject to review by a GATT Working Party, which may report on its views. This procedure would be in addition to that of Article XXIII under which a specific party may complain. (John H. Jackson, *The Law of GATT*, 752 (1969))

[91] Article XXI may thus be compared to the famous Connally Reservation to the US Declaration Recognizing as Compulsory the Jurisdiction of the International Court of Justice (1946), stating that the declaration shall not apply to

disputes with regard to matters which are essentially within the domestic jurisdiction of the United States of America as determined by the United States of America.

[92] As summarized in Robert E. Hudec, *Enforcing International Trade Law*, Appendix, 420 (1993).

[93] Quoted (again without specific attribution) in *Analytic Index of the GATT* (n. 86 supra), 600, also John H. Jackson (n. 90 supra), 749.

[94] Robert E. Hudec, *The GATT Legal System and World Trade Diplomacy*, 77 (2nd edn. 1990).

[95] Decision of 8 June, 1949, GATT Doc. II BISD, 28 (1952).

In 1951, when the Korean War was in full swing and the Cold War was at its chilliest, the US Congress adopted an amendment requiring the President to deny the benefits of most-favoured-nation treatment to the products of any country 'dominated or controlled by Communism'.[96] With respect to the Soviet Union, Bulgaria, Poland, and Hungary, the United States just gave the required notice; Czechoslovakia, however, was entitled to MFN treatment under GATT. The United States sought a waiver under Article XXV, arguing that 'fruitful economic relations between any two countries . . . must presuppose some reasonable degree of mutual respect, some reasonable degree of good faith by each in its dealings with the other. . . . If there is no genuine means of communication between the two governments, then what possible basis can there be for the fulfillment of commercial policy obligations such as we find in the General Agreement on Tariffs and Trade?'[97] The Contracting Parties did not expressly grant a waiver, but agreed on a declaration submitted by the United States stating that

the governments of the United States and Czechoslovakia shall be free to suspend, each with respect to the other, the obligations of the General Agreements on Tariffs and Trade.[98]

It was stated at the time that 'the present case could on no account provide a precedent.' In fact Ghana announced in 1961 that it was banning all imports from Portugal because of the situation in Angola, and the United States proclaimed an embargo against Cuba in 1962, without serious repercussion in the GATT.[99]

(d)   The Argentine Crisis and the GATT Decision (1982)

In April 1982, as described above,[100] the European Community, as well as Canada and Australia, imposed an embargo on imports against Argentina following Argentina's invasion of the Falkand Islands (Islas Malvinas). The EC notified the GATT, stating that

they have taken certain measures in the light of the situation addressed in the [UN] Security Council Resolution 502 [the Falkland/Malvinas issue]; they have taken these measures on the basis of their inherent rights of which Article XXI of the General Agreement is a reflection.[101]

---

[96] Trade Agreements Extension Act of 1951, ch. 141, §5, 65 Stat. 73 (1951).

[97] Statement by the Chairman of the US Delegation at the Sixth Session of the Contracting Parties, quoted in Gerard Curzon, *Multilateral Commercial Diplomacy: The General Agreement on Tariffs and Trade and its Impact on National Commercial Policies and Techniques*, 299 (1965).

[98] Declaration of 27 Sept. 1951: Suspension of Obligations between Czechoslovakia and the United States under the Agreement, GATT Doc. II BISD 36 (1952).

[99] See Jackson (n. 90 supra), 750.   [100] See Sect. 23.2(b).

[101] GATT Doc. L/5319/Rev. 1 (1982).

Argentina filed a complaint, asserting that except for the United Kingdom, the EC embargo completely lacked justification under the national security exception of Article XXI, and therefore violated Articles I, II, XI(1), XIII and the principles of Part IV (Trade and Development). Though the embargo was suspended at the end of June, the discussion was carried on in the GATT Council for another six months, as Argentina sought an interpretation of Article XXI. The Chairman of the Council noted that there were widely differing viewing as to whether the trade measures against Argentina violated GATT obligations, whether notification, justification, or approval was necessary, and whether the matter under consideration was within the competence of GATT.[102]

Eventually, Argentina's efforts found recognition of sorts in the 1982 GATT Ministerial Declaration that led, four years later, to initiation of the Uruguay Round. Article 7 of the Ministerial Declaration reads, in pertinent part:

In drawing up the work programme and priorities for the 1980s, the contracting parties undertake, individually and jointly

. . .

(iii) to abstain from taking restrictive trade measures, for reasons of a non-economic character, not consistent with the General Agreement.[103]

In addition, the Contracting Parties adopted a Decision Concerning Article XXI of the General Agreement, recording their failure to agree on an interpretation of the Article, and calling only for notification:

Considering that the exceptions envisaged in Article XXI of the General Agreement constitute an important element for safeguarding the rights of contracting parties when they consider that reasons of security are involved;

Noting that recourse to Article XXI could constitute, in certain circumstances, an element of disruption and uncertainty for international trade and affect benefits accruing to contracting parties under the General Agreement;

Recognizing that in taking action in terms of the exceptions provided in Article XXI of the General Agreement, contracting parties should take into consideration the interests of third parties which may be affected;

That until such time as the CONTRACTING PARTIES may decide to make a formal interpretation of Article XXI it is appropriate to set procedural guidelines for its application;

The CONTRACTING PARTIES decide that:

1. Subject to the exception in Article XXI:a, contracting parties should be informed to the fullest extent possible of trade measures taken under Article XXI.

2. When action is taken under Article XXI, all contracting parties affected by such action retain their full rights under the General Agreement.

---

[102] See *GATT Activities 1982*, 72–3 (1983).
[103] Ministerial Declaration of 29 Nov. 1982 GATT Doc. L/5424, L/5426 (30 Nov. 1982), BISD, 29th Supp. 9 at 11 (1983).

3. The Council may be requested to give further consideration to this matter in due course.[104]

(e)   The Nicaragua Question (1983, 1985)

The closest the GATT has come (as of year-end 2000) to looking at the merits of an economic sanction imposed by one GATT member against another came in two complaints filed on behalf of Nicaragua against the United States. The underlying controversy is well known—opposition (and more) by the United States to the Sandinista regime that governed Nicaragua in the 1980s. In 1983, the United States announced that as from October of that year Nicaragua's allocation under the US import quota for sugar would be reduced from 58,000 to 6,000 tons per year. This was not a protectionist measure, in that Nicaragua's prior share of the quota would be reallocated to Honduras, Costa Rica, and El Salvador, which according to President Reagan, 'are experiencing enormous problems, caused in considerable part by Nicaragua-supported subversion and extremist violence.'[105] Nicaragua contended that the US action violated Article XIII(2)(d) of the GATT which requires non-discriminatory administration of quotas, as well as Article II and Part IV. The US representative did not approve establishment of a panel, but stated that 'the reasons for the US decision were well known but more appropriately discussed in other fora.'[106]

A panel was created, and issued a ruling that the action by the United States had violated Article XIII(2)(d) of the GATT. The panel noted that the challenged measures were but one aspect of a more general problem, but said that it was concerning itself only with the trade issue. The Council adopted the report of the Panel without objection from the United States,[107] but the United States did not modify its policy or restore the quota to Nicaragua.

In 1985 the United States proclaimed a total embargo against trade with Nicaragua.[108] Nicaragua again brought a complaint before the GATT Council. The US representative said the measures had been taken for national security reasons and were therefore justified under Article XXI, which left to each contracting party the judgment of any action necessary for national security interests.[109] The Nicaragua delegate said:

[104] GATT Doc. BISD, 29th Supp. 23 (1983), repr. in *Analytical Index of the GATT* (n. 86 supra), 605–6.
[105] See 19 *Weekly Comp. Pres. Docs.* 695, 10 May 1983, 'United States Imports of Sugar from Central America', implemented in *Modification of Country Allocation of Quotas on Certain Sugars, Syrups and Molasses*, Pres. Proclamation 5107 of 23 Sept. 1983, 48 Fed. Reg. 44057 (27 Sept. 1983).
[106] As reported in *GATT Activities 1983*, 47 (1984).
[107] GATT BISD, 31st Supp. 67 (13 Mar. 1984), Pescatore, *Handbook*, case 55.
[108] Exec. Order 12513 of 1 May 1985 Prohibiting Trade and Certain Other Transactions Involving Nicaragua, 50 Fed. Reg. 18629, (1985), implemented in Nicaraguan Trade Control Regulations, 31 C.F.R., Part 540, 50 Fed. Reg. 19890 (10 May 1985).
[109] *GATT Activities 1985*, 47 (1986); 2 BNA Int'l Trade Rptr. 765 (5 June 1985).

The United States cannot convince this Council that Nicaragua is a threat to American national security. This is not a case of economic policy but a straight use of coercion.[110]

The ambassador of the European Community regretted the US decision, but agreed with the United States that 'it is not the role of GATT to resolve disputes in the field of national security.[111]

After considerable debate, the United States withdrew its objection to creation of a panel, provided that the panel would not be authorized to examine or judge the validity of or motivation for the invocation of Article XXI. A panel was established under the chairmanship of a delegate from Norway, but concluded that

as it was not authorized to examine the justification for the U.S. invocation of a general exception to the obligations under the General Agreement, it could find the United States neither to be complying with its obligations under the General Agreement nor to be failing to carry out its obligations under that Agreement.[112]

The panel did add that 'embargoes such as the one imposed by the United States, independent of whether or not they were justified under Article XXI, run counter to the basic aims of the GATT.'[113]

The United States favoured adopting the panel report as written; Nicaragua opposed adoption of the report unless it were amended to recommend removal of the embargo and confiscation for the losses it had suffered. The impasse was not resolved until the Sandinistas lost power in 1990 and the embargo was rescinded.[114]

(f)   The Helms-Burton Act: EU v. USA

In March 1996, the US Congress passed the Cuban Liberty and Democratic Solidarity (Libertad) Act of 1996, generally known by the names of its principal sponsors as the Helms-Burton Act.[115] The Act had two principal aspects. On the one hand, it was a legislative codification of existing economic sanctions previously imposed pursuant to executive orders, which Congress feared might be relaxed by a President with doubts about the continued usefulness of sanctions; on the other hand, the act provided in Title III that persons from third countries that did business with Cuba and 'trafficked' in property confiscated from US nationals could be held liable in an action in the United States for the value of the property in question, and if the trafficking continued, for three times the value of the property.[116] Thus

---

[110] Ibid.   [111] Ibid.   [112] As quoted in *GATT Activities 1986*, 58 (1987).
[113] Ibid.
[114] See GATT Doc. L/6661 (23 Mar. 1990) (Communication from Nicaragua); C/M/240 (Meeting of 3 Apr. 1990), 30–2.
[115] Pub. L. No. 104–114, 110 Stat. 785 (12 Mar. 1996).
[116] Helms-Burton Act, §302(a). 'Trafficking', a word heretofore applied in legislation almost exclusively to dealing in narcotics, was defined to indicate not only selling, transferring, buying

the Act contemplated that if, say, an English company purchased sugar from a Cuban state enterprise and it also did business in the United States and therefore was amenable to judicial jurisdiction in the United States, it would be liable to a US national who could show that some of the English company's purchases consisted of sugar grown on the plantation that the plaintiff once owned. There would be no necessary connection between the value of the property on which the claim was based and the value of the transaction on which the assertion of trafficking rested.[117]

The proponents of Helms-Burton asserted that the Act was designed to provide a remedy—long overdue—for persons whose property had been taken without compensation by the Cuban government under Castro, primarily in the years 1959–62.[118] A more likely outcome—and probably purpose—was to deter persons and companies that did business with the United States from doing business with Cuba—a classical secondary boycott similar to the Arab League boycott of Israel. Unless the English company in the example given above—or a company in Canada, Mexico, Argentina, France, etc.—was prepared to abandon its business and presence in the huge American market, it would be well advised to keep away from business in or with Cuba.[119]

Many commentators, including the present author, considered the Helms-Burton Act to violate international law, on the ground that it purported (albeit indirectly) to prescribe conduct beyond the jurisdiction of the United States.[120] The reaction outside the United States, and particularly within the European Community, was similar to the reaction in the *Pipeline* case discussed in Section 23.4(d) above. Once more the United States was exercising extraterritorial jurisdiction on an unprecedented and unacceptable basis. The European Commission even drafted a regulation to prevent European companies from complying with Helms-Burton and to enable them to recover amounts awarded against them by American courts.

---

or leasing the property in question, but also 'engaging in a commercial activity arising or otherwise benefiting from confiscated property.' Helms-Burton Act, §4(13).

[117] In addition, Title IV of the Act ordered the Secretary of State to deny an entry visa to any person (including officers of corporations) who has trafficked in confiscated property to which a claim is owned by a US national, and including the spouse and minor children of such person.

[118] See e.g. Brice M. Clagett, 'Title III of the Helms-Burton Act Is Consistent with International Law', 90 *Am. J. Int'l L.* 434 (1996).

[119] One might have thought that the act of state doctrine, Chapter 14, Sect. 14.3(b), would provide a defense to an action of this kind, but the drafters of Helms-Burton expressly provided, in §302(a)(6), that the act of state doctrine shall not be applicable to actions brought under the Act.

[120] See e.g. A Lowenfeld, 'Congress and Cuba: The Helms-Burton Act', 90 *Am. J. Int'l L.* 419, esp. 428–32 (1996); Brigitte Stern, 'Can the United States Set Rules for the World? A French View', 31 *J. World Trade* 4, p. 5 (1997); also Brigitte Stern, 'Vers la Mondialisation Juridique? Les Lois Helms-Burton et d'Amato-Kennedy', 100 *Rev. Générale de Droit International Public* 979 (1996).

What was different this time, relevant to the present focus, was that the European Commission on behalf of the European Union, brought a formal complaint to the WTO, asserting that Helms-Burton violated several provisions of the GATT, and also of GATS.[121] Even though Title III of Helms-Burton included a provision authorizing the President to suspend its application for six months and President Clinton had already done so once, the EU asserted that suspension was not good enough, because the very threat of suits under the Act, like the sword of Damocles, creates a disincentive to investment or long-term trading relationships.

The United States, as it had done on other occasions, objected to the GATT/WTO as the proper forum,[122] but under the disputes procedures established in the Uruguay Round,[123] the United States could no longer block establishment of a panel, and in November 1996 a disputes panel was established.

Neither the United States nor the European Union, however, had an incentive to test the reach of Article XXI of the GATT, and both had reason to settle out of court. In April 1997, a Memorandum of Understanding was agreed to whereby the United States agreed to postpone enforcement of Title III of Helms-Burton during the remainder of President Clinton's term 'so long as the EU and other allies continue their stepped up efforts to promote democracy in Cuba.'[124]

Following a summit meeting between President Clinton and Prime Minister Blair (at the time President of the European Council) just before the celebration of the fiftieth anniversary of the GATT, it was announced that a breakthrough had been achieved. The waiver promised by President Clinton in the 1997 Memorandum would be extended, and the WTO panel procedure would be called off.[125]

---

[121] WTO DOC.WT/DS38/2/Corr. 1 (14 Oct. 1996).

[122] *Financial Times*, London, 17 Oct. 1996, p. 15; 13 *BNA Int'l Trade Rptr.* No. 47, p. 1828 (2 Nov. 1996). Also Werner Meng, 'Extraterritoriale Jurisdiktion in der US-Amerikanischen Sanktionsgesetzgebung', 1997 *Europäische Zeitschrift für Wirtschaftsrecht* 423, 426 (1997).

[123] See Ch. 8, Sect. 8.1.

[124] Memorandum of Understanding concerning the US Helms-Burton Act and the US Iran Libya Sanctions Act, 1 Apr. 1997, repr. in 36 *I.L.M.* 529 (1997). The Memorandum also stated:

> Similarly, and in parallel, the EU and U.S. will work together to address and resolve through agreed principles the issue of conflicting jurisdictions, including issues affecting investors of another party because of their investments in third countries.

[125] *Financial Times*, London, 19 May 1998, p. 1. President Clinton continued to grant the waiver at six-months intervals to the end of his term, January 2001. On July 16, 2001, President Bush also issued the required waiver, 'taking into account that it is necessary for the national interest of the United States and will expedite the transition to democracy in Cuba.'

For a critical discussion of the understanding between the EU and the United States, addressing also the so-called Iran–Libya Sanctions Act of 1996, Pub. L. 104–172, see Stefan Smis and Kim van der Borght, 'The EU–U.S. Compromise on the Helms-Burton and D'Amato Acts', 93 *Am. J. Int'l L.* 227 (1999).

Thus the still young WTO was spared a difficult issue, which might have irritated the Congress if the decision had gone against the United States, and the EU and others if self-judging under Article XXI had been upheld.[126] The United States neither prevailed on nor surrendered its interpretation of Article XXI. On the other hand, the *Helms-Burton* episode, like the *Fruehauf* case and the *Pipeline* case demonstrated the limits on action by one country—even the United States—seeking to impose its political will on companies acting outside its territory in relations with third countries.

SUMMARY

Well before the UN Security Council began to use economic sanctions as a primary tool, individual countries used economic sanctions as an important instrument of foreign policy, less dangerous than military force, but more serious—and sometimes more effective—than diplomacy alone. The assertion that economic sanctions are coercive and therefore unlawful, while still heard from time to time, is unpersuasive in light of a long record of resort to such measures and legal challenges only in particular respects, notably concerning exercise of extraterritorial jurisdiction.

A variety of sanctions have been employed, from total embargoes to selective controls on exports and imports, to freezing of assets, blocking of financial transactions, and restrictions on shipping and aviation. In some instances, groups of states have acted jointly; in other instances, states have acted on their own—notably the United States but also the United Kingdom and the European Community. When the United States has taken measures to control behaviour outside its own territory or by its own nationals, such measures have been resisted, and in several instances have led to confrontations with states that regarded the measures as infringement on their sovereignty. While no precise rules have been formulated, it seems that in the area of sanctions, more even than in other areas such as antitrust or securities regulation, customary international law places limits on unilateral extraterritorial measures.

A few challenges to economic sanctions have been raised in the GATT and WTO, but the challenged measures have been defended on the basis of the national security exception to GATT (as well as related Agreements).[127] So long as the measures do not appear to be disguised efforts at economic protectionism, the consensus has been that the GATT/WTO system is not the appropriate forum for resolving controversies about trade controls for political ends.

---

[126] While the controversy was in progress, the present writer, in a joint piece with Prof. John H. Jackson, wrote:

> It seems to us that the greatest threat is not to the EU from Helms-Burton or to the United States from Cuba, but to the world trading system and its firm but still fragile system for compulsory adjudication and enforcement of trade disputes. (Jackson and Lowenfeld, 'Helms-Burton, the U.S., and the WTO', *ASIL Insight*, Mar. 1997).

[127] See e.g. GATS Art. XIV*bis* and TRIPs Art. 73, both tracking Art. XXI of the GATT.

Index of Subjects

Afterword

One may ask, after exploring the many different subjects addressed in this volume, whether there is indeed an International Economic Law, a connection among the several strands. I believe there is, even if it is not capable of irrefutable proof.

Certain concepts run through all of the subjects—discrimination, for example, sovereignty, jurisdiction, the interrelation of law and politics, national and international. I believe that understanding of the subjects here addressed is helpful in working in areas not covered, regional arrangements for example, or foreign assistance. A highly technical subject such as dumping and anti-dumping has a political aspect, and a highly political subject such as the treatment of foreign investment has technical aspects. Almost everywhere, private and governmental activities intersect, neither ever fully independent of the other.

All of the subjects covered contain elements of ambiguity. Reliance only on the written 'black letter' texts leads to misunderstanding, but proceeding without reference to the texts leads to breach and to loss of credibility.

It is evident that this book has made more use of narrative and illustration, and less of flat normative statements than might have been expected from a treatise. This approach reflects the author's belief that the answers cannot be understood without the questions, and that abstract statements cannot be comprehended without awareness of the underlying facts and the continuing controversies.

This is not to deny the normative character of international economic law. But international economic law—like all law but perhaps more so—is a process. Any attempt to define the law as of a given moment cannot help but distort. The process continues, and the hope is that this book has illuminated the path.

Index of Persons